Adalyn
Avery D

Beginning DICTIONARY

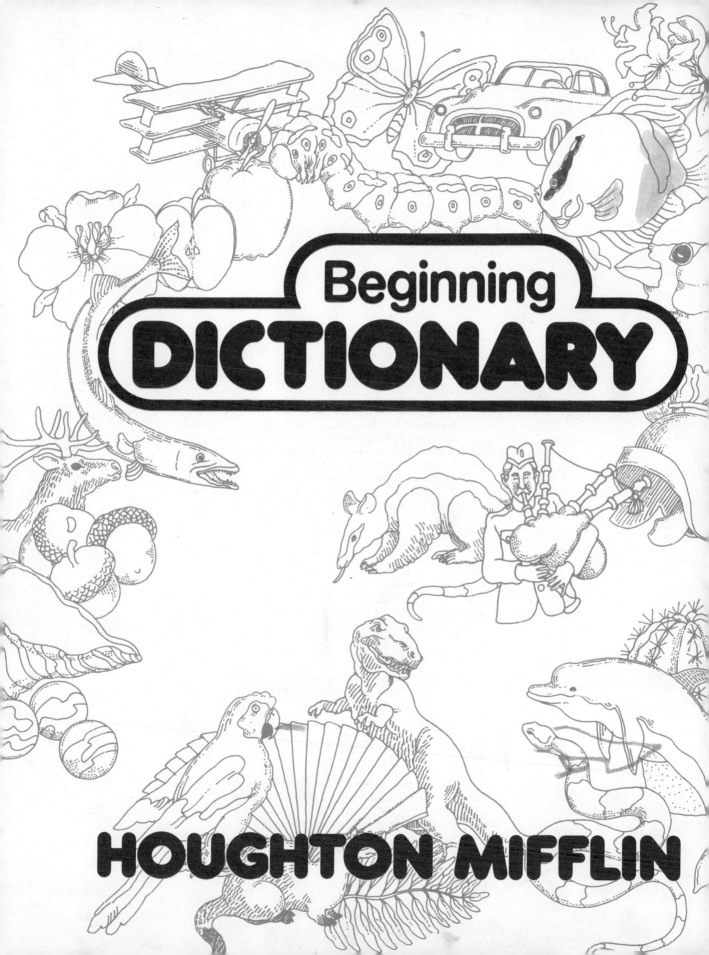

Beginning DICTIONARY

HOUGHTON MIFFLIN

All correspondence and inquiries should be directed to
Reference Division, Houghton Mifflin Company
Two Park Street, Boston, MA 02107

Library of Congress Cataloging in Publication Data
Main entry under title:
Beginning dictionary.
     SUMMARY: A dictionary for grades three to six which
features illustrative sentences as part of many of the
definitions.
     1. English language—Dictionaries, Juvenile.
[1. English language—Dictionaries]
PE1628.5.B44   1979   423   78-27760
ISBN 0-395-27400-1

Contents

Staff

Editorial Director
Fernando de Mello Vianna

Project Editor
Timothy J. Baehr

Art Director
Geoffrey Hodgkinson

Supervising Editor
Anne D. Steinhardt

Illustrator
George Ulrich

Associate Editors
Mark Boyer
Pamela B. DeVinne
Walter M. Havighurst

Picture and Research Editor
Carole LaMond

Contributing Editors
Olga Coren *(Plants and Animals)*
Eden Force Eskin

Definitions
Linda Ward Beech, Robert B. Costello, Bruce Dale,
Eleanor Eccleston, Kathleen Gerard, Frances M. Halsey,
Michele A. Roberts, Dorothy Z. Seymour, Barry Shannon,
Eugene F. Shewmaker, Andrea Denson Wechsler

Manuscript Coding and Composition
Joanne L. Nichols
Brenda Bregoli Sturtevant

Cross Reference
Barbara Collins
Sally Hehir
David Lovler

Computer Analysis
Milton D. Jacobson

Picture Researcher
Paula Rubenstein

Cover Design
Dorothea Sierra
George Ulrich

Proofreading
Kendra K. Ho, Doris Scarpello

Consultants

William K. Durr
Senior Author, Houghton Mifflin Reading Series
Professor of Education
Michigan State University
East Lansing, Michigan

Hugh D. Schoephoerster
Reading and Language Arts Consultant
Houghton Mifflin Company
Boston, Massachusetts

Kate Bell
Former Assistant Superintendent for Basic Skills
Houston Independent School District
Houston, Texas

Bernice M. Christenson
Instructional Specialist, English/Reading
Los Angeles Unified School District
Los Angeles, California

Shirley J. Mann
Director of Reading
Columbus Public Schools
Columbus, Ohio

Leonard Olguín
Professor, School of Education
California State University
Long Beach, California

John Reddick
Instructional Consultant, Elementary Language Arts
Denver Public Schools
Denver, Colorado

Contributing Author
Stephen Krensky

Preface

The *Beginning Dictionary* is a completely new work in the Houghton Mifflin series of dictionaries. Houghton Mifflin, the publishers of *The American Heritage Dictionary of the English Language* and of *The American Heritage School Dictionary,* continues its commitment to sound lexicography with the *Beginning Dictionary.* It is the product of many years of planning, research, writing, and editing by a large and experienced staff of lexicographers and teachers.

The *Beginning Dictionary* is intended for use in schools in grades 3 through 6 and has the distinctive advantage of being the first dictionary ever published in complete harmony with a highly successful reading series and language arts series. Houghton Mifflin's pre-eminence in these areas is in itself a guarantee of the *Beginning Dictionary*'s special usefulness to both teacher and student.

The words included in the Houghton Mifflin *Beginning Dictionary* strike a careful balance between familiar words and unfamiliar words the student is likely to encounter in reading. Compilation of the list of words included in the *Beginning Dictionary* was based on careful evaluation of the Dictionary Division's citation files, textbook glossaries, and other school materials. The final selection was determined by a comparison of this list with *The American Heritage Word Frequency Book* (Houghton Mifflin, 1971), a tabulation of five million words from a thousand different books and magazines encountered by students in grades 3 through 9, and *The Living Word Vocabulary*, a national vocabulary inventory by Edgar Dale and Joseph O'Rourke (Field Enterprises Educational Corporation, 1976).

The Living Word Vocabulary is the result of testing students for vocabulary recognition at grades 4, 6, 8, 10, 12, 13 (high-school graduates), and 16 (college seniors). Each word was presented with three possible meanings, and the student was to select the correct meaning. A word was usually assigned to a given grade level if more than 66 per cent and fewer than 85 per cent of the students at that grade level correctly identified the word with its meaning. For the *Beginning Dictionary* words were selected from grades 4 and 6 and sometimes from 8 and up, depending on their frequency of occurrence as determined by *The American Heritage Word Frequency Book.*

Control of the words used in the *Beginning Dictionary* extends to definitions as well. Computer analysis of all definitions was carried out under the direction of Dr. Milton D. Jacobson to ensure that every word used in the definitions is defined in the dictionary, to prevent confusing and frustrating dead ends.

The *Beginning Dictionary* is lavishly illustrated. More than eight hundred four-color illustrations were especially commissioned for this dictionary. The illustrations are realistic enough to convey all necessary information and yet fanciful enough to capture the attention and imagination of young readers. In all there are more than 1,500 illustrations, many of them photographs depicting children of various ages pursuing different activities.

Word histories and a short pronunciation key are attractively interspersed with the illustrations in the wide margins of the dictionary. A comprehensive front-matter section has been especially prepared to help young people become acquainted with this dictionary. It contains special activities that will enable readers to derive the maximum benefits from the book.

The editors of the *Beginning Dictionary* have sought to create a book that is attractive and stimulating to young readers while providing a solid foundation for the improvement of reading and writing skills.

A Guide to the Dictionary

A dictionary is a book about words. When you learn how to use it, a dictionary can tell you everything you want to know about a word.

Most people think of a dictionary as a book that you use to find out what a word means. But there are many other important things you can learn about a word from a dictionary: how to spell a word, how to say a word, and how a word can change in form when it is used in different ways. All of this information comes at the beginning of the entry, before the meaning. The entries in your dictionary are organized in the same way as they are in most dictionaries for grownups. Once you understand the special way this information is organized, you can find out anything you want to know about a word quickly and easily.

The Entry

The word that you look up in a dictionary is called an *entry word*. The entry word is printed in heavy, dark letters and placed a little to the left of the rest of the column. All of the information about an entry word comes right after it. The entry word and all the information about it make up the *entry*.

> **moat** |mōt| —*noun, plural* **moats** A wide, deep ditch, usually filled with water. In the Middle Ages a moat was dug around castles and towns to protect them from enemies. A bridge could be lowered over the moat so people could cross over.

Alphabetical Order

There are more than thirteen thousand entry words listed in your dictionary. To help you find the word you are looking for quickly, all of the entry words are listed in alphabetical order. The words beginning with the letter *a* come first. The words beginning with the letter *z* come last.

You will see right away that knowing the first letter of a word is not enough to help you find the word quickly. Suppose you are looking up the word *bake*. You know it will be listed near the front of the book, since it begins with the letter *b*. But there are more than fifty pages of words that begin with *b*. You do not have to look through all fifty pages to find the entry word *bake*.

Words that begin with the same letter are put into alphabetical order using the second and often third or fourth letter. Since there are many words beginning with the letters *ba,* you have to use the third letter, *k,* to find *bake. Bake* comes right after *bait* in the dictionary because the letter *k* comes after the letter *i* in the alphabet.

bait
bake
baker

To find *baker* you have to use the fifth letter, *r.* This is because *baker* has the same letters as *bake* and in the same order. Since the *r* in *baker* is an additional letter, *baker* must come after *bake.*

Some entry words are made up of more than one word. These can be *phrases,* such as *blue jay* and *water color,* that are written as two separate words. Or they can be *compounds,* such as *baby-sit* and *worn-out,* that are joined together with a hyphen. These phrases and compounds are put into alphabetical order as if they were written as one word. That is, phrases and compounds are alphabetized as if the space or hyphen between the words were not there.

blueish   **wormy**
blue jay   **worn**
blue jeans   **worn-out**
blueprint   **worry**

Practice

A. Copy the letters below and fill in the missing capital letters to form the alphabet.

A B C ▪ E ▪ ▪ H ▪ ▪ ▪ L M N ▪ ▪ Q R ▪ T ▪ V W ▪ ▪ Z

B. Copy the letters below. Leave a space before and after each one. Before each letter write the letter that comes just before it in the alphabet. After each letter write the letter that comes just after it in the alphabet.

c	h	t	e	s
v	u	b	n	l
j	o	q	x	p

C. Write the words in each group in alphabetical order.

1. egg
   event
   elementary school
   echo
   eyebrow

2. laugh
   left-hand
   legend
   laundry
   Latin America

3. part-time
   pleasure
   plead
   prank
   partly

Entry Words That Are Spelled Alike

When you look through your dictionary, you will see that some entry words are spelled alike. Small numbers are printed after them and above the line.

bail[1]   mean[1]
bail[2]   mean[2]
                 mean[3]

bill[1]   bill[2]

These words that are spelled alike have different meanings. Sometimes they also have different pronunciations. They are listed separately because each word has a different history. When you see different words that are spelled alike in this dictionary, you will also see a note in the margin that tells you where the words came from. These are called *word histories*.

> **pick[1], pick[2]**
> **Pick[1]** is probably from an old French word that meant "to prick or pierce."
> **Pick[2]** comes from an old English word that was used to mean "sharp object."

Practice

Copy these sentences. Look up the five entry words spelled *bay*. Decide which one has the correct definition for *bay* as it is used in each sentence. Write the number of the correct entry word next to each sentence.

1. We went swimming in the **bay**.
2. Our dog always **bays** at the moon.
3. The **bay** lets a lot of light into the room.
4. We planted a **bay** under the window.
5. I rode on the **bay** horse.

Words That Can Be Spelled in More Than One Way

Sometimes a word can be spelled in more than one way. Most of the time these words are listed in the dictionary as separate entry words. But if they are pronounced the same way and if there are no other entry words that come between them in alphabetical order, they are listed together at the same entry word.

ax or **axe**   **coconut** or **cocoanut**

Guide Words

There are two words printed together with a page number at the top of almost every page in the dictionary. These words are called *guide words* because they help you to find the word you are looking for. They can guide you to the right page. Find the word *bone* in the dictionary. Look at the guide words at the top of the page. They are printed in dark letters and have a bar between them.

bolt|**book**   **84**

The word on the left, *bolt,* tells you the first entry word on the page. The word on the right, *book,* tells you the last entry word on the page. Every word that comes between *bolt* and *book* in alphabetical order is listed on this page.

The next time you look up the word *bone,* you should be able to find it more quickly by using the guide words. Suppose you have found the word *bone* and now you want to find the word *bath.* The guide words **bolt**|**book** tell you that you have to go all the way back to the beginning of the words in the letter *b* to find *bath.* Words beginning with the letters *ba* come before words beginning with the letters *bo* in alphabetical order.

Practice

A. Copy this list of entry words. Beside each one there are three sets of guide words. Next to each entry word write the one set of guide words that would be at the top of the page in the dictionary where you would find the entry word.

1. brute	barber|barracks	been|begonia	brunet|buckle
2. diagram	depict|description	devise|diamond	domain|doorway
3. human	harsh|haul	hint|hit	huge|hump
4. lagoon	lacy|lance	length|lessen	loose|lot
5. remember	raven|readily	release|remark	remarkable|repay

● B. Copy this list of words. Look them up, and next to each write the guide words that are at the top of the page where you found the word.

1. fuel
2. grease
3. incubator
4. mechanic
5. salt

● C. Copy this list of words. Look them up. Next to each word that is a guide word in the dictionary, write the other guide word that is on the same page.

1. cement
2. hitch
3. link
4. society
5. thunder

The Entry Word

One of the most important things you want to find out from a dictionary is how to spell a word. As you have already seen, the entry word is printed in heavy, dark letters and shows you the correct spelling of the word.

The entry word is divided into syllables; the syllables are separated by black dots. Some words have two or more syllables; others have only one. A word with one syllable cannot be divided.

at·mos·phere   girl

pas·sen·ger   mess·y

Seeing how a word is divided into syllables can show

you how to divide a word when you are writing. If a word with two or more syllables will not fit on a line, you can divide it and put part of the word on the next line. You can divide a word the same way it is divided as an entry word.

Practice

A. Look up these words. Write them as they are divided into syllables in the dictionary.

1. magic	3. excellent	5. rifle	7. expand	9. gigantic
2. recess	4. goal	6. value	8. terrible	10. muscle

B. Look up these words. Write them as they are divided into syllables in the dictionary.

1. theater	5. opposite	9. acorn	13. journalism
2. umbrella	6. unfriendly	10. advertisement	14. raspberry
3. satisfactory	7. Indiana	11. flight	15. pancreas
4. reign	8. kitchen	12. management	16. kaleidoscope

Pronunciation

Another important thing you can learn from a dictionary is how to say a word. The way a word is pronounced is called its *pronunciation.* In the *Beginning Dictionary* the pronunciation comes right after the entry word so that when you look up a new word you will know how to say it correctly. The pronunciation has vertical lines on each side of it and looks like this:

o·be·di·ent |ō bē′dē ənt|

Some words can be pronounced in different ways. For these words all the pronunciations are entered. The most common pronunciation is listed first, but all are correct.

ketch·up |kĕch′əp| or |kăch′əp|

There are also some words that are pronounced in different ways depending on how they are used. Think about the word *record.* It can be used as a noun and also as a verb, but it has a different pronunciation for each use. For such words each pronunciation is given.

> **rec·ord** |rĕk′ərd| —*noun, plural* **records** **1.** Facts or other information set down in writing . . .
> —*verb* **re·cord** |rĭ kôrd′| **recorded, recording**

The Pronunciation Key and Symbols

You can see from these examples that the pronunciations look different from the entry words. In English the way a word is spelled does not always tell you how it is pronounced. This is because there are twenty-six letters in the alphabet that we use for writing, but there are about forty different sounds that we use when we speak. In order to show in print how a word is pronounced we have to use a special system.

The pronunciation system uses the letters of the alphabet and some other symbols and marks. If you turn to page **B-38** you will see a chart that lists all these marks. A special section that explains how to read them begins on page **B-31**.

The Part of Speech

How a word is used in a sentence determines its *part of speech*. A word that is used to name something is called a *noun*. A word that shows action is called a *verb*. Here is a list of the parts of speech used in this dictionary:

noun	*adverb*	*conjunction*
verb	*pronoun*	*interjection*
adjective	*preposition*	

Knowing the part of speech of a word can help you understand how to use it. In this dictionary the part of speech is printed in italics and listed right after the pronunciation.

house | hous | —*noun*
pol·ish | pŏl′ĭsh | —*verb*
beau·ti·ful | byōo′tə fəl | —*adjective*
al·read·y | ôl rĕd′ē | —*adverb*
them | *th*ĕm | —*pronoun*
in | ĭn | —*preposition*
or | ôr | or | ər | —*conjunction*
hi | hī | —*interjection*

Sometimes a word can be labeled as more than one part of speech. For example, the word *paint* can be used as a noun: *I bought blue paint for my bedroom.* And it can also be used as a verb: *She painted that picture.* When a word like this is entered in the dictionary, each part of speech is listed with its separate definition.

res·cue | rĕs′kyōo | —*verb* **rescued, rescuing** To save from danger or harm: *The lifeguard rescued the boy from drowning.* —*noun, plural* **rescues** The act of rescuing or saving.

Practice

A. Copy this list of words. Next to each word write down its part or parts of speech. Check the dictionary if you are not sure. The first one is done for you.

1. animal *noun*	6. pretty	11. under
2. funny	7. window	12. you
3. bicycle	8. oh	13. tooth
4. at	9. us	14. bald
5. chew	10. nearly	15. wary

B. Copy this list of words. Next to each word write down its part of speech. Remember that some words can be labeled as more than one part of speech. Check the dictionary if you are not sure.

1. happiness	6. wow	11. shove
2. once	7. miserable	12. round
3. walk	8. she	13. hey
4. jack	9. deserve	14. hammer
5. absence	10. into	15. barely

Different Forms of Words

Many forms of words that you use all the time are not separate entry words in the dictionary. For example, nouns have different forms to show singular and plural. Verbs have different forms to show present and past tense. Adjectives have different forms when they are used to make comparisons.

Suppose you read the sentence "I'm sorry I was late, but I lingered at my friend's house." You don't understand the sentence and want to look up *lingered* in the dictionary. To find the meaning of *lingered* you have to look up the word to which the ending *-ed* was added.

> **lin·ger** |lĭng′gər| —*verb* **lingered, lingering** To stay on longer than usual, as if not willing to leave: *The guests lingered in the dining room long after dinner was over.*

All the different forms of every word are listed in the *Beginning Dictionary*. They are printed in dark letters right after the part of speech.

Nouns   A word is a *noun* when it is used to name a person, a place, or a thing. You use the plural form of a noun when you want to name more than one person, place, or thing. The word *plural* follows the part of speech *noun*. The plural form of the entry word is then printed in dark letters.

The plural of most nouns is formed by adding *-s* or *-es* to the word. The spelling of the noun itself is not changed. These are called *regular plurals* and are given only at the entry word.

> **gown** |goun| —*noun, plural* **gowns**
> **box¹** |bŏks| —*noun, plural* **boxes**

The spelling and pronunciation of some nouns change when the plural is formed. Such nouns have *irregular plurals*. Irregular plurals are given at two places. They are listed at the main entry, and they are also listed as entry words with their own pronunciations.

> **goose** |gōōs| —*noun, plural* **geese**
> **geese** |gēs| The plural of the noun **goose.**
>
> **child** |chīld| —*noun, plural* **children**
> **chil·dren** |chĭl′drən| The plural of the noun **child.**

Some irregular plurals are spelled and pronounced the same way as the singular form; these are given only at the main entry.

deer |dîr| —*noun, plural* **deer**

Some nouns have no plural form, and some can be used only as plurals. When a noun has no plural, no plural is given.

mac·a·ro·ni |măk′ə rō′nē| —*noun*

When a noun can be used only as a plural, it is called a *plural noun.*

cat·tle |kăt′l| —*plural noun*
goods |go͝odz| —*plural noun*

Practice

A. Copy this list of nouns. Find the plural form of each word and write it next to the singular. If a word has no plural, write an *X* next to it.

1. nation	6. sky	11. Wednesday
2. prairie	7. loaf	12. fun
3. snow	8. people	13. country
4. fish	9. banana	14. mouse
5. mackerel	10. purpose	15. heart

B. Copy this list of nouns. Find the singular form of each word and write it next to the plural. If a word has no singular, write an *X* next to it.

1. pickles	6. enemies	11. women
2. peaches	7. teeth	12. costs
3. oxen	8. riches	13. increases
4. lunches	9. wolves	14. lives
5. keys	10. ladies	15. paragraphs

Verbs A word is a *verb* when it is used to show action. Verbs change their form to show the time when an action takes place. All the different forms of a verb are printed in dark letters after the part of speech.

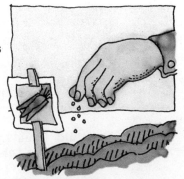

For most verbs the different forms are made by adding *-ed* or *-d* and *-ing* to the word. The spelling of the verb itself is not changed. Such verbs are called *regular verbs*.

> **talk** |tôk| —*verb* **talked, talking**
> **hope** |hōp| —*verb* **hoped, hoping**

The first form following the part of speech is used when you talk or write about something that has already taken place. This is called the *past tense: I talked to her yesterday.* Another form of the verb is called the *past participle.* The past participle of all regular verbs has the same form as the past tense, but a past participle is always used with a form of the auxiliary verb *have: I had already talked to her. We had hoped that Laura would arrive on Saturday.* The past participle often may be used as an adjective: *a restored house.*

The second form following the part of speech is used when you talk or write about something that is still going on. This form is called the *present participle.* It is always used with a form of the auxiliary verb *be: He is still talking on the telephone. I am hoping to get a sled for my birthday.* The present participle may also be used as an adjective: *a filling dinner.*

For some verbs the spelling of the verb form changes or the same form is used for two tenses. Such verbs are called *irregular verbs.* These forms are also printed in dark letters after the part of speech. If the irregular form of a verb has a different spelling, it is given in two places. It is listed at the main entry, and it is also listed as an entry word itself with its own pronunciation.

> **make** |māk| —*verb* **made, making**
> **made** |mād| The past tense and past participle of the verb **make.**

Some irregular verbs have different forms for the past tense and the past participle. For such verbs both forms are listed before the present participle.

> **give** |gĭv| —*verb* **gave, given, giving**
> **see** |sē| —*verb* **saw, seen, seeing**

You will find the words *gave, given, saw,* and *seen* as entry words with their own pronunciations because they are irregular forms with different spellings. You will not find the words *giving* and *seeing* as entry words because they are regular forms. The spelling of the verb does not change when the *-ing* ending is added, except that sometimes a final *e* is dropped or a final consonant is doubled.

Irregular forms of verbs that are spelled and pronounced the same way as the main verb are given only at the main entry.

put |po͞ot| —*verb* **put, putting**

Practice

A. Copy this list of verbs. Next to each write down the word you would look up to find its meaning.

1. **cheering**   6. **riding**
2. **fished**   7. **eating**
3. **leaked**   8. **decorated**
4. **writing**   9. **selling**
5. **washed**   10. **skating**

B. Look up these irregular verbs. Write down the sentences and put in the correct form of the verb.

1. **run**   After the game yesterday I _____ all the way home.
2. **grow**   The plant has _____ six inches.
3. **do**   I haven't _____ anything all day.
4. **come**   She _____ to see me when I was sick.
5. **think** Have you _____ about what I said?
6. **go**   When the movie had ended, we _____ and had a soda.

Adjectives   A word is an *adjective* when it is used to describe a noun. Adjectives can change form when they are used to make comparisons. The different forms of an adjective are printed in dark letters after the part of speech.

The different forms of most adjectives are made by adding *-er* and *-est* to the word. The spelling of the adjective does not change. These are called *regular adjectives*.

slow |slō| —*adjective* **slower, slowest**
nice |nīs| —*adjective* **nicer, nicest**
big |bĭg| —*adjective* **bigger, biggest**
like·ly |līk′lē| —*adjective* **likelier, likeliest**

The first form means "more": *This is a slower car than your car. He is a nicer person than she is.* An adjective having the -*er* ending is called the *comparative* form of the adjective.

The second form means "most": *This is the slowest car I ever saw. He is the nicest person I know.* An adjective having the -*est* ending is called the *superlative* form of the adjective.

For some adjectives the spelling and pronunciation change when the comparative and superlative are formed. These are called *irregular adjectives*. Irregular adjectives are given in two places. They are listed at the main entry, and they are also listed as entry words with their own pronunciations.

much |mŭch| —*adjective* **more, most**
more |môr| or |mōr| The comparative of the adjective **much.**
most |mōst| The superlative of the adjective **much.**

Some adjectives have no comparative and superlative forms. These are given with only the part of speech.

beau·ti·ful |byōō′tə fəl| —*adjective*
ter·rif·ic |tə rĭf′ĭk| —*adjective*

To make comparisons using these adjectives the words *more* and *most* are put in front of the adjective itself: *The brown horse is more beautiful than the white horse. That was the most terrific movie I ever saw.*

Practice

A. Copy this list of adjectives. Find the comparative and superlative forms of each and write them next to the adjective. If a word has no comparative and superlative forms, write an *X* next to it.

1. clear
2. ugly
3. silent
4. soft
5. tall
6. fast
7. large
8. loud
9. handsome
10. difficult
11. quiet
12. delightful
13. red
14. alive
15. pretty

B. Copy this list of comparatives and superlatives. Next to each write down the adjective you would look up to find its meaning.

1. hardest
2. drier
3. toughest
4. greater
5. fatter

6. braver
7. happier
8. thinnest
9. brittlest
10. quickest

11. sicker
12. brightest
13. greener
14. smoothest
15. angrier

The Definition

Most people use a dictionary when they want to find out what a word means. The meaning of a word is given in its *definition*. The definitions in the *Beginning Dictionary* have several different parts. All these parts are designed to make the meaning of a word as clear and exact as possible.

The definition is the second section of the entry. It comes after the entry word, the pronunciation, the part of speech, and the different forms of the entry word.

ca·boose |kə bōos′| —*noun, plural* **cabooses** The last car on a freight train. The train crew can eat and sleep in the caboose.

The first part of a definition is always a short sentence or phrase. This tells you in clear, simple language what you need to know about a word. With some words, such as *caboose*, there is a second sentence that gives you more information.

Synonyms Many words can be explained easily in just a sentence or phrase. But for some words the dictionary also gives you other kinds of information to help you understand the meaning. You will see that in some definitions the sentence or phrase is followed by one or more single words.

heap |hēp| —*noun, plural* **heaps** A collection of things lying or thrown together; pile: *a rubbish heap.*

The single word that you find in a definition is called a *synonym*. A synonym is a word that has almost the same meaning as another word. In this definition *heap* and *pile* are synonyms. They mean almost the same thing.

Synonyms are very helpful when you look up a word. Most of the time the synonym will be a word you already know. This can help you to understand the meaning of the word you are checking.

Synonyms can also be helpful when you write. You can use a synonym to say something in a different way so that you do not have to use the same word over and over. For example, you could say "There is a heap of leaves in the yard" or "There is a pile of leaves in the yard."

Words That Have More Than One Meaning   There are a lot of words that can mean many different things. For example, there are six meanings for the adjective *mad* and twenty-five meanings for the verb *take*. When a word has more than one meaning, the different definitions are numbered.

> **flash** |flăsh| —*verb* **flashed, flashing 1.** To burst or cause to burst suddenly into light or flame: *The bulb in the camera flashed. The ship flashed its signal lights.* **2.** To appear suddenly or only for a short time: *An idea flashed in his mind.* **3.** To be lighted on and off: *The lighthouse flashed in the distance.* **4.** To move rapidly: *A car flashed by.*

Often the meaning you are looking for will be listed first. But always read through all the different meanings to make sure you find the one you want.

Practice

Copy these sentences. In each sentence look up the word printed in dark letters. After the sentence write the number of the definition that fits the sentence.

1. You should drink the orange juice because it's **healthy**.
2. I made a **note** of what I was supposed to do, but I lost it.
3. Jane isn't very **practical** with money.
4. We have **lived** in Chicago for ten years.
5. I'm **free** for two hours after school.

Examples in Definitions   Have you ever skated on roller skates? You probably know that a roller skate is a metal device with four wheels on the bottom that you attach to your shoe. The wheels roll over a hard surface, so you can "skate" or "glide" down a street or sidewalk. But even if you know this, you don't really know how it feels to roller-skate until you have done it.

Words work the same way. You can understand many words better if you see them used in a sentence. In fact, you already know a lot of words that you learned by hearing people use them. Suppose you heard this sentence: "The heavy wheels of the wagon left deep grooves in the earth." You might not know the word *groove*. But you can figure out from the sentence that a groove is a long, narrow cut.

It is easy to see how helpful examples can be when you are trying to understand the meaning of a word. Look at the following definitions. The examples have been taken out.

> **fraud** |frôd| —*noun, plural* **frauds** **1.** A dishonest act in which someone is cheated . . . **2.** . . .
> **el·o·quent** |ĕl′ə kwənt| —*adjective* Using words well and effectively . . .
> **a·bout** |ə bout′| —*preposition* **1.** Of or having to do with; concerning . . . **2.** Near in time to; close to . . . **3.** All around . . . **4.** Around in . . .
> **if** |ĭf| —*conjunction* **1.** On the condition that . . . **2.** Supposing that; in case that . . . **3.** Whether . . . **4.** Even though . . .

Some of these words you may never have seen before. Others may be words you see all the time. But all of them can be difficult to understand even though you have the definitions. You will probably understand their meanings right away, however, when you read the examples that go with them. Here are the complete entries.

> **fraud** |frôd| —*noun, plural* **frauds** **1.** A dishonest act in which someone is cheated: *The businessman was accused of fraud when the car he sold us wouldn't run.* . . . **2.** . . .
> **el·o·quent** |ĕl′ə kwənt| —*adjective* Using words well and effectively: *an eloquent speaker.*
> **a·bout** |ə bout′| —*preposition* **1.** Of or having to do with; concerning: *She wrote many stories about animals.* **2.** Near in time to; close to: *I will leave about noon.* **3.** All around: *Look about you before dark for a good campsite.* **4.** Around in: *We saw a bear prowling about the woods.*
> **if** |ĭf| —*conjunction* **1.** On the condition that: *I will come only if you do.* **2.** Supposing that; in case that: *Even if his story is true, what can we do about it?* **3.** Whether: *I wonder if she is coming.* **4.** Even though: *This is a useless if interesting gadget.*

By reading these definitions with the examples you should be able to understand the meanings more easily. You may have noticed that you already knew what some of these words mean. You probably use the words *about* and *if* every day. The examples in this dictionary can help you learn because they are written as people speak. They can also show you how much you already know about certain words and how to use them.

Phrases in Entries

In addition to the entry words, certain kinds of special phrases are defined in the *Beginning Dictionary*. One of these is a verb phrase in which the meaning of the phrase cannot be figured out from knowing the meanings of each of the words that make up the phrase. Suppose you read this sentence: "Gary looks up to his older sister." This does not mean that Gary is small and has to lift his head up when he speaks to his sister. The phrase *look up to* means "to admire and respect." Phrases like this are called *phrasal verbs*.

The first word in a phrasal verb is always the verb, and the phrasal verb is listed under the main-entry word for that verb. The phrasal verb *look up to* is listed under the verb *look*. But phrasal verbs have their own definitions. Phrasal verbs are entered right after all the definitions of the main-entry verb. First, the words *phrasal verb* are printed in dark italics. These words are followed by the phrase itself, which is printed in dark letters. Then a sentence or phrase explains its meaning or meanings.

> **pol·ish** |pŏl′ish| —*verb* **polished, polishing** To make or become smooth and shiny, especially by rubbing with a special substance: *Polish your shoes. The new car polishes easily.*
>   **Phrasal verb polish off** To finish or use up something quickly: *We polished off our dinner in ten minutes.*
> —*noun, plural* **polishes 1.** A substance that is rubbed on the surface of something to make it smooth and shiny: *shoe polish; silver polish.* **2.** A smooth and shiny surface; a shine: *The kitchen floor has a bright polish.*

Practice

Copy these phrasal verbs. Look them up. After each phrase write down the verb you looked up to find the meaning of the phrase.

1. **get away with**
2. **make up**
3. **give away**
4. **blow up**

Phrases That Do Not Mean What They Say

Many phrases do not mean what they seem to say. That is, the meaning of the phrase is different from the sum of the meanings of the words in the phrase. Suppose someone tells you a story: Two brothers were having an argument over who was going to use the bicycle. Jim lost his head and punched his little brother.

pssst! over here!

You know that the phrase *lose one's head* does not mean what the separate words mean. Jim's head did not fall off. And Jim did not take his head off and forget where he put it. The phrase means that Jim got so angry that he did something foolish. To *lose one's head* means "to lose one's composure or calm." A phrase like this is called an *idiom*.

All idioms in this dictionary are listed under the entry word of the most important word in the phrase. You will find the definition of *lose one's head* under the entry word *head*. Every idiom has its own definition. All idiom definitions are listed at the very end of an entry, after all the other parts of the entry.

The definition of an idiom is set up like this. First, the word *idiom* is printed in dark italics. It is followed by the phrase itself, which is printed in dark letters. The idiom is then defined like all other words. It has a sentence or phrase that explains its meaning. Many idioms have examples.

> **blue** | blōo | —*noun, plural* **blues** The color of the sky on a clear day. Blue, red, and green are called primary colors.
>   *Idiom* **out of the blue** Suddenly and at an unexpected time or place: *We were in a strange town when out of the blue we met an old friend.*

Practice

Copy these idioms. Look them up. After each idiom write down the word you looked up to find the meaning of the idiom.

1. **make fun of**
2. **close call**
3. **up in the air**
4. **on pins and needles**
5. **as the crow flies**

Words That Sound Alike

One of the things that can be confusing about language is that there are words that are spelled differently but that sound the same — for example, *son* and *sun*; *right* and *write*; *to, too,* and *two.*

All the words that sound like an entry word are listed at the very end of the entry. They have a black diamond (♦) in front of them to let you know that there is another word or words that sound like the entry word. The entry word and the word or words that sound like it are all printed in dark letters.

heir |âr| —*noun, plural* **heirs** Someone who gets the money, property, or title of another person after that person dies.
♦ *These sound alike* **heir, air.**
air |âr| —*noun, plural* **airs** **1.** The mixture of gases around the earth. . . . **2.** . . .
♦ *These sound alike* **air, heir.**

Parts of Words That Are Used to Make Other Words

Two other kinds of entries are listed in the *Beginning Dictionary.* These are parts of words that are added to other words in order to make new words. The word *unfriendly* is made by adding the beginning *un-* to the word *friendly.* The word *quickly* is made by adding the ending *-ly* to the word *quick.* A beginning that is added to a word is called a *prefix.* An ending that is added to a word is called a *suffix.* The different prefixes and suffixes are listed in the dictionary like this:

pre- A prefix that means "before": *prehistoric.*
-ness A suffix that forms nouns. The suffix "-ness" means "a state, condition, or quality": *kindness; politeness; rudeness.*

It is important to know about prefixes and suffixes because

we use them all the time to make new words. In fact, so many words are made by adding prefixes or suffixes to other words that if all the new words were listed in the dictionary, the book would be twice as big as it is.

What do you do if you read a word like *builder* and you can't find it in the dictionary? Since you will find the word *build,* you then look up the suffix *-er.*

build | bĭld | —*verb* **built, building 1.** To make or form something by putting parts or materials together; construct; erect. **2.** . . .

-er² A suffix that forms nouns: *eraser; foreigner; maker; photographer.*

By reading both of these definitions you will figure out that a builder is a person who makes or constructs things.

Practice

A. Copy the words below each prefix. Then add the prefix to the words and see what new words are made.

un-	pre-
1. happy	1. pay
2. wrap	2. historic
3. likely	3. fabricate
4. lucky	4. cook
5. cover	5. date

B. Copy the words below each suffix. Then add the suffix to the words and see what new words are made.

-ment	-ly
1. govern	1. brave
2. arrange	2. cautious
3. enjoy	3. quiet
4. require	4. pleasant
5. excite	5. rough

Pictures in Definitions

A dictionary is a book about words. It uses words to explain other words. But sometimes, no matter how well a word is described, a picture can tell you more.

puf·fin |pŭf'ĭn| —*noun, plural* **puffins** A sea bird of northern regions. The puffin has a plump body, black and white feathers, and a heavy, brightly colored bill.

The definition of *puffin* tells you what it is, what it looks like, and where it lives. There are, however, many birds with black and white feathers and a colored bill. You can get a much better idea of what a puffin looks like if you look at the picture after you read the definition.

A picture can help explain what something does or what it looks like. There are more than fifteen hundred pictures in the *Beginning Dictionary*. These are photographs and drawings in color and in black and white that were created especially for this dictionary.

The Pronunciation Key

Long ago words were spelled the way they were spoken. Each letter of the alphabet stood for a different sound. A person could figure out how to say a word from the way it was spelled.

Many words in English are still spelled with letters that stand for their sounds. You know that just about any word that begins with the letter *b* will have the same beginning sound that you can hear in the word *bib*. But many other words no longer have such a simple spelling. Their pronunciations have changed over the years, but their spelling has not. The spelling of words like *tough, thought,* and *though* no longer tells us enough about how they are pronounced. This is no problem for words you already know how to say, but sometimes you will see a word that is new to you. Your dictionary can tell you how to pronounce it.

In order to show how words are pronounced, your dictionary uses a special spelling system. This system uses letters of the alphabet and other special symbols to stand for the sounds in each word. The system looks a little complicated at first, but it's really quite simple. You may even find it easier to learn than the regular spelling system.

A special spelling, called the *pronunciation*, is used at almost every entry in the dictionary to show how each word is pronounced. The pronunciation comes between two heavy black lines, like this:

dic·tion·ar·y |dĭk′shə nĕr′ē|

All of the letters and symbols of the pronunciation system are shown together in the *pronunciation key*. The pronunciation key shows the letter or symbol for each sound in English. And for each sound you will find one or more *key words*. The key words are ones that you should know very well. Since you already know how to say them, the key words can show you how to say the sounds in the pronunciation key.

ă	pat	ĕ	pet	î	fierce
ā	pay	ē	be	ŏ	pot
â	care	ĭ	pit	ō	go
ä	father	ī	pie	ô	paw, for
oi	oil	ŭ	cut	zh	vision
o͝o	book	û	fur	ə	ago, item,
o͞o	boot	*th*	the		pencil, atom,
yo͞o	abuse	th	thin		circus
ou	out	hw	which	ər	butter

Consonants   Most of the consonant letters stand for just one consonant sound. You have nothing really new to learn about them. These are the consonants that are used in the pronunciations:

b d f g h j k l m n p r s t v w y z

There are some two-letter combinations that are also very familiar:

ch   sh   th

You can see that you already know a lot about the pronunciation key, especially about consonants. In fact, there are only four more consonant sounds you have to learn about:

hw   as in **wh**ich   *th*   as in bo**th**er and **th**is
ng   as in thi**ng**   zh   as in gara**g**e, plea**s**ure, and vi**s**ion

Practice

A. Listed below are the letters used in the pronunciation key for some of the consonant sounds. Write each letter and after it write a word that begins with the sound it stands for. Use the pronunciation key if you need help.

1. b	6. h	11. n	16. v
2. ch	7. j	12. p	17. w
3. d	8. k	13. r	18. y
4. f	9. l	14. s	19. z
5. g	10. m	15. t	20. hw

B. Copy these words. Say each one to yourself. Decide which letter in the pronunciation key stands for the beginning sound. Write that letter next to the word. Use the pronunciation key to help you decide.

1. civil	6. church
2. phonograph	7. money
3. bunch	8. giggle
4. gem	9. chorus
5. cover	10. jam

Vowels   Only five vowel letters are used in regular spelling: *a, e, i, o,* and *u*. Your dictionary shows the many vowel sounds of English by using just the five vowel letters from the alphabet along with some marks over the letters. These marks show short and long vowel sounds, and vowel sounds with *r*.

Letters for short vowel sounds have a curved line over them:

ă ĕ ĭ ŏ ŭ

If you say the key words, you can hear that all the vowel sounds in them are short: *pat, pet, pit, pot, cut*.

The letters for long vowel sounds all have a straight line over them:

ā ē ī ō

These are the same sounds you would use to name the vowel letters when you recite the alphabet. Say the key words and listen for the long vowels: *pay, be, pie, go*.

When the *r* sound follows some vowel sounds, the vowel sound is neither long nor short. To show this your dictionary uses a bent line over the vowel letter:

â î ô û

Listen for the vowel sounds as you say these key words: *care, fierce, for, fur.* The ô is also used for the vowel sound you hear in *paw.*

Just one letter in the pronunciation key has dots over it. The ä stands for the sound you hear for the *a* in *father.*

Two vowel sounds are shown as double vowel letters:

ŏŏ o͞o

The vowel sounds are the ones you hear in *book* and *boot.* The o͞o is also used with *y* for yo͞o, the sound you hear for the *u* in *abuse.*

The letters *oi* and *ou* are used for the sounds they most commonly stand for. You can hear them in the key words, *oil* and *out.*

Practice

Write the numbers 1 to 10 on your paper. Read each question. Beside each number write the letter of the correct answer. The letters and symbols from the pronunciation key will help you find the answers.

1. Which word means "a grassy place"?

   a. lôn   b. lōn   c. lēn

2. Which of these is a large body of water?

   a. līk   b. lăk   c. lāk

3. Which of these would you wear on your head?

   a. kŭp   b. kăp   c. kāp

4. Which of these can you ride on?

   a. bāk   b. bīk   c. bēk

5. What is the opposite of *near*?

   a. fär   b. fîr   c. fâr

6. What is the opposite of *girl*?

   a. bou   b. boi   c. bo͞o

7. Which word names a large animal?

   a. bâr   b. bär   c. bûr

8. What is the opposite of *empty*?

   a. foil   b. foul   c. fo͞ol

9. Which of these is a kind of weapon?

   a. spîr   b. spâr   c. spûr

10. What connects your head to the rest of your body?

   a. nŏk   b. nĭk   c. nĕk

Schwa   When a vowel sound falls in a syllable that has no stress, it is often very hard to tell it apart from other vowel sounds. To show this your dictionary uses a symbol that looks like an upside-down *e* and is called a *schwa:* ə . You can hear the ə used for *a* in *ago, e* in *item, i* in *pencil, o* in *atom,* and *u* in *circus.*

When an *r* sound follows a vowel in a syllable that has no stress, the schwa is followed by *r.* Listen for it in the last syllable of *butter.*

Practice

Copy these words. Look them up and copy their pronunciations. Then circle each schwa you see in the pronunciations you copied.

1. parlor
2. centipede
3. brilliant
4. surface
5. imagination
6. babble
7. circus
8. bachelor
9. radius
10. blossom

Stress   When a word has more than one syllable, one of the syllables is usually spoken more loudly than the others. The louder syllable is called the *stressed syllable.* In your diction-

ary stressed syllables are shown by a heavy, dark accent mark
(′) following the stressed syllable. The syllable itself is also
shown in heavy, dark letters:

bat·tle |băt′l|

in·struct |ĭn strŭkt′|

Some longer words have one or more syllables that are
louder than the rest of the word but not as loud as the stressed
syllable. These words are shown with a lighter accent mark (′):

rep·re·sent |rĕp′rĭ zĕnt′|

Practice

A. Copy these words. Look up each word
   and then write the number of syllables
   it has.

1. jump
2. parasol
3. bachelor
4. excellent
5. moon
6. opposite
7. umbrella
8. tiger
9. buffalo
10. thorough
11. dolphin
12. thought
13. anteater
14. boomerang
15. tyrannosaur

B. Following are some words and their pronunciations. Copy
   them exactly as you see them. Then look up the words to
   find where the accents should go. Put the accents in the
   pronunciations you have written. Draw a line under the
   syllable that has the strongest stress. That syllable is
   printed in heavy, dark type in your dictionary.

1. **mystery**   mĭs tə rē
2. **intimidate**   ĭn tĭm ĭ dāt
3. **biscuit**   bĭs kĭt
4. **ordinary**   ôr dn ĕr ē
5. **preserve**   prĭ zûrv

Variations in Pronunciation   For some entry words two or
more pronunciations are given. While the first one is usually
the most common one, all are correct.

bath |băth| or |bäth|

Using a pronunciation key does not mean that everyone

must talk alike or that there is only one correct way to say each word. When you say one of the key words, you are using your own way of talking, not someone else's. And since the key words are your guide to how words in the dictionary are pronounced, you will naturally pronounce any word in your own way. Educated people from different parts of the country speak in different ways that are correct for them, and they will say the key words in ways that are correct for them.

A Smaller Pronunciation Key A shorter form of the pronunciation key appears on every left-hand page of the dictionary.

The Spelling Table

To look up a word that you don't know how to spell, you use the spelling table found on pages **B-40−B-43**. As you have read before, there are about forty sounds we use when we speak. The spelling table shows you all the different ways these sounds can be spelled when they are used in words.

Suppose someone told you that she had seen a *llama* at the zoo. You don't know what kind of animal a llama is and want to look it up in the dictionary. But you have only heard the word and don't know how to spell it. Since the first sound is *l*, you might look it up under such spellings as *lama* or *lahma*. You would still not find the word.

If you look in the spelling table, you will find that words beginning with an *l* sound can be spelled *l* or *ll*. If you check under these spellings, you will find *llama*.

Practice

These words are spelled wrong in at least two places. They might be the spellings you would think of if you had just heard the words. You won't find them in the dictionary because their spellings are so far from the correct ones. Use the spelling table to help you find the words in your dictionary. Then write the words, correcting all of the parts that are not spelled correctly.

1. terradactil   2. tiranosour   3. dynosore
4. Phairlnheight   5. pherit

Pronunciation Key

ă	rat
ā	aid, pay
â	air, care, wear
ä	father
b	bib
ch	church
d	deed
ĕ	pet, pleasure
ē	be, bee, easy, leisure

f	fast, fife, off, phrase, rough
g	gag
h	hat

hw	which
ĭ	pit
ī	by, pie
î	dear, deer, fierce, mere

j	judge
k	cat, kick

kw	choir, quick
l	lid, needle
m	am, man

n	**n**o, sudde**n**
ng	thi**ng**
ŏ	h**o**rrible, p**o**t
ō	g**o**, r**ow**, t**oe**
ô	**a**lter, c**au**ght, f**o**r, p**aw**
oi	b**oy**, n**oi**se, **oi**l
ou	c**ow**, **ou**t

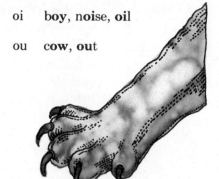

ŏŏ	t**oo**k
ōō	b**oo**t, fr**ui**t

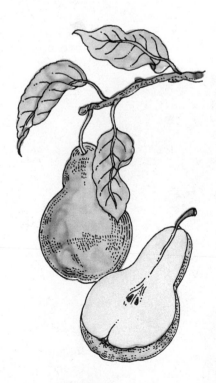

p	**p**o**p**
r	**r**oa**r**
s	mi**ss**, **s**au**c**e, **s**ee
sh	di**sh**, **sh**ip
t	**t**igh**t**
th	pa**th**, **th**in
th	ba**th**e, **th**is
ŭ	c**u**t, r**ou**gh
û	c**i**rcle, f**i**rm, h**ea**rd, t**e**rm, t**u**rn, **u**rge, w**o**rd
v	ca**v**e, **v**al**v**e, **v**ine
w	**w**ith
y	**y**es
yōō	ab**u**se, **u**se
z	ro**s**e, **s**i**z**e, **x**ylophone, **z**ebra

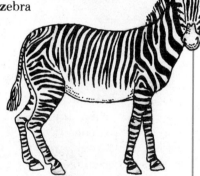

zh	gara**g**e, plea**s**ure, vi**s**ion
ə	**a**bout, sil**e**nt, penc**i**l, lem**o**n, circ**u**s
ər	butt**er**

Stress
Shown by accent marks ′ and ′
and by heavy, dark letters.

dic·tion·ar·y |dĭk′shə ner′ē|

Spelling Table

Sound and Key Word	Spelling	Sample Words
ă pat	a ai al au	pat plaid calf, half, salve laugh
ā aid	a ai	mane aid
	au ay e ea ei eig eigh et ey	gauge clay, day suede break, great reindeer, veil reign eight, neighbor bouquet obey, they
â air	ae ai ay e ea ei	aerosol air, fair prayer there, where bear, pear heir, their
ä father	a ah	father ah

Sound and Key Word	Spelling	Sample Words
	al e ea	calm, palm sergeant heart, hearth
b bib	b bb pb	bib blubber, cabbage cupboard, raspberry
ch church	c ch tch ti tu	cello church batch, stitch question, suggestion nature, pasture
d deed	d ed dd	deed mailed bladder, saddle
ĕ pet	a ae ai ay e ea ei eo ie u	any, many aesthetic again, said says pet measure, thread heifer leopard friend burial

Sound and Key Word	Spelling	Sample Words
ē be	ay	quay
	e	be
	ea	beach, leap
	ee	beet, meek
	ei	receive
	eo	people
	ey	key, monkey
	i	piano
	ie	believe, fiend
	oe	amoeba
	y	comedy, quality
f fast	f	fast
	ff	stiff, sniffle
	gh	enough, trough
	lf	calf, half
	ph	alphabet, graph
g gag	g	gag
	gg	bragged, sluggish
	gh	ghost
	gu	guess, guest
	gue	catalogue
h hat	h	hat
	wh	who

Sound and Key Word	Spelling	Sample Words
hw which		which, when
ĭ pit	a	certificate, village
	e	enough, recite
	ee	been
	i	pit
	ia	carriage, marriage
	ie	sieve
	o	women
	u	busy
	ui	built
	y	mystery, symbol
ī pie	ai	aisle
	ay	bayou
	ei	height
	ey	eye
	i	kite
	ie	die, lie, tie
	igh	right, sigh, thigh
	is	island
	uy	buy
	y	sky, try
	ye	rye
î dear	e	cereal, here, series
	ca	clear, ear, smear
	ee	beer, steer
	ei	weird
	ie	pier
j judge	d	graduate, individual
	dg	judgment, lodging
	di	soldier
	dj	adjective
	g	agitate, gem
	ge	revenge
	gg	exaggerate
	j	judge, jar
k kick	c	call, copy
	cc	account, succotash
	ch	schedule, school
	ck	crack, package
	cqu	lacquer
	cu	biscuit, circuit
	k	kick

Sound and Key Word	Spelling	Sample Words
	lk	talk, walk
	qu	quay
	que	plaque
kw quick	ch	choir
	cqu	acquaint
	qu	quick
l lid	l	lid
	ll	llama, tall
m am	lm	balm, calm
	m	am
	mb	dumb
	mm	hammer, mammoth
	mn	autumn, hymn
n no	gn	align, gnat
	kn	knee, knife
	n	no
	nn	inn, banner
	pn	pneumonia
ng thing	n	anchor, ink
	ng	thing
	ngue	tongue
ŏ pot	a	waffle, watch
	ho	honest
	o	pot
ō go	eau	bureau
	ew	sew
	o	go
	oa	croak, foam
	oe	foe
	oh	oh
	oo	brooch
	ou	boulder, shoulder
	ough	dough, thorough
	ow	crow, low
	owe	owe
ô for, paw	a	all, water
	al	balk, talk, walk
	ah	Utah
	as	Arkansas
	au	caught, daughter
	aw	awful, awning
	o	for
	oa	broad, oar

Sound and Key Word	Spelling	Sample Words
	ough	brought, thought
oi boy	oy	boy, royal
ou cow	au	sauerkraut
	hou	hour
	ou	out
	ough	bough
	ow	cow, fowl
o͝o took	o	woman, wolf
	oo	took, book
	ou	could, should, would
	u	bush, full
o͞o boot	eu	maneuver
	ew	drew, flew
	ieu	lieutenant
	o	do, move, two
	oe	canoe
	oo	boot
	ou	group, soup
	ough	through
	u	prudence, rude
	ue	blue
	ui	bruise, fruit
p pop	p	pop
	pp	happy
r roar	r	roar
	rh	rhythm
	rr	cherry, marriage
	wr	wrinkle, write

Sound and Key Word	Spelling	Sample Words
s **see**	c ce ps s sc ss sth	**c**ellar, **c**ent practi**ce**, sau**ce** **ps**alm, **ps**ychology bu**s**, **s**ee fa**sc**inate, **sc**ene la**ss**, pa**ss** i**sth**mus
sh **ship**	ce ch ci s sc sh si ss ti	o**ce**an **ch**andelier musi**ci**an, spe**ci**al **s**ugar, **s**ure con**sc**ience di**sh**, **sh**ip pen**si**on mi**ss**ion, ti**ss**ue elec**ti**on, na**ti**on
t **tight**	ed ght pt t th tt tw	bump**ed**, crash**ed**, stopp**ed** bou**ght**, cau**ght** **pt**armigan, **pt**erodactyl **t**igh**t** **th**yme be**tt**er, le**tt**uce **tw**o
th **thin**	th	pa**th**, **th**in
th **this**	th the	**th**is, **th**at, o**th**er ba**the**
ŭ cut	o oe oo ou u	inc**o**me, s**o**me, s**o**n d**oe**s bl**oo**d, fl**oo**d c**ou**ple, tr**ou**ble c**u**t
yo͞o **use**	eau eu ew iew u ue you yu	b**eau**tiful f**eu**d f**ew**, p**ew**ter v**iew** ab**u**se, **u**se c**ue** **you** **yu**le
û **turn**	ear er	**ear**n, l**ear**n c**er**tain, f**er**n

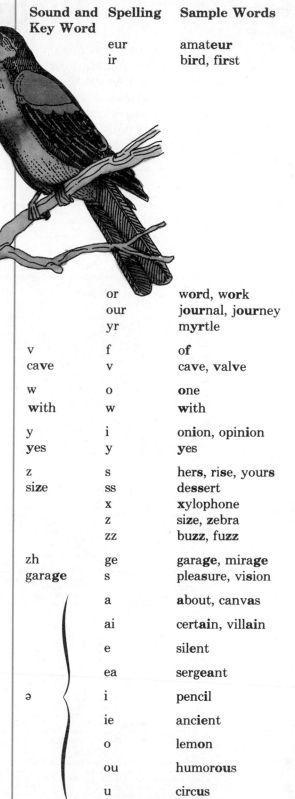

Sound and Key Word	Spelling	Sample Words
	eur ir	amat**eur** b**ir**d, f**ir**st
	or our yr	w**or**d, w**or**k j**our**nal, j**our**ney m**yr**tle
v cave	f v	o**f** **c**a**v**e, **v**al**v**e
w **with**	o w	**o**ne **w**ith
y **yes**	i y	on**i**on, op**i**nion **y**es
z size	s ss x z zz	her**s**, ri**s**e, your**s** de**ss**ert **x**ylophone **s**ize, **z**ebra bu**zz**, fu**zz**
zh **garage**	ge s	gara**ge**, mira**ge** plea**s**ure, vi**s**ion
ə	a ai e ea i ie o ou u	**a**bout, canv**a**s cert**ai**n, vill**ai**n sil**e**nt serg**ea**nt penc**i**l anc**ie**nt lem**o**n humor**ou**s circ**u**s

Picture Credits

The following list of credits includes the names of organizations and individuals who helped secure illustrations for this dictionary. The editors wish to thank all of them—as well as others not specifically mentioned—for their assistance. The credits are arranged alphabetically by entry word, which is printed in boldface type. In those cases where two or more illustrations are credited for the same entry word, dashes are used to separate them sequentially from top to bottom. The abbreviations BTA, MFA, and LC stand for, respectively, the British Tourist Authority, the Museum of Fine Arts, Boston, and the Library of Congress.

abacus Allen J. Smith; **abbey** BTA; **aborigine** LC; **academy** U.S. Military Academy; **accessory** Oster; **accordion** M. Hohner, Inc.; **acrobat** Ringling Brothers and Barnum & Bailey Circus; **actor** and **actress** Martha Swope; **agile** Cary Wolinsky, Stock, Boston; **agriculture** USDA, Soil Conservation Service; **Airedale** Evelyn M. Shafer; **airplane** Boeing Photo; **akimbo** Ron Schick; **altar** George Robinson, Carmel Mission; **ambulance** Allen J. Smith; **amphitheater** Mount Holyoke College; **anchor** U.S. Navy; **andirons** MFA, Boston; **antique** MFA, Boston; **anvil** *Steelways,* American Iron and Steel Institute; **apparatus** Jean-Claude Lejeune, Stock, Boston; **appliance** Oster; **apron** MFA, Boston; **aqueduct** French Government Tourist Office; **arch** Convention and Visitors Board of Greater St. Louis—French Government Tourist Office; **arena** Spanish National Tourist Office; **armor** MFA, Boston; **assassination** LC; **assortment** BTA; **astride** Jon Chase; **astronaut** NASA; **athlete** Jon Chase; **atomic bomb** U.S. Air Force; **auction** Sotheby Parke Bernet, Inc., New York; **audience** Chicago Symphony Orchestra; **automobile** LC; **aviator** LC; **awl** Stanley Tools.

backpack George Bellerose, Stock, Boston; **backhand** Peter Southwick, Stock, Boston; **backboard** Medford High *Mustang News;* **banjo** Allen J. Smith; **barge** F. D. Perdue, Republic Steel Corp.; **barn** Webb Photos; **baseball** Medford High *Mustang News;* **bassoon** Ron Schick; **battlement** BTA; **battleship** U.S. Navy; **bayonet** U.S. Navy; **beard** LC; **bell** Philadelphia Convention and Visitors Bureau; **bench** Medford High *Mustang News;* **berth** Japan Air Lines; **beret** U.S. Navy; **bicycle** AMF Inc.; **binoculars** Frank Siteman; **bit** Stanley Tools; **bleachers** Medford High *Mustang News;* **blimp** Goodyear Tire & Rubber Company; **blindfold** Ron Schick; **bloodhound** Evelyn M. Shafer; **blowtorch** Bettmann Archives; **boar** USDA; **bog** Ocean Spray Cranberries, Inc.; **boll weevil** USDA; **bongo drums** George Cohen, Stock, Boston; **bonnet** National Gallery of Art, Index of American Design; **booth** AT&T; **bottle** The Coca-Cola Company; **bow**[1] AMF Inc.; **boxcar** Union Pacific Railroad; **boxer**[2] Evelyn M. Shafer; **brace** Peter Vandermark, Stock, Boston; **Braille** John Urban; **brave** LC; **bread** Frank Siteman; **breaker** Medford High *Mustang News;* **breeches** LC; **bridge** George Cooper, State of New Hampshire—Elizabeth Hamlin, Stock, Boston; **brooch** DeScenza Diamonds, Boston; **Brownie** Mary Hale, Girl Scouts of America; **buckle** Frank Siteman; **Buddha** Information Service of India; **bulldog** Evelyn M. Shafer; **bulldozer** International Harvester; **bullfight** Bettmann Archives; **burro** LC; **bust** MFA, Boston.

cable car Swiss National Tourist Office; **calculator** Hewlett-Packard; **camper** Winnebago Industries, Inc.; **candlestick** MFA, Boston; **cannon** U.S. Military Academy; **canoe** Great Canadian; **cap** Jon Chase; **capitol** LC; **car** LC—Pullman Standard—Allen J. Smith; **cart** Staten Island Historical Society; **cartwheel** Allen J. Smith; **castle** French Government Tourist Office—Donald Dietz, Stock, Boston; **cat** Allen J. Smith; **catcher** Boston Red Sox; **cavern** National Park Service; **cello** Ron Schick; **cent** Chase Manhattan Bank, New York—Allen J. Smith; **chain** Allen J. Smith; **chair** MFA, Boston; **chandelier** Old North Church, Boston; **chariot** Metropolitan Museum of Art, New York; **charm** MFA, Boston; **cheerleader** Jon Chase; **chef** Jon Chase; **chicken** Cary Wolinsky, Stock, Boston; **chin** Ron Schick; **chisel** Stanley Tools; **choir** Ellis Herwig, Stock, Boston; **chopsticks** Allen J. Smith; **chorus** Martha Swope, N.Y. Shakespeare Festival; **Christmas tree** Allen J. Smith; **church** Samuel Chamberlain; **churn** Old Sturbridge Village, Mass.; **circus** Ringling Brothers and Barnum & Bailey Circus; **clamp** Stanley Tools; **clarinet** Ron Schick; **class** Bohdan J. Hrynewych, Stock, Boston; **claw hammer** Stanley Tools; **cleaver** R. H. Forschner Co.; **cliff** BTA; **clock** Sony; **clown** Ringling Brothers and Barnum & Bailey Circus; **coach** BTA; **coin** Chase Manhattan Bank, New York; **college** Bradford F. Herzog, Wellesley College; **collie** Evelyn M. Shafer; **column** Italian Government Tourist Office; **combine** International Harvester; **comet** NASA; **comic** United Features Syndicate, Inc.; **common** Allen J. Smith; **compass** Allen J. Smith; **competitor** Jeff Albertson, Stock, Boston; **computer** Digital Equipment Corp.; **concert** Chicago Symphony Orchestra; **conductor** Chicago Symphony Orchestra—Jon Chase; **Confederate** LC; **Congress** Keith Jewell; **console**[2] Sony; **constable** BTA; **construction** Peter Vandermark, Stock, Boston; **contact lens** Bausch & Lomb Soflens Division; **control tower** Allen J. Smith; **convention** UPI; **convertible** Museum of Transportation, Brookline, Mass.—Cadillac Motor Car Division; **coronation** Wide World Photos; **corral** Montana Chamber of Commerce; **costume** Allen J. Smith; **counter**[1] Allen J. Smith; **courthouse** Allen J. Smith; **courtroom** Ellis Herwig, Stock, Boston; **covered wagon** LC; **cowboy** Standard Oil Co.; **cradle** MFA, Boston; **crater** NASA; **crossbow** Metropolitan Museum of Art, New York; **crossword puzzle** Allen J. Smith; **crown** BTA; **crow's-nest** U.S. Navy; **cruiser** Allen J. Smith; **Cub Scout** Peter Southwick, Stock, Boston; **cultivate** International Harvester; **cup** Owen Franken, Stock, Boston; **currency** Steve Potter, Stock, Boston; **curve** Dept. of Transportation, Washington, D.C.; **cymbal** Ron Schick.

dachshund Evelyn M. Shafer; **dagger** Metropolitan Museum of Art, New York; **Dalmatian** Evelyn M. Shafer; **daring** Wide World Photos; **dashboard** Allen J. Smith; **debate** LC; **decanter** Waterford Glass, Inc.; **deck** U.S. Navy; **Declaration of Independence** LC; **decoration** LC; **decoy** L. L. Bean Co.; **Democratic Party** UPI; **demonstration** National Archives; **dentist** Elizabeth Hamlin, Stock, Boston; **department store** Allen J. Smith; **depot** Union Pacific Railroad; **derrick** Mobil Oil Corp.; **desert**[1] Union Pacific Railroad; **desk** Donald Dietz, Stock, Boston; **destroyer** U.S. Navy; **destruction** U.S. Army; **development** Peter Vandermark, Stock, Boston; **dial** AT&T; **diamond** Boston Red Sox; **diner** Allen J. Smith; **diploma** Jonathan Rawle, Stock, Boston; **disc jockey** Allen J. Smith; **dish** MFA, Boston; **dishwasher** Allen J. Smith; **display** BTA; **distort** Philip Kimball—Jon Chase; **diver** Peter Shaw, New England Divers Inc.; **Doberman pinscher** Evelyn M. Shafer; **dome** State House Library, Boston; **drawbridge** BTA; **dribble** Boston Celtics; **driftwood** George Bellerose, Stock, Boston; **drill** Allen J. Smith; **drum major** Owen Franken, Stock, Boston; **drum majorette** News & Information Service, University of Texas; **duck**[1] Allen J. Smith; **dugout** Boston Red Sox; **dump** Jon Chase; **dune** Cape Cod Chamber of Commerce; **dust** LC.

earphone AT&T; **earthquake** LC; **eclipse** NASA; **egg**[1] Patricia Hollander Gross, Stock, Boston; **embankment** Cape Cod Chamber of Commerce; **embassy** U.S. State Dept.; **emergency** D.C. Fire Dept., Washington; **emigrant** LC; **engrave** MFA, Boston; **equipment** Walter Hendricks; **eraser** Ron Schick; **Eskimo** Alaska Historical Society; **estate** John T. Hopf, courtesy of Newport County Chamber of Commerce; **excavate** USDA, Soil Conservation Service; **exchange** LC; **exercise** Frank Siteman, Stock, Boston—Cliff Garboden, Stock, Boston; **exhibit** UPI; **expedition** UPI; **exploit** UPI; **explorer** UPI; **expressway** Dept. of Transportation, Washington, D.C.; **extinguisher** Allen J. Smith.

factory Hershey Foods Corp.; **falls** National Park Service, Yosemite National Park; **fife** Peter Southwick, Stock, Boston; **fire escape** Allen J. Smith; **firefighter** Jon Chase; **flipper** Peter Shaw, New England Divers Inc.; **flood** USDA, Soil Conservation Service; **flute** Ron Schick; **foil**[3] Bruce Repko, Salle d'Armes Richards Fencing Club, Watertown, Mass.; **font** MFA, Boston; **football** Jeff Adler, Medford High *Mustang News;* **forehand** Christopher Morrow, Stock, Boston; **forge**[1] Old Sturbridge Village, Mass.; **fort** LC; **fossil** American Museum of Natural History; **fountain** The White House; **framework** Allen J. Smith; **French horn** Ron Schick; **funnel** United States Lines.

gable House of the Seven Gables, Salem, Mass.; **galaxy** Hale Observatories; **gem** DeScenza Diamonds, Boston; **generator** Ellis Herwig, Stock, Boston; **German shepherd** Evelyn M. Shafer; **geyser** National Park Service, Yellowstone National Park; **glacier** Alaska State Library; **glider** John Gussman, Uniphoto; **glove** Spalding; **goblet** Waterford Glass, Inc.; **gorilla** San Diego Zoological Society; **graduation** Owen Franken, Stock, Boston; **graveyard** Allen J. Smith; **Great Dane** Evelyn M. Shafer; **greenhouse** Lord & Burnham; **greyhound** Evelyn M. Shafer; **guard** Allen J. Smith—BTA; **guided missile** U.S. Army; **guitar** Allen J. Smith.

habit Allen J. Smith; **halo** MFA, Boston; **handbill** International Harvester; **handicraft** MFA, Boston; **handiwork** MFA, Boston; **hang-glide** Jon Chase; **harbor** Geoffrey Hodgkinson; **harmonica** M. Hohner, Inc.; **harvest** USDA, Soil Conservation Service; **haystack** Montana Chamber of Commerce; **headline** Herbert H. Randle; **hedge** Allen J. Smith; **helicopter** U.S. Army; **helmet** Elizabeth Hamlin, Stock, Boston; **hilt** MFA, Boston; **hockey** Medford High *Mustang News*—Mount Holyoke College; **holster** Allen J. Smith; **homestead** USDA, Soil Conservation Service; **hoop** Allen J. Smith; **hothouse** Lord & Burnham; **House of Representatives** Keith Jewell; **hurdle** Stuart Cohen, Stock, Boston; **husky**[2] Evelyn M. Shafer.

icebreaker U.S. Coast Guard; **ice-skate** Mike Mazzaschi, Stock, Boston; **icy** Jon Chase; **igloo** Steve McCutcheon, Alaska Pictorial Service; **illuminate** Empire State Building Co.; **immigrant** LC; **implement** J. I. Case Co.; **inauguration** John F. Kennedy Library; **incubator** Joseph Marchetti, Narco Air-Shields; **industry** American Iron & Steel Institute; **infantry** U.S. Signal Corps; **instrument** Allen J. Smith; **insulate** James Percy, Uniphoto; **interior** The Solomon R. Guggenheim Museum; **invention** Polaroid Corp.; **inventor** Collections of Greenfield Village and the Henry Ford Museum; **invitation** The White House; **Irish setter** Evelyn M. Shafer; **ivory** Allen J. Smith.

jeep American Motors Corp.; **jetty** Allen J. Smith; **jewelry** Shreve, Crump & Low Co.; **jockey** Suffolk Downs; **judge** LC.

keg © Anheuser-Busch, Inc.; **kennel** Evelyn M. Shafer; **key** MFA, Boston—Allen J. Smith; **kickoff** Frank Siteman, Stock, Boston; **kilt** BTA; **kitten** Allen J. Smith; **knocker** Allen J. Smith.

lace Allen J. Smith; **lacrosse** Medford High *Mustang News;* **lasso** Montana Chamber of Commerce; **lattice** Allen J. Smith; **leash** Allen J. Smith; **leather** John J. Riley Co.—Allen J. Smith; **ledge** Ira Kirschenbaum, Stock, Boston; **leotard** Danskin, Inc.; **library** Mount Holyoke College—The Pierpont Morgan Library; **liftoff** NASA; **lighthouse** Fredrik Bodin, Stock, Boston; **lightning** Frank Siteman, Stock, Boston;

litter Evelyn M. Shafer; livery BTA; locomotive Union Pacific Railroad; luggage American Tourister; lumberjack Weyerhaeuser Company; lunar module NASA; lute MFA, Boston.

magician Peter Menzel, Stock, Boston; mandolin MFA, Boston; manor BTA; mansion John T. Hopf, courtesy of Newport County Chamber of Commerce; mask MFA, Boston—Peter Shaw, New England Divers Inc.; massacre LC; mastiff Evelyn M. Shafer; medal Allen J. Smith; merchandise Bill Browning, Montana Chamber of Commerce; microscope Allen J. Smith; migration LC; mill Allen J. Smith—American Iron & Steel Institute; miner Jon Chase; mirror MFA, Boston—French Government Tourist Office; mission George Robinson, Carmel Mission; mitt Spalding; moccasin Allen J. Smith; monogram Allen J. Smith; monument Allen J. Smith; motorboat AMF Inc.; mummy MFA, Boston; mural J. Berndt, Stock, Boston.

nail *Popular Mechanics;* navigator U.S. Navy; neckerchief Boy Scouts of America; nobleman Wide World Photos; notions Allen J. Smith.

oboe Ron Schick; observatory Hale Observatories; officer Allen J. Smith—U.S. Navy; offspring San Diego Zoological Society; operator AT&T; organ New England Conservatory of Music; outboard motor Allen J. Smith; overalls Rick Smolan, Stock, Boston; overpass Allen J. Smith.

pad Al Ruelle, Boston Bruins; pagoda Consulate General of Japan, New York; painter Jon Chase; palace BTA; parachute NASA; paratrooper U.S. Air Force; parchment The Jewish Theological Seminary of America, New York; passport Allen J. Smith; pasture Bill Browning, Montana Chamber of Commerce; patio Isabella Stewart Gardner Museum, Boston; pedestal Allen J. Smith; Pekingese Evelyn M. Shafer; percussion Chicago Symphony Orchestra; pewter MFA, Boston; piano Steinway & Sons; picket Donald Dietz, Stock, Boston—Peter Simon, Stock, Boston; pier The Port Authority of N.Y. & N.J.; pillar John T. Hopf, Newport County Chamber of Commerce; pipeline Mobil Oil Co.—Steve McCutcheon, Alaska Pictorial Service; pitcher¹ N.Y. Yankees, Inc.; pitcher² MFA, Boston; planet NASA; plantation National Coffee Association of the U.S.A., Inc.; platform Allen D. Moore; plaza Dept. of Transportation, Washington, D.C.; plume U.S. Army; pocketknife Allen J. Smith; pointer Evelyn M. Shafer; polar bear San Diego Zoological Society; pond S. L. Tinsley, USDA, Soil Conservation Service; poodle Evelyn M. Shafer; porcelain MFA, Boston; porpoise New England Aquarium; postage stamp U.S. Post Office, Boston; postmark U.S. Post Office, Boston; potter Old Sturbridge Village, Mass.; poultry Cary Wolinsky, Stock, Boston; prank Peter Menzel, Stock, Boston; press Christopher Morrow, Stock, Boston; print FBI—UPI; prize John Running, Stock, Boston; probe NASA; produce Allen J. Smith; profile MFA, Boston; program Allen J. Smith; projectile U.S. Navy; propeller NASA—Cessna Aircraft Co.; prospector Los Angeles County Museum of Natural History; puppet Allen J. Smith, courtesy of Cranberry Puppets, Brookline, Mass.; puppy Evelyn M. Shafer.

queen Lou Jones; quilt Allen D. Moore; quiver² George Bellerose, Stock, Boston.

railroad Union Pacific Railroad; ramrod Allen D. Moore; reactor UPI; reaper International Harvester; rebellion LC; recruit LC; reel¹ Allen J. Smith; referee Medford High *Mustang News;* refinery Gulf Oil Corp.; reflect Allen J. Smith; register NCR Corp.; rehearsal Louis Perez; relay UPI; relic Metropolitan Museum of Art, New York; relief MFA, Boston; reservoir Idaho Power Co.; resort Miami Beach Tourist Development Authority—Pocono Mts. Vacation Bureau; retriever Evelyn M. Shafer; reunion Mount Holyoke College; rice George Bellerose, Stock, Boston; rider Jon Chase; rifle U.S. Army; ring¹ Allen J. Smith; rink Allen D. Moore; robe Colonial Williamsburg; robot copyright © 1977 STAR WARS Twentieth Century-Fox Film Corp. All rights reserved; roller coaster Magic Mountain, Valencia, Calif.; roller-skate Allen D. Moore; route Allen D. Moore; row¹ USDA, Soil Conservation Service; ruin LC; rural USDA, Soil Conservation Service.

saddle Allen J. Smith; sailboat John T. Hopf, Newport County Chamber of Commerce; salute Allen D. Moore; sandal Allen D. Moore; sash¹ LC; Saturn NASA; saw¹ Jon Chase; saxophone Ron Schick; scaffold Daniel S. Brody, Stock, Boston; scale³ Ohaus Scale Corp.; scallop MFA, Boston; school¹ Allen D. Moore; schooner Mystic Seaport Museum, Inc.; scoop Allen D. Moore; score Allen D. Moore; scroll The

Jewish Theological Seminary of America, New York; seat-belt Davis Aircraft Products Co., Inc.; secretary MFA, Boston; seesaw Frank Siteman; seismograph Seismograph Stations, Univ. of California, Berkeley; semaphore General Railway Signal Co.—Boy Scouts of America; senate Keith Jewell; sentry BTA; sequoia U.S. Forest Service; service International Silver Co.; setter Evelyn M. Shafer; settlement LC; shaggy Wendy Quinones; shawl Burton Historical Collection, Detroit Public Library; sheep dog Evelyn M. Shafer; shell U.S. Navy; ship Cunard Line Ltd.; shore Cape Cod Chamber of Commerce; shotgun Smith & Wesson; shovel Allen D. Moore; shrubbery John T. Hopf, Newport County Chamber of Commerce; silo Bill Browning, Montana Chamber of Commerce; silver MFA, Boston; silversmith MFA, Boston—French Government Tourist Office; sister Lattanzio Studio; ski Vermont Development Agency; skin diving Paul J. Tzimoulis; sky diving U.S. Air Force; skyline The Port Authority of N.Y. & N.J.; skyscraper Empire State Building Co.; sled Steve McCutcheon, Alaska Pictorial Service; sledgehammer Stanley Tools; sleigh Massachusetts Historical Society; slide Frank Siteman; sluice Idaho Power Co.; smokestack Union Pacific Railroad; snorkel Walter Hendricks; snowmobile Vermont Development Agency; snowshoe L. L. Bean Co.; soccer AMF Inc.; soda fountain Allen J. Smith; sofa Allen D. Moore; soldier U.S. Army; soot LC; spaniel Evelyn M. Shafer; spectator Boston Red Sox; spinning wheel Old Sturbridge Village, Mass.; spoke¹ Museum of Transportation, Brookline, Mass.; spout MFA, Boston; sprinkler USDA, Soil Conservation Service; stadium Convention and Visitors Board of Greater St. Louis; stalactite and stalagmite National Park Service; stamp Allen J. Smith; statue The Port Authority of N.Y. & N.J.; St. Bernard Evelyn M. Shafer; steeple Old North Church, Boston; stilt Ringling Brothers and Barnum & Bailey Circus; stirrup Allen D. Moore; stove Allen D. Moore; streetcar Frank Siteman; structure The Port Authority of N.Y. & N.J.; submarine U.S. Navy; subway Allen D. Moore; suitcase American Tourister; Supreme Court LC; surfing Cary Wolinsky, Stock, Boston; suspenders Allen J. Smith; suspension bridge Elizabeth Hamlin, Stock, Boston; swimmer Harvard Sports News Bureau; swing Allen D. Moore; switchboard AT&T; synagogue Arnold Jarmak, Chelsea Press, Inc.; syrup Vermont Development Agency; system Sony.

tackle M. Sharf & Co., Inc.; takeoff British Airways; tank U.S. Navy; tanker Pullman Trailmobile; taxicab Allen J. Smith; team Medford High *Mustang News*—© Anheuser-Busch, Inc.; telephone AT&T; telescope U.S. Navy; tennis Tom McDermott, Pocono Mts. Vacation Bureau; tentacle Mary Price, New England Aquarium; tepee LC; terrier Evelyn M. Shafer; theater Allen D. Moore; thimble MFA, Boston; throne Pictorial Parade; tide G. Blouin, NFB Phototheque, Ottawa, Canada; tile Allen D. Moore; timber Weyerhaeuser Company; tiptoe Ron Schick; tongs MFA, Boston; tool Christopher S. Johnson, Stock, Boston; totem pole Alaska Historical Library; tower French Government Tourist Office; tractor International Harvester; train Union Pacific Railroad; trainer Bruce Lederer, New England Aquarium; trampoline Jon Chase; translate Ira Kirschenbaum, Stock, Boston; trapeze Ringling Brothers and Barnum & Bailey Circus; tread J. I. Case Co.; treaty U.S. Army; triangle Ron Schick; tricycle AMF Inc.; tripod Allen D. Moore; trolley Allen D. Moore; trombone Ron Schick; trough Old Sturbridge Village, Mass.; truck Pullman Trailmobile; trumpet Ron Schick; tuba Ron Schick; turban Information Service of India; turnpike Allen J. Smith; turret Geoffrey Hodgkinson; type Herbert H. Randle.

underpass Dept. of Transportation, Washington, D.C.; underwater Ron Church; unicorn Allen D. Moore; United Nations United Nations; upholster Allen D. Moore; uproot Frank Siteman; upside-down Ron Schick; urn MFA, Boston; utensil Allen D. Moore.

vaccinate Frank Siteman; vault¹ Frank Siteman; vault² Pamela Schuyler, Stock, Boston; veil Frank Siteman; vending machine Frank Siteman; Venetian blind Allen D. Moore; Viking LC; vineyard Owen Franken, Stock, Boston; viola Ron Schick; violin Mrs. Gerhard R. Schade, Jr., New England Conservatory of Music; visor LC; volleyball Medford High *Mustang News.*

warship U.S. Navy; water-ski Cypress Gardens, Winter Haven, Florida; weapon U.S. Navy; weightless NASA; weld Jon Chase; whisker New England Aquarium—Allen J. Smith; whistle MFA, Boston; wicker Allen D. Moore; wig BTA; wintry Allen D. Moore; workbench Allen D. Moore; worker Jon Chase; workout Allen D. Moore; world NASA; wrestling Jay Zagorsky, Medford High *Mustang News.*

xylophone Ron Schick; yoke Jon Chase; zither MFA, Boston.

B

Sample Column

Index tab

Entry word

Pronunciation

Verb forms

Sample sentence

Phrasal verb

Words that are spelled alike

Plural

Part of speech

blouse |blous| or |blouz| —*noun, plural* **blouses** A loose shirt or garment worn on the upper part of the body. Most blouses are worn by women or girls.

blow¹ |blō| —*verb* **blew, blown, blowing** **1.** To be in motion, as air: *The wind blew all night. It was blowing hard.* **2.** To move or cause to move by means of a current of air: *His hat blew off his head. The high winds blew the ship off course.* **3.** To send out a current of air or gas: *Blow on your soup to cool it.* **4.** To make a noise by forcing air through: *Can you blow the bugle? The factory whistle blows at noon.* **5.** To shape by forcing air or gas into or through: *We watched the man blow glass vases.* **6.** To melt a fuse: *We used too many appliances and blew a fuse.* **7.** To spout water: *How often does that whale blow?* **8.** To destroy or break by an explosion: *The bomb blew the building to pieces.*
    Phrasal verbs **blow out** **1.** To put out or go out by blowing: *Let's make a wish and blow out the candles. The candle blew out.* **2.** To burst suddenly: *The tire blew out.* **blow up** **1.** To fill with air or gas; inflate: *We blew up the balloons with helium.* **2.** To make larger: *The photographer will blow up the picture.* **3.** To explode: *The grenade blew up and wrecked the enemy tank.* **4.** To get angry: *She blew up at me for not telling her our plans.*
    —*noun, plural* **blows** A strong wind or gale: *A blow came out of the west and took the roof off the shack.*

blow² |blō| —*noun, plural* **blows** **1.** A sudden hard hit with a fist or weapon: *The man gave the thief a sharp blow with his cane.* **2.** A sudden shock, disappointment, or misfortune: *Losing his job was a blow to him.*

blow·torch |blō′tôrch′| —*noun, plural* **blowtorches** A small torch that can give off a very hot flame. Blowtorches are used for melting metal, soldering, and burning off old paint.

blub·ber |blŭb′ər| —*noun* The thick layer of fat under the skin of whales, seals, and some other sea animals.

blue |bloo| —*noun, plural* **blues** The color of the sky on a clear day. Blue, red, and green are called primary colors.
    —*adjective* **bluer, bluest** **1.** Of the color blue: *She wore a blue skirt.* **2.** Unhappy; gloomy; sad: *They were in a blue mood because their plans had been spoiled by the weather.* **3.** Having a slight blue tint: *Her lips were blue from swimming too long.*
    ♦ *These sound alike* **blue, blew.**
    Idiom **out of the blue** Suddenly and at an unexpected time or place: *We were in a strange town when out of the blue we met an old friend.*

blue·bird |bloo′bûrd′| —*noun, plural* **bluebirds** A North American bird with a blue back and a reddish breast.

Part of speech

bluebird

Illustration

Definition

Words that sound alike

Word history

Photograph

Pronunciation key

ă	pat	ĕ	pet	î	fierce
ā	pay	ē	be	ŏ	pot
â	care	ĭ	pit	ō	go
ä	father	ī	pie	ô	paw, for

oi	oil	ŭ	cut	zh	vision
ŏŏ	book	û	fur	ə	ago, item,
ōō	boot	th	the		pencil, atom,
yōō	abuse, th	thin			circus
ou	out	hw	which	ər	butter

blowtorch

blow¹, blow²
Blow¹ comes from a word used long ago in English to mean "to blow." **Blow²** comes from a word used by northern English people. It may have come from a Germanic word meaning "to strike," but this is not certain.

A-Z

Phoenician — The letter *A* comes originally from a Phoenician symbol named *'aleph,* meaning "ox," in use about 3,000 years ago.

Greek — The Greeks borrowed the symbol from the Phoenicians and changed its form. They also changed its name to *alpha.*

Roman — The Romans took the letter and adapted it for carving into stone. This became the model for our modern printed capital *A.*

Medieval — The hand-written form of about 1,200 years ago became the basis of the modern small letter.

Modern — The modern capital and small letters are based on the Roman capital and later hand-written forms.

a or **A** |ā| —*noun, plural* **a's** or **A's** The first letter of the English alphabet.

a |ə| or |ā| —*indefinite article* **1.** Any: *A kind person would not say that.* **2.** One: *I didn't say a word.* **3.** A kind of: *Orange juice is a fruit drink.* **4.** Each; every: *He goes to New York once a month.* The indefinite article **a** belongs to a class of words called **determiners.** They signal that a noun is coming.

a- A prefix that means "in" or "on": *aboard; afire.*

ab·a·cus |ăb′ə kəs| —*noun, plural* **abacuses** An old-fashioned calculator used especially for adding and subtracting. It is made up of a frame on which beads slide back and forth.

a·ban·don |ə băn′dən| —*verb* **abandoned, abandoning** **1.** To leave for good; desert: *"Abandon ship!" ordered the captain. Her parents abandoned their farm and moved to the city.* **2.** To give up completely: *She abandoned all hope of being a doctor.*

ab·bey |ăb′ē| —*noun, plural* **abbeys** **1.** A building or set of buildings occupied by a group of nuns or monks. **2.** A group of nuns or monks who live in an abbey.

ab·bre·vi·ate |ə brē′vē āt′| —*verb* **abbreviated, abbreviating** To make shorter by leaving out letters: *She abbreviates "Avenue" to "Ave." on envelopes.*

ab·bre·vi·a·tion |ə brē′vē ā′shən| —*noun, plural* **abbreviations** A short way of writing a word of group of words: *"U.S.A." is an abbreviation for "United States of America."*

ab·di·cate |ăb′dĭ kāt′| —*verb* **abdicated, abdicating** To give up in a formal way: *The king abdicated the throne. Queen Wilhelmina of the Netherlands abdicated in 1948.*

ab·do·men |ăb′də mən| or |ăb dō′mən| —*noun, plural* **abdomens** **1.** In human beings and other mammals, the front part of the body from below the chest to about where the legs join. The stomach, the intestines, and other important organs are in the abdomen. **2.** One of the three main parts of an insect's body. It is at the hind end.

a·bide |ə bīd′| —*verb* **abided, abiding** To put up with; bear; stand: *I cannot abide that noise.*

Phrasal verb **abide by** To agree to live up to; obey: *We must abide by the judge's decision.*

abacus

abbey

a·bil·i·ty |ə bĭl′ĭ tē| —*noun, plural* **abilities** The power or skill to do something: *Birds have the ability to fly. Human beings have the ability to speak.*

a·ble |ā′bəl| —*adjective* **abler, ablest 1.** Having the power or means to do something: *He is able to lift heavy objects.* **2.** Having skill or talent; capable: *She is an able painter. He is an able nurse.*

a·board |ə bôrd′| or |ə bōrd′| —*adverb* On, onto, or inside a ship, train, airplane, or other vehicle: *We climbed aboard as soon as the train stopped.*

a·bol·ish |ə bŏl′ĭsh| —*verb* **abolished, abolishing** To put an end to or do away with: *Abraham Lincoln abolished slavery.*

ab·o·li·tion |ăb′ə lĭsh′ən| —*noun* The act of abolishing: *Many people had to fight for the abolition of slavery.*

ab·o·rig·i·ne |ăb′ə rĭj′ə nē| —*noun, plural* **aborigines** Any member of a group of people who are the first known to have lived in a particular region: *There were aborigines in Australia long before the Europeans arrived.*

a·bound |ə bound′| —*verb* **abounded, abounding** To be plentiful or have plenty of: *Wild animals abound in the forest. The forest abounds in wild animals.*

a·bout |ə bout′| —*preposition* **1.** Of or having to do with; concerning: *She wrote many stories about animals.* **2.** Near in time to; close to: *I will leave about noon.* **3.** All around: *Look about you before dark for a good campsite.* **4.** Around in: *We saw a bear prowling about the woods.*
—*adverb* **1.** Nearly; approximately: *The hummingbird's egg is about the size of a pea. There were about ten people standing in line.* **2.** Around: *Look about for a good hiding place.*

a·bove |ə bŭv′| —*adverb* In or to a higher place or position; overhead: *Look at the stars above.*
—*preposition* **1.** Over or higher than: *Andy saw the seagulls hovering just above the water. The President is above all military officers.* **2.** More than: *Last week's spending was above normal.* **3.** Beyond: *The road is snowed in above this point.*

a·bove·board |ə bŭv′bôrd′| or |ə bŭv′bōrd′| —*adjective* Without deceit; honest; open; straightforward: *His way of playing cards is fair and aboveboard.*

a·breast |ə brĕst′| —*adverb* and *adjective* **1.** Standing or moving side by side: *The soldiers marched four abreast.* **2.** Up to date with: *abreast of the new fashions.*

a·bridge |ə brĭj′| —*verb* **abridged, abridging** To make shorter by using fewer words; condense; shorten: *The writer abridged the book for use in the magazine.*

a·broad |ə brôd′| —*adverb* and *adjective* **1.** In or to a foreign country: *Her mother is going abroad to England on a business trip. She wrote of her trip abroad.* **2.** Over a broad area; all around; here and there: *They scattered seeds abroad.* **3.** Out of doors: *Do you walk abroad in bad weather?*

a·brupt |ə brŭpt′| —*adjective* **1.** Not expected; sudden: *an abrupt change of plans.* **2.** Very steep: *an abrupt cliff.* **3.** So short as to seem rude: *an abrupt answer to a question.*

ab·scess |ăb′sĕs′| —*noun, plural* **abscesses** A mass of pus that forms and collects at one place in the body. An abscess usually comes from an infection and feels sore.

ab·sence |ăb′səns| —*noun, plural* **absences 1.** The condition of being away: *Everyone noticed my absence from school.* **2.** The

aborigine
Drawings made about 1585 of
Florida Indians

ă	pat	ĕ	pet	î	fierce
ā	pay	ē	be	ŏ	pot
â	care	ĭ	pit	ō	go
ä	father	ī	pie	ô	paw, for
oi	oil	ŭ	cut	zh	vision
ōō	book	û	fur	ə	ago, item,
ōō	boot	*th*	the		pencil, atom,
yōō	abuse	th	thin		circus
ou	out	hw	which	ər	butter

period of time that one is away: *an absence of four days.* **3.** A lack: *The absence of a good defense made their team lose the game.*

ab·sent | ăb′sənt | —*adjective* **1.** Not present; away: *Two students are absent today.* **2.** Lacking; missing: *Horns are absent in some cows.*

ab·sent-mind·ed | ăb′sənt mīn′dĭd | —*adjective* Likely to be lost in thought and to forget what one is doing: *The absent-minded cook left the towel in the freezer and the ice cream on the stove.*

ab·so·lute | ăb′sə lōot′ | —*adjective* **1.** Complete; total: *They sat in absolute silence. He has my absolute trust.* **2.** Not limited in any way: *The king was an absolute ruler. He has absolute freedom.*

ab·so·lute·ly | ăb′sə lōot′lē | or | ăb′sə lōot′lē | —*adverb* **1.** Completely; perfectly; entirely; fully: *They stood absolutely still.* **2.** Without any doubt; positively: *She is absolutely my best friend.*

ab·sorb | ăb sôrb′ | or | ăb zôrb′ | —*verb* **absorbed, absorbing** **1.** To take in or soak up: *Plants absorb energy from the sun. A sponge absorbs moisture. He absorbs information quickly.* **2.** To take the full attention of: *The comic books absorbed his little brother during the weekend. My work absorbs all of my time.*

ab·sorp·tion | ăb sôrp′shən | or | ăb zôrp′shən | —*noun* **1.** The act or process of absorbing: *Paper towels dry dishes by absorption.* **2.** The ability to absorb: *Some towels have very good absorption.* **3.** The condition of being very much interested: *Their great absorption in the football game made them forget to eat lunch.*

ab·stain | ăb stān′ | —*verb* **abstained, abstaining** To keep oneself from doing something; hold oneself back: *Some people abstain from eating meat.*

ab·stract | ăb′străkt′ | or | ăb străkt′ | —*adjective* **1.** Having a quality that is not connected with any person, thing, or action. The words "truth" and "justice" are abstract because they are not connected with any person, thing, or action. A farmer, a glass of water, and a ride on a bicycle are not abstract because they are connected with persons, things, or actions. **2.** Very hard to understand; difficult: *Your explanation is too abstract for me.*

ab·surd | ăb sûrd′ | or | ăb zûrd′ | —*adjective* Very silly; foolish; ridiculous: *The clown looks absurd with the pumpkin on his head and the prune on his nose.*

a·bun·dance | ə bŭn′dəns | —*noun* A supply that is more than enough; a great amount: *The oceans have an abundance of minerals. The apples grew in abundance.*

a·bun·dant | ə bŭn′dənt | —*adjective* In great amounts; plentiful: *Jungles receive abundant rainfall.*

a·buse | ə byōoz′ | —*verb* **abused, abusing** **1.** To put to bad or wrong use: *The king abused his power when he burned all the books in the kingdom.* **2.** To hurt or injure by treating in a bad or cruel way: *He abused his eyes by reading in poor light. The man abused his horse by beating it.* **3.** To attack or injure with words: *They abused the child with scolding.*
—*noun* | ə byōos′ |, *plural* **abuses** **1.** Bad or wrong use: *a tyrant's abuse of power.* **2.** Bad or rough treatment: *The gym's equipment gets lots of abuse.* **3.** Language that insults; scolding or cursing: *He could not listen to their abuse any longer.*

a·byss | ə bĭs′ | —*noun, plural* **abysses** **1.** A very deep and large hole. **2.** A huge empty space.

a·cad·e·my | ə kăd′ə mē | —*noun, plural* **academies** **1.** A school

academy
U.S. Military Academy

for a special kind of study: *a music academy; the Naval Academy.*
2. A private high school.

ac·cel·er·ate | ăk sĕl′ə rāt′ | —*verb* **accelerated, accelerating** To increase in speed; speed up; move faster: *He accelerated the car. The bicycle accelerated going down the hill.*

ac·cel·er·a·tion | ăk sĕl′ə rā′shən | —*noun* An increase in speed; faster movement: *the acceleration of a windmill as the wind grows stronger.*

ac·cel·er·a·tor | ăk sĕl′ə rā′tər | —*noun, plural* **accelerators** Anything that increases speed. In a car the accelerator is a pedal that a person steps on to make the car go faster.

ac·cent | ăk′sĕnt′ | —*noun, plural* **accents 1.** More force or stronger tone of voice given to a syllable or syllables of a word. The accent is on the first syllable in "funny"; it is on the second syllable in "alone." **2.** A mark used in pronunciations to show which syllable or syllables have an accent. In this dictionary the mark ′ and darker type are used for the syllable of a word with the strongest tone. The mark ′ is used to show a syllable with an accent that is not quite so strong. For example, the pronunciation of the word "accent" has two accents: | ăk′sĕnt′ | . **3.** A style of speech or pronunciation that shows the speaker comes from a particular part of a country or from another country: *a Boston accent; a French accent.*
—*verb* **accented, accenting** To pronounce a syllable in a word with more force or a stronger tone: *Some people accent the first syllable in "hello," and some people accent the second syllable.*

ac·cept | ăk sĕpt′ | —*verb* **accepted, accepting 1.** To take something that is offered; agree to take: *She accepted his compliments but would not accept the gift.* **2.** To say yes to; agree to: *We accept your invitation to the party.* **3.** To think of as true; believe: *Few people accepted Columbus' idea that the world was round.* **4.** To receive in a friendly manner: *The club quickly accepted the new member.*

ac·cept·a·ble | ăk sĕp′tə bəl | —*adjective* Capable of being good enough to be accepted; satisfactory: *The book report was acceptable in place of the assigned homework.*

ac·cept·ance | ăk sĕp′təns | —*noun* **1.** The act of taking something that is offered: *the acceptance of tokens instead of money. Her acceptance of the award was greeted by wild applause.* **2.** The condition of being accepted or liked; approval: *We were hoping for the acceptance of our plan.*

ac·cess | ăk′sĕs′ | —*noun, plural* **accesses 1.** The act of entering; entrance: *The thief gained access through a broken window.* **2.** A way to get into or reach a place: *The drawbridge was the only access to the castle.* **3.** The means to get or reach something: *Books give us access to a great deal of information. The spy gained access to the secret files.*

ac·ces·so·ry | ăk sĕs′ə rē | —*noun, plural* **accessories 1.** An extra item that goes with and improves a main item. Scarves, hats, pins, and belts are accessories to women's clothing. Air conditioners, radios, and clocks are accessories in cars. **2.** A person who helps someone carry out a crime but who is not actually there when the crime is committed.
—*adjective* Adding to something more important; not the main part; extra: *The school has a main building and three accessory buildings.*

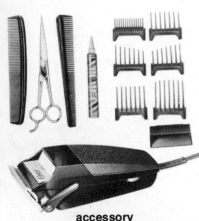

accessory
Accessories for cutting hair

ă	pat	ĕ	pet	î	fierce
ā	pay	ē	be	ŏ	pot
â	care	ĭ	pit	ō	go
ä	father	ī	pie	ô	paw, for
oi	oil	ŭ	cut	zh	vision
ōō	book	û	fur	ə	ago, item,
ōō	boot	*th*	the		pencil, atom,
yōō	abuse	th	thin		circus
ou	out	hw	which	ər	butter

ac·ci·dent |ăk′sĭ dənt| —*noun, plural* **accidents 1.** Something bad or unlucky that happens without being planned, intended, or expected: *I broke my arm in an ice-skating accident.* **2.** Anything that happens without being planned, intended, or expected: *Meeting my friend at the beach was a lucky accident.*

ac·ci·den·tal |ăk′sĭ dĕn′tl| —*adjective* Happening without being planned, intended, or expected; not on purpose: *Our accidental discovery of the missing jewels surprised everybody.*

ac·claim |ə klām′| —*verb* **acclaimed, acclaiming** To greet with loud approval; praise; hail: *The people acclaimed their hero. Her new movie has been acclaimed by all the critics.*
—*noun* Loud or enthusiastic praise, applause, or approval: *The winning football team was greeted with great acclaim.*

ac·com·mo·date |ə kŏm′ə dāt′| —*verb* **accommodated, accommodating 1.** To do a favor for; help out: *He accommodated me by putting out his cigar.* **2.** To have room for; hold: *The tree house accommodates five children or two adults.* **3.** To provide with a place to stay or sleep: *The new hotel at the beach will accommodate 800 weekend guests.*

ac·com·mo·da·tion |ə kŏm′ə dā′shən| —*noun, plural* **accommodations 1.** An act that helps someone out; a favor: *The bus driver does not usually stop at my corner; he stopped there as an accommodation for me.* **2. accommodations** A place to stay or sleep: *accommodations for two on a train.*

ac·com·pa·ni·ment |ə kŭm′pə nĭ mənt| or |ə kŭmp′nĭ mənt| —*noun, plural* **accompaniments 1.** Anything that goes along with or adds to something else: *Crackers are a good accompaniment to soup. A sore throat is often an accompaniment to a cold.* **2.** Music that is played to go along with singing, dancing, other music, or any other activity: *We danced and the teacher played an accompaniment.*

ac·com·pa·ny |ə kŭm′pə nē| —*verb* **accompanied, accompanying, accompanies 1.** To go along with: *I accompanied Terry when he went shopping.* **2.** To happen along with: *Thunder often accompanies lightning.* **3.** To play an accompaniment for: *Can you accompany this song? Janet sang, and Paul accompanied.*

ac·com·plice |ə kŏm′plĭs| —*noun, plural* **accomplices** A person who helps someone else in a crime. An accomplice may or may not be there when the crime is committed: *Pete and two accomplices robbed the jewelry store.*

ac·com·plish |ə kŏm′plĭsh| —*verb* **accomplished, accomplishing** To finish after setting out to do; achieve; complete: *We accomplished our assignment in half the time we thought it would take.*

ac·com·plish·ment |ə kŏm′plĭsh mənt| —*noun, plural* **accomplishments 1.** The act of finishing what one has set out to do; completion: *She rested after the accomplishment of the task. The accomplishment of the job took five hours.* **2.** Something that has been done with skill and success: *Winning the game was a great accomplishment for the team.* **3.** A skill that has been learned well: *Singing and embroidery are among their many accomplishments.*

ac·cord |ə kôrd′| —*verb* **accorded, according** To be in agreement; agree: *His side of the story does not accord with hers. Their stories do not accord.*
—*noun* Agreement; harmony: *His ideas are in accord with mine.*
Idiom **of (one's) own accord** Without assistance or suggestions

accordion

ace

from anybody else; by oneself: *She decided to enter the contest of her own accord. The balloon came down of its own accord.*

ac·cord·ing to |ə kôr′dĭng| **1.** As stated or indicated by; on the authority of: *The car was blue according to John, but Tim said it was green.* **2.** In agreement with; in keeping with: *We filled out the forms according to the instructions.* **3.** With reference to; in proportion to: *We were paid according to the amount of berries we had picked, not according to the time we had spent.*

ac·cor·di·on |ə kôr′dē ən| —*noun, plural* **accordions** A musical instrument with a keyboard, buttons, bellows, and metal reeds. The sound is created when the player operates the bellows to force air through the reeds.

ac·count |ə kount′| —*noun, plural* **accounts 1.** A written or spoken description; a report: *They gave an exciting account of their canoe trip.* **2.** A set of reasons; explanation: *You need to give an account of your strange behavior.* **3.** A record of business and money spent or received: *My brother keeps an account of all his money from baby-sitting.* **4.** Importance; value; worth: *Their complaints are of little account.*

—*verb* **accounted, accounting** To believe to be; consider: *We account him innocent unless he is proved guilty.*

Phrasal verb account for 1. To give a reason for; explain: *Can you account for the strange noises?* **2.** To take into consideration: *You must account for all the facts in your answer.* **3.** To be responsible for: *Careless driving accounts for many accidents.*

Idiom on account of Because of: *We were late on account of traffic.*

ac·count·ant |ə koun′tənt| —*noun, plural* **accountants** A person who keeps or inspects the money records of a business or a person.

ac·cu·mu·late |ə kyōō′myə lāt′| —*verb* **accumulated, accumulating** To gather together; pile up; collect: *He accumulated a large collection of stamps in a short period of time. Snow accumulated quickly on the lawn.*

ac·cu·mu·la·tion |ə kyōō′myə lā′shən| —*noun, plural* **accumulations 1.** The act of accumulating: *The accumulation of knowledge can take a lifetime.* **2.** Things that have accumulated; a collection: *Under my bed there is an accumulation of toys.*

ac·cu·ra·cy |ăk′yər ə sē| —*noun* The condition of being correct and exact: *Each morning I check the accuracy of my watch with the time given on the radio.*

ac·cu·rate |ăk′yər ĭt| —*adjective* Free from errors; correct; exact: *She gave an accurate description of what I wore yesterday.*

ac·cu·sa·tion |ăk′yōō zā′shən| —*noun, plural* **accusations** A statement that a person has done something wrong: *The accusations that he lied hurt him because he had told the truth.*

ac·cuse |ə kyōōz′| —*verb* **accused, accusing** To state that someone has done something wrong: *He accused me of cheating.*

ac·cus·tom |ə kŭs′təm| —*verb* **accustomed, accustoming** To make familiar by practice, use, or habit: *We had to accustom ourselves to the dark when the electricity failed.*

ac·cus·tomed |ə kŭs′təmd| —*adjective* Usual; familiar: *The frogs were making their accustomed noises.*

accustomed to Familiar with; in the habit of: *She is not accustomed to the city noises.*

ace |ās| —*noun, plural* **aces 1.** A playing card with one heart, spade, diamond, or club in the center. **2.** A person who is outstanding or an expert in his field: *He is the class spelling ace.*

ache |ăk| —*verb* **ached, aching 1.** To feel or hurt with a dull, steady pain: *I ache all over. My tooth aches.* **2.** To want very much; to long: *I am aching to see her again.*
—*noun, plural* **aches** A dull, steady pain: *For a week after playing ball he had an ache in his back.*

a·chieve |ə chēv′| —*verb* **achieved, achieving 1.** To accomplish something desired or attempted: *Few people achieve all that they expected to in their lifetime. He achieved a country look in his city home.* **2.** To get as a result of effort; win; gain: *Babe Ruth achieved fame as a baseball player.*

a·chieve·ment |ə chēv′mənt| —*noun, plural* **achievements 1.** An outstanding act or accomplishment: *The doctor received a medal for her achievements in public health.* **2.** The act of doing something with skill and effort: *Lily is proud of her achievement of a perfect score on the test.*

ac·id |ăs′ĭd| —*noun, plural* **acids** A chemical substance that is capable of joining with a base to form water and a salt. An acid can turn blue litmus paper red. Acids have a sour taste, but many acids cause burns and should not be tasted or touched.
—*adjective* **1.** Containing acid or like acid; sharp and sour: *Lemons are an acid fruit.* **2.** Sharp in manner: *Her acid remarks hurt people's feelings.*

ac·knowl·edge |ăk nŏl′ĭj| —*verb* **acknowledged, acknowledging 1.** To admit or agree that something is true: *He acknowledges that he made a mistake.* **2.** To recognize the authority or position of: *They acknowledged him supreme ruler. Everybody acknowledges her to be the best tennis player.* **3.** To say that one has received something: *She acknowledged the letter right away.*

ac·knowl·edg·ment |ăk nŏl′ĭj mənt| —*noun, plural* **acknowledgments 1.** The act of admitting the truth of something: *He bowed his head in acknowledgment of guilt.* **2.** Something done to answer, thank, or recognize someone else's action: *My telephone call was an acknowledgment of the invitation. She received many gifts and sent out many acknowledgments.*

ac·ne |ăk′nē| —*noun* A skin condition in which the oil glands of the skin become infected and form pimples.

a·corn |ā′kôrn′| or |ā′kərn| —*noun, plural* **acorns** The nut of an oak tree.

ac·quaint |ə kwānt′| —*verb* **acquainted, acquainting** To make familiar: *When we go to a different country, we must acquaint ourselves with new ways of doing things.*

ac·quaint·ance |ə kwān′təns| —*noun, plural* **acquaintances 1.** A person one knows but not very well: *I have a few good friends and many acquaintances.* **2.** A knowledge of something: *Do you have any acquaintance with the game of soccer?*

ac·quire |ə kwīr′| —*verb* **acquired, acquiring** To get as one's own; gain; obtain: *She acquired knowledge and skills in her job.*

ac·quit |ə kwĭt′| —*verb* **acquitted, acquitting 1.** To declare not guilty: *The jury acquitted him of the crime.* **2. acquit oneself** To conduct oneself; behave: *The warriors acquitted themselves bravely in battle.*

a·cre |ā′kər| —*noun, plural* **acres** A unit for measuring land. An acre is the same as 43,560 square feet, or 4,840 square yards. The acre is not used in the metric system.

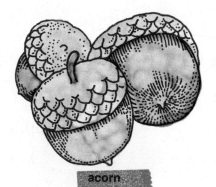

acorn

acrobat

actress and actor

a·cre·age |ā′kər ĭj| —*noun* Land as measured in acres.

ac·ro·bat |ăk′rə băt′| —*noun, plural* **acrobats** A person who is skilled in performing on a trapeze, walking a tightrope, and tumbling. The stunts that acrobats do require great strength and balance.

a·cross |ə krôs′| or |ə krŏs′| —*preposition* **1.** To or from the other side of; over: *He spent the summer driving across the country.* **2.** On the other side of; beyond: *Through the fog we could barely see the hills across the valley.*
—*adverb* **1.** From one side to the other: *A tornado may be only 100 feet across.* **2.** Over: *I want to get my point across.*

act |ăkt| —*noun, plural* **acts** **1.** Something that is done; a deed; action: *an act of bravery; a wise act.* **2.** The process of doing something: *He was caught in the act of stealing.* **3.** A performance for an audience: *a magician's act.* **4.** A main division of a play or other dramatic work: *The opera has four acts.* **5.** A pretense; false show: *She is not really angry; it's only an act.* **6.** A law that has been passed: *an act of Congress.*
—*verb* **acted, acting** **1.** To do something; perform an action: *He acted quickly to save her life.* **2.** To conduct oneself; behave: *She acts like an adult. The heart acts like a pump.* **3.** To perform, play a part, or pretend to be: *We all acted in the play. He acted brave although he was frightened.* **4.** To have the effect that is expected; work properly: *The heat acted on the sore leg.*

ac·tion |ăk′shən| —*noun, plural* **actions** **1.** The activity, process, or fact of doing something: *Verbs show action.* **2.** A thing that is done; a deed; act: *a generous action.* **3.** Activity; motion: *The firefighters sprang into action.* **4.** The way something works or affects another thing: *the action of sunlight on plants.* **5.** Battle; combat: *The general put the troops into action.*

ac·ti·vate |ăk′tə vāt′| —*verb* **activated, activating** To set in operation or motion: *A press of the button activates the machine.*

ac·tive |ăk′tĭv| —*adjective* **1.** Moving about much of the time; engaged in physical action: *Athletes are more active than office workers.* **2.** Full of energy; busy: *He led a full and active life.* **3.** In operation or in action; working: *an active volcano.*

active voice A form of a verb or phrasal verb that shows the subject of the sentence is performing or causing the action expressed by the verb. In the sentence "John bought the book", the verb, "bought," is in the active voice.

ac·tiv·i·ty |ăk tĭv′ĭ tē| —*noun, plural* **activities** **1.** The condition or process of being active; action: *The store was a scene of great activity. He enjoys activity and does not like to sit still.* **2.** Something to do or to be done: *Music lessons and soccer club are his activities after school.*

ac·tor |ăk′tər| —*noun, plural* **actors** A man or boy who performs dramatic roles in plays, motion pictures, or television or radio stories.

ac·tress |ăk′trĭs| —*noun, plural* **actresses** A woman or girl who performs dramatic roles in plays, motion pictures, or television or radio stories.

ac·tu·al |ăk′chōō əl| —*adjective* Existing in fact; real: *The actual living conditions at the explorer's camp were very poor.*

ac·tu·al·ly |ăk′chōō ə lē| —*adverb* In fact; really: *She actually tried to eat three ice-cream sundaes!*

a·cute |ə kyōot′| —*adjective* **1.** Sharp and intense: *an acute*

ă	pat	ĕ	pet	î	fierce
ā	pay	ē	be	ŏ	pot
â	care	ĭ	pit	ō	go
ä	father	ī	pie	ô	paw, for
oi	oil	ŭ	cut	zh	vision
ŏŏ	book	û	fur	ə	ago, item,
ōō	boot	th	the		pencil, atom,
yōō	abuse	th	thin		circus
ou	out	hw	which	ər	butter

pain in the chest. **2.** Sharp and quick in noticing things: *She has
an acute sense of smell* **3.** Very serious; extremely bad: *The
school has an acute need for money. She had an acute attack of the
flu.*

acute angle An angle that is smaller than a right angle. An
acute angle measures between zero and ninety degrees.

ad |ăd| —*noun, plural* **ads** An advertisement.
♦ *These sound alike* **ad, add.**

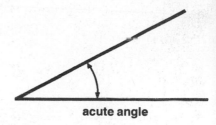
acute angle

A.D. An abbreviation for the Latin words *anno Domini,* which
mean "in the year of the Lord." "A.D." is used in giving dates
after the birth of Christ: *This vase was made around A.D. 32.*

ad·age |ăd′ĭj| —*noun, plural* **adages** A short saying that many
people consider to be wise and true; a proverb. "Haste makes
waste" is an adage.

ad·a·mant |ăd′ə mənt| —*adjective* Not willing to change one's
mind; very firm in an inflexible way: *She was adamant that she
would not join the other girls at the beach.*

Ad·am's apple |ăd′əmz| The lump at the front of a person's
throat made by the larynx. It is easier to notice an Adam's apple
on a man than on a woman or child.

a·dapt |ə dăpt′| —*verb* **adapted, adapting** To change or adjust
to fit different conditions: *He adapted the car for camping trips. We
adapted quickly to life in the desert.*

add |ăd| —*verb* **added, adding** **1.** To find the sum of two or
more numbers: *If you add 8 and 5, you get 13. She added correctly.*
2. To put something more in, on, or next to: *Did you add salt to
the stew? They added a room to the house. Add "s" to "cat" to form
the plural.* **3.** To say or write something more: *She waved good-by
and added, "Be careful."*
♦ *These sound alike* **add, ad.**

ad·dend |ăd′ĕnd′| or |ə dĕnd′| —*noun, plural* **addends** Any
one of a set of numbers that are to be added. In 4 + 5 + 2 = 11
the numbers 4, 5, and 2 are addends.

ad·der |ăd′ər| —*noun, plural* **adders** **1.** A poisonous snake of
Europe or Africa. **2.** A nonpoisonous snake that is thought to be
harmful.

ad·dict |ăd′ĭkt| —*noun, plural* **addicts** A person who has
developed a need for something harmful, as drugs or tobacco.

ad·di·tion |ə dĭsh′ən| —*noun, plural* **additions** **1.** The process
of finding the sum of two or more numbers; 4 + 5 + 2 = 11 is
an example of addition. **2.** The act of adding one thing to
another: *The addition of sugar to the carrots made them less bitter.*
3. An added thing, part, or person: *He built an addition to the
garage. The baby is an addition to the family.*

   Idiom **in addition** or **in addition to** Also; besides: *They cleaned up
the alley and painted the fence in addition. In addition to flowers, they
grew vegetables.*

adder

ad·di·tion·al |ə dĭsh′ə nəl| —*adjective* Added; extra; more: *Do
you have additional news besides what we saw in the paper?*

ad·dress |ə drĕs′| —*noun, plural* **addresses** **1.** |*also* ăd′rĕs′|
The house number, street name, city, state, and zip code where a
person lives, works, or receives mail: *We wanted to visit them, but
we forgot their address. The address of the White House is 1600
Pennsylvania Avenue, Washington, D.C. 20506.* **2.** |*also* ăd′rĕs′|
The information on an envelope or other piece of mail that shows

where mail is going to or sent from: *The mail was lost because the address was wrong and there was no return address.* **3.** A formal speech: *The governor gave an address to the state.*

—*verb* **addressed, addressing 1.** To put the house number, street name, city, state, and zip code on mail: *She addressed all the envelopes for the invitations.* **2.** To speak to or give a speech to: *Did you address me? The President addressed the nation.*

ad·e·noids | ăd′n oidz′ | —*plural noun* Growths at the back of the nose, above the throat. When adenoids are swollen, it may be difficult to breathe and speak.

a·dept | ə dĕpt′ | —*adjective* Very good at something; skillful: *She is adept at whittling and sewing.*

ad·e·quate | ăd′ĭ kwĭt | —*adjective* Enough to meet needs; sufficient: *We have adequate supplies to last the winter. The food was adequate but not plentiful.*

ad·here | ăd hîr′ | —*verb* **adhered, adhering 1.** To hold fast; stick: *The stamp did not adhere to the envelope.* **2.** To follow closely, without changes: *They adhered to the original plan.*

ad·he·sive | ăd hē′sĭv | —*noun, plural* **adhesives** Anything that sticks or makes things stick. Glue and paste are adhesives.
—*adjective* Made to stick to something; sticky: *an adhesive tape.*

a·di·os | ä′dē ōs′ | or | ăd′ē ōs′ | —*interjection* The Spanish word for good-by.

ad·ja·cent | ăd jā′sənt | —*adjective* Next to; adjoining; near: *My sister's room is adjacent to mine. We visited the city and the adjacent suburbs.*

ad·jec·tive | ăj′ĭk tĭv | —*noun, plural* **adjectives** A word that is used to describe a noun or to give it a special meaning. For example, in the sentence "The big red dog chased the dirty old cat" the adjectives are "big," "red," "dirty," and "old."

ad·join | ə join′ | —*verb* **adjoined, adjoining** To be next to; be side by side: *The football field adjoins the school. Their offices adjoin.*

ad·journ | ə jûrn′ | —*verb* **adjourned, adjourning** To stop and plan to continue at another time; end for the time being: *They adjourned the meeting until next week. The meeting adjourned for the day.*

ad·just | ə jŭst′ | —*verb* **adjusted, adjusting 1.** To change in order to make right or better: *He adjusted the television picture.* **2.** To move into a different position: *The table adjusts to three heights.* **3.** To become used to new conditions; adapt: *She soon adjusted to life on a farm.*

ad·just·ment | ə jŭst′mənt | —*noun, plural* **adjustments 1.** The act, condition, or process of changing to make right or better: *The store made an adjustment on the incorrect bill. An adjustment of the motor made the car run well.* **2.** The act or process of getting used to something: *She made a rapid adjustment to the new camp.*

ad·min·is·ter | ăd mĭn′ĭ stər | —*verb* **administered, administering 1.** To be in charge of; direct; manage: *Mrs. Smith administers her family's business.* **2. a.** To give as a remedy or treatment: *The lifeguard administered artificial respiration to the swimmer.* **b.** To give or deal out: *The sheriff administered a public scolding to his deputy.* **3.** To give in a formal or official way: *The court clerk administered the oath to the witness.*

ad·min·is·tra·tion | ăd mĭn′ĭ strā′shən | —*noun, plural* **administrations 1.** The act or job of managing a company, business, or other organization; management: *The administration of* a large corporation is a very demanding task. She used to be an engineer, but now she works in administration. **2.** The people who manage a business, organization, or government: *The president, vice presidents, secretary, and treasurer are part of a company's administration. The principal and assistant principal are part of a school's administration.* **3.** The act of giving or supplying: *a nurse's administration of good care; a judge's administration of justice.* **4. the Administration** The President of the United States, along with the Vice President, the cabinet officers, and the departments they are in charge of; the executive branch of the government. **5.** Often **Administration** The period of time during which a government is in power: *The Eisenhower Administration lasted eight years.*

ad·mi·ral |ăd′mər əl| —*noun, plural* **admirals 1.** The commander in chief of a navy or fleet. **2.** An officer of high rank in the United States Navy. There are four ranks of admirals: fleet admiral, admiral, vice admiral, and rear admiral.

ad·mi·ra·tion |ăd′mə rā′shən| —*noun* A feeling of pleasure, wonder, respect, and approval caused by something good or beautiful: *They looked at his statue with admiration.*

ad·mire |ăd mīr′| —*verb* **admired, admiring 1.** To look at or think of with pleasure, wonder, respect, and approval: *We admired the view from the top of the mountain.* **2.** To have a high opinion of; feel respect for: *We all admire her courage.*

ad·mis·sion |ăd mĭsh′ən| —*noun, plural* **admissions 1.a.** The fact of being allowed to enter or join: *The admission of a new state to the Union comes through an act of Congress.* **b.** The right to enter or join: *He hoped for admission to the college.* **2.** A price charged or paid to enter a place: *The admission to the play was raised to four dollars.* **3.** A statement that something is true; a confession: *By her own admission she had broken the watch.*

ad·mit |ăd mĭt′| —*verb* **admitted, admitting 1.** To say that something is true; confess as a fact: *He admitted that he had painted the windows black.* **2.** To allow to enter; let in: *The pass admits one person free.*

ad·mit·tance |ăd mĭt′ns| —*noun* Permission or right to enter; entrance: *The sign said "No admittance."*

a·do·be |ə dō′bē| —*noun, plural* **adobes 1.** Brick or bricks made of clay and straw that dry and harden in the sun. **2.** A building made of these bricks.

ad·o·les·cent |ăd′l ĕs′ənt| —*noun, plural* **adolescents** A boy or girl who is older than a child but not yet an adult; a teen-ager.

a·dopt |ə dŏpt′| —*verb* **adopted, adopting 1.** To take someone else's child and by law make that child one's own: *They adopted two children. His stepfather adopted him and gave him his name.* **2.** To take a person or animal into one's family or group: *The children adopted a dog and a cat.* **3.** To take and use as one's own: *Samuel Clemens adopted the name Mark Twain. She adopted her friend's style of dressing.* **4.** To pass by a vote or accept in an official way: *The government adopted a new constitution.*

a·dop·tion |ə dŏp′shən| —*noun, plural* **adoptions** The act or condition of adopting or being adopted: *The adoption of the new law presented problems. The boy's adoption changed his life.*

a·dore |ə dôr′| or |ə dōr′| —*verb* **adored, adoring** To love deeply and with great respect: *He adores his grandfather and follows him about.*

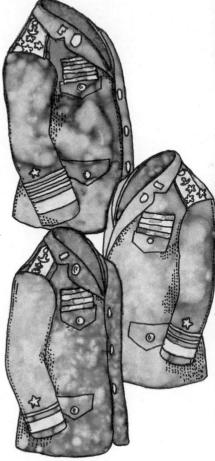

admirals' insignias
Above: Admiral
Center: Vice admiral
Below: Rear admiral

adobe

a·dorn |ə dôrn′| —*verb* **adorned, adorning** **1.** To decorate with something beautiful: *She adorned her fingers with gold rings.* **2.** To be an ornament to: *Flowers adorned the table.*

a·drift |ə drĭft′| —*adverb* and *adjective* Drifting or floating without direction; not guided: *The storm set the boat adrift. The boat was adrift in the water. She felt adrift in the strange city.*

a·dult |ə dŭlt′| or |ăd′ŭlt′| —*noun, plural* **adults** **1.** A person who is fully grown; a grown-up: *Children will not be admitted without an adult.* **2.** A plant or animal that is fully grown. —*adjective* Fully grown; grown-up; mature: *A tadpole becomes an adult frog.*

a·dul·ter·ate |ə dŭl′tə rāt′| —*verb* **adulterated, adulterating** To make weaker or impure by adding something: *She adulterated the milk with water.*

ad·vance |ăd văns′| or |ăd väns′| —*verb* **advanced, advancing** **1.** To move forward, onward, or upward: *The army advanced across the river. The team advanced the ball. Prices advanced quickly.* **2.** To make or help make progress; improve: *Our work advances quickly. The space flight advanced our knowledge of the universe.* **3.** To raise or rise in rank or position; promote or be promoted: *They advanced him from private to sergeant. She advanced to captain.* **4.** To put forward; propose; offer: *He advanced an idea for earning money for the team's uniforms.* **5.** To pay money ahead of time: *Dad advanced me a week's allowance so I could buy Mom a present.* —*noun, plural* **advances** **1.** A movement forward, onward, or upward; progress: *our slow advance through the jungle. The doctor made many advances in medicine.* **2.** A rise in prices or value: *an advance in the cost of eggs; an advance in the stock market.* **3.** Money paid ahead of time: *an advance on my allowance.* **4.** **advances** Efforts to win someone's favor or friendship: *After the fight, I made the first advances to make up.*

ad·vance·ment |ăd văns′mənt| or |ăd väns′mənt| —*noun, plural* **advancements** **1.** A forward step; progress: *He made great advancements in airplane design.* **2.** A move ahead in position; promotion: *a job with a chance for advancement.*

ad·van·tage |ăd văn′tĭj| or |ăd vän′tĭj| —*noun, plural* **advantages** Anything that is helpful or useful: *His knowledge of French was an advantage in getting the job.*

Idiom **take advantage of** **1.** To put to good use; benefit by: *Let's take advantage of the warm weather by going swimming.* **2.** To treat in an unfair manner for selfish reasons: *That bully always takes advantage of the little children.*

ad·van·ta·geous |ăd′văn tā′jəs| —*adjective* Giving an advantage; favorable; useful: *Our seats gave us an advantageous view of the football field.*

ad·ven·ture |ăd vĕn′chər| —*noun, plural* **adventures** **1.** A bold, unusual, or dangerous act or experience: *They set out on a daring space adventure.* **2.** An unusual or exciting experience: *The day at the amusement park was a delightful adventure.*

ad·ven·tur·ous |ăd vĕn′chər əs| —*adjective* **1.** Interested in new and daring deeds; willing to take risks; bold; daring: *The adventurous children explored the old gold mine.* **2.** Full of danger or excitement: *They took an adventurous canoe trip.*

ad·verb |ăd′vûrb′| —*noun, plural* **adverbs** A word that is used to describe a verb, an adjective, or another adverb. Adverbs usually tell when, where, and how and give information about

ă	pat	ĕ	pet	î	fierce
ā	pay	ē	be	ŏ	pot
â	care	ĭ	pit	ō	go
ä	father	ī	pie	ô	paw, for
oi	oil	ŭ	cut	zh	vision
ōō	book	û	fur	ə	ago, item,
ōō	boot	*th*	the		pencil, atom,
yōō	abuse	th	thin		circus
ou	out	hw	which	ər	butter

time, place, manner, or degree. In the sentence "The very small boy ran upstairs quickly and arrived too early," "very," "upstairs," "quickly," "too," and "early" are adverbs.

ad·ver·sar·y |ăd′vər sĕr′ē| —*noun, plural* **adversaries** Someone on the opposite side in a war or contest; an enemy or opponent: *Germany and the Soviet Union were adversaries in World War II. His best friend is his adversary in the chess match.*

ad·verse |ăd **vûrs′**| or |**ăd′**vûrs′| —*adjective* **1.** Not favorable; not friendly: *Their adverse comments on my work make me unhappy.* **2.** Opposite to what is wanted or expected: *The adverse currents make swimming difficult. The medicine had an adverse effect on her.*

ad·ver·si·ty |ăd **vûr′**sĭ tē| —*noun, plural* **adversities** Great misfortune; hardship; trouble: *In spite of many adversities, he finished the trip around the world in his sailboat.*

ad·ver·tise |**ăd′**vər tīz′| —*verb* **advertised, advertising** **1.** To call public attention to, especially by placing paid notices in magazines and newspapers, on radio and television, and in other public places: *Companies advertise their products to increase sales. That company does not advertise.* **2.** To call attention to; make known: *She advertised her happiness with a smile.*

ad·ver·tise·ment |ăd′vər **tīz′**mənt| or |ăd **vûr′**tĭs mənt| or |ăd **vûr′**tĭz mənt| —*noun, plural* **advertisements** A public notice in a newspaper or magazine, on radio or television, or in any public place. An advertisement may be used to sell a product, find or offer work, or find or offer a service.

ad·vice |ăd **vīs′**| —*noun* Opinion about what to do; guidance: *My advice is to follow the doctor's orders.*

ad·vis·a·ble |ăd **vī′**zə bəl| —*adjective* Worth doing; wise; sensible: *It is advisable to dress warmly when you play in the snow.*

ad·vise |ăd **vīz′**| —*verb* **advised, advising** **1.** To offer an opinion about what to do; give advice to: *He advised me to ask for help in building the model plane.* **2.** To give notice to; inform; tell: *The weather reporter advised us that it would rain all day.*

ad·vis·er or **ad·vi·sor** |ăd **vī′**zər| —*noun, plural* **advisers** or **advisors** A person who gives advice: *Two teachers were my advisers on the science project.*

ad·vo·cate |**ăd′**və kāt′| —*verb* **advocated, advocating** To be or speak in favor of; recommend; urge: *He advocates stronger punishment of criminals.*
—*noun* |**ăd′**və kĭt| or |**ăd′**və kāt′|, *plural* **advocates** A person who is or speaks in favor of something; someone who supports a cause: *Thomas Jefferson was an advocate of independence for America.*

adz or **adze** |ădz| —*noun, plural* **adzes** A tool that looks like an ax with its blade set at an angle. An adz is used for shaping logs and other heavy pieces of wood.

aer·i·al |**âr′**ē əl| —*noun, plural* **aerials** An antenna for radio or television.
—*adjective* In the air: *the aerial flights of birds.*

aer·o·nau·tics |âr′ə **nô′**tĭks| —*noun* (Used with a singular verb.) The science and art of flight. Aeronautics includes designing, making, and flying aircraft.

aer·o·sol |**âr′**ə sôl′| or |**âr′**ə sŏl′| or |**âr′**ə sōl′| —*noun, plural* **aerosols** A mass of tiny drops of a liquid or pieces of solid material suspended in air or another gas. Some aerosols are natural, like smoke or smog. Other aerosols are manufactured and

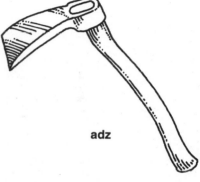

adz

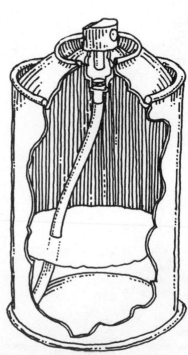

aerosol
Inside view of an aerosol can

sold in containers. Paints, furniture polish, and hair sprays are often sold as aerosols.

aer·o·space |âr′ə spās′| —*noun* **1.** The region that is made up of the earth's atmosphere and outer space. **2.** The science of the flight of aircraft and spacecraft both in the earth's atmosphere and in outer space.

af·fa·ble |ăf′ə bəl| —*adjective* Pleasant and friendly; easy to talk to; gentle: *We were surprised that the famous man was so affable.*

af·fair |ə fâr′| —*noun, plural* **affairs 1.** Something to be done; a piece of business: *We have many affairs to settle before we move.* **2.** An event, action, or happening: *The wedding was a simple affair.*

af·fect¹ |ə fĕkt′| —*verb* **affected, affecting 1.** To have an influence on; bring about a change in: *The weather affects my moods. Poor eating habits affected his health.* **2.** To touch the feelings of: *The sad movie affected her deeply.*

af·fect² |ə fĕkt′| —*verb* **affected, affecting** To pretend to feel or have: *He affected sorrow. He affected an English accent because he liked the sound.*

af·fec·tion |ə fĕk′shən| —*noun, plural* **affections** A loving feeling: *Their parents have a great deal of affection for them.*

af·fec·tion·ate |ə fĕk′shə nĭt| —*adjective* Having or showing love or affection: *Her brother gave her an affectionate pat on the shoulder.*

af·fil·i·ate |ə fĭl′ē āt′| —*verb* **affiliated, affiliating** To join with a larger or more important group, person, or company: *Our club affiliated with the national organization.*
—*noun* |ə fĭl′ə ĭt| or |ə fĭl′ə āt′|, *plural* **affiliates** A person or company that is connected to a larger or more important group, person, or company: *The television network had affiliates in small cities and towns.*

af·firm·a·tive |ə fûr′mə tĭv| —*adjective* Saying that something is so; indicating "yes": *an affirmative answer to a question.*

af·fix |ə fĭks′| —*verb* **affixed, affixing** To add on; attach: *He affixed a stamp to the envelope.*
—*noun* |ăf′ĭks′|, *plural* **affixes** Something added on or attached, especially a prefix or a suffix.

af·flict |ə flĭkt′| —*verb* **afflicted, afflicting** To cause pain or sorrow to; trouble greatly: *His illness afflicts him badly.*

af·flic·tion |ə flĭk′shən| —*noun, plural* **afflictions 1.** Pain or sorrow; suffering; trouble: *The country felt the affliction of a drought.* **2.** A cause of pain, sorrow, suffering, and trouble: *Polio was a common affliction before vaccine for it was found.*

af·flu·ent |ăf′lōō ənt| —*adjective* Having plenty of money; prosperous; wealthy: *In that affluent suburb everyone has a large house and two cars.*

af·ford |ə fôrd′| or |ə fōrd′| —*verb* **afforded, affording 1.** To be able to pay for, spare, or spend: *We can afford the small car but not the large one. I can't afford the time for vacation.* **2.** To be able to do or be without: *This is one game we can't afford to lose.* **3.** To give; provide: *The barn afforded some protection from the storm.*

af·front |ə frŭnt′| —*noun, plural* **affronts** An insult made on purpose: *His rude remarks were an affront to us all.*
—*verb* **affronted, affronting** To insult on purpose; offend strongly: *That song's words affront our sense of what is proper.*

---

affect¹, affect²
Affect¹ comes from a Latin word meaning "to strive after" or "to aim at." **Affect²** comes from a related Latin word meaning "to have an effect on" or "to apply oneself to."

ă	pat	ĕ	pet	î	fierce
ā	pay	ē	be	ŏ	pot
â	care	ĭ	pit	ō	go
ä	father	ī	pie	ô	paw, for

oi	oil	ŭ	cut	zh	vision
ōō	book	û	fur	ə	ago, item,
ōō	boot	*th*	the		pencil, atom,
yōō	abuse	th	thin		circus
ou	out	hw	which	ər	butter

a·fire | ə fīr′ | —*adverb* and *adjective* On fire or as if on fire; burning: *He set the fields afire. His mind was afire with plans.*

a·float | ə flōt′ | —*adjective* and *adverb* **1.** Floating on a liquid or in the air: *The raft was afloat on the lake. A life jacket kept him afloat. The balloon is afloat.* **2.** In circulation; around: *There were many false stories afloat after the shocking news.*

a·foot | ə fŏot′ | —*adjective* and *adverb* **1.** On foot; walking: *They left the car and went afoot.* **2.** In the process of happening; going on: *Something strange is afoot in the empty house.*

a·fraid | ə frād′ | —*adjective* **1.** Filled with fear; frightened: *She is not afraid of the big dog. He is afraid to climb the tower.* **2.** Filled with regret; sorry: *I'm afraid you don't understand.*

Af·ri·ca | ăf′rĭ kə | A continent that is south of Europe between the Atlantic Ocean and the Indian Ocean.

Af·ri·can | ăf′rĭ kən | —*noun, plural* **Africans** A person born in Africa and belonging to the Negroid ethnic group.
—*adjective* Of Africa or the Africans: *an African village; African folk songs.*

African violet A plant with flowers that look like violets. It is often grown as a house plant.

aft | ăft | or | äft | —*adverb* and *adjective* Toward or near the rear of a ship: *He went aft. She slept in the aft cabin.*

af·ter | ăf′tər | or | äf′tər | —*preposition* **1.** In a place or order following: *The caboose comes after the freight cars.* **2.** At a later time than; following: *After school we can go to the movies.* **3.** Past the hour of: *five minutes after three.* **4.** In pursuit or in search of: *All the kids were running after the fire engine.*
—*adverb* **1.** At a later time; afterward: *We arrived shortly after.* **2.** Behind: *And Jill came tumbling after.*
—*conjunction* As soon as or following the time that: *We can eat after we get home.*

af·ter·math | ăf′tər măth′ | or | äf′tər măth′ | —*noun, plural* **aftermaths** Something that follows as a result: *in the aftermath of war. The hurricane left an aftermath of spoiled crops and ruined homes.*

af·ter·noon | ăf′tər nōon′ | or | äf′tər nōon′ | —*noun, plural* **afternoons** The part of the day from noon until sunset.

af·ter·ward | ăf′tər wərd | or | äf′tər wərd | —*adverb* At a later time: *We napped and afterward we swam.* Another form of this adverb is **afterwards.**

af·ter·wards | ăf′tər wərdz | or | äf′tər wərdz | A form of the adverb **afterward.**

a·gain | ə gĕn′ | —*adverb* Once more; another time: *Nobody answered, so we rang again.*

a·gainst | ə gĕnst′ | —*preposition* **1.** In a direction or course opposite to: *They were sailing against the wind.* **2.** So as to come into contact with: *The waves were crashing against the shore. The rain was beating against the window.* **3.** In opposition or resistance to: *They were always fighting against any change in the rules.* **4.** Contrary to: *I went to the game against my better judgment.* **5.** As a defense or protection from: *The little girl was wearing gloves against the chill.*

ag·ate | ăg′ĭt | —*noun, plural* **agates** **1.** A stone that is a type of quartz. Agate is striped with different colors and is often cloudy. **2.** A playing marble that is made of agate or something that looks like agate.

African violet

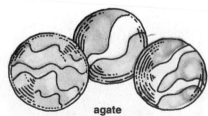

agate
Marbles made from agate

age | āj | —*noun, plural* **ages** **1.** The amount of time a person, plant, animal, or thing has lived or existed: *His age is ninety-two. What is the age of that antique?* **2.** A particular time of life: *At age four he could play the piano.* **3.** The time or condition of being old: *Wisdom sometimes comes with age.* **4.** A particular period of time when some special thing is important: *the space age; the Age of Reptiles.* **5.** A long time: *It is an age since I last saw you. He has not danced in ages.* **6.** The time when the law says a person may take on adult rights and responsibilities: *He cannot vote because he is under age. She came of age yesterday.*
—*verb* **aged, aging** **1.** To grow old: *He aged quickly after his wife died.* **2.** To cause to become or appear old: *His wife's death aged him.*

ag·ed | ā′jĭd | —*adjective* Having lived for a long time; old; elderly: *An aged tree still stands in the yard.*

a·gen·cy | ā′jən sē | —*noun, plural* **agencies** A business or organization that acts for another person or business: *A real-estate agency buys and sells land and houses for people. A detective agency finds information for people. A government agency does work for the government.*

a·gent | ā′jənt | —*noun, plural* **agents** **1.** A person or group that handles business matters for another: *The actor's agent found him a good movie part. His company was the local agent for foreign cars.* **2.** A means by which something is done or caused: *Wind and water are agents of erosion.*

ag·gra·vate | ăg′rə vāt′ | —*verb* **aggravated, aggravating** **1.** To make worse: *Use of his arm aggravated the injury.* **2.** To irritate; annoy: *His constant whining aggravates her.*

ag·gres·sion | ə grĕsh′ən | —*noun, plural* **aggressions** An action that is likely to start a war, cause a fight, or create bad feelings: *Their raid into the neighboring country was an act of aggression.*

ag·gres·sive | ə grĕs′ĭv | —*adjective* **1.** Quick to attack or start a fight: *The aggressive country began many wars. The aggressive boy often argued with his friends.* **2.** Full of energy; very active in getting things done: *an aggressive salesman; an aggressive campaign against crime.*

a·ghast | ə găst′ | or | ə gäst′ | —*adjective* Shocked by something terrible or wrong: *We were aghast when we saw what the rains had done.*

ag·ile | ăj′əl | or | ăj′īl′ | —*adjective* Capable of moving quickly and easily; nimble: *the dancer's agile movements; her agile mind.*

a·gil·i·ty | ə jĭl′ĭ tē | —*noun* The ability to move quickly and easily: *an acrobat's agility.*

ag·i·tate | ăj′ĭ tāt′ | —*verb* **agitated, agitating** **1.** To shake or stir up strongly: *The storm agitated the sea.* **2.** To upset the mind or feelings of; disturb: *The news of his arrest agitated his family a great deal.*

ag·i·ta·tion | ăj′ĭ tā′shən | —*noun* **1.** The act of agitating: *the agitation of the milk by the churn; the agitation of the curtains by the wind.* **2.** Great disturbance of mind; the condition of being very upset: *her agitation at the theft of her purse.*

a·go | ə gō′ | —*adjective* Gone by; past: *It was two years ago that we met.*
—*adverb* In the past: *They lived there long ago.*

ag·o·ny | ăg′ə nē | —*noun, plural* **agonies** Very great pain of

agile
Performing gymnastics

ă	pat	ĕ	pet	î	fierce
ā	pay	ē	be	ŏ	pot
â	care	ĭ	pit	ō	go
ä	father	ī	pie	ô	paw, for

oi	oil	ŭ	cut	zh	vision
ōō	book	û	fur	ə	ago, item,
ōō	boot	*th*	the		pencil, atom,
yōō	abuse	th	thin		circus
ou	out	hw	which	ər	butter

body or mind; deep suffering: *the agony of a broken back; the agony of seeing a friend die.*

a·gree |ə grē′| —*verb* **agreed, agreeing** **1.** To have the same opinion: *He likes cats and she agrees.* **2.** To say "yes"; consent: *He agreed to visit us soon.* **3.** To be the same; be in harmony: *Their stories do not agree.* **4.** In grammar, to have the same person and number: *The verb "is" agrees with "he," "she," and "it"; it does not agree with "I", "they," "you," or "we."*

    Phrasal verb **agree with** To be good or healthful for: *Onions do not agree with me. The climate agrees with him.*

a·gree·a·ble |ə grē′ə bəl| —*adjective* **1.** Pleasant; pleasing: *an agreeable odor; an agreeable friendship.* **2.** Willing to agree; ready to say "yes": *He is agreeable to our plan.*

a·gree·ment |ə grē′mənt| —*noun, plural* **agreements** **1.** The act or condition of agreeing; harmony of opinions or ideas: *We are in agreement on what to do next.* **2.** An arrangement or understanding between two or more people or groups: *The boxer signed an agreement to fight the champion. The countries made an agreement on their boundaries.*

ag·ri·cul·tur·al |ăg′rĭ **kŭl′**chər əl| —*adjective* Of farms or farming: *an agricultural region; agricultural studies.*

ag·ri·cul·ture |ăg′rĭ kŭl′chər| —*noun* The science, art, and business of farming.

a·head |ə hĕd′| —*adverb* and *adjective* **1.** At or to the front; farther forward: *Please move ahead in line. The road ahead is full of dust.* **2.** In advance; beforehand: *Phone ahead for tickets.* **3.** Onward; forward: *Go ahead with the work.*

aid |ād| —*verb* **aided, aiding** To help or assist: *Glasses aid my sight. A map aids us in finding our way.*
—*noun, plural* **aids** **1.** Help; assistance: *She offered aid to the victims of the fire.* **2.** Something that helps or is helpful: *A dictionary is an aid to finding out meanings of words.*
♦ *These sound alike* **aid, aide.**

aide |ād| —*noun, plural* **aides** A person who helps someone more important carry out a job; an official assistant: *the general's aide. She is an aide to the President.*
♦ *These sound alike* **aide, aid.**

ail |āl| —*verb* **ailed, ailing** **1.** To be ill; feel sick: *She has been ailing since she fell.* **2.** To cause pain to; make ill; trouble: *What ails you?*
♦ *These sound alike* **ail, ale.**

ai·lan·thus |ā lăn′thəs| —*noun, plural* **ailanthuses** A tree that has small, pointed leaves shaped like feathers. The ailanthus is very common in cities and grows where other trees fail to grow.

ail·ment |āl′mənt| —*noun, plural* **ailments** An illness or sickness that may last a long time.

aim |ām| —*verb* **aimed, aiming** **1.** To point or direct one thing at another: *He aimed his camera at me and took a picture. She aimed the gun at the target. They aimed and fired. He aimed his criticism at a few people in the audience.* **2.** To have a purpose or goal: *We aim to please our customers.*
—*noun, plural* **aims** **1.** The act of pointing or directing one thing at another: *He takes careful aim with darts.* **2.** A purpose; goal: *Her aim is to become a doctor.*

aim·less |ām′lĭs| —*adjective* Without direction or purpose: *her aimless wandering through town.*

agriculture
A dairy farm in Michigan

ailanthus
Tree *(above)* and leaves *(below)*

Airedale

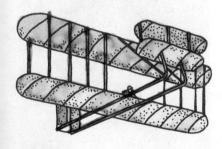

airplane

ain't |ānt| A contraction of the words "am not," "is not," "are not," "have not," and "has not." The word **ain't** is not considered to be correct English.

air |âr| —*noun, plural* **airs** **1.** The mixture of gases around the earth. The two main gases in air are nitrogen and oxygen. There are other gases, too. Air also has water vapor, dust, pollen, and some pollutants. Air itself has no color, no odor, and no taste. **2.** Fresh air that is moving: *This room has no air; it's stuffy.* **3.** The open space above the earth; the sky: *The bird flew into the air.* **4.** A melody; tune: *She played old Scottish airs on the piano.* **5.** Look, style, or manner; appearance: *There was an air of mystery about the old house. The judge had a dignified air about him.* **6. airs** Manners used to make oneself seem better than others: *She puts on airs as if she were a princess.*
—*verb* **aired, airing** **1.** To let fresh air in or through: *Let's air this room.* **2.** To become fresh or cool by letting air in, on, or through: *Open the windows and give the room time to air out.* **3.** To talk about; make known: *It is sometimes good to air one's feelings.*
Idioms **off the air** Not broadcasting or being broadcast by radio or television: *The station will be off the air until tomorrow morning. After tonight the show will be off the air.* **on the air** Broadcasting or being broadcast by radio or television: *Quiet, we are now on the air! Is that quiz show still on the air?* **up in the air** Not settled or decided: *Our vacation plans are still up in the air.*
♦ *These sound alike* **air, heir.**

air con·di·tion·er |kən dĭsh′ə nər| A machine that cools, and sometimes cleans and dries, the air in a room, car, or other closed place.

air·craft |âr′krăft′| or |âr′kräft′| —*noun, plural* **aircraft** Any machine that is made for flying. Airplanes, helicopters, gliders, and dirigibles are all aircraft.

aircraft carrier A large ship that is part of a navy and is used as an air base. An aircraft carrier has a long, flat deck on which aircraft can take off and land.

Aire·dale |âr′dāl′| —*noun, plural* **Airedales** A large dog with a wiry black and tan coat. The Airedale is a kind of terrier.

air·field |âr′fēld′| —*noun, plural* **airfields** A place where aircraft can take off and land. An airfield usually has paved runways.

air force or **Air Force** The branch of a country's military forces that is equipped with aircraft.

air·line |âr′līn′| —*noun, plural* **airlines** A company whose business is to carry passengers and cargo in airplanes.

air·mail |âr′māl′| —*adjective* For or of mail sent by aircraft: *an air-mail stamp; an air-mail package.*

air mail **1.** Letters or packages that are sent by aircraft. **2.** The system of sending mail by aircraft.

air·man |âr′mən| —*noun, plural* **airmen** A person of the lowest rank in the United States Air Force.

air·plane |âr′plān′| —*noun, plural* **airplanes** A vehicle that is heavier than air but is capable of flying. An airplane has wings and is driven by propellers or jet engines.

air·port |âr′pôrt′| or |âr′pōrt′| —*noun, plural* **airports** A place with runways where aircraft can land and take off. An airport has buildings for storing aircraft and repairing them. It also has buildings for passengers who are arriving and leaving.

air pressure The force of air pressing on anything it touches.

ă	pat	ē	pet	î	fierce
ā	pay	ē	be	ŏ	pot
â	care	ĭ	pit	ō	go
ä	father	ī	pie	ô	paw, for
oi	oil	ŭ	cut	zh	vision
ōō	book	û	fur	ə	ago, item,
ōō	boot	*th*	the		pencil, atom,
yōō	abuse	th	thin		circus
ou	out	hw	which	ər	butter

Air pressure is created by the weight of higher air pressing down on the air below.

air·ship | âr′shĭp′ | —*noun, plural* **airships** An aircraft that is lighter than air, can be steered, and has engines; a dirigible.

air·tight | âr′tīt′ | —*adjective* **1.** Closed or closing so tightly that no air or other gases can get into or out of: *Place the food in an airtight container.* **2.** Having no weak points; not able to be attacked with success: *He has an airtight excuse to prove that he was elsewhere when the windows were smashed.*

air·y | âr′ē | —*adjective* **airier, airiest 1.** Built so that air can move freely: *a light and airy cottage.* **2.** Light as air; delicate: *an airy spider web.*

aisle | īl | —*noun, plural* **aisles** A narrow passage through which one may walk, as between rows of seats in a church or theater or between counters in a store.
♦ *These sound alike* **aisle, I'll, isle.**

a·jar | ə jär′ | —*adjective* and *adverb* Not closed all the way; partly open: *The door is ajar. Please leave the door ajar.*

a·kim·bo | ə kĭm′bō | —*adjective* and *adverb* With the hands on the hips and the elbows bent outward.

a·kin | ə kĭn′ | —*adjective* **1.** Having a common origin; related: *My cousins are akin to me. The word "mother" is akin to the word "maternal."* **2.** Of the same sort; similar: *Her taste in books is akin to mine.*

Al·a·bam·a | ăl′ə băm′ə | A state in the southern United States. The capital of Alabama is Montgomery.

al·a·bas·ter | ăl′ə băs′tər | or | ăl′ə bä′stər | —*noun* A kind of smooth stone sometimes carved for decoration. Alabaster may be white, pink, or pale yellow.

a·larm | ə lärm′ | —*noun, plural* **alarms 1.** Sudden fear caused by a feeling of danger: *Our eyes were wide with alarm when the burning building collapsed.* **2.** A warning that danger is near: *The explosions were an alarm that the volcano would erupt.* **3.** A bell, buzzer, flashing light, or other signal sounded to warn people or to wake them up: *a fire alarm; a burglar alarm; set the alarm for eight o'clock.*
—*verb* **alarmed, alarming** To fill with fear; frighten: *The sound of thunder alarmed him.*

a·las | ə lăs′ | or | ə läs′ | —*interjection* A word used to express sorrow, regret, or grief.

A·las·ka | ə lăs′kə | The largest state of the United States. Alaska is in northwestern North America. The capital of Alaska is Juneau.

Al·ba·ny | ôl′bə nē | The capital of New York State.

al·ba·tross | ăl′bə trôs′ | or | ăl′bə trŏs′ | —*noun, plural* **albatrosses** A large sea bird with webbed feet, a hooked beak, and very long wings.

Al·ber·ta | ăl bûr′tə | A province of western Canada. The capital of Alberta is Edmonton.

al·bum | ăl′bəm | —*noun, plural* **albums 1.** A book with blank pages in which collections of photographs, stamps, or other things may be kept. **2.** A long-playing phonograph record or a set of such records in one case: *He bought a one-record album of folk songs and a three-record album of classical music.*

al·che·my | ăl′kə mē | —*noun* An old kind of science and magic that existed before chemistry. People who practiced alchemy tried

akimbo

Alabama
The name **Alabama** probably comes from two Indian words meaning "I make a clearing." The state was named for the river.

Alaska
Alaska comes from an Eskimo word meaning "peninsula." In 1867 the United States bought the land from Russia.

Alberta
The province of **Alberta** was named for Princess Louise Caroline Alberta, the daughter of Prince Albert and Queen Victoria of England.

to find a way to turn common metals into gold. They also tried to find a magic formula that would keep people young and healthy forever.

al·co·hol |ăl′kə hôl′| or |ăl′kə hŏl′| —*noun, plural* **alcohols** **1.** Any of several related liquids that are clear, burn easily, and evaporate quickly. One kind of alcohol is made from fruits, grains, or sugar and is found in drinks like wine, beer, and whiskey. Other kinds of alcohol are now made by combining chemicals. Alcohols are used in medicines, in skin lotions, in paints, and in many manufactured products. **2.** Any drink, like wine, beer, and whiskey, that contains alcohol; liquor.

al·co·hol·ic |ăl′kə hô′lĭk| or |ăl′kə hŏl′ĭk| —*adjective* Of or containing alcohol: *Wine is an alcoholic drink.*
—*noun, plural* **alcoholics** A person who has a strong need for drinks containing alcohol. Alcoholics have little control over how much alcohol they drink.

al·co·hol·ism |ăl′kə hô lĭz′əm| —*noun* A disease in which people cannot control how much alcohol they consume.

al·cove |ăl′kōv′| —*noun, plural* **alcoves** A small room that opens on a larger one without being separated from it by a wall.

al·der |ôl′dər| —*noun, plural* **alders** A tree or shrub that grows in cool, damp places. Alders have rough bark and rounded leaves.

ale |āl| —*noun, plural* **ales** An alcoholic drink made of malt and hops. Ale is like beer but heavier.
♦ *These sound alike* **ale, ail.**

a·lert |ə lûrt′| —*adjective* Quick to notice or understand: *an alert watchman; an alert student.*
—*verb* **alerted, alerting** To warn or make aware of: *A siren alerted us to danger. We alerted him to the change in schedule.*
—*noun, plural* **alerts** **1.** A signal, such as a bell or siren, sounded to warn of danger or attack: *a fire alert.* **2.** A period of time when people watch for possible danger: *during a hurricane alert.*

al·fal·fa |ăl făl′fə| —*noun* A plant with purple flowers and leaves that look like clover. Alfalfa is grown as food for cattle and other animals. Chemicals that make the soil richer are produced on alfalfa roots.

al·gae |ăl′jē| —*plural noun* Plants that do not have true roots, stems, and leaves but often have green coloring. Most algae grow in water. There are many kinds of algae. Some are tiny single cells. Others are large seaweeds.

al·ge·bra |ăl′jə brə| —*noun* A branch of mathematics in which letters or other symbols are used to represent numbers or sets of numbers.

a·li·as |ā′lē əs| —*noun, plural* **aliases** A name that a person takes to hide his or her real name: *Jesse James used the alias "Thomas Howard."*
—*adverb* Also known as; otherwise named: *Martha Jane Canary, alias Calamity Jane, was a famous Western character.*

al·i·bi |ăl′ə bī′| —*noun, plural* **alibis** **1.** A claim offered in an attempt to prove that a person was somewhere else when a crime was committed: *Her alibi is that she was away on a trip when the safe was robbed.* **2.** An excuse: *He has dozens of alibis for not doing his work.*

a·li·en |ā′lē ən| or |āl′yən| —*adjective* **1.** Of or from another country; foreign: *The F.B.I. made an effort to expel all alien spies.* **2.** Opposed; contrary: *Lying is alien to his nature.*

alfalfa

ă	pat	ĕ	pet	î	fierce
ā	pay	ē	be	ŏ	pot
â	care	ĭ	pit	ō	go
ä	father	ī	pie	ô	paw, for
oi	oil	ŭ	cut	zh	vision
ōō	book	û	fur	ə	ago, item,
ōō	boot	th	the		pencil, atom,
yōō	abuse	th	thin		circus
ou	out	hw	which	ər	butter

—*noun, plural* **aliens** **1.** A person who lives in one country although a citizen of another country; a foreigner. **2.** In science fiction, an intelligent being not from Earth.

al·ien·ate | ãl′yə nãt′ | or | ā′lē ə nãt′ | —*verb* **alienated, alienating** To lose the friendship of; make others become unfriendly: *His angry shouting alienated almost everybody.*

a·light[1] | ə līt′ | —*adjective* **1.** Lighted; sparkling: *His eyes were alight with happiness.* **2.** On fire; burning: *The house was alight before the firefighters arrived.*

a·light[2] | ə līt′ | —*verb* **alighted** or **alit, alighting** **1.** To come down and settle gently: *A bird alighted on the branch.* **2.** To get off; get down: *The train stopped and he alighted.*

a·lign | ə līn′ | —*verb* **aligned, aligning** To bring into a straight line; line up: *Let's align the chairs in two rows.*

a·like | ə līk′ | —*adjective* Having a close resemblance; similar: *Alice and her mother are alike in many ways.*
—*adverb* In the same way or manner: *Bob and his father walk and talk alike.*

al·i·men·ta·ry canal | ăl′ə měn′tə rē | or | ăl′ə měn′trē | The tube in the body through which food passes, is digested, and leaves as waste. The alimentary canal begins at the mouth and includes the esophagus, the stomach, and the intestines.

al·i·mo·ny | ăl′ə mō′nē | —*noun, plural* **alimonies** Money that must be paid regularly to support a person's former wife or husband after a divorce.

a·lit | ə līt′ | A past tense and past participle of the verb **alight** (to get down): *He alit from the train carefully. The bird had already alit on the branch when the storm began.*

a·live | ə līv′ | —*adjective* **1.** Having life; living: *We were surprised to find our plants alive after such hot, dry weather.* **2.** In existence or operation; active: *The team's hopes for the championship were still alive.*

all | ôl | —*adjective* **1.** The whole of; the entire quantity of: *He ate all the candy in the house.* **2.** Every one of; each of: *All the children are healthy.* **3.** Any: *She hoped beyond all chance that she would win.*
—*pronoun* Each and every one: *All were rescued.*
—*noun* Everything one has: *He gave his all in the contest.*
—*adverb* **1.** Wholly; entirely; completely: *She is all wrong.* **2.** Each; apiece: *The score is tied one all.*
♦ *These sound alike* **all, awl.**

Al·lah | ăl′ə | or | ä′lə | —*noun* The name of God in the Moslem religion.

al·lege | ə lěj′ | —*verb* **alleged, alleging** To declare something to be true without definite proof: *She alleged that he was the thief, and the jury will decide whether he is.*

al·le·giance | ə lē′jəns | —*noun, plural* **allegiances** Loyal and faithful devotion to someone or something: *allegiance to the flag; allegiance to one's country; allegiance to the king.*

al·ler·gic | ə lûr′jĭk | —*adjective* **1.** Having one or more allergies: *He is allergic to chocolate, nuts, and cats.* **2.** Resulting from an allergy: *She had an allergic reaction to the medicine.*

al·ler·gy | ăl′ər jē | —*noun, plural* **allergies** An unpleasant physical reaction to certain foods, pollens, furs, animals, or other things. A person with an allergy may develop a rash, hives, watery eyes, or other problems.

---

alight¹, alight²
Alight¹ comes from an old English phrase, *on light,* in the same way that *afire* comes from *on fire.* **Alight²** comes from an old English word meaning "to lighten" or "to take the weight off something." **Alight¹** is related to **light¹** (brightness), while **alight²** is related to **light²** (not heavy).

al·ley | ăl′ē | —*noun, plural* **alleys** **1.** A narrow street or passage between or behind buildings. **2.** A long, smooth, narrow lane down which one rolls bowling balls.

al·li·ance | ə lī′əns | —*noun, plural* **alliances** An agreement to join together for a common purpose: *The three countries made an alliance and signed the treaty.*

al·lied | ə līd′ | or | ăl′īd′ | —*adjective* Joined together in an alliance: *Three allied families took over the business.*

al·li·ga·tor | ăl′ĭ gā′tər | —*noun, plural* **alligators** **1.** A large reptile with sharp teeth and strong jaws. Alligators look like crocodiles but have a shorter, wider snout. True alligators live only in wet places in the southeastern United States and in China. **2.** Leather made from the skin of an alligator.

al·lot | ə lŏt′ | —*verb* **allotted, allotting** **1.** To give out in parts or shares: *She allotted the money equally to the three workers. He allotted us each a piece of cake and a glass of milk.* **2.** To put aside part of something for a special purpose: *He allotted two hours of his time for homework and three hours for sports.*

al·low | ə lou′ | —*verb* **allowed, allowing** **1.** To let do or happen; permit: *He allowed us to leave early. Do they allow dancing here?* **2.** To let have: *Mom allows me money for movies.* **3.** To admit the possibility or truth of: *I'll allow that I've made some mistakes.* **4.** To let in; permit the presence of: *No dogs are allowed in the restaurant.* **5.** To subtract or add for a special reason: *The salesman allowed $15 on my old bicycle, so I paid $85 for the new $100 bicycle. The judge allowed him time off for good behavior.*

al·low·ance | ə lou′əns | —*noun, plural* **allowances** **1.** Money, food, or other things given at regular times or for a special purpose: *an allowance of fifty cents a week; an allowance of two cookies a day.* **2.** Money subtracted from a price for a special reason; a discount: *The new fifty-dollar coat needed to be cleaned, so the salesperson gave her an allowance of five dollars and she bought it for forty-five dollars.*

Idiom **make allowance (or allowances) for** To take into account; allow for: *They made allowances for the fact that he was new at the job and had to learn everything.*

al·loy | ăl′oi′ | or | ə loi′ | —*noun, plural* **alloys** A metal made by melting together two or more other metals. Some alloys offer qualities that are an improvement for some purposes over the metals that were mixed. Brass, bronze, and pewter are examples of this. Other alloys allow a valuable metal to be combined with a cheaper one to lower the cost.

all right **1.** Satisfactory but not excellent; good enough; acceptable: *The food is all right, but I've tasted better.* **2.** Free from error; correct: *My answer was all right.* **3.** Not sick or injured; safe: *Are you all right after that nasty fall?* **4.** Very well; yes: *All right, I'll go with you.*

al·lude | ə lōōd′ | —*verb* **alluded, alluding** To refer to in an indirect way; mention in passing: *Did you allude to me when you said that someone had lied?*

al·ly | ə lī′ | —*verb* **allied, allying, allies** To join or unite for a special purpose: *Small countries often ally themselves to be strong against their enemies.*

—*noun* | ăl′ī′ | or | ə lī′ |, *plural* **allies** A person or country that has united with another for a special purpose: *The mayor was his ally in the campaign against crime.*

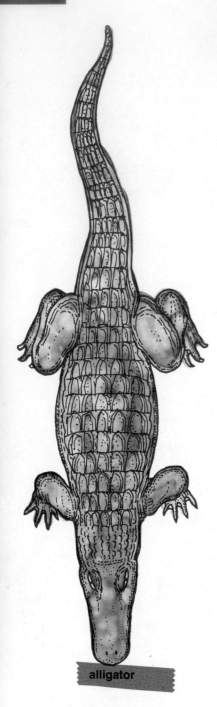

alligator

ă	pat	ĕ	pet	î	fierce
ā	pay	ē	be	ŏ	pot
â	care	ĭ	pit	ō	go
ä	father	ī	pie	ô	paw, for

oi	oil	ŭ	cut	zh	vision
ōō	book	û	fur	ə	ago, item,
ōō	boot	*th*	the		pencil, atom,
yōō	abuse	th	thin		circus
ou	out	hw	which	ər	butter

al·ma·nac |ôl′ mə năk′| or |ăl′ mə năk′| —*noun, plural* almanacs A book published once a year containing facts and information on many different subjects. Some almanacs are arranged like calendars and give facts about weather, tides, the moon, and the sun. Other almanacs have lists of important dates, people, and reference materials in many fields.

al·mond |ä′ mənd| or |ăm′ ənd| —*noun, plural* almonds **1.** An oval nut with a soft, light-brown shell. Almonds are good to eat. **2.** A tree on which almonds grow.

al·most |ôl′ mōst′| or |ôl mōst′| —*adverb* Nearly but not quite: *We are almost finished with the job. It is almost spring.*

a·loft |ə lôft′| or |ə lŏft′| —*adverb* **1.** In or into a high place; up in or into the air: *The gulls soared aloft.* **2.** High on the mast and rigging of a sailing ship: *The sailor climbed aloft to see if land was near.*

a·lo·ha |ä lō′hä′| —*interjection* A Hawaiian word that is used to say "greetings," "hello," or "good-by." Aloha means "love" in Hawaiian.

a·lone |ə lōn′| —*adjective* **1.** Without another person; by oneself: *She lives alone.* **2.** Only: *The magician alone knew the secret. The noise alone is enough to scare him.*
—*adverb* Without help: *I can finish it alone.*
Idioms **leave** (or **let**) **alone** To keep from bothering, disturbing, or interrupting: *Please leave him alone until he finishes his work.*

a·long |ə lông′| or |ə lŏng′| —*preposition* In a line with; following the length or path of: *The band marched along the main street of the town.*
—*adverb* **1.** In a line with something; following the length or path: *Trees grew along by the river.* **2.** Forward; onward; ahead: *Run along and I'll follow.* **3.** As company or in company: *Bring a friend along to the picnic. Come along with us to the beach and enjoy the fun.*

a·long·side |ə lông′ sīd′| or |ə lŏng′ sīd′| —*preposition* and *adverb* By the side of; side by side with: *The boat pulled up alongside the dock. The boat pulled alongside for a while.*

a·loof |ə lōōf′| —*adjective* Cool and distant; not very friendly: *His aloof manner keeps people away.*
—*adverb* At a distance from others; apart: *She stood aloof as the others fought.*

a·loud |ə loud′| —*adverb* Loud enough to be heard; out loud: *Don't whisper; say it aloud. She read the story aloud to the class.*

al·pac·a |ăl păk′ə| —*noun, plural* alpacas A South American animal with long, silky wool. The alpaca is related to the llama.

al·pha·bet |ăl′ fə bĕt′| —*noun, plural* alphabets The letters used to stand for the different sounds of a language. The letters of the alphabet are arranged in a set order.

al·pha·bet·i·cal |ăl′ fə bĕt′ ĭ kəl| —*adjective* Arranged in the order of the letters of the alphabet: *an alphabetical list of words. The book has an alphabetical index.*

al·pha·bet·ize |ăl′ fə bĭ tīz′| —*verb* alphabetized, alphabetizing To arrange in the order of the letters of the alphabet: *Please alphabetize these words.*

al·read·y |ôl rĕd′ ē| —*adverb* By this or that time: *It is early, but she has already finished the job. When I arrived, he had already left.*

al·so |ôl′ sō| —*adverb* In addition; besides; too: *He is an artist and a musician also.*

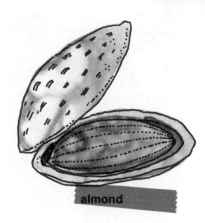
almond

alpaca

altar

al·tar |ôl′tər| —*noun, plural* **altars** A table or a raised place used for religious ceremonies: *an altar in a church; a pagan altar.*
♦ *These sound alike* **altar, alter.**

al·ter |ôl′tər| —*verb* **altered, altering** To change or make changes in: *His appearance altered when he shaved off his beard. The woman altered the dress so that it fit better.*
♦ *These sound alike* **alter, altar.**

al·ter·nate |ôl′tər nāt′| or |ăl′tər nāt′| —*verb* **alternated, alternating 1.** To take turns by allowing first one, then the other to go: *Dots alternate with dashes in the pattern . - . - . Day alternates with night. The two children alternate taking out the garbage.* **2.** To pass back and forth: *She alternates between happy and sad moods.*
—*adjective* |ôl′tər nĭt| or |ăl′tər nĭt| **1.** Happening in turns; one after the other: *We had alternate years of rain and drought.*
2. Every other; skipping one between each: *She goes swimming on alternate Fridays.* **3.** In place of another: *The highway was closed, so we took an alternate route.*
—*noun* |ôl′tər nĭt| or |ăl′tər nĭt |, *plural* **alternates** A person or thing that is available to take the place of another; a substitute: *The jury had twelve people and two alternates in case any took sick during the trial.*

al·ter·nat·ing current |ôl′tər nā′tĭng| An electric current that flows first in one direction, then in the opposite direction, at regular intervals.

al·ter·na·tive |ôl tûr′nə tĭv| or |ăl tûr′nə tĭv| —*noun, plural* **alternatives 1.** A choice between two or more things or ways of doing things: *The state has to face the alternative of high taxes or poor schools. The judge gave him the alternative of paying a fine or going to jail.* **2.** One of the things or ways of doing things that can be chosen: *The governor favors the alternative of high taxes. He took the alternative of paying the fine.*

al·though |ôl thō′| —*conjunction* Even though: *She won't swim although she knows how.*

al·tim·e·ter |ăl tĭm′ĭ tər| —*noun, plural* **altimeters** An instrument that measures altitude. Altimeters are used in aircraft to find how high they are flying.

al·ti·tude |ăl′tĭ tōōd′| or |ăl′tĭ tyōōd′| —*noun, plural* **altitudes** A height measured from sea level or from the surface of the ground: *Denver, at an altitude of 5,280 feet, is called the Mile-High City. The plane flew at an altitude of 12,000 feet.*

al·to |ăl′tō| —*noun, plural* **altos 1.** A low singing voice of a woman or boy or a man's high singing voice in the same range. An alto is lower than a soprano and higher than a tenor. **2.** A person who has this singing voice. **3.** A musical instrument with the same range as this voice.

al·to·geth·er |ôl′tə gĕth′ər| or |ôl′tə gĕth′ər| —*adverb*
1. Completely; entirely: *She is altogether mistaken.* **2.** With all included or counted: *Altogether there are thirty-six teachers in the school* **3.** On the whole; considering everything: *There were some bad moments, but altogether Mark had a good time.*

a·lu·mi·num |ə lōō′mə nəm| —*noun* A lightweight, silver-white metal. It is used for pots and pans, kitchen foil, tools, airplanes, and many other items. Aluminum is the most plentiful metal in the earth's crust. It is a chemical element.

al·ways |ôl′wāz| or |ôl′wĕz| —*adverb* **1.** On every occasion; every single time: *He always leaves work at exactly five o'clock.*

ă	pat	ĕ	pet	î	fierce
ā	pay	ē	be	ŏ	pot
â	care	ĭ	pit	ō	go
ä	father	ī	pie	ô	paw, for
oi	oil	ŭ	cut	zh	vision
ōō	book	û	fur	ə	ago, item,
ōō	boot	*th*	the		pencil, atom,
yōō	abuse	th	thin		circus
ou	out	hw	which	ər	butter

2. For all the time one can imagine; forever: *There will always be a sun in the sky. We shall always have a place for you.*

am | ăm | The first person singular present tense of the verb **be:** *Marilyn said: "I am glad to meet you."*

a.m. or **A.M** Before noon or between midnight and noon: *Breakfast is at 8:00 a.m.* A.M. is an abbreviation for the Latin words *ante meridiem,* meaning "before noon."

am·a·ryl·lis | ăm′ə **rĭl′**ĭs | —*noun, plural* **amaryllises** A plant with very large reddish or white flowers. It grows from a bulb and is often used as a house plant.

am·a·teur | ăm′ə chŏŏr′ | or | ăm′ə chər | or | ăm′ə tyŏŏr′ | —*noun, plural* **amateurs 1.** A person who does something just for pleasure and does not get paid; someone who is not a professional: *Only amateurs are allowed to play college football.* **2.** A person who does something without much skill: *The sloppy paint job is the work of an amateur.*

a·maze | ə **māz′** | —*verb* **amazed, amazing** To fill with surprise or wonder; astonish: *The speed of the hummingbird's wings amazed us.*

a·maze·ment | ə **māz′**mənt | —*noun* Great surprise; astonishment: *her amazement at the size and beauty of the canyon.*

am·bas·sa·dor | ăm **băs′**ə dər | —*noun, plural* **ambassadors** An official of the highest rank who goes to another country to represent his own country or government.

am·ber | ăm′bər | —*noun* A light or brownish-yellow material that looks like stone. Amber is a hardened fossil resin from ancient pine trees. It sometimes has insects or leaves that were trapped in it and is used for making jewelry and ornaments.

am·big·u·ous | ăm **bĭg′**yŏŏ əs | —*adjective* Having two or more possible meanings; not clear. The sentence "He only eats pickles" is ambiguous because it could mean "Only he eats pickles" (nobody else eats them) or "He eats pickles only" (and no other food) or "He only eats pickles" (and does not drink them or grow them).

am·bi·tion | ăm **bĭsh′**ən | —*noun, plural* **ambitions 1.** A strong desire to get or become something: *His ambition is to be a great detective.* **2.** The thing desired: *She spent a lot of time and money to achieve her great ambition.*

am·bi·tious | ăm **bĭsh′**əs | —*adjective* **1.** Eager for success, fame, money, or power: *The ambitious boy started a business while he was still in school.* **2.** Needing a lot of work to succeed: *He has an ambitious plan to build a city in the desert.*

am·bu·lance | ăm′byə ləns | —*noun, plural* **ambulances** A large vehicle that is used to rush people who are sick or hurt to a hospital. An ambulance has special medical equipment and trained people to help on the way to the hospital.

am·bush | ăm′bŏŏsh′ | —*noun, plural* **ambushes 1.** A surprise attack made from a place of hiding: *The soldiers planned an ambush against the enemy.* **2.** The place of hiding from which a surprise attack is made: *The tiger crouched in ambush.*
—*verb* **ambushed, ambushing** To attack from a hidden position: *The enemy soldiers ambushed the supply train.*

a·me·ba | ə **mē′**bə | —*noun, plural* **amebas** A very small animal that has only one cell. Amebas can be seen only through a microscope. The shape of an ameba is always changing. Another form of this word is **amoeba.**

a·men | ā′mĕn′ | or | ä′mĕn′ | —*interjection* A word that means

amaryllis

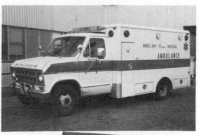

ambulance

"so be it" or "truly." **Amen** is often said at the end of a prayer. It is also said at the end of a statement with which one agrees.

a·mend |ə **měnd′** | —*verb* **amended, amending** To change for the better; improve; correct: *He amended his speech to include the new information.*

a·mend·ment |ə **měnd′**mənt| —*noun, plural* **amendments** A change in a law, a group of laws, or an official document: *An amendment to the Constitution limits a President to two full terms in office.*

a·mends |ə **měndz′**| —*plural noun* **make amends** To make up for an insult, injury, or wrong: *He sent her flowers to make amends for his rude remarks.*

A·mer·i·ca |ə **měr′**ĭ kə| **1.** The United States of America. **2.** North America. **3. the Americas** North America, Central America, and South America.

A·mer·i·can |ə **měr′**ĭ kən| —*noun, plural* **Americans 1.** A person who was born in or is a citizen of the United States. **2.** A person who was born in North America, Central America, or South America.
—*adjective* **1.** Of the United States or the people of the United States: *Thanksgiving Day is an American holiday. Washington, Lincoln, and Roosevelt are important names in American history.* **2.** Of North America, Central America, or South America or their peoples: *The American land masses stretch from the extreme north to the extreme south of the Western Hemisphere. The rattlesnake is an American snake. Maize, chocolate, and the potato were originally American foods and were not known anywhere else in the world.*

American English The English language as it is spoken in the United States.

American Indian 1. A member of any of the groups of peoples except the Eskimos, who had been living in North America, South America, or the West Indies before the European explorers first arrived. **2.** Any descendants of these peoples.

A·mer·i·can·ism |ə **měr′**ĭ kə nĭz′əm| —*noun, plural* **Americanisms** A word, phrase, or spelling that comes from American English or is used mainly in American English. "Muskrat," "typewriter," "rock'n' roll," and "aluminum" are Americanisms.

am·e·thyst |**ăm′**ə thĭst| —*noun, plural* **amethysts** A purple or violet form of quartz used as a gemstone.

a·mi·a·ble |**ā′**mē ə bəl| —*adjective* Friendly and good-natured; pleasant: *an amiable person. It was an amiable meeting even though we disagreed on some things.*

am·i·ca·ble |**ăm′**ĭ kə bəl| —*adjective* Friendly in tone; peaceful: *Let's try to settle our quarrel in an amicable way.*

a·mid |ə **mĭd′**| —*preposition* In the middle of; among: *The ship appeared amid the waves. We heard her calling amid the noise of the crowd.*

a·mi·go |ə **mē′**gō| —*noun, plural* **amigos** A Spanish word meaning "friend."

a·miss |ə **mĭs′**| —*adjective* Not the way it should be; not proper; wrong: *The strange silence told us something was amiss.*

am·mo·nia |ə **mōn′**yə| or |ə **mō′**nē ə| —*noun* **1.** A gas made up of nitrogen and hydrogen. Ammonia has a strong, irritating smell and no color. **2.** Ammonia that has been dissolved in water. It is very useful for cleaning.

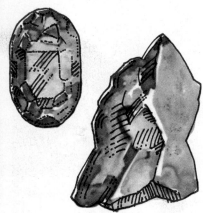

amethyst
As a cut stone *(left)* and in rock form *(right)*

ă	pat	ě	pet	î	fierce
ā	pay	ē	be	ŏ	pot
â	care	ĭ	pit	ō	go
ä	father	ī	pie	ô	paw, for
oi	oil	ŭ	cut	zh	vision
ŏŏ	book	û	fur	ə	ago, item,
ōō	boot	*th*	the		pencil, atom,
yōō	abuse	th	thin		circus
ou	out	hw	which	ər	butter

am·mu·ni·tion |ăm′yə nĭsh′ən| —*noun* **1.** Bullets, explosives, bombs, grenades, or anything else that can be fired from a gun or weapon or can explode and cause damage. **2.** Anything that can help support an argument or cause: *The riot in the park gave the mayor ammunition to announce a curfew.*

am·ne·sia |ăm nē′zhə| —*noun* A partial or complete loss of memory. Amnesia can be caused by a shock, a brain injury, or an illness.

a·moe·ba |ə mē′bə| —*noun, plural* **amoebas** A form of the word **ameba.**

a·mong |ə mŭng′| —*preposition* **1.** In the company of; with: *He was glad to be among friends again.* **2.** With a portion to each of: *They shared the cake among the six of them.* **3.** Between one and another of: *There is often arguing among the four brothers.* **4.** In the group of: *Football and basketball are among my favorite sports.* **5.** Through all or most of: *The illness spread among the students.*

a·mount |ə mount′| —*noun, plural* **amounts** **1.** The whole sum; total: *The amount of the grocery bill was $21.76.* **2.** Quantity: *We had a small amount of rain this year.*
—*verb* **amounted, amounting** **1.** To add up in total; reach a sum of: *The check for lunch amounted to $8.50.* **2.** To be equal; be the same as: *His story amounted to a proposal of marriage.*

am·phib·i·an |ăm fĭb′ē ən| —*noun, plural* **amphibians** **1.** One of a group of animals with smooth, moist skin. Frogs, toads, and salamanders are amphibians. Amphibians have gills and live in water when they are young. Later they develop lungs and breathe air. **2.** A vehicle that can travel on both land and water. **3.** An aircraft that can take off from and land on either land or water.

am·phib·i·ous |ăm fĭb′ē əs| —*adjective* **1.** Able to live both on land and in water: *An alligator is an amphibious animal, but it is not an amphibian.* **2.** Able to travel on land and water: *an amphibious tank.*

am·phi·the·a·ter |ăm′fə thē′ə tər| —*noun, plural* **amphitheaters** An oval or round structure with a stage or arena in the center and rows of seats all around. Each row is higher and farther back than the row in front of it.

am·ple |ăm′pəl| —*adjective* **ampler, amplest** **1.** Generously sufficient; abundant: *We had ample rainfall this year. We have ample time for a full dinner.* **2.** Large; roomy: *a building remarkable for the ample space of its public halls; an ample room.*

am·pli·fy |ăm′plə fī′| —*verb* **amplified, amplifying, amplifies** **1.** To add to; expand on; make fuller: *The magazine article amplified the details given in the newspaper item about the earthquake.* **2.** To make an electric signal, especially a sound signal, stronger: *A public-address system amplified the speaker's voice.*

am·pu·tate |ăm′pyŏŏ tāt′| —*verb* **amputated, amputating** To cut off all or part of an arm, leg, finger, or other part of the body.

a·muse |ə myŏoz′| —*verb* **amused, amusing** **1.** To cause enjoyment; entertain: *Playing checkers amuses me. Her riddles amused us for hours.* **2.** To cause to laugh or smile: *The clown's tricks amused the audience.*

a·muse·ment |ə myŏoz′mənt| —*noun, plural* **amusements** **1.** The condition of being amused: *We laughed in amusement at the clown's tricks.* **2.** Something that provides enjoyment or

amphibian
Above: Salamander
Below: Vehicle

amphitheater

anaconda

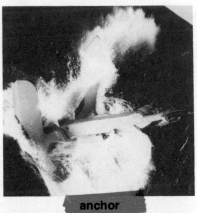

anchor

andirons

ă	pat	ĕ	pet	î	fierce
ā	pay	ē	be	ŏ	pot
â	care	ĭ	pit	ō	go
ä	father	ī	pie	ô	paw, for

oi	oil	ŭ	cut	zh	vision
ŏŏ	book	û	fur	ə	ago, item,
ōō	boot	th	the		pencil, atom,
yŏŏ	abuse	th	thin		circus
ou	out	hw	which	ər	butter

entertainment: *Her favorite amusements in the summer are tennis and swimming.*

an | ən | or | ăn | —*indefinite article* A form of **a** used before words beginning with a vowel or with an *h* that is not pronounced: *an apple; an elephant; an ice-cream cone; an orange; an umbrella; an hour.*

an·a·con·da | ăn′ə kŏn′də | —*noun, plural* **anacondas** A large, nonpoisonous snake of South America. It coils around and crushes the animals it eats.

a·nal·y·ses | ə năl′ĭ sēz′ | The plural of the noun **analysis.**

a·nal·y·sis | ə năl′ĭ sĭs | —*noun, plural* **analyses** **1.** The separation of something into its basic parts to find out what it is made of: *An analysis of the lake water revealed hydrogen, oxygen, microscopic plants, and chemical pollutants.* **2.** Any careful study of a subject and its details: *An analysis of his report showed he had used long words to say very little.*

an·a·lyze | ăn′ə līz′ | —*verb* **analyzed, analyzing** **1.** To separate something into its basic parts to find out what it is made of: *The laboratory workers analyzed the lake water into hydrogen, oxygen, microscopic plants, and chemical pollutants.* **2.** To examine very carefully: *They analyzed the reasons their project had failed and wrote a report to the mayor.*

an·ar·chy | ăn′ər kē | —*noun, plural* **anarchies** The absence of any form of law, government, or order, and the confusion that goes with this absence.

a·nat·o·my | ə năt′ə mē | —*noun, plural* **anatomies** **1.** The scientific study of the structure of animals and plants. **2.** The structure of an animal or plant: *The anatomies of butterflies and moths are similar.*

an·ces·tor | ăn′sĕs′tər | —*noun, plural* **ancestors** Any person from whom one is descended. Grandparents, great-grandparents, and great-great-grandparents as far back as one can go are one's ancestors.

an·chor | ăng′kər | —*noun, plural* **anchors** **1.** A heavy weight, usually of metal, that can be dropped from a rope to keep a ship from floating away. **2.** Any device used to keep another thing in place.
—*verb* **anchored, anchoring** **1.** To hold in place by means of an anchor: *The captain anchored the ship in the harbor.* **2.** To hold in place; fix firmly: *The stones anchored the beach blanket and they played cards on it.*

an·cient | ān′shənt | —*adjective* **1.** Of times long ago, especially before A.D. 500: *the history of ancient Greece.* **2.** Very old: *He found an ancient chair in the museum's attic.*

and | ənd | or | ən | or | ănd | —*conjunction* **1.** Together with or along with: *He and his son were here.* **2.** As well as: *She is tall and thin.* **3.** Added to; plus: *Two and two makes four.*

and·i·ron | ănd′ī′ərn | —*noun, plural* **andirons** One of a pair of metal pieces for holding up logs in a fireplace.

an·ec·dote | ăn′ĭk dōt′ | —*noun, plural* **anecdotes** A short tale that is interesting or amusing.

a·ne·mi·a | ə nē′mē ə | —*noun* An unhealthy condition in which the body has too few red blood cells. Anemia can make a person feel tired and weak.

a·ne·mic | ə nē′mĭk | —*adjective* Of or suffering from anemia: *anemic blood.*

a·nem·o·ne | ə **něm**′ə nē | —*noun, plural* **anemones** A plant with white, purple, or red flowers shaped like cups.

an·es·thet·ic | ăn′ĭs **thĕt**′ĭk | —*noun, plural* **anesthetics** A drug or other substance that makes the body or part of the body unable to feel pain, heat, cold, or other sensations.

a·new | ə **nōō**′ | or | ə **nyōō**′ | —*adverb* Over again; once more: *I lost my book report and had to write it anew.*

an·gel | **ăn**′gəl | —*noun, plural* **angels** **1.** A heavenly being who serves as an attendant and messenger of God. **2.** Any person who is considered especially good: *You are an angel to look after your sick neighbors.*

an·gel·ic | ăn **gĕl**′ĭk | —*adjective* Of or like an angel: *angelic voices; an angelic smile.*

an·ger | **ăng**′gər | —*noun* The strong feeling that comes from believing that one has been treated badly; a feeling of wanting to quarrel or fight: *We were filled with anger because they ruined our park.*
—*verb* **angered, angering** To make or become angry: *The insult angered him. She angers slowly, but when she does, watch out!*

an·gle | **ăng**′gəl | —*noun, plural* **angles** **1.** The space between two lines or two surfaces that meet. **2.** The place, position, or direction from which an object is presented to view; a point of view: *The building is handsome from any angle.* **3.** A way of looking at something: *Do you have a new angle to solve the problem?*
—*verb* **angled, angling** To move at an angle: *The car angled sharply to the left.*

an·gry | **ăng**′grē | —*adjective* **angrier, angriest** **1.** Feeling or showing anger: *We were angry at her for telling our secret. The angry crowd threatened to break down the doors.* **2.** Seeming ready to cause trouble: *The angry clouds threatened rain.* **3.** Red, sore, and painful: *He had an angry wound that did not heal.*

an·guish | **ăng**′gwĭsh | —*noun* Very great pain or suffering of body or mind.

an·i·mal | **ăn**′ə məl | —*noun, plural* **animals** A living thing that is not a plant. Animals can usually move from place to place; they eat plants or other animals as food. Worms, ants, fish, turtles, birds, cats, elephants, and human beings are animals.

an·i·mat·ed | **ăn**′ə mā′tĭd | —*adjective* **1.** Full of spirit; lively: *We had an animated talk about our vacation plans.* **2.** Made to move and appear alive: *animated puppets.*

an·i·mos·i·ty | ăn′ə **mŏs**′ĭ tē | —*noun, plural* **animosities** Strong hatred that shows: *Their animosity toward us led to a fist fight.*

an·kle | **ăng**′kəl | —*noun, plural* **ankles** The joint where the foot meets the leg.

an·klet | **ăng**′klĭt | —*noun, plural* **anklets** A short sock that reaches just above the ankle.

An·nap·o·lis | ə **năp**′ə lĭs | The capital of Maryland.

an·nex | ə **něks**′ | —*verb* **annexed, annexing** To add something to a larger thing: *The city will annex two of the suburbs.*
—*noun* | **ăn**′ěks′ |, *plural* **annexes** A building or structure that is added to another building and used for a related purpose: *Our library has a science annex. We built an annex onto our house.*

an·ni·hi·late | ə **nī**′ə lāt′ | —*verb* **annihilated, annihilating** To destroy completely; wipe out: *Six straight losses annihilated our team's hopes for the championship.*

an·ni·ver·sa·ry | ăn′ə **vûr**′sə rē | —*noun, plural* **anniversaries**

anemone

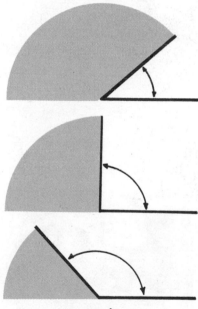

angle
Different kinds of angles

The return each year of the date on which an event happened: *Their wedding anniversary is September fourth. It was the fiftieth anniversary of the opening of the bridge.*

an·nounce | ə **nouns'** | —*verb* **announced, announcing** **1.** To give public notice of: *The principal announced that he would retire in June.* **2.** To make a presence or arrival known: *He announced us by house telephone.* **3.** To speak to the public, especially on radio, television, or over a public-address system; serve as an announcer of: *He announces hockey games on television.*

an·nounce·ment | ə **nouns'**mənt | —*noun, plural* **announcements** A public statement or notice in writing or speech: *a newspaper announcement of an auction.*

an·nounc·er | ə **noun'**sər | —*noun, plural* **announcers** A person whose job is to speak to the public on radio, television, or over a public-address system. Announcers usually introduce programs or read news on the radio or television.

an·noy | ə **noi'** | —*verb* **annoyed, annoying** To bother; irritate; pester: *The ants and flies annoyed us at the picnic.*

an·noy·ance | ə **noi'**əns | —*noun, plural* **annoyances** **1.** Something or someone that bothers or irritates: *The sirens were an annoyance during the concert.* **2.** The feeling of being bothered or irritated: *our annoyance at having to wait two hours in the doctor's office.*

an·nu·al | ăn'yo͞o əl | —*adjective* **1.** Happening or done every year: *Our club has an annual barbecue in June.* **2.** For one year; in one year's time: *an annual income of $10,000.* **3.** Living and growing for only one year or season: *an annual plant.*

a·non·y·mous | ə nŏn'ə məs | —*adjective* **1.** From or by a person whose identity is not known to anybody: *Many nursery rhymes are anonymous.* **2.** From or by a person who wants his or her name to be kept secret: *The wealthy man made an anonymous gift to the charity.*

an·oth·er | ə nŭth'ər | —*adjective* **1.** Different: *He has another version of that story.* **2.** One more; additional: *Have another glass of milk.* **3.** Of the same kind as: *He thinks he's another Reggie Jackson.*
—*pronoun* An additional or different one: *I finished my hamburger and ordered another.*

an·swer | ăn'sər | or | än'sər | —*noun, plural* **answers** **1.** A reply to a question, statement, request, invitation, or letter: *My answer is "no." As soon as she got my letter, she sent an answer.* **2.** A response to a signal: *I telephoned but there was no answer.* **3.** A solution to a problem: *The teacher has the answers to the multiplication test.*
—*verb* **answered, answering** **1.** To speak or write in reply to something said or written: *She answered "maybe" to all my questions.* **2.** To act in response to a signal: *If I knock three times, please answer the door.* **3.** To be liable or responsible for: *Who will answer for my safety?* **4.** To correspond; match: *He answers to the description on the "Wanted" poster.*

ant | ănt | —*noun, plural* **ants** An insect that lives with others of the same kind in large colonies. Ants often dig tunnels in the ground or in wood. Most have no wings. There are many kinds of ants.
♦ *These sound alike* **ant, aunt.**

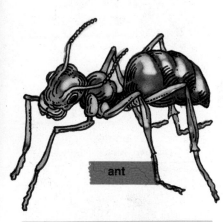

ant

ă	pat	ĕ	pet	î	fierce
ā	pay	ē	be	ŏ	pot
â	care	ĭ	pit	ō	go
ä	father	ī	pie	ô	paw, for
oi	oil	ŭ	cut	zh	vision
o͞o	book	û	fur	ə	ago, item,
o͞o	boot	*th*	the		pencil, atom,
yo͞o	abuse	th	thin		circus
ou	out	hw	which	ər	butter

an·tag·o·nism | ăn **tăg′** ə nĭz′ əm | —*noun* An unfriendly or
hostile feeling; opposition: *There was antagonism between the
cattlemen and the farmers in the old West*

an·tag·o·nize | ăn **tăg′** ə nĭz′ | —*verb* **antagonized, antagonizing**
To earn the dislike of; make an enemy of: *If you want his help,
don't antagonize him with threats.*

Ant·arc·tic | ănt **ärk′** tĭk | or | ănt **är′** tĭk | —*adjective* Of or in the
region around the South Pole: *the Antarctic weather.*
—*noun* **the Antarctic** Antarctica and the waters around it.

Ant·arc·ti·ca | ănt **ärk′** tĭ kə | or | ănt **är′** tĭ kə | The continent
surrounding the South Pole. It is almost covered with ice.

Antarctic Ocean The waters around Antarctica. This ocean is
made up of the southern parts of the Atlantic, Pacific, and Indian
oceans. The Antarctic Ocean appears to be a separate ocean on
most world maps.

ant·eat·er | ănt′ ē′tər | —*noun, plural* **anteaters** An animal that
feeds on ants and other insects. It has a long snout and a long,
sticky tongue that it uses to catch its food.

an·te·lope | ăn′ tl ōp′ | —*noun, plural* **antelope** or **antelopes**
1. A horned animal of Africa or Asia that can run very fast.
There are many kinds of antelopes. **2.** The pronghorn of western
North America.

an·ten·na | ăn **tĕn′** ə | —*noun* **1.** *plural* **antennae** One of a pair
of long, thin feelers on the head of some animals. Insects,
lobsters, and shrimps have antennae. **2.** *plural* **antennas** An
aerial for sending or receiving radio, television, and other signals.

an·ten·nae | ăn **tĕn′** ē | A plural of the noun **antenna** (feelers).

an·them | ăn′ thəm | —*noun, plural* **anthems** **1.** A song of loyalty
or praise: *The band played the national anthems of both teams'
countries.* **2.** A sacred song, usually having words from the Bible.

an·ther | ăn′ thər | —*noun, plural* **anthers** A part of a flower that
produces pollen. It is at the tip of a stamen.

ant·hill | ănt′ hĭl′ | —*noun, plural* **anthills** A mound of earth
formed by ants when they dig a tunnel or build a nest.

an·thol·o·gy | ăn **thŏl′** ə jē | —*noun, plural* **anthologies** A book
containing a collection of poems or stories written by many
different authors.

an·thra·cite | ăn′ thrə sīt′ | A kind of coal that is hard and makes
little smoke when it burns.

anti- A prefix that means: **1.** Opposed to or not liking
something: *antislavery; antisocial.* **2.** Acting against the effect of
something: *antitoxin.*

an·ti·bi·ot·ic | ăn′ tē bī ŏt′ ĭk | —*noun, plural* **antibiotics** Any of a
group of substances made by certain molds or bacteria.
Antibiotics can kill or slow the growth of germs that cause
disease. Penicillin is an antibiotic that is used in treating diseases
and infections.

an·ti·bod·y | ăn′ tĭ bŏd′ē | —*noun, plural* **antibodies** A substance
found in the blood of human beings and animals. Antibodies are
produced by the blood to destroy or weaken germs.

an·tic·i·pate | ăn tĭs′ ə pāt′ | —*verb* **anticipated, anticipating 1.** To
consider or imagine in advance; expect: *We had not anticipated so
many guests.* **2.** To deal with in advance: *I try to anticipate trouble.*

an·tic·i·pa·tion | ăn tĭs′ ə **pā′**shən | —*noun, plural* **anticipations**
The act of anticipating; expectation: *He frowned in anticipation of
the pain.*

anteater

antelope

anther

antique
A box made about 1835

antler

anvil

ă	pat	ĕ	pet	î	fierce
ā	pay	ē	be	ŏ	pot
â	care	ĭ	pit	ō	go
ä	father	ī	pie	ô	paw, for
oi	oil	ŭ	cut	zh	vision
ōō	book	û	fur	ə	ago, item,
ōō	boot	th	the		pencil, atom,
yōō	abuse	th	thin		circus
ou	out	hw	which	ər	butter

an·ti·dote | ăn′tĭ dōt′ | —*noun, plural* **antidotes** A medicine that acts against the harmful effects of a poison.

an·tique | ăn tēk′ | —*noun* Something made a long time ago: *Her family has a valuable collection of Colonial antiques such as pewter plates, silver candlesticks, and Chinese porcelain.*
—*adjective* **1.** Being an antique: *antique silver objects; antique furniture; an antique automobile.* **2.** Of times long ago: *the ruins of an antique city.*

an·ti·sep·tic | ăn′tĭ sĕp′tĭk | —*adjective* Able to destroy harmful bacteria or stop them from growing: *Iodine is an antiseptic liquid.*
—*noun, plural* **antiseptics** Something that destroys harmful bacteria or stops them from growing. *Alcohol is often used as an antiseptic.*

an·ti·slav·er·y | ăn′tē slā′və rē | or | ăn′tē slāv′rē | —*adjective* Against slavery: *an antislavery meeting.*

an·ti·so·cial | ăn′tē sō′shəl | —*adjective* **1.** Not liking to be with other people; not sociable: *Some people who seem antisocial are only shy.* **2.** Against the best interests of other people: *Selling harmful drugs is antisocial behavior.*

an·ti·tox·in | ăn′tē tŏk′sĭn | —*noun, plural* **antitoxins** A substance or antibody that can protect a person against certain diseases.

ant·ler | ănt′lər | —*noun, plural* **antlers** One of the bony growths on the head of a deer or related animal. Antlers grow in pairs and are often branched. They grow out each year and are shed at the end of a season. Usually only males have antlers.

an·to·nym | ăn′tə nĭm′ | —*noun, plural* **antonyms** A word that means the opposite of a certain other word. For example, "thin" is an antonym of "thick."

an·vil | ăn′vĭl | —*noun, plural* **anvils** A heavy block of iron or steel with a smooth, flat top. Certain metal articles are hammered into shape on an anvil.

anx·i·e·ty | ăng zī′ĭ tē | —*noun, plural* **anxieties** **1.** An uneasy feeling about what will happen; worry: *Darkness increased our anxiety about the hikers.* **2.** An eager feeling mixed with worry: *My anxiety to pass the test made me study late the night before.*

anx·ious | ăngk′shəs | or | ăng′shəs | —*adjective* **1.** Having an uneasy feeling about what will happen; worried: *When they were three hours late, we were anxious about the hikers.* **2.** Eager: *I was truly anxious to pass that test.*

an·y | ĕn′ē | —*adjective* **1.** One out of three or more: *Take any book you want.* **2.** Every: *Any kid on our team would do the same to win the match.* **3.** Some: *Is there any soda?* **4.** Much: *He doesn't need any strength to chop kindling.* The adjective **any** belongs to a class of words called **determiners.** They signal that a noun is coming.
—*pronoun* Anything or anybody: *Did you buy apples? No, I didn't buy any.*
—*adverb* At all: *He doesn't feel any better.*

an·y·bod·y | ĕn′ē bŏd′ē | or | ĕn′ē bŭd′ē | —*pronoun* Any person; anyone: *Has anybody called you today?*
—*noun* An important person: *Everybody who is anybody was at the party last night.*

an·y·how | ĕn′ē hou′ | —*adverb* **1.** In any case; at any rate; anyway: *The twins were sick, but they were too little to play with anyhow.* **2.** Just the same; nevertheless; anyway: *You may know these words, but study them anyhow.*

an·y·one |ĕn′ē wŭn′| or |ĕn′ē wən| —*pronoun* Any person; anybody: *Has anyone seen Louise today?*

an·y·place |ĕn′ē plās′| —*adverb* To, in, or at any place; anywhere: *I can go anyplace I like.*

an·y·thing |ĕn′ē thĭng′| —*pronoun* Any thing: *The band will play anything you ask them to. Is there anything left in the box?* —*adverb* At all: *His house isn't anything like ours.*

an·y·time |ĕn′ē tīm′| —*adverb* At any time: *You may go to the store anytime you want to.*

an·y·way |ĕn′ē wā′| —*adverb* **1.** In any case; at any rate; anyhow: *Both girls would wear, or anyway carry, white gloves.* **2.** Just the same; nevertheless; anyhow: *The ball was slippery, but Henry caught it anyway.*

an·y·where |ĕn′ē hwâr′| or |ĕn′ē wâr′| —*adverb* **1.** To, in, or at any place: *They travel anywhere they want to.* **2.** At all: *Before my hand was anywhere near him, he was gone.*

a·or·ta |ā ôr′tə| —*noun, plural* **aortas** The largest artery of the body. It begins at the left ventricle of the heart and divides into branches to carry blood to all the organs of the body except the lungs.

a·part |ə pärt′| —*adverb* **1.** Away from each other in time or place: *The trains leave two hours apart. Those trees are about ten feet apart.* **2.** To one side or in the opposite direction from each other: *She kept the pennies apart from the dimes.* **3.** In or into separate pieces; to pieces: *His old car was falling apart. He took the engine apart to fix it.*

Idiom **apart from** Other than; aside from: *Apart from her temper, she is all right to work with.*

a·part·ment |ə pärt′mənt| —*noun, plural* **apartments** A room or set of rooms for one household. An apartment is in a building or house that usually has other rooms or sets of rooms like it.

ap·a·thy |ăp′ə thē| —*noun* Lack of feeling or interest; indifference: *The audience watched the new play with apathy.*

ape |āp| —*noun, plural* **apes** A large animal that has no tail and is related to the monkeys. Gorillas, chimpanzees, and orangutans are apes. —*verb* **aped, aping** To copy the actions of; imitate: *John's little brother aped the clown they had seen at the circus.*

a·phid |ā′fĭd| or |ăf′ĭd| —*noun, plural* **aphids** A small insect that sucks juices from plants.

a·piece |ə pēs′| —*adverb* To or for each one; each: *Give them an apple apiece.*

a·pol·o·gize |ə pŏl′ə jīz′| —*verb* **apologized, apologizing** To say one is sorry; make an apology: *When we bumped into each other, we both apologized.*

a·pol·o·gy |ə pŏl′ə jē| —*noun, plural* **apologies** A statement that one is sorry for something that one has done wrong or that bothers, hurts, or angers someone: *I made an apology to Frank for being late for our lunch date. Joan accepted Marie's apologies for talking about her behind her back.*

A·pos·tle |ə pŏs′əl| —*noun, plural* **Apostles** One of the twelve original disciples of Christ.

a·pos·tro·phe |ə pŏs′trə fē| —*noun, plural* **apostrophes** A punctuation mark (') that: **1.** Shows that one or more letters have been left out of a word: *aren't* for *are not; can't* for *cannot.* **2.** Shows possession or ownership: *Tom's hat* is *the hat of Tom.*

ape
An orangutan

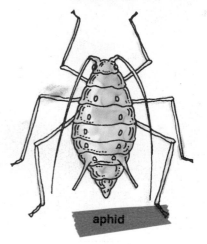

aphid

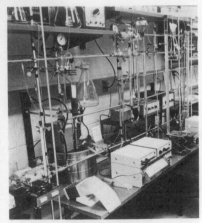

apparatus

3. Forms the plurals of numbers and letters: *I got two 100's on my tests.*

a·poth·e·car·y |ə pŏth′ĭ kĕr′ē| —*noun, plural* **apothecaries** A person who prepares and sells medicine; a druggist; pharmacist.

ap·pa·ra·tus |ăp′ə rā′təs| or |ăp′ə răt′əs| —*noun, plural* **apparatus** or **apparatuses** Anything, such as equipment or tools, that is used to do or perform a particular task: *Musical instruments are the apparatus of an orchestra.*

ap·par·ent |ə păr′ənt| or |ə pâr′ənt| —*adjective* **1. a.** Easily seen; obvious. *His limp was apparent even though he tried to hide it.* **b.** Easily understood; obvious: *It was apparent to his father that Joey was unhappy with the cut in his allowance.* **2.** Appearing to be true or real even though it may not be so; seeming: *His size was an apparent advantage in the tug of war, but the smaller boy was really stronger.*

ap·peal |ə pēl′| —*verb* **appealed, appealing 1.** To make a strong or urgent request, especially for help or sympathy; ask for or beg: *I appeal to you to help him.* **2.** To be attractive or interesting: *That dress appeals to her.* **3.** In law, to ask that a case be tried again by a higher court: *After the jury found him guilty, his lawyer appealed the conviction.*
—*noun, plural* **appeals 1.** An urgent request: *During the blizzard the governor made an appeal for everyone to stay home.* **2.** The power or ability of attracting or interesting: *Comic books have a great appeal to children.* **3.** A request to have a law case tried again by a higher court.

ap·pear |ə pîr′| —*verb* **appeared, appearing 1.** To come into view; be seen: *A car appeared at the top of the hill.* **2.** To seem or look: *The coat appears to be dark blue.* **3.** To come before the public: *She has appeared in three television shows.*

ap·pear·ance |ə pîr′əns| —*noun, plural* **appearances 1.** The act of coming into view: *They were frightened by the sudden appearance of pirate ships in the harbor.* **2.** The way someone or something looks: *A good appearance makes other people want to know you better.* **3.** The act of coming before the public: *It has been nine years since the singer's last appearance in Denver.*

ap·pease |ə pēz′| —*verb* **appeased, appeasing 1.** To make calm or quiet, especially by giving what is demanded: *She appeased the child by giving him a cookie.* **2.** To satisfy or relieve: *A glass of water will appease your thirst.*

ap·pen·di·ci·tis |ə pĕn′dĭ sī′tĭs| —*noun* A swelling or inflammation of the appendix that causes pain.

ap·pen·dix |ə pĕn′dĭks| —*noun, plural* **appendixes 1.** A section at the end of a book that gives more information about the subject or subjects of the book. An appendix may contain such things as charts, tables, and lists. **2.** A thin, closed tube that is attached to the large intestine.

ap·pe·tite |ăp′ĭ tīt′| —*noun, plural* **appetites 1.** The desire for food: *After hiking through the woods Ellen and Jennifer each had a big appetite.* **2.** A strong desire for something: *Joan has a great appetite for work.*

ap·plaud |ə plôd′| —*verb* **applauded, applauding 1.** To show approval or enjoyment by clapping the hands: *The audience applauded for ten minutes. The students applauded the band concert.* **2.** To praise or approve: *The neighbors applauded the children's effort to clean up the playground.*

ă	pat	ĕ	pet	î	fierce
ā	pay	ē	be	ŏ	pot
â	care	ĭ	pit	ō	go
ä	father	ī	pie	ô	paw, for

oi	oil	ŭ	cut	zh	vision
ŏŏ	book	û	fur	ə	ago, item,
ōō	boot	*th*	the		pencil, atom,
yōō	abuse	th	thin		circus
ou	out	hw	which	ər	butter

ap·plause | ə plôz′ | —*noun* Approval or enjoyment shown by clapping the hands.

ap·ple | ăp′əl | —*noun, plural* **apples** A firm, rounded fruit that is good to eat. Apples usually have red skin.

ap·pli·ance | ə plī′əns | —*noun, plural* **appliances** A small machine used to do a special job around the house more easily. Toasters, vacuum cleaners, and washing machines are appliances.

ap·ply | ə plī′ | —*verb* **applied, applying, applies 1.** To put on: *Pam applied glue to the back of the picture before putting it in the album.* **2.** To put into action; use: *To stop the bicycle you must apply the hand brakes.* **3.** To devote oneself to something; work hard at: *Larry applied himself to playing the guitar.* **4.** To be suitable or useful; have to do with: *This rule does not apply to you.* **5.** To ask or request employment, acceptance, or admission: *He applied for a job. She applied to a college.*

ap·point | ə point′ | —*verb* **appointed, appointing 1.** To choose someone for a job, office, or position; select: *The mayor appointed Mr. Cataldo to be the new chief of police.* **2.** To decide on a time or place: *They appointed three o'clock at the library for the meeting.*

ap·point·ment | ə point′mənt | —*noun, plural* **appointments 1.a.** The act of appointing to a job, office, or position: *The appointment of a Chief Justice of the Supreme Court is an important decision.* **b.** The job, office, or position to which a person has been appointed: *David accepted the appointment as chairman of the refreshment committee.* **2.** An arrangement to meet with someone at a particular time and place: *Dr. Jones cannot change the time of your appointment.*

ap·praise | ə prāz′ | —*verb* **appraised, appraising 1.** To set a value on; fix a price for: *The expert appraised the gold bracelet at $500.* **2.** To estimate or judge the value, quality, amount, or size of: *The coach appraised him as the most important member of the team.*

ap·pre·ci·ate | ə prē′shē āt′ | —*verb* **appreciated, appreciating 1.** To recognize the worth or importance of; value highly: *Most Americans appreciate the freedoms they have. She appreciated the opportunity to go to college.* **2.** To be grateful for: *We appreciate your help.*

ap·pre·ci·a·tion | ə prē′shē ā′shən | —*noun* **1.** The act of recognizing the worth or importance of: *an appreciation of the scientist's accomplishments.* **2.** Gratitude: *Roberta showed her appreciation of our help by sending us a thank-you letter.*

ap·pre·hend | ăp′rĭ hĕnd′ | —*verb* **apprehended, apprehending** To arrest or capture; seize: *The police apprehended the robbers after a long chase.*

ap·pre·hen·sion | ăp′rĭ hĕn′shən | —*noun, plural* **apprehensions 1.** Fear of what may happen: *Going into the dark, empty house filled us with apprehension.* **2.** The act of capturing; an arrest: *The apprehension of the murderer made everyone feel safer.*

ap·pre·hen·sive | ăp′rĭ hĕn′sĭv | —*adjective* Afraid or fearful; nervous: *Mark was apprehensive about doing well in his job.*

ap·pren·tice | ə prĕn′tĭs | —*noun, plural* **apprentices** A person who learns a skill or trade by working for a skilled craftsman. Because they are learning and studying, apprentices are paid a very small salary.
—*verb* **apprenticed, apprenticing** To place or hire as an apprentice: *Leonard's father apprenticed him to a silversmith.*

apple
Above: Tree
Center: Blossom
Below: Fruit

appliance

ap·proach | ə prōch' | —*verb* **approached, approaching 1.** To come near or nearer to: *We tried to approach the dog as it was keeping watch over the puppies. You can tell spring is approaching because it's getting warmer every day.* **2.** To go and speak to someone about a plan or request; make a proposal to: *Larry approached the store manager for a job.*
—*noun, plural* **approaches 1.** The act of approaching: *The barking dogs announced his approach.* **2.** A way of doing or handling a problem or job; a method: *A good approach to sound health is to exercise every day.* **3.** A way to reach a place; an access: *The only approach to the lake is a dirt road.*

ap·pro·pri·ate | ə prō'prē ĭt | —*adjective* Suitable for a particular person, place, or event; proper: *the appropriate clothes for a cold day. Turkey is an appropriate food for Thanksgiving.*
—*verb* | ə prō'prē āt' | **appropriated, appropriating** To set apart for a special use: *The committee appropriated money for new books.*

ap·prov·al | ə prōo'vəl | —*noun, plural* **approvals 1.** A favorable opinion; praise: *The audience showed their approval of the concert by applauding for ten minutes.* **2.** Official permission or consent: *The voters gave their approval for a new town recreation center.*

ap·prove | ə prōov' | —*verb* **approved, approving 1.** To have a favorable opinion of; think right or good: *My parents approved my plan to get a part-time job. Cindy did not approve of Mark's bad language.* **2.** To give consent or permission to; confirm: *The Senate approved the treaty.*

ap·prox·i·mate | ə prŏk'sə mĭt | —*adjective* Almost exact; nearly correct: *The approximate weight of the car is 3,000 pounds.*
—*verb* | ə prŏk'sə māt' | **approximated, approximating** To come close to; be nearly the same as: *The temperature of the gym's pool approximates that of the ocean.*

ap·ri·cot | ăp'rĭ kŏt' | or | ā'prĭ kŏt' | —*noun, plural* **apricots** A juicy, yellowish fruit that looks like a small peach. Apricots are good to eat.

A·pril | ā'prəl | —*noun, plural* **Aprils** The fourth month of the year, after March and before May. April has 30 days.

a·pron | ā'prən | —*noun, plural* **aprons** A garment tied around the waist to keep a person's clothes clean. Some aprons have a section that covers the chest or upper part of the body.

apt | ăpt | —*adjective* **1.** Exactly suitable; appropriate or fitting: *an apt reply to the question.* **2.** Having or showing good probability; likely: *People are apt to be impressed by fancy new cars. Where are seashells most apt to be found?* **3.** Having a tendency or leaning; inclined: *People are apt to believe what they like to believe.* **4.** Quick to learn; bright: *He is more apt in science than his brothers.*

ap·ti·tude | ăp'tĭ tōod' | or | ăp'tĭ tyōod' | —*noun, plural* **aptitudes 1.** A natural ability or talent: *Kathy has an aptitude for picking the right person for the job.* **2.** The ability to learn and understand quickly: *a good aptitude for algebra.*

aq·ua·ma·rine | ăk'wə mə rēn' | or | ä'kwə mə rēn' | —*noun, plural* **aquamarines 1.** A blue-green gemstone. **2.** A greenish blue.
—*adjective* Greenish-blue.

a·quar·i·um | ə kwâr'ē əm | —*noun, plural* **aquariums 1.** A tank, glass bowl, or other container filled with water in which living fish, other water animals, and water plants are kept and

apricot
Fruit and blossom

apron

ă	pat	ĕ	pet	î	fierce
ā	pay	ē	be	ŏ	pot
â	care	ĭ	pit	ō	go
ä	father	ī	pie	ô	paw, for
oi	oil	ŭ	cut	zh	vision
ōō	book	û	fur	ə	ago, item,
ōō	boot	th	the		pencil, atom,
yōō	abuse	th	thin		circus
ou	out	hw	which	ər	butter

shown. **2.** A building in which collections of different kinds of living fish, other water animals, and water plants are kept so the public may see them.

aq·ue·duct |ăk′wĭ dŭkt′| —*noun, plural* **aqueducts** **1.** A large pipe or channel that carries water over a long distance. **2.** A structure like a bridge made to hold up such a pipe when it crosses low ground or a river.

Ar·ab |ăr′əb| —*noun, plural* **Arabs** **1.** A person who was born in or is a citizen of Arabia. **2.** A member of any of the various Arabic-speaking peoples of Asia and Africa.
—*adjective* Of Arabia or the Arabs.

A·ra·bi·a |ə rā′bē ə| A large peninsula in the Middle East.

Ar·a·bic |ăr′ə bĭk| —*noun* The language of the Arabs.
—*adjective* Of the Arabs or their language.

Arabic numerals The numerical figures 1, 2, 3, 4, 5, 6, 7, 8, 9, and 0. These numerals are called Arabic because they were introduced to Europeans by the Arabs.

ar·bi·trar·y |är′bĭ trĕr′ē| —*adjective* Based on someone's wishes or feelings and not on law or good judgment: *The lifeguard made an arbitrary decision that no children can go in the water today.*

ar·bi·trate |är′bĭ trāt′| —*verb* **arbitrated, arbitrating** To make a decision that settles an argument; decide: *Michael had to arbitrate the fight between his sisters over who would wear the green sweater.*

ar·bi·tra·tion |är′bĭ trā′shən| —*noun, plural* **arbitrations** The act or process of settling an argument by letting an outside person listen to both sides and make a decision.

ar·bor |är′bər| —*noun, plural* **arbors** A shaded place or garden area closed in by trees, bushes, or vines growing on lattices.

arc |ärk| —*noun, plural* **arcs** **1.** Any part of the curved line of a circle. **2.** Any part of a curved line or curved thing: *The rainbow was a large arc in the sky.*
♦ *These sound alike* **arc, ark.**

arch |ärch| —*noun, plural* **arches** **1.** An open, curved structure that supports the weight of the building material on top of it. Arches are often used to hold up bridges. They are also used for doorways and windows in many buildings. **2.** A large monument that is built in the shape of an arch. **3.** Something that is curved like an arch: *the arch of the foot; the arch of a rainbow.*
—*verb* **arched, arching** To make or cause to make an arch; curve or bend: *I knew the cat would arch his back when he saw the dog.*

ar·chae·ol·o·gist |är′kē ŏl′ə jĭst| —*noun, plural* **archaeologists** A person who practices archaeology. Another form of this word is **archeologist.**

ar·chae·ol·o·gy |är′kē ŏl′ə jē| —*noun* The scientific study of ancient societies and the way of life and customs of their people. Scientists dig up and study their tools, pottery, weapons, household items, and the ruins of their buildings. Another form of this word is **archeology.**

arch·bish·op |ärch′bĭsh′əp| —*noun, plural* **archbishops** A bishop of the highest rank.

ar·che·ol·o·gist |är′kē ŏl′ə jĭst| —*noun, plural* **archeologists** A form of the word **archaeologist.**

ar·che·ol·o·gy |är′kē ŏl′ə jē| —*noun* A form of the word **archaeology.**

arch·er |är′chər| —*noun, plural* **archers** A person who shoots with a bow and arrows.

aqueduct

arbor

arch

Above: A steel arch in Missouri
Below: A stone arch in France

arch·er·y | är′chə rē | —*noun* The sport or skill of shooting with a bow and arrows.

ar·chi·tect | är′kĭ tĕkt′ | —*noun, plural* **architects** A person who designs buildings and other large structures. Architects also work with people who build to make sure that the buildings are constructed the way they designed them.

ar·chi·tec·ture | är′kĭ tĕk′chər | —*noun* **1.** The skill or business of designing and planning buildings. **2.** A style or special method of building: *In Greek architecture most large buildings were made of marble.*

arc·tic | ärk′tĭk | or | är′tĭk | —*adjective* Of or in the region around the North Pole: *arctic waters.*
—*noun* **the Arctic.** The north polar region.

Arctic Ocean The ocean surrounding the North Pole.

are | är | **1.** The second person singular present tense of **be:** *I am tall and you are thin.* **2.** The first, second, and third person plural present tense of the verb **be:** *We are tired. "You are wrong," she said to the boys. They are smart.*

ar·e·a | âr′ē ə | —*noun, plural* **areas** **1.** A section or region of land: *a farming area. The southwestern area of the United States is mostly desert.* **2.** A space set aside for a particular use; a special place or section: *The kitchen and dining room are eating areas. We'll use the area behind the school for a soccer field.* **3.** The measure of a surface: *The area of our driveway is 500 square feet.* **4.** A field or range of study, interest, knowledge, or activity: *Sandy is an expert in the area of fixing up old houses.*

Area code or **area code** A set or series of three numbers given to each telephone area in the United States. Area codes are used in calling from one part of the country to another.

a·re·na | ə rē′nə | —*noun, plural* **arenas** An enclosed area or stadium for sports events and large shows such as circuses and concerts. Arenas can be either covered or open buildings. The first arenas were in ancient Rome, where gladiators fought as a form of entertainment.

aren't | ärnt | or | är′ənt | A contraction of "are not."

ar·gue | är′gyoō | —*verb* **argued, arguing** **1.** To have a quarrel or disagreement; to dispute; bicker: *Tom was always arguing with his friends. Frank and Larry argued about who was going to sit in the front seat of the car.* **2.** To give reasons for or against something: *The lawyer argued the case in court. Rachel argued against building a parking lot over the playground.*

ar·gu·ment | är′gyə mənt | —*noun, plural* **arguments** **1.** A quarrel or dispute: *The teacher had to break up the argument when the girls started yelling.* **2.** A reason or reasons given for or against something: *Jeannie and Pam believed Dad's argument that with a new lawnmower he could cut the grass twice as fast.*

ar·id | ăr′ĭd | —*adjective* Having little or no rainfall; dry: *an arid desert.*

a·rise | ə rīz′ | —*verb* **arose, arisen, arising** **1.** To get up; rise up: *He arose from his chair.* **2.** To move upward: *Smoke is arising from the pile of burning leaves.* **3.** To come into being; appear: *When the chance to go to the zoo arose, he took it.*

a·ris·en | ə rĭz′ən | The past participle of the verb **arise:** *We had arisen long before the sun came up.*

ar·is·toc·ra·cy | ăr′ĭ stŏk′rə sē | —*noun, plural* **aristocracies** **1.** A class of people who have a high position in society because

arena

ă	pat	ĕ	pet	î	fierce
ā	pay	ē	be	ŏ	pot
â	care	ĭ	pit	ō	go
ä	father	ī	pie	ô	paw, for
oi	oil	ŭ	cut	zh	vision
ōo	book	û	fur	ə	ago, item,
ōo	boot	*th*	the		pencil, atom,
yōo	abuse	th	thin		circus
ou	out	hw	which	ər	butter

they are born into families with great wealth and sometimes titles. Kings, queens, knights, dukes, and duchesses all belong to the aristocracy. **2.** A class of people who are thought to be superior or better because of their intelligence or wealth.

a·ris·to·crat | ə rĭs′tə krăt′ | or | ăr′ĭs tə krăt′ | —*noun, plural* **aristocrats** A person who belongs to the aristocracy.

a·rith·me·tic | ə rĭth′mə tĭk | —*noun* **1.** The study of numbers and their use in addition, subtraction, multiplication, and division. **2.** The act of adding, subtracting, multiplying, or dividing.

Ar·i·zo·na | ăr′ĭ zō′nə | A state in the southwestern United States. The capital of Arizona is Phoenix.

ark | ärk | —*noun* **1.** In the Bible, the large ship built to save a few people chosen by God and also two of every kind of animal from the great flood. **2.** The cabinet in a synagogue in which the Torah is stored when it is not being used during religious worship.

♦ *These sound alike* **ark, arc.**

Ar·kan·sas | är′kən sô′ | A state in the southern United States. The capital of Arkansas is Little Rock.

arm¹ | ärm | —*noun, plural* **arms** **1.** The part of the body between the shoulder and the hand. A person has two arms. **2.** Any part shaped or used like an arm; a part that comes out or extends from a larger body as an arm does: *the arms of a chair; the arms of a starfish. A bay is an arm of the sea.*

arm² | ärm | —*noun* **arms** Weapons of all kinds that are used in war or for defense. Guns, tanks, bombs, and missiles are all arms. —*verb* **armed, arming** **1.** To supply with weapons or another means of defense: *The villagers armed themselves with sticks and faced the wild mountain lion. Porcupines are armed with sharp quills.* **2.** To prepare for war by collecting weapons and training soldiers. **3.** To supply with something that is useful or that protects: *When she came home late from the party, she was armed with an excuse.*

ar·ma·dil·lo | är′mə dĭl′ō | —*noun, plural* **armadillos** A burrowing animal whose body has a bony covering that looks like armor. Armadillos live in South America and southern North America.

armed forces | ärmd | The complete military forces of a country. The Army, Navy, Marine Corps, and Air Force are all part of the armed forces of the United States.

ar·mi·stice | är′mĭ stĭs | —*noun, plural* **armistices** An agreement by both sides in a war to a temporary stop in fighting; a truce.

ar·mor | är′mər | —*noun* **1.** A covering or suit for the body, usually made of metal. In the Middle Ages knights wore armor to protect their bodies in battle. **2.** Any kind of protective covering. The hard shell of a turtle and the metal plates on a warship are armor.

ar·mored | är′mərd | —*adjective* Covered with or having armor: *an armored car; an armored battalion.*

ar·mor·y | är′mə rē | —*noun, plural* **armories** **1.** A storehouse where military weapons are kept. **2.** A building where military units train and have their headquarters.

arm·pit | ärm′pĭt′ | —*noun, plural* **armpits** The curved, hollow part under the arm at the shoulder.

ar·my | är′mē | —*noun, plural* **armies** **1.** A large group of soldiers organized and trained to fight on land. **2.** The complete

---

Arizona
The name **Arizona** probably comes from an Indian word that means "small springs" or "few springs."

Arkansas
Arkansas comes from the name of an Indian tribe.

arm¹, arm²
Arm¹, like most of the words for basic parts of the body, is a native English word; it has hardly changed in 1,200 years. **Arm²** was borrowed from a French word, which is itself from a Latin word meaning "arms" or "weapons." The English and Latin words both come from the same word used by the prehistoric people whose language is the source of many languages spoken today. The original meaning was that of **arm¹**; the meaning "weapon" developed later.

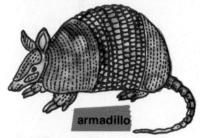
armadillo

armor

group or force of soldiers trained to fight on land for a country.
3. Any large group of people organized for a purpose: *An army of people marched to Washington to protest high taxes.* **4.** Any large group of people or animals: *An army of ants ruined the picnic.*

a·ro·ma |ə rō′mə| —*noun, plural* **aromas** A pleasant smell; fragrance: *From the living room we could smell the aroma of the apple pie baking in the oven.*

a·rose |ə rōz′| The past tense of the verb **arise:** *She arose from the table.*

a·round |ə round′| —*preposition* **1.** In a circle surrounding: *The elves were dancing around the magic oak tree. We ran around the block.* **2.** In a group or groups surrounding: *The Indian tribes around the Great Lakes were helping the explorers.* **3.** All about; all over in: *The reporter looked around the room.* **4.** Near in time to; close to: *I'll call you around noon.* **5.** Round about so as to surround or enclose: *She was wearing a belt around her waist.*
6. On or to the farther side of: *The gas station is just around the corner.*
—*adverb* **1.** All about; all over: *Come up to the shop and I'll take you around.* **2.** In a circle: *The workmen gathered around to get paid off.* **3.** On or to the farther side: *After a stop at the corner, the car finally got around.* **4.** So as to face in the reverse direction: *The trolley cars were turned around as they reached the end of the line.*

a·rouse |ə rouz′| —*verb* **aroused, arousing** **1.** To awaken from sleep: *The noise of the trucks arouses me every morning.* **2.** To stir up; excite: *When Barry complains, it always arouses my anger.*

ar·range |ə rānj′| —*verb* **arranged, arranging** **1.** To put in order or in a special order: *He arranged the desk by putting the books on one side and the paper and pencils on the other side. Arrange these words alphabetically.* **2.** To plan; prepare: *David is arranging the picnic.* **3.** To adapt a piece of music so that it can be performed by instruments or voices other than those for which it was originally written.

ar·range·ment |ə rānj′mənt| —*noun, plural* **arrangements**
1. The act of putting in order: *The arrangement of the flowers for the wedding took special planning.* **2.** The order in which persons or things are arranged: *an alphabetical arrangement of the students' names.* **3.** A group or set of things that have been arranged in a special way: *a flower arrangement of daisies and carnations; a jazz arrangement of an opera; an old-fashioned arrangement of furniture in the living room.* **4.** **arrangements** Plans or preparations: *We made arrangements to go to the movies.*

ar·ray |ə rā′| —*noun, plural* **arrays** **1.** An orderly arrangement; order: *The soldiers were lined up in battle array.* **2.** An impressive display or collection: *The zoo has a wide array of different animals. The array of talent on our basketball team is tremendous.*
—*verb* **arrayed, arraying** To put in order; arrange: *The sergeant arrayed the soldiers for inspection.*

ar·rest |ə rěst′| —*verb* **arrested, arresting** **1.** To seize and hold under the law: *The sheriff arrested the bandit.* **2.** To stop the movement or development of; hold back; check: *We must arrest the rust on the car so it doesn't spread. The dam arrested the flow of water.*
—*noun, plural* **arrests** The act of arresting: *ten arrests made last night only.*

ar·ri·val |ə rī′vəl| —*noun, plural* **arrivals** **1.** The act of arriving:

ă	pat	ĕ	pet	î	fierce
ā	pay	ē	be	ŏ	pot
â	care	ĭ	pit	ō	go
ä	father	ī	pie	ô	paw, for
oi	oil	ŭ	cut	zh	vision
ōō	book	û	fur	ə	ago, item,
ōō	boot	*th*	the		pencil, atom,
yōō	abuse	th	thin		circus
ou	out	hw	which	ər	butter

We waited at the airport for the arrival of the movie star. **2.** Someone or something that arrives or has arrived: *There are many new arrivals at the hotel every week.*

ar·rive | ə rīv′ | —*verb* **arrived, arriving** **1.** To come to a place: *They arrived in the city on time.* **2.** To come: *The children were waiting for summer to arrive so they could go swimming.* **3.** To reach or come to a goal or decision: *The jury arrived at a verdict.*

ar·ro·gant | ăr′ə gənt | —*adjective* Feeling that one is a lot better or more important than everyone else; having too much pride: *Helen was very arrogant after she won the science prize.*

ar·row | ăr′ō | —*noun, plural* **arrows** **1.** A thin, straight shaft or stick with feathers on one end and a sharp point at the other. It is shot from a bow. **2.** Anything that is shaped like an arrow, especially a sign or mark used to show direction: *The arrow on the road sign tells you to turn right to go to Austin and left to Atlanta.*

ar·row·head | ăr′ō hĕd′ | —*noun, plural* **arrowheads** A pointed tip that is attached to the end of an arrow. An arrowhead is usually made of stone or metal.

ar·se·nal | är′sə nəl | —*noun, plural* **arsenals** A building where weapons and ammunition are made and stored.

ar·se·nic | är′sə nĭk | —*noun* A very dangerous white poison without any taste. Arsenic is used to kill weeds, rats, and insects that destroy crops.

art | ärt | —*noun, plural* **arts** **1.** Painting, sculpture, poetry, music, dance, or any other activity in which a person makes or does something that is beautiful. **2.** The work or object made in these activities: *His art is on display at the museum.* **3.** A practical craft or skill: *the art of cooking; the art of building a campfire.* **4.** A special ability to do something easily: *the art of making friends.*

ar·ter·y | är′tə rē | —*noun, plural* **arteries** **1.** Any of the tubes that carry blood away from the heart to all parts of the body. **2.** A main road or way: *Washington Street is a major artery.*

ar·thri·tis | är thrī′tĭs | —*noun* A swelling and feeling of pain in a joint or joints of the body.

ar·thro·pod | är′thrə pŏd′ | —*noun, plural* **arthropods** Any of a large group of animals with bodies made up of two or three parts and legs having joints. Insects, spiders, lobsters, and crabs are arthropods.

ar·ti·choke | är′tĭ chōk′ | —*noun, plural* **artichokes** The flower of a plant like a thistle. It is covered with thick, leafy scales and is eaten as a vegetable.

ar·ti·cle | är′tĭ kəl | —*noun, plural* **articles** **1.** A written composition or piece in a newspaper, magazine, or book: *Did you read the article on the war in Africa that was in the Sunday newspaper?* **2.** An individual or separate section of a written document, such as a treaty or contract: *an article of the Constitution.* **3.** A particular thing; an item: *A bed is an article of furniture.* **4.** Any of the words *a, an,* or *the,* as in *a* dog, *an* apple, *the* snow. *A* and *an* are indefinite articles. *The* is the definite article.

ar·tic·u·late | är tĭk′yə lĭt | —*adjective* Able to express oneself clearly and effectively: *The senator was very articulate about his health insurance plan.*
—*verb* | är tĭk′yə lāt′ | **articulated, articulating** To express oneself clearly and effectively: *He articulated the sentiments of the group to the tour guide.*

arrowhead

arthropod
A garden spider

artichoke

ar·ti·fi·cial | är′tə fǐsh′əl | —*adjective* **1.** Made or manufactured by people and not made or produced by nature; not natural: *Light bulbs give off artificial light. There was a bowl of artificial fruit on the table.* **2.** Not natural, honest, or real; not sincere; pretended: *Wendy's happiness at seeing George was artificial; she really was sick and wanted to go to sleep.*

artificial respiration A way or method of helping a living person who has stopped breathing to start breathing again. Artificial respiration is the forcing of air in and out of the lungs until the person can breathe normally again.

ar·til·ler·y | är tǐl′ə rē | —*noun* **1.** Large guns or cannons that are too heavy to be carried. Artillery is usually pulled on a cart with large wheels. **2.** The part of an army that uses such guns.

art·ist | är′tǐst | —*noun, plural* **artists** **1.** A person who is skilled in any form of art. Painters, sculptors, writers, and musicians are all artists. **2.** A person who publicly performs in such activities as singing, dancing, or acting; an entertainer.

ar·tis·tic | är tǐs′tǐk | —*adjective* **1.** Of art or artists: *Ann's artistic works are sold in many galleries and shops.* **2.** Done or made with skill and good taste: *an artistic flower arrangement. Her drawing is very artistic.*

as | ăz | or | əz | —*adverb* **1.** To the same degree; equally: *Jane is as smart as Mary.* **2.** For example: *The zoo has many large animals, as tigers, elephants, and bears.*
—*conjunction* **1.** To the same degree that; equally with: *a syrup sweet as sugar.* **2.** In the same way that: *Her hair is brown, as are her eyes. During his stay at the island he lived as a native.* **3.** At the same time that; while: *She winked as our eyes met.* **4.** Since; because: *He stayed home, as he was ill.*
—*pronoun* **1.** That; who; which: *I got the same grade as you did.* **2.** A fact that: *Roses are red, as we all know.*
—*preposition* **1.** The same as; like: *He stared at her as a man filled with jealousy.* **2.** Doing the work of: *Mr. Jones was acting as a marshal.*

as·bes·tos | ăs bĕs′təs | —*noun* A gray mineral or substance that does not burn. Asbestos fibers can be woven into fireproof cloth for suits to protect firefighters and astronauts.

as·cend | ə sĕnd′ | —*verb* **ascended, ascending** To go or move upward; rise; climb: *We watched the balloon ascend higher and higher. The hikers ascended the mountain.*

as·cent | ə sĕnt′ | —*noun, plural* **ascents** **1.** The act of ascending or moving upward; a going up: *I lost sight of the rocket during its quick ascent into the sky.* **2.** The act of climbing up: *Our ascent of the mountain took five hours.*

as·cer·tain | ăs′ər tān′ | —*verb* **ascertained, ascertaining** To find out; discover: *ascertain the facts. We were able to ascertain why the car was always breaking down.*

ash¹ | ăsh | —*noun, plural* **ashes** The grayish, solid material left over after something has burned completely: *Roberta swept up the ashes in the fireplace. He spotted his shirt with an ash from his cigar.*

ash² | ăsh | —*noun, plural* **ashes** A tree that has leaves with many leaflets. It has strong, tough wood that is often used for making baseball bats.

a·shamed | ə shāmd′ | —*adjective* **1.** Feeling shame because one has done something wrong, bad, or silly: *Diane was ashamed because she had lied to her sister.* **2.** Not wanting or willing to do

---

ash¹, ash²

Ash¹ and **ash²** have always meant what they mean now. They began as two different words in the prehistoric language from which English and many other languages have developed, and they still have separate meanings today.

ă	pat	ĕ	pet	î	fîerce
ā	pay	ē	be	ŏ	pot
â	care	ĭ	pit	ō	go
ä	father	ī	pie	ô	paw, for

oi	oil	ŭ	cut	zh	vision
ōō	book	û	fur	ə	ago, item,
ōō	boot	*th*	the		pencil, atom,
yōō	abuse	th	thin		circus
ou	out	hw	which	ər	butter

something because of fear of being embarrassed: *Wayne was ashamed to tell anyone that a little girl had knocked him down.*

a·shore |ə **shôr'** | or |ə **shŏr'** | —*adverb* On or to the shore or land: *The sailors stepped ashore on the island. We rowed the boat ashore.*

A·sia |**ā'**zhə| or |**ā'**shə| —*noun* The largest continent on earth. Asia extends from Europe and Africa on the west to the Pacific Ocean on the east.

A·sian |**ā'**zhən| or |**ā'**shən| —*noun, plural* **Asians** A person born in Asia and belonging to one of the various ethnic groups native to Asia.
—*adjective* Of Asia or the Asians: *Asian architecture.*

a·side |ə **sīd'** | —*adverb* **1.** To one side; on one side: *I stepped aside so the children could pass. I pulled the curtain aside.* **2.** Apart for a special purpose or reason: *We set Sunday aside to have a big party. I put some money aside to buy a new suit.*

ask |ăsk| or |äsk| —*verb* **asked, asking** **1.** To put a question to; inquire: *Her mother asked her why she was crying.* **2.** To look or call for an answer to: *My father asked me where I put the shovel. You can only learn by asking questions.* **3.** To request: *The President asked everyone to use less gasoline. I wanted to ask for another hamburger.* **4.** To look for information about: *If you get lost, ask the way. Mildred asked Tom where he was going on his vacation.* **5.** To invite: *Jill and I were asked to the party.*

a·skew |ə **skyōō'** | —*adverb* and *adjective* At or to one side; not lined up or straight; crooked: *She always wears her hat askew. The picture is askew.*

a·sleep |ə **slēp'** | —*adjective* **1.** Not awake; sleeping: *You must have been asleep when the phone rang.* **2.** Without feeling; numb: *My foot is asleep.*
—*adverb* Into a condition of sleep: *He fell asleep quickly after the long hike.*

asp |ăsp| —*noun, plural* **asps** A poisonous snake of northern Africa and southwestern Asia.

as·par·a·gus |ə **spăr'**ə gəs| —*noun* **1.** A plant grown for its young, tender green stalks. **2.** The stalks of this plant, eaten as a vegetable.

as·pect |**ăs'**pĕkt' | —*noun, plural* **aspects** **1.** One of many ways of looking at or thinking about something or someone; a side or part of something: *We considered every aspect of our plan to move to another city.* **2.** Look or appearance: *The old, wrinkled raincoat gave John a sloppy aspect. The modern aspect of the new store made it very different from the old buildings on each side of it.*

as·pen |**ăs'**pən| —*noun, plural* **aspens** A poplar tree with leaves that flutter in even the lightest breeze.

as·phalt |**ăs'**fôlt' | —*noun* **1.** A thick, sticky, brownish-black substance that is found under the ground in some parts of the world. Asphalt can also be made by refining petroleum. Asphalt is used on roofs and gutters to make them waterproof. **2.** A hard, smooth material made by mixing asphalt with sand, small stones, and gravel. Asphalt is often used to pave roads.

as·pi·ra·tion |ăs'pə **rā'**shən| —*noun, plural* **aspirations** A strong desire to achieve or do something important.

as·pire |ə **spīr'** | —*verb* **aspired, aspiring** To have a great ambition; strive toward a goal: *He's practicing the flute because he aspires to play in the school orchestra.*

asparagus
Plant *(left)* and stalks *(right)*

assassination
The assassination of President
James A. Garfield, July, 1881

as·pi·rin | ăs′pə rĭn | or | ăs′prĭn | —*noun, plural* **aspirins** A drug used to ease pain and lower fever.

ass | ăs | —*noun, plural* **asses** **1.** A donkey or similar animal having hoofs. **2.** A silly or stupid person.

as·sas·sin | ə săs′ĭn | —*noun, plural* **assassins** A person who murders someone who is of political or public importance.

as·sas·si·nate | ə săs′ə nāt′ | —*verb* **assassinated, assassinating** To murder someone who is of political or public importance.

as·sas·si·na·tion | ə săs′ə nā′shən | —*noun, plural* **assassinations** The act of assassinating; a murder: *Presidents Lincoln, McKinley, and Kennedy all died by assassination.*

as·sault | ə sôlt′ | —*noun, plural* **assaults** A violent attack: *The army decided to make an assault on the enemy camp the next day.* —*verb* **assaulted, assaulting** To attack violently: *The robber assaulted my uncle in the park.*

as·sem·ble | ə sĕm′bəl | —*verb* **assembled, assembling** **1.** To bring or come together in a group; gather together: *The teachers assembled their classes in the auditorium. Three policemen assembled in the hall.* **2.** To fit or put together the parts of: *I watched my mother assemble the jigsaw puzzle.*

as·sem·bly | ə sĕm′blē | —*noun, plural* **assemblies** **1.** A group of people gathered together for a special purpose or reason: *The last school assembly before vacation will be on Friday.* **2. Assembly** A group or body of lawmakers in some state governments of the United States and in many foreign countries: *The Connecticut Assembly met in Hartford last month.* **3.** The act of fitting or putting together the parts of an object to make up a whole or complete thing: *The assembly of the swings, the slide, and the sandbox didn't take very long.* **4.** All the parts that are needed to put something together: *in the steering assembly of a truck.*

as·sert | ə sûrt′ | —*verb* **asserted, asserting** **1.** To state or declare strongly and positively; to claim: *The woman asserted again and again that she did not steal the necklace.* **2.** To defend or insist on a right, claim, or privilege: *Ellen asserted her independence by refusing to go to the doctor.*

as·sess | ə sĕs′ | —*verb* **assessed, assessing** **1.** To figure out or estimate the value of property for taxes: *Mr. Graham's house was assessed at $12,000.* **2.** To charge with a tax, fine, or special payment: *Each member of the club will be assessed fifty cents.*

as·set | ăs′ĕt′ | —*noun, plural* **assets** **1.** Something that is useful or valuable: *Marjorie's ability to make people feel comfortable is an asset. The large supply of oil is the country's most important asset.* **2. assets** All of the objects and property owned by a person, business, or group that are worth money: *His assets include some bonds, a house, and two cars.*

as·sign | ə sīn′ | —*verb* **assigned, assigning** **1.** To give out a task or job: *The teacher assigned us two books to read. I was assigned the job of getting wood for the fire.* **2.** To choose for something; appoint: *Paul was assigned to the entertainment committee.* **3.** To set aside for a particular purpose; fix: *The judge will assign a day for the trial.* **4.** To give out; distribute: *Different bunks were assigned to the campers.*

as·sign·ment | ə sīn′mənt | —*noun, plural* **assignments** **1.** Something that is assigned: *The English assignment was easy.* **2.** The act of assigning: *The coach's assignment of the new player to the starting line was well received by all.*

ă	pat	ĕ	pet	î	fierce
ā	pay	ē	be	ŏ	pot
â	care	ĭ	pit	ō	go
ä	father	ī	pie	ô	paw, for
oi	oil	ŭ	cut	zh	vision
ŏŏ	book	û	fur	ə	ago, item,
ōō	boot	*th*	the		pencil, atom,
yōō	abuse	th	thin		circus
ou	out	hw	which	ər	butter

as·sist | ə sĭst′ | —*verb* **assisted, assisting** To give help; aid: *The whole neighborhood assisted in cleaning up the park. Please assist me.*

as·sis·tance | ə sĭs′təns | —*noun* Help; aid: *I needed your assistance to move the picnic table.*

as·sis·tant | ə sĭs′tənt | —*noun, plural* **assistants** Someone who assists or helps: *My uncle is an assistant to the mayor.*
—*adjective* Helping or working under another person: *an assistant coach.*

as·so·ci·ate | ə sō′shē āt′ | or | ə sō′sē āt′ | —*verb* **associated, associating 1.** To bring together or connect in one's mind: *I associate birthdays with presents.* **2.** To join as a friend, member, or partner: *Rachel usually associates with women her own age. Mrs. Elkins is associated with her cousins in business.*
—*noun* | ə sō′shē ĭt | or | ə sō′sē ĭt | or | ə sō′shē āt′ | or | ə sō′sē āt′ |, *plural* **associates** A partner or friend: *My mother brought her business associate home for dinner.*

as·so·ci·a·tion | ə sō′sē ā′shən | or | ə sō′shē ā′shən | —*noun, plural* **associations 1.** A group of people joined together for a special purpose: *I joined an association that tries to find homes for stray dogs and cats.* **2.** A partnership or friendship: *People admired him because of his association with the governor.* **3.** The connection of thoughts or ideas: *What associations does the word "vacation" bring to your mind?*

as·sort·ment | ə sôrt′mənt | —*noun, plural* **assortments** A collection of different kinds; a variety: *an assortment of colors; an assortment of silver objects.*

as·sume | ə soōm′ | —*verb* **assumed, assuming 1.** To believe something is true without even thinking about it: *I assume you know how to fix a flat tire. He assumed the plane would be on time, but he was wrong.* **2.** To take upon oneself; undertake: *I assumed responsibility for my brother when my parents went to the store.* **3.** To take completely for oneself: *The king assumed the right to put anybody he didn't like in prison.*

as·sump·tion | ə sŭmp′shən | —*noun, plural* **assumptions 1.** The act of assuming: *his assumption of responsibility for his little brother.* **2.** Something that is assumed: *My assumption that it would rain today turned out to be wrong.*

as·sur·ance | ə shoŏr′əns | —*noun, plural* **assurances 1.** A statement made to make someone feel certain; a guarantee: *He gave me his assurance that he would pay back the money he borrowed.* **2.** Belief in one's ability to do something; confidence: *All my practicing on the piano gave me the assurance to play in front of the class.*

as·sure | ə shoŏr′ | —*verb* **assured, assuring 1.** To say positively; declare: *I can assure you that we will be home by eight o'clock.* **2.** To make certain; guarantee: *He checked the clock just to assure that the alarm was set.*

as·ter | ăs′tər | —*noun, plural* **asters** A plant with purple, white, or pink flowers that look like daisies. There are many kinds of asters.

as·ter·isk | ăs′tə rĭsk′ | —*noun, plural* **asterisks** A symbol or mark shaped like a star (*) used in printing or writing. An asterisk is placed after a word or a name or at the end of a sentence, and it tells the reader that there is more information about the subject printed somewhere else on the page.

assortment
Silver pieces on display

aster

astride

astronaut

athlete

ă	pat	ĕ	pet	î	fierce
ā	pay	ē	be	ŏ	pot
â	care	ĭ	pit	ō	go
ä	father	ī	pie	ô	paw, for

oi	oil	ŭ	cut	zh	vision
ōō	book	û	fur	ə	ago, item,
ōō	boot	th	the		pencil, atom,
yōō	abuse	th	thin		circus
ou	out	hw	which	ər	butter

as·ter·oid | ăs′tə roid′ | —*noun, plural* **asteroids** Any of the thousands of small rocky objects that revolve around the sun, mostly in the region between Mars and Jupiter. Asteroids are of many different sizes.

asth·ma | ăz′mə | or | ăs′mə | —*noun* A disease that causes coughing and makes it hard to breathe.

as·ton·ish | ə stŏn′ĭsh | —*verb* **astonished, astonishing** To surprise greatly; amaze: *It astonished me when my grandmother gave me a hundred dollars for my birthday. That we could send men to the moon in a spacecraft astonished many people.*

as·ton·ish·ment | ə stŏn′ĭsh mənt | —*noun* Great surprise; amazement; wonder: *The circus audience was filled with astonishment when the lion tamer put his head inside the lion's mouth.*

a·stound | ə stound′ | —*verb* **astounded, astounding** To fill or strike with surprise or sudden wonder; astonish: *Our victory completely astounded him.*

a·stray | ə strā′ | —*adverb* **1.** Away from the right path or direction: *I went astray in the forest and got lost.* **2.** Away from the right thing to do: *I didn't think she would skip school, but the older girls led her astray.*

a·stride | ə strīd′ | —*preposition* With one leg on each side of: *The cowboy sat astride the horse.*

as·trol·o·gy | ə strŏl′ə jē | —*noun* The study of the positions of the stars and planets to try to tell what influence or effect they have on things that happen and on people's lives. Some people believe that astrology can be used to tell what the future will be.

as·tro·naut | ăs′trə nôt′ | —*noun, plural* **astronauts** A person who is trained to fly in a spacecraft: *The United States is the only country that has sent astronauts to the moon.*

as·tron·o·mer | ə strŏn′ə mər | —*noun, plural* **astronomers** A scientist who practices astronomy.

as·tron·o·my | ə strŏn′ə mē | —*noun* The science that observes and studies the sun, moon, planets, stars, comets, galaxies, and other heavenly bodies.

a·sy·lum | ə sī′ləm | —*noun, plural* **asylums 1.** A place or institution that takes care of people who cannot take care of themselves. There are asylums for orphans and the insane or mentally ill. An asylum is often also a hospital. **2.** A place where someone can find protection or safety; shelter. One country may give asylum to someone from another country who has been accused of a political crime.

at | ăt | or | ət | —*preposition* **1.** In, on, by, or near: *Call me when I'm at home. The line starts at the side door.* **2.** In a condition of: *Germany and Japan were at war with the United States.* **3.** In the direction of; toward; to: *Look at us.* **4.** Near or on the time of: *We always eat at noon.* **5.** For: *We bought the furniture at a very reasonable price.*

ate | āt | The past tense of the verb **eat:** *We ate dinner at my aunt's house.*

♦ *These sound alike* **ate, eight.**

ath·lete | ăth′lēt′ | —*noun, plural* **athletes** A person who is trained for and takes part in sports or physical exercises that require strength, speed, and agility. Skiers, basketball players, and swimmers are athletes.

ath·let·ic | ăth lĕt′ĭk | —*adjective* **1.** Of or for athletics: *athletic ability. The new athletic building opens this fall.* **2.** Of or for athletes: *a good athletic build for basketball; an athletic club at school.* **3.** Strong and having good muscles: *All the boys and girls in that family are very athletic.*

ath·let·ics |ăth lĕt′ĭks| —*noun* (Used with a plural verb.) Athletic activities; sports: *Athletics are an important part of our school's program.*

At·lan·ta |ăt lăn′tə| The capital of Georgia.

At·lan·tic Ocean |ăt lăn′tĭk| The ocean extending between the Americas on one side and Africa and Europe on the other.

at·las |ăt′ləs| —*noun, plural* **atlases** A book of maps or a collection of maps fastened between covers.

at·mos·phere |ăt′mə sfîr′| —*noun, plural* **atmospheres** **1.** The gas that surrounds a body in space, especially the air around the earth: *The earth's atmosphere is different from the atmosphere of Mars.* **2.** The climate of a place: *the dry atmosphere of the desert.* **3.** Surroundings that have an effect on the mind or body: *A hospital should have a quiet atmosphere.* **4.** A general feeling or mood: *the atmosphere of a ghost story.*

at·mos·pher·ic |ăt′mə sfĕr′ĭk| —*adjective* Of, in, or from the atmosphere: *atmospheric pressure; atmospheric flight; atmospheric smog.*

at·oll |ăt′ôl′| or |ăt′ŏl′| or |ā′tôl′| or |ā′tŏl′| —*noun, plural* **atolls** A coral island or a string of coral islands and coral reefs. An atoll makes a partial or complete ring around a lagoon.

at·om |ăt′əm| —*noun, plural* **atoms** **1. a.** The smallest unit of a chemical element, made up of neutrons and protons with a main nucleus with electrons surrounding it. An atom stays the same in chemical reactions except for the taking away or exchanging of certain electrons. Everything in the universe is made up of atoms. **b.** A unit of this kind thought of as a source of nuclear energy. **2.** A small piece or amount; a bit: *There is not an atom of sense in what he says.*

a·tom·ic |ə tŏm′ĭk| —*adjective* **1.** Of an atom or atoms. **2.** Of or using nuclear energy; nuclear: *an atomic power plant.*

atomic bomb A bomb that gets its explosive power from nuclear energy. The explosion of an atomic bomb has enormous force, heat, light, and harmful radioactivity.

atomic energy Energy that is produced as a result of reactions in the nuclei of atoms.

at·tach |ə tăch′| —*verb* **attached, attaching** **1.** To fasten on or join; connect: *We attached the wires. The wires attach here.* **2.** To fasten with ties of love or loyalty: *She is very attached to her parents.* **3.** To think of as having or belonging to: *I attach no importance to his opinions.* **4.** To add something at the end: *He attached his signature to the document.*

at·tach·ment |ə tăch′mənt| —*noun, plural* **attachments** **1.** The act of attaching or condition of being attached: *The attachment of those wires is not safe.* **2.** Something that attaches as an extra part; an accessory: *The vacuum cleaner has several attachments.* **3.** Love, affection, or loyalty: *a strong attachment to a friend.*

at·tack |ə tăk′| —*verb* **attacked, attacking** **1.** To set upon with violent force: *Even large animals were usually afraid to attack a buffalo herd. Germany attacked the Soviet Union in 1941. The troops attacked at dawn.* **2.** To speak or write about in an unfriendly way: *The candidates attacked each other in the debate.* **3.** To be harmful to; afflict: *Flu attacked thousands of people in the city.*

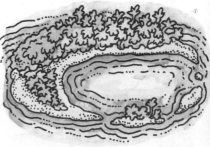

atoll

atomic bomb
Explosion over Japan on August 9, 1945

—*noun, plural* **attacks** **1.** The act of attacking: *There have been five attacks on the fort.* **2.** The occurrence or beginning of a disease, especially when it is sudden: *a heart attack.*

at·tain |ə tān'| —*verb* **attained, attaining** **1.** To get, do, or bring about by trying hard: *Correct grammar is a magic tool for attaining confidence in writing and speaking.* **2.** To arrive at through time and growth; reach: *He attained the age of 80.*

at·tempt |ə tĕmpt'| —*verb* **attempted, attempting** To make an effort; try: *They will fight if anyone attempts to steal their cargo.* —*noun, plural* **attempts** **1.** An effort or try: *He had made the first attempt to win back the championship.* **2.** A violent or forceful attack: *An attempt was made on the President's life.*

at·tend |ə tĕnd'| —*verb* **attended, attending** **1.** To be present at; go to: *Some students attend school in the morning only.* **2.** To wait upon or be in waiting; serve: *Many knights attended the king.* **3.** To take care of: *Nurses attended the victims of the fire.* **4.** To give care and thought; apply oneself: *attend to one's business. Please attend to the matter at hand.*

at·ten·dance |ə tĕn'dəns| —*noun* **1.** The act or practice of being present: *His attendance at school is regular.* **2.** The act of waiting upon someone or something: *a doctor in attendance at the hospital; the engineer in attendance in the boiler room.* **3.** The persons or number of persons present: *an attendance of 50,000 at the football game.*

at·ten·dant |ə tĕn'dənt| —*noun, plural* **attendants** A person who attends or waits on another: *An attendant in the garage parked the car. The queen had four attendants.* —*adjective* Going along with: *the death of the President and its attendant confusion.*

at·ten·tion |ə tĕn'shən| —*noun, plural* **attentions** **1.** Mental concentration; thinking, watching, or listening carefully to or about something or someone: *Read the article and pay attention to the details about forests. The speaker kept the audience's attention for more than an hour.* **2.** Consideration; notice: *Your interesting suggestion has come to our attention.* **3.** **attentions** Polite or considerate acts, especially in trying to win a person's love: *The girl seemed to return his attentions.*

at·tic |ăt'ĭk| —*noun, plural* **attics** The space in a house just under the roof. Attics are used for storage and are sometimes made into extra rooms.

at·tire |ə tīr'| —*verb* **attired, attiring** To dress, especially in fine or formal clothing: *an emperor attired in embroidered robes.* —*noun* Clothing or costume: *white tennis attire.*

at·ti·tude |ăt'ĭ tōod'| or |ăt'ĭ tyōod'| —*noun, plural* **attitudes** **1.** A way of thinking, feeling, or acting about someone or something; a point of view: *What is the principal's attitude toward building a new swimming pool?* **2.** A position of the body: *Beth sat at the table in a stiff, upright attitude.*

at·tor·ney |ə tûr'nē| —*noun, plural* **attorneys** A person legally appointed to act for another; a lawyer.

at·tract |ə trăkt'| —*verb* **attracted, attracting** To draw or pull to oneself or itself by some special quality or action: *A magnet attracts nails. Clean beaches attract many people in the summer.*

at·trac·tion |ə trăk'shən| —*noun, plural* **attractions** **1.** The act or power of attracting: *the attraction of a magnet.* **2.** Something or someone that attracts: *The Old North Church is one of Boston's*

ă	pat	ĕ	pet	î	fierce
ā	pay	ē	be	ŏ	pot
â	care	ĭ	pit	ō	go
ä	father	ī	pie	ô	paw, for

oi	oil	ŭ	cut	zh	vision
ōo	book	û	fur	ə	ago, item,
ōo	boot	*th*	the		pencil, atom,
yōo	abuse	th	thin		circus
ou	out	hw	which	ər	butter

many attractions. The clown is the attraction in the center ring at the circus.

at·trac·tive |ə trăk′tĭv| —*adjective* **1.** Having the power of attracting: *the attractive force of magnetism.* **2.** Pleasing to the eye, mind, or senses: *an attractive girl; an attractive offer of a new job.*

at·trib·ute |ə trĭb′yo͞ot| —*verb* **attributed, attributing** To think of as belonging to or coming from someone or something: *We attribute the air pollution partly to the heavy use of cars and trucks.* —*noun* |ăt′rə byo͞ot′|, *plural* **attributes** A quality or characteristic that belongs to a person or thing: *Among Jim's attributes are honesty and courtesy.*

auc·tion |ôk′shən| —*noun, plural* **auctions** A public sale at which goods and property are sold to the person who bids the highest amount of money. —*verb* **auctioned, auctioning** To sell at an auction: *auction off a diamond ring. He auctioned his house with all its furnishings.*

auction

au·di·ble |ô′də bəl| —*adjective* Loud enough to be heard: *an audible whisper.*

au·di·ence |ô′dē əns| —*noun, plural* **audiences** **1.** The people gathered together to see and hear a play, movie, concert, sports event, or other performance. **2.** The readers, listeners, or viewers reached by a book, radio broadcast, or television program. **3.** A formal hearing or conference: *an audience with the pope.*

au·di·o |ô′dē ō′| —*adjective* Of sound or hearing: *We can't get the audio part of our television set to work.*

au·di·to·ri·um |ô′dĭ tôr′ē əm| or |ô′dĭ tōr′ē əm| —*noun, plural* **auditoriums** A large room or building that holds a big audience.

audience

au·ger |ô′gər| —*noun, plural* **augers** A tool for boring holes.

Au·gust |ô′gəst| —*noun, plural* **Augusts** The eighth month of the year, after July and before September. August has 31 days.

Au·gus·ta |ô gŭs′tə| The capital of Maine.

auk |ôk| —*noun, plural* **auks** A black and white sea bird with a thick body and short wings. Auks live along northern shores.

aunt |ănt| or |änt| —*noun, plural* **aunts** **1.** The sister of one's father or mother. **2.** The wife of one's father's or mother's brother.
♦ *These sound alike* **aunt, ant.**

au·ri·cle |ôr′ĭ kəl| —*noun, plural* **auricles** **1.** The outside part of the ear. **2.** A chamber of the heart that receives blood from a vein. A heart has two auricles.
♦ *These sound alike* **auricle, oracle.**

Aus·tin |ô′stən| The capital of Texas.

Aus·tra·lia |ô strāl′yə| **1.** A continent southeast of Asia between the Pacific and Indian oceans. **2.** A country made up of this continent and nearby islands.

au·then·tic |ô thĕn′tĭk| —*adjective* **1.** Worthy of belief; true; correct: *His story about the old West has authentic characters.* **2.** Not copied, counterfeit, or fake: *an authentic cave painting.*

au·thor |ô′thər| —*noun, plural* **authors** **1.** A person who writes a book, story, article, play, or other work. **2.** The beginner or creator of something: *the author of an idea for a new park for the town.*

au·thor·i·ty |ə thôr′ĭ tē| or |ə thŏr′ĭ tē| —*noun, plural* **authorities** **1.a.** The power and right to order, to decide, and to enforce laws or rules. **b.** A person who has this power and right: *School authorities decided to buy more books for the library.* **2.** A

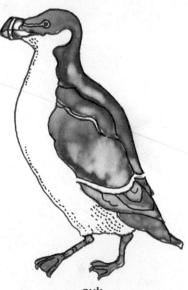

auk

source of correct or expert information: *an authority on American history.*

au·thor·ize | ô′thə rīz′ | —*verb* **authorized, authorizing** **1.** To give power or authority to: *The mayor authorized him to form a committee to make plans for a new city hall.* **2.** To give permission for; approve: *He authorized Janet's absence from the meeting because of illness.*

au·to | ô′tō | —*noun, plural* **autos** An automobile.

au·to·bi·og·ra·phy | ô′tō bī ŏg′rə fē | or | ô′tō bē ŏg′rə fē | —*noun, plural* **autobiographies** The story of a person's life written by himself or herself.

au·to·graph | ô′tə grăf′ | or | ô′tə gräf′ | —*noun, plural* **autographs** A written name or signature of a famous person. Autographs are saved by fans or collectors.
—*verb* **autographed, autographing** To write one's name or signature on: *The actor autographed the program of the play for me.*

au·to·mat·ic | ô′tə măt′ĭk | —*adjective* **1.** Working, moving, or acting by itself: *an automatic elevator.* **2.** Done or made by the body without thinking or control: *The heartbeat is automatic.*
—*noun, plural* **automatics** A device or machine that is all or partly automatic. Many firearms are automatics and fire until they run out of ammunition.

au·to·ma·tion | ô′tə mā′shən | —*noun* The automatic working of a machine, process, or system. Automation makes it possible for many jobs to be done by machines instead of people.

au·to·mo·bile | ô′tə mə bēl′ | or | ô′tə mō′bēl′ | or | ô′tə mə bēl′ | —*noun, plural* **automobiles** A land vehicle that has four wheels and is moved by an engine that usually uses gasoline; a car. An automobile has room for the driver and other passengers.

au·tumn | ô′təm | —*noun, plural* **autumns** The season of the year between summer and winter; fall.

aux·il·ia·ry | ôg zĭl′yə rē | or | ôg zĭl′ə rē | —*adjective* Giving help or support: *Some kinds of racing cars need auxiliary parachutes to come to a stop.*
—*noun, plural* **auxiliaries** **1.** A person or thing that helps; an aid: *The guide's auxiliary will take you on the shorter canoe trip.* **2.** A small group that is part of a larger group: *an auxiliary of volunteer firefighters.* **3.** An auxiliary verb.

auxiliary verb A verb that comes first in a verb phrase and helps form the tense, mood, or voice of the main verb. *Have, may, can, must,* and *will* are some auxiliary verbs.

automobile

a·vail·a·ble | ə vā′lə bəl | —*adjective* **1.** Able to be purchased or obtained: *fifty available tickets for the ball game. There are three available lengths of those curtains.* **2.** Ready to serve or be used: *There are three available people for the jobs.*

av·a·lanche | ăv′ə lănch′ | or | ăv′ə länch′ | —*noun, plural* **avalanches** A large mass of material that falls or slides down the side of a mountain. An avalanche is usually made up of snow, ice, earth, or rocks.

av·e·nue | ăv′ə nōo′ | or | ăv′ə nyōo′ | —*noun, plural* **avenues** **1.** A wide street or main road. There are often trees along each side of an avenue. **2.** A way of reaching or getting something.

av·er·age | ăv′ər ĭj | or | ăv′rĭj | —*noun, plural* **averages** A number found by adding up two or more quantities and dividing the total by the number of quantities. The average of 1, 3, 5, and 7 is 4 or $1 + 3 + 5 + 7 = 16 \div 4 = 4$.

ă	pat	ĕ	pet	î	fierce
ā	pay	ē	be	ŏ	pot
â	care	ĭ	pit	ō	go
ä	father	ī	pie	ô	paw, for

oi	oil	ŭ	cut	zh	vision
ŏŏ	book	û	fur	ə	ago, item,
ōō	boot	*th*	the		pencil, atom,
yōō	abuse	th	thin		circus
ou	out	hw	which	ər	butter

—*verb* **averaged, averaging 1.** To find the average of: *We averaged our daily sales for the month.* **2.** To have as an average: *The temperature in June averaged 76 degrees last year.*

—*adjective* **1.** Found as an average; being an average: *On the trip to Florida we had an average speed of 50 miles an hour.* **2.** Not very good and not very bad; normal; ordinary: *He is just an average student and about in the middle of his class.*

a·vert |ə vûrt′| —*verb* **averted, averting 1.** To turn away or aside: *She averted her eyes from the accident.* **2.** To keep from happening; prevent: *She had to jam on the brakes to avert the accident.*

a·vi·a·tion |ā′vē ā′shən| —*noun* The science, business, or operation of aircraft.

a·vi·a·tor |ā′vē ā′tər| —*noun, plural* **aviators** A person who flies or can fly aircraft; a pilot.

av·o·ca·do |ăv′ə kä′dō| or |ä′və kä′dō| —*noun, plural* **avocados** A tropical American fruit with leathery green or blackish skin. It has smooth, yellowish-green pulp and a large seed. Avocados are often eaten in salads.

a·void |ə void′| —*verb* **avoided, avoiding** To keep away from: *We left the game early and avoided the crowds.*

a·wait |ə wāt′| —*verb* **awaited, awaiting 1.** To wait for someone or something: *He awaited news of their safe arrival home.* **2.** To be in store for: *No one knows for sure what awaits him in life.*

a·wake |ə wāk′| —*verb* **awoke, awaked, awaking** To rouse from sleep; wake up: *The alarm clock awakes me at seven.*

—*adjective* Not sleeping: *He was awake all night.*

a·wak·en |ə wā′kən| —*verb* **awakened, awakening** To wake up; rouse; awake: *The clatter of a passing truck awakened me. I awakened early because of the noise.*

a·ward |ə wôrd′| —*verb* **awarded, awarding 1.** To give a prize for special quality or performance: *The committee awarded him the medal for the best paper.* **2.** To give by legal or governmental decision: *The judge awarded a settlement to the victim of the accident. The town awarded the contract for building a new fire house to our company.*

—*noun, plural* **awards 1.** Something given for special quality or performance. **2.** Something given by legal decision.

a·ware |ə wâr′| —*adjective* Being conscious of; knowing: *He is aware of his faults.*

a·ware·ness |ə wâr′nĭs| —*noun* The state or quality of being aware: *His awareness of the danger saved their lives.*

a·way |ə wā′| —*adverb* **1.** At or to a distance: *a house two miles away.* **2.** In or to a different place or direction: *Don't look away now.* **3.** From someone's presence or possession: *Take these things away. Her old bicycle was given away by the janitor.* **4.** Out of existence: *The noise died away.* **5.** All the time; without stopping: *He was working away at his homework.* **6.** At once; immediately: *Fire away!*

—*adjective* **1.** Absent: *He's away from home.* **2.** At a distance: *She's miles away.*

awe |ô| —*noun* A feeling of wonder, fear, or respect about something that is mighty or majestic: *We looked in awe at the hidden waterfall we came upon in the forest.*

—*verb* **awed, awing** To fill with awe: *The size of the plane awed everyone.*

aviator
Above: Charles Lindbergh
Below: Amelia Earhart

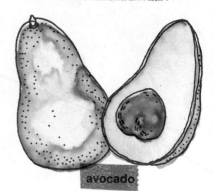

avocado

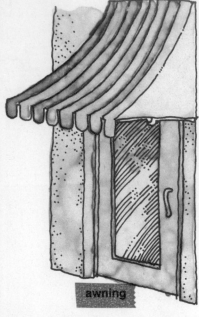

awning

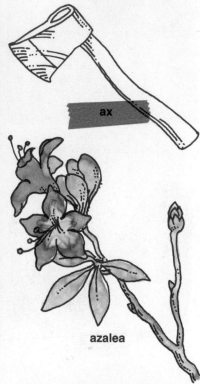

ax

azalea

aw·ful |ô′fəl| —*adjective* **1.** Causing awe or fear: *There is an awful stillness before a tornado.* **2.** Very bad or unpleasant; horrible: *an awful pain in my arm; awful weather; an awful movie.* **3.** Very big; great; considerable: *I have an awful lot of homework to do before tomorrow.*

aw·ful·ly |ô′fə lē| or |ô′flē| —*adverb* **1.** Very much; terribly: *When Pat broke her arm, it hurt awfully.* **2.** Very: *He did seem awfully confused.* **3.** Very badly: *She behaved awfully in front of her mother's guests.*

a·while |ə hwīl′| or |ə wīl′| —*adverb* For a short time: *We waited awhile but he did not arrive, and we went to the fair without him.*

awk·ward |ôk′wərd| —*adjective* **1.** Not moving in a graceful way; clumsy: *She is a very awkward dancer.* **2.** Not natural in speech or behavior: *Jill became shy and awkward whenever Bob was around.* **3.** Hard to move, handle, or manage: *an awkward bundle to carry; an awkward dress to put on.*

awl |ôl| —*noun, plural* **awls** A pointed tool that is used to make small holes in wood or leather.
♦ *These sound alike* **awl, all.**

awn·ing |ô′nĭng| —*noun, plural* **awnings** A canvas or plastic screen that looks like a roof. An awning is put up over a window or door. Awnings protect the inside of houses from the sun and rain.

a·woke |ə wōk′| The past tense of the verb **awake:** *Billy awoke at five-thirty this morning to prepare for the picnic.*

ax or **axe** |ăks| —*noun, plural* **axes** A chopping or cutting tool with a head that has a sharp blade. An ax is fixed on a long handle.

ax·es 1. |ăk′sēz′| The plural of the noun **axis. 2.** |ăk′sĭz| The plural of the noun **ax.**

ax·is |ăk′sĭs| —*noun, plural* **axes** A straight line around which an object turns or can be imagined to turn: *The axis of the earth passes through both of its poles, the North Pole and the South Pole.*

ax·le |ăk′səl| —*noun, plural* **axles** A bar or shaft on which one or more wheels turn.

aye or **ay** |ī| —*adverb* Yes: *All in favor say "aye."*
—*noun, plural* **ayes 1.** A vote of "yes." **2. the ayes** The people who vote "yes": *The ayes have it; the town will get a new road.*
♦ *These sound alike* **aye, eye, I.**

a·zal·ea |ə zāl′yə| —*noun, plural* **azaleas** A shrub with clusters of flowers that are usually pink, red, or white. Azaleas are often grown in gardens or as house plants.

az·ure |ăzh′ər| —*noun, plural* **azures** A light to medium blue, like that of the sky on a clear day.
—*adjective* Light to medium blue.

ă	pat	ĕ	pet	î	fierce
ā	pay	ē	be	ŏ	pot
â	care	ĭ	pit	ō	go
ä	father	ī	pie	ô	paw, for

oi	oil	ŭ	cut	zh	vision
ŏŏ	book	û	fur	ə	ago, item,
ōō	boot	*th*	the		pencil, atom,
yōō	abuse	th	thin		circus
ou	out	hw	which	ər	butter

⟨	**Phoenician** — The letter *B* comes originally from a Phoenician symbol named *beth*, meaning "house," in use about 3,000 years ago.
ß	**Greek** — The Greeks borrowed the symbol from the Phoenicians and changed its form. They also changed its name to *bēta*.
B	**Roman** — The Romans took the letter and adapted it for carving into stone. This became the model for our modern printed capital *B*.
b	**Medieval** — The hand-written form of about 1,200 years ago became the basis of the modern small letter.
Bb	**Modern** — The modern capital and small letters are based on the Roman capital and later hand-written forms.

Bb

b or **B** | bē | —*noun, plural* **b's** or **B's** The second letter of the English alphabet.

baa | bă | or | bä | —*noun, plural* **baas** The sound made by a sheep.
—*verb* **baaed, baaing** To make this sound.

bab·ble | băb'əl | —*verb* **babbled, babbling** **1.** To make sounds that have no meaning: *The baby babbles when he sees his mother.* **2.** To talk a long time about something that is not important; to chatter: *He babbled on and on about the new television show.* **3.** To make a steady, low gurgling sound, as a brook does.
—*noun* **1.** Sounds that have no meaning: *All we could hear in the auditorium was the babble of voices.* **2.** A steady, low gurgling sound: *the babble of the brook under the bridge.*

babe | bāb | —*noun, plural* **babes** A baby; an infant.

ba·boon | bă bōon' | —*noun, plural* **baboons** A large African monkey with a long, narrow face.

ba·by | bā'bē | —*noun, plural* **babies** **1.** A very young child; an infant. **2.** The youngest member of a family. **3.** A person who behaves in a childish way.
—*verb* **babied, babying, babies** To treat like a baby; pamper.

ba·by-sat | bā'bē săt' | The past tense and past participle of the verb **baby-sit**: *Last night I baby-sat for the family next door. I have baby-sat for them for the past five years.*

ba·by-sit | bā'bē sĭt' | —*verb* **baby-sat, baby-sitting** To take care of a child or children when the parents are not at home.

bach·e·lor | băch'ə lər | or | băch'lər | —*noun, plural* **bachelors** A man who has not married.

back | băk | —*noun, plural* **backs** **1.** The part of the human body from the bottom of the neck to the top of the buttocks. **2.** The upper part of an animal's body that is closest to the spine. **3.** The spine; backbone. **4.a.** The reverse side of something: *the back of the hand.* **b.** Something opposite the front: *The doctor's office is in the back of the building.* **5.** The part of a chair, bench, couch, or seat that one's back rests against while one is sitting.
—*adverb* **1.** To a direction opposite the front: *Everyone move back, please.* **2.** To a former place, time, or condition: *They went back to their old home. Think back to last week.*
—*adjective* **1.** Opposite the front: *the back porch.* **2.** Old; past:

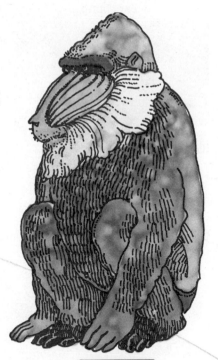

baboon

backboard

backhand

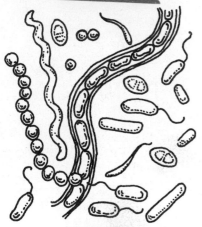

backpack

bacteria

ă	pat	ĕ	pet	î	fierce
ā	pay	ē	be	ŏ	pot
â	care	ĭ	pit	ō	go
ä	father	ī	pie	ô	paw, for

oi	oil	ŭ	cut	zh	vision
ōō	book	û	fur	ə	ago, item,
ōō	boot	th	the		pencil, atom,
yōō	abuse	th	thin		circus
ou	out	hw	which	ər	butter

Ted keeps all back copies of his sports magazine.
—*verb* **backed, backing** **1.** To move or cause to move backward: *As she said good-by, she backed slowly toward the door. John backed the car into the garage.* **2.** To be in favor of; support: *The whole team backed him for captain. Everyone backed her plan.*

back·board |băk′bôrd′| or |băk′bōrd′| —*noun, plural* **backboards** In basketball, a flat sheet of wood or hard plastic to which the basket is attached.

back·bone |băk′bōn′| —*noun, plural* **backbones** **1.** The series of jointed bones, called vertebras, in the middle of the back; the spinal column; spine. The backbone is found in human beings and in other mammals, reptiles, amphibians, and fish. The backbone is the main support of the body. **2.** Strength of character; courage: *To face that bully took plenty of backbone.*

back·ground |băk′ground′| —*noun, plural* **backgrounds** **1.** The part of a scene, view, or picture that is at the back and looks far away: *mountains painted in the background.* **2.** The general surface on which other things are shown: *white stars on a blue background.* **3.** A person's past experience, education, and training: *He has the right background for the job.*

back·hand |băk′hănd′| —*noun, plural* **backhands** In tennis and other sports, a stroke made with the back of the hand facing forward.

back·pack |băk′păk′| —*noun, plural* **backpacks** A knapsack or heavy cloth bag that is worn on the back and used to carry camping equipment.

back·ward |băk′wərd| —*adverb* **1.** Toward the back: *He looked backward when he heard the horn of the car.* **2.** With the back first: *Helicopters can fly backward.* **3.** In reverse order or direction; opposite to the usual or regular way: *Say the alphabet backward.* **4.** From good to bad or from bad to worse: *Our team hasn't improved, it has gone backward.* **5.** Into or toward the past: *Older people sometimes look backward to when they were young.* Another form of this adverb is **backwards.**
—*adjective* **1.** Directed or moving toward the back: *a backward glance; a backward fall.* **2.** Behind others in development: *a backward country.*

back·wards |băk′wərdz| A form of the adverb **backward.**

ba·con |bā′kən| —*noun* The salted and smoked meat from the back and sides of a pig.

bac·te·ri·a |băk tîr′ē ə| —*plural noun* Tiny plants that can be seen only with a microscope. Some bacteria cause diseases.

bad |băd| —*adjective* **worse, worst** **1.** Not good; *a bad book; a bad driver.* **2. a.** Not favorable: *bad weather.* **b.** Not convenient: *The movie starts at a bad time.* **3.** Disagreeable; unpleasant: *a bad smell; He is in a bad mood.* **4.** Causing distress: *bad news; a bad dream.* **5.** Incorrect; improper: *bad grammar; bad manners.* **6.** Disobedient; naughty: *Johnny was a bad boy today.* **7.** Harmful: *Candy is bad for your teeth.* **8.** In poor health; sick: *Jim feels bad today.* **9.** Severe; violent: *a bad storm.* **10.** Sorry: *I feel bad about what happened.* **11.** Rotten; spoiled: *a bad apple.*
♦ *These sound alike* **bad, bade.**

bade |băd| or |bād| A past tense of the verb **bid:** *He bade them enter.*
♦ *These sound alike* **bade, bad.**

badge |băj| —*noun, plural* **badges** Something worn to show that a person belongs to a certain group, school, profession, or club: *a sheriff's badge; a mail carrier's badge.*

bad·ger |băj′ər| —*noun, plural* **badgers** An animal with short legs and thick, grayish fur. Badgers live underground.
—*verb* **badgered, badgering** To annoy or confuse by or as if by asking many questions; pester; bother: *The reporter badgered the mayor about higher taxes.*

bad·ly |băd′lē| —*adverb* **1.** In a bad way or manner: *The painting was badly done. He swims badly.* **2.** Very much; greatly: *Nobody was badly hurt in the accident.*

bad·min·ton |băd′mĭn′tən| —*noun* A game for two or four players. Light, long-handled rackets are used by the players to hit a small rubber and plastic object back and forth over a high net.

baf·fle |băf′əl| —*verb* **baffled, baffling** To be so confusing or difficult to someone that understanding is hard: *This math problem baffles me.*

bag |băg| —*noun, plural* **bags** **1.** A container made of paper, cloth, plastic, or leather, used for holding things. **2.a.** A bag with something in it: *a bag of onions.* **b.** The amount that a bag holds: *Who ate the bag of peanuts?* **3.** Something, such as a suitcase or a purse, that can be used like a bag.

bag·gage |băg′ĭj| —*noun* The suitcases, trunks, and bags that a person carries when traveling.

bag·gy |băg′ē| —*adjective* **baggier, baggiest** Fitting loosely; sagging: *baggy pants.*

bag·pipe |băg′pīp′| —*noun, plural* **bagpipes** A musical instrument made of a leather bag and four pipes. A player blows air into the bag through a mouthpiece and then forces the air through the pipes by squeezing the bag.

bail¹ |bāl| —*noun* Money given to set free an arrested person from jail until a trial takes place. The money is held by the court and returned when the person appears for trial.
—*verb* **bailed, bailing** To set free by giving bail: *The lawyer bailed his client out of jail.*
♦ *These sound alike* **bail, bale.**

bail² |bāl| —*verb* **bailed, bailing** **1.** To empty water from a boat: *We bailed the leaky rowboat with a coffee can.* **2.** **bail out** To escape from an aircraft by jumping with a parachute.
♦ *These sound alike* **bail, bale.**

bait |bāt| —*noun* **1.** Something, especially food, used to attract fish or animals so they can be caught. **2.** Anything that attracts or lures a person or animal.
—*verb* **baited, baiting** **1.** To put bait on: *He baited the fishhook with a worm.* **2.** To tease in a cruel way: *The children were baiting each other by shouting insults.*

bake |bāk| —*verb* **baked, baking** **1.** To cook in an oven with steady, dry heat: *We baked bread. The muffins baked quickly.* **2.** To harden or dry by heating: *After she painted the clay pot, she baked it to make it stronger. Mud bakes in the hot sun.*

bak·er |bā′kər| —*noun, plural* **bakers** A person who bakes or sells bread, rolls, pies, and cakes.

bak·e·ry |bā′kə rē| —*noun, plural* **bakeries** A place where bread, rolls, pies, and cakes are baked or sold.

bak·ing powder |bā′kĭng| A powder used in baking to cause breads and cakes to rise.

baking soda A white powder used in cooking and in medicine.

badger

bagpipe

bail¹, bail²
Bail¹ comes from a word used long ago by English-speaking people to mean "custody," which is the right or duty to take care of someone or something. Earlier still it came from a French word meaning "to take charge of" and from the Latin word for "a person who carries." **Bail²** comes from a word used long ago by English- and French-speaking people to mean "a bucket." Its earlier source may also be the Latin word meaning "a person who carries."

balance

bald eagle

ball¹, ball²

Ball¹ comes from a word used very long ago by people who lived in Scandinavia; the word is related to our words **boulder** and **balloon**. **Ball²** comes from an old Greek word meaning "to dance." Like many other words in our language, **ball²** traveled through Latin and French before it arrived in English.

ă	pat	ĕ	pet	î	fierce
ā	pay	ē	be	ŏ	pot
â	care	ĭ	pit	ō	go
ä	father	ī	pie	ô	paw, for

oi	oil	ŭ	cut	zh	vision
ŏŏ	book	û	fur	ə	ago, item,
ōō	boot	th	the		pencil, atom,
yōō	abuse	th	thin		circus
ou	out	hw	which	ər	butter

bal·ance |băl′əns| —*noun, plural* **balances** **1.** An instrument for weighing things. **2.** A condition in which things such as amount, weight, force, or power are equal: *There is a balance in the number of boys and girls in my class, twelve boys and twelve girls.* **3.** A steady or stable position: *I lost my balance and fell.* **4.** Something that is left over; remainder: *When we finished our work, we spent the balance of the afternoon swimming.* —*verb* **balanced, balancing** To put or hold in a steady or stable position: *I balanced the ball on my head.*

bal·co·ny |băl′kə nē| —*noun, plural* **balconies** **1.** A platform that juts out from the side of a building. Balconies have railings around them. **2.** An upper floor or section of seats that juts out over the main floor of a theater or auditorium.

bald |bôld| —*adjective* **balder, baldest** **1.** Without hair on the head. **2.** Without natural covering: *a bald spot in the lawn.*

bald ea·gle |ē′gəl| A North American eagle with a dark body and a white head and tail. It is often called the American eagle and is the national emblem of the United States.

bale |bāl| —*noun, plural* **bales** A large, tightly wrapped bundle of raw or finished material: *a bale of hay; a bale of silk cloth.*
♦ *These sound alike* **bale, bail.**

balk |bôk| —*verb* **balked, balking** **1.** To stop short and refuse to go on: *The mule balked when it saw the rattlesnake.* **2.** To keep from happening; check: *The police balked their escape plans.*

ball¹ |bôl| —*noun, plural* **balls** **1.** Something round or nearly round: *a ball of string; the ball of the foot.* **2.** A round or oval object used in sports and games: *a tennis ball.* **3.** A game, especially baseball, that is played with a ball. **4.** In baseball, a pitch that the batter does not swing at and is not thrown over home plate in the area between the batter's knees and shoulders.
♦ *These sound alike* **ball, bawl.**

ball² |bôl| —*noun, plural* **balls** A large, formal party for social dancing.
♦ *These sound alike* **ball, bawl.**

bal·lad |băl′əd| —*noun, plural* **ballads** A poem that tells a story in a simple manner. Ballads are often sung.

bal·last |băl′əst| —*noun* Any heavy material carried in a vehicle to give it weight. Ballast helps to control balance.

ball bear·ing |bâr′ĭng| A bearing in which the moving part turns or slides upon freely turning steel balls. Ball bearings lessen friction between the parts.

bal·le·ri·na |băl′ə rē′nə| —*noun, plural* **ballerinas** A woman or girl who dances ballet, especially the leading part.

bal·let |bă lā′| or |băl′ā′| —*noun, plural* **ballets** A kind of dancing with formal jumps, turns, and poses. It requires great accuracy and grace. A ballet usually tells a story through the dancing and music.

bal·loon |bə lōōn′| —*noun, plural* **balloons** **1.** A large bag filled with hot air or another gas that is lighter than regular air. It often has a basket to lift passengers and loads into the air. **2.** A small, brightly colored rubber bag that floats when it is filled with air or another gas. Balloons are used as children's toys. —*verb* **ballooned, ballooning** To swell or puff out like a balloon: *The clown's baggy jacket ballooned in the wind.*

bal·lot |băl′ət| —*noun, plural* **ballots** A piece of paper or another object used in an election. Voters mark their choices on them, usually in secret in the privacy of a booth.

ball-point pen |bôl′point′| A pen with a small metal ball for its writing point. The ball turns in its socket and inks itself by touching an ink container inside the pen.

ball·room |bôl′rōōm′| or |bôl′rŏŏm′| —*noun, plural* **ballrooms** A large room for dancing.

bal·sa |bôl′sə| —*noun* **1.** A tropical American tree with very light, strong wood. **2.** The wood of this tree. It is used to make rafts and model airplanes.

bal·sam |bôl′səm| —*noun, plural* **balsams** A fir tree of North America. Balsams are often used for Christmas trees.

bam·boo |băm bōō′| —*noun, plural* **bamboos** A tall grass that looks like a tree. It has hollow, woody stems that are used to make window blinds and many other things.

ban |băn| —*verb* **banned, banning** To forbid by law or decree; prohibit: *The governor banned the parking of cars in the city.*
—*noun, plural* **bans** An official order or decree that does not allow something to be done: *a ban on smoking in public places.*

ba·na·na |bə năn′ə| —*noun, plural* **bananas** A curved fruit with sweet, soft flesh. It has yellow or red skin that peels off easily. Bananas grow in the tropics on plants that look like trees.

band¹ |bănd| —*noun, plural* **bands** **1.** A strip of cloth, rubber, metal, or other material that binds or ties together: *a trunk fastened with leather bands.* **2.** A stripe of color or material: *the band of colors forming the rainbow.*
—*verb* **banded, banding** To put a band on: *Betty banded the duck's leg so it could be counted with others of the same kind.*

band² |bănd| —*noun, plural* **bands** **1.** A group of people or animals acting together: *a band of explorers.* **2.** A group of musicians who play together: *a marching band.*
—*verb* To form or gather in a group: *The Indians banded together for protection.*

band·age |băn′dĭj| —*noun, plural* **bandages** A strip of cloth or other material used to bind, or cover a wound or injury.
—*verb* **bandaged, bandaging** To cover or bind with a bandage.

ban·dan·na or **ban·dan·a** |băn dăn′ə| —*noun, plural* **bandannas** or **bandanas** A large, brightly colored handkerchief, often worn around the neck.

ban·dit |băn′dĭt| —*noun, plural* **bandits** A robber, often one who is a member of a gang of outlaws.

bang |băng| —*noun, plural* **bangs** A loud, sharp, sudden noise: *the bang of the guns; The door shut with a bang.*
—*verb* **banged, banging** **1.** To make a loud, sharp, sudden noise: *The guns banged in the distance.* **2.** To strike, hit, or move suddenly or with great force: *I banged my knee against the table.*

bangs |băngz| —*plural noun* Hair that is cut straight across the forehead.

ban·ish |băn′ish| —*verb* **banished, banishing** **1.** To force someone officially to leave a country or place; exile: *The king banished the outlaws.* **2.** To drive away; force away; expel: *We banished her from the game because she cheated.*

ban·is·ter |băn′ĭ stər| —*noun, plural* **banisters** The railing supported by posts along a staircase.

ban·jo |băn′jō| —*noun, plural* **banjos** or **banjoes** A musical instrument somewhat like a guitar. A banjo has four or five strings that are played by plucking.

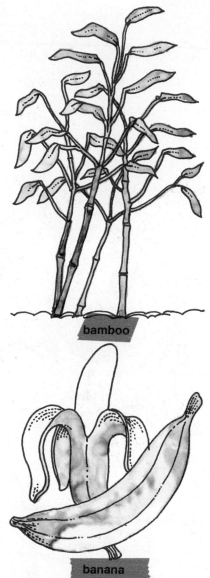

bamboo

banana

band¹, band²
Band¹ comes from a word used by prehistoric peoples who spoke Germanic; the word meant "a bond, tie, or link." **Band²** comes from a Germanic word that meant "a sign, a banner" or "a troop of men under one banner."

banjo

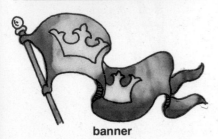

banner

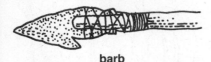

barb

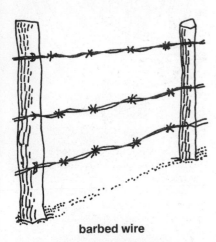

barbed wire

ă	pat	ĕ	pet	î	fierce
ā	pay	ē	be	ŏ	pot
â	care	ĭ	pit	ō	go
ä	father	ī	pie	ô	paw, for

oi	oil	ŭ	cut	zh	vision
ŏŏ	book	û	fur	ə	ago, item,
ōō	boot	th	the		pencil, atom,
yōō	abuse	th	thin		circus
ou	out	hw	which	ər	butter

bank¹ | băngk | —*noun, plural* **banks 1.** The sloping ground at the edge of a river or lake. **2.** A sloping pile or heap: *a snow bank.*
—*verb* **banked, banking** To form into a bank; pile; heap.

bank² | băngk | —*noun, plural* **banks 1.** A place of business where people's money is kept for them and money is lent for a charge. Banks also help in the transfer and exchange of money between persons and other banks. **2.** A small container used for saving money, especially coins.
—*verb* **banked, banking 1.** To put in a bank: *She banked her full rent check today.* **2.** To have an account or savings at a particular bank: *His father banks at the Provident.*

bank·er | băng′kər | —*noun, plural* **bankers 1.** An owner or manager of a bank. **2.** Someone who works in a bank.

bank·rupt | băngk′rŭpt′ | —*adjective* **1.** Legally declared unable to pay one's debts. **2.** Without money; financially ruined.
—*verb* **bankrupted, bankrupting** To make bankrupt.

ban·ner | băn′ər | —*noun, plural* **banners** A flag or other piece of cloth that has words or a special design on it.
—*adjective* Extremely good: *a banner year for our team.*

ban·quet | băng′kwĭt | —*noun, plural* **banquets** A large, formal meal, usually given to mark some special occasion; a feast.

bap·tism | băp′tĭz′əm | —*noun, plural* **baptisms** The religious ceremony in which a person is sprinkled with water or dipped in water as a sign of having sins washed away. Through baptism a person is admitted to a Christian church.

bap·tize | băp tīz′ | or | băp′tīz′ | —*verb* **baptized, baptizing** To sprinkle with water or dip in water in baptism.

bar | bär | —*noun, plural* **bars 1.** A straight piece of wood or metal that is longer than it is wide. Bars may be used to fasten doors, windows, or other openings. Some bars can be removed and some cannot. **2.** A solid, rectangular block of a substance: *a chocolate bar; a bar of soap.* **3.** Something that blocks the way or makes progress difficult; an obstacle: *Long sentences are a bar to easy reading.* **4.** A stripe, band, or other narrow marking: *The bars of the major's uniform show that he has served overseas.* **5. a.** One of the upright lines drawn across a musical staff to divide it into equal measures of time. Double bars at the end of the music show that the music has ended. **b.** A unit of music between two such lines; a measure. **6.** The occupation of a lawyer: *Doris passed her law examinations and was admitted to the bar.* **7. a.** A counter where alcoholic drinks, and sometimes food, are served or sold: *leaning on the bar ordering a drink; a salad bar.* **b.** The place that has such a counter.
—*verb* **barred, barring 1.** To close and fasten with a bar: *The watchman barred the warehouse gate.* **2.** To keep out; exclude: *New regulations barred hunters from national parks.*

barb | bärb | —*noun, plural* **barbs** A sharp point that sticks out backward. Fishhooks and porcupine quills have barbs.

bar·bar·i·an | bär bâr′ē ən | —*noun, plural* **barbarians** A person from a group or tribe that is primitive and not civilized.

bar·be·cue | bär′bĭ kyōō′ | —*noun, plural* **barbecues 1.** An open pit or fireplace used for cooking meat, usually outdoors. **2.** A social gathering at which food is prepared on a barbecue.
—*verb* **barbecued, barbecuing** To cook on a barbecue.

barbed wire Twisted strands of wire having sharp hooks or barbs at regular intervals. Barbed wire is used in fences.

bar·ber |bär′bər| —*noun, plural* **barbers** A person whose work is cutting hair and shaving or trimming beards.

bare |bâr| —*adjective* **barer, barest** **1.** Without covering or clothing; naked: *a bare hillside; bare feet.* **2.** Without the usual supplies or furnishings; empty: *a store with bare shelves.* **3.** Just enough and no more: *He earns a bare living by his work.*
—*verb* **bared, baring** To open up to view; uncover: *The dog bared its teeth and growled. He bared his head to the sun.*
♦ *These sound alike* **bare, bear.**

bare·back |bâr′băk′| —*adjective* On the back of a horse without a saddle: *a bareback rider.*
—*adverb* Without a saddle: *riding a horse bareback.*

bare·foot |bâr′fŏot′| —*adjective* Without shoes or other covering on the feet: *A barefoot boy is playing on the beach.*
—*adverb* Without shoes on: *The boy played barefoot on the beach.*

bare·ly |bâr′lē| —*adverb* Almost not; hardly; only just: *We could barely see the shore in the fog.*

bar·gain |bär′gĭn| —*noun, plural* **bargains** **1.** An agreement between two sides; a deal: *We made a bargain that he would cut the grass for two dollars.* **2.** Something offered or bought at a low price: *At one dollar this book is a bargain.*
—*verb* **bargained, bargaining** To discuss a price to be paid: *She bargained with the carpenter to lower the price of the chairs.*

barge |bärj| —*noun, plural* **barges** A boat with a flat bottom used to carry freight on rivers and canals.

bar·i·tone |băr′ĭ tōn′| —*noun, plural* **baritones** **1.** A man's singing voice, higher than a bass and lower than a tenor. **2.** A singer who has such a voice.

bark¹ |bärk| —*noun, plural* **barks** The short, gruff sound made by a dog and certain other animals.
—*verb* **barked, barking** To make the sound of a bark: *The seal barked for his food.*

bark² |bärk| —*noun, plural* **barks** The outer covering of the trunks, branches, and roots of trees. Bark can be thick and rough or thin and smooth.
—*verb* **barked, barking** To scrape the skin from: *He tripped and barked his knee on a rock.*

bar·ley |bär′lē| —*noun* A plant that is like grass and bears seeds. Barley is used as food and in making beer and whiskey.

barn |bärn| —*noun, plural* **barns** A large farm building used for storing grain, hay, and other farm products. A barn is also used for sheltering cattle and other livestock.

barn·yard |bärn′yärd′| —*noun, plural* **barnyards** The yard around a barn.

ba·rom·e·ter |bə rŏm′ĭ tər| —*noun, plural* **barometers** An instrument that measures the pressure of the atmosphere. A barometer shows changes in the weather.

bar·on |băr′ən| —*noun, plural* **barons** **1.** A nobleman of the lowest rank. **2.** In the Middle Ages, a man with lands and a title received directly from a king.
♦ *These sound alike* **baron, barren.**

bar·on·ess |băr′ə nĭs| —*noun, plural* **baronesses** **1.** The wife of a baron. **2.** A woman with a rank equal to that of a baron in her own right.

bar·racks |băr′əks| —*plural noun* A building or group of buildings where soldiers live.

barge

barley

barn

barracuda

bar·ra·cu·da |băr′ə kōō′də| —*noun, plural* **barracudas** or **barracuda** A sea fish with a long, narrow body and very sharp teeth. Barracudas are found mostly in tropical waters.

bar·rel |băr′əl| —*noun, plural* **barrels** **1.** A large wooden container with a flat, round top and bottom and curved sides. **2. a.** A barrel with something in it: *a barrel of apples.* **b.** The amount held by a barrel: *The cook peeled a barrel of potatoes.* **3.** A unit of measure, especially 31.5 gallons of oil. **4.** The metal tube of a gun. Bullets are fired through the barrel.

bar·ren |băr′ən| —*adjective* **1.** Not producing anything: *a barren field.* **2.** Not able to bear offspring: *a barren animal.*
♦ *These sound alike* **barren, baron.**

bar·rette |bə rět′| or |bä rět′| —*noun, plural* **barrettes** A clip used to hold hair in place.

bar·ri·cade |băr′ĭ kād′| or |băr′ĭ kād′| —*noun, plural* **barricades** A quickly built fence set up for defense.
—*verb* **barricaded, barricading** To close off, block, or protect with a barricade.

bar·ri·er |băr′ē ər| —*noun, plural* **barriers** Something that holds back or stops movement or passage: *The ditch in the road was a barrier to traffic.*

bar·ter |bär′tər| —*verb* **bartered, bartering** To trade one thing for another without using money: *We bartered our fresh corn for the neighbor's apples.*
—*noun* The act of bartering: *trade carried on by barter.*

base¹ |bās| —*noun, plural* **bases** **1.** The lowest part; the bottom: *the base of the stairs.* **2.** A part on which something rests: *the base of the lamp.* **3.** The main part of something: *This soup has a chicken base.* **4.** A starting point or main place; headquarters: *The explorers set up a base at the foot of the mountain.* **5.** In baseball, one of the four corners of the infield. A runner must touch four bases to score. **6.** A place to which ships, aircraft, or other military or naval forces return for supplies, repairs, orders, or shelter: *The plane returned to its base safely.* **7.** A chemical substance that joins with an acid to make a salt. A base will turn red litmus paper blue.
—*verb* **based, basing** To use as a base or foundation for; support: *I will base my opinion on the facts.*
♦ *These sound alike* **base, bass².**

base² |bās| —*adjective* **baser, basest** **1.** Not honorable; shameful, mean, or low: *Taking someone's money is a base thing to do.* **2.** Not of great value: *Iron is a base metal.*
♦ *These sound alike* **base, bass².**

base·ball |bās′bôl′| —*noun, plural* **baseballs** **1.** A game played with a bat and ball by two teams of nine players each. Baseball is played on a field with four bases. Runs are scored when a player is able to go around and touch all the bases. **2.** The ball used in this game.

base·ment |bās′mənt| —*noun, plural* **basements** The lowest floor of a building, often below ground.

ba·ses¹ |bā′sēz′| The plural of the noun **basis.**

bas·es² |bā′sĭz| The plural of the noun **base.**

bash·ful |băsh′fəl| —*adjective* Timid and embarrassed with other people; shy: *The child is bashful when we have company.*

ba·sic |bā′sĭk| —*adjective* **1.** Forming the main part of something; essential: *Flour and eggs are the basic ingredients of a*

---

base¹, base²

Base¹ comes from an old Greek word meaning "a platform" or "a pedestal." **Base²** comes from a word used long ago by English-speaking people to mean "low." Those people got the word from an old Latin word that also meant "low."

baseball

ă	pat	ĕ	pet	î	fierce
ā	pay	ē	be	ŏ	pot
â	care	ĭ	pit	ō	go
ä	father	ī	pie	ô	paw, for

oi	oil	ŭ	cut	zh	vision
ŏŏ	book	û	fur	ə	ago, item,
ōō	boot	*th*	the		pencil, atom,
yōō	abuse	th	thin		circus
ou	out	hw	which	ər	butter

cake mixture. **2.** Necessary before something else: *basic training.*
—*noun, plural* **basics** Basic knowledge or skills: *learning the basics of drawing.*

ba·sin | bā′sən | —*noun, plural* **basins** **1.** A round, shallow bowl often used for holding water to wash in. **2. a.** A basin with something in it: *a basin of water.* **b.** The amount that a basin holds: *Bill used up a basin of water to wash his face.* **3.** A natural or man-made hollow filled with water: *We sailed into the boat basin.* **4.** The land drained by a river and all the streams that flow into it: *the basin of the Mississippi River.*

ba·sis | bā′sĭs | —*noun, plural* **bases** The part on which other parts rest or depend; foundation: *The prisoner claimed that the charges against him had no basis in fact.*

bask | băsk | *or* | bäsk | —*verb* **basked, basking** **1.** To rest and enjoy a pleasant warmth: *The dog basked by the fire.* **2.** To feel pleasure: *He basked in his children's love.*

bas·ket | băs′kĭt | *or* | bä′skĭt | —*noun, plural* **baskets** **1.** A container to hold things. Baskets are made of woven twigs, grasses, fibers, or strips of wood. **2. a.** A basket with something in it: *a basket of flowers.* **b.** The amount that a basket holds: *They ate a basket of strawberries.* **3.** In basketball: **a.** A metal hoop with a net that is open at the bottom. The ball is thrown through the basket to score a goal. **b.** A goal scored by such a throw.

bas·ket·ball | băs′kĭt bôl′ | *or* | bä′skĭt bôl′ | —*noun, plural* **basketballs** **1.** A game played with a large ball and two raised baskets. Two teams of five players each try to throw the ball through the basket on their opponent's side. **2.** The ball used in this game.

bass¹ | băs | —*noun, plural* **bass** *or* **basses** Any of several North American fishes caught for food or sport. Bass can be found in the sea or in streams and lakes.

bass² | bās | —*noun, plural* **basses** **1.** The lowest musical notes. **2.** The lowest man's singing voice. **3.** A singer who has such a voice.
♦ *These sound alike* **bass, base.**

bas·soon | bə sōōn′ | *or* | bă sōōn′ | —*noun, plural* **bassoons** A musical instrument of the woodwind family. A bassoon has a long wooden body that is connected to the mouthpiece by a curved metal tube. It makes a low, deep tone when played.

baste¹ | bāst | —*verb* **basted, basting** To sew with large, loose stitches that can easily be taken out when the final sewing is done: *The tailor basted the hem before sewing it on the machine.*

baste² | bāst | —*verb* **basted, basting** To pour melted fat or other liquid over food while roasting it: *basting the turkey.*

bat¹ | băt | —*noun, plural* **bats** A wooden stick or club used to hit the ball in games such as baseball.
—*verb* **batted, batting** To hit with or as if with a bat; hit: *He batted the ball out of the park. The cat batted at the ball with his paw.*
Idiom **at bat.** Having a turn as a hitter in baseball: *Mark was at bat in the ninth inning.*

bat² | băt | —*noun, plural* **bats** An animal with a furry body and thin, leathery wings. Bats sleep during the day and fly at night. They are the only mammals that can fly.

batch | băch | —*noun, plural* **batches** **1.** An amount prepared at one time: *a batch of cookies; a batch of cement.* **2.** A group of things: *We burned a batch of old papers.*

---

bass¹, bass²
Bass¹ comes from a word used long ago by English-speaking people to mean "a fish with a spiny back" or "a prickly fish." **Bass²** comes from a word used long ago by English-speaking people to mean "low." Those people got the word from an old Latin word that also meant "low." Even though **bass¹** and **bass²** are spelled the same way, they are pronounced differently.

bassoon

baste¹, baste²
Baste¹ comes from a word used long ago by English-speaking people to mean "to sew with fiber." Those people got the word from the French, who also used it in the meaning "to sew with fiber." **Baste²** is a word whose original source is not known. There are still several thousand words in English whose roots are unknown. Many more can only be traced back a short way.

bat¹, bat²
Bat¹ comes from a word used long ago by English-speaking people to mean "a club." This word came from a still older English word that in turn came from an old Latin word meaning "to beat." **Bat²** comes from a word that was also used long ago by English-speaking people. But this word came from Scandinavia, where it meant "the bat, the leather-flapper."

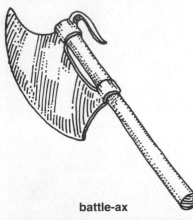

battle-ax

battlement

ă	pat	ĕ	pet	î	fierce
ā	pay	ē	be	ŏ	pot
â	care	ĭ	pit	ō	go
ä	father	ī	pie	ô	paw, for
oi	oil	ŭ	cut	zh	vision
ŏŏ	book	û	fur	ə	ago, item,
ōō	boot	*th*	the		pencil, atom,
yōō	abuse	th	thin		circus
ou	out	hw	which	ər	butter

bath | băth | or | bäth | —*noun, plural* **baths** | băthz | or | bäthz | or | băths | or | bäths | **1.** The act of washing the body in water. **2.** The water used for a bath: *Mary got the bath ready for the baby.* **3.** A bathroom: *Louise's parents rented an apartment with three rooms and a bath.*

bathe | bāth | —*verb* **bathed, bathing 1.** To give a bath to or take a bath: *Mary is going to bathe the baby. Do you bathe every day?* **2.** To soak in a liquid: *Florence bathed her swollen leg.* **3.** To seem to wash or pour over; flood: *Sunlight bathed the living room when the window shades were lifted.* **4.** To go swimming.

bath·ing suit | bā′ thĭng | A piece of clothing worn for swimming.

bath·room | băth′ rŏŏm′ | or | băth′ rŏŏm′ | or | bäth′ rŏŏm′ | or | bäth′ rŏŏm′ | —*noun, plural* **bathrooms 1.** A room for taking a bath or shower, usually also containing a sink and toilet. **2.** A room with a toilet in it.

bath·tub | băth′ tŭb′ | or | bäth′ tŭb′ | —*noun, plural* **bathtubs** A tub to bathe in.

ba·ton | bə tŏn′ | or | băt′n | —*noun, plural* **batons 1.** A thin stick used by the leader of a band, chorus, or orchestra. **2.** A stick or staff twirled by a drum major or majorette.

Bat·on Rouge | băt′n rōōzh′ | The capital of Louisiana.

bat·tal·ion | bə tăl′ yən | —*noun, plural* **battalions 1.** A large group of soldiers organized as a unit. Two or more companies make a battalion. **2.** A large group of people.

bat·ter¹ | băt′ ər | —*verb* **battered, battering 1.** To strike or pound again and again with heavy blows: *The boxer battered the punching bag. Waves battered against the pier.* **2.** To hurt or damage by rough treatment or hard wear: *The weather had battered the paint on his car so that it had lost its finish.*

bat·ter² | băt′ ər | —*noun, plural* **batters** In baseball, a player who is or will be batting.

bat·ter³ | băt′ ər | —*noun, plural* **batters** A beaten, liquid mixture of flour, eggs, and milk or water. Batter becomes solid when fried or baked. Pancakes, biscuits, and cakes are made of batter.

bat·ter·ing-ram or **bat·ter·ing ram** | băt′ ər ĭng răm′ | —*noun, plural* **battering-rams** or **battering rams** A heavy wooden pole with an iron head. It was used in ancient times to batter down walls and gates.

bat·ter·y | băt′ ər ē | —*noun, plural* **batteries 1.** A small, sealed can with a chemical paste inside that makes or stores electricity; a dry cell: *Please put fresh batteries in the flashlight.* **2.** A group of things or people that do something together: *a battery of photographers.* **3.** A set of large artillery guns.

bat·tle | băt′l | —*noun, plural* **battles 1.** A fight between two armed groups, usually in war. **2.** Any hard struggle or contest: *The spelling bee between the schools was quite a battle.*
—*verb* **battled, battling 1.** To fight; to struggle: *The troops battled bravely.* **2.** To fight against: *We battled the storm for hours.*

bat·tle-ax or **bat·tle-axe** | băt′l ăks′ | —*noun, plural* **battle-axes** A heavy ax with a broad head. It was used as a weapon long ago.

bat·tle·field | băt′l fēld′ | —*noun, plural* **battlefields** A field or area where a battle is fought.

bat·tle·ment | băt′l mənt | —*noun, plural* **battlements** A wall along the top edge of a tower, castle, or fort. Battlements had openings for soldiers to shoot through.

bat·tle·ship | băt′l shĭp′ | —*noun, plural* **battleships** A large warship having very heavy guns and armor.

bawl | bôl | —*verb* **bawled, bawling** **1.** To cry or sob loudly; howl: *The unhappy baby kicked and bawled.* **2.** To cry out or call in a loud, strong voice; bellow: *"Who goes there?" bawled the soldier.*
   Phrasal verb **bawl out** To scold loudly or harshly: *Mom bawled Jane out for losing her allowance.*
   —*noun, plural* **bawls** A loud cry or shout: *the bawl of a stray calf.*
♦ *These sound alike* **bawl, ball.**

bay¹ | bā | —*noun, plural* **bays** A broad part of a sea or lake partly surrounded by land.

bay² | bā | —*noun, plural* **bays** A part of a room or building that juts out beyond the main outside wall. It often has windows on three sides.

bay³ | bā | —*adjective* Reddish-brown: *a bay horse.*

bay⁴ | bā | —*noun, plural* **bays** The long, deep barking of a dog.
   —*verb* **bayed, baying** To bark with long, deep cries.

bay⁵ | bā | —*noun, plural* **bays** A tree or shrub with shiny evergreen leaves that are often used as spice; a laurel.

bay·o·net | bā′ə nĭt | or | bā′ə nĕt′ | or | bā′ə **nĕt′** | —*noun, plural* **bayonets** A knife attached to the front end of a rifle. A bayonet is used in close combat.

bay·ou | bī′ōō | or | bī′ō | —*noun, plural* **bayous** A stream that moves slowly through a marsh and into or out of a lake or river. Bayous are common in the southern United States.

ba·zaar | bə zär′ | —*noun, plural* **bazaars** **1.** A market found in Oriental countries and made up of a street lined with shops and stalls. **2.** A fair or sale, usually to raise money for a charity.

BB | bē′bē′ | —*noun, plural* **BB's** A small round ball of steel or lead that can be shot from a rifle or pistol.

B.C. The abbreviation for "Before Christ." This abbreviation is used after a number to name any particular year before the birth of Christ: *We learned that 400 B.C. is 250 years earlier than 150 B.C.*

be | bē |

battleship

bay¹, bay², bay³,
bay⁴, bay⁵

All five words spelled **bay** come from words used very long ago in French. Earlier than that all five had different sources. **Bay¹** comes from the Spanish word meaning "a gulf." **Bay²**, **bay³**, **bay⁴**, and **bay⁵** all come from different Latin words: **bay²** from the word meaning "to yawn or gape"; **bay³** from the word meaning "chestnut brown"; **bay⁴** from the word meaning "to howl"; and **bay⁵** from the word meaning "berry." It is interesting that these five words are spelled and pronounced alike, although they have different histories. They make up the largest such group in English.

Inflected Forms of the Verb *Be*

	1st person	2nd person	3rd person
Present Tense singular	am	are	is
plural	are	are	are
Present Participle	being	being	being
Past Participle	been	been	been
Past Tense singular	was	were	was
plural	were	were	were

bayonet

The verb **be** does not show action. It shows that something exists, it describes relationships in place, space, or time, and it functions as a linking verb and as a helping, or auxiliary, verb.

1. To be real; exist: *How can such things be?* In this sense the verb **be** is often used with the pronoun *there: There is a lot of excitement in our class.* **2.** To occupy a certain position in place, space, or time: *The groceries are on the table. The plane is in the air. Her birthday is on Tuesday.* In this sense the prepositional phrase (for example, *on the table, in the air, on Tuesday*) describes the place, space, or time. **3.** To take place; occur: *When is the show?*
—*linking verb* As a linking verb **be** is used to connect, or link, a noun or pronoun with a word that describes it, or with another noun that names the same thing: *Mr. Walker is tall. Mr. Walker is the librarian. That book is mine.*
—*helping,* or *auxiliary, verb* As a helping verb **be** is used:
1. With the present participle of a verb to show continuing action: *I am drawing the plans for a kite. You are drinking coffee. Ms. Bennett is building a house. We are waiting patiently. Miguel was painting his bicycle. Sally and Lois were playing tennis.* **2.** With the past participle of a verb to show the passive voice: *I am held responsible for my actions by my superiors. You are blamed unfairly by your friends. He is surprised by her arrival. We are amazed at the beauty of the landscape. I was struck by the ball. You were blinded by the sun. She was pleased by the results of the test. They were wounded by the explosion.* **3.** With the preposition **to** and the infinitive of another verb to indicate: **a.** duty or necessity: *She is to tell you when the package arrives.* **b.** supposition: *How am I to know the answer?* **c.** the fact that something has not yet happened: *She was to become the first woman doctor.*
♦ *These sound alike* **be, bee.**

beach |bēch| —*noun, plural* **beaches** The shore of a body of water. Beaches are full of sand or of pebbles.
—*verb* **beached, beaching** To haul or drive a boat onto a shore.
♦ *These sound alike* **beach, beech.**

bea·con |bē′kən| —*noun, plural* **beacons** A fire, light, radio signal, or anything used to guide or warn.

bead |bēd| —*noun, plural* **beads** **1.** A small, round piece of glass, metal, wood, or other material. A bead has a hole in it through which a string can be pulled: *a necklace of glass beads.* **2.** Any small, round object: *a bead of sweat.*

bea·gle |bē′gəl| —*noun, plural* **beagles** A small dog with a smooth coat and drooping ears. It is often used as a hunting dog.

beak |bēk| —*noun, plural* **beaks** **1.** The hard, projecting mouth parts of a bird; a bill. **2.** A part that looks like a bird's beak.

beak·er |bē′kər| —*noun, plural* **beakers** A container used in a laboratory. It has straight sides, and a lip for pouring.

beam |bēm| —*noun, plural* **beams** **1.** A long, sturdy piece of wood or metal. Beams are used in building as horizontal supports for floors or ceilings. **2.** Light sent out into space: *The plane was guided by the beams of the searchlights.*
—*verb* **beamed, beaming** **1.** To send off light; shine: *the sun beaming in the sky.* **2.** To smile widely: *His face beamed with delight.*

bean |bēn| —*noun, plural* **beans** **1.** An oval, often flat seed, used as food. There are several kinds of beans, and some, such as lima beans or kidney beans, are eaten as vegetables. **2.** A pod in which beans grow. Bean pods are usually long and narrow. Some kinds of bean pods are eaten as vegetables. **3.** A plant on which

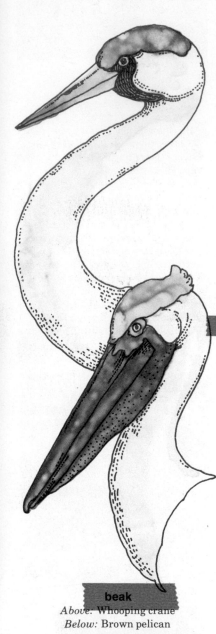

beak
Above: Whooping crane
Below: Brown pelican

ă	pat	ĕ	pet	î	fierce
ā	pay	ē	be	ŏ	pot
â	care	ĭ	pit	ō	go
ä	father	ī	pie	ô	paw, for
oi	oil	ŭ	cut	zh	vision
ōō	book	û	fur	ə	ago, item,
ōō	boot	*th*	the		pencil, atom,
yōō	abuse	th	thin		circus
ou	out	hw	which	ər	butter

beans grow. **4.** A seed or pod that is like a bean, such as coffee beans.

bear¹ |bâr| —*verb* **bore, borne, bearing** **1.** To hold up; support: *That broken chair won't bear your weight.* **2.** To carry: *That train bears people from far away. This letter bears good news.* **3.** To show: *The stamp bears a picture of a famous writer. The girls bear a resemblance to their mother.* **4.** To put up with; endure: *He couldn't bear the pain any longer.* **5.** To produce; yield: *trees that bear fruit.* **6.** To give birth to: *She has borne six children. Six children were borne by her.* In this sense the verb **bear** has another form for the past participle. This other form is **born.** It is mainly used when the verb **bear** indicates the fact of birth: *a daughter born to her. The twins were born in Boston.*
♦ *These sound alike* **bear, bare.**

bear² |bâr| —*noun, plural* **bears** A large animal with a shaggy coat and a very short tail. There are several kinds of bears, such as the polar bear and the grizzly bear.
♦ *These sound alike* **bear, bare.**

beard |bîrd| —*noun, plural* **beards** **1.** The hair on a man's face. **2.** Something that looks like a beard: *a goat's beard.*

bear·ing |bâr′ĭng| —*noun, plural* **bearings** **1.** The way a person looks, acts, and moves: *a tall, handsome man with the bearing of an actor.* **2.** A part on a machine that holds a moving part and allows it to move or turn with little resistance. **3.** Relationship in thought or meaning; connection: *His remarks had no bearing on the subject of the discussion.* **4. bearings** Sense or knowledge of direction: *We lost our bearings and didn't get back to camp until after dinner.*

beast |bēst| —*noun, plural* **beasts** **1.** Any animal that is not a human being, especially a large animal with four feet. **2.** A cruel or savage person.

beat |bēt| —*verb* **beat, beaten** or **beat, beating** **1.** To hit or strike again and again: *The gang beat him with fists and clubs.* **2.** To pound again and again; dash: *The angry waves beat against the coast.* **3.** To make a sound by striking again and again: *The clown was beating a giant drum in the circus parade.* **4.** To shape or flatten by pounding: *The Eskimos beat copper into arrowheads.* **5.** To move up and down; flap: *Hummingbirds beat their wings very quickly.* **6.** To pound heavily and fast; throb: *After the race his heart was beating very fast.* **7.** To mix or whip rapidly: *Beat the eggs as you add the sugar.* **8.** To win against: *Our team always beats every other team in town.*
—*noun, plural* **beats** **1.** A sound, stroke, or blow made again and again: *We heard the beat of distant drums.* **2. a.** The regular action of the heart pumping blood; a throb: *Can you feel the beat of your heart?* **b.** The sound made by this: *He was so frightened that he could hear the beat of his heart.* **3.** In music, the basic unit of time: *There are four beats in this measure.* **4.** A route or round that is followed regularly by someone: *The officer knows everyone on his beat.*
♦ *These sound alike* **beat, beet.**

beat·en |bēt′n| A past participle of the verb **beat:** *Our football team had beaten all the other teams in town.*
—*adjective* **1.** Thinned or formed by hammering: *beaten tin.* **2.** Much traveled: *beaten paths.*

beau·ti·ful |byōō′tə fəl| —*adjective* Delightful to look at, listen

bear¹, bear²
Bear¹ comes from a word used long ago in English to mean "to carry" or "to have a child." Earlier still it came from a word used by a prehistoric people whose language was the source of many languages spoken today. **Bear²** comes from a different old English word. The word's earlier source was the word for "brown" used by the same prehistoric people.

bear²

beard

to, or think about; pleasing: *a beautiful baby; beautiful music.*

beau·ty |byōō′tē| —*noun, plural* **beauties 1.** A quality that is delightful or pleasing to look at, listen to, or think about: *glaciers adding beauty to the scenery; the beauty of the singer's voice; the beauty in a poem.* **2.** A person or thing that is beautiful: *That car was a beauty in its day.*

bea·ver |bē′vər| —*noun, plural* **beavers 1.** An animal with thick fur, a broad, flat tail, and large, strong front teeth. Beavers live in and near lakes and streams. They gnaw down trees to build dams and homes in the water. **2.** The fur of a beaver.

beaver

be·came |bǐ kām′| The past tense of the verb **become:** *The sky became red as the sun went down.*

be·cause |bǐ kôz′| or |bǐ kŭz′| —*conjunction* For the reason that: *He left because he was sick.*

because of On account of: *He stayed home because of illness.*

beck·on |běk′ən| —*verb* **beckoned, beckoning** To signal to someone with the head or hand: *The captain beckoned us over to watch him. The waiter beckoned to us when he found an empty table.*

be·come |bǐ kŭm′| —*verb* **became, become, becoming 1.** To grow or come to be: *The town became a city. She became angry.* **2.** To look good on: *The new suit becomes you.* **3. become of** To happen to: *What has become of our old car?*

be·com·ing |bǐ kŭm′ing| —*adjective* **1.** Appropriate; fitting; proper: *She fixed the alarm clock with the skill becoming to an expert.* **2.** Attractive; pleasing to look at: *a becoming hat.*

bed |běd| —*noun, plural* **beds 1.a.** A piece of furniture for resting and sleeping. **b.** Any place or surface upon which animals or people may sleep or rest: *The farmer made a bed of straw for his cows.* **2.** A small area of land for growing things: *a bed of roses.* **3.** Anything that forms a bottom or supporting part: *the bed of a river; lobster meat on a bed of rice; the bed of a pickup truck.* —*verb* **bedded, bedding** To provide with a place to sleep: *They were unable to bed all their guests.*

bee

bed·ding |běd′ing| —*noun* Things used on a bed, such as sheets, blankets, and pillows.

bed·room |běd′rōōm′| or |běd′rŏom′| —*noun, plural* **bedrooms** A room for sleeping.

bed·spread |běd′sprěd′| —*noun, plural* **bedspreads** A cover for a bed. It goes on over the sheets and blanket.

bed·time |běd′tīm′| —*noun, plural* **bedtimes** The time when a person usually goes to bed.

bee |bē| —*noun, plural* **bees** A winged insect that gathers pollen and nectar from flowers. There are several kinds of bees. Most of them can sting. Some bees live together in large groups.
♦ *These sound alike* **bee, be.**

beech |bēch| —*noun, plural* **beeches 1.** A tree with smooth, light-gray bark and strong wood. **2.** The wood of this tree.
♦ *These sound alike* **beech, beach.**

beef |bēf| —*noun* The meat from a full-grown steer, bull, ox, or cow.

beef·steak |bēf′stāk′| —*noun, plural* **beefsteaks** A slice of beef that can be broiled, fried, or grilled.

bee·hive |bē′hīv′| —*noun, plural* **beehives 1.** A place where a swarm of bees lives. A beehive may be made by bees or by humans. **2.** A very busy place: *The toy factory was a beehive of activity before Christmas.*

beech

ă	pat	ě	pet	î	fierce
ā	pay	ē	be	ŏ	pot
â	care	ĭ	pit	ō	go
ä	father	ī	pie	ô	paw, for

oi	oil	ŭ	cut	zh	vision
ōo	book	û	fur	ə	ago, item,
ōō	boot	*th*	the		pencil, atom,
yōō	abuse	th	thin		circus
ou	out	hw	which	ər	butter

been |bĭn| The past participle of the verb **be:** *Sally and Dick have been out of town since May.*
♦ *These sound alike* **been, bin.**

beer |bîr| —*noun, plural* **beers 1.** An alcoholic drink made from malt and hops. **2.** Any of several soft drinks: *root beer.*

bees·wax |bēz′wăks′| —*noun* The yellow or brown wax made by honeybees to build their honeycombs. Beeswax is used to make candles, furniture polish, and other things.

beet |bēt| —*noun, plural* **beets 1.** A plant with a rounded dark-red root that is eaten as a vegetable. **2.** A form of this plant with a large, white root used to make sugar. This kind of beet is also called **sugar beet. 3.** The root of either of these plants.
♦ *These sound alike* **beet, beat.**

bee·tle |bēt′l| —*noun, plural* **beetles** An insect that has hard, glossy front wings. When a beetle is not flying, the hind wings are hidden under the front wings. There are many kinds of beetles. Some are harmful to plants.

be·fall |bĭ fôl′| —*verb* **befell, befallen, befalling** To happen to: *Many adventures behall explorers.*

be·fall·en |bĭ fôl′ən| The past participle of the verb **befall:** *Many strange adventures had befallen the knights.*

be·fell |bĭ fĕl′| The past tense of the verb **befall:** *What befell the king on his journey?*

be·fore |bĭ fôr′| or |bĭ fōr′| —*adverb* **1.** Earlier: *Class will start at 3 o'clock, not before.* **2.** At any time in the past; until now: *Our teams have never played against each other before.*
—*preposition* **1.** Earlier than; ahead of: *He got there before me.* **2.** In front of: *Stand before the fire.* **3.** Preceding someone or something in time: *He now lives in Washington as his brother did before him. Gone were the good old days before the war.*
—*conjunction* In advance of the time when: *Eat your breakfast before you go to the beach.*

be·fore·hand |bĭ fôr′hănd′| or |bĭ fōr′hănd′| —*adverb* Ahead of time; at an earlier time: *School starts at 8:30, but the teacher is always there beforehand.*

beg |bĕg| —*verb* **begged, begging 1.** To ask for in a humble way: *She begged for mercy. He begged us to forgive his behavior.* **2.** To ask or ask for as charity: *They begged in the streets for food. They begged money to buy food.*

be·gan |bĭ găn′| The past tense of the verb **begin:** *She began to read for the class.*

beg·gar |bĕg′ər| —*noun, plural* **beggars 1.** A person who begs for a living. **2.** A very poor person.

be·gin |bĭ gĭn′| —*verb* **began, begun, beginning 1.** To have as a starting point; commence; start: *The book begins in the middle of the story. Does your name begin with a G or a J?* **2.** To do the first part of: *He begins many projects and never finishes them.*

be·gin·ner |bĭ gĭn′ər| —*noun, plural* **beginners** A person who is just starting to learn or to do something: *The easy ski trail is for beginners.*

be·gin·ning |bĭ gĭn′ĭng| —*noun, plural* **beginnings 1.** The first part: *They came late and missed the beginning of the movie.* **2.** The starting point; the time or place when something begins: *a book about the Wright brothers and the beginning of airplanes. The beginning of the story is on page 25.*

be·go·nia |bĭ gōn′yə| —*noun, plural* **begonias** A plant with

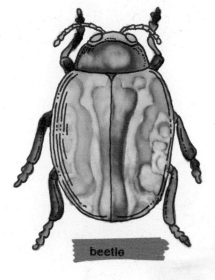

beetle

begonia

many brightly colored flowers or colorful leaves. There are several kinds of begonias. They are often grown as house plants.

be·gun | bǐ **gŭn′** | The past participle of the verb **begin:** *The leaves on the trees have begun to fall.*

be·half | bǐ **hăf′** | or | bǐ **häf′** | —*noun* Interest; benefit: *The lawyer will act in our behalf.*

    Idioms **in behalf of** In the interest of; for: *He bought the land in behalf of the bank.* **on behalf of** Acting for: *The captain accepted the trophy on behalf of her team.*

be·have | bǐ **hāv′** | —*verb* **behaved, behaving** **1.** To act or work in a certain way: *The car behaves smoothly on the highway.* **2.** To act properly; be good: *If you behave, you may stay up late to watch the football game.*

be·hav·ior | bǐ **hāv′** yər | —*noun* A way of acting; conduct: *His mother was pleased by his behavior at the concert.*

be·head | bǐ **hĕd′** | —*verb* **beheaded, beheading** To cut someone's head off: *The angry people beheaded their king.*

be·held | bǐ **hĕld′** | The past tense and past participle of the verb **behold:** *The explorers beheld the ruins of the ancient city. We have beheld a miracle.*

be·hind | bǐ **hīnd′** | —*preposition* **1.** At the back of or in the rear of: *the shed behind the barn. He glanced quickly behind him.* **2.** Later than: *The train is running behind schedule.* **3. a.** Following: *An ambulance drove close behind the fire engine.* **b.** In pursuit of; after: *His heart beat faster as he heard the sound of footsteps behind him.* **4.** In support of: *Most of the voters were behind the governor.*
  —*adverb* **1.** At the back: *He sneaked up on us from behind.* **2.** In the place or situation that is left: *With good-bys for the children who stayed behind, the parents left on vacation.* **3.** Falling back or backward; late: *He was behind in his homework.*

be·hold | bǐ **hōld′** | —*verb* **beheld, beholding** To look at; see: *The crew was happy to behold the last port of their voyage.*

beige | bāzh | —*noun* A very light shade of brown or tan.
  —*adjective* Of the color beige: *a beige skirt.*

be·ing | bē′ĭng | —*noun, plural* **beings** **1.** A living creature. **2.** Existence: *When did scissors come into being?*

be·lat·ed | bǐ **lā′** tǐd | —*adjective* Late or too late; tardy: *Our belated wedding gift arrived after the reception.*

bel·fry | bĕl′frē | —*noun, plural* **belfries** **1.** A tower or steeple where bells are hung. **2.** A place in a tower or steeple where bells are hung.

be·lief | bǐ **lēf′** | —*noun, plural* **beliefs** **1.** A thing or idea that is considered to be true or real: *his belief that solar power can heat the world.* **2.** The acceptance of something as true or real; strong conviction: *a belief in one's religion; a belief in one's form of government.* **3.** A strong opinion or expectation: *It is his belief that we will win the game.*

be·lieve | bǐ **lēv′** | —*verb* **believed, believing** **1.** To accept as true or real: *Everyone in the club believed that Binky had seen a monster.* **2.** To have faith or confidence in: *They don't believe her promises. We believe in your idea and we'll help you.* **3.** To expect; think or suppose: *I believe it will snow tomorrow.*

be·lit·tle | bǐ **lĭt′** l | —*verb* **belittled, belittling** To make someone or something seem small or unimportant: *The teen-agers belittled our clubhouse and called it kid stuff.*

belfry

ă	pat	ĕ	pet	î	fierce
ā	pay	ē	be	ŏ	pot
â	care	ĭ	pit	ō	go
ä	father	ī	pie	ô	paw, for
oi	oil	ŭ	cut	zh	vision
ōō	book	û	fur	ə	ago, item,
ōō	boot	*th*	the		pencil, atom,
yōō	abuse	th	thin		circus
ou	out	hw	which	ər	butter

bell |bĕl| —*noun, plural* **bells 1.** A hollow piece of metal that is usually shaped like a cup. It makes a ringing, musical sound when it is struck. **2.** An object that is shaped like a bell: *the bell of a tulip; the bell of a trumpet; a diving bell.*

bel·lig·er·ent |bə lĭj′ər ənt| —*adjective* **1.** Likely to start a fight or quarrel: *a belligerent bully.* **2.** Engaged in warfare; at war: *a belligerent nation.*

bel·low |bĕl′ō| —*verb* **bellowed, bellowing** To make a loud roaring noise like a bull: *A strange animal bellowed.*
—*noun, plural* **bellows** A loud roar: *a bellow of pain.*

bel·lows |bĕl′ōz| or |bĕl′əz| —*plural noun* A simple air pump, often made of leather and wood. Some bellows are used for making fires burn hotter. Others are used in musical instruments like organs and accordions.

bel·ly |bĕl′ē| —*noun, plural* **bellies 1.** The front part of the body below the chest of a human being or other mammal; abdomen. **2.** The stomach. **3.** The deep, hollow part inside of something: *They loaded cargo into the belly of the ship.* **4.** The bulging part underneath something.
—*verb* **bellied, bellying, bellies** To swell; bulge: *The sails bellied in the breeze. A puff of wind bellied the sails.*

be·long |bĭ lông′| or |bĭ lŏng′| —*verb* **belonged, belonging 1.** To have a proper place: *The suit belongs in the closet. The cap belongs on the bottle.* **2. belong to** To be the property of; be owned by: *This ranch belongs to my uncle.* **3. belong to** To be a member of: *She belongs to the music club and the soccer team.*

be·long·ings |bĭ lông′ĭngs| or |bĭ lŏng′ĭngs| —*plural noun* The things a person owns; possessions.

be·lov·ed |bĭ lŭv′ĭd| or |bĭ lŭvd′| —*adjective* Dearly loved: *a beloved old teddy bear.*
—*noun* A person who is dearly loved.

be·low |bĭ lō′| —*adverb* **1.** In or to a lower place or level: *The girls stopped at the bridge to look at the river below.* **2.** Lower on a scale than zero: *temperatures of 20° below.*
—*preposition* **1.** Underneath; under; beneath: *We stood at the window and watched the people in the street below us.* **2.** Lower than: *We use negative numbers to show temperatures below zero.*

belt |bĕlt| —*noun, plural* **belts 1.** A band or strap of leather, cloth, plastic, or any other material. It is worn around the waist to hold up clothing or for decoration. **2.** A region or area that has some common feature: *There was a belt of farms near the city.* **3.** A band that goes around wheels or pulleys. A belt helps transfer motion from one wheel or pulley to another.

bench |bĕnch| —*noun, plural* **benches 1.** A long seat for two or more people. A bench may or may not have a back. **2.** A sturdy table on which a person may work at a craft; workbench: *a carpenter's bench; a cobbler's bench.* **3.** A judge or the position of judge: *The lawyers argued before the bench. He was elected to the bench.* **4.** The place where members of a sports team sit when they are not playing.
—*verb* **benched, benching** To keep a team's player from playing: *His sprained ankle benched him for the week.*

bend |bĕnd| —*verb* **bent, bending 1.** To make or become curved, crooked, or angled: *He bent his elbows. The branches bend when the wind blows.* **2.** To move part of the body lower; bow: *He bent his head. Can you bend to pick up the ball?* **3.** To take or cause to take

bell

bellows
Air is pumped through the nozzle by pressing the handles.

bench

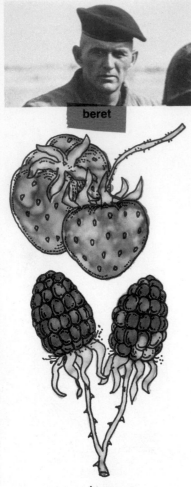

beret

berry
Above: Strawberry
Below: Raspberry

berth
Aboard a Boeing 747 jet

ă	pat	ĕ	pet	î	fierce
ā	pay	ē	be	ŏ	pot
â	care	ĭ	pit	ō	go
ä	father	ī	pie	ô	paw, for
oi	oil	ŭ	cut	zh	vision
ŏŏ	book	û	fur	ə	ago, item,
ōō	boot	*th*	the		pencil, atom,
yōō	abuse	th	thin		circus
ou	out	hw	which	ər	butter

a new direction: *The road bends to the left here. Water bends light rays that pass through it.*
—*noun, plural* **bends** A turn, curve, angle, or bent part: *The car came around the bend in the road.*

be·neath | bĭ nēth′ | —*preposition* **1.** Underneath; below; under: *The cat is sleeping beneath the stove.* **2.** At a lower level than or farther down from: *We found a spring just beneath the top of the mountain.*
—*adverb* Below; under: *The picture is explained in the caption printed beneath.*

ben·e·fit | bĕn′ə fĭt | —*noun, plural* **benefits** Something that is good or helpful; an advantage: *The new pitcher is a great benefit to the team.*
—*verb* **benefited, benefiting** **1.** To be helpful or useful to: *A vacation will benefit the whole family.* **2.** To receive help or useful service: *We all benefited from the town's new water system.*

bent | bĕnt | The past tense and past participle of the verb **bend:** *The electrician bent the wire with a pair of pliers. He has bent the wire.*
—*adjective* **1.** Not in a straight line; curved; crooked: *A bent pin can be used as a fishhook.* **2.** Determined: *He is bent on doing everything his own way.*

be·ret | bə rā′ | or | bĕr′ā′ | —*noun, plural* **berets** A soft, round, flat cap, usually made of wool or felt.

ber·ry | bĕr′ē | —*noun, plural* **berries** A small, juicy fruit with many seeds. Blueberries and cranberries are berries.
♦ *These sound alike* **berry, bury.**

berth | bûrth | —*noun, plural* **berths** **1.** A bed or bunk on a ship, aircraft, or train. **2.** A space for a ship to dock.
♦ *These sound alike* **berth, birth.**

be·seech | bĭ sēch′ | —*verb* **besought** or **beseeched, beseeching** To ask in a serious way; beg: *I beseech you to let him live.*

be·set | bĭ sĕt′ | —*verb* **beset, besetting** To attack from all sides: *Wild dogs suddenly beset the travelers.*

be·side | bĭ sīd′ | —*preposition* At the side of: *She sat down beside her parents.*

be·sides | bĭ sīdz′ | —*adverb* **1.** In addition: *The teacher made sure that every child had a lunch box and an apple besides.* **2.** Beyond what has been said; moreover: *They didn't want to go to the beach, and besides it was raining.*
—*preposition* **1.** In addition to: *Mrs. Chandler did other things besides teaching second grade.* **2.** Other than; except for: *There's nothing to eat in the refrigerator besides a little ham.*

be·siege | bĭ sēj′ | —*verb* **besieged, besieging** **1.** To surround in order to capture: *The enemy besieged the fortress for two years.* **2.** To crowd around and hem in: *The admirers besieged the singer as he came out of his hotel.*

be·sought | bĭ sôt′ | A past tense and past participle of the verb **beseech:** *The prisoner besought the judge to have pity on him. We had besought his mercy.*

best | bĕst | —*adjective* The superlative of the adjective **good.** **1.** Most excellent or suitable: *My answer was good, yours was better, and his was best. She is the best athlete in school.* **2.** The largest: *We have completed the best part of this job.* **3.** Closest; favorite: *Who is your best friend? This is my best doll.*
—*adverb* The superlative of the adverb **well.** **1.** In the most

excellent or suitable way: *I work best when I have had a good breakfast. Use the tool that best fits the job.* **2.** In or to the highest degree; most: *What dessert do you like best?*

—*singular* or *plural noun* **1.** The most excellent or suitable person or persons: *Even the best make mistakes. We picked the best in the group to go on the mission.* **2.** The finest effort or appearance: *Do your best. He always looks his best on weekends.* **3.** Good wishes or regards: *Give your family my best.*

be·stow | bĭ stō′ | —*verb* **bestowed, bestowing** To give as a gift or an honor: *The mayor bestowed medals on the contest winners.*

bet | bĕt | —*noun, plural* **bets 1.** An agreement between two people or groups that the one who is wrong about something will give money or something of value to the one who is right: *He lost the bet and had to pay his friend 50¢.* **2.** The money or thing at risk in such an agreement: *His bet was 50¢.*

—*verb* **bet, betting 1.** To risk something on a bet; make a bet: *He bet a dollar that his frog would beat mine. I don't like to bet on card games.* **2.** To say with certainty; be sure: *I bet you don't know what the surprise is.*

be·tray | bĭ trā′ | —*verb* **betrayed, betraying 1.** To give away or sell to an enemy; be a traitor to: *He betrayed his country by spying for the enemy.* **2.** To be disloyal to; be false to: *He betrayed his friends' trust by telling their secrets.*

bet·ter | bĕt′ər | —*adjective* The comparative of the adjective **good. 1.** More excellent or suitable than another: *He is a better skater than his father. This is a better place for the desk than near the window.* **2.** Improved in condition or health: *Better roads help reduce accidents. Do you feel better today?*

—*adverb* The comparative of the adverb **well. 1.** In a more excellent or suitable way: *Jim reads better than John, but not as well as Harry. The wrench is better for this job than the pliers.* **2.** In or to a higher degree; more: *a book written better than 20 years ago.*

—*noun, plural* **betters** The finer of two: *Of these two paintings, this is the better.*

be·tween | bĭ twēn′ | —*preposition* **1.** In the time, space, or position separating two points, things, places, persons: *When I was neither man nor boy, but between both, I wanted to be a truck driver. The bookcase is between the windows. The bus makes three stops between New York and Albany. There is a desk between the teacher and the students.* **2.** After a comparison of: *There was not much to choose between the two cars.* **3.** Linking: *a canal between the two cities.* **4.** Involving or done by two or more people; engaged in by two or more people: *The job was completed between the two of them. This morning there was a long meeting between faculty members and parents.* **5.** Either one or the other of: *I can't buy skates for both of you, so decide between you which stands the better chance of making the team.*

—*adverb* In the time, space, or position separating two points, things, places, or persons: *The bus was scheduled to stop in New York, Albany, and several towns between.*

bev·er·age | bĕv′ər ĭj | or | bĕv′rĭj | —*noun, plural* **beverages** Any liquid for drinking. Milk, tea, and cider are beverages.

be·ware | bĭ wâr′ | —*verb* To watch out for; be on guard against: *Beware of the dog! He was told to beware of pickpockets.*

be·wil·der | bĭ wĭl′dər | —*verb* **bewildered, bewildering** To confuse very much; to puzzle: *All their questions bewildered him.*

bicycle

The bicycle at the bottom was called a high-wheeler or penny-farthing and was popular from about 1870 to the 1890's.

ă	pat	ĕ	pet	î	fierce
ā	pay	ē	be	ŏ	pot
â	care	ĭ	pit	ō	go
ä	father	ī	pie	ô	paw, for
oi	oil	ŭ	cut	zh	vision
ōō	book	û	fur	ə	ago, item,
ōō	boot	th	the		pencil, atom,
yōō	abuse	th	thin		circus
ou	out	hw	which	ər	butter

be·witch | bĭ wĭch′ | —*verb* **bewitched, bewitching** **1.** To cast a magic spell over: *She bewitched the boy and turned him into a tree.* **2.** To charm a great deal: *The pianist bewitched the audience with his magnificent playing.*

be·yond | bē ŏnd′ | or | bĭ yŏnd′ | —*preposition* **1.** On the far side of: *The ocean is just beyond the dunes.* **2.** Farther on than: *Place a ruler on the desk so that half of it sticks out beyond the desk.* **3.** Later than; after; past: *No papers will be accepted beyond this deadline.* **4.** Outside the limit of: *The fans' enthusiasm was beyond control. Her health is beyond hope.*
—*adverb* Farther away: *We sailed through the fog into the bright sunlight beyond.*

bi·as | bī′əs | —*noun, plural* **biases** **1.** A line that slants or is diagonal: *Cut the cloth on the bias across the weave.* **2.** A strong feeling for or against something without enough reason; a prejudice: *The manager has a bias against girl pitchers.*
—*verb* **biased, biasing** To cause to have a prejudiced opinion: *His report biased many people against the movie.*

Bi·ble | bī′bəl | —*noun, plural* **Bibles** **1.** The Old Testament and the New Testament, which together make up the sacred book of the Christian religion. **2.** The Old Testament alone, which is the sacred book of the Jewish religion.

Bib·li·cal or **bib·li·cal** | bĭb′lĭ kəl | —*adjective* Of, from, or in keeping with the Bible: *a Biblical prophet; their biblical customs.*

bib·li·og·ra·phy | bĭb′lē ŏg′rə fē | —*noun, plural* **bibliographies** A list of books on a particular subject or by a particular writer.

bi·car·bo·nate of soda | bī kär′bə nĭt | or | bī kär′bə nāt′ | A white powder containing sodium.

bi·ceps | bī′sĕps′ | —*noun, plural* **biceps** The large muscle in the upper arm that bends the elbow.

bick·er | bĭk′ər | —*verb* **bickered, bickering** To argue over small or unimportant matters: *The children always bicker over whose turn it is to set the table.*

bi·cus·pid | bī kŭs′pĭd | —*noun, plural* **bicuspids** A tooth that has two points. An adult should have eight bicuspids.

bi·cy·cle | bī′sĭ kəl | or | bī′sĭk′əl | —*noun, plural* **bicycles** A vehicle that has two wheels, a seat, pedals, handlebars, and a frame to hold them together. The rider makes a bicycle move by pushing the pedals to turn the rear wheel and steers the bicycle by directing the handlebars.
—*verb* **bicycled, bicycling** To ride a bicycle.

bid | bĭd | —*verb* **bid** or **bade, bidden** or **bid, bidding** **1.** To tell someone to do something; command: *My mother bade me wash my face.* **2.** To say as a greeting or farewell: *Did you bid your aunt good morning?* **3.** *Past tense* and *past participle* **bid** To offer to pay a certain price or do a job for a certain price: *I bid $25 for this chair at the auction.*
—*noun, plural* **bids** **1.** An offer to pay or receive a certain price for something: *The man wanted to receive a higher bid for the paintings.* **2.** The amount offered: *a bid of $10.*

bid·den | bĭd′n | A past participle of the verb **bid:** *We had bidden the children to remain in their seats until the end of the trip.*

bid·ding | bĭd′ĭng | —*noun, plural* **biddings** **1.** A command, order, or request: *He went to the store at his brother's bidding.* **2.** The act of making offers to buy: *The bidding went quickly at the horse auction.*

bide | bīd | —*verb* **bided, biding** —**bide (one's) time** To wait patiently for the right moment.

big | bĭg | —*adjective* **bigger, biggest** **1.** Of great size; large: *An elephant is a big animal. His house is bigger than mine.* **2.** Grown-up or older: *You're a big girl now. My big brother is thirteen.* **3.** Important: *On Saturday we have a big game.*

bike | bīk | —*noun, plural* **bikes** A bicycle. —*verb* **biked, biking** To ride a bicycle: *He biked into town on Saturday to see his parents.*

bile | bīl | —*noun* A bitter yellow-green liquid that is made by the liver. It helps the body digest fats.

bill¹ | bĭl | —*noun, plural* **bills** **1.** A written statement saying how much money is to be paid for things that have been bought or work that has been done: *a telephone bill; a doctor's bill.* **2.** A piece of paper money worth a certain amount: *a ten-dollar bill.* **3.** A poster or public announcement: *Post no bills!* **4.** A list of what is offered: *a theater bill.* **5.** A formal proposal containing rules or regulations that is offered to a legislative body in the hope it will become a law. A bill becomes a law if the lawmakers vote to pass it. —*verb* **billed, billing** To send a statement of what is owed: *The store will bill us for the things we charged today.*

bill² | bĭl | —*noun, plural* **bills** **1.** The hard, projecting mouth parts of a bird; a beak. **2.** A part that looks like a bird's bill.

bill·board | bĭl′bôrd′ | or | bĭl′bŏrd′ | —*noun, plural* **billboards** A large board for displaying advertising posters in public places and along highways.

bill·fold | bĭl′fōld′ | —*noun, plural* **billfolds** A small folding case for carrying paper money or cards in a pocket or handbag; wallet.

bil·liards | bĭl′yərdz | —*noun* (Used with a singular verb.) A game of skill played on a cloth-covered table that has raised, cushioned edges. Billiards is played with a stick called a cue. The player uses the cue to hit three hard balls against one another or against the side cushions of the table.

bil·lion | bĭl′yən | —*noun, plural* **billions** **1.** In the United States and Canada, one thousand million; 1,000,000,000 (1 followed by 9 zeros). **2.** In Great Britain and some other countries, one million million; 1,000,000,000,000 (1 followed by 12 zeros).

bil·low | bĭl′ō | —*noun, plural* **billows** **1.** A great wave or swelling of the sea. **2.** A great rising mass of anything: *Billows of smoke came from the chimney.* —*verb* **billowed, billowing** To rise or swell in billows: *The waves billowed. Flames and smoke billowed over the prairie.*

bil·ly goat | bĭl′ē | A male goat.

bin | bĭn | —*noun, plural* **bins** An enclosed space for keeping or storing food, coal, or other items.
♦ *These sound alike* **bin, been.**

bi·na·ry | bī′nə rē | Of a system of numbers in which any numeral may be written using just the symbols 1 and 0.

bind | bīnd | —*verb* **bound, binding** **1.** To fasten together; tie up: *Let's bind the twigs together with string.* **2.** To wrap a bandage around: *He bound the dog's paw with gauze.* **3.** To hold together because of feelings, custom, promises, duty, or law: *Their love binds them although they are apart.* **4.** To fasten pages together between covers: *They bound the book in leather.*

bi·noc·u·lars | bə nŏk′yə lərz | or | bī nŏk′yə lərz | —*plural noun*

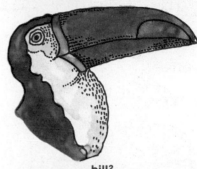

bill¹, bill²
Bill¹ comes to English from a French word that had as its source a word of the Latin language spoken in the Middle Ages; the word meant "a seal" or "a sealed document." Bill² comes from an old English word; it has always meant "a bird's beak."

bill²
Toucan

billboard

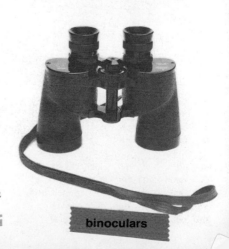
binoculars

A device that a person looks through with both eyes. Binoculars look like two small telescopes attached to each other. They make distant objects seem closer and larger.

bi·o·graph·i·cal | bī′ə **grăf′** ĭ kəl | —*adjective* Of or about a person's life: *biographical information about the poet.*

bi·og·ra·phy | bī ŏg′rə fē | —*noun, plural* **biographies** A written story of a person's life.

bi·o·log·i·cal | bī′ə lŏj′ĭ kəl | —*adjective* **1.** Of the scientific study of living things: *Botany is a biological science.* **2.** Of or affecting living things: *Growth is a biological process.*

bi·ol·o·gy | bī ŏl′ə jē | —*noun* The scientific study of living things. Biology deals with the origin, growth, structure, and distribution of plants and animals. Some branches of biology are botany, zoology, and ecology.

bi·on·ic | bī ŏn′ĭk | —*adjective* Using or containing mechanical equipment to strengthen or replace part of a living creature: *The man had lost his arm and had a bionic arm to replace it.*

bi·on·ics | bī ŏn′ĭks | —*noun* (Used with a singular verb.) The study and use of mechanical parts to help living things or make them stronger. For example, bionics may help develop artificial arms that perform for people who have lost their own.

birch | bûrch | —*noun, plural* **birches** **1.** A tree with smooth bark that peels off easily. There are several kinds of birch tree. **2.** The hard wood of a birch.

bird | bûrd | —*noun, plural* **birds** One of a large group of animals that lay eggs and have feathers and wings. Most birds can fly. Some birds, such as hummingbirds, are only a few inches long. Some, such as the ostrich, are larger than a human being.

birth | bûrth | —*noun, plural* **births** **1.** The beginning of a life; the act or time of being born: *What was the baby's weight at birth?* **2.** A beginning of anything; origin: *the birth of an idea.*
♦ *These sound alike* **birth, berth.**

birth·day | bûrth′dā′ | —*noun, plural* **birthdays** **1.** The day that someone is born. **2.** The return each year of this day.

birth·mark | bûrth′märk′ | —*noun, plural* **birthmarks** A mark or spot on a person's body that was there from the time of birth.

birth·place | bûrth′plās′ | —*noun, plural* **birthplaces** The place where someone was born or where something began.

bis·cuit | bĭs′kĭt | —*noun, plural* **biscuits** A small bread, roll, or cake that is made with flour and baking soda or baking powder.

bish·op | bĭsh′əp | —*noun, plural* **bishops** **1.** A Christian clergyman of high rank. A bishop is in charge of a district of the church. **2.** A chess piece that can move in a diagonal line across squares of one color that have no pieces on them.

Bis·marck | bĭz′märk′ | The capital of North Dakota.

bi·son | bī′sən | or | bī′zən | —*noun, plural* **bison** A large animal of western North America. It has a shaggy, dark-brown mane and short, curved horns. Another name for this animal is **buffalo.**

bit¹ | bĭt | —*noun, plural* **bits** **1.** A small piece or amount: *The toy fell and broke into bits. Add a bit of blue to the paint.* **2.** A small amount of time; a moment: *Please stay a bit.*
Idioms **a bit** A little; somewhat; slightly: *I am a bit hungry. He is a bit late for his date.*

bit² | bĭt | —*noun, plural* **bits** **1.** A tool used for drilling holes. A bit fits into a brace or an electric drill. **2.** A shaped piece of metal that is part of a horse's bridle. The bit goes into the horse's

birch

bison
American bison

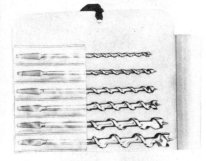

bit²

ă	pat	ĕ	pet	î	fierce
ā	pay	ē	be	ŏ	pot
â	care	ĭ	pit	ō	go
ä	father	ī	pie	ô	paw, for

oi	oil	ŭ	cut	zh	vision
ōō	book	û	fur	ə	ago, item,
ōō	boot	*th*	**the**		pencil, atom,
yōō	abuse	th	thin		circus
ou	out	hw	which	ər	butter

mouth and is used to help control the animal.

bit³ |bĭt| The past tense and a past participle of the verb **bite:** *The dog chased the boy on the bicycle and bit him. The same dog had bit him before.*

bite |bīt| —*verb* **bit, bitten** or **bit, biting** **1.** To cut or tear with the teeth: *I told him not to bite off a piece of the apple. Mary bit the thread in two. He bit off a piece of bread.* **2.** To pierce the skin of a person or animal with fangs, a stinger, or teeth: *A snake bit him in the leg. The mosquitoes kept biting all night. That dog bites!* **3.** To cause a sharp pain to; to sting; to smart: *The cold wind bit his face.* **4.** To take or swallow bait: *The trout bit the fly.*
—*noun, plural* **bites** **1.** A wound or injury that comes from biting: *a mosquito bite.* **2.** An amount of food taken into the mouth at one time: *Let me have a bite of your sandwich.* **3.** A light meal or snack: *We'll have a bite before we go to the movies.* **4.** A sharp pain; a sting: *the bite of the winter wind.*

bit·ten |bĭt′n| A past participle of the verb **bite:** *Have you been bitten by the black flies?*

bit·ter |bĭt′ər| —*adjective* **bitterer, bitterest** **1.** Having a sharp or unpleasant taste: *a bitter medicine.* **2.** Causing sharp pain to the body, mind, or feelings: *a bitter wind; bitter tears; bitter memories.* **3.** Showing or coming from bad feelings or hatred: *He had bitter words about his rival.*

bi·tu·mi·nous coal |bĭ tōō′mə nəs| or |bĭ tyōō′mə nəs| A kind of coal that burns with a smoky flame; soft coal.

black |blăk| —*noun, plural* **blacks** **1.** The darkest of all colors; the color of the printing on this page; the opposite of white. **2.** A member of the Negroid ethnic group; a Negro.
—*adjective* **blacker, blackest** **1.** Having the darkest of all colors; of the color of the printing on this page: *a black car; a black umbrella.* **2.** Of or belonging to the Negroid ethnic group; Negro. **3.** Without light; dark: *a black night; a black room.*

black·ber·ry |blăk′bĕr′ē| —*noun, plural* **blackberries** A shiny black berry that grows on a thorny plant.

black·bird |blăk′bûrd′| —*noun, plural* **blackbirds** Any of several kinds of birds that have black or mostly black feathers.

black·board |blăk′bôrd′| or |blăk′bōrd′| —*noun, plural* **blackboards** A surface for writing on with chalk. Blackboards are made of slate or other smooth, hard materials and may be green, or another color.

black·en |blăk′ən| —*verb* **blackened, blackening** **1.** To make or become black or dark: *Smoke blackened the sky. The sky blackened before the storm.* **2.** To speak evil of; give a bad reputation to: *The nasty rumors blackened the officer's name.*

black-eyed Su·san |blăk′ĭd sōō′zən| —*plural,* **black-eyed Susans** A plant that has flowers with narrow orange-yellow petals around a dark-brown center.

black·ish |blăk′ĭsh| —*adjective* Somewhat black.

black·mail |blăk′māl′| —*verb* **blackmailed, blackmailing** To try to force a person to pay something or do something by threatening to tell a secret that could hurt the person.
—*noun* An act of blackmailing.

black·smith |blăk′smĭth′| —*noun, plural* **blacksmiths** A person who makes things out of iron. A blacksmith heats the iron and shapes and hammers it into horseshoes, tools, and other objects.

black widow A black spider. The female has a red mark on the

bit¹, bit²
Bit¹ comes from a word used long ago in English to mean "a piece bitten off." **Bit²** comes from another old English word that meant "a bite" or "a sting." Later this word came to refer to the mouthpiece of a horse's bridle.

blackberry

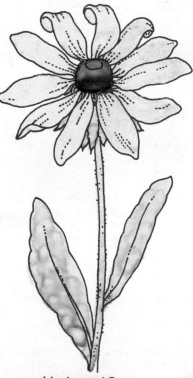

black-eyed Susan

underside of the abdomen and has a poisonous bite.

blad·der | blăd′ər | —*noun, plural* **bladders** A small structure like a bag in the body. It stores urine from the kidneys.

blade | blād | —*noun, plural* **blades** **1.** The flat, sharp part of a tool that cuts: *a knife blade; a saw blade.* **2.** A thin, narrow leaf of grass. **3.** A broad, flat part of a leaf that grows from a stalk. **4.** The thin, flat part of something: *a shoulder blade; the blade of an oar.* **5.** The metal part of an ice skate.

blame | blām | —*verb* **blamed, blaming** **1.** To consider someone or something guilty or responsible: *Farmers often blame coyotes for more harm than they really do.* **2.** To find fault with: *I don't blame you for wanting to play outdoors.*
—*noun* Responsibility or guilt for something wrong: *He took all the blame for the mischief, although others were involved.*

bland | blănd | —*adjective* **blander, blandest** Pleasant and soothing; not irritating, spicy, or especially interesting: *a bland climate; bland foods; a bland remark.*

blank | blăngk | —*adjective* **blanker, blankest** **1.** Without writing, decoration, or objects on it: *a blank paper; a blank wall; a blank desk top.* **2.** Without expression or ideas: *He gave me a blank stare.*
—*noun, plural* **blanks** **1.** An empty space, sometimes with a line, where a letter, word, or sentence is missing: *Write the correct words in the blanks.* **2.** A paper or form with empty spaces to be written in: *an order blank for a magazine subscription.* **3.** A cartridge containing gunpowder but no bullet.

blank·et | blăng′kĭt | —*noun, plural* **blankets** **1.** A warm covering of soft, thick cloth, used on a bed or to keep a person or animal warm. **2.** Any thick cover: *a blanket of snow.*
—*verb* **blanketed, blanketing** To cover with a blanket: *We blanketed ourselves from chin to toe. Snow blanketed the fields.*

blare | blâr | —*noun, plural* **blares** A loud, shrill sound, as a trumpet or horn makes: *the blare of a brass band.*
—*verb* **blared, blaring** To make a loud, shrill sound: *The trumpets blared.*

blast | blăst | or | bläst | —*noun, plural* **blasts** **1.** A strong gust of wind, air, or gas: *a sudden blast of cold air.* **2.** A loud noise: *the blast of a neighbor's radio.* **3.** The action of blowing up; an explosion: *Blast after blast shook the factory and destroyed it.*
—*verb* **blasted, blasting** **1.** To blow up with explosives: *They blasted the mountainside to build a road.* **2.** To destroy or ruin: *The defeat blasted our hopes for the championship.*
　***Phrasal verb* blast off** To move into flight with great speed, propelled by rockets: *The space vehicle blasted off at three o'clock.*

blaze¹ | blāz | —*noun, plural* **blazes** **1.** A burning fire or flame: *There was a warm blaze in the fireplace. The firefighters battled the blaze all night.* **2.** A bright light or glow: *The blaze of the spotlight was on her.* **3.** A brilliant display: *The flowers were a blaze of color.*
—*verb* **blazed, blazing** **1.** To burn with a bright flame: *A fire blazed on the hearth.* **2.** To shine with bright light or color: *The main street blazed with electric signs. The garden blazed with red tulips.* **3.** To show strong feelings: *Her temper blazed up again.*

blaze² | blāz | —*noun, plural* **blazes** A mark cut into the bark of a tree to show where a trail is.
—*verb* **blazed, blazing** To mark trees or trails by cutting into the bark of a tree: *The scouts blazed a trail through the forest.*

bleach | blēch | —*verb* **bleached, bleaching** To make or become

blanket
Navaho blanket

blaze¹, blaze²
Blaze¹ comes from an old English word that meant "torch" or "bright fire." **Blaze²** comes from a word used a very long time ago in a form of German to mean "white mark." Both **blaze¹** and **blaze²** originally came from the prehistoric Germanic word for "a bright or white object."

ă	pat	ĕ	pet	î	fierce
ā	pay	ē	be	ŏ	pot
â	care	ĭ	pit	ō	go
ä	father	ī	pie	ô	paw, for
oi	oil	ŭ	cut	zh	vision
ōō	book	û	fur	ə	ago, item,
ōō	boot	*th*	the		pencil, atom,
	house	th	thin		circus
		hw	which	ər	butter

lighter or white by exposing to the sun or certain chemicals: *She bleached the laundry. The summer sun bleached his hair.*
—*noun, plural* **bleaches** Any substance used for bleaching.

bleach·ers |blē'chǝrz| —*plural noun* Wooden benches for people to sit on at ball games, parades, and other public events.

bleak |blēk| —*adjective* **bleaker, bleakest 1.** Without cheer; dreary: *a bleak life of poverty.* **2.** Cold and harsh: *a damp, bleak wind.* **3.** Exposed to the winds: *a bleak hillside.*

bled |blĕd| The past tense and past participle of the verb **bleed:** *He cut his thumb and it bled. It had bled on his shirt.*

bleed |blēd| —*verb* **bled, bleeding 1.** To lose blood: *Did your finger bleed when you cut it?* **2.** To lose sap or liquid: *Milkweed bleeds when you cut it.*

blem·ish |blĕm'ĭsh| —*noun, plural* **blemishes** A mark on something that spoils its appearance or quality: *She tried to get rid of the pimples and other blemishes on her face.*
— *verb* **blemished, blemishing** To spoil the appearance or quality of: *Scratches blemished the table.*

blend |blĕnd| —*verb* **blended, blending 1.** To mix together so well that one part cannot be recognized from another: *The cook blended the milk and eggs. Sugar blends easily into the batter.* **2.** To have a color or shade of color that goes well with another: *The sofa blends well with the colors of the room.*
—*noun, plural* **blends** Something that has been blended; a mixture: *a blend of colors; a blend of tea.*

bless |blĕs| —*verb* **blessed** or **blest, blessing 1.** To make holy: *The Lord blessed the Sabbath.* **2.** To ask God's favor for: *The woman blessed them for helping her.* **3.** To praise as holy; glorify: *They blessed the Lord in their prayers and hymns.* **4.** To grant good fortune to: *The passing years blessed them with good health.*

bless·ing |blĕs'ĭng| —*noun, plural* **blessings 1.** A short prayer for God's favor or to thank God. **2.** A wish for happiness or success; approval: *He had his parents' blessing to seek his fortune in foreign lands.* **3.** Something that brings happiness or well-being: *The air conditioner is a blessing in this hot weather.*

blest |blĕst| A past tense and a past participle of the verb **bless:** *They were blest with strong bodies and good minds. She had been blest with good teeth.*

blew |blo͞o| The past tense of the verb **blow:** *He blew the horn to call the officer. A strong wind blew outside.*
♦ *These sound alike* **blew, blue.**

blight |blīt| —*noun, plural* **blights 1.** A disease that withers or destroys plants. **2.** Anything that is harmful or destroys: *The crime wave is a blight on the city.*
—*verb* **blighted, blighting** To cause harm to; ruin; destroy: *The flood waters blighted the crops on the river banks.*

blimp |blĭmp| —*noun, plural* **blimps** A kind of balloon that can be steered and can carry people and cargo.

blind |blīnd| —*adjective* **blinder, blindest 1.** Having no sense of sight; unable to see: *The blind woman had a dog to help her get around.* **2.** Depending on instruments and not on one's eyes: *The pilot made a blind landing in the fog.* **3.** Hidden from sight; hard to see: *There is a blind crossing just beyond the curve in the road.* **4.** Not willing or able to notice: *She is blind to his faults.* **5.** Without reason or good sense: *He has blind faith in his friend.* **6.** Closed at one end: *a blind alley.*

bleachers

blimp

blindfold

block

blockhouse

—*noun, plural* **blinds** Something that shuts out light or gets in the way of vision: *He closed the window blinds to darken the room.*
—*verb* **blinded, blinding** 1. To cause to lose the sense of sight: *The head injury blinded him for a while.* 2. To cause to lose judgment or good sense: *Her beauty blinds him to her faults.*

blind·fold | blīnd′fōld′ | —*verb* **blindfolded, blindfolding** To cover the eyes of someone: *They blindfolded her and then asked her to identify objects by touch.*
—*noun, plural* **blindfolds** A piece of cloth put over the eyes and tied around the head to keep someone from seeing.

blind·ness | blīnd′nĭs | —*noun* The condition of having no sense of sight; a lack of the ability to see.

blink | blĭngk | —*verb* **blinked, blinking** 1. To close and open the eyes quickly; wink with both eyes: *He blinked as he came out from a dark room into the bright sunlight.* 2. To flash off and on; shine in an unsteady way: *His flashlight blinked because the battery had to be changed.*

bliss | blĭs | —*noun* Very great joy; extreme happiness: *Her grandparents lived in perfect loving bliss after years of marriage.*

blis·ter | blĭs′tər | —*noun, plural* **blisters** 1. A small swelling on the skin that is sore and is filled with fluid. Burns and rubbing may cause blisters. 2. Any small swelling or bubble: *The heat created blisters in the paint.*
—*verb* **blistered, blistering** To form or cause to form blisters: *Her skin blistered from poison ivy. Tight shoes blistered his feet.*

bliz·zard | blĭz′ərd | —*noun, plural* **blizzards** A very heavy snowstorm with strong winds.

bloat | blōt | —*verb* **bloated, bloating** To cause to swell: *Eating too much clover bloated the stomachs of the sheep.*

blob | blŏb | —*noun, plural* **blobs** A soft lump or spot without a definite shape: *a blob of clay; a blob of paint.*

block | blŏk | —*noun, plural* **blocks** 1. A solid piece of wood, stone, ice, or any other hard material: *He carved the statue from a block of marble.* 2. Something that gets in the way so that other things cannot pass or move: *The beaver dam caused a block in the flow of the stream.* 3. An area in a city or town with streets on all sides; a square: *He ran around the block three times.* 4. The length of one side of a city block from one crossing to the next: *I live five blocks from school.* 5. A group of things that are connected in some way: *a block of tickets.* 6. A pulley or a set of pulleys in a wooden or metal case.
—*verb* **blocked, blocking** To stop the passage or movement of: *A fallen tree blocked the entrance to the house.*

block·ade | blŏ kād′ | —*noun, plural* **blockades** The closing off of an area, a city, or a harbor to keep people and supplies from going in or out.
—*verb* **blockaded, blockading** To close off with a blockade: *The fleet blockaded the enemy's ports so the people ran out of food and medical supplies.*

block·house | blŏk′hous′ | —*noun, plural* **block·hous·es** | blŏk′hou′zĭz | 1. A fort built of heavy material with holes through which to fire at the enemy. Some blockhouses are made of heavy timber and have upper stories that stick out over the lower part. Others are made of stone or concrete. 2. A strong building near a launching pad. People can safely control and watch the launching of a rocket from a blockhouse.

ă	pat	ĕ	pet	î	fierce
ā	pay	ē	be	ŏ	pot
â	care	ĭ	pit	ō	go
ä	father	ī	pie	ô	paw, for

oi	oil	ŭ	cut	zh	vision
ŏŏ	book	û	fur	ə	ago, item,
ōō	boot	*th*	the		pencil, atom,
	house	th	thin		circus
		hw	which	ər	butter

blond or **blonde** | blŏnd | —*adjective* **blonder, blondest**
1. Having hair that is light in color and pale skin: *a blond boy; a blonde girl.* **2.** Light in color: *blond hair; blond furniture.*
—*noun, plural* **blonds** or **blondes** A person with hair that is light in color and pale skin. Often the spelling **blond** is used for males and **blonde** for females. Either spelling may be used for wood or furniture.

blood | blŭd | —*noun, plural* **bloods** **1.** The red fluid that the heart pumps through the veins and arteries. Blood carries oxygen, food, minerals, and other useful things to all parts of the body, and it carries away waste materials. **2.** Ancestry; kinship: *Are they related by blood or by marriage?*
Idiom **in cold blood** Without any feelings; cruelly and without pity: *The thief shot the bank guard in cold blood.*

blood·hound | blŭd′hound′ | —*noun, plural* **bloodhounds** A large dog with a smooth coat, drooping ears, and loose folds of skin around the face. Bloodhounds have a keen sense of smell. They are sometimes used to track down people who are lost or who are wanted by the police.

blood·shed | blŭd′shĕd′ | —*noun* The loss of blood by killing or wounding: *The soldiers captured the town without bloodshed.*

blood·stream | blŭd′strĕm′ | —*noun, plural* **bloodstreams** The blood flowing through a living body.

blood·thirst·y | blŭd′thûr′stē | —*adjective* **bloodthirstier, bloodthirstiest** Eager to cause or see bloodshed or violence; extremely cruel: *The bloodthirsty mob stormed the fort.*

blood vessel Any tube in the body through which blood circulates. Arteries and veins are blood vessels.

blood·y | blŭd′ē | —*adjective* **bloodier, bloodiest** **1.** Bleeding: *a bloody nose.* **2.** Stained or covered with blood: *bloody bandages.* **3.** Causing or marked by bloodshed: *During the bloody fight, many people were hurt. The bloody revolution killed many people.*

bloom | blo͞om | —*noun, plural* **blooms** **1.** The flowers or blossoms of a plant: *The rose blooms are starting to come out.* **2.** The time or condition of flowering: *The lilacs are in bloom now.*
—*verb* **bloomed, blooming** To bear flowers; to blossom: *The apple trees bloomed all along the street.*

blos·som | blŏs′əm | —*noun, plural* **blossoms** **1.** A flower or cluster of flowers, especially of a fruit tree: *We picked apple blossoms.* **2.** The time or condition of flowering: *The peach trees are in blossom.*
—*verb* **blossomed, blossoming** **1.** To bear flowers; to bloom: *The orange trees blossomed late this year.* **2.** To grow and develop; flourish; thrive: *His talent blossomed as he continued to paint.*

blot | blŏt | —*noun, plural* **blots** **1.** A stain or spot: *an ink blot.* **2.** Something that spoils beauty or perfection; a blemish: *The failing grade was a blot on his school record.*
—*verb* **blotted, blotting** **1.** To spot or stain: *The ink spilled and blotted the drawing.* **2.** To dry or soak up: *He blotted the spill with an old rag.*

blotch | blŏch | —*noun, plural* **blotches** A large, irregular spot or blot: *He made big blotches of color on the canvas.*
—*verb* **blotched, blotching** To mark or become marked with spots: *The rash blotched his arm. Her face blotched in the sun.*

blot·ter | blŏt′ər | —*noun, plural* **blotters** A piece of absorbent paper used to soak up wet ink.

bloodhound

blossom
Peach blossoms

blow¹, blow²
Blow¹ comes from a word used long ago in English to mean "to blow." **Blow²** comes from a word used by northern English people. It may have come from a Germanic word meaning "to strike," but this is not certain.

blowtorch

blueberry

bluebird

ă	pat	ĕ	pet	î	fierce
ā	pay	ē	be	ŏ	pot
â	care	ĭ	pit	ō	go
ä	father	ī	pie	ô	paw, for
oi	oil	ŭ	cut	zh	vision
ŏŏ	book	û	fur	ə	ago, item,
ōō	boot	th	the		pencil, atom,
yōō	abuse	th	thin		circus
ou	out	hw	which	ər	butter

blouse | blous | or | blouz | —*noun, plural* **blouses** A loose shirt or garment worn on the upper part of the body. Most blouses are worn by women or girls.

blow¹ | blō | —*verb* **blew, blown, blowing** **1.** To be in motion, as air: *The wind blew all night. It was blowing hard.* **2.** To move or cause to move by means of a current of air: *His hat blew off his head. The high winds blew the ship off course.* **3.** To send out a current of air or gas: *Blow on your soup to cool it.* **4.** To make a noise by forcing air through: *Can you blow the bugle? The factory whistle blows at noon.* **5.** To shape by forcing air or gas into or through: *We watched the man blow glass vases.* **6.** To melt a fuse: *We used too many appliances and blew a fuse.* **7.** To spout water: *How often does that whale blow?* **8.** To destroy or break by an explosion: *The blast blew the building to pieces.*
   Phrasal verbs **blow out** **1.** To put out or go out by blowing: *Let's make a wish and blow out the candles. The candle blew out.* **2.** To burst suddenly: *The tire blew out.* **blow up** **1.** To fill with air or gas; inflate: *We blew up the balloons with helium.* **2.** To make larger: *The photographer will blow up the picture.* **3.** To explode: *The grenade blew up and wrecked the enemy tank.* **4.** To get angry: *She blew up at me for not telling her our plans.*
   —*noun, plural* **blows** A strong wind or gale: *A blow came out of the west and took the roof off the shack.*

blow² | blō | —*noun, plural* **blows** **1.** A sudden hard hit with a fist or weapon: *The man gave the thief a sharp blow with his cane.* **2.** A sudden shock, disappointment, or misfortune: *Losing his job was a blow to him.*

blow·er | blō'ər | —*noun, plural* **blowers** A device that creates a flow of air or gas: *She used the blower to dry her hair.*

blown | blōn | The past participle of the verb **blow:** *The wind has blown the neighbor's leaves into our yard.*

blow·torch | blō'tôrch' | —*noun, plural* **blowtorches** A small torch that can give off a very hot flame. Blowtorches are used for melting metal, soldering, and burning off old paint.

blub·ber | blŭb'ər | —*noun* The thick layer of fat under the skin of whales, seals, and some other sea animals.

blue | blōō | —*noun, plural* **blues** The color of the sky on a clear day.
   —*adjective* **bluer, bluest** **1.** Of the color blue: *She wore a blue skirt.* **2.** Unhappy; gloomy; sad: *They were in a blue mood because their plans had been spoiled by the weather.* **3.** Having a slight blue tint: *Her lips were blue from swimming too long.*
   ♦ *These sound alike* **blue, blew.**
   Idiom **out of the blue** Suddenly and at an unexpected time or place: *We were in a strange town when out of the blue we met an old friend.*

blue·bell | blōō'bĕl' | —*noun, plural* **bluebells** One of several kinds of plants with blue flowers shaped like bells.

blue·ber·ry | blōō'bĕr'ē | —*noun, plural* **blueberries** A round, juicy blue or purplish berry that grows on a bush.

blue·bird | blōō'bûrd' | —*noun, plural* **bluebirds** A North American bird with a blue back and a reddish breast.

blue·grass | blōō'grăs' | or | blōō'gräs' | —*noun* A grass with bluish or grayish leaves and stems. Bluegrass is grown on lawns and pastures.

blue·ish | blōō'ĭsh | A form of the adjective **bluish.**

blue jay |jā| A North American bird that has a crest on its head and blue feathers with white and black markings.

blue jeans |jēnz| Pants made out of blue denim or a similar sturdy cloth; jeans; dungarees.

blue·print |blōo′prĭnt′| —*noun, plural* **blueprints** A photographic copy of a drawing in which the original drawing shows as white lines on blue paper. Blueprints are used for designs of buildings, machines, and other things.

blues |blōoz| —*plural noun* **1.** A kind of music that is slow and sad and has a jazz rhythm. **2.** Unhappy feeling; low spirits: *He has had the blues ever since he lost his dog.*

bluff¹ |blŭf| —*verb* **bluffed, bluffing** To try to mislead or fool others by pretending to have, do, or be something: *He bluffed his friends into thinking his cousin was a famous tennis player. He is only bluffing about being a prince.*
—*noun, plural* **bluffs** A pretense or show made to mislead or fool others: *Is he really going to tell the teacher or is it just a bluff?*

bluff² |blŭf| —*noun, plural* **bluffs** A steep cliff, hill, or river bank.
—*adjective* **bluffer, bluffest** Gruff in manner but not unkind: *He had a bluff and hearty laugh.*

blu·ish |blōo′ĭsh| —*adjective* Somewhat blue: *The grass was a bluish green.* Another form of this adjective is **blueish.**

blun·der |blŭn′dər| —*noun, plural* **blunders** A foolish or stupid mistake: *He made the blunder of introducing the speaker by the wrong name.*
—*verb* **blundered, blundering 1.** To make a foolish or stupid mistake: *She blundered when she said the dolphin was a fish.* **2.** To move or do something in a clumsy way: *We blundered through the woods without a compass or flashlight.*

blun·der·buss |blŭn′dər bŭs′| —*noun, plural* **blunderbusses** An old type of gun with a wide muzzle. It was used to shoot at close range without exact aim.

blunt |blŭnt| —*adjective* **blunter, bluntest 1.** Having an edge or point that is not sharp: *The knife is too blunt to cut properly. The point of this pencil is blunt and should be sharpened.* **2.** Very direct and frank without being too polite: *a blunt answer.*
—*verb* **blunted, blunting** To make less sharp or effective: *Daily use blunts a scissors' edge. A snack just before dinner blunted his appetite.*

blur |blûr| —*verb* **blurred, blurring** To make or become less distinct or clear: *Smoke blurred the shapes of the houses. Her vision blurred as her eyes filled with tears.*
—*noun, plural* **blurs** Something that is not distinct or clear: *The distant crowd was a blur of faces.*

blurt |blûrt| —*verb* **blurted, blurting** To say suddenly and without thinking: *Before he knew it, he had blurted out the secret.*

blush |blŭsh| —*verb* **blushed, blushing** To become suddenly red in the face from embarrassment, confusion, or shame: *She blushed when he said she was beautiful.*
—*noun, plural* **blushes** A sudden reddening of the face from embarrassment, confusion, or shame: *The blush rose in his face when he realized what he had said.*

blus·ter |blŭs′tər| —*verb* **blustered, blustering 1.** To blow in noisy, violent gusts: *The wind blustered around the house.* **2.** To make loud boasts, threats, or noises: *The bully blustered that he*

blue jay

bluff¹, bluff²
Bluff¹ comes from a Dutch word that originally meant "to swell up" and then "to boast." The origin of **bluff²** is uncertain, but it might have come from an old Dutch word meaning "broad" or "flat."

blunderbuss

could beat the three of us with his hands tied behind his back.
—*noun, plural* **blusters** **1.** A noisy, gusty wind. **2.** Loud boasts, threats, or noises: *The dog's growling is only bluster.*

bo·a |bō′ə| —*noun, plural* **boas** **1.** A boa constrictor or similar snake. **2.** A long, fluffy scarf usually made of feathers or fur.

boa con·stric·tor |kən strĭk′tər| A large snake of tropical America. The boa constrictor is not poisonous. It coils itself around the animals it eats and crushes them.

boa constrictor

boar |bôr| or |bōr| —*noun, plural* **boars** or **boar** **1.** A wild pig with a thick coat of dark bristles. **2.** A male pig.
♦ *These sound alike* **boar, bore.**

board |bôrd| or |bōrd| —*noun, plural* **boards** **1.** A flat, long piece of sawed wood; a plank: *We made a bookcase of boards and bricks.* **2.** A flat piece of wood or other material used for a special purpose: *a chess board; a diving board; a bulletin board.* **3.** Food served daily to paying guests: *The school offers room and board to students from out of town.* **4.** A group of people who take care of the business of a company, school, or other organization: *The board of directors voted to raise the cost for tuition.*
—*verb* **boarded, boarding** **1.** To close or cover with boards: *We boarded up the broken window until it could be repaired.* **2.** To receive or give daily meals for pay: *He lives in a hotel but boards at the school. The woman boards three paying guests.* **3.** To go onto a ship, train, or other vehicle: *We boarded the bus just before the door closed. The plane leaves at 2:30, but we can board at 2:15.*

boast |bōst| —*verb* **boasted, boasting** **1.** To praise oneself, one's possessions, and one's achievements; to brag: *He boasted that he was the best athlete in the class, but he wasn't.* **2.** To have something to be proud of: *The valley boasts beautiful gardens of flowers and fruit.*
—*noun, plural* **boasts** Talk that is too full of praise for oneself, one's possessions, and one's achievements: *He made the foolish boast that he could finish three sundaes in one sitting.*

boar

A wild boar

boat |bōt| —*noun, plural* **boats** **1.** A small open craft for traveling on water. A boat may have sails, oars, or a motor to make it move. **2.** A ship.
—*verb* **boated, boating** To travel by boat: *Let's boat across the lake.*

bob |bŏb| —*noun, plural* **bobs** A quick up-and-down motion: *He gave a bob of his head to show he understood.*
—*verb* **bobbed, bobbing** **1.** To move up and down in quick motions: *The cork bobbed on the water. She bobbed her head to indicate "yes."* **2.** To grab at floating objects with the teeth: *We bobbed for apples at the Halloween party.*

bob·bin |bŏb′ĭn| —*noun, plural* **bobbins** A spool that holds thread or yarn. Some kinds of bobbins are used in sewing machines. Other kinds are used for spinning thread, making lace, or weaving cloth.

bob·cat |bŏb′kăt′| —*noun, plural* **bobcats** A wild cat of North America. It has spotted, reddish-brown fur and a short tail.

bob·o·link |bŏb′ə lĭngk′| —*noun, plural* **bobolinks** An American songbird with black, white, and tan feathers.

bob·sled |bŏb′slĕd′| —*noun, plural* **bobsleds** A long racing sled with two sets of runners, a steering wheel, and brakes. A bobsled usually holds several people.
—*verb* **bobsledded, bobsledding** To ride or race in a bobsled.

bobcat

ă	pat	ĕ	pet	î	fierce
ā	pay	ē	be	ŏ	pot
â	care	ĭ	pit	ō	go
ä	father	ī	pie	ô	paw, for
oi	oil	ŭ	cut	zh	vision
ōō	book	û	fur	ə	ago, item,
ōō	boot	*th*	the		pencil, atom,
yōō	abuse	th	thin		circus
ou	out	hw	which	ər	butter

bob·white | bŏb **hwīt′** | or | bŏb **wīt′** | —*noun, plural* **bobwhites**
A plump brown and white bird of North America. It has a call
that sounds like its name. The bobwhite is a kind of quail.

bode | bōd | —*verb* **boded, boding** To be a sign or omen of: *The
choppy sea boded an uncomfortable voyage.*

bod·i·ly | bŏd′l ē | —*adjective* Of or in the body: *The heart and
lungs are bodily organs.*

bod·y | bŏd′ē | —*noun, plural* **bodies 1.** All of a person or
animal other than the mind: *a sound mind in a sound body. An
elephant's body is gray and wrinkled. He washed his whole body in
the shower.* **2.** A dead person or animal; corpse: *The firemen found
two bodies in the house.* **3.** The main part of a person or animal,
not including the head, arms, legs, or tail; trunk; torso: *The cat's
tail is almost as long as its body.* **4.** A mass of something: *a body of
water.* **5.** The main or central part of anything: *The wings were
set at an angle to the airplane's body.*

bod·y·guard | bŏd′ē gärd′ | —*noun, plural* **bodyguards** One or
more persons who are responsible for protecting someone.

bog | bôg | or | bŏg | —*noun, plural* **bogs** A soft, wet area of land;
marsh; swamp.
—*verb* **bogged, bogging** To sink or cause to sink in or as if in a
bog: *Rain had bogged the village in a sea of mud. He bogged down in
too much work.*

boil¹ | boil | —*verb* **boiled, boiling 1. a.** To reach a temperature
where bubbles form and steam is given off: *The water boiled in the
teakettle. At sea level water boils at 100 degrees Celsius (212 degrees
Fahrenheit).* **b.** To cause a liquid to boil: *The cook boiled water for
the coffee.* **2.** To cook or be cooked in boiling liquid: *She boiled
some eggs. The eggs boiled.*
—*noun* The condition of boiling; boiling point: *The soup came to
a boil.*

boil² | boil | —*noun, plural* **boils** A painful, infected swelling on
the skin, filled with pus.

boil·er | boi′lər | —*noun, plural* **boilers 1.** A large tank for
heating water, often until it turns to steam. Boilers run engines
and heat buildings. **2.** A large container or pot for boiling liquids,
usually water: *We need a boiler to cook eight lobsters.*

boil·ing point | boi′lĭng | The temperature at which a liquid
starts to boil. At sea level the boiling point of water is 100
degrees Celsius or 212 degrees Fahrenheit. The boiling point of
water is lower on a mountain.

Boi·se | boi′zē | or | boi′sē | The capital of Idaho.

bold | bōld | —*adjective* **bolder, boldest 1.** Not having or showing
fear; brave: *The bold explorers traveled down the unknown river.*
2. Showing or needing courage; daring: *He had a bold plan to
rescue the princess.* **3.** Not polite; rude: *He used bold language to
his brothers.*

boll | bōl | —*noun, plural* **bolls** The rounded seed pod of the
cotton plant.
♦ *These sound alike* **boll, bowl.**

boll weevil A beetle with a long snout. Boll weevils cause great
damage to cotton plants.

bol·ster | bōl′stər | —*noun, plural* **bolsters** A long, narrow pillow
or cushion.
—*verb* **bolstered, bolstering** To keep from falling; strengthen: *The
pillars bolster the roof. The applause bolstered his courage.*

bobwhite

bog
Cranberry bog

boil¹, boil²
Boil¹ comes from an old French word
whose source was the Latin word
meaning "to bubble." **Boil²** is an old
English word that has not changed
in meaning. It is likely that both
boil¹ and **boil²** came from the same
form, meaning "to swell," in the prehistoric language that was the
source of many languages spoken
today.

boll weevil

bolt

bongo drums

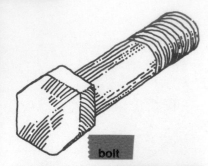

bonnet

ă	pat	ĕ	pet	î	fierce
ā	pay	ē	be	ŏ	pot
â	care	ĭ	pit	ō	go
ä	father	ī	pie	ô	paw, for
oi	oil	ŭ	cut	zh	vision
ōō	book	û	fur	ə	ago, item,
ōō	boot	th	the		pencil, atom,
yōō	abuse	th	thin		circus
ou	out	hw	which	ər	butter

bolt |bōlt| —*noun, plural* **bolts** **1.** A rod or pin with spiral grooves cut around it so that a nut may be screwed onto it. Bolts hold things together. **2.** A rod that slides to fasten a door, window, or gate. **3.** The part of a lock that is turned by a key. **4.** A flash of lightning; thunderbolt. **5.** A sudden dash from or to something: *The dog made a bolt for the door, but he was caught.* **6.** A large roll of cloth or paper.
—*verb* **bolted, bolting** **1.** To fasten or lock with a bolt or bolts: *He bolted the leg to the bed. We bolted the doors and windows when we went out.* **2.** To dash away suddenly: *The horse turned and bolted off in fright.* **3.** To eat too quickly without chewing enough: *He bolted down his lunch and got a stomach ache.*

bomb |bŏm| —*noun, plural* **bombs** A container filled with a material that can explode or blow up. A bomb blows up when it hits something after being dropped or thrown, or when a timing device in it sets it off. Bombs are used as weapons.
—*verb* **bombed, bombing** To attack, damage, harm, or destroy with a bomb or bombs: *The airplanes bombed the city.*

bom·bard |bŏm bärd′| —*verb* **bombarded, bombarding** **1.** To attack with bombs or heavy gunfire; *The soldiers bombarded the enemy's position.* **2.** To attack or bother with words or remarks: *My friends bombarded me with questions about my vacation.*

bond |bŏnd| —*noun, plural* **bonds** **1.** Anything that binds, ties, fastens, or unites: *The prisoner was kept from escaping by bonds of iron. There is a strong bond of love between the two sisters.* **2.** A certificate issued by a government or a company for borrowing money. The bond is a promise that the money will be paid back with interest to the person who buys it.

bon·dage |bŏn′dĭj| —*noun* The condition of being a slave; slavery: *Slaves were freed from bondage by President Lincoln.*

bone |bōn| —*noun, plural* **bones** One of the hard pieces that make up the skeleton of an animal with a backbone: *There is one long bone in the upper arm. There are many small bones in the hand.*
—*verb* **boned, boning** To remove the bones from a fish or piece of meat: *The butcher boned the roast.*

bon·fire |bŏn′fīr′| —*noun, plural* **bonfires** A large outdoor fire.

bon·go drums |bŏng′gō| or |bông′gō| A pair of drums attached to each other. One drum is usually larger than the other and has a lower sound. Bongo drums are held between the knees and played with the hands.

bon·net |bŏn′ĭt| —*noun, plural* **bonnets** **1.** A hat for a woman, girl, or baby. A bonnet usually has a wide brim and ribbons that tie under the chin. **2.** A headdress made of feathers, worn by some American Indians.

bo·nus |bō′nəs| —*noun, plural* **bonuses** Something extra in addition to what is usual or expected: *She received $100 as a bonus for finishing the job a week early.*

bon·y |bō′nē| —*adjective* **bonier, boniest** **1.** Of or like bone: *The skull is the bony part of the head.* **2.** Full of bones; having many bones: *a bony piece of fish.* **3.** Having bones that stick out; very thin; gaunt: *a bony old horse.*

boo |bōō| —*interjection* A word used to scare or surprise people: *He shouted, "Boo!" as he jumped out from behind the tree.*
—*verb* **booed, booing** To say "boo" as a sign of dislike or disapproval: *The fans booed the umpire.*

book |bŏŏk| —*noun, plural* **books** **1.a.** A set of pages with

writing or printing that are fastened on one side and placed between covers: *This dictionary is a book.* **b.** A set of blank pages fastened together between covers. These pages may be used for writing or printing on: *an address book; a homework book.* **2.** A main division of a bigger written or printed work: *the books of the Bible in order.*
—*verb* **booked, booking** To arrange for ahead of time; make reservations: *They have booked tickets for the play.*

book·case | bŏŏk′kās′ | —*noun, plural* **bookcases** A piece of furniture with shelves for holding books.

book·keep·er | bŏŏk′kē′pər | —*noun, plural* **bookkeepers** A person who keeps records of the money paid, received, and owed by a business.

book·let | bŏŏk′lĭt | —*noun, plural* **booklets** A small book that usually has paper covers.

boom[1] | bōōm | —*noun, plural* **booms** **1.** A deep, hollow sound, like the sound of an explosion: *We heard the boom of a cannon.* **2.** A period of time when business is growing rapidly: *The city had a boom after oil was discovered nearby.*
—*verb* **boomed, booming** **1. a.** To make a deep, hollow sound: *The thunder boomed during the storm.* **b.** To speak in a deep, hollow voice: *"No!" boomed the giant.* **2.** To grow rapidly; thrive; flourish: *Business boomed and people grew richer.*

boom[2] | bōōm | —*noun, plural* **booms** **1.** A long pole used to stretch out the bottom of a sail. **2.** A long pole that holds an object being lifted by a derrick.

boo·mer·ang | bōō′mə răng′ | —*noun, plural* **boomerangs** A flat, curved piece of wood that can be thrown so that it circles and returns to the thrower. Boomerangs can be used as weapons and were first used by the native people of Australia.

boon | bōōn | —*noun, plural* **boons** A help or blessing: *The compass was a boon to us when we were lost in the forest.*

boost | bōōst | —*verb* **boosted, boosting** To lift by pushing from below: *He boosted his brother into the saddle.*
—*noun, plural* **boosts** A push upward or ahead: *Give her a boost over the fence. The advertisement gave the sales a boost.*

boot | bōōt | —*noun, plural* **boots** A kind of shoe that covers the foot and ankle and often part of the leg as well. Boots are usually made of leather, rubber, or vinyl. Some are worn instead of shoes, and others are worn over shoes.
—*verb* **booted, booting** To kick: *He booted the football.*

booth | bōōth | —*noun, plural* **booths** | bōō*th*z | or | bōōths | **1.** A small enclosed compartment: *a telephone booth; a voting booth.* **2.** A place or stand for selling or displaying things: *a lemonade booth; a crafts booth.*

bor·der | bôr′dər | —*noun, plural* **borders** **1.** The line where one thing ends and another begins: *The river is the border between the two states.* **2.** An edge, margin, or rim: *The plate has a pattern of flowers around the border.* **3.** A strip that makes an edge or a trim to an edge: *a border of lace on a skirt.*
—*verb* **bordered, bordering** **1.** To share a boundary with: *Canada borders the United States.* **2.** To form an edge for: *Mountains border the valley.* **3.** To put an edging on: *She bordered the quilt with a ruffle.*

bore[1] | bôr | or | bōr | —*verb* **bored, boring** **1.** To make by drilling or digging: *I bored a hole in the wood with a hand drill. The mole*

boomerang

booth
Telephone booth

bored through the garden. **2.** To make a hole or holes in: *Worms bored the apple. The carpenter bored the wood.*
♦ *These sound alike* **bore, boar.**

bore² |bôr| or |bōr| —*verb* **bored, boring** To make or become weary by failing to interest or being dull: *The long speech bored the audience. She bores easily if nothing is planned.*
—*noun, plural* **bores** A person or thing that is dull, tiresome, and not interesting: *That old bore talks for hours about her cats. The movie was such a bore that we left before it ended.*
♦ *These sound alike* **bore, boar.**

bore³ |bôr| or |bōr| The past tense of the verb **bear:** *They bore the hero on their shoulders.*
♦ *These sound alike* **bore, boar.**

born |bôrn| or |bōrn| A past participle of the verb **bear** (to give birth to). This form of the past participle is used mainly when the verb **bear** indicates the fact of birth: *She was born on Mother's Day in 1970.*
—*adjective* **1.** By birth or natural ability: *He was a born singer who could carry a tune when he was very young.* **2.** Brought into being; coming from: *an invention born of need.*
♦ *These sound alike* **born, borne.**

borne |bôrn| or |bōrn| A past participle of the verb **bear:** *The leaf was borne on the wind. She has borne three children.*
♦ *These sound alike* **borne, born.**

bor·ough |bûr′ō| or |bŭr′ō| —*noun, plural* **boroughs** **1.** In some parts of the United States, a town that governs itself.
2. One of the five main parts of New York City.
♦ *These sound alike* **borough, burro, burrow.**

bor·row |bŏr′ō| or |bôr′ō| —*verb* **borrowed, borrowing** **1.** To take something from someone else with the understanding that it will be given back or replaced later: *I borrowed a book from the library. My mother borrowed a cup of sugar from our neighbor.* **2.** To take something and use it as one's own: *We borrowed the word "kindergarten" from German.*

bos·om |bŏŏz′əm| or |bōō′zəm| —*noun, plural* **bosoms** The human chest or breast: *She clasped her daughter to her bosom to keep her warm.*
—*adjective* Very close and deep: *bosom friends.*

boss |bôs| or |bŏs| —*noun, plural* **bosses** A person who is in charge, who makes decisions, and who supervises other people.
—*verb* **bossed, bossing** To give orders to; order around: *She always bosses her younger sisters around.*

Bos·ton |bô′stən| or |bŏs′tən| The capital of Massachusetts.

bo·tan·i·cal |bə tăn′ĭ kəl| —*adjective* For or of the study of plants; of botany: *We have a botanical garden near the zoo.*

bot·a·ny |bŏt′n ē| —*noun* The scientific study of plants. Botany is a branch of biology.

both |bōth| —*adjective* The two; the one as well as the other: *She painted both sides of the house. Instead of plain blue and yellow she chose a paint that combined both these colors. Both my parents are gone.* The adjective **both** belongs to a class of words called **determiners.** They signal that a noun is coming.
—*pronoun* The two alike; the one as well as the other: *If one is guilty, both are. I talked to both of them. You both skate well.*
—*conjunction* **Both** is used with the conjunction **and** to show that two of anything are to be mentioned and to give special

---

ă	pat	ĕ	pet	î	fierce
ā	pay	ē	be	ŏ	pot
â	care	ĭ	pit	ō	go
ä	father	ī	pie	ô	paw, for
oi	oil	ŭ	cut	zh	vision
ōō	book	û	fur	ə	ago, item,
ōō	boot	*th*	the		pencil, atom,
yōō	abuse	th	thin		circus
ou	out	hw	which	ər	butter

importance to this fact: *Both New York and Washington are big cities. The class includes both boys and girls.*

both·er | bŏ*th*′ər | —*verb* **bothered, bothering** **1.** To give trouble to; annoy: *The flies bothered the horse. Don't let his behavior bother you.* **2.** To take the trouble: *Please don't bother to get up.*
—*noun, plural* **bothers** **1.** Something that annoys or worries: *Having to wait is a bother.* **2.** Trouble or fuss: *They made a big bother about the decorations for the party.*

bot·tle | bŏt′l | —*noun, plural* **bottles** **1.** A container with a narrow neck that can be closed with a cap or cork. Bottles are usually made of glass or plastic and can hold liquids. **2. a.** A bottle with something in it: *She bought a bottle of soda.* **b.** The amount that a bottle holds: *He drank two bottles of milk today.*
—*verb* **bottled, bottling** To place in a bottle or bottles.

bot·tom | bŏt′əm | —*noun, plural* **bottoms** **1.** The lowest part of anything: *the bottom of the page.* **2.** The lowest outside part; underside: *The bottom of the jar left a wet circle on the table.* **3.** The lowest inside part: *Chocolate syrup was left in the bottom of the glass.* **4.** The land under a body of water: *She dove to the bottom of the lake and came up with weeds.* **5.** The basic truth or cause; main part: *Can we get to the bottom of the mystery?*

bough | bou | —*noun, plural* **boughs** A large branch of a tree.
♦ *These sound alike* **bough, bow², bow³.**

bought | bôt | The past tense and past participle of the verb **buy**: *They bought a stove at the garage sale. We have bought from that store since it opened.*

boul·der | bōl′dər | —*noun, plural* **boulders** A large round rock on or in the ground.

boul·e·vard | bŏŏl′ə värd′ | or | bōō′lə värd′ | —*noun, plural* **boulevards** A broad street in a city.

bounce | bouns | —*verb* **bounced, bouncing** **1.** To hit a surface and spring back one or more times: *The ball bounced across the street.* **2.** To cause something to hit a surface and spring back: *She bounced the ball on the ground.* **3.** To move up and down in a lively or jumpy way: *She bounced on the bed.*
—*noun, plural* **bounces** A bounding movement; a spring: *The ball crossed the street in three bounces.*

bound¹ | bound | —*verb* **bounded, bounding** **1.** To leap, jump, or spring: *He bounded over the barrel and finished the race.* **2.** To hit a surface and spring back; bounce: *The ball went over the fence and bounded off the top of a car.*
—*noun, plural* **bounds** A leap, jump, or spring: *The horse cleared the fence with a bound and galloped off.*

bound² | bound | —*noun, plural* **bounds** Often **bounds** The farthest edge; boundary; limit: *He stayed inside the bounds of the city. His imagination traveled beyond the bounds of the universe.*
—*verb* **bounded, bounding** To mark the limiting edge of; be the boundary of: *Rivers bounded the city on three sides.*

bound³ | bound | The past tense and past participle of the verb **bind**: *She bound the twigs together with string. She had bound the package with a ribbon.*
—*adjective* **1.** Certain; sure: *We are bound to be late because of this traffic.* **2.** Under obligation; obliged: *He felt bound by his duty to his country.* **3.** In a cover or binding: *She bought a set of bound books for Christmas.*

bound⁴ | bound | —*adjective* Ready to go; going in the direction:

bottle
Above: Bottles on a conveyer belt
Below: Inside a bottling plant

bound¹, bound², bound⁴
Bound¹ comes from a French word meaning "to bounce." Earlier this French word meant "to resound"; it came from a Latin word meaning "to buzz" or "a deep, hollow sound." The source of the Latin word was one used a very long time ago by the Greeks. **Bound²** also comes from an old French word, one that meant "a boundary." **Bound⁴** comes from a word used long ago in English to mean "prepared or ready to go." Earlier still it came from a word used by people who lived in Scandinavia to mean "to dwell" or "to prepare."

bouquet

bow¹

bow¹, bow², bow³
Bow¹ and bow² have always meant pretty much what they mean today. Bow¹ meant "an arch," and bow² meant "to bend." Both came from the same form in the prehistoric language from which English and many other languages spoken today descended. Bow³ was used long ago in English but came to English from a form of German spoken in northern Germany. There the word was, of course, spelled and pronounced differently; it meant both "shoulder" and "bow of a ship."

bowl¹, bowl²
Bowl¹ comes from an old English word that meant "a pot" or "a bowl." Bowl² originally came from a French word meaning "a ball." The French word came from a Latin one meaning "a ball" or "a bubble."

ă	pat	ĕ	pet	î	fierce
ā	pay	ē	be	ŏ	pot
â	care	ĭ	pit	ō	go
ä	father	ī	pie	ô	paw, for
oi	oil	ŭ	cut	zh	vision
ōō	book	û	fur	ə	ago, item,
ōō	boot	th	the		pencil, atom,
yōō	abuse	th	thin		circus
ou	out	hw	which	ər	butter

Take the eastward-bound train. We are bound for Mexico.

bound·a·ry |boun′də rē| or |boun′drē| —*noun, plural* **boundaries** An edge, limit, or dividing line between one place or thing and another; a border: *A bridge took us across the boundary between Canada and the United States.*

boun·ti·ful |boun′tə fəl| —*adjective* Providing more than enough; plentiful; abundant: *The crops are bountiful this year.*

bou·quet |bō kā′| or |bōō kā′| —*noun, plural* **bouquets** A bunch of flowers, especially when they are tied together.

bout |bout| —*noun, plural* **bouts** **1.** A contest: *a boxing bout.* **2.** A period of time; a spell: *a bout of illness.*

bow¹ |bō| —*noun, plural* **bows** **1.** A weapon for shooting arrows. A bow is made of a curved piece of wood or other material with a string stretched tightly from one tip to the other. **2.a.** A knot tied with loops: *He tied the string in a bow.* **b.** A ribbon tied with loops and used as a decoration. **3.** A slender stick with horsehair stretched from end to end, used to play a violin, viola, cello, and some other stringed instruments.

bow² |bou| —*verb* **bowed, bowing** **1.** To bend the body, head, or knee to show greeting, respect, or worship: *They bowed their heads in prayer. He bowed to his partner after the waltz.* **2.** To give in; yield; submit: *Because they refused to bow to the king's wishes, they were jailed.*
—*noun, plural* **bows** The act of bending the body or head as a sign of respect, thanks, greeting, or worship: *The actor made several bows as the audience applauded.*
♦ *These sound alike* **bow²**, **bough**, **bow³**.

bow³ |bou| —*noun, plural* **bows** The front part of a ship or boat.
♦ *These sound alike* **bow³**, **bough**, **bow²**.

bow·els |bou′əlz| or |boulz| —*plural noun* **1.** The intestines. The bowels carry matter through the body. **2.** The part deep inside of something: *in the bowels of the earth.*

bowl¹ |bōl| —*noun, plural* **bowls** **1.** A round, hollow dish or container: *a salad bowl; a mixing bowl; a goldfish bowl.* **2.a.** A bowl with something in it: *a bowl of cherries.* **b.** The amount that a bowl holds: *He ate two bowls of chili for lunch.* **3.** The curved, hollow part of an object: *the bowl of a spoon; the bowl of a pipe.* **4.** A bowl-shaped stadium or arena for sports or entertainment.
♦ *These sound alike* **bowl, boll.**

bowl² |bōl| —*verb* **bowled, bowling** **1.** To play the game of bowling: *He bowls well and often wins.* **2.** To take a turn or roll a ball in bowling: *You bowl first.*
♦ *These sound alike* **bowl, boll.**

bow·leg·ged |bō′lĕg′ĭd| or |bō′lĕgd| —*adjective* Having legs that curve outward at the knees.

bowl·ing |bō′lĭng| —*noun* Any of several games in which a large, heavy ball is rolled down a wooden alley to try to knock over wooden pins. Some games of bowling use ten wooden pins, others use nine.

bow·man |bō′mən| —*noun, plural* **bowmen** A person who shoots with a bow and arrow; an archer.

bow·string |bō′strĭng′| —*noun, plural* **bowstrings** The string of a bow, stretched tight for shooting arrows.

box¹ |bŏks| —*noun, plural* **boxes** **1.** A container made of a stiff material such as cardboard, wood, metal, or plastic. A box often

has four sides, a bottom, and a lid or cover: *a cereal box; a hat box; a shoe box.* **2. a.** A box with something in it: *He bought a box of crayons.* **b.** The amount a box holds: *He ate a whole box of cookies.* **3.** Anything shaped like a box or closed in like a box: *a theater box; a sentry box.* **4.** A rectangle or square: *She drew a box around her name on the drawing.*
—*verb* **boxed, boxing 1.** To put or pack in a box: *She boxed the gift and wrapped it.* **2.** To draw a rectangle or square around: *He boxed the correct answers on the test.*

box² | bŏks | —*verb* **boxed, boxing 1.** To fight with the fists: *Whom will the champion box next time?* **2.** To hit or slap with the hand, especially on the ear.
—*noun, plural* **boxes** A blow with the hand: *a box on the ear.*

box·car | bŏks′kär′ | —*noun, plural* **boxcars** A railway car that is closed on all sides and on the top. It is used to carry freight.

box·er¹ | bŏk′sər | —*noun, plural* **boxers** A person who fights with his fists.

box·er² | bŏk′sər | —*noun, plural* **boxers** A medium-sized dog with a short, smooth, brownish coat and a short, square face.

box·ing | bŏk′sĭng | —*noun* The sport of fighting an opponent with the fists, usually with padded gloves, following special rules.

boy | boi | —*noun, plural* **boys** A male child who is not yet a man.

boy·cott | boi′kŏt′ | —*noun, plural* **boycotts** The effort of a group of people working together to refuse to use, buy from, or deal with a store, company, person, or nation. A boycott is used as a way of protesting or forcing a change.
—*verb* **boycotted, boycotting** To take part in a boycott against: *Students boycotted the store because it charged unfair prices.*

boy·hood | boi′hŏŏd′ | —*noun, plural* **boyhoods** The time of life when one is a boy: *He had a happy boyhood.*

boy·ish | boi′ĭsh | —*adjective* Of, like, or suitable for a boy: *The man gave a boyish grin when he spotted the electric trains.*

boy scout A member of the Boy Scouts.

Boy Scouts An organization for boys to help them develop good citizenship, good character, and outdoor skills.

brace | brās | —*noun, plural* **braces 1.** A device that holds two or more parts together or that helps to support something: *We added a brace to the loose leg of the table.* **2.** A medical device used to support an injured part of the body: *He had to wear a brace on his leg after the accident.* **3. braces** An arrangement of wires and bands used for straightening a person's teeth. **4.** A handle used to hold the bit of a drill. **5.** A pair: *He caught a brace of pheasants.*
—*verb* **braced, bracing 1.** To support or strengthen: *We braced the old walls with timbers.* **2.** To prepare for something difficult or unpleasant: *They braced themselves for the dive into the icy water.* **3.** To fill with energy or strength; refresh: *The clear air braced the skiers for the run down the hill.*

brace·let | brās′lĭt | —*noun, plural* **bracelets** A band or chain that is worn around the wrist or arm as jewelry or for identification.

brack·et | brăk′ĭt | —*noun, plural* **brackets 1.** A support that is fastened to a wall to hold something up. Brackets may be used to support a shelf. **2.** Either of the symbols [ ], used to enclose letters, words, or numerals in written or printed material. **3.** A

box¹, box²
Box¹ has been used — and spelled — the same way in English ever since about the eighth century. Earlier still it came from a Latin word that itself came from a Greek word meaning "box tree." A box tree was a tree whose hard wood may have been used in making boxes. We know that **box²** was in use in English about the years 1100 to 1500, but we do not know anything about its history before that time.

boxcar

boxer²

boxer¹, boxer²
Boxer¹ is related to **box²** by the addition of the ending **-er**, which here shows that someone does the action of the verb to which the ending is added. So **boxer¹** is someone who boxes. **Boxer²** is related to **boxer¹**; the word was borrowed from English into German to refer to a kind of dog with a quarrelsome nature.

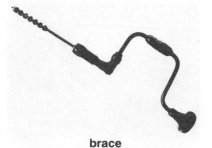

brace

group or category: *The pupils are in the 7-to-12 age bracket.*
—*verb* **bracketed, bracketing** **1.** To put brackets around words or numbers. **2.** To consider as a group or category: *He bracketed the 2-to-4-year-olds as the nursery group.*

brad |brăd| —*noun, plural* **brads** A thin nail with a small head.

brag |brăg| —*verb* **bragged, bragging** To praise oneself or the things one owns or has done; to boast: *She often brags about her house. He brags so much that nobody wants to listen to him.*

braid |brād| —*verb* **braided, braiding** To weave three or more strands together into a rope shape: *The baker braided the dough to make a fancy loaf. She braided her daughter's hair.*
—*noun, plural* **braids** **1.** A piece of hair that has been braided like a rope: *She wore her hair in braids.* **2.** A strip of braided material: *a trim of blue braid around the edge of the draperies.*

Braille or **braille** |brāl| —*noun* A system of writing and printing for blind people. In Braille, different patterns of raised dots represent letters, words, numbers, and punctuation marks. A blind person reads by feeling the dot patterns with the finger tips.

brain |brān| —*noun, plural* **brains** **1.** The large mass of gray nerve tissue inside the skull of an animal with a backbone. The brain is the center of thinking, feeling, learning, and remembering. It also controls many of the body's activities. **2.** The human mind: *The plan took shape slowly in his brain.* **3.** **brains** Intelligence: *She has both brains and good sense.*
—*verb* **brained, braining** To hit hard on the head.

brake |brāk| —*noun, plural* **brakes** A part of a vehicle, wheel, or machine that can stop or slow down its motion.
—*verb* **braked, braking** To slow down or stop by using one or more brakes: *He braked the train as it entered the station.*
♦ *These sound alike* **brake, break.**

bram·ble |brăm′bəl| —*noun, plural* **brambles** A prickly plant or shrub. Blackberry and raspberry plants are brambles.

bran |brăn| —*noun* The outer covering of grains like wheat, rye, and oats. When flour is made, the bran is usually sifted out. It is used in some cereals and breads, and in animal foods.

branch |brănch| or |bränch| —*noun, plural* **branches** **1.** One of the parts that grow out from the trunk or limbs of a tree or shrub. A large branch may have smaller branches growing from it. **2.** Any part that is a division of a larger thing: *the judicial branch of government. One branch of our family lives in Ohio.*
—*verb* **branched, branching** To divide or spread into branches: *The road branches into two forks.*

brand |brănd| —*noun, plural* **brands** **1.a.** A name or symbol that identifies a product; a trademark: *Look for the "Yellowsweet" brand on every banana you buy.* **b.** The make of a product marked in this way: *a new brand of soup* **2.** A style or type; a kind: *her strange brand of humor.* **3.** A mark burned into the skin. Brands are used on cattle to show who owns them. Brands were once used on criminals as a sign of shame or disgrace.
—*verb* **branded, branding** **1.** To mark with a brand: *Cowboys branded the calves.* **2.** To mark or label with shame or disgrace: *The people branded him a liar.*

brand-new |brănd′nōo′| or |brănd′nyōo′| —*adjective* Completely new; not used.

brass |brăs| —*noun, plural* **brasses** **1.** A yellowish metal that contains copper and zinc. **2.** Things made of brass, such as

Braille
The fingertips are used to feel the dot patterns.

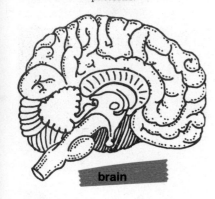

brain

ă	pat	ĕ	pet	î	fierce
ā	pay	ē	be	ŏ	pot
â	care	ĭ	pit	ō	go
ä	father	ī	pie	ô	paw, for
oi	oil	ŭ	cut	zh	vision
ōō	book	û	fur	ə	ago, item,
ōō	boot	*th*	the		pencil, atom,
yōō	abuse	th	thin		circus
ou	out	hw	which	ər	butter

candlesticks, bowls, and furniture: *She polishes the brass every Wednesday.* **3.** Often **brasses** The group of musical instruments that includes the trumpet, trombone, French horn, and tuba.

brat | brăt | —*noun, plural* **brats** A nasty or spoiled child.

brave | brāv | —*adjective* **braver, bravest** Having or showing courage; able to overcome fear or pain: *brave people.*
—*noun, plural* **braves** A North American Indian warrior.
—*verb* **braved, braving** To face danger in a courageous way: *They braved the winter storm to rescue the trapped skiers.*

brav·er·y | brā′ və rē | or | brāv′ rē | —*noun* The quality of being brave; courage: *He received an award after the war for his bravery.*

breach | brēch | —*noun, plural* **breaches** A gap or a hole that makes a break in something solid: *Water poured through the breach in the dike.*
—*verb* **breached, breaching** To make a hole or gap in; break through: *Soldiers breached the enemy's line.*

bread | brĕd | —*noun, plural* **breads** **1.** A food made from flour or meal mixed with water or milk and baked in an oven.
2. a. Food in general: *"Give us this day our daily bread." (The Bible, Matthew 6:11).* **b.** The things one needs to stay alive; livelihood: *He earned his bread as a farm laborer.*
♦ *These sound alike* **bread, bred.**

breadth | brĕdth | —*noun, plural* **breadths** The distance from side to side; width: *He measured the length and breadth of the table.*

break | brāk | —*verb* **broke, broken, breaking** **1.** To crack, split, or burst into two or more pieces; come apart or take apart: *The mirror broke when she dropped it. Glass breaks easily.* **2.** To pull apart; to separate: *Don't break the branch from the tree.* **3.** To crack a bone of: *He broke his leg in a skiing accident. His arm broke and he had to wear a cast.* **4.** To damage or become damaged; ruin or become ruined: *Dad broke the electric trains. Her watch broke and couldn't be fixed.* **5.** To fail to keep or follow: *She broke her promise. I did not break the law.* **6.** To appear or come about suddenly: *Will the sun break through the clouds? A storm broke and drenched us all.* **7.** To stop; end: *He is trying to break his habit of smoking.* **8.** To change pitch suddenly: *His voice broke as he told the sad story* **9.** To do better than; go beyond; surpass: *Will he break the record for the pole vault?* **10.** To make or become known: *Who will break the bad news to mother? The story of the victory broke in all the newspapers.* **11.** To fill or be filled with sorrow: *The sad news broke her heart. His heart broke when she died.*

 Phrasal verbs **break down 1.** To fail to work properly: *The car broke down on the highway.* **2.** To separate into parts; itemize: *He broke down the project into individual jobs.* **3.** To become very upset: *She broke down and cried.* **break in 1.** To enter by force; force one's way in: *Burglars broke in and stole our television set.* **2.** To train or prepare for a new job or for new use: *She broke in a new secretary. He will break in his new shoes slowly.* **break into** To enter by force; force one's way into: *Burglars broke into the house and stole jewelry and money.* **break up 1.** To separate into smaller parts: *Can you break up "unusual" into its syllables? The crowd broke up after the game ended.* **2.** To bring to an end or come to an end: *He broke up the fight in the yard. The marriage broke up.* **3.** To end a friendship or marriage: *They broke up after the argument.* **4.** To burst or cause to burst into laughter: *The audience broke up during the funny scene. The clown broke up the audience.*

brave
An Indian brave

bread

—*noun, plural* **breaks** **1.** A broken place; an opening, crack, or gap: *a break in a bone; a break in the clouds.* **2.** An interruption; a pause or rest: *a break in the talks; a break in an electric circuit; a break for lunch.* **3.** An attempt to escape: *a jail break.* **4.** A sudden run: *a break for freedom.* **5.** A sudden change: *a break in the weather; a break with the past.* **6.** An unexpected chance or event: *He got a lucky break and became the star of the show.*
♦ *These sound alike* **break, brake.**

break·down | brāk′doun′ | —*noun, plural* **breakdowns** **1.** A failure to work properly: *the breakdown of a truck on the highway.* **2.** A loss of health of the body or mind or both: *Too much hard work led to the man's breakdown.*

break·er | brā′kər | —*noun, plural* **breakers** A wave that breaks into foam when it reaches shore.

break·fast | brĕk′fəst | —*noun, plural* **breakfasts** The first meal of the day.
—*verb* **breakfasted, breakfasting:** To eat breakfast: *They breakfasted on fruit and rolls.*

breast | brĕst | —*noun, plural* **breasts** **1.** The front part of the body from the neck to the abdomen; chest; bosom. **2.** A gland in a female mammal that produces milk. **3.** The center of feelings and emotions; heart; bosom: *He felt love awakening in his breast.*

breast·bone | brĕst′bōn′ | —*noun, plural* **breastbones** The bone in the center of the breast, to which the ribs and collarbones are attached.

breath | brĕth | —*noun, plural* **breaths** **1.** The air that is taken into the lungs and forced out when one breathes. **2.** The ability to breathe easily: *He lost his breath after the fast run.* **3.** The act of breathing. **4.** A single instance of taking in air: *The singer took a deep breath.* **5.** A slight breeze: *There was not a breath of air on that hot day.*

breathe | brēth | —*verb* **breathed, breathing** **1.** To take in and force out air from the lungs: *All mammals must breathe to stay alive.* **2.** To say in a most quiet way; whisper: *Don't breathe a word of our plan to anybody.*

breath·less | brĕth′lĭs | —*adjective* **1.** Out of breath; panting: *He was breathless after running all the way home.* **2.** Holding the breath because of fear, excitement, or interest: *The passengers were breathless as the plane attempted the emergency landing.*

breath·tak·ing | brĕth′tā′kĭng | —*adjective* Filling with wonder; very exciting: *a breathtaking view from an airplane. She gave a breathtaking performance.*

bred | brĕd | The past tense and past participle of the verb **breed:** *We bred gerbils for the pet store. They have bred horses on their farm for over a hundred years.*
♦ *These sound alike* **bred, bread.**

breech·es | brĭch′ĭz | —*plural noun* **1.** Short trousers that are fastened at or just below the knees. **2.** Any trousers.

breed | brēd | —*verb* **bred, breeding** **1.** To produce offspring: *Mosquitoes breed rapidly. This mare has bred some champion race horses.* **2.** To raise animals or plants: *Mr. Jones breeds cattle, and his brother breeds roses.* **3.** To rear or train; bring up: *His parents tried to breed him to behave like a gentleman.*
—*noun, plural* **breeds** A particular type or variety of animal or plant that has been produced from a selected group of parents: *Poodles and beagles are breeds of dog.*

breaker

breeches

ă	pat	ĕ	pet	î	fierce
ā	pay	ē	be	ŏ	pot
â	care	ĭ	pit	ō	go
ä	father	ī	pie	ô	paw, for
oi	oil	ŭ	cut	zh	vision
ŏŏ	book	û	fur	ə	ago, item,
ōō	boot	*th*	the		pencil, atom,
yōō	abuse	th	thin		circus
ou	out	hw	which	ər	butter

breed·ing |brē′dĭng| —*noun* The way someone is trained in the proper forms of behavior and conduct: *Rosalie's good manners with the elderly ladies showed her good breeding.*

breeze |brēz| —*noun, plural* **breezes** A gentle movement of air. —*verb* **breezed, breezing** To move quickly and easily: *The girls breezed into the room. He breezed through the test and did well.*

breve |brĕv| or |brēv| —*noun, plural* **breves** A mark (˘) placed over a vowel in a pronunciation to show that the vowel is short. In the pronunciation of the word "bat," (băt), the breve is placed over the "a".

brew |brōō| —*verb* **brewed, brewing** **1.** To make beer or ale. Beer and ale are made by soaking, boiling and fermenting malt and hops. **2.** To make other drinks by soaking, boiling, or mixing: *The longer you brew tea, the stronger it gets. The coffee is brewing in the pot.* **3.** To think up; plan or plot: *He brewed a scheme for making money during his vacation.* **4.** To begin to take form; threaten to occur: *A storm is brewing.*
—*noun, plural* **brews** A drink made by brewing.

bri·ar |brī′ər| —*noun, plural* **briars** A form of the word **brier.**

bribe |brīb| —*noun, plural* **bribes** Money or something else valuable that is offered or given to make a person do something dishonest: *The policeman refused to take a bribe to let the thief go.*
—*verb* **bribed, bribing** To offer or give a bribe to: *He bribed the reporter not to write the story.*

brick |brĭk| —*noun, plural* **bricks** **1.** A block of clay that has been baked by the sun or in an oven until hard. Bricks are used for building and for paving. **2.** Bricks considered together or as a kind of building material: *The house is made of red brick.* **3.** Any object shaped like a brick: *a brick of cheese.*

bride |brīd| —*noun, plural* **brides** A woman who is about to be married or who has just been married.

bride·groom |brīd′grōōm′| or |brīd′grŏŏm′| —*noun, plural* **bridegrooms** A man who is about to be married or who has just been married; a groom.

bridge |brĭj| —*noun, plural* **bridges** **1.** Something built across a river, railroad track, road, or other obstacle so that people or vehicles can cross over from one side to the other; a span. **2.** The upper bony part of the human nose. **3.** A platform above the main deck of a ship. The officer in charge controls the ship from the bridge.
—*verb* **bridged, bridging** To build a bridge over or across: *The Army has made plans to bridge the river before the waterfall.*

bri·dle |brī′dl| —*noun, plural* **bridles** The straps, bit, and reins that fit over a horse's head and are used to control the animal.
—*verb* **bridled, bridling** **1.** To put a bridle on: *He always bridles his own horse.* **2.** To control: *It is hard to bridle my anger.*

brief |brēf| —*adjective* **briefer, briefest** Short in time or length: *a brief rest; a brief letter.*
—*verb* **briefed, briefing** To give detailed instructions, information, or advice to: *The staff briefed the President about the country he was about to visit. The police captain briefed his officers before the raid.*

bri·er |brī′ər| —*noun, plural* **briers** A thorny plant or bush, especially a rosebush with prickly stems. Another form of this word is **briar.**

brig |brĭg| —*noun, plural* **brigs** **1.** A sailing ship with two masts and square sails. **2.** A prison on a ship.

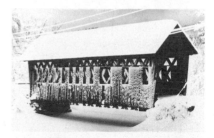

bridge

Above: New England covered bridge
Below: The Golden Gate Bridge, San Francisco

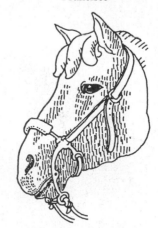

bridle

brig

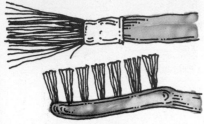

bristle

Above: Bristles on a walrus
Below: Brushes with bristles

ă	pat	ĕ	pet	î	fierce
ā	pay	ē	be	ŏ	pot
â	care	ĭ	pit	ō	go
ä	father	ī	pie	ô	paw, for
oi	oil	ŭ	cut	zh	vision
ŏŏ	book	û	fur	ə	ago, item,
ōō	boot	*th*	the		pencil, atom,
yōō	abuse	th	thin		circus
ou	out	hw	which	ər	butter

bri·gade | brĭ gād′ | —*noun, plural* **brigades** **1.** A large army unit. In the United States Army a brigade has two or more regiments. **2.** A group organized for a special purpose: *Our town's fire brigade fights fires.*

bright | brīt | —*adjective* **brighter, brightest** **1.** Giving off much light; shining: *The bright sun shone through the branches. The bright silver and crystal made the table sparkle.* **2.** Vivid or strong in color; having little or no black, gray, or white: *a clear bright green; the bright colors of the beach umbrella.* **3.** Smart; clever: *He's a bright boy with many bright ideas.* **4.** Happy; cheerful: *a bright, smiling face; a bright tune; a bright view of the future.*

bright·ness | brīt′ nĭs | —*noun* **1.** The condition or quality of being bright: *We were pleased with the brightness of the day.* **2.** The measure of how bright a color or object is.

bril·liant | brĭl′ yənt | —*adjective* **1.** Full of light; shining brightly; very bright: *a brilliant sun blazing in the sky.* **2.** Magnificent; splendid; excellent: *She gave a brilliant concert.* **3.** Very high in intelligence or ability: *He is a brilliant inventor.*

brim | brĭm | —*noun, plural* **brims** **1.** The rim or upper edge of a cup, glass, or other hollow object: *He filled the glass to the brim.* **2.** The part of a hat that stands out from the crown.
—*verb* **brimmed, brimming** To be full to the brim or to seem to be full to the brim: *Her eyes brimmed with tears.*

brine | brīn | —*noun* Water that contains a lot of salt and is used to prepare certain foods: *The pickles were packed in brine.*

bring | brĭng | —*verb* **brought, bringing** **1.** To take or carry along with oneself: *Please bring me a glass of water. He brought a friend to the party. Did you remember to bring your lunch?* **2.** To be accompanied by: *Spring brings flowers. The flood brought death to many. The story brought tears to her eyes.*
Phrasal verbs **bring about** To be the cause of; cause: *Good food and lots of rest brought about a change in her health.* **bring forth** To produce or to bear: *The trees brought forth fruit, and the animals brought forth their young.* **bring up** To raise or rear a child: *After his parents died, his aunt brought him up.*

brink | brĭngk | —*noun, plural* **brinks** **1.** The upper edge of a high or steep place: *The boy stood at the brink of the canyon.* **2.** The very edge of something; verge: *at the brink of disaster.*

brisk | brĭsk | —*adjective* **brisker, briskest** **1.** Fast and lively; active: *We took a brisk trot along the road. The store made some brisk sales of umbrellas on the rainy day.* **2.** Fresh and keen; sharp: *It was a brisk morning, cold and windy.*

bris·tle | brĭs′əl | —*noun, plural* **bristles** A short, coarse, stiff hair. Hog bristles are often used to make brushes.
—*verb* **bristled, bristling** **1.** To raise the bristles stiffly: *The dog bristled and showed his teeth.* **2.** To stand up straight and stiff, like bristles: *His short hair bristled.* **3.** To show anger or irritation: *The boy bristled when she called him sweetheart.*

Brit·ain | brĭt′n | Great Britain.

Brit·ish | brĭt′ĭsh | —*adjective* Of Great Britain, its people, or their language: *The British word for "elevator" is "lift."*
—*noun* **the British** (Used with a plural verb.) The people of Great Britain.

British Co·lum·bi·a | kə lŭm′bē ə | The province of Canada that is farthest to the west. Capital, Victoria.

brit·tle | brĭt′l | —*adjective* **brittler, brittlest** Hard and easy to break; not flexible: *brittle bones; brittle crystal ornaments.*

broad |brôd| —*adjective* **broader, broadest 1.** Large from side to side; wide: *Four of us could sit on the broad bench.* **2.** Covering a wide range; having few limits: *We have a broad view of the road from here. He has a broad vocabulary.* **3.** Clear; bright: *I saw the accident in broad daylight.*

broad·cast |brôd′kăst′| or |brôd′käst′| —*verb* **broadcast** or **broadcasted, broadcasting 1.** To send out over radio or television: *The networks will broadcast the President's speech. The radio station broadcasts from noon to midnight.* **2.** To make known over a wide area: *He loves to broadcast rumors through the town.*
—*noun, plural* **broadcasts** Something that is sent out by radio or television; a radio or television program.

bro·cade |brō kād′| —*noun* A thick cloth with a rich, raised pattern woven into it. Brocade often has threads of silver, gold, or silk.

broc·co·li |brŏk′ə lē| —*noun* A plant with dark green stalks and flower buds that are eaten as a vegetable. Broccoli is related to the cabbage and the cauliflower.

broil |broil| —*verb* **broiled, broiling 1.** To cook directly under or over heat: *She broiled the chicken in the broiler. The fish broiled for 10 minutes.* **2.** To become or make very hot: *We broiled in the hot sun. The desert sun broiled the men in the caravan.*

broil·er |broi′lər| —*noun, plural* **broilers** A pan, open rack, or a part of a stove for broiling foods.

broke |brōk| The past tense of the verb **break:** *Louise broke her mirror.*

bro·ken |brō′kən| The past participle of the verb **break:** *The dishes were broken in the dishwasher.*
—*adjective* **1.** Not whole; in pieces; shattered: *a broken cup; a broken chair.* **2.** Not working properly; out of order: *a broken watch.* **3.** Not kept: *a broken promise.* **4.** Overcome by sadness or difficulty: *a broken heart; a broken spirit.* **5.** Rough; uneven: *patches of broken ground.*

bron·chi·al tube |brŏng′kē əl| Any of the large or small tubes in the lungs that form branches of the windpipe. The bronchial tubes help us breathe.

bron·chi·tis |brŏng kī′tĭs| —*noun* An illness caused by an infection or swelling of the bronchial tubes. People who have bronchitis may have a severe cough, a hoarse voice, and a fever.

bron·co |brŏng′kō| —*noun, plural* **broncos** A small wild or partly tamed horse of western North America.

bron·to·saur |brŏn′tə sôr′| —*noun, plural* **brontosaurs** A very large dinosaur with a long neck and a long tail. Brontosaurs lived in swamps and streams and ate plants.

bronze |brŏnz| —*noun* **1.** A hard metal made of copper and tin and sometimes other elements. Bronze is used for statues, machine parts, bells, and many other useful items. **2.** A yellowish brown color. ◊ The noun **bronze** can be used like an adjective for things made of bronze: *a bronze medal for third place.*
—*adjective* Yellowish brown: *a bronze silk dress.*
—*verb* **bronzed, bronzing** To make or become the color of bronze: *The sun bronzed her skin. Her skin bronzes easily.*

brooch |brōch| or |broōch| —*noun, plural* **brooches** A large pin worn as an ornament. A brooch is fastened with a clasp.

brood |broōd| —*noun, plural* **broods 1.** A group of young birds

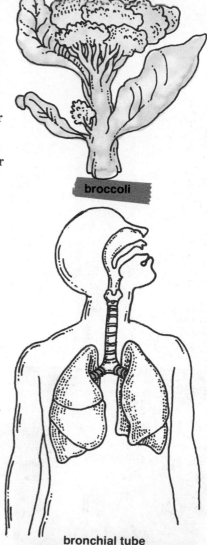

broccoli

bronchial tube

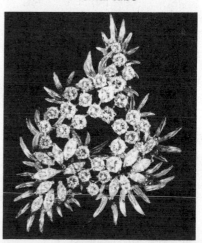

brooch

that are hatched from eggs laid at the same time by one mother.
2. The children in one family.
—*verb* **brooded, brooding 1.** To sit on eggs so they will hatch.
2. To worry or think about in an unhappy way for a long time:
He brooded about the test he had failed.

brook | brŏok | —*noun, plural* **brooks** A small natural stream of fresh water.

broom | brōom | or | brŏom | —*noun, plural* **brooms 1.** A tool used for sweeping. A broom has a long handle with straw bristles or a brush at one end. **2.** A shrub with yellow flowers, small leaves, and many straight, slender branches.

broth | brôth | or | brŏth | —*noun, plural* **broths 1.** The water in which meat, fish, or vegetables have been boiled or simmered.
2. A thin soup made from this water.

broth·er | brŭ*th*′ ər | —*noun, plural* **brothers 1.** A boy or man who has the same parents as another person. **2.a.** A fellow man.
b. A male member of the same group, club, profession, or religion.

broth·er·hood | brŭ*th*′ ər hŏod′ | —*noun* **1.** The close feeling or friendship between brothers or other men. **2.** A group of men who are united in an organization or club.

broth·er·in·law | brŭ*th*′ ər ĭn lô′ | —*noun, plural* **brothers-in-law**
1. The brother of one's husband or wife. **2.** The husband of one's sister. **3.** The husband of the sister of one's husband or wife.

broth·er·ly | brŭ*th*′ ər lē | —*adjective* Of or appropriate to a brother; warm and friendly: *brotherly advice.*

brought | brôt | The past tense and past participle of the verb **bring:** *She brought her lunch to school with her. I have brought a friend to the party.*

brow | brou | —*noun, plural* **brows 1.** The part of the face between the eyes and the line of the hair; forehead: *He wiped the sweat from his brow.* **2.** One of the two arches of hair above the eyes; an eyebrow.

brown | broun | —*noun, plural* **browns** The color of chocolate, coffee, or most kinds of soil.
—*adjective* **browner, brownest** Of the color brown: *a brown leather belt; brown velvet.*
—*verb* **browned, browning 1.** To cook until the outside is brown: *He browned the chicken in oil.* **2.** To make or become brown: *The sun browned his skin. The leaves browned in the hot weather.*

brown·ie | brou′nē | —*noun, plural* **brownies 1.** A small imaginary creature like an elf. A brownie is supposed to do helpful deeds while people sleep. **2.** A small, chewy chocolate cake that often has nuts in it.

Brown·ie | brou′nē | —*noun, plural* **Brownies** A girl who is a member of the Brownies, a junior division of the Girl Scouts.

brown·ish | brou′nĭsh | —*adjective* Somewhat brown: *The leaves had a brownish color at the edges.*

browse | brouz | —*verb* **browsed, browsing** To look at or read in a casual way: *He likes to browse before buying anything. She browsed through some books in the library.*

bruise | brōoz | —*noun, plural* **bruises 1.** An injury that leaves a mark on the skin but does not break the skin: *He received some bad bruises but no broken bones from his accident.* **2.** An injury to the outside of a fruit or vegetable, caused by dropping or rough handling.

Brownie

ă	pat	ĕ	pet	î	fierce
ā	pay	ē	be	ŏ	pot
â	care	ĭ	pit	ō	go
ä	father	ī	pie	ô	paw, for
oi	oil	ŭ	cut	zh	vision
ōo	book	û	fur	ə	ago, item,
ōo	boot	*th*	the		pencil, atom,
yōo	abuse	th	thin		circus
ou	out	hw	which	ər	butter

—*verb* **bruised, bruising** To make or receive bruises on: *The fall bruised his face and knees. Pears bruise easily.*

brunet or **brunette** | broo nĕt' | —*adjective* Having hair that is dark or dark brown in color: *a brunet boy; a brunette girl.*
—*noun, plural* **brunets** or **brunettes** A person with hair that is dark or dark brown in color. Often the spelling **brunet** is used for males and **brunette** for females.

brush¹ | brŭsh | —*noun, plural* **brushes** **1.** A tool for scrubbing, grooming, or applying liquids. A brush usually is made of bristles attached to a hard back or a handle. **2.** The act of using a brush: *Give the coat a good brush to remove the lint.* **3.** Something that resembles a brush, especially the tail of a fox or other animal. **4.** A light touch in passing: *I felt the brush of his cape going by.*
—*verb* **brushed, brushing** **1.** To clean, polish, sweep, or groom with a brush: *He brushes his teeth three times a day.* **2.** To put on or take off with a brush: *Brush the corn with melted butter. He brushed on some paint.* **3.** To give a light touch in passing: *The ball just brushed her shoulder, so it didn't hurt her.*

brush² | brŭsh | —*noun* **1.** An area with a thick growth of shrubs and small trees. **2.** Branches and twigs that have broken off or been cut off: *They gathered some brush for a fire.*

Brus·sels sprouts | brŭs'əlz | The buds of a kind of cabbage. They grow on a thick stalk and look like small heads of cabbage. Brussels sprouts are cooked and eaten as a vegetable.

bru·tal | broot'l | —*adjective* Cruel and harsh like a brute; savage: *They made a brutal attack on the enemy.*

brute | broot | —*noun, plural* **brutes** **1.** An animal other than a human being; a beast. **2.** A cruel and harsh person who does not seem to have human feelings.

bub·ble | bŭb'əl | —*noun, plural* **bubbles** **1.** A thin film of liquid, shaped like a ball, that has air or gas trapped inside it. Bubbles often form from soapy water and can float in the air. They also form in boiling water. **2.** A round pocket of air or gas inside a liquid or solid. This type of bubble can be found in plastic, glass, and other solids. **3.** A dome of glass or plastic: *We play tennis under a bubble in cold weather.*
—*verb* **bubbled, bubbling** To form or rise in bubbles: *The soup bubbled on the stove. My soda is bubbling.*

buck | bŭk | —*noun, plural* **bucks** A male deer or antelope. A male rabbit is also called a buck.
—*verb* **bucked, bucking** **1.** To leap upward and forward suddenly with the head down: *The bronco bucked and kicked.* **2.** To charge into; go or work against: *The little boat bucked a strong wind. We will have to buck heavy traffic to get home.*

buck·et | bŭk'ĭt | —*noun, plural* **buckets** **1.** A round, open container with a handle, used for carrying such things as water, coal, sand, and milk; a pail. **2. a.** A bucket with something in it: *Please hand me that bucket of water.* **b.** The amount a bucket can hold: *The cow gave two buckets of milk.*

buck·le | bŭk'əl | —*noun, plural* **buckles** **1.** A clasp used to fasten one end of a belt or strap to the other. **2.** An ornament that looks like such a clasp: *She has silver buckles on her shoes.* **3.** A bend, bulge, or twist: *The heat caused a buckle in the sidewalk.*
—*verb* **buckled, buckling** **1.** To fasten with a buckle: *I can't buckle my sandal. Does your belt buckle or tie?* **2.** To bend, bulge,

brush¹, brush²
Brush¹ comes from an old French word meaning "a broom" or "a brush." **Brush²** comes from a word used long ago in French to mean "twigs" or "brushwood." Brooms and brushes have often been made of twigs. These two words may both have come from the same form in the prehistoric language from which many languages spoken today are descended.

Brussels sprouts

buckle
Ski boot with buckles

or twist: *My knees buckled when I tried to stand. The earthquake buckled the earth in many places.*

Phrasal verb **buckle down** To begin to work hard: *We finally buckled down and made some progress.*

buck·skin | bŭk′skĭn′ | —*noun, plural* **buckskins** A soft, strong, pale yellow leather made from the skin of a deer or sheep.

buck·wheat | bŭk′hwēt′ | or | bŭk′wēt′ | —*noun* A plant with seeds that are often ground into flour.

bud | bŭd | —*noun, plural* **buds** **1.** A plant part that contains a flower, stem, or leaves that have not yet developed. A bud usually looks like a small swelling on a stem or branch. **2.** A flower or leaf that has just begun to grow.

—*verb* **budded, budding** To form or produce a bud or buds: *The trees will soon bud.*

Bud·dha | bōō′də | or | bŏŏd′ə | The title of a great religious leader who lived in India about 2,500 years ago. The title means "the Enlightened One."

Bud·dhism | bōō′dĭz′əm | or | bŏŏd′ĭz′əm | —*noun* The beliefs and religion that are based on the teachings of Buddha. Buddhism is one of the major religions of Asia.

Bud·dhist | bōō′dĭst | or | bŏŏd′ĭst | —*noun, plural* **Buddhists** A person who believes in or practices the religion of Buddhism. —*adjective* Of Buddha or Buddhism: *a Buddhist priest.*

bud·dy | bŭd′ē | —*noun, plural* **buddies** A close friend; a pal.

budge | bŭj | —*verb* **budged, budging** To move or cause to move slightly: *The heavy rock would not budge. The strong men could not budge the door. His ideas are firm and he will not budge.*

bud·get | bŭj′ĭt | —*noun, plural* **budgets** A plan for how money will be spent. A household budget must include rent, food, clothing, and other expenses.

—*verb* **budgeted, budgeting** To plan in advance how to spend money or time: *He budgeted $50 for clothing this month but did not use it. She budgets her time so that she can finish her work.*

buff | bŭf | —*noun, plural* **buffs** **1.** A soft, thick, yellowish leather made from the skin of a buffalo, elk, or ox. **2.** The color of this leather; a yellowish tan. **3.** A tool that is used for polishing. A buff is usually a hard piece of wood or plastic covered with leather or with any strong, soft material.

—*adjective* Yellowish tan: *She wore buff cotton gloves.*

—*verb* **buffed, buffing** To polish or shine with a buff: *We buffed the car to a bright shine.*

buf·fa·lo | bŭf′ə lō′ | —*noun, plural* **buffaloes** or **buffalos** or **buffalo** **1.** An animal, the bison of North America. **2.** An African or Asian animal with curved, spreading horns. Another name for the animal is **water buffalo.**

buf·fet | bə fā′ | or | bōō fā′ | —*noun, plural* **buffets** **1.** A piece of furniture with a flat top from which food may be served. It also has drawers and shelves for holding china, silverware, and table linens. **2.** A meal at which guests may serve themselves from food set out on a table or buffet.

bug | bŭg | —*noun, plural* **bugs** **1.** A kind of insect that has mouth parts used for sucking. Some bugs have no wings, and some have four wings. **2.** Any insect or animal like an insect. Cockroaches, beetles, and spiders are often called bugs. **3.** A germ that causes a disease: *He was sick all winter from a bug he had caught.* **4.** Something wrong with a machine or a system; a fault:

Buddha

buffalo
Asian water buffalo

ă	pat	ĕ	pet	î	fierce
ā	pay	ē	be	ŏ	pot
â	care	ĭ	pit	ō	go
ä	father	ī	pie	ô	paw, for
oi	oil	ŭ	cut	zh	vision
ōō	book	û	fur	ə	ago, item,
ōō	boot	th	the		pencil, atom,
yōō	abuse	th	thin		circus
ou	out	hw	which	ər	butter

He must eliminate the bugs before he shows off his new invention. There are still some bugs in our plan. **5.** A small microphone that can be hidden to allow private conversations to be overheard: *The spy placed a bug in the telephone.*

—*verb* **bugged, bugging** To hide one or more microphones in a place to listen in on conversations: *The police bugged the home of the man they believed to be a gangster.*

bug·gy |bŭg′ē| —*noun, plural* **buggies 1.** A small, light carriage pulled by a horse. **2.** A baby carriage.

bu·gle |byōō′gəl| —*noun, plural* **bugles** A brass instrument that is like a trumpet. Bugles are used in the army and navy and at camps to call people for meals and other activities.

bu·gler |byōō′glər| —*noun, plural* **buglers** A person who plays a bugle.

build |bĭld| —*verb* **built, building 1.** To make or form something by putting parts or materials together; construct; erect: *Let's build a house out of wood and stone. The nation built a system of bridges and roads.* **2.** To make or form little by little; create and add to; develop: *Reading helps you build a better vocabulary.*

—*noun, plural* **builds** The way a person or thing is shaped or put together: *The dog has a square, sturdy build.*

build·ing |bĭl′dĭng| —*noun, plural* **buildings 1.** Something that is built. A house, store, school, barn, church, and a theater are buildings. **2.** The business or work of putting up or constructing buildings, railways, ships, bridges, and other structures.

built |bĭlt| The past tense and past participle of the verb **build**: *We built sand castles at the beach. My sister has built a very big stamp collection.*

bulb |bŭlb| —*noun, plural* **bulbs 1.** A rounded plant part that develops under the ground. A new plant grows from it. Tulips, daffodils, and onions grow from bulbs. **2.** A rounded part of anything: *the bulb of a thermometer.* **3.** A rounded glass lamp that fits into an electrical socket: *an electric light bulb.*

bulge |bŭlj| —*noun, plural* **bulges** A rounded part that swells out: *An apple made a bulge in his lunch bag.*

—*verb* **bulged, bulging** To swell or cause to swell beyond the usual size: *His suitcases bulged with things he had bought. Her eyes bulged with wonder. The stolen seeds bulged the chipmunk's cheeks.*

bulk |bŭlk| —*noun* **1.** Great size, volume, or mass: *A whale's bulk makes it look clumsier than it is.* **2.** The largest part of; greatest portion: *The bulk of his wealth went to charity.*

bull |bŏŏl| —*noun, plural* **bulls 1.** The full-grown male of cattle. **2.** The male of certain other large animals, such as the elephant.

bull·dog |bŏŏl′dôg′| or |bŏŏl′dŏg′| —*noun, plural* **bulldogs** A dog with short hair, a thick body, and short legs. It has a large head and strong, square jaws.

bull·doz·er |bŏŏl′dō′zər| —*noun, plural* **bulldozers** A large, powerful tractor with a heavy metal blade in front. Bulldozers are used for moving earth, rocks, and small trees.

bul·let |bŏŏl′ĭt| —*noun, plural* **bullets** A piece of metal made to be shot from a pistol, rifle, or other small gun.

bul·le·tin |bŏŏl′ĭ tn| or |bŏŏl′ĭ tĭn| —*noun, plural* **bulletins 1.** A short public announcement that gives the latest news about something: *The hospital issued a bulletin about the senator's health.* **2.** A small magazine or pamphlet published by an organization: *Our club bulletin appears four times a year.*

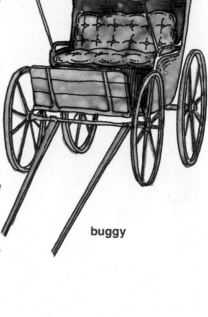

buggy

bulldog

bulldozer

bullfight

bumblebee

bull·fight | bŏŏl′fīt′ | —*noun, plural* **bullfights** A performance in which a person with assistants challenges and tries to kill a bull in an arena. Bullfights are popular in Spain, Mexico, and some parts of South America.

bull·frog | bŏŏl′frôg′ | or | bŏŏl′frŏg′ | —*noun, plural* **bullfrogs** A large frog with a loud, deep croak.

bull's eye **1.** The small circle that is the center of a target. **2.** A shot that lands in that small circle. Another form of this phrase is **bull's-eye.**

bull's-eye | bŏŏlz′ī′ | —*noun, plural* **bull's-eyes** A form of the phrase **bull's eye.**

bul·ly | bŏŏl′ē | —*noun, plural* **bullies** A person who likes to pick fights with, tease, or beat up smaller and weaker people.
—*verb* **bullied, bullying, bullies** To use strength or threats to hurt someone or to get what one wants: *She always bullies her little brother. He bullied her into doing his homework for him.*

bul·rush | bŏŏl′rŭsh′ | —*noun, plural* **bulrushes** A tall plant that grows in wet places. It has long leaves that look like grass.

bum·ble·bee | bŭm′bəl bē′ | —*noun, plural* **bumblebees** A large, hairy bee that flies with a humming sound.

bump | bŭmp | —*verb* **bumped, bumping** **1.** To knock or hit against: *He bumped into the wall. She bumped her head on the table.* **2.** To move with jerks and jolts: *The old car bumped down the road.*
—*noun, plural* **bumps** **1.** A knock, blow, hit, or jolt: *He gave me a bump on the head with his tennis racket.* **2.** A swelling from a blow or sting: *The blow left a bump on my forehead. My arm is full of bumps from mosquito bites.*

bump·er | bŭm′pər | —*noun, plural* **bumpers** Something used to soften a blow or protect against being hit or struck. The bumpers on a car usually are metal bars attached to the front and back.
—*adjective* Very large; abundant; plentiful: *The country grew a bumper crop of corn this year.*

bun | bŭn | —*noun, plural* **buns** **1.** A small bread roll. Many buns are sweet and have raisins, nuts, or spices. **2.** A roll of hair worn at the back or on the top of the head.

bunch | bŭnch | —*noun, plural* **bunches** **1.** A group of similar things that are growing, fastened, or placed together: *a bunch of daisies; a bunch of carrots; a bunch of keys.* **2.** A small group of people: *His friends are a pleasant bunch.*
—*verb* **bunched, bunching** To gather together in a group or cluster: *She bunched the flowers according to color.*

bun·dle | bŭn′dl | —*noun, plural* **bundles** **1.** A number of objects tied or wrapped together: *a bundle of sticks; a bundle of newspapers.* **2.** A package tied up for carrying: *We made up holiday bundles for the children in the hospital.*
—*verb* **bundled, bundling** **1.** To tie, wrap, or package together: *We bundled the logs for carrying.* **2.** To send or go quickly: *His mother bundled him off to school.* **3.** To dress in warm clothes: *It's cold today, so be sure to bundle up.*

bun·ga·low | bŭng′gə lō′ | —*noun, plural* **bungalows** A small house or cottage that is one story high.

bunk | bŭngk | —*noun, plural* **bunks** A narrow bed, often built like a shelf against the wall.

bun·ny | bŭn′ē | —*noun, plural* **bunnies** A rabbit: *the Easter bunny.*

ă	pat	ĕ	pet	î	fierce
ā	pay	ē	be	ŏ	pot
â	care	ĭ	pit	ō	go
ä	father	ī	pie	ô	paw, for
oi	oil	ŭ	cut	zh	vision
ŏŏ	book	û	fur	ə	ago, item,
ōō	boot	*th*	the		pencil, atom,
yōō	abuse	th	thin		circus
ou	out	hw	which	ər	butter

Bun·sen burner |bŭn′sən| A kind of small burner used in a laboratory. A Bunsen burner produces a very hot flame by using a mixture of gas and air.

bunt |bŭnt| —*verb* **bunted, bunting** To bat a baseball lightly so that it rolls slowly and does not go very far.
—*noun, plural* **bunts 1.** The act or result of bunting: *Jackson's bunt sent a runner to third base.* **2.** A ball that has been bunted.

bun·ting |bŭn′tĭng| —*noun, plural* **buntings 1.** A thin cotton or woolen cloth used for making flags **2.** Long strips of cloth using colors and decorations from a flag. Bunting is used for decoration on holidays and on special occasions.

buoy |bōō′ē| or |boi| —*noun, plural* **buoys 1.** A float used to mark dangerous places in a river, sea, or other body of water or to show where boats may safely go. **2.** A ring made of some material that floats.

bur |bûr| —*noun, plural* **burs** A seed or other plant part with a rough, prickly covering. Another form of this word is **burr**.

bur·den |bûr′dn| —*noun, plural* **burdens 1.** Something that is carried; a load: *The hikers carried their heavy burden up the mountain.* **2.** A duty; responsibility: *The children share the burden of cleaning up.* **3.** Something that is considered very hard to bear: *Supporting two families was a great burden to him.*
—*verb* **burdened, burdening** To load with something that is difficult to bear: *Too much heavy, wet snow burdened the branches of the tiny pine tree. Don't burden your memory with useless information.*

bu·reau |byŏŏr′ō| —*noun, plural* **bureaus 1.** A chest of drawers; dresser. **2.** An office for a particular kind of business: *a news bureau.* **3.** A department of a government: *the Federal Bureau of Investigation.*

bur·glar |bûr′glər| —*noun, plural* **burglars** A person who breaks into a house or other place to steal.

bur·i·al |bĕr′ē əl| —*noun, plural* **burials** The act of placing a dead body in a grave, the sea, or another final resting place.

bur·lap |bûr′lăp′| —*noun* A coarse cloth woven of thick fibers of hemp, jute, or flax. Burlap is used to make bags, sacks, curtains, and wrappings.

burn |bûrn| —*verb* **burned** or **burnt, burning 1.** To set fire to or be on fire: *He burned charcoal to cook the steaks. The logs burned in the fireplace.* **2.** To hurt, damage, or destroy with fire or heat: *She burned her hand on the hot stove.* **3.** To be hurt, damaged, or destroyed by fire, heat, or chemicals: *The house burned to the ground.* **4.** To injure or destroy with certain chemicals: *The acid burned the cloth.* **5.** To feel or cause to feel hot: *Her forehead burned with fever. The spicy food burned his mouth.* **6.** To use as fuel: *Does your furnace burn gas or oil?* **7.** To make or produce by fire, heat, or chemicals: *The sparks burned holes in his jacket. She burned her name on the piece of wood. The acid burned a design on the piece of copper.*
—*noun, plural* **burns** Damage or an injury caused by something that burns: *There was a burn on the table from a cigarette.*

burn·er |bûr′nər| —*noun, plural* **burners** The part of a stove top on which a pot or pan may be heated.

burnt |bûrnt| A past tense and a past participle of the verb **burn:** *I burnt my finger on the stove. Who has burnt the dinner?*

burr |bûr| —*noun, plural* **burrs** A form of the word **bur**.

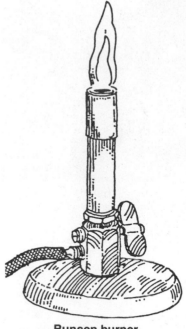
Bunsen burner

bunting

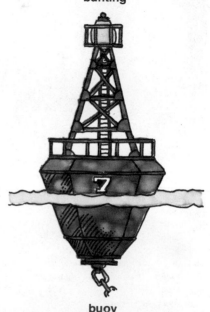
buoy

burro
California miner with burro

bur·ro |bûr′ō| or |bŏŏr′ō| or |bŭr′ō| —*noun, plural* **burros** A small donkey, usually used for riding or carrying loads.
♦ *These sound alike* **burro, borough, burrow**

bur·row |bûr′ō| or |bŭr′ō| —*noun, plural* **burrows** A hole, tunnel, or opening dug in the ground by a small animal such as a rabbit or mole.
—*verb* **burrowed, burrowing 1.** To make a hole, tunnel, or opening by digging: *Gophers burrowed in the fields. A mole burrowed tunnels in the garden* **2.** To search as if digging under things: *She burrowed in the library for books to help her.*
♦ *These sound alike* **burrow, borough, burro.**

burst |bûrst| —*verb* **burst, bursting 1.** To break open or cause to break open suddenly: *The balloon hit a nail and burst. Ice can burst water pipes.* **2.** To come in or go out suddenly and with much noise or fuss: *She burst into the room without knocking.* **3.** To be or seem to be full enough to break open: *His suitcase is bursting.* **4.** To begin abruptly: *Please don't burst out laughing.*
—*noun, plural* **bursts** A sudden outbreak or rush: *a burst of laughter; a burst of speed.*

bur·y |bĕr′ē| —*verb* **buried, burying, buries 1.** To place a dead body in a grave, the sea, or another final resting place: *They buried the sailor's body in the sea. Some Indians buried their dead on platforms.* **2.** To put in the ground and cover with earth: *Squirrels bury acorns.* **3.** To hide something as if by burying: *He buried his homework under toys and games.*
♦ *These sound alike* **bury, berry.**

bus |bŭs| —*noun, plural* **buses** or **busses** A long vehicle with seats for many passengers. Most buses travel on regular routes.
—*verb* **bused** or **bussed, busing** or **bussing** To send or go by bus: *The town buses children to school.*

bush |bŏŏsh| —*noun, plural* **bushes** A woody plant that is smaller than a tree and has many branches; a shrub: *a lilac bush.*

bush·el |bŏŏsh′əl| —*noun, plural* **bushels** A unit used in the United States to measure grain, fruit, vegetables, and other dry foods. A bushel is equal to 4 pecks or 32 dry quarts.

bush·y |bŏŏsh′ē| —*adjective* **bushier, bushiest 1.** Covered with bushes: *a bushy patch full of berries.* **2.** Thick and shaggy: *a squirrel's bushy tail; the man's bushy eyebrows.*

busi·ness |bĭz′nĭs| —*noun, plural* **businesses 1.** The work a person does for money; a job or occupation: *What business is he in? He was in the shoe business before he became an actor.* **2.** A company, such as a store or factory, that buys or sells goods or services: *She took over her father's business when he retired.* **3.** The amount of buying and selling: *Is business good or bad this year?* **4.** The things that a person can or should be interested in: *What they said to each other is not your business.*

bus·ing or **bus·sing** |bŭs′ĭng| —*noun* The act or practice of sending children to schools outside their neighborhoods in order to change the balance of races in the schools.

bus·ses |bŭs′ĭz| **1.** A plural of the noun **bus.** **2.** A third person singular present tense of the verb **bus.**

bust |bŭst| —*noun, plural* **busts** A sculpture of a person's head, shoulders, and the upper part of the chest.

bus·tle |bŭs′əl| —*verb* **bustled, bustling** To hurry and move around in a busy and excited way: *They bustled about packing for the vacation.*

bust

ă	pat	ĕ	pet	î	fierce
ā	pay	ē	be	ŏ	pot
â	care	ĭ	pit	ō	go
ä	father	ī	pie	ô	paw, for
oi	oil	ŭ	cut	zh	vision
ŏŏ	book	û	fur	ə	ago, item,
ōō	boot	th	the		pencil, atom,
yōō	abuse	th	thin		circus
ou	out	hw	which	ər	butter

—noun Busy, excited activity: *much bustle in the market.*

bus·y |bĭz′ē| —*adjective* **busier, busiest** **1.** Having plenty to do; active: *He was busy all day finishing up the paint job.* **2.** Crowded with activity: *We had a busy day at the zoo.* **3.** In use: *Her telephone is always busy when I call.*
—*verb* **busied, busying, busies** To keep oneself occupied: *She busied herself with some sewing.*

but |bŭt| —*conjunction* **1.** On the contrary: *Their family name was not Smith but Smythe.* **2.** Yet; nevertheless: *Mr. Gardner was thought to be wealthy, but he had no money.*
—*adverb* Only; merely: *She said good-by to him but minutes ago.*
—*preposition* **1.** Except: *The new game plan worked in all but a few plays.* **2.** Other than: *the whole truth and nothing but the truth.*
♦ *These sound alike* **but, butt.**

butch·er |bŏŏch′ər| —*noun, plural* **butchers** **1.** A person who cuts and sells meat. **2.** A cruel person who likes to kill.

but·ler |bŭt′lər| —*noun, plural* **butlers** A male servant in a house. The butler often directs the work of other servants.

butt¹ |bŭt| —*noun, plural* **butts** Someone who is the target of jokes and teasing: *The bully made the little boy the butt of his jokes.*
♦ *These sound alike* **butt, but.**

butt² |bŭt| —*verb* **butted, butting** To hit or push with the head or horns: *The goat butted the fence.*
—*noun, plural* **butts** A push or blow with the head or horns.
♦ *These sound alike* **butt, but.**

butt³ |bŭt| —*noun, plural* **butts** **1.** The thicker end of a tool, weapon, or piece of meat: *the butt of a rifle.* **2.** The end of something that is left over: *cigarette butts.*
♦ *These sound alike* **butt, but.**

but·ter |bŭt′ər| —*noun, plural* **butters** **1.** A soft, yellow fat that is made by churning cream. Butter is used to spread on bread, to fry foods, and to add flavor to foods. **2.** A smooth food that can be spread easily: *peanut butter; apple butter.*
—*verb* **buttered, buttering** To spread butter on.

but·ter·cup |bŭt′ər kŭp′| —*noun, plural* **buttercups** A flower that is shaped like a cup and has shiny yellow petals.

but·ter·fly |bŭt′ər flī′| —*noun, plural* **butterflies** An insect with four large wings that are often brightly colored. There are many kinds of butterflies.

but·ter·milk |bŭt′ər mĭlk′| —*noun* **1.** The thick, somewhat sour liquid that remains after butter has been churned. **2.** Milk that has been made sour by the addition of special bacteria.

but·ter·nut |bŭt′ər nŭt′| —*noun, plural* **butternuts** The oily nut of a North American tree that is related to the walnut.

but·ter·scotch |bŭt′ər skŏch′| —*noun* A flavoring or a candy made from brown sugar and butter.

but·tocks |bŭt′əks| —*plural noun* The rounded part of the body on which a person sits; the rump.

but·ton |bŭt′n| —*noun, plural* **buttons** **1.** A round disk or knob that is sewn onto clothing. A button may be used to fasten clothing or as an ornament. **2.** A part that is pushed to work a switch. A button may ring a doorbell or start something that works by electricity. **3.** A round, flat pin with a design or words on it: *buttons that said "Vote for lower taxes."*
—*verb* **buttoned, buttoning** To fasten with a button or buttons: *She buttoned her jacket. This dress buttons in the back.*

butt¹, butt², butt³
Butt¹ comes from a word used long ago in English to mean "a target." Earlier still it came from a French word. **Butt²** originally came from a Germanic word; it came into English through a word meaning "to strike" or "to push" in a form of French. It is likely that **butt³** originally came from Scandinavia, where it meant "a block of wood."

buttercup

butterfly

buttress

buzzard

but·tress |bŭt′rĭs| —*noun, plural* **buttresses** Something that is built against a wall to support or strengthen it.
—*verb* **buttressed, buttressing** To support or strengthen with a buttress or buttresses: *They buttressed the wall with bricks.*

buy |bī| —*verb* **bought, buying** To give money to get goods or services; to purchase: *He bought a watch.*
—*noun, plural* **buys** Something that costs less than usual; a bargain: *His house was a real buy.*
♦ *These sound alike* **buy, by.**

buy·er |bī′ər| —*noun, plural* **buyers** **1.** A person who buys goods; a customer. **2.** A person whose job is to buy things for a store or company.

buzz |bŭz| —*verb* **buzzed, buzzing** **1.** To make a low, humming sound like that of a bee or other insect: *A fly buzzed somewhere in the room. The alarm clock buzzed.* **2.** To signal with a buzzer: *The doctor buzzed for the nurse. The doctor buzzed her nurse.* **3.** To be full of activity and talk: *The room buzzed with excitement.* **4.** To fly a plane low over something: *The pilot buzzed the buildings.*
—*noun, plural* **buzzes** **1.** A low, humming sound like that of a bee or other insect: *the buzz of a mosquito; the buzz of machines at work.* **2.** A call on the telephone: *Give me a buzz when you return.*

buz·zard |bŭz′ərd| —*noun, plural* **buzzards** A large bird with dark feathers, broad wings, and a head without feathers. A buzzard is a kind of vulture.

buzz·er |bŭz′ər| —*noun, plural* **buzzers** An electrical device that makes a buzzing sound as a signal or warning: *the door buzzer; the buzzer on an alarm clock.*

by |bī| —*preposition* **1.** Through the action of: *The family's picture was taken by the butler.* **2.** Through the efforts, work, talent, or ability of: *"Alice in Wonderland" was written by Lewis Carroll. "The Last Supper" was painted by Leonardo da Vinci.* **3.** With the help or use of: *We crossed the river by ferry.* **4.** According to: *We always play by the rules.* **5.** Through the means of: *He succeeded by working hard.* **6.** Through the route of; via: *She got home by a shorter route.* **7.** During: *working at night and sleeping by day.* **8.** In the measure or amount of: *Do you sell onions by the pound?* **9.** Not later than: *You must finish this job by noon.* **10.** Past: *A car drove by us.* **11.** After: *day by day.* **12.** Along: *We always go jogging by the river.* **13.** To, in, or at someone's place: *Come by our house.*
—*adverb* **1.** Past: *The jeep raced by.* **2.** To, in, or at someone's place: *Come by when you feel like it.* **3.** Aside or away: *You must put some money by for later.*
♦ *These sound alike* **by, buy.**

by·gone |bī′gôn′| or |bī′gŏn′| —*adjective* Of the past; gone by; past; former: *the bygone days of horses and wagons.*

by-pass or **bypass** |bī′păs| —*noun, plural* **by-passes** or **bypasses** A road that passes around a city or other crowded area.
—*verb* **by-passed** or **bypassed, by-passing** or **bypassing** To go or send around the main or usual route by another route.

by-prod·uct |bī′prŏd′əkt| —*noun, plural* **by-products** Something useful or harmful that is the result of making something else: *Feathers are a by-product of the chicken business.*

by·stand·er |bī′stănd′ər| —*noun, plural* **bystanders** A person who is present when something happens but who does not take part in the action.

ă	pat	ĕ	pet	î	fierce
ā	pay	ē	be	ŏ	pot
â	care	ĭ	pit	ō	go
ä	father	ī	pie	ô	paw, for
oi	oil	ŭ	cut	zh	vision
ŏŏ	book	û	fur	ə	ago, item,
ōō	boot	*th*	the		pencil, atom,
yōō	abuse	th	thin		circus
ou	out	hw	which	ər	butter

c or **C** |sē| —*noun, plural* **c's** or **C's** The third letter of the English alphabet.

cab |kăb| —*noun, plural* **cabs** **1.** An automobile that carries passengers for a charge; taxicab. **2.** A one-horse carriage that carries passengers. **3.** A compartment for the operator or driver at the front of a train, truck, crane, or other machine.

cab·bage |kăb′ĭj| —*noun, plural* **cabbages** A vegetable with a rounded head of overlapping green or reddish leaves.

cab·in |kăb′ĭn| —*noun, plural* **cabins** **1.** A small, simply built house; cottage; hut: *Early settlers lived in cabins made of logs.* **2.** A room that a passenger or member of the crew lives in on a ship or boat. **3.** The space for carrying passengers in an aircraft.

cab·i·net |kăb′ə nĭt| —*noun, plural* **cabinets** **1.** A case or cupboard with drawers, compartments, or shelves for storing or showing objects: *a kitchen cabinet for dishes and glasses; a file cabinet.* **2.** Often **Cabinet** A group of people chosen by the head of a government to serve as advisers and to be in charge of important departments of state.

ca·ble |kā′bəl| —*noun, plural* **cables** **1.** A thick, strong rope made of twisted wire or fiber. **2.** A bundle of protected wires that carry or conduct electric current: *Telegraph messages are sent by cable.* **3.** A message sent by means of a cable under the ocean.
—*verb* **cabled, cabling** To send a telegraph message to a person or place by cable: *We cabled our grandfather on his birthday.*

cable car **1.** A small car or bus that goes on tracks and is pulled along by a cable. **2.** A small car or bus that hangs from a cable and is pulled along by it.

ca·boose |kə bōōs′| —*noun, plural* **cabooses** The last car on a freight train. The train crew eat and sleep in the caboose.

ca·ca·o |kə kä′ō| or |kə kā′ō| —*noun* The seeds from the pods of a tropical American tree. They are used to make chocolate and cocoa.

cack·le |kăk′əl| —*verb* **cackled, cackling** **1.** To make the harsh, broken cry of a hen that has just laid an egg. **2.** To laugh or speak with a sound like this.
—*noun, plural* **cackles** The harsh, broken cry of a hen or a sound like it.

cac·ti |kăk′tī′| A plural of the noun **cactus**.

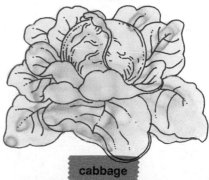

cabbage

cable car

caboose

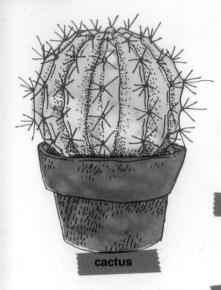

cactus

calculator

calf¹, calf²

Calf¹ comes from an old English word that meant the same thing it does today. That word came from Germanic. Calf² comes from a word used a very long time ago by people who lived in Scandinavia. Its meaning has always been the same.

ă	pat	ĕ	pet	î	fierce		
ā	pay	ē	be	ŏ	pot		
â	care	ĭ	pit	ō	go		
ä	father	ī	pie	ô	paw, for		
oi	oil	ŭ	cut		zh	vision	
ŏŏ	book	û	fur		ə	ago, item,	
ōō	boot	th	the			pencil, atom,	
yōō	abuse	th	thin			circus	
ou	out	hw	which		ər	butter	

cac·tus |kăk′təs| —*noun, plural* **cactuses** or **cacti** A plant that has thick stems with spines and no leaves. There are many kinds of cactuses. They grow in hot, dry places.

ca·det |kə dĕt′| —*noun, plural* **cadets** A student at a military or navy academy who is training to be an officer.

ca·fé |kă fā′| or |kə fā′| —*noun, plural* **cafés** A small restaurant or tavern.

caf·e·te·ri·a |kăf′ĭ tîr′ē ə| —*noun, plural* **cafeterias** A restaurant in which customers carry their food from a counter to their table.

caf·feine or **caf·fein** |kă fēn′| or |kăf′ēn′| —*noun, plural* **caffeines** or **caffeins** A slightly bitter, stimulating substance found in coffee, tea, and some soft drinks. Too much caffeine can keep a person from sleeping.

cage |kāj| —*noun, plural* **cages** **1.** A structure for keeping or carrying birds and animals. Cages have bars or wire screens for letting in light and air. **2.** Something that looks like a cage: *He went to the cashier's cage for his check.*
—*verb* **caged, caging** To put or keep in a cage: *The trainer cages the circus animals for the night.*

cake |kāk| —*noun, plural* **cakes** **1.** A baked mixture of flour, sugar, liquid, eggs, and other ingredients, often covered with icing. **2.** A thin mixture of batter that is baked or fried. It is usually round and flat in shape: *buckwheat cakes; fish cakes.* **3.** A solid, shaped mass of something: *a cake of soap.*
—*verb* **caked, caking** To cover with or become a solid, hardened mass: *Mud caked his boots. Clay cakes as it dries.*

ca·lam·i·ty |kə lăm′ĭ tē| —*noun, plural* **calamities** Something that causes great misfortune and suffering; disaster: *The loss of their home in the fire was a calamity.*

cal·ci·um |kăl′sē əm| —*noun* A silvery, somewhat hard metal that is found in milk, bone, shells, and other substances and is important in growing strong bones and teeth.

cal·cu·late |kăl′kyə lāt′| —*verb* **calculated, calculating** **1.** To find out an answer or result by using mathematics: *We calculated the money we took in by adding up the sales slips.* **2.** To estimate beforehand; figure out: *The campers calculated that their water supply would last ten days.* **3.** To plan deliberately; intend: *The movie was calculated to frighten people.*

cal·cu·lat·ed |kăl′kyə lā′tĭd| —*adjective* Carefully thought out ahead of time: *a calculated risk.*

cal·cu·la·tion |kăl′kyə lā′shən| —*noun, plural* **calculations** The act, process, or result of calculating: *The teacher checked my calculations to make sure they were correct.*

cal·cu·la·tor |kăl′kyə lā′tər| —*noun, plural* **calculators** **1.** A person who calculates. **2.** A machine with a keyboard for automatically performing arithmetic operations.

cal·en·dar |kăl′ən dər| —*noun, plural* **calendars** **1.** A chart showing each month, week, and day of the year. **2.** A list of events planned to take place at special times: *a calendar of holidays.*

calf¹ |kăf| or |käf| —*noun, plural* **calves** **1.** The young of cattle; a young cow or bull. **2.** The young of certain other large animals, such as the whale or elephant. **3.** Leather made from the skin of a calf; calfskin.

calf² |kăf| or |käf| —*noun, plural* **calves** The fleshy back part of the leg between the knee and the ankle.

cal·i·co |kăl′ĭ kō| —*noun, plural* **calicoes** or **calicos** A cotton cloth printed with a brightly colored design.
—*adjective* Having spots of a different color: *a calico cat.*

Cal·i·for·nia |kăl′ə fôr′nyə| or |kăl′ə fôr′nē ə| A state in the western United States. The capital of California is Sacramento.

call |kôl| —*verb* **called, calling 1.** To say or speak in a loud voice; shout; cry out: *Call the names in alphabetical order. They swam for some time, calling for help.* **2.** To send for; summon: *Call the guards to help us.* **3.** To refer to by a certain name: *Let's call the puppy Ginger.* **4.** To describe as: *They called the police officers heroes.* **5.** To telephone: *Call the office.* **6.** To make a short stop; visit: *Let's call at our neighbors' house before we leave.* **7.** To halt or postpone: *The officials called the game on account of rain.*

   Phrasal verbs **call back** To return a telephone call. **call for 1.** To go and get; pick up: *We will call for you at your house.* **2.** To require; demand; need: *The job calls for patience. The recipe calls for three eggs.* **3.** To ask for; request; appeal: *The chairman called for an immediate vote.* **call off** To cancel: *call off a trip.* **call on 1.** To ask someone to speak: *The teacher called on me.* **2.** To make an appeal to: *We call on each citizen to help.*

   —*noun, plural* **calls 1.** A shout or loud cry: *a call for help from the woods.* **2.** The usual cry of a bird or animal. **3.** An act or instance of calling on the telephone: *Were there any calls while I was out?* **4.** A short visit: *We paid a call on the minister.*

   Idioms **call to mind** To serve as a reminder of: *That picture calls to mind an old story.* **close call** A dangerous situation that one barely gets out of: *The plane landed safely, but it was a close call.*

call·er |kô′lər| —*noun, plural* **callers** A person who calls.

cal·lus |kăl′əs| —*noun, plural* **calluses** A small area of skin that has become hard and thick. Calluses usually form on the hands and feet.

calm |käm| —*adjective* **calmer, calmest 1.** Peacefully quiet; not excited: *She spoke in a calm voice.* **2.** Not moving; still; serene: *The ship sailed smoothly on the calm sea.*
—*noun, plural* **calms 1.** A condition of quiet; peace: *A loud noise broke the calm of the evening.* **2.** Lack of motion; stillness: *the calm of the sea after a storm.*
—*verb* **calmed, calming** To make or become calm: *Lullabies calm the baby. The high wind began to calm.*

cal·o·rie |kăl′ə rē| —*noun, plural* **calories 1.** A unit for measuring the amount of heat in something. **2.** A unit for measuring the amount of energy in food: *An apple has about one hundred calories.*

calves |kăvz| The plural of the noun **calf.**

came |kām| The past tense of the verb **come:** *Eloise came to New York for her vacation.*

cam·el |kăm′əl| —*noun, plural* **camels** An animal with a long neck and one or two humps. Camels live in northern Africa and western Asia. They are used in dry, sandy deserts for riding and carrying loads.

cam·er·a |kăm′ər ə| or |kăm′rə| —*noun, plural* **cameras 1.** A device that can take photographs or motion pictures. Most cameras consist of a box that has a lens that lets in light and forms a picture that is recorded on film. **2.** A similar device that forms pictures and changes them into electrical signals for television.

calico cat

California
The name **California** seems to have been taken from the name of a make-believe island in an old Spanish story. The name itself is thought to have come either from a Spanish word meaning "chief of state in a monarchy" or from one meaning "succession." It may also have come from a combination of Latin words meaning "hot furnace."

camel
The camel with one hump is found in Africa and Asia. The camel with two humps is found only in Asia.

cam·ou·flage |kăm′ə fläzh′| —*noun, plural* **camouflages** A way of hiding or disguising people, animals, or things with colors and patterns that make them look like their surroundings.
—*verb* **camouflaged, camouflaging** To hide or disguise by camouflages: *The twins camouflaged their tree house by painting it brown and green.*

camp |kămp| —*noun, plural* **camps** An outdoor area with tents, cabins, or other simple places to live and sleep.
—*verb* **camped, camping** 1. To live in a camp: *The travelers put up tents and camped by the side of the trail.* 2. To live in a simple way, as if in a camp: *We camped in the garage until the workers finished our house.*

cam·paign |kăm pān′| —*noun, plural* **campaigns** 1. A series of military operations aimed at gaining a specific victory.
2. Organized activity to achieve a particular goal: *a campaign to elect a mayor; an advertising campaign to sell a new car.*
—*verb* **campaigned, campaigning** To take part in a campaign.

camp·er |kăm′pər| —*noun, plural* **campers** 1. A person who camps outdoors. 2. A boy or girl attending summer camp. 3. A car or trailer specially designed for camping or long trips.

camp·fire |kămp′fīr′| —*noun, plural* **campfires** An outdoor fire for cooking or keeping people warm.

cam·phor |kăm′fər| —*noun, plural* **camphors** A white, strong-smelling substance used in medicine and in making plastics and small pellets to keep away moths.

cam·pus |kăm′pəs| —*noun, plural* **campuses** The buildings and grounds of a university, college, or school.

can¹ |kăn| or |kən| —*helping,* or *auxiliary, verb* Past tense **could** As a helping verb **can** is used to indicate that the subject:
1. Knows how to: *She can skate well.* 2. **a.** Is able or is enabled to: *Can you fix the bicycle? Find a place where I can put all these books. Green plants can make their own food.* **b.** Will be able to: *I'll take you where you can find out about him.* 3. Has permission to: *She said we can go to the movies.* 4. Is asked or invited to: *If you want to come, you can meet us at the corner.* 5. Has to or will have to: *If you don't behave, you can leave the room.*

can² |kăn| —*noun, plural* **cans** 1. An airtight metal container for storing foods or liquids. 2. **a.** A can with something in it: *a can of peaches.* **b.** The amount that a can holds: *Add three cans of water to the recipe.* 3. A large container, usually with a lid: *a garbage can.*
—*verb* **canned, canning** To preserve food in a jar or other sealed container: *We can summer vegetables for use in the winter.*

Ca·na·da |kăn′ə də| A country in North America. Canada is located north of the United States and extends from the Atlantic to the Pacific Ocean. The capital of Canada is Ottawa.

Ca·na·di·an |kə nā′dē ən| —*adjective* Of or about Canada: *a Canadian river.*
—*noun, plural* **Canadians** A person who was born in or is a citizen of Canada.

ca·nal |kə năl′| —*noun, plural* **canals** 1. A body of water, usually created by digging, that connects two or more points. Canals are used for travel, shipping, irrigation, or drainage. 2. A tube in the body that carries food, liquid, or air: *the alimentary canal.*

ca·nar·y |kə nâr′ē| —*noun, plural* **canaries** 1. A yellow bird

camper

can¹, can²
Can¹ comes from the old English word meaning "he knows how," which was a form of the verb meaning "to know." **Can¹** is related to the word **know**. **Can²** also comes from an old English word, one meaning "a cup." This word came from one used by prehistoric peoples who spoke Germanic.

canary

ă	pat	ĕ	pet	î	fierce
ā	pay	ē	be	ŏ	pot
â	care	ĭ	pit	ō	go
ä	father	ī	pie	ô	paw, for
oi	oil	ŭ	cut	zh	vision
ŏŏ	book	û	fur	ə	ago, item,
ōō	boot	*th*	the		pencil, atom,
yōō	abuse	th	thin		circus
ou	out	hw	which	ər	butter

that sings and is popular as a pet. **2.** A light, bright yellow color.

can·cel |kăn′səl| —*verb* **canceled** or **canceling** **1.** To give up; call off: *cancel an appointment.* **2.** To mark a postage stamp or check to show that it may no longer be used.

can·cer |kăn′sər| —*noun, plural* **cancers** A disease in which some cells of the body grow too rapidly, destroying healthy tissues and organs.

can·di·date |kăn′dĭ dāt′| —*noun, plural* **candidates** A person who seeks or is nominated for a prize, honor, or office: *Sheila is our room's candidate for student council.*

can·died |kăn′dēd| —*adjective* Coated with or cooked in a glaze of sugar: *candied apples; candied sweet potatoes.*

can·dle |kăn′dl| —*noun, plural* **candles** A solid stick of wax, tallow, or other fatty substance with a wick inside. Candles are burned to give light or heat.

can·dle·stick |kăn′dl stĭk′| —*noun, plural* **candlesticks** An object that holds one or more candles.

can·dy |kăn′dē| —*noun, plural* **candies** A sweet food made from sugar or syrup, often mixed with chocolate, fruit, nuts, or other things.
—*verb* **candied, candying, candies** To cook, coat, or preserve with sugar or syrup: *Let's candy the apples for the party.*

cane |kān| —*noun, plural* **canes** **1.** A stick used for help in walking: *The man is using a cane until his leg is better.* **2.** Something shaped like a cane: *a candy cane.* **3.** A hollow, woody plant stem. Cane is often used to make furniture. **4.** A plant having such stems, such as bamboo or sugar cane.

canned |kănd| —*adjective* Preserved or sealed in an airtight can or jar: *canned fruits and vegetables.*

can·ni·bal |kăn′ə bəl| —*noun, plural* **cannibals** **1.** A person who eats human flesh. **2.** An animal that feeds on others of its own kind.

can·non |kăn′ən| —*noun, plural* **cannons** or **cannon** A large gun mounted on wheels or on a heavy base.

can·non·ball |kăn′ən bôl′| —*noun, plural* **cannonballs** A heavy, round ball fired from a cannon.

can·not |kăn′ŏt′| or |kă nŏt′| or |kə nŏt′| The negative form of **can** (to be able or know how).

ca·noe |kə nōō′| —*noun, plural* **canoes** A light, narrow boat that is pointed at the ends and is moved with paddles.
—*verb* **canoed, canoeing** To travel in or paddle a canoe.

can·o·py |kăn′ə pē| —*noun, plural* **canopies** **1.** A covering like a tent held up over a bed, entrance, or important person. **2.** A similar covering: *A canopy of branches arched over the path.*
—*verb* **canopied, canopying, canopies** To spread over with a canopy.

can't |kănt| or |känt| A contraction of "cannot."

can·ta·loupe |kăn′tl ōp′| —*noun, plural* **cantaloupes** A melon with sweet, orange flesh and a rough rind.

can·teen |kăn tēn′| —*noun, plural* **canteens** **1.** A container for carrying drinking water or other liquids. **2.** A store within a school, factory, or office. Food and beverages are sold there, often from vending machines.

can·ter |kăn′tər| —*noun, plural* **canters** A slow, easy gallop: *The rider slowed her horse to a canter.*

candlestick

cannon

canoe

cantaloupe

—*verb* **cantered, cantering** To ride or run at a canter: *He cantered the horse into the stable. The stallion cantered across the prairie.*

can·vas |kăn′vəs| —*noun, plural* **canvases** 1. A heavy, coarse cloth used for making tents, sails, etc. 2. An oil painting on canvas. 3. A piece of canvas stretched on a frame and used for an oil painting.

can·yon |kăn′yən| —*noun, plural* **canyons** A deep valley with steep cliffs on both sides and often a stream running through it.

cap |kăp| —*noun, plural* **caps** 1. A covering for the head, especially one that fits closely. Some caps have no brims and some have a visor. Baseball players and nurses wear caps. 2. A small, circular, tight-fitting cover: *a bottle cap.* 3. A circular top attached to a stem: *a mushroom cap.* 4. A small amount of explosive powder wrapped in paper.
—*verb* **capped, capping** 1. To put a cap on; cover the top of: *cap a bottle; Snow capped the mountain.* 2. To outdo; improve on: *His joke capped all the others.*

ca·pa·bil·i·ty |kā′pə bĭl′ĭ tē| —*noun, plural* **capabilities** 1. The quality of being capable; ability: *Do you have the capability for the job?* 2. Often **capabilities** Natural ability: *a smart boy who doesn't live up to his capabilities.*

ca·pa·ble |kā′pə bl| —*adjective* 1. Able; skilled: *a capable teacher.* 2. **capable of** Having a certain ability or capacity: *She is capable of great kindness.*

ca·pac·i·ty |kə păs′ə tē| —*noun, plural* **capacities** 1. The amount that can be held: *a bottle with the capacity of one quart.* 2. Ability; capability: *She has a capacity to learn easily.* 3. Position; role: *She is here for two weeks in the capacity of substitute teacher.*

cape¹ |kāp| —*noun, plural* **capes** A piece of clothing that is worn hanging loose over the shoulders and is often fastened at the neck. A cape does not have sleeves.

cape² |kāp| —*noun, plural* **capes** A point of land extending into the sea or other body of water.

cap·i·tal |kăp′ĭ tl| —*noun, plural* **capitals** 1. A city where the government of a state or country is located. 2. Money or property that is invested to produce more money. 3. A capital letter.
—*adjective* 1. Most important: *a capital city.* 2. Calling for a penalty of death: *capital punishment.*
♦ *These sound alike* **capital, capitol.**

cap·i·tal·ize |kăp′ĭ tl īze′| —*verb* **capitalized, capitalizing** 1. To begin with a capital letter: *Capitalize the first word in each sentence.* 2. To write or print in capital letters.

capital letter A letter, such as A, B, or C, written or printed in a size larger than the same smaller letter, such as a, b, or c. A capital letter often has a form that is different from the smaller letter.

cap·i·tol |kăp′ĭ tl| —*noun, plural* **capitols** 1. **Capitol** The building in Washington, D.C., occupied by the Congress of the United States. 2. The building in which a state legislature meets.
♦ *These sound alike* **capitol, capital.**

cap·size |kăp′sīz′| or |kăp sīz′| —*verb* **capsized, capsizing** To turn bottom side up; overturn: *A huge wave capsized our boat. The ship capsized in the storm.*

cap·sule |kăp′səl| or |kăp′syōol| —*noun, plural* **capsules** 1. A

cap

cape¹, cape²
Cape¹ and **cape²** both came into English through French. Both came from the Latin word meaning "head." The development of **cape²** is easy to understand: the meaning grew from "head" to "head of land." In the case of **cape¹**, the Latin source word developed another form, which meant "hat" and later also came to mean "cloak."

capitol
The U.S. Capitol in Washington, D.C.

ă	pat	ĕ	pet	î	fierce
ā	pay	ē	be	ŏ	pot
â	care	ĭ	pit	ō	go
ä	father	ī	pie	ô	paw, for
oi	oil	ŭ	cut	zh	vision
ŏŏ	book	û	fur	ə	ago, item,
ōō	boot	*th*	the		pencil, atom,
yōō	abuse	th	thin		circus
ou	out	hw	which	ər	butter

small container, usually made of gelatin, containing medicine to be swallowed. **2.** A place on a spacecraft for the crew. The capsule can be separated from the rest of the spacecraft.

cap·tain |kăp′tən| —*noun, plural* **captains 1.** The leader of a group: *the captain of the football team.* **2.** The officer in charge of a ship. **3.** An Army, Air Force, or Marine Corps officer ranking above a first lieutenant. **4.** A Navy officer ranking above a commander.

cap·tion |kăp′shən| —*noun, plural* **captions** A title or explanation that goes with an illustration or photograph.

cap·tive |kăp′tĭv| —*adjective* Held prisoner; not free: *a captive mountain lion.*
—*noun, plural* **captives** A person or animal held captive; prisoner.

cap·tiv·i·ty |kăp tĭv′ĭ tē| —*noun, plural* **captivities** A period of being held captive, or the condition of being captive: *Their captivity lasted six years. Many zoo animals are born in captivity.*

cap·ture |kăp′chər| —*verb* **captured, capturing 1.** To get hold of; seize: *capture a city during a war; We captured a raccoon under the porch.* **2.** To hold the attention or interest of: *The idea captured his imagination.*
—*noun, plural* **captures** The act of capturing: *The thieves stole thousands of dollars until their capture.*

car |kär| —*noun, plural* **cars 1.** An automobile. **2.** A vehicle with wheels that moves along rails or tracks: *A railroad train usually has many cars.* **3.** The part of an elevator in which the passengers ride.

car·a·mel |kăr′ə məl| or |kăr′ə měl′| or |kär′məl| —*noun, plural* **caramels 1.** A smooth, chewy candy. **2.** A brown syrup made by cooking sugar. Caramel is used to color and flavor foods.

car·at |kăr′ət| —*noun, plural* **carats** A unit of weight for diamonds, rubies, and other precious stones. Another form of this word is **karat.**
♦ *These sound alike* **carat, carrot, karat.**

car·a·van |kăr′ə văn′| —*noun, plural* **caravans** A group of people, animals, or vehicles traveling together, usually in a long line: *a caravan of Arab merchants crossing the desert; a caravan of army trucks on the highway.*

car·a·way |kăr′ə wā′| —*noun* A plant that has small, curved seeds with a strong taste. Caraway seeds are used in cooking, especially to flavor rye bread.

car·bo·hy·drate |kär′bō hī′drāt′| or |kär′bə hī′drāt′| —*noun, plural* **carbohydrates** Any substance made up of carbon, hydrogen, and oxygen. Carbohydrates are produced by plants and include sugars and starches.

car·bon |kär′bən| —*noun* A substance found in all living things. Coal and charcoal contain large amounts of carbon, and diamonds are pure carbon in crystal form. Carbon is one of the chemical elements.

car·bon·ated |kär′bə nā′tĭd| —*adjective* Having or mixed with carbon dioxide: *carbonated water.*

carbon di·ox·ide |dī ŏk′sīd′| A gas that is present in the air and is made up of carbon and oxygen. Carbon dioxide has no color or odor. It is formed when animals breathe and when any fuel containing carbon burns. Carbon dioxide is used in soft drinks.

car
Railroad cars from 1830 to 1978

car·bon mo·nox·ide | mŏ **nŏk′**sīd′ | or | mə **nŏk′**sīd′ | A gas that is very poisonous and has no color or odor. Carbon monoxide is formed when any substance containing carbon does not burn completely. Fumes that come from the exhaust pipes of cars contain carbon monoxide.

car·bu·re·tor | **kär′**bə rā′tər | or | **kär′**byə rā′tər | —*noun, plural* **carburetors** A part of a gasoline engine that mixes the gasoline with air so that it will burn properly.

car·cass | **kär′**kəs | —*noun, plural* **carcasses** 1. The dead body of an animal. 2. The framework or worthless remains of an object: *the rusted carcass of an old car.*

card | kärd | —*noun, plural* **cards** 1. A small, thin piece of stiff paper, plastic, or cardboard that is usually rectangular in shape. Cards have many uses and usually bear writing, pictures, names, or information: *a library card; a greeting card; a calling card; a file card.* 2. One of a set or pack of 52 cards marked with numbers, pictures, and designs and used to play games; a playing card.

card·board | **kärd′**bôrd | or | **kärd′**bōrd | —*noun* A stiff, heavy paper made by pressing sheets of paper or layers of paper pulp together.

car·di·nal | **kär′**dn əl | —*adjective* Of greatest or first importance; chief; foremost: *the cardinal issue in the campaign for governor.*
—*noun, plural* **cardinals** 1. An official of the Roman Catholic Church whose rank is just below that of pope. 2. A North American songbird that has bright red feathers and a crest on its head.

care | kâr | —*noun, plural* **cares** 1. A feeling of worry or concern: *free from care; troubled by the cares of raising a family.* 2. Serious attention; caution: *You should do your work with more care.* 3. Supervision; charge; keeping: *in the care of a nurse.*
—*verb* **cared, caring** 1. To be worried or concerned; to have interest: *She cares about her friends. I don't care what happens.* 2. To be willing or wish; to want: *Would you care to dance?*
 Phrasal verb **care for** 1. To like: *He doesn't care for music.* 2. To take charge of; look after: *Who will care for the baby?*
 Idioms **take care** To be careful: *Take care that you don't fall down the steps.* **take care of** To attend to; look after: *His secretary takes care of getting him plane reservations. They hire a nurse to take care of the children.*

ca·reer | kə **rîr′** | —*noun, plural* **careers** 1. The kind of work or occupation that a person chooses to do; a profession: *a medical career.* 2. The progress or general course of action of a person through life: *an officer with a fine career.*

care·free | **kâr′**frē′ | —*adjective* Without worries or responsibilities: *a carefree life.*

care·ful | **kâr′**fəl | —*adjective* 1. Taking time to think before acting; cautious; prudent: *Be careful about crossing the street.* 2. Done with care; thorough: *a careful job on a science project.* 3. Showing concern; considerate: *Being polite means being careful of other people's feelings.*

care·less | **kâr′**lĭs | —*adjective* 1. Not taking care; failing to pay attention: *a careless worker; a careless mistake; careless about one's appearance.* 2. Done or made without care; not thorough: *The painters did a careless job.* 3. Said or done without thought: *He made a careless remark.*

cardinal

ă	pat	ĕ	pet	î	fierce
ā	pay	ē	be	ŏ	pot
â	care	ĭ	pit	ō	go
ä	father	ī	pie	ô	paw, for

oi	oil	ŭ	cut	zh	vision
ōō	book	û	fur	ə	ago, item,
ōō	boot	*th*	the		pencil, atom,
yōō	abuse	th	thin		circus
ou	out	hw	which	ər	butter

ca·ress | kə rĕs′ | —*noun, plural* **caresses** A gentle touch or gesture that shows a fond or tender feeling.
—*verb* **caressed, caressing** To touch or stroke in a way that shows fond or tender feeling.

care·tak·er | kâr′tā′kər | —*noun, plural* **caretakers** A person who has the job of looking after and taking care of a house, an estate, or other property that belongs to another.

car·go | kär′gō | —*noun, plural* **cargoes** or **cargos** The freight carried by a ship, airplane, or other vehicle.

car·i·bou | kăr′ə boō′ | —*noun, plural* **caribou** or **caribous** A large deer of northern North America. Both the males and the females have large, spreading antlers.

car·na·tion | kär nā′shən | —*noun, plural* **carnations** A flower with a spicy smell and many petals of different colors. Carnations are often grown in gardens or sold by florists.

car·ni·val | kär′nə vəl | —*noun, plural* **carnivals** An outdoor show that has rides, games, side shows, and other entertainment; a fair or festival.

car·ni·vore | kär′nə vôr′ | —*noun, plural* **carnivores** An animal that feeds on the flesh of other animals. Lions, tigers, and weasels are carnivores.

car·ni·vor·ous | kär nĭv′ər əs | —*adjective* Feeding on the flesh of other animals: *Lions, tigers, and weasels are carnivorous animals.*

car·ol | kăr′əl | —*noun, plural* **carols** A song of joy or praise, especially one that is sung at Christmas.
—*verb* **caroled, caroling** To celebrate with joyful song: *The choir caroled the Lord's praises.*

car·ou·sel | kăr′ə sĕl′ | or | kăr′ə zĕl′ | —*noun, plural* **carousels** A merry-go-round. Another form of this word is **carrousel**.

carp | kärp | —*noun, plural* **carp** or **carps** A fish that lives in fresh water, especially in ponds. It is often used as food.

car·pen·ter | kär′pən tər | —*noun, plural* **carpenters** A person who builds or repairs things that are made of wood.

car·pet | kär′pĭt | —*noun, plural* **carpets** **1.** A thick, heavy covering for a floor, usually made of a woven fabric. **2.** Anything that covers a surface like a carpet: *A carpet of leaves covered the grass.*
—*verb* **carpeted, carpeting** To cover with or as if with a carpet: *We carpeted our living room last year. The ground we walked on was carpeted with pine needles.*

car·pet·ing | kär′pĭ tĭng | —*noun* **1.** Material or fabric used for carpets. **2.** A carpet or carpets: *a room with wall-to-wall carpeting.*

car·riage | kăr′ĭj | —*noun, plural* **carriages** **1.** A passenger vehicle that has four wheels and is usually pulled by horses. **2.** A small vehicle for a baby or a doll. It is usually pushed along by a person. **3.** A movable part of a machine. A carriage holds or carries another structure or part. The carriage of a typewriter holds and moves a piece of paper back and forth. **4.** The way in which the body is held; posture: *A dancer must have good carriage.*

car·ri·er | kăr′ē ər | —*noun, plural* **carriers** A person or thing that moves or transports something. Mailmen, trains, and buses are all carriers.

car·rot | kăr′ət | —*noun, plural* **carrots** The long, tapering, yellow-orange root of a plant with feathery leaves. Carrots are eaten as a vegetable.
♦ *These sound alike* **carrot, carat, karat.**

caribou

carnation

carrot

car·rou·sel | kăr′ə sĕl′ | or | kăr′ə zĕl′ | —*noun, plural* **carrousels**
A form of the word **carousel.**

car·ry | kăr′ē | —*verb* **carried, carrying, carries 1.** To take from one place to another: *He carried the groceries into the house. Trains carry coal.* **2.** To keep, wear, or have with oneself: *He never carries much money. A police officer carries a gun.* **3.** To hold up or support; bear the major burden of: *Marble columns carry the roof of the church. The star of the show carried the whole production.* **4.** To be or act as the means for transporting or moving someone or something: *Pipes carry water. The balloon carried us high into the air.* **5.** To transmit a disease: *Some insects carry malaria.* **6.** To make something known; communicate: *Books carry ideas to millions of people.* **7.** To project or travel in space: *Her voice carries very well. The baseball carried deep into left field.* **8.** To hold or move the body or a part of the body in a certain way: *She carries herself like a dancer.* **9.** To have in stock or for sale: *Department stores carry a variety of goods.* **10.** To sing on key: *Can you carry a tune?* **11.** To bring forward or place a number in the next column of figures in addition. **12.** To extend or continue: *The fence carries all the way around the field. Her brother carried his teasing too far.* **13.** To win or gain approval by a majority of votes: *John carried the election for class president. The motion to buy new band uniforms carried.*

Phrasal verbs **carry away** To arouse strong emotion or enthusiasm: *He was carried away by the music.* **carry on 1.** To engage in; conduct: *They carried on a conversation. Does she carry on an occupation?* **2.** To continue in a course of action; keep going: *The workers carried on their efforts in spite of the rising flood waters.* **carry out** To fulfill; execute; accomplish: *He carried out our orders perfectly.*

Car·son City | kär′sən | The capital of Nevada.

cart | kärt | —*noun, plural* **carts 1.** A wooden vehicle that has two wheels and is pulled by a horse or other animal. A cart is used to carry people or goods from one place to another. **2.** Any small, light vehicle with wheels that can be pushed or pulled by hand: *a grocery cart; a golf cart.*
—*verb* **carted, carting 1.** To move or transport in or as if in a cart: *The farmers carted their tomatoes to market.* **2.** To carry with effort; drag; lug: *They carted their books home from school.*

car·ti·lage | kär′tl ĭj | —*noun* A tough, white substance that is attached to bones near the joints and helps to hold them in position.

car·ton | kär′tn | —*noun, plural* **cartons 1.** A cardboard box made in many sizes and used to hold goods, liquids, and other objects. **2. a.** A carton with something in it: *Please buy me a carton of milk.* **b.** The amount that a carton holds: *It will take two cartons of milk to make all those cupcakes.*

car·toon | kär tōon′ | —*noun, plural* **cartoons 1.** A sketch or drawing that shows people or events in a way that is supposed to be funny; a joke in the form of a picture. Cartoons usually appear in magazines and newspapers. **2.** A movie made up of such drawings; an animated cartoon. **3.** A group of such drawings arranged in sequence; comic strip.

car·toon·ist | kär tōo′nĭst | —*noun, plural* **cartoonists** A person who draws cartoons.

car·tridge | kär′trĭj | —*noun, plural* **cartridges 1. a.** The metal

cart

ă	pat	ĕ	pet	î	fierce
ā	pay	ē	be	ŏ	pot
â	care	ĭ	pit	ō	go
ä	father	ī	pie	ô	paw, for

oi	oil	ŭ	cut	zh	vision
ŏŏ	book	û	fur	ə	ago, item,
ōō	boot	*th*	the		pencil, atom,
yōō	abuse	th	thin		circus
ou	out	hw	which	ər	butter

or metal and cardboard case that holds the gunpowder for a bullet. **b.** Such a case plus the bullet or pellets that are fitted into it. **2.** Any container or case that holds something and can be easily inserted into another object. A cartridge may hold ink for a pen, film for a camera, or tape for a tape recorder.

cart·wheel |kärt′hwēl′| or |kärt′wēl′| —*noun, plural* **cartwheels** **1.** The wheel of a cart. **2.** A kind of somersault in which the arms and legs are spread like the spokes of a wheel.

carve |kärv| —*verb* **carved, carving** **1.** To slice or cut into pieces: *We carved the turkey for Thanksgiving dinner.* **2.** To make something by cutting a solid material: *The sculptor carved a statue from marble.*

cas·cade |kăs kād′| —*noun, plural* **cascades** **1.** A waterfall or group of waterfalls that flows over steep rocks. **2.** Something that falls like a cascade: *a cascade of stars from the skyrockets.* —*verb* **cascaded, cascading** To fall in a cascade or like a cascade: *The water cascaded over the rocks.*

case[1] |kās| —*noun, plural* **cases** **1.** An example or instance of something: *a case of mistaken identity.* **2.** A situation or state of affairs; event: *In that case there is nothing to be done.* **3.** An instance of illness or injury: *Mary has a case of the flu.* **4.** Something that is being investigated: *the case of the missing fortune.* **5.** Something that is to be decided in a court of law: *His case comes to trial next month.*

   Idioms **in case** If it should happen that; if: *In case I'm late, you start the meeting without me.* **in case of** In the event of; if there should be: *In case of fire, leave the building.*

case[2] |kās| —*noun, plural* **cases** **1.** A large box or carton for shipping things in: *a packing case.* **2. a.** A case with something in it: *Please bring home a case of root beer.* **b.** The amount that a case holds: *The boys and girls drank three cases of root beer at our party.* **3.** An outer covering: *The knife has a leather case.*

cash |kăsh| —*noun* **1.** Money in the form of bills or coins: *How much cash do you have on you?* **2.** Money paid at the time something is bought: *Will you pay cash for this, or do you want to charge it?* —*verb* **cashed, cashing** To exchange for or convert into cash: *Will the bank cash this check? Mother cashed her check.*

cash·ew |kăsh′ōō| or |kə shōō′| —*noun, plural* **cashews** The curved nut of a tropical American tree. Cashews are good to eat.

cash·ier |kă shîr′| —*noun, plural* **cashiers** Someone who has the job of receiving and paying out money for a bank, store, restaurant, or other business.

cash·mere |kăzh′mîr′| or |kăsh′mîr′| —*noun, plural* **cashmeres** A fine, soft, wool obtained from a goat of Asia.

cask |kăsk| or |käsk| —*noun, plural* **casks** **1.** A barrel of any size for holding liquids. **2. a.** A cask with something in it: *A cask of olive oil rolled off the shelf.* **b.** The amount that a cask holds: *He spilled a cask of olive oil.*

cas·ket |kăs′kĭt| or |käs′kĭt| —*noun, plural* **caskets** **1.** A small box or chest used to hold jewelry or other valuable things. **2.** A box in which a dead person is buried; a coffin.

cas·se·role |kăs′ə rōl′| —*noun, plural* **casseroles** **1.** A heavy dish of glass or pottery in which food is baked and served. **2.** The food that is baked in this kind of dish: *We had a macaroni and cheese casserole for dinner.*

cartwheel

case[1]**, case**[2]

Case[1] comes from the Latin word meaning "an event or occurrence." It traveled through French before arriving in English. **Case**[2] followed a similar route. Coming from a Latin word meaning "a container or box," it appeared in French before English-speaking people started using it.

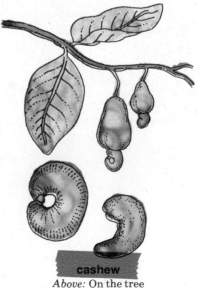

cashew

Above: On the tree
Below: Nut

castle

Above: A castle in France
Below: A castle made of sand

cat

ă	pat	ĕ	pet	î	fierce
ā	pay	ē	be	ŏ	pot
â	care	ĭ	pit	ō	go
ä	father	ī	pie	ô	paw, for

oi	oil	ŭ	cut	zh	vision
ōō	book	û	fur	ə	ago, item,
ōō	boot	*th*	the		pencil, atom,
yōō	abuse	th	thin		circus
ou	out	hw	which	ər	butter

cast |kăst| or |käst| —*verb* **cast, casting 1.** To throw or fling: *We watched the fishermen cast nets into the water.* **2.** To cause to fall upon something: *The moon cast shadows on the ground.* **3.** To make or form something by pouring a liquid or soft material into a mold so it will harden: *The artist melted bronze and cast a statue of a man.* **4.** To deposit a ballot; give a vote: *Father and Mother cast their votes for President.* **5.** To choose for a part in a play: *The teacher cast Mary in the role of Betsy Ross.*
Phrasal verbs **cast about for** To search or look for: *We were casting about for a way to escape.* **cast aside** To throw away; discard: *They cast aside their old clothes.*
—*noun, plural* **casts 1.** The act of throwing or casting: *He won the game by a cast of the dice.* **2.** The actors in a play: *The members of the club gave a party for members of the cast.* **3.** A stiff bandage, usually made of gauze coated with plaster: *His broken arm is in a cast.* **4.** Something that is cast in a mold: *The artist made a plaster cast of President Lincoln's face.* **5.** A slight squint. It occurs when a person's eyes are unable to focus together: *She has a cast in her left eye.*
Idioms **cast down** Unhappy or dejected: *The team was cast down after their defeat.* **cast one's lot with** To join or take sides with: *He cast his lot with the losing party.*

cas·ta·nets |kăs′tə nĕts′| —*plural noun* A pair of small pieces of wood shaped like a shell that make a sharp, sudden sound when struck together. Castanets are used by Spanish dancers and singers.

cast iron A very hard and brittle form of iron made by mixing melted iron with other elements and pouring it into a mold.

cas·tle |kăs′əl| or |käs′əl| —*noun, plural* **castles 1.** A large fort or group of buildings that are strong enough to resist attack. In the Middle Ages, castles were built with thick walls and places to shoot arrows from. They were sometimes surrounded by a deep ditch filled with water. The castle was usually the home of a king or queen, or of someone important who was loyal to the king or queen. **2.** A large and impressive home; a mansion. **3.** A playing piece in chess; a rook.

cas·u·al |kăzh′ōō əl| —*adjective* **1.** Not planned; happening by chance; accidental: *a casual meeting of two old friends.* **2.** Not formal: *The speaker made a few casual remarks.* **3.** Suitable for everyday or informal wear: *He changed into casual clothes after church.* **4.** Not intimate or close: *casual friends.*

cas·u·al·ty |kăzh′ōō əl tē| —*noun, plural* **casualties 1.** A person who is killed or injured in an accident: *The flood was responsible for many casualties.* **2.** A member of the armed forces who is killed, wounded, captured, or missing in a military action.

cat |kăt| —*noun, plural* **cats 1.** A small, furry animal with sharp claws, whiskers at each side of the mouth, and usually a long tail. Cats are kept as pets or for catching rats and mice. **2.** A larger animal, related to the cat, such as the lion, tiger, leopard, or wildcat.
Idiom **let the cat out of the bag** To give away a secret: *The party was to be a secret, but somebody let the cat out of the bag.*

cat·a·log or **cat·a·logue** |kăt′l ôg′| or |kăt′l ŏg′| —*noun, plural* **catalogs** or **catalogues 1.** A list, usually in alphabetical order and having a short description of each item: *Look in the catalog to see if the library has the book.* **2.** A book containing such

a list: *I ordered a pair of leather boots from the store's catalog.*
—*verb* **cataloged** or **catalogued, cataloging** or **cataloguing** To list in a catalog; make a catalog of: *He spent weeks cataloging his phonograph records.*

cat·a·ract |kăt′ə răkt′| —*noun, plural* **cataracts** A very large waterfall.

ca·tas·tro·phe |kə tăs′trə fē| —*noun, plural* **catastrophes** A sudden disaster that causes much damage, such as a flood or earthquake.

cat·bird |kăt′ bûrd′| —*noun, plural* **catbirds** A dark-gray North American songbird. It can make a sound like the mewing of a cat.

catch |kăch| —*verb* **caught, catching** **1.** To receive into the hands; grasp something that is moving: *I'll throw the ball and you catch it.* **2.** To capture or seize; trap: *The cat will catch the mouse. We caught the thief.* **3.** To come upon suddenly; take by surprise: *They caught the guard asleep in his office.* **4.** To arrive in time for: *We barely caught the train.* **5.** To become stuck or lodged: *A bone caught in her throat.* **6.** To entangle or become entangled in: *He caught his foot in the fence. The rosebush caught her dress.* **7.** To become ill with: *She caught a cold last week.* **8.** To attract: *He's trying to catch your attention.* **9.** To take or get: *catch sight of someone.* **10.** To ignite; begin to burn: *The fire won't catch with this damp wood.* **11.** To hear: *I didn't catch what you said just now.* **12.** To see a play, movie, or similar entertainment: *Did you catch the new TV show last night?*

　　Phrasal verbs **catch on** **1.** To understand; grasp the meaning: *She explained it, but I didn't catch on.* **2.** To become popular: *That new song has really caught on.* **catch up** To overtake; come up even with someone or something: *They ran so fast I couldn't catch up.* **catch up on** To bring up to date; make up for a lack in: *Tonight I'm going to catch up on my sleep.*
—*noun, plural* **catches** **1.** The act of grasping or getting hold of: *The fielder made a great catch.* **2.** A device for holding or securing; fastener: *the catch on a bracelet.* **3.** An amount of something caught: *a large catch of fish.* **4.** A drawback or disadvantage: *There must be a catch to his sudden friendship.* **5.** A game of throwing a ball back and forth between two or more people.

　　Idiom **catch (one's) breath** To rest until one is able to go on: *I have to sit down a minute and catch my breath.*

catcher

catch·er |kăch′ər| —*noun, plural* **catchers** **1.** Someone or something that catches. **2.** A baseball player who stands behind home plate to catch balls thrown by the pitcher.

catch·ing |kăch′ ĭng| —*adjective* Easily spread by infection; contagious: *Flu is one of the most catching diseases.*

catch·y |kăch′ē| —*adjective* **catchier, catchiest** **1.** Easy to remember: *a catchy tune.* **2.** Likely to deceive or confuse; tricky: *The quiz was full of catchy questions.*

cat·e·go·ry |kăt′ə gôr′ē| or |kăt′ə gōr′ē| —*noun, plural* **categories** A division or group within a system; a class: *The strings are one category of musical instruments.*

ca·ter |kā′ tər| —*verb* **catered, catering** **1.** To provide with food and services: *Which company catered the banquet?* **2.** To show preference; give whatever is needed or desired: *The store caters to wealthy customers.* **3.** To show prejudice; give special or unfair advantage: *He says the President caters to the big industries.*

cat·er·pil·lar |kăt′ ər pĭl′ ər| or |kăt′ə pĭl′ər| —*noun, plural*

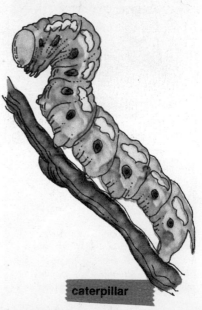

caterpillar

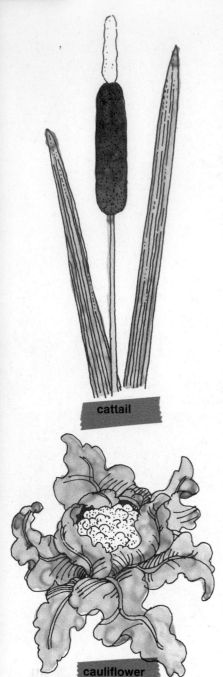

cattail

cauliflower

caterpillars The young of a butterfly or moth, after it has hatched from an egg. Caterpillars have a soft, long body like that of a worm. They are often covered with hair or bristles.

cat·fish |kăt′fĭsh′| —*noun, plural* **catfish** or **catfishes** A fish with feelers that look like whiskers around its mouth. Catfish have no scales. There are several kinds of catfish. Most of them live in fresh water.

ca·the·dral |kə thē′drəl| —*noun, plural* **cathedrals** 1. The principal church of the district under the authority of a bishop. 2. Any large or important church.

Cath·o·lic |kăth′ə lĭk| or |kăth′lĭk| —*adjective* Of or belonging to the Roman Catholic Church or one of the Christian churches related to it.

—*noun, plural* **Catholics** A member of the Roman Catholic faith or one of the Christian faiths related to it.

cat·sup |kăt′səp| or |kăch′əp| or |kĕch′əp| —*noun, plural* **catsups** A form of the word **ketchup.**

cat·tail |kăt′tāl′| —*noun, plural* **cattails** A tall plant that grows in wet places. It has long, narrow leaves and a long, dense cluster of tiny brown flowers.

cat·tle |kăt′l| —*plural noun* Animals that have horns and hoofs and are raised for meat and milk; cows, bulls, and oxen.

cat·tle·man |kăt′l mən| or |kăt′l măn′| —*noun, plural* **cattlemen** A person who raises cattle.

Cau·ca·soid |kô′kə soid′| —*adjective* Of a major division of the human species whose members have very light to brown skin color, light-blue to brown eyes, and straight or curly hair.

caught |kôt| The past tense and past participle of the verb **catch:** *She caught the ball and ran for a touchdown. He has caught all the fish he can carry.*

cau·li·flow·er |kô′lĭ flou′ər| or |kŏl′ĭ flou′ər| —*noun* A vegetable with a rounded head of small, closely clustered whitish flowers. Cauliflower is related to cabbage and broccoli.

cause |kôz| —*noun, plural* **causes** 1. Someone or something that makes something happen: *She is the cause of all my trouble. What was the cause of the fire?* 2. The reason for a certain action or feeling: *There is no cause for alarm.* 3. A goal or ideal that a person works toward: *the cause of human rights.*

—*verb* **caused, causing** To be the cause of; make happen; bring about: *The storm caused a lot of damage. What caused the fire?*

cau·tion |kô′shən| —*noun, plural* **cautions** 1. The act or condition of being careful in order to avoid trouble or danger: *Always cross a busy street with caution.* 2. A warning against trouble or danger: *He's sorry he ignored my caution.*

—*verb* **cautioned, cautioning** To warn against possible trouble or danger: *He cautioned us to stay away from the lions.*

cau·tious |kô′shəs| —*adjective* Showing or having caution; careful: *Be cautious when you climb that tree.*

cav·al·ry |kăv′əl rē| —*noun, plural* **cavalries** Military troops that formerly were trained to fight on horseback. Now the cavalry fights in armored vehicles.

cave |kāv| —*noun, plural* **caves** A hollow area in the earth or in the side of a hill or mountain, with an opening to the outside.

—*verb* **caved, caving** —**cave in** To fall in or cause to fall in; collapse: *The tunnel caved in during the earthquake.*

cave-in |kāv′ĭn′| —*noun, plural* **cave-ins** The action of

ă	pat	ĕ	pet	î	fierce
ā	pay	ē	be	ŏ	pot
â	care	ĭ	pit	ō	go
ä	father	ī	pie	ô	paw, for
oi	oil	ŭ	cut	zh	vision
ŏŏ	book	û	fur	ə	ago, item,
ōō	boot	th	the		pencil, atom,
yōō	abuse	th	thin		circus
ou	out	hw	which	ər	butter

collapsing or caving in: *The miners were trapped in the cave-in.*

cave man A human being who lived thousands of years ago in caves.

cav·ern |kăv′ərn| —*noun, plural* **caverns** A large cave.

cav·i·ty |kăv′ĭ tē| —*noun, plural* **cavities** **1.** A hollow or hole. **2.** A hollow place in a tooth, usually caused by decay: *The dentist filled two of my cavities.*

caw |kô| —*noun, plural* **caws** The loud, hoarse cry of a crow or raven.
—*verb* **cawed, cawing** To make this sound.

cease |sēs| —*verb* **ceased, ceasing** To bring or come to an end; stop: *He warned us to cease talking. The storm ceased at daybreak.*

ce·dar |sē′dər| —*noun, plural* **cedars** An evergreen tree with reddish wood that has a pleasant smell. Cedars are related to pines and firs.

ceil·ing |sē′lĭng| —*noun, plural* **ceilings** **1.** The inside upper surface in a room: *All the rooms have high ceilings.* **2.** The highest altitude at which an aircraft can fly. **3.** The greatest or upper limit: *to put a ceiling on food prices.*

cel·e·brate |sĕl′ə brāt′| —*verb* **celebrated, celebrating** **1.** To have a party or other festivity in honor of a special occasion: *We always celebrate my birthday. They celebrated by having a big party.* **2.** To perform a religious ceremony: *The priest celebrated Mass.* **3.** To praise or honor: *The book celebrates several famous women.*

cel·e·bra·tion |sĕl′ə brā′shən| —*noun, plural* **celebrations** The act of celebrating: *the celebration of his anniversary.*

ce·leb·ri·ty |sə lĕb′rĭ tē| —*noun, plural* **celebrities** A famous or well-known person.

cel·er·y |sĕl′ər ē| —*noun* A plant with crisp, juicy, whitish or green stems. The stems are eaten raw or cooked. Celery seeds are used as seasoning.

cell |sĕl| —*noun, plural* **cells** **1.** A small room in which a person is confined: *a prison cell; a monastery cell.* **2.** The smallest part of any living plant or animal. A cell has a thin membrane that encloses a substance called protoplasm and a small central mass called a nucleus. Most living plants and animals consist of great numbers of related and connected cells. **3.** A small part of an object or substance: *the cells of a honeycomb.* **4.** A container holding chemicals that produce electricity: *The battery is made up of dry cells.*
♦ *These sound alike* **cell, sell.**

cel·lar |sĕl′ər| —*noun, plural* **cellars** A room under a building where things are stored.
♦ *These sound alike* **cellar, seller.**

cel·lo |chĕl′ō| —*noun, plural* **cellos** A musical instrument of the violin family. A cello is much larger than a violin and held between the knees when played. It has a deep, mellow tone.

cel·lo·phane |sĕl′ə fān′| —*noun* A thin, clear material like flexible paper. Cellophane is made from wood pulp. It is used as a wrapping to keep food fresh.

cel·lu·lose |sĕl′yə lōs′| —*noun* A substance that forms the cell walls of plants and trees. Cellulose is used to make paper, cloth, plastics, and explosives.

Cel·si·us |sĕl′sē əs| or |sĕl′shəs| —*adjective* Of the Celsius scale.

Celsius scale A temperature scale on which the freezing point

cavern

celery

cello

of water is 0°C and the boiling point is 100°C. It is the official name for the centigrade scale.

ce·ment |sĭ **mĕnt´**| —*noun, plural* **cements 1.** A mixture of powders made from clay and limestone, to which water is added to form a paste. Cement becomes hard like stone. It is used as a building material, to make sidewalks and streets, and to hold bricks and stones together. **2.** Any material, such as glue, that hardens to hold things together.
—*verb* **cemented, cementing 1.** To join or cover with cement: *Judy cemented the handle to the jar.* **2.** To bind or strengthen: *They cemented their friendship with a handshake.*

cem·e·ter·y |**sĕm´**ĭ tĕr´ē| —*noun, plural* **cemeteries** A place where dead people are buried; graveyard.

cen·sus |**sĕn´**səs| —*noun, plural* **censuses** An official count, usually by a government, of the people living in a given area. A census may also include the age, sex, job, and other information about the people being counted.

cent |sĕnt| —*noun, plural* **cents** A coin of the United States, Canada, and other countries, equal to 1/100 of the country's basic unit of money. In the United States and Canada, 100 cents equal one dollar.
♦ *These sound alike* **cent, scent, sent.**

cen·ten·ni·al |sĕn **tĕn´**ē əl| —*noun, plural* **centennials** A 100th anniversary or a celebration of it.
—*adjective* **1.** Of a period of 100 years: *a centennial year.* **2.** Happening once every 100 years: *a centennial celebration.*

cen·ter |**sĕn´**tər| —*noun, plural* **centers 1.** A point that is the same distance from every point of a circle or sphere; the exact middle. **2.** The middle point, place, or part of something: *the center of the table.* **3.** A place where many things or activities are gathered together: *a shopping center; a recreation center.* **4.** A main or principal person, place, or thing: *the center of attraction.* **5.** A player on a team who has the middle position: *She plays center on her hockey team.*
—*verb* **centered, centering** To place in or at the center: *We centered the gate in the fence.*

centi- A prefix that means "a hundredth": *centigram.*

cen·ti·grade |**sĕn´**tĭ grād´| —*adjective* Of a temperature scale divided into 100 degrees between the freezing and boiling points of water; Celsius: *The centigrade thermometer shows zero degrees as the temperature at which water freezes.*

cen·ti·gram |**sĕn´**tĭ grăm´| —*noun, plural* **centigrams** A unit of weight in the metric system equal to 1/100 gram.

cen·ti·me·ter |**sĕn´**tĭ mē´tər| —*noun, plural* **centimeters** A unit of length in the metric system equal to 1/100 meter.

cen·ti·pede |**sĕn´**tĭ pēd| —*noun, plural* **centipedes** An animal that looks something like a worm. It has a long, flat body and many pairs of legs. A centipede can give a painful bite.

cen·tral |**sĕn´**trəl| —*adjective* **1.** At or near the center: *the central part of the city.* **2.** Most important; main; chief: *Decisions are made at the central office.*

Central America The part of North America between Mexico and South America.

cen·tu·ry |**sĕn´**chər ē| —*noun, plural* **centuries** A period of one hundred years: *The years 1801 to 1900 make up the nineteenth century.*

cent
Above: Both sides of the first U.S. cent
Below: Both sides of a modern U.S. cent

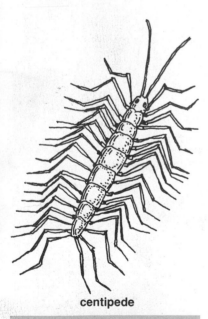

centipede

ă	pat	ĕ	pet	î	fierce
ā	pay	ē	be	ŏ	pot
â	care	ĭ	pit	ō	go
ä	father	ī	pie	ô	paw, for
oi	oil	ŭ	cut	zh	vision
ŏŏ	book	û	fur	ə	ago, item,
ōō	boot	*th*	the		pencil, atom,
yōō	abuse	th	thin		circus
ou	out	hw	which	ər	butter

ce·ram·ic | sə răm′ĭc | —*noun, plural* **ceramics** **1.** A hard, brittle material made by treating clay or other substance to extremely high heat. Ceramic is used in making pottery and many other things. **2.** Often **ceramics** Objects made of this ceramic: *Pack the ceramics carefully so they won't break.* **3. ceramics** (In this sense used with a singular verb.) The art or technique of making things from ceramic: *Ceramics is his hobby.*

ce·re·al | sîr′ē əl | —*noun, plural* **cereals** **1.** The seeds of certain grasses, such as wheat, oats, corn, or rice, used as food. **2.** A food made from the seeds of such plants: *What kind of cereal do you want for breakfast, corn flakes or oatmeal?*

cer·e·mo·ni·al | sĕr′ə mō′nē əl | —*adjective* Of a ceremony: *They performed a ceremonial dance.*
—*noun, plural* **ceremonials** A ceremony: *The ceremonial included several parts.*

cer·e·mo·ny | sĕr′ə mō′nē | —*noun, plural* **ceremonies** **1.** A formal act or series of acts in honor of an event or special occasion: *a wedding ceremony.* **2.** Very polite or formal behavior: *She spoke with great ceremony.*

cer·tain | sûr′tn | —*adjective* **1.** Having no doubt; positive; sure: *Are you certain that you left your book on the subway?* **2.** Beyond doubt; proven; definite: *Whether we will be there is not certain.* **3.** Sure to come or happen: *The team faced certain defeat.* **4.** Not named but assumed to be known: *There are certain laws protecting us.* **5.** Some: *to a certain degree.*
   Idiom **for certain** Surely; without doubt: *It will happen for certain.*

cer·tain·ly | sûr′tn lē | —*adverb* Surely or definitely: *He will certainly come.*

cer·tain·ty | sûr′tn tē | —*noun, plural* **certainties** **1.** The condition of being certain or sure: *She answered the question with certainty.* **2.** A sure or established fact: *It is a certainty that the sun will rise.*

cer·tif·i·cate | sər tĭf′ĭ kĭt | —*noun, plural* **certificates** **1.** An official statement or document that gives information. A birth certificate states the date and place of birth of a person. **2.** A document that someone may do special jobs: *He has earned a certificate for teaching.*

chain | chān | —*noun, plural* **chains** **1.** A row of connected rings or loops, usually made of metal. One kind of chain is used to hold or fasten things. Another kind of chain is used for ornaments: *The men held the logs together with a chain. She wore a chain around her neck.* **2.** A series of connected or related things: *a chain of events; a chain of food stores; a chain of mountains.*
—*verb* **chained, chaining** To hold or fasten with a chain: *He chained the elephant to a post.*

chair | châr | —*noun, plural* **chairs** **1.** A piece of furniture on which a person sits. A chair usually has a back, seat, four legs, and some have arms. **2.** A position of authority: *Mrs. Green holds the chair of French Art in this college.*

chair·man | châr′mən | —*noun, plural* **chairmen** A man in charge of a meeting or who directs the work of a committee or other group.

chair·per·son | châr′pûr′sən | —*noun, plural* **chairpersons** A person in charge of a meeting or who directs the work of a committee or other group.

chair·wom·an | châr′wŏom′ən | —*noun, plural* **chairwomen** A

chain

chair

woman in charge of a meeting or who directs the work of a committee or other group.

chalk |chŏk| —*noun, plural* **chalks** **1.** A soft mineral made up mostly of tiny fossil seashells. **2.** A piece of this substance used especially for making marks on a blackboard: *The teacher wrote the lesson with chalks of different colors.*

Phrasal verb **chalk up** To earn or score: *The points you win will be chalked up for your team.*

chal·lenge |chăl′ənj| —*noun, plural* **challenges** **1.** A call or invitation to take part in a contest or fight to see who is the better, stronger, or faster: *The Red Team will meet the challenge of the Blue Team.* **2.** A call to find out who someone is: *The guard called out a challenge to the stranger.* **3.** Something that needs all of a person's efforts and skills: *The new job will be a challenge.*

—*verb* **challenged, challenging** **1.** To call to take part in a contest or fight. **2.** To order to stop and say who you are. **3.** To call for all a person's efforts and skills: *This assignment challenges the workers.* **4.** To question the truth or right of: *The customer challenged the salesperson's claim about the product.*

cham·ber |chām′bər| —*noun, plural* **chambers** **1.** A private room in a house, especially a bedroom. **2.** **chambers** A judge's office in a courthouse. **3.** The room or hall where lawmakers meet: *Members of the Senate met in the Senate chambers.* **4.** The lawmaking group itself: *The Senate is the upper chamber of Congress.* **5.** An enclosed space in a plant or animal body: *a seashell divided into chambers; the three chambers of a bird's heart.* **6.** The place in a gun where a bullet is put, ready for firing: *He loaded the chamber with another bullet.*

cha·me·leon |kə mēl′yən| *or* |kə mē′lē ən| —*noun, plural* **chameleons** A small lizard that can change its color quickly. It may turn green, brown, or gray, to blend in with its surroundings.

cham·pi·on |chăm′pē ən| —*noun, plural* **champions** **1.** Someone or something who has won a game or contest against all others: *Judy won the race and is the new champion.* **2.** Someone who fights for or defends something he or she believes in: *Don is a champion of animal rights.*

—*verb* **championed, championing** To fight for or defend something one believes in: *The new representatives championed the rights of poor people.*

cham·pi·on·ship |chăm′pē ən shĭp′| —*noun, plural* **championships** **1.** The title or position of champion: *He won the spelling championship.* **2.** Defense or support: *her championship of women's rights.*

chance |chăns| *or* |chäns| —*noun, plural* **chances** **1.** The happening of things without any cause that can be seen or understood; fate; luck; accident: *They found the treasure by chance.* **2.** The possibility or probability that something will happen: *He has a good chance of recovering.* **3.** An opportunity: *The salesman saw a chance to make some money.* **4.** A risk or gamble: *He took a chance and left his umbrella at home.*

—*verb* **chanced, chancing** **1.** To happen by accident: *She chanced to call when we were out.* **2.** To take a chance with; risk: *The robbers decided to chance an escape.*

Phrasal verb **chance on** or **upon** To come upon or meet accidentally: *Dan chanced upon Mary in the park.*

chameleon

ă	pat	ĕ	pet	î	fierce
ā	pay	ē	be	ŏ	pot
â	care	ĭ	pit	ō	go
ä	father	ī	pie	ô	paw, for
oi	oil	ŭ	cut	zh	vision
ŏŏ	book	û	fur	ə	ago, item,
ōō	boot	th	the		pencil, atom,
yōō	abuse	th	thin		circus
ou	out	hw	which	ər	butter

chan·de·lier |shăn′də **lîr′** | —*noun, plural* **chandeliers** A light fixture with several arms or branches that hold light bulbs or candles. A chandelier hangs from the ceiling.

change |chānj| —*verb* **changed, changing** **1.** To make or become different: *Let's change the color of the room. You have changed since last year.* **2.** To take, put, or use something in place of another; replace; exchange: *change these shoes for more comfortable ones; change this dollar bill for some coins; change into more comfortable clothing.* **3.** To put fresh clothing or coverings on: *change a baby; change a bed.*
—*noun, plural* **changes** **1.** The act or result of changing: *a change in plans; a change in seasons.* **2.** Something that is put in place of something else: *a change of sheets on the bed. Rinse the vegetables in three changes of water.* **3. a.** The money returned when the amount given in payment is more than the amount owed: *The pad cost eighty cents so Jane got back change from her dollar.* **b.** Coins: *She needs change to operate the machine.* **4.** A fresh set of clothing: *You will need two changes of clothing for camp.*

chan·nel |chăn′əl| —*noun, plural* **channels** **1.** The deepest part of a river or harbor through which ships can pass. **2.** A body of water that connects two larger bodies: *The English Channel connects the Atlantic Ocean with the North Sea.* **3.** A band of radio waves used for broadcasting or communicating: *truck drivers talking to one another on Channel 19; a television channel.*
—*verb* **channeled, channeling** To form a channel in or through something: *The river had channeled a deep valley.*

chant |chănt| or |chänt| —*noun, plural* **chants** **1.** A song or melody with many words sung on the same note: *In some religious services, people sing chants.* **2.** A shouting or calling of words over and over: *The football team could hear the school chant.*
—*verb* **chanted, chanting** **1.** To sing the words to a chant. **2.** To call out in a chant: *The students chanted as the score went higher.*

Cha·nu·kah |hä′nŏŏ kä′| —*noun, plural* **Chanukahs** A Jewish festival. Chanukah comes in December or late November and lasts eight days. Another form of this word is **Hanukkah.**

cha·os |kā′ŏs| —*noun* Great confusion; disorder: *The living room was in chaos after the party.*

chap¹ |chăp| —*verb* **chapped, chapping** To make or become rough, dry, and cracked: *Her lips chap in the cold. Harsh soap will chap your hands.*

chap² |chăp| —*noun, plural* **chaps** A man or boy; fellow: *He is a fine chap.*

chap·el |chăp′əl| —*noun, plural* **chapels** **1.** A small church. **2.** A room or other place in a building for worship.

chap·lain |chăp′lən| —*noun, plural* **chaplains** A clergyman who holds religious services for a school, prison, military unit, or other group.

chaps |chăps| —*plural noun* Heavy leather pants without a seat, worn over regular pants by cowboys to protect their legs.

chap·ter |chăp′tər| —*noun, plural* **chapters** **1.** A main division of a book. A chapter may have a title, a number, or both. **2.** A local branch of a club or other group: *The downtown chapter of mom's business club meets on Thursdays.*

char·ac·ter |kăr′ĭk tər| —*noun, plural* **characters** **1.** The combination of qualities that makes one person or thing different

chandelier

---

chap¹, chap²
Chap¹ first appeared in the fourteenth century. It may have been borrowed from a word used in a form of German. **Chap²** was a slang word in the sixteenth century. It is short for *chapman,* which in England even now refers to a peddler or dealer.

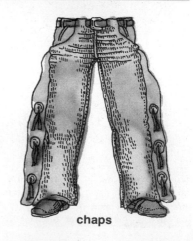

chaps

from another: *The character of this town is quiet and sleepy.* **2.** A person's moral nature: *A leader's character is judged by the way he or she talks, thinks, and acts.* **3.** Moral strength; honesty: *a man of character.* **4.** A person in a book, story, play, or movie: *My favorite character is Mary Poppins.* **5.** Someone who is different, odd, and often funny: *That child is really a character.*

char·ac·ter·is·tic |kăr′ĭk tər ĭs′tĭk| —*adjective* Showing a special feature of a person or thing: *Laughing was a characteristic action of hers.*

—*noun, plural* **characteristics** A special feature or quality: *A characteristic of a beaver is the way it builds its home.*

char·ac·ter·ize |kăr′ĭk tə rīz′| —*verb* **characterized, characterizing 1.** To describe the character or qualities of; portray: *He characterized his aunt as lively and kind.* **2.** To be a characteristic or quality of: *Strength characterizes steel.*

cha·rades |shə rādz′| —*plural noun* A game in which words and phrases are acted out silently until guessed by other players.

char·coal |chär′kōl′| —*noun* A black material made mostly of carbon. Charcoal is produced by heating wood or other plant or animal matter. Charcoal is used as fuel, as a filtering material, and for drawing.

charge |chärj| —*verb* **charged, charging 1.** To ask as payment: *The ice cream shop charged forty cents for a cone.* **2.** To put off paying for something, with an arrangement to pay later: *Do you want to pay for this now, or will you charge it to your account?* **3.** To rush at or into with force, as if attacking: *He charged into the room without knocking.* **4.** To accuse; blame: *The police charged him with speeding.* **5.** To trust with a duty: *The nurse was charged with the care of the children.* **6.** To put or take electrical energy into a battery: *Please charge the car's battery. Is the battery charging?*

—*noun, plural* **charges 1.** The amount asked or made as payment: *The charge is two dollars for this service.* **2.** Care; supervision; control: *The children are in his charge. She is in charge of the meeting.* **3.** An accusation, especially one made formally: *He was fired on a charge of cheating.* **4.** An attack: *the charge of an angry bull.* **5.** Electrical energy that is or can be stored in a battery: *This old battery won't hold a charge any more.*

charge account An arrangement with a store or other business in which a customer receives goods or services and pays for them at a later time.

char·i·ot |chăr′ē ət| —*noun, plural* **chariots** A two-wheeled vehicle pulled by horses. In ancient times chariots were used in battles, races, and parades.

char·i·ta·ble |chăr′ĭ tə bəl| —*adjective* **1.** Showing love or kindness: *His father has a very warm, charitable nature.* **2.** Generous in giving help to needy people. **3.** Tolerant and understanding: *Be more charitable when you speak of him; he has his own problems.* **4.** Of charity; for charity: *Some hospitals are charitable institutions.*

char·i·ty |chăr′ĭ tē| —*noun, plural* **charities 1.** Good will or love toward others. **2.** The condition or quality of being understanding in judging others: *Although Al broke a dish, his aunt showed great charity toward him.* **3.** Money or other help given to the needy. **4.** A group that is organized to help the poor or needy: *Give money to your favorite charity.*

chariot
On a Greek vase

ă	pat	ĕ	pet	î	fierce
ā	pay	ē	be	ŏ	pot
â	care	ĭ	pit	ō	go
ä	father	ī	pie	ô	paw, for
oi	oil	ŭ	cut	zh	vision
ŏŏ	book	û	fur	ə	ago, item,
ōō	boot	*th*	the		pencil, atom,
yōō	abuse	th	thin		circus
ou	out	hw	which	ər	butter

Charles·ton |chärl′stən| The capital of West Virginia.

Char·lotte·town |shär′lət toun′| The capital of Prince Edward Island.

charm |chärm| —*noun, plural* **charms** **1.** The power to please or delight; great appeal: *There was great charm in her voice.* **2.** A magic spell, act, or saying: *The wizard cast a charm on us.* **3.** An object kept or worn for its magic power: *They think a rabbit's foot is a lucky charm.* **4.** A small ornament worn on a necklace or bracelet.
—*verb* **charmed, charming** **1.** To please or delight. **2.** To win over; bewitch: *She charmed us into getting her own way.*

charm·ing |chär′mĭng| —*adjective* Delightful; attractive; very pleasing: *a charming man.*

chart |chärt| —*noun, plural* **charts** **1.** A paper giving information in the form of graphs and tables. **2.** A map for sailors showing the coast, water depth, and other information.
—*verb* **charted, charting** To show or plot on a chart; make a chart of: *Chart the sales for the lemonade stand.*

chase |chās| —*verb* **chased, chasing** **1.** To go quickly after and try to catch or catch up with; pursue: *My father chased my baby sister.* **2.** To drive away: *Our dog chased the stranger away.*
—*noun, plural* **chases** The act of chasing: *There is a wild chase in that movie.*

chasm |kăz′əm| —*noun, plural* **chasms** **1.** A deep crack in the earth's surface. **2.** A wide difference of views: *Their different opinions caused a chasm among the members of the club.*

chat |chăt| —*verb* **chatted, chatting** To talk in a friendly way: *They chatted about the weather.*
—*noun, plural* **chats** A friendly talk: *They had a little chat while waiting for the bus.*

chat·ter |chăt′ər| —*verb* **chattered, chattering** **1.** To make rapid noises that sound like speech: *The birds chatter at dawn.* **2.** To talk fast about unimportant things: *She chattered about nothing.* **3.** To make quick, rattling noises: *Joe's teeth chattered in the cold.*
—*noun, plural* **chatters** **1.** The sharp, quick sounds made by some animals: *the chatter of squirrels.* **2.** Unimportant talk. **3.** Any series of quick, rattling sounds: *the chatter of machines.*

chauf·feur |shō′fər| or |shō fûr′| —*noun, plural* **chauffeurs** Someone who drives a car for pay.

cheap |chēp| —*adjective* **cheaper, cheapest** **1.** Low in price; inexpensive: *Eggs are cheap this week.* **2.** Charging low prices: *a cheap restaurant.* **3.** Of low or poor quality: *cheap shoes.* **4.** Not willing to spend or give money; stingy: *She is too cheap to buy her own copy of the book.*

cheat |chēt| —*verb* **cheated, cheating** **1.** To take something away from someone dishonestly; to swindle: *They cheated the Indians of their land.* **2.** To act in a dishonest way; to fool or mislead: *cheat at sports.*
—*noun, plural* **cheats** A person who cheats.

check |chĕk| —*verb* **checked, checking** **1.** To stop; hold back: *The driver checked the horses as we came around the bend. She checked her anger and smiled.* **2.** To test, examine, or compare to make sure something is right or in good condition: *We checked our answers. The pilot checked her plane before taking off.* **3.** To note or consult for information or permission: *Check with the librarian for that book. Check the dictionary for the spelling of that*

charm
Both sides of a silver charm

word. **4.** To mark with a sign to show that something has been chosen, noted, or is correct. **5.** To leave something to be kept: *They checked their bags at the airport.*

Phrasal verbs **check in** To sign in at a hotel, hospital, or other place that keeps a record of people who stay there. **check out** To leave after paying: *They checked out of the hotel.*
—*noun, plural* **checks 1.** A stop; halt: *The accident put a check on our game.* **2.** A careful examination or test to make sure something is right: *Make a check of your addition.* **3.** A mark made to show something has been chosen, noted, or is correct. **4.** A written order to a bank to pay money from an account: *pay bills by check.* **5.** A ticket, slip, or tag given in return for something that has been left to be kept or for repairs: *a baggage check.* **6.** A bill at a restaurant. **7. a.** A pattern made of squares: *Did you wear the striped shirt or the one with checks?* **b.** A single square in such a pattern: *The checks in his shirt are yellow.*

check·er |chĕk′ər| —*noun, plural* **checkers 1.** Someone or something that checks for accuracy: *She is a checker at the factory.* **2. a. checkers** (In this sense used with a singular verb.) A game played on a checkerboard by two players. Each player has twelve round, flat disks. Players take turns moving their disks on the board. They try to capture or block each other's disks. **b.** One of the disks used in the game of checkers: *Put the red checker on the black square.*

check·er·board |chĕk′ər bôrd′| or |chĕk′ər bōrd′| —*noun, plural* **checkerboards** A board divided into 64 squares of alternating colors. Checkers and chess are played on a checkerboard.

check·up |chĕk′ŭp′| —*noun, plural* **checkups** A careful examination to find out what condition a person or thing is in: *a health checkup; a car checkup.*

cheek |chēk| —*noun, plural* **cheeks 1.** The part of the face on either side below the eye and between the nose and ear. **2.** A rude or fresh way of acting: *She had the cheek to ask why she wasn't invited.*

cheer |chîr| —*verb* **cheered, cheering 1.** To shout in happiness, praise, approval, or encouragement: *We clapped and cheered as the runners crossed the finish line.* **2.** To praise, encourage, or urge by shouting: *Crowds gathered to cheer the President. We cheered the runners on.* **3.** To make happier: *Her laughter cheered us up.*
—*noun, plural* **cheers 1.** A shout or chant of happiness, praise, approval, or encouragement. **2.** Happiness; gaiety; good spirits: *Grandfather was always full of cheer and good stories.*

cheer·ful |chîr′fəl| —*adjective* **1.** In good spirits; happy: *She was cheerful at work.* **2.** Causing a feeling of cheer; pleasant and bright: *a cheerful room; a cheerful smile.*

cheer·lead·er |chîr′lē′dər| —*noun, plural* **cheerleaders** A person who leads cheers at sports events.

cheer·y |chîr′ē| —*adjective* **cheerier, cheeriest** Bright and pleasant; gay: *She had a cheery smile.*

cheese |chēz| —*noun, plural* **cheeses** A food made from milk. A solid material, called curds, is separated from the milk and then pressed together to make cheese.

cheese·burg·er |chēz′bûr′gər| —*noun, plural* **cheeseburgers** A hamburger cooked with melted cheese on top.

chee·tah |chē′tə| —*noun, plural* **cheetahs** A spotted wild cat of

checkerboard

cheerleader

cheetah

ă	pat	ĕ	pet	î	fierce
ā	pay	ē	be	ŏ	pot
â	care	ĭ	pit	ō	go
ä	father	ī	pie	ô	paw, for

oi	oil	ŭ	cut	zh	vision
ŏŏ	book	û	fur	ə	ago, item,
ōō	boot	*th*	the		pencil, atom,
yōō	abuse	th	thin		circus
ou	out	hw	which	ər	butter

Africa and southern Asia. Cheetahs have long legs and can run very fast.

chef |shĕf| —*noun, plural* **chefs** A cook, especially the head cook of a restaurant.

chem·i·cal |kĕm′ĭ kəl| —*adjective* **1.** Of chemistry: *a chemical discovery.* **2.** Used in or produced by chemistry: *a chemical formula; a chemical change.*
—*noun, plural* **chemicals** Any substance produced by or used in chemistry; an element or compound.

chem·ist |kĕm′ĭst| —*noun, plural* **chemists** A scientist who knows a lot about chemistry.

chem·is·try |kĕm′ĭ strē| —*noun* The scientific study of substances to see what they are made of, what is special about them, how they change when combined with other substances, and what happens to them under various conditions such as heat or cold.

cher·ish |chĕr′ĭsh| —*verb* **cherished, cherishing** **1.** To care for tenderly and affectionately; love: *We cherished our little cousin as if she were our own sister.* **2.** To keep or think of fondly; think of as very valuable; hold dear: *They cherished their freedom above all else.*

cher·ry |chĕr′ē| —*noun, plural* **cherries** **1.** A small, round red fruit with smooth skin and a hard pit. **2.** A tree on which cherries grow. Cherry trees have white or pink flowers that bloom in spring. **3.** A deep or bright-red color. ◊ The noun **cherry** can be used like an adjective for things made from the wood or fruit of a cherry tree: *a cherry table; a cherry pie.*
—*adjective* Deep or bright red.

chess |chĕs| —*noun* A game for two played on a chessboard or checkerboard. Each player starts with sixteen pieces that are allowed to move in various ways. The object of chess is to capture the other player's king.

chess·board |chĕs′bôrd′| or |chĕs′bōrd′| —*noun, plural* **chessboards** A board with 64 squares in alternating colors. Chess or checkers can be played on it.

chess·man |chĕs′măn′| or |chĕs′mən| —*noun, plural* **chessmen** One of the pieces used in the game of chess. The chessmen are king, queen, bishop, knight, rook, and pawn.

chest |chĕst| —*noun, plural* **chests** **1.** The upper front part of the body between the neck and abdomen. The chest is enclosed by the ribs and breastbone. **2.** A strong box with a lid, used for holding things: *a tool chest; a treasure chest.* **3.** A piece of furniture with several drawers, used mostly for holding clothing; a bureau or dresser: *She found her sweater in the chest of drawers.*

chest·nut |chĕs′nŭt′| or |chĕs′nət| —*noun, plural* **chestnuts**
1. A smooth reddish-brown nut that grows inside a prickly bur.
2. A tree on which chestnuts grow. **3.** A reddish-brown color.
—*adjective* Reddish-brown.

chew |chōo| —*verb* **chewed, chewing** To grind, crush, or gnaw with the teeth or jaws: *Food should be chewed carefully before you swallow it. Grasshoppers chew with a sideways motion.*
—*noun, plural* **chews** The act of chewing; a bite.

chew·ing gum |chōo′ĭng| Gum for chewing, usually sweet and flavored mint, fruit, or spices.

chew·y |chōo′ē| —*adjective* **chewier, chewiest** Needing much chewing: *chewy candy.*

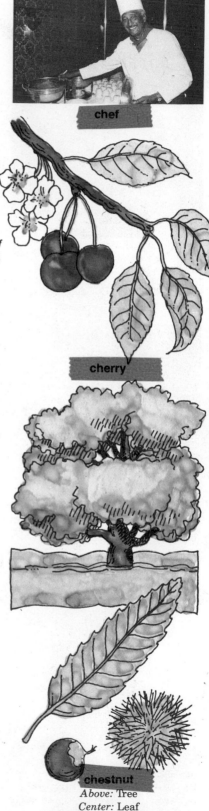

chef

cherry

chestnut
Above: Tree
Center: Leaf
Below: Chestnut *(left)* and bur *(right)*

Chey·enne |shī ăn′| or |shī ĕn′| The capital of Wyoming.
Chi·ca·no |shĭ kä′nō| or |chĭ kä′nō| —*noun, plural* **Chicanos**
An American who was born in Mexico or whose parents or
ancestors were from Mexico.
chick |chĭk| —*noun, plural* **chicks 1.** A young chicken. **2.** A
young bird.
chick·a·dee |chĭk′ə dē′| —*noun, plural* **chickadees** A small,
plump bird with gray, black, and white feathers. It has a call that
sounds like its name.
chick·en |chĭk′ən| —*noun, plural* **chickens 1.** A large bird
commonly raised for its eggs or as food; a hen or a rooster.
2. The meat of this bird.
chicken pox A children's disease that spreads to others easily.
In chicken pox the skin breaks out in spots and fever occurs.
chick·pea |chĭk′pē′| —*noun, plural* **chickpeas** A round seed
that grows on a bushy plant. Chickpeas are good to eat.
chief |chēf| —*noun, plural* **chiefs** A person with the highest
rank; a leader: *the chief of the police department.*
—*adjective* **1.** Highest in rank: *the chief engineer.* **2.** Most
important; main: *Two of that country's chief products are steel and
automobiles.*
chief·ly |chēf′lē| —*adverb* Mainly; mostly; especially: *His
questions were chiefly about food.*
chief·tain |chēf′tən| —*noun, plural* **chieftains** The leader of a
tribe or clan.
child |chīld| —*noun, plural* **children 1.** A young girl or boy.
2. Someone who acts childish or young. **3.** A son or daughter;
offspring: *The parents came to pick up their child from school.*
child·hood |chīld′hŏŏd′| —*noun, plural* **childhoods** The
condition of being a child; the time when a person is a child: *My
mother often speaks of her childhood. During their childhood many
things had happened in the world.*
child·ish |chīl′dĭsh| —*adjective* **1.** Of, typical of, or for a child:
a high, childish voice; childish clothes. **2.** Foolish in a way that is
like someone much younger; immature: *You're too old for such
childish pouting and crying.*
chil·dren |chĭl′drən| The plural of the noun **child.**
chil·e con car·ne |chĭl′ē kŏn kär′nē| A spicy food made of
chili, meat, and often beans.
chil·i |chĭl′ē| —*noun* **1.** A spice with a sharp, hot taste, made
from the pods of a kind of red pepper. **2.** Chile con carne.
♦ *These sound alike* **chili, chilly.**
chill |chĭl| —*noun, plural* **chills 1.** A sharp or penetrating cold:
In October there is a chill in the air. **2.** A feeling of cold from illness
or fear: *Jan went home with chills and a runny nose. A chill went up
his back from the ghost story.*
—*adjective* **chiller, chillest** Unpleasantly cold; chilly: *a chill wind.*
—*verb* **chilled, chilling 1.** To make or become cold: *Dad chilled the
juice. The salad is chilling in the refrigerator.* **2.** To cause a feeling
of cold or fear: *The ghost story chilled all who heard it.*
chill·y |chĭl′ē| —*adjective* **chillier, chilliest 1.** Fairly cold; cold
enough to be uncomfortable: *It was a chilly November day. Six chilly
campers huddled in front of the fire.* **2.** Not very interested or
eager; not friendly: *Our plans for a giant tree house got a chilly
reaction from our parents.*
♦ *These sound alike* **chilly, chili.**

chicken

ă	pat	ĕ	pet	î	fierce
ā	pay	ē	be	ŏ	pot
â	care	ĭ	pit	ō	go
ä	father	ī	pie	ô	paw, for
oi	oil	ŭ	cut	zh	vision
ŏŏ	book	û	fur	ə	ago, item,
ōō	boot	*th*	the		pencil, atom,
yōō	abuse	th	thin		circus
ou	out	hw	which	ər	butter

chime |chīm| —*noun, plural* **chimes 1. chimes** A set of bells, pipes, or metal rods that make musical sounds. Some chimes are used as signals, as in doorbells or clocks. Some chimes are built as a musical instrument and are tuned to a musical scale. To play chimes a musician usually strikes them with a small hammer. **2.** A musical sound made by bells or chimes: *the chime of the steeple bells.*
—*verb* **chimed, chiming** To ring or make a musical sound: *The old clock chimed in the hallway. The bells chimed the hour.*
  Phrasal verb **chime in** To join in: *When we were talking, Dan chimed in too.*

chim·ney |chĭm′nē| —*noun, plural* **chimneys 1.** A hollow, upright structure through which smoke passes from a fireplace, stove, or furnace. **2.** A glass tube placed around the flame of a candle or lamp.

chim·pan·zee |chĭm′păn zē′| or |chĭm păn′zē| —*noun, plural* **chimpanzees** An African ape with dark hair. Chimpanzees are very intelligent. In captivity they can be trained to do many things.

chimpanzee

chin |chĭn| —*noun, plural* **chins** The front of the lower jaw between the mouth and the neck.
—*verb* **chinned, chinning** To hang by a bar and pull oneself up with the arms until the chin is just higher than the bar.

chi·na |chī′nə| —*noun* **1.** A fine, hard pottery made from white clay and often decorated with bright colors. Originally such pottery came from China. **2.** Objects made from this pottery, such as dishes and small statues.

Chi·na |chī′nə| A country in eastern and central Asia. More people live in China than in any other country in the world.

Chi·nese |chī nēz′| or |chī nēs′| —*noun, plural* **Chinese 1.** A person who was born in China or who is a citizen of China. **2.** A person whose ancestors were born in China. **3.** Any of the several languages of China.
—*adjective* Of China, the Chinese, or their languages or culture.

chink |chĭngk| —*noun, plural* **chinks** A narrow crack or opening: *a chink in the wall.*

chip |chĭp| —*noun, plural* **chips 1.** A small piece that has been cut or broken off: *a chip of wood.* **2.** A mark left when a small piece is broken off: *a chip in the bowl.* **3.** A small disk used in some games. **4.** A thin slice of food: *a potato chip.*
—*verb* **chipped, chipping** To break off a piece by hitting, bumping, or cutting: *Chip the bark with an ax.*
  Phrasal verb **chip in** To give or contribute money: *The team chipped in to buy a new banner.*

chin
Exercising on a chinning bar

chip·munk |chĭp′mŭngk′| —*noun, plural* **chipmunks** A small North American animal with brown fur and a striped back. Chipmunks are related to squirrels.

chirp |chûrp| —*noun, plural* **chirps** A short, high sound such as that made by a small bird or a cricket.
—*verb* **chirped, chirping** To make such a sound: *The birds chirp early in the morning.*

chis·el |chĭz′əl| —*noun, plural* **chisels** A metal tool with a sharp edge. A chisel is used with a hammer to cut or shape wood, stone, or metal.
—*verb* **chiseled, chiseling** To shape or cut with a chisel: *The carpenter chiseled a groove in the cabinet.*

chipmunk

chisel

chiv·al·ry |shĭv′əl rē| —*noun* **1.** The customs and actions of the knights of the Middle Ages. **2.** The qualities that an ideal knight might have, including bravery, honor, courtesy, and being helpful to the weak.

chlo·rine |klôr′ēn′| or |klôr′ĭn| or |klōr′ēn′| or |klōr′ĭn| —*noun, plural* **chlorines** A greenish-yellow gas with an unpleasant odor. Compounds of chlorine are used to purify water for drinking and for swimming pools. Chlorine is one of the chemical elements.

chlo·ro·phyll or **chlo·ro·phyl** |klôr′ə fĭl| or |klōr′ə fĭl| —*noun* A substance in the leaves and other parts of green plants. It gives them their green color. Chlorophyll helps plants make sugar from elements in air and water.

choc·o·late |chô′kə lĭt| or |chŏk′ə lĭt| or |chôk′lĭt| or |chŏk′lĭt| —*noun, plural* **chocolates** **1.** A food made from roasted and ground cacao beans. **2.** A sweet drink made with chocolate: *a cup of hot chocolate.* **3.** Candy made with chocolate: *My brother bought chocolates for my birthday.*

choice |chois| —*noun, plural* **choices** **1.** The act of choosing: *I must make a choice between two books.* **2.** The power, right, or chance to choose: *Mom gave us a choice of rice or potatoes.* **3.** Someone or something chosen: *My choice was a green shirt.* **4.** A variety of things to choose from: *a wide choice of fruits and vegetables.*
—*adjective* **choicer, choicest** Of fine quality; very good; excellent: *choice meat.*

choir |kwīr| —*noun, plural* **choirs** A group of singers that meet regularly and perform together, often in a church.

choke |chōk| —*verb* **choked, choking** **1.** To stop or block the breathing of a person or animal by squeezing or blocking the windpipe. **2.** To be unable to breathe, swallow, or speak normally because the throat is blocked: *He choked on a peanut.* **3.** To reduce the air that goes to an engine so that it will start more easily. **4.** To hold back; stop: *choke back tears.* **5.** To fill up; clog: *Hair choked the sink drain.*

choose |chōoz| —*verb* **chose, chosen, choosing** **1.** To select or pick from a group: *She will choose a partner. He chose a book.* **2.** To decide or prefer something: *She did not choose to leave.*

choos·y |chōo′zē| —*adjective* **choosier, choosiest** Hard to please; fussy: *You would have more friends if you weren't so choosy.*

chop |chŏp| —*verb* **chopped, chopping** **1.** To cut by hitting with a heavy, sharp tool such as an ax: *chop wood; chop down a tree.* **2.** To cut into little pieces: *chop up nuts; chop onions.* **3.** To stop suddenly; cut something short: *She chopped off her sentence in the middle of a word.*
—*noun, plural* **chops** **1.** A quick, short blow. **2.** A small cut of meat with a piece of bone: *a lamb chop.*

chop·sticks |chŏp′stĭks| —*plural noun* A pair of thin sticks used as eating tools in some Asian countries.

chord |kôrd| —*noun, plural* **chords** A combination of three or more musical notes sounded at the same time.
♦ *These sound alike* **chord, cord.**

chore |chôr| or |chōr| —*noun, plural* **chores** **1.** A small job, usually done on a regular schedule: *One of my chores is feeding the cat every day.* **2.** An unpleasant task or duty: *Cleaning out the garage was a real chore.*

choir

chopsticks

ă	pat	ĕ	pet	î	fierce
ā	pay	ē	be	ŏ	pot
â	care	ĭ	pit	ō	go
ä	father	ī	pie	ô	paw, for
oi	oil	ŭ	cut	zh	vision
ōō	book	û	fur	ə	ago, item,
ōō	boot	th	the		pencil, atom,
yōō	abuse	th	thin		circus
ou	out	hw	which	ər	butter

cho·rus |kôr′əs| or |kōr′əs| —*noun, plural* **choruses** **1.** A group of singers or dancers who perform together. **2.** A part of a song repeated after each verse. **3.** Something said by many people at the same time: *a chorus of protests.*
—*verb* **chorused, chorusing** To sing or speak at the same time: *When the teacher asked us what time it was, we all chorused, "Lunch time!"*

chose |chōz| The past tense of the verb **choose:** *He chose a dark suit to wear at the party.*

chos·en |chō′zən| The past participle of the verb **choose:** *She was chosen by her classmates to be queen of the ball.*

chow·der |chou′dər| —*noun, plural* **chowders** A thick soup made with seafood or vegetables, usually with potatoes and milk: *clam chowder; fish chowder; corn chowder.*

Christ |krīst| —*noun* Jesus, regarded by Christians as the Son of God. He is the founder of the Christian religion.

chris·ten |krĭs′ən| —*verb* **christened, christening** **1.** To baptize and receive into a Christian church. **2.** To give a name to at baptism: *They christened me Robert, but they call me Chip.* **3.** To name at a ceremony: *christen a ship.*

chris·ten·ing |krĭs′ə nĭng| —*noun, plural* **christenings** The Christian ceremony of baptism, in which a child is named.

Chris·tian |krĭs′chən| —*noun, plural* **Christians** Someone who believes in Jesus Christ or follows a religion based on his teachings.
—*adjective* **1.** Believing in Christ or in a religion based on his teachings. **2.** Of Christ, Christianity, or Christians. **3.** Following the example of Christ; showing a gentle, loving, unselfish spirit.

Chris·ti·an·i·ty |krĭs′chē ăn′ĭ tē| —*noun* **1.** The religion of Christians. **2.** The condition or fact of being a Christian.

Christ·mas |krĭs′məs| —*noun, plural* **Christmases** A holiday on December 25 to celebrate the birth of Christ.

Christmas tree An evergreen tree, real or artificial, decorated with lights or ornaments to celebrate Christmas.

chro·mi·um |krō′mē əm| —*noun* A hard, gray metal, one of the chemical elements. Chromium does not rust. It can be polished to a bright shine.

chrys·a·lis |krĭs′ə lĭs| —*noun, plural* **chrysalises** A stage in the development of a moth or butterfly from a caterpillar. The caterpillar spins a tough case around itself and changes into a butterfly or moth during the months that it is inside. Each kind of caterpillar becomes a different kind of butterfly or moth.

chry·san·the·mum |krĭ săn′thə məm| —*noun, plural* **chrysanthemums** A flower with many closely clustered petals. Chrysanthemums come in many colors and are often grown in gardens or sold by florists.

chub·by |chŭb′ē| —*adjective* **chubbier, chubbiest** Round and plump: *The baby had a chubby face and a happy smile.*

chuck·le |chŭk′əl| —*verb* **chuckled, chuckling** To laugh quietly: *Dad chuckled as he read the comics.*
—*noun, plural* **chuckles** A quiet laugh: *We could hear the baby's chuckles as she played with her toes.*

chuck wagon |chŭk| A wagon with food and cooking equipment for a group of workers who move from place to place. Chuck wagons are often used on cattle drives.

chum |chŭm| —*noun, plural* **chums** A good friend or pal.

chorus

Christmas tree

chrysanthemum

church

churn

circle

ă	pat	ĕ	pet	î	fierce
ā	pay	ē	be	ŏ	pot
â	care	ĭ	pit	ō	go
ä	father	ī	pie	ô	paw, for

oi	oil	ŭ	cut	zh	vision
ŏŏ	book	û	fur	ə	ago, item,
ōō	boot	th	the		pencil, atom,
yōō	abuse	th	thin		circus
ou	out	hw	which	ər	butter

—*verb* **chummed, chumming** To do things together as close friends; pal around with: *Jill and Sue chum around together.*

chunk |chŭngk| —*noun, plural* **chunks 1.** A thick piece of something; a lump: *a chunk of ice.* **2.** A large amount: *a chunk of time.*

church |chûrch| —*noun, plural* **churches 1.** A building for religious worship. **2.** Religious services in a church: *going to church.* **3. Church** A group of people with the same religious beliefs; denomination: *the Catholic Church.* **4.** The power of organized religions, as opposed to government or personal power: *separation of church and state.*

churn |chûrn| —*noun, plural* **churns** A container in which cream is beaten to make butter.
—*verb* **churned, churning 1.** To beat cream in a churn to make butter. **2.** To move or swirl violently: *The storm churned the water in the harbor.*

chute |shoot| —*noun, plural* **chutes** A long passage or tube through which things can be dropped or slid to an opening at the other end: *a mail chute; a laundry chute.*
♦ *These sound alike* **chute, shoot.**

ci·der |sī′dər| —*noun, plural* **ciders** The juice that is made from apples that have been ground up and pressed. Cider is used as a drink or to make vinegar.

ci·gar |sĭ gär′| —*noun, plural* **cigars** A small roll of tobacco leaves used for smoking.

cig·a·rette |sĭg′ə rĕt′| or |sĭg′ə rĕt′| —*noun, plural* **cigarettes** A small roll of finely chopped tobacco leaves for smoking, enclosed in a wrapper of thin paper.

cin·der |sĭn′dər| —*noun, plural* **cinders** A piece of partly burned coal or wood that cannot be burned further.

cin·e·ma |sĭn′ə mə| —*noun, plural* **cinemas** A theater where motion pictures are shown.

cin·na·mon |sĭn′ə mən| —*noun* **1.** A reddish-brown spice made from the bark of a tropical tree. **2.** A reddish-brown color.
—*adjective* Reddish-brown.

cir·cle |sûr′kəl| —*noun, plural* **circles 1.** A curve that is closed. Every point on the curve is at the same distance from a fixed point in the center. **2.** Anything that has the general shape of a circle; a ring: *Stand in a circle for this game.* **3.** A group of people having the same interests: *a circle of friends.*
—*verb* **circled, circling 1.** To draw or form a circle: *Circle the correct answer.* **2. a.** To move or travel around something in a circle: *The bird circled its nest.* **b.** To move in a circle: *The airplane circled, waiting for its turn to land.*

cir·cuit |sûr′kĭt| —*noun, plural* **circuits 1. a.** A path that follows a closed curve such as a circle or an ellipse: *Each planet follows its own circuit around the sun.* **b.** Motion that goes along such a path: *The cars made a circuit of the racetrack before the race started.* **2.** A closed path through which electricity can flow: *This air conditioner must be connected to its own circuit.* **3. a.** A regular route followed by a judge from town to town in order to hear cases in each of them. **b.** A similar route, such as that followed by a salesperson or people in a particular sport: *Mr. Jones made a circuit of all the small towns. She now joined the professional golf circuit.*

cir·cu·lar |sûr′kyə lər| —*adjective* **1.** Of, shaped like, or shaped nearly like a circle: *circular path.* **2.** Forming or moving in a circle: *circular motion.*

—noun, plural **circulars** A printed letter, announcement, or advertisement given out or mailed to the public.

cir·cu·late |sûr′kyə lāt′| *—verb* **circulated, circulating 1.** To move or cause to move in a closed path: *Blood circulates through the body. The heart circulates the blood.* **2.** To move, flow, or spread easily: *The message circulated among everyone in the class.*

cir·cu·la·tion |sûr′kyə lā′shən| *—noun, plural* **circulations 1.** The act or process of circulating: *Something is blocking the circulation of air in this building.* **2.** The movement of blood through the blood vessels of the body: *Exercise helps your circulation.* **3.** The movement of things from place to place or person to person: *circulation of money; circulation of books.*

cir·cu·la·to·ry system |sûr′kyə lə tôr′ē| or |sûr′kyə lə tōr′ē| The system for moving fluids through the body. The heart and blood vessels are part of the circulatory system.

cir·cum·fer·ence |sər kŭm′fər əns| *—noun, plural* **circumferences 1. a.** The outside edge of a circle. **b.** The distance around the outside edge of a circle. **2.** The distance around the edge of something: *the circumference of the yard.*

cir·cum·flex |sûr′kəm flĕks′| *—noun, plural* **circumflexes** A mark used over a vowel to show how it is pronounced. A vowel with a circumflex looks like this: â.

cir·cum·stance |sûr′kəm stăns′| *—noun, plural* **circumstances 1.** A condition, fact, or event that goes along with and usually affects something or someone else: *Sickness and bad weather were two circumstances that caused poor attendance at the play.* **2. circumstances** Financial condition: *They live in comfortable circumstances.*

Idioms **under no circumstances** In no case; never: *Under no circumstances should the baby cross the street alone.* **under the circumstances** This being the situation; given the conditions: *Under the circumstances I had no choice.*

cir·cus |sûr′kəs| *—noun, plural* **circuses** A colorful show put on by clowns, acrobats, and trained animals. A circus often travels from city to city and performs under a big tent.

cite |sīt| *—verb* **cited, citing 1.** To mention as an authority; quote: *She cited two articles in a magazine that confirmed her statement.* **2.** To bring up as an example; refer to: *Let me cite two cases of extreme good planning*

♦ *These sound alike* **cite, sight, site.**

cit·i·zen |sĭt′ĭ zən| *—noun, plural* **citizens 1.** Someone who is a member of a country, either by being born there or by choosing to become a member. A citizen has certain rights from his or her country and also some responsibilities. **2.** Anyone who lives in a city or town; a resident.

cit·i·zen·ship |sĭt′ĭ zən shĭp′| *—noun* The duties and rights of a citizen: *A person born in the United States receives automatic citizenship. We practice good citizenship by taking part in our town government.*

cit·rus |sĭt′rəs| *—adjective* Of or belonging to a certain group of fruits or fruit trees. Oranges, lemons, limes, and grapefruits are citrus fruits.

—noun, plural **citruses** A citrus tree.

cit·y |sĭt′ē| *—noun, plural* **cities 1.** An important center where

circus

many people live and work. **2.** All the people living in a city: *The city celebrated its anniversary with a big parade.*

civ·il |sĭv′əl| —*adjective* **1.** Of a citizen or people within a community: *The laws of our country protect our civil rights.* **2.** Not related to military or church activities: *Labor Day is a civil holiday.* **3.** Of the events happening within a country or community: *civil war.* **4.** Having or showing good manners; polite: *a civil answer to a question.*

ci·vil·ian |sĭ vĭl′yən| —*noun, plural* **civilians** A person who is not serving in the armed forces.

civ·i·li·za·tion |sĭv′ə lĭ zā′shən| —*noun, plural* **civilizations 1.** A condition of human beings in which people are far along in their knowledge of art, science, religion, and government: *Civilization took thousands of years to develop.* **2.** The way a people of a nation or area live: *We are studying early American civilization.*

civ·i·lize |sĭv′ə līz′| —*verb* **civilized, civilizing** To change from a primitive condition of life to a more highly developed one; educate: *The Romans tried to civilize the nations they captured.*

civil war 1. A war between groups of people or areas within one country. **2. Civil War** The war in the United States between the North and the South that took place from 1861 to 1865. Also called *War Between the States.*

clad |klăd| A past tense and past participle of the verb **clothe:** *We clad ourselves in bright colors for the party. Autumn has clad the trees in gold and red.*

claim |klām| —*verb* **claimed, claiming 1.** To ask for something one owns or deserves: *We claimed our luggage at the airport. The winner claimed her prize.* **2.** To say that something is true; assert: *The doctor claims the disease is cured.*
—*noun, plural* **claims 1.** A demand or request for something one owns or deserves: *a claim for car damages.* **2.** A statement that something is true: *an advertisement that makes false claims about certain foods.* **3.** Something that has been claimed, especially land: *The miners were hoping to find gold on their claims.*

clam |klăm| —*noun, plural* **clams** A water animal that has a soft body and a shell with two parts hinged together. Many kinds of clams are used as food.

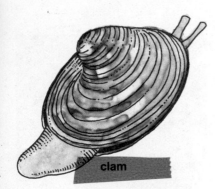
clam

clam·bake |klăm′bāk′| —*noun, plural* **clambakes** A picnic at which clams and other foods are baked.

clam·my |klăm′ē| —*adjective* **clammier, clammiest** Damp, sticky, and usually cold: *clammy clothes; clammy hands.*

clamp |klămp| —*noun, plural* **clamps** A device used for gripping or keeping things together. It is usually made up of two parts that can be brought together by turning a screw.
—*verb* **clamped, clamping** To hold together with a clamp: *The carpenter clamped the wooden planks together.*

clamp

clan |klăn| —*noun, plural* **clans 1.** A group of families that claim to be related to the same ancestor. **2.** Any group of relatives or friends: *a reunion of the clan.*

clang |klăng| —*verb* **clanged, clanging** To make a loud, ringing sound like metal objects hitting one another: *We clanged a bell to announce our victory. The bells clanged to welcome the mayor.*
—*noun, plural* **clangs** A clanging sound: *The wrench fell to the floor with a clang.*

clank |klăngk| —*noun, plural* **clanks** A loud, ringing sound like metal objects hitting one another: *The gate closed with a clank.*

ă	pat	ĕ	pet	î	fierce
ā	pay	ē	be	ŏ	pot
â	care	ĭ	pit	ō	go
ä	father	ī	pie	ô	paw, for
oi	oil	ŭ	cut	zh	vision
ōŏ	book	û	fur	ə	ago, item,
ōō	boot	*th*	the		pencil, atom,
yōō	abuse	th	thin		circus
ou	out	hw	which	ər	butter

—*verb* **clanked, clanking** To make a clank: *The baby was marching around and clanking a spoon against a pan. The rope clanked against the pole in the wind.*

clap |klăp| —*verb* **clapped, clapping 1.** To hit the hands together quickly and loudly: *The crowd clapped to the music. The teacher clapped his hands to get the children's attention.* **2.** To come together quickly with a loud noise: *The door clapped shut.* **3.** To tap with an open hand: *clap him on the shoulder.*
—*noun, plural* **claps 1.** A loud, sudden noise: *a clap of thunder.* **2.** A slap: *He gave his son a friendly clap on the back.*

clar·i·fy |klăr′ĭ fī′| —*verb* **clarified, clarifying, clarifies** To make something clear or easier to understand: *The additional instructions clarified the rules of the game.*

clar·i·net |klăr′ĭ nĕt′| —*noun, plural* **clarinets** A musical instrument made up of a mouthpiece and a long body shaped like a tube, with a bottom shaped like a bell. It is played by blowing into the mouthpiece and covering holes in its body with the fingers and with pads that are operated by the fingers.

clar·i·ty |klăr′ĭ tē| —*noun* **1.** The condition or quality of being clear and distinct in shape, outline, or sound: *an actor known for the clarity of his speech; a photograph of great clarity and depth.* **2.** Showing an ability to be clear in thoughts or ideas: *She gave the complicated instructions with great clarity.*

clash |klăsh| —*verb* **clashed, clashing 1.** To hit or come together with a loud, harsh noise: *The knights clashed their swords. The cymbals clashed loudly.* **2.** To hit or come together violently: *Warm air clashed against cold air, and a thunderstorm followed. The armies clashed in battle.* **3.** To disagree strongly; not match: *The candidates clashed over their ideas. Orange and purple clash.*
—*noun, plural* **clashes 1.** A strong disagreement: *a clash between two countries.* **2.** A loud, harsh sound like metal objects hitting one another: *the clash of swords.*

clasp |klăsp| or |kläsp| —*noun, plural* **clasps 1.** A buckle or hook used to hold two objects or parts together: *the clasp on a necklace.* **2.** A strong grasp or hold: *The mother's clasp stopped her child from turning into the traffic.*
—*verb* **clasped, clasping 1.** To fasten with a clasp: *He clasped a bracelet on his wrist.* **2.** To grasp or hold tightly: *Clasp the handlebars.*

class |klăs| or |kläs| —*noun, plural* **classes 1.** A group or collection of objects or people alike in some way: *As a class, people who exercise a lot seem to enjoy better health.* **2.** A group of people who earn about the same amount of money and live very much alike: *the middle class; the working class.* **3.** A group of animals or plants that are alike in many ways: *All mammals belong to the same class of animals.* **4.a.** A group of students learning together in the same classroom: *a third-grade class.* **b.** The time in which a lesson is taught: *No talking during class.* **5.a.** A type or grade of mail: *a letter sent first class.* **b.** The grade or quality of seats, service, food, and other things received when traveling: *We always travel first class. That hotel is only second class.*
—*verb* **classed, classing** To put an animal, plant, or object into a class; classify: *How would you class that insect? I would class that book as a biography.*

clas·sic |klăs′ĭk| —*adjective* **1.** Thought for a long time to be the best of its kind: *a classic automobile.* **2.** Well known and not

clarinet

class

surprising: *a classic case of measles.* **3.** Of ancient Greece and Rome or their writings and art: *classic times; a classic statue.*
—*noun, plural* **classics** **1.** An artist, writer, or object thought to be the best of its kind: *Shakespeare is a classic.* **2. the classics** The writings of ancient Greece and Rome.

clas·si·cal |klăs′ĭ kəl| —*adjective* **1.a.** Of the art, writings, and way of life of ancient Greece and Rome: *classical buildings; the classical languages.* **b.** In the style of the art and writings of ancient Greece and Rome: *a modern building with classical designs.* **2.** Of concert music or all music other than popular music and folk music: *The symphony follows classical music rules.*

clas·si·fi·ca·tion |klăs′ə fĭ kā′shən| —*noun, plural* **classifications** **1.** The act or result of classifying; arrangement: *the classification of books by their subject.* **2.** A category, group, or rating: *Our team placed in the "B" classification for the play-offs.*

clas·si·fy |klăs′ə fī′| —*verb* **classified, classifying, classifies** To put into classes or groups; sort: *A librarian classifies books.*

class·mate |klăs′māt′| or |kläs′māt′| —*noun, plural* **classmates** A member of the same class in a school.

class·room |klăs′rōōm′| or |klăs′rŏŏm′| or |kläs′rōōm′| or |kläs′rŏŏm′| —*noun, plural* **classrooms** A room in a school where classes take place.

clat·ter |klăt′ər| —*verb* **clattered, clattering** To make a noisy, rattling sound; move in a noisy, rattling way: *The two youngsters clattered along on their roller skates.*
—*noun* A noisy, rattling sound: *The clatter at the town meeting stopped when the mayor began her speech.*

claw |klô| —*noun, plural* **claws** **1.** A sharp, curved nail on the toe of an animal or bird. **2.** One of the grasping parts shaped like a claw of a lobster or crab.
—*verb* **clawed, clawing** To scratch or dig with the claws or hands: *The cats clawed the furniture. The trapped miners clawed their way to safety.*

claw hammer A hammer having a head with one end split like a fork for removing nails.

clay |klā| —*noun, plural* **clays** A firm kind of fine earth that is soft and can be shaped when wet. After heating, it becomes a hard material. Clay is used in making bricks and pottery.

clean |klēn| —*adjective* **cleaner, cleanest** **1.** Free from dirt or stain: *clean clothes; a clean glass; clean water.* **2.** Free from guilt or wrongdoing; innocent: *a clean life; a clean record.* **3.** Having a smooth edge or top; even; regular: *a clean break in a bone; a clean line.* **4.** Complete; total: *a clean escape.*
—*adverb* Entirely; completely: *I clean forgot your birthday.*
—*verb* **cleaned, cleaning** To get rid of dirt or stain: *I must clean my room. Saturday is the day we clean.*
   Phrasal verbs **clean out** To get rid of dirt or trash: *Let's clean out the closet.* **clean up** To get rid of dirt or clutter: *I must clean up my room.*

clean·er |klēn′ər| —*noun, plural* **cleaners** **1.** A person or business whose job it is to clean: *I took my suit to the cleaner.* **2.a.** A machine used in cleaning: *a vacuum cleaner.* **b.** A material or liquid used in cleaning: *What kind of cleaner did you use to get the stain out of the rug?*

clean·li·ness |klĕn′lē nĭs| —*noun* The condition or quality of being clean: *We stayed at that motel because of its cleanliness.*

claw
Above: Crab
Center: Bird
Below: Lion

claw hammer

ă	pat	ĕ	pet	î	fierce
ā	pay	ē	be	ŏ	pot
â	care	ĭ	pit	ō	go
ä	father	ī	pie	ô	paw, for
oi	oil	ŭ	cut	zh	vision
ŏŏ	book	û	fur	ə	ago, item,
ōō	boot	*th*	the		pencil, atom,
yŏŏ	abuse	th	thin		circus
ou	out	hw	which	ər	butter

clean·ly | klĕn′lē | —*adjective* **cleanlier, cleanliest** Always carefully neat and clean: *A cat is a very cleanly animal.*
—*adverb* | klĕn′lē | In a clean, neat way: *The fruit stems have been cut cleanly by a knife.*

cleanse | klĕnz | —*verb* **cleansed, cleansing** To make clean: *The doctor cleansed the wound.*

clean·ser | klĕn′zər | —*noun, plural* **cleansers** A material or liquid used for cleaning: *a tooth cleanser; a bathroom cleanser.*

clear | klîr | —*adjective* **clearer, clearest** **1.** Free from anything that dims, darkens, or blocks: *a clear day; clear water; a clear road.* **2.** Easily seen or heard: *a clear picture; a clear sound.* **3.** Plainly or easily understood: *a clear explanation.* **4.** Free from guilt; not troubled: *a clear conscience.*
—*adverb* **1.** Out of the way: *He jumped clear of the oncoming car.* **2.** In a clear way: *Speak loud and clear before an audience.*
—*verb* **cleared, clearing** **1.** To make or become clear, light, or bright: *Please clear the window of mist. The day cleared.* **2.** To move people or objects out of the way: *Clear the way. The settlers cleared the land of trees.* **3.** To remove or get rid of: *They cleared snow from the roads. She cleared the mud from her goggles.* **4.** To pass by, under, or over without touching: *The jumper cleared the fence.* **5.** To free from a charge or an accusation: *The jury cleared him of the charge.*
   Phrasal verbs **clear away** To take away; remove: *Please clear away the dishes.* **clear off** To remove something from to make clear: *Let's clear off the table.* **clear up** To make or become clear: *clear up a mystery; His skin cleared up. The sky cleared up.*

clear·ance | klîr′əns | —*noun, plural* **clearances** **1.** The act of clearing: *The clearance of snow from the roads took all night.* **2.** A sale, at cheaper prices, to get rid of things that have been around too long in a store: *a summer clearance at the department store.* **3.** Distance or space between two things, such as a road and the ceiling of a tunnel: *There is not enough clearance for trucks to pass under this bridge.*

clear·ing | klîr′ĭng | —*noun, plural* **clearings** An area of land where trees are not growing or have been removed: *a clearing in a forest.*

clear·ly | klîr′lē | —*adverb* **1.** In a way that is easy to understand; plainly: *Speak clearly.* **2.** Without doubt or beyond doubt: *Clearly, we need the money.*

cleat | klēt | —*noun, plural* **cleats** **1.** A piece of metal, rubber, plastic, or leather attached to the sole or heel of a shoe to keep it from slipping on the ground: *cleats on a football shoe.* **2. cleats** A pair of shoes with cleats attached to them.

cleav·er | klē′vər | —*noun, plural* **cleavers** A tool used by butchers for cutting meat. A cleaver has a broad, heavy blade and a short handle.

clef | klĕf | —*noun, plural* **clefs** A printed mark on a musical scale that tells the pitch for each line and space.

clench | klĕnch | —*verb* **clenched, clenching** **1.** To close a hand or the teeth tightly: *clench one's fist.* **2.** To grasp or grip tightly: *The football player clenched the football.*

cler·gy | klûr′jē | —*noun, plural* **clergies** Ministers, priests, and rabbis in general; people whose job it is to do religious work.

cler·gy·man | klûr′jē mən | —*noun, plural* **clergymen** A member of the clergy; a minister, priest, or rabbi.

cleaver

clef

clerk | klûrk | —*noun, plural* **clerks** **1.** A person who works in an office and keeps records and other papers in correct order. **2.** A person who sells things in a store: *a grocery clerk.*

clev·er | klĕv′ər | —*adjective* **cleverer, cleverest** **1.** Having a quick mind; smart; bright: *a clever student.* **2.** Showing skill or quick thinking: *a clever plan; a clever trick.*

click | klĭk | —*noun, plural* **clicks** A short, sharp sound: *the click of train wheels.*
—*verb* **clicked, clicking** To make or cause to make such a sound: *The door clicked as it shut. He was nervously clicking his heels together as he stood waiting for the train.*

cli·ent | klī′ənt | —*noun, plural* **clients** **1.** A person who uses the services of a professional person: *Lawyers and accountants have many clients. His public relations firm has many clients.* **2.** A customer or patron: *a store with few clients.*

cliff | klĭf | —*noun, plural* **cliffs** A high, steep, or overhanging face of earth or rock: *Boys were diving from the cliff into the water far below.*

cli·mate | klī′mĭt | —*noun, plural* **climates** **1.** The usual weather a place has all year, including its temperature, rainfall, and wind: *a climate of four seasons.* **2.** A section of a country with a certain type of weather: *We moved to a colder climate and had to buy warmer clothing.*

climb | klīm | —*verb* **climbed, climbing** **1.a.** To go up, over, or through something by using the hands and feet: *climb a ladder; climb over a fence. Monkeys climb well.* **b.** To move downward using the hands and feet: *climb down a ladder.* **2.** To go higher; rise: *The sun climbed in the sky. The rocket climbed speedily. Food prices are climbing fast.* **3.** To get in or out of: *climb aboard a train; climb out of bed.* **4.** To grow upward by holding on to something: *The vine climbs the brick wall.*
—*noun, plural* **climbs** **1.** The act of climbing: *a climb up the mountain trail; a climb in prices.* **2.** A place to be climbed: *That hill was a good climb.*

clinch | klĭnch | —*verb* **clinched, clinching** **1.** To nail or bolt something tightly: *The carpenter clinched boards onto the windows of the empty building.* **2.** To come to a final agreement: *clinch a deal.* **3.** In boxing, to hold the other boxer's body with one or both arms to keep him from punching.
—*noun, plural* **clinches** In boxing, the act of clinching: *a tight clinch.*

cling | klĭng | —*verb* **clung, clinging** **1.** To hold tight or stick to something: *cling to a rope. Dirt was clinging to her boots.* **2.** To stay near or close: *The children cling to their mother.* **3.** To stay attached to something; refuse to give up: *cling to old beliefs; cling to a hope.*

clin·ic | klĭn′ĭk | —*noun, plural* **clinics** **1.** A place, usually connected with a hospital, that gives medical help to patients not staying in the hospital: *We took the baby to the clinic for a flu shot.* **2.** A school or course that gives special training or advice: *a reading clinic; a basketball clinic.*

clip¹ | klĭp | —*verb* **clipped, clipping** To cut with scissors or shears; cut short; trim: *She clipped an ad out of the newspaper. Please clip the hedge. The barber will clip his beard.*
—*noun, plural* **clips** A fast rate of moving: *They walked along at a good clip.*

cliff

clip¹, clip²

Clip¹ comes from a word used a very long time ago by people living in Scandinavia to mean "to cut short." Clip² comes from an old English word that meant "to embrace or fasten."

ă	pat	ĕ	pet	î	fierce
ā	pay	ē	be	ŏ	pot
â	care	ĭ	pit	ō	go
ä	father	ī	pie	ô	paw, for
oi	oil	ŭ	cut	zh	vision
ōŏ	book	û	fur	ə	ago, item,
ōō	boot	*th*	the		pencil, atom,
yōō	abuse	th	thin		circus
ou	out	hw	which	ər	butter

clip² |klĭp| —*noun, plural* **clips 1.** An object used to hold things together: *a paper clip.* **2.** A piece of jewelry that closes with a clasp or clip: *a tie clip.*
—*verb* **clipped, clipping** To hold together with a clip: *clip on an earring; clip the papers together.*

clip·per |klĭp′ər| —*noun, plural* **clippers 1. clippers** A tool for clipping or cutting: *nail clippers; a barber's clippers.* **2.** A sailing ship built for fast speed: *Clippers were replaced by steamships.*

clip·ping |klĭp′ĭng| —*noun, plural* **clippings 1.** Something cut or trimmed off: *a plant clipping; fingernail clippings.* **2.** An article, advertisement, or photograph cut from a newspaper or magazine: *Grandmother sent us clippings of stories and pictures of the big storm in her state.*

cloak |klōk| —*noun, plural* **cloaks 1.** A loose piece of outer clothing, usually having no sleeves: *a warm, woolen cloak.* **2.** Something that covers or hides: *His frowning and shouting were just a cloak for his fears.*
—*verb* **cloaked, cloaking** To cover up; hide: *I cloaked my anger with a smile.*

clock |klŏk| —*noun, plural* **clocks** An instrument that tells the time. Some clocks have a face with numerals and moving hands or pointers. Other clocks show the time directly in numerals.
—*verb* **clocked, clocking** To measure or record the time or speed of something: *We clocked the runners in the second race.*

clock·wise |klŏk′wīz′| —*adverb* In the same direction as the moving hands of a clock: *Turn the key clockwise.*
—*adjective* Moving in the same direction as the hands of a clock: *a clockwise movement.*

clog |klŏg| —*verb* **clogged, clogging** To become or cause to become blocked up: *The pipes clogged with hair. Heavy traffic clogged the highway.*

clone |klōn| —*noun, plural* **clones** A living plant or animal that has been produced from a single cell of another plant or animal. A clone is identical in many ways to the plant or animal it has been taken from.
—*verb* **cloned, cloning** To create a clone: *Scientists were trying to clone a frog.*

close |klōs| —*adjective* **closer, closest 1.** Near in space or time: *The airport is close to town. My birthday is close to yours.* **2.** Near within a family or in relationship: *close relatives; close friends.* **3.** With little or no space between; tight: *a close fit; a close weave.* **4.** Having little room; narrow; crowded: *close living quarters.* **5.** Without enough fresh air; stuffy: *It's very close in this room.* **6.** Almost even or equal: *a close race; a close election.* **7.** Careful; complete: *Pay close attention.*
—*verb* |klōz| **closed, closing 1.** To shut: *Close your eyes. Please close the door.* **2.** To be or cause to be not open for its usual purpose: *The store closes at six o'clock. The mayor closed all streets so that the snowplows could work.* **3.** To bring or come to an end: *He closed his letter with a joke. School closed in June.* **4.** To pull together or come together: *It took eight stitches to close the wound. His arms closed around the grocery bag.*
—*noun* |klōz| An ending: *The meeting came to a close.*
♦ *These sound alike* **close** (*verb* and *noun*), **clothes.**

Idiom a close call An escape that almost failed or could easily have failed; a narrow escape.

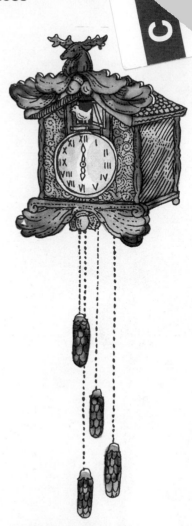

clock
Above: Cuckoo clock
Below: Modern alarm clock

clover

clown

ă	pat	ĕ	pet	î	fierce
ā	pay	ē	be	ŏ	pot
â	care	ĭ	pit	ō	go
ä	father	ī	pie	ô	paw, for

oi	oil	ŭ	cut	zh	vision
ŏŏ	book	û	fur	ə	ago, item,
ōō	boot	th	the		pencil, atom,
yōō	abuse	th	thin		circus
ou	out	hw	which	ər	butter

clos·et | klŏz′ĭt | —*noun, plural* **closets** A small room or cabinet
for hanging clothes or storing supplies.

clot | klŏt | —*noun, plural* **clots** A thick or solid material formed
from a liquid: *a blood clot.*
—*verb* **clotted, clotting** To form into clots: *Blood will clot more
slowly in some wounds.*

cloth | klôth | or | klŏth | —*noun, plural* **cloths** | klô*thz* | or
| klŏ*thz* | or | klôths | or | klŏths | **1.** Material made by weaving
or knitting cotton, wool, silk, flax, nylon, or other fibers together:
Silk cloth is expensive. **2.** A piece of cloth used for a special
purpose, such as a tablecloth or a washcloth.

clothe | klō*th* | —*verb* **clothed** or **clad, clothing 1.** To put clothes
on or provide clothes for; dress: *feed and clothe a family.* **2.** To
cover: *Trees were clothed in autumn colors.*

clothes | klōz | or | klō*thz* | —*plural noun* Coverings worn on the
body: *Shirts, pants, and dresses are clothes.*
♦ *These sound alike* **clothes, close** (*verb* and *noun*).

cloth·ing | klō′*th*ĭng | —*noun* Coverings worn on the body;
clothes: *new clothing for the party.*

cloud | kloud | —*noun, plural* **clouds 1. a.** A large white or gray
object in the sky made up of a collection of very small drops of
water or tiny pieces of ice held in the air: *a storm cloud.* **b.** Any
object made up of a collection of tiny pieces held in the air, such
as dust, steam, or smoke: *A cloud of dust rose behind the horses as
they galloped along the road.* **2.** A moving group of things that is
so large that it looks like a cloud: *a cloud of bees.* **3.** Something
that saddens or makes gloomy: *The bad news brought a cloud over
our happy day.*
—*verb* **clouded, clouding 1.** To cover or become covered with
clouds: *Heavy mist clouded the hills. The sky clouded over. Car fumes
clouded the air.* **2.** To make gloomy, dark, or confused: *The puzzle
clouded my mind. My feelings clouded at once.*

cloud·less | kloud′lĭs | —*adjective* Without clouds; clear: *a
cloudless day.*

cloud·y | kloud′ē | —*adjective* **cloudier, cloudiest 1.** Full of or
covered with clouds: *a cloudy sky; a cloudy day.* **2.** Not clear: *The
water of the brook was so cloudy you couldn't see the fish.*

clout | klout | —*noun, plural* **clouts 1.** A strong punch with the
fist: *The baby gave her brother a surprise clout.* **2.** In baseball, a
long, powerful hit.
—*verb* **clouted, clouting** To hit hard: *The twins clouted each other.*

clove¹ | klōv | —*noun, plural* **cloves** One of the dried flower buds
of a tropical plant. Cloves have a strong smell and taste. They are
used as a spice, either ground into a powder or whole.

clove² | klōv | —*noun, plural* **cloves** One of the sections of a bulb
of garlic.

clo·ver | klō′vər | —*noun* A plant with leaves made up of three
leaflets and small flowers in round, tight clusters. There are
several kinds of clover.

clown | kloun | —*noun, plural* **clowns 1.** A person who has a
job, usually with a circus, doing tricks and telling jokes to make
people laugh: *a circus clown.* **2.** A person who is always making
jokes or acting foolishly: *the class clown.*
—*verb* **clowned, clowning 1.** To perform as a clown in a circus or
show: *The chimpanzees clowned in the center ring of the circus.*
2. To behave like a clown: *My friend clowns around too much.*

club | klŭb | —*noun, plural* **clubs** **1.** A heavy stick, usually thicker at one end than at the other, used as a weapon. **2.** A stick used to strike a ball in certain games: *a golf club.* **3. a.** A black figure that looks like a clover leaf found on a playing card. **b.** A playing card marked with this figure. **c.** **clubs** The suit of cards that has this figure: *ace of clubs.* **4. a.** A group of people who have joined together to do the same thing: *a tennis club.* **b.** The room or building used by the members of such a group. —*verb* **clubbed, clubbing** To hit or beat with a stick or club.

club·house | klŭb'hous' | —*noun, plural* **clubhouses** **1.** A building used by members of a club. **2.** A locker room used by an athletic team.

cluck | klŭk | —*noun, plural* **clucks** The sound made by a hen sitting on eggs or caring for young chicks. —*verb* **clucked, clucking** To make such a sound.

clue | klōō | —*noun, plural* **clues** An object, footprint, fingerprint, or other information that helps to solve a problem or mystery.

clump | klŭmp | —*noun, plural* **clumps** **1.** A thick group of trees or bushes. **2.** A thick piece of dirt or earth. **3.** A heavy, dull sound: *the clump of heavy footsteps.* —*verb* **clumped, clumping** To walk with a heavy, dull sound: *Every time the giant clumped around, the earth shook.*

clum·sy | klŭm'zē | —*adjective* **clumsier, clumsiest** **1.** Uneven in movement; awkward: *a clumsy walk; clumsy animals.* **2.** Hard to use or control: *clumsy wooden shoes.* **3.** Done without skill; careless: *a clumsy try for a part in the play.*

clung | klŭng | The past tense and past participle of the verb **cling:** *The baby opossums clung to their mother's back. We have clung faithfully to our old beliefs.*

clus·ter | klŭs'tər | —*noun, plural* **clusters** A group of similar things growing or grouped close together: *a cluster of flowers; a cluster of stars.* —*verb* **clustered, clustering** To gather or grow in clusters: *Everyone clustered around the fire.*

clutch | klŭch | —*verb* **clutched, clutching** To hold or grasp tightly: *She was clutching a baby in her arms.* —*noun, plural* **clutches** **1.** A tight hold or grip: *He had a good clutch on the hammer.* **2. a.** A part of a machine, used to connect and disconnect the motor that makes the machine work. **b.** The lever or pedal that controls this part: *an automobile clutch.*

clut·ter | klŭt'ər | —*noun* A group of things scattered about in a messy way; a jumble; disorder: *a clutter of garbage cans in the alley.* —*verb* **cluttered, cluttering** To scatter things about in a messy way, making it difficult to move around: *clutter up a room with toys.*

coach | kōch | —*noun, plural* **coaches** **1.** A large, closed carriage with four wheels pulled by horses: *the Queen's golden coach.* **2.** A bus or a railroad passenger car: *We toured the country in a coach for tourists.* **3.** A less expensive section of seats on a train, airplane, or bus: *Coach was full, so we had to pay extra to go first class.* **4. a.** A person in charge of a football, basketball, or other athletic team. **b.** A person who gives private lessons in a certain sport, or in singing, acting, or other kinds of performing: *a tennis coach; a drama coach.*

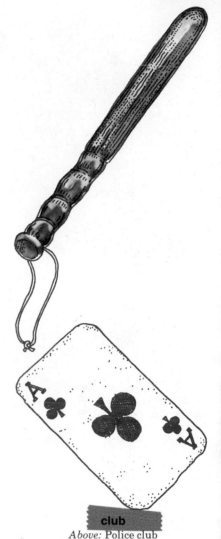

club
Above: Police club
Below: Playing card

coach

coat of arms

—verb **coached, coaching** To teach or train: *coach a football team; coach actors for play tryouts; coach for the state university.*

coal | kōl | *—noun, plural* **coals** **1.a.** A black, natural material taken from the ground. It is made up mainly of carbon and is used as a fuel. **b.** A piece of this material. **2.** A glowing or burned piece of wood, coal, or charcoal: *The coals glowed.*

coarse | kôrs | or | kōrs | *—adjective* **coarser, coarsest** **1.** Not smooth; rough: *coarse skin; coarse material.* **2.** Made up of large parts or pieces: *coarse sand.* **3.** Not having or showing good manners; rude; crude: *coarse language.*
♦ *These sound alike* **coarse, course.**

coast | kōst | *—noun, plural* **coasts** **1.** The edge of the land touching the sea: *walking along a rocky coast.* **2.** The area next to or near the sea: *The coast was cleared out because of high waves.*
—verb **coasted, coasting** To move down a hill without any power: *Let's coast down the hill on a sled! The car coasted to a stop.*

coast·al | kō′stəl | *—adjective* On, along, or near a coast: *a coastal village.*

coast guard or **Coast Guard** A military group that guards the coast of a country, rescues boats and ships in trouble, and sees that laws that have to do with the sea and with entering and leaving a country are obeyed.

coat | kōt | *—noun, plural* **coats** **1.** A piece of outer clothing with sleeves, usually worn to keep warm or to protect against the weather: *a fur coat.* **2.** The hair or fur of an animal: *a shaggy coat on a dog.* **3.** A thin layer of something spread over an area: *a coat of paint.*
—verb **coated, coating** To cover with a thin layer of something: *Dust coated the table.*

coat·ing | kō′tĭng | *—noun, plural* **coatings** A layer of something spread over an object to decorate it or protect it: *A coating of light oil will keep tools from rusting.*

coat of arms *—plural* **coats of arms** The design on a shield that shows the symbols of a country, family, school, or other organization.

coax | kōks | *—verb* **coaxed, coaxing** **1.** To try in a gentle or pleasant way to get someone to do something: *He coaxed the monkey into the cage.* **2.** To get something by being nice: *The police officer coaxed a smile from the lost child.*

cob | kŏb | *—noun, plural* **cobs** The long, hard center part of an ear of corn; a corncob.

co·balt | kō′bôlt′ | *—noun* A hard, brittle metal that looks like nickel or iron. Cobalt is one of the chemical elements. It is used in making steel and paint.

cob·ble | kŏb′əl | *—noun, plural* **cobbles** A round stone once used to cover streets; a cobblestone.
—verb **cobbled, cobbling** To cover a street with cobblestones.

cob·bler¹ | kŏb′lər | *—noun, plural* **cobblers** A person who makes or repairs shoes.

cob·bler² | kŏb′lər | *—noun, plural* **cobblers** A fruit pie baked in a deep dish with a biscuit crust on top.

cob·ble·stone | kŏb′əl stōn′ | *—noun, plural* **cobblestones** A round stone once used to cover streets.

co·bra | kō′brə | *—noun, plural* **cobras** A poisonous snake of Asia or Africa. A cobra can spread out the skin of its neck to form a flattened hood.

---

cobbler¹, cobbler²
Cobbler¹ comes from a word used in English a long time ago. We do not know the origin of that word. **Cobbler²** may come from **cobbler¹**.

cobra

ă	pat	ĕ	pet	î	fierce
ā	pay	ē	be	ŏ	pot
â	care	ĭ	pit	ō	go
ä	father	ī	pie	ô	paw, for
oi	oil	ŭ	cut	zh	vision
o͝o	book	û	fur	ə	ago, item,
o͞o	boot	*th*	the		pencil, atom,
yo͞o	abuse	th	thin		circus
ou	out	hw	which	ər	butter

cob·web | kŏb′wĕb′ | —*noun, plural* **cobwebs** A web spun by a spider or a strand from a spider's web.

cock | kŏk | —*noun, plural* **cocks** **1.** A fully grown male chicken; a rooster. **2.** The male of other birds: *"Who killed Cock Robin?"* —*verb* **cocked, cocking** **1.** To set the hammer of a gun into position so that the gun can be fired: *She cocked the rifle and aimed carefully at the target. She cocked and fired the rifle.* **2.** To set something into a tight position so that it can be released suddenly: *You must cock the shutter on the camera before taking a picture.* **3.** To tilt or turn up to one side: *The puppy cocked an ear at us.*

cock·a·too | kŏk′ə tōō′ | or | kŏk′ə tōō′ | —*noun, plural* **cockatoos** A parrot that has a crest. It is found in Australia.

cock·le | kŏk′əl | —*noun, plural* **cockles** A small sea animal that has a pair of shells shaped something like a heart. Cockles are sometimes eaten as food.

cock·pit | kŏk′pĭt′ | —*noun, plural* **cockpits** The part of an airplane where the pilot and copilot sit.

cock·roach | kŏk′rōch′ | —*noun, plural* **cockroaches** A brown insect with a flat, oval body. Cockroaches are often pests in homes.

cock·tail | kŏk′tāl′ | —*noun, plural* **cocktails** **1.** An alcoholic drink made with a liquor or wine and fruit juice or other ingredients. **2.** A seafood or fruit eaten before dinner: *a shrimp cocktail; fruit cocktail.*

co·coa | kō′kō′ | —*noun* **1.** A powder made from cacao seeds that have been roasted and ground, and from which most of the fat has been removed. **2.** A sweet drink made with cocoa and milk or water: *hot cocoa with marshmallows.*

co·co·nut or **co·coa·nut** | kō′kə nŭt′ | or | kō′kə nət | —*noun, plural* **coconuts** or **cocoanuts** The large, round nut of a tropical palm tree. A coconut has a hard, brown, hairy shell and sweet white meat. It has a hollow center filled with sweet, watery liquid called coconut milk.

co·coon | kə kōōn′ | —*noun, plural* **cocoons** A covering of silky strands made by a caterpillar. The cocoon protects the insect until it turns into a fully developed adult with wings.

cod | kŏd | —*noun, plural* **cod** or **cods** A fish of northern ocean waters. Cod are caught in large numbers for food.

code | kōd | —*noun, plural* **codes** **1.** A system of signals that stand for letters and numerals in a message: *a code for telegrams.* **2.** A system of words, marks, or letters used to keep messages secret or short: *a club's secret code; a computer code.* **3.** A collection of laws or rules and regulations: *a building code; a military code.* —*verb* **coded, coding** To put something into a code: *The secret agent coded the message before she sent it.*

cod·fish | kŏd′fĭsh | —*noun, plural* **codfish** or **codfishes** **1.** A cod. **2.** The flesh of a cod, used as food.

cof·fee | kô′fē | or | kŏf′ē | —*noun* **1.** A dark-brown drink made from the ground, roasted seeds of a tropical tree. **2.** The ground or whole seeds of this tree.

cof·fin | kô′fĭn | or | kŏf′ĭn | —*noun, plural* **coffins** A box in which a dead person is buried.

coil | koil | —*noun, plural* **coils** **1.** Anything made by winding something long and flexible around a center a number of times: *a*

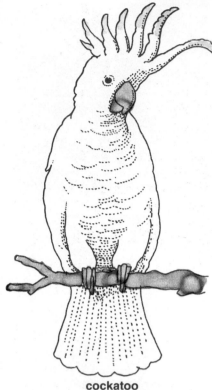

cockatoo

coconut
Tree *(left)* and nut *(right)*

coin
Early U.S. coins

coil of rope. **2.** One in a group of turns: *Each coil is bigger than the one inside it.*
—*verb* **coiled, coiling** To wind into a coil or into the shape of a coil: *The sailor coiled the rope on the deck.*

coin | koin | —*noun, plural* **coins** A piece of flat, round metal issued by a government for use as money.
—*verb* **coined, coining 1.** To make coins from metal: *The United States once coined pennies from steel.* **2.** To make up; invent: *coin a new word.*

co·in·cide | kō′ĭn sīd′ | —*verb* **coincided, coinciding 1.** To be in the same space at the same time: *Fold the sheets so that the top coincides with the bottom.* **2.** To correspond exactly; be identical: *Both students' stories coincide.* **3.** To happen at the same time: *Our birthdays coincide.*

co·in·ci·dence | kō ĭn′sĭ dəns | —*noun, plural* **coincidences** A happening or a group of happenings that seem to have been planned or arranged, but have not been: *By a strange coincidence, Presidents John Adams and Thomas Jefferson both died on the 50th anniversary of the signing of the Declaration of Independence.*

coke | kōk | —*noun* A solid black material that remains after coal is heated with almost no air present. Coke is mostly carbon and is used as a fuel and in making steel.

cold | kōld | —*adjective* **colder, coldest 1.** Having a low temperature: *cold water; cold air. Tuesday was a cold day.* **2.** Feeling no warmth; chilly: *I am cold in this house.* **3.** Not cordial or friendly: *I got a cold look from the woman.*
—*noun, plural* **colds 1. a.** A lack of heat: *The cold made all the rivers freeze.* **b.** The feeling caused by this: *The cold made us shiver.* **2.** A common sickness that causes sneezing, a running nose, and cough: *I was in bed with a cold.*

cold-blood·ed | kōld′blŭd′ĭd | —*adjective* **1.** Having a body temperature that becomes colder or warmer as the surrounding air or water becomes colder or warmer. Fish, frogs, turtles, and snakes are cold-blooded. **2.** Having no feeling or emotion: *He was a cold-blooded killer.*

col·i·se·um | kŏl′ĭ sē′əm | —*noun, plural* **coliseums** A large stadium or building used for sports events, exhibitions, and other entertainments.

col·lage | kō läzh′ | or | kə läzh′ | —*noun, plural* **collages** A collection of different materials pasted or glued onto a surface to make a picture or design.

col·lapse | kə lăps′ | —*verb* **collapsed, collapsing 1.** To fall down or inward suddenly; cave in: *The building collapsed because of poor construction. The balloon collapsed when she stuck a pin into it.* **2.** To break down or fail suddenly: *We almost collapsed from the heavy work.* **3.** To fold together: *Please collapse the tent. This chair collapses very easily.*
—*noun, plural* **collapses 1.** The act of collapsing or an example of collapsing: *The collapse of the building was caused by a mistake in design.* **2.** A breakdown; failure: *The man suffered a collapse from too much work.*

col·lar | kŏl′ər | —*noun, plural* **collars 1.** The band around the neck of a coat, dress, or shirt. **2.** A leather or metal band for the neck of an animal. **3.** The part of a harness that fits around a horse's neck and over its shoulders to help it pull heavy objects.
—*verb* **collared, collaring** To catch and hold by or as if by the

ă	pat	ĕ	pet	î	fierce
ā	pay	ē	be	ŏ	pot
â	care	ĭ	pit	ō	go
ä	father	ī	pie	ô	paw, for
oi	oil	ŭ	cut	zh	vision
ŏŏ	book	û	fur	ə	ago, item,
ōō	boot	*th*	the		pencil, atom,
yōō	abuse	th	thin		circus
ou	out	hw	which	ər	butter

collar; capture; arrest: *The police collared the burglar as he climbed in by the window.*

col·lar·bone |kŏl′ər bōn′| —*noun, plural* **collarbones** A bone that connects the shoulder blade and the breastbone.

col·league |kŏl′ēg′| —*noun, plural* **colleagues** An associate.

col·lect |kə lĕkt′| —*verb* **collected, collecting 1.** To bring or come together in a group; gather: *He collects wild flowers to use in floral arrangements. She collects old coins as a hobby. The students collected on the playground before school each morning.* **2.** To pick up and take away: *collect garbage.* **3.** To obtain payment of: *He wanted to collect the money the woman owed him.*

col·lec·tion |kə lĕk′shən| —*noun, plural* **collections 1.** The act or process of collecting: *collection of pollen by bees; collection of garbage; collection of money.* **2.** A group of things gathered or kept together as a hobby: *My neighbor has an antique automobile collection.*

col·lec·tor |kə lĕk′tər| —*noun, plural* **collectors** Someone or something that collects: *He's an art collector. That man is the tax collector. An electric dryer has a lint collector.*

col·lege |kŏl′ĭj| —*noun, plural* **colleges 1.** A school attended after high school. A college usually has a program of studies that lasts two, four, or five years. A student is given a diploma to show that he or she has completed the program successfully. **2.** Any of several special schools within a university: *He graduated from the medical college of New York University.*

col·lide |kə līd′| —*verb* **collided, colliding 1.** To strike or bump together violently; to crash: *Two planes collided on the runway.* **2.** To disagree strongly: *The workers collided with management over their pay.*

col·lie |kŏl′ē| —*noun, plural* **collies** A large dog with long hair and a narrow face. Collies were first raised to herd sheep.

col·li·sion |kə lĭzh′ən| —*noun, plural* **collisions 1.** The act or process of colliding; a crash: *There was a bad collision on our street, but no one was hurt.* **2.** A clash of ideas or interests; a conflict.

co·lon¹ |kō′lən| —*noun, plural* **colons** A punctuation mark (:) used after a word that introduces a list, explanation, quotation, or example.

co·lon² |kō′lən| —*noun, plural* **colons** The lower part of the large intestine.

colo·nel |kûr′nəl| —*noun, plural* **colonels** An officer in the Army, Air Force, or Marine Corps. A colonel ranks above a major and below a general.
♦ *These sound alike* **colonel, kernel.**

co·lo·ni·al |kə lō′nē əl| —*adjective* **1.** Of or possessing colonies: *colonial rule. France was once a colonial power.* **2.** Having to do with the thirteen original American colonies: *In colonial times children were not required to go to school.*

col·o·nist |kŏl′ə nĭst| —*noun, plural* **colonists 1.** An original settler of a colony or someone who helped establish one. **2.** A person who lives in a colony.

col·o·ny |kŏl′ə nē| —*noun, plural* **colonies 1.** A group of people who settle in another land but are still citizens of their native country: *A colony of English Puritans settled in America.* **2.** A territory that is ruled by a country that is far away from it: *America once was a British colony.* **3. the colonies** The thirteen British colonies that became the original states of the United

college

collie

---

colon¹, colon²
Colon¹ and **colon²** both came into English after traveling through Latin from Greek. In Greek **colon¹** originally meant "link" or "piece." **Colon²** meant "large intestine."

States. They were Connecticut, Delaware, Georgia, Maryland, Massachusetts, New Hampshire, New Jersey, New York, North Carolina, Pennsylvania, Rhode Island, South Carolina, and Virginia. **4.** A group of the same kind of animals or plants living closely together: *a colony of ants.*

col·or |kŭl′ər| —*noun, plural* **colors** **1.** The property by which our sense of sight can tell things apart, such as a red rose and a yellow rose, that may be alike in size and feel. **2.** A dye, paint, or other coloring substance. **3.** The way the skin looks: *He has a healthy color since he has been getting a lot of fresh air and exercise. They hire people without regard to color.* **4.** **colors** A flag or banner of a country or military unit: *She carried the colors in the Memorial Day parade.*
—*verb* **colored, coloring** To give color to or change the color of: *He drew a giraffe and colored it purple.*
Idioms **show one's true colors** To reveal one's real personality. **with flying colors** With great success: *She passed the test with flying colors.*

Col·o·ra·do |kŏl′ə rä′dō| or |kŏl′ə răd′ō| —*noun* A state in the western United States. The capital of Colorado is Denver.

col·or·ful |kŭl′ər fəl| —*adjective* **1.** Full of color. **2.** Interesting; exciting to the imagination: *a colorful description.*

col·or·ing |kŭl′ər ĭng| —*noun, plural* **colorings** **1.** The way color is applied: *The coloring of food is controlled by laws.* **2.** A substance used to color something: *food coloring; hair coloring.* **3.** Appearance having to do with color: *Some animals are protected by their coloring.*

col·or·less |kŭl′ər lĭs| —*adjective* **1.** Without color: *Water appears colorless.* **2.** Weak in color: *Her colorless face indicated she was sick.* **3.** Not having variety or interest; dull: *The story was colorless and boring to me.*

colt |kōlt| —*noun, plural* **colts** A young horse, especially a male.

Co·lum·bi·a |kə lŭm′bē ə| The capital of South Carolina.

Co·lum·bus |kə lŭm′bəs| The capital of Ohio.

Columbus Day A holiday in honor of Christopher Columbus. It is celebrated on the second Monday in October.

col·umn |kŏl′əm| —*noun, plural* **columns** **1.** A support or decoration for a building, shaped like a thin, upright cylinder; a pillar. **2.** Anything resembling a pillar in shape or in use: *a column of figures; spinal column; column of smoke.* **3.** A narrow vertical section of printed words on a page: *The story is continued in the third column on page five.* **4.** An article that appears regularly in a newspaper or magazine: *the daily sports column.* **5.** A long line of things or people following one behind the other: *A column of ants marched toward our picnic basket.*

comb |kōm| —*noun, plural* **combs** **1.** A thin strip of stiff material having teeth and used to arrange or fasten the hair. **2.** A bright-red strip of flesh on the head of a rooster, hen, or some other birds. **3.** An object used to straighten out fibers of wool or cotton before spinning. **4.** A bee's honeycomb.
—*verb* **combed, combing** **1.** To dress or arrange hair. **2.** To search thoroughly; look everywhere in: *They combed the area looking for the lost boy.*

com·bat |kəm băt′| or |kŏm′băt′| —*verb* **combated** or **combating** To fight or struggle against: *They discovered a new drug that combats infection.*

Colorado
Colorado comes from a Spanish word meaning "reddish." The word was first used to describe the color of the river running through the region that is today the state of Colorado, and the state was named after the river.

column

ă	pat	ĕ	pet	î	fierce
ā	pay	ē	be	ŏ	pot
â	care	ĭ	pit	ō	go
ä	father	ī	pie	ô	paw, for
oi	oil	ŭ	cut	zh	vision
ŏŏ	book	û	fur	ə	ago, item,
ōō	boot	*th*	the		pencil, atom,
yōō	abuse	th	thin		circus
ou	out	hw	which	ər	butter

—*noun* |kŏm′băt |, *plural* **combats** A fight or battle using weapons: *He was injured in combat during the war.*

com·bi·na·tion |kŏm′bĭ **nā′**shən | —*noun, plural* **combinations** **1.** The act or process of combining: *The combination of hydrogen and oxygen can produce water.* **2.** The result of combining: *Vanilla ice cream with strawberry topping is a good combination.* **3.** A series of numbers or letters used to open a lock: *Only the manager of the store knew the combination to the safe.*

com·bine |kəm **bīn′** | —*verb* **combined, combining** **1.** To bring or come together; unite; join: *The author combined real events with make-believe characters. The twins combined to cause all sorts of trouble for their brother.* **2.** To join two or more substances together to make a single substance: *Water and dirt combine to make mud. I combined sugar, water, and eggs to make icing for the chocolate cookies.*
—*noun* |**kŏm′**bīn′ |, *plural* **combines** A machine that cuts and cleans grain: *The farmer drove the combine into the field to begin the harvest.*

com·bus·tion |kəm **bŭs′**chən | —*noun, plural* **combustions** The process of burning: *The combustion of coal is important for heating many homes.*

come |kŭm | —*verb* **came, come, coming** **1.** To move toward the person who is speaking; to approach: *Will the kittens come when you call them? Come here for a moment, please.* **2.** To arrive at a particular point or result: *Please come to my party. They came to an agreement.* **3.** To move or be brought to a particular position: *We came to a stop in front of the store.* **4.** To extend; reach: *The water came up to her waist.* **5.** To exist or belong at a particular point in time or space: *Your name comes last on this form. My birthday comes a week after yours. Your work comes first.* **6.** To be from: *He comes from a famous family. She comes from Boston. That word comes from Latin.* **7.** To become: *His tie came undone. Their dream had come true.* **8.** To be available: *Those shoes come in many sizes.*

  Phrasal verbs **come about** To occur: *How did it come about that you arrived too early at school?* **come across** To meet by chance: *We just happened to come across your name on the list.* **come in for** To receive; get: *This behavior may come in for a lot of criticism.* **come off** To happen; occur: *The class trip may never come off if we don't get more money.* **come out** To become known: *It finally came out that she is a famous person.* **come to** **1.** To get consciousness back; revive: *He came to in the hospital after they gave him a drink of water.* **2.** To add up to; amount to: *The bill comes to fifty-one dollars. We never thought that dog would come to much.*

co·me·di·an |kə **mē′**dē ən | —*noun, plural* **comedians** **1.** A person who makes other people laugh by telling jokes or doing funny things. **2.** An actor in comedy.

com·e·dy |**kŏm′**ĭ dē | —*noun, plural* **comedies** **1.** A play, movie, or other entertainment that is funny and has a happy ending. **2.** A happening or event in real life that resembles a comedy.

com·et |**kŏm′**ĭt | —*noun, plural* **comets** A mass of material that travels around the sun on a long path. When a comet comes close to the sun, it looks like a bright ball with a long, bright tail.

com·fort |**kŭm′**fərt | —*verb* **comforted, comforting** To soothe someone in a time of grief, pain, or fear: *We tried to comfort the hurt child until the doctor arrived.*

combine

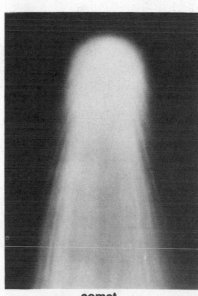

comet

© 1960 UNITED FEATURES SYNDICATE, INC.

SCHULZ

comic strip

ă	pat	ē	pet	î	fierce		
ā	pay	ē	be	ŏ	pot		
â	care	ĭ	pit	ō	go		
ä	father	ī	pie	ô	paw, for		
oi	oil	ŭ	cut		zh vision		
ōō	book	û	fur	ə	ago, item,		
ōō	boot	th	the		pencil, atom,		
yōō	abuse	th	thin		circus		
ou	out	hw	which	ər	butter		

—*noun, plural* **comforts** **1.** A feeling of ease or well-being that is without grief, pain, or fear: *The store is cooled during the summer for your comfort.* **2.** A person or thing that makes grief, pain, or fear easier to stand: *The child was a comfort to us. The frightened boy held the toy bear for comfort.* **3.** A thing or quality that makes people feel well or at ease: *The hotel had many facilities and all the comforts of home.*

com·fort·a·ble |kŭmf′tə bəl| or |kŭm′fər tə bəl| —*adjective* **1.** Giving comfort: *This chair is soft and very comfortable.* **2.** In a state of comfort; at ease: *I feel very comfortable with my friend's family.*

com·ic |kŏm′ĭk| —*adjective* **1.** Funny; amusing: *The mask with the giant nose was a comic sight.* **2.** Having to do with comedy: *a comic opera.*
—*noun, plural* **comics** **1.** A person who is funny. **2. comics** Comic strips.

com·i·cal |kŏm′ĭ kəl| —*adjective* Causing laughter; funny; amusing: *We laughed at the squirrel's comical tricks on the garden statues.*

comic book A booklet of comic strips.

comic strip A series of cartoons or drawings that tell a joke, a story, or part of a story: *The Sunday newspaper has a large section of comic strips.*

com·ma |kŏm′ə| —*noun, plural* **commas** A punctuation mark (,) used to separate things or ideas in a sentence.

com·mand |kə mănd′| or |kə mänd′| —*verb* **commanded, commanding** **1.** To direct; give orders to: *He commanded us to leave.* **2.** To have control or authority over; rule: *The general commanded a large army.*
—*noun, plural* **commands** **1.** An order or direction: *We received the command to march.* **2.** The ability or authority to give orders: *The boat captain was in command of a large crew.* **3.** The ability to control or use: *She has command of four languages.*

com·mand·er |kə măn′dər| or |kə män′dər| —*noun, plural* **commanders** **1.** A person in charge; a leader. **2.** An officer in the Navy who is below a captain. **3.** An officer who is in command of a military unit.

com·mand·ment |kə mănd′mənt| or |kə mänd′mənt| —*noun, plural* **commandments** **1.** A command; order. **2. Commandment** Any of the Ten Commandments.

com·mence |kə mĕns′| —*verb* **commenced, commencing** To begin; start: *The ball game commenced with the singing of the national anthem.*

com·mence·ment |kə mĕns′mənt| —*noun, plural* **commencements** **1.** A beginning; start: *The commencement of the county fair is Saturday.* **2.** A graduation ceremony in which school and college students receive their diplomas.

com·ment |kŏm′ĕnt| —*noun, plural* **comments** A note or remark that gives an opinion about something or explains something: *The teacher asked the class for their comments on the film they saw.*
—*verb* **commented, commenting** To make a comment; remark: *My friends commented that I did a good job in the school play.*

com·merce |kŏm′ərs| —*noun* The buying and selling of goods; trade; business: *The United States has a lot of commerce with other countries.*

com·mer·cial | kə **mûr′**shəl | —*adjective* Having to do with business or trade: *The scientist thought her new invention would be a big commercial success and make lots of money.*
—*noun, plural* **commercials** An advertisement on television or radio: *I enjoyed the program, but there were too many commercials.*

com·mis·sion | kə **mĭsh′**ən | —*noun, plural* **commissions** **1.** A group of people who have been chosen to do a certain job: *The Mayor named a commission to pick the best location in the city to build a new library.* **2.** The job assigned to such a group of people: *Your commission is to find a way to clean up the pollution in the river.* **3.** The act of committing or doing something: *the commission of a crime.* **4.** Money paid to someone for work done: *His commission was twenty cents on every box of candy he sold.* **5.** The appointment of a person to one of several ranks in the military: *He got a commission as a captain in the army.*
—*verb* **commissioned, commissioning** To give someone the power or right to do something; give a commission to: *They commissioned an artist to paint a portrait of the President.*

   Idiom **out of commission** Not in working condition: *I received no calls while my telephone was out of commission. The flu put me out of commission for a week.*

com·mis·sion·er | kə **mĭsh′**ə nər | —*noun, plural* **commissioners** A person who is in charge of a department of the government: *a police commissioner; a commissioner of parks and recreation.*

com·mit | kə **mĭt′** | —*verb* **committed, committing** **1.** To do or perform, especially to make a mistake or do something wrong: *commit a crime; commit an error.* **2.** To pledge or devote oneself to; promise: *We committed ourselves to obey the rules.*

com·mit·tee | kə **mĭt′**ē | —*noun, plural* **committees** A group of people chosen to do a particular job: *A committee of ten people was set up to suggest activities for our class picnic.*

com·mod·i·ty | kə **mŏd′**ĭ tē | —*noun, plural* **commodities** Anything that can be bought and sold: *The price of corn and other commodities will go up next year.*

com·mon | **kŏm′**ən | —*adjective* **commoner, commonest** **1.** Belonging to all or shared equally by all: *common interests; the common wall between two apartments.* **2.** Of the community as a whole; public: *The law was created for the common good.* **3.** Usual; widespread: *the common cold.* **4.** Most widely known of its kind; average; ordinary: *a common cat; a common housefly.* **5.** Of low quality: *common cloth.*
—*noun, plural* **commons** An area of land belonging to a community and used by the people in the community: *There was a concert on the town common last Sunday.*

   Idiom **in common** Jointly; equally shared with another: *They had several qualities in common.*

common

com·mon·place | **kŏm′**ən plās′ | —*adjective* Ordinary; usual; common: *Cold days are commonplace in Maine.*

common sense Good judgment that cannot be taught: *Closing the windows when it rains is just common sense.*

com·mon·wealth | **kŏm′**ən wĕlth′ | —*noun, plural* **commonwealths** **1.** A nation or state governed by the people: *The United States is a commonwealth.* **2.** The people of a nation or state. **3.** Any of certain states of the United States: *Kentucky, Maryland, Massachusetts, Pennsylvania, and Virginia are commonwealths.*

com·mo·tion |kə mō′shən| —*noun, plural* **commotions** Violent motion; noisy activity; confusion: *The squirrel and the cardinal were causing quite a commotion in the garden.*

com·mu·ni·cate |kə myōō′nĭ kāt′| —*verb* **communicated, communicating** To speak or write to; to pass along or exchange thoughts, ideas, opinions, or information: *They were good friends because they could communicate well.*

com·mu·ni·ca·tion |kə myōō′nĭ **kā′**shən| —*noun, plural* **communications 1.** The act of communicating. **2.** The exchange of thoughts, information, or messages: *The telephone is useful for quick communication over long distances.* **3.** Something communicated; a message. **4. communications** A system for sending and receiving messages, such as by telephone, mail, radio, or television.

com·mun·ion |kə myōōn′yən| —*noun, plural* **communions 1.** The act or condition of sharing feelings or thoughts. **2.** Spiritual or religious fellowship. **3. a. Communion** A religious ceremony in memory of the last meal of Jesus with his apostles on the night before he was crucified. **b.** The blessed bread and wine used in such a ceremony. **c.** The part of a Christian service in which this bread and wine is received.

com·mu·nism |kŏm′yə nĭz′əm| —*noun* A social system in which there are no social classes and in which property, goods, products, and labor are shared by everyone. The governments of some countries are based on this system.

Com·mu·nist |kŏm′yə nĭst| —*noun, plural* **Communists 1.** A member of the Communist Party. **2.** Often **communist** A person who believes in communism as a way of life.
—*adjective* **1.** Of the Communist Party or its members. **2.** Often **communist** Of communism in general: *That country has a communist society.*

Communist Party A political party that promotes communism.

com·mu·ni·ty |kə myōō′nĭ tē| —*noun, plural* **communities 1.** A group of people living in the same area and under the same government. **2.** The area in which they live; town.

com·mute |kə myōōt′| —*verb* **commuted, commuting** To travel to and from work or school: *We commute to Washington every day by train.*

com·pact |kəm păkt′| or |kŏm păkt′| or |kŏm′păkt′| —*adjective* **1.** Packed together tightly: *We went skiing on compact snow.* **2.** Taking up a small amount of space: *a compact apartment.*
—*verb* |kəm păkt′| **compacted, compacting** To pack or press together: *The trash truck has a machine that compacts the trash.*
—*noun* |kŏm′păkt′|, *plural* **compacts 1.** A small case containing face powder. **2.** A small car.

com·pan·ion |kəm păn′yən| —*noun, plural* **companions** A person who is often with another person; a friend; a comrade.

com·pan·ion·ship |kəm păn′yən shĭp′| —*noun, plural* **companionships** The relationship of companions: *The girl and her grandfather enjoyed a close companionship for years.*

com·pa·ny |kŭm′pə nē| —*noun, plural* **companies 1.** A guest or guests: *We are expecting company over the holidays.* **2.** Companionship; fellowship: *I'm grateful for his company.* **3.** One's friends or associates: *You are sometimes judged by the company you keep.* **4.** A business; a firm: *The company employed over a thousand people.*

ă	pat	ĕ	pet	î	fierce
ā	pay	ē	be	ŏ	pot
â	care	ĭ	pit	ō	go
ä	father	ī	pie	ô	paw, for
oi	oil	ŭ	cut	zh	vision
ōō	book	û	fur	ə	ago, item,
ōō	boot	*th*	the		pencil, atom,
yōō	abuse	th	thin		circus
ou	out	hw	which	ər	butter

com·par·a·tive |kəm **păr′**ə tĭv| —*adjective* **1.** Based on or making a comparison: *a comparative study of religions.*
2. Measured in relation to something else; relative: *the comparative sizes of the earth and the sun.*
—*noun, plural* **comparatives** The form of an adjective or adverb that gives the idea of an increase in quantity, quality, or other relation expressed by the adjective or adverb. Most comparatives are formed by adding the ending *-er* to the adjective or adverb, as in "larger," "greater," and "earlier." Some, however, are completely different from the original adjective or adverb. For example, the comparatives of the adjectives "good" and "bad" are "better" and "worse," and the comparative of the adverb "well" is "better." Many adjectives do not have a true comparative; the comparatives of such adjectives are formed by placing the word "more" before the adjective, as in the sentence *The plane is more comfortable than the train.* The comparative of most adverbs is also formed in the same way. For example, in the sentence *My car seats five more comfortably than yours,* the adverb "comfortably" shows comparison.

com·pare |kəm **pâr′**| —*verb* **compared, comparing** **1.** To say that something is similar: *The writer compared the lawn to a large emerald.* **2.** To examine the differences and similarities of two or more things or people: *Compare the skills of an astronaut with those of an airplane pilot.* **3.** To be worthy of comparison: *In what ways does the swan compare to the duck?*

com·par·i·son |kəm **pâr′**ĭ sən| —*noun, plural* **comparisons** **1.** The act of comparing: *A scientist measures and makes comparisons.* **2.** The result of comparing; a statement of similarities and differences: *a comparison of prices.*

com·part·ment |kəm **pärt′**mənt| —*noun, plural* **compartments** A separate section: *My desk has a compartment for large files.*

com·pass |**kŭm′**pəs| or |**kŏm′**pəs| —*noun, plural* **compasses** **1.** An instrument used to show directions. A compass has a magnetic needle that looks like the hand of a clock. The needle can turn freely so that it always points to the north. **2.** An instrument used for drawing circles or measuring distances. It is made up of two pieces joined together at the top. One of the pieces ends in a point and the other holds a pencil.

com·pas·sion |kəm **păsh′**ən| —*noun* A feeling of sharing someone else's suffering or misfortune, along with a desire to help.

com·pel |kəm **pĕl′**| —*verb* **compelled, compelling** To force someone to do something: *The sudden storm compelled us to go indoors.*

com·pen·sate |**kŏm′**pən sāt′| —*verb* **compensated, compensating** **1.** To make up for something: *A baseball player who is not a speedy runner can compensate by powerful hitting.* **2.** To pay: *He worked hard, and the company compensated him very well.*

com·pete |kəm **pēt′**| —*verb* **competed, competing** To take part in a contest; to try to win something: *The two teams competed for the championship. How many will compete in the spelling bee?*

com·pe·ti·tion |kŏm′pĭ **tĭsh′**ən| —*noun, plural* **competitions** **1.** The act of taking part in a contest: *The competition for the awards is fierce.* **2.** A contest or other test of skill and ability: *a skating competition; a swimming competition.*

com·pet·i·tive |kəm **pĕt′**ĭ tĭv| —*adjective* **1.** Of, in, or decided

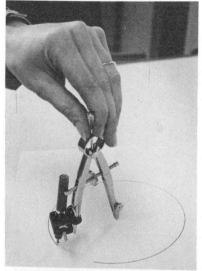

compass
Above: A compass to draw circles
Below: A compass to show direction

competitor

by competition: *Chess is a very competitive game.* **2.** Liking to compete: *a competitive person.*

com·pet·i·tor |kəm **pĕt′** ĭ tər| —*noun, plural* **competitors** A person, team, or other group that competes with another person or group; a contestant; a rival; opponent: *Bobby's competitor for first prize was his sister.*

com·pla·cent |kəm **plā′**sənt| —*adjective* Pleased with oneself; satisfied; contented: *She was a good runner, but she became so complacent that she lost her next two races.*

com·plain |kəm **plān′**| —*verb* **complained, complaining 1.** To say that one is unhappy or annoyed about something: *He complained that he had too much homework.* **2.** To make a statement or report about something that is wrong: *I complained to the telephone company about a mistake in my bill.*

com·plaint |kəm **plānt′**| —*noun, plural* **complaints 1.** A statement or other act that expresses that one is unhappy or annoyed about something: *He worked hard, with never a complaint.* **2.** A cause or reason for complaining: *"Too much wind!" that's my only complaint.* **3.** A formal statement or report: *The store owner signed a complaint against the man who broke into the store.*

com·ple·ment |**kŏm′**plə mənt| —*noun, plural* **complements 1.** Something that completes, makes up a whole, or makes something perfect: *Fresh flowers are a complement to a fine dinner table.* **2.** The amount needed to make something complete: *The library shelves now have a full complement of books.*
—*verb* **complemented, complementing** To make something complete; add to the effect of: *That sweater complements the rest of your outfit.*
♦ *These sound alike* **complement, compliment.**

com·ple·men·ta·ry |kŏm′plə **mĕn′**tə rē| or |kŏm′plə **mĕn′**trē| —*adjective* Completing something; supplying what is lacking or needed: *Two countries are complementary if each country produces what the other needs.*
♦ *These sound alike* **complementary, complimentary.**

com·plete |kəm **plēt′**| —*adjective* **1.** Not lacking anything; having everything that is necessary; whole: *I own a complete set of tools for repairing bicycles.* **2.** Ended; finished: *He could not go out to play until his homework was complete.* **3.** Thorough; full; perfect: *The news came as a complete surprise to us.*
—*verb* **completed, completing 1.** To make something whole; to add what is missing: *Complete this form by filling in the blanks.* **2.** To finish; end: *We were very happy when we completed painting our house.*

com·plete·ly |kəm **plēt′**lē| —*adverb* Totally; entirely; wholly: *Carol was completely honest about her feelings toward him.*

com·ple·tion |kəm **plē′**shən| —*noun, plural* **completions 1.** The act or process of completing: *We helped him with the completion of his paper route so he could come to the baseball game with us.* **2.** The condition of being completed: *carry plans through to completion.*

com·plex |kəm **plĕks′**| or |**kŏm′**plĕks′| —*adjective* **1.** Made up of many parts: *We have a system of complex highways. A computer is a complex machine.* **2.** Difficult to understand or do: *complex problems in arithmetic.*

com·plex·ion |kəm **plĕk′**shən| —*noun, plural* **complexions 1.** The natural look and color of a person's skin, especially that of the face: *She had a lovely complexion.* **2.** The general appearance or nature of something: *The complexion of the contest changed when last year's champion dropped out.*

com·plex·i·ty |kəm **plĕk'**sĭ tē| —*noun, plural* **complexities** The condition of being complex: *The complexity of that machine made it break down a lot.*

com·pli·cate |**kŏm'**plĭ kāt'| —*verb* **complicated, complicating** To make something hard to understand or do; make something confusing: *Too many long words complicate the meaning of the story.*

com·pli·ca·ted |**kŏm'**plĭ kā'tĭd| —*adjective* **1.** Having parts that are tangled or put together in a confusing way: *a complicated machine.* **2.** Not easy to understand or do; confusing: *The math problems were too complicated for me to do.*

com·pli·ca·tion |kŏm'plĭ **kā'**shən| —*noun, plural* **complications** Something that complicates; an unexpected difficulty or obstacle: *Rain was a real complication for the farmers' work.*

com·pli·ment |**kŏm'**plə mənt| —*noun, plural* **compliments** Something good said to show praise or admiration: *Jeanne won many compliments for the way she handled the business deal.*
—*verb* **complimented, complimenting** To say something that shows praise or admiration; pay a compliment: *We complimented the pianist for his great performance.*
♦ *These sound alike* **compliment, complement.**

com·pli·men·ta·ry |kŏm'plĭ **mĕn'**tə rē| or |kŏm'plə **mĕn'**trē| —*adjective* **1.** Expressing or containing compliments or praise: *The high school received many complimentary remarks about its band.* **2.** Given free: *We received two complimentary tickets to the movies.*
♦ *These sound alike* **complimentary, complementary.**

com·pose |kəm **pōz'**| —*verb* **composed, composing** **1.** To make up; form: *A jury is composed of twelve people.* **2.** To write; create: *He composed many operas. She composed mostly for the piano.* **3.** To make calm or controlled: *She tried to compose herself after the boy insulted her.*

com·pos·er |kəm **pō'**zər| —*noun, plural* **composers** A person who composes, especially a creator of musical works.

com·pos·ite |kəm **pŏz'**ĭt| —*adjective* Made up of many different parts: *a composite picture.*

com·po·si·tion |kŏm'pə **zĭsh'**ən| —*noun, plural* **compositions** **1.** The act or process of composing; the putting together of things to form a whole: *The composition of music takes years to learn.* **2.** A work that has been composed, especially a musical work: *She played one of her own compositions on the guitar.* **3.** A short story or essay: *She got a good grade on her composition from her English teacher.* **4.** The parts of something and the way in which they are put together: *We admired the composition of the painting. They studied the composition of minerals.*

com·po·sure |kəm **pō'**zhər| —*noun* Control over one's emotions; a calm manner; self-control: *He felt his anger and fear rise up, but then he got his composure back.*

com·pound |**kŏm'**pound'| —*noun, plural* **compounds** **1.** Something made by the mixture or combination of two or more things, parts, or ingredients: *The meal was a compound of good food and good conversation.* **2.** A substance formed by the chemical combination of two or more elements: *Water is a compound made up of two parts hydrogen to one part oxygen.*
—*verb* |kŏm **pound'**| or |kəm **pound'**| **compounded,**

compounding To make up or put together by mixing or combining parts or ingredients: *A druggist compounds medicines.*
—*adjective* | kŏm′pound′ | or | kəm **pound′** | Made up of two or more things, parts, or ingredients: *"Everyone" is a compound word. A compound sentence has two or more sentences in it.*

com·pre·hend | kŏm′prĭ **hĕnd′** | —*verb* **comprehended, comprehending** To understand: *Do you comprehend the question?*

com·pre·hen·sion | kŏm′prĭ **hĕn′**shən | —*noun, plural* **comprehensions 1.** The act of understanding: *Can you read with good comprehension?* **2.** The ability to understand: *problems that are beyond our comprehension.*

com·press | kəm **prĕs′** | —*verb* **compressed, compressing** To press or squeeze together: *Some garbage trucks are equipped to compress garbage.*
—*noun* | kŏm′prĕs′ |, *plural* **compresses** A soft pad of material that is put against a wound or injury. A compress may have medicine on it, or it may be soaked in hot or cold water.

com·prise | kəm **prīz′** | —*verb* **comprised, comprising** To consist of; be composed of; include: *In the beginning, the United States comprised thirteen states.*

com·pro·mise | kŏm′prə mīz′ | —*noun, plural* **compromises** A settlement of differences or of an argument. A compromise is reached when each side gives up some of its demands.
—*verb* **compromised, compromising** To give up certain demands in order to settle an argument: *Neither of us wanted to do the dishes, but we compromised, with one washing and the other drying.*

com·pute | kəm **pyōot′** | —*verb* **computed, computing** To work out by mathematics; calculate: *We computed how much our new car will cost per year.*

com·put·er | kəm **pyōo′**tər | —*noun, plural* **computers** Any of several kinds of complex electronic devices. Computers can do arithmetic at very high speeds. They are used for storing and processing information, making decisions, and controlling machinery.

com·rade | kŏm′răd′ | —*noun, plural* **comrades** A companion who shares one's activities.

con·cave | kŏn **kāv′** | or | kŏn′kāv′ | —*adjective* Curved inward: *That salad bowl is concave on the inside.*

con·ceal | kən **sēl′** | —*verb* **concealed, concealing** To keep from being seen, noticed, or known; hide: *The magician concealed a coin in the palm of her hand. I tried to conceal my fear.*

con·cede | kən **sēd′** | —*verb* **conceded, conceding 1.** To admit that something is true, often without wanting to: *He conceded that the boy won the award fair and square.* **2.** To give up on: *The man running for office conceded the election before all the votes had been counted.*

con·ceit | kən **sēt′** | —*noun, plural* **conceits** Too high an opinion of oneself and one's abilities; vanity.

con·ceit·ed | kən **sē′**tĭd | —*adjective* Too proud of oneself or one's abilities; vain: *She had no friends because she was so conceited.*

con·cen·trate | kŏn′sən trāt′ | —*verb* **concentrated, concentrating 1.** To keep one's mind, attention, or efforts on something: *Barbara couldn't concentrate on her homework because the TV was on. Farmers were concentrating on corn that year.* **2.** To gather or bring together in one place: *Our population is concentrated in the*

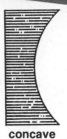

computer

concave

ă	pat	ĕ	pet	î	fierce
ā	pay	ē	be	ŏ	pot
â	care	ĭ	pit	ō	go
ä	father	ī	pie	ô	paw, for

oi	oil	ŭ	cut	zh	vision
ōō	book	û	fur	ə	ago, item,
ōō	boot	*th*	the		pencil, atom,
yōō	abuse	th	thin		circus
ou	out	hw	which	ər	butter

cities. **3.** To make a solution stronger: *Orange juice is concentrated and sold in cans.*

con·cen·tra·tion |kŏn′sən **trā′**shən| —*noun, plural* **concentrations** **1.** Close attention: *Concentration is important when you are doing your homework.* **2.** A close gathering or dense grouping: *the concentration of people in large cities.*

con·cept |**kŏn′**sĕpt′| —*noun, plural* **concepts** A general idea or understanding: *Very young children have no concept of time.*

con·cep·tion |kən **sĕp′**shən| —*noun, plural* **conceptions** **1.** A mental picture; an idea: *The study of astronomy gives us some conception of what the universe is about.* **2.** A beginning of an idea; origin: *We studied the automobile from its earliest conception.*

con·cern |kən **sûrn′**| —*verb* **concerned, concerning** **1.** To be about; have to do with: *I heard something that concerns you and your best friend.* **2.** To worry: *The child's high temperature concerned the mother greatly.*
—*noun, plural* **concerns** **1.** Something of interest or importance: *My chief concern was to get the child to safety.* **2.** Serious care or interest: *The doctor's concern helped the patient feel less worried.* **3.** Anxiety; worry: *He made his speech without the slightest concern.* **4.** A business; a firm: *Many concerns deal in services rather than in goods.*

con·cerned |kən **sûrnd′**| —*adjective* **1.** Interested; involved: *As far as I'm concerned you made the right choice.* **2.** Worried; anxious: *She had a concerned expression on her face.*

con·cern·ing |kən **sûr′**nĭng| —*preposition* About; regarding: *I like to read weird stories concerning visitors from outer space.*

con·cert |**kŏn′**sûrt′| or |**kŏn′**sərt| —*noun, plural* **concerts** A performance of music given by a number of musicians.

concert

con·cer·to |kən **chĕr′**tō| —*noun, plural* **concertos** A piece of music written for one or more instruments to be accompanied by an orchestra.

conch |kŏngk| or |kŏnch| —*noun, plural* **conchs** |kŏngks| or **conches** |**kŏn′**chĭz| A tropical sea animal with a large spiral shell. Conch shells are often brightly colored.

con·clude |kən **klōōd′**| —*verb* **concluded, concluding** **1.** To bring or come to an end: *The speaker concluded his speech and sat down. The movie concluded with a wild chase.* **2.** To think over and decide: *After listening to all the arguments, I conclude that no one is entirely right.*

con·clu·sion |kən **klōō′**zhən| —*noun, plural* **conclusions** **1.** The end of something: *the conclusion of a story.* **2.** A decision or judgment made after careful thought: *We can draw only one conclusion: you were right in the first place.*

Con·cord |**kŏng′**kərd| The capital of New Hampshire.

con·crete |**kŏn′**krēt′| or |kŏn **krēt′**| —*noun* A building material made of cement, pebbles, sand, and water. Concrete becomes very hard when it dries. Buildings, roads, sidewalks, and bridges can be made from concrete.
—*adjective* Able to be seen, heard, touched, or otherwise sensed; real: *Shoes and trees are concrete objects.*

con·cus·sion |kən **kŭsh′**ən| —*noun, plural* **concussions** **1.** A violent jarring; a shock. **2.** An injury, especially to the brain, caused by a hard blow.

con·demn |kən **dĕm′**| —*verb* **condemned, condemning** **1.** To disapprove of strongly: *The parents condemned violence on*

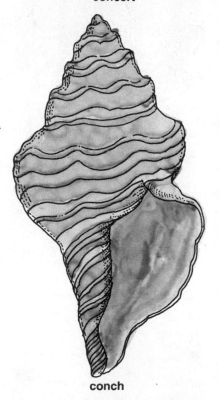
conch

conductor
Above: Orchestra conductor
Below: Train conductor

cone
Ice-cream cone *(left)* and rocket nose cone *(right)*

ă	pat	ĕ	pet	î	fierce
ā	pay	ē	be	ŏ	pot
â	care	ĭ	pit	ō	go
ä	father	ī	pie	ô	paw, for

oi	oil	ŭ	cut	zh	vision
ŏŏ	book	û	fur	ə	ago, item,
ōō	boot	*th*	the		pencil, atom,
yōō	abuse	th	thin		circus
ou	out	hw	which	ər	butter

television. **2.** To find someone guilty and say what the punishment is: *The judge condemned the prisoner to thirty days in jail.* **3.** To declare unsafe or no longer fit for use: *The city condemned the old jail on Water Street.*

con·den·sa·tion |kŏn′dĕn sā′shən| or |kŏn′dən sā′shən| —*noun, plural* **condensations** **1.** The process of changing or being changed from a gas to a liquid or a solid: *Condensation caused moisture to collect as frost on our windows.* **2.** A liquid or solid formed by this process: *Please wipe the condensation off the bathroom mirror.* **3.** A brief or shortened form of something: *the condensation of a novel.*

con·dense |kən dĕns′| —*verb* **condensed, condensing** **1.** To change from a gas to a liquid or solid form: *Steam condenses to water when cooled.* **2.** To make thicker or more dense, usually by boiling away a liquid or allowing it to evaporate: *We learned how they condense milk into a thick syrup.* **3.** To put into a brief or short form: *The author condensed her book into a magazine article.*

con·di·tion |kən dĭsh′ən| —*noun, plural* **conditions** **1.** The way something or someone is: *The house was in good condition after the storm. Under the evil king, the condition of the people became worse.* **2.** General health and physical ability: *Exercise every day to stay in good condition.* **3.** Something said to be necessary or desirable; a requirement: *Being able to write clearly is one of the conditions for passing this course.* **4.** Often **conditions** Something that affects an activity or event; circumstances: *They are trying to improve working conditions at the factory.*
—*verb* **conditioned, conditioning** **1.** To put into good condition; make fit: *They ran every day to condition themselves for the race.* **2.** To adapt; accustom: *Years of getting up at the same time had conditioned her to awake every morning at six.*

con·di·tion·er |kən dĭsh′ə nər| —*noun, plural* **conditioners** Something that is used to improve something in some way: *an air conditioner. Put conditioner in your hair after washing it.*

con·do·min·i·um |kŏn′də mĭn′ē əm| —*noun, plural* **condominiums** An apartment building in which the apartments are owned by the people living in them.

con·dor |kŏn′dôr′| or |kŏn′dər| —*noun, plural* **condors** A very large bird of the mountains of California and South America. The condor is a kind of vulture.

con·duct |kən dŭkt′| —*verb* **conducted, conducting** **1.** To lead; guide; direct: *She conducted a tour of her factory. He conducted the orchestra.* **2.** To manage: *He conducted the meeting. The brothers conduct a gardening business in the summer.* **3.** To act as a path for electricity, heat, or other forms of energy: *Most metals conduct heat well.* **4.** **conduct oneself** To act properly; do what is right: *How did the twins conduct themselves at the movie?*
—*noun* |kŏn′dŭkt′|, *plural* **conducts** The way a person acts; behavior: *The teacher wants to see you about your conduct in class.*

con·duc·tor |kən dŭk′tər| —*noun, plural* **conductors** **1.** A person who leads or conducts: *the conductor of the orchestra.* **2.** The person in charge of a bus or train. A conductor usually collects fares: *The conductor told me when it was time for me to get off the train.* **3.** Something that provides an easy path for the flow of heat, electricity, or other forms of energy: *Copper is a good conductor.*

cone |kōn| —*noun, plural* **cones** **1.** A solid object that has a flat base in the shape of a curve, such as a circle, and is pointed at the other end. **2.** Anything shaped like a cone: *an ice-cream cone.* **3.** A cluster of overlapping scales that grows on a pine or related tree. It contains the seeds of the tree.

con·fed·er·a·cy |kən fĕd′ər ə sē| —*noun, plural* **confederacies**
1. A group of people or countries joined together for a common purpose. **2. the Confederacy** The group of eleven southern states that left the United States in 1860 and 1861. They were Alabama, Arkansas, Florida, Georgia, Louisiana, Mississippi, North Carolina, South Carolina, Tennessee, Texas, and Virginia.

con·fed·er·ate |kən fĕd′ər ĭt| —*adjective* **1.** Belonging to a confederacy. **2. Confederate** Of the Confederacy: *a Confederate soldier.*
—*noun, plural* **confederates 1.** A person who helps another keep a secret or commit a crime. **2.** A member of a confederacy.
3. Confederate A person who supported the Confederacy.

con·fed·er·a·tion |kən fĕd′ə rā′shən| —*noun, plural* **confederations** A confederacy: *a confederation of Indian tribes.*

con·fer |kən fûr′| —*verb* **conferred, conferring 1.** To take part in a conference; discuss together: *The doctors conferred about their patient.* **2.** To give; award: *They conferred a gold medal on the best athlete in the competition.*

con·fer·ence |kŏn′fər əns| or |kŏn′frəns| —*noun, plural* **conferences** A meeting to discuss something: *a peace conference.*

con·fess |kən fĕs′| —*verb* **confessed, confessing 1.** To say that one has committed a crime or done something bad; admit: *He confessed that he had broken the window.* **2.** To admit: *I must confess he was a good speaker.* **3.** To tell one's sins to God or to a priest.

con·fes·sion |kən fĕsh′ən| —*noun, plural* **confessions** The act of confessing or admitting guilt: *His confession was sincere.*

con·fet·ti |kən fĕt′ē| —*noun* (Used with a singular verb.) Small pieces of colored paper that are scattered around at celebrations, parades, parties, and some sports events.

con·fide |kən fīd′| —*verb* **confided, confiding 1.** To tell someone something, knowing that it will be kept secret: *She confided her worries to her father.* **2. confide in** To tell or share one's secrets with: *I always confide in my best friend.*

con·fi·dence |kŏn′fĭ dəns| —*noun, plural* **confidences 1.** A feeling of faith in oneself. **2.** Trust or faith in others: *You have won my confidence.* **3.** Faith or trust that someone will keep a secret: *I am telling you this in confidence.*

con·fi·dent |kŏn′fĭ dənt| —*adjective* Having confidence; feeling sure of oneself: *I am confident I will pass the course.*

con·fi·den·tial |kŏn′fĭ dĕn′shəl| —*adjective* Told in confidence; secret: *a confidential report.*

con·fine |kən fīn′| —*verb* **confined, confining 1.** To keep from moving freely: *He was confined to bed for a week.* **2.** To put into prison: *Several people were confined after the fight.*

con·firm |kən fûrm′| —*verb* **confirmed, confirming 1.** To agree that something is true: *The mayor confirmed the newspaper report that he was quitting.* **2.** To give or get definite evidence: *We have confirmed that humans can live on the moon.* **3.** To make sure of an appointment or other arrangement: *We confirmed the plane reservations.* **4.** To admit as a full member of a church or synagogue.

Confederate
General Robert E. Lee, leader of the Confederate army

con·fir·ma·tion |kŏn′fər mā′shən| —*noun, plural* **confirmations**
1. The act of confirming: *His secretary called for a confirmation of our travel plans.* **2.** Something that confirms; proof: *This was confirmation of the rumor.* **3.** A ceremony in which a person is made a full member of a church or synagogue.

con·fis·cate |kŏn′fĭ skāt′| —*verb* **confiscated, confiscating** To take something away from someone because one has the right to do so: *The police confiscated the stolen television.*

con·flict |kŏn′flĭkt′| —*noun, plural* **conflicts 1.** Long fighting; warfare: *armed conflict between the two nations.* **2.** A clash or struggle of ideas or interests: *There are two television shows I want to see, but there is a conflict in the schedule.*
—*verb* |kən flĭkt′| **conflicted, conflicting** To clash; be different: *What people do often conflicts with what they say.*

con·form |kən fôrm′| —*verb* **conformed, conforming** To follow a set rule or standard: *If you don't conform to the traffic laws, you may be hurt.*

con·front |kən frŭnt′| —*verb* **confronted, confronting 1.** To come face to face with: *He was allowed to confront the man who accused him. Many problems confront us.* **2.** To bring face to face; challenge to accept or deny: *The girl confessed when she was confronted with the evidence.*

con·fuse |kən fyōoz′| —*verb* **confused, confusing 1.** To mix up; mislead: *These two signs confuse me: I still don't know which way to go.* **2.** To mistake for something else: *It is easy to confuse a donkey for a mule.*

con·fu·sion |kən fyōo′zhən| —*noun, plural* **confusions 1.** The act of confusing or mixing up: *You can prevent confusion by writing clearly.* **2.** The condition of being confused: *In my confusion I took the wrong bus.*

con·grat·u·late |kən grăch′ə lāt′| —*verb* **congratulated, congratulating** To praise someone for something the person has done or for any good event: *We congratulated the actress.*

con·grat·u·la·tion |kən grăch′ə lā′shən| —*noun, plural* **congratulations 1.** The act of congratulating: *He spoke a few words of congratulation.* **2. congratulations** Praise given to someone for something the person has done or for any good event: *We shouted our congratulations to the runners as they crossed the finish line.*

con·gre·gate |kŏng′grə gāt′| —*verb* **congregated, congregating** To gather together; assemble: *The people congregated on the village green.*

con·gre·ga·tion |kŏng′grə gā′shən| —*noun, plural* **congregations 1.** A gathering of people or things. **2.** A group of people gathered for religious worship.

con·gress |kŏng′grĭs| —*noun, plural* **congresses 1.** A group of people who make laws in a republic. **2. Congress** In the United States, the Senate and House of Representatives. Members are elected to each of these groups from their own states. They make the laws of the nation.

con·gress·man or **Con·gress·man** |kŏng′grĭs mən| —*noun, plural* **congressmen** or **Congressmen** A member of the United States Congress, especially of the House of Representatives.

con·gress·wom·an or **Con·gress·wom·an** |kŏng′grĭs wŏom′ən| —*noun, plural* **congresswomen** or **Congresswomen** A woman who is a member of the United States Congress, especially of the House of Representatives.

Congress

ă	pat	ĕ	pet	î	fierce
ā	pay	ē	be	ŏ	pot
â	care	ĭ	pit	ō	go
ä	father	ī	pie	ô	paw, for
oi	oil	ŭ	cut	zh	vision
ōō	book	û	fur	ə	ago, item,
ōō	boot	th	the		pencil, atom,
yōō	abuse	th	thin		circus
ou	out	hw	which	ər	butter

con·junc·tion | kən **jŭngk'** shən | —*noun, plural* **conjunctions** **1.** A word used to join together words or groups of words in a sentence. *If, or, but,* and *and* are conjunctions. **2.** A combination or association: *The local police worked in conjunction with the fire department.*

con·nect | kə **nĕkt'** | —*verb* **connected, connecting** **1.** To join or come together: *They connected the water pipe to our new house. Route 11 connects with route 20 just outside town.* **2.** To think of as related; associate: *She always connects the word "blue" with the color of the sky.* **3.** To link by telephone: *The operator connected us.* **4.** To plug into an electrical circuit: *Please connect the radio.*

Con·nect·i·cut | kə **nĕt'** ĭ kət | A state in the northeastern United States. The capital of Connecticut is Hartford.

con·nec·tion | kə **nĕk'** shən | —*noun, plural* **connections** **1.** The act of connecting or the condition of being connected: *This special plug makes connection of the antenna easy.* **2.** A relationship: *the connection between the sun and the seasons.*

con·quer | **kŏng'** kər | —*verb* **conquered, conquering** **1.** To defeat in war: *Has a smaller country ever conquered a larger one?* **2.** To get control over; overcome: *The girl tried to conquer her fear.*

con·quer·or | **kŏng'** kər ər | —*noun, plural* **conquerors** Someone who conquers: *The conquerors entered the city they had defeated.*

con·quest | **kŏn'** kwĕst' | or | **kŏng'** kwĕst' | —*noun, plural* **conquests** **1.** The act of conquering: *Our conquest against disease has been successful.* **2.** Something conquered: *Spain made some conquests in South America.*

con·science | **kŏn'** shəns | —*noun, plural* **consciences** An inner feeling that tells a person right from wrong.

con·scious | **kŏn'** shəs | —*adjective* **1.** Able to see, feel, and hear, and to understand what is happening: *He is badly injured but still conscious.* **2.** Able to know; aware: *She was conscious of her faults.* **3.** Done with awareness; intentional: *Please make a conscious effort to speak more clearly.*

con·scious·ness | **kŏn'** shəs nĭs | —*noun* **1.** The condition of being conscious: *He lost consciousness after he had been hit on the head.* **2.** Awareness: *They had no consciousness of how far they had walked that day.* **3.** All the ideas, opinions, and feelings held by a person or group: *We cannot believe that cheating has become a part of students' consciousness.*

con·sec·u·tive | kən **sĕk'** yə tĭv | —*adjective* Following in order without a break or interruption: *four consecutive phone calls.*

con·sent | kən **sĕnt'** | —*verb* **consented, consenting** To give permission; agree: *She consented to let him go to the movies.* —*noun, plural* **consents** Permission; agreement: *The queen gave her consent to her son's marriage.*

con·se·quence | **kŏn'** sĭ kwĕns' | —*noun, plural* **consequences** **1.** Something that happens as a result of another action or condition; effect: *What were the consequences of your meeting?* **2.** Importance: *That is a matter of no consequence to me. He is a man of consequence.*

con·se·quent | **kŏn'** sĭ kwĕnt' | or | **kŏn'** sĭ kwənt | —*adjective* Following as an effect or result: *The newspaper printed an article about the heavy rains and the consequent flooding of the lowlands.*

con·se·quent·ly | **kŏn'** sĭ kwĕnt'lē | or | **kŏn'** sĭ kwənt lē | —*adverb* As a result; therefore: *He didn't study, consequently he failed the test.*

Connecticut
The name **Connecticut** probably comes from an Indian word meaning "at the long river." The state was named for the river.

con·ser·va·tion |kŏn′sər vā′shən| —*noun* **1.** The act of conserving or saving: *These new gadgets will help in the conservation of time and effort. The conservation of his money made it possible to buy a car.* **2.** The careful use and protection of natural elements and resources: *Conservation is one way to make sure we will have enough energy in the future.*

con·ser·va·tion·ist |kŏn′sər vā′shə nĭst| —*noun, plural* **conservationists** A person who is in favor of or a trained worker in conservation.

con·serv·a·tive |kən sûr′və tĭv| —*adjective* **1.** Tending to be against change; in favor of traditional values. **2.** Cautious; careful: *a conservative attitude.*
—*noun, plural* **conservatives** Someone who is conservative.

con·serve |kən sûrv′| —*verb* **conserved, conserving** **1.** To use carefully, without waste: *Try to conserve your energy on a very hot day.* **2.** To take measures to keep resources in good condition: *Science and common sense teach us to conserve our forests.*

con·sid·er |kən sĭd′ər| —*verb* **considered, considering** **1.** To think over: *I'm considering your suggestion.* **2.** To regard as; believe to be: *I consider you an excellent pianist.* **3.** To take into account; keep in mind: *He plays well if you consider that he has never had any lessons.* **4.** To be thoughtful of: *Try to consider the feelings of others.*

con·sid·er·a·ble |kən sĭd′ər ə bəl| —*adjective* Fairly large: *He agreed to paint her portrait for a considerable fee.*

con·sid·er·ate |kən sĭd′ər ĭt| —*adjective* Thinking of other people's feelings; thoughtful: *A considerate person will not gossip.*

con·sid·er·a·tion |kən sĭd′ə rā′shən| —*noun, plural* **considerations** **1.** Careful thought: *He gave the idea some consideration.* **2.** Something to be considered in making a decision: *The weather is an important consideration when you plan a vacation.* **3.** Thoughtful concern for other people: *He shows no consideration for people's feelings.*

con·sid·er·ing |kən sĭd′ər ĭng| —*preposition* In view of: *Considering their ages, they did a wonderful job.*

con·sist |kən sĭst′| —*verb* **consisted, consisting** To be made up: *A week consists of seven days.*

con·sis·ten·cy |kən sĭs′tən sē| —*noun, plural* **consistencies** **1.** The degree of how stiff, thick, or firm something is: *He mixed flour and water to the consistency of paste.* **2.** The ability or quality of staying with the same ideas or actions: *His statements do not have consistency; first he says one thing and then its opposite.*

con·sist·ent |kən sĭs′tənt| —*adjective* **1.** Staying always with the same ideas or actions: *It helps to have consistent habits for studying.* **2.** In agreement: *What she said is not consistent with what actually happened.*

con·so·la·tion |kŏn′sə lā′shən| —*noun* **1.** Comfort during a time of disappointment or sorrow: *We tried to offer some consolation after her uncle died.* **2.** Something that gives consolation: *The toys seemed to be the boy's only consolation.*

con·sole¹ |kən sōl′| —*verb* **consoled, consoling** To comfort during a time of disappointment or sorrow: *Faithful fans consoled the team with their cheers after it lost the game.*

con·sole² |kŏn′sōl′| —*noun, plural* **consoles** A cabinet that contains a radio, record player, or television and is designed to sit on the floor.

---

console¹, console²
Both of these words come from a Latin word meaning "to comfort." Both came to English through French.

console²

ă	pat	ĕ	pet	î	fierce
ā	pay	ē	be	ŏ	pot
â	care	ĭ	pit	ō	go
ä	father	ī	pie	ô	paw, for
oi	oil	ŭ	cut	zh	vision
ōō	book	û	fur	ə	ago, item,
ōō	boot	*th*	the		pencil, atom,
yōō	abuse	th	thin		circus
ou	out	hw	which	ər	butter

con·so·nant |**kŏn′**sə nənt| —*noun, plural* **consonants** **1.** A speech sound that is made when two parts of the mouth touch each other or are very close together. **2.** A letter of the alphabet that can stand for such a sound. The consonants *p, b, f, v,* and *m* stand for sounds in which the lips touch each other or the teeth. The tongue and teeth come together to make sounds that *t, d, s, z, ch, j, n,* and *l* stand for.

con·spic·u·ous |kən **spĭk′**yōō əs| —*adjective* Attracting attention; easy to notice: *a conspicuous dress.*

con·spir·a·cy |kən **spîr′**ə sē| —*noun, plural* **conspiracies** A secret plan to do something that is against the law.

con·spire |kən **spīr′**| —*verb* **conspired, conspiring** To plan together secretly to do something wrong or against the law: *The men conspired to kidnap the senator.*

con·sta·ble |**kŏn′**stə bəl| —*noun, plural* **constables** A member of a police force in a town or village.

con·stant |**kŏn′**stənt| —*adjective* **1.** Not changing; staying the same: *the constant sound of a waterfall.* **2.** Happening all the time: *constant interruptions.* **3.** Without interruption; continuous: *The patient needs constant care.*

con·stel·la·tion |kŏn′stə **lā′**shən| —*noun, plural* **constellations** Any of 88 groups of stars that reminded people long ago of animals, people, or objects.

con·sti·tute |**kŏn′**stĭ tōōt′| or |**kŏn′**stĭ tyōōt′| —*verb* **constituted, constituting** To make up; form: *Twelve units constitute a dozen.*

con·sti·tu·tion |kŏn′stĭ **tōō′**shən| or |kŏn′stĭ **tyōō′**shən| —*noun, plural* **constitutions** **1.** The basic law or plan under which a government is organized: *Our state constitution does not allow the governor more than two terms in office.* **2.** **the Constitution** The written constitution of the United States, adopted in 1787 and put into effect in 1789. **3.** The way in which something or someone is made up: *a girl with a strong constitution.*

con·sti·tu·tion·al |kŏn′stĭ **tōō′**shə nəl| or |kŏn′stĭ **tyōō′**shə nəl| —*adjective* **1.** Of, according to, or permitted by a constitution: *a constitutional amendment; a law that is not constitutional; a constitutional right.* **2.** Operating under a constitution: *a constitutional government.*

con·strict |kən **strĭkt′**| —*verb* **constricted, constricting** To make or become smaller or narrower; to contract: *The doctor used a clamp to constrict the blood vessel. When his throat muscles constricted, he couldn't breathe.*

con·struct |kən **strŭkt′**| —*verb* **constructed, constructing** To build or put together: *The company will construct a skyscraper for its offices. Can you construct a sentence from these words?*

con·struc·tion |kən **strŭk′**shən| —*noun, plural* **constructions** **1.** The act or process of constructing: *Two new hotels are under construction.* **2.** The business or work of building. **3.** Something that is put together; a structure: *The tower was a construction of steel and glass.* **4.** The way in which something is put together; design: *A chisel is a tool of simple construction.*

con·struc·tive |kən **strŭk′**tĭv| —*adjective* Serving a useful purpose or helping to make something better: *The tennis coach gave him some constructive suggestions on how to improve his game.*

con·sult |kən **sŭlt′**| —*verb* **consulted, consulting** To go to or turn to for advice, an opinion, or information: *You must consult a*

constable

construction

doctor. If you don't know the meaning of a word, you should consult a dictionary.

con·sume |kən sōōm′| —*verb* **consumed, consuming** **1.** To eat or drink: *You probably consume iron in many of your foods.* **2.** To use up: *Big cars consume more fuel than small cars do. Arguing over details consumed precious time.* **3.** To destroy by burning or as if by burning: *The moth flew too near the candle and was consumed in its flame. His hate consumed him.*

con·sum·er |kən sōō′mər| —*noun, plural* **consumers** Someone who buys and uses goods and services.

con·sump·tion |kən sŭmp′shən| —*noun* **1.** The act of consuming: *Consumption of the wrong kind of food can lead to illness.* **2.** A quantity or amount used: *We want a car with low gas consumption.*

con·tact |kŏn′tăkt′| —*noun, plural* **contacts** **1.** The act or condition of touching or coming together: *We could feel the contact of the plane's wheels on the runway.* **2.** The condition or fact of being in touch: *He put me in contact with the right people. They kept radio contact with the pilot.*
—*verb* |kŏn′tăkt′| or |kən tăkt′| **contacted, contacting** **1.** To come into contact with; touch: *Suddenly we felt the bottom of our boat contact the sandy ocean floor.* **2.** To get in touch with; communicate with: *He contacted his wife by telephone.*

contact lens A small, thin plastic lens worn directly on the eye in order to correct poor vision.

con·ta·gious |kən tā′jəs| —*adjective* **1.** Easily spread by direct or indirect contact; catching: *a contagious disease; contagious laughter.* **2.** Carrying or able to carry disease: *That patient is still contagious.*

con·tain |kən tān′| —*verb* **contained, containing** **1.** To have within itself; hold: *The carton contains milk. That book contains important information.* **2.** To consist of; be made up of: *A quart contains two pints.* **3.** To hold back; restrain: *I could not contain my laughter.*

con·tain·er |kən tā′nər| —*noun, plural* **containers** Anything used to hold something else. Boxes, jars, cans, and barrels are containers.

con·tam·in·ate |kən tăm′ə nāt′| —*verb* **contaminated, contaminating** To make impure by mixing or touching; pollute: *Dumping chemicals into a lake contaminates the water.*

con·tem·po·rar·y |kən tĕm′pə rĕr′ē| —*adjective* **1.** Living or happening in the same period of time: *Please report on the American Revolution and on a contemporary event somewhere else in the world.* **2.** Current; modern: *contemporary history.*
—*noun, plural* **contemporaries** **1.** A person of about the same age as another: *John's younger sister is my contemporary.* **2.** A person living at the same time as another: *The author was greatly admired by his contemporaries.*

con·tempt |kən tĕmpt′| —*noun* **1.** A feeling that someone or something is of little value, worthless, or not wanted; scorn; disdain: *He has only contempt for cheating and for the people who do it.* **2.** The condition of being scorned or despised: *People held him in contempt for betraying his friend.*

con·tend |kən tĕnd′| —*verb* **contended, contending** **1.** To fight or battle: *We had to contend with bad weather on our hike.* **2.** To compete: *Seven students will contend in the final round of the*

contact lens

ă	pat	ĕ	pet	î	fierce
ā	pay	ē	be	ŏ	pot
â	care	ĭ	pit	ō	go
ä	father	ī	pie	ô	paw, for

oi	oil	ŭ	cut	zh	vision
ŏŏ	book	û	fur	ə	ago, item,
ōō	boot	*th*	the		pencil, atom,
yōō	abuse	th	thin		circus
ou	out	hw	which	ər	butter

spelling bee. **3.** To argue against; be opposed to: *We contended the judge's decision.* **4.** To say that something is true; claim: *The workers contend that they are not paid enough money.*

con·tent¹ |kŏn′tĕnt′| —*noun, plural* **contents** **1.** Often **contents** Something that is inside a container: *We opened the jar and emptied its contents onto the table.* **2.** Often **contents** The information that is contained in a book, letter, film, or other form of communication: *The film's content was considered appropriate for children. The contents of the letter were kept secret.*

con·tent² |kən tĕnt′| —*adjective* Pleased with what one has or is; satisfied: *He is content to be a farmer.*
—*noun* A feeling of happiness or satisfaction: *The baby lay in complete content in his father's arms.*
—*verb* **contented, contenting** To make content; satisfy: *He contents himself with collecting stamps and visiting his grandchildren.*
  Idiom **to one's heart's content** As much as one wishes: *He wished that he could eat ice cream to his heart's content.*

con·tent·ed |kən tĕn′tĭd| —*adjective* **1.** Satisfied with things as they are; content: *A contented dog dozed by the fire.* **2.** Showing happiness or satisfaction: *a contented look on her face.*

con·test |kŏn′tĕst′| —*noun, plural* **contests** **1.** A struggle or fight between two or more people or groups: *The election turned into a contest between two popular students.* **2.** A race, game, or other trial; a competition: *a beauty contest; a skating contest.*

con·test·ant |kən tĕs′tənt| —*noun, plural* **contestants** Someone who takes part in a contest; competitor.

con·ti·nent |kŏn′tə nənt| —*noun, plural* **continents** One of the main land masses of the earth. The seven continents are Africa, Antarctica, Asia, Australia, Europe, North America, and South America.

con·ti·nen·tal |kŏn′tə nĕn′tl| —*adjective* Of, like, or belonging to a continent: *the continental boundaries of the United States.*

con·tin·u·al |kən tĭn′yŏŏ əl| —*adjective* **1.** Happening again and again; frequent: *the continual banging of the shutters.* **2.** Not interrupted or broken; steady: *two weeks of continual rain.*

con·tin·ue |kən tĭn′yŏŏ| —*verb* **continued, continuing** **1.** To go on without stopping; keep on: *The storm continued for days. The police continued their investigation.* **2.** To begin again after stopping; resume: *Our program will continue after a short commercial.* **3.** To stay in the same place, condition, or situation; remain: *She will continue as our school principal for another year. The weather continued stormy for another week.*

con·tin·u·ous |kən tĭn′yŏŏ əs| —*adjective* Going on without interruption or break: *A continuous line of traffic went on for miles.*

con·tour |kŏn′tŏŏr′| —*noun, plural* **contours** The outline of something: *the contour of the United States.*

con·tract |kŏn′trăkt′| —*noun, plural* **contracts** An agreement, often written down, between two or more persons or groups to do or not to do something.
—*verb* |kən trăkt′| **contracted, contracting** **1.** To draw together; make or become smaller in length, width, or size: *He contracted his muscles and jumped. The pupils of his eyes contracted.* **2.** To arrange or make by a contract: *We contracted to build a new house. He contracted a marriage with his neighbor's niece.* **3.** To get: *contract the mumps.*

con·trac·tion |kən trăk′shən| —*noun, plural* **contractions**

content¹, content²
Content¹ and **content²** both come from the same Latin word, which originally meant "to hold together." But that word also meant "to contain or hold" and then "something contained" (**content¹**). And it meant "to restrain, hold back" and then "restrained, satisfied" (**content²**).

1. The act or process of contracting: *We studied the contraction of muscles in science class.* **2.** A shortened form of a word or pair of words. "Isn't" is a contraction of "is not."

con·tra·dict | kŏn'trə **dĭkt'** | —*verb* **contradicted, contradicting**
1. To say the opposite of: *You have just contradicted what you said earlier.* **2.** To say that something is not true or that someone is not telling the truth: *She contradicted her friend.*

con·tra·dic·tion | kŏn'trə **dĭk'** shən | —*noun, plural* **contradictions**
An act or example of contradicting or of being contradicted: *He can't stand contradiction. What you're doing is a contradiction of what you promised.*

con·tral·to | kən **trăl'** tō | —*noun, plural* **contraltos** **1.** The lowest female singing voice. **2.** A singer who has such a voice.

con·tra·ry | kŏn' trĕr'ē | —*adjective* **1.** Completely different; opposite; opposed: *His sisters had contrary points of view on politics. The two dancers were moving in contrary directions, away from each other.* **2.** | kŏn'trĕr'ē | or | kən **trâr'** ē | Stubborn and opposed to others: *He was the most contrary child in the class.*
—*noun, plural* **contraries** Something that is opposite: *I believe the contrary to be true.*

con·trast | kən **trăst'** | —*verb* **contrasted, contrasting** **1.** To compare in order to show differences: *The story contrasts the good and evil in people.* **2.** To show differences when a comparison is made: *Light contrasts with dark.*
—*noun* | kŏn' trăst' |, *plural* **contrasts** **1.** Comparison, especially when it is used to show differences: *In contrast to the dry plains of the western United States, the eastern states are green and fertile.* **2.** A great difference: *the contrast between deserts and jungles.*

con·tri·bute | kən **trĭb'** yōot | —*verb* **contributed, contributing** To give or supply; donate: *He contributed his services without charge. We contribute to several charities.*

con·tri·bu·tion | kŏn'trĭ **byōo'** shən | —*noun, plural* **contributions**
1. The act of contributing: *Please help in the contribution of money for the needy.* **2.** Something contributed; a donation: *He gave a small contribution to the fund.*

con·trol | kən **trōl'** | —*verb* **controlled, controlling** **1.** To have authority over; to direct; command: *The ancient Romans controlled a huge empire. The pilot controlled the plane.* **2.** To hold in check; restrain: *She controlled her emotions.*
—*noun, plural* **controls** **1.** Authority or power: *The coach has a strong control over the team.* **2.** Something that restrains; a check: *a price control. He has no control over his temper.* **3.** Usually **controls** The knobs, levers, pedals, and other instruments used to operate a machine.

control tower A high tower at an airport. Workers in a control tower observe and direct the landing and taking off of aircraft.

con·tro·ver·sial | kŏn'trə **vûr'** shəl | —*adjective* Causing or able to cause arguments: *a controversial decision.*

con·tro·ver·sy | kŏn' trə **vûr'** sē | —*noun, plural* **controversies**
Argument; debate; disagreement: *The new traffic light at Forest Street caused a lot of controversy.*

con·ven·ience | kən **vēn'** yəns | —*noun, plural* **conveniences**
1. Comfort or advantage; ease: *the convenience of airplane travel. A car and driver were provided for his convenience.* **2.** Anything that saves time and effort: *An automatic dishwasher is one of the conveniences of modern living.*

control tower

ă	pat	ĕ	pet	î	fierce
ā	pay	ē	be	ŏ	pot
â	care	ĭ	pit	ō	go
ä	father	ī	pie	ô	paw, for
oi	oil	ŭ	cut	zh	vision
ōo	book	û	fur	ə	ago, item,
ōo	boot	*th*	the		pencil, atom,
yōo	abuse	th	thin		circus
ou	out	hw	which	ər	butter

con·ven·ient |kən **vēn′**yənt| —*adjective* **1.** Easy to reach; handy: *a convenient location; a house that is convenient to shopping.* **2.** To someone's liking or comfort; suitable: *We'll meet at a time that is convenient for you.*

con·vent |**kŏn′**vənt| or |**kŏn′**vĕnt′| —*noun, plural* **convents** **1.** A group of nuns living together. **2.** A building that nuns live in.

con·ven·tion |kən **vĕn′**shən| —*noun, plural* **conventions** **1.** A formal meeting of people who have something in common: *a political convention; a convention of army veterans.* **2.** A way of acting or of doing something that most people accept; custom: *Wearing a tie is a convention of male dress.*

convention
A political convention

con·ven·tion·al |kən **vĕn′**shə nəl| —*adjective* Following accepted practice, customs, or taste; ordinary: *a conventional greeting; a conventional design for a house.*

con·ver·sa·tion |kŏn′vər **sā′**shən| —*noun, plural* **conversations** An informal talk in which people share ideas and feelings.

con·verse |kən **vûrs′**| —*verb* **conversed, conversing** To talk informally with another person or persons: *We conversed about our family.*

con·ver·sion |kən **vûr′**zhən| or |kən **vûr′**shən| —*noun, plural* **conversions** **1.** The act or process of changing or being changed: *the conversion of electricity to heat; the conversion of the warehouse into an office building.* **2.** A change in which a person adopts a new religion or beliefs: *her conversion to Judaism.*

con·vert |kən **vûrt′**| —*verb* **converted, converting** **1.** To change something into something else: *Electricity converts easily into other forms of energy. The first problem is to convert 100 yards into meters. We voted to convert the President's home into a museum.* **2.** To convince a person or persons to adopt a new religion or belief: *The missionaries converted the pagans to Christianity.*

con·vert·i·ble |kən **vûr′**tə bəl| —*adjective* Able to be changed into something else: *These convertible sofas can be made into beds for overnight guests.*
—*noun, plural* **convertibles** An automobile with a top that can be folded back or taken off.

convertible

con·vex |kŏn **vĕks′**| or |**kŏn′**vĕks| or |kən **vĕks′**| —*adjective* Curved outward: *The outside of a bowl is convex.*

con·vey |kən **vā′**| —*verb* **conveyed, conveying** **1.** To take or carry from one place to another: *A helicopter conveyed us to the city. Cables convey electrical power.* **2.** To make something known; communicate: *Words convey meaning. Please convey my best wishes to your grandmother.*

convex

con·vict |kən **vĭkt′**| —*verb* **convicted, convicting** To prove that someone is guilty: *The court convicted him of bombing the building.*
—*noun* |**kŏn′**vĭkt′|, *plural* **convicts** Someone who has been proven guilty of a crime and sent to jail.

con·vic·tion |kən **vĭk′**shən| —*noun, plural* **convictions** **1.** The act or process of proving that someone is guilty: *The surprising evidence given by the last witness resulted in the conviction of the housekeeper.* **2.** A strong feeling or belief about something: *He acted according to his true convictions when he decided to vote against the new school regulations.*

con·vince |kən **vĭns′**| —*verb* **convinced, convincing** To make someone believe something; persuade: *Our actions finally convinced him that we were ready to talk about an agreement.*

con·voy |kŏn′voi′| or |kən **voi′** | —*verb* **convoyed, convoying** To go with in order to protect: *The destroyers convoyed the aircraft carrier.*
—*noun* |kŏn′voi′ |, *plural* **convoys 1. a.** A group of ships or vehicles that are protected by an armed escort that travels with it. **b.** The armed escort itself. **2.** A group of vehicles traveling together for convenience: *We formed a convoy with our campers and traveled on to the next park.*

cook |kŏŏk| —*verb* **cooked, cooking 1.** To get food ready for eating by using heat: *You can cook the chops by frying or grilling.* **2.** To be cooked: *The chops will cook in twenty minutes.*
—*noun, plural* **cooks** A person who cooks.

cook·y or **cook·ie** |kŏŏk′ē| —*noun, plural* **cookies** A small, sweet cake, usually flat.

cool |kōōl| —*adjective* **cooler, coolest 1.** Not very warm or cold: *cool weather; a cool plate.* **2.** Not excited; calm: *She stayed cool when everyone else was shouting.* **3.** Not friendly or enthusiastic; indifferent: *a cool hello.*
—*verb* **cooled, cooling** To make or become less warm: *The fan cooled the room. Let the pie cool before you cut it.*
—*noun* Something that is cool: *The animals found relief from the heat in the cool of the forest.*

coop |kōōp| —*noun, plural* **coops** A cage or pen for chickens, rabbits, or other small animals.
—*verb* **cooped, cooping** To put or shut in a coop or other closed space: *Jesse has been cooped up in his room all day.*

co·op·er·ate |kō ŏp′ə rāt′ | —*verb* **cooperated, cooperating** To work or act together: *We can clean this campsite up quickly if we all cooperate.*

co·op·er·a·tion |kō ŏp′ə **rā′**shən | —*noun* The act of cooperating or working together: *Cooperation between different countries can help avoid war. The principal asked for the cooperation of the students.*

co·op·er·a·tive |kō ŏp′ər ə tĭv | or |kō **ŏp′**ə rā′tĭv | —*adjective* Willing to help or work together: *She's not very cooperative when there is work to be done around the house.*

co·or·di·nate |kō ôr′dn āt′ | —*verb* **coordinated, coordinating** To work or cause to work together well or efficiently: *When a tightrope walker's muscles no longer coordinate perfectly, he should stay off the tightrope. The brain coordinates all of the body's movements.*

cope |kōp| —*verb* **coped, coping** To struggle with successfully: *He coped with heavy traffic all the way home.*

co·pi·lot |kō′pī′lət | —*noun, plural* **copilots** The second pilot or assistant pilot of an airplane.

cop·per |kŏp′ər| —*noun* **1.** A reddish-brown metal that is easy to work with and is a good conductor of heat and electricity. Copper is one of the chemical elements. **2.** A reddish-brown color. ◊ The noun **copper** can be used like an adjective for things made of copper: *a copper wire; a copper pot.*
—*adjective* Reddish brown.

cop·per·head |kŏp′ər hĕd′ | —*noun, plural* **copperheads** A poisonous reddish-brown snake of the eastern United States.

cop·y |kŏp′ē| —*noun, plural* **copies 1.** Something that is made to be like or look like something else; reproduction or duplicate: *a copy of a letter; a copy of a famous painting.* **2.** One of a number of

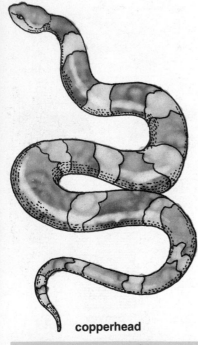

copperhead

ă	pat	ĕ	pet	î	fierce
ā	pay	ē	be	ŏ	pot
â	care	ĭ	pit	ō	go
ä	father	ī	pie	ô	paw, for

oi	oil	ŭ	cut	zh	vision
ōō	book	û	fur	ə	ago, item,
ōō	boot	*th*	the		pencil, atom,
yōō	abuse	th	thin		circus
ou	out	hw	which	ər	butter

things that have been printed at the same time: *I bought my copy of the June issue of the magazine.*
—*verb* **copied, copying, copies** **1.** To make a copy or copies of: *He copied part of your letter. Copy this drawing.* **2.** To follow someone or something as a model or example; imitate: *Her friends copied the way she wore her hair. She's always copying whatever I do.*

cor·al |**kôr′**əl| or |**kŏr′**əl| —*noun* **1.** A substance, as hard as stone, that is formed by the skeletons of tiny sea animals. Large groups of these animals form rounded or branching masses. Coral is often brightly colored. Some kinds are used to make jewelry. **2.** A yellowish-pink or reddish-orange color. ◊ The noun **coral** can be used like an adjective for things made of coral: *a coral necklace.*
—*adjective* Yellowish pink or reddish orange.

coral snake A poisonous snake of the southern United States. It is marked with red, yellow, and black bands.

cord |**kôrd**| —*noun, plural* **cords** **1.** A strong string or thin rope. Cord is made of a number of smaller strings twisted together: *Tie the package with cord before you mail it.* **2.** An electric wire covered with protecting material and having a plug at one or both ends. **3.** A part of the body that is like a cord: *the spinal cord.* **4.** A unit of measure for cut firewood. A cord of wood is equal to a stack that is four feet high, four feet wide, and eight feet long.
♦ *These sound alike* **cord, chord.**

cor·dial |**kôr′**jəl| —*adjective* Cheerful and friendly; sincere: *a cordial greeting. The two countries enjoy a cordial relationship.*

cor·du·roy |**kôr′**də roi′| —*noun* A heavy cotton cloth with a smooth surface of raised ridges. Corduroy is usually used for making clothes, especially jackets, pants, and skirts.

core |**kôr**| or |**kōr**| —*noun, plural* **cores** **1.** The tough center part of an apple, pear, or some other fruits. The seeds of the fruit are in the core. **2.** The central or most important part of anything; heart: *The core of her work was writing.*
—*verb* **cored, coring** To take or cut out the core of: *You must peel and core apples before you can use them to bake a pie.*
♦ *These sound alike* **core, corps.**

cork |**kôrk**| —*noun, plural* **corks** **1.** The light, soft outer bark of a kind of oak tree. It is used to make bottle stoppers, rafts, floor covering, and other things. **2.** A stopper for a bottle or jar, made from cork or another soft material.
—*verb* **corked, corking** To close or stop up with a cork: *cork a bottle.*

cork·screw |**kôrk′**skrōō′| —*noun, plural* **corkscrews** A tool or device used to pull corks out of bottles. A corkscrew is made of a pointed metal spiral attached to a handle.

corn |**kôrn**| —*noun* **1.** A tall plant that has large ears with many kernels. Corn is grown as food for people and animals. **2.** The ears or kernels of the corn plant.

corn bread A kind of bread made with cornmeal.

corn·cob |**kôrn′**kŏb′| —*noun, plural* **corncobs** The long, hard center part of an ear of corn.

cor·ne·a |**kôr′**nē ə| —*noun, plural* **corneas** The transparent outer coat or covering of the eyeball. The cornea covers the iris and lens.

cor·ner |**kôr′**nər| —*noun, plural* **corners** **1.** The place where

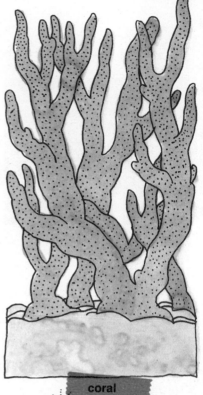

coral

corn
Plant *(left)* and ear *(right)*

cornea

two lines or surfaces meet: *the upper left-hand corner of the page; the corner of a table.* **2.** The place where two roads or streets meet: *Meet me in front of the drugstore at the corner of Washington and Main.* **3.** A difficult position or situation: *He has me in a corner because I can't pay back the money I owe him.*
—*verb* **cornered, cornering** To place or force into a difficult position or situation: *The dog cornered the cat.*

corn·meal |kôrn′mēl| —*noun* Coarsely ground dried corn kernels.

cor·o·na·tion |kôr′ə nā′shən| or |kŏr′ə nā′shən| —*noun, plural* **coronations** The act or ceremony of crowning a king, queen, or other monarch: *My parents went to England for the coronation of Queen Elizabeth II.*

coronation

cor·po·ral |kôr′pər əl| or |kôr′prəl| —*noun, plural* **corporals** An officer in the United States Army or Marine Corps. A corporal ranks above a private and below a sergeant.

cor·po·ra·tion |kôr′pə rā′shən| —*noun, plural* **corporations** A business or other organization that is allowed by law to act as a single person. A corporation is formed by a group of people acting under a legal arrangement.

corps |kôr| or |kōr| —*noun, plural* **corps** |kôrz| or |kōrz| **1.** Often **Corps** A section of the armed forces having a special function: *The Marine Corps captured the town.* **2.** Any group of people acting or working together: *The reporter is a member of the press corps.*
♦ *These sound alike* **corps, core.**

corpse |kôrps| —*noun, plural* **corpses** A dead body, usually of a human being.

cor·pus·cle |kôr′pə səl| or |kôr′pŭs′əl| —*noun, plural* **corpuscles** A cell of the body, such as a red or white blood cell, that can move about freely.

cor·ral |kə răl′| —*noun, plural* **corrals** A pen or a place with a fence for keeping cattle or horses.
—*verb* **corralled, corralling** **1.** To put or drive into a corral: *They corralled the wild horses by stampeding them.* **2.** To get hold of; round up; seize: *They corralled four students to hand out programs.*

corral

cor·rect |kə rĕkt′| —*verb* **corrected, correcting** **1.** To remove errors from: *We corrected our homework.* **2.** To mark errors in: *The teacher corrected our papers.* **3.** To make something right by changing or adjusting: *These new glasses will correct my poor vision.* **4.** To scold or punish: *A parent should correct a child who misbehaves.*
—*adjective* **1.** Free from error; accurate: *Was my answer correct?* **2.** Following rules; proper: *His behavior is always correct.*

cor·rec·tion |kə rĕk′shən| —*noun, plural* **corrections** **1.** The act or process of correcting: *The correction of the tests took the teacher two hours.* **2.** Something put in place of a mistake or error; an improvement: *The corrections on your test are in red.*

cor·rec·tive |kə rĕk′tĭv| —*adjective* Made or used to correct: *He wears corrective shoes.*

cor·re·spond |kôr′ĭ spŏnd′| or |kŏr′ĭ spŏnd′| —*verb* **corresponded, corresponding** **1.** To be in agreement; to match: *His rude manner didn't correspond with his usual behavior.* **2.** To be similar or the same: *The eye corresponds to the lens of a camera.* **3.** To write and send letters: *I corresponded for years with him.*

cor·re·spond·ence |kôr′ĭ spŏn′dəns| or |kŏr′ĭ spŏn′dəns|

ă	pat	ĕ	pet	î	fierce
ā	pay	ē	be	ŏ	pot
â	care	ĭ	pit	ō	go
ä	father	ī	pie	ô	paw, for
oi	oil	ŭ	cut	zh	vision
ōō	book	û	fur	ə	ago, item,
ōō	boot	*th*	the		pencil, atom,
yōō	abuse	th	thin		circus
ou	out	hw	which	ər	butter

—*noun, plural* **correspondences** **1.** Agreement, similarity, or likeness: *Some words have very little correspondence between their sound and their spelling.* **2. a.** Communication by writing and sending letters: *my correspondence with my cousin.* **b.** The letters themselves: *I let him read my correspondence.*

cor·re·spond·ent |kôr´ĭ **spŏn**´dənt| or |kŏr´ĭ **spŏn**´dənt| —*noun, plural* **correspondents** **1.** Someone to whom one writes regularly. **2.** Someone hired by a newspaper or television station to report on news in distant places: *Here's our correspondent with the latest news from China.*

cor·ri·dor |kôr´ĭ dər| or |kôr´ĭ dôr´| or |kŏr´ĭ dər| or |kŏr´ĭ dôr´| —*noun, plural* **corridors** A narrow hallway or passage in a building, with doors opening onto it.

cor·rode |kə rōd´| —*verb* **corroded, corroding** To wear away or be worn away, especially by chemical action: *Water will corrode many metals. Some kinds of steel do not corrode easily.*

cor·rupt |kə **rŭpt**´| —*adjective* **1.** Having no morals; wicked: *the corrupt court of the emperor.* **2.** Capable of being bribed; dishonest: *a corrupt official.*
—*verb* **corrupted, corrupting** **1.** To ruin the morals of; make wicked. **2.** To make dishonest; bribe: *The foreign agent tried to corrupt the government official.*

cor·sage |kôr **säzh**´| —*noun, plural* **corsages** A small bouquet of flowers worn by a woman, usually at the shoulder.

cor·set |kôr´sĭt| —*noun, plural* **corsets** **1.** Tight underwear worn by women to shape the waist and hips. **2.** A similar piece of underwear, containing strong elastic, worn by men or women to support weak or injured muscles in the back.

cos·met·ic |kŏz **mĕt**´ĭk| —*noun, plural* **cosmetics** A preparation, such as lotion or powder, used on the body.

cos·mic |kŏz´mĭk| —*adjective* Of the universe, especially the heavens as distinguished from the earth: *cosmic laws.*

cost |kôst| —*noun, plural* **costs** **1.** The amount paid or charged for a purchase: *The cost of milk is going up.* **2.** Something given up; a loss or penalty: *He refused treatment at the cost of his health.*
—*verb* **cost, costing** **1.** To have as a price: *A new scarf will cost seven dollars.* **2.** To cause the loss of: *Being late every day cost her the job.*

Idiom **at all costs** Regardless of the cost or effort: *At all costs I have to pass that test.*

cost·ly |kôst´lē| —*adjective* **costlier, costliest** **1.** Of great cost; having a high price; expensive: *A car is a costly purchase.* **2.** Resulting in great loss or sacrifice: *a costly winter storm.*

cos·tume |kŏs´tōōm´| or |kŏs´tyōōm´| —*noun, plural* **costumes** **1.** Clothing that is typical of a certain place, group of people, or period of history: *The peasants danced in their national costume.* **2.** Clothing worn for a particular activity or occasion: *a skating costume.* **3.** Clothing worn when playing a part or dressing up in disguise: *a Halloween costume.*

cot |kŏt| —*noun, plural* **cots** A narrow bed, usually made of canvas stretched over a folding frame.

cot·tage |kŏt´ĭj| —*noun, plural* **cottages** **1.** A small house in the country. **2.** A summer home, usually near the sea or in the mountains.

cottage cheese A soft white cheese with a mild flavor. Cottage cheese is made of the curds of skim milk.

corsage

costume

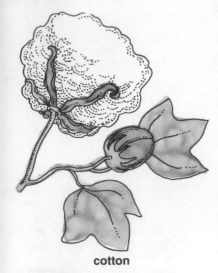
cotton

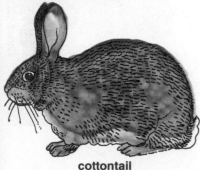
cottontail

cougar

cot·ton |kŏt′n| —*noun* **1.** A plant that has seeds covered with soft, fluffy white fibers. Cotton is grown in warm places. **2.** The soft, fine fibers of this plant. They are used to make thread or cloth. **3.** Cloth or thread made from these fibers.

cotton gin A machine that separates cotton fibers from the seeds.

cot·ton·mouth |kŏt′n mouth′| —*noun, plural* **cottonmouths** |kŏt′n mouths′| or |kŏt′n mout/hz| A poisonous snake. Another name for this snake is **water moccasin.**

cot·ton·tail |kŏt′n tāl| —*noun, plural* **cottontails** An American rabbit with a short, fluffy white tail.

cot·ton·wood |kŏt′n wŏod′| —*noun, plural* **cottonwoods** A tree that has seeds with white tufts that look like cotton.

couch |kouch| —*noun, plural* **couches** A piece of furniture, usually upholstered and having a back, for seating two or more persons; sofa.

cou·gar |kōo′gər| —*noun, plural* **cougars** A large wild cat. Another name for this animal is **mountain lion.**

cough |kôf| or |kŏf| —*verb* **coughed, coughing** To force air from the lungs in a sudden, noisy way: *I couldn't help coughing during the concert.*
—*noun, plural* **coughs** **1.** The act or sound of coughing. **2.** An illness that causes much coughing.

could |kŏod| or |kəd| The past tense of the verb **can**: *I could see that the child was hurt.*

couldn't |kŏod′nt| A contraction of "could not."

coun·cil |koun′səl| —*noun, plural* **councils** **1.** A group of persons brought together to discuss or settle a problem or question: *a council of religious leaders.* **2.** A group of people chosen to make laws or rules: *the city council; student council.*
♦ *These sound alike* **council, counsel.**

coun·cil·or |koun′sə lər| or |koun′slər| —*noun, plural* **councilors** A member of a council.
♦ *These sound alike* **councilor, counselor.**

coun·sel |koun′səl| —*noun, plural* **counsels** **1.** Advice; guidance: *Thank you for your counsel when I was in trouble.* **2.** A lawyer or group of lawyers: *the counsel for the defense.*
—*verb* **counseled, counseling** To give advice: *We counseled him to refuse the offer.*
♦ *These sound alike* **counsel, council.**

coun·sel·or |koun′sə lər| or |koun′slər| —*noun, plural* **counselors** **1.** A person who advises or guides; adviser: *My teacher is a school counselor.* **2.** A lawyer. **3.** A person who supervises children at a summer camp.
♦ *These sound alike* **counselor, councilor.**

count[1] |kount| —*verb* **counted, counting** **1.** To find the total number of; add up: *Count the sandwiches and napkins.* **2.** To jot down or say numbers in order: *Count up to 100.* **3.** To include; take account of: *There are six of us, counting me.* **4.** To be important; be of value: *It's how you play the game that counts.* **5.** To regard; consider: *I count myself lucky to be on the team.* **6.** To take or be taken into account: *We won't count that game because we couldn't finish it.*
—*noun, plural* **counts** **1.** The act of counting: *By my count, you have already eaten too many cookies.* **2.** The number reached by counting: *We will all start on the count of three.*

ă	pat	ĕ	pet	î	fierce
ā	pay	ē	be	ŏ	pot
â	care	ĭ	pit	ō	go
ä	father	ī	pie	ô	paw, for
oi	oil	ŭ	cut	zh	vision
ŏŏ	book	û	fur	ə	ago, item,
ōō	boot	th	the		pencil, atom,
yōō	abuse	th	thin		circus
ou	out	hw	which	ər	butter

count² | kount | —*noun, plural* **counts** A nobleman in some countries. The rank of count is equal to the English rank of earl.

count·down | kount′doun′ | —*noun, plural* **countdowns** The act of counting backward to zero to indicate how many minutes and seconds are left until the beginning of an event: *the countdown for the rocket launching.*

count·er¹ | koun′tər | —*noun, plural* **counters** **1.** A narrow table on which things are sold or food is prepared, served, or eaten. Counters are found in most kitchens and stores, and in some restaurants: *She left her purse on the tie counter.* **2.** A small disk or other object used in some games to keep score.

count·er² | koun′tər | —*adjective* Contrary; opposing or opposite: *His opinions are counter to mine.*
—*verb* **countered, countering** To act against; oppose: *He countered my idea with the suggestion that we stop for lunch.*
—*adverb* In the opposite manner or direction: *You acted counter to my wishes.*

coun·ter·clock·wise | koun′tər **klŏk**′wīz | —*adverb* In a direction opposite to the direction in which a clock's hands move: *Twist the jar's lid counterclockwise.*
—*adjective* Moving in a counterclockwise direction: *to skate in a counterclockwise circle.*

coun·ter·feit | **koun**′tər fĭt | —*verb* **counterfeited, counterfeiting** To make a copy of something in order to fool or cheat people; to forge; imitate: *She was put in jail because she had counterfeited some rare stamps.*
—*adjective* Made as a copy or imitation in order to fool or cheat people: *counterfeit money.*
—*noun, plural* **counterfeits** Something that has been copied; an imitation: *The gold coin was a counterfeit.*

coun·ter·part | **koun**′tər pärt′ | —*noun, plural* **counterparts** Someone or something that is exactly like or closely resembles another: *A car is the modern counterpart of the horse and buggy.*

count·ess | **koun**′tĭs | —*noun, plural* **countesses** **1.** The wife of a count. **2.** A woman with a rank equal to that of a count in her own right.

count·less | kount′lĭs | —*adjective* Too many to be counted: *Countless fans were unable to get tickets for the big game.*

coun·try | **kŭn**′trē | —*noun, plural* **countries** **1.a.** A group of people living under a single independent government; a nation or state: *The country voted him president.* **b.** The territory occupied by such a group of people: *All across our country new industries are developing.* **2.** The nation a person was born in or belongs to: *to love one's country.* **3.** The land away from cities and large towns, especially land used for farming: *a vacation in the country.* **4.** A region having certain characteristics: *hilly country; cow country.*

coun·try·man | **kŭn**′trē mən | —*noun, plural* **countrymen** A person from one's own country.

coun·try·side | **kŭn**′trē sīd′ | —*noun, plural* **countrysides** The land away from cities and large towns; a rural area or region.

coun·ty | **koun**′tē | —*noun, plural* **counties** One of the divisions of a state or country.

cou·ple | **kŭp**′əl | —*noun, plural* **couples** **1.** Two things of the same kind; a pair. **2.** A man and a woman who are married or engaged: *Two couples shared the pizza.* **3.** A small number; a few: *I'll see you in a couple of hours.*

count¹, count²
Count¹ comes from a Latin word meaning "to add up" or "to sum up." Our word **compute** also comes from this same Latin word. **Count²** comes from a Latin word that meant "companion" and that later came to refer to a person holding state office. Both **count¹** and **count²** traveled through French before arriving in English.

counter¹, counter²
Counter¹ comes from a Latin word meaning "to count." **Counter²** comes from a Latin word that means "against." Both words came to English through French.

counter¹

—verb **coupled, coupling** To link together; join or attach: *The engineer coupled the engine to the train.*

cou·pon |**ko͞o′**pŏn| or |**kyo͞o′**pŏn| *—noun, plural* **coupons** A part of a ticket or advertisement that can be exchanged for a gift or money.

cour·age |**kûr′**ĭj| or |**kŭr′**ĭj| *—noun* A quality of mind or character that makes a person able to face danger or hardship without fear; bravery: *It took courage to face the enemy.*

cou·ra·geous |kə **rā′**jəs| *—adjective* Having or showing courage; brave: *a courageous woman.*

course |kôrs| or |kōrs| *—noun, plural* **courses 1.** Forward or onward movement in a particular direction or in time; progress or advance: *events that changed the course of history; in the course of a week.* **2.** The direction taken by someone or something: *Due west is the course of the river. The captain set the course for the islands.* **3.** A way of acting or behaving: *Your best course is to do your homework now.* **4.** A series of classes in school: *She is taking a course in geography.* **5.** An area of land or water on which races or other sports take place: *a golf course.* **6.** A dish or other part of a meal: *Meat was the main course.*

Idioms **in due course** At the right or proper time. **of course** Without a doubt; certainly; naturally: *Of course we will be there.*

♦ *These sound alike* **course, coarse.**

court |kôrt| or |kōrt| *—noun, plural* **courts 1.** An open space surrounded by walls or buildings; a courtyard: *Our only window faces the court.* **2.** A short street, especially an alley having buildings on three sides. **3.** An area marked off and provided with equipment for certain games: *a tennis court; a basketball court.* **4.** The attendants, advisers, and other people who work for or with a king, queen, or other ruler. **5.** An official meeting of government advisers and their king, queen, or other ruler: *The king held court to decide how to defend his land against his enemies.* **6.** A judge or group of officials who hear legal cases and make decisions. **7.** The room or building in which such cases are heard. *—verb* **courted, courting 1.** To treat with flattery and attention; try to win the favor of: *The mayor was courting powerful and rich people in the state capital.* **2.** To try to win the love or affections of: *Dad courted Mother for three years.*

cour·te·ous |**kûr′**tē əs| *—adjective* Considerate toward others; polite; gracious.

cour·te·sy |**kûr′**tĭ sē| *—noun, plural* **courtesies 1.** Polite or thoughtful behavior. **2.** An act that shows a polite manner: *The soldier saluted, and the general returned the courtesy.*

court·house |**kôrt′**hous′| or |**kōrt′**hous′| *—noun, plural* **courthouses** A building in which trials and other legal matters take place.

court·room |**kôrt′**ro͞om′| or |**kôrt′**ro͝om′| or |**kōrt′**ro͞om′| or |**kōrt′**ro͝om′| *—noun, plural* **courtrooms** A room in which trials and other legal matters take place.

court·yard |**kôrt′**yärd′| or |**kōrt′**yärd′| *—noun, plural* **courtyards** An open space surrounded by walls or buildings: *Their house is built around a courtyard.*

cous·in |**kŭz′**ən| *—noun, plural* **cousins** A child of one's aunt or uncle.

cove |kōv| *—noun, plural* **coves** A small bay that is protected from the wind by high land that surrounds it.

courthouse

courtroom

ă	pat	ĕ	pet	î	fierce
ā	pay	ē	be	ŏ	pot
â	care	ĭ	pit	ō	go
ä	father	ī	pie	ô	paw, for
oi	oil	ŭ	cut	zh	vision
o͞o	book	û	fur	ə	ago, item,
o͞o	boot	*th*	the		pencil, atom,
yo͞o	abuse	th	thin		circus
ou	out	hw	which	ər	butter

cov·er |kŭv′ər| —*verb* **covered, covering** **1.** To place something over or upon: *We covered the plants to keep the frost from hurting them. Clouds covered the mountains. He covered his ears with his hands.* **2.** To spread over the surface of: *Water covered the floor.* **3.** To have a certain distance, area, or duration of: *The farm covers 100 acres. The book covers the first seven years of our history.* **4.** To learn and report the details of: *She covered the story for a newspaper.* **5.** To travel over: *We covered 200 miles a day this summer.* **6.** To guard or defend: *Her job is to cover second base.* **7.** To hide or conceal: *He couldn't cover his anger.*
—*noun, plural* **covers** **1.** Something that covers another thing: *Put the cover on the pan. Don't throw away the cover of the book. You must arrange the covers on the bed.* **2.** Shelter of any kind: *We found cover during the storm.* **3.** Something that hides or disguises something else: *His laughter is just a cover for his tears.*

cov·ered wagon |kŭv′ərd| A large wagon covered with canvas stretched over hoops. These wagons, pulled by horses or oxen, were used by American pioneers traveling westward across the country.

cov·er·ing |kŭv′ər ĭng| —*noun, plural* **coverings** Something that covers, protects, or hides: *plastic coverings for the porch furniture.*

cov·et |kŭv′ĭt| —*verb* **coveted, coveting** To want something very much, especially something that belongs to another: *My dog sat staring at me, coveting each chocolate I ate.*

cow |kou| —*noun, plural* **cows** **1.** The fully grown female of cattle. **2.** The female of some other large animals, such as the elephant or moose.

cow·ard |kou′ərd| —*noun, plural* **cowards** A person who lacks courage or is easily frightened.

cow·ard·ice |kou′ər dĭs| —*noun* Lack of courage or a show of fear.

cow·ard·ly |kou′ərd lē| —*adjective* Lacking courage or showing fear easily: *a cowardly act; the cowardly lion.*

cow·boy |kou′boi′| —*noun, plural* **cowboys** A hired man, usually working on horseback, who tends cattle on a ranch.

coy·o·te |kī ō′tē| or |kī′ōt′| —*noun, plural* **coyotes** A North American animal that looks like a wolf. Coyotes are common in the western parts of the United States and Canada.

co·zy |kō′zē| —*adjective* **cozier, coziest** Snug and comfortable: *a cozy room; a cozy fire.*

crab |krăb| —*noun, plural* **crabs** A water animal that has a broad, flat body covered with a tough shell. Its front legs have large claws. Many kinds of crabs are used as food.

crab apple **1.** A small, sour fruit that looks like an apple. **2.** A tree on which crab apples grow.

crab·by |krăb′ē| —*adjective* **crabbier, crabbiest** Always complaining; grouchy or irritable: *He's crabby when anyone steps on his lawn.*

crack |krăk| —*verb* **cracked, cracking** **1.** To break or split suddenly and with a sharp sound: *The limb cracked under his weight. She cracked the shell of the coconut.* **2.** To make a sharp, snapping sound: *She heard the rifle crack. The cowboys cracked the whips at the rodeo.* **3.** To break without separating; split: *The cup cracked in the boiling water.* **4.** To strike sharply: *She cracked her head on the curtain rod.* **5.** To break down or give way: *He*

covered wagon

cowboy

cradle

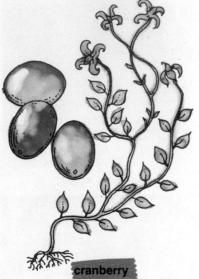

cranberry

Berries *(left)* and plant *(right)*

crane

ă	pat	ĕ	pet	î	fierce
ā	pay	ē	be	ŏ	pot
â	care	ĭ	pit	ō	go
ä	father	ī	pie	ô	paw, for
oi	oil	ŭ	cut	zh	vision
ōō	book	û	fur	ə	ago, item,
ōō	boot	*th*	the		pencil, atom,
yōō	abuse	th	thin		circus
ou	out	hw	which	ər	butter

cracked under the strain of so much work. **6.** To solve: *We cracked the enemy's secret code.*

Phrasal verbs **crack down** To become more strict: *The police are cracking down on thieves.* **crack up** **1.** To crash; collide: *Several cars cracked up in the fog.* **2.** To begin or cause to begin to laugh suddenly: *I cracked up when I saw your funny mask. That joke really cracked me up.*

—*noun, plural* **cracks** **1.** A sharp, snapping sound: *a crack of thunder.* **2.** A small split or break: *The old paint had many cracks in it.* **3.** A narrow space: *Please open the window a crack.* **4.** A sharp blow: *a crack on the head.* **5.** A joke, especially one that is insulting: *She made a crack about my hair.*

—*adjective* Excellent: *He's a crack shot with any target.*

crack·er |krăk′ər| —*noun, plural* **crackers** A thin, crisp wafer or biscuit: *cheese and crackers.*

crack·le |krăk′əl| —*verb* **crackled, crackling** To make slight sharp, snapping sounds: *A fire was crackling in the fireplace.* —*noun* The act or sound of crackling: *the crackle of crushed paper.*

cra·dle |krād′l| —*noun, plural* **cradles** A small bed for a baby, usually on rockers: *Dad rocked the baby to sleep in the cradle.* —*verb* **cradled, cradling** To hold closely: *He cradled the baby in his arms.*

craft |krăft| or |kräft| —*noun, plural* **crafts** **1.** Skill or ability in doing something with the hands: *The carpenter developed his craft working with his father.* **2.** Skill in fooling or tricking others; cunning: *the craft of a successful spy.* **3.** An occupation or trade: *the plumber's craft.* **4.** *plural* **craft** A boat, ship, aircraft, or spacecraft.

crafts·man |krăfts′mən| or |kräfts′mən| —*noun, plural* **craftsmen** A worker skilled in doing something with the hands: *He is a craftsman who makes beautiful cabinets.*

crag |krăg| —*noun, plural* **crags** A steep part that juts out of a cliff or mountain.

cramp |krămp| —*noun, plural* **cramps** **1.** A sharp, painful contraction of a muscle, usually caused by strain or a chill: *A leg cramp kept the runner out of the race.* **2.** **cramps** Sharp pains in one's stomach or abdomen.

cramped |krămpt| —*adjective* Too small or restricted: *to live in cramped quarters.*

cran·ber·ry |krăn′běr′ē| —*noun, plural* **cranberries** A sour, shiny red berry used to make sauce, jelly, and juice. Cranberries grow in wet places.

crane |krān| —*noun, plural* **cranes** **1.** A large bird with a long neck, long legs, and a long bill. Cranes usually live near water. **2.** A large machine for lifting heavy objects. A crane has a long arm and uses cables to do the lifting. —*verb* **craned, craning** To stretch or strain for a better view: *She craned forward to look. We craned our necks at the game.*

crank |krăngk| —*noun, plural* **cranks** **1.** A device that has a handle or a rod for making a part of a machine turn: *Dad turned the crank on the ice-cream machine.* **2. a.** A person who has a bad temper; a grouch. **b.** A person whose ideas are considered odd or strange: *He's become a crank on the subject of health foods.* —*verb* **cranked, cranking** To start or operate with a crank.

crash |krăsh| —*verb* **crashed, crashing** **1.** To fall, strike, or

collide violently and with noise: *The tray of dishes crashed to the floor. Several cars crashed in the fog.* **2.** To go through violently: *The elephants crashed through the forest.* **3.** To make a sudden, loud noise: *Can you hear the cymbals crash?*
—*noun, plural* **crashes** **1.** A sudden, loud noise like things hitting one another: *a crash of thunder.* **2.** A violent collision: *a car crash; a plane crash.*

crate |krāt| —*noun, plural* **crates** A large box made of slats of wood: *Our new refrigerator arrived in a crate.*
—*verb* **crated, crating** To pack into a crate: *My books were crated for shipment.*

cra·ter |krā′ tər| —*noun, plural* **craters** A depression or low place in the ground, shaped like a bowl. The mouth of a volcano is a crater. A crater may be formed by an explosion or by a meteor. There are craters on the moon that may have been caused by meteors hitting it.

crawl |krôl| —*verb* **crawled, crawling** **1.** To move slowly on the hands and knees; creep: *The baby crawled across the room.* **2.** To go forward slowly or with great effort: *The cars crawled along in the heavy traffic.* **3.** To be covered with crawling things: *The new shopping center was crawling with people.*
—*noun* **1.** A very slow pace: *Traffic slowed to a crawl.* **2.** A swimming stroke in which arm strokes alternate and the legs kick rapidly.

cray·fish |krā′ fĭsh′| —*noun, plural* **crayfish** or **crayfishes** A water animal that looks like a lobster but is much smaller. Crayfish live in fresh water.

cray·on |krā′ ŏn′| or |krā′ ən| —*noun, plural* **crayons** A stick of colored wax or chalk used for drawing.

cra·zy |krā′ zē| —*adjective* **crazier, craziest** **1.** Sick in the mind; insane. **2.** Not sensible; not practical; foolish: *Making gasoline from water was a crazy idea. You're crazy to go out in this snow without boots.* **3.** Full of enthusiasm; excited: *I'm crazy about tacos.*

creak |krēk| —*verb* **creaked, creaking** To make a harsh grating or squeaking sound: *The door creaked when I opened it.*
—*noun, plural* **creaks** A harsh grating or squeaking sound: *The rusty gate opened with a loud creak.*
♦ *These sound alike* **creak, creek.**

cream |krēm| —*noun, plural* **creams** **1.** The yellowish part of milk that contains fat. It can be separated from milk and is used in cooking, with coffee, and to make butter. **2.** The color of cream; a yellowish white: *We did the bedroom walls in cream.* **3.** A lotion or other cosmetic that looks like cream: *face cream; shaving cream.* **4.** The best part: *the cream of the crop.*
—*adjective* Yellowish white: *She was dressed in cream satin.*

crease |krēs| —*noun, plural* **creases** A fold, wrinkle, or line, often formed by pressure or heat: *Dad put the crease back in his slacks with a hot iron.*
—*verb* **creased, creasing** To make or become creased, folded, or wrinkled: *Leaning against the radiator creased my skirt. This jacket creases every time I wear it. Her face has creased with age.*

cre·ate |krē āt′| —*verb* **created, creating** **1.** To cause to exist; originate or produce: *How was the world created? Who created that TV show?* **2.** To cause; make happen: *The newspaper story created a lot of talk.*

crater
On the moon

cre·a·tion | krē ā′shən | —*noun, plural* **creations** **1.** The act or process of creating: *the creation of a new chemical.* **2.** Something invented or produced by a person's imagination: *The phonograph was an important creation.* **3. the Creation** The story of the earth's beginning as told in the Bible.

cre·a·tive | krē ā′tĭv | —*adjective* Having the ability to create things; having original ideas: *the creative work of a painter or writer.*

cre·a·tor | krē ā′tər | —*noun, plural* **creators** **1.** A person who creates: *the creators of the Declaration of Independence.* **2. the Creator** God.

crea·ture | krē′chər | —*noun, plural* **creatures** **1.** A living being, especially an animal. **2.** A human being; a person: *Your grandmother is a lovely creature. The poor creature has no home.* **3.** A strange or frightening being: *creatures from outer space.*

cred·it | krĕd′ĭt | —*noun, plural* **credits** **1.** Belief or confidence; trust: *We put complete credit in his story.* **2.** Reputation; good will felt by others: *It is to your credit that you told the truth.* **3.** A source of honor: *She is a credit to her team.* **4.** Recognition; honor; praise: *We did all the work and she got all the credit.* **5. a.** A system of buying things and paying for them later: *They bought a car on credit.* **b.** Trust that the buyer will be able to pay at a later time: *Your credit is good at this store.*

—*verb* **credited, crediting** **1.** To believe; trust: *He could not credit her explanation.* **2.** To give recognition, honor, or praise to: *They credit her with discovering a cure for the disease.*

credit card A card given out by a store or company that allows a person to buy on credit: *He bought gas with his credit card.*

creed | krēd | —*noun, plural* **creeds** **1.** A formal statement of religious belief. **2.** Any set of beliefs or principles that guide a person's actions: *His creed has always been to help others.*

creek | krēk | or | krĭk | —*noun, plural* **creeks** A small stream, often one that flows into a river.

♦ *These sound alike* **creek, creak.**

creep | krēp | —*verb* **crept, creeping** **1.** To move slowly or cautiously with the body close to the ground; crawl: *The cat was creeping toward the mouse.* **2.** To move or spread slowly: *A note of warning crept into his voice. The colors of the sunset were creeping across the sky.* **3.** To have a tingling sensation, as if covered with crawling things: *It made my flesh creep to hear the chalk scrape on the blackboard.* **4.** To grow along the ground or by clinging to a wall or other surface: *Ivy creeps down the hill in our front yard.*

—*noun* **the creeps** A feeling of fear and disgust, as if things were crawling on one's skin: *This old house gives me the creeps.*

crepe or **crêpe** | krāp | —*noun, plural* **crepes** or **crêpes** A soft, thin cloth with a crinkled surface.

crepe paper Paper like crepe with crinkles in it. Crepe paper is made in colors and used in decoration.

crept | krĕpt | The past tense and past participle of the verb **creep:** *A blush crept over his face. The cat has crept under the porch and won't come out.*

cres·cent | krĕs′ənt | —*noun, plural* **crescents** **1.** The moon as it appears in its first quarter, with curved edges ending in points. **2.** Anything shaped like this: *A smile, almost a perfect crescent, formed on her lips.*

crest | krĕst | —*noun, plural* **crests** **1.** A tuft of feathers on a bird's head. **2.** A band of feathers on top of a warrior's helmet.

crest
Of a bird *(above)* and on a helmet
(below)

ă	pat	ĕ	pet	î	fierce
ā	pay	ē	be	ŏ	pot
â	care	ĭ	pit	ō	go
ä	father	ī	pie	ô	paw, for
oi	oil	ŭ	cut	zh	vision
ōō	book	û	fur	ə	ago, item,
ōō	boot	*th*	the		pencil, atom,
yōō	abuse	th	thin		circus
ou	out	hw	which	ər	butter

3. The top of something, such as a mountain or a wave.

crew |krōō| —*noun, plural* **crews 1.** All the persons who operate a boat, ship, or aircraft. **2.** Any group or team of people who work together: *A crew of four operates the lighthouse.*

crib |krĭb| —*noun, plural* **cribs 1.** A child's or infant's bed, enclosed on four sides. **2.** A small building for storing corn or other grain. **3.** A rack or trough from which cattle or horses eat.

crick·et¹ |krĭk'ĭt| —*noun, plural* **crickets** An insect that looks like a small, dark grasshopper. The male makes a chirping sound by rubbing the front wings together.

crick·et² |krĭk'ĭt| —*noun* An outdoor game for two teams of eleven players each, played with bats, a ball, and wickets. Cricket is popular in Great Britain.

crime |krīm| —*noun, plural* **crimes 1.** An action that is against the law. Usually, a crime is something done on purpose to harm a person or to destroy or take a person's property. **2.** Activity that is not legal: *a life of crime; a police department fighting crime.* **3.** Any action that is foolish or makes no sense; a shame; a pity: *It's a crime the way you waste money.*

crim·i·nal |krĭm'ə nəl| —*noun, plural* **criminals** A person who has committed a crime or been convicted of one: *The prison holds hundreds of criminals.*
—*adjective* Having to do with crime: *The criminal act was punished. A criminal lawyer can make sure that someone accused of a crime gets a fair trial.*

crim·son |krĭm'zən| or |krĭm'sən| —*noun, plural* **crimsons** A bright purplish-red color.
—*adjective* Bright purplish red: *The king wore a crimson robe.*

crin·kle |krĭng'kəl| —*verb* **crinkled, crinkling 1.** To make or become wrinkled or creased: *This dress crinkles too easily. The corners of her eyes crinkle when she smiles.* **2.** To make a soft, crackling sound; rustle: *The aluminum foil crinkles when I shake it.*

crip·ple |krĭp'əl| —*noun, plural* **cripples** A person or animal that cannot move normally because some part of the body is injured or defective.
—*verb* **crippled, crippling 1.** To make into a cripple: *An accident crippled him for life.* **2.** To damage; make helpless or useless: *The storm crippled the ship.*

cri·ses |krī'sēz'| The plural of the noun **crisis.**

cri·sis |krī'sĭs| —*noun, plural* **crises 1.** A time of danger or difficulty in which great changes can take place: *There was a crisis in our town when the big factory closed and nearly everyone was out of work.* **2.** A sudden change in a serious illness: *The crisis has passed, and her temperature is coming down.*

crisp |krĭsp| —*adjective* **crisper, crispest 1.** Pleasantly dry and hard from cooking: *He likes crisp toast and crisp bacon.* **2.** Fresh and firm; not wilted or limp: *crisp lettuce; crisp celery.* **3.** Cool and refreshing; bracing: *a crisp fall day.* **4.** Short and clear: *A crisp answer stopped my foolish questions.*

criss·cross |krĭs'krôs'| or |krĭs'krŏs'| —*verb* **crisscrossed, crisscrossing 1.** To mark with or make a pattern of crossing lines: *Animal trails crisscrossed the woods. Our paths crisscrossed in the snow.* **2.** To move back and forth across: *Ships crisscrossed the sea between England and America.*
—*noun, plural* **crisscrosses** A mark or pattern made of crossing lines.

cricket¹, cricket²
It is possible that **cricket¹** and **cricket²** come from two old French words that also look alike but mean different things. **Cricket¹** comes from *criquet,* meaning "grasshopper." This noun came from the verb *criquer,* which meant both "to click" and "to make a sharp sound." **Cricket²** may be from *criquet,* a different noun that referred to a kind of bat used in a ball game. This noun also came from *criquer* as it applied to the sound made by the bat when it hit the ball.

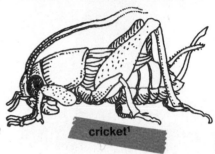
cricket¹

—adjective Crossing one another: *the crisscross lines of a puzzle.*
—adverb In a crisscross pattern or arrangement: *The pencils lay crisscross on the table.*

crit·ic |**krĭt′ĭk**| *—noun, plural* **critics** A person whose job is judging books, plays, and other artistic efforts: *a book critic; a movie critic.*

crit·i·cal |**krĭt′ĭ kəl**| *—adjective* **1.** Of a critic or critics: *critical reviews of new movies.* **2.** Likely to criticize or find fault: *She is always critical of anything I wear.* **3.** Extremely important: *a critical need to clean up our rivers and lakes.* **4.** Very serious or dangerous: *a critical injury.*

crit·i·cism |**krĭt′ĭ sĭz′əm**| *—noun, plural* **criticisms 1.** The act of making and expressing judgments about the good and bad qualities of things. **2.** An opinion that is not favorable: *I didn't like his criticism of the way I played ball.* **3.** The act or practice of judging books, plays, art, or other artistic work: *literary criticism; dramatic criticism.*

crit·i·cize |**krĭt′ĭ sīz**| *—verb* **criticized, criticizing 1.** To judge whether something is good or bad; evaluate: *Please criticize the speech I just made.* **2.** To find something wrong with; judge severely: *Stop criticizing everything I do!*

croak |krōk| *—noun, plural* **croaks** A low, hoarse sound, such as that made by a frog or crow.
—verb **croaked, croaking** To make this or a similar sound: *a chorus of bullfrogs croaking in the swamp.*

cro·chet |krō shā′| *—verb* **cro·cheted** |krō shād′|, **cro·chet·ing** |krō shā′ĭng| To make clothing, lace, or other articles by connecting loops of thread with a hooked needle called a crochet hook: *Will you teach me to crochet a sweater?*

croc·o·dile |krŏk′ə dīl′| *—noun, plural* **crocodiles** A large reptile with thick skin, sharp teeth, and long, narrow jaws. Crocodiles live in wet places throughout the tropics. Alligators and crocodiles look very much alike, but crocodiles have narrower jaws.

cro·cus |krō′kəs| *—noun, plural* **crocuses** A small garden plant with purple, yellow, or white flowers that bloom early in spring.

crook |krŏŏk| *—noun, plural* **crooks 1.** Something bent or curved: *He held the baby in the crook of his arm.* **2.** A long staff with a bent or curved part: *a shepherd's crook.* **3.** A dishonest person; a thief: *The crook stole my bicycle.*
—verb **crooked, crooking** To bend or curve: *He crooked his arm around the package. The path crooks through the forest.*

crook·ed |krŏŏk′ĭd| *—adjective* **1.a.** Bent; twisted: *a crooked tail.* **b.** Following a bent or twisted path: *a crooked street.* **c.** Not straight or regular: *a crooked picture; a crooked smile; crooked teeth.* **2.** Dishonest: *Don't do business with crooked merchants.*

crop |krŏp| *—noun, plural* **crops 1.** Plants grown for their grain, fruit, or other parts that can be eaten: *Wheat is a leading crop in the United States and Canada.* **2.** The amount of one of the products grown or harvested in one season: *a record corn crop.* **3.** A group of things appearing at one time: *He produced a crop of new ideas.* **4.** A pouch in the neck of a bird where food is stored and partially digested. **5.** A short whip used in horseback riding.
—verb **cropped, cropping 1.** To cut or bite off the tops of: *They kept sheep to crop the grass.* **2.** To cut short: *She crops her hair every summer.*

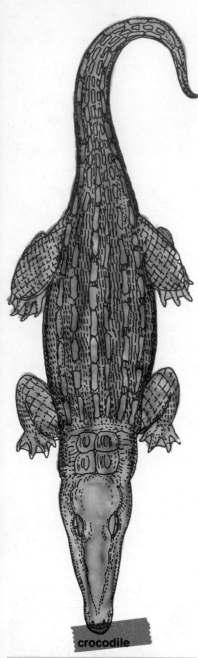

crocodile

ă	pat	ĕ	pet	î	fierce
ā	pay	ē	be	ŏ	pot
â	care	ĭ	pit	ō	go
ä	father	ī	pie	ô	paw, for
oi	oil	ŭ	cut	zh	vision
ŏŏ	book	û	fur	ə	ago, item,
ōō	boot	th	the		pencil, atom,
yōō	abuse	th	thin		circus
ou	out	hw	which	ər	butter

cro·quet | krō kā' | —*noun* A lawn game in which each player uses a large mallet to hit a wooden ball through a series of wickets.

cross | krôs | or | krŏs | —*noun, plural* **crosses 1.** An upright post with a horizontal bar at the top or near the top. In ancient times certain types of criminals were put to death by nailing or tying them to a cross. **2. the Cross** The cross upon which Christ was crucified. **3.** An emblem, medal, or badge in the shape of a cross: *Around her neck was a gold chain with a small cross.* **4.** A mark or pattern formed by two lines that come together and pass beyond each other. **5.** The result of combining two things: *My dog is a cross between a boxer and a bulldog.*
—*verb* **crossed, crossing 1.** To go to the other side of: *We crossed the street. The bridge crosses the river.* **2.** To come together and pass beyond each other: *The two streets cross in the center of town.* **3.** To disagree with; contradict: *She's pleasant enough, but don't ever cross her.* **4.** To draw a line across: *Cross your t's.* **5.** To move or cause to move the eyes toward the nose: *He crossed his eyes and made a face. My eyes crossed.* **6.** To place across: *She crossed her legs as she sat down.*
   Phrasal verb **cross out** To eliminate by drawing a line through: *Cross out the old address and put in the new one.*
—*adjective* **1.** Lying or placed across: *Turn off the avenue onto a cross street.* **2.** In a bad mood: *She's always cross when she first wakes up.*

cross·bow | krôs'bō' | or | krŏs'bō' | —*noun, plural* **crossbows** A weapon for shooting arrows or darts. A crossbow has a bow fixed across a wooden stock, with grooves on the stock to direct the arrow or dart. Crossbows were used by hunters and soldiers long ago. Modern crossbows are still used for hunting.

cross-eyed | krôs'īd' | or | krŏs'īd' | —*adjective* Having one or both eyes turned in toward the nose.

cross·ing | krô'sĭng | or | krŏs'ĭng | —*noun, plural* **crossings 1.** A place at which a street, railroad, river, or other route may be crossed: *Cross at the crossing, not in the middle of the block.* **2.** The place where two or more things cross; an intersection. **3.** A trip across an ocean.

cross·road | krôs'rōd' | or | krŏs'rōd' | —*noun, plural* **crossroads 1.** A road that crosses another road. **2. crossroads** A place, especially in the countryside, where two or more roads meet: *A town grew up at the crossroads.*

cross section 1. A straight cut or slice through a solid object, often done in order to show what is inside it: *The museum has a cross section of an automobile engine.* **2.** A picture or drawing of such a slice. **3.** A sampling or a selection of people or things that is thought to represent a larger group: *His stories show a cross section of the many kinds of people who live in cities.*

cross·word puzzle | krôs'wûrd' | or | krŏs'wûrd' | A puzzle in which one is given clues to words that are to be fitted into numbered squares, one letter to a square. Words cross through one another and may be read across or down.

crotch | krŏch | —*noun, plural* **crotches 1.** The point at which a branch grows out from the trunk or another branch of a tree. **2.** The point at which one's legs branch off from one's body. **3.** The part of a garment where the leg seams meet.

crouch | krouch | —*verb* **crouched, crouching** To bend low; stoop;

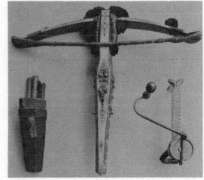
crossbow

crossword puzzle

squat: *He had to crouch to get into Freddie's small car.*

crow¹ | krō | —*noun, plural* **crows** A large, glossy black bird with a harsh, hoarse call.

    Idiom **as the crow flies** In a straight line: *It's only three miles to town as the crow flies, but on the road it's almost five miles.*

crow² | krō | —*noun, plural* **crows** 1. The loud cry of a rooster. 2. A loud cry of delight.

    —*verb* **crowed, crowing** 1. To utter the loud cry of a rooster: *That rooster started to crow at five a.m.* 2. To utter a cry of delight: *The baby gurgled and crowed.*

crow·bar | krō′bär′ | —*noun, plural* **crowbars** A bar of iron or steel, bent slightly at one end, used as a lever for lifting or prying.

crowd | kroud | —*noun, plural* **crowds** A large number of people gathered together: *A crowd gathered around the speaker.*

    —*verb* **crowded, crowding** 1. To fill with many people or things: *Hundreds crowded into the shop. Fans crowded the stadium. Many delicious foods crowded the shelves.* 2. To press tightly; cram: *I crowded several more books onto the shelf.*

crown | kroun | —*noun, plural* **crowns** 1. A covering for the head, often made of gold and set with jewels. Crowns are worn by kings, queens, and other rulers as a symbol of their power. 2. The person, authority, or government of a king or queen: *a servant of the crown; heir to the crown.* 3. A wreath worn on the head as a symbol of victory or honor: *The winner of the race was presented with a crown of laurel.* 4. The top part of something: *the crown of a person's head.* 5. a. The part of a tooth that is above the gums. b. A covering of gold or other substance for the crown of a tooth.

    —*verb* **crowned, crowning** 1. To place a crown on the head of a person while giving the power that goes with it: *The queen was crowned in a long ceremony.* 2. To cover the top of: *Snow crowned the mountain peak.*

crow's-nest | krōz′něst′ | —*noun, plural* **crow's-nests** A small platform located near the top of a ship's mast, used by sailors for seeing long distances.

cru·cial | krōō′shəl | —*adjective* Of the greatest importance; critical: *The governor faces a crucial test of his power.*

cru·ci·fix | krōō′sə fĭks′ | —*noun, plural* **crucifixes** A cross with the figure of Christ on it.

cru·ci·fix·ion | krōō′sə fĭk′shən | —*noun, plural* **crucifixions** 1. The act of dying or putting a person to death on a cross. 2. **the Crucifixion** The death of Christ on the Cross.

cru·ci·fy | krōō′sə fī′ | —*verb* **crucified, crucifying, crucifies** To put a person to death by nailing or tying to a cross.

crude | krōōd | —*adjective* **cruder, crudest** 1. In a raw or natural state; not refined: *crude oil.* 2. Not done or made with skill; rough: *a crude drawing; a crude attempt to repair a clock.* 3. Without consideration for others; lacking good manners; vulgar: *a crude person; a crude remark.*

cru·el | krōō′əl | —*adjective* **crueler, cruelest** 1. Liking to cause pain or suffering; unkind: *a cruel man.* 2. Causing suffering; painful: *a cruel storm; a cruel trap.*

cru·el·ty | krōō′əl tē | —*noun, plural* **cruelties** 1. The condition or quality of being cruel: *He was jailed for his cruelty to animals.* 2. A cruel act or remark.

crown

crow's-nest

ă	pat	ĕ	pet	î	fierce
ā	pay	ē	be	ŏ	pot
â	care	ĭ	pit	ō	go
ä	father	ī	pie	ô	paw, for

oi	oil	ŭ	cut	zh	vision
ōō	book	û	fur	ə	ago, item,
ōō	boot	*th*	the		pencil, atom,
yōō	abuse	th	thin		circus
ou	out	hw	which	ər	butter

cruise | krōoz | —*verb* **cruised, cruising** **1.** To sail or travel about for pleasure: *We cruised around the island in a sailboat last summer.* **2.** To patrol an area by automobile: *The police car cruised the neighborhood.*
—*noun, plural* **cruises** A sea voyage for pleasure: *We took a cruise to the islands.*

cruis·er | krōo′zər | —*noun, plural* **cruisers** **1.** A warship capable of high speeds and long cruising range. A cruiser is usually smaller than a battleship and has less armor and less powerful guns. **2.** A police car.

cruiser
Police cruiser

crumb | krŭm | —*noun, plural* **crumbs** **1.** A tiny piece or particle of food, especially of pastry, bread, or a cracker. **2.** A small piece or scrap: *crumbs of information.*

crum·ble | krŭm′bəl | —*verb* **crumbled, crumbling** To break or fall into pieces or crumbs: *He crumbled crackers into his soup.*

crum·ple | krŭm′pəl | —*verb* **crumpled, crumpling** **1.** To crush out of shape, forming creases or wrinkles; rumple: *Try not to crumple your new dress. Aluminum foil crumples easily.* **2.** To fall down: *He felt sick and crumpled to the floor.*

crunch | krŭnch | —*verb* **crunched, crunching** **1.** To grind or crush with a noisy or cracking sound; chew noisily: *He crunched peanuts all through the movie.* **2.** To make a crunching sound: *The snow crunched under our boots.*
—*noun, plural* **crunches** The act or sound of crunching: *He ate the celery with loud crunches.*

cru·sade | krōo sād′ | —*noun, plural* **crusades** **1. Crusade** Any of the military expeditions that European Christians undertook in the 11th, 12th, and 13th centuries to take the Holy Land from the Moslems. **2.** Any campaign or movement for reform, a cause, or an ideal: *a crusade for better housing; a crusade against crime.*
—*verb* **crusaded, crusading** To take part in a crusade: *He crusaded for equal rights.*

cru·sad·er | krōo sā′dər | —*noun, plural* **crusaders** Often **Crusader** A person who takes part in a crusade: *They are crusaders for solar power.*

crush | krŭsh | —*verb* **crushed, crushing** **1.** To press or squeeze with enough force to break or injure: *A landslide crushed many of the town's houses.* **2.** To grind or pound into very fine bits: *That machine can crush rocks into powder.* **3.** To wrinkle; crumple: *Try not to crush your pretty dress. This cloth crushes easily.* **4.** To defeat, put down, or destroy: *All the queen's soldiers could not crush the rebellion.*
—*noun, plural* **crushes** **1.** A dense crowd of people in motion: *We were caught in the crush and nearly trampled.* **2.** A strong liking, usually lasting only a short time: *She had a crush on my brother last summer.*

crust | krŭst | —*noun, plural* **crusts** **1.** The hard outer layer of bread. **2.** The shell of a pie or other pastry: *She ate the cherry filling but left the crust.* **3.** Any hard outer layer or covering: *The earth's crust is twenty miles deep.*
—*verb* **crusted, crusting** To cover or become covered with a crust: *The pond crusted with ice.*

crus·ta·cean | krŭ stā′shən | —*noun, plural* **crustaceans** One of a group of animals with a body that has a hard outer covering. Most crustaceans live in the water. Lobsters, crabs, and shrimps are crustaceans.

Cub Scout

cucumber
On the vine

---

cue¹, cue²
We do not know the origin of **cue¹**, but we can trace its use back to about the sixteenth century. **Cue²** is from the French word meaning "tail," which came from Latin.

ă	pat	ĕ	pet	î	fierce
ā	pay	ē	be	ŏ	pot
â	care	ĭ	pit	ō	go
ä	father	ī	pie	ô	paw, for
oi	oil	ŭ	cut	zh	vision
ōō	book	û	fur	ə	ago, item,
ōō	boot	th	the		pencil, atom,
yōō	abuse	th	thin		circus
ou	out	hw	which	ər	butter

---

crutch | krŭch | —*noun, plural* **crutches** A support, often one of a pair, used by lame or injured persons as an aid in walking. A crutch usually has a padded part at the top that fits under the armpit.

cry | krī | —*verb* **cried, crying, cries** **1.** To shed tears because of pain or a strong feeling such as anger, sorrow, or joy; weep: *She always cries at weddings.* **2.** To call loudly; shout: *"Look out for the car!" she cried.* **3.** To give a call or sound that can identify a particular animal: *A wolf cried in the distance.*
—*noun, plural* **cries** **1.** A loud call; a shout: *We heard his cries for help.* **2.** A loud expression of fear, distress, or pain: *a cry of anger.* **3.** A fit of weeping: *We had a good cry at that sad movie.* **4.** The sound or call of an animal: *the cry of a wolf.*

crys·tal | krĭs′təl | —*noun, plural* **crystals** **1.** A solid substance with sides and angles that naturally form a regular pattern. Snow is formed from ice crystals. **2.** A piece of quartz or other transparent mineral, often having flat surfaces and angles. **3.** A clear glass of high quality, or an object made from it: *The bowl is made of fine crystal. Where did you buy all that beautiful crystal?* **4.** The clear covering that protects the face of a clock or watch.

cub | kŭb | —*noun, plural* **cubs** **1.** A young bear, wolf, or lion. The young of some other animals are also called cubs. **2. Cub** A Cub Scout.

cube | kyōob | —*noun, plural* **cubes** **1.** A solid figure having six flat, square sides of equal size, which meet at right angles. **2.** Anything having this shape: *a cube of sugar.* **3.** The result of multiplying a number by itself twice. The cube of 2 is 2 × 2 × 2, or 8.
—*verb* **cubed, cubing** **1.** To form the cube of a number: *If you cube 4, your answer is 64.* **2.** To cut or form into cubes: *Cube the apples before putting them into the salad.*

cu·bic | kyōo′bĭk | —*adjective* **1.** Having the shape of a cube. **2.** Having to do with volume or the measurement of volume: *What is the volume of the swimming pool in cubic feet?*

Cub Scout A member of the junior division of the Boy Scouts.

cuck·oo | kōo′kōo | or | kŏok′ōo | —*noun, plural* **cuckoos** **1.** A European bird with grayish feathers and a call that sounds like its name. It lays its eggs in the nests of other birds. **2.** An American bird that is related to the European cuckoo.

cuckoo clock A wall clock with a small mechanical cuckoo that pops out to announce the time, usually on the hour and half hour.

cu·cum·ber | kyōo′kŭm′bər | —*noun, plural* **cucumbers** A long vegetable with green skin and white flesh. Cucumbers grow on vines. They are eaten in salads or made into pickles.

cud | kŭd | —*noun, plural* **cuds** Food that has been swallowed by a cow, sheep, or other animal, and then brought up to the mouth to be chewed again.

cue¹ | kyōo | —*noun, plural* **cues** **1.** A word, sound, or other signal to an actor or performer to begin a speech or movement: *The doorbell is your cue to hide in the closet.* **2.** Any hint or reminder: *When they start arguing, that's my cue to leave.*
—*verb* **cued, cuing** To give a person a cue: *The conductor cued the violins to begin.*

cue² | kyōo | —*noun, plural* **cues** A long, tapered stick used to strike a ball in billiards or pool.

cuff¹ |kŭf| —*noun, plural* **cuffs** A band or fold of cloth at the bottom of a sleeve or trouser leg: *I prefer my pants without a cuff.*

cuff² |kŭf| —*verb* **cuffed, cuffing** To strike with the open hand; slap; hit: *The bear cuffed her cubs when they played too roughly.* —*noun, plural* **cuffs** A blow or slap: *a cuff on the ear.*

cul·prit |kŭl′prĭt| —*noun, plural* **culprits** A person who is suspected or found guilty of a crime.

cul·ti·vate |kŭl′tə vāt′| —*verb* **cultivated, cultivating** **1.** To prepare and tend soil to grow plants: *The farmer cultivated the field with a large tractor.* **2.** To develop by study or teaching: *He reads a lot to cultivate his mind.*

cul·tur·al |kŭl′chər əl| —*adjective* Having to do with culture: *This city is the cultural center of the state.*

cul·ture |kŭl′chər| —*noun, plural* **cultures** **1.** The result of education and a great amount of interest in the arts, history, literature, and other areas of learning: *a woman of great culture and intelligence.* **2.** The customs, beliefs, arts, and institutions of a group of people: *the various cultures of North American Indians.* **3.** Development of the mind or body through special training: *Jogging is part of his physical culture.*

cun·ning |kŭn′ĭng| —*adjective* Sly or clever: *He has a cunning scheme for earning some extra money. The fox is a cunning animal.* —*noun* The act or condition of being sly: *The weasel is an animal of great cunning.*

cup |kŭp| —*noun, plural* **cups** **1.** A small, open container, usually with a handle. Cups are used for drinking coffee, tea, or other liquids: *A cup and saucer were beside each plate.* **2.a.** A cup with something in it: *How about a cup of tea?* **b.** The amount that a cup can hold: *I've had three cups already.* **3.** Something with the shape of a cup: *She was given a gold cup for winning the race.* —*verb* **cupped, cupping** To form something to look like a cup: *He cupped his hand behind his ear to hear better.*

cup·board |kŭb′ərd| —*noun, plural* **cupboards** A closet or cabinet, usually with shelves. A cupboard is used for storing dishes, food, or other household items.

cup·cake |kŭp′kāk′| —*noun, plural* **cupcakes** A small cake that is baked in a pan that is shaped into one or more cups.

curb |kûrb| —*noun, plural* **curbs** **1.** A rim of stone, concrete, or other material along the edge of a road or sidewalk. **2.** Something that stops or holds back: *a curb on spending.* —*verb* **curbed, curbing** To hold back or keep under control: *She tried to curb her temper.*

curd |kûrd| —*noun, plural* **curds** A thick substance that separates from milk when it turns sour. Curds are used to make cheese.

cure |kyŏŏr| —*noun, plural* **cures** **1.** A medical treatment or series of such treatments for the purpose of regaining one's health: *There is no cure for the common cold.* **2.** A drug or medicine. **3.** A return to good health: *The cure was slow but completely successful.* —*verb* **cured, curing** **1.** To bring back to good health: *The veterinarian cured my dog.* **2.** To get rid of something bad or harmful: *A smile will often cure another person's anger.* **3.** To preserve food by drying, salting, smoking, or by other means: *They cured the meat by salting it and drying it in the sun.*

cuff¹, cuff²
Cuff¹ goes back to the fourteenth century; it originally meant "glove, mitten." **Cuff²** goes back to the sixteenth century. Both are of unknown origin.

cultivate

cup
The winners of a tennis match

cur·few |kûr′fyōō| —*noun, plural* **curfews** A fixed time at night when people have to stay off the streets: *a curfew of eleven o'clock for teenagers.*

cu·ri·os·i·ty |kyŏŏr′ē ŏs′ĭ tē| —*noun, plural* **curiosities 1.** A desire to know or learn: *My curiosity made me peek into the room.* **2.** Something unusual or remarkable: *The attic was full of old clothes and other curiosities.*

cu·ri·ous |kyŏŏr′ē əs| —*adjective* **1.** Eager to learn or know: *An intelligent person is always curious.* **2.** Unusual or remarkable: *It is a curious fact that many intelligent students fail in school.* **3.** Too nosy; prying: *She's always curious about what I'm doing.*

curl |kûrl| —*verb* **curled, curling** To twist or form into rings or coils: *It took her all afternoon to curl her hair. My hair curls naturally. Smoke curled from the chimney.*
—*noun, plural* **curls 1.** A ring or coil of hair: *Her long curls covered her shoulders.* **2.** Something with a spiral or coiled shape: *We saw a curl of smoke over the houses.*

curl·y |kûr′lē| —*adjective* **curlier, curliest** Having curls or tending to curl: *curly hair.*

cur·rant |kûr′ənt| or |kŭr′ənt| —*noun, plural* **currants 1.** A small, sour red or blackish berry that grows on a prickly bush. Currants are used for making jelly. **2.** A small raisin without seeds, used mostly in baking.
♦ *These sound alike* **currant, current.**

cur·ren·cy |kûr′ən sē| or |kŭr′ən sē| —*noun, plural* **currencies** The form of money that a country uses: *England's currency usually shows a picture of the Queen.*

cur·rent |kûr′ənt| or |kŭr′ənt| —*adjective* **1.** Belonging to the present time; of the present day: *current events.* **2.** Widely accepted; widely used: *"Groovy" is a word that is no longer current.*
—*noun, plural* **currents 1.** Liquid or gas that is moving: *a current of air; the strong current of a river.* **2.** A flow of electricity: *When you turn on the switch, the current passes through the cord.* **3.** A general tendency or trend: *the current of public opinion.*
♦ *These sound alike* **current, currant.**

curse |kûrs| —*noun, plural* **curses 1.** An appeal to heaven to send down evil or harm on someone: *The old woman shouted a curse at the burglars.* **2.** Evil or harm that is suffered: *Poor health was the family's curse.* **3.** A word or group of words expressing great anger or hatred.
—*verb* **cursed, cursing 1.** To call down a curse on a person: *The old wizard cursed the prince and turned him into a frog.* **2.** To bring evil to; harm: *Illness and bad weather cursed the explorers from the start.* **3.** To swear at; use bad language: *The citizens cursed the tax collectors.*

cur·tain |kûr′tn| —*noun, plural* **curtains 1.** A piece of cloth or other material hung at a window to shut out the light, provide privacy, or as a decoration: *She opened the curtains and let in the morning light.* **2.** A large, movable screen of cloth or other material that hides the stage from the audience in a theater. **3.** Something that acts as a screen or cover: *a curtain of secrecy; a curtain of smoke.*
—*verb* **curtained, curtaining** To decorate, cover, or hide with a curtain: *Let's curtain that doorway. The enemy ships were curtained with smoke.*

curt·sy |kûrt′sē| —*noun, plural* **curtsies** A way of showing

currency

ă	pat	ĕ	pet	î	fierce
ā	pay	ē	be	ŏ	pot
â	care	ĭ	pit	ō	go
ä	father	ī	pie	ô	paw, for
oi	oil	ŭ	cut	zh	vision
ŏŏ	book	û	fur	ə	ago, item,
ōō	boot	*th*	the		pencil, atom,
yōō	abuse	th	thin		circus
ou	out	hw	which	ər	butter

respect to a person by bending one's knees and lowering the body
while keeping one foot forward.
—*verb* **curtsied, curtsying, curtsies** To make a curtsy.

curve |kûrv| —*noun, plural* **curves** **1.** A line or surface that
bends smoothly and continuously. **2.** Anything having the shape
of a curve: *a curve in the road; a curve in the back of a chair.* **3.** A
pitched baseball that turns sharply downward or to one side as it
nears the batter. Also called *curve ball.*
—*verb* **curved, curving** **1.** To move in or have the shape of a
curve: *The road curves at the bottom of the hill.* **2.** To cause to
curve: *He taught me how to curve metal bands around a barrel.*

curve

cush·ion |kŏŏsh'ən| —*noun, plural* **cushions** **1.** A pad or
pillow with a soft filling, used to sit, rest, or lie on: *The chairs
need new cushions.* **2.** Anything used to reduce shocks or soften
blows: *A carpet will act as a cushion for your feet.*
—*verb* **cushioned, cushioning** **1.** To supply with a cushion or
cushions: *to cushion a chair.* **2.** To soften a blow from; reduce the
effect of: *The soft dirt cushioned his fall.*

cus·tard |kŭs'tərd| —*noun, plural* **custards** A dessert, similar
to pudding, made of eggs, milk, sugar, and flavoring.

cus·to·di·an |kŭ stō'dē ən| —*noun, plural* **custodians** **1.** A
person in charge of something; a caretaker: *He works at the
museum as custodian of the mineral collection.* **2.** A person who
takes care of a building; a janitor: *The custodian went to the closet
for his broom.*

cus·to·dy |kŭs'tə dē| —*noun* **1.** The right or duty to take care
of someone or something: *The court gave the father the custody of
the children.* **2.** The condition of being held by police or under
guard: *The suspect was in the custody of the sheriff.*

cus·tom |kŭs'təm| —*noun, plural* **customs** **1.** Something
people do that is widely accepted or has become a tradition: *Many
people have the custom of shaking hands when meeting someone.*
2. Something a person usually does; a habit: *It is her custom to
clear her throat before speaking.*
—*adjective* Made especially to fit a buyer or according to a
buyer's instructions or desires: *a custom suit; a custom car.*

cus·tom·ar·y |kŭs'tə měr'ē| —*adjective* According to custom or
habit; usual: *Sit at your customary desk.*

cus·tom·er |kŭs'tə mər| —*noun, plural* **customers** A person
who buys goods or services: *The store gives a discount to its best
customers.*

cus·toms |kŭs'təmz| —*noun* (Used with a singular verb.) **1.** A
tax that must be paid on things brought into a country that were
bought outside that country: *The customs on that watch was $6.00.*
2. The organization, buildings, people, and equipment used to
collect such taxes: *We had to stop at customs when we arrived.*

cut |kŭt| —*verb* **cut, cutting** **1.** To go through or into with a
knife or with something as sharp as a knife: *The broken glass cut
his hand. The wind cut right through my jacket.* **2.** To form, shape,
or divide by using a sharp instrument: *The children cut out paper
dolls. We cut the cake in half.* **3.** To separate from the main part
of something: *Please cut a piece of chicken for me.* **4.** To shorten
or trim: *Who cut your hair?* **5.** To grow teeth through the gums:
The baby is cutting a new tooth. **6.** To reduce the size or amount
of: *a plan to cut taxes.* **7.** To remove; eliminate: *We cut the magic
act from the program.*

***Phrasal verbs* cut off 1.** To separate: *The soldiers were cut off from their supplies.* **2.** To stop: *He cut off the power to the engine.*
cut out 1. To be suited or good enough: *I'm not cut out to be a scientist.* **2.** To stop; cease: *Cut that out or you'll get hurt.*
—*noun, plural* **cuts 1.** The result of cutting; a slit, wound, or other opening: *a cut in her skirt; a cut on one's hand.* **2.** A piece of meat that has been cut from an animal: *a good cut of beef.* **3.** A reduction: *a cut in one's pay.* **4.** A part of something cut out to shorten or improve it: *The movie was shown without cuts.*
—*adjective* Having been cut or separated: *cut flowers.*

cute |kyōōt| —*adjective* **cuter, cutest 1.** Delightfully pretty; charming: *a cute baby; a cute dress.* **2.** Clever: *a cute trick to get out of working.*

cu·ti·cle |kyōō′tĭ kəl| —*noun, plural* **cuticles** The strip of hardened skin at the base of a fingernail or toenail.

cut·lass |kŭt′ləs| —*noun, plural* **cutlasses** A heavy sword with a curved blade that is sharpened along one edge. Cutlasses were once used as weapons.

cut·ter |kŭt′ər| —*noun, plural* **cutters 1.** A worker whose job is to cut material, such as cloth, glass, or stone. **2.** A device or machine for cutting: *a cooky cutter.*

cut·ting |kŭt′ĭng| —*noun, plural* **cuttings 1.** A part cut off from a main body; a clipping: *She saves cuttings from the newspapers.*
2. A stem, leaf, or twig cut from a plant and placed in sand, soil, or water to form roots and develop into a new plant: *She gave me a cutting from her prize begonia.*
—*adjective* **1.** Used for cutting: *a cutting blade.* **2.** Mean and insulting: *a cutting remark.*

cy·cle |sī′kəl| —*noun, plural* **cycles 1.** An event or series of events that is repeated regularly: *the yearly cycle of the seasons.*
2. A series of operations necessary for the completion of a process: *the cycle of a washing machine or dishwasher.*
—*verb* **cycled, cycling** To ride a bicycle or motorcycle: *Last summer we cycled from one side of the state to the other.*

cy·clone |sī′klōn| —*noun, plural* **cyclones 1.** A mass of rapidly rotating air surrounding an area of low pressure. **2.** Any violent rotating wind storm, such as a tornado.

cyl·in·der |sĭl′ən dər| —*noun, plural* **cylinders** A hollow or solid object shaped like a tube, pipe, or tree trunk. Each end of a cylinder is usually a circle. The circles are parallel to each other: *The rollers on a printing press are cylinders.*

cym·bal |sĭm′bəl| —*noun, plural* **cymbals** A musical instrument that is a circular sheet of brass. The cymbal is sounded by being struck against another cymbal or with a drumstick.
♦ *These sound alike* **cymbal, symbol.**

cy·press |sī′prəs| —*noun, plural* **cypresses 1.** An evergreen tree that has small needles that look like scales. **2.** A related tree that grows in swamps and sheds its needles every year. **3.** The wood of a cypress tree.

cymbals

ă	pat	ĕ	pet	î	fierce
ā	pay	ē	be	ŏ	pot
â	care	ĭ	pit	ō	go
ä	father	ī	pie	ô	paw, for

oi	oil	ŭ	cut	zh	vision
ōō	book	û	fur	ə	ago, item,
ōō	boot	*th*	the		pencil, atom,
yōō	abuse	th	thin		circus
ou	out	hw	which	ər	butter

Dd

d or **D** |dē| —*noun, plural* **d's** or **D's** The fourth letter of the English alphabet.

dab |dăb| —*verb* **dabbed, dabbing** To put on with soft, light touches: *The nurse dabbed cooling lotion on the sore spot.*
—*noun, plural* **dabs** A very small amount of something: *We put a dab of butter on the piece of bread.*

dab·ble |dăb'əl| —*verb* **dabbled, dabbling** **1.** To splash or spatter: *Raindrops dabbled her freshly ironed dress.* **2.** To splash in and out of water playfully: *The children dabbled their feet in the pool.* **3.** To do or work on something, but not seriously: *He dabbled at carpentry.*

dachs·hund |däks'hŏont'| or |däks'hŏond'| —*noun, plural* **dachshunds** A small dog with a long body, drooping ears, and very short legs.

dachshund

dad |dăd| —*noun, plural* **dads** Father.

dad·dy |dăd'ē| —*noun, plural* **daddies** Father.

daddy long·legs |lông'lĕgz'| or |lŏng'lĕgz'| —*plural* **daddy longlegs** An animal related to the spiders. It has a small, round body and eight long, slender legs.

daf·fo·dil |dăf'ə dĭl| —*noun, plural* **daffodils** A plant with long, narrow leaves and flowers that are usually yellow. The flowers have a center part shaped like a trumpet.

dag·ger |dăg'ər| —*noun, plural* **daggers** A short, pointed weapon with sharp edges, used like a knife.

dai·ly |dā'lē| —*adjective* Done or happening every day: *The family takes a daily walk in the woods.*
—*adverb* Once each day: *You must feed the cat daily.*
—*noun, plural* **dailies** A newspaper published every day.

dain·ty |dān'tē| —*adjective* **daintier, daintiest** **1.** Very fine and delicate: *The dress was covered with dainty embroidery.* **2.** Light and graceful: *The dancer took small, dainty steps.* **3.** Careful in choosing; fussy: *The kitten is dainty about what she eats.*

dai·ry |dâr'ē| —*noun, plural* **dairies** **1.** A place where milk and cream are prepared for use or made into butter and cheese. **2.** A business that makes or sells milk, cream, butter, and cheese.

da·is |dā'ĭs| or |dās| —*noun, plural* **daises** A platform for a throne, a speaker, or group of special guests. A dais is often at the front of an auditorium.

daffodil

dagger

daisy

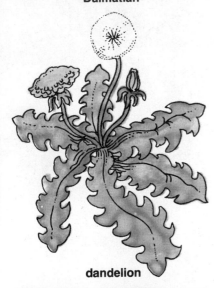

Dalmatian

dandelion

dai·sy |dā′zē| —*noun, plural* **daisies** A plant with flowers that have narrow petals around a yellow center. The common wild daisy of North America has flowers with white petals.

Dal·ma·tian |dăl mā′shən| —*noun, plural* **Dalmatians** A dog that has a smooth white coat with many small black spots.

dam |dăm| —*noun, plural* **dams** A wall built across a river or other body of water. A dam controls the flow or raises the level of the water.
—*verb* **dammed, damming** To build a dam.
♦ *These sound alike* **dam, damn.**

dam·age |dăm′ĭj| —*noun, plural* **damages** Harm or injury that causes a loss or makes something less useful or valuable: *The hurricane did much damage to their summer house at the beach.*
—*verb* **damaged, damaging** To harm or injure: *The cold spring weather damaged the apple blossoms.*

dame |dām| —*noun, plural* **dames** 1. **Dame** A title of honor in England given to a woman for some worthwhile accomplishment. It is equal to a knight's title of "Sir." 2. Any lady or wife.

damn |dăm| —*verb* **damned, damning** To describe as being very bad: *The audience damned the school play because they couldn't hear the actors.*
—*interjection* A word used to express anger or disappointment.
♦ *These sound alike* **damn, dam.**

damp |dămp| —*adjective* **damper, dampest** Being a little wet; moist; humid: *The clothes were still damp several hours after we washed them. It is a damp evening with fog and drizzle.*
—*noun, plural* **damps** Moisture in the air or on the surface of or throughout something: *Don't go out in the damp.*

damp·en |dăm′pən| —*verb* **dampened, dampening** 1. To make moist or wet: *Before you wipe the windshield, dampen the sponge.* 2. To lower or lessen: *The long wait dampened their excitement.*

dance |dăns| or |däns| —*verb* **danced, dancing** 1. To move the body or parts of the body with rhythmic steps and motion: *The band began to play a lively tune and the people began to dance.* 2. To move actively or with excitement: *When the boy burned his foot, he danced up and down in pain.*
—*noun, plural* **dances** 1. A special set of steps and motions, usually done in time to music. 2. A party at which people dance.

dan·cer |dăn′sər| or |dän′sər| —*noun, plural* **dancers** 1. A person who dances. 2. A performer who dances in front of an audience.

dan·de·li·on |dăn′dl ī′ən| —*noun, plural* **dandelions** A common plant with bright yellow flowers and leaves with ragged edges. The leaves are sometimes eaten in salads. The seeds of a dandelion form a fluffy cluster shaped like a ball.

dan·druff |dăn′drəf| —*noun* Small white pieces of dead skin that fall from the scalp.

dan·dy |dăn′dē| —*noun, plural* **dandies** 1. A man who is very proud of his fine clothes and his appearance. 2. Something very good of its kind: *Your new car is a dandy.*

dan·ger |dān′jər| —*noun, plural* **dangers** 1. The chance or threat of something harmful happening: *The jungle is full of danger at night.* 2. The condition of being exposed to harm or loss: *He was in danger of falling from the ledge.* 3. Something that threatens safety: *Fog is a danger to pilots.*

dan·ger·ous |dān′jər əs| —*adjective* 1. Full of threat of harm or injury; risky; hazardous: *The ocean is dangerous in stormy weather.* **2.** Able or likely to cause harm: *Snakes can be dangerous creatures.*

dan·gle | dăng′ gəl | —*verb* **dangled, dangling** To hang loosely and swing and sway: *The key dangled from a chain.*

Dan·ish | dā′ nĭsh | —*adjective* Of Denmark, the Danish people, or their language.
—*noun* The Germanic language of Denmark.

dare | dâr | —*verb* **dared, daring** **1.** To be brave enough to do or try to do something: *She doesn't dare speak up in class. The swimmers dared the powerful waves.* **2.** To have courage or strength for something: *I'd like to help you but I don't dare.* **3.** To challenge: *He dared me to climb over the fence.*
—*noun, plural* **dares** A challenge: *We accepted his dare to jump from the bridge.*

dar·ing | dâr′ ĭng | —*adjective* Willing to take chances; bold; adventurous: *a daring deep-sea diver.*
—*noun* Great courage; bravery: *the daring of the firefighters.*

dark | därk | —*adjective* **darker, darkest** **1.** Without light or with very little light: *a dark tunnel.* **2.** Dim, cloudy, or gray rather than bright: *a dark winter day.* **3.** Of a deep color closer to black or brown than to white: *dark hair; a dark storm cloud.*
—*noun* **1.** Lack of light: *They stepped from the bright lights into the dark outside.* **2.** Night; nightfall: *Be home before dark.*

dark·en | där′ kən | —*verb* **darkened, darkening** To make or become dark or darker: *Rain clouds darkened the afternoon. As the sun sets, the day darkens.*

dark·ness | därk′ nĭs | —*noun, plural* **darknesses** **1.** Lack of light: *They were lost in the darkness without a flashlight.* **2.** Night; nighttime: *Darkness comes quickly after sundown.*

dar·ling | där′ lĭng | —*noun, plural* **darlings** A dearly loved person.
—*adjective* **1.** Loved very much: *my darling children.* **2.** Very charming and attractive; cute: *What darling puppies!*

darn | därn | —*verb* **darned, darning** To mend cloth by making stitches with yarn or thread across a hole: *Let me darn the heel of your sock.*

dart | därt | —*verb* **darted, darting** **1.** To move suddenly and quickly: *A squirrel darted in front of the car.* **2.** To shoot out or send forth with a quick, sudden movement: *The snake darted its tongue at us. They darted furious glances at us.*
—*noun, plural* **darts** **1.** A thin, pointed weapon that looks like a small arrow. Darts are usually thrown by hand. **2.** **darts** (In this sense used with a singular verb.) A game in which darts are thrown at a board or other target. **3.** A quick, sudden movement: *With a dart the chipmunk ran behind a tree.*

dash | dăsh | —*verb* **dashed, dashing** **1.** To rush or race with sudden speed: *They dashed for the house when it began to rain.* **2.** To hit, knock, or throw with great force: *Huge waves dashed against the shore. The storm dashed the boat against the rocks.* **3.** To spoil; ruin: *His injury dashed our hopes of winning the game.*
—*noun, plural* **dashes** **1.** A quick run or rush: *We made a dash for shelter from the rain.* **2.** A short, fast race: *a 100-yard dash.* **3.** A small amount: *a dash of salt.* **4.** A punctuation mark (—) used to set off part of a sentence from the rest or to show a pause or break in a sentence. A dash is also used to show that a word or

daring
Above: Walking on a tightrope high above city streets
Below: Performing a motorcycle feat

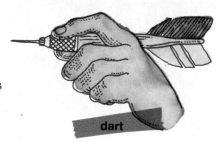

dart

dashboard

letters in a word have been left out.

dash·board | dăsh′bôrd′ | or | dăsh′bōrd′ | —*noun, plural* **dashboards** The panel below the windshield and behind the steering wheel in an automobile. The dashboard has instruments, dials, and controls that show if the automobile is working properly, and how much gasoline, oil, and water are in it.

dash·ing | dăsh′ĭng | —*adjective* **1.** Brave, bold, and daring: *a dashing hero.* **2.** Very handsome or elegant: *The soldiers wore dashing uniforms in the parade.*

da·ta | dā′tə | or | dăt′ə | or | dä′tə | —*plural noun* Facts; information: *The data show the age, height, weight, and past medical history of all patients.*

date¹ | dāt | —*noun, plural* **dates** **1.** The time when something happened or will happen. A date is given by the month, day, and year or any of these: *They set the wedding date for May 15. The date of the meeting was April 20, 1975. You should memorize important dates in history.* **2.** An appointment to meet someone or be somewhere: *He has a date with a girl in your class. You have a date at the dentist's office on Thursday.* **3.** The person with whom one has the appointment: *He asked his date if she would like to dance or have some refreshments.*
—*verb* **dated, dating** **1.** To mark with a date: *He dated his letter March 1, 1978.* **2.** To find out the age, time, or origin of: *The scientists dated the rock by studying the fossils in it. This gun dates from the American Revolution.* **3.** To go out with socially: *She has been dating the same boy all year.*

Idioms **out of date** No longer in use or fashion: *That style of dress is out of date.* **up to date** In use or style now; modern: *All our information is very up to date.*

date² | dāt | —*noun, plural* **dates** The sweet fruit of a kind of palm tree. It has a hard, narrow seed.

daugh·ter | dô′tər | —*noun, plural* **daughters** A female child.

daugh·ter-in-law | dô′tər ĭn lô′ | —*noun, plural* **daughters-in-law** The wife of a person's son.

daw·dle | dô′dəl | —*verb* **dawdled, dawdling** To take more time than is needed; dally: *If you dawdle over breakfast, you'll be late for school.*

dawn | dôn | —*noun, plural* **dawns** **1.** The first light that shows in the morning; daybreak. **2.** The first appearance; beginning: *They found stone tools dating from the dawn of civilization.*
—*verb* **dawned, dawning** To begin to grow light in the morning: *We left the house when day dawned.*

Phrasal verb **dawn on** To become clear to: *It finally dawned on us that he wasn't joking, but was serious.*

day | dā | —*noun, plural* **days** **1.** The time of light between sunrise and sunset. **2.** The period that includes one day and one night. A day has twenty-four hours. **3.** One of the seven divisions of the week: *What day was May 21?* **4.** The part of a day spent in work or other activity: *He works eight hours a day. The school day usually ends at three o'clock in the afternoon.* **5.** A period or time: *The day of the horse and buggy is gone forever. This harpoon goes back to the days of the whaling ships.* **6. days** Life; lifetime: *They lived happily for the rest of their days.*

day·break | dā′brāk′ | —*noun, plural* **daybreaks** The time each morning when light first shows; dawn.

day·light | dā′līt′ | —*noun* **1.** The light of day; direct light of the

date¹, date²
Date¹ comes through French from a Latin verb meaning "to give." Date² also comes through French, from the Latin word meaning "finger" (from the shape of the fruit). The Latin word comes from Greek.

date²
Tree *(left)* and fruit *(right)*

ă	pat	ĕ	pet	î	fierce
ā	pay	ē	be	ŏ	pot
â	care	ĭ	pit	ō	go
ä	father	ī	pie	ô	paw, for

oi	oil	ŭ	cut	zh	vision
ŏŏ	book	û	fur	ə	ago, item,
ōō	boot	*th*	the		pencil, atom,
yōō	abuse	th	thin		circus
ou	out	hw	which	ər	butter

sun: *The garden looks cheerful in the daylight.* **2.** Dawn; daybreak: *The cows have to be milked before daylight.* **3.** Daytime: *We plan to drive home while it is still daylight.*

day·light·sav·ing time |dā′līt′sāv′ĭng| Time during which clocks are set one hour ahead of standard time, used in late spring, summer, and early fall to give extra daylight.

day·time |dā′tīm′| —*noun* The time between dawn and dark; day; daylight.

daze |dāz| —*verb* **dazed, dazing** To confuse or stun; bewilder: *The loud explosion frightened and dazed us.*
—*noun, plural* **dazes** A state of not realizing what is going on around oneself; a confused condition: *He walked around in a daze after being hit by the baseball.*

daz·zle |dăz′əl| —*verb* **dazzled, dazzling** To make nearly blind or blind for a short time with too much bright light: *The sunlight dazzled her, and she covered her eyes..*

de- A prefix that means "to remove": *defrost.*

dea·con |dē′kən| —*noun, plural* **deacons** **1.** An officer of a church who helps the minister. **2.** In some churches, a clergyman ranking below a priest.

dead |dĕd| —*adjective* **deader, deadest** **1.** No longer alive or living: *The gardener removed the dead tree from the yard. They found many deer dead from the cold winter.* **2.** Without life or living things: *We don't know if Mars is a dead planet.* **3.** Without any feeling; numb: *His arm felt dead from pulling on the rope.* **4.** Without any motion; not moving or circulating: *Flies buzzed in the dead summer air.* **5.** No longer used or needed: *Latin is a dead language. You must throw out your dead files.* **6.** No longer working or operating: *Our telephone went dead during the thunderstorm.* **7.** Without activity, interest, or excitement: *The town is dead after 9 p.m.* **8.** Complete; total; absolute: *In the room there was dead silence.* **9.** Sudden; abrupt: *The car came to a dead stop.* **10.** Exact; sure; certain: *The arrow hit the target at dead center.*
—*noun* **1.** Those who have died; dead people: *After the battle the soldiers buried their dead.* **2.** The darkest, coldest, or most quiet part: *The boat sailed in the dead of night.*
—*adverb* **1.** Completely; absolutely: *We are dead tired from working so hard.* **2.** Suddenly; abruptly: *They stopped dead in their tracks.* **3.** Straight; directly: *The center of town lies dead ahead.*

dead·en |dĕd′n| —*verb* **deadened, deadening** To make less strong, loud, or sharp: *The doctor gave him a medicine to deaden the pain. The studio has a special ceiling to deaden sound.*

dead end A street or other passage that is closed off at one end.

dead·line |dĕd′līn′| —*noun, plural* **deadlines** A set time by which something must be done, finished, or settled: *The deadline for your homework assignment is noon on Monday.*

dead·ly |dĕd′lē| —*adjective* **deadlier, deadliest** **1.** Causing or capable of causing death: *Guns are deadly weapons. The berries on that tree are deadly.* **2.** Dangerous or violent enough to kill: *The gangsters had many deadly enemies in that town.*
—*adverb* Completely; absolutely: *deadly serious.*

deaf |dĕf| —*adjective* **deafer, deafest** **1.** Not being able to hear well or to hear at all: *Some deaf people learn to read lips.* **2.** Not willing to listen: *His parents were deaf to his request for a new bike.*

deaf·en |dĕf′ən| —*verb* **deafened, deafening** To make deaf, especially for a short time: *The explosion deafened him.*

debate
Abraham Lincoln speaks in a
debate.

decanter

ă	pat	ě	pet	î	fierce
ā	pay	ē	be	ŏ	pot
â	care	ĭ	pit	ō	go
ä	father	ī	pie	ô	paw, for
oi	oil	ŭ	cut	zh	vision
ōō	book	û	fur	ə	ago, item,
ōō	boot	*th*	the		pencil, atom,
yōō	abuse	th	thin		circus
ou	out	hw	which	ər	butter

deal |dēl| —*verb* **dealt, dealing** **1.** To have to do with; be about: *Astronomy deals with stars and planets.* **2.** To do business; trade: *a store that deals in used furniture.* **3.** To give; strike: *Bill dealt Joe a blow.* **4.** To hand out cards to players in a card game.
　　Phrasal verb **deal with** **1.** To behave toward; treat: *He deals with everyone fairly.* **2.** To take care of; handle or manage: *ready to deal with all emergencies.*
　　—*noun, plural* **deals** An agreement or bargain: *Let's make a deal to trade bicycles for a month.*
　　Idiom **a good** or **great deal** **1.** A considerable amount; a lot: *We learned a good deal in class today.* **2.** Much; considerably: *You look a great deal thinner after dieting.*

dealt |dĕlt| The past tense and past participle of **deal**: *The science class dealt with whales yesterday. We have dealt with this store for many years.*

dear |dîr| —*adjective* **dearer, dearest** **1.** Loved and cherished; beloved: *I miss my dear family. We must take care of those dearest to us.* **2.** Greatly admired or respected: *"My Dear Mr. Mayor," his letter began.* In writing letters we put "Dear" before a person's name as a polite way of beginning to write to that person.
　　—*noun, plural* **dears** A person one likes or is grateful to: *You are a dear for helping me.*
　　—*interjection* A word used to express trouble or surprise: *Oh, dear! Dear me!*
　　♦ *These sound alike* **dear, deer.**

dear·ly |dîr′lē| —*adverb* Very much; greatly: *Jimmy loves his dog dearly.*

death |dĕth| —*noun, plural* **deaths** **1.** The act or fact of dying: *Her mind was clear till the hour of her death.* **2. a.** The end of life: *The lovers remained faithful until death.* **b.** The condition of being dead: *He lay still, pretending death.* **3.** A cause of dying: *Such a fall is certain death.* **4.** The ending or destruction of something: *Wars caused the death of many great ancient empires.*

de·bate |dĭ bāt′| —*noun, plural* **debates** A discussion of the arguments for or against something: *The town held a debate about opening a new school.*
　　—*verb* **debated, debating** **1.** To present or discuss arguments for or against something: *The House of Representatives debated the new tax bill before adopting it.* **2.** To consider carefully before deciding: *We debated having a picnic on the last day of school.*

de·bris |də brē′| or |dā′brē′| —*noun* The scattered pieces or remains of something that has been broken, destroyed, or thrown away; rubble: *The tornado left the streets of the town full of debris.*

debt |dĕt| —*noun, plural* **debts** **1.** Something that is owed to another: *We paid our $200 debt to the bank. The city owes the police force a debt of thanks.* **2.** The condition of owing: *The loss of her job left them in severe debt.*

debt·or |dĕt′ər| —*noun, plural* **debtors** A person who owes something to another.

dec·ade |dĕk′ād′| —*noun, plural* **decades** A period of ten years. When you are ten years old, you have lived one decade.

de·cant·er |dĭ kăn′tər| —*noun, plural* **decanters** An ornamental glass bottle used to hold liquids, especially wine.

de·cay |dĭ kā′| —*verb* **decayed, decaying** To rot or cause to become rotten: *Damp caused the wood to decay. Bacteria decay garbage.*

—*noun, plural* **decays** The slow rotting of animal or plant matter: *Brush your teeth after every meal to prevent tooth decay.*

de·ceased | dĭ sēst′ | —*adjective* No longer living; dead: *Their parents have been deceased for ten years.*
—*noun* **the deceased** A dead person or persons.

de·ceit | dĭ sēt′ | —*noun, plural* **deceits** The act or practice of deceiving: *He was guilty of deceit when he sold them an old television set as a new one.*

de·ceive | dĭ sēv′ | —*verb* **deceived, deceiving** To make a person believe something that is not true; mislead: *He deceived you when he told you he would help and didn't.*

De·cem·ber | dĭ sĕm′bər | —*noun, plural* **Decembers** The 12th and last month of the year. December comes after November and before January. It has 31 days.

de·cent | dē′sənt | —*adjective* According to accepted standards of behavior; proper; respectable: *The language the angry man used was not decent. It is not decent behavior to cheat on your school tests.*

de·cep·tive | dĭ sĕp′tĭv | —*adjective* Trying or meant to deceive; misleading: *The salesmen were guilty of deceptive business practices.*

deci- A prefix that means "one tenth": *deciliter; decimeter.*

de·cide | dĭ sīd′ | —*verb* **decided, deciding** **1.** To make up one's mind: *Have you decided what to do? What decided you to come with us? She decided to become a doctor.* **2.** To judge or settle: *The jury decided in favor of the accused woman.*

de·cid·ed | dĭ sī′dĭd | —*adjective* Definite or certain; sure: *They have a decided preference for tennis over golf.*

dec·i·li·ter | dĕs′ə lē′tər | —*noun, plural* **deciliters** A unit of volume in the metric system equal to 1/10 of a liter.

dec·i·mal | dĕs′ə məl | —*noun, plural* **decimals** **1.** A numeral in the decimal system of numbers. **2.** A numeral based on 10, used in expressing a **decimal fraction.**
—*adjective* Of or based on 10: *The United States has a decimal system of money.*

decimal fraction A fraction in which the denominator is 10 or a power of 10. In the decimal system of numbers, 29/100 would be written .29 and 29/1000 would be written .029.

dec·i·me·ter | dĕs′ə mē′tər | —*noun, plural* **decimeters** A unit of length in the metric system equal to 1/10 of a meter.

de·ci·sion | dĭ sĭzh′ən | —*noun, plural* **decisions** **1.** A final or definite conclusion; a judgment: *The decision of the judges in the contest is final.* **2.** A strong, determined way of thinking or acting: *The president of the company is a man of decision.*

deck | dĕk | —*noun, plural* **decks** **1.** One of the floors dividing a boat or ship into different levels. **2.** A platform that is like a deck of a ship: *There is a sun deck on the roof of the house.* **3.** A set of playing cards.
—*verb* **decked, decking** To decorate or adorn: *We decked the room with paper streamers for the party.*

dec·la·ra·tion | dĕk′lə rā′shən | —*noun, plural* **declarations** A formal statement or announcement: *The governor made a declaration that Friday will be a holiday.*

Declaration of Independence A statement, made on July 4, 1776, declaring the thirteen American colonies independent of Great Britain.

deck

Declaration of Independence
The signing of the Declaration of Independence

decoration
Medals given as honors

decoy

de·clare | dĭ klâr′ | —*verb* **declared, declaring** **1.** To state strongly; stress; affirm: *We declared our aim to help them wherever possible.* **2.** To announce officially or formally: *Congress declared war on the enemy country.*

de·cline | dĭ klīn′ | —*verb* **declined, declining** **1.** To refuse to take, accept, or do: *She politely declined the invitation to the ball. We asked him to help but he declined.* **2.** To become less or weaker; decrease slowly: *School attendance declined because of the bad weather. His health has declined since the accident.*
—*noun, plural* **declines** The process or result of declining; a slow lessening or weakening: *Good crops caused the decline in food prices. The decline in his health caused him to give up his job.*

de·com·pose | dē′kəm pōz′ | —*verb* **decomposed, decomposing** To decay; rot: *The tomatoes decomposed after days in the hot sun.*

dec·o·rate | dĕk′ə rāt′ | —*verb* **decorated, decorating** **1.** To furnish with something attractive or beautiful; adorn: *I will help you decorate the Christmas tree.* **2.** To give a medal to: *The general decorated the corporal for bravery.*

dec·o·ra·tion | dĕk′ə rā′shən | —*noun, plural* **decorations** **1.** The act or process of decorating: *The decoration of the house for the party took a long time.* **2.** Something that decorates: *The hall was hung with cheerful decorations.* **3.** A medal, badge, or ribbon given as an honor: *The general had many battle decorations.*

dec·o·ra·tive | dĕk′ər ə tĭv | or | dĕk′ə rā′tĭv | —*adjective* Helping to make attractive or beautiful; ornamental: *a decorative necklace; decorative rugs.*

dec·o·ra·tor | dĕk′ə rā′tər | —*noun, plural* **decorators** A person who chooses the paint, wallpaper, and furnishings for the inside of a building.

de·coy | dē′koi′ | or | dĭ koi′ | —*noun, plural* **decoys** **1.** A model of a duck or other bird used by hunters to attract wild birds or animals. **2.** A person who leads another person into danger or a trap: *She acted as a decoy for the police to catch the thieves.*
—*verb* | dĭ koi′ | **decoyed, decoying** To lure into danger or a trap: *The thief decoyed us out of the store by yelling "Fire."*

de·crease | dĭ krēs′ | —*verb* **decreased, decreasing** To make or become slowly less or smaller; diminish: *He decreased the amount they spent on food. The company's profits have decreased.*
—*noun* | dē′krēs′ | or | dĭ krēs′ |, *plural* **decreases** The act or process of decreasing; a decline: *We do not know why there is a decrease in the number of eggs the hens are laying.*

de·cree | dĭ krē′ | —*noun, plural* **decrees** An official order; a law: *The king issued a decree that all prisoners were to be released.*
—*verb* **decreed, decreeing** To settle or decide by decree: *The emperor decreed that all war veterans would receive special benefits.*

ded·i·cate | dĕd′ĭ kāt′ | —*verb* **dedicated, dedicating** To set apart for a special use or purpose: *The bishop dedicated the new church.*

ded·i·ca·tion | dĕd′ĭ kā′shən | —*noun, plural* **dedications** The act of dedicating: *The bishop came for the dedication of the old building as the new church.*

de·duct | dĭ dŭkt′ | —*verb* **deducted, deducting** To take away an amount from another; subtract: *They deduct money from his salary every week for health insurance.*

de·duc·tion | dĭ dŭk′shən | —*noun, plural* **deductions** **1.** The act of deducting; subtraction: *The deduction of ten dollars that we spent at the fair leaves us only five dollars.* **2.** An amount deducted:

ă	pat	ĕ	pet	î	fierce
ā	pay	ē	be	ŏ	pot
â	care	ĭ	pit	ō	go
ä	father	ī	pie	ô	paw, for
oi	oil	ŭ	cut	zh	vision
ōō	book	û	fur	ə	ago, item,
ōō	boot	*th*	the		pencil, atom,
yōō	abuse	th	thin		circus
ou	out	hw	which	ər	butter

The sales clerk gave them a deduction of thirty dollars on all their purchases.

deed |dēd| —*noun, plural* **deeds** **1.** An act or thing done; an action: *He tries to do a good deed each day.* **2.** A legal document that shows who owns a special piece of property.
—*verb* **deeded, deeding** To give or transfer property by means of a deed: *My father deeded the house to us.*

deep |dēp| —*adjective* **deeper, deepest** **1.** Going far down from the top or the surface: *a deep hole in the ground. The stream is very deep in the middle.* **2.** Going far in from the front to the back: *a deep closet.* **3.** Far distant down or in: *They walked in the deep woods.* **4.** Extreme, intense, or profound: *a deep sleep; a deep silence.* **5.** Concentrated; absorbed: *He is deep in thought about his new job.* **6.** Hard to understand: *a deep mystery.* **7.** Not pale; dark and rich: *a deep red; the deep blue of the sea.* **8.** Low in pitch: *a deep voice.*
—*adverb* Far down or into: *You must dig deep to find coal.*
—*noun* **the deep** The ocean; sea: *Many strange fish live in the deep.*

deep·en |dē′pən| —*verb* **deepened, deepening** To make or become deep or deeper: *We helped him deepen the hole for the fence post. The water deepened offshore.*

deer |dîr| —*noun, plural* **deer** An animal that can run very fast. Deer have hoofs. Most male deer have antlers. There are many kinds of deer.
♦ *These sound alike* **deer, dear.**

de·face |dĭ fās′| —*verb* **defaced, defacing** To spoil or mar the surface or appearance of: *He defaced a wall with crayon.*

de·feat |dĭ fēt′| —*verb* **defeated, defeating** To win victory over; overcome: *Our team defeated the visitors 10 to 2.*
—*noun, plural* **defeats** **1.** The condition of being defeated: *It is not easy to be gracious in defeat.* **2.** The act of defeating: *We watched the defeat of our baseball team by the visitors.*

de·fect |dē′fĕkt′| or |dĭ fĕkt′| —*noun, plural* **defects** A lack of something that is needed for completion or perfection; a flaw: *The engine has too many defects to run at all.*

de·fec·tive |dĭ fĕk′tĭv| —*adjective* Having a defect or flaw; imperfect: *This radio is defective because a part is missing.*

de·fend |dĭ fĕnd′| —*verb* **defended, defending** **1.** To protect from attack, harm, or challenge; guard: *The boy defended himself by punching back. The football team will defend its title.* **2.** To argue or speak in support of: *A famous lawyer will defend him in his case against the landlord.*

de·fense |dĭ fĕns′| —*noun, plural* **defenses** **1.** The act of defending: *The soldiers are fighting in defense of their country.* **2.** Something that defends: *The citizens put high walls and other defenses around the city.* **3.** A team or part of a team that tries to stop the opposing team from scoring.

de·fen·sive |dĭ fĕn′sĭv| —*adjective* Of or for defense; protecting from attack: *defensive walls; a defensive football player.*

de·fer¹ |dĭ fûr′| —*verb* **deferred, deferring** To put off until a later time; postpone; delay: *The rally has been deferred until Friday.*

de·fer² |dĭ fûr′| —*verb* **deferred, deferring** To give in to the judgment or opinion of another; yield: *She deferred to wiser people on the matter of going on a trip alone.*

de·fi·ance |dĭ fī′əns| —*noun, plural* **defiances** Outright refusal to obey authority: *He raised his fist in a gesture of defiance.*

deer

defer¹, defer²
Defer¹ comes from a Latin word that meant "to carry in various directions" or "to scatter, to separate." The word **differ** comes from the same Latin word. **Defer²** comes from a different Latin verb. At first it meant "to carry away"; later it came to mean "to report to someone, to seek someone else's judgment." Both **defer¹** and **defer²** traveled through French before arriving in English.

de·fi·cien·cy |dǐ fǐsh′ ən sē| —*noun, plural* **deficiencies** **1.** A lack of something that is needed or important: *He is feeling sick from a vitamin deficiency.* **2.** The amount lacking; shortage: *There is a deficiency of twenty dollars in the club funds.*

de·fi·cient |dǐ fǐsh′ ənt| —*adjective* Lacking something needed or important: *The doctor told him that his diet is deficient in vitamins.*

de·fine |dǐ fīn′| —*verb* **defined, defining** **1.** To give or tell the exact meaning or meanings of: *Your dictionary defines words so you can use them correctly in writing and speaking.* **2.** To describe or tell exactly; make clear: *These instructions define the duties you must fulfill.* **3.** To mark or fix the limits of: *The hedge defines our property from our neighbors'.*

def·i·nite |děf′ ə nǐt| —*adjective* Known with certainty; beyond doubt; exact; clear: *a definite time and place to meet.*

definite article The word **the**, used to introduce a noun or noun phrase: *The rain has stopped. The large dog barked at the boy.* The word **the** belongs to a class of words called **determiners.** They signal that a noun is coming.

def·i·ni·tion |děf′ ə nǐsh′ ən| —*noun, plural* **definitions** An explanation of the exact meaning or meanings of a word or phrase: *Look up the definition of "get" in this dictionary.*

de·form |dǐ fôrm′| —*verb* **deformed, deforming** To spoil the appearance of; make ugly: *Heavy snows and ice deformed the young tree. Anger deformed his face.*

de·frost |dē frôst′| or |dē frŏst′| —*verb* **defrosted, defrosting** To make or become free of ice or frost; thaw: *He had to defrost the windshield of the car after the blizzard. This refrigerator defrosts automatically.*

deft |děft| —*adjective* **defter, deftest** Quick and skillful: *She knitted with deft movements of her fingers.*

de·fy |dǐ fī′| —*verb* **defied, defying, defies** To go against openly; challenge boldly: *Outlaws defy the laws of the land.*

de·grade |dǐ grād′| —*verb* **degraded, degrading** To lower in rank, standing, or character; bring shame or disgrace upon: *Your bad behavior degrades the whole class.*

de·gree |dǐ grē′| —*noun, plural* **degrees** **1.** One of a series of steps in a process or course of action: *They learned the hard lessons slowly and by degrees.* **2.** Relative amount or extent: *There are various degrees of reading ability in a class.* **3.** A title given by a college or university to a person who finishes a course of study. **4.** One of the equal units into which a temperature scale is divided: *Water boils at 212 degrees (212°) Fahrenheit or 100 degrees (100°) Celsius.* **5.** A unit for measuring arcs of a circle or angles: *A square has four angles of 90 degrees (90°).*

de·i·ty |dē′ ǐ tē| —*noun, plural* **deities** A god or goddess.

de·ject·ed |dǐ jěk′ tǐd| —*adjective* Sad or depressed: *He felt dejected at the low grade he received on the test.*

Del·a·ware |děl′ ə wâr′| A state in the eastern United States. The capital of Delaware is Dover.

de·lay |dǐ lā′| —*verb* **delayed, delaying** **1.** To put off until a later time; postpone: *We will have to delay dinner an hour.* **2.** To cause to be late: *Heavy rain delayed the start of the game.* —*noun, plural* **delays** **1.** The act of delaying or the condition of being delayed: *Your grocery order will be filled without delay.* **2.** A period of time during which someone or something is delayed: *There will be a delay of two weeks in filling your order.*

Delaware

Delaware comes from the name of Virginia's first governor, Lord De La Warr. Delaware Bay, an inlet of the Atlantic Ocean between Delaware and New Jersey, was named for Lord De La Warr; the state was named after the bay.

ă	pat	ě	pet	î	fierce
ā	pay	ē	be	ŏ	pot
â	care	ĭ	pit	ō	go
ä	father	ī	pie	ô	paw, for
oi	oil	ŭ	cut	zh	vision
ōō	book	û	fur	ə	ago, item,
ōō	boot	th	the		pencil, atom,
yōō	abuse	th	thin		circus
ou	out	hw	which	ər	butter

del·e·gate |dĕl′ə gāt′| or |dĕl′ə gĭt| —*noun, plural* **delegates** A person chosen to speak and act for another person or for a group; a representative: *Three members of the class were named as delegates to the school convention.*

—*verb* |dĕl′ə gāt′| **delegated, delegating 1.** To choose a person as a delegate: *The class delegated him to think up ideas for the party.* **2.** To give over to someone else to do: *A leader must know what jobs he can delegate to others.*

de·lib·er·ate |dĭ lĭb′ər ĭt| —*adjective* **1.** Done or said on purpose: *He told a deliberate lie.* **2.** Not hurried or quick; careful; cautious: *She is a very deliberate person who always plans ahead.*

—*verb* |dĭ lĭb′ə rāt′| **deliberated, deliberating 1.** To give a lot of careful thought to something before deciding what to do or say: *He deliberated whether or not to spend his money on a new car.* **2.** To discuss carefully: *The committee deliberated the problem for two days. The Senate deliberated throughout the night.*

del·i·ca·cy |dĕl′ĭ kə sē| —*noun, plural* **delicacies 1.** The condition or quality of being delicate: *Her lace handkerchiefs are of the greatest delicacy.* **2.** A very special food: *Certain kinds of fish eggs are thought to be a delicacy by some people.*

del·i·cate |dĕl′ĭ kĭt| —*adjective* **1.** Very finely made: *delicate lace; a delicate spider web.* **2.** Pleasing to the senses; very subtle: *This food has a delicate flavor. Mary wears a very delicate perfume.* **3.** Having a soft, pale tint: *The roses are of a very delicate pink.* **4.** Requiring or needing great skill: *a delicate secret mission; delicate eye surgery.* **5.** Easily spoiled or broken; fragile: *delicate crystal goblets.* **6.** Very sensitive: *There are delicate instruments for recording heartbeats.*

del·i·ca·tes·sen |dĕl′ĭ kə tĕs′ən| —*noun, plural* **delicatessens** A store that sells foods that are ready to eat. Cheeses, salads, smoked meats, sandwiches, and pastries are sold in a delicatessen.

de·li·cious |dĭ lĭsh′əs| —*adjective* Very pleasing to the taste and smell: *My brother bakes delicious cookies.*

de·light |dĭ līt′| —*noun, plural* **delights 1.** Great pleasure; joy: *He smiled with delight at the news.* **2.** Someone or something that gives great pleasure or enjoyment: *She is a delight to have around. The summer day was a delight.*

—*verb* **delighted, delighting** To please greatly: *The music delighted the audience.*

de·light·ful |dĭ līt′fəl| —*adjective* Giving delight; very pleasing: *We had a delightful time at the party.*

de·lir·i·ous |dĭ lîr′ē əs| —*adjective* **1.** Out of one's senses; raving: *The high fever made the patient delirious.* **2.** Wildly excited: *She was delirious with joy when she won the race.*

de·liv·er |dĭ lĭv′ər| —*verb* **delivered, delivering 1.** To carry and give out; distribute: *The mailman delivers mail to our house every day.* **2.** To send against; throw: *He delivered a punch to his opponent.* **3.** To give or utter: *He delivered a speech.*

de·liv·er·y |dĭ lĭv′ə rē| —*noun, plural* **deliveries 1.** The act of delivering: *It was hard to wait for the delivery of the new piano.* **2.** A manner of speaking or singing: *It is important for an actor to have a good delivery.*

del·phin·i·um |dĕl fĭn′ē əm| —*noun, plural* **delphiniums** A tall garden plant with long clusters of flowers. The flowers are usually blue, but are sometimes white or pink.

del·ta |dĕl′tə| —*noun, plural* **deltas** A mass of sand, mud, and

delphinium

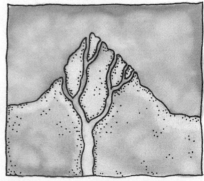

delta

Democratic Party
Above: Symbol of the party
Below: Badges from a Democratic convention

demonstration
A demonstration in Washington, D.C.

ă	pat	ĕ	pet	î	fierce
ā	pay	ē	be	ŏ	pot
â	care	ĭ	pit	ō	go
ä	father	ī	pie	ô	paw, for
oi	oil	ŭ	cut	zh	vision
ōō	book	û	fur	ə	ago, item,
ōō	boot	*th*	the		pencil, atom,
yōō	abuse	th	thin		circus
ou	out	hw	which	ər	butter

soil that settles at the mouth of a river. A delta is often shaped like a triangle.

de·mand | dĭ mănd′ | or | dĭ mänd′ | —*verb* **demanded, demanding** **1.** To ask for very strongly: *The workers demanded better working conditions.* **2.** To need or require: *This leaking roof demands attention right away.*
—*noun, plural* **demands** **1.** A very strong request: *a demand for an answer.* **2.** Something that is needed or required: *His job makes many demands on his time.* **3.** The condition of being needed or wanted very much: *Doctors are always in great demand.*

de·moc·ra·cy | dĭ mŏk′rə sē | —*noun, plural* **democracies** **1.** A form of government in which the power belongs to the people, who express what they want through representatives they have elected. **2.** A country with this kind of government. The United States of America is a democracy.

dem·o·crat | dĕm′ə krăt′ | —*noun, plural* **democrats** **1.** A person who believes in and supports democracy. **2.** **Democrat** A person who is a member of the Democratic Party.

dem·o·crat·ic | dĕm′ə krăt′ | —*adjective* **1.** Of, like, or for a democracy: *a democratic government.* **2.** Based on the idea of equal rights for all: *The Bill of Rights is a strong democratic statement.* **3.** **Democratic** Of the Democratic Party.

Democratic Party One of the two main political parties of the United States.

de·mol·ish | dĭ mŏl′ĭsh | —*verb* **demolished, demolishing** To tear down completely; wreck: *Many buildings were demolished by the explosion.*

de·mon | dē′mən | —*noun, plural* **demons** **1.** An evil spirit; devil. **2.** A person with great energy or enthusiasm: *He is a demon for hard work.*

dem·on·strate | dĕm′ən strāt′ | —*verb* **demonstrated, demonstrating** **1.** To show clearly; leave no doubt about; prove: *She demonstrated her ability to play the flute well.* **2.** To show, operate, or explain: *He demonstrated the speeds of the new washing machine.* **3.** To take part in a demonstration: *The students demonstrated against the new highway near the campus.*

dem·on·stra·tion | dĕm′ən strā′shən | —*noun, plural* **demonstrations** The act or process of demonstrating: *The teacher gave a demonstration of the law of gravity. The salesman gave us a demonstration of a new car. The students joined in a demonstration against the war.*

den | dĕn | —*noun, plural* **dens** **1.** The home or shelter of a wild animal; a lair. **2.** A small room set apart for study or relaxing. **3.** A unit of about eight Cub Scouts.

de·ni·al | dĭ nī′əl | —*noun, plural* **denials** The act of denying: *She was very insistent in her denial of the charges against her.*

den·im | dĕn′ĭm | —*noun, plural* **denims** **1.** A heavy cotton cloth used for work clothes and sport clothes. **2.** **denims** Overalls or trousers made of denim.

Den·mark | dĕn′märk′ | A country in Europe that extends north from Germany.

de·nom·i·na·tion | dĭ nŏm′ə nā′shən | —*noun, plural* **denominations** **1.** An organized religious group. The Protestants formed many different denominations. **2.** A unit in a system of money. A dollar and a nickel are denominations of the U.S. money.

de·nom·in·a·tor | dĭ **nŏm′**ə nā′tər | —*noun, plural* **denominators**
The number written below or to the right of the line in a
fraction. In the fraction ½, 2 is the denominator.

de·note | dĭ **nōt′** | —*verb* **denoted, denoting** **1.** To mean exactly;
signify: *The prefix "non-" denotes "not."* **2.** To be a sign of;
indicate: *The blue areas on the map denote water.*

de·nounce | dĭ **nouns′** | —*verb* **denounced, denouncing** To show
or express very strong lack of approval of; accuse in public: *The
press denounced the poor condition of the schools.*

dense | dĕns | —*adjective* **denser, densest** Packed closely
together; thick: *a dense fog.*

den·si·ty | **dĕn′**sĭ tē | —*noun, plural* **densities** The condition of
being thick or close together: *Molasses has a higher density than
water.*

dent | dĕnt | —*noun, plural* **dents** A hollow place in a surface,
usually caused by a blow or pressure: *After the accident our car
was full of dents.*
—*verb* **dented, denting** To make a dent in or get dents: *The other
car dented one of our fenders. Some metals dent easily.*

den·tal | **dĕn′**tl | —*adjective* **1.** Of or for the teeth: *a dental drill; a
dental cleaning powder.* **2.** Having to do with the work of a
dentist: *a dental clinic.*

den·tine | **dĕn′**tēn′ | —*noun* The hard part of a tooth
underneath the outer enamel.

den·tist | **dĕn′**tĭst | —*noun, plural* **dentists** A doctor who treats
people's teeth. A dentist cleans teeth, pulls teeth when necessary,
fills cavities, and does all kinds of work related to the teeth and
mouth tissues.

Den·ver | **dĕn′**vər | The capital of Colorado.

de·ny | dĭ **nī′** | —*verb* **denied, denying, denies** **1.** To say that
something is not true; contradict: *He denied the accusation of
lying.* **2.** To refuse to give; turn down: *Congress denied aid to the
other country. She denied the request.*

de·part | dĭ **pärt′** | —*verb* **departed, departing** **1.** To go away;
leave: *Your train departs at noon.* **2.** To change from the usual
course or way; vary: *The teacher departed from the lesson plan and
announced a surprise test.*

de·part·ment | dĭ **pärt′**mənt | —*noun, plural* **departments** A
separate division of an organization that has a special purpose or
function: *the music department of a school.*

department store A large store that sells many kinds of goods.

de·par·ture | dĭ **pär′**chər | —*noun, plural* **departures** The act of
departing: *The train's departure will be at 2 p.m. The coach's
departure from the usual maneuvers confused the players.*

de·pend | dĭ **pĕnd′** | —*verb* **depended, depending** **1.** To be
decided or determined: *Your reward depends on how much work
you get done.* **2.** To be certain about; trust: *Can I depend on you
not to tell the secret?* **3.** To rely on: *Farmers must depend on rainfall
for healthy crops.*

de·pend·a·ble | dĭ **pĕn′**də bəl | —*adjective* Able to be depended
upon; reliable: *a dependable friend; a dependable car.*

de·pend·ence | dĭ **pĕn′**dəns | —*noun* The condition of being
dependent: *A farmer knows the dependence of crops upon rainfall.*

de·pend·ent | dĭ **pĕn′**dənt | —*adjective* **1.** Relying on someone
or something else: *The success of this project is dependent on the
help of all students.* **2.** Needing the help of someone or something

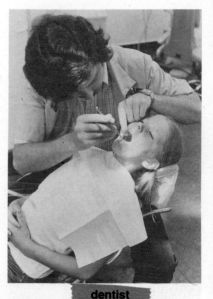

dentist

department store

else: *Plants are dependent on the sun for their growth.*
—*noun, plural* dependents A person who depends on another for support.

de·pict | dĭ pĭkt′ | —*verb* **depicted, depicting** To show in words, drawings, or by other ways; describe: *This book depicts life in ancient Rome. This painting depicts life in the country.*

de·pos·it | dĭ pŏz′ĭt | —*verb* **deposited, depositing** **1.** To put down; lay down: *She deposited the package on the chair.* **2.** To place money in a bank.
—*noun, plural* deposits **1.** An amount of money in a bank or ready to be put in a bank. **2.** An amount of money given as part of a full payment: *We left a deposit of ten dollars so they wouldn't sell the radio to anyone else.* **3.** A mass of material that builds up by a natural process: *The river left a deposit of mud on the fields.*

de·pot | dē′pō | —*noun, plural* **depots** A railroad or bus station.

de·press | dĭ prĕs′ | —*verb* **depressed, depressing** To make gloomy or sad: *News of the accident depressed everyone.*

de·pres·sion | dĭ prĕsh′ən | —*noun, plural* **depressions** **1.** An unhappy state of mind: *The loss of the dog caused her depression.* **2.** An area that is lower than its surroundings; a hollow: *a depression in the lawn.* **3.** A period when business is bad and many people are out of work.

de·prive | dĭ prīv′ | —*verb* **deprived, depriving** To take something away from; keep or prevent from having or doing: *The law deprived the people of their right to travel.*

depth | dĕpth | —*noun, plural* **depths** **1.** The distance from top to bottom or front to back of something: *the depth of a wall; the depth of a shelf.* **2.** Deep learning, thought, or feeling: *a man of great depth. She wrote a novel of great depth.*

dep·u·ty | dĕp′yə tē | —*noun, plural* **deputies** A person appointed to assist or act in the place of another: *The sheriff has three deputies.*

de·rive | dĭ rīv′ | —*verb* **derived, deriving** To get or receive from a source: *I derive great pleasure from music.*

der·rick | dĕr′ĭk | —*noun, plural* **derricks** **1.** A large machine for lifting and moving heavy objects. It consists of a long, movable arm with pulleys and cables that is connected to the base of an upright beam that doesn't move. **2.** A tall framework used to support the equipment used to drill an oil well.

de·scend | dĭ sĕnd′ | —*verb* **descended, descending** **1.** To move from a higher to a lower place or position; go or come down: *She descended the stairs. The airplane descended quickly.* **2.** To come down or along from a source or origin: *The ruler is descended from a long line of kings.*

de·scen·dant | dĭ sĕn′dənt | —*noun, plural* **descendants** A person or animal that comes from a certain ancestor or ancestors: *She is a descendant of German and Dutch immigrants.*

de·scent | dĭ sĕnt′ | —*noun, plural* **descents** **1.** The act of descending: *The airplane made a rapid descent.* **2.** A downward slope: *The hill has a sharp descent that is good for skiing.* **3.** Family origin: *Their family is of French descent.*
♦ *These sound alike* **descent, dissent.**

de·scribe | dĭ skrīb′ | —*verb* **described, describing** To give an account of in words: *Describe the highlights of your summer vacation for us. The book describes city life.*

de·scrip·tion | dĭ skrĭp′shən | —*noun, plural* **descriptions**

depot

derrick
Drilling for oil in the ocean

ă	pat	ĕ	pet	î	fierce
ā	pay	ē	be	ŏ	pot
â	care	ĭ	pit	ō	go
ä	father	ī	pie	ô	paw, for

oi	oil	ŭ	cut	zh	vision
ōo	book	û	fur	ə	ago, item,
ōo	boot	*th*	the		pencil, atom,
yōo	abuse	th	thin		circus
ou	out	hw	which	ər	butter

1. The act or process of describing: *That writer is not good at description.* **2.** An account in words describing something: *a good description of play.* **3.** A kind or variety; sort: *People of every description come to the fair.*

de·scrip·tive |dĭ skrĭp′tĭv| —*adjective* Giving a description; describing: *a descriptive booklet about sailing.*

de·seg·re·gate |dē sĕg′rĭ gāt′| —*verb* **desegregated, desegregating** To put an end to the forced separation of races in public schools and other facilities.

des·ert[1] |dĕz′ərt| —*noun, plural* **deserts** A dry region usually covered with sand. A desert has few or no plants.
—*adjective* Without people: *a desert island.*

de·sert[2] |dĭ zûrt′| —*verb* **deserted, deserting** To leave or abandon: *The soldier deserted his battalion. The players deserted the team.*

♦ *These sound alike* **desert, dessert.**

de·serve |dĭ zûrv′| —*verb* **deserved, deserving** To be worthy of; have a right to; merit: *They deserve all the honors given to them.*

de·sign |dĭ zīn′| —*verb* **designed, designing** **1.** To prepare a plan for something, especially by sketching or drawing: *The architect designs buildings. I like to design my own dresses.* **2.** To plan or intend for a special purpose: *Parks are designed for the enjoyment of the people.*
—*noun, plural* **designs** **1.** A drawing or sketch showing how something is to be made: *the design for a new library.* **2.** An arrangement of lines, figures, or objects into a pattern: *This wallpaper has pretty designs in blue and green.*

des·ig·nate |dĕz′ĭg nāt′| —*verb* **designated, designating** **1.** To point out; show: *A sign designates where to park your car.* **2.** To call by a name or title: *Our period of history is often designated the Space Age.* **3.** To choose; appoint: *We designated Mr. Jones to represent us at the meeting.*

de·sir·a·ble |dĭ zīr′ə bəl| —*adjective* Of such quality as to be wanted; worth having; pleasing: *a desirable spot for camping.*

de·sire |dĭ zīr′| —*verb* **desired, desiring** To wish or long for; want: *For your birthday, you may have anything your heart desires.*
—*noun, plural* **desires** A wish or longing: *She has a desire for chocolate.*

desk |dĕsk| —*noun, plural* **desks** A piece of furniture with a flat top used for writing or reading. A desk usually has drawers for papers, pencils, and other things.

Des Moines |də moin′| or |də moinz′| The capital of Iowa.

des·o·late |dĕs′ə lĭt| —*adjective* **1.** Without people; empty; deserted: *a desolate beach.* **2.** In bad condition; ruined: *a desolate castle.* **3.** Lonely and sad; miserable: *an orphan with a desolate expression.*

des·pair |dĭ spâr′| —*noun, plural* **despairs** Lack of all hope: *They gave up in despair of ever winning the game.*
—*verb* **despaired, despairing** To lose all hope: *I despaired of ever finding my wristwatch again.*

des·per·ate |dĕs′pər ĭt| —*adjective* **1.** Being in a situation without hope and ready to do anything: *The desperate criminal was cornered by the police.* **2.** Needing something or someone urgently: *desperate for food and water.* **3.** Almost beyond hope; very bad: *The survivors of the crash were in a desperate position stranded on a desert island.*

desert[1], desert[2]
Desert[1] and **desert[2]** are relatives. **Desert[1]** comes from an old French word that came from a Latin word meaning "wasteland." That was related to the verb meaning "to abandon," from which **desert[2]** comes. **Desert[2]** also traveled through French before arriving in English.

desert[1]

desk

des·per·a·tion |dĕs′pə rā′shən| —*noun, plural* **desperations** A reckless feeling that comes from needing something very badly or from losing all hope: *Desperation made the poor man rob the bank.*

de·spise |dĭ spīz′| —*verb* **despised, despising** To look down on with scorn; hate: *We despise people who try to cheat the poor.*

de·spite |dĭ spīt′| —*preposition* In spite of: *We went sailing despite the strong winds.*

des·sert |dĭ zûrt′| —*noun, plural* **desserts** The last part of a lunch or dinner. Ice cream and fruit are desserts.
♦ *These sound alike* **dessert, desert²**.

des·ti·na·tion |dĕs′tə nā′shən| —*noun, plural* **destinations** The place to which someone is going or something is sent.

des·tine |dĕs′tĭn| —*verb* **destined, destining** To determine or establish ahead of time: *He was destined as a small child to become a great singer.*

des·ti·ny |dĕs′tə nē| —*noun, plural* **destinies** The fate or fortune of a person or thing. Destiny is thought of as decided or determined ahead of time.

de·stroy |dĭ stroi′| —*verb* **destroyed, destroying 1.** To ruin completely; wipe out: *The fire destroyed the whole village.* **2.** To put to death; kill: *A mad dog has to be destroyed.*

de·stroy·er |dĭ stroi′ər| —*noun, plural* **destroyers** A fast warship that carries guns, torpedoes, and other weapons.

de·struc·tion |dĭ strŭk′shən| —*noun* **1.** The act of destroying: *The gang was accused of the destruction of the school garden.* **2.** Heavy or serious harm: *The tornado created widespread destruction in the town.*

de·struc·tive |dĭ strŭk′tĭv| —*adjective* Causing destruction: *destructive people; a destructive hurricane.*

de·tach |dĭ tăch′| —*verb* **detached, detaching** To separate or disconnect: *You must detach the cord from the wall outlet before repairing the lamp.*

de·tached |dĭ tăcht′| —*adjective* **1.** Standing apart; not attached; separated: *The pieces of the puzzle are detached when you first open the package.* **2.** Free from strong feeling or emotion: *Her father had a detached view of the regulations.*

de·tail |dĭ tāl′| or |dē′tāl′| —*noun, plural* **details 1.** A small or less important part or item: *Don't concern yourself with details.* **2.** Such items in relation to something larger: *A small map usually has less detail than a large map.* **3.** A small group of soldiers or sailors given a special duty or mission.
—*verb* |dĭ tāl′| **detailed, detailing** To tell or relate very precisely: *The teacher detailed exactly how the work was to be done.*

de·tain |dĭ tān′| —*verb* **detained, detaining 1.** To make late; delay: *The thunderstorms detained our plane from landing on time.* **2.** To keep in custody; confine: *The police detained the burglar for questioning.*

de·tect |dĭ tĕkt′| —*verb* **detected, detecting** To notice or find the presence of: *I detected anger in his voice. This device can detect the presence of harmful gases in the air.*

de·tec·tive |dĭ tĕk′tĭv| —*noun, plural* **detectives** A person, usually a police officer, whose work is getting information about crimes and trying to solve them.

de·ter |dĭ tûr′| —*verb* **deterred, deterring** To prevent from doing something; discourage: *Fear deterred them from going into the cave.*

de·ter·gent |dĭ tûr′jənt| —*noun, plural* **detergents** A cleaning

destroyer

destruction
A city bombed during World War II

ă	pat	ĕ	pet	î	fierce
ā	pay	ē	be	ŏ	pot
â	care	ĭ	pit	ō	go
ä	father	ī	pie	ô	paw, for
oi	oil	ŭ	cut	zh	vision
o͞o	book	û	fur	ə	ago, item,
o͞o	boot	*th*	the		pencil, atom,
yo͞o	abuse	th	thin		circus
ou	out	hw	which	ər	butter

powder or liquid used instead of soap. Detergents are used especially for cleaning oily, greasy, or very dirty surfaces or materials.

de·te·ri·o·rate |dǐ tîr′ē ə rāt′| —*verb* **deteriorated, deteriorating** To make or become worse: *Moisture deteriorates powder. The railroads deteriorated as air travel grew.*

de·ter·mi·na·tion |dǐ tûr′mə nā′shən| —*noun, plural* **determinations** **1.** The act of coming to a decision: *The determination of a name for their club took hours.* **2.** A strong and firm purpose: *Our team has a real determination to win the final game.*

de·ter·mine |dǐ tûr′mǐn| —*verb* **determined, determining** **1.** To decide or settle: *On the test you must determine if the figures are circles, squares, or rectangles.* **2.** To be the cause of; influence: *Your ability to work determines your chances of getting ahead.* **3.** To find out; establish: *The voting in an election determines how the citizens really feel.*

de·ter·min·er |dǐ tûr′mə nər| —*noun, plural* **determiners** A word that belongs to a special class of noun modifiers. This class includes articles and certain pronouns and adjectives. A determiner signals that a noun is coming. Some of the determiners are: *a, an, the, my, his, our, this, that, each, every, several, first, second, hundred,* and *some.*

de·test |dǐ tĕst′| —*verb* **detested, detesting** To dislike strongly; hate; loathe: *I detest having to get up early on Monday mornings.*

de·tour |dē′tŏŏr′| or |dǐ tŏŏr′| —*noun, plural* **detours** A road or path used while the main one is out of use or being repaired. A detour is often longer and not as convenient as the regular way. —*verb* **detoured, detouring** To take or cause to take a detour: *We detoured around the accident. The police detoured the truck.*

de·tract |dǐ trăkt′| —*verb* **detracted, detracting** To take away the value or pleasing nature of: *Dirty hands detract from an otherwise good appearance.*

dev·as·tate |dĕv′ə stāt′| —*verb* **devastated, devastating** To destroy completely; ruin: *Fires and storms devastated the county.*

de·vel·op |dǐ vĕl′əp| —*verb* **developed, developing** **1.** To grow or cause to grow: *Nations develop in many different ways. Water and sunlight help to develop plants.* **2.** To bring into being; help grow: *You should try to develop good reading habits.* **3.** To treat a photographic plate, film, or print with chemicals so that the picture can be seen.

de·vel·op·ment |dǐ vĕl′əp mənt| —*noun, plural* **developments** **1.** The act or process of developing: *The development of this area into a park will take a year.* **2.** An event or happening: *Because of new developments our plans had to be changed.* **3.** A group of buildings or houses built in a similar manner, usually by the same person.

de·vi·ate |dē′vē āt′| —*verb* **deviated, deviating** To differ from the usual way of doing something: *You must not deviate from the rules of the game.*

de·vice |dǐ vīs′| —*noun, plural* **devices** **1.** Something that is made or used for a special purpose, especially a machine that does one or more jobs: *This new device can chop vegetables in seconds.* **2.** A plan, scheme, or trick: *His tears were just a device to make us feel sorry for him.*

dev·il |dĕv′əl| —*noun, plural* **devils** **1.** Often **Devil** The ruler of

development
Housing development

Hell. The devil is often shown as someone with horns, a tail, and hoofs. **2.** A person who is wicked or has a bad temper.

de·vise | dĭ vīz′ | —*verb* **devised, devising** To form or arrange in the mind; plan; invent: *They devised a way to get down the cliff.*

de·vote | dĭ vōt′ | —*verb* **devoted, devoting** To give one's time, attention, or effort to someone or some purpose: *She devoted her life to the ballet. He devoted himself to bringing up his family.*

de·vo·tion | dĭ vō′shən | —*noun, plural* **devotions** Loyal feeling; loyalty: *The parents' life was one of devotion to their children.*

de·vour | dĭ vour′ | —*verb* **devoured, devouring** To swallow or eat up eagerly: *The hungry campers devoured the food in no time.*

de·vout | dĭ vout′ | —*adjective* **1.** Deeply religious: *a devout man.* **2.** Sincere; earnest: *devout wishes for success.*

dew | dōō | or | dyōō | —*noun, plural* **dews** Small drops of water that form from the air and collect on a surface, usually during the night: *As the sun came up, dew sparkled on the grass and flowers.*
♦ *These sound alike* **dew, do, due.**

dew·lap | dōō′lăp′ | or | dyōō′lăp′ | —*noun, plural* **dewlaps** A loose fold of skin hanging from the neck of an animal. Some dogs and cattle have dewlaps.

di·a·crit·i·cal mark | dī′ə krĭt′ĭ kəl | Any of different marks added to a letter or letters, used to show a certain kind of pronunciation. The long mark over the *i* in the pronunciation of **bite** | bīt | is a diacritical mark.

di·ag·no·ses | dī′əg nō′sēz′ | The plural of the noun **diagnosis.**

di·ag·no·sis | dī′əg nō′sĭs | —*noun, plural* **diagnoses** The act or process of examining persons, animals, or things carefully to find out what is wrong with them.

di·ag·o·nal | dī ăg′ə nəl | —*adjective* Slanting downward from one corner or side to another.
—*noun, plural* **diagonals** A diagonal line.

di·a·gram | dī′ə grăm′ | —*noun, plural* **diagrams** A drawing or sketch that shows how something works: *Here is the diagram that will help us put this toy together quickly.*
—*verb* **diagrammed, diagramming** To draw or show by a diagram.

di·al | dī′əl | —*noun, plural* **dials** **1.** A round part on the face of an instrument that is marked with numbers or figures. It has pointers that move and show the measurements to be read or chosen. Clocks and telephones have dials. **2.** A device that points to the station where a radio or television set is tuned.
—*verb* **dialed, dialing** To control or choose by means of a dial: *I dialed the wrong number the first time I tried to phone you.*

di·a·lect | dī′ə lĕkt′ | —*noun, plural* **dialects** A way of speaking a language in different places or parts of a country. Dialects usually differ in the pronunciation of certain words and in how certain words are used or chosen.

di·a·logue | dī′ə lôg′ | or | dī′ə lŏg′ | —*noun, plural* **dialogues** **1.** A conversation between two or more people. **2.** The words spoken by the characters in a play or story.

dial tone A sound in a telephone receiver that goes on without a break when the receiver is lifted. The dial tone tells that a call can be dialed.

di·am·e·ter | dī ăm′ĭ tər | —*noun, plural* **diameters** The part of a straight line that goes through the center of a circle or other round object from one side to the other.

di·a·mond | dī′mənd | or | dī′ə mənd | —*noun, plural* **diamonds**

dial

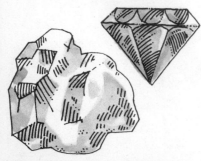

diamond
Above: In rock form *(left)* and as a cut stone *(right)*
Below: Baseball diamond

ă	pat	ĕ	pet	î	fierce
ā	pay	ē	be	ŏ	pot
â	care	ĭ	pit	ō	go
ä	father	ī	pie	ô	paw, for
oi	oil	ŭ	cut	zh	vision
ōō	book	û	fur	ə	ago, item,
ōō	boot	*th*	the		pencil, atom,
yōō	abuse	th	thin		circus
ou	out	hw	which	ər	butter

1. A mineral that is a crystal form of carbon. Diamond is the hardest of all known substances. Diamonds are used for cutting and grinding in industry. They are polished, cut, and used as jewels. **2.a.** A red figure (♦) that is formed with four equal sides, found on a playing card. **b.** A playing card marked with this figure. **c. diamonds** The suit of cards marked with this figure. **3.** In baseball, the infield.

di·amond·back |dī′mənd băk′| or |dī′ə mənd băk′| —*noun, plural* **diamondbacks 1.** A large rattlesnake of the southern United States. It has markings shaped like diamonds on its back. **2.** A turtle of the eastern coast of the United States.

di·a·per |dī′ə pər| or |dī′pər| —*noun, plural* **diapers** A soft cloth or other material that is folded and fastened around a baby to serve as underpants.

di·a·phragm |dī′ə frăm′| —*noun, plural* **diaphragms 1.** A wall of muscle that separates the organs of the chest from the organs of the abdomen. The diaphragm is used in breathing and acts in forcing air into and out of the lungs. **2.** A thin disk, as in a microphone or telephone that changes electric signals into sound.

di·a·ry |dī′ə rē| —*noun, plural* **diaries 1.** A record written each day of a person's own experiences and thoughts: *I kept a diary when I spent the year in England.* **2.** A book with blank pages for keeping such a record.

dice |dīs| —*plural noun* Small cubes marked on each side with from one to six dots. Dice are used in different games by being tossed onto a flat surface.
—*verb* **diced, dicing** To cut into small cubes: *We diced celery and cucumber for a salad.*

dic·tate |dĭk′tāt′| or |dĭk tāt′| —*verb* **dictated, dictating 1.** To say or read aloud so that another person can write down or a machine can record what is said: *The principal dictated letters to the school secretary. He usually dictates after he opens the mail.* **2.** To order with authority: *The coach dictated the rules to be followed in the game.*
—*noun, plural* **dictates** An order, command, or direction: *The people should follow the dictates of the government.*

dic·ta·tor |dĭk′tā′tər| or |dĭk tā′tər| —*noun, plural* **dictators** A ruler who has complete power over the government of a country.

dic·tion·ar·y |dĭk′shə nĕr′ē| —*noun, plural* **dictionaries** A book in which the words of a language are arranged in alphabetical order, with information given about each word. A dictionary includes the spelling, the pronunciation, the meaning or meanings, and the history of a word.

did |dĭd| The past tense of the verb **do:** *I did a lot of work yesterday.*

did·n't |dĭd′nt| A contraction of "did not."

die¹ |dī| —*verb* **died, dying 1.** To stop living; become dead: *Our cat died of old age.* **2.** To become weak: *The wind died away and the sun came out. The noise died down.* **3.** To want very much: *The audience is dying to hear you play.*
♦ *These sound alike* **die, dye.**

die² |dī| —*noun* **1.** *plural* **dies** A machine part or device for stamping designs on coins, making raised patterns on paper, or cutting and shaping leather or metal. **2.** *plural* **dice** One of a pair of dice.
♦ *These sound alike* **die, dye.**

diamondback

dice

die¹, die²
Die¹ and **die²** have entirely different sources. **Die¹** was being used in English as it was spoken in about the eighth to twelfth century. But it was borrowed from a word used by people who lived in Scandinavia. The words **dead** and **death** are related to it. **Die²** comes from an old French word whose earlier source was a Latin word meaning "playing piece."

die·sel engine |dē′zəl| An engine that burns oil in its cylinders. The oil is burned by the heat of air compressed in the cylinders, instead of by an electric spark as in an engine that burns gasoline.

di·et |dī′ĭt| —*noun, plural* **diets 1.** The usual food and drink taken in by a person or animal: *A good diet of meat, vegetables, and milk will keep you healthy.* **2.** Special foods eaten for medical reasons or to gain or lose weight.

dif·fer |dĭf′ər| —*verb* **differed, differing 1.** To not be the same in form, quality, or amount: *The spoken language of people often differs from one area to another.* **2.** To have another opinion of; to disagree: *They differed over the amount to give their church.*

dif·fer·ence |dĭf′ər əns| or |dĭf′rəns| —*noun, plural* **differences 1.** The condition of being different: *The class learned the difference between a mule and a horse.* **2.** The amount of being different: *Our figures show a difference of three feet in the measurements.* **3.** A disagreement; quarrel: *We have had many differences about the furnishings for our house.* **4.** The amount left after one number is subtracted from another: *The difference between 6 and 9 is 3.*

dif·fer·ent |dĭf′ər ənt| or |dĭf′rənt| —*adjective* **1.** Not being the same; unlike: *The seahorse is different from any other fish.* **2.** Separate or distinct: *He visited us on two different days.*

dif·fi·cult |dĭf′ĭ kŭlt′| or |dĭf′ĭ kəlt| —*adjective* **1.** Hard to do, understand, or get the answer to: *a difficult task; a difficult word; a difficult math assignment.* **2.** Hard to please or manage: *He seems to be a difficult person to get along with.*

dif·fi·cul·ty |dĭf′ĭ kŭl′tē| or |dĭf′ĭ kəl tē| —*noun, plural* **difficulties 1.** The condition or quality of being difficult: *We were surprised at the difficulty of the science experiment. After breaking his leg, he could walk only with difficulty.* **2.** Something that causes trouble or worry: *Keeping quiet is a big difficulty for him.*

dig |dĭg| —*verb* **dug, digging 1.** To break up, turn over, or take away earth with a tool, hands, or paws: *It is time to dig the ground so we can plant the cabbages.* **2.** To make a hole by digging: *They have to dig a tunnel through the mountain.* **3.** To get by digging: *The miners dig coal from the ground.* **4.** To get by looking for or studying: *He has to dig information from a textbook for his report.* **5.** To push hard against or go into or through something: *Thorns dug into his arms when he was cutting the roses.*

di·gest |dĭ jĕst′| or |dī jĕst′| —*verb* **digested, digesting** To change food into simple substances that are easily taken into the body.
—*noun* |dī′jĕst′|, *plural* **digests** A shortening or summary of a written work: *a brief digest of the reports from last year's meetings.*

di·gest·i·ble |dĭ jĕs′tə bəl| or |dī jĕs′tə bəl| —*adjective* Able to be digested: *easily digestible food.*

di·ges·tion |dĭ jĕs′chən| or |dī jĕs′chən| —*noun, plural* **digestions** The process of digesting.

di·ges·tive |dĭ jĕs′tĭv| or |dī jĕs′tĭv| —*adjective* Of, helping, or active in the digestion of food: *a digestive pill.*

digestive system The alimentary canal together with certain other organs of the body, such as the liver and pancreas, that produce substances needed for digestion.

di·git |dĭj′ĭt| —*noun, plural* **digits 1.** A finger or toe. **2.** One of the numerals 1, 2, 3, 4, 5, 6, 7, 8, 9, and sometimes 0.

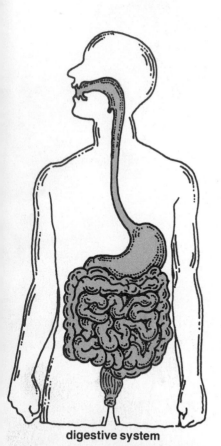

digestive system

ă	pat	ĕ	pet	î	fierce
ā	pay	ē	be	ŏ	pot
â	care	ĭ	pit	ō	go
ä	father	ī	pie	ô	paw, for

oi	oil	ŭ	cut	zh	vision
ŏŏ	book	û	fur	ə	ago, item,
ōō	boot	*th*	the		pencil, atom,
yōō	abuse	th	thin		circus
ou	out	hw	which	ər	butter

dig·ni·fied |dǐg′nə fīd′| —*adjective* Having or showing dignity; serious and stately: *in a dignified manner.*

dig·ni·ty |dǐg′nǐ tē| —*noun, plural* **dignities** The condition of being worthy or honorable: *The leader was interested in preserving human dignity for his people.*

dike |dīk| —*noun, plural* **dikes** A wall, dam, or embankment that is built to hold back water and prevent flooding.

di·lap·i·dat·ed |dǐ lǎp′ǐ dā′tǐd| —*adjective* Being in a state of poor repair or almost ruined: *a dilapidated barn with a leaky roof and no doors.*

dil·i·gent |dǐl′ə jənt| —*adjective* Working hard; careful; industrious: *a diligent student; a diligent search for the lost keys.*

dill |dǐl| —*noun* A plant with very fine, feathery leaves and spicy seeds. Both the leaves and the seeds are used for seasoning foods.

di·lute |dǐ lōōt′| or |dī lōōt′| —*verb* **diluted, diluting** To make thinner or weaker by adding a liquid: *You have to dilute this can of soup with water or milk.*

dim |dǐm| —*adjective* **dimmer, dimmest 1.** Faintly lighted or giving little light: *a dim closet. This flashlight is too dim to let us see anything.* **2.** Not clear: *the dim outline of a building against the evening sky.* **3.** Not sharp or keen: *dim eyesight.*
—*verb* **dimmed, dimming** To make or become dim: *Dim the lights in the dining room.*

dime |dīm| —*noun, plural* **dimes** A U.S. or Canadian coin worth ten cents.

di·men·sion |dǐ mĕn′shən| —*noun, plural* **dimensions** The measure of how far something extends in space. The dimensions of a room are its length, width, and height.

di·min·ish |dǐ mǐn′ǐsh| —*verb* **diminished, diminishing** To make or become smaller or less: *The more they ate, the more the birds diminished the supply of seeds.*

di·min·u·tive |dǐ mǐn′yə tǐv| —*adjective* Of very small size; tiny: *diminutive fingers.*

dim·ple |dǐm′pəl| —*noun, plural* **dimples** A small hollow in the flesh of the body, as in the cheek or chin.

din |dǐn| —*noun, plural* **dins** Loud, confusing noise: *The falling pots and pans made a terrible din.*
—*verb* **dinned, dinning** To cause to understand something by repeating it over and over: *Our parents dinned it into us that it is dangerous to jaywalk.*

dine |dīn| —*verb* **dined, dining** To eat dinner: *We dined on chicken and boiled potatoes.*

din·er |dī′nər| —*noun, plural* **diners 1.** A person who is eating a meal: *The restaurant was filled with diners.* **2.** A railroad car in which meals are served. **3.** A small restaurant usually having the shape of a railroad car.

din·ghy |dǐng′ē| —*noun, plural* **dinghies** A small rowboat. A dinghy is often carried on a larger boat.

din·gy |dǐn′jē| —*adjective* **dingier, dingiest** Dirty or soiled: *a dingy white shirt.*

din·ing room |dī′nǐng| A room in which meals are served.

din·ner |dǐn′ər| —*noun, plural* **dinners 1.** The main meal of the day, served at noon or in the evening. **2.** A formal meal in honor of a person or a special occasion: *The president gave a dinner for the visiting ambassador.*

diner

dinghy

dinosaur

diploma

dipper

ă	pat	ĕ	pet	î	fierce
ā	pay	ē	be	ŏ	pot
â	care	ĭ	pit	ō	go
ä	father	ī	pie	ô	paw, for
oi	oil	ŭ	cut	zh	vision
ŏŏ	book	û	fur	ə	ago, item,
ōō	boot	*th*	the		pencil, atom,
yōō	abuse	th	thin		circus
ou	out	hw	which	ər	butter

di·no·saur |dī′nə sôr′| —*noun, plural* **dinosaurs** One of many kinds of reptiles that lived millions of years ago. Some dinosaurs were the largest land animals that have ever lived.

di·o·cese |dī′ə sĭs| or |dī′ə sēs′| —*noun, plural* **dioceses** The churches or district under the direction of a bishop.

dip |dĭp| —*verb* **dipped, dipping** **1.** To put briefly in or into a liquid: *I like to dip bread into melted butter. Six pairs of oars dipped at the same time.* **2.** To reach into to get something: *The children dipped into the cookie jar.* **3.** To lower and raise in salute: *The soldiers dipped the flags as the Queen rode by.* **4.** To go down; sink: *The sun dipped below the horizon.*
—*noun, plural* **dips** **1.** A brief plunge or swim: *take a dip in the ocean.* **2.** A liquid into which something is dipped. **3.** A soft food mixture into which other foods may be dipped: *a cheese and onion dip.* **4.** A sudden slope downward: *a dip in the road.*

diph·thong |dĭf′thông′| or |dĭp′thông′| —*noun, plural* **diphthongs** A speech sound beginning with one vowel sound and moving to another within the same syllable. In the word "boy" *oy* is a diphthong.

di·plo·ma |dĭ plō′mə| —*noun, plural* **diplomas** A document given to a student who graduates from a school or college or finishes a course of study.

dip·lo·mat |dĭp′lə măt′| —*noun, plural* **diplomats** A person who is appointed to represent his or her country in its relations with other countries. A diplomat is trained to be an expert in dealing with people or situations.

dip·per |dĭp′ər| —*noun, plural* **dippers** A cup with a long handle for scooping up liquids.

di·rect |dĭ rĕkt′| or |dī rĕkt′| —*verb* **directed, directing** **1.** To manage the affairs of: *Our neighbor directs a large company.* **2.** To instruct, order, or command: *We were directed to finish the job by five o'clock.* **3.** To aim, point, or guide someone or something to or toward: *Can you direct me to his house? The fire fighters directed the water at the fire.*
—*adjective* **1.** Going or lying in a straight way or line: *This street is a direct route into town.* **2.** Straightforward; honest: *a direct answer.*
—*adverb* In a straight line; directly: *We fly direct to New York from Boston.*

direct current An electric current that does not change its direction of flow.

di·rec·tion |dĭ rĕk′shən| or |dī rĕk′shən| —*noun, plural* **directions** **1.** Control, management, and guidance. **2.** **directions** The manner or way to do something or way to get to some place. **3.** An order or command: *a direction to begin immediately.* **4.** The line or course along which someone or something lies, faces, or moves: *Walk in the direction of town.*

di·rect·ly |dĭ rĕkt′lē| or |dī rĕkt′lē| —*adverb* **1.** In a direct line; straight: *Go directly to your room.* **2.** Exactly: *This town is directly south of Washington.* **3.** Without delay; at once; immediately: *I will see you directly after the meeting.*

di·rec·tor |dĭ rĕk′tər| or |dī rĕk′tər| —*noun, plural* **directors** **1.** A person who manages or guides something, especially the affairs of a business. **2.** A person who directs the performers in a play, motion picture, or television show.

di·rec·to·ry |dĭ rĕk′tə rē| or |dī rĕk′tə rē| —*noun, plural*

directories A list of names, addresses, or other information: *a telephone directory.*

dir·i·gi·ble |dîr′ ə jə bəl| or |dĭ rĭj′ə bəl| —*noun, plural* **dirigibles** A large airship shaped like a cigar. A dirigible has a motor and a steering mechanism.

dirt |dûrt| —*noun* **1.** Earth or soil: *My hands are covered with dirt from digging in the garden.* **2.** Mud, grease, or other filthy material that soils: *We'll never get the dirt out of these clothes.*

dirt·y |dûr′tē| —*adjective* **dirtier, dirtiest** Not clean; soiled: *dirty dishes; dirty hands.*
—*verb* **dirtied, dirtying, dirties** To make or become soiled: *He dirtied his hands. White clothes dirty easily.*

dis- A prefix that means: **1.** Not; the opposite of: *disadvantage.* **2.** To do the opposite of: *disagree.*

dis·a·ble |dĭs ā′bəl| —*verb* **disabled, disabling** To make weak or take away the normal abilities of; cripple: *The wound disabled him.*

dis·ad·van·tage |dĭs′əd văn′tĭj| or |dĭs′əd vän′tĭj| —*noun, plural* **disadvantages** **1.** Something that makes it harder to do something; a handicap: *It is a disadvantage not to speak the language of the country where you are living.* **2.** Damage or harm: *The new rules worked to our disadvantage.*

dis·a·gree |dĭs′ə grē′| —*verb* **disagreed, disagreeing** **1.** To fail to match or agree: *Your answer to the problem disagrees with mine.* **2.** To have a different opinion: *I disagree on how many to invite.*

dis·a·gree·ment |dĭs′ə grē′mənt| —*noun, plural* **disagreements** A difference of opinion; quarrel; dispute: *They had a disagreement over the color of the walls.*

dis·ap·pear |dĭs′ə pîr′| —*verb* **disappeared, disappearing** To pass out of sight either little by little or suddenly; vanish: *The ship disappeared over the horizon.*

dis·ap·pear·ance |dĭs′ə pîr′əns| —*noun, plural* **disappearances** The act or an example of disappearing: *The disappearance of the dinosaurs is often thought to be a mystery.*

dis·ap·point |dĭs′ə point′| —*verb* **disappointed, disappointing** To fail to satisfy the hopes or wishes of: *The actor's performance disappointed the audience.*

dis·ap·point·ment |dĭs′ə point′mənt| —*noun, plural* **disappointments** **1.** The act of disappointing or the feeling of being disappointed: *Her disappointment at not going to the dance was great.* **2.** A person or thing that disappoints: *The picnic was a disappointment.*

dis·ap·prove |dĭs′ə prōōv′| —*verb* **disapproved, disapproving** **1.** To have an opinion that is not favorable: *He always disapproves of what I say.* **2.** To refuse to approve: *disapprove a request.*

dis·as·ter |dĭ zăs′tər| —*noun, plural* **disasters** Something that causes great destruction or misfortune. A tornado is a disaster.

dis·be·lief |dĭs′bĭ lēf′| —*noun, plural* **disbeliefs** The refusal to believe: *Disbelief showed in his face.*

disc |dĭsk| —*noun, plural* **discs** A phonograph record.

dis·card |dĭs kärd′| —*verb* **discarded, discarding** To throw away: *He discarded the old magazines.*

dis·charge |dĭs chärj′| —*verb* **discharged, discharging** **1.** To release from work, service, or jail; dismiss; let go: *Mr. Jones discharged the secretary because he was always tardy. The Army discharged him in 1974. The spies were discharged from prison.*

2. To get rid of passengers or cargo; unload: *The bus discharges all passengers at the end of the line. The ship discharged its cargo at the wharf.* **3.** To fire or shoot: *The cadets discharged the cannon as a salute to the academy's visitors.* **4. a.** To let flow or escape; give off: *He opened the outlet that discharges water from the tank.* **b.** To flow out; empty: *Many mountain streams discharge into the lake.* —*noun* |**dĭs′**chärj| or |dĭs **chärj′**|, *plural* **discharges 1. a.** A release from work, service, or jail: *His family was present at his discharge from the army.* **b.** A certificate showing such release: *He framed his discharge from the army.* **2.** The act of unloading: *The discharge of the cargo will be finished by noon.*

dis·ci·ple |dĭ **sī′**pəl| —*noun, plural* **disciples** A person who believes in the teachings of a leader and helps to spread them.

dis·ci·pline |**dĭs′**ə plĭn| —*noun, plural* **disciplines 1.** Training of the mind, body, or character that demands great obedience to rules: *It takes years of discipline to become a ballet dancer. In the boarding school they still believed in military discipline.* **2.** Controlled behavior that results from this training; orderly conduct: *The troops showed great discipline and courage under fire. It was hard to maintain discipline in that classroom.* —*verb* **disciplined, disciplining 1. a.** To train by instruction or exercise: *Years of practice have disciplined his muscles to act with great control. Reading has disciplined his mind.* **b.** To train to be obedient; keep under control: *The sergeant disciplined the new troops.* **2.** To punish in order to train or correct: *The major disciplined the cadets by confining them to their quarters.*

disc jockey A person who chooses and plays phonograph records for a radio station or discotheque.

dis·close |dĭs **klōz′**| —*verb* **disclosed, disclosing** To make known: *The couple disclosed the date of their wedding.*

dis·co |**dĭs′**kō′| —*noun, plural* **discos** A form of the word **discotheque.**

dis·con·nect |dĭs′kə **nĕkt′**| —*verb* **disconnected, disconnecting** To break the connection of or between: *Jim disconnected the lamp by pulling the plug out of its socket.*

dis·con·tent·ed |dĭs′kən **tĕn′**tĭd| —*adjective* Not happy or satisfied: *She was discontented with her salary.*

dis·con·tin·ue |dĭs′kən **tĭn′**yōō| —*verb* **discontinued, discontinuing** To bring to an end; stop or give up: *Lack of time made her discontinue her Spanish lessons. The railroad discontinued train service between the two cities.*

dis·co·theque |**dĭs′**kō tĕk′| —*noun, plural* **discotheques** A club or dance hall where people dance to amplified recorded music. Another form of this word is **disco.**

dis·count |**dĭs′**kount′| or |dĭs **kount′**| —*noun, plural* **discounts** An amount that is less than the full or regular price: *The store was selling all appliances at a 30 per cent discount.*

dis·cour·age |dĭ **skûr′**ĭj| or |dĭ **skŭr′**ĭj| —*verb* **discouraged, discouraging 1.** To cause to lose courage, hope, or enthusiasm: *The size of the problem discouraged me.* **2.** To try to stop: *She tried to discourage Tim from going swimming when it was so cold.*

dis·cour·te·ous |dĭs **kûr′**tē əs| —*adjective* Lacking courtesy; impolite; rude: *It is discourteous to interrupt people.*

dis·cov·er |dĭ **skŭv′**ər| —*verb* **discovered, discovering** To find or come upon anything for the first time: *Christopher Columbus discovered America in 1492.*

disc jockey

ă	pat	ĕ	pet	î	fierce
ā	pay	ē	be	ŏ	pot
â	care	ĭ	pit	ō	go
ä	father	ī	pie	ô	paw, for
oi	oil	ŭ	cut	zh	vision
ōō	book	û	fur	ə	ago, item,
ōō	boot	*th*	the		pencil, atom,
yōō	abuse	th	thin		circus
ou	out	hw	which	ər	butter

dis·cov·er·y |dĭ skŭv′ə rē| —*noun, plural* **discoveries** **1.** The act of discovering: *The day that honors Columbus and his discovery of America is in October.* **2.** Something discovered: *Penicillin was a great scientific discovery.*

dis·crim·i·nate |dĭ skrĭm′ə nāt′| —*verb* **discriminated, discriminating** To treat people differently and often badly because of their color, religion, sex, or age: *The company was sued for discriminating against minority groups.*

dis·crim·i·na·tion |dĭ skrĭm′ə **nā**′shən| —*noun* Behavior marked by unfairness or injustice toward others because of color, religion, sex, or age.

dis·cuss |dĭ skŭs′| —*verb* **discussed, discussing** To speak together about; talk over: *Let's discuss our plans for the holidays.*

dis·cus·sion |dĭ skŭsh′ən| —*noun, plural* **discussions** A serious talk about something by two or more persons: *The players had a lively discussion about Sunday's game.*

dis·dain |dĭs dān′| —*noun* A feeling of mild contempt; scorn: *He treated his colleagues with disdain.*
—*verb* **disdained, disdaining** To show contempt for; look down upon: *She disdained all her brother's friends.*

dis·ease |dĭ zēz′| —*noun, plural* **diseases** A condition that does not let the body or the mind function normally; sickness; illness. People, animals, and plants can all get diseases.

dis·grace |dĭs grās′| —*noun, plural* **disgraces** **1.** A loss of honor or good name; shame: *The family fight over Mr. Shaw's will ended in disgrace for all.* **2.** A cause of shame or dishonor: *These dirty streets are a disgrace to the city.*
—*verb* **disgraced, disgracing** To be a cause of shame or dishonor to: *His arrest for stealing disgraced his family.*

dis·grace·ful |dĭs grās′fəl| —*adjective* Causing shame or embarrassment: *his disgraceful behavior at the party.*

dis·guise |dĭs gīz′| —*noun, plural* **disguises** Something that changes or hides a person's appearance: *He went to the party wearing the disguise of a wolf. Her calm manner was just a disguise.*
—*verb* **disguised, disguising** **1.** To change the appearance of in order to look like someone or something else: *At Halloween, they disguised themselves as witches and goblins.* **2.** To hide; conceal: *He disguised his anger with a smile.*

dis·gust |dĭs gŭst′| —*verb* **disgusted, disgusting** To cause a feeling of strong dislike or loathing in; sicken: *The smell of burning rubber disgusted us.*
—*noun, plural* **disgusts** A feeling of strong dislike that makes a person feel sick: *He showed his disgust when he saw the rat.*

dish |dĭsh| —*noun, plural* **dishes** **1.a.** A flat or shallow container for holding or serving food. **b.** A dish with something in it: *She set the dish of tomatoes on the table.* **c.** The amount that a dish holds: *He ate a full dish of stew.* **2.** Food made or cooked in a special way: *Fried chicken is his favorite dish.*
—*verb* **dished, dishing** To put in dishes; serve: *As soon as everyone was seated, the food was dished out.*

dis·hon·est |dĭs ŏn′ĭst| —*adjective* Not honest; likely to lie, cheat, or deceive: *a dishonest person; a dishonest report.*

dis·hon·or |dĭs ŏn′ər| —*noun* Loss of honor or good name; shame: *The general, once hailed as a hero, is now in dishonor. His career will never recover from the dishonor of having surrendered to the enemy.*

dish
An ornamental dish

dishwasher
In a restaurant

—*verb* **dishonored, dishonoring** To bring shame upon; disgrace: *Bob would not dishonor his school by cheating in the spelling contest.*

dish·wash·er | dĭsh′wŏsh′ər | —*noun, plural* **dishwashers** A machine or person that washes dishes, pots, pans, glasses, and other kitchen equipment.

dis·in·fect | dĭs′ĭn fĕkt′ | —*verb* **disinfected, disinfecting** To destroy with chemicals or heat germs that are capable of causing disease: *The nurse disinfected his wound. The doctor disinfected his instruments by boiling them.*

dis·in·te·grate | dĭs ĭn′tĭ grāt′ | —*verb* **disintegrated, disintegrating** To break into many separate pieces: *The clay pot disintegrated when I dropped it.*

dis·in·ter·est·ed | dĭs ĭn′trĭ stĭd | or | dĭs ĭn′tə rĕs′tĭd | —*adjective* Free from any personal interest; impartial: *A judge should be disinterested and listen to both sides in a case.*

disk | dĭsk | —*noun, plural* **disks** A thin, flat, round object. Phonograph records, coins, and some kinds of candy are disks.

dis·like | dĭs līk′ | —*verb* **disliked, disliking** To have a feeling of not liking: *Father dislikes people who are not honest.*
—*noun, plural* **dislikes** A feeling of not liking: *a dislike of rats.*

dis·lo·cate | dĭs′lō kāt | or | dĭs lō′kāt′ | —*verb* **dislocated, dislocating** To put or force a bone out of joint: *He was tackled and dislocated his left shoulder.*

dis·lodge | dĭs lŏj′ | —*verb* **dislodged, dislodging** To move or force out of position: *The earthquake dislodged many rocks.*

dis·loy·al | dĭs loi′əl | —*adjective* Lacking in loyalty; not faithful: *He was disloyal to his friends.*

dis·mal | dĭz′məl | —*adjective* **1.** Causing gloom or depression; dreary: *a dismal, rainy day.* **2.** Showing gloom; depressed; sad: *a dismal look on his face. She was in a dismal mood that morning.*

dis·may | dĭs mā′ | —*verb* **dismayed, dismaying** To cause to lose courage or confidence in the face of danger or trouble: *The surprise attack dismayed the enemy's troops.*
—*noun* A sudden loss of courage or confidence in the face of danger or trouble: *Our football team faced with dismay the powerful passing game of the visitors.*

dis·miss | dĭs mĭs′ | —*verb* **dismissed, dismissing** **1.** To allow to leave; send away: *It is time to dismiss the music class.* **2.** To let go; fire; discharge: *The automobile factory dismissed fifty workers.* **3.** To put out of one's mind: *He dismissed the idea as impossible.*

dis·miss·al | dĭs mĭs′əl | —*noun, plural* **dismissals** **1.** The act of allowing to leave: *The principal ordered an early dismissal from school because of the snowstorm.* **2.** The act of firing from a job; a discharge: *She requested the dismissal of the new typist.*

dis·mount | dĭs mount′ | —*verb* **dismounted, dismounting** To get off or down: *He dismounted from the horse.*

dis·o·be·di·ent | dĭs′ə bē′dē ənt | —*adjective* Not following orders; not obedient: *a disobedient child.*

dis·o·bey | dĭs′ə bā′ | —*verb* **disobeyed, disobeying** To fail or refuse to obey: *Anyone who disobeys the rules will have to pay a fine.*

dis·or·der | dĭs ôr′dər | —*noun, plural* **disorders** Lack of order; confusion: *The classroom was in complete disorder after recess..*

dis·patch | dĭ spăch′ | —*verb* **dispatched, dispatching** To send off quickly to some person or place: *The sheriff dispatched a message to the marshal.*
—*noun, plural* **dispatches** **1.** A written message or report sent

ă	pat	ĕ	pet	î	fierce
ā	pay	ē	be	ŏ	pot
â	care	ĭ	pit	ō	go
ä	father	ī	pie	ô	paw, for
oi	oil	ŭ	cut	zh	vision
ōō	book	û	fur	ə	ago, item,
ōō	boot	*th*	the		pencil, atom,
yōō	abuse	th	thin		circus
ou	out	hw	which	ər	butter

with speed: *The reporter sent a dispatch to his paper.* **2.** Quick action and efficiency: *I'll take care of your order with dispatch so we can close the office on time.*

dis·pel | dĭ spĕl′ | —*verb* **dispelled, dispelling** To make disappear; drive away: *Her good spirits dispelled the sadness of the occasion.*

dis·perse | dĭ spûrs′ | —*verb* **dispersed, dispersing** To move or scatter in different directions: *The police dispersed the crowd. The crowd dispersed quickly after the movie.*

dis·place | dĭs plās′ | —*verb* **displaced, displacing** **1.** To put out of the usual place: *A disaster like a flood displaces many people.* **2.** To take the place of: *Modern machinery has displaced workers in many industries.*

dis·play | dĭ splā′ | —*verb* **displayed, displaying** To put on view; exhibit; show: *In the store models displayed the latest fashions.* —*noun, plural* **displays** A public showing or exhibition: *The museum is announcing a display of American paintings. He was embarrassed by his display of anger in front of his children.*

dis·please | dĭs plēz′ | —*verb* **displeased, displeasing** To make angry; offend; annoy: *Noisy behavior displeases her.*

dis·pos·a·ble | dĭ spō′zə bəl | —*adjective* Designed to be thrown away after use: *a disposable container; disposable paper towels.*

dis·pos·al | dĭ spō′zəl | —*noun, plural* **disposals** **1.** The act of throwing something out or away: *The proper disposal of rubbish is in a garbage can.* **2.** The freedom to use something: *Our school facilities are at your disposal.*

dis·pose | dĭ spōz′ | —*verb* **disposed, disposing** —**dispose of** To get rid of: *Please dispose of this trash. The boy greedily disposed of his food.*

dis·po·si·tion | dĭs′pə zĭsh′ən | —*noun, plural* **dispositions** A person's usual mood: *She has a generous disposition.*

dis·pute | dĭ spyo͞ot′ | —*verb* **disputed, disputing** To question the truth of; deny; doubt: *The scientist disputed the report that there was life on Mars.* —*noun, plural* **disputes** A quarrel; an argument: *The brothers had a dispute over the use of the car.*

dis·qual·i·fy | dĭs kwŏl′ə fī′ | —*verb* **disqualified, disqualifying** To make or declare unfit: *Poor eyesight disqualified him for military service. The school disqualified several athletes for low grades.*

dis·re·gard | dĭs′rĭ gärd′ | —*verb* **disregarded, disregarding** To pay little or no attention to: *Don't disregard traffic signals.* —*noun* Lack of attention to or respect for something: *She has a careless disregard for rules of safety on the road.*

dis·rupt | dĭs rŭpt′ | —*verb* **disrupted, disrupting** To throw into confusion; upset: *The blizzard disrupted the lives of hundreds of people.*

dis·sat·is·fied | dĭs săt′ĭs fīd′ | —*adjective* Not pleased; discontented: *She is always dissatisfied with her work.*

dis·sect | dĭ sĕkt′ | or | dī sĕkt′ | —*verb* **dissected, dissecting** To cut apart or separate in order to examine: *We dissected a lobster in biology class.*

dis·sent | dĭ sĕnt′ | —*verb* **dissented, dissenting** To think or feel differently; disagree: *You have a right to dissent from the opinion of others.* —*noun* Difference of opinion; disagreement: *He voiced his dissent to the group's plans.*

♦ *These sound alike* **dissent, descent.**

display
Monarch's jewels on display

dis·solve | dĭ zŏlv′ | —*verb* **dissolved, dissolving** **1.** To mix or become mixed into a liquid: *Dissolve the powder in water. Sugar dissolves in water.* **2.** To break up; end: *We dissolved our partnership at the end of the boating season.*

dis·tance | dĭs′təns | —*noun, plural* **distances** The length of the space between two things, places, or points: *What is the distance between New York and Washington?*

dis·tant | dĭs′tənt | —*adjective* **1.** Not near; far away in space or time: *a distant mountain; a distant memory of childhood.* **2.** Not friendly: *Our neighbors remain cold and distant despite our efforts.* —*adverb* At or to a distance; away: *She lives two blocks distant from John's house.*

dis·till | dĭ stĭl′ | —*verb* **distilled, distilling** To make pure or separate out by distillation: *The factory bought machinery to distill alcohol.*

dis·til·la·tion | dĭs′tə lā′shən | —*noun* The process of heating a liquid until it becomes a vapor and then cooling it until it becomes a liquid again. Distillation is used to make liquids pure or to separate out various chemical compounds.

dis·tinct | dĭ stĭngkt′ | —*adjective* **1.** Not identical; not the same; different: *Zebras and tigers are two distinct kinds of animals.* **2.** Easily perceived by the senses; clear: *Ether has a distinct odor. The building has a distinct outline against the sky.* **3.** Very definite: *His marks show a distinct improvement.*

dis·tinc·tion | dĭ stĭngk′shən | —*noun, plural* **distinctions** **1.** The act of making a difference between things: *You should treat everybody alike without distinction as to age, race, or creed.* **2.** Something that makes one different; difference: *Observe the distinction between mice and rats.*

dis·tinc·tive | dĭ stĭngk′tĭv | —*adjective* Marking or showing a difference from others: *the distinctive sound of the robin. The nurses wore distinctive uniforms.*

dis·tin·guish | dĭ stĭng′gwĭsh | —*verb* **distinguished, distinguishing** **1.** To make different; set apart: *Their uniforms distinguish soldiers, sailors, and firefighters from police officers.* **2.** To know or see clearly the difference between two things: *Can you distinguish ants from spiders?* **3.** To hear or see clearly; make out: *The ear has the ability to distinguish musical tones. The captain could not distinguish the lighthouse through the fog.* **4.** To make oneself well known: *He distinguished himself by his discoveries in the field of chemistry.*

dis·tort | dĭ stôrt′ | —*verb* **distorted, distorting** **1.** To bend or twist out of the usual shape: *Anger distorted their faces.* **2.** To change the original meaning of: *Several newspapers distorted the senator's speech.*

dis·tract | dĭ străkt′ | —*verb* **distracted, distracting** To draw away the mind or attention of; divert: *Music distracts him from his troubles. The noise of the parade distracted her from her chores.*

dis·trac·tion | dĭ străk′shən | —*noun, plural* **distractions** Something that draws away the mind or attention of someone: *Television is a distraction when you are trying to study.*

dis·tress | dĭ strĕs′ | —*noun, plural* **distresses** **1.** Great grief or suffering; misery; sorrow: *He is in great distress over the illness of his father.* **2.** Serious danger or trouble: *a ship in distress.* —*verb* **distressed, distressing** To cause grief or suffering: *News of the accident distressed Mrs. Jones.*

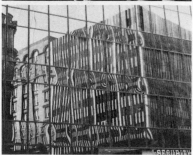

distort
Above: A girl's image in a trick mirror
Below: Buildings reflected in nearby windows

ă	pat	ĕ	pet	î	fierce
ā	pay	ē	be	ŏ	pot
â	care	ĭ	pit	ō	go
ä	father	ī	pie	ô	paw, for

oi	oil	ŭ	cut	zh	vision
ōō	book	û	fur	ə	ago, item,
ōō	boot	*th*	the		pencil, atom,
yōō	abuse	th	thin		circus
ou	out	hw	which	ər	butter

dis·trib·ute | dĭ strĭb′yo͞ot | —*verb* **distributed, distributing 1.** To divide something and give it out in portions: *Take these flowers and distribute them among the guests.* **2.** To spread out; scatter: *Television networks distribute news all over the globe.* **3.** To put into groups; arrange; sort: *Mail is distributed each morning.*

dis·tri·bu·tion | dĭs′trə byo͞o′shən | —*noun, plural* **distributions** The act of distributing: *The distribution of the report cards took a long time.*

dis·trict | dĭs′trĭkt | —*noun, plural* **districts 1.** A part of a country, state, or city marked out for a special purpose: *Our school district covers ten miles.* **2.** An area that has a special use: *New York's theater district.*

District of Co·lum·bi·a | kə lŭm′bē ə | The Federal District of the United States. It is entirely occupied by the city of Washington, the capital of the United States.

dis·turb | dĭ stûrb′ | —*verb* **disturbed, disturbing 1.** To make uneasy, upset, or nervous: *Rumors of the team's defeat disturbed the coach greatly.* **2.** To put into disorder; change the arrangement of: *Don't disturb the papers on my desk.* **3.** To break in upon; interrupt: *The noise will disturb his sleep.*

dis·turb·ance | dĭ stûr′bəns | —*noun, plural* **disturbances 1.** The act of disturbing: *The cats made a terrible disturbance outside our window last night.* **2.** Something that disturbs: *Television can be a great disturbance when you want to read.* **3.** Public disorder: *The police have been checking up on disturbances in the neighborhood.*

ditch | dĭch | —*noun, plural* **ditches** A long, narrow trench dug in the ground.

dive | dīv | —*verb* **dived** or **dove, diving 1.** To plunge headfirst into water: *He dived from the cliffs into the sea below.* **2.** To go underwater to search for something: *The island's natives dive for pearls.* **3.** To plunge downward at a steep angle: *The eagle dived out of the clouds.* **4.** To go, move, or drop suddenly and quickly: *We all dived for cover when the storm started.*
—*noun, plural* **dives 1.** A headfirst plunge into water: *She won the prize for her dive from the high board.* **2.** A sudden downward plunge: *The eagle made a dive at the squirrel.*

di·ver | dī′vər | —*noun, plural* **divers 1.** A person who dives. **2.** A person who works or explores underwater with special equipment. This equipment lets a person breathe and stay underwater for a while.

di·verse | dĭ vûrs′ | or | dī vûrs′ | or | dī′vûrs′ | —*adjective* Clearly different; of several or many kinds: *America is a land of diverse peoples.*

di·ver·sion | dĭ vûr′zhən | or | dī vûr′shən | or | dī vûr′zhən | or | dī vûr′shən | —*noun, plural* **diversions 1.** A change in the direction in which something moves: *A diversion of traffic to a side road was necessary because of the accident.* **2.** Something that relaxes or amuses; a pastime: *Movies and sports are his favorite diversions.* **3.** Something that draws the attention to another direction: *The enemy created a diversion with a surprise attack from the back.*

di·ver·si·ty | dĭ vûr′sĭ tē | or | dī vûr′sĭ tē | —*noun, plural* **diversities** Difference; variety: *a great diversity of opinion; the diversity of colors on a butterfly's wings.*

di·vert | dĭ vûrt′ | or | dī vûrt′ | —*verb* **diverted, diverting 1.** To

diver

change the direction in which something moves: *Traffic was diverted until the highway was repaired.* **2.** To draw the attention to another direction: *The band diverted our attention from the football game.* **3.** To amuse or entertain: *We were diverted by the puppet show.*

di·vide | dǐ vīd′ | —*verb* **divided, dividing** **1.** To separate or become separated into parts, groups, or branches; split: *Dad divided the cake into slices. The river divides here.* **2.** To separate into parts that are against each other: *Bad feelings divided the team.* **3.** To separate from; cut off: *A high fence divides their garden from ours.* **4.** To give out in equal amounts; share: *We will divide the reward money between us.* **5.** To find out how many times a number contains another number: *10 divided by 2 is 5. This machine can multiply and divide.*

div·i·dend | dǐv′ĭ dĕnd′ | —*noun, plural* **dividends** **1.** A number that is to be divided: *When you divide 10 by 2, the dividend is 10.* **2.** Money that is earned by a company as profit and shared among the people who own stock in the company.

di·vine | dǐ vīn′ | —*adjective* **1.** Of or from God or a god: *divine love.* **2.** Sacred; holy: *divine services; divine worship.*

di·vis·i·ble | dǐ vǐz′ ə bəl | —*adjective* Able to be divided: *16 is divisible by 2, 4, and 8.*

di·vi·sion | dǐ vǐzh′ən | —*noun, plural* **divisions** **1.** The act of dividing or the state of being divided: *We approved the division of the farm into small plots of land.* **2.** One of the parts into which something is divided: *Our team is in the first division in the tournament.* **3.** Something that divides or separates: *This street is the division between the east and west sides of town.* **4.** The process of dividing one number by another. **5.** An army unit that is made up of a number of battalions.

di·vi·sor | dǐ vī′zər | —*noun, plural* **divisors** The number by which another number is to be divided: *When you divide 10 by 2, the divisor is 2.*

di·vorce | dǐ vôrs′ | or | dǐ vōrs′ | —*noun, plural* **divorces** The legal ending of a marriage.
—*verb* **divorced, divorcing** To end a marriage legally.

diz·zy | dǐz′ē | —*adjective* **dizzier, dizziest** Having a feeling that one is spinning and about to fall.

do | dōō | —*verb* **did, done, doing, does** **1.** To perform or make; carry out; complete: *Try to do a good job. Do your duty. Do five copies of this letter.* **2.** To give; grant: *Please do me a favor.* **3.** To bring about; be the cause of: *Crying won't do you any good. Be careful, the gun can do you harm.* **4.** To work on; set in order; arrange: *Who will do your hair today?* **5.** To figure out; solve: *Do all the arithmetic problems on this page.* **6.** To be good enough; be adequate: *These shoes won't do for running.* **7.** To work at for a living: *What do you do?* **8.** To get along; succeed; fare: *She will do very well in business.*
—*helping,* or *auxiliary, verb* As a helping verb **do** is used: **1.** To show present or past tense when asking a question: *Do you want this hat? Did you see her car?* **2.** To show present and past tense when making a negative statement: *He does not drive. I did not sleep very well.* **3.** To take the place of the verb mentioned just before: *Who owns this store? I do.* **4.** To make what one says more forceful: *I do want to be sure.*
♦ *These sound alike* **do, dew, due.**

ă	pat	ĕ	pet	î	fierce
ā	pay	ē	be	ŏ	pot
â	care	ĭ	pit	ō	go
ä	father	ī	pie	ô	paw, for
oi	oil	ŭ	cut	zh	vision
ōō	book	û	fur	ə	ago, item,
ōō	boot	*th*	the		pencil, atom,
yōō	abuse	th	thin		circus
ou	out	hw	which	ər	butter

Do·ber·man pin·scher |dō′bər mən **pĭn′**shər| A large dog with a smooth black or brown coat.

doc·ile |dŏs′əl| —*adjective* Easy to handle or train: *a docile kitten.*

dock¹ |dŏk| —*noun, plural* **docks** A platform extending into the water where ships may tie up to load and unload; a slip. —*verb* **docked, docking** **1.** To come up to a dock: *The captain docked his boat to get fuel.* **2.** To join together while in space: *The two spacecraft will dock on their second orbit of the moon.*

dock² |dŏk| —*verb* **docked, docking** **1.** To cut off the end of: *The veterinarian docked the horse's tail.* **2.** To take part off: *The company docks a day's pay for missing work.*

doc·tor |dŏk′tər| —*noun, plural* **doctors** **1.** A person who is trained and licensed to treat diseases and injuries. A surgeon, a dentist, and a veterinarian are all doctors. **2.** A person who has the highest degree that a university gives.

doc·trine |dŏk′trĭn| —*noun, plural* **doctrines** A belief or set of beliefs held by a group of people: *a religious doctrine.*

doc·u·ment |dŏk′yə mənt| —*noun, plural* **documents** An official paper that can be used to give information or proof of something. A birth certificate, a marriage certificate, and a driver's license are documents.

dodge |dŏj| —*verb* **dodged, dodging** **1.** To avoid by moving quickly out of the way: *She dodged the pillow that Mary threw at her. He dodged when I tried to catch him.* **2.** To avoid by being clever or cunning: *Mr. Larsen dodged the reporter's questions during his interview.*

do·do |dō′dō| —*noun, plural* **dodoes** or **dodos** A large bird that used to live on an island in the Indian Ocean. It had a heavy body and short wings and was not able to fly. There are no dodoes living now.

doe |dō| —*noun, plural* **does** **1.** A female deer. **2.** The female of some other animals, such as the rabbit or antelope.
♦ *These sound alike* **doe, dough.**

does |dŭz| The third person singular present tense of the verb **do:** *He does a very good job as sheriff.*

does·n't |dŭz′ənt| A contraction of "does not."

dog |dôg| or |dŏg| —*noun, plural* **dogs** An animal that is related to the wolves and foxes. There are many breeds of dogs. —*verb* **dogged, dogging** To follow closely: *My little brother has been dogging me all day.*

dog·wood |dôg′wŏŏd′| or |dŏg′wŏŏd′| —*noun, plural* **dogwoods** A tree that blooms in spring. It has small greenish flowers surrounded by white or pink leaves that look like petals.

doi·ly |doi′lē| —*noun, plural* **doilies** A small, fancy mat of lace, paper, or other material placed under a dish or vase to protect or decorate furniture.

doll |dŏl| —*noun, plural* **dolls** A child's toy that is made to look like a baby or other human being.

dol·lar |dŏl′ər| —*noun, plural* **dollars** A unit of money equal to 100 cents in the United States and Canada and some other countries.

dol·phin |dŏl′fĭn| or |dôl′fĭn| —*noun, plural* **dolphins** **1.** A sea animal related to the whales, but smaller. It has a snout shaped like a beak. Dolphins can be trained to do many things. **2.** A large, brightly colored ocean fish.

Doberman pinscher

dock¹, dock²
Dock¹ is from a Dutch word that probably came from a Latin word meaning "channel." **Dock²** comes from a word used long ago in English to mean "trimmed hair of a tail." It probably came from a Germanic word meaning "bundle, lump."

dogwood
Tree *(above)* and blossom *(below)*

dome

domino

donkey

do·main |dō mān′| —*noun, plural* **domains** All the lands under the rule or control of one person, animal, or government: *the duke's domain; the lion's domain; British domains.*

dome |dōm| —*noun, plural* **domes** A large, rounded roof that fits on a round base. A dome looks like an upside-down bowl.

do·mes·tic |də měs′tĭk| —*adjective* **1.** Of a home, household, or family life: *domestic chores; domestic comfort.* **2.** Used to living with human beings; not wild; tame: *Dogs and cats are domestic animals.* **3.** Of one's own country: *The President must always be informed on both domestic and foreign matters.*

do·mes·ti·cate |də měs′tĭ kāt′| —*verb* **domesticated, domesticating** To train to live with and be useful to human beings; tame: *The cowboys domesticated horses.*

dom·i·nant |dŏm′ə nənt| —*adjective* Most important or powerful; ruling; controlling: *The president is the dominant person in the company. The dominant color in her dress is red.*

dom·i·nate |dŏm′ə nāt′| —*verb* **dominated, dominating** To govern or rule by will or strength: *The large country dominated its smaller neighbors for centuries.*

do·min·ion |də mĭn′yən| —*noun, plural* **dominions** All lands under the control of one ruler or government; realm: *the Queen's dominions.*

Dominion Day A Canadian national holiday on July 1. It celebrates the anniversary of the beginning of Canada as a country.

dom·i·no |dŏm′ə nō| —*noun, plural* **dominoes** or **dominos** **1.** A thin block of wood, bone, or other material used in playing a game called dominoes. The face of each block is divided in half and marked with from 1 to 6 dots. **2.** **dominoes** (Used with a singular verb.) A game played with a set of these blocks.

do·nate |dō′nāt′| or |dō nāt′| —*verb* **donated, donating** To present as a gift; contribute.

do·na·tion |dō nā′shən| —*noun, plural* **donations** A gift or contribution: *Please put your donation in the box in the lobby.*

done |dŭn| The past participle of **do:** *You have done a good job.* —*adjective* **1.** Completely finished: *All the work is done.* **2.** Cooked enough: *The meat is done and ready to serve.*

don·key |dŏng′kē| or |dŭng′kē| or |dông′kē| —*noun, plural* **donkeys** An animal related to the horse, but smaller and with longer ears.

don't |dōnt| A contraction of "do not."

doom |do͞om| —*noun, plural* **dooms** A terrible fate, especially death: *The sailors met their doom in the raging seas.* —*verb* **doomed, dooming** **1.** To come to an unhappy end: *The ship was doomed because of the storm.* **2.** To fix or decree ahead of time; destine: *Their project was doomed to fail.*

door |dôr| or |dōr| —*noun, plural* **doors** A movable panel that is used to open or close an entrance to a room, building, or vehicle. Doors are usually made of wood, metal, or glass. They are on hinges or slide open or shut.

door·bell |dôr′běl′| or |dōr′běl′| —*noun, plural* **doorbells** A bell or buzzer outside a door.

door·step |dôr′stěp′| or |dōr′stěp′| —*noun, plural* **doorsteps** A step or flight of steps leading up to an outside door.

door·way |dôr′wā′| or |dōr′wā′| —*noun, plural* **doorways** The entrance to a room or building in which a door may be placed.

ă	pat	ĕ	pet	î	fierce
ā	pay	ē	be	ŏ	pot
â	care	ĭ	pit	ō	go
ä	father	ī	pie	ô	paw, for
oi	oil	ŭ	cut	zh	vision
o͞o	book	û	fur	ə	ago, item,
o͞o	boot	*th*	the		pencil, atom,
yo͞o	abuse	th	thin		circus
ou	out	hw	which	ər	butter

dope |dōp| —*noun, plural* **dopes** A varnish or similar liquid preparation. Dope is used to put together things that are made out of wood, especially model planes, trains, and cars.

dor·mant |dôr′mənt| —*adjective* Not active for a period of time: *a dormant volcano. Some animals remain dormant during the winter months.*

dor·mi·to·ry |dôr′mĭ tôr′ē| or |dôr′mĭ tōr′ē| —*noun, plural* **dormitories** A building containing many bedrooms. College students often live in dormitories.

dor·mouse |dôr′mous′| —*noun, plural* **dor·mice** |dôr′mīs′| An animal that looks like a small squirrel. Dormice live in Europe, Asia, and Africa. They sleep during the day and are active at night.

dose |dōs| —*noun, plural* **doses** The amount of medicine taken at one time: *Take a dose of cough syrup every four hours.*

dot |dŏt| —*noun, plural* **dots** A small, rounded spot or mark; a speck: *paint dots on the floor.*
—*verb* **dotted, dotting** **1.** To mark with a dot; cover with dots: *Don't forget to dot the i's.* **2.** To be scattered here and there on: *The field was dotted with haystacks.*

dote |dōt| —*verb* **doted, doting** To show too much love or affection: *He is a spoiled child because his grandparents dote on him.*

dou·ble |dŭb′əl| —*adjective* **1.** Two times as much in size, strength, number, or amount: *a double dose of medicine.* **2.** Having two parts that are the same: *double doors.* **3.** Designed for two: *a double bed.* **4.** Living or acting two parts: *He leads a double life as a spy and a diplomat.*
—*adverb* **1.** Two together: *They are going to ride double on a horse.* **2.** In two's or in pairs: *His eyeglasses make her see double.*
—*noun, plural* **doubles** **1.** Someone or something that looks like another; a duplicate. **2.** A hit in baseball that lets the batter get to second base safely.
—*verb* **doubled, doubling** **1.** To make or become twice as great: *The population has doubled in this town.* **2.** To fold in two: *We doubled the blankets for warmth.* **3.** To hit a double in baseball.

dou·ble-cross |dŭb′əl krôs′| or |dŭb′əl krŏs′| —*verb* **double-crossed, double-crossing** To betray someone by not doing what was agreed on: *One crook double-crossed his partner and kept all the money.*

doubt |dout| —*verb* **doubted, doubting** To not be sure or certain about: *We doubt that he will really make the trip.*
—*noun, plural* **doubts** **1.** A feeling of not being sure or certain: *We have doubts about the success of our plan.* **2.** A state of not being sure or certain: *When in doubt ask the teacher.*

doubt·ful |dout′fəl| —*adjective* **1.** Not sure or certain: *The game's outcome looks doubtful.* **2.** Having or showing doubt: *a doubtful expression on his face.*

dough |dō| —*noun, plural* **doughs** A soft, thick mixture of flour, water or milk, and other ingredients. Dough is used to make bread, pastry, and other baked goods.
♦ *These sound alike* **dough, doe.**

dough·nut |dō′nŭt′| or |dō′nət| —*noun, plural* **doughnuts** A small cake made of sweetened dough fried in deep fat. Doughnuts are often shaped like rings.

dove[1] |dŭv| —*noun, plural* **doves** A bird with a plump body, short legs, and a cooing voice. Doves and pigeons are related.

dormouse

dove[1]

down¹, down²

Down¹ comes from an expression used in English long ago to mean "from the hill," that is, "downward." **Down²** was borrowed from a word in the language spoken a very long time ago by people living in Scandinavia; the meaning has never changed.

dove² | dōv | A past tense and past participle of **dive:** *They dove into the pool. They had dove from the rock into the lake.*

Do·ver | dō′vər | The capital of Delaware.

down¹ | doun | —*adverb* **1.** From a higher to a lower place: *We pulled down the shades. He climbed down from the roof.* **2.** In, at, or to a lower position, point, or condition: *He is getting ready to sit down. The temperature is going down tonight. Store prices are coming down. Tell the driver to slow down.* **3.** From an earlier to a later time: *The name Evangeline was passed down in her family.* **4.** From a larger to a smaller quantity: *Make sure to boil down the syrup.* **5.** In writing: *Please put down your phone number.* **6.** In cash at the time of purchase: *Pay ten dollars down and the rest in weekly payments.* **7.** In a serious way: *Let's get down to work.*
—*adjective* **1.** Moving or directed downward: *a down elevator.* **2.** In a lower position; not up: *The shades are down.* **3.** Not feeling well; sick: *He is down with the mumps.* **4.** Being the first in a series of payments; in cash: *a down payment on the new car.*
—*preposition* From a higher to a lower place or position in or on: *We must row down the stream. She fell down the staircase. Walk down the street to the grocery store.*
—*noun, plural* **downs 1.** Any of four plays in football during which a team must move the ball forward by at least ten yards. If it fails to do so, the other team gets possession of the ball. **2. downs** Bad times: *There are ups and downs in life.*
—*verb* **downed, downing 1.** To bring or put down; defeat: *The fighter downed his opponent in the second round.* **2.** To swallow quickly; gulp: *He downed his milk and ran out.*

down² | doun | —*noun* **1.** Fine, soft, fluffy feathers: *the down on a newly hatched chick.* **2.** Fine, soft fluff or hair: *the down on a peach.*

down·pour | doun′pôr′ | or | doun′pōr′ | —*noun, plural* **downpours** A heavy fall of rain.

down·right | doun′rīt | —*adjective* Complete: *a downright lie.*
—*adverb* Thoroughly; absolutely: *They're downright crazy.*

down·stairs | doun′stârz′ | —*adverb* **1.** Down the stairs: *He fell downstairs.* **2.** On or to a lower floor: *You'll find the book downstairs in the den.*
—*adjective* | doun′stârz′ | On a lower floor: *a downstairs bedroom.*
—*noun* | doun′stârz′ | (Used with a singular verb.) The lower floor of a building: *She has the whole downstairs for herself.*

down·stream | doun′strēm′ | —*adverb* In the direction of flow of a stream: *He swam downstream.*
—*adjective* | doun′strēm′ | In the direction of flow of a stream: *a downstream current.*

down·town | doun′toun′ | —*adverb* Toward or in the main or business part of a town or city: *She went downtown. He shops downtown.*
—*adjective* | doun′toun′ | Of the main or business part of a town or city: *the downtown office buildings; a downtown shopping center.*

down·ward | doun′wərd | —*adverb* **1.** From a higher to a lower place, level, or condition: *Cool air moves downward. The kite glided downward.* **2.** From an earlier time: *Knowledge has come to us downward through the ages.* Another form of this adverb is **downwards.**
—*adjective* Moving from a higher to a lower place, level, or condition: *the downward movement of the kite.*

ă	pat	ĕ	pet	î	fierce
ā	pay	ē	be	ŏ	pot
â	care	ĭ	pit	ō	go
ä	father	ī	pie	ô	paw, for
oi	oil	ŭ	cut	zh	vision
ŏŏ	book	û	fur	ə	ago, item,
ōō	boot	th	the		pencil, atom,
yōō	abuse	th	thin		circus
ou	out	hw	which	ər	butter

down·wards |doun'wərdz| A form of the adverb **downward.**

dow·ry |dou'rē| —*noun, plural* **dowries** Money or property brought by a bride to the man she is going to marry.

doze |dōz| —*verb* **dozed, dozing** To sleep lightly; to nap: *The cat likes to doze in the sun.*

doz·en |dŭz'ən| —*noun, plural* **dozens** or **dozen** A group of twelve: *How many eggs are there in a dozen?*
—*adjective* Twelve: *a dozen eggs.* The adjective **dozen** belongs to a class of words called **determiners.** They signal that a noun is coming.

drab |drăb| —*adjective* **drabber, drabbest** Not bright or cheerful; dull; dreary: *a drab, old house. He is tired of his drab existence.*

draft |drăft| or |dräft| —*noun, plural* **drafts** **1.** A current of air: *I can feel a draft coming from the open window.* **2.** A device for controlling the flow of air in a fireplace, furnace, and some stoves. **3.** A rough sketch, plan, or outline for something: *He wrote several drafts of his speech before he had it typed up. This is only a draft of the architect's plans.* **4.** The picking of someone for a special job or duty: *the draft of a fine quarterback.*
—*verb* **drafted, drafting** **1.** To make a rough sketch, plan, or outline for something: *Several writers helped him draft the speech.* **2.** To pick someone for a special job or duty: *The coach drafted many good players for the hockey team.*
—*adjective* Used for pulling loads: *a team of draft horses.*

drafts·man |drăfts'mən| or |dräfts'mən| —*noun, plural* **draftsmen** A person whose work is drawing plans or designs for buildings, machines, and other things.

drag |drăg| —*verb* **dragged, dragging** **1.** To draw or pull along with force: *It is easier to roll a log than to drag it.* **2.** To move or go too slowly: *His speech dragged on and on. Janice dragged behind the other girls.* **3.** To trail or cause to trail along the ground: *Her coat drags behind her because it is too long. Don't drag the clothes in the mud.* **4.** To search the bottom of a river or lake for sunken objects: *They dragged the lake today looking for the missing bus.*

drag·on |drăg'ən| —*noun, plural* **dragons** An imaginary monster who breathes fire. A dragon is usually pictured as a giant lizard with wings and claws.

drag·on·fly |drăg'ən flī'| —*noun, plural* **dragonflies** A large insect with a long body and four narrow wings. Dragonflies catch and eat other insects.

drain |drān| —*verb* **drained, draining** **1.** To draw off slowly: *We drained the water from the swimming pool.* **2.** To draw off liquid from: *The army engineers drained the swamp.* **3.** To become dry: *Wash the dishes and leave them on the counter to drain.* **4.** To discharge a liquid; flow off: *The river drains into the sea.* **5.** To use up completely: *The day's activities drained her energy.*
—*noun, plural* **drains** **1.** A pipe, ditch, sewer, or other device for carrying away liquids that are not wanted: *a street drain; a sink drain.* **2.** Something that uses up completely: *Holding two jobs was a drain on his strength.*

drain·age |drā'nĭj| —*noun, plural* **drainages** The act or process of draining off water or waste material: *The army engineers supervised the drainage of the swamp.*

drake |drāk| —*noun, plural* **drakes** A male duck.

dra·ma |drä'mə| or |drăm'ə| —*noun, plural* **dramas** **1.** A story written for actors to perform on a stage; a play. **2.** A

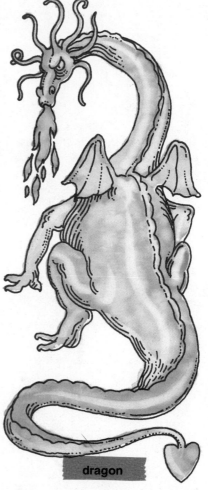

dragon

dragonfly

situation in real life that has the excitement and interest of a play: *The lawyer enjoyed the drama of a murder trial.*

dra·mat·ic |drə **măt′** ĭk | —*adjective* **1.** Of drama or the theater: *a dramatic coach.* **2.** Like a drama; interesting and exciting: *the dramatic events that led to his election.*

dram·a·tize |**drăm′** ə tīz | or |**drä′** mə tīz | —*verb* **dramatized, dramatizing 1.** To make something into a play for the stage, motion pictures, or television: *He always wanted to dramatize that story.* **2.** To do or see things in a dramatic way: *She likes to dramatize her problems.*

drank |drăngk | The past tense of **drink:** *He drank his milk.*

drape |drāp | —*verb* **draped, draping 1.** To cover or hang with cloth in loose folds: *He draped the partially finished painting.* **2.** To arrange or hang cloth in folds: *She draped the veil over her head.* **3.** To spread casually; sprawl: *He draped his legs over the side of the chair.*
—*noun, plural* **drapes** Often **drapes** Long, heavy curtains that hang straight in loose folds.

drap·er·y |**drā′** pə rē | —*noun, plural* **draperies** Often **draperies** Long, heavy curtains; drapes.

dras·tic |**drăs′** tĭk | —*adjective* Extreme or severe: *Drastic measures must be taken to prevent crime.*

draw |drô | —*verb* **drew, drawn, drawing 1.** To pull or haul: *Two horses drew the farmer's cart.* **2.** To pull out; haul off; remove: *We drew two buckets of water from the well.* **3.** To take or bring out: *She drew the cork of the bottle. The sheriff drew his gun and fired.* **4.a.** To withdraw; take out: *Pedro drew ten dollars from his savings account. Louise drew the lucky number in the lottery.* **b.** To take a chance: *She will draw for a prize.* **5.** To cause to come; attract: *Beautiful weather and fine beaches draw many summer visitors to our state.* **6.** To move or cause to move in a given direction: *The boat drew near the shore. She drew him aside.* **7.** To pull or move so as to close: *It is too light, so draw the curtains.* **8.** To write out in suitable form: *The lawyers drew up her will.* **9.** To get as a response; bring forth: *His act drew laughter from the audience.* **10.** To get; receive: *He draws a big salary.* **11.** To make a picture, likeness, or design with pen or pencil, chalk, or other similar object: *He drew a landscape on her notebook. She draws well.* **12.** To allow a current of air to pass: *Our fireplace draws well.* **13.** To breathe in; inhale: *Sheila drew a deep breath.*
—*noun, plural* **draws 1.** The act of taking out and aiming a firearm: *The outlaw was quick on the draw.* **2.** A contest that ends in a tie: *The race was a draw between the two leading runners.*

draw·back |**drô′** băk′ | —*noun, plural* **drawbacks** A disadvantage or inconvenience.

draw·bridge |**drô′** brĭj′ | —*noun, plural* **drawbridges** A bridge that can be raised or turned to prevent someone from crossing it. Another kind of drawbridge can be raised or turned to permit boats to pass through.

draw·er |drôr | —*noun, plural* **drawers** A box fitted with handles that slides in and out of a desk, bureau, or table.

draw·ing |**drô′** ĭng | —*noun, plural* **drawings 1.** A picture, likeness, or design made on a surface with a pen or pencil, chalk, or other similar object. **2.** The choosing of a winning ticket, number, or chance in a lottery: *The drawing for the winning ticket is on Wednesdays.*

drawbridge

ă	pat	ĕ	pet	î	fierce
ā	pay	ē	be	ŏ	pot
â	care	ĭ	pit	ō	go
ä	father	ī	pie	ô	paw, for
oi	oil	ŭ	cut	zh	vision
ŏŏ	book	û	fur	ə	ago, item,
ōō	boot	th	the		pencil, atom,
yōō	abuse	th	thin		circus
ou	out	hw	which	ər	butter

drawl |drôl| —*verb* **drawled, drawling** To speak in a slow way.
—*noun, plural* **drawls** A slow way of speaking.

drawn |drôn| The past participle of **draw:** *He has drawn many pictures this week.*

dread |drĕd| —*noun, plural* **dreads** A great fear of something that may happen: *They live in dread of forest fires.*
—*verb* **dreaded, dreading** To live in fear of; become frightened by: *Some people dread flying in airplanes.*
—*adjective* Causing fear: *Smallpox is a dread disease.*

dread·ful |drĕd′fəl| —*adjective* **1.** Filling with great fear; terrible: *He told dreadful stories about ghosts.* **2.** Of poor quality or in poor taste: *The house is painted a dreadful color.*

dream |drēm| —*noun, plural* **dreams** **1.** A series of pictures, thoughts, and emotions that a person sees or feels during sleep. **2.** Something like this that happens when a person is awake: *She has dreams of great wealth.*
—*verb* **dreamed** or **dreamt, dreaming** **1.** To have a dream or dreams while sleeping: *Normally a person dreams from one to two hours a night. I dreamed I was a police officer.* **2.** To think of as possible: *She never dreamed she would win the award.*

dreamt |drĕmt| A past tense and past participle of **dream:** *He dreamt of a big castle that belonged to him. I have dreamt every night for a week.*

drear·y |drîr′ē| —*adjective* **drearier, dreariest** **1.** Gloomy or dismal: *a dreary January day.* **2.** Boring or dull: *They tried to do the dreary kitchen chores cheerfully.*

dredge |drĕj| —*noun, plural* **dredges** A large machine that uses scooping devices to bring up mud, silt, or other material from the bottom of a body of water.
—*verb* **dredged, dredging** To clean out or deepen the bottom of a channel or harbor.

dregs |drĕgz| —*plural noun* Small bits of material that settle to the bottom of a liquid: *the dregs of coffee.*

drench |drĕnch| —*verb* **drenched, drenching** To wet completely; soak: *The sudden cloudburst drenched us.*

dress |drĕs| —*noun, plural* **dresses** **1.** An outer garment worn by women and girls. A dress usually has a top and skirt and is made in one piece. **2.** Any type of clothing: *fancy dress. You can come to my party in casual dress.*
—*verb* **dressed, dressing** **1.** To put clothes on; clothe: *She dressed the baby in a warm outfit. She dressed in a hurry.* **2.** To get something ready for cooking: *Dad dressed the turkey for Thanksgiving dinner.* **3.** To clean and treat a wound: *The nurse dressed my cut knee.*

dress·er |drĕs′ər| —*noun, plural* **dressers** A piece of furniture that has drawers and often a mirror above it. A dresser is used for storing clothes and other objects.

dress·ing |drĕs′ĭng| —*noun, plural* **dressings** **1.** A sauce for salads and some other foods. **2.** A stuffing made of bread crumbs and seasonings. Dressing is used to stuff poultry, fish, and meat. **3.** Medicine and bandages that are put on a wound.

drew |drōō| The past tense of **draw:** *He drew a picture.*

drib·ble |drĭb′əl| —*verb* **dribbled, dribbling** **1.** To drip or cause to drip; trickle: *Water dribbled from the faucet. He dribbled a little water into the pan.* **2.** To move a ball along by bouncing or kicking it many times in basketball or in soccer.

dress

dribble

—*noun, plural* **dribbles** A small quantity; drop: *There's only a dribble of milk left in the carton.*

dried | drīd | The past tense and past participle of the verb **dry**: *We dried the sheets in the sun. I had dried the floor before I waxed it.*

dri·er[1] | drī′ər | —*noun, plural* **driers** A form of the word **dryer**.

dri·er[2] | drī′ər | The comparative of the adjective **dry**.

dri·est | drī′ĭst | The superlative of the adjective **dry**.

drift | drĭft | —*verb* **drifted, drifting** **1.** To be carried along by a current of water or air: *The boat drifted toward shore. Dark storm clouds drifted by. The smoke drifted out through the window.* **2.** To cause to pile up: *The wind drifted the snow.*

—*noun, plural* **drifts** Something that has been carried along or piled up by a current of water or air: *snow drifts.*

drift·wood | drĭft′wŏŏd′ | —*noun* Wood floating in the water or washed ashore by water. Driftwood is sometimes used as a decoration.

drill | drĭl | —*noun, plural* **drills** **1.** A tool that is used to make holes in wood, rocks, plastic, or other solid materials. **2.** Training or teaching by repeating something again and again; practice: *For our daily English drill we have to spell twenty words correctly.*

—*verb* **drilled, drilling** **1.** To make a hole with a drill: *She drilled a hole in the wall. The farmer had to drill thirty feet to reach water for his new well.* **2.** To train or teach by repeating something again and again: *The teacher drilled us on the multiplication tables.*

drink | drĭngk | —*verb* **drank, drunk, drinking** **1.** To take liquid into the mouth and swallow: *Jim drinks a quart of milk a day.* **2.** To soak up; absorb: *Plants drink water.* **3.** To use alcoholic beverages: *If you drink, you shouldn't drive a car.*

—*noun, plural* **drinks** **1.** A liquid for drinking; beverage: *Milk is a nourishing drink.* **2.** An amount of a beverage: *Give each guest a drink of orange juice.* **3.** An amount of an alcoholic beverage: *Mother and Dad had a drink to welcome the New Year.*

drip | drĭp | —*verb* **dripped, dripping** To fall or let fall in drops: *Water dripped from the faucet. You're dripping hot wax on the table.*

—*noun, plural* **drips** **1.** Liquid or moisture that falls in drops. **2.** The sound made by dripping liquid: *I love to hear the drip of the rain on the roof.*

drive | drīv | —*verb* **drove, driven, driving** **1.** To steer or operate a vehicle, especially a car: *Dad drives to work every day. Please drive carefully.* **2.** To carry in a vehicle: *She drove me to school.* **3.** To put into and keep in motion; move by force: *The wind drove the sailboat. The soldiers drove the enemy all the way back to the river. Drive the cows down to the pasture.* **4.** To force someone into feeling or acting in a certain way: *Your complaining is driving me crazy. He's driving himself hard in school because he wants to go to college.* **5.** To force; make penetrate: *Drive the nail into the wood.*

—*noun, plural* **drives** **1.** A ride or trip in a car or other vehicle: *We took a drive to my aunt's house on Sunday.* **2.** A road or driveway: *Whose red car is parked in the drive?* **3.** A special, organized effort to do something: *The school is having a drive to raise money for charity.* **4.** A strong wish or instinct: *She has the drive and ambition to become a doctor.* **5.** A ball hit hard in a game: *He hit a drive over the fence.*

drive-in | drīv′ĭn′ | —*noun, plural* **drive-ins** A restaurant, movie theater, or bank that customers can use without leaving their cars.

driftwood

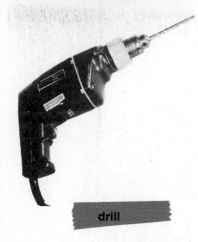

drill

ă	pat	ĕ	pet	î	fierce
ā	pay	ē	be	ŏ	pot
â	care	ĭ	pit	ō	go
ä	father	ī	pie	ô	paw, for
oi	oil	ŭ	cut	zh	vision
ŏŏ	book	û	fur	ə	ago, item,
ōō	boot	*th*	the		pencil, atom,
yōō	abuse	th	thin		circus
ou	out	hw	which	ər	butter

driv·er |drī′vər| —*noun, plural* **drivers** A person who drives a car, truck, or other vehicle.

drive·way |drīv′wā′| —*noun, plural* **driveways** A private road leading from a house or other building to the street; a drive.

driz·zle |drĭz′əl| —*verb* **drizzled, drizzling** To rain in gentle drops like mist.
—*noun, plural* **drizzles** A gentle rain like mist.

drom·e·dar·y |drŏm′ĭ dĕr′ē| or |drŭm′ĭ dĕr′ē| —*noun, plural* **dromedaries** A camel with one hump. It is used in certain parts of northern Africa and southwestern Asia for riding and carrying loads.

drone¹ |drōn| —*noun, plural* **drones** A male bee. Drones have no stings, do no work, and do not make honey.

drone² |drōn| —*verb* **droned, droning** **1.** To make a low, humming noise: *An airplane droned far overhead.* **2.** To talk in a boring, dull way: *The speaker droned on for a long time.*
—*noun, plural* **drones** A low, humming sound: *I could hear the drone of the machinery as I approached the factory.*

drool |drool| —*verb* **drooled, drooling** To let saliva dribble from the mouth, as a baby does.

droop |droop| —*verb* **drooped, drooping** To bend or hang downward; sag: *The flowers drooped for lack of water.*

drop |drŏp| —*verb* **dropped, dropping** **1.** To fall or let fall from a higher to a lower place: *A penny dropped from his pocket. She dropped a dish on the floor.* **2.** To lower; let down: *Drop the anchor.* **3.** To decrease; become less: *The temperature has dropped ten degrees since this morning.* **4.** To go down; sink: *The sun dropped behind the trees. Be careful; those cliffs drop straight down to the ocean.* **5.** To leave out; omit: *You dropped the second "t" from the word "little."* **6.** To put down or let out at a particular place; deliver: *Would you drop me at the store?* **7.** To take away one's right to be a member of; remove or let go: *He was angry when the coach dropped him from the team.* **8.** To put an end to; stop: *I said you can't go, so now let's drop the subject.*
—*noun, plural* **drops** **1.a.** A tiny mass or amount of liquid. It usually has a round or oval shape: *I felt a drop of rain.* **b.** Something that is shaped like this: *a cough drop.* **2.** A small amount of liquid: *Drink your milk to the last drop.* **3.** A sudden fall or decrease: *a drop in temperature; a drop in car prices.* **4.** The distance between something and what is below it: *It's a three-hundred-foot drop from the roof down to the street.*

drought |drout| —*noun, plural* **droughts** A long period with little or no rain.

drove¹ |drōv| The past tense of **drive**: *He drove the car carefully.*

drove² |drōv| —*noun, plural* **droves** **1.** A number of cattle, sheep, or other animals that are herded together. **2.** A crowd: *Visitors arrived in droves for the rodeo.*

drown |droun| —*verb* **drowned, drowning** **1.** To die underwater for lack of air to breathe: *When the ship sank, many sailors drowned.* **2.** To kill by keeping underwater: *The high tides caused by the hurricane drowned many animals.* **3.** To cover up sound by a louder sound: *A fire siren drowned out the sound of their voices.*

drows·y |drou′zē| —*adjective* **drowsier, drowsiest** Partly asleep; sleepy: *Sitting in the sun made me drowsy.*

drug |drŭg| —*noun, plural* **drugs** **1.** A substance that is used to treat or cure disease or pain; medicine. **2.** A substance that

dromedary

drone¹, drone²
Drone¹ comes from an old English word that comes from a root meaning "to buzz." **Drone²** first appears in the sixteenth century. It seems to be related to the original meaning of the root from which **drone¹** comes.

drum major

drum majorette

duck¹, duck²

Duck¹ meant "diving bird" to English-speaking people of long ago. It is probably from **duck²**, which originally meant "to dive," although we have no written documents to prove this.

duck¹

ă	pat	ĕ	pet	î	fierce
ā	pay	ē	be	ŏ	pot
â	care	ĭ	pit	ō	go
ä	father	ī	pie	ô	paw, for

oi	oil	ŭ	cut	zh	vision
ōō	book	û	fur	ə	ago, item,
ōō	boot	th	the		pencil, atom,
yōō	abuse	th	thin		circus
ou	out	hw	which	ər	butter

affects the nervous system and can become habit forming. Heroin and alcohol are drugs of this kind.
—verb **drugged, drugging** To give a drug to: *The doctor drugged the patient before the operation.*

drug·gist |drŭg′ĭst| *—noun, plural* **druggists 1.** A person who owns and runs a drugstore. **2.** A pharmacist.

drug·store |drŭg′stôr′| or |drŭg′stōr′| *—noun, plural* **drugstores** A store where medicines are sold. Drugstores often sell magazines, cosmetics, and sometimes ice cream and food.

drum |drŭm| *—noun, plural* **drums 1.** A musical instrument that makes a sound when it is beaten. It is a hollow container, such as a tube or bowl, with material stretched tightly across one or more of its openings. The sides of a drum are struck with the hands or sticks to produce sound. **2.** A container shaped like a drum: *an oil drum.*
—verb **drummed, drumming 1.** To play a drum. **2.** To tap again and again: *He drummed his fingers on the table.* **3.** To force into by repeating: *Father finally drummed the idea into my brother's head.*

drum major A person in a costume and tall helmet who leads a marching band.

drum ma·jor·ette |mā′jə rĕt′| A girl in a costume who twirls a baton at the head of a marching band.

drum·stick |drŭm′stĭk′| *—noun, plural* **drumsticks 1.** A stick for beating a drum. **2.** The lower part of the leg of a cooked fowl.

drunk |drŭngk| The past participle of **drink:** *He has drunk all the milk.*
—adjective **drunker, drunkest** Having had too much alcoholic liquor to drink.
—noun, plural **drunks** A person who drinks too much alcoholic liquor.

dry |drī| *—adjective* **drier, driest 1.** Free from liquid or moisture; not wet or damp: *dry clothes; dry weather.* **2.** Not liquid; solid: *dry foods.* **3.** Not underwater: *He swam for dry land.* **4.** Thirsty: *We're very dry after the hike.*
—verb **dried, drying, dries** To make or become dry: *It's your turn to dry the dishes. His socks dried off.*

dry cell An electric cell in which the negative and positive poles are separated by a moist paste rather than a liquid. A dry cell is sealed to prevent spilling.

dry·er |drī′ər| *—noun, plural* **dryers** An electrical appliance that removes moisture: *a hair dryer; a clothes dryer.* Another form of this word is **drier.**

du·al |dōō′əl| or |dyōō′əl| *—adjective* Having or made up of two parts; double: *a plane with dual controls. She acted a dual role in the play: Mrs. Stevens and her twin sister.*
♦ *These sound alike* **dual, duel.**

duch·ess |dŭch′ĭs| *—noun, plural* **duchesses 1.** The wife of a duke. **2.** A woman with a rank equal to that of a duke in her own right.

duck¹ |dŭk| *—noun, plural* **ducks 1.** A water bird with a broad, flat bill, short legs, and webbed feet. There are several kinds of ducks. Some are raised for food. **2.** The meat of a duck, used as food.

duck² |dŭk| *—verb* **ducked, ducking 1.** To lower the head and body quickly to avoid being hit or seen: *They all ducked as they passed through the entrance to the tunnel.* **2.** To push suddenly under water: *In the pool, someone ducked me from behind.*

duck·ling | dŭk′lĭng | —*noun, plural* **ducklings** A young duck.

duct | dŭkt | —*noun, plural* **ducts** Any tube or pipe through which a liquid or air can flow.

due | dōo | or | dyōo | —*adjective* **1.** Owed as a debt; owing: *The telephone bill is due.* **2.** Requiring payment on demand: *The bank loan is due on November 15.* **3.** Expected or supposed to arrive, happen, or be ready: *The plane is due at noon. He is due for a promotion in June.*

—*noun, plural* **dues 1.** Something that is owed; something that must be given to another: *You must pay the man his due. He was denied a promotion that his colleagues thought his due.* **2. dues** A charge or fee paid by a person to a club or institution for the right of being a member.

—*adverb* Directly; straight: *The ship traveled due north.*

♦ *These sound alike* **due, dew, do.**

   Idiom due to 1. Caused by: *a shy manner due to fear of strangers.* **2.** Because of: *The game was called off due to rain.*

du·el | dōo′əl | or | dyōo′əl | —*noun, plural* **duels** A fight arranged ahead of time between two men with swords or pistols.

—*verb* **dueled, dueling** To fight a duel.

♦ *These sound alike* **duel, dual.**

du·et | dōo ĕt′ | or | dyōo ĕt′ | —*noun, plural* **duets** A musical piece for two voices or two instruments.

dug | dŭg | The past tense and past participle of **dig**: *He dug a tunnel through the hill. He has dug many ditches around the farm.*

dug·out | dŭg′out′ | —*noun, plural* **dugouts 1.** A boat or canoe made by hollowing out a log. **2.** A long, low shelter at the side of a baseball field for the players.

duke | dōok | or | dyōok | —*noun, plural* **dukes** A nobleman who has the highest rank below a prince.

dull | dŭl | —*adjective* **duller, dullest 1.** Not having a sharp edge or point; blunt: *I can't cut anything with this dull knife.* **2.** Not exciting; not interesting; boring: *a dull book.* **3.** Not bright or clear: *Her car is a dull color. The sky is so dull today.* **4.** Slow to learn: *The dull student is having trouble with multiplication.* **5.** Not sharply or strongly felt: *I have a dull ache in my arm.*

—*verb* **dulled, dulling** To make or become dull: *Cutting all that wood dulled the knife. These scissors dull easily.*

dumb | dŭm | —*adjective* **dumber, dumbest 1.** Not able to speak; mute: *a deaf and dumb person.* **2.** Stupid or silly: *a dumb remark.*

dum·my | dŭm′ē | —*noun, plural* **dummies 1.** A model of the human figure. Dummies are used to show clothes or to shoot at or tackle as a target. **2.** An object that looks like and takes the place of a real one: *wooden dummies instead of rifles.*

dump | dŭmp | —*verb* **dumped, dumping** To let fall in a mass; unload: *The trucks dumped the rubbish into a pit.*

—*noun, plural* **dumps** A place where trash is thrown out.

dune | dōon | or | dyōon | —*noun, plural* **dunes** A hill of sand that has been made by the blowing of the wind.

dun·ga·ree | dŭng′gə rē′ | —*noun, plural* **dungarees 1.** A sturdy blue cotton fabric. **2. dungarees** Overalls or pants made of this fabric; blue jeans.

dun·geon | dŭn′jən | —*noun, plural* **dungeons** A dark, underground prison.

du·pli·cate | dōo′plĭ kĭt | or | dyōo′plĭ kĭt | —*noun, plural*

dugout

dump

dune

duplicates Something that is exactly like another: *The file holds a duplicate of the original letter.*
—*adjective* Exactly like another: *a duplicate key.*
—*verb* |dōō′plĭ kāt′| or |dyōō′plĭ kāt′| **duplicated, duplicating** To make an exact copy of.

dur·a·ble |dŏŏr′ə bəl| or |dyŏŏr′ə bəl| —*adjective* Able to stand wear and heavy use: *durable clothes.*

du·ra·tion |dŏŏ rā′shən| or |dyŏŏ rā′shən| —*noun* The length of time during which something goes on or continues: *We stayed in the cellar for the duration of the storm.*

dur·ing |dŏŏr′ĭng| or |dyŏŏr′ĭng| —*preposition* **1.** Throughout the time of: *She goes skiing during the winter.* **2.** At some point of time in; in the course of: *He called me during the evening.*

dusk |dŭsk| —*noun* The time of evening just before darkness.

dust |dŭst| —*noun* Matter in the form of tiny, dry particles.
—*verb* **dusted, dusting** To remove the dust from by wiping, brushing, or beating: *Sally dusted the books. She dusts every day.*

Dutch |dŭch| —*noun* **1. the Dutch** (Used with a plural verb.) The people of the Netherlands. **2.** The Germanic language of the Netherlands.
—*adjective* Of the Netherlands, its people, or their language.

du·ty |dōō′tē| or |dyōō′tē| —*noun, plural* **duties 1.** Something that a person must or should do: *It is your duty to defend your country.* **2.** A task, chore, or function: *household duties; the duties of a senator.* **3.** A tax paid to a government on goods brought into or taken out of a country.

dwarf |dwôrf| —*noun, plural* **dwarfs** or **dwarves 1.** A person, animal, or plant whose size is very much smaller than normal. **2.** In fairy tales, a tiny man with magic powers.
—*verb* **dwarfed, dwarfing** To make seem small beside someone or something else: *The ocean liner dwarfed the tugboat.*

dwarves |dwôrvz| A plural of the noun **dwarf.**

dwell |dwĕl| —*verb* **dwelt** or **dwelled, dwelling** To live in; reside: *We plan to dwell in this house for many years.*

dwell·ing |dwĕl′ĭng| —*noun, plural* **dwellings** A place to live in; a residence.

dwelt |dwĕlt| A past tense and past participle of the verb **dwell:** *They dwelt in that town for many years. Our family has dwelt in this house for years.*

dwin·dle |dwĭn′dəl| —*verb* **dwindled, dwindling** To grow less; become smaller; diminish: *His savings dwindled away.*

dye |dī| —*noun, plural* **dyes** A substance or coloring matter that is used to change the color of something.
—*verb* **dyed, dyeing** To color with or become colored by a dye: *She dyed her hair red. This fabric dyes easily.*
♦ *These sound alike* **dye, die.**

dy·nam·ic |dī năm′ĭk| —*adjective* Full of energy; active; forceful: *She has a dynamic personality and gets a lot of work done.*

dy·na·mite |dī′nə mīt′| —*noun, plural* **dynamites** A powerful explosive that is used especially to blow up rocks.
—*verb* **dynamited, dynamiting** To blow up with or as if with dynamite.

dy·na·mo |dī′nə mō′| —*noun, plural* **dynamos** An electric generator that produces direct current.

dy·nas·ty |dī′nə stē| —*noun, plural* **dynasties** A line of kings or rulers who belong to the same family.

dust
A dust storm in Kansas, 1937

ă	pat	ĕ	pet	î	fierce
ā	pay	ē	be	ŏ	pot
â	care	ĭ	pit	ō	go
ä	father	ī	pie	ô	paw, for
oi	oil	ŭ	cut	zh	vision
ōō	book	û	fur	ə	ago, item,
ōō	boot	*th*	the		pencil, atom,
yōō	abuse	th	thin		circus
ou	out	hw	which	ər	butter

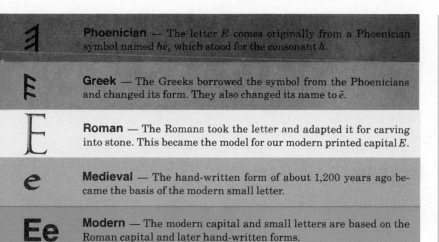

Phoenician — The letter *E* comes originally from a Phoenician symbol named *hē*, which stood for the consonant *h*.

Greek — The Greeks borrowed the symbol from the Phoenicians and changed its form. They also changed its name to *ē*.

Roman — The Romans took the letter and adapted it for carving into stone. This became the model for our modern printed capital *E*.

Medieval — The hand-written form of about 1,200 years ago became the basis of the modern small letter.

Modern — The modern capital and small letters are based on the Roman capital and later hand-written forms.

Ee

e or **E** |ē| —*noun, plural* **e's** or **E's** The fifth letter of the English alphabet.

each |ēch| —*adjective* One of two or more persons or things; every: *Look each way before crossing.* The adjective **each** belongs to a class of words called **determiners.** They signal that a noun is coming.
—*pronoun* Every one: *Each of us had a turn at bat.*
—*adverb* For or to each one; apiece: *He gave the three boys a dollar each.*

each other One another: *The new girl and I liked each other right away.*

ea·ger |ē′ gər| —*adjective* **eagerer, eagerest** Wanting something very much; full of desire: *Bill is so eager to learn that he asks for extra homework. We're ready and eager to get started.*

ea·gle |ē′ gəl| —*noun, plural* **eagles** A large bird with a hooked bill and broad, strong wings. Eagles fly high and have very good eyesight.

ear¹ |îr| —*noun, plural* **ears** **1.** The part of the body with which people and animals hear; especially, the outer part on each side of a person's head. **2.** The sense of hearing: *If you can hear the cat purr in the next room, you have a good ear.*

ear² |îr| —*noun, plural* **ears** The part of a grain plant on which the seeds grow: *an ear of corn; an ear of wheat.*

ear·drum |îr′ drŭm′| —*noun, plural* **eardrums** A layer of thin tissue that separates the middle and outer parts of the ear. The eardrum vibrates when sound waves strike it.

earl |ûrl| —*noun, plural* **earls** A British nobleman.

ear·ly |ûr′ lē| —*adjective* **earlier, earliest** **1.** Of or happening near the beginning; first: *Birds sing during the early part of the morning.* **2.** Of a time long ago; ancient: *Early humans learned to make and use stone tools.* **3.** Before the usual time: *an early dinner.*
—*adverb* **earlier, earliest** **1.** At or near the beginning: *The hikers set out early in the morning. He was wounded early in the battle.* **2.** Before the usual or expected time: *We arrived early for the dentist's appointment.* **3.** Far back in time; long ago: *Their religion was practiced as early as the twelfth century B.C.*

ear·muffs |îr′ mŭfs′| —*plural noun* A pair of warm coverings for the ears.

eagle

ear¹, ear²
Ear¹ and **ear²** are both native English words. The original words had the same meanings they do today, but they sounded different and were spelled differently. The two are not related at all.

earphone

earthquake

Fires after an earthquake, 1906

easel

earn | ûrn | —*verb* **earned, earning 1.** To get in return for work; be paid: *My brother earns money by baby-sitting.* **2.** To deserve or win by one's efforts: *They earned their good grades.*
♦ *These sound alike* **earn, urn.**

ear·nest | ûr′nĭst | —*adjective* Serious and sincere: *The congregation joined in earnest prayer to end the fighting between the countries. Really earnest students often ask questions in class.*

earn·ings | ûr′nĭngz | —*plural noun* Money that has been earned in payment for work or as a profit.

ear·phone | îr′fōn′ | —*noun, plural* **earphones** A device that carries sound to the ear. It is designed to be worn over the ear.

ear·ring | îr′rĭng | or | îr′ĭng | —*noun, plural* **earrings** A piece of jewelry hanging from or clipped to the ear.

earth | ûrth | —*noun, plural* **earths 1.** Often **Earth** The planet on which human beings live. It is the fifth largest planet in the solar system and the third in distance from the sun. **2.** The surface of the land; ground: *The snowflakes fell slowly to earth.* **3.** Dirt; soil: *The seeds sprouted from the moist earth.*

Idiom **down to earth** Sensible; simple: *The teacher's explanation was very clear and down to earth.*

earth·ly | ûrth′lē | —*adjective* **1.** Of or from the earth rather than heaven; physical: *The old priest's only earthly possessions were the clothes on his back.* **2.** Possible; practical: *That broken tennis racket in your closet is of no earthly use.*

earth·quake | ûrth′kwāk′ | —*noun, plural* **earthquakes** A shaking of the ground. Earthquakes are caused by sudden movements in masses of rock far below the earth's surface.

earth·worm | ûrth′wûrm′ | —*noun, plural* **earthworms** A common worm that lives in the ground. Its body is made up of many narrow parts shaped like rings.

ease | ēz | —*noun, plural* **eases 1.** Freedom from difficulty, trouble, strain, or hard work: *She won the race with ease.* **2.** Relief; rest: *His mother's soft words gave ease to his troubled mind.* **3.** Comfort; luxury: *a life of ease and pleasure.*
—*verb* **eased, easing 1.** To make easier: *Use short cuts to ease your work.* **2.** To relieve and give comfort to: *The nurse gave medicine to the sick man to ease his pain.* **3.** To move slowly and carefully: *Use a shoehorn to ease your foot into a tight shoe.*

ea·sel | ē′zəl | —*noun, plural* **easels** A stand for holding a painting or displaying a sign or picture.

eas·i·ly | ē′zə lē | —*adverb* **1.** Without difficulty: *Libraries are arranged so you can find books easily.* **2.** Without doubt; definitely: *That is easily the best meal I have eaten this month.* **3.** Possibly; very likely: *He might easily slip and fall.*

east | ēst | —*noun* **1.** The direction from which the sun is seen rising in the morning. **2.** Often **East** A region in this direction. **3. the East** The part of the United States along or near the coast of the Atlantic Ocean. **4. the East** Asia and the islands near it; the Orient.
—*adjective* **1.** Of, in, or toward the east: *the east bank of the river.* **2.** Coming from the east: *an east wind.*
—*adverb* Toward the east: *This river flows east to the sea.*

Eas·ter | ē′stər | —*noun, plural* **Easters** A Christian holiday that celebrates Christ's return to life from the grave. Easter falls on the first Sunday after the first full moon on or after March 21.

ă	pat	ĕ	pet	î	fierce
ā	pay	ē	be	ŏ	pot
â	care	ĭ	pit	ō	go
ä	father	ī	pie	ô	paw, for
oi	oil	ŭ	cut	zh	vision
ŏŏ	book	û	fur	ə	ago, item,
ōō	boot	*th*	the		pencil, atom,
yōō	abuse	th	thin		circus
ou	out	hw	which	ər	butter

east·er·ly | ē′stər lē | —*adjective* **1.** In or toward the east: *The ship took an easterly course.* **2.** From the east: *easterly winds.* —*adverb* **1.** In or toward the east: *The plane flew easterly.* **2.** From the east: *winds blowing easterly.*

east·ern | ē′stərn | —*adjective* **1.** Often **Eastern** Of, in, or toward the east: *eastern Europe.* **2.** From the east: *an eastern wind.*

east·ward | ēst′wərd | —*adverb* To or toward the east: *The river flows eastward.* Another form of this word is **eastwards.** —*adjective* Moving to or toward the east: *The storm took an eastward turn.*

east·wards | ēst′wərds | A form of the adverb **eastward.**

easy | ē′zē | —*adjective* **easier, easiest** **1.** Needing very little work; not hard: *It's easy to ride a tricycle. Good handwriting is easy to read.* **2.** Free from worry or trouble; carefree: *Dogs have an easy life.* **3.** Not hurried; leisurely: *walking at an easy pace.*

eat | ēt | —*verb* **ate, eaten, eating** **1.** To take food into the body by swallowing: *Robins eat worms. Eat slowly and chew well.* **2.** To have a meal: *We usually eat at 6 o'clock in the evening. Let's eat breakfast.* **3.** To destroy; consume; use up: *Rust ate away the iron pipes.*

eat·en | ēt′n | The past participle of the verb **eat:** *We have eaten everything that was on our plates.*

eaves | ēvz | —*plural noun* The part of a roof that forms the lower edge and juts out over the side of a building.

eaves·drop | ēvz′drŏp′ | —*verb* **eavesdropped, eavesdropping** To listen secretly to other people talking: *He stepped behind the curtains and eavesdropped on what his friends were saying.*

ebb | ĕb | —*verb* **ebbed, ebbing** **1.** To flow out from the seashore: *After the tide has risen to its highest point, it begins to ebb.* **2.** To fade; weaken: *My strength began to ebb toward the end of the long climb.* —*noun, plural* **ebbs** The motion or condition of flowing out from the seashore: *You can find seashells during the ebb of the tide.*

eb·on·y | ĕb′ə nē | —*noun* The hard, black wood of a tree that grows in the tropics. Ebony is used to make the black keys of pianos.

ec·cen·tric | ĭk sĕn′trĭk | —*adjective* Odd or unusual in appearance or behavior; strange; peculiar: *Our eccentric neighbor always carries an open umbrella on sunny days.* —*noun, plural* **eccentrics** A person who often behaves oddly.

ech·o | ĕk′ō | —*noun, plural* **echoes** A sound that is reflected off something so that it is heard again. —*verb* **echoed, echoing** To repeat a sound in an echo: *The sound of the guns echoed through the valley.*

e·clipse | ĭ klĭps′ | —*noun, plural* **eclipses** The darkening of the moon or sun that happens when light coming from it is blocked. In an eclipse of the moon, the earth casts its shadow on the moon as it passes between the sun and the moon. In an eclipse of the sun, the moon blocks the light from the sun as it passes between the sun and the earth. —*verb* **eclipsed, eclipsing** **1.** To block the light from; darken: *The earth will partly eclipse the moon tonight.* **2.** To do better than; overshadow: *The performer's skill eclipsed that of his competitors.*

e·col·o·gy | ĭ kŏl′ə jē | —*noun, plural* **ecologies** The study of living things in relation to each other and to their environment.

eaves

eclipse
Of the sun

e·co·nom·ic |ēʹkə nŏmʹĭk| or |ĕkʹə nŏmʹĭk| —*adjective* Of economics: *economic policies.*

e·co·nom·i·cal |ēʹkə nŏmʹĭ kəl| or |ĕkʹə nŏmʹĭ kəl| —*adjective* Careful about spending money; not wasteful; saving money: *Sometimes it is more economical to buy the large size of a product instead of two of the smaller size. That car has an economical engine that uses very little gas.*

e·co·nom·ics |ēʹkə nŏmʹĭks| or |ĕkʹə nŏmʹĭks| —*noun* (Used with a singular verb.) The science that deals with money, goods, and services, and how they are related to one another.

e·con·o·mize |ĭ kŏnʹə mīz| —*verb* **economized, economizing** To save money; spend less: *She decided to economize and bring her lunch to school.*

e·con·o·my |ĭ kŏnʹə mē| —*noun, plural* **economies 1.** The way a country develops, divides up, and uses its money, goods, and services. **2.** The careful use of money; thrift: *By practicing economy, he was able to save enough to buy Christmas presents.*

ec·sta·sy |ĕkʹstə sē| —*noun, plural* **ecstasies** A feeling of great happiness or delight.

–ed¹ A suffix that forms the past tense and past participle of verbs: *cared; carried; lingered.*

–ed² A suffix that forms adjectives from nouns: *a footed vase.*

edge |ĕdj| —*noun, plural* **edges 1.** The line or place where an object or area ends; side: *The ball rolled off the edge of the table.* **2.** The sharpened side of a blade or any other tool that cuts: *a hatchet with a sharp edge.* **3.** An advantage: *Our basketball team has an edge on the visitors because our players are taller.*
—*verb* **edged, edging 1.** To move slowly: *He edged his way through the crowd.* **2.** To form an edge for; to border: *Tall trees edged the lawn.*

ed·i·ble |ĕdʹə bəl| —*adjective* Good or safe to eat: *This peach is too ripe to be edible.*

ed·it |ĕdʹĭt| —*verb* **edited, editing** To make written material ready for publication by selecting, correcting, revising, and checking: *We will have to edit your story before it appears in print.*

e·di·tion |ĭ dĭshʹən| —*noun, plural* **editions 1. a.** The entire number of copies of a book, newspaper, or magazine printed at one time. **b.** A single copy of such a number. **2.** The form in which something is printed: *a paperback edition.*

ed·i·tor |ĕdʹĭ tər| —*noun, plural* **editors** A person who chooses, corrects, revises, and checks the material that goes into a book or other publication.

ed·i·to·ri·al |ĕdʹĭ tôrʹē əl| or |ĕdʹĭ tōrʹē əl| —*noun, plural* **editorials** An article printed in a newspaper or a statement broadcast on radio or television, giving the opinions of the editors or management.
—*adjective* Of editors or their work.

Ed·mon·ton |ĕdʹmən tən| The capital of Alberta.

ed·u·cate |ĕjʹo͞o kāt| —*verb* **educated, educating** To give knowledge or training to; teach.

ed·u·ca·tion |ĕjʹo͞o kāʹshən| —*noun, plural* **educations 1.** The process of gaining knowledge or of giving knowledge; training in school. **2.** The knowledge gained through education; learning: *People without education are not always ignorant.*

eel |ēl| —*noun, plural* **eels** A long, slippery fish that looks like a snake.

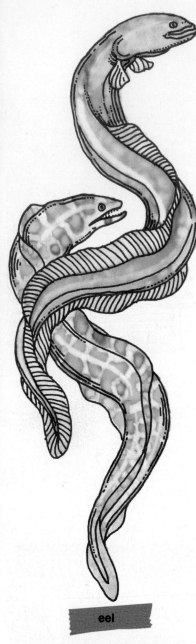

eel

ă	pat	ĕ	pet	î	fierce
ā	pay	ē	be	ŏ	pot
â	care	ĭ	pit	ō	go
ä	father	ī	pie	ô	paw, for

oi	oil	ŭ	cut	zh	vision
o͞o	book	û	fur	ə	ago, item,
o͞o	boot	*th*	the		pencil, atom,
yo͞o	abuse	th	thin		circus
ou	out	hw	which	ər	butter

ee·rie or **ee·ry** |îr′ē| —*adjective* **eerier, eeriest** Causing fear or dread; strange; weird: *An eerie blue light appeared suddenly in an attic window of the dark house.*

ef·fect |ĭ fĕkt′| —*noun, plural* **effects 1.** Something that happens because of something else; result: *The effect of too much sun can be a bad sunburn.* **2.** The power to bring about a desired result: *All our good advice has no effect on him.* **3. effects** Belongings; property: *He packed all his effects and left town.*

ef·fec·tive |ĭ fĕk′tĭv| —*adjective* **1.** Bringing about a desired effect; successful: *There are two kinds of vaccine effective against polio.* **2.** In force; in effect: *The law becomes effective immediately.*

ef·fi·cien·cy |ĭ fĭsh′ən sē| —*noun* The condition or quality of being efficient.

ef·fi·cient |ĭ fĭsh′ənt| —*adjective* Getting good results without wasting time, materials, or effort: *An efficient engine runs on very little fuel. It is more efficient to feed the whole family at once.*

ef·fort |ĕf′ərt| —*noun, plural* **efforts 1.** The use of energy to do something; work: *Doing a job the proper way will save time and effort.* **2.** A serious attempt; hard try: *Make an effort to arrive at school on time.*

egg¹ |ĕg| —*noun, plural* **eggs 1.** One of the special cells formed in the body of a female animal. A young animal develops inside the egg. Many animals lay eggs that hatch outside the female's body. Birds, turtles, frogs, fish, and insects lay eggs. **2.** The egg of a chicken, with its hard shell. The part inside the shell is used as food.

egg² |ĕg| —*verb* **egged, egging** —**egg on** To urge; encourage: *The fight began after the two boys were egged on by their friends.*

egg·plant |ĕg′plănt′| or |ĕg′plänt′| —*noun, plural* **eggplants** A vegetable that has shiny purple skin and is shaped like a large egg.

e·gret |ē′grĭt| or |ĕg′rĭt| —*noun, plural* **egrets** A wading bird with a long neck and a long, pointed bill. Most egrets are white. Sometimes they have lacy, drooping feathers on the neck and back.

E·gypt |ē′jĭpt| A country in northeastern Africa.

E·gyp·tian |ĭ jĭp′shən| —*noun, plural* **Egyptians 1.** A person who was born in or is a citizen of Egypt. **2.** The language of ancient Egyptians.
—*adjective* Of Egypt, the Egyptians, or their language.

eight |āt| —*noun, plural* **eights** A number, written 8, that is equal to the sum of 7 + 1.
—*adjective* Being one more than seven in number: *eight books.* The adjective **eight** belongs to a class of words called **determiners.** They signal that a noun is coming.
♦ *These sound alike* **eight, ate.**

eight·een |ā′tēn′| —*noun, plural* **eighteens** A number, written 18, that is equal to the sum of 10 + 8.
—*adjective* Being one more than seventeen in number: *eighteen years.* The adjective **eighteen** belongs to a class of words called **determiners.** They signal that a noun is coming.

eight·eenth |ā′tēnth′| —*noun, plural* **eighteenths 1.** In a group of people or things that are in numbered order, the one that matches the number eighteen. **2.** One of eighteen equal parts, written ¹⁄₁₈.
—*adjective: the eighteenth girl in line.*

egg¹, egg²
Egg¹ and **egg²** both came from the language of people who lived long ago in Scandinavia. **Egg¹** meant the same as it does today. **Egg²** had the meaning "to goad, to dare."

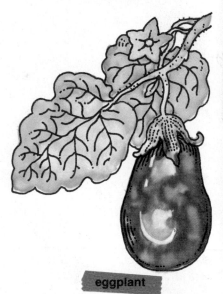

egg¹
Eggs on display at a state fair

eggplant

eighth |ātth| —*noun, plural* **eighths** **1.** In a group of people or things that are in numbered order, the one that matches the number eight. **2.** One of eight equal parts, written ⅛.
—*adjective: the eighth boy in line.*

eight·i·eth |ā′tē ĭth| —*noun, plural* **eightieths** **1.** In a group of people or things that are in numbered order, the one that matches the number eighty. **2.** One of eighty equal parts, written ⅟₈₀.
—*adjective: the eightieth bus in line.*

eight·y |ā′tē| —*noun, plural* **eighties** A number, written 80, that is equal to the product of 8 × 10.
—*adjective* Being ten more than seventy in number: *eighty days.* The adjective **eighty** belongs to a class of words called **determiners.** They signal that a noun is coming.

ei·ther |ē′thər| or |ī′thər| —*adjective* **1.** One or the other; any one of two: *You may take either seat.* **2.** Each of the two: *Elm trees lined either side of the street.* The adjective **either** belongs to a class of words called **determiners.** They signal that a noun is coming.
—*pronoun* One or the other of two: *She looked at two dresses, but didn't buy either.*
—*adverb* Likewise; also: *We didn't go and she didn't go, either.* The adverb **either** is only used following a negative statement.
—*conjunction* The conjunction **either** is used with **or** to present two alternatives: *They will leave on vacation either today or tomorrow.*

e·lab·o·rate |ĭ lăb′ər ĭt| —*adjective* Having many parts or made in great detail: *We built an elaborate sand castle with towers, doors, windows, and a moat. They made elaborate plans for their trip.*
—*verb* |ĭ lăb′ə rāt′| **elaborated, elaborating** To say more on a subject; give details: *If your answer is too short, we will ask you to elaborate on it.*

e·lapse |ĭ lăps′| —*verb* **elapsed, elapsing** To go by; pass: *Months elapsed before I heard from my friend again.*

e·las·tic |ĭ lăs′tĭk| —*adjective* Returning to normal shape after being stretched or pressed together: *Rubber bands and metal springs are elastic.*
—*noun, plural* **elastics** A fabric or tape that can stretch and fit tightly: *The pants are held up by elastic in the waist band.*

el·bow |ĕl′bō| —*noun, plural* **elbows** **1.** The joint or bend between the lower arm and the upper arm. **2.** Something that has a sharp bend in it, such as a piece of pipe.
—*verb* **elbowed, elbowing** To push or shove with the elbows: *The police officers elbowed their way through the crowd.*

el·der |ĕl′dər| —*adjective* A comparative of the adjective **old.** The word **elder** is used only to refer to persons who are relatives: *my elder sister.*
—*noun, plural* **elders** A person who is older: *Children can learn from the experience of their elders.*

eld·er·ly |ĕl′dər lē| —*adjective* Approaching old age: *I gave my seat on the bus to an elderly woman.*

eld·est |ĕl′dĭst| —*adjective* A superlative of the adjective **old.** The word **eldest** is used only to refer to persons who are relatives: *his eldest daughter.*

e·lect |ĭ lĕkt′| —*verb* **elected, electing** **1.** To choose by voting: *We elect a president every four years.* **2.** To choose or make a choice: *After careful thought, I elected to go with them.*

ă	pat	ĕ	pet	î	fierce
ā	pay	ē	be	ŏ	pot
â	care	ĭ	pit	ō	go
ä	father	ī	pie	ô	paw, for
oi	oil	ŭ	cut	zh	vision
ōō	book	û	fur	ə	ago, item,
ōō	boot	th	the		pencil, atom,
yōō	abuse	th	thin		circus
ou	out	hw	which	ər	butter

e·lec·tion | ĭ lĕk′shən | —*noun, plural* **elections** **1.** The act of choosing someone for an office or position by voting. **2.** The fact of being chosen by voting: *His election to Congress pleased all his supporters.*

e·lec·tric | ĭ lĕk′trĭk | —*adjective* Of, coming from, produced, or run by electricity: *an electric current; an electric shock; an electric train; an electric guitar.*

e·lec·tri·cal | ĭ lĕk′trĭ kəl | —*adjective* Of someone or something having to do with electricity: *an electrical engineer; electrical appliances; electrical repairs.*

e·lec·tri·cian | ĭ lĕk trĭsh′ən | —*noun, plural* **electricians** A person whose work is installing, repairing, or operating electric equipment.

e·lec·tric·i·ty | ĭ lĕk trĭs′ĭ tē | —*noun* **1.** A form of energy that can be sent through wires in a flow of tiny particles. Electricity is used to produce light and heat and to run motors. **2.** Electric current: *Be sure to turn off the electricity by pulling the plug before you clean the toaster.*

e·lec·tro·cute | ĭ lĕk′trə kyōot′ | —*verb* **electrocuted, electrocuting** To kill with very strong electric current.

e·lec·trode | ĭ lĕk′trōd′ | —*noun, plural* **electrodes** **1.** Either end of an electric battery or any other source of electricity. **2.** Any one of the parts that give off, collect, or control the flow of electricity in an electrical device. Transistors have electrodes.

e·lec·tro·mag·net | ĭ lĕk′trō măg′nĭt | —*noun, plural* **electromagnets** A piece of iron that becomes a magnet when an electric current is passed through a wire wound around it.

e·lec·tron | ĭ lĕk′trŏn′ | —*noun, plural* **electrons** One of the smallest possible pieces of matter. Electrons are usually found in an atom outside the nucleus.

e·lec·tron·ic | ĭ lĕk trŏn′ĭk | or | ē′lĕk trŏn′ĭk | —*adjective* Of or relating to electrons or electronics.

e·lec·tron·ics | ĭ lĕk trŏn′ĭks | or | ē′lĕk trŏn′ĭks | —*noun* (Used with a singular verb.) The study of electrons and their use in radio, television, computers, and other such devices.

el·e·gance | ĕl′ĭ gəns | —*noun, plural* **elegances** Good taste and grace in appearance or manner.

el·e·gant | ĕl′ĭ gənt | —*adjective* Tastefully beautiful; refined: *We dined in an elegant restaurant.*

el·e·ment | ĕl′ə mənt | —*noun, plural* **elements** **1.** Any of the more than 100 basic materials from which all other things are made. Elements cannot be broken down into simpler substances by using chemicals, but electrons and protons can sometimes be split off from their atoms. Water consists of the elements hydrogen and oxygen. **2.** A basic part of something: *Vegetables and dairy products are elements of a good diet.* **3.** A natural or preferred place to be: *Out of water, which is their element, fish quickly die.* **4. the elements** The outdoor forces of nature, such as rain, wind, and cold: *He braved the elements to walk ten miles to the railroad station.*

el·e·men·ta·ry | ĕl′ə mĕn′tə rē | or | ĕl′ə mĕn′trē | —*adjective* Having to do with the basic or simplest parts of a subject: *We learned spelling, grammar, and other fundamentals of writing in an elementary textbook.*

elementary school A school attended for the first six to eight years of a child's classroom instruction.

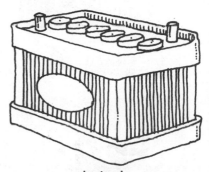

electrode
At each end of a battery

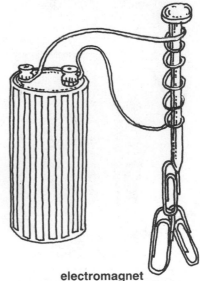

electromagnet
Wires attach electrodes to a nail.

el·e·phant | ĕl′ə fənt | —*noun, plural* **elephants** A very large animal of Africa or Asia. It has long tusks and a long trunk that it uses to pick things up. Elephants are the largest animals now living on land.

el·e·vate | ĕl′ə vāt′ | —*verb* **elevated, elevating** To raise to a higher place or position; lift up: *The nurse elevated his head by putting a pillow under it.*

el·e·va·tion | ĕl′ə vā′shən | —*noun, plural* **elevations** **1.** A raised place; hill: *A baseball pitcher stands on a slight elevation called the mound.* **2.** Height above the earth's surface or above sea level: *The mountain rises to an elevation of 3,000 feet.* **3.** The act of raising or lifting.

el·e·va·tor | ĕl′ə vā′tər | —*noun, plural* **elevators** **1.** A platform or small room that can be raised or lowered to carry people or things from one level to another in a building, mine, or other place. **2.** A building for storing grain.

e·lev·en | ĭ lĕv′ən | —*noun, plural* **elevens** A number, written 11, that is equal to the sum of 10 + 1.
—*adjective* Being one more than ten in number: *eleven pencils.* The adjective **eleven** belongs to a class of words called **determiners.** They signal that a noun is coming.

e·lev·enth | ĭ lĕv′ənth | —*noun, plural* **elevenths** **1.** In a group of people or things that are in numbered order, the one that matches the number eleven. **2.** One of eleven equal parts, written 1/11.
—*adjective: the eleventh girl in line.*

elf | ĕlf | —*noun, plural* **elves** A tiny being of folklore who has magical powers. Elves love to make mischief but rarely hurt people.

el·i·gi·ble | ĕl′ĭ jə bəl | —*adjective* Suitable or qualified to be in a group, hold a position, or have a privilege: *We will be eligible to vote at the age of eighteen.*

e·lim·i·nate | ĭ lĭm′ə nāt′ | —*verb* **eliminated, eliminating** **1.** To get rid of; remove: *The city government is trying to eliminate poverty by giving poor people jobs.* **2.** To leave out; omit; reject: *Make a list of your clothes and eliminate those you don't want to take on the trip.*

elk | ĕlk | —*noun, plural* **elk** or **elks** **1.** A large deer of North America. The male has large, branching antlers. This animal is also called **wapiti. 2.** The European moose.

el·lipse | ĭ lĭps′ | —*noun, plural* **ellipses** A figure shaped like a narrow or flattened circle.

elm | ĕlm | —*noun, plural* **elms** A tall shade tree with arching or curving branches. Elms have strong, hard wood that is used to make crates and boxes.

e·lope | ĭ lōp′ | —*verb* **eloped, eloping** To go away to get married without the consent of one's parents: *Janet and Paul eloped last month.*

el·o·quent | ĕl′ə kwənt | —*adjective* Using words well and effectively: *an eloquent speaker.*

else | ĕls | —*adjective* **1.** Other; different: *I would rather you invited somebody else than your brother.* **2.** More; additional: *Would you like anything else?*
—*adverb* **1.** Differently: *How else could the job have been done?* **2.** Otherwise: *Run, or else you will be caught in the rain and will ruin your new clothes.*

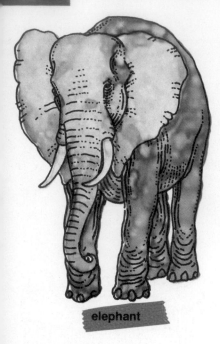

elephant

elk

ă	pat	ĕ	pet	î	fierce
ā	pay	ē	be	ŏ	pot
â	care	ĭ	pit	ō	go
ä	father	ī	pie	ô	paw, for
oi	oil	ŭ	cut	zh	vision
ōō	book	û	fur	ə	ago, item,
ōō	boot	th	the		pencil, atom,
yōō	abuse	th	thin		circus
ou	out	hw	which	ər	butter

else·where |ĕls′hwâr′| —*adverb* Somewhere else: *The boys were so noisy that Frank decided to play elsewhere.*

e·lude |ĭ lōōd′| —*verb* **eluded, eluding** To avoid or escape through tricks, speed, or by being daring and clever: *The runner eluded the tag.*

elves |ĕlvz| The plural of the noun **elf.**

e·man·ci·pate |ĭ măn′sə pāt′| —*verb* **emancipated, emancipating** To free from slavery; liberate.

em·bank·ment |ĕm băngk′mənt| —*noun, plural* **embankments** A mound of earth or stone built up to hold back water or hold up a road.

em·bark |ĕm bärk′| —*verb* **embarked, embarking 1.** To go on board a ship: *The passengers embarked for a cruise to Europe.* **2.** To set out on an adventure: *We embarked on a trip.*

em·bar·rass |ĕm băr′əs| —*verb* **embarrassed, embarrassing** To cause to feel uncomfortable and nervous: *They embarrassed him by joking about his cute red curly hair.*

em·bar·rass·ment |ĕm băr′əs mənt| —*noun, plural* **embarrassments 1.** The condition of being embarrassed: *Her face turned red with embarrassment when Doug asked her to dance.* **2.** Something that embarrasses: *Having to cough at a concert can be a great embarrassment.*

em·bas·sy |ĕm′bə sē| —*noun, plural* **embassies** The official home and office of an ambassador and the ambassador's staff.

em·bed |ĕm bĕd′| —*verb* **embedded, embedding** To set or fix firmly in something: *The thorns from the prickly bush embedded themselves in our skin.*

em·ber |ĕm′bər| —*noun, plural* **embers** A piece of glowing coal or wood, as in a fire that is going out.

em·bez·zle |ĕm bĕz′əl| —*verb* **embezzled, embezzling** To steal money put in one's care in the course of a job: *The cashier embezzled thousands of dollars from the bank.*

em·blem |ĕm′bləm| —*noun, plural* **emblems** An object or picture that represents something else; a symbol: *The maple leaf is the emblem of Canada.*

em·boss |ĕm bôs′| or |ĕm bŏs′| —*verb* **embossed, embossing** To decorate with a design that is raised up a little from the surface.

em·brace |ĕm brās′| —*verb* **embraced, embracing** To grasp or hold in the arms as a sign of affection; hug: *The mother embraced her child with affection.*
—*noun, plural* **embraces** A hug.

em·broi·der |ĕm broi′dər| —*verb* **embroidered, embroidering 1.** To decorate cloth by sewing on designs: *Nancy embroidered the pillow cover with a flower pattern.* **2.** To make up extra details for; exaggerate: *Pedro embroidered the story of his adventures to make his own part in them seem more heroic.*

em·broi·der·y |ĕm broi′də rē| —*noun, plural* **embroideries 1.** The art or act of embroidering: *I worked on my embroidery after supper.* **2.** Decorative designs that have been sewn on cloth: *The embroidery on those curtains is very beautiful.*

em·bry·o |ĕm′brē ō| —*noun, plural* **embryos** A plant or animal when it is just beginning to develop from a seed or egg.

em·er·ald |ĕm′ər əld| or |ĕm′rəld| —*noun, plural* **emeralds 1.** A bright-green, clear stone that is valuable as a gem, especially in jewelry. **2.** A dark yellowish green color. ◊ The noun **emerald**

embankment

embassy
The U.S. embassy in Greece

embroider

emergency

emigrant
Emigrants traveling to the
American West

can be used like an adjective for things made with emeralds: *an emerald necklace.*
—*adjective* Dark yellowish green.

e·merge | ĭ mûrj′ | —*verb* **emerged, emerging** **1.** To come into view; appear: *The monster emerged from the lake and crawled up the shore toward us.* **2.** To come into existence; be born: *A new spirit of freedom emerged from the American Revolution.* **3.** To become known: *New problems emerged as the scientists worked.*

e·mer·gen·cy | ĭ mûr′jən sē | —*noun, plural* **emergencies** Something serious that happens suddenly and calls for quick action.

em·er·y | ĕm′ə rē | or | ĕm′rē | —*noun, plural* **emeries** A hard brown mineral that is used as a powder for grinding and polishing.

em·i·grant | ĕm′ĭ grənt | —*noun, plural* **emigrants** Someone who leaves his or her own country or region to settle in another: *Wagon trains carried emigrants from the East to the West.*

em·i·grate | ĕm′ĭ grāt′ | —*verb* **emigrated, emigrating** To leave one's own country or region and settle in another: *The United States was settled by millions of people who emigrated from Europe and other parts of the world.*

em·i·nent | ĕm′ə nənt | —*adjective* Famous and respected; outstanding: *an eminent scientist.*

e·mit | ĭ mĭt′ | —*verb* **emitted, emitting** To send forth; give out: *The huge street lamp emitted a brilliant light. The baby emitted a series of happy gurgles.*

e·mo·tion | ĭ mō′shən | —*noun, plural* **emotions** A strong feeling: *Fright, rage, love, joy, and sorrow are all emotions.*

e·mo·tion·al | ĭ mō′shə nəl | —*adjective* **1.** Having to do with a person's emotions: *That boy's problem with math is emotional; he's afraid of it.* **2.** Easily moved by emotion: *My parents are emotional people who can laugh or cry very easily.* **3.** Arousing emotion; moving: *The retiring leader gave an emotional speech of farewell.*

em·per·or | ĕm′pər ər | —*noun, plural* **emperors** A man who rules an empire.

em·pha·ses | ĕm′fə sēz | The plural of the noun **emphasis.**

em·pha·sis | ĕm′fə sĭs | —*noun, plural* **emphases** **1.** Special importance given to something: *There is an emphasis on running in our gym class.* **2.** Special force of voice given to a particular syllable, word, or phrase; stress: *Give that word extra emphasis.*

em·pha·size | ĕm′fə sīz′ | —*verb* **emphasized, emphasizing** To give emphasis to; stress: *I tried to emphasize my hunger by staring at the cookies. He emphasized all the important words in his song.*

em·pire | ĕm′pīr | —*noun, plural* **empires** A group of countries under one ruler or government.

em·ploy | ĕm ploi′ | —*verb* **employed, employing** **1.** To give a job to; hire: *The factory employs hundreds of people.* **2.** To make use of: *They employed all their skills to build the bridge.*
—*noun, plural* **employs** The condition of being employed: *My father spent years in the employ of the school system.*

em·ploy·ee | ĕm ploi′ē | or | ĕm′ploi ē′ | —*noun, plural* **employees** A person who works for another person or for an organization in return for pay.

em·ploy·er | ĕm ploi′ər | —*noun, plural* **employers** A person or organization that pays people to work.

em·ploy·ment | ĕm ploi′mənt | —*noun, plural* **employments**

1. The act of employing or the condition of being employed: *The company was interested in the employment of handicapped workers. The man retired after fifty years of employment.* **2.** Work for pay; job: *He found employment at the local grocery store.*

em·press | ĕm′prĭs | —*noun, plural* **empresses** A woman who rules an empire.

emp·ty | ĕmp′tē | —*adjective* **emptier, emptiest 1.** Containing nothing or nobody: *an empty box; an empty house.* **2.** Lacking purpose or interest: *an empty life.*
—*verb* **emptied, emptying, empties 1.** To make or become empty: *At the shout of "fire" the theater emptied immediately.* **2.** To pour out or off: *Empty the water from the pail into the sink.* **3.** To flow; discharge: *The Ohio River empties into the Mississippi.*

e·mu | ē′myōō | —*noun, plural* **emus** A large bird of Australia.

en- A prefix that forms verbs and means; **1.** To put into: *endanger.* **2.** To cause to be; make: *enable.* When *en-* is followed by *b, m,* or *p,* it becomes *em-: embed.*

-en¹ A suffix that forms verbs from adjectives and means "to make" or "to become": *thicken.*

-en² A suffix that forms adjectives from nouns and means "made of": *wooden.*

en·a·ble | ĕn ā′bəl | —*verb* **enabled, enabling** To make it possible for; give the ability to: *This money will enable you to take the trip.*

en·act | ĕn ăkt′ | —*verb* **enacted, enacting 1.** To make into law; pass: *The city council enacted a new tax bill.* **2.** To act out on a stage: *The children enacted the final scene of the play.*

e·nam·el | ĭ năm′əl | —*noun, plural* **enamels 1.** A smooth, hard coating that is baked onto pottery or other surfaces to protect or decorate them. **2.** A paint that forms a hard, shiny surface when it dries. **3.** The hard, white outer layer of a tooth.

en·chant | ĕn chănt′ | or | ĕn chänt′ | —*verb* **enchanted, enchanting 1.** To put under a magical spell; bewitch: *The music from the magic flute enchanted all the children of the town, and the man led them away.* **2.** To please completely; charm: *His beautiful voice enchanted the audience.*

en·cir·cle | ĕn sûr′kəl | —*verb* **encircled, encircling 1.** To form a circle around; surround: *Excited fans encircled the winning team.* **2.** To move in a circle around: *The moon encircles the earth.*

en·close | ĕn klōz′ | —*verb* **enclosed, enclosing 1.** To go completely around; surround; shut in: *A high fence encloses the football field.* **2.** To put into the same envelope: *I am enclosing a check for $10 with this letter.*

en·clos·ure | ĕn klō′zhər | —*noun, plural* **enclosures 1.** Something that encloses, such as a wall or fence. **2.** An additional item in a letter or package.

en·com·pass | ĕn kŭm′pəs | —*verb* **encompassed, encompassing** To form a circle or ring around; surround: *An old wooden fence encompasses the vacant lot.*

en·core | äng′kôr′ | or | äng′kōr′ | or | än′kôr′ | or | än′kōr′ | —*noun, plural* **encores 1.** A request by an audience for an extra performance from someone on a stage. It is made by clapping for a long time or calling out "encore!" **2.** An extra performance in answer to such a request.

en·coun·ter | ĕn koun′tər | —*verb* **encountered, encountering** To come upon or meet: *She encountered many new words in the science book. The players encountered difficulties during the game.*

emu

—*noun, plural* **encounters** The act of encountering; a meeting: *an encounter with a bear in the woods.*

en·cour·age | ĕn kûr′ĭj | —*verb* **encouraged, encouraging 1.** To give hope or confidence to: *Bruce looked very sick, but the doctor's good report encouraged us.* **2.** To urge; inspire: *The teacher encouraged the students to make use of the library.* **3.** To help make something happen: *Does violence on television encourage real violence?*

en·cour·age·ment | ĕn kûr′ĭj mənt | —*noun, plural* **encouragements 1.** The act of encouraging: *The quarterback needed the coach's encouragement to throw passes more often.* **2.** Something that encourages: *We got tired looking for the lost wallet, but the thought of the reward was an encouragement.*

en·cy·clo·pe·di·a | ĕn sī′klə pē′dē ə | —*noun, plural* **encyclopedias** A book or set of books containing many articles on a wide variety of subjects.

end | ĕnd | —*noun, plural* **ends 1.** The part where a thing stops: *Grandfather was seated at one end of the table.* **2.** The finish of something: *Summer is coming to an end.* **3.** A purpose; goal: *To what end are you doing all that work?*
—*verb* **ended, ending** To bring or come to an end: *The group song was a nice way to end the play. The story ends happily.*

en·dan·ger | ĕn dān′jər | —*verb* **endangered, endangering** To put in danger: *The oil spill endangered thousands of birds.*

endangered species Any of various kinds of animals that are in danger of disappearing from the earth.

en·deav·or | ĕn dĕv′ər | —*verb* **endeavored, endeavoring** To make an effort; attempt: *The three men endeavored to cross the Atlantic Ocean in a balloon, and they succeeded.*
—*noun, plural* **endeavors** A major effort or attempt: *Good luck in all your endeavors.*

end·ing | ĕn′dĭng | —*noun, plural* **endings** The last part: *The book has a happy ending.*

end·less | ĕnd′lĭs | —*adjective* Having or seeming to have no end: *endless stretches of sandy beach; endless arguments.*

en·dorse | ĕn dôrs′ | —*verb* **endorsed, endorsing 1.** To sign one's name on the back of: *First endorse the check, then the bank will give you cash for it.* **2.** To support publicly: *The candidate got many famous people to endorse him for president.*

en·dur·ance | ĕn do͝or′əns | or | ĕn dyo͝or′əns | —*noun, plural* **endurances** The ability to stand strain, hardship, or use and not break down: *That hike was a real test of our endurance.*

en·dure | ĕn do͝or′ | or | ĕn dyo͝or′ | —*verb* **endured, enduring 1.** To put up with; stand; bear: *The early settlers in America endured great hardships.* **2.** To continue to exist; last: *His fame will endure forever.*

en·e·my | ĕn′ə mē | —*noun, plural* **enemies 1.** Someone opposed to or wishing harm to another. **2.** A country that is at war with another country. **3.** Something harmful in its effects: *Weather is sometimes the farmer's worst enemy.*

en·er·get·ic | ĕn′ər jĕt′ĭk | —*adjective* Full of energy; vigorous: *Our gym teacher is so energetic that he does all the exercises with us.*

en·er·gy | ĕn′ər jē | —*noun, plural* **energies 1.** The strength or desire to be doing things; will to work or play: *I woke up rested and full of energy.* **2.** Effort; work: *After their own children grew up, the couple devoted their energies to helping orphans.* **3.** Power to

endangered species
Whooping crane *(above)* and endangered species of frog and turtle *(below)*

ă	pat	ĕ	pet	î	fierce
ā	pay	ē	be	ŏ	pot
â	care	ĭ	pit	ō	go
ä	father	ī	pie	ô	paw, for
oi	oil	ŭ	cut	zh	vision
o͝o	book	û	fur	ə	ago, item,
o͞o	boot	th	the		pencil, atom,
yo͞o	abuse	th	thin		circus
ou	out	hw	which	ər	butter

move objects or do other kinds of physical work. Electricity, heat, and oil are all sources of energy.

en·force | ĕn fôrs′ | or | ĕn fōrs′ | —*verb* **enforced, enforcing** To make sure that a law or rule is obeyed: *The police will enforce the speed limit with extra care during the holiday weekend.*

en·gage | ĕn gāj′ | —*verb* **engaged, engaging 1.** To employ; hire: *She engaged a staff of workers.* **2.** To take up the attention or time of: *A friend engaged him in conversation for over an hour.* **3.** To take part: *You're too young to engage in business deals.* **4.** To promise or agree to marry: *Linda and Joe are engaged.*

en·gage·ment | ĕn gāj′mənt | —*noun, plural* **engagements 1.** The act of engaging or the condition of being engaged. **2.** A promise to marry. **3.** The time during which one is promised to marry. **4.** An agreement with someone to meet or do something; date.

en·gine | ĕn′jən | —*noun, plural* **engines 1.** A machine that uses energy to make something run or move; motor. **2.** A railroad locomotive.

en·gin·eer | ĕn′jə nîr′ | —*noun, plural* **engineers 1.** A person who is trained in engineering. **2.** A person who runs a locomotive.

en·gi·neer·ing | ĕn′jə nîr′ĭng | —*noun* The work of planning and building complicated structures that require a lot of scientific knowledge, such as bridges, canals, and oil wells.

Eng·land | ĭng′glənd | The larger, southern part of the island of Great Britain.

Eng·lish | ĭng′glĭsh | —*noun* The language of Great Britain, the United States, Canada, Australia, and various other countries throughout the world.
—*adjective* Of the English language or the people of England: *English grammar; English customs.*

en·grave | ĕn grāv′ | —*verb* **engraved, engraving 1.** To carve or cut a design or letters into a surface. **2.** To fix firmly: *The accident is engraved in my memory.*

en·gross | ĕn grōs′ | —*verb* **engrossed, engrossing** To take up all the attention of; absorb: *The boys were too engrossed in the ball game to eat lunch.*

en·hance | ĕn hăns′ | or | ĕn häns′ | —*verb* **enhanced, enhancing** To make greater; improve: *Age enhances the value of antiques.*

en·joy | ĕn joi′ | —*verb* **enjoyed, enjoying 1.** To get pleasure from; like to do: *Do you enjoy hikes in the woods?* **2.** To have the benefit of: *He has enjoyed good health all his life.*

en·joy·ment | ĕn joi′mənt | —*noun, plural* **enjoyments 1.** The act or condition of enjoying something: *It was fun watching his enjoyment of good food.* **2.** Pleasure; joy: *My father works in the garden for enjoyment.*

en·large | ĕn lärj′ | —*verb* **enlarged, enlarging** To make or become larger: *enlarge a house; enlarge a picture.*

en·list | ĕn lĭst′ | —*verb* **enlisted, enlisting 1.** To join or get to join the armed forces: *My brother enlisted in the navy. A recruiting officer enlisted him in the National Guard.* **2.** To seek and gain: *Stamp collectors should enlist the aid of their friends.*

e·nor·mous | ĭ nôr′məs | —*adjective* Very large; huge: *an enormous dog; the enormous cost of the building.*

e·nough | ĭ nŭf′ | —*adjective* As many or as much as needed; sufficient: *Is there enough food for everybody?*

engrave
Engraving on a silver mug

—*adverb* To a satisfactory amount or degree: *Are you warm enough?*

—*noun* An adequate quantity: *He ate enough for two.*

en·rage | ĕn rāj′ | —*verb* **enraged, enraging** To make very angry: *My father was enraged when he learned that someone had stolen his golf clubs.*

en·rich | ĕn rĭch′ | —*verb* **enriched, enriching** 1. To make rich or richer: *The family was greatly enriched by the discovery of oil on their property.* 2. To improve by adding something; make better: *Fertilizer enriches the soil.*

en·roll | ĕn rōl′ | —*verb* **enrolled, enrolling** To sign up; register: *Four new students are enrolled in our class.*

en·roll·ment | ĕn rōl′mənt | —*noun, plural* **enrollments** 1. The act of enrolling: *High school enrollment starts next week.* 2. The number of people enrolled: *The school expects to have an enrollment of six hundred.*

en·sign | ĕn′sən | —*noun, plural* **ensigns** 1. A flag or banner: *The ship displayed the British naval ensign.* 2. An officer in the U.S. Navy of the lowest rank.

en·sure | ĕn shŏŏr′ | —*verb* **ensured, ensuring** To make sure or certain of; guarantee: *Hot weather ensured the success of our lemonade stand.*

en·tan·gle | ĕn tăng′gəl | —*verb* **entangled, entangling** 1. To make twisted and tangled: *Please don't entangle the yarn.* 2. To involve: *He became entangled in a long legal battle.*

en·ter | ĕn′tər | —*verb* **entered, entering** 1. To go in or into: *Knock before entering. We stood up when she entered the room.* 2. To start out on; begin: *Cancer research is entering a new phase.* 3. To register or enroll: *We entered our son in a new school this September.* 4. To put down in a book; record: *Enter the expenses in this book.*

en·ter·prise | ĕn′tər prīz′ | —*noun, plural* **enterprises** A big, important project or undertaking. An enterprise is usually difficult, complicated, or involves a great amount of risk.

en·ter·tain | ĕn′tər tān′ | —*verb* **entertained, entertaining** 1. To hold the attention of in a pleasant way; amuse: *He entertained us with several songs.* 2. To have a person as a guest: *They entertained me at dinner. They entertain often.* 3. To consider: *The star is entertaining several offers for her next movie.*

en·ter·tain·er | ĕn′tər tā′nər | —*noun, plural* **entertainers** A person, such as a singer or dancer, who performs for an audience.

en·ter·tain·ment | ĕn′tər tān′mənt | —*noun, plural* **entertainments** 1. Something intended to amuse a gathering of people: *There will be some entertainment after dinner.* 2. Enjoyment; fun: *This puzzle has given the whole family a lot of entertainment.*

en·thrall | ĕn thrôl′ | —*verb* **enthralled, enthralling** To hold the attention of completely; fascinate: *The boy enthralled the class with a description of the parade.*

en·thu·si·asm | ĕn thŏŏ′zē ăz′əm | —*noun, plural* **enthusiasms** Great interest or excitement: *The teacher's enthusiasm for poetry was so strong that everyone began to listen.*

en·thu·si·as·tic | ĕn thŏŏ′zē ăs′tĭk | —*adjective* Full of enthusiasm; warmly interested: *The cheering crowd gave the marathon runner an enthusiastic welcome when he crossed the finish line.*

ensign
Of the U.S. Coast Guard

ă	pat	ĕ	pet	î	fierce
ā	pay	ē	be	ŏ	pot
â	care	ĭ	pit	ō	go
ä	father	ī	pie	ô	paw, for
oi	oil	ŭ	cut	zh	vision
ŏŏ	book	û	fur	ə	ago, item,
ōō	boot	th	the		pencil, atom,
yŏŏ	abuse	th	thin		circus
ou	out	hw	which	ər	butter

en·tire | ĕn tīr′ | —*adjective* **1.** Having no part missing; complete; whole: *Sing us the entire song.* **2.** Without any limit; total: *You have my entire approval.*

en·tire·ly | ĕn tīr′lē | —*adverb* Fully; completely: *It's entirely too late for you to go out.*

en·ti·tle | ĕn tīt′l | —*verb* **entitled, entitling 1.** To give a title to; call: *Walt Whitman entitled his book "Leaves of Grass."* **2.** To give someone a right: *The coupon entitles you to free ice cream.*

en·trance¹ | ĕn′trəns | —*noun, plural* **entrances 1.** The act of entering: *The audience applauded the actor's entrance.* **2.** A door or passageway through which one enters.

en·trance² | ĕn trăns′ | or | ĕn träns′ | —*verb* **entranced, entrancing** To fill with wonder; fascinate; charm: *The speaker's powerful voice entranced the audience.*

en·treat | ĕn trēt′ | —*verb* **entreated, entreating** To ask earnestly; beg: *I entreated the doctor to let me see my brother.*

en·try | ĕn′trē | —*noun, plural* **entries 1.** The act or right of entering: *Your passport gives you entry into foreign countries.* **2.** A passage or opening that provides a way in: *The canyon had one narrow entry.* **3.** An item entered in a book or list: *I made an entry in my diary about the party.* **4.** Someone or something entered in a contest.

en·vel·op | ĕn vĕl′əp | —*verb* **enveloped, enveloping** To enclose completely; cover all over: *The big coat enveloped her.*

en·ve·lope | ĕn′və lōp′ | —*noun, plural* **envelopes** A flat paper wrapper with a gummed flap, used chiefly for mailing letters.

en·vi·ous | ĕn′vē əs | —*adjective* Wanting something that someone else has; feeling envy: *He was always envious of his brother's good grades.*

en·vi·ron·ment | ĕn vī′rən mənt | —*noun, plural* **environments** The surroundings in which a plant or animal lives: *Penguins are well adapted to the harsh environment of the Antarctic.*

en·vy | ĕn′vē | —*noun, plural* **envies 1.** A feeling of resentment at someone who has what you want; jealousy: *I was full of envy when he got to go to Europe.* **2.** Someone or something that gives you this feeling: *Her new bicycle is the envy of all her friends.* —*verb* **envied, envying, envies** To feel envy toward.

ep·au·let | ĕp′ə lĕt′ | —*noun, plural* **epaulets** A strap worn on the shoulder of an officer's uniform.

ep·ic | ĕp′ĭk | —*noun, plural* **epics 1.** A long poem about the adventures of heroes. **2.** Any long story or movie with lots of characters and events. —*adjective* **1.** Of or like an epic: *an epic poem about the discovery of the New World.* **2.** Impressive; tremendous: *Swimming the English Channel was an epic achievement.*

ep·i·dem·ic | ĕp′ĭ dĕm′ĭk | —*adjective* Spreading rapidly and widely among the people of an area: *an epidemic disease.* —*noun, plural* **epidemics 1.** A disease that spreads rapidly and widely: *The influenza epidemic of 1918 infected about 200,000,000 people around the world.* **2.** A rapid spread or development of anything: *There has been an epidemic of auto accidents.*

ep·i·sode | ĕp′ĭ sōd′ | —*noun, plural* **episodes 1.** An event in one's life or experience: *She told about an episode in her childhood when she got lost.* **2.** An incident in a story, or one part of a continuing story: *In tonight's episode of this television show the family inherits a million dollars.*

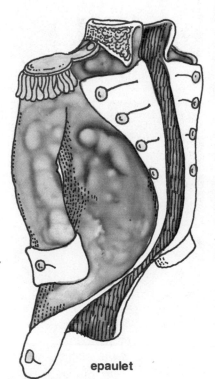

epaulet

entrance¹, entrance²
Entrance¹ is from **enter. Entrance²** is formed from **trance**. It is interesting that in the pronunciation of each word the stress is on the part that contains the main idea.

equipment
Diving equipment

eraser

ă	pat	ĕ	pet	î	fierce
ā	pay	ē	be	ŏ	pot
â	care	ĭ	pit	ō	go
ä	father	ī	pie	ô	paw, for
oi	oil	ŭ	cut	zh	vision
ŏŏ	book	û	fur	ə	ago, item,
ōō	boot	th	the		pencil, atom,
yōō	abuse	th	thin		circus
ou	out	hw	which	ər	butter

ep·och | ĕp′ək | —*noun, plural* **epochs** A particular period in history; era: *We live in the epoch of space exploration.*

e·qual | ē′kwəl | —*adjective* **1.** Having the same size, amount, or capacity as another: *The boys are equal in height. One meter is equal to 39.37 inches.* **2.** Having the necessary strength or ability; capable: *The exhausted boy was not equal to the task of playing another game.*
—*noun, plural* **equals** Someone or something equal to another: *He's still a child, but they treat him as an equal.*
—*verb* **equaled, equaling** **1.** To be the same as: *Four quarts equal one gallon.* **2.** To do something equal to: *Mary sold ten books of stamps, and Jean equaled her.*

e·qual·i·ty | ĭ kwŏl′ĭ tē | —*noun* The condition of being equal, especially in political, social, or economic rights: *Black people have worked hard to achieve equality.*

e·qua·tion | ĭ kwā′zhən | or | ĭ kwā′shən | —*noun, plural* **equations** A statement expressed in mathematical terms that two sets of values are equal: *3 × 2 = 6 and 3 + 2 = 5 are equations.*

e·qua·tor | ĭ kwā′tər | —*noun, plural* **equators** The imaginary line that goes around the middle of the earth at an equal distance from the North and South Poles. The equator divides the earth into the Northern Hemisphere and the Southern Hemisphere.

e·qua·to·ri·al | ē′kwə tôr′ē əl | —*adjective* **1.** Of or near the equator. **2.** Showing or having the characteristics of the areas along the equator: *In that equatorial heat you should always wear a hat.*

e·qui·lib·ri·um | ē′kwə lĭb′rē əm | —*noun* A state of balance: *When the weight on each side of a scale is exactly even, it is in equilibrium.*

e·qui·nox | ē′kwə nŏks′ | or | ĕk′wə nŏks′ | —*noun, plural* **equinoxes** Either of the times of the year in which the sun is exactly above the equator and day and night are about equal in length. The equinoxes take place at about September 23 and March 21.

e·quip | ĭ kwĭp′ | —*verb* **equipped, equipping** To supply with things that are needed; provide: *We equipped ourselves with boots and canteens for the hike.*

e·quip·ment | ĭ kwĭp′mənt | —*noun* The things needed or used for a particular purpose: *We bought camping equipment for our vacation.*

e·quiv·a·lent | ĭ kwĭv′ə lənt | —*adjective* Equal: *The dollar is equivalent to 100 cents.*
—*noun, plural* **equivalents** Something that is equal: *Her failure to answer the invitation was the equivalent of saying "no."*

–er[1] A suffix that forms the comparative of adjectives and adverbs: *neater; whiter; slower.*

–er[2] A suffix that forms nouns: *eraser; foreigner; marker; photographer.*

e·ra | îr′ə | or | ĕr′ə | —*noun, plural* **eras** A period of history: *the atomic era; the Colonial era of early America.*

e·rase | ĭ rās′ | —*verb* **erased, erasing** **1.** To remove by rubbing or wiping: *Toby erased the whole sentence and started a new one.* **2.** To remove writing or a recording from: *Please erase the blackboard. I erased the old tape and made a new recording.*

e·ras·er | ĭ rā′sər | —*noun, plural* **erasers** Something used to rub out marks on paper or blackboards.

e·rect | ĭ rĕkt′ | —*adjective* Not bent or stooped; upright: *Try to have an erect posture.*
—*verb* **erected, erecting 1.** To build or construct; put up: *They are erecting many new buildings downtown.* **2.** To make upright; set on end: *It took five boys to erect the heavy tent pole.*

er·mine | ûr′mĭn | —*noun, plural* **ermines** or **ermine 1.** An animal whose fur in winter is white with a black tail tip. For the rest of the year, its fur is brown. The ermine is a kind of weasel. **2.** The white fur of an ermine. It often has spots made with the black tail tips.

e·rode | ĭ rōd′ | —*verb* **eroded, eroding** To wear away bit by bit: *Water and wind erode soil when it is not held in place by plant roots. Exposed rock gradually erodes.*

e·ro·sion | ĭ rō′zhən | —*noun, plural* **erosions** The process of being worn away slowly, as by wind or water: *Soil erosion is a major problem of farmers in the Great Plains.*

er·rand | ĕr′ənd | —*noun, plural* **errands** A short trip taken to perform a task: *I sent him to mail a letter and do several other errands.*

er·ror | ĕr′ər | —*noun, plural* **errors 1.** Something that is wrong or incorrect; a mistake: *There's an error in your addition.* **2.** In baseball, a fielder's mistake that allows a batter to get on base or a runner to advance.

e·rupt | ĭ rŭpt′ | —*verb* **erupted, erupting 1.** To burst out violently: *The volcano erupted and covered the ground with lava.* **2.** To appear or develop suddenly: *A fight erupted among the soldiers.*

es·ca·la·tor | ĕs′kə lā′tər | —*noun, plural* **escalators** A moving staircase, as in a store or public building, that carries people up and down.

es·cape | ĭ skāp′ | —*verb* **escaped, escaping 1.** To get free; break loose: *The prisoner escaped by climbing a wall.* **2.** To succeed in avoiding something: *The driver was hurt, but the passenger escaped injury.*
—*noun, plural* **escapes 1.** The act of escaping: *The prisoners planned their escape for months.* **2.** A way of avoiding care or worry: *Television is Father's escape after a busy day.*

es·cort | ĕs′kôrt′ | —*noun, plural* **escorts 1.** A person or group that goes along with another to protect or show respect to the person or group: *The visiting king was given a large police escort.* **2.** A plane or ship that travels with another for protection: *The battleship had an escort of four fighter planes.* **3.** A man who goes along with a woman to a party or other social event: *Her escort to the dance brought her roses.*
—*verb* | ĭ skôrt′ | **escorted, escorting** To go with as an escort: *My brother escorted me to the dance.*

Es·ki·mo | ĕs′kə mō | —*noun, plural* **Eskimos** or **Eskimo 1.** A member of a people that live in the Arctic regions of North America and Asia. **2.** The language of these people.
—*adjective* Of the Eskimos or their language.

e·soph·a·gus | ĭ sŏf′ə gəs | —*noun* The tube that connects the throat with the stomach.

es·pe·cial·ly | ĭ spĕsh′ə lē | —*adverb* **1.** In a special way; more than usually; very: *You've been especially nice to us.* **2.** More than others; particularly: *This dress is especially designed for a tall girl.*

Eskimo

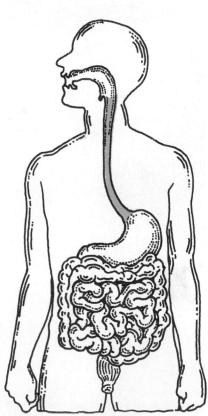

esophagus

es·say | ĕs′ā | —*noun, plural* **essays** A short piece of writing giving the author's views on a certain subject; composition: *Write an essay describing your best friend.*

es·sence | ĕs′əns | —*noun, plural* **essences** **1.** The basic or most important part of something: *The essence of friendship is mutual trust.* **2.** The concentrated liquid form of a plant, herb, or other substance: *essence of peppermint.*

es·sen·tial | ĭ sĕn′shəl | —*adjective* Of the greatest importance; basic; fundamental: *Eating the right foods is essential to health.*
—*noun, plural* **essentials** A basic or necessary thing: *Just bring a small suitcase for your toothbrush and other essentials.*

–est A suffix that forms the superlative of adjectives and adverbs: *warmest; latest.*

es·tab·lish | ĭ stăb′lĭsh | —*verb* **established, establishing** **1.** To begin or start; set up; create: *My father established this business in 1910.* **2.** To show to be true; prove: *The new boy quickly established his superiority by fighting back when teased.*

es·tab·lish·ment | ĭ stăb′lĭsh mənt | —*noun, plural* **establishments** **1.** The act of establishing: *the money paid for the establishment of a new business.* **2.** Something established, such as a business firm or club: *The hotel is one of the oldest establishments in town.*

es·tate | ĭ stāt′ | —*noun, plural* **estates** **1.** A large piece of land, usually with a large house and other buildings. **2.** Everything owned by a person, especially the property left by someone who has died.

es·teem | ĭ stēm′ | —*verb* **esteemed, esteeming** To think highly of; respect: *I esteem him for his honesty and courage.*
—*noun* Respect; honor: *The old judge was held in great esteem.*

es·ti·mate | ĕs′tə māt′ | —*verb* **estimated, estimating** To make a guess about; calculate or judge roughly: *The plumber estimated that the repair would cost $25.*
—*noun* | ĕs′tə mĭt | or | ĕs′tə māt′ |, *plural* **estimates** A rough calculation; a guess: *The painter gave an estimate on what it would cost to do the whole house.*

es·ti·ma·tion | ĕs′tə mā′shən | —*noun, plural* **estimations** An opinion; judgment: *In my estimation it was an awful show.*

etc. An abbreviation for the Latin phrase **et cetera.**

et cet·er·a | ĕt sĕt′ər ə | or | ĕt sĕt′rə | And other things of the same kind; and so forth. This was originally a Latin phrase meaning "and the rest." Now it is used chiefly in its abbreviated form: *Don't forget to bring pencils, paper, etc., on the first day of school.*

etch | ĕch | —*verb* **etched, etching** To make a drawing or design by cutting lines with acid on a metal plate. The lines are then filled with ink so that they leave an impression on paper pressed against the plate.

etch·ing | ĕch′ĭng | —*noun, plural* **etchings** **1.** The art or technique of making etched metal plates and using them to print pictures or designs. **2.** A picture or design made this way.

e·ter·nal | ĭ tûr′nəl | —*adjective* **1.** Continuing forever: *God is eternal.* **2.** Not affected by time; lasting: *She kept her eternal good humor through the disaster.* **3.** Going on and on; constant: *their eternal quarreling.*

e·ter·ni·ty | ĭ tûr′nĭ tē | —*noun, plural* **eternities** **1.** All of time without beginning or end: *Ancient kings tried to build tombs that*

estate

ă	pat	ĕ	pet	î	fierce
ā	pay	ē	be	ŏ	pot
â	care	ĭ	pit	ō	go
ä	father	ī	pie	ô	paw, for
oi	oil	ŭ	cut	zh	vision
ŏŏ	book	û	fur	ə	ago, item,
ōō	boot	*th*	the		pencil, atom,
yōō	abuse	th	thin		circus
ou	out	hw	which	ər	butter

would last for eternity. **2.** A very long time: *I had to wait an eternity for him to get a haircut.*

e·ther |ē′thər| —*noun, plural* **ethers** A liquid that evaporates easily and is used in medicine to make people unconscious for medical operations.

eth·nic |ĕth′nĭk| —*adjective* Of a group within a larger society who continue to speak a foreign language and share a way of life: *Italians, Germans, and Chinese are among the ethnic groups living in New York City.*

et·i·quette |ĕt′ĭ kĭt| —*noun, plural* **etiquettes** A set of rules that tell you how to behave in various social situations: *It is not good etiquette to put your elbows on the dinner table.*

et·y·mol·o·gy |ĕt′ə mŏl′ə jē| —*noun, plural* **etymologies** The history of a word, including where it came from and how it got its present form and meaning.

eu·ca·lyp·tus |yōō′kə lĭp′təs| —*noun, plural* **eucalyptuses** A tall tree that grows in Australia and other warm regions. An oil with a strong smell is made from its leaves. Its wood is used for building.

Eu·rope |yōōr′əp| The continent that is between the Atlantic Ocean and Asia.

Eu·ro·pe·an |yōōr′ə pē′ən| —*noun, plural* **Europeans** A person from Europe.
—*adjective* Of Europe or its people: *How many European countries did you visit?*

e·vac·u·ate |ĭ văk′yōō āt′| —*verb* **evacuated, evacuating 1.** To send away; withdraw: *They evacuated the farmers when the volcano began to erupt.* **2.** To depart from; leave: *Residents evacuated the building when the fire alarm sounded.*

e·vade |ĭ vād′| —*verb* **evaded, evading** To escape or avoid, especially by smart planning: *I evaded arrest by wearing a disguise.*

e·val·u·ate |ĭ văl′yōō āt′| —*verb* **evaluated, evaluating** To judge or figure out the value of; appraise: *They evaluated our property at $2,000.*

e·vap·o·rate |ĭ văp′ə rāt′| —*verb* **evaporated, evaporating** To change from a liquid into a vapor or gas: *Alcohol evaporates quickly. The sun evaporates moisture from the soil.*

e·vap·o·ra·tion |ĭ văp′ə rā′shən| —*noun, plural* **evaporations** The action or process of evaporating: *We can get salt from the evaporation of sea water.*

eve |ēv| —*noun, plural* **eves** The evening or day before a special day: *There was excitement on the eve of the big game.*

e·ven |ē′vən| —*adjective* **1.** Having a flat surface; level; smooth: *We sanded the floor to make it even.* **2.** Located at the same height or level: *The picture is even with the top of the window.* **3.** Not changing suddenly; steady: *an even disposition.* **4.** Equal: *Use even amounts of oil and vinegar for the dressing.* **5.** Having the same score: *The teams were even at the half.* **6.** Owing nothing; square: *Give me a dollar and we're even.* **7.** Exact: *an even pound of flour.* **8.** Capable of being divided by two without a remainder: *12, 4, and 108 are even numbers.*
—*adverb* **1.** To a greater degree; yet; still: *Your room is in even worse condition than last week.* **2.** At the same time as; just: *Even as we watched, the tornado struck the barn.* **3.** In spite of; despite: *Even with his head start, I won the race.* **4.** Though it seems unlikely: *Even grownups cry sometimes.*

eucalyptus
Leaves and flowers *(above)* and tree *(below)*

evergreen
Above: Rhododendron
Center: Holly
Below: Pine

ă	pat	ĕ	pet	î	fierce
ā	pay	ē	be	ŏ	pot
â	care	ĭ	pit	ō	go
ä	father	ī	pie	ô	paw, for

oi	oil	ŭ	cut	zh	vision
ŏŏ	book	û	fur	ə	ago, item,
ōō	boot	*th*	the		pencil, atom,
yōō	abuse	th	thin		circus
ou	out	hw	which	ər	butter

—*verb* **evened, evening** To make or become even: *Even the sheet on that side of the bed. The scores will even out in the end.*

  Idioms **break even** To finish without losses or gains: *With so many expenses, we barely broke even.* **get even** To have revenge: *He got even with her for telling on him.*

eve·ning |ēv′nĭng| —*noun, plural* **evenings** **1.** The time around sunset and just afterward. **2.** The time between sunset and midnight.

e·vent |ĭ vĕnt′| —*noun, plural* **events** **1.** Something that happens; an occurrence: *Birth, marriage, and death are perhaps the most important events in a person's life.* **2.** One contest in a program of sports: *The swimmers got ready for the next event.*

  Idiom **in the event of** In case: *In the event of bad weather, we'll hold the picnic indoors.*

e·ven·tu·al |ĭ vĕn′chōō əl| —*adjective* Happening in the end; ultimate or final: *We always believed in our eventual victory.*

ev·er |ĕv′ər| —*adverb* **1.** At all times; always: *My dog is ever faithful.* **2.** At any time: *Have you ever met her?* **3.** By any chance; in any possible way: *Why did you ever buy that dress?*

ev·er·green |ĕv′ər grēn′| —*adjective* Having green leaves or needles all through the year: *Pines and hollies are evergreen trees.* —*noun, plural* **evergreens** A tree, shrub, or plant with leaves or needles that stay green all year.

ev·er·last·ing |ĕv′ər lăs′tĭng| —*adjective* Lasting forever: *Christians believe in everlasting life.*

eve·ry |ĕv′rē| —*adjective* **1.** Each with no exceptions: *There is a book for every student in the class.* **2.** Each in a particular series: *Every third student will step out of line.*

  Idioms **every bit** Entirely; in all ways: *He's every bit as mean as we thought.* **every other** Each second; every alternate: *I go to dancing class every other week.*

eve·ry·bod·y |ĕv′rē bŏd′ē| —*pronoun* Each person without exception; everyone: *Come to dinner, everybody!*

eve·ry·day |ĕv′rē dā′| —*adjective* Ordinary; usual: *everyday clothes; everyday problems.*

eve·ry·one |ĕv′rē wŭn′| —*pronoun* Every person; everybody: *Does everyone have a pencil?*

eve·ry·thing |ĕv′rē thĭng′| —*pronoun* **1.** All things: *Everything we own is in this room. Tell me everything that happened.* **2.** A great deal; a lot: *Your friendship means everything to me.*

eve·ry·where |ĕv′rē hwâr′| —*adverb* In all places: *We looked everywhere for him.*

e·vict |ĭ vĭkt′| —*verb* **evicted, evicting** To put out a tenant by lawful means: *He was evicted for not paying rent.*

ev·i·dence |ĕv′ĭ dəns| —*noun, plural* **evidences** Facts or signs that help one to form an opinion; indication: *Her broad smile was clear evidence that she liked the gift.*

  Idiom **in evidence** Clearly visible; obvious: *We thought we heard barking, but no dog was in evidence.*

ev·i·dent |ĕv′ĭ dənt| —*adjective* Easy to see or understand; obvious; plain: *It's evident you're not listening.*

e·vil |ē′vəl| —*adjective* **1.** Morally bad; wicked: *We were taught that cheating, lying, and stealing are evil. He's made mistakes, but he's not an evil man.* **2.** Causing harm or misfortune; harmful: *Drinking can have evil effects.* —*noun, plural* **evils** **1.** The condition of being wicked; sin:

Deliver us from evil. **2.** Anything bad or harmful: *Poverty is a social evil.*

ev·o·lu·tion | ĕv′ə lōō′shən | —*noun, plural* **evolutions** Slow, gradual development: *Some believe that fossil remains show the evolution of plants and animals from earlier, extinct forms.*

e·volve | ĭ vŏlv′ | —*verb* **evolved, evolving** **1.** To arrive at gradually; develop: *We evolved a method of washing dishes very quickly.* **2.** To develop gradually, as new types of plants and animals may do: *Modern horses may have evolved from smaller animals that existed millions of years ago.*

ewe | yōō | —*noun, plural* **ewes** A female sheep.
♦ *These sound alike* **ewe, yew, you.**

ex– A prefix that means "former": *an ex-congressman.*

ex·act | ĭg zăkt′ | —*adjective* Correct or accurate in every detail: *Give me an exact copy of the letter. What were his exact words?*

ex·act·ly | ĭg zăkt′lē | —*adverb* **1.** Without any change or mistake; precisely; accurately: *Be sure to follow the recipe exactly.* **2.** In every respect; just: *You may do exactly as you please.*

ex·ag·ger·ate | ĭg zăj′ə rāt′ | —*verb* **exaggerated, exaggerating** To describe something as larger than it really is: *To gain sympathy, Tania always exaggerates the amount of homework she has to do over the weekend.*

ex·am | ĭg zăm′ | —*noun, plural* **exams** An examination; test.

ex·am·i·na·tion | ĭg zăm′ə nā′shən | —*noun, plural* **examinations** **1.** The act of examining; inspection: *A close examination of the gloves showed faint oil stains.* **2.** A test: *You have to pass physical and mental examinations to join the army.*

ex·am·ine | ĭg zăm′ĭn | —*verb* **examined, examining** **1.** To look at carefully; check; inspect: *We went closer to examine the details of the painting.* **2.** To test the knowledge of: *The teacher examined the students in arithmetic.*

ex·am·ple | ĭg zăm′pəl | —*noun, plural* **examples** **1.** Something that is singled out or studied because it is like other things of the same kind; sample: *This is an example of good handwriting.* **2.** A person or thing that is worth imitating; model: *He should be an example to all of us.* **3.** A warning; lesson: *Let his punishment be an example to you.*

ex·ca·vate | ĕks′kə vāt′ | —*verb* **excavated, excavating** **1.** To dig or dig out: *excavate a swimming pool; excavate a tunnel.* **2.** To uncover by digging; expose to view: *Archaeologists have excavated the ancient city.*

ex·ceed | ĭk sēd′ | —*verb* **exceeded, exceeding** **1.** To be greater than; surpass: *My expenses have exceeded my allowance again.* **2.** To go beyond: *He got a ticket for exceeding the speed limit.*

ex·cel | ĭk sĕl′ | —*verb* **excelled, excelling** To be or do better than others: *She excels us all in sports. Frank excels in swimming and football.*

ex·cel·lence | ĕk′sə ləns | —*noun* The quality or condition of being excellent: *the excellence of Jane's essay.*

ex·cel·lent | ĕk′sə lənt | —*adjective* Of the highest quality; superior: *an excellent car; an excellent team.*

ex·cept | ĭk sĕpt′ | —*preposition* Not including; leaving out; but: *All the eggs except one are broken. They invited everyone except me.* —*conjunction* **1.** But; only: *I'd lend you my bicycle except I need it.* **2.** But for the purpose of: *He never came to visit except to borrow something.*

excavate
Coal mine in Wyoming

ex·cep·tion |ĭk sĕp′shən| —*noun, plural* **exceptions 1.** The fact of being excluded; omission: *Everyone was on time with the exception of Helen.* **2.** A person or thing that is different from most others: *Most of us like sports, but Phil is an exception.*

ex·cep·tion·al |ĭk sĕp′shə nəl| —*adjective* Unusual; outstanding: *The performances were all good, but hers was exceptional.*

ex·cerpt |ĕk′sûrpt| —*noun, plural* **excerpts** A passage taken out of a longer work; sample: *I copied excerpts of my diary into my letter home.*

ex·cess |ĭk sĕs′| or |ĕk′sĕs′| —*noun, plural* **excesses 1.** An amount that is too much or more than usual: *She suffers from an excess of self-confidence.* **2.** The amount by which one thing is more than another: *I expected to count fifty marbles, but there was an excess of eight.*
—*adjective* Greater than necessary or normal; extra: *Shake off the excess water and dice the celery.*

ex·ces·sive |ĭk sĕs′ĭv| —*adjective* Greater than necessary, proper, or normal; extreme: *an excessive amount of time; an excessive number of phone calls.*

ex·change |ĭks chānj′| —*verb* **exchanged, exchanging 1.** To give one thing for another; trade: *I exchanged my marbles for his baseball.* **2.** To give and get back: *We exchanged letters.*
—*noun, plural* **exchanges 1.** An act of exchanging: *an exchange of gifts.* **2.** A place where things are traded; market: *the New York Stock Exchange.* **3.** A central office; center: *A telephone exchange connects calls within a given area.*

ex·cite |ĭk sīt′| —*verb* **excited, exciting** To arouse or stir up: *Ghost stories excited the children.*

ex·cite·ment |ĭk sīt′mənt| —*noun, plural* **excitements 1.** The condition of being excited: *The excitement among the spectators increased as the runners neared the finish line.* **2.** Commotion or confusion: *Several were injured in the excitement.* **3.** Something that excites: *All the excitements at the circus had worn the children out.*

ex·cit·ing |ĭk sī′tĭng| —*adjective* Causing excitement; thrilling: *We took an exciting trip down the Colorado River in a rubber boat.*

ex·claim |ĭk sklām′| —*verb* **exclaimed, exclaiming** To speak out suddenly and loudly, as from surprise: *"Look who's here!" she exclaimed.*

ex·cla·ma·tion |ĕk′sklə mā′shən| —*noun, plural* **exclamations** Something said suddenly and loudly, as in surprise.

exclamation point A mark of punctuation (!) used after an exclamation, as in "Help!" or "Hurrah!"

ex·clude |ĭk sklōōd′| —*verb* **excluded, excluding** To keep or leave out; bar: *He was excluded from the school's basketball team.*

ex·clu·sive |ĭk sklōō′sĭv| —*adjective* **1.** Not shared; complete; whole: *His family has exclusive ownership of the beach.* **2.** Admitting only some people and rejecting others: *Exclusive clubs are forbidden in my school. Many rich people live in exclusive neighborhoods.*
Idiom **exclusive of** Not including; besides: *The price of the motorcycle is exclusive of headlights and horn.*

ex·cur·sion |ĭk skûr′zhən| —*noun, plural* **excursions** A short trip for pleasure; an outing: *Last Sunday we took an excursion on a ferryboat.*

exchange
The New York Stock Exchange

ă	pat	ĕ	pet	î	fierce
ā	pay	ē	be	ŏ	pot
â	care	ĭ	pit	ō	go
ä	father	ī	pie	ô	paw, for
oi	oil	ŭ	cut	zh	vision
ōō	book	û	fur	ə	ago, item,
ōō	boot	*th*	the		pencil, atom,
yōō	abuse	th	thin		circus
ou	out	hw	which	ər	butter

ex·cuse | ĭk skyōōz' | —*verb* **excused, excusing** **1.** To pardon; forgive: *I can't excuse such lack of good manners. Excuse my appearance.* **2.** To free from a duty or obligation: *I got the school nurse to excuse me from gym.*
—*noun* | ĭk skyōōs' |, *plural* **excuses** Something that serves to excuse; an explanation: *You'll need a written excuse if you're absent.*

ex·e·cute | ĕk'sĭ kyōōt' | —*verb* **executed, executing** **1.** To perform; do: *Can you execute a figure 8 on ice skates?* **2.** To carry out; put into effect: *The captain gives orders, and the sailors execute them.* **3.** To put to death: *execute a criminal.*

ex·e·cu·tion | ĕk'sĭ kyōō'shən | —*noun, plural* **executions** **1.** The act of executing; performance: *I hope our emergency plans to evacuate the building never have to be put into execution.* **2.** The act of putting to death: *The murderer died by execution.*

ex·e·cu·tion·er | ĕk'sĭ kyōō'shə nər | —*noun, plural* **executioners** Someone who puts condemned prisoners to death.

ex·ec·u·tive | ĭg zĕk'yə tĭv | —*noun, plural* **executives** **1.** A person who helps to manage and make decisions for a company or organization: *The business executives met to discuss ways of increasing the firm's profits.* **2.** The branch of government responsible for managing the affairs of the nation and for putting laws into effect.
—*adjective* **1.** Having to do with management and the making of decisions: *The club is run by an executive committee.* **2.** Of or working for an executive: *She's an executive secretary and works in the executive offices.* **3.** Of the branch of government responsible for managing the affairs of the nation and for putting laws into effect: *The President issued an executive order.*

ex·empt | ĭg zĕmpt' | —*verb* **exempted, exempting** To free from a duty or obligation required of others; excuse: *The law exempts churches and charities from taxes.*
—*adjective* Released from an obligation required of others: *Father was exempt from military service because of poor eyesight.*

ex·er·cise | ĕk'sər sīz' | —*noun, plural* **exercises** **1.** Use; employment: *With the proper exercise of caution, you can enjoy a campfire safely.* **2.** Physical activity, usually done for the good of the body: *A little exercise is a good way to start the day.* **3.** A problem or task that helps a student learn or gives him practice: *Do the exercises at the end of the chapter.* **4.** **exercises** A ceremony: *graduation exercises.*
—*verb* **exercised, exercising** **1.** To do physical activity for the good of one's body: *I exercise for an hour every morning.* **2.** To put through a series of exercises: *exercise a horse; exercise one's stiff muscles.* **3.** To put into practice; use: *Don't forget to exercise your right to vote.*

ex·ert | ĭg zûrt' | —*verb* **exerted, exerting** To bring into use; apply: *He had to exert all his strength to move the stone.*

ex·er·tion | ĭg zûr'shən | —*noun, plural* **exertions** Strenuous effort; hard work: *It required exertion to get the table upstairs.*

ex·hale | ĕks hāl' | or | ĕk sāl' | —*verb* **exhaled, exhaling** To breathe out.

ex·haust | ĭg zôst' | —*verb* **exhausted, exhausting** **1.** To use up; consume: *The astronauts nearly exhausted their supply of oxygen.* **2.** To make very tired; wear out: *That long walk exhausted me.*
—*noun, plural* **exhausts** The gases and other matter released from a running engine.

exercise
Above: Keeping fit
Below: College graduation

exhibit
In a museum

ex·haus·tion | ĭg zôs′ chən | —*noun, plural* **exhaustions**
1. Extreme or great fatigue: *It took me two days to get over my exhaustion.* **2.** The act of exhausting or the condition of being exhausted: *The gradual exhaustion of our fuel.*

ex·hib·it | ĭg zĭb′ĭt | —*verb* **exhibited, exhibiting 1.** To show; demonstrate: *The soldiers exhibited much courage in battle.* **2.** To put on display: *She exhibited her paintings at the gallery.*
—*noun, plural* **exhibits** Something exhibited; a display: *We saw an exhibit of good behavior at the children's party.*

ex·hi·bi·tion | ĕk′sə bĭsh′ən | —*noun, plural* **exhibitions 1.** The act of exhibiting; display: *He struck the dog in an ugly exhibition of cruelty.* **2.** A public display: *an exhibition of the latest model cars.*

ex·hil·a·rate | ĭg zĭl′ə rāt′ | —*verb* **exhilarated, exhilarating** To make cheerful or excited; refresh; invigorate: *The cool air of fall exhilarates me.*

ex·ile | ĕg′zīl | or | ĕk′sīl | —*noun, plural* **exiles 1.** Forced removal from one's country; a banishing: *His punishment was exile.* **2.** A person who has been forced to leave his country: *He met many exiles in Florida.*
—*verb* **exiled, exiling** To send into exile; banish: *The dictator exiled many of his political rivals.*

ex·ist | ĭg zĭst′ | —*verb* **existed, existing 1.** To be real: *Do flying saucers exist?* **2.** To live: *Dinosaurs existed millions of years ago.*

ex·is·tence | ĭg zĭs′təns | —*noun, plural* **existences 1.** The condition of being real; reality: *Do you believe in the existence of life on other planets?* **2.** The fact of being alive; life: *Human progress sometimes threatens the existence of wild animals.*

ex·it | ĕg′zĭt | or | ĕk′sĭt | —*noun, plural* **exits 1.** A passage or way out: *The theater exits are marked with red lights.* **2.** The act of leaving: *I hope my exit didn't stop the party.*
—*verb* **exited, exiting** To make one's exit; depart: *We exited fast when the bell rang.*

ex·o·dus | ĕk′sə dəs | —*noun, plural* **exoduses** A departure, especially by a large number of people: *On summer weekends there is an exodus of city people for the beaches.*

ex·ot·ic | ĭg zŏt′ĭk | —*adjective* From another part of the world; foreign: *exotic birds from South American jungles.*

ex·pand | ĭk spănd′ | —*verb* **expanded, expanding** To make or become larger: *The balloon expanded slowly. Jean expanded her essay into a longer composition.*

ex·panse | ĭk spăns′ | —*noun, plural* **expanses** A wide and open area; a broad, smooth stretch: *an expanse of desert.*

ex·pan·sion | ĭk spăn′shən | —*noun, plural* **expansions 1.** The act of expanding or the condition of being expanded; increase in size: *The science teacher demonstrated the expansion of gas when heated.* **2.** Something formed by making another thing bigger or longer: *The book is an expansion of his short story.*

ex·pect | ĭk spĕkt′ | —*verb* **expected, expecting 1.** To look for as likely to happen; foresee: *The farmers are expecting rain.* **2.** To want as something proper or due: *The teacher expects an apology from you.* **3.** To suppose; think: *I expect you're hungry.*

ex·pec·ta·tion | ĕk′spĕk tā′shən | —*noun, plural* **expectations 1.** The act or condition of expecting; anticipation: *The dog wagged his tail in expectation.* **2. expectations** Hopes or prospects: *Our vacation fell short of expectations.*

ex·pe·di·tion | ĕk′spĭ dĭsh′ən | —*noun, plural* **expeditions 1.** A

exotic
Exotic animal

ă	pat	ĕ	pet	î	fierce
ā	pay	ē	be	ŏ	pot
â	care	ĭ	pit	ō	go
ä	father	ī	pie	ô	paw, for
oi	oil	ŭ	cut	zh	vision
ŏŏ	book	û	fur	ə	ago, item,
ōō	boot	*th*	the		pencil, atom,
yōō	abuse	th	thin		circus
ou	out	hw	which	ər	butter

long trip, usually for exploring or studying something not known or far away: *President Thomas Jefferson sent the explorers on a large expedition across the continent to the Pacific Ocean.* **2.** The group making such a trip: *In 1519 a Spanish expedition set out to be the first to sail around the world.*

ex·pel | ĭk spĕl' | —*verb* **expelled, expelling 1.** To force out: *expel air from the lungs.* **2.** To remove by official decision; dismiss: *expel a student from school.*

ex·pense | ĭk spĕns' | —*noun, plural* **expenses 1.** Cost; price: *Can you afford the expense of a long vacation?* **2.** Something that requires the spending of money: *A car can be a heavy expense.* **3.** Loss or sacrifice: *He worked long hours at the expense of his health.*

ex·pen·sive | ĭk spĕn'sĭv | —*adjective* Having a high price; costly: *It's the most expensive dress I ever owned.*

ex·pe·ri·ence | ĭk spîr'ē əns | —*noun, plural* **experiences 1.** Something that one lives through; an event in one's life: *Seeing the tall snowy peaks was one of my greatest experiences.* **2.** Knowledge or skill that one gains by practice: *You can't get a good job without experience.*
—*verb* **experienced, experiencing** To live through; undergo: *We all experienced hunger and thirst while lost in the forest.*

ex·per·i·ment | ĭk spĕr'ə mənt | —*noun, plural* **experiments** Something done to show a fact, test a theory, or find out what might happen: *We did an experiment to show that plants need light to grow. As an experiment, I let the dog off the leash to see if she could find the way home.*
—*verb* **experimented, experimenting** To do an experiment or experiments: *He was one of the first scientists to experiment with rockets.*

ex·per·i·men·tal | ĭk spĕr'ə mĕn'tl | —*adjective* **1.** Of or based on experiments: *an experimental science.* **2.** New and still being tested: *an experimental drug.*

ex·pert | ĕk'spûrt' | —*noun, plural* **experts** A person who knows a lot about a subject or is very good at it: *Bill studied boxing till he became an expert.*
—*adjective* **1.** Skilled in a particular field: *an expert photographer.* **2.** Given by an expert: *You need some expert advice.*

ex·pire | ĭk spīr' | —*verb* **expired, expiring 1.** To die: *The old man expired at 92.* **2.** To come to an end: *My library card expires next week.*

ex·plain | ĭk splān' | —*verb* **explained, explaining 1.** To tell about in a way that makes a listener or reader understand; make clear: *Can you explain electricity to me?* **2.** To give a reason for; account for: *You'd better explain your idea.*

ex·pla·na·tion | ĕk'splə nā'shən | —*noun, plural* **explanations 1.** The act or process of explaining: *He gave a lengthy explanation of his new theory.* **2.** Something that serves to explain; reason: *There seemed to be no explanation for the sudden change.*

ex·plan·a·to·ry | ĭk splăn'ə tôr'ē | —*adjective* Helping to explain; clarifying: *There are explanatory notes on this page.*

ex·plic·it | ĭk splĭs'ĭt | —*adjective* Clearly stated; openly expressed: *Instead of just telling us to review our work at home, the teacher gave us an explicit assignment today.*

ex·plode | ĭk splōd' | —*verb* **exploded, exploding 1.** To burst with a loud noise; blow up: *The mines exploded in the ground.*

expedition
Near the North Pole, 1909

2. To burst forth suddenly: *The news caused Father to explode with anger.* **3.** To increase beyond control: *a country where the birth rate is exploding.*

ex·ploit |ĕk′sploit′| —*noun, plural* **exploits** A heroic or daring act; deed: *the exploits of Robin Hood.*
—*verb* |ĭk sploit′| **exploited, exploiting 1.** To use to the greatest advantage: *The mining company hopes to exploit coal reserves deep underground.* **2.** To take unfair advantage of: *The owners exploited their slaves cruelly.*

ex·plo·ra·tion |ĕk′splə rā′shən| —*noun, plural* **explorations** The act of exploring: *The exploration of the New World was done mainly by Spaniards.*

ex·plore |ĭk splôr′| or |ĭk splōr′| —*verb* **explored, exploring 1.** To travel through an unfamiliar place for the purpose of discovery: *They explored the unknown upper Missouri River. The children explored the attic of the old house.* **2.** To look into closely; investigate: *Today scientists are exploring different ways of removing salt from sea water.*

ex·plor·er |ĭk splôr′ər| or |ĭk splōr′ər| —*noun, plural* **explorers** A person who explores unknown places.

ex·plo·sion |ĭk splō′zhən| —*noun, plural* **explosions 1.** The act of breaking apart violently with great force and noise: *We were startled by the explosion of a giant firecracker.* **2.** A sudden outbreak: *an explosion of laughter.* **3.** A sudden and sharp increase: *a population explosion.*

ex·plo·sive |ĭk splō′sĭv| —*noun, plural* **explosives** A substance that can explode: *Dynamite is a powerful explosive.*
—*adjective* Capable of exploding or tending to explode: *an explosive gas.*

ex·port |ĭk spôrt′| or |ĭk spōrt′| —*verb* **exported, exporting** To send goods to another country for trade or sale: *The United States exports wheat but imports oil.*
—*noun* |ĕk′spôrt′| or |ĕk′spōrt′|, *plural* **exports 1.** The act or process of exporting: *Many Middle Eastern nations depend on the export of oil.* **2.** Something that is exported: *Automobiles were a major Japanese export last year.*

ex·pose |ĭk spōz′| —*verb* **exposed, exposing 1.** To uncover; reveal: *She lifted the veil to expose her pale face.* **2.** To leave open; subject: *By visiting his sick friend, he exposed himself to flu germs.* **3.** To make known; disclose: *The detectives exposed a ring of gangsters.*

ex·po·si·tion |ĕk′spə zĭsh′ən| —*noun, plural* **expositions** A public show; exhibition.

ex·po·sure |ĭk spō′zhər| —*noun, plural* **exposures 1.** The act of exposing or the condition of being exposed: *The newspaper's exposure of a scandal won it an award. Long exposure to heat has cracked the cement.* **2.** The front or open side of a structure or room: *The dining room has a southern exposure.*

ex·press |ĭk sprĕs′| —*verb* **expressed, expressing 1.** To show; reveal: *His face expressed great joy.* **2.** To put into words; state: *Try to express your ideas more clearly.*
—*adjective* **1.** Clearly stated; definite: *It is my express wish that you do not go.* **2.** Meant for fast travel: *an express train; an express highway.*
—*noun, plural* **expresses 1.** An express train, bus, or other vehicle. **2.** A fast system for delivering goods and mail.

exploit
Climbing a skyscraper

explorer
Admiral Robert E. Peary

ă	pat	ĕ	pet	î	fierce
ā	pay	ē	be	ŏ	pot
â	care	ĭ	pit	ō	go
ä	father	ī	pie	ô	paw, for

oi	oil	ŭ	cut	zh	vision
ŏŏ	book	û	fur	ə	ago, item,
ōō	boot	*th*	the		pencil, atom,
yōō	abuse	th	thin		circus
ou	out	hw	which	ər	butter

ex·pres·sion | ĭk **sprĕsh′**ən | —*noun, plural* **expressions 1.** The act of expressing: *I hope the meeting allows for the expression of unpopular opinions.* **2.** A way of expressing something; sign: *A yawn is an expression of anger among baboons.* **3.** A look that expresses a person's mood or feeling: *John has a worried expression.* **4.** A common word, phrase, or saying: *"Sleep like a log" is a familiar expression.*

ex·press·way | ĭk **sprĕs′**wā′ | —*noun, plural* **expressways** A wide highway with many lanes built for high-speed travel.

ex·qui·site | **ĕk′**skwĭz ĭt | or | ĭk **skwĭz′**ĭt | —*adjective* **1.** Of special beauty or charm: *an exquisite bouquet of roses.* **2.** Very sensitive; refined: *She has exquisite taste in clothes.*

ex·tend | ĭk **stĕnd′** | —*verb* **extended, extending 1.** To make longer; lengthen: *We extended the table to seat four more guests. She extended her stay another day.* **2.** To reach; stretch: *The mountains extend from the United States into Canada.* **3.** To offer or grant: *Let's extend our greetings to the newcomers.*

ex·ten·sion | ĭk **stĕn′**shən | —*noun, plural* **extensions 1.** The act of extending or the condition of being extended: *the extension of a deadline for another day.* **2.** Something that extends or enlarges; addition: *We built a new extension to our house.* **3.** An additional telephone linked with the main one.

ex·ten·sive | ĭk **stĕn′**sĭv | —*adjective* Large in area or amount; wide: *There's an extensive forest near our house.*

ex·tent | ĭk **stĕnt′** | —*noun, plural* **extents 1.** The area or distance over which something extends; size: *What is the extent of your land?* **2.** The point or degree to which something extends: *To some extent we agree with you.*

ex·te·ri·or | ĭk **stîr′**ē ər | —*adjective* Outer or outside; external: *an exterior wall.*
—*noun, plural* **exteriors 1.** An outer part or surface: *the exterior of a house.* **2.** An outward appearance: *Don't be deceived by his friendly exterior.*

ex·ter·mi·nate | ĭk **stûr′**mə nāt′ | —*verb* **exterminated, exterminating** To destroy; kill; wipe out: *We hired a man to exterminate the cockroaches.*

ex·ter·nal | ĭk **stûr′**nəl | —*adjective* **1.** Of the outside or an outer part: *The bark is the external layer of a tree trunk.* **2.** Intended for the outer surface of the body: *a medicine for external use only.*

ex·tinct | ĭk **stĭngkt′** | —*adjective* **1.** No longer in existence: *The dinosaur is an extinct animal.* **2.** Inactive; not likely to erupt: *an extinct volcano.*

ex·tinc·tion | ĭk **stĭngk′**shən | —*noun, plural* **extinctions 1.** The condition of being extinct: *The buffalo was hunted almost to extinction.* **2.** Ending: *Scientists do extensive research and work for the cure and eventual extinction of diseases.*

ex·tin·guish | ĭk **stĭng′**gwĭsh | —*verb* **extinguished, extinguishing** To put out a fire or flame: *extinguish a candle.*

ex·tin·guish·er | ĭk **stĭng′**gwĭ shər | —*noun, plural* **extinguishers** A device used to put out fires, often a sealed container from which a liquid is sprayed.

ex·tra | **ĕk′**strə | —*adjective* More than what is usual or expected; additional: *When everyone else went home, Joe stayed in the store to do extra work.*
—*noun, plural* **extras** Something additional, as an accessory that

expressway

extinct
The dodo, an extinct bird

extinguisher

one must pay more for: *a new car with all the extras.*

ex·tract |ĭk străkt′| —*verb* **extracted, extracting 1.** To pull out with force: *The dentist might have to extract a tooth.* **2.** To obtain with some effort or difficulty: *The Indians extract medicines from plant leaves and roots.*
—*noun* |ĕk′străkt′|, *plural* **extracts** Something that is drawn out or refined from larger or less pure matter: *vanilla extract.*

ex·traor·di·nar·y |ĭk strôr′dn ĕr′ē| or |ĕk′strə ôr′dn ĕr′ē| —*adjective* Very unusual; remarkable; exceptional: *His grandfather was an extraordinary man.*

ex·trav·a·gance |ĭk străv′ə gəns| —*noun, plural* **extravagances** A tendency to spend too much money on unnecessary things: *Helen spent her first salary check on a new hat, but then was immediately sorry for her extravagance.*

ex·trav·a·gant |ĭk străv′ə gənt| —*adjective* Spending lavishly; wasteful: *an extravagant buying spree.*

ex·treme |ĭk strēm′| —*adjective* **1.** Very great or intense: *extreme cold; extreme caution.* **2.** Very far; farthest: *They live in the extreme end of town.* **3.** Drastic; severe: *extreme measures.*
—*noun, plural* **extremes 1.** Either of two ends of a scale or range: *the extremes of happiness and sadness.* **2.** The greatest or utmost degree of something: *He is always polite in the extreme.* **3.** A drastic method or measure: *In the emergency we had to resort to extremes.*

ex·treme·ly |ĭk strēm′lē| —*adverb* Very; especially: *She has always been extremely kind to me.*

ex·trem·i·ty |ĭk strĕm′ĭ tē| —*noun, plural* **extremities 1.** The farthest point; end: *the southern extremity of South America.* **2. extremities** A person's hands and feet.

eye |ī| —*noun, plural* **eyes 1.** Either of a pair of round, hollow organs by which a person or animal sees. **2.** The outer, visible part of this organ: *She has brown eyes.* **3.** A look or gaze: *She cast an adoring eye at her father.* **4.** Ability to see or to tell things apart: *You need a good eye to see that far.* **5. a.** A hole for a hook or lace to go in. **b.** The hole in a needle.
—*verb* **eyed, eyeing** To look at; watch: *He eyed me suspiciously.*
♦ *These sound alike* **eye, aye, I**

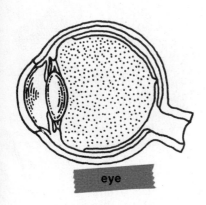

eye

eye·ball |ī′bôl′| —*noun, plural* **eyeballs** The round part of the eye covered in front by the eyelid.

eye·brow |ī′brou′| —*noun, plural* **eyebrows** The short hair covering the bony ridge above each eye.

eye·glass·es |ī′glăs′ĭz| or |ī′glä′sĭz| —*plural noun* A pair of lenses worn on a frame in front of the eyes to improve one's vision; glasses.

eye·lash |ī′lăsh′| —*noun, plural* **eyelashes 1.** A row of hairs along the edge of each eyelid. **2.** Any one of the hairs in this row.

eye·let |ī′lĭt| —*noun, plural* **eyelets** A small hole for a lace, cord, or hook to fit through.

eye·lid |ī′lĭd′| —*noun, plural* **eyelids** Either of a pair of folds of skin that can be brought together to cover an eye.

eye·sight |ī′sīt′| —*noun* The ability to see; vision.

eye·tooth |ī′tooth′| —*noun, plural* **eyeteeth** Either of the two pointed teeth in a person's upper jaw.

eye·wit·ness |ī′wĭt′nĭs| —*noun, plural* **eyewitnesses** A person who was present when something happened, as a crime or accident.

ă	pat	ĕ	pet	î	fierce
ā	pay	ē	be	ŏ	pot
â	care	ĭ	pit	ō	go
ä	father	ī	pie	ô	paw, for
oi	oil	ŭ	cut	zh	vision
ŏŏ	book	û	fur	ə	ago, item,
ōō	boot	*th*	the		pencil, atom,
yōō	abuse	th	thin		circus
ou	out	hw	which	ər	butter

Y	**Phoenician** — The letter *F* comes originally from a Phoenician symbol named *wāw*, which is the basis for *U, V, W, Y,* and *F*.
F	**Greek** — The Greeks borrowed the symbol from the Phoenicians and changed its form. One form they used was called *digamma*.
F	**Roman** — The Romans took the letter and adapted it for carving into stone. This became the model for our modern printed capital *F*.
f	**Medieval** — The hand-written form of about 1,200 years ago became the basis of the modern small letter.
Ff	**Modern** — The modern capital and small letters are based on the Roman capital and later hand-written forms.

f or **F** |ĕf| —*noun, plural* **f's** or **F's** The sixth letter of the English alphabet.

fa·ble |fā′bəl| —*noun, plural* **fables** A story that teaches a lesson. Often the characters in fables are animals that talk and act like people.

fab·ric |făb′rĭk| —*noun, plural* **fabrics** A material made by weaving or knitting threads together; cloth.

fab·u·lous |făb′yə ləs| —*adjective* **1.** Belonging to fables; legendary: *The dragon is a fabulous creature.* **2.** Very extraordinary; fantastic: *a fabulous jewel.*

face |fās| —*noun, plural* **faces** **1. a.** The front part of the head. **b.** The expression of this part of the head: *a sad face; make a face.* **2.** The front or outer part of something: *the face of a building; the snowy face of a mountain.* **3.** The upper or marked side of something: *the face of the card.*
—*verb* **faced, facing** **1.** To turn the face to: *Please face the front of the room.* **2.** To have the front looking out on; front on: *The house faces the park.* **3.** To deal with directly or boldly: *Some people run away from their problems, while others face them.*

fac·et |făs′ĭt| —*noun, plural* **facets** **1.** A flat, polished surface on a cut gem. **2.** Aspect; side: *Mr. Arnold is a complicated guy with many facets to his character.*

fa·cial |fā′shəl| —*adjective* Of the face: *a facial expression.*

fa·cil·i·ty |fə sĭl′ĭ tē| —*noun, plural* **facilities** **1.** Skill without effort; ease: *He speaks Italian with such facility that he could pass for a native.* **2. facilities** Things provided for people to use: *The school's athletic facilities include a large gym and a pool.*

fact |făkt| —*noun, plural* **facts** Something that is known to be true or to have really happened: *It is a fact that the sun is a star.*

fac·tor |făk′tər| —*noun, plural* **factors** **1.** Something that helps bring about or influence a certain result: *Air pollution was an important factor in our decision to move away from the city.* **2.** One of two or more numbers that when multiplied together form a product: *2 and 3 are factors of 6.*

fac·to·ry |făk′tə rē| —*noun, plural* **factories** A building or group of buildings where things are made; a plant.

fac·tu·al |făk′chōō əl| —*adjective* Based on or including facts: *a factual story.*

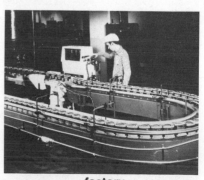

factory
Filling cocoa cans in a chocolate factory

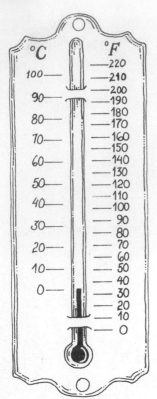

Fahrenheit
Thermometer showing degrees
on the Celsius scale *(left)* and the
Fahrenheit scale *(right)*

ă	pat	ĕ	pet	î	fierce		
ā	pay	ē	be	ŏ	pot		
â	care	ĭ	pit	ō	go		
ä	father	ī	pie	ô	paw, for		
oi	oil	ŭ	cut	zh	vision		
ŏŏ	book	û	fur	ə	ago, item,		
ōō	boot	*th*	the		pencil, atom,		
yōō	abuse	th	thin		circus		
ou	out	hw	which	ər	butter		

fac·ul·ty |făk′əl tē| —*noun, plural* **faculties** **1.** A power of the mind: *The shock of the news took away her faculty of speech.* **2.** The talent or skill to do something: *He has a great faculty for cheering people up.* **3.** The teaching staff of a school or college.

fad |făd| —*noun, plural* **fads** Something that is very popular for a short time; a craze: *Blue lipstick was a fad in my sister's class.*

fade |fād| —*verb* **faded, fading** **1.** To lose or cause to lose a bright look: *Her shirt faded in the laundry. Hot water will fade this fabric.* **2.** To lose or cause to lose a fresh look: *The flowers faded.* **3.** To become faint; die out: *Her footsteps faded as she left.* **4.** To disappear slowly: *His anger faded.*

Fahr·en·heit |făr′ən hīt′| —*adjective* Of a temperature scale on which 32 degrees is the freezing point of water and 212 degrees is the boiling point.

fail |fāl| —*verb* **failed, failing** **1.** To not succeed; not do what one attempts: *She tried to be on time but failed. He failed to appear for dinner.* **2.** To break down; stop: *The electric power failed and all the lights went out.* **3.** To disappoint; let down: *Her friends failed her when she needed them most.* **4.** To become weaker; decline: *His hearing failed as he grew older.* **5.** To get less than a passing grade in: *Three students failed math this year.*

fail·ure |fāl′yər| —*noun, plural* **failures** **1.** The act or fact of failing: *My failure to arrive on time was due to bad planning.* **2.** Someone or something that fails: *When my Dad couldn't get a job, he considered himself a failure. The new shop was a failure and soon closed.* **3.** The condition of being no longer available or in operation: *heart failure; a power failure.*

faint |fānt| —*adjective* **fainter, faintest** **1.** Not clearly seen, sensed, or heard; weak: *a faint light; a faint smell.* **2.** Dizzy and weak: *Her illness made her feel faint.*
—*noun, plural* **faints** A condition in which a person suddenly seems to fall asleep for a little while. Sickness, bad air, or a sudden shock can cause someone to fall into a faint.
—*verb* **fainted, fainting** To fall into a faint.

fair¹ |fâr| —*adjective* **fairer, fairest** **1.** Pleasing to look at; beautiful: *a fair lady.* **2.** Light in color: *fair hair; fair skin.* **3.** Clear; sunny: *a fair day.* **4.** Not favoring one more than another; just: *a fair judge; a fair rule.* **5.** Not too good or too bad; average: *The book was only fair.* **6.** Following the rules: *fair play.*
—*adverb* In a fair way; properly: *The team played fair.*
♦ *These sound alike* **fair, fare.**

fair² |fâr| —*noun, plural* **fairs** **1.** A gathering for the buying and selling of goods; a market. **2.** A large public display of farm or industrial products. County and state fairs often have entertainment and contests.
♦ *These sound alike* **fair, fare.**

fair·ly |fâr′lē| —*adverb* **1.** In a fair or just manner: *treating people fairly.* **2.** Rather; somewhat: *a fairly good summer job.*

fair·y |fâr′ē| —*noun, plural* **fairies** A tiny make-believe being that has magical powers and can be good or evil.

faith |fāth| —*noun, plural* **faiths** **1.** Confident belief; trust: *She had great faith in her father.* **2.** Belief in God: *a person of faith.* **3.** A religion: *People of all faiths were at the meeting.*

faith·ful |fāth′fəl| —*adjective* **1.** Worthy of trust; loyal: *My faithful friends stood by me.* **2.** True to fact; exact: *a faithful copy.*

fake |fāk| —*verb* **faked, faking** **1.** To pretend: *Some kids fake*

illness to get out of school. *The boy didn't look at all scared, but he was faking.* **2.** To make up and pass off as true and real: *The actor forgot his lines and had to fake them.* **3.** To move so as to mislead one's opponent during a game: *Jerry faked to the left and ran down the center for a pass.*
—*noun, plural* **fakes 1.** Someone or something that is not what it pretends to be: *That gun is a fake made of plastic.* **2.** A deceptive move meant to mislead one's opponent.
—*adjective* Not genuine; false: *fake money.*

fal·con |făl′kən| *or* |fôl′kən| *or* |fô′kən| —*noun, plural* **falcons** A hawk that has long wings and can fly very fast. Falcons have been trained to hunt for small animals and birds.

fall |fôl| —*verb* **fell, fallen, falling 1.** To drop or come down from a higher place: *Snow fell last night. In the play she falls to the ground and asks for help.* **2.** To be wounded or killed: *Many soldiers fall in battle.* **3.** To come suddenly: *Darkness fell on the city. A hush fell over the crowd.* **4.** To become lower; go down: *Prices fell on the stock market.* **5.** To be defeated or captured: *France fell in 1940.* **6.** To come to rest: *His eyes fell on the dog.* **7.** To pass from one state or condition to another; become: *fall asleep; fall in love.* **8.** To come by chance: *fall into a trap; fall into bad company.*
—*noun, plural* **falls 1.** The act of coming down from a higher place, especially a drop through the air: *He took a hard fall.* **2.** The season after summer; autumn. **3. falls** A place on a river where water drops sharply. **4.** A reduction; decline: *a fall in prices.* **5.** A collapse: *the fall of a government.*

fall·en |fô′lən| The past participle of the verb **fall:** *I have fallen on the ice many times.*

fall·out |fôl′out′| —*noun* The radioactive dust that slowly falls to the earth after a nuclear bomb is exploded.

fal·low |făl′ō| —*adjective* Not planted: *a fallow field.*

false |fôls| —*adjective* **falser, falsest 1.** Not true or correct; wrong: *I gave an answer, but I knew it was false.* **2.** Not real; artificial: *false teeth; false laughter.* **3.** Not to be trusted; full of deceit; insincere: *false promises; a false friend.*

fal·ter |fôl′tər| —*verb* **faltered, faltering** To move unsteadily; to stumble: *The old man faltered and groped about for a helping arm.*

fame |fām| —*noun* The quality of being very well known.

fa·mil·iar |fə mĭl′yər| —*adjective* **1.** Often seen or heard; common: *Frisbee players are a familiar sight in the park.* **2.** Knowing something fairly well; acquainted: *Since he wasn't familiar with the neighborhood, he had to be careful not to get lost.* **3.** Friendly; informal: *She's on familiar terms with Mr. Jones.*

fam·i·ly |făm′ə lē| *or* |făm′lē| —*noun, plural* **families 1.** A mother and father and their children: *I come from a family of five, including three children.* **2.** The children of a mother and father: *The newly married couple decided to wait a while before raising a family.* **3.** A group of related persons; relatives: *Our whole family, including aunts and uncles, gets together every summer.* **4.** A group of related animals or plants. Dogs, wolves, coyotes, and foxes belong to the same animal family. Daisies, dandelions, and asters belong to the same plant family. **5.** A group of similar or slightly different things: *The violin and the cello are members of the stringed family of musical instruments.*

fam·ine |făm′ĭn| —*noun, plural* **famines** A bad shortage of food in an area.

falcon

falls

fan¹, fan²

Fan¹ comes from a Latin word used to describe a device that made an artificial draft. **Fan²** is a fairly recent American word. It is a shortened form of **fanatic**, used to refer to a supporter who is extremely enthusiastic.

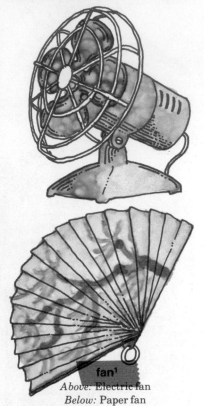

fan¹

Above: Electric fan
Below: Paper fan

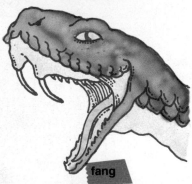

fang

ă	pat	ĕ	pet	î	fierce
ā	pay	ē	be	ŏ	pot
â	care	ĭ	pit	ō	go
ä	father	ī	pie	ô	paw, for
oi	oil	ŭ	cut	zh	vision
ōō	book	û	fur	ə	ago, item,
ōō	boot	*th*	the		pencil, atom,
yōō	abuse	th	thin		circus
ou	out	hw	which	ər	butter

fa·mous | fā′məs | —*adjective* Widely known; celebrated: *The famous singer was recognized by people everywhere he went.*

fan¹ | făn | —*noun, plural* **fans 1.** A stiff, flat piece of material that is waved back and forth to make air move in a cooling breeze. Most fans are shaped like triangles with the longest side curved. **2.** An electrical device with several blades that turn fast and blow air.
—*verb* **fanned, fanning** To make air blow on or toward, as with a fan: *She fanned herself with a folded newspaper.*

fan² | făn | —*noun, plural* **fans** Someone who loves an activity and follows it closely: *a baseball fan; a movie fan.*

fa·nat·ic | fə năt′ĭk | —*noun, plural* **fanatics** A person who believes in or loves something so much that he does foolish things for it: *My aunt is a fanatic for natural foods.*

fan·cy | făn′sē | —*noun, plural* **fancies 1.** The ability to form pictures in the mind; make-believe; imagination: *Her story is partly fact and partly fancy.* **2.** Something made up; fantasy: *In some of her childhood fancies she had an invisible playmate.* **3.** A funny idea or wish; a whim: *Joe had a sudden fancy to stand on his head.* **4.** A liking; fondness: *The two girls took a fancy to each other.*
—*verb* **fancied, fancying, fancies 1.** To picture in the mind; imagine: *Tim fancies himself a great athlete, but I can outrun him.* **2.** To like; prefer: *She fancies long skirts and big hats.*
—*adjective* **fancier, fanciest** Not plain; elaborate or special; fine: *fancy food; fancy clothes; fancy steps on the dance floor.*

fang | făng | —*noun, plural* **fangs** A long, pointed tooth. When some snakes bite, their fangs inject poison.

fan·tas·tic | făn tăs′tĭk | —*adjective* **1.** Very strange; weird: *The sun and water had twisted the driftwood into fantastic shapes.* **2.** Very good; wonderful: *We just saw a fantastic movie.*

fan·ta·sy | făn′tə sē | or | făn′tə zē | —*noun, plural* **fantasies 1.** Imagination; fiction: *His claim to be a prince is pure fantasy.* **2.** A story with a lot of make-believe; an unlikely tale: *"The Time Machine" is a fantasy about a man who travels backward in time.* **3.** A wishful picture in the mind; a daydream: *We walked on in the sun and had fantasies of drinks full of ice.*

far | fär | —*adverb* **farther** or **further, farthest** or **furthest 1.** To, from, or at a great distance: *She has to walk far to get to school each day. That promising boy will go far in life.* **2.** To a certain distance, place, or time: *I'm riding the train only as far as the next station. The meeting lasted far into the night.* **3.** Considerably; much: *This size fits far more comfortably.*
—*adjective* **farther** or **further, farthest** or **furthest 1.** Distant: *a far country.* **2.** More distant: *the far corner.*

fare | fâr | —*noun, plural* **fares** The price of a ride on a bus, train, or other vehicle.
—*verb* **fared, faring** To get along; do: *He's faring well at his new home.*
♦ *These sound alike* **fare, fair.**

fare·well | fâr wĕl′ | —*interjection* Good-by.
—*noun, plural* **farewells** An expression of good wishes to someone about to leave.

farm | färm | —*noun, plural* **farms** A piece of land where food crops and animals are raised.
—*verb* **farmed, farming** To raise food crops and animals; run a farm: *Not many people farm for a living any more.*

farm·er | fär′mər | —*noun, plural* **farmers** A person who runs a farm.

farm·ing | fär′mĭng | —*noun* The work of raising food crops or animals on a farm.

far·sight·ed | fär′sī′tĭd | —*adjective* Seeing distant things more clearly than near things. Far-sighted people sometimes have to wear glasses to read.

far·ther | fär′thər | —*adverb* A comparative of the adverb **far.** To a greater distance or extent: *She has to walk farther to school than I do.*
—*adjective* A comparative of the adjective **far.** More distant: *Of the two towns Boston is farther from here.*

far·thest | fär′thĭst | —*adverb* A superlative of the adverb **far.** To the greatest distance or extent: *Allen has to walk farthest to school of all of us.*
—*adjective* A superlative of the adjective **far.** Most distant: *The farthest mountain we can see is also the highest.*

fas·ci·nate | făs′ə nāt′ | —*verb* **fascinated, fascinating** To attract and interest very strongly; to charm: *The lifelike figures in the puppet show fascinated the children.*

fash·ion | făsh′ən | —*noun, plural* **fashions** **1.** Way; manner: *Hold your racket in this fashion.* **2.** A way of dressing, acting, or talking that many people imitate; style: *Short skirts are out of fashion now. It's the fashion these days to ride a bicycle to school.*
—*verb* **fashioned, fashioning** To make by shaping or putting together; to form: *The boys fashioned a raft out of a few logs.*

fash·ion·a·ble | făsh′ə nə bəl | —*adjective* In fashion; stylish: *fashionable clothes; a fashionable restaurant.*

fast¹ | făst | or | fäst | —*adjective* **faster, fastest** **1.** Acting or moving quickly; swift: *a fast driver; a fast car; a fast reply; a fast breakfast.* **2.** Running ahead of the correct time: *My watch must be fast.* **3.** Close; faithful: *They were fast friends in no time.*
—*adverb* **faster, fastest** **1.** Quickly: *Run fast and you'll catch him.* **2.** Tightly; firmly: *The lifeboats were held fast to the ship's deck by cables.* **3.** Thoroughly; deeply: *We were fast asleep by ten o'clock.*

fast² | făst | or | fäst | —*verb* **fasted, fasting** To stop eating food or certain kinds of food: *Some people fast on holy days.*
—*noun, plural* **fasts** An act or time of fasting: *We broke our fast with a light meal.*

fas·ten | făs′ən | or | fä′sən | —*verb* **fastened, fastening** **1.** To make something hold or stick; attach: *She fastened her apron by tying it in back.* **2.** To become attached: *The door fastens with a hook.* **3.** To apply; fix: *Fasten your attention on your work.*

fas·ten·er | făs′ə nər | or | fä′sə nər | —*noun, plural* **fasteners** Something used to fasten things together.

fat | făt | —*noun, plural* **fats** A soft white or yellow substance found in the bodies of animals and in the seeds, nuts, and fruits of plants.
—*adjective* **fatter, fattest** **1.** Too heavy; plump: *a fat person; a fat arm.* **2.** Full; ample: *a fat wallet.*

fa·tal | fāt′l | —*adjective* Causing death: *The airplane accident was fatal to everyone aboard.*

fate | fāt | —*noun, plural* **fates** **1. a.** A power no one can see or control that is believed to decide everything that happens in the future: *We thought we'd just start walking and leave our goal to fate.* **b.** An event or future that cannot be avoided and is decided by

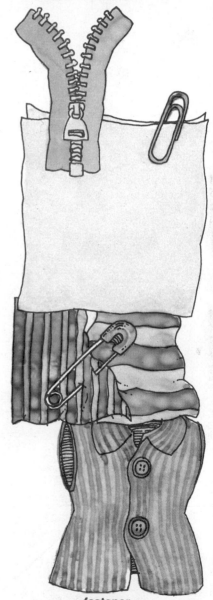

fast¹, fast²
Fast¹ and fast² come from two different meanings of the same old English word. As an adjective **fast¹** meant "firm, steady." As an adverb it originally meant "firmly, immediately"; it also came to mean "swiftly." **Fast²** had the meaning "to hold firm, to keep steady," which came to mean "to abstain from food."

fastener
A zipper, paper clip, safety pin, and button (*above*) are kinds of fasteners.

this power: *It was his fate to endure many sorrows during his life.*
2. Something that happens to a person or thing: *Everyone knows the fate of snowmen when it gets warmer.*

fa·ther |fä′ thər| —*noun, plural* **fathers** **1.** The male parent of a child. **2.** Father God. **3.** A priest.

fa·ther-in-law |fä′ thər ĭn lô′| —*noun, plural* **fathers-in-law** The father of one's husband or wife.

fa·ther·ly |fä′ thər lē| —*adjective* Like a father; affectionate and guiding: *The coach took me aside and gave me some fatherly advice.*

Father's Day A holiday celebrated on the third Sunday in June, in honor of fathers.

fath·om |făth′ əm| —*noun, plural* **fathoms** A unit of length equal to six feet. Fathoms are used mainly for expressing the depth of water.

fa·tigue |fə tēg′| —*noun* A feeling of needing rest or sleep; exhaustion.
—*verb* **fatigued, fatiguing** To make tired; wear out: *Painting her room took a long time and fatigued her.*

fat·ten |făt′n| —*verb* **fattened, fattening** To make or become fat: *Farmers fatten cattle for the market. We'll all fatten on this rich food.*

fat·ty |făt′ē| —*adjective* **fattier, fattiest** Of, full of, or like fat: *fatty body tissues; fatty foods.*

fau·cet |fô′sĭt| —*noun, plural* **faucets** A device with a handle for turning on and off a flow of liquid from a pipe or container.

fault |fôlt| —*noun, plural* **faults** **1.** A bad habit or quality; a weakness; defect: *Not being on time and laziness are my two worst faults.* **2.** Responsibility for something that shouldn't have happened: *The child was struck by a car, and it was the driver's fault.* **3.** A mistake; error: *many faults in grammar.*

faun |fôn| —*noun, plural* **fauns** A minor god in Roman myths who lived in the woods and fields. Fauns looked like men but had the horns, ears, tail, and legs of a goat.
♦ *These sound alike* **faun, fawn.**

fa·vor |fā′ vər| —*noun, plural* **favors** **1.** An act that helps someone: *Will you do me a favor and zip up my dress?* **2.** Approval; acceptance: *Metal bats are slowly gaining favor with children who play baseball.* **3.** Special treatment to one over another: *The teacher at the nursery school was careful not to show favor to her own child in the class.* **4.** A little party gift: *Paper hats and sacks of candy were among the favors.*
—*verb* **favored, favoring** **1.** To do a favor for; oblige: *Please favor us with your company for dinner.* **2.** To be for; support: *My parents favor a change in the tax laws.* **3.** To look like; take after: *In her face and build Jennie favors her mother.* **4.** To treat kindly; be gentle with: *The athlete ran carefully, favoring his injured leg.*

fa·vor·a·ble |fā′ vər ə bəl| —*adjective* **1.** Helping a plan or cause: *With favorable winds, the ship crossed the ocean rapidly.* **2.** Pointing to success; encouraging: *a favorable sign.* **3.** Approving or agreeing; saying "yes": *We invited him and the children to the party and received a favorable reply.*

fa·vor·ite |fā′ vər ĭt| —*noun, plural* **favorites** Someone or something liked above all others: *Cheese is a favorite of hers.*
—*adjective* Liked best: *My favorite color is yellow.*

fawn |fôn| —*noun, plural* **fawns** A young deer.
♦ *These sound alike* **fawn, faun.**

fear |fîr| —*noun, plural* **fears** A bad feeling caused by the

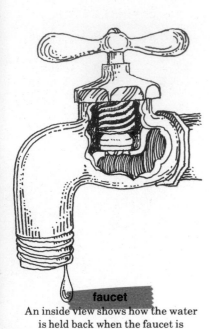

faucet

An inside view shows how the water is held back when the faucet is turned off.

fawn

ă	pat	ĕ	pet	î	fierce
ā	pay	ē	be	ŏ	pot
â	care	ĭ	pit	ō	go
ä	father	ī	pie	ô	paw, for

oi	oil	ŭ	cut	zh	vision
ŏŏ	book	û	fur	ə	ago, item,
ōō	boot	th	the		pencil, atom,
yōō	abuse	th	thin		circus
ou	out	hw	which	ər	butter

nearness of danger or pain or something unknown; terror; dread: *I have a fear of high places.*

—*verb* **feared, fearing** **1.** To be afraid of; be scared of: *Jill feared snakes.* **2.** To suspect unhappily: *I fear that there is a storm up ahead.*

fear·ful |fîr′fəl| —*adjective* **1.** Feeling fear; afraid: *Hal was fearful of heights.* **2.** Causing fear; scary: *A fearful scream woke us all up suddenly.* **3.** Very bad: *a fearful headache.*

feast |fēst| —*noun, plural* **feasts** A large, fancy meal: *a wedding feast.*

—*verb* **feasted, feasting** **1.** To eat well: *We feasted on ham and sweet potatoes.* **2.** To give pleasure to; to delight: *Feast your eyes on those flowers.*

feat |fēt| —*noun, plural* **feats** An act or deed, especially a skillful one: *That golf shot was a great feat.*

♦ *These sound alike* **feat, feet.**

feath·er |fĕth′ ər| —*noun, plural* **feathers** One of the light special parts that grow from the skin of birds. Feathers protect birds and help them fly.

feath·er·y |fĕth′ ə rē| —*adjective* Made of or covered with feathers: *a feathery cape; a feathery pillow.*

fea·ture |fē′chər| —*noun, plural* **features** **1.** A part or quality that stands out; something that can be noticed: *The large kitchen was one feature Dad liked about the house.* **2.** A part of the face. The nose, eyes, mouth, chin, cheeks, and forehead are features. **3.** The main film of a movie program.

—*verb* **featured, featuring** To give special attention to; to offer: *The menu featured fish.*

Feb·ru·ar·y |fĕb′rōō ĕr′ē| or |fĕb′yōō ĕr′ē| —*noun, plural* **Februarys** The second month of the year, after January and before March. February has 28 days except in leap year, when it has 29.

fed |fĕd| The past tense and past participle of the verb **feed:** *Jane fed her cat. She has fed him every kind of canned food.*

fed·er·al |fĕd′ər əl| —*adjective* **1.** Formed by an agreement of different states to unite under one central authority. The United States has a federal government. **2.** Of the central government rather than the states: *a federal power.*

fee |fē| —*noun, plural* **fees** An amount of money asked or paid for a service or right; a charge: *The dentist's fee is $20 for a visit.*

fee·ble |fē′bəl| —*adjective* **feebler, feeblest** Lacking strength or force; weak: *The patient was too feeble to feed himself. Joe made a few feeble attempts at humor but no one laughed.*

feed |fēd| —*verb* **fed, feeding** **1.** To give food to: *Please feed the dog.* **2.** To give as food: *We feed lettuce to the hamster.* **3.** To serve as food for: *A large chicken will feed the family.* **4.** To eat: *The cows fed on grass.*

—*noun, plural* **feeds** Food for animals or birds; fodder.

feel |fēl| —*verb* **felt, feeling** **1.** To touch: *He felt the rough cloth with his fingers. She felt his forehead to see if he was ill.* **2.** To find or detect by touching: *Can you feel my pulse?* **3.** To search by touching; grope: *He felt in the drawer for the key.* **4.** To seem to the touch; have a texture: *The cat's fur feels like velvet.* **5.** To be aware of; sense: *He felt a stab of pain. They could feel the waiter's impatience.* **6.** To have a sensation of being: *He felt like a fool.* **7.** To have a feeling or emotion: *I feel sorry for you.* **8.** To hold an

feather

Above: Feather *(left)* and magnified section *(right)*
Below: Birds with unusual feathers

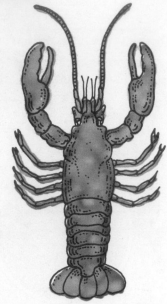

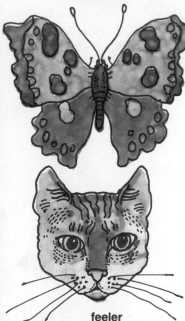

feeler
Above: On a lobster
Center: On a butterfly
Below: On a cat

opinion; believe: *She feels that TV is a bad influence.*
—*noun, plural* **feels** The way something seems when touched:
Bark has a rough feel.

feel·er |fē′lər| —*noun, plural* **feelers** A part of an animal that is used for touching or feeling. A cat's whiskers and an insect's antennae are feelers.

feel·ing |fē′lĭng| —*noun, plural* **feelings 1.** The ability to feel; the sense of touch: *It was so cold that there was no feeling in her feet.* **2.** A physical sensation: *a sick feeling in his stomach.* **3.** An emotion or mood: *Madge had a feeling of joy when she saw her dog.* **4. feelings** The tender part of one's nature; one's pride: *Their remarks hurt my feelings.* **5.** An impression: *We all got a feeling of peace from the church.* **6.** An opinion or belief: *These are my feelings about unions.*

feet |fēt| The plural of the noun **foot.**
♦ *These sound alike* **feet, feat.**

feign |fān| —*verb* **feigned, feigning** To give a false appearance of; pretend: *I almost feigned illness to avoid school that day.*

fell¹ |fĕl| —*verb* **felled, felling** To cut or knock down: *They felled trees to make a fence.*

fell² |fĕl| The past tense of the verb **fall:** *Jim fell on the rocks.*

fel·low |fĕl′ō| —*noun, plural* **fellows 1.** A man or boy. **2.** A companion or associate: *He likes the company of his fellows.*

fel·low·ship |fĕl′ō shĭp′| —*noun, plural* **fellowships** The friendship among a group; companionship: *Their fellowship made him feel welcome.*

felt¹ |fĕlt| —*noun, plural* **felts** A cloth made by pressing wool, hair, or other fibers together instead of weaving them.

felt² |fĕlt| The past tense and past participle of the verb **feel:** *Joan felt the kitten's fur. Pat had felt sick before the party.*

fe·male |fē′māl′| —*adjective* Of or belonging to the sex that can give birth to young or produce eggs. A hen is a female chicken.
—*noun, plural* **females** A female person or animal. Girls and women are females.

fem·i·nine |fĕm′ə nĭn| —*adjective* Of or belonging to women or girls rather than men: *We guessed it was a girl's bedroom because the furniture and decorations seemed feminine.*

fence |fĕns| —*noun, plural* **fences** A structure set up around an area to protect it or mark it off. Fences are often made of wire, posts, or stones.
—*verb* **fenced, fencing 1.** To surround or separate with a fence. **2.** To fight with long, slender swords.

fenc·ing |fĕn′sĭng| —*noun* The art or sport of fighting with long, slender swords.

fen·der |fĕn′dər| —*noun, plural* **fenders** A metal cover or guard above and around the wheel of a car, truck, or bicycle.

fer·ment |fûr′mĕnt′| —*noun, plural* **ferments 1.** Something that causes fermentation. Yeasts and molds are ferments. **2.** A state of excitement or unrest: *The new teacher encouraged a ferment of ideas and new projects among his students.*
—*verb* |fər mĕnt′| **fermented, fermenting** To undergo or cause fermentation: *When fruit juice is left standing, it ferments.*

fer·men·ta·tion |fûr′mĕn tā′shən| —*noun, plural* **fermentations** A process by which the sugar in a liquid gradually turns into alcohol and a gas. A little yeast or mold added to fruit juice can cause fermentation.

ă	pat	ĕ	pet	î	fierce
ā	pay	ē	be	ŏ	pot
â	care	ĭ	pit	ō	go
ä	father	ī	pie	ô	paw, for
oi	oil	ŭ	cut	zh	vision
ŏŏ	book	û	fur	ə	ago, item,
ōō	boot	*th*	the		pencil, atom,
yōō	abuse	th	thin		circus
ou	out	hw	which	ər	butter

fern |fûrn| —*noun, plural* **ferns** One of a group of plants that usually have feathery leaves with many leaflets. Ferns do not have flowers and seeds. They produce tiny spores from which new plants grow.

fe·ro·cious |fə rō′shəs| —*adjective* Very cruel and fierce; savage: *a ferocious lion.*

fer·ret |fĕr′ĭt| —*noun, plural* **ferrets** An animal related to the weasels. Ferrets have yellowish or white fur. In Europe they are often trained to hunt for rats and rabbits.
—*verb* **ferreted, ferreting** To hunt; search: *The cat finally ferreted out the mouse.*

Fer·ris wheel |fĕr′ĭs| A large, revolving wheel with two rims from which seats are suspended in which people ride for fun. Ferris wheels are found at fairs and amusement parks.

fer·ry |fĕr′ē| —*noun, plural* **ferries** A boat used to carry people, cars, or goods across a narrow body of water.
—*verb* **ferried, ferrying, ferries** **1.** To carry across a narrow body of water: *Mat ferried them from the island to the mainland in his motorboat.* **2.** To take a ferry: *We'll ferry to the island tomorrow.*

fer·tile |fûr′tl| —*adjective* **1.** Good for plants to grow in; promoting plant growth: *fertile soil.* **2.** Capable of having offspring: *If your dog is still fertile, she can have puppies.* **3.** Capable of developing into a complete person, plant, or animal: *a fertile egg; a fertile seed.* **4.** Creative; imaginative: *a fertile mind.*

fer·til·ize |fûr′tl īz′| —*verb* **fertilized, fertilizing** **1.** To make an egg cell or plant flower fertile by providing sperm or pollen. **2.** To use fertilizer on soil.

fer·til·iz·er |fûr′tl ī′zər| —*noun, plural* **fertilizers** A substance that is added to soil to make it better for the growing of plants.

fes·ti·val |fĕs′tə vəl| —*noun, plural* **festivals** **1.** A day or time of celebrating; a holiday. **2.** A series of special cultural events: *a film festival; a music festival.*

fetch |fĕch| —*verb* **fetched, fetching** **1.** To go and get; bring back: *Please fetch my purse.* **2.** To be sold for; bring in: *The corn will fetch a good price.*

fet·ter |fĕt′ər| —*noun, plural* **fetters** A chain attached to the ankles to restrain movement.

feud |fyo͞od| —*noun, plural* **feuds** A long, bitter quarrel between two people or groups.
—*verb* **feuded, feuding** To carry on a feud: *We've been feuding with our neighbors ever since they stole our firewood.*

fe·ver |fē′vər| —*noun, plural* **fevers** A body temperature that is higher than normal. For most people normal body temperature is 98.6°F.

few |fyo͞o| —*adjective* **fewer, fewest** Not many; a small number of: *a few things.*
—*noun* (Used with a plural verb.) A small number: *Most children go home after school, but a few remain to read or study.*
—*pronoun* (Used with a plural verb.) A small number of persons or things: *Few were able to read.*

fez |fĕz| —*noun, plural* **fezzes** A felt cap shaped like an upside-down flower pot. Fezzes are worn by men in certain parts of the Middle East.

fi·an·cé |fē′än sā′| or |fē än′sā′| —*noun, plural* **fiancés** A man to whom a woman is engaged to be married.

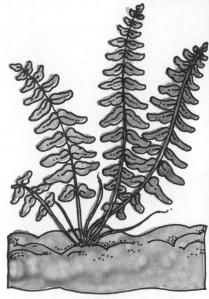

fern

ferret

fez

fi·an·cée |fē′än sā′ | or | fē än′sā′ | —*noun, plural* **fiancées** A woman to whom a man is engaged to be married.

fib |fĭb| —*noun, plural* **fibs** A small lie: *Sue told a fib and said she hadn't touched the cookies.*
—*verb* **fibbed, fibbing** To tell a small lie.

fi·ber |fī′bər| —*noun, plural* **fibers** A long, thin strand; a thread: *Cotton, wool, and silk fibers are spun together to make this yarn.*

fic·tion |fĭk′shən| —*noun, plural* **fictions** **1.** Something imaginary; made-up events: *Legends and myths are often a mixture of fact and fiction.* **2.** Written works, such as novels and short stories, that tell about characters and events that are not real.

fid·dle |fĭd′l| —*noun, plural* **fiddles** A violin.
—*verb* **fiddled, fiddling** **1.** To play the violin. **2.** To play idly with something: *He fiddled with the keys.*

field |fēld| —*noun, plural* **fields** **1.** A large area of open or cleared land: *The boys used the field for football practice.* **2.** An area of land where a crop is grown or a resource is obtained: *a field of corn; a gold field.* **3.** An area of interest; subject: *the field of medicine.* **4.** A large marked-out area where a game is played: *a football field.*
—*verb* **fielded, fielding** To catch or pick up a batted ball in baseball.

field·er |fēl′dər| —*noun, plural* **fielders** A baseball player who has a position out in the field.

field glass·es |glăs′ĭz| or |glä′sĭz| A pair of binoculars for outdoor use.

field trip A trip made by a group of students, as to a museum.

fierce |fîrs| —*adjective* **fiercer, fiercest** **1.** Wild and savage; dangerous: *a fierce animal.* **2.** Very strong; raging: *a fierce storm.*

fi·es·ta |fē ĕs′tə| —*noun, plural* **fiestas** A celebration or festival, especially in a Spanish-speaking country.

fife |fīf| —*noun, plural* **fifes** A musical instrument similar to a flute but smaller. It makes a high-pitched sound and is used mainly in marching bands.

fif·teen |fĭf tēn′| —*noun, plural* **fifteens** A number, written 15, that is equal to the sum of 10 + 5.
—*adjective* Being one more than fourteen in number: *fifteen years.* The adjective **fifteen** belongs to a class of words called **determiners.** They signal that a noun is coming.

fif·teenth |fĭf tēnth′| —*noun, plural* **fifteenths** **1.** In a group of people or things that are in numbered order, the one that matches the number fifteen. **2.** One of fifteen equal parts, written 1/15.
—*adjective: the fifteenth boy in line.*

fifth |fĭfth| —*noun, plural* **fifths** **1.** In a group of people or things that are in numbered order, the one that matches the number five. **2.** One of five equal parts, written 1/5.
—*adjective: the fifth girl in line.*

fif·ti·eth |fĭf′tē ĭth| —*noun, plural* **fiftieths** **1.** In a group of people or things that are in numbered order, the one that matches the number fifty. **2.** One of fifty equal parts, written 1/50.
—*adjective: the fiftieth person in line.*

fif·ty |fĭf′tē| —*noun, plural* **fifties** A number, written 50, that is equal to the product of 10 × 5.

fife

ă	pat	ĕ	pet	î	fierce
ā	pay	ē	be	ŏ	pot
â	care	ĭ	pit	ō	go
ä	father	ī	pie	ô	paw, for
oi	oil	ŭ	cut	zh	vision
ōō	book	û	fur	ə	ago, item,
ōō	boot	*th*	the		pencil, atom,
yōō	abuse	th	thin		circus
ou	out	hw	which	ər	butter

—*adjective* Being ten more than forty in number: *fifty years.* The adjective **fifty** belongs to a class of words that are called **determiners.** They signal that a noun is coming.

fig |fĭg| —*noun, plural* **figs** A sweet fruit that is shaped like a pear and has many small seeds. Figs grow on trees and shrubs in warm parts of the world.

fight |fīt| —*verb* **fought, fighting** **1.** To use the fists or weapons against an opponent; struggle against: *The Allied nations fought Germany in World War II. He fought with the boy to get back his cap.* **2.** To try to stop or defeat; oppose: *Medicine fights disease. We must fight our weaknesses.* **3.** To work hard: *We fought to keep the leaky boat afloat.* **4.** To engage in: *fighting a duel.* **5.** To quarrel: *We fought over what TV program to watch.*
—*noun, plural* **fights** **1.** A physical struggle with fists or weapons; a battle: *a fist fight; a dog fight.* **2.** Any struggle: *The sick man is undergoing a brave fight for his life.* **3.** A quarrel: *My sister and I had a fight over who would do the dishes.*

fight·er |fī′tər| —*noun, plural* **fighters** **1.** A person or animal who fights: *The fish they hooked was quite a fighter.* **2.** A boxer.

fig·ur·a·tive |fĭg′yər ə tĭv| —*adjective* Using words in a way that stretches their actual meaning. "I've told you a million times not to do that" and "She cried her eyes out when she got the news" are figurative expressions because they do not really mean what the words say.

fig·ure |fĭg′yər| —*noun, plural* **figures** **1.** A symbol that stands for a number. "1," "12," and "457" are figures. **2.** Calculations that involve numbers: *He's good at figures.* **3.** An amount represented in numbers: *a population figure.* **4.** A diagram or picture: *Look at that figure of a dog on page 23.* **5.** The shape of the human body: *That dress suited her figure.* **6.** A form; shape: *Who is that figure in the distance?* **7.** A person, especially a well-known one: *the governor and some other public figures.*
—*verb* **figured, figuring** **1.** To work out by using numbers: *Let's figure our budget for the month.* **2.** To believe; assume: *I figured you would say that.* **Phrasal verb figure out** To find an explanation for; solve: *We looked at a bus map and figured out how to go all the way across town.*

fig·ure·head |fĭg′yər hĕd′| —*noun, plural* **figureheads** **1.** A person who seems to be the leader but has no real power: *The king was just a figurehead.* **2.** A carved figure placed on the bow of a ship for decoration.

figure of speech An expression in which words are used not with their real meanings but in a way that adds color or drama. Here are some figures of speech: "The team bowed" (the team lost). "Please give me a hand" (please help me). "She's walking on air" (she's very happy).

fil·a·ment |fĭl′ə mənt| —*noun, plural* **filaments** A very fine wire or thread. The filament in a light bulb is heated by an electric current until it gives off light.

fil·bert |fĭl′bərt| —*noun, plural* **filberts** A hazelnut.

file¹ |fīl| —*noun, plural* **files** **1.** A container in which papers are kept and arranged in order: *Your school records are in the file.* **2.** A collection of papers, cards, or other information arranged in order: *a recipe file; a picture file.* **3.** A line of people, animals, or things placed one behind the other: *Stay in single file.*
—*verb* **filed, filing** **1.** To store or put away in a file: *Please file*

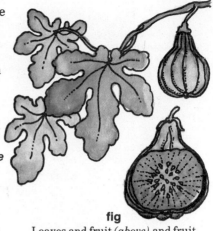

fig
Leaves and fruit *(above)* and fruit cut in half *(below)*

figurehead

filament
In a light bulb

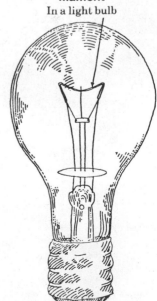

file²
Two kinds of file

fin

ă	pat	ĕ	pet	î	fierce
ā	pay	ē	be	ŏ	pot
â	care	ĭ	pit	ō	go
ä	father	ī	pie	ô	paw, for

oi	oil	ŭ	cut	zh	vision
ŏŏ	book	û	fur	ə	ago, item,
ōō	boot	*th*	the		pencil, atom,
yŏŏ	abuse	th	thin		circus
ou	out	hw	which	ər	butter

these papers where I can find them easily. **2.** To send in; submit:
After the theft we filed an insurance claim.

file² |fīl| —*noun, plural* **files** A tool with a rough surface, used
for smoothing, scraping, and cutting.
—*verb* **filed, filing** To smooth, scrape, cut, or grind down with a
file: *She filed her fingernails.*

fi·let |fĭ lā′| or |fĭl′ā′| —*noun, plural* **filets** A form of the word
fillet.

fil·ing |fī′lĭng| —*noun, plural* **filings** A particle scraped off by a
file.

fill |fĭl| —*verb* **filled, filling** **1.** To make or become full: *Fill the
pitcher with milk. The kitchen filled with smoke when the toast burned.*
2. To take up the whole space of: *Smoke filled the room. People
filled the auditorium.* **3.** To give what is asked for; supply: *Pete
filled the grocery order.* **4.** To supply a blank space with writing
or pictures: *He filled his sketch pad with drawings.* **5.** To stop up or
plug up: *The dentist will fill her teeth. He filled a hole in the yard with
cement.* **6.** To satisfy; fulfill: *She filled the requirements for the job.*

fil·let |fĭ lā′| or |fĭl′ā′| —*noun, plural* **fillets** A piece of meat or
fish that has had the bones removed. Another form of this word
is **filet.**

fill·ing |fĭl′ĭng| —*noun, plural* **fillings** Something used to fill a
space or container: *a silver filling in a tooth; custard filling in a pie.*

fil·ly |fĭl′ē| —*noun, plural* **fillies** A young female horse.

film |fĭlm| —*noun, plural* **films** **1.** A thin strip of material
coated with a delicate substance that changes when light hits it.
Film is used in photography. **2.** A motion picture. **3.** A very
thin coating: *The kitten's eyes were covered with a bluish film.*
—*verb* **filmed, filming** To make a motion picture of: *He filmed the
school soccer game.*

fil·ter |fĭl′tər| —*noun, plural* **filters** A device or material
through which a liquid or air is passed in order to clean out any
dirt or other matter that is not wanted: *Her swimming pool has a
filter. Cloth, charcoal, and gravel are used as filters.*
—*verb* **filtered, filtering** **1.** To pass through a filter: *We filtered the
water before drinking it.* **2.** To separate by a filter: *The screen
filters leaves from the water.* **3.** To pass slowly; seep: *Sunlight
filtered through the clouds.*

filth |fĭlth| —*noun* Disgusting, dirty matter: *Beaches were
covered with filth after the ship spilled oil into the water.*

filth·y |fĭl′thē| —*adjective* **filthier, filthiest** Extremely dirty:
These glasses are filthy.

fin |fĭn| —*noun, plural* **fins** **1.** One of the thin, flat parts that
stick out from the body of a fish. Fish and other water animals
use their fins for swimming and for keeping their balance. **2.** A
part shaped or used like a fin. Some airplanes and boats have fins
that help them keep their balance.

fi·nal |fī′nəl| —*adjective* **1.** Last: *final preparations for the trip.*
2. Not likely to change; definite: *You are not going to take the car
and that's final!*
—*noun, plural* **finals** **1.** The last game in a series of games: *He
won the final and received a gold medal.* **2.** The last examination
or test of a school course or subject.

fi·nal·ly |fī′nə lē| —*adverb* At last: *Finally the taxi arrived.*

fi·nance |fĭ năns′| or |fī′năns′| —*noun, plural* **finances** **1.** The
management and use of money: *I'd like to take a course in finance.*

2. finances The money resources or funds of a person, business, or government: *The accountant handled the company's finances.*
—*verb* **financed, financing** To provide money for: *They financed their son's college education.*

fi·nan·cial |fĭ **năn′**shəl| or |fī **năn′**shəl| —*adjective* Having to do with finance: *the financial page of the newspaper.*

finch |fĭnch| —*noun, plural* **finches** A bird with a short, thick bill that is used for cracking seeds. The cardinal, canary, and common house sparrow are finches.

find |fīnd| —*verb* **found, finding** **1.** To come upon by accident: *She found a penny on the floor.* **2.** To look for and discover: *They found a cure for polio.* **3.** To learn: *Are you surprised to find that whales and dolphins breathe air?* **4.** To determine: *Find the answer to that problem.* **5.** To meet with; encounter: *They found a lot of mosquitoes in the marshes.* **6.** To get back; recover: *Did you find your dog?Phrasal verb* **find out** To get information about; discover: *Doctors try to find out why a person is feeling sick.*
—*noun, plural* **finds** Something found; a discovery: *These old pictures from the attic are a wonderful find.*

fine¹ |fīn| —*adjective* **finer, finest** **1.** Very good; excellent: *Barbara is a fine athlete.* **2.** Very thin or small: *fine lines; fine embroidery.* **3.** Very sharp: *The blade has a fine edge.* **4.** Careful; painstaking: *Making that tapestry was fine work.* **5.** In good health: *I'm feeling fine today, thank you.*
—*adverb* Well; excellently: *doing fine.*

fine² |fīn| —*noun, plural* **fines** An amount of money that has to be paid as a penalty for breaking a rule or law.
—*verb* **fined, fining** To order to pay a fine of: *The judge fined him $25 for speeding.*

fin·ger |fĭng′gər| —*noun, plural* **fingers** Any one of the five body parts that extend outward from the hand. Usually a person is said to have four fingers and a thumb on each hand.
—*verb* **fingered, fingering** **1.** To feel or handle with the fingers; to touch: *She fingered the soft, smooth material.* **2.** To play a musical instrument by using the fingers.

fin·ger·nail |fĭng′gər nāl′| —*noun, plural* **fingernails** The thin layer of hard, transparent material at the end of each finger.

fin·ger·print |fĭng′gər prĭnt′| —*noun, plural* **fingerprints** A mark with many fine, curved lines made by the fleshy end of a finger. No two people have exactly the same fingerprints, so they are used as a method of identifying people.
—*verb* **fingerprinted, fingerprinting** To record the fingerprints of.

fin·ish |fĭn′ĭsh| —*verb* **finished, finishing** **1.** To bring to an end; complete: *When will you finish doing the dishes?* **2.** To use up: *We finished a whole box of popcorn.* **3.** To destroy or wear out completely: *The long bike ride almost finished me.* **4.** To treat the surface of: *We finished the chair with a dark varnish.*
—*noun, plural* **finishes** **1.** The end: *I'll fight to the finish.* **2.** The final coating or treatment of a surface: *a smooth finish on a table.*

fir |fûr| —*noun, plural* **firs** **1.** An evergreen tree with rather flat needles. **2.** The wood of a fir tree.
♦ *These sound alike* **fir, fur.**

fire |fīr| —*noun, plural* **fires** **1.** The flame, heat, and light given off when something burns. **2.** Something burning: *Throw that piece of wood into the fire.* **3.** A burning that causes damage: *The*

finch

fir
Tree *(above)* and needles and cone *(below)*

school has an extinguisher for putting out fires. **4.** Strong emotion or enthusiasm: *The angry woman's words blazed with fire.* **5.** The shooting of firearms: *We heard the sound of rifle fire in the woods.* —*verb* **fired, firing 1.** To set on fire; burn: *We fired the coals for the barbecue.* **2.** To dismiss from a job: *The store owner fired the clerk for always being late.* **3.** To stir up; excite: *He fired the child's imagination with detective stories.* **4.** To shoot a gun: *She fired a rifle at the target. The policeman fired twice.*

fire·arm | fīr′ärm′ | —*noun, plural* **firearms** Any weapon used for shooting, especially one that can be carried and fired by one person. Shotguns, rifles, and pistols are firearms.

fire·crack·er | fīr′krăk′ər | —*noun, plural* **firecrackers** A paper tube containing an explosive and a fuse. Firecrackers are used to make noise during celebrations. They are dangerous and are illegal in many states.

fire engine A truck that carries firefighters and equipment to fight a fire.

fire escape An outside flight of stairs attached to a building and used as an emergency exit in case of fire.

fire·fight·er | fīr′fī′tər | —*noun, plural* **firefighters** A person who fights fires.

fire·fly | fīr′flī′ | —*noun, plural* **fireflies** An insect that gives off a flashing light from the rear part of its body.

fire·house | fīr′hous′ | —*noun, plural* **firehouses** A building for fire engines and firefighters.

fire·man | fīr′mən | —*noun, plural* **firemen 1.** A man who fights fires; a firefighter. **2.** A man who takes care of a fire in a furnace or steam engine.

fire·place | fīr′plās′ | —*noun, plural* **fireplaces** An opening in the wall of a room for holding a fire. Fireplaces have chimneys leading up from them to get rid of smoke.

fire·proof | fīr′proŏf′ | —*adjective* Designed not to burn: *Our new house is fireproof.*

fire·side | fīr′sīd′ | —*noun, plural* **firesides 1.** The area around a fireplace. **2.** A home: *People have a right to the peace and comfort of their own fireside.*

fire·works | fīr′wûrks′ | —*plural noun* Firecrackers and other explosives that are used to produce colored lights, smoke, and noise for entertainment at celebrations.

firm¹ | fûrm | —*adjective* **firmer, firmest 1.** Not giving way to pressure; solid; hard: *a firm mattress; firm ground.* **2.** Not easily moved: *The post was firm in the ground.* **3.** Not changing; steady: *a firm belief; a firm friend.* **4.** Strong: *a firm grasp.* **5.** Showing strength of will: *a firm voice.*

firm² | fûrm | —*noun, plural* **firms** A company formed by two or more people who go into business together.

first | fûrst | —*adjective* Before any others in place or time: *I was first in line. John Adams was the first Vice President.* —*adverb* **1.** Before any others: *You go first.* **2.** For the first time: *I first rode a bike when I was seven.* —*noun, plural* **firsts 1.** In a group of people or things that are in numbered order, the one that matches the number one. **2.** The beginning: *At first I really liked the job.*

first aid Emergency care given to an injured or sick person before a doctor comes.

first-class | fûrst′klăs′ | or | fûrst′kläs′ | —*adjective* **1.** Of the

fire escape

firefighter

firm¹, firm²

Firm¹ comes from a Latin word that meant "firm, steady, certain." A related Latin word meaning "to make firm, to confirm" was the original source of **firm².** The Latin word remained in Italian and came to mean "to confirm something by signature." A noun was formed from this, meaning "trademark, name of a business or partnership." This was borrowed into English as **firm².**

ă	pat	ĕ	pet	î	fierce
ā	pay	ē	be	ŏ	pot
â	care	ĭ	pit	ō	go
ä	father	ī	pie	ô	paw, for

oi	oil	ŭ	cut	zh	vision
ŏŏ	book	û	fur	ə	ago, item,
ōō	boot	*th*	the		pencil, atom,
yōō	abuse	th	thin		circus
ou	out	hw	which	ər	butter

best quality: *The pianist gave a first-class performance.* **2.** Of or for the best class of seats or rooms: *first-class tickets.*
—*adverb* With first-class seats or rooms: *traveling first-class.*

first·hand | fûrst′hănd′ | —*adjective* Gotten from the original source; direct: *Since he talked to one of the drivers, he has firsthand information about the accident.*

fish | fĭsh | —*noun, plural* **fish** or **fishes** One of a large group of animals that have fins and live in the water. Fish have gills for breathing and are usually covered with scales.
—*verb* **fished, fishing** **1.** To catch or try to catch fish. **2.** To search; hunt: *I fished in the crowded closet for a dress that might fit me.* **3.** To draw up or out; pull: *The traveler fished a train schedule out of his bag and studied it.*

fish·er·man | fĭsh′ər mən | —*noun, plural* **fishermen** Someone who fishes.

fish·er·y | fĭsh′ə rē | —*noun, plural* **fisheries** A place where fish are bred.

fish·y | fĭsh′ē | —*adjective* **fishier, fishiest** **1.** Tasting or smelling of fish. **2.** Unlikely; doubtful: *The suspect's story seemed fishy because he knew exactly what he was doing at the time of the crime.*

fis·sion | fĭsh′ən | —*noun* The breaking up of the nucleus of an atom. Nuclear fission releases large amounts of energy.

fist | fĭst | —*noun, plural* **fists** The hand closed tightly, with the fingers bent in against the palm.

fit¹ | fĭt | —*verb* **fitted, fitting** **1.** To be the proper size and shape for someone or something: *The shoe fits perfectly.* **2.** To be suitable or right for: *That style just doesn't fit you.* **3.** To make suitable; adjust: *The tailor fitted the suit to him.* **4.** To place snugly; insert: *Can we fit all the food in one lunch bag?* **5.** To equip; provide: *We fitted the truck with snow tires.*
—*noun, plural* **fits** The way something fits: *a perfect fit.*
—*adjective* **fitter, fittest** **1.** Suitable: *We must think of a fit ceremony for the new members.* **2.** Proper; appropriate: *Do what you think fit.* **3.** Healthy: *She certainly is looking fit lately.*

fit² | fĭt | —*noun, plural* **fits** **1.** A sudden onset of a strong emotion or physical reaction: *a fit of laughter; a fit of coughing.* **2.** A sudden attack of a disease: *a fit of malaria.*

five | fīv | —*noun, plural* **fives** A number, written 5, that is equal to the sum of 1 + 4.
—*adjective* Being one more than four in number: *five bottles.* The adjective **five** belongs to a class of words called **determiners.** They signal that a noun is coming.

fix | fĭks | —*verb* **fixed, fixing** **1.** To fasten tightly; secure: *They fixed the posts for a fence in a cement base.* **2.** To arrange definitely; settle: *Let's fix the time of the party.* **3.** To direct steadily: *She fixed her eyes on the screen.* **4.** To place; put: *fix the blame.* **5.** To repair: *fix a faucet; fix a car.* **6.** To prepare: *She will fix dinner for us tonight.*
—*noun, plural* **fixes** A difficult situation; trouble: *He got himself into a fix and had to ask his father to help him out.*

fix·ture | fĭks′chər | —*noun, plural* **fixtures** Something firmly fastened in place for permanent use: *The plumbing fixtures included a toilet and a sink.*

flag | flăg | —*noun, plural* **flags** A piece of cloth with a special color or design on it. Flags are flown as symbols of countries and are also used for giving signals.

fit¹, fit²
Fit¹ may come from an old English word that meant "to maneuver soldiers," and thus perhaps "to arrange, to fit." **Fit²** comes from a different old English word that meant "a hardship" or "a painful experience."

flag
Above: Flag used by the American colonial navy about 1776
Center: Flag used by the American colonies until 1777
Below: Flag used by the American colonists in a Revolutionary War battle in 1777

—*verb* **flagged, flagging** To signal with or as if with a flag: *We flagged down a taxi.*

flair |flâr| —*noun, plural* **flairs** A natural talent: *a flair for music.*
♦ *These sound alike* **flair, flare.**

flake |flāk| —*noun, plural* **flakes** A small, thin piece or particle: *a soap flake; a snow flake.*
—*verb* **flaked, flaking** To come off or chip off in flakes: *The paint is flaking.*

flame |flām| —*noun, plural* **flames** **1.** One of the glowing masses of light given off by a burning substance. **2.** Often **flames** The condition of burning: *The house burst into flames.*
—*verb* **flamed, flaming** **1.** To burn brightly. **2.** To glow fiercely: *Hatred flamed in his eyes.*

fla·min·go |flə mǐng′gō| —*noun, plural* **flamingos** or **flamingoes** A large bird with a very long neck and legs and pink or reddish feathers. Flamingos live near water in warm parts of the world.

flank |flăngk| —*noun, plural* **flanks** The part between the hip and the ribs on either side of the body of an animal or person; the side.
—*verb* **flanked, flanking** To be placed at the side of: *Two chairs flanked the couch.*

flan·nel |flăn′əl| —*noun, plural* **flannels** **1.** A soft cloth made of cotton or wool. **2.** **flannels.** Trousers, underwear, or other garments made of flannel.

flap |flăp| —*verb* **flapped, flapping** **1.** To move up and down: *The bird flapped its wings.* **2.** To wave loosely; flutter: *The sail flapped in the breeze.*
—*noun, plural* **flaps** **1.** The sound or action of flapping: *We listened to the flap of the shutters in the wind.* **2.** A piece fastened at one edge and meant to fold over and cover or seal something: *This cap has flaps to keep your ears warm.*

flare |flâr| —*verb* **flared, flaring** **1.** To burn with a sudden flame: *The fire flared up when we fanned it.* **2.** To burst out with sudden or violent feeling: *Tempers flared during the argument.* **3.** To spread outward: *Her skirt flares from the waist.*
—*noun, plural* **flares** **1.** A sudden blaze of light. **2.** A bright light that can be shot into the air as a signal. **3.** A shape that spreads out: *the flare of a trumpet.*
♦ *These sound alike* **flare, flair.**

flash |flăsh| —*verb* **flashed, flashing** **1.** To burst or cause to burst suddenly into light or flame: *The bulb in the camera flashed. The ship flashed its signal lights.* **2.** To appear suddenly or only for a short time: *An idea flashed in his mind.* **3.** To be lighted on and off: *The lighthouse flashed in the distance.* **4.** To move rapidly: *A car flashed by.*
—*noun, plural* **flashes** **1.** A sudden burst of light: *a flash of lightning.* **2.** A sudden, brief burst: *a flash of humor.* **3.** An instant: *I'll be there in a flash.*

flash·light |flăsh′līt′| —*noun, plural* **flashlights** An electric light powered by batteries and small enough for a person to carry around.

flask |flăsk| or |fläsk| —*noun, plural* **flasks** A small bottle with a narrow neck.

flat |flăt| —*adjective* **flatter, flattest** **1.** Having a smooth, even surface; level: *a flat road; flat land.* **2.** Lying stretched out; spread out: *He was flat on his back.* **3.** Not deep; shallow: *a flat dish.*

flamingo

flask
Two kinds of flask

ă	pat	ĕ	pet	î	fierce
ā	pay	ē	be	ŏ	pot
â	care	ĭ	pit	ō	go
ä	father	ī	pie	ô	paw, for
oi	oil	ŭ	cut	zh	vision
ōō	book	û	fur	ə	ago, item,
ōō	boot	*th*	the		pencil, atom,
yōō	abuse	th	thin		circus
ou	out	hw	which	ər	butter

4. Having lost air: *a flat tire.* **5.** Dull: *a flat performance.*
6. Downright; absolute: *a flat refusal.* **7.** Not shiny: *flat paint.*
8. Lower in musical pitch than is correct: *a flat note.*
—*noun, plural* **flats 1.** A flat surface or part. **2.** A flat tire.

flat·car |flăt′kär′| —*noun, plural* **flatcars** A railroad car without
sides or a roof, used for carrying freight.

flat·fish |flăt′fĭsh′| —*noun, plural* **flatfish** or **flatfishes** A fish
that has a flat body with the eyes on the upper side. The
flounder, sole, and halibut are flatfish.

flat·ten |flăt′n| —*verb* **flattened, flattening 1.** To make or
become flat or flatter. **2.** To knock down, as in a fight.

flat·ter[1] |flăt′ər| —*verb* **flattered, flattering 1.** To try to please
with praise and compliments: *She flattered her husband by telling
him that he was the best player on the team.* **2.** To make more
attractive than is actually true: *The photograph flatters her.* **3.** To
please or gratify: *Receiving the award flattered me.*

flat·ter[2] |flăt′ər| The comparative of the adjective **flat.**

flat·ter·y |flăt′ə rē| —*noun, plural* **flatteries** Insincere praise.

flat·test |flăt′ĭst| The superlative of the adjective **flat.**

fla·vor |flā′vər| —*noun, plural* **flavors 1.** A taste: *The candy had
a chocolate flavor.* **2.** A special quality or impression: *the
mysterious flavor of the Orient.*
—*verb* **flavored, flavoring** To give flavor to: *We flavored the ice
cream with vanilla.*

flaw |flô| —*noun, plural* **flaws** A defect: *There is a flaw in this
crystal glass. He has several flaws in his character.*
—*verb* **flawed, flawing** To make or become defective; spoil; mar:
The movie was flawed by a confusing ending.

flax |flăks| —*noun* **1.** A plant that has blue flowers and slender
stems. Linen is made from a fiber taken from the stems. Linseed
oil is made from the seeds of flax. **2.** The whitish fibers from the
stems of this plant.

flea |flē| —*noun, plural* **fleas** A small, jumping insect that has
no wings. Fleas live on the bodies of animals and human beings
and suck their blood.
♦ *These sound alike* **flea, flee.**

fled |flĕd| The past tense and past participle of the verb **flee:** *He
fled from the burning house. She had fled by the time they missed her.*

flee |flē| —*verb* **fled, fleeing 1.** To run away or run away from:
*The family fled the burning house. The burglar tried to flee when he
heard the sirens.* **2.** To move quickly; vanish: *His hopes fled when
he learned what had happened.*
♦ *These sound alike* **flee, flea.**

fleece |flēs| —*noun* The wool forming the coat of a sheep.
—*verb* **fleeced, fleecing** To cut the fleece from.

fleet[1] |flēt| —*noun, plural* **fleets 1.** A group of warships. **2.** A
large group of ships, cars, or other vehicles traveling or working
together: *a fishing fleet; a fleet of taxicabs.*

fleet[2] |flēt| —*adjective* **fleeter, fleetest** Moving quickly; swift: *a
fleet animal.*

flesh |flĕsh| —*noun* **1.** The soft material of the body that covers
the bones and is itself covered by the skin. **2.** The meat of
animals used as food. **3.** The soft part of a fruit or vegetable that
can usually be eaten.

flesh·y |flĕsh′ē| —*adjective* **fleshier, fleshiest** Having too much
flesh; plump.

flax

fleet[1], **fleet**[2]
An old English verb meaning "to
float" is the source of both of these
words. This verb formed a noun
meaning "a floating, a collection of
ships," which became **fleet**[1]. It also
formed another verb, meaning "to
flow, go swiftly," which later became
fleet[2].

flicker²

ă	pat	ĕ	pet	î	fierce
ā	pay	ē	be	ŏ	pot
â	care	ĭ	pit	ō	go
ä	father	ī	pie	ô	paw, for
oi	oil	ŭ	cut	zh	vision
ōŏ	book	û	fur	ə	ago, item,
ōō	boot	th	the		pencil, atom,
yōō	abuse	th	thin		circus
ou	out	hw	which	ər	butter

flew | flōō | The past tense of the verb **fly**: *The bat flew in the window.*
♦ *These sound alike* **flew, flu, flue.**

flex | flĕks | —*verb* **flexed, flexing** **1.** To bend: *flex your elbow.* **2.** To tighten; contract: *Look at him flex his muscles.*

flex·i·ble | flĕk′sə bəl | —*adjective* **1.** Capable of being bent without breaking: *This strip of plastic is flexible.* **2.** Open to change or new ideas: *flexible plans.*

flick | flĭk | —*noun, plural* **flicks** A light, quick blow or hit: *With a flick of her hand the pianist turned the page of her music.*
—*verb* **flicked, flicking** **1.** To hit quickly and lightly: *She flicked the dust off his shoes.* **2.** To move with a flick: *The snake flicked its tongue.*

flick·er¹ | flĭk′ər | —*verb* **flickered, flickering** **1.** To give off a weak, unsteady light: *The candle flickered and finally went out.* **2.** To move back and forth quickly; flutter: *Shadows flickered on the wall.*
—*noun, plural* **flickers** **1.** A weak, unsteady light. **2.** A quick back-and-forth movement; a flutter. **3.** A small, faint occurrence or expression: *He spoke coldly, without a flicker of emotion.*

flick·er² | flĭk′ər | —*noun, plural* **flickers** A North American woodpecker with a brown back and a spotted breast.

flied | flīd | A past tense and past participle of the verb **fly** (to hit a baseball): *He flied to left field.*

fli·er | flī′ər | —*noun, plural* **fliers** Someone or something that flies: *He owned an airplane and was a very good flier.* Another form of this word is **flyer.**

flight¹ | flīt | —*noun, plural* **flights** **1.** The act or process of flying. **2.** An airplane trip: *The flight was due to arrive at three o'clock in the afternoon.* **3.** A group, especially of birds or aircraft, flying together: *We saw a V-shaped flight of geese heading south.* **4.** A swift movement: *the flight of time.* **5.** A series of stairs between landings or floors of a building: *We walked up five flights to the roof.*

flight² | flīt | —*noun, plural* **flights** The act of running away; escape: *The beach was filled with city people in flight from the heat.*

flim·sy | flĭm′zē | —*adjective* **flimsier, flimsiest** Thin, light, and weak; not strong or solid: *Her flimsy dress was not warm enough in the evening chill. She gave a flimsy excuse for being late.*

flinch | flĭnch | —*verb* **flinched, flinching** To pull back quickly in pain or fear; to wince: *He flinched when the dentist pulled his tooth.*

fling | flĭng | —*verb* **flung, flinging** To throw hard; hurl: *He flung his coat on the chair.*
—*noun, plural* **flings** **1.** A hard throw: *He gave the ball a fling at the basket.* **2.** A short time of doing what one wants or of trying something out: *He had a fling at skiing.*

flint | flĭnt | —*noun, plural* **flints** A very hard stone that makes sparks when it strikes against steel. Flint is a kind of quartz and is usually gray. Before there were matches, flint was used for starting fires.

flip | flĭp | —*verb* **flipped, flipping** **1.** To throw so as to cause to turn over in the air: *The cook flipped the pancakes. The team captains flipped a coin to choose sides.* **2.** To move with a snap or jerk: *He flipped the pages of the magazine until he found the story he wanted.*
—*noun, plural* **flips** **1.** An act of flipping; a toss: *Give the coin a flip to see if it lands heads or tails.* **2.** A somersault made from a

standing position. In a flip, the person turns heels over head and usually lands on the feet.

flip·per |flĭp′ər| —*noun, plural* **flippers** **1.** A wide, flat body part used for swimming. Flippers look like fins but have the same kinds of bones as legs and feet. Seals and walruses have flippers. **2.** A wide, flat rubber shoe that swimmers wear. Flippers help skin divers go faster and farther when they kick their legs.

flirt |flûrt| —*verb* **flirted, flirting** **1.** To be friendly and playful and pretend to be interested in romance: *He likes to flirt with pretty girls.* **2.** To play; to toy: *He flirted with the idea of starting his own business.*
—*noun, plural* **flirts** A person who likes to flirt.

flit |flĭt| —*verb* **flitted, flitting** To move in a quick and light way: *Bees flit from flower to flower.*

float |flōt| —*verb* **floated, floating** **1.** To be held up by liquid or air: *Will the boat float or sink? The balloon floated above the trees.* **2.** To move on a current of air or water: *The leaves floated on the wind. They floated logs down the river.*
—*noun, plural* **floats** **1.** An object designed to float. Some examples of floats are a cork on a fishing line, a raft used by swimmers, and a hollow ball on a rope marking the edge of a swimming area. **2.** A large platform on wheels that carries an exhibit in a parade.

flock |flŏk| —*noun, plural* **flocks** **1.** A group of one kind of animal that lives, travels, or feeds together: *a flock of geese; a flock of sheep.* **2.** A group of people who follow one leader, especially a religious leader. **3.** A large number; a big group: *Flocks of people came to see the art exhibition.*
—*verb* **flocked, flocking** To gather or travel in a flock: *The birds flocked together. People flocked to see the new movie.*

floe |flō| —*noun, plural* **floes** A large, flat area of ice floating on water.
♦ *These sound alike* **floe, flow.**

flood |flŭd| —*noun, plural* **floods** **1.** A great overflow of water onto a place that is usually dry: *Heavy rain caused a flood along the river bank.* **2.** Any large flow; a pouring out: *a flood of tears; a flood of new settlers on the land.*
—*verb* **flooded, flooding** **1.** To cover or fill with water: *Water from the river floods the land when it rains too much. The cellar flooded during the big storm.* **2.** To overflow: *The river floods every spring.* **3.** To come pouring into; fill: *Suddenly lights flooded the room and we all blinked. Letters flooded the mayor's office with complaints.*

floor |flôr| or |flōr| —*noun, plural* **floors** **1.** The surface of a room that a person stands or walks on: *The palace has a marble floor.* **2.** The solid ground underneath an ocean or forest: *A sunken ship lay on the floor of the sea.* **3.** A story or level of a building: *The elevator took him to the tenth floor.*
—*verb* **floored, flooring** **1.** To put a floor on: *He floored the kitchen with linoleum.* **2.** To knock down to the floor: *The boxer floored his opponent twice.* **3.** To overwhelm; stun: *The news floored us.*

flop |flŏp| —*verb* **flopped, flopping** **1.** To fall in a noisy and heavy way; to plop: *He flopped onto his bed.* **2.** To move about in a loose, noisy way; to flap: *The dog's ears flopped as she ran.* **3.** To fail completely: *The show flopped after its first performance.*
—*noun, plural* **flops** **1.** The noise and motion of flopping: *He sat down with a flop.* **2.** A complete failure: *The experiment was a flop.*

flipper

flood
A city damaged by a flood

Florida

The name **Florida** comes from a Spanish word meaning "flowering." The name was given to the place by Ponce de León, who landed there in 1513 on Easter Sunday (the Spanish "holiday of flowers").

flounder¹, flounder²

Flounder¹ is thought to have come from a blend of **blunder** and **founder²**. **Flounder²** probably comes from an old Scandinavian word meaning "flat fish." The word traveled through French before it arrived in English.

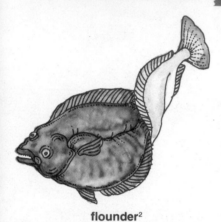

flounder²

flo·ral |flôr′əl| or |flōr′əl| —*adjective* Of or like flowers: *a floral arrangement; a floral perfume.*

Flor·i·da |flôr′ĭ də| or |flōr′ĭ də| A state in the southeastern United States. The capital of Florida is Tallahassee.

flo·rist |flôr′ĭst| or |flōr′ĭst| or |flŏr′ĭst| —*noun, plural* **florists** A person whose work is raising or selling flowers and small plants.

floss |flôs| or |flŏs| —*noun, plural* **flosses** **1.** A soft, shiny thread of cotton or silk, used in embroidery. **2.** A strong thread used to clean between the teeth.
—*verb* **flossed, flossing** To use dental floss on the teeth: *Dentists recommend brushing and flossing well at least once a day.*

floun·der¹ |floun′dər| —*verb* **floundered, floundering** To move in a clumsy way or with difficulty; to struggle: *They floundered through the deep snow.*

floun·der² |floun′dər| —*noun, plural* **flounder** or **flounders** A flatfish often used as food.

flour |flour| —*noun, plural* **flours** A fine powder made by grinding wheat or another grain. Flour can also be made from potatoes and beans. It is used to make bread, spaghetti, pancakes, desserts, and many other foods.
—*verb* **floured, flouring** To cover or coat with flour: *She floured the board before kneading the bread.*
♦ *These sound alike* **flour, flower.**

flour·ish |flûr′ĭsh| or |flŭr′ĭsh| —*verb* **flourished, flourishing 1.** To grow well and strong; thrive: *Most plants flourish in full sunlight. The town flourished with the coming of the railroad.* **2.** To wave in a bold or showy way: *The conductor flourished his baton.*
—*noun, plural* **flourishes 1.** A vigorous wave, gesture, or display: *The duel began with a flourish of swords.* **2.** A decoration or fancy touch: *His handwriting has many flourishes.*

flow |flō| —*verb* **flowed, flowing 1.** To move freely in a steady stream: *Water flowed over the dam. Air flowed in through the window.* **2.** To keep moving in a steady way: *Traffic flowed through the tunnel.* **3.** To hang or fall smoothly: *Her hair flowed over her shoulders.*
—*noun, plural* **flows 1.** The act or process of flowing: *The dam stopped the flow of water.* **2.** A moving mass: *A hot flow of lava poured from the volcano.*
♦ *These sound alike* **flow, floe.**

flow·er |flou′ər| —*noun, plural* **flowers 1.a.** The part of a plant that produces seeds. Flowers often have colorful petals, but many kinds of plants have small flowers that can hardly be noticed. **b.** A plant with colorful flowers: *We planted pansies, marigolds, and other flowers.* **2.** The best or finest part or time: *These bright young people are the flower of their generation. He played the trumpet in the 1920's, when jazz was in flower.*
—*verb* **flowered, flowering 1.** To produce flowers; to bloom. **2.** To reach a peak; flourish: *She had painted for many years, but her work flowered that summer on the island.*
♦ *These sound alike* **flower, flour.**

flown |flōn| The past participle of the verb **fly:** *We have often flown to Florida.*

flu |flōō| —*noun, plural* **flus** A disease like a bad cold, caused by viruses; influenza. Some symptoms of the flu are fever, cough, and sore muscles.
♦ *These sound alike* **flu, flew, flue.**

flue |floo| —*noun, plural* **flues** A pipe, tube, or passage through which smoke or hot air can escape.
♦ *These sound alike* **flue, flew, flu.**

fluff |flŭf| —*noun, plural* **fluffs** Soft, light material like down: *The baby birds were round balls of fluff.*
—*verb* **fluffed, fluffing** To make soft and light by letting air in: *Let's fluff up the pillows. Fluff the rice with a fork.*

fluff·y |flŭf′ē| —*adjective* **fluffier, fluffiest 1.** Soft and light; airy: *some fluffy rice; fluffy cotton balls.* **2.** Covered with fluff: *a fluffy kitten; a fluffy robe.*

flu·id |floo′ĭd| —*noun, plural* **fluids** A liquid or a gas. A fluid flows easily and takes the shape of its container.
—*adjective* Flowing, like a liquid or gas: *The lake waters remained fluid even through the winter.*

flung |flŭng| The past tense and past participle of the verb **fling:** *Jane flung her doll on the floor. After Jim had flung his coat on the chair, his mother scolded him.*

flunk |flŭngk| —*verb* **flunked, flunking** To fail a test.

flur·ry |flûr′ē| or |flŭr′ē| —*noun, plural* **flurries 1.** A sudden gust: *a flurry of wind.* **2.** A short, light fall of snow or rain. **3.** A sudden outburst; a stir: *A flurry of excitement went through the crowd when the astronauts entered the room.*

flush |flŭsh| —*verb* **flushed, flushing 1.** To turn red; to blush: *He flushed with embarrassment. The fever flushed her cheeks.* **2.** To wash or empty out with a flow of water: *Please flush the toilet. Rain flushed the streets and left them clean.* **3.** To flow suddenly: *Blood flushed into his face.*
—*noun, plural* **flushes 1.** A blush or rosy glow: *a healthy flush on the runner's cheeks.* **2.** A washing out with a sudden flow of water: *He forgot to give the toilet a flush.*
—*adjective* On the same level; even: *The milk was just flush with the top of the glass. The sofa was flush with the table.*

flus·ter |flŭs′tər| —*verb* **flustered, flustering** To make nervous, excited, or confused: *The embarrassing questions flustered her.*
—*noun, plural* **flusters** A nervous, excited, or confused condition: *She was in a fluster when he kissed her hand.*

flute |floot| —*noun, plural* **flutes** A stick-shaped musical instrument that makes high, clear tones. It is held out to one side and played by blowing across the mouthpiece and covering different holes with the fingers or with keys.

flut·ter |flŭt′ər| —*verb* **fluttered, fluttering 1.** To flap the wings lightly in flying: *A butterfly fluttered by.* **2.** To move or wave about in a light, rapid, uneven way: *Leaves and petals fluttered to the ground. The flag fluttered on the pole.*
—*noun, plural* **flutters 1.** A quick flapping motion: *With a flutter of wings, the bird was gone.* **2.** Excitement: *There was a flutter in the room as the ballerina entered.*

fly¹ |flī| —*verb* **flew, flown, flying, flies 1.** To move through the air with the aid of wings or of parts like wings: *The bird flew up to the tree. An airplane flies to Denver each morning.* **2.** To travel, carry, or send in an aircraft or spacecraft: *I'll fly home tomorrow. Helicopters flew in supplies.* **3.** To pilot an aircraft or spacecraft: *He flies his own small plane.* **4.** To display, wave, or float in air: *The ship flew the pirate flag. The banner flew from the pole. He flew his new kite. The kite flies well.* **5.** *Past tense and past participle* **flied** To bat a baseball high into the air: *Rivers flied out to the*

flute

fly¹, fly²
Both words spelled **fly** came from one Germanic root meaning "to go quickly, to fly." The root formed a verb that meant "to fly through the air," which became **fly¹** in modern English. The verb then formed a noun meaning "the one that flies, a fly," **fly².**

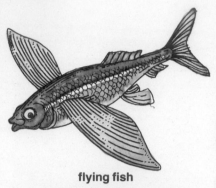

flying fish

foil³

ă	pat	ĕ	pet	î	fierce
ā	pay	ē	be	ŏ	pot
â	care	ĭ	pit	ō	go
ä	father	ī	pie	ô	paw, for
oi	oil	ŭ	cut	zh	vision
ŏŏ	book	û	fur	ə	ago, item,
ōō	boot	*th*	the		pencil, atom,
yōō	abuse	th	thin		circus
ou	out	hw	which	ər	butter

center fielder. **6.** To be carried away by moving air: *Her hat flew off her head.* **7.** To move quickly; rush: *She flew to the door.*
—*noun, plural* **flies 1.** A cloth flap that covers a zipper or a set of buttons on clothing, especially on the front of trousers. **2.** A baseball that is batted high in the air. Also called *fly ball.*

fly² | flī | —*noun, plural* **flies** One of a large group of insects that have one pair of thin, clear wings. The common housefly belongs to this group.

fly·er | flī′ər | —*noun, plural* **flyers** A form of the word **flier.**

fly·ing fish | flī′ĭng | An ocean fish with large side fins. Flying fish use these fins like wings as they leap out of the water and glide through the air.

foal | fōl | —*noun, plural* **foals** A young horse, zebra, or donkey.

foam | fōm | —*noun, plural* **foams** A mass of tiny bubbles; froth: *The waves became foam at the beach.*
—*verb* **foamed, foaming** To form foam; to froth: *The soap suds foamed in the tub.*

foam rubber A light kind of rubber like sponge, used for pillows, mattresses, and cushions.

fo·cus | fō′kəs | —*noun, plural* **focuses 1.** A point where rays of light meet after being bent by a lens. **2.** The distance from the surface of the lens to the point where the rays of light meet. **3.** The condition in which a lens, an eye, or a camera gets the sharpest image: *Now the camera is in focus. My eyes are not in focus because the doctor has put drops in them.* **4.** A center of activity or interest: *Our club's focus is ecology. She was the focus of attention when she sang.*
—*verb* **focused, focusing 1.** To adjust an instrument or the eyes so as to get a clear image: *She focused the camera for a close shot.* **2.** To make light rays come to a point or travel in a particular direction: *A magnifying glass focused the light and burnt a hole in the leaf. The spotlight focused on the star performer.* **3.** To concentrate; fix: *They focused their attention on the speech.*

fod·der | fŏd′ər | —*noun, plural* **fodders** Chopped corn stalks, hay, and other dry food for farm animals.

foe | fō | —*noun, plural* **foes** An enemy; opponent: *The wizard was the king's greatest foe.*

fog | fôg | or | fŏg | —*noun, plural* **fogs 1.** A mass of tiny drops of water that looks like a cloud and is on or near the ground. **2.** A confused condition: *The head cold put my mind in a fog all day.*
—*verb* **fogged, fogging** To cover or be covered with a fog or with something like a fog: *Steam fogged the bathroom mirror. The car windows fogged up.*

fog·gy | fô′gē | or | fŏg′ē | —*adjective* **foggier, foggiest 1.** Full of or covered with fog: *a foggy day; foggy islands.* **2.** Blurred or clouded; vague: *The photograph was very foggy. She had only a foggy idea of where she had been.*

foil¹ | foil | —*verb* **foiled, foiling** To prevent from being successful; defeat: *The hero foiled the villain's plans by marrying the heroine.*

foil² | foil | —*noun, plural* **foils** A very thin sheet of a metal: *Some people wrap potatoes in aluminum foil before baking them.*

foil³ | foil | —*noun, plural* **foils** A long, light, thin sword used in fencing. A button on the tip of the foil prevents injuries.

fold¹ | fōld | —*verb* **folded, folding 1.** To bend over or double up so that one part lies on another: *Fold your paper in half. This cardboard does not fold well.* **2.** To press close to the body: *The*

bird folded its wings. **3.** To clasp or embrace: *He folded the baby in his arms.* **4.** To give way; collapse: *The foal's weak legs folded under him.* **5.** To fail and close: *His business folded.*
—*noun, plural* **folds** A crease, line, pleat, or hollow made by folding: *The skirt hung in loose folds.*

fold² |fōld| —*noun, plural* **folds** An area that is closed in, used to keep sheep; a pen.

fold·er |fōl'dər| —*noun, plural* **folders** **1.** A piece of heavy paper folded in the middle and used to hold loose papers. **2.** A small booklet or pamphlet: *We picked up some travel folders to help us plan our vacation.*

fo·li·age |fō'lē ĭj| —*noun* The leaves of plants or trees.

folk |fōk| —*noun, plural* **folk** or **folks** **1.** People of a particular kind: *City folk are used to noise and bustle.* **2.** **folks** People in general: *The sign "Beware!" scared folks away.* **3.** **folks** Family; relatives: *Give my regards to your folks.*
—*adjective* Of or coming from the common people, who remember and pass along legends, traditions, songs, and skills: *a folk hero; the folk art of decorating eggs.*

folk·lore |fōk'lôr'| or |fōk'lōr'| —*noun* The old beliefs, legends, and customs of a people.

fol·low |fōl'ō| —*verb* **followed, following** **1.** To go or come after: *You lead; I'll follow. Who will follow him as president? Night follows day.* **2.** To move or go along: *They followed the trail into the forest.* **3.** To come as a result: *If you break the rules, trouble will follow.* **4.** To obey; stick to: *Just follow the instructions. Did you follow a recipe for the cake?* **5.** To listen to or watch closely: *Will you follow the game on radio or TV?* **6.** To understand; grasp: *I can't follow his argument.*

fol·low·er |fōl'ō ər| —*noun, plural* **followers** **1.** A person or thing that follows another. **2.** An attendant or servant: *The prince and his followers went hunting.* **3.** Someone who believes in or supports something: *a follower of Buddhism.*

fol·low·ing |fōl'ō ĭng| —*adjective* Coming just after; next: *He went home the following afternoon.*
—*noun, plural* **followings** **1.** A group of fans or supporters: *The soccer team has a very large following.* **2.** **the following** The things mentioned next: *Buy the following: milk, bread, and eggs.*

fol·ly |fōl'ē| —*noun, plural* **follies** **1.** Lack of good sense and judgment; foolish behavior: *People once said it was folly to buy Alaska, but they were wrong.* **2.** A foolish idea or action: *Buying a hat when she needed food was just one of her many follies.*

fond |fŏnd| —*adjective* **fonder, fondest** Loving; affectionate: *She gave him a fond kiss on the forehead. Idiom* **fond of** Having a liking for: *He is fond of pets. She is fond of fighting.*

fon·dle |fŏn'dl| —*verb* **fondled, fondling** To touch or pat in a loving way; to caress: *He fondled the puppy.*

fond·ness |fŏnd'nĭs| —*noun* A feeling of liking or being fond of someone or something: *a fondness for her friend.*

font |fŏnt| —*noun, plural* **fonts** A basin that holds water used for baptizing.

food |fōōd| —*noun, plural* **foods** **1.** Anything that plants, animals, or people can eat or take in to keep them alive and healthy; nourishment. **2.** Anything that encourages an activity or growth: *The speech gave them food for thought.*

font

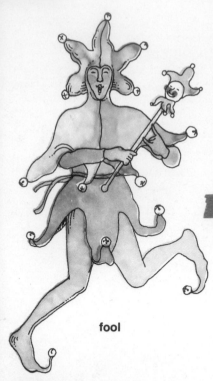

fool

football

fool | fōol | —*noun, plural* **fools** **1.** A person without good sense: *He is a fool to swim out into the ocean alone.* **2.** A person who used to amuse a king, queen, or noble by telling jokes and clowning; a jester.
—*verb* **fooled, fooling** **1.** To trick; mislead: *You can't fool me by changing your voice; I know you.* **2.** To joke, pretend, or tease: *I'm not fooling; it really did happen.* **3.** To waste time; play: *He fooled around instead of doing his homework.* **4.** To play; toy: *We were told not to fool with matches.*

fool·ish | fōo′lĭsh | —*adjective* **1.** Not having or showing good sense; not wise: *The foolish boy sold his cow for some beans.* **2.** Like a fool; silly: *He felt foolish when he realized he had called the strange woman "Mother."*

foot | fōot | —*noun, plural* **feet** **1.** The end part of a leg, used for standing or walking. **2.** The lowest part of something high or long; the bottom: *the foot of the stairs; the foot of a page; the foot of a cliff.* **3.** The part that is opposite the head: *He folded the blankets at the foot of his bed. The children sat at the foot of the table.* **4.** A unit of length that equals 12 inches. In the metric system, a foot equals 30.4 centimeters.
—*verb* **footed, footing** To pay: *Who will foot the bill for this party?*
Idiom on foot Walking or running, not riding.

foot·ball | fōot′bôl′ | —*noun, plural* **footballs** **1.** A game in which two teams of 11 players each try to carry or kick a ball over the other team's goal. **2.** The oval ball used in this game.

foot·ing | fōot′ĭng | —*noun, plural* **footings** **1.** A firm placing of the feet: *It is easy to lose one's footing and slip on those icy streets.* **2.** A safe place to walk or stand: *The steep cliff offered no footing.* **3.** A position or standing; status: *The new member was on an equal footing with the others.*

foot·note | fōot′nōt′ | —*noun, plural* **footnotes** A note at the bottom of a page that tells more about something on the page.

foot·print | fōot′prĭnt′ | —*noun, plural* **footprints** A mark or hollow place left by a foot or shoe: *We followed the deer's footprints in the snow.*

foot·step | fōot′stĕp′ | —*noun, plural* **footsteps** **1.** A step taken in walking or running: *She took a few footsteps and fell.* **2.** The sound made by a foot stepping: *We heard footsteps in the attic.* **3.** A footprint.

foot·stool | fōot′stōol′ | —*noun, plural* **footstools** A low stool on which to rest the feet while sitting.

for | fôr | or | fər | —*preposition* **1.** As long as; during: *He had to sit still for an hour.* **2.** To the extent of; as far as: *They ran for three miles in the rain.* **3.** Mailed or sent to: *There is a letter for you in the desk.* **4.** In place of; instead of: *They used their hands for paddles.* **5.** In support of: *The senator stands for lower taxes.* **6.** At the price of: *She bought a kitten for ten dollars.* **7.** With the purpose of having: *He plays tennis for fun.* **8.** In order to find, get, have, help, or save: *She is always looking for bargains. The soldiers were fighting for their lives.* **9.** In order to go to or reach: *Her father left for California today.* **10.** Limited to: *These are books for children.* **11.** On behalf or in honor of: *We will start a collection for the poor. The mayor gave a party for the players.* **12.** As a result of: *He was punished for lying.* **13.** As being: *Don't take him for a fool.* **14.** Up to: *This is for you to decide.*
—*conjunction* Because; since: *She can't hear, for she is deaf.*

ă	pat	ĕ	pet	î	fierce
ā	pay	ē	be	ŏ	pot
â	care	ĭ	pit	ō	go
ä	father	ī	pie	ô	paw, for
oi	oil	ŭ	cut	zh	vision
ŏŏ	book	û	fur	ə	ago, item,
ōō	boot	*th*	the		pencil, atom,
yōō	abuse	th	thin		circus
ou	out	hw	which	ər	butter

♦ *These sound alike* **for, four.**

for·age | fôr′ĭj | or | fŏr′ĭj | —*noun* Food for horses, cattle, and other animals, as grass or plants eaten while grazing: *The ranch had acres of good forage.*
—*verb* **foraged, foraging** **1.** To search for food: *Raccoons foraged in the garbage cans.* **2.** To search or hunt: *He foraged in his drawer.*

for·bade | fər băd′ | or | fər bād′ | or | fôr băd′ | or | fôr bād′ | The past tense of the verb **forbid:** *Mother forbade me to leave the house before finishing my homework.*

for·bid | fər bĭd′ | or | fôr bĭd′ | —*verb* **forbade, forbidden, forbidding** To refuse to allow; order not to do; prohibit: *The new law forbids smoking in elevators. I forbid you to go out tonight.*

for·bid·den | fər bĭd′n | or | fôr bĭd′n | The past participle of the verb **forbid:** *Father had forbidden us to take the car, so we were in real trouble when we dented the fender.*
—*adjective* Not permitted for use or entry: *a forbidden cave.*

force | fôrs | or | fōrs | —*noun, plural* **forces** **1.** Strength; power; energy: *The force of the explosion shattered windows and made cracks in buildings. The force of his argument convinced us.*
2. Physical strength used on someone or something: *The police had to use force to open the door. You need force to open that jar.*
3. A push or pull that can start or stop motion: *The force of gravity keeps us on earth.* **4.** A group of people who are organized for action or are available for service: *the police force; a large force of workers.* **5.** **forces** An army: *Our forces landed in Europe.*
—*verb* **forced, forcing** **1.** To make someone do something that he or she does not want to do: *The robbers forced the manager to turn over the money.* **2.** To move or push by pressure: *The pump forces water up into the pipe. The police forced their way through the crowd.*
3. To make happen by a great effort: *She forced a smile, although she was unhappy.* **4.** To use force on; break or pry: *He forced open the door. If the lock won't work, don't force it.*

force·ful | fôrs′fəl | or | fōrs′fəl | —*adjective* Full of force; strong; powerful: *a forceful person.*

ford | fôrd | or | fōrd | —*noun, plural* **fords** A place in a river shallow enough to walk or ride across.
—*verb* **forded, fording** To cross by wading or riding through shallow water: *They forded the river on horseback.*

fore- A prefix that means: **1.** Earlier; before: *forefather; foretell.*
2. In front; front: *foreleg.* **3.** The front or first part of: *forehead; forearm.* **4.** First: *forefinger.*

fore·arm | fôr′ärm′ | or | fōr′ärm′ | —*noun, plural* **forearms** The part of the arm between the wrist and the elbow.

fore·cast | fôr′kăst′ | or | fôr′käst′ | or | fōr′kăst′ | or | fōr′käst′ | —*verb* **forecast** or **forecasted, forecasting** To say what will happen ahead of time; predict: *The weather report forecasts snow for tomorrow. He tried to forecast the future.*
—*noun, plural* **forecasts** A prediction of things to come: *a weather forecast; a forecast of higher prices for food.*

fore·fath·er | fôr′fä′thər | or | fōr′fä′thər | —*noun, plural* **forefathers** An ancestor.

fore·fin·ger | fôr′fĭng′gər | or | fōr′fĭng′gər | —*noun, plural* **forefingers** The finger next to the thumb; the index finger.

fore·foot | fôr′fŏŏt′ | or | fōr′fŏŏt′ | —*noun, plural* **forefeet** One of the front feet of an animal.

fore·gone | fôr′gôn′ | or | fôr′gŏn′ | or | fōr′gôn′ | or | fōr′gŏn′ |

forehand

—*adjective* Already decided or done: *Violet's election as club president was a foregone conclusion, since no one opposed her and she was very popular.*

fore·ground |fôr′ground′| or |fōr′ground′| —*noun, plural* **foregrounds** The part of a scene or picture that is or seems to be closest to the person looking at it.

fore·hand |fôr′hănd′| or |fōr′hănd′| —*noun, plural* **forehands** In tennis and other sports, a stroke made with the palm of the hand turned forward.

fore·head |fôr′ĭd| or |fōr′ĭd| or |fôr′hĕd′| or |fōr′hĕd′| —*noun, plural* **foreheads** The part of the face above the eyes; the brow.

for·eign |fôr′ĭn| or |fŏr′ĭn| —*adjective* **1.** Outside or different from one's own country: *a foreign country.* **2.** Of, from, or for a different country: *a foreign language; a foreign government; foreign trade.* **3.** Not belonging by nature: *Jealousy is foreign to her character.*

for·eign·er |fôr′ə nər| or |fŏr′ə nər| —*noun, plural* **foreigners** A person from another country.

fore·leg |fôr′lĕg′| or |fōr′lĕg′| —*noun, plural* **forelegs** One of the front legs of an animal.

fore·man |fôr′mən| or |fōr′mən| —*noun, plural* **foremen** **1.** A person who is in charge of a group of workers: *He is the new foreman at the ranch.* **2.** The member of a jury who is its chairman.

fore·most |fôr′mōst′| or |fōr′mōst′| —*adjective* Most important in rank or position; leading: *He is the world's foremost authority on snails*

fore·run·ner |fôr′rŭn′ər| or |fōr′rŭn′ər| —*noun, plural* **forerunners** Something that comes before another thing: *Adding machines were the forerunners of modern computers.*

fore·saw |fôr sô′| or |fōr sô′| The past tense of the verb **foresee:** *I foresaw trouble, and I was right.*

fore·see |fôr sē′| or |fōr sē′| —*verb* **foresaw, foreseen, foreseeing** To see, imagine, or realize in advance: *Joe must have foreseen that it would snow, because he wore his woolen hat and mittens.*

fore·seen |fôr sēn′| or |fōr sēn′| The past participle of the verb **foresee:** *Pat had foreseen the need for an umbrella.*

fore·sight |fôr′sīt′| or |fōr′sīt′| —*noun* The ability to look ahead and plan for the future: *She had the foresight to buy extra cloth in case she wanted to make a matching vest.*

for·est |fôr′ĭst| or |fŏr′ĭst| —*noun, plural* **forests** A large area with many trees, plants, and living creatures; woods.

for·est·ry |fôr′ĭ strē| or |fŏr′ĭ strē| —*noun* The study or work of improving forests, helping them grow, and looking after them.

fore·tell |fôr tĕl′| or |fōr tĕl′| —*verb* **foretold, foretelling** To tell beforehand; predict: *Can anybody foretell the future?*

fore·told |fôr tōld′| or |fōr tōld′| The past tense and past participle of the verb **foretell:** *The fortuneteller foretold the accident. Many witches had foretold the death of the king.*

for·ev·er |fôr ĕv′ər| or |fər ĕv′ər| —*adverb* **1.** Without ever stopping; always: *I'll love you forever.* **2.** All or most of the time; very often: *She is forever whining.*

for·feit |fôr′fĭt| —*verb* **forfeited, forfeiting** To lose or give up because of a mistake or the breaking of an agreement: *The team*

ă	pat	ĕ	pet	î	fierce
ā	pay	ē	be	ŏ	pot
â	care	ĭ	pit	ō	go
ä	father	ī	pie	ô	paw, for
oi	oil	ŭ	cut	zh	vision
ōō	book	û	fur	ə	ago, item,
ōō	boot	*th*	the		pencil, atom,
yōō	abuse	th	thin		circus
ou	out	hw	which	ər	butter

forfeited the basketball game when it failed to show up Saturday.
—*noun, plural* **forfeits** Something lost, given up, or paid as a penalty or fine: *The loss of the library book resulted in the forfeit of her deposit.*

for·gave |fər **gāv′** | or |fôr **gāv′** | The past tense of the verb **forgive:** *Melinda forgave me for being rude.*

forge¹ |fôrj| or |fōrj| —*noun, plural* **forges** **1.** A furnace or fire where metal is heated so that it can be hammered or bent into shape. **2.** A blacksmith's workshop, with its fire and tools.
—*verb* **forged, forging** **1.** To work or shape metal by heating and hammering it: *He forged iron into chains. She forged a ring of gold.* **2.** To make or form with effort: *The coach forged his team into champions. They forged a town out of the wilderness.* **3.** To copy or imitate with the intention of presenting the copy as the real thing: *She forged her mother's signature. He forged some paintings and tried to sell them to a museum.*

forge² |fôrj| or |fōrj| —*verb* **forged, forging** To move ahead in a slow and steady way or with a final burst of speed: *They forged through the swamp. He suddenly forged ahead in the race.*

for·get |fər **gĕt′** | —*verb* **forgot, forgotten** or **forgot, forgetting** **1.** To be unable to remember; fail to bring to mind: *He forgot his own address. She often forgets what she is about to do.* **2.** To fail to think of doing, taking, or using; to neglect: *He forgot his coat at the office. She often forgets her manners.*

for·get·ful |fər **gĕt′** fəl | —*adjective* Tending not to remember; likely to forget: *The forgetful boy often leaves home without his keys.*

for·get-me-not |fər **gĕt′** mē nŏt′ | —*noun, plural* **forget-me-nots** A plant with clusters of small blue flowers.

for·give |fər **gĭv′** | —*verb* **forgave, forgiven, forgiving** To stop being angry at; pardon or excuse: *She forgave him for behaving badly.*

for·giv·en |fər **gĭv′** ən | The past participle of the verb **forgive:** *I have never forgiven him for meddling.*

for·got |fər **gŏt′** | The past tense and a past participle of the verb **forget:** *I forgot where I put my keys. She had forgot to lock the door one day last year and some of her things had been stolen.*

for·got·ten |fər **gŏt′** n | A past participle of the verb **forget:** *John had forgotten to feed the cat.*

fork |fôrk| —*noun, plural* **forks** **1.** A tool for picking up food. A fork has two or more sharp points at one end and a handle at the other. **2.** A large farm tool with a long handle and several sharp prongs; a pitchfork. **3.** A place where something separates into two or more parts: *a nest in the fork of a tree. We came to a fork in the road.*
—*verb* **forked, forking** **1.** To pick up, throw, or stab with a fork: *They forked the hay into the wagon. He forked his meat.* **2.** To divide into two or more branches: *The river forked, and we took the left branch. The snake's tongue forks at the tip.*

form |fôrm| —*noun, plural* **forms** **1.** The shape, structure, or outline of something: *a ring in the form of a snake biting its tail; the human form; vague forms seen through the fog.* **2.** Kind; variety: *Light is one form of energy.* **3.** A way of doing something; manner; style: *He plays tennis well, but his form is awkward.* **4.** A paper or set of papers with blanks to be filled in: *a medical form; an income-tax form.* **5.** Any of the different appearances a word may take: *"Flyer" is a form of the word "flier."*

forge¹, forge²
Forge¹ comes from an old word in French that in turn came from a Latin word meaning "blacksmith's workshop." We are not certain of the origin of **forge²**. One possibility is that it is a variant of the verb **force**, but there is no proof of this.

forge¹

forget-me-not

—*verb* **formed, forming** **1.** To give shape to; put together; make: *She formed the cooky dough into balls.* **2.** To come into being or cause to come into being: *Buds form in the spring. Ice crystals formed rings around the moon.* **3.** To make up; create: *The three boys formed a trio to play folk music.*

for·mal |fôr′məl| —*adjective* **1.** Correct, official, and proper; following strict rules and forms; not casual: *a formal wedding invitation; an ambassador's formal visit to the king.* **2.** Stiff and cold: *He gave his enemy a formal nod of greeting.* **3.** Of or for occasions where elegant clothes are worn and fine manners are expected: *a formal dance; a formal table setting.*
—*noun, plural* **formals** **1.** A dance at which people are expected to wear elegant clothing. **2.** An evening gown.

for·ma·tion |fôr mā′shən| —*noun, plural* **formations** **1.** The act or process of forming; development: *The formation of a new volcano is a rare event.* **2.** Something that has been formed: *a cloud formation.* **3.** A particular arrangement: *The geese flew in a V formation.*

for·mer |fôr′mər| —*adjective* **1.** From or belonging to an earlier time: *She is my former teacher. In former days there were no telephones and automobiles.* **2.** Being the first mentioned of two: *She tried swimming and golf but enjoyed only the former activity.*
—*noun* **the former** The one mentioned first: *Jim and Fred cleared a garden on the former's land.*

for·mu·la |fôr′myə lə| —*noun, plural* **formulas** **1.** A fixed way of doing something; a method or pattern: *She wrote all her books according to the same formula.* **2.** A recipe or set of ingredients: *a formula for a new medicine.* **3.** A special food made for a baby to drink from a bottle. **4.** A set of symbols used in chemistry that tells what is in a compound. For example, the formula for table salt is NaCl. **5.** A rule in mathematics, often written in symbols. For example, the formula for finding area is $w \times l$ (width times length).

for·sake |fôr sāk′| —*verb* **forsook, forsaken, forsaking** To give up; leave; abandon: *He forsook his old friends when he became rich and famous.*

for·sak·en |fôr sā′kən| The past participle of the verb **forsake:** *Bill had forsaken his art studies by the time he married.*

for·sook |fôr sŏŏk′| The past tense of the verb **forsake:** *They forsook their friends by refusing to help them.*

for·syth·i·a |fôr sĭth′ē ə| or |fər sĭth′ē ə| —*noun, plural* **forsythias** A garden shrub with yellow flowers that bloom early in spring.

fort |fôrt| or |fōrt| —*noun, plural* **forts** An area or building that has been made strong against possible attacks by enemies. A fort often has troops stationed at it.

forth |fôrth| or |fōrth| —*adverb* **1.** Into full sight; out: *The bushes put forth leaves and flowers.* **2.** Forward or onward: *They went forth to build a new life.*
♦ *These sound alike* **forth, fourth.**

for·ti·eth |fôr′tē ĭth| —*noun, plural* **fortieths** **1.** In a group of people or things that are in numbered order, the one that matches number forty. **2.** One of forty equal parts, written 1/40.
—*adjective: her fortieth birthday.*

for·ti·fy |fôr′tə fī′| —*verb* **fortified, fortifying, fortifies** **1.** To make stronger or more secure: *They fortified their city by building a wall of*

forsythia

fort
Built in Ohio, 1790

ă	pat	ĕ	pet	î	fierce
ā	pay	ē	be	ŏ	pot
â	care	ĭ	pit	ō	go
ä	father	ī	pie	ô	paw, for
oi	oil	ŭ	cut	zh	vision
ŏŏ	book	û	fur	ə	ago, item,
ōō	boot	*th*	the		pencil, atom,
yōō	abuse	th	thin		circus
ou	out	hw	which	ər	butter

stone around it. **2.** To add vitamins or minerals to: *The bakery fortifies its bread.*

for·tress | fôr′trĭs | —*noun, plural* **fortresses** A fort or other strong place built to resist attacks.

for·tu·nate | fôr′chə nĭt | —*adjective* Having or bringing good fortune; lucky: *He's a fortunate man to have lived through two world wars. The chef's salad was a fortunate choice, for it was delicious.*

for·tune | fôr′chən | —*noun, plural* **fortunes** **1.** Luck; chance: *I had the good fortune to meet many nice people.* **2.** What will happen in the future; fate; destiny: *She says she can tell my fortune by reading my palm.* **3.** A large amount of money or property; wealth: *He made a fortune in the movie business.*

for·tune·tell·er | fôr′chən tĕl′ər | —*noun, plural* **fortunetellers** A person who claims to be able to tell what is going to happen to other people, often by looking at their palms.

for·ty | fôr′tē | —*noun, plural* **forties** A number, written 40, that is equal to the product of 4 × 10.

—*adjective* Being ten more than thirty in number. The adjective **forty** belongs to a class of words called **determiners.** They signal that a noun is coming.

fo·rum | fôr′əm | or | fōr′əm | —*noun, plural* **forums** **1.** The main public square of an ancient Roman city. The forum was a market and a place for public assemblies. **2.** A place or meeting where things are discussed in public: *The town meeting was a forum for the hearing of all kinds of complaints and suggestions.*

for·ward | fôr′wərd | —*adjective* **1.** At, near, or belonging to the front of something: *He walked to the forward part of the train.* **2.** Going or moving toward the front: *a forward leap.* **3.** Toward the future: *from this time forward.* **4.** Bold; rude: *I thought his manners were a bit forward.*

—*adverb* **1.** Toward the front: *Please step forward.* **2.** In or toward the future: *I look forward to seeing you.* Another form of this adverb is **forwards.**

—*verb* **forwarded, forwarding** **1.** To send on something mailed to someone who has moved to a new address: *She forwarded the letters to her son in college.* **2.** To send something ordered by a buyer: *We will forward the garden tools after we receive your check.* **3.** To cause something to progress; promote: *He is always trying to forward his own interests.*

for·wards | fôr′wərdz | A form of the adverb **forward.**

fos·sil | fŏs′əl | —*noun, plural* **fossils** The remains or traces of a plant or animal that lived long ago. Fossils are found in rocks and other substances that form the earth's crust. The bones and footprints of dinosaurs are fossils.

fos·ter | fô′stər | or | fŏs′tər | —*verb* **fostered, fostering** **1.** To raise; bring up: *foster a child.* **2.** To help grow or develop; encourage: *The book on ships fostered Bob's interest in the sea.*

—*adjective* Receiving or giving care in a family that is not related by blood or adoption: *a foster child; foster parents.*

fought | fôt | The past tense and past participle of the verb **fight:** *Paul fought for justice. The two brothers have fought often, but they are fond of each other just the same.*

foul | foul | —*adjective* **fouler, foulest** **1.** Bad to smell or taste; disgusting; rotten: *a foul odor of decaying garbage; a foul flavor.* **2.** Dirty; filthy: *Foul rags lay about the room.* **3.** Evil; wicked: *There were rumors of foul deeds in the old castle.* **4.** Unpleasant;

fossil
Above: Plant fossil
Below: Animal fossil

nasty: *We had a week of foul weather.* **5.** Not according to the rules or standards: *He struck a foul blow beneath the belt.*
6. Outside the foul lines in a baseball game: *a foul ball.* **7.** Not acceptable among polite people; vulgar: *He uses foul language.*
—*noun, plural* **fouls 1.** A move or play that is against the rules of a game: *The basketball player committed a foul by pushing his opponent.* **2.** A ball hit outside the foul lines in baseball.
—*verb* **fouled, fouling 1.** To make foul: *The smoke fouled the air.*
2. To break a rule in a game. **3.** To hit a baseball outside the foul lines: *He fouled twice before he hit a home run.*
♦ *These sound alike* **foul, fowl.**

foul line Either of the two straight lines that run from home plate through first or third base to the end of a baseball field.

found¹ |found| The past tense and past participle of the verb **find:** *Joan found her watch. We have never found our keys.*

found² |found| —*verb* **founded, founding** To bring into being; establish; start: *He founded a company.*

foun·da·tion |foun dā′shən| —*noun, plural* **foundations 1.** The act of founding; creation: *Basketball's foundation occurred at the YMCA in Springfield, Massachusetts.* **2.** The lowest part of a structure; the base: *the foundation of a house.* **3.** Supporting facts or reasons; basis: *The charges against me lack all foundation.*

foun·dry |foun′drē| —*noun, plural* **foundries** A place where metal is melted and cast into different shapes.

foun·tain |foun′tən| —*noun, plural* **fountains 1.** A flow of water from the earth. **2.** A man-made stream of water that is made to shoot up into the air or flow among specially designed statues and pools: *The city parks have many beautiful fountains.* **3.** An object providing a stream of water for drinking. **4.** A good source: *My sister is a fountain of information about movie stars.*

fountain pen A pen, used for writing, that must be filled with ink.

four |fôr| or |fōr| —*noun, plural* **fours** A number, written 4, that is equal to the sum of 3 + 1.
—*adjective* Being one more than three in number: *four books.* The adjective **four** belongs to a class of words called **determiners.** They signal that a noun is coming.
♦ *These sound alike* **four, for.**

four·teen |fôr′tēn′| or |fōr′tēn′| —*noun, plural* **fourteens** A number, written 14, that is equal to the sum of 13 + 1.
—*adjective* Being one more than thirteen in number: *fourteen bicycles.* The number **fourteen** belongs to a class of words called **determiners.** They signal that a noun is coming.

four·teenth |fôr′tēnth′| or |fōr′tēnth′| —*noun, plural* **fourteenths 1.** In a group of people or things that are in numbered order, the one that matches the number fourteen.
2. One of fourteen equal parts, written $\frac{1}{14}$.
—*adjective: the fourteenth bus to stop by the gas station.*

fourth |fôrth| or |fōrth| —*noun, plural* **fourths 1.** In a group of people or things that are in numbered order, the one that matches the number four. **2.** One of four equal parts, written $\frac{1}{4}$.
—*adjective: the fourth girl in line.*
♦ *These sound alike* **fourth, forth.**

Fourth of July A holiday in honor of the adoption of the Declaration of Independence in 1776. Another name for this holiday is **Independence Day.**

fountain

ă	pat	ĕ	pet	î	fierce
ā	pay	ē	be	ŏ	pot
â	care	ĭ	pit	ō	go
ä	father	ī	pie	ô	paw, for
oi	oil	ŭ	cut	zh	vision
ŏŏ	book	û	fur	ə	ago, item,
ōō	boot	*th*	the		pencil, atom,
yōō	abuse	th	thin		circus
ou	out	hw	which	ər	butter

fowl | foul | —*noun, plural* **fowl** or **fowls** **1.** A bird that is raised or hunted for food. Chickens, ducks, turkeys, and pheasants are fowl. **2.** A large fully grown chicken used for cooking.

♦ *These sound alike* **fowl, foul.**

fox | fŏks | —*noun, plural* **foxes** **1.** An animal with a pointed snout and a long, bushy tail. Foxes are related to dogs and wolves. **2.** The fur of a fox.

fox

frac·tion | frăk'shən | —*noun, plural* **fractions** **1.** A small part or amount: *Only a fraction of the eggs laid by a fish survive to become adults.* **2.** Two numbers with a line between them that express a part of a whole. The fraction $^7/_{10}$ means that the whole is divided into 10 equal amounts, and 7 of them make up the part expressed by the fraction. The 10 is called the denominator and the 7 is called the numerator of the fraction.

frac·ture | frăk'chər | —*noun, plural* **fractures** A break or crack, often in a bone: *a leg fracture.*

—*verb* **fractured, fracturing** To break; crack: *The fall fractured the vase in three places. The bones of old people fracture easily.*

frag·ile | frăj'əl | or | frăj'īl' | —*adjective* Easy to break or harm: *a fragile drinking glass.*

frag·ment | frăg'mənt | —*noun, plural* **fragments** A piece broken off from a whole object: *a fragment of a broken plate.*

fra·grance | frā'grəns | —*noun, plural* **fragrances** A sweet or pleasant smell: *the fragrance of roses.*

fra·grant | frā'grənt | —*adjective* Having a sweet or pleasant smell: *a fragrant apple pie.*

frail | frāl | —*adjective* **frailer, frailest** **1.** Thin and weak in body: *a frail old man.* **2.** Easily broken; fragile: *a frail flower.*

frame | frām | —*noun, plural* **frames** **1.** A form that holds up or puts a border around something; a supporting structure: *a window frame; a picture frame.* **2.** The structure of a human body: *He has a small frame.*

—*verb* **framed, framing** **1.** To put a frame around; to border: *frame a picture. Her hair framed her face perfectly.* **2.** To build or design; draw up: *The diplomats framed a peace treaty.* **3.** To put into words; to phrase: *The lawyer framed his questions carefully.*

frame·work | frām'wûrk' | —*noun, plural* **frameworks** A form with connected parts that shapes or holds up something.

France | frăns | or | fräns | A country in western Europe.

frank | frăngk | —*adjective* **franker, frankest** Honest in telling one's real thoughts and feelings; open and sincere: *a frank talk.*

Frank·fort | frăngk'fərt | The capital of Kentucky.

frank·furt·er | frăngk'fər tər | —*noun, plural* **frankfurters** A pink sausage made of beef or beef and pork. Frankfurters are often served in a roll with mustard, relish, or other seasonings. Another name for this food is **hot dog.**

fran·tic | frăn'tĭk | —*adjective* Very excited with fear or worry: *a frantic scream. There was a frantic rush to get a seat on the subway.*

fra·ter·ni·ty | frə tûr'nĭ tē | —*noun, plural* **fraternities** **1.** Close feeling between people; brotherhood. **2.** A social club for boys or men.

fraud | frôd | —*noun, plural* **frauds** **1.** A dishonest act in which someone is cheated: *The businessman was accused of fraud when the car he sold us wouldn't run.* **2.** Someone or something that is not real or genuine; a fake: *The woman claims to be a princess, but she's a fraud.*

framework
Steel framework of a building

fray | frā | —*verb* **frayed, fraying** To wear away at the edge so that loose threads show: *The cuffs of his only white shirt frayed.*

freak | frēk | —*noun, plural* **freaks 1.** A person or thing that looks strange because of some unusual growth or feature: *The freaks in the circus included a giant man and a fat lady.* **2.** A very unusual thing or event: *Snow in July is a freak.*

freck·le | frĕk′əl | —*noun, plural* **freckles** A small brown spot on the skin: *Alice's face gets covered with freckles every summer.*

Fred·er·ic·ton | frĕd′rĭk tən | The capital of New Brunswick.

free | frē | —*adjective* **freer, freest 1.** Not under someone else's power; acting according to one's own will: *a free people; a free press.* **2.** Not prevented or forbidden; at liberty: *You are free to disagree with me.* **3.** Not affected by something; clear; exempt: *free of germs; free of worry.* **4.** Not tied; loose: *the free end of a chain.* **5.** Not filled or busy; available: *free space; a free hour.* **6.** Costing nothing: *free meals.*
—*adverb* Without having to pay: *Children can ride free.*
—*verb* **freed, freeing 1.** To set free; let loose: *We opened the cages and freed the birds.* **2.** To untie or release: *Our dog got entangled in his leash, and we had to free him.* **3.** To show to be innocent; to clear: *The police freed him of all charges.*

free·dom | frē′dəm | —*noun, plural* **freedoms 1.** The condition of being free: *The slaves were given their freedom.* **2.** Ease in moving: *These gym shorts give my legs freedom for running.* **3.** The right to use something: *We were given the freedom of the house.*

free·si·a | frē′zhē ə | or | frē′zhə | or | frē′zē ə | —*noun, plural* **freesias** A plant that has clusters of fragrant white, yellow, or purple flowers.

free·way | frē′wā′ | —*noun, plural* **freeways** A highway with no tolls to pay.

freeze | frēz | —*verb* **froze, frozen, freezing 1.** To change from a liquid to a solid by losing heat; harden with cold: *Water freezes at 32°F. We froze the orange juice in ice trays to make orange cubes.* **2.** To become covered or filled with ice: *The river froze.* **3.** To make or become motionless: *The scream froze us in our steps. I heard a noise and froze.* **4.** To make or become painfully cold; to chill: *The wind froze us. We stood outside freezing.*
—*noun, plural* **freezes** A time of very cold weather.

freez·er | frē′zər | —*noun, plural* **freezers 1.** A refrigerator. **2.** A very cold refrigerator or very cold part of a refrigerator for freezing foods and storing frozen foods.

freight | frāt | —*noun, plural* **freights 1.** Goods carried in a train, truck, or other vehicle. **2.** The act or business of transporting goods: *Oranges are sent by freight from Florida.* **3.** A railway train carrying goods only: *The freight came into the station.*

freight·er | frā′tər | —*noun, plural* **freighters** A ship that carries goods.

French | frĕnch | —*noun* **1.** The Romance language of France and some other countries. **2. the French** (Used with a plural verb.) The people of France.
—*adjective* Of France, the French, or their language.

French fries Potatoes that are sliced into thin strips and fried in deep fat until golden.

French horn A brass musical instrument with a coiled tube, played by blowing into a mouthpiece and pressing valves. The French horn widens out to a bell at the end.

freesia

French horn

ă	pat	ĕ	pet	î	fierce
ā	pay	ē	be	ŏ	pot
â	care	ĭ	pit	ō	go
ä	father	ī	pie	ô	paw, for

oi	oil	ŭ	cut	zh	vision
ŏŏ	book	û	fur	ə	ago, item,
ōō	boot	*th*	the		pencil, atom,
yōō	abuse	th	thin		circus
ou	out	hw	which	ər	butter

fren·zy |frĕn′zē| —*noun, plural* **frenzies** Wild, energetic excitement in which people can't think clearly or stay still: *The crowd went into a frenzy when their team won the pennant.*

fre·quen·cy |frē′kwən sē| —*noun, plural* **frequencies 1.** The number of times an event happens within a certain amount of time: *The frequency with which a monthly magazine comes out is 12 times a year.* **2.** The condition of happening over and over during a short time: *the frequency of forest fires.*

fre·quent |frē′kwənt| —*adjective* Happening again and again; appearing or occurring often: *My grandmother is a frequent visitor here. Rain is frequent in tropical forests.*
—*verb* |frĭ kwĕnt′| or |frē′kwənt| **frequented, frequenting** To visit often: *I met him because we frequent the same club.*

fresh |frĕsh| —*adjective* **fresher, freshest 1.** Just made, grown, or gathered; not stale or spoiled: *fresh bread; fresh wolf tracks.* **2.** Not salty: *fresh water.* **3.** New; additional: *a fresh start; fresh clues.* **4.** Different; original: *a fresh solution to old problems.* **5.** Not yet used or dirtied; clean: *fresh paper towels.* **6.** Bright and clear; not dull or faded: *a fresh memory.* **7.** Refreshing: *fresh air; a fresh breeze.* **8.** Rude; impolite: *a fresh remark.*

fresh·man |frĕsh′mən| —*noun, plural* **freshmen** A student in the first year of high school or college.

fresh·wa·ter |frĕsh′wô′tər| or |frĕsh′wŏt′ər| —*adjective* Of or living in water that is not salty: *a freshwater fish.*

fri·ar |frī′ər| —*noun, plural* **friars** A man who is a member of a group devoted to religious service and prayer in the Roman Catholic Church.

fric·tion |frĭk′shən| —*noun, plural* **frictions 1.** The rubbing of one object against another: *Matches are lit by friction. Constant friction wore holes in the elbows of my shirt.* **2.** A force that slows down or stops the motion of two objects touching each other: *Friction causes a rolling ball to stop eventually.* **3.** Disagreement; conflict: *There is sometimes friction in our family over money matters.*

Fri·day |frī′dē| or |frī′dā′| —*noun, plural* **Fridays** The sixth day of the week, after Thursday and before Saturday.

fried |frīd| The past tense and past participle of the verb **fry:** *Jim fried the trout he caught Sunday. He had fried fish before, so he knew how.*

friend |frĕnd| —*noun, plural* **friends 1.** A person one knows and likes: *Joan is my friend.* **2.** A person who helps or supports someone or something: *a friend of the poor.*

friend·ly |frĕnd′lē| —*adjective* **friendlier, friendliest 1.** Showing friendship; warm and kind: *friendly advice; a friendly smile.* **2.** Liking to meet or talk pleasantly with others; companionable; sociable: *Our friendly neighbors are always dropping by.* **3.** Not hostile or fighting; cordial: *Japan and the United States became friendly nations after World War II.*

friend·ship |frĕnd′shĭp′| —*noun, plural* **friendships** The close feeling or relationship between friends: *Dave and I show our friendship by always helping each other.*

fright |frīt| —*noun, plural* **frights** Sudden, deep fear: *The noise from the darkness filled us with fright.*

fright·en |frīt′n| —*verb* **frightened, frightening 1.** To make or become suddenly afraid; alarm suddenly: *frighten a child. Her children frighten easily.* **2.** To force or drive by scaring: *Loud noises frighten birds away.*

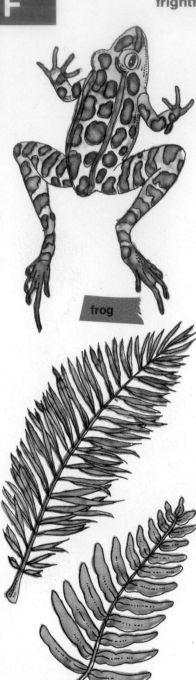

frog

frond

Above: Palm frond
Below: Fern frond

ă	pat	ĕ	pet	î	fierce
ā	pay	ē	be	ŏ	pot
â	care	ĭ	pit	ō	go
ä	father	ī	pie	ô	paw, for
oi	oil	ŭ	cut	zh	vision
o͞o	book	û	fur	ə	ago, item,
o͞o	boot	*th*	the		pencil, atom,
yo͞o	abuse	th	thin		circus
ou	out	hw	which	ər	butter

fright·ful | frīt′fəl | —*adjective* **1.** Causing fear; terrifying: *frightful masks.* **2.** Upsetting; shocking: *a frightful accident.*

frig·id | frĭj′ĭd | —*adjective* **1.** Very cold: *a frigid climate; frigid north winds.* **2.** Cold in manner; unfriendly; stiff: *When we whispered, the librarian silenced us with a frigid glance.*

frill | frĭl | —*noun, plural* **frills 1.** A piece of fancy trimming: *frills on a doll's dress.* **2.** An extra little feature, ornament, or service: *I want a banana split with nuts and all the other frills.*

fringe | frĭnj | —*noun, plural* **fringes 1.** An edge made of hanging threads, cords, or strips. Fringes are used on bedspreads and curtains. **2.** Something like a fringe along an edge: *a fringe of eyelashes.* **3.** A border; edge: *on the fringe of the crowd.*
—*verb* **fringed, fringing** To decorate with a fringe: *We fringed the hem of the dress. Long lashes fringed her eyes.*

friv·o·lous | frĭv′ə ləs | —*adjective* Not serious or important; silly: *frivolous matters like clothes and parties.*

fro | frō | —*adverb* **to and fro** Back and forth: *pushing the swing to and fro.*

frog | frôg | or | frŏg | —*noun, plural* **frogs** A small animal with smooth skin, webbed feet, and long hind legs. Frogs live in or near water. They swim well and can make long jumps.

frog·man | frôg′măn′ | or | frôg′mən | or | frŏg′măn′ | or | frŏg′mən | —*noun, plural* **frogmen** A swimmer who wears an oxygen tank and other equipment to work under water.

frol·ic | frŏl′ĭk | —*noun, plural* **frolics 1.** A playful game; a romp: *We enjoyed a frolic in the snow.* **2.** Fun; merriment.
—*verb* **frolicked, frolicking, frolics** To behave playfully; to romp: *When we set them free, the two dogs frolicked happily in the tall grass.*

from | frŭm | or | frŏm | or | frəm | —*preposition* **1.** Starting at; beginning with: *We walked home from the station. He flew from Boston to Denver. The book was recommended for children from age four to age eight.* **2.** Originating in or with: *We import coffee from South America. I received a letter from my cousin.* **3.** Out of: *He took some coins from his pocket.* **4.** At a distance measured in relation to: *There was a mark three inches away from the edge of the page.* **5.** Out of the possession of: *Take the ball away from him.* **6.** Because of: *He is weak from hunger.* **7.** As being unlike; as distinguished from: *She doesn't know one flower from another.*

frond | frŏnd | —*noun, plural* **fronds** The leaf of a fern or palm tree.

front | frŭnt | —*noun, plural* **fronts 1.** The forward part of a thing or place: *a blouse with lace down the front; a desk at the front of the room; a crowd in front of the monkey's cage.* **2.** Land lying next to a lake, river, ocean, or street: *a lake front.* **3.** A place where fighting is happening during a war: *More troops were sent to the front.* **4.** An outward appearance: *He was frightened but kept up a brave front.*
—*adjective* In or facing the front: *the front door; the front pages.*
—*verb* **fronted, fronting** To face or look out: *We live in a building fronting on the river.*

fron·tier | frŭn tîr′ | —*noun, plural* **frontiers 1.** The edge between countries or the land along it; a border: *We crossed the frontier into Mexico by car.* **2.** A distant area that marks the last point where people live: *The American frontier gradually moved westward. Alaska is our last frontier.* **3.** Any place or subject not yet completely studied: *exploring new frontiers in space.*

frost |frôst| or |frŏst| —*noun, plural* **frosts 1.** A covering of thin ice formed by the freezing of water vapor in the air: *Our car windows were covered with frost.* **2.** Air temperatures below freezing: *The frost killed the orange crop.*
—*verb* **frosted, frosting 1.** To cover with or as if with frost: *At the glass factory they frosted the drinking glasses with a special tool.* **2.** To cover a cake with frosting or icing.

frost·bit |frôst'bĭt'| or |frŏst'bĭt'| The past tense of the verb **frostbite:** *The temperature was below zero yesterday and frostbit everyone who went outdoors.*

frost·bite |frôst'bĭt'| or |frŏst'bĭt'| —*noun, plural* **frostbites** Damage to a part of the body caused by freezing temperatures.
—*verb* **frostbit, frostbitten, frostbiting** To injure by extreme cold: *The very cold air frostbit the Arctic explorers' fingers.*

frost·bit·ten |frôst'bĭt'n| or |frŏst'bĭt'n| The past participle of the verb **frostbite:** *Because he had gone without gloves, his hands had been frostbitten.*

frost·ing |frô'stĭng| or |frŏs'tĭng| —*noun, plural* **frostings** A sweet covering of sugar and other ingredients, used to decorate cakes and cookies; icing.

frost·y |frô'stē| or |frŏs'tē| —*adjective* **frostier, frostiest 1.** Cold enough for frost; chilly: *a frosty night.* **2.** Covered with frost: *a frosty window.* **3.** Unfriendly: *a frosty hello.*

froth |frôth| or |frŏth| —*noun, plural* **froths** A group of bubbles in or on a liquid; foam: *The froth on the soda spilled over the glass.*
—*verb* **frothed, frothing** To pour out froth; to foam: *They knew the dog was sick when it frothed at the mouth.*

frown |froun| —*verb* **frowned, frowning 1.** To wrinkle the forehead when thinking, confused, or unhappy: *The teacher frowned when no one could answer the question.* **2.** To be against; disapprove of: *Mother and Dad frown on our staying out after dark.*
—*noun, plural* **frowns** The act of wrinkling the forehead when thinking, confused, or unhappy: *A frown crossed the old woman's face.*

froze |frōz| The past tense of the verb **freeze:** *When the lake froze, we went skating.*

fro·zen |frō'zən| The past participle of the verb **freeze:** *Mother had frozen the strawberries and had to let them thaw.*

fru·gal |frōō'gəl| —*adjective* **1.** Not willing to spend much money; not wasteful; thrifty: *Frugal people compare prices at different stores before buying.* **2.** Costing little; modest: *We ate a frugal meal of leftovers.*

fruit |frōōt| —*noun, plural* **fruit** or **fruits 1.** The part of a flowering plant that contains the seeds. Many kinds are sweet and are used as food. Apples, oranges, peaches, and bananas are kinds of fruit. Berries, pods, nuts, and burs are also fruits. **2.** A result; product: *Janet's science award was the fruit of many months of work building and studying an ant colony.*
—*verb* **fruited, fruiting** To produce fruit.

frus·trate |frŭs'trāt'| —*verb* **frustrated, frustrating 1.** To keep from achieving a goal; prevent: *Lack of money frustrated her plans to paint the dining room.* **2.** To cause to feel helpless or useless; discourage: *Constant failure at school frustrated the boy.*

fry |frī| —*verb* **fried, frying, fries** To cook over heat in hot oil or fat: *He fried the chicken and the potatoes.*
—*noun, plural* **fries** A meal of fried food: *a fish fry.*

froth
On an ice-cream soda

fuchsia

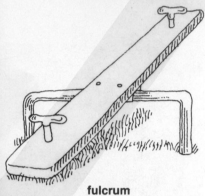

fulcrum

The middle of a seesaw is a fulcrum.

fuch·sia |fyoo′shə| —*noun, plural* **fuchsias** A plant with drooping flowers that are usually purple and red. Fuchsias are often grown as house plants.

fudge |fŭj| —*noun, plural* **fudges** A soft candy, usually flavored with chocolate.

fu·el |fyoo′əl| —*noun, plural* **fuels** Anything that is burned to give off heat or energy. Fires need fuels like wood, coal, and oil. The engines of cars usually use gasoline as fuel.

fu·gi·tive |fyoo′jĭ tĭv| —*noun, plural* **fugitives** A person running away, especially from the law: *The fugitives were captured.*

-ful A suffix that means: **1.** Full of or having: *playful; useful.* **2.** An amount that will fill: *handful.*

ful·crum |fool′krəm| or |fŭl′krəm| —*noun, plural* **fulcrums** The point on which a lever turns.

ful·fill |fool fĭl′| —*verb* **fulfilled, fulfilling** **1.** To do or carry out: *You may leave when you fulfill all your duties. The birth of the child fulfilled a prophecy.* **2.** To satisfy; meet: *The swim team fulfilled all requirements to enter the finals.*

full |fool| —*adjective* **fuller, fullest** **1.** Holding all that is possible: *a full bucket.* **2.** Not missing any parts; complete: *a full set of teeth; your full attention* **3.** Having many or a lot: *shelves full of books.* **4.** Rounded in shape: *a full figure.* **5.** Not tight or narrow; wide: *a full skirt.* **6.** Appearing as a fully lighted circle: *The moon is full tonight.*
—*adverb* Entirely; completely: *He knew full well what it was.*

full·back |fool′băk′| —*noun, plural* **fullbacks** A player on a football or soccer team who stands farthest behind the front line.

full·y |fool′ē| —*adverb* **1.** Totally; completely: *He was fully grown at sixteen. He was fully aware that he was breaking a school rule.* **2.** At least; no less than: *To have good common sense is fully as important as to have a good education.*

fum·ble |fŭm′bəl| —*verb* **fumbled, fumbling** **1.** To grope or feel about clumsily: *He fumbled in his pockets for change.* **2.** To handle clumsily or without skill: *He fumbled his first important job.* **3.** To lose one's grasp on; drop: *The fullback fumbled the ball.*
—*noun, plural* **fumbles** **1.** An act of fumbling. **2.** A ball that has been dropped during play.

fume |fyoom| —*noun, plural* **fumes** Any smoke or gas, especially one that is harmful or smells bad.
—*verb* **fumed, fuming** **1.** To produce or give off fumes: *Certain chemicals fume when exposed to air.* **2.** To be very angry: *The man fumed over the insult for weeks.*

fun |fŭn| —*noun* Enjoyment; pleasure; amusement.
Idioms **in fun** As a joke; in jest: *We teased him only in fun.* **make fun of** To ridicule: *The other children make fun of the way he speaks.* **poke fun at** To ridicule: *Don't poke fun at her.*

func·tion |fŭngk′shən| —*noun, plural* **functions** **1.** The normal or proper activity of a person or thing; purpose; role: *A teacher's function is to educate.* **2.** Something that is related to or dependent upon something else: *Proper growth is a function of sound diet.* **3.** A formal social gathering or ceremony: *Her wedding was the social function of the year.*
—*verb* **functioned, functioning** To have or perform a function; serve; operate: *That column functions as a support. This typewriter functions poorly.*

fund |fŭnd| —*noun, plural* **funds** **1.** A sum of money raised or

ă	pat	ĕ	pet	î	fierce
ā	pay	ē	be	ŏ	pot
â	care	ĭ	pit	ō	go
ä	father	ī	pie	ô	paw, for
oi	oil	ŭ	cut	zh	vision
oo	book	û	fur	ə	ago, item,
oo	boot	th	the		pencil, atom,
yoo	abuse	th	thin		circus
ou	out	hw	which	ər	butter

set aside for a certain purpose: *a retirement fund.* **2. funds** Available money; ready cash: *Our club has no funds to buy new uniforms.* **3.** A source of supply; a stock: *He has an enormous fund of knowledge.*

fun·da·men·tal |fŭn′də **měn**′tl| —*adjective* Forming a foundation or basis; basic; primary: *Food and shelter are fundamental human needs.*
—*noun, plural* **fundamentals** A basic principle, fact, or skill: *A good writer must master the fundamentals of grammar, punctuation, and spelling.*

fu·ner·al |fyōō′nər əl| —*noun, plural* **funerals** The ceremonies held at the time of the burial of a dead person.

fun·gi |fŭn′jī′| A plural of the noun **fungus.**

fun·gus |fŭng′gəs| —*noun, plural* **fungi** or **funguses** One of a group of plants that have no flowers and leaves and no green coloring. Mushrooms, molds, and yeast are fungi.

fun·nel |fŭn′əl| —*noun, plural* **funnels** **1.** A utensil shaped like a cone or cup that narrows to a small, open tube at the bottom. A funnel is used to pour a liquid or other substance into a container with a small opening. **2.** The smokestack of a steamship or locomotive.

fun·nies |fŭn′ēz| —*plural noun* Comic strips.

fun·ny |fŭn′ē| —*adjective* **funnier, funniest** **1.** Causing laughter or amusement; humorous: *a funny clown; a funny show.* **2.** Strange; odd; curious: *"Pee Wee" is a very funny name for such a tall man.*

fur |fûr| —*noun, plural* **furs** **1.** The thick, soft hair that covers the body of some animals. Cats, rabbits, and foxes have fur. **2.** The skin and hair of such animals.
♦ *These sound alike* **fur, fir.**

fu·ri·ous |fyŏor′ē əs| —*adjective* **1.** Full of or showing extreme anger; raging: *He was furious over the theft of his car.* **2.** Violent; intense: *a furious battle; a furious speed.*

fur·nace |fûr′nĭs| —*noun, plural* **furnaces** An enclosed chamber in which fuel is burned to produce heat.

fur·nish |fûr′nĭsh| —*verb* **furnished, furnishing** **1.** To equip with furniture: *furnishing a new home.* **2.** To supply; give: *The church will furnish food, bats, and balls for our Sunday picnic.*

fur·nish·ings |fûr′nĭ shĭngz| —*plural noun* **1.** Furniture and other equipment for a home or office. **2.** Clothes and accessories: *men's furnishings.*

fur·ni·ture |fûr′nə chər| —*noun* The movable items used to make a home or office fit for living or working. Chairs, tables, and desks are pieces of furniture.

fur·row |fûr′ō| or |fŭr′ō| —*noun, plural* **furrows** **1.** A long, narrow cut or groove made in the ground by a plow or other tool. Farmers plow furrows and plant seeds in them. **2.** Any narrow groove; a deep line: *furrows in the old man's face.*

fur·ry |fûr′ē| —*adjective* **furrier, furriest** **1.** Made of or covered with fur: *a furry coat; a furry animal.* **2.** Resembling fur; thick, soft, and fluffy: *cloth with a furry nap.*

fur·ther |fûr′thər| —*adjective* A comparative of the adjective **far.** **1.** More distant: *You could not be further from the right idea.* **2.** Additional: *Keep tuned for further bulletins.*
—*adverb* A comparative of the adverb **far.** **1.** To a greater extent; more: *He was going to explore the matter further.* **2.** In

funnel
Above: Utensil
Below: Ship smokestack

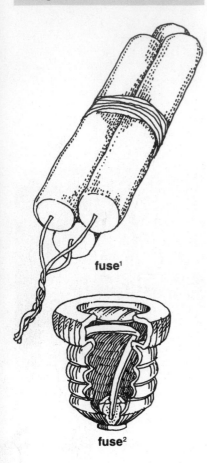

fuse¹, fuse²

Fuse¹ and fuse² both originated long ago in Latin, **fuse¹** meaning "spindle" and **fuse²** coming from a verb that meant "to pour, to melt." **Fuse¹** appeared in Italian before arriving in English.

fuse¹

fuse²

addition; furthermore; also: *We further see the importance of careful preparation for a game.* **3.** At or to a more distant point: *Her house is further from school than my house is.*
—*verb* **furthered, furthering** To help the progress of; to advance: *He furthered the careers of many young writers.*

fur·ther·more |fûr′ *th*ər môr′| or |fûr′ *th*ər môr′| —*adverb* Moreover; in addition: *We are not ready to leave now; furthermore, we want to finish our dinner first.*

fur·thest |fûr′ *th*ist| —*adjective* A superlative of the adjective **far.** Most distant: *the furthest corner of the earth.*
—*adverb* A superlative of the adverb **far. 1.** To the greatest extent or degree: *He went furthest toward finding an eventual solution.* **2.** At or to the most distant point: *Of all her sons Ronald traveled furthest from home.*

fu·ry |fyŏŏr′ē| —*noun, plural* **furies 1.** Violent anger; rage. **2.** Violent action; turbulence: *the blizzard's fury.*

fuse¹ |fyŏŏz| —*noun, plural* **fuses** A length of easily burned material used to set off an explosive charge. It is lighted at one end to carry a flame to and explode the charge at the other end.

fuse² |fyŏŏz| —*verb* **fused, fusing 1.** To soften by heating; melt: *High temperatures fuse gold. Rock in an active volcano often fuses.* **2.** To combine or unite by or as if by melting; to blend: *The photographer fused two images to make one picture.*
—*noun, plural* **fuses** A protective device in an electrical circuit. It contains a wire that melts and breaks the circuit when the current becomes too strong.

fu·se·lage |fyŏŏ′sə läzh′| or |fyŏŏ′zə läzh′| —*noun, plural* **fuselages** The body of an airplane, to which the wings and tail are attached.

fu·sion |fyŏŏ′zhən| —*noun, plural* **fusions 1.** The act or process of melting or combining different things into one. **2.** A mixture; blend; union: *An alloy is a fusion of several metals. The new ruling party in the country is a fusion of several political parties.*

fuss |fŭs| —*noun, plural* **fusses** A lot of bother over some little thing; unnecessary excitement; commotion: *In case of fire we should leave the building without noise or fuss.*
—*verb* **fussed, fussing** To get excited or concerned without a real need for it; make a fuss: *She fussed over the dinner.*

fuss·y |fŭs′ē| —*adjective* **fussier, fussiest 1.** Given to fussing; easily upset over small matters: *a fussy old lady.* **2.** Hard to please; demanding: *a fussy baby.*

fu·tile |fyŏŏt′l| or |fyŏŏ′tīl′| —*adjective* Having no useful result; ineffective: *futile efforts.*

fu·ture |fyŏŏ′chər| —*noun, plural* **futures 1.** The time that is yet to come: *We're making plans for the future. These science students are the doctors of the future.* **2.** Prospects; outlook; fate: *That company's future looks shaky.* **3.** The future tense.
—*adjective* Occurring in the future; coming: *some future date.*

future tense A verb tense used to express action in the future. It is formed in English with the help of the auxiliary verbs **shall** and **will:** *I shall be back tonight. They will leave in half an hour.*

fuzz |fŭz| —*noun* Soft, short fibers or hairs; fine down: *the fuzz on a peach.*

fuzz·y |fŭz′ē| —*adjective* **fuzzier, fuzziest 1.** Like or covered with fuzz: *fuzzy hair; a fuzzy peach.* **2.** Not clear; hazy or blurred: *a fuzzy snapshot.*

1   **Phoenician** — The letter G, like C, comes from a Phoenician symbol named *gimel*, meaning "camel," in use about 3,000 years ago.

‹   **Greek** — The Greeks borrowed the symbol from the Phoenicians and changed its form. They also changed its name to *gamma*.

G   **Roman** — The Romans took the letter and added a bar to distinguish it from *C*. This became the model for our modern capital *G*.

ꝿ   **Medieval** — The hand-written form of about 1,200 years ago became the basis of the modern small letter.

Gg   **Modern** — The modern capital and small letters are based on the Roman capital and later hand-written forms.

g or **G** |jē| —*noun, plural* **g's** or **G's** The seventh letter of the English alphabet.

ga·ble |gā′bəl| —*noun, plural* **gables** The triangular section of wall between the two slopes of a roof.

gadg·et |găj′ĭt| —*noun, plural* **gadgets** A small, unusual tool or mechanical device: *We bought a kitchen gadget for loosening stuck bottle tops.*

gag |găg| —*noun, plural* **gags** **1.** Something put into or over the mouth to keep a person from talking or crying out. **2.** A joke: *The comedian told a lot of gags.*
—*verb* **gagged, gagging** **1.** To put a gag on; stop up the mouth of: *The bank robbers tied up and gagged the guard.* **2.** To feel a tightening in the throat and stomach, as a person does before vomiting: *The bad-tasting medicine made me gag.*

gai·e·ty |gā′ĭ tē| —*noun, plural* **gaieties** The quality or condition of being gay; cheer; joy: *The gaiety of the festival made even the most solemn of the citizens smile and dance.*

gai·ly |gā′lē| —*adverb* **1.** In a cheerful manner; merrily; joyfully: *She danced gaily to the music.* **2.** In a bright or colorful manner: *a gaily decorated room.*

gain |gān| —*verb* **gained, gaining** **1.** To get possession of; obtain or win: *We've gained experience in hiking this summer. Sue gained the victory in the tennis match.* **2.** To increase: *She gained weight. The car gained speed.* **3.** To come nearer; get closer: *Our team is ahead, but they are gaining on us.*
—*noun, plural* **gains** **1.** Something obtained or won: *The quarterback ran for a gain of 20 yards. The winning card player counted up his gains.* **2.** An increase: *I showed a weight gain of five pounds in one week.*

gait |gāt| —*noun, plural* **gaits** A way of walking or running: *a slow gait; a clumsy gait.*
♦ *These sound alike* **gait, gate.**

gal·ax·y |găl′ək sē| —*noun, plural* **galaxies** A very large group of stars. Our Earth, the other planets, and the sun are in a galaxy called the Milky Way.

gale |gāl| —*noun, plural* **gales** **1.** A very strong wind: *The gale blew several trees down.* **2.** A noisy outburst: *We heard gales of laughter coming from the living room.*

gable

galaxy

gal·lant |găl′ənt| —*adjective* **1.** Brave and good; courageous: *a gallant knight; a gallant try.* **2.** Polite; courteous: *He greeted the lady with a gallant compliment.*

gall·blad·der |gôl′blăd′ər| —*noun, plural* **gallbladders** A small body part shaped like a bag that is found near the liver. The gallbladder stores bile.

gal·le·on |găl′ē ən| or |găl′yən| —*noun, plural* **galleons** A large sailing ship with three masts that was most often used during the sixteenth century. The Pilgrims' ship, the *Mayflower*, was a galleon.

gal·ler·y |găl′ə rē| or |găl′rē| —*noun, plural* **galleries** **1.** A room or building where works of art are shown. **2.** A narrow hall or corridor, especially one used for a certain purpose: *a shooting gallery.* **3.** The highest balcony of a theater, hall, or church.

gal·ley |găl′ē| —*noun, plural* **galleys** **1.** A low, long ship, driven by sails and oars, used until the seventeenth century. **2.** The kitchen of a ship or airplane.

gal·lon |găl′ən| —*noun, plural* **gallons** A unit of measure for liquids. A gallon equals four quarts or 3.785 liters.

gal·lop |găl′əp| —*noun, plural* **gallops** The fastest gait of an animal with four feet: *The horse broke into a gallop.*
—*verb* **galloped, galloping** To ride or run at a gallop: *The horse galloped over the pasture.*

gal·lows |găl′ōz| —*noun, plural* **gallowses** or **gallows** **1.** A frame from which criminals are hanged. The typical gallows is made up of two upright posts with a beam across them. A noose is tied to the beam. **2. the gallows** Execution by hanging.

ga·losh·es |gə lŏsh′ĭz| —*plural noun* Waterproof overshoes or boots that are worn in wet weather to protect a person's shoes.

gam·ble |găm′bəl| —*verb* **gambled, gambling** **1.** To play a game for money; bet: *He gambles on the horse races.* **2.** To take a chance: *The sign says that the bridge is safe for a car, but I wouldn't gamble on it.*

game |gām| —*noun, plural* **games** **1.** A way of playing or having fun; an amusement: *As a game, we tried not to step on any of the cracks in the sidewalk. The baby tossed his food around as if eating was just a game.* **2.** A contest with rules and a purpose or goal that each side tries to achieve: *a football game; a game of cards.* **3.** Wild animals, birds, or fish that are hunted for food or sport.
—*adjective* **gamer, gamest** **1.** Full of courage; brave; courageous: *He's a game boxer who'll never give up.* **2.** Ready; willing: *Are you game for a long walk?* **3.** Of or among animals hunted for sport or food: *The pheasant is a game bird.*

gan·der |găn′dər| —*noun, plural* **ganders** A male goose.

gang |găng| —*noun, plural* **gangs** A group of people who do things together regularly: *a gang of criminals; a gang of rough boys; a gang of workers repairing a road.*

gang·plank |găng′plăngk′| —*noun, plural* **gangplanks** A movable board used as a bridge for getting on and off a ship.

gang·ster |găng′stər| —*noun, plural* **gangsters** A member of a group of criminals.

gap |găp| —*noun, plural* **gaps** An opening, crack, or break: *a gap in the fence; a gap in the rocks.*

ga·rage |gə räzh′| or |gə räj′| —*noun, plural* **garages** A building where cars and trucks are repaired or parked.

galley

ă	pat	ē	pet	î	fierce
ā	pay	ē	be	ŏ	pot
â	care	ĭ	pit	ō	go
ä	father	ī	pie	ô	paw, for

oi	oil	ŭ	cut	zh	vision
ōō	book	û	fur	ə	ago, item,
ōō	boot	*th*	the		pencil, atom,
yōō	abuse	th	thin		circus
ou	out	hw	which	ər	butter

gar·bage |gär′bĭj| —*noun, plural* **garbages** Things like food scraps and wrappers that are thrown out from a kitchen.

gar·den |gär′dn| —*noun, plural* **gardens** A piece of land where flowers or vegetables are grown: *There were tulips, roses, and carnations in the garden. We planted tomatoes in our garden this year.* —*verb* **gardened, gardening** To take care of a garden: *We spent all day Saturday gardening.*

gar·den·er |gär′dn ər| —*noun, plural* **gardeners** A person who takes care of a garden.

gar·de·nia |gär dē′nyə| or |gär dē′nē ə| —*noun, plural* **gardenias** A flower with whitish petals and a very sweet fragrance.

gar·lic |gär′lĭk| —*noun* The bulb of a plant related to the onion. It has a strong taste and smell, and is divided into sections. Garlic is used in cooking to flavor foods.

gar·ment |gär′mənt| —*noun, plural* **garments** Any piece of clothing.

gar·nish |gär′nĭsh| —*verb* **garnished, garnishing** To decorate food with something colorful and tasty: *We garnished the iced tea with lemon slices and mint leaves.*

gar·ri·son |gär′ĭ sən| —*noun, plural* **garrisons** **1.** A fort or other place where troops are stationed. **2.** The troops who are living in a garrison.

gar·ter |gär′tər| —*noun, plural* **garters** An elastic band used for holding up stockings or socks.

garter snake A North American snake with lengthwise stripes. Garter snakes are not poisonous.

gas |găs| —*noun, plural* **gases** or **gasses** **1.** A form of matter that does not have a shape of its own and so fills and takes the shape of its container. Air is made up of gases. When some gases cool, they turn into liquids and then solids. **2.** A mixture of gases used as a fuel for cooking and heating. **3.** Gasoline: *We put ten gallons of gas in the car.*

gas·e·ous |găs′ē əs| or |găs′yəs| or |găsh′əs| —*adjective* Of or like gas: *Car engines give off both solid and gaseous exhaust products.*

gas·o·line |găs′ə lēn′| or |găs′ə lēn′| —*noun, plural* **gasolines** A liquid that burns easily and is used as a fuel to run cars, trucks, and other vehicles. Gasoline is made mostly from petroleum.

gasp |găsp| or |gäsp| —*verb* **gasped, gasping** To breathe in suddenly: *He gasped in amazement at the magician's tricks. She gasped for breath after running the fifty-yard dash.* —*noun, plural* **gasps** An act or noise of gasping: *With a gasp of admiration, she held the diamond in her hand.*

gas station A building where cars, trucks, and other vehicles are repaired or serviced.

gate |gāt| —*noun, plural* **gates** A part like a door in a wall or fence.

♦ *These sound alike* **gate, gait.**

gate·way |gāt′wā′| —*noun, plural* **gateways** An opening in a wall or fence that may be closed with a gate.

gath·er |găth′ər| —*verb* **gathered, gathering** **1.** To bring or come together: *Let's gather the dirty dishes and put them in the sink. A crowd gathered to watch the performance.* **2.** To collect from many sources; pick: *They were gathering flowers in the garden. The*

gardenia

garter snake

gazelle

gear

gem

Diamond *(left)* and diamond ring *(right)*

ă	pat	ĕ	pet	î	fierce
ā	pay	ē	be	ŏ	pot
â	care	ĭ	pit	ō	go
ä	father	ī	pie	ô	paw, for

oi	oil	ŭ	cut	zh	vision
ŏŏ	book	û	fur	ə	ago, item,
ōō	boot	th	the		pencil, atom,
yōō	abuse	th	thin		circus
ou	out	hw	which	ər	butter

reporter *gathered information about the contest.* **3.** To reach an opinion; conclude: *I gather you didn't get my telephone message.* **4.** To bring cloth together into small folds or pleats: *A pleated skirt is gathered at the waist.*

gath·er·ing | gă*th*′ər ĭng | —*noun, plural* **gatherings** A group of people; a meeting: *a family gathering.*

gau·dy | gô′dē | —*adjective* **gaudier, gaudiest** Cheap and too bright: *She wore a gaudy dress to the dance.*

gauge | gāj | —*noun, plural* **gauges** **1.** A standard length, quantity, or dimension; a measure. There are gauges for the distance between the rails on a railroad track, for the diameter of shotgun barrels, and for the thickness of wire. **2.** A measuring instrument: *A thermometer is a gauge for measuring degrees of heat.* —*verb* **gauged, gauging** **1.** To measure: *We gauged the air pressure in our bicycle tires with a special device.* **2.** To judge or evaluate: *It is too early to gauge the damage caused by the hurricane.*

gaunt | gônt | —*adjective* **gaunter, gauntest** Thin and bony: *The sick old man had a gaunt face.*

gauze | gôz | —*noun, plural* **gauzes** A thin, loosely woven cloth: *Let's use this gauze to bandage his cut.*

gave | gāv | The past tense of the verb **give:** *She gave him a new tennis racket.*

gay | gā | —*adjective* **gayer, gayest** **1.** Happy; cheerful: *I was in a gay mood when I found I had made the honor roll.* **2.** Bright or lively: *The room was decorated in gay colors.*

gaze | gāz | —*verb* **gazed, gazing** To look steadily; stare: *The mother gazed at her child with love.* —*noun, plural* **gazes** A long, steady look; a stare.

ga·zelle | gə zĕl′ | —*noun, plural* **gazelles** A horned animal of Asia and Africa. Gazelles have slender legs and can run very fast.

gear | gîr | —*noun, plural* **gears** **1.** A wheel with teeth around the edge that fit into the teeth of another wheel. Gears are used to send motion or power from one machine part to another. **2.** A group of connected machine parts: *the landing gear of an airplane.* **3.** Equipment needed for a special purpose: *fishing gear; camping gear.* —*verb* **geared, gearing** **1.** To provide with or connect with gears. **2.** To adjust or adapt: *The teachers gear their classes to fit the needs of their students.*

gear·shift | gîr′shĭft′ | —*noun, plural* **gearshifts** A device that connects a motor, as in a car, to any of a set of gears.

geck·o | gĕk′ō | —*noun, plural* **geckos** A lizard that has pads on its toes and can walk on walls and ceilings. Geckos live in warm regions.

geese | gēs | The plural of the noun **goose.**

Gei·ger counter | gī′gər | A device used to find and measure radioactivity.

gel·a·tin | jĕl′ə tən | —*noun, plural* **gelatins** A substance like jelly that is made from the skin, bones, and other parts of animals. Gelatin is used in glues, drugs, jellies, and desserts.

gem | jĕm | —*noun, plural* **gems** A precious stone that has been cut and polished to be used as a jewel: *a necklace made of diamonds, emeralds, and other precious gems.*

gem·stone | jĕm′stōn′ | —*noun, plural* **gemstones** A precious stone that may be used as a jewel when cut and polished.

gene | jēn | —*noun, plural* **genes** A tiny part of a plant or animal cell that determines a characteristic that will be passed on to the plant's or animal's offspring.

gen·er·al |jĕn′ər əl| —*adjective* **1.** Of or for everyone; for all: *a general meeting; a general strike.* **2.** By all or many; widespread: *general panic.*

—*noun, plural* **generals** A high-ranking army officer. There are several kinds of generals. The highest-ranking is a **general of the army,** followed by **general, lieutenant general, major general,** and **brigadier general.** All of these rank above a colonel.

gen·er·al·ly |jĕn′ər ə lē| —*adverb* **1.** Usually: *I generally take a walk before breakfast.* **2.** Commonly; widely: *That fact is not generally known.* **3.** In broad, general terms; not going into details: *Generally speaking, there are two ways to handle the problem.*

gen·er·ate |jĕn′ə rāt′| —*verb* **generated, generating** To bring about; produce: *Flowing water can be used to generate electric power. The foreign boy generated a lot of interest when he visited our class.*

gen·e·ra·tion |jĕn′ə rā′shən| —*noun, plural* **generations 1.** The act or process of generating: *the generation of electric power.* **2.** A group of people born around the same time, who usually grow up with similar ideas and customs: *The younger generation often has trouble understanding the older generation.* **3.** A period of about thirty years, or the time between the birth of parents and the birth of their children: *A generation ago we did things differently.*

gen·er·a·tor |jĕn′ə rā′tər| —*noun, plural* **generators** A machine that produces electricity: *The hospital had its own generator in case of a power failure.*

generator

gen·er·ous |jĕn′ər əs| —*adjective* **1.** Willing and happy to give to others; unselfish: *The little girl is generous and lets everyone play with her toys.* **2.** Large; ample; plentiful: *We have a generous supply of clothes for the winter.* **3.** Kind; tolerant: *a generous judge; a generous critic.*

ge·nie |jē′nē| —*noun, plural* **genies** A magical spirit in Arab folklore: *Aladdin rubbed the magic lamp and a genie appeared.*

gen·ius |jĕn′yəs| —*noun, plural* **geniuses 1.** The ability to think and create or invent in an outstanding way: *the genius of the scientist.* **2.** A person who has this ability: *A great scientist, writer, painter, or musician is a genius.* **3.** A strong natural talent or ability: *She has a genius for organization.*

Gen·tile or **gen·tile** |jĕn′tīl′| —*noun, plural* **Gentiles** or **gentiles** A person who is not a Jew.

—*adjective* Of the Gentiles; not Jewish.

gen·tle |jĕn′tl| —*adjective* **1.** Soft or mild; moderate: *a gentle breeze.* **2.** Light and tender; not forceful: *gentle hands; a gentle push; a gentle touch.* **3.** Kindly; considerate: *a gentle girl who seldom got angry. His gentle words soothed his grief.* **4.** Gradual; not steep or sudden: *gentle hills; a gentle descent to the ocean floor.*

gen·tle·man |jĕn′tl mən| —*noun, plural* **gen·tle·men** |jĕn′tl mən| **1.** A man who is polite, considerate, honorable, and kind. **2.** A man of high birth or social standing. **3.** Any man: *He's a nice old gentleman.*

gen·u·ine |jĕn′yōo ĭn| —*adjective* Not false; real; true: *a genuine antique; genuine leather; genuine concern.*

ge·o·graph·ic |jē′ə grăf′ĭk| —*adjective* A form of the word **geographical.**

ge·o·graph·i·cal | jē′ə **grăf′** ĭ kəl | —*adjective* Of or having to do with geography: *geographical boundaries; geographical names.* Another form of this word is **geographic.**

ge·og·ra·phy | jē ŏg′rə fē | —*noun, plural* **geographies** The study of the earth's surface and its use by human beings, plants, and animals. In geography you learn about the various countries, peoples, products, climates, and natural features and resources around the world.

ge·o·log·ic | jē′ə **lŏj′** ĭk | —*adjective* A form of the word **geological.**

ge·o·log·i·cal | jē′ə **lŏj′** ĭ kəl | —*adjective* Of or having to do with geology. Another form of this word is **geologic.**

ge·ol·o·gy | jē ŏl′ə jē | —*noun, plural* **geologies** The study of the origin and history of the earth. In geology you learn about the layers of soil, rock, and minerals that make up the earth's crust. You also learn how the earth's surface came to look as it does today.

ge·o·met·ric | jē′ə **mĕt′** rĭk | —*adjective* **1.** Of geometry: *a geometric problem.* **2.** Using straight lines, circles, or rectangles: *The rug had a geometric pattern.* Another form of this word is **geometrical.**

ge·o·met·ri·cal | jē′ə **mĕt′** rĭ kəl | —*adjective* A form of the word **geometric.**

ge·om·e·try | jē ŏm′ĭ trē | —*noun* A part of mathematics that deals with the measurement and comparison of lines, angles, points, planes, and surfaces and of plane figures and solids composed of combinations of them.

Geor·gia | jôr′jə | A state in the southeastern United States. The capital of Georgia is Atlanta.

ge·ra·ni·um | jĭ rā′nē əm | —*noun, plural* **geraniums 1.** A plant with rounded clusters of red, pink, or white flowers. Geraniums are often grown in flower pots. **2.** A related plant with pink or purplish flowers.

ger·bil | jûr′bĭl | —*noun, plural* **gerbils** A small animal with a long tail and long hind legs. It looks rather like a mouse. Gerbils are sometimes kept as pets.

germ | jûrm | —*noun, plural* **germs 1.** One of many kinds of tiny animals or plants that can cause disease. Germs are so small that they can be seen only with a microscope. **2.** Something in its earliest or beginning stage: *the germ of an idea.* **3.** The part of a seed of grain that can sprout into a new plant.

Ger·man | jûr′mən | —*noun, plural* **Germans 1.** A person who was born in or is a citizen of Germany. **2.** The Germanic language of Germany and some other European countries. —*adjective* Of Germany, the Germans, or their language.

Ger·man·ic | jər **măn′** ĭk | —*noun* A prehistoric language that is the ancestor of English, German, the Scandinavian languages, and several others. —*adjective* Of Germanic: *a language with Germanic roots.*

German shepherd A large dog with a blackish or brownish coat. German shepherds are often trained to help police workers or blind people.

Ger·ma·ny | jûr′mə nē | A country in central Europe, divided into East Germany and West Germany.

ges·ture | jĕs′chər | —*noun, plural* **gestures 1.** A movement of a body part, made to help express a feeling or idea: *She shook her*

Georgia

Georgia comes from the name of King George II of England. George II granted a royal charter to some settlers to start a colony in the region that is today the state of Georgia.

geranium

German shepherd

ă	pat	ĕ	pet	î	fierce
ā	pay	ē	be	ŏ	pot
â	care	ĭ	pit	ō	go
ä	father	ī	pie	ô	paw, for
oi	oil	ŭ	cut	zh	vision
ŏŏ	book	û	fur	ə	ago, item,
ōō	boot	*th*	the		pencil, atom,
yōō	abuse	th	thin		circus
ou	out	hw	which	ər	butter

head in a gesture of disgust. The police officer stopped traffic and made a beckoning gesture to the children. **2.** An act or show of courtesy, friendship, or respect: *It was a thoughtful gesture of our new neighbors to welcome us with fruit.*
—*verb* **gestured, gesturing** To make a gesture; to signal: *The usher gestured for us to follow him down the aisle.*

get | gĕt | —*verb* **got, got** or **gotten, getting** **1.** To receive; to gain: *Mary is hoping that she will get a bike for her birthday. My mother thought she would get first prize in the baking contest.* **2.** To become: *You are getting to be a pest. Jimmy is getting better at the piano.* **3.** To arrive; reach: *We got home late. We never got to the end of the book.* **4.** To obtain; acquire: *He is trying to get the money for a new car.* **5.** To have to: *I've got to go now.* **6.** To go after: *Please get my books.* **7.** To be allowed: *When will I get to see that movie?* **8.** To come down with a sickness: *I'm getting a cold.* **9.** To catch; capture: *We chased him until we got him.* **10.** To understand: *Do you get what I'm saying?* **11.** To make ready; prepare: *I'll get dinner tonight.* **12.** To move, bring, or take; send: *Get that cat out of the house!* **13.** To go; pass: *Let's get to the park before we play catch. I got through some hard times.*

  Phrasal verbs get across To make understood; make clear: *The math teacher got the new idea across with many examples.* **get along** To be on friendly terms with: *I get along with Nancy very well.* **get around** **1.** To go places; be active: *She really gets around.* **2.** To spread or travel: *Bad news gets around fast.* **get away** To escape: *He went fishing to get away from his worries.* **get away with** To succeed in doing something bad without being punished or found out. **get by** **1.** To manage somehow: *We don't have much money but we'll get by.* **2.** To pass: *Try to get by that slow car.* **get out of** To avoid: *He was trying to get out of his homework.* **get over** To recover from an illness: *He'll get over the measles.* **get through to** To make contact with: *We couldn't get through to you by phone.* **get through with** To be finished with: *When are you going to get through with the newspaper?* **get together** To meet: *Let's get together tonight.* **get up** **1.** To leave the bed: *At what time do you get up?* **2.** To rise from a sitting or lying position: *Please get up and give your seat to your grandmother.*

  Idiom get it To understand: *Tell me the joke again; I didn't get it.*

gey·ser | gī′ zər | —*noun, plural* **geysers** A natural hot spring that shoots steam and hot water into the air from time to time.

ghast·ly | găst′ lē | or | gäst′ lē | —*adjective* **ghastlier, ghastliest** **1.** Terrible; horrible; terrifying: *That scene in the movie was ghastly.* **2.** Very pale and sick: *She looked ghastly.*

ghost | gōst | —*noun, plural* **ghosts** The spirit of a dead person, supposed to appear to living persons.

ghost·ly | gōst′ lē | —*adjective* **ghostlier, ghostliest** Of or like a ghost: *Jean managed to look very ghostly by wearing a sheet and gliding through the darkened room.*

gi·ant | jī′ ənt | —*noun, plural* **giants** **1.** Someone or something that is very large, powerful, or important: *the three musical giants of the century. The company he works for is a giant in the field of electronics.* **2.** An imaginary creature like a huge man: *When the ground began to shake, Jack knew the giant was approaching.*
—*adjective* Very large; huge: *a giant shark.*

gib·bon | gĭb′ ən | —*noun, plural* **gibbons** An Asian ape with a

geyser

Gila monster

giraffe

slender body and long arms. Gibbons live in trees, and swing from branch to branch with their arms.

gid·dy |gĭd′ē| —*adjective* **giddier, giddiest** **1.** Dizzy; feeling the head spin: *She felt giddy when she got off the merry-go-round.* **2.** Playful; silly: *a giddy mood.*

gift |gĭft| —*noun, plural* **gifts** **1.** Something given; a present. **2.** A special talent or ability: *She had a gift for mathematics.*

gift·ed |gĭf′tĭd| —*adjective* Having a special ability or talent: *She is a gifted athlete. Jimmy is a gifted pianist.*

gi·gan·tic |jĭ găn′tĭk| —*adjective* Like a giant in size or power; huge: *Bears look gigantic when they rise up on their hind legs.*

gig·gle |gĭg′əl| —*verb* **giggled, giggling** To laugh in a silly way: *When Sally starts giggling in class, I have to giggle too.*
—*noun, plural* **giggles** A short, silly laugh: *I knew you were hiding in the closet because I heard a giggle. He had a fit of the giggles.*

Gi·la monster |hē′lə| A poisonous lizard of the southwestern United States. It has a thick body with black and pinkish markings.

gild |gĭld| —*verb* **gilded, gilding** To cover with a thin layer of gold: *The artist gilded the frame of the mirror.*
♦ *These sound alike* **gild, guild.**

gill |gĭl| —*noun, plural* **gills** A body part with which fish and many other water animals breathe.

gin |jĭn| —*noun, plural* **gins** A machine that separates the seeds from the fibers of cotton.

gin·ger |jĭn′jər| —*noun* A tropical plant root with a strong, sharp taste. Ginger is often powdered and used as a spice. It is also candied and made into preserves.

ginger ale A soft drink flavored with ginger.

gin·ger·bread |jĭn′jər brĕd′| —*noun, plural* **gingerbreads** A cake flavored with ginger and molasses.

ging·ham |gĭng′əm| —*noun, plural* **ginghams** A cotton fabric that usually has a pattern of stripes, checks, or plaids.

gi·raffe |jĭ răf′| or |jĭ räf′| —*noun, plural* **giraffes** A tall African animal with a very long neck and legs. It has a coat covered with brown blotches.

gird·er |gûr′dər| —*noun, plural* **girders** A large, long beam made of steel or wood that is used to support floors and frameworks of buildings, bridges, and other structures.

girl |gûrl| —*noun, plural* **girls** A female child who has not yet become a woman.

girl scout A member of the Girl Scouts.

Girl Scouts An organization for girls to help them develop good citizenship, good character, and outdoor skills.

give |gĭv| —*verb* **gave, given, giving** **1.** To make a present of: *We give gifts at Christmas. We gave a large amount of money to the church.* **2.** To hand over; convey or grant: *I gave the salt to Bob. England gave the American colonies their freedom after the Revolutionary War.* **3.** To deliver in exchange; pay: *What will you give me for the car?* **4.** To apply: *The school gives special attention to reading.* **5.** To supply; provide: *Vegetables give us vitamins and minerals.* **6.** To be a source of; cause: *He will not give you any more trouble, I assure you!* **7.** To permit; allow: *My job gives me no time to rest.* **8.** To name; indicate: *Give a starting time for the race.* **9.** To offer: *She gave a prayer of thanks.* **10.** To produce; yield: *Cows give milk.* **11.** To perform: *The girl gave a little dance step.*

ă	pat	ĕ	pet	î	fierce
ā	pay	ē	be	ŏ	pot
â	care	ĭ	pit	ō	go
ä	father	ī	pie	ô	paw, for

oi	oil	ŭ	cut	zh	vision
ŏŏ	book	û	fur	ə	ago, item,
ōō	boot	*th*	the		pencil, atom,
yōō	abuse	th	thin		circus
ou	out	hw	which	ər	butter

12. To break down; collapse: *The bridge gave under the pressure of the hurricane winds.*

   Phrasal verbs **give away** To reveal a secret, often by accident. **give in** To surrender. **give out** **1.** To make known; announce: *When can we give out the good news?* **2.** To distribute: *This charity gives out food to the needy.* **3.** To break down; fail: *The dryer finally gave out.* **4.** To run out: *Our savings gave out.* **give up** **1.** To admit defeat; surrender: *She tried very hard and never gave up.* **2.** To stop: *He gave up smoking.*

giv·en |gĭv′ən| The past participle of the verb **give:** *She had given her books to her sister.*
   —adjective **1.** Named; specified; stated: *You must obtain all the facts on a given country for your report.* **2.** Tending; inclined: *He is given to temper tantrums.*

gla·cial |glā′shəl| *—adjective* Of or having to do with glaciers.

gla·cier |glā′shər| *—noun, plural* **glaciers** A large mass of ice that is moving very slowly down a valley or the side of a mountain. Glaciers are formed by tightly packed snow.

glad |glăd| *—adjective* **gladder, gladdest** Pleased; happy: *The tired boy was glad to be home. I was glad to do it for her.*

glad·i·o·li |glăd′ē ō′lī| A plural of the noun **gladiolus.**

glad·i·o·lus |glăd′ē ō′ləs| *—noun, plural* **gladioli** or **gladioluses** A plant with large, colorful flowers that grow in a long cluster.

glance |glăns| or |gläns| *—verb* **glanced, glancing** To look quickly: *He glanced at his watch as he drove.*
   —noun, plural **glances** A quick look.

gland |glănd| *—noun, plural* **glands** An organ in the body that makes and releases a substance. Glands control the growth and functioning of the body. Glands make tears for crying, juices for digesting food, and cells for fighting germs when you are sick.

glare |glâr| *—verb* **glared, glaring** **1.** To stare angrily: *He glared at the man who had insulted him.* **2.** To shine brightly and unpleasantly: *Without a shade, that lamp glares down on the desk.*
   —noun, plural **glares** **1.** An angry stare. **2.** A strong and blinding light: *The glare from snow can blind a skier.*

glass |glăs| or |gläs| *—noun, plural* **glasses** **1.** A hard, clear material used for making window panes and containers. Glass is made of various kinds of melted sand. **2.** A container made of glass and used for drinking. **3. a.** A glass with something in it: *Please give me a glass of water.* **b.** The amount that a glass holds: *She drank two glasses of milk.* **4. glasses** A pair of lenses set into a frame and worn or held over the eyes to aid vision; eyeglasses.

glaze |glāz| *—noun, plural* **glazes** **1.** A thin, shiny coating: *the glaze on pottery.* **2.** A thin coating of ice.
   —verb **glazed, glazing** **1.** To put glass into: *The carpenter glazed all our windows.* **2.** To apply a glaze to: *She was learning to glaze pottery in her ceramics class.*

gleam |glēm| *—noun, plural* **gleams** **1.** A bright beam or flash of light: *A gleam of sunshine through the window threw light into the room.* **2.** A brief appearance; a trace: *A gleam of hope showed in David's eyes.*
   —verb **gleamed, gleaming** To shine brightly: *Snow-covered trees gleamed in the sun.*

glee |glē| *—noun, plural* **glees** Merriment; delight: *She laughed with glee when she found the hidden candy.*

glen |glĕn| *—noun, plural* **glens** A small valley.

glacier
In Alaska

gladiolus

glider

globe

glide | glīd | —*verb* **glided, gliding** **1.** To move smoothly and easily: *The skaters glided over the ice.* **2.** To happen or go by without notice: *The summer days glided by.* **3.** To come down slowly on air currents without a motor: *The plane glided the last few miles to the airport.*

glid·er | glī′dər | —*noun, plural* **gliders** A special airplane without an engine. It is towed into the air by a regular airplane, then allowed to come down slowly by itself on air currents.

glim·mer | glĭm′ər | —*noun, plural* **glimmers** **1.** A dim, flickering light: *The glimmer of flashlights through the woods told us the hunters were coming home.* **2.** A trace or glimpse: *A glimmer of fear showed in his eyes.*
—*verb* **glimmered, glimmering** To give off a dim, flickering light: *Candles glimmered on the cake.*

glimpse | glĭmps | —*noun, plural* **glimpses** A quick view or look: *We caught a glimpse of the house as we rode by.*
—*verb* **glimpsed, glimpsing** To get a quick view of: *She glimpsed the mouse as it ran behind the stove.*

glis·ten | glĭs′ən | —*verb* **glistened, glistening** To shine with reflected light: *Sunshine made the snow glisten.*

glit·ter | glĭt′ər | —*noun* **1.** A sparkling light: *The glitter of the moon on the newly fallen snow could be seen through the window.* **2.** Brightly colored or sparkling little bits of material used for decorating: *She had fun spreading the glitter on the wings of her butterfly costume.*
—*verb* **glittered, glittering** To sparkle brightly: *Frost glittered on the windowpane.*

gloat | glōt | —*verb* **gloated, gloating** To feel or show great selfish satisfaction; be proud of in a malicious way: *A good sport doesn't gloat over his victory.*

glob | glŏb | —*noun, plural* **globs** A small drop or lump: *a glob of butter.*

glob·al | glō′bəl | —*adjective* **1.** Having a round shape like a ball. **2.** Of or involving the whole world; worldwide: *Air pollution is of global importance. Global war was threatened.*

globe | glōb | —*noun, plural* **globes** **1.** Any object with a round shape; ball. **2.** A map of the world that is shaped like a ball. **3.** The earth.

gloom | glōōm | —*noun, plural* **glooms** **1.** Partial or total darkness: *The gloom of the rainy afternoon made us turn the lights on early.* **2.** Low spirits; sadness: *When his friend went away, he fell into gloom.*

gloom·y | glōō′mē | —*adjective* **gloomier, gloomiest** **1.** Dark, dismal, or dreary: *It's hard to feel happy on a gloomy winter day.* **2.** In low spirits; discouraged; sad: *Mary is gloomy about her future.*

glo·ri·fy | glôr′ə fī′ | or | glōr′ə fī′ | —*verb* **glorified, glorifying, glorifies** To give praise or glory to: *They glorified their queen with songs about her good deeds. The church members glorified God with prayers and hymns.*

glo·ri·ous | glôr′ē əs | or | glōr′ē əs | —*adjective* **1.** Having or deserving great praise or glory: *Their glorious deeds won them fame.* **2.** Magnificent: *The weather that day was glorious.*

glo·ry | glôr′ē | or | glōr′ē | —*noun, plural* **glories** **1.** Great honor or praise; fame: *The team's top player got all the glory for the victory.* **2.** Praise offered in worship: *Glory to God in the highest.* **3.** Great beauty; splendor: *The sun rose over the ocean in a scene of glory.*

—*verb* **gloried, glorying, glories** To be joyful or proud; rejoice: *The mother gloried in her daughter's achievements.*

gloss |glôs| or |glŏs| —*noun, plural* **glosses** A bright, smooth shine on a surface: *He polished the table until an even gloss appeared.*

glos·sa·ry |glô′sə rē| or |glŏs′ə rē| —*noun, plural* **glossaries** A list of hard or special words with explanations, usually found at the end of a book.

gloss·y |glô′sē| or |glŏs′ē| —*adjective* **glossier, glossiest** Having a smooth, bright surface; shiny: *glossy paper; a dog's glossy coat.*

glove |glŭv| —*noun, plural* **gloves** 1. A covering for the hand with a separate section for each finger and the thumb. 2. A padded covering worn to protect the hand in sports like baseball and boxing.

glove
Baseball glove

glow |glō| —*verb* **glowed, glowing** 1. To give off a steady light; shine: *The embers glowed in the fireplace. The clock's dial glowed in the dark.* 2. To have a warm, healthy color: *His cheeks glowed when he came in from outdoors.*
—*noun, plural* **glows** 1. A steady, usually soft light; shine: *the glow of the stars; the glow of the lamp.* 2. A brightness or warmth of color: *The glow of the gold coins caught her eye.* 3. A rosy, healthy color caused by emotion: *A glow spread over the child's face.*

glue |glōō| —*noun, plural* **glues** A thick liquid used to stick things together.
—*verb* **glued, gluing** 1. To stick together with glue: *Marie glued the pieces of paper together.* 2. To fix or hold tightly: *Steve glued his eyes to the television when his favorite program was on.*

glum |glŭm| —*adjective* **glummer, glummest** In low spirits; sad and silent; gloomy: *Don't look so glum; it can't rain forever!*

gnat |năt| —*noun, plural* **gnats** A biting insect that looks like a very small fly or mosquito.

gnaw |nô| —*verb* **gnawed, gnawing** 1. To bite or chew over and over: *The puppy gnawed the shoe.* 2. To make by gnawing: *Mice gnawed a hole in the grain sack.*

gnu |nōō| or |nyōō| —*noun, plural* **gnus** A large African antelope with a mane and curved horns.
♦ *These sound alike* **gnu, knew, new.**

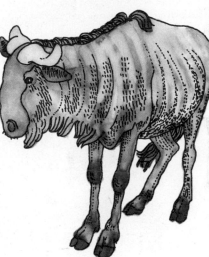
gnu

go |gō| —*verb* **went, gone, going** 1. To pass from one place to another; move along: *We're going to the store in the afternoon. I have to go to Washington tomorrow. She went shopping with her mother.* 2. To move from a place; move away; leave; depart: *We must go at once.* 3. To be free or move freely after being held: *She let the dog go.* 4. To run, work, or operate: *The car wouldn't go despite all his efforts.* 5. To make a certain sound: *The cannon went boom.* 6. To have a place; belong: *This book goes here.* 7.a. To stretch; reach or extend: *The drapes go from the ceiling to the floor.* b. To lead: *The highway goes west after Boston.* 8. To be given: *Mr. Lockwood's money went to his niece Helen. The award goes to Sue Ann.* 9. To serve; help: *It all goes to show he was right in the first place.* 10. To be suited; fit: *These colors go well with your furniture.* 11. To continue; proceed: *How does the rest of the story go?* 12. To pass by: *An hour goes quickly.* 13. To collapse or fail: *That wall looks just about ready to go. My eyes are going fast.* 14. To be sold: *This shirt goes for eight dollars.* 15. To be or

goat

gobble¹, gobble²

Gobble¹ comes from a word of the same meaning used in English as it was spoken from about 1100 to about 1500. **Gobble²** is a word formed in imitation of the sound it describes.

goblet

ă	pat	ě	pet	î	fierce
ā	pay	ē	be	ŏ	pot
â	care	ĭ	pit	ō	go
ä	father	ī	pie	ô	paw, for

oi	oil	ŭ	cut	zh	vision
ŏŏ	book	û	fur	ə	ago, item,
ōō	boot	th	the		pencil, atom,
yōō	abuse	th	thin		circus
ou	out	hw	which	ər	butter

become: *You will go hungry if you don't take enough food with you. Louise went blind after the fire. Jeff goes to sleep at nine o'clock. The tire went flat.* **16.** The verb **go** is used with the present participle of another verb to indicate the act of doing something: *Let's go swimming. She went shopping with her mother.* **17.** The verb **go** in the form **be going** followed by an infinitive indicates future: *I'm going to be a doctor when I grow up.*

Phrasal Verbs **go along with** To agree with: *I'll go along with you on that idea.* **go at** To work at very hard: *When he does get down to work, he goes at it.* **go away** To come to an end: *I wish this fever would go away.* **go back** To be traced back; date from: *The custom of shaking hands goes back to ancient times.* **go back on** To break a promise: *I could never go back on my word.* **go down** To be remembered: *She will go down as one of the great stars of our age.* **go in for** To take part in: *She never did go in for the beach.* **go off** **1.** To be fired; explode: *The pistol went off by accident.* **2.** To start ringing: *The alarm went off at six o'clock.* **3.** To happen: *Our party was very improvised, but everything went off fine.* **go on** To happen: *Read the newspaper and find out what's going on.* **go out** To go to parties or other places for entertainment: *My parents no longer get someone to stay with me when they go out.* **go through** To endure; undergo: *The survivors of the plane crash went through a terrible experience.* **go through with** To complete: *They decided to go through with the first wedding plans.*

goal | gōl | —*noun, plural* **goals** **1.** Something wanted and worked for; purpose; aim: *My goal in life is to be happy.* **2.** A place a person is trying to reach: *His goal was California.* **3.** The finish line of a race. **4.** A place in certain games to which a player must get the ball or puck in order to score. **5.** A point given for this: *three goals ahead.*

goat | gōt | —*noun, plural* **goats** An animal that has hoofs, horns, and a beard. Goats are raised in many parts of the world for their milk, meat, and wool.

goat·ee | gō tē′ | —*noun, plural* **goatees** A small beard that comes to a point just below a man's chin.

gob·ble¹ | gŏb′əl | —*verb* **gobbled, gobbling** To eat quickly without chewing.

gob·ble² | gŏb′əl | —*noun, plural* **gobbles** The sound made by a male turkey.
—*verb* **gobbled, gobbling** To make the sound that a turkey makes.

gob·let | gŏb′lĭt | —*noun, plural* **goblets** A drinking glass with a long, thin stem and a flat base.

god | gŏd | —*noun, plural* **gods** **1.** **God** A being thought of as having great power and always present everywhere, worshiped as the ruler of the universe. **2.** A being who is supposed to live forever and to be able to do things that people can't possibly do. Gods are worshiped and prayed to.

god·child | gŏd′chīld′ | —*noun, plural* **god·chil·dren** | gŏd′chĭl′drən | A child other than one's own for whom one acts as a witness at baptism. The religious training of a godchild becomes one of the responsibilities of the godfather and the godmother.

god·dess | gŏd′ĭs | —*noun, plural* **goddesses** A female god: *The ancient Greeks had many goddesses.*

god·fa·ther | gŏd′fä′thər | —*noun, plural* **godfathers** A man who

acts as a witness for a child at its baptism. A godfather promises
to supervise the child's religious training.

god·moth·er |gŏd′mŭ*th*′ər| —*noun, plural* **godmothers** A
woman who acts as a witness for a child at its baptism. A
godmother promises to supervise the child's religious training.

gold |gōld| —*noun, plural* **golds** 1. A soft, yellow precious
metal used to make ornaments, jewelry, and coins. Gold is one of
the chemical elements. 2. A bright yellow color. 3. Something
thought to have great value or goodness: *a heart of gold.* ◊ The
noun **gold** can be used like an adjective for things made of gold:
a gold ring; a gold coin.
—*adjective* Bright yellow.

gold·en |gōl′dən| —*adjective* 1. Made of gold: *golden earrings.*
2. Having the color of gold: *She had golden hair as a baby.*
3. Very valuable; precious: *We treasure our golden memories of
summer camp.* 4. Peaceful and prosperous: *a golden age.*

gold·en·rod |gōl′dən rŏd′| —*noun* A plant with branching
clusters of small yellow flowers. Goldenrod blooms in the late
summer and fall.

gold·finch |gōld′fĭnch′| —*noun, plural* **goldfinches** A small
North American bird that is mostly yellow. It has a black tail,
wings, and head patch.

gold·fish |gōld′fĭsh′| —*noun, plural* **goldfish** or **goldfishes** A
small fish that is usually golden-orange or reddish. Goldfish live
in fresh water. They are often kept in home aquariums.

golf |gŏlf| or |gôlf| —*noun* A game played with a small, hard
ball and long, thin clubs on a large outdoor course. A player tries
to hit the ball into each of a series of holes, using as few strokes
as possible.
—*verb* **golfed, golfing** To play golf.

gone |gôn| or |gŏn| The past participle of the verb **go**: *Johnny
had already gone to the movies when his brother called him.*

gong |gông| or |gŏng| —*noun, plural* **gongs** A circular plate of
metal that makes a deep, ringing sound when struck with a
hammer. Gongs are used for signaling and as musical instruments
in Asia.

good |gŏŏd| —*adjective* **better, best** 1. High in quality; not bad
or poor: *a good book; a good player; good food.* 2. Useful;
suitable: *a good wood for building ships.* 3. Helpful: *Earthworms
are good for our soil.* 4. Favorable: *good luck.* 5. Causing
pleasure; pleasant: *a good time. The soup smells good.* 6. Strong;
sound: *good health; a good reason.* 7. Doing what is right;
honorable; moral: *a good person.* 8. Well-behaved; obedient:
good children. 9. Proper; correct: *good manners; good grammar.*
10. Complete; full: *a good mile to the station; a good cry.*
—*noun* 1. Something that is good: *You must learn to accept the
bad with the good.* 2. Benefit; advantage: *He acted for the good of
the country.*
　　Idioms **a good deal** A lot; a big amount: *You learn a good deal
when you collect stamps.* **as good as** Nearly; almost: *This car is as
good as new.* **for good** Permanently; forever: *We broke up for
good.* **make good** To be successful: *He could never make good as
an athlete.* **no good** Useless: *It's no good arguing with him.*

good-by or **good-bye** |gŏŏd′bī′| —*interjection* A word said to
express good wishes when people are leaving one another: *She
turned and called out "Good-by!" as she walked off.*

goldenrod

goldfinch

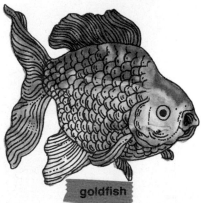

goldfish

—*noun, plural* **good-bys** or **good-byes** A farewell: *We kept our good-bys short.*

Good Friday A Christian holiday in memory of Christ's death on the Cross. Good Friday is the Friday before Easter.

good-na·tured |gŏod′ nā′ chərd| —*adjective* Having an easy manner; pleasant by nature; kindly; obliging: *Jerry is so good-natured that he'll pick up his sister's toys without complaining.*

good·ness |gŏod′ nĭs| —*noun, plural* **goodnesses** **1.** The quality of being good; excellence: *the goodness of fruit.* **2.** Kindness: *He's helping us out of sheer goodness.* —*interjection* A word used to show surprise: *My goodness!*

goods |gŏodz| —*plural noun* **1.** Things that can be bought and sold; wares: *These goods are not on sale.* **2.** Possessions; belongings: *household goods.* **3.** Cloth; fabric: *a store that sells imported goods for women's dresses.*

goo·ey |gŏo′ ē| —*adjective* **gooier, gooiest** Sticky: *a cake with gooey chocolate frosting.*

goose |gŏos| —*noun, plural* **geese** **1.** A water bird that has webbed feet and looks rather like a duck. Geese are usually larger than ducks and have a longer neck and a shorter bill. Some geese are raised for food. **2.** The meat of a goose. **3.** A silly person.

goose

go·pher |gō′ fər| —*noun, plural* **gophers** A small North American animal that has pouches like pockets in its cheeks. Gophers live in burrows that they dig in the ground.

gorge |gôrj| —*noun, plural* **gorges** A deep, narrow valley with high, rocky sides. —*verb* **gorged, gorging** To stuff with food: *The woodchuck gorges himself in summer and sleeps in winter.*

gor·geous |gôr′ jəs| —*adjective* Extremely beautiful; magnificent: *gorgeous jewels; a gorgeous wedding dress.*

go·ril·la |gə rĭl′ ə| —*noun, plural* **gorillas** An African ape with a broad, heavy body and dark hair. Gorillas are the largest and most powerful of the apes.

♦ *These sound alike* **gorilla, guerrilla.**

gos·pel |gŏs′ pəl| —*noun, plural* **gospels** **1.** The teachings of Christ and his Apostles. **2. Gospel** Any of the four stories of the life of Christ in the New Testament. **3.** Something that is never doubted or questioned: *He took his father's words as gospel.*

gos·sip |gŏs′ əp| —*noun, plural* **gossips** **1.** Stories and news, often not true, that people repeat; idle talk; rumors: *People say that Ann's parents won't let her marry Edward, but it's just gossip.* **2.** A person who likes to tell and hear such stories and news: *Jim and Harriet are the town gossips.* —*verb* **gossiped, gossiping** To exchange stories and rumors about people; spread gossip: *We gossiped all afternoon on the telephone.*

got |gŏt| The past tense and a past participle of the verb **get:** *She got a new car for her birthday. He had got tired of asking for an answer.*

got·ten |gŏt′ n| A past participle of the verb **get:** *It has gotten to be quite cold outside.*

gouge |gouj| —*noun, plural* **gouges** **1.** A metal tool with a rounded blade for cutting grooves in wood. **2.** A hole or groove dug in the ground. —*verb* **gouged, gouging** **1.** To cut or mark with a gouge or other sharp object: *Who gouged this desk top?* **2.** To remove with a sharp object; dig or pry out.

gopher

gorilla

ă	pat	ĕ	pet	î	fierce
ā	pay	ē	be	ŏ	pot
â	care	ĭ	pit	ō	go
ä	father	ī	pie	ô	paw, for

oi	oil	ŭ	cut	zh	vision
ŏŏ	book	û	fur	ə	ago, item,
ōō	boot	*th*	the		pencil, atom,
yōō	abuse	th	thin		circus
ou	out	hw	which	ər	butter

gourd |gôrd| or |gōrd| or |gŏord| —*noun, plural* **gourds** **1.** A fruit that is related to the pumpkin and squash. It has a hard rind and grows in many shapes. **2.** A bowl, ladle, or cup made from the rind of a gourd.

gov·ern |gŭv′ərn| —*verb* **governed, governing** **1.** To be in charge of a country, state, or city; rule; manage: *The king governed wisely. Congress and the President govern the nation.* **2.** To guide; determine; direct: *Food prices were governed by the size of the crops.*

gov·ern·ment |gŭv′ərn mənt| —*noun, plural* **governments** **1.** The act of governing; rule: *the government of a state.* **2.** A plan or system of governing: *Under democratic government, elected representatives make the decisions.* **3.** A group of people who govern: *She joined the government as a Presidential adviser.*

gov·er·nor |gŭv′ər nər| —*noun, plural* **governors** **1.** The person elected as the head of a state in the United States. **2.** A person placed in charge of a colony or an area of land. **3.** A device that controls the working or speed of a machine.

gown |goun| —*noun, plural* **gowns** **1.** A woman's long, usually formal dress. **2.** A long, outer robe for important ceremonies, worn by graduates, judges, and ministers.

grab |grăb| —*verb* **grabbed, grabbing** To take suddenly; seize; snatch: *The elephant grabbed the peanut out of her hand.* —*noun, plural* **grabs** An act of grabbing: *I made a grab at the tray of sandwiches as it passed.*

grace |grās| —*noun, plural* **graces** **1.** Beauty of movement or form without seeming to try hard: *The cat sprang up to the shelf with natural grace.* **2.** A pleasing quality; a charm: *His cheerfulness is one of his true graces.* **3.** Courtesy; polite manners. **4.** Favor; good will: *I tried to get in my parents' graces by cleaning my room well.* **5.** A short prayer of blessing or thanks before or after a meal. —*verb* **graced, gracing** **1.** To honor; favor: *She graced the meeting with her lovely presence.* **2.** To add beauty to; decorate: *Bowls of fruit and flowers graced the banquet table.*

grace·ful |grās′fəl| —*adjective* **1.** Smoothly beautiful: *a graceful dance.* **2.** Simple and pleasing: *a graceful apology.*

gra·cious |grā′shəs| —*adjective* Courteous and kind; well-mannered: *a gracious host.*

grack·le |grăk′əl| —*noun, plural* **grackles** An American blackbird with glossy blackish feathers and a long tail. Grackles have a harsh, husky voice.

grade |grād| —*noun, plural* **grades** **1.** A step on a scale of quality, value, or rank; level: *a poor grade of wood; the highest grade of beef.* **2.** A class or category: *Eggs are put into grades according to size.* **3.** A class or year in a school: *the fourth grade.* **4.** A mark showing how well a student has done: *He got a good grade in science.* **5.** The amount of slope in a road or other surface. —*verb* **graded, grading** **1.** To put into grades; class; sort: *The farmer graded the peas by size.* **2.** To give a mark to: *The teachers grade all the tests.*

grade school A school for young persons; elementary school.

grad·u·al |grăj′ōō əl| —*adjective* Happening slowly and steadily; little by little: *Jack pulled the bathtub's plug and watched the gradual lowering of the water level around his body.*

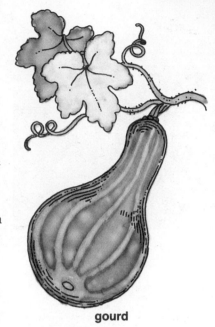

gourd

grackle

graduation

grad·u·ate | grăj′ o͞o āt′ | —*verb* **graduated, graduating 1.** To finish a course of study at a school or college and get a diploma: *He graduated from high school.* **2.** To give a diploma to: *The college graduated 100 students.* **3.** To mark with evenly spaced lines for measuring: *We graduated our paper rulers in exactly the same way as our real, wooden rulers.*
—*noun* | grăj′ o͞o ĭt | or | grăj′ o͞o āt′ |, *plural* **graduates** A person who has graduated from a school or college.

grad·u·a·tion | grăj′o͞o ā′shən | —*noun, plural* **graduations 1.** The act of graduating; completion of a course of study. **2.** A ceremony for giving out diplomas to graduating students: *Are your parents coming to your graduation?*

graft | grăft | or | gräft | —*verb* **grafted, grafting 1.** To join a plant shoot or bud to another plant so that the two grow together. **2.** To take body tissue and attach it to a different place in the body or to another person's body: *The surgeons grafted skin from the boy's leg onto the burned area of his face.*
—*noun, plural* **grafts 1.** A shoot or bud that has been grafted onto another plant. **2.** Body tissue that has been grafted by surgery onto a different place in the body or to another person's body: *The burned area was covered with a skin graft.*

grain | grān | —*noun, plural* **grains 1.** The seed or seeds of wheat, corn, rice, or other cereal plants: *a grain of wheat; flour made from grain.* **2.** A tiny particle of something: *a grain of salt; grains of sand.* **3.** Marks or lines that form a pattern or texture in wood and other substances.

gram | grăm | —*noun, plural* **grams** A unit of weight in the metric system. One gram equals .035 of an ounce.

gram·mar | grăm′ər | —*noun, plural* **grammars 1.** The study of how words are used in sentences so that their meaning is clear. **2.** A group of rules for using words in sentences. **3.** The use of words and word forms according to these rules: *Many English teachers think that "It's me" is bad grammar and "It's I" is good grammar.*

grammar school A school for young persons; an elementary school.

gram·mat·i·cal | grə măt′ĭ kəl | —*adjective* Of or following the rules of grammar. The sentence "I given friend me a candies" is not grammatical, but "I gave my friend some candy" is.

grand | grănd | —*adjective* **grander, grandest 1.** Very pleasing; wonderful; fine: *a grand time.* **2.** Very large and impressive: *The river is spanned by a grand bridge.* **3.** Magnificent; splendid: *a grand church ceremony.* **4.** Most important; main: *the grand prize; a grand ballroom.* **5.** Complete; final: *She was sick for two days and then three for a grand total of five.*

grand·child | grănd′chīld′ | or | grăn′chīld′ | —*noun, plural* **grand·chil·dren** | grănd′chĭl′drən | or | grăn′chĭl′drən | A child of a person's son or daughter.

grand·daugh·ter | grăn′dô′tər | —*noun, plural* **granddaughters** The daughter of a person's son or daughter.

grand·fa·ther | grănd′fä′thər | or | grăn′fä′thər | —*noun, plural* **grandfathers** The father of a person's mother or father.

grand jury A kind of jury that meets to study the facts of a case and decide whether someone should be officially accused of a crime and put on trial.

grand·moth·er | grănd′mŭth′ər | or | grăn′mŭth′ər | —*noun,* *plural* **grandmothers** The mother of a person's father or mother.

grand·par·ent | **grănd′**pâr′ənt | or | **grănd′**păr′ənt | —*noun, plural* **grandparents** A mother or father of a person's mother or father.

grand·son | **grănd′**sŭn′ | or | **grăn′**sŭn′ | —*noun, plural* **grandsons** The son of a person's son or daughter.

grand·stand | **grănd′**stănd′ | or | **grăn′**stănd′ | —*noun, plural* **grandstands** A seating area at a playing field or stadium. Grandstands are made of sloping rows of seats and are sometimes covered with a roof.

gran·ite | **grăn′**ĭt | —*noun, plural* **granites** A hard rock used in buildings and monuments.

grant | grănt | or | gränt | —*verb* **granted, granting** **1.** To give or allow: *She asked him to grant her favor. He will grant permission for them to travel.* **2.** To admit as true; agree: *I'll grant that he looks a lot better now.*
—*noun, plural* **grants** **1.** The act of granting. **2.** Something granted: *His grant of land from the government covers five acres.*

  Idiom **take for granted** **1.** To believe to be true without proof: *The teacher takes for granted that we complete our homework.* **2.** To accept without full appreciation: *We take for granted many of the wonders of electricity.*

grape | grāp | —*noun, plural* **grapes** A small, juicy fruit that grows in clusters on a vine. Grapes are eaten raw and are used to make wine, raisins, and jelly or jam.

grape·fruit | **grāp′**frōōt′ | —*noun, plural* **grapefruit** or **grapefruits** A large, round fruit with a yellow skin and a rather sour taste. The grapefruit is related to the orange and the lemon.

grape·vine | **grāp′**vīn′ | —*noun, plural* **grapevines** **1.** A vine on which grapes grow. **2.** An informal way of spreading gossip, rumor, or information: *We heard through the grapevine that he was getting married.*

graph | grăf | or | gräf | —*noun, plural* **graphs** A chart or drawing that shows the relationship between changing things. A bar graph shows quantities as thick lines of different lengths. A pie chart is a graph that shows parts of a whole as larger or smaller pieces of a pie.

grasp | grăsp | or | gräsp | —*verb* **grasped, grasping** **1.** To seize and hold firmly with the hands: *He grasped the fish by the tail.* **2.** To understand: *You fail to grasp the problem.*
—*noun, plural* **grasps** **1.** A firm hold or grip: *The pirate wriggled out of his grasp.* **2.** The ability to get hold of something; reach: *The victory seemed within the team's grasp.* **3.** Understanding; comprehension: *He has a thorough grasp of our problems.*

grass | grăs | or | gräs | —*noun, plural* **grasses** **1.** One of a large group of plants with narrow leaves. Grasses have jointed stems and clusters of small flowers. Some kinds of grass grow in lawns and pastures. Corn, wheat, rice, bamboo, and sugar cane are grasses. **2.** Ground covered with grass: *The park sign said "Keep off the grass."*

grass·hop·per | **grăs′**hŏp′ər | or | **gräs′**hŏp′ər | —*noun, plural* **grasshoppers** A large insect with two pairs of wings and long hind legs. Grasshoppers can jump long distances.

grass·land | **grăs′**lănd′ | or | **gräs′**lănd′ | —*noun, plural* **grasslands** Open land covered with grass. Meadows and prairies are grasslands.

grape
On a vine

grapefruit
Cut in half *(above)* and whole *(below)*

grasshopper

graveyard

ă	pat	ĕ	pet	î	fierce
ā	pay	ē	be	ŏ	pot
â	care	ĭ	pit	ō	go
ä	father	ī	pie	ô	paw, for
oi	oil	ŭ	cut	zh	vision
ŏŏ	book	û	fur	ə	ago, item,
ōō	boot	*th*	the		pencil, atom,
yōō	abuse	th	thin		circus
ou	out	hw	which	ər	butter

grass·y | grăs′ē | or | grä′sē | —*adjective* **grassier, grassiest** Of or covered with grass: *a grassy hillside.*

grate¹ | grāt | —*verb* **grated, grating 1.** To break into tiny pieces or shreds by rubbing or scraping against a rough surface: *Grate the nutmegs into a fine powder.* **2.** To make or cause to make a harsh grinding or scraping sound by rubbing: *The rusty old wagon grated and squeaked down the road. He grated the two rocks together.* **3.** To be harsh or irritating: *That sound grates on my nerves.*
♦ *These sound alike* **grate, great.**

grate² | grāt | —*noun, plural* **grates 1.** A frame of parallel bars or crossed wires over a window, sewer, or other opening. **2.** A framework of bars or wires used to hold the fuel in a furnace, fireplace, or stove.
♦ *These sound alike* **grate, great.**

grate·ful | grāt′fəl | —*adjective* Full of gratitude; showing appreciation; thankful: *The explorer was grateful to the Indian maiden for her help. She gave her doctor a grateful smile.*

grat·i·fy | grăt′ə fī′ | —*verb* **gratified, gratifying, gratifies** To give or be a source of pleasure to; please: *The results of the charity drive gratified us all.*

grat·ing¹ | grā′tĭng | —*adjective* **1.** Harsh or scraping in sound: *The chalk made a grating noise on the blackboard.* **2.** Not pleasant; irritating: *a grating personality.*

gra·ting² | grā′tĭng | —*noun, plural* **gratings** A frame of parallel bars or crossed wires set across an opening. Windows on the ground floor often have gratings to protect them.

grat·i·tude | grăt′ĭ tōōd′ | or | grăt′ĭ tyōōd′ | —*noun* The quality or a feeling of being grateful for some gift, favor, or kindness; appreciation.

grave¹ | grāv | —*noun, plural* **graves 1.** A hole dug in the ground in which a corpse is buried. **2.** Any place of burial; tomb: *The sea was the dead sailor's grave.*

grave² | grāv | —*adjective* **graver, gravest 1.** Extremely serious; important: *grave doubts; a grave responsibility.* **2.** Threatening life or safety; critical: *a grave illness; a grave error.* **3.** Solemn; dignified: *grave words; a grave expression on his face.*

grav·el | grăv′əl | —*noun* A loose mixture of pebbles or small pieces of rock, used to cover roads and paths.

grave·yard | grāv′yärd | —*noun, plural* **graveyards** A cemetery.

grav·i·ta·tion | grăv′ĭ tā′shən | —*noun* The force that makes all the objects in the universe tend to move toward one another; gravity. Gravitation keeps the planets from flying out of their orbits around the sun.

grav·i·ty | grăv′ĭ tē | —*noun, plural* **gravities 1.** The force by which the earth or another heavenly body pulls smaller objects on or near its surface toward its center. Gravity gives people and things weight. It is what makes a ball tossed in the air fall back to earth. **2.** Serious nature; importance: *It was then that we realized the gravity of our deed.*

gra·vy | grā′vē | —*noun, plural* **gravies** The juices that drip from cooking meat or a sauce made from these juices.

gray | grā | —*noun, plural* **grays** Any of the colors that can be made by mixing black and white in differing amounts.
—*adjective* **grayer, grayest** Of the color gray.

gray·ish | grā′ĭsh | —*adjective* Somewhat gray.

graze¹ | grāz | —*verb* **grazed, grazing** To feed on growing grass: *Cattle grazed lazily in the pasture.*

graze² | grāz | —*verb* **grazed, grazing** To touch or scrape lightly in passing: *The suitcase grazed her leg and tore her stocking.*

grease | grēs | —*noun, plural* **greases** **1.** Animal fat that is melted or soft. Grease is used in cooking. **2.** Thick oil or a similar substance. This kind of grease is put on the moving parts of machines to make them run more smoothly.
—*verb* **greased, greasing** To smear or put grease on: *Always grease a cake pan before using it. He greased the rusty bolts before trying to remove them.*

greas·y | grē′sē | or | grē′zē | —*adjective* **greasier, greasiest** **1.** Covered or soiled with grease: *greasy pots and pans.* **2.** Containing grease; oily: *greasy chicken soup.*

great | grāt | —*adjective* **greater, greatest** **1.** Very large; big: *a great, shaggy dog; great herds of animals.* **2.** More than usual; exceptional: *a great surprise; a great beauty.* **3.** Important; outstanding; famous: *a great work of art; a great man.* **4.** Exceptionally good; wonderful: *a great party; great news.*
—*noun, plural* **greats** An outstanding person or thing: *one of the greats of football.*
♦ *These sound alike* **great, grate.**

Great Britain A large island just off the coast of western Europe. It contains England, Scotland, and Wales.

Great Dane A large, strong dog with a short coat.

great·ly | grāt′lē | —*adverb* To a large degree; very much: *He will be missed greatly. Families vary greatly in size.*

Greece | grēs | A country in southeastern Europe.

greed | grēd | —*noun* A selfish desire to get more and more of something, especially money or food: *Greed made the farmer buy more land that he couldn't use.*

greed·y | grē′dē | —*adjective* **greedier, greediest** Wanting all one can get; filled with greed: *a man greedy for money and power.*

Greek | grēk | —*noun, plural* **Greeks** **1.** A person who was born in or is a citizen of Greece. **2.** Either the old or the modern language of the Greeks.
—*adjective* Of Greece, its people, or their language.

green | grēn | —*noun, plural* **greens** **1.** The color of most plant leaves and growing grass. **2.** **greens** The leaves and branches of green plants used for decoration; greenery: *Christmas greens.* **3.** **greens** Green leaves and stems of plants eaten as vegetables: *salad greens; turnip greens.* **4.** A grassy area or park in the center of a town: *the village green.* **5.** The area of smooth, short grass around a hole on a golf course.
—*adjective* **greener, greenest** **1.** Of the color green. **2.** Covered with grass, trees, or other plant growth: *green meadows.* **3.** Not ripe: *a green banana.* **4.** Without training; not experienced: *an army of green recruits.* **5.** Pale and looking sick: *He turned green with fear.*

green·er·y | grē′nə rē | —*noun* Green plants or leaves.

green·house | grēn′hous′ | —*noun, plural* **greenhouses** A room or building made of glass in which plants needing a warm, even temperature are grown.

green·ish | grē′nĭsh | —*adjective* Somewhat green.

greet | grēt | —*verb* **greeted, greeting** **1.** To welcome with a friendly or polite word or action: *The hostess greeted her guests.*

graze¹, graze²
Graze¹ is from an old English verb that came from the noun meaning "grass." **Graze²** is perhaps from **graze¹**, but this is not certain.

Great Dane

greenhouse

2. To meet or receive: *Our parents greeted the news with great joy.*

greet·ing | **grēt′ĭng** | —*noun, plural* **greetings 1.** An act or expression of welcome: *He nodded his head in greeting. We received a warm greeting by our host.* **2. greetings** A message of friendly wishes: *In her letter to me, she sends greetings to you.*

gre·nade | grə **nād′** | —*noun, plural* **grenades** A small bomb usually thrown by hand.

grew | grōō | The past tense of the verb **grow:** *Weeds grew wild in the garden.*

grey·hound | **grā′**hound′ | —*noun, plural* **greyhounds** A slender dog with long legs, a smooth coat, and a narrow head. Greyhounds can run very fast.

grid·dle | **grĭd′l** | —*noun, plural* **griddles** A flat, metal surface or pan for cooking pancakes, bacon, and other foods.

grief | grēf | —*noun, plural* **griefs** Great sadness over a loss or misfortune; deep sorrow: *We all felt grief over the death of our favorite aunt.*

grieve | grēv | —*verb* **grieved, grieving 1.** To feel grief; mourn: *She grieved for her dead child.* **2.** To cause to feel grief; distress: *The news grieved her deeply.*

grill | grĭl | —*noun, plural* **grills** A cooking utensil with parallel metal bars on which food is placed for broiling. —*verb* **grilled, grilling** To cook on a grill: *We grilled a steak.*

grim | grĭm | —*adjective* **grimmer, grimmest 1.** Harsh; forbidding; stern: *a man with a grim face.* **2.** Not giving up; firm: *a grim determination to win.* **3.** Ghastly; sinister: *grim jokes about death.*

grim·ace | **grĭm′**əs | or | grĭ **mās′** | —*noun, plural* **grimaces** A tightening and twisting of the face muscles. —*verb* **grimaced, grimacing** To make a grimace: *Father grimaced when he saw my report card.*

grime | grīm | —*noun* Heavy dirt covering or rubbed into a surface: *The hands of the workers were covered with grime.*

grin | grĭn | —*verb* **grinned, grinning** To smile broadly: *She grinned with delight.* —*noun, plural* **grins** A very broad, happy smile: *The grin on his face stretched from ear to ear when he heard the good news.*

grind | grīnd | —*verb* **ground, grinding 1.** To turn into very small pieces or powder by crushing, pounding, or rubbing: *a machine that grinds coffee beans.* **2.** To shape, sharpen, or make smooth by rubbing: *Grind new lenses for these eyeglasses. He grinds knife blades for a living.* **3.** To rub together noisily; grate: *He ground his teeth in anger.*

grind·stone | **grīnd′**stōn′ | —*noun, plural* **grindstones** A flat, stone wheel that spins on a rod set in a frame. It is used to grind, polish, and sharpen tools.

grip | grĭp | —*noun, plural* **grips 1.** The act, power, or manner of grasping; firm hold: *Get a good grip on the steering wheel. With age, his hands had lost their grip.* **2.** A part to be grasped and held; a handle: *a hammer with a metal grip.* **3.** Full hold; control: *She told him to keep a grip on his emotions.* —*verb* **gripped, gripping** To seize and hold on to; grasp firmly: *The child gripped his mother's hand when he saw the big dog.*

gris·tle | **grĭs′**əl | —*noun* Strands of tough white tissue in meat.

grit | grĭt | —*noun* **1.** Tiny, rough bits of sand or stone. **2.** Great spirit; courage: *It took a lot of grit to keep studying a subject that was so hard for her.*

grenade

greyhound

ă	pat	ĕ	pet	î	fierce
ā	pay	ē	be	ŏ	pot
â	care	ĭ	pit	ō	go
ä	father	ī	pie	ô	paw, for
oi	oil	ŭ	cut	zh	vision
ōō	book	û	fur	ə	ago, item,
ōō	boot	*th*	the		pencil, atom,
yōō	abuse	th	thin		circus
ou	out	hw	which	ər	butter

—*verb* **gritted, gritting** To clamp or grind together: *He gritted his teeth against the pain.*

grits |grĭts| —*plural noun.* Coarsely ground grain, especially corn.

griz·zled |grĭz′əld| —*adjective* Streaked or marked with gray: *a grizzled beard.*

grizzly bear A large grayish or brownish bear of western North America.

groan |grōn| —*verb* **groaned, groaning** To make a deep sound low in the throat showing pain, grief, or annoyance: *He groaned and groaned, but his pain wouldn't go away. The audience groaned at the clown's bad jokes.*
—*noun, plural* **groans** The deep, sad sound made in groaning; a moan: *the groans of wounded soldiers.*
♦ *These sound alike* **groan, grown.**

gro·cer |grō′sər| —*noun, plural* **grocers** A person who sells fresh food, canned goods, and household supplies.

gro·cer·y |grō′sə rē| —*noun, plural* **groceries 1.** A store that sells fresh food, canned goods, and household supplies.
2. groceries Things sold by a grocer.

groom |grōōm| or |grŏŏm| —*noun, plural* **grooms 1.** A person who takes care of horses. **2.** A bridegroom.
—*verb* **groomed, grooming 1.** To make neat: *He groomed his hair.*
2. To clean and brush horses.

groove |grōōv| —*noun, plural* **grooves 1.** A long, narrow cut or channel: *The heavy wheels of the wagon left deep grooves in the earth.* **2.** The track on a phonograph record that the needle follows.
—*verb* **grooved, grooving** To cut a groove in: *They groove the edge of a carving board so it will catch gravy.*

grope |grōp| —*verb* **groped, groping 1.** To feel about or search blindly or uncertainly: *He groped for the light switch. He groped for an answer to her question.* **2.** To feel one's way without seeing clearly: *The crying child groped his way to his room.*

gross |grōs| —*adjective* **grosser, grossest 1.** Without anything taken out; total: *His gross income is $10,000.* **2.** Extreme; obvious: *a gross error; a gross injustice.* **3.** Disgusting; coarse: *a gross remark.*
—*noun* **1.** *plural* **grosses** A total amount received: *The theater's gross for the evening was high.* **2.** *plural* **gross** Twelve dozen; a group of 144: *We ordered three gross of pencils.*

gro·tesque |grō tĕsk′| —*adjective* Distorted, odd, or unnatural; very ugly or strange: *a grotesque monster.*

grouch |grouch| —*noun, plural* **grouches** A person who is always cross and complaining.

ground¹ |ground| —*noun, plural* **grounds 1.** The solid part of the earth's surface; land; soil. **2.** Often **grounds** An area or plot of land set aside and used for a special purpose: *a burial ground.*
3. Often **grounds** The land around and belonging to a house or other building: *the school grounds; the grounds of an estate.*
4. Often **grounds** The reason for a belief, action, or thought; basis: *What grounds does she have to think that he was guilty?*
5. grounds The small pieces of solid material at the bottom of a liquid, especially coffee; sediment.
—*verb* **grounded, grounding 1.** To touch or cause to touch the bottom of a river, lake, or other body of water: *The schooner*

grizzly bear

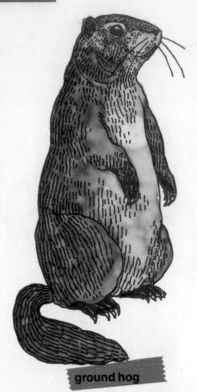

ground hog

grouse

grounded in shallow water. *We grounded our boat by accident.* **2.** To teach basic principles to; instruct: *She grounds her pupils in the rules of spelling.* **3.** To base; establish: *He grounded his argument on hard facts.* **4.** To connect an electric wire to the ground. **5.** To stop an airplane or pilot from flying. **6.** In baseball, to hit a ball so that it bounces on the ground.

ground² | ground | The past tense and past participle of the verb **grind:** *The mill ground the wheat for the farmer. The machine had ground the coffee beans.*

ground hog An animal, the woodchuck.

group | gro͞op | —*noun, plural* **groups** **1.** A number of persons or things together: *a group of men on a street corner; a group of islands off the coast of Alaska.* **2.** A number of persons or things classified or belonging together: *a children's group.*

—*verb* **grouped, grouping** To gather or arrange in a group or groups: *She grouped the chairs in a circle. We grouped on the steps of the library.*

grouse | grous | —*noun, plural* **grouse** A bird that has a plump body and brownish or grayish feathers. Grouse are often hunted for food.

grove | grōv | —*noun, plural* **groves** A group of trees with open ground between them.

grow | grō | —*verb* **grew, grown, growing** **1.** To become larger in size because of some natural process: *A wart grew on his finger. Our class studied how crystals grow.* **2.** To be produced: *Banana trees grow only in tropical countries.* **3.** To plant and raise; produce: *We grow vegetables in our garden. Many farms in this area grow tobacco.* **4.** To increase or spread: *The singer's fame grew until millions of people knew and loved him.* **5.** To become: *It grows dark early in winter.*

   Phrasal verb grow up To become an adult: *Tom wants to be a lawyer when he grows up.*

growl | groul | —*noun, plural* **growls** A low, deep sound such as the one made by an angry dog.

—*verb* **growled, growling** **1.** To make such a sound: *The dog growled every time someone came near him.* **2.** To speak in a gruff, angry way: *"You're not paying attention to the game," growled the coach.*

grown | grōn | The past participle of the verb **grow:** *The tree had grown to ten feet.*

—*adjective* Having reached adult age; mature: *He's a grown man now.*

♦ *These sound alike* **grown, groan.**

grown·up or **grown-up** | grōn′ŭp′ | —*noun, plural* **grownups** or **grown-ups** A fully grown person; an adult.

grown-up | grōn′ŭp′ | —*adjective* Adult; mature: *She's become a grown-up woman. That little girl behaves in a grown-up manner on the telephone.*

growth | grōth | —*noun, plural* **growths** **1.** The process of growing: *the growth of a child; the growth of the country's population.* **2.** Complete development; mature age: *The dog has reached full growth.* **3.** Something that grows or has grown: *A thick growth of weeds covered the yard.*

grub | grŭb | —*noun, plural* **grubs** A beetle after it has hatched from an egg and before it is a fully grown insect. It looks like a small, thick worm.

ă	pat	ĕ	pet	î	fierce
ā	pay	ē	be	ŏ	pot
â	care	ĭ	pit	ō	go
ä	father	ī	pie	ô	paw, for
oi	oil	ŭ	cut	zh	vision
o͝o	book	û	fur	ə	ago, item,
o͞o	boot	*th*	the		pencil, atom,
yo͞o	abuse	th	thin		circus
ou	out	hw	which	ər	butter

—*verb* **grubbed, grubbing** To dig in the ground: *The children grubbed for potatoes.*

grudge |grŭj| —*noun, plural* **grudges** Anger because of some old grievance; resentment felt a long time: *She held a grudge against her cousin and wouldn't let him forget it.*
—*verb* **grudged, grudging** To refuse to give or allow; deny something deserved: *Don't grudge him his enjoyment of his new car just because you don't have one.*

gru·el |grōō'əl| —*noun* A thin watery porridge.

gru·el·ing |grōō'ə lĭng| —*adjective* Exhausting: *a grueling race.*

grue·some |grōō'səm| —*adjective* Causing shock or horror; awful: *The scene of the accident was gruesome.*

gruff |grŭf| —*adjective* **gruffer, gruffest** 1. Having a harsh and deep sound: *The judge had a gruff voice.* 2. Not friendly; rough; impolite: *The old sailor had a gruff manner, but he was really very nice.*

grum·ble |grŭm'bəl| —*verb* **grumbled, grumbling** To complain in a low, discontented voice; mutter discontentedly: *The students grumbled about their weekend homework assignment.*

grump·y |grŭm'pē| —*adjective* **grumpier, grumpiest** Getting angry over little things; in a bad mood; irritable: *Martha is grumpy when she's very tired.*

grunt |grŭnt| —*noun, plural* **grunts** A short, deep, harsh sound: *The pig's grunts made the children laugh.*
—*verb* **grunted, grunting** 1. To make a short, deep, harsh sound: *The man grunted as he lifted the heavy box.* 2. To speak or say with such a sound: *My sleepy brother came in for breakfast and grunted a good morning to us.*

guar·an·tee |găr'ən tē| —*noun, plural* **guarantees** 1. A way of being sure of a certain result: *Buying a ticket ahead of time is a guarantee of a good seat at the play.* 2. A personal promise: *She gave her guarantee that the newspapers would be delivered that evening.* 3. A promise that a product made by someone will be repaired or replaced if anything goes wrong with it during a certain amount of time: *Dad's new car came with a two-year guarantee.*
—*verb* **guaranteed, guaranteeing** 1. To make certain: *Hard work and musical talent guaranteed her a place in the band.* 2. To promise: *Paul guaranteed that his homework would be finished by tomorrow.* 3. To give a guarantee for: *The company guarantees this watch for a year.*

guard |gärd| —*verb* **guarded, guarding** 1. To keep from harm; protect: *A soldier guarded the entrance to the palace. This cap will guard your eyes from the sun's glare.* 2. To watch over; keep from escaping: *They guarded the prisoner closely.* 3. To take precautions: *Guard against a head cold by keeping warm and dry in the rain.*
—*noun, plural* **guards** 1. A person or group that keeps watch or protects: *Mary is a guard at the bank. The palace guard stood in a line at attention.* 2. Protection; control: *The house is under guard by the police.* 3. Any device that protects or shields the user: *The bicycle had mud guards. White-colored oils are used by swimmers as guards against sunburn.* 4. Either of the two players on a football team's line next to the center. 5. Either of the two players on a basketball team stationed farthest from the opponents' basket.

guard
Above: A building guard
Below: A palace guard

guard·i·an |gär′dē ən| —*noun, plural* **guardians** 1. Someone or something that guards or protects: *An army is the guardian of a country.* 2. A person who is appointed by a court of law to look after someone who is too young, too old, or too sick to take care of himself: *When the boy's parents died, his aunt became his guardian.*

guer·ril·la |gə rĭl′ə| —*noun, plural* **guerrillas** A member of a small, loosely organized group of soldiers fighting to overthrow an established government. Guerrillas move and attack quickly. They try to disrupt their enemy and win the people over to their side.
♦ *These sound alike* **guerrilla, gorilla.**

guess |gĕs| —*verb* **guessed, guessing** 1. To form an opinion without enough information to be sure of it: *I can only guess at the size of this crowd.* 2. To form such an opinion and be right; choose correctly: *Susan guessed where the kitten was hiding. You guessed the answer to the riddle.* 3. To suppose; assume: *I guess he understood us because he nodded his head.*
—*noun, plural* **guesses** An opinion formed without enough information to be sure of it: *My guess is that the world will survive somehow.*

guest |gĕst| —*noun, plural* **guests** 1. Someone who goes to another person's home for a visit or a meal: *We cooked a special meal for our dinner guests.* 2. Someone who visits a hotel or restaurant: *The servant showed the guests to their room. The restaurant's guests were served their meal on the terrace.*

guid·ance |gīd′ns| —*noun* 1. The act of guiding or showing the way: *The expedition depended on the guidance of the Indian scouts.* 2. Help or advice; counsel: *It is often useful to receive guidance in choosing a career.* 3. Leadership; supervision: *The space flight was under the guidance of skillful experts.*

guide |gīd| —*noun, plural* **guides** 1. Someone or something that shows the way: *Our guide led us safely out of the woods. The recipe was his guide in making the cake.* 2. Someone whose job is to lead a tour or expedition: *Our guide in France spoke Italian, French, and English fluently.* 3. A book of information for travelers or tourists; a manual.
—*verb* **guided, guiding** 1. To show the way to; direct: *She guided her friend through the dance steps.* 2. To steer: *He guided his bike through the crowd.*

guided missile A missile whose course can be controlled while it is in flight.

guide·word |gīd′wûrd′| A word that appears at the top of a page in a dictionary. It tells you what the first or last word is on that page.

guild |gĭld| —*noun, plural* **guilds** 1. An association of people who share a trade, interest, or cause. 2. A union of merchants or craftsmen in the Middle Ages. Guilds set standards of workmanship and looked after the welfare of their members.
♦ *These sound alike* **guild, gild.**

guil·lo·tine |gĭl′ə tēn′| or |gē′ə tēn′| —*noun, plural* **guillotines** A machine for executing people by cutting off their heads. A guillotine is made of a heavy blade that slides up and down between two posts.

guilt |gĭlt| —*noun* 1. The fact of having done wrong; blame for a crime or offense: *The police believed that Sykes was a thief, but*

guided missile

ă	pat	ĕ	pet	î	fierce
ā	pay	ē	be	ŏ	pot
â	care	ĭ	pit	ō	go
ä	father	ī	pie	ô	paw, for
oi	oil	ŭ	cut	zh	vision
ŏŏ	book	û	fur	ə	ago, item,
ōō	boot	th	the		pencil, atom,
yōō	abuse	th	thin		circus
ou	out	hw	which	ər	butter

they couldn't prove his guilt. **2.** Painful awareness of having done something wrong; shame: *He felt a great deal of guilt for having quarreled with his friend.*

guilt·y |gĭl′tē| —*adjective* **guiltier, guiltiest 1.** Having committed a crime or offense: *He was found guilty of stealing.* **2.** Feeling shame: *She felt guilty after stealing the money.*

guin·ea pig |gĭn′ē| An animal with short ears, short legs, and a tail so short that it cannot be seen. Guinea pigs are related to squirrels, mice, and woodchucks. They are often kept as pets or used in scientific experiments.

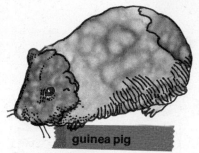

guinea pig

gui·tar |gĭ tär′| —*noun, plural* **guitars** A musical instrument having a long neck attached to a sound box shaped like a pear with a flat back. It usually has six strings, which are plucked with the fingers or a pick.

gulf |gŭlf| —*noun, plural* **gulfs 1.** A large area of ocean or sea that is partly enclosed by land. **2.** A large, deep hole. **3.** A big difference: *They talked about common experiences to bridge the gulf between them.*

gull |gŭl| —*noun, plural* **gulls** A bird with webbed feet, gray and white feathers, and long wings. Gulls live on or near coasts, lakes, and rivers.

guitar

gul·li·ble |gŭl′ə bəl| —*adjective* Easily tricked or fooled: *John is so gullible he'll believe anything.*

gul·ly |gŭl′ē| —*noun, plural* **gullies** A ditch cut in the earth by flowing water.

gulp |gŭlp| —*verb* **gulped, gulping 1.** To swallow quickly or greedily: *She was so hungry she gulped down her dinner.* **2.** To swallow air out of fear or from being nervous: *She gulped when she saw the figure that looked like a ghost approaching.*
—*noun, plural* **gulps** A large, quick swallow: *The giant swallowed the watermelon in one gulp. Lisa took a gulp of air before plunging into the pool.*

gum¹ |gŭm| —*noun, plural* **gums 1.** A thick, sticky juice produced by different trees and plants. One kind of gum is sticky only when it is moistened. It is used to coat envelope seals and the backs of stamps. Other gums are used to make candies and chemicals. **2.** Chewing gum.

gum² |gŭm| —*noun, plural* **gums** The firm flesh in the mouth that holds the teeth in place.

gum·drop |gŭm′drŏp| —*noun, plural* **gumdrops** A small jellied candy covered with sugar.

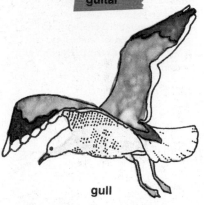

gull

gum¹, gum²
Gum¹ can be traced back to a very old Egyptian word. It traveled through Greek, Latin, and French before arriving in English. **Gum²** comes from an old English word that meant "jaw" or "roof of the mouth."

gun |gŭn| —*noun, plural* **guns 1.** A weapon that shoots bullets or other missiles through a metal tube. Pistols, rifles, and cannons are guns. **2.** Any device that shoots something out: *He painted the walls with a spray gun.*
—*verb* **gunned, gunning 1.** To shoot with a gun: *The space pilot gunned down the charging monster.* **2.** To direct one's efforts; aim: *Sheila is gunning for the class presidency.*

gun·fire |gŭn′fīr′| —*noun* The shooting of guns.

gun·pow·der |gŭn′pou′dər| —*noun, plural* **gunpowders** An explosive powder used to shoot bullets out of guns.

gun·shot |gŭn′shŏt′| —*noun, plural* **gunshots** A shot fired from a gun: *We heard a gunshot, and the race began.*

gup·py |gŭp′ē| —*noun, plural* **guppies** A small, brightly colored tropical fish. Guppies are often kept in home aquariums.

gur·gle |gûr′gəl| —*verb* **gurgled, gurgling 1.** To flow with a low, bubbling sound: *The milk gurgled out of the bottle.* **2.** To make low, bubbling sounds: *The baby gurgled whenever she saw her father.*

—*noun, plural* **gurgles** A low, bubbling sound.

gush | gŭsh | —*verb* **gushed, gushing** **1.** To flow or pour out all of a sudden and in great quantity: *Oil gushed out of the ground.* **2.** To show too much feeling or enthusiasm: *Grandmother gushed over the new baby.*

—*noun, plural* **gushes** A sudden or large flow: *The pipe burst open with a gush of hot water.*

gust | gŭst | —*noun, plural* **gusts** **1.** A sudden, strong breeze. **2.** A sudden outburst of feeling: *He exploded in a gust of laughter.*

gut | gŭt | —*noun, plural* **guts** **1.** The stomach or intestines. **2.** String made from certain animals' intestines. Gut is used in musical instruments and tennis rackets.

gut·ter | gŭt′ər | —*noun, plural* **gutters** **1.** A ditch along the side of a street for carrying off water: *The ball rolled off the sidewalk and into the gutter.* **2.** A pipe or trough along the edge of a roof for carrying off rain water.

guy¹ | gī | —*noun, plural* **guys** A rope or cord used to steady, hold, or guide something.

guy² | gī | —*noun, plural* **guys** A man or boy.

guz·zle | gŭz′əl | —*verb* **guzzled, guzzling** To drink rapidly or greedily: *The athlete guzzled water after his long run.*

gym | jĭm | —*noun, plural* **gyms** **1.** A room or building for gymnastics or sports; a gymnasium. **2.** A class in gymnastics and sports.

gym·na·si·um | jĭm nā′zē əm | —*noun, plural* **gymnasiums** A room or building made especially for gymnastics and indoor sports.

gym·nas·tics | jĭm năs′tĭks | —*noun* Exercises and physical feats done with the use of the bars, mats, and other equipment in a gymnasium. Gymnastics is an Olympic sport that calls for great skill and concentration.

Gyp·sy | jĭp′sē | —*noun, plural* **Gypsies** A member of a wandering group of people who came from India in the 14th and 15th centuries and now live everywhere.

—*adjective* Of the Gypsies: *a Gypsy caravan; Gypsy music.*

gypsy moth A small brownish moth. It has hairy caterpillars that feed on leaves. The caterpillars often do great damage to trees.

gy·ro·scope | jī′rə skōp′ | —*noun, plural* **gyroscopes** A wheel mounted on a vertical axis that can tilt at various angles to its base. When the base is tilted, the gyroscope's axis tends to tilt the opposite way. Large gyroscopes are used to keep ships and airplanes steady. Small ones make interesting toys.

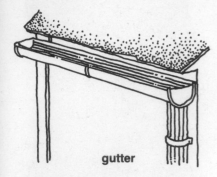

gutter

guy¹, guy²

Guy¹ is thought to have come from a Dutch word meaning "rope used in sail rigging." **Guy²** comes from the first name of an Englishman who long ago led a plot to blow up the king of England. The meaning of **guy²**, "man," developed after the word was borrowed into English as it is spoken in America.

ă	pat	ĕ	pet	î	fierce
ā	pay	ē	be	ŏ	pot
â	care	ĭ	pit	ō	go
ä	father	ī	pie	ô	paw, for

oi	oil	ŭ	cut	zh	vision
ōō	book	û	fur	ə	ago, item,
ōō	boot	th	the		pencil, atom,
yōō	abuse	th	thin		circus
ou	out	hw	which	ər	butter

⊟	**Phoenician** — The letter *H* comes originally from a Phoenician symbol named *hêth*, standing for an *h* sound.
H	**Greek** — The Greeks borrowed the symbol from the Phoenicians and changed its form. They also changed its name to *ēta*.
H	**Roman** — The Romans took the letter and adapted it for carving into stone. This became the model for our modern printed capital *H*.
h	**Medieval** — The hand-written form of about 1,200 years ago became the basis of the modern small letter.
Hh	**Modern** — The modern capital and small letters are based on the Roman capital and later hand-written forms.

Hh

h or **H** |āch| —*noun, plural* **h's** or **H's** The eighth letter of the English alphabet.

ha |hä| —*interjection* A word used to express laughter, surprise, or triumph: *Ha! I found the answer at last!*

hab·it |hăb'ĭt| —*noun, plural* **habits** 1. An action done so often that one does it without thinking: *He has a habit of scratching his ear when he's thinking.* 2. A person's usual practice or custom: *It was my habit to walk to work every day.* 3. The condition of being addicted to; dependence: *a drug habit.* 4. Clothing worn for a special activity or by a particular profession: *riding habit; a nun's habit.*

hab·i·tat |hăb'ĭ tăt'| —*noun, plural* **habitats** The place or kind of place where an animal or plant usually lives or grows: *The ocean is the habitat of whales.*

ha·bit·u·al |hə bĭch'ōo əl| —*adjective* 1. Being a habit; done over and over again: *habitual lying.* 2. By habit; continual: *a habitual smoker.* 3. Done or used regularly; customary; usual: *John wasn't in his habitual place this morning.*

hack |hăk| —*verb* **hacked, hacking** 1. To cut with heavy blows; chop roughly: *Using a cleaver, the butcher hacked the beef into pieces. We had to hack our way through the dense underbrush.* 2. To cough harshly.

had |hăd| The past tense and past participle of the verb **have:** *She had a bad dream last night. She has had several jobs since June.*

had·dock |hăd'ək| —*noun, plural* **haddock** or **haddocks** An ocean fish related to the cod. It is often used as food.

had·n't |hăd'nt| A contraction of "had not."

hag |hăg| —*noun, plural* **hags** 1. An ugly, mean old woman. 2. A witch.

hail¹ |hāl| —*noun* 1. Small, rounded pieces of ice that fall to earth, usually during thunderstorms. 2. Something like hail in force or quantity: *a hail of acorns from the tree.*
—*verb* **hailed, hailing** 1. To fall as hail: *It hailed during the rainstorm.* 2. To pour down or forth like hail: *Sheila hailed blows upon the locked door.*
♦ *These sound alike* **hail, hale.**

hail² |hāl| —*verb* **hailed, hailing** 1. To call to in greeting or welcome: *He hailed his friend across the street.* 2. To attract the

habit
Above: Riding habit
Below: Nun's habit

hail¹, hail²
Both words spelled **hail** appeared long ago in English. **Hail¹** has always meant the same thing. **Hail²** originally meant "Be healthy!" It can be traced back to the language spoken long ago by people living in Scandinavia, where it meant "healthy."

attention of; signal to: *She waved her arm to hail a passing cab.*

Phrasal verb **hail from** To come or originate from: *We hail from Ohio.*

♦ *These sound alike* **hail, hale.**

hair |hâr| —*noun, plural* **hairs** **1.** One of the thin, fine strands that grow from the skin of animals and human beings. **2.** A mass or covering of these strands: *Liza has red hair. A camel has soft, thick hair.* **3.** A growth like a hair on a plant or insect.

♦ *These sound alike* **hair, hare.**

hair·cut |hâr′kŭt′| —*noun, plural* **haircuts** An act or style of cutting a person's hair.

hair·less |hâr′lĭs| —*adjective* Without hair; bald.

hair·y |hâr′ē| —*adjective* **hairier, hairiest** Covered with hair: *Gorillas are hairy animals.*

hale |hāl| —*adjective* **haler, halest** Healthy; robust: *My grandmother is 86 and still hale and hearty.*

♦ *These sound alike* **hale, hail.**

half |hăf| or |häf| —*noun, plural* **halves** **1.** Either of two equal parts into which a thing can be divided: *Do you want half of my dessert?* **2.** Either of two time periods that make up a game: *The football game was in its second half.*

—*adjective* **1.** Being a half: *a half hour.* **2.** Being so in part only; incomplete: *a half truth.* **3.** Related through one parent only: *He is my half brother.*

—*adverb* **1.** To the extent of one half: *The gas tank is half empty.* **2.** Not completely or fully; partly: *I was half asleep.*

Idioms **go halves** To share the expense of equally: *Want to go halves on a pizza?* **in half** Into halves: *Cut the apple in half.*

half·heart·ed |hăf′här′tĭd| or |häf′här′tĭd| —*adjective* Showing little enthusiasm; not really trying or caring: *Joe pulled the spread over the sheets in a halfhearted attempt to make his bed.*

half-mast |hăf′măst′| or |häf′măst′| —*noun* The position of a flag when it is about halfway up a mast or pole. Flags are flown at half-mast to honor someone who has just died.

half·way |hăf′wā′| or |häf′wā′| —*adjective* **1.** Midway between two points; in the middle: *The town is halfway between New York and Boston.* **2.** Incomplete; partial: *Don't be satisfied with halfway measures.*

—*adverb* |hăf′wā′| or |häf′wā′| **1.** To or at half the distance: *I'll meet you halfway between your house and mine.* **2.** Partly; somewhat: *I'm halfway inclined to go with you.*

hal·i·but |hăl′ə bət| or |hŏl′ə bət| —*noun, plural* **halibut** or **halibuts** A very large ocean flatfish. It is often used as food.

Hal·i·fax |hăl′ə făks′| The capital of Nova Scotia.

hall |hôl| —*noun, plural* **halls** **1.** A passageway in a house, hotel, or other building; corridor: *Our classroom is on the right at the end of the hall.* **2.** A large entrance room in a building; a lobby. **3.** A large building or room for public gatherings: *a concert hall; a dining hall.*

♦ *These sound alike* **hall, haul.**

Hal·low·een |hăl′ō ēn′| or |hŏl′ō ēn′| —*noun, plural* **Halloweens** October 31. Children often celebrate Halloween by dressing up in strange costumes and begging for treats.

hall·way |hôl′wā′| —*noun, plural* **hallways** **1.** A hall or corridor in a building; passageway. **2.** A room at the entrance of a building or home: *Leave your raincoat and umbrella in the hallway.*

ă	pat	ĕ	pet	î	fierce
ā	pay	ē	be	ŏ	pot
â	care	ĭ	pit	ō	go
ä	father	ī	pie	ô	paw, for
oi	oil	ŭ	cut	zh	vision
ōō	book	û	fur	ə	ago, item,
ōō	boot	th	the		pencil, atom,
yōō	abuse	th	thin		circus
ou	out	hw	which	ər	butter

halo |hā′lō| —*noun, plural* **halos** **1.** A ring of light or bright haze surrounding the sun, moon, or other shining object. **2.** A ring of light drawn around or above the head of a saint or angel in a religious painting.

halt |hôlt| —*noun, plural* **halts** A stop; a pause: *Traffic came to a halt at the red light.*
—*verb* **halted, halting** To come or bring to a stop: *The police officer attempted to halt traffic. On command the policeman's horse halted.*

hal·ter |hôl′tər| —*noun, plural* **halters** A set of ropes or straps for leading or tying an animal. A halter fits around an animal's nose and its neck just behind the ears.

halve |hăv| or |häv| —*verb* **halved, halving** **1.** To divide into two equal portions: *We halved the cupcake.* **2.** To reduce by half: *During its big sale the clothing store is halving prices.*
♦ *These sound alike* **halve, have.**

halves |hăvz| or |hävz| The plural of the noun **half.**

ham |hăm| —*noun, plural* **hams** **1.** The thigh of the hind leg of a hog or other animal. **2.** The meat from the thigh of a hog, often smoked or cured.

ham·burg·er |hăm′bûr′gər| —*noun, plural* **hamburgers** **1.** Ground beef. **2.** A round, flat portion of ground beef, usually fried or broiled and served in a roll or bun.

ham·let |hăm′lĭt| —*noun, plural* **hamlets** A small village.

ham·mer |hăm′ər| —*noun, plural* **hammers** **1.** A hand tool made of an iron head attached to a wooden handle. A hammer is used chiefly for driving in nails and for shaping metals. **2.** The part of a gun that strikes the firing pin, causing the gun to go off.
—*verb* **hammered, hammering** **1.** To pound or drive in with a hammer: *hammer a nail.* **2.** To shape or flatten with a hammer: *hammer designs in a brass tray.* **3.** To strike or pound with repeated blows: *He hammered on the door to awaken the family.*

ham·mock |hăm′ək| —*noun, plural* **hammocks** A swinging bed made of rope or strong fabric and hung in the air between two supports.

ham·per¹ |hăm′pər| —*verb* **hampered, hampering** To get in the way of; impede; block: *Heavy fog hampered efforts to find the lost hikers.*

ham·per² |hăm′pər| —*noun, plural* **hampers** A large basket or similar container for holding laundry or carrying food: *a hamper full of dirty clothes; a picnic hamper.*

ham·ster |hăm′stər| —*noun, plural* **hamsters** A small animal with soft fur, large cheek pouches, and a short tail. Hamsters are often kept as pets. They are also used in scientific experiments.

hand |hănd| —*noun, plural* **hands** **1.** The part of the arm below the wrist. Each hand has a palm, four fingers, and a thumb. **2.** A pointer that moves around a circular dial, as on a clock or gauge. **3.** A style of handwriting: *She writes a fine hand.* **4.** Physical assistance; help: *Give me a hand with this box.* **5.** Often **hands** Possession; control: *The criminal is now in the hands of the police.* **6.** A person who does manual labor: *a farm hand; a hired hand.* **7.** A round of applause: *Give the little girl a great big hand.* **8.** An active part in something; a role or share: *All students had a hand in organizing the picnic.* **9. a.** The cards dealt to a player in a card game. **b.** One round of a card game. **10.** A unit of length equal to four inches. It is used to indicate the height of a horse.

halo
On an embroidered picture of a saint

halter

hamster

hamper¹, hamper²
Hamper¹ first appeared in the fourteenth century; its origin is unknown. **Hamper²** is from a French word meaning "a kind of wicker basket."

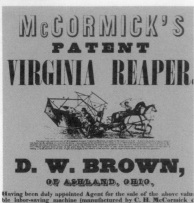

handbill
An advertisement for farm
equipment, 1850

handicraft
Baskets made by hand

handiwork
An embroidered cloth

ă	pat	ĕ	pet	î	fierce
ā	pay	ē	be	ŏ	pot
â	care	ĭ	pit	ō	go
ä	father	ī	pie	ô	paw, for
oi	oil	ŭ	cut	zh	vision
ŏŏ	book	û	fur	ə	ago, item,
ōō	boot	*th*	the		pencil, atom,
yōō	abuse	th	thin		circus
ou	out	hw	which	ər	butter

—*verb* **handed, handing** To give or pass with the hand: *Hand me the flashlight.*

  Phrasal verbs **hand down** To pass along; transmit: *Folk tales and songs are handed down from generation to generation.* **hand in** To turn in; submit: *Did you hand in your homework assignment?* **hand over** To give possession of; deliver up: *Hand over the money.*

  Idioms **at hand** Close by; near: *Keep an eraser at hand when you do math problems.* **by hand** By using one's hands: *The dresses were sewn by hand.* **hand it to** To give credit to: *You've got to hand it to him for sheer determination.* **on hand** Ready when needed; available: *We keep extra food on hand for surprise guests.* **on the other hand** In spite of this; nevertheless: *I hate spinach, but on the other hand, maybe it's good for me.*

hand·bag | hănd′băg′ | —*noun, plural* **handbags** A woman's pocketbook carried in the hand or on the arm.

hand·ball | hănd′bôl′ | —*noun, plural* **handballs** **1.** A game played by two or four players, in which a ball is hit against a wall with the hand. **2.** The small, hard, rubber ball used in this game.

hand·bill | hănd′bĭl′ | —*noun, plural* **handbills** A sheet of paper, usually containing advertising and distributed by hand: *The handbill announced the opening of a new drugstore.*

hand·book | hănd′bŏŏk′ | —*noun, plural* **handbooks** A small book of instructions or information on a particular subject: *the Boy Scout handbook.*

hand·cuff | hănd′kŭf′ | —*noun, plural* **handcuffs** One of a pair of sturdy metal rings held together by a chain. Handcuffs are fastened around the wrists of a prisoner to keep him from using his hands.

  —*verb* **handcuffed, handcuffing** To put handcuffs on: *The sheriff handcuffed the prisoner.*

hand·ful | hănd′fŏŏl′ | —*noun, plural* **handfuls** **1.** An amount that can be held in the hand: *a handful of peanuts.* **2.** A small number: *Only a handful of people came to the game.*

hand·i·cap | hăn′dē kăp′ | —*noun, plural* **handicaps** **1.** A defect of the mind or body: *He's confined to a hospital bed because of his handicap.* **2.** A disadvantage; hindrance: *Lack of experience can be a handicap in getting a job.*

  —*verb* **handicapped, handicapping** To put at a disadvantage; hinder or impede: *A heavy pack will handicap you during a long hike.*

hand·i·capped | hăn′dē kăpt′ | —*adjective* Disabled or crippled: *Handicapped workers are known to be dependable.*

  —*noun* **the handicapped** Handicapped persons in general: *funds to aid the handicapped.*

hand·i·craft | hăn′dē krăft′ | or | hăn′dē kräft′ | —*noun, plural* **handicrafts** A trade, craft, or occupation requiring skilled use of the hands. Weaving and pottery are handicrafts.

hand·i·work | hăn′dē wûrk′ | —*noun, plural* **handiworks** **1.** Work performed by hand: *The quilt is her grandmother's handiwork.* **2.** The result of a person's efforts: *This messy kitchen looks like your handiwork.*

hand·ker·chief | hăng′kər chĭf′ | or | hăng′kər chēf′ | —*noun, plural* **handkerchiefs** A small square of cloth used to wipe the nose or face.

han·dle | hăn′dl | —*noun, plural* **handles** The part of a tool, door, or container that is made to be held by the hand.

  —*verb* **handled, handling** **1.** To touch or hold with the hands:

Please do not handle the tomatoes. **2.** To use with the hands: *Can you handle this large saw?* **3.** To be capable of being operated: *The new car handled easily.* **4.** To deal in; buy and sell: *Does the store handle this brand of soap?* **5.** To deal with; cope with: *How do you handle him when he behaves this way?*

han·dle·bar |**hăn′**dl bär′| —*noun, plural* **handlebars** A curved metal bar for steering a bicycle or motorcycle.

hand·made |**hănd′măd′**| —*adjective* Made by hand rather than by machine: *Her dress was trimmed with handmade lace.*

hand·shake |**hănd′**shāk′| —*noun, plural* **handshakes** The act of grasping a person's right hand as a gesture of greeting, congratulations, or agreement.

hand·some |**hăn′**səm| —*adjective* **handsomer, handsomest** **1.** Of a pleasing appearance; good-looking: *a handsome young man; a handsome new suit.* **2.** Generous; liberal: *a handsome present.*

hand·writ·ing |**hănd′**rī′tĭng| —*noun, plural* **handwritings** **1.** Writing done with the hand. **2.** The style of writing of a particular person: *Her handwriting is very small and neat.*

hand·y |**hăn′**dē| —*adjective* **handier, handiest** **1.** Skilled in the use of one's hands: *He is very handy at making repairs.* **2.** Within easy reach: *Keep the hair lotion handy.* **3.** Useful; convenient: *A flashlight is a handy thing to have.* **4.** Easy to use or handle: *A dictionary is a handy reference book.*

hang |hăng| —*verb* **hung** or **hanged, hanging** **1.** To fasten or be fastened at the upper end only: *Hang the clothes on the line. A sign hung over the door.* **2.** *Past tense and past participle* **hanged** To execute by suspending from a rope tied around the neck: *Nathan Hale was hanged as a spy.* **3.** To hold or bend downward; let droop: *The boy hung his head in shame.* **4.** To remain suspended over a place; hover: *Fog hung over the city all day.*

Phrasal verbs **hang around** **1.** To spend time idly; loaf: *Hang around a while longer.* **2.** To loiter at or near: *We hung around the ball park all afternoon.* **hang on** **1.** To cling tightly: *Hang on to the rope.* **2.** To remain on the telephone: *Hang on, I'll see if he's here.* **3.** To last; linger: *Your cough is still hanging on.* **hang up** To end a telephone conversation: *It's late, so I'd better hang up.*

han·gar |**hăng′**ər| —*noun, plural* **hangars** A large building used to house aircraft.

♦ *These sound alike* **hangar, hanger.**

hang·er |**hăng′**ər| —*noun, plural* **hangers** A wire or wooden frame on which a garment is draped for hanging from a hook or rod: *Pick up your coat and put it on a hanger.*

♦ *These sound alike* **hanger, hangar.**

hang-glide |**hăng′**glīd′| —*verb* **hang-glided, hang-gliding** To glide through the air on a large kite. A person is strapped to a frame which is attached to and used to steer the kite.

Ha·nuk·kah |**hä′**nŏŏ kä′| or |**hä′**nə kə| A form of the word **Chanukah.**

hap·haz·ard |hăp **hăz′**ərd| —*adjective* Having no definite plan or order; random: *She opened a drawer or two in a haphazard search for the lost earring.*

hap·pen |**hăp′**ən| —*verb* **happened, happening** **1.** To take place; occur: *What happened at school today?* **2.** To come by accident; to chance: *I just happened to be passing by your house. My mother happened on an old friend in the supermarket.* **3.** To be done; cause a change: *Something must have happened to the toaster, because it*

hang-glide

doesn't work. **4.** To be the fate; become: *What ever happened to Thelma?*

hap·pen·ing |hăp′ə nĭng| —*noun, plural* **happenings** Something that happens; an event or occurrence: *At the dinner table we all talk about the happenings of the day.*

hap·pi·ly |hăp′ə lē| —*adverb* In a happy manner; contentedly: *Cinderella and her prince lived happily ever after.*

hap·pi·ness |hăp′ĭ nĭs| —*noun* The condition of being happy; joy: *She found happiness working among Indian children.*

hap·py |hăp′ē| —*adjective* **happier, happiest 1.** Having a good time with no big worries; enjoying oneself: *The happy children played and sang. She works hard, but she is happy in what she does.* **2.** Showing pleasure; contented; satisfied; glad: *a happy smile.* **3.** Fortunate; favorable: *The story has a happy ending.*

har·ass |hăr′əs| or |hə răs′| —*verb* **harassed, harassing** To bother again and again; trouble constantly; torment: *The students harassed the speaker. Flies and mosquitoes harassed us during the picnic.*

har·bor |här′bər| —*noun, plural* **harbors** A sheltered place along a coast serving as a port for ships: *Many ships anchored in the nearest harbor as the storm approached.*
—*verb* **harbored, harboring 1.** To give shelter to; take in: *They were guilty of harboring an escaped convict.* **2.** To have and keep; hold: *She's been harboring a grudge against her best friend.*

hard |härd| —*adjective* **harder, hardest 1.** Not giving when touched; firm; rigid: *Cement is hard when it dries.* **2.** Difficult to understand or express: *You asked me a hard question.* **3.** Requiring great effort: *years of hard work.* **4.** Difficult to endure; trying: *He's had a hard life.* **5.** Difficult to please; stern or strict: *a hard teacher.* **6.** Containing substances that keep soap suds from forming: *hard water.* **7.** Having or showing no feelings; cold: *Years of suffering had made her hard.*
—*adverb* **harder, hardest 1.** With great effort: *We all worked very hard on the party preparations.* **2.** With great force; heavily: *It rained hard all day long.* **3.** Firmly; tightly: *Press hard and the seat belt will open.* **4.** With difficulty or reluctantly: *Old habits die hard.*
 Idioms **hard of hearing** Slightly deaf; having defective hearing.
hard up Needing money; poor: *Many people were hard up during the 1930's.*

hard-boiled |härd′boild′| —*adjective* Boiled until the yolk and white are hard: *hard-boiled eggs.*

hard·en |härd′dn| —*verb* **hardened, hardening** To make or become hard: *The new process hardens steel more quickly. The liquid hardens as it cools.*

hard·ly |härd′lē| —*adverb* **1.** Barely; only just; scarcely: *He hardly noticed me.* **2.** Surely not: *You would hardly expect a favor from such mean people.*

hard·ness |härd′nĭs| —*noun, plural* **hardnesses** The quality or condition of being hard: *The hardness of that bed makes it impossible to sleep.*

hard·ship |härd′shĭp′| —*noun, plural* **hardships** Something that causes suffering or difficulty: *It was a hardship to go without a winter coat.*

hard·ware |härd′wâr′| —*noun* Metal articles used for making and repairing things around the house. Tools, nails, bolts, locks, and keys are hardware.

harbor

ă	pat	ē	pet	î	fierce
ā	pay	ē	be	ŏ	pot
â	care	ĭ	pit	ō	go
ä	father	ī	pie	ô	paw, for
oi	oil	ŭ	cut	zh	vision
ŏŏ	book	û	fur	ə	ago, item,
ōō	boot	th	the		pencil, atom,
yōō	abuse	th	thin		circus
ou	out	hw	which	ər	butter

hard·wood | härd′wŏŏd′ | —*noun, plural* **hardwoods** The wood of a tree that has leaves and flowers rather than needles and cones. This kind of wood is often hard and strong. It can be used to make furniture, floors, and other things. Oak, maple, and mahogany are hardwoods.

har·dy | här′dē | —*adjective* **hardier, hardiest** Strong and healthy; robust: *Hardy young people like to climb mountains.*

hare | hâr | —*noun, plural* **hares** An animal that looks very much like a rabbit. Hares are larger than rabbits, and have longer ears and legs.
♦ *These sound alike* **hare, hair.**

harm | härm | —*noun* Injury or damage: *Locusts can cause harm to crops.*
—*verb* **harmed, harming** To cause harm to; injure; hurt: *Lack of proper food can harm your health.*

harm·ful | härm′fəl | —*adjective* Causing harm; having bad effects: *harmful insects; a harmful drug.*

harm·less | härm′lĭs | —*adjective* Causing no harm: *a harmless snake; a harmless joke.*

har·mon·i·ca | här mŏn′ĭ kə | —*noun, plural* **harmonicas** A small rectangular musical instrument containing one or more rows of metal reeds. It is played by blowing in and out through a set of holes.

har·mo·nize | här′mə nīz′ | —*verb* **harmonized, harmonizing**
1. To provide the harmony or accompaniment for a melody.
2. To sing or play in harmony: *The four brothers harmonized in a group of songs.* **3.** To be in harmony or agreement: *The curtains should harmonize with the carpet.*

har·mo·ny | här′mə nē | —*noun, plural* **harmonies 1.** A series of notes or tones that accompany a melody: *As she sang, a piano and guitar supplied the harmony.* **2.** Music or a musical sound made up of different tones sounded together. **3.** A pleasing combination of the different parts that make up a whole; balance: *The harmony of the picture would be spoiled if all the figures were on one side.*
4. Agreement in opinion or feeling; good will; accord: *Cats and dogs can live in harmony in the same household.*

har·ness | här′nĭs | —*noun, plural* **harnesses** A set of leather straps and metal pieces by which a horse, ox, or other animal is attached to a vehicle or plow.
—*verb* **harnessed, harnessing 1.** To put a harness on. **2.** To attach by means of a harness: *We harnessed the dog team to the sled.* **3.** To bring under control for use; make use of: *The dam harnesses the power of the river.*

harp | härp | —*noun, plural* **harps** A large, stringed musical instrument that is plucked with the fingers by a player seated next to it.

har·poon | här pōōn′ | —*noun, plural* **harpoons** A spear with a rope attached to it, used in hunting whales and other large sea animals. Harpoons are thrown by hand or shot from a gun.
—*verb* **harpooned, harpooning** To strike or kill with a harpoon.

harp·si·chord | härp′sĭ kôrd′ | —*noun, plural* **harpsichords** A keyboard instrument similar to the piano. A harpsichord's strings are plucked by quills or picks rather than being struck by little hammers.

Har·ris·burg | hăr′ĭs bûrg′ | The capital of Pennsylvania.

har·row | hăr′ō | —*noun, plural* **harrows** A farm implement

hare

harmonica

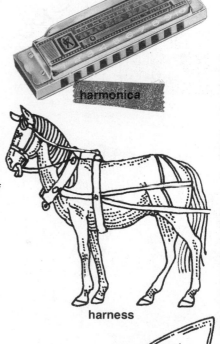
harness

harpoon

made of a heavy frame with rows of metal teeth or disks. A harrow is used to break up and level off plowed ground.

harsh |härsh| —*adjective* **harsher, harshest** **1.** Rough and unpleasant: *a cold, harsh wind; a harsh voice.* **2.** Severe; stern: *The teacher seemed harsh, but he really wanted us to do well.* **3.** Cruel; unkind: *Weak animals meet with a harsh fate.*

Hart·ford |härt′fərd| The capital of Connecticut.

har·vest |här′vĭst| —*noun, plural* **harvests** **1.** The act or process of gathering in a crop: *The wheat was grown and ready for harvest in October.* **2.** The crop that is gathered: *It took a week to bring in the harvest.*

—*verb* **harvested, harvesting** To gather in: *We harvested a bumper crop of apples.*

has |hăz| The third person singular present tense of the verb **have:** *He has a new bicycle.*

hash |hăsh| —*noun, plural* **hashes** **1.** Chopped meat and potatoes browned and cooked together. **2.** A confused mess; jumble: *Father made a hash of today's newspaper.*

has·n't |hăz′ənt| A contraction of "has not."

haste |hāst| —*noun* **1.** Speed in moving or in getting something done; hurry: *The fire engines left the station in haste.* **2.** Careless speed: *I regretted that I acted in haste.*

has·ten |hā′sən| —*verb* **hastened, hastening** **1.** To move or act swiftly; hurry: *We all hastened to the ball park after school.* **2.** To cause to happen faster or sooner; speed up: *When we heard about the storm we hastened our departure.*

hast·y |hā′stē| —*adjective* **hastier, hastiest** **1.** Quick; speedy; rapid: *The crowd made a hasty exit from the stadium.* **2.** Done too quickly to be accurate; rash: *a hasty choice; hasty judgments.*

hat |hăt| —*noun, plural* **hats** A covering for the head, especially one with a crown and a brim.

hatch¹ |hăch| —*verb* **hatched, hatching** **1.** To cause to come out of an egg or eggs: *The hen hatched several chicks.* **2.** To break open and produce young: *When will the eggs hatch?* **3.** To come out of the egg: *These chicks hatched yesterday.*

hatch² |hăch| —*noun, plural* **hatches** **1.** A small door: *an escape hatch.* **2.** An opening in the deck of a ship that leads to a lower deck or to the hold.

hatch·et |hăch′ĭt| —*noun, plural* **hatchets** A small ax with a short handle, used with one hand.

hate |hāt| —*verb* **hated, hating** To dislike very much; detest: *I hate her for lying about me. He has always hated oatmeal.*

—*noun, plural* **hates** **1.** Strong dislike; hatred: *a person who is full of hate and gloom.* **2.** A person or thing that one hates: *Spinach is one of my pet hates.*

hate·ful |hāt′fəl| —*adjective* **1.** Arousing or deserving hatred: *Stealing from a friend is a hateful act.* **2.** Full of hate: *She gave me a hateful look.*

ha·tred |hā′trĭd| —*noun* A very strong dislike; hate: *I feel hatred for anyone who is cruel to animals.*

haugh·ty |hô′tē| —*adjective* **haughtier, haughtiest** Too proud of oneself; superior in one's own mind; arrogant: *That haughty lady only speaks to rich people from old families.*

haul |hôl| —*verb* **hauled, hauling** **1.** To pull or drag with force: *It took all four of us to haul the wood to the shed.* **2.** To transport; carry; cart: *They hauled away the trash in a huge truck.*

harvest
Harvesting wheat

hatch¹, hatch²
In old English **hatch¹** meant "to produce chicks from eggs." **Hatch²** comes from another old English word, one that meant "small doorway." The two words are not related.

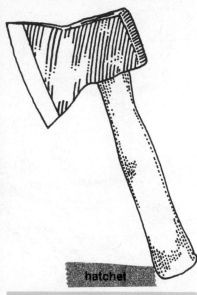

hatchet

ă	pat	ĕ	pet	î	fierce
ā	pay	ē	be	ŏ	pot
â	care	ĭ	pit	ō	go
ä	father	ī	pie	ô	paw, for

oi	oil	ŭ	cut	zh	vision
ōō	book	û	fur	ə	ago, item,
ōō	boot	*th*	the		pencil, atom,
yōō	abuse	th	thin		circus
ou	out	hw	which	ər	butter

—*noun, plural* **hauls** **1.** The act of hauling; a strong pull. **2.** A distance over which something is transported: *It's a long haul from California to New York.* **2.** An amount won, caught, or taken in: *He made a big haul at the races.*

♦ *These sound alike* **haul, hall.**

haunt |hônt| or |hänt| —*verb* **haunted, haunting** **1.** To visit or return to regularly as a ghost or spirit: *They say an old sea captain haunts the house.* **2.** To stay in the mind of; be thought of often by: *The music has haunted me ever since I heard it.*

—*noun, plural* **haunts** A place often visited: *The island is a favorite haunt of scuba divers.*

have |hăv| —*verb* **had, having, has** **1.** To be in possession of; own: *I have a bicycle. She has a new dog.* **2.** To take; accept: *Will you have an apple?* **3.** To get; receive: *She had a letter from her mother yesterday.* **4.** To arrange for; cause to do or to be done: *He had his brother help him with the gardening. Mrs. Sanchez had a cake made for her son's birthday.* **5.** To be related to: *I have two brothers and one sister.* **6.** To keep or harbor in one's mind: *He has a new plan. She has a grudge against Sue Ann.* **7.** To cause to take place; hold: *We will have a spelling contest next Friday.* **8.** To go through; experience: *She had a good time at the party. We had an accident on the road.* **9.** To be ill with: *Father has a cold.* **10.** To give birth to: *She had a baby girl. The dog had pups.*

—*helping,* or *auxiliary, verb* As a helping verb **have** is used: **1.** With a past participle to form several verb tenses that show completed action: **a.** The action was completed before a certain time in the past: *We had just finished supper when they arrived.* **b.** The action has been completed in the present, at the time of speaking: *They have already had their supper.* **c.** The action will be completed by a certain time in the future: *I will have finished supper by the time they arrive.* **2.** With the infinitive of another verb to indicate need or obligation: *I have to go. She has to stay. They have to work late every Monday night.*

♦ *These sound alike* **have, halve.**

  Idioms **have on** To be wearing: *Is that a new sweater you have on?* **have it out** To fight it out to the end: *The two teams had it out in the state championship game.* **have to do with** To deal with; be concerned with: *The book has to do with the discovery of America.*

ha·ven |hā′vən| —*noun, plural* **havens** A place of safety or rest; shelter: *Home is always a haven.*

have·n't |hăv′ənt| A contraction of "have not."

Ha·wai·i |hə wä′ē| or |hə wä′yə| A state of the United States made up of a group of islands in the Pacific Ocean. The capital of Hawaii is Honolulu.

Ha·wai·ian |hə wä′yən| —*noun, plural* **Hawaiians** **1.** Someone who was born or lives in Hawaii. **2.** The native language of the Hawaiians.

—*adjective* Of Hawaii, the Hawaiians, or their language.

hawk¹ |hôk| —*noun, plural* **hawks** A bird with a short, hooked bill and strong claws. Hawks catch small animals for food.

hawk² |hôk| —*verb* **hawked, hawking** To offer goods for sale by shouting in the street; peddle: *He made a few dollars hawking balloons at the fair.*

haw·thorn |hô′thôrn′| —*noun, plural* **hawthorns** A thorny shrub with white or pink flowers and red berries.

hay |hā| —*noun* Grass, clover, or other plants that have been

hawk¹

hawthorn
Shrub (*above*) and branch showing leaves, thorns, and berries (*below*)

haystack
Above: On a cart
Below: In a field

headdress
Indian headdress

cut and dried. Hay is used as food for horses, cattle, and other animals.

♦ *These sound alike* **hay, hey.**

hay fever An allergy caused by the pollen of certain plants. People with hay fever sneeze and have crying, itching eyes and running noses.

hay·stack | hā′stăk′ | —*noun, plural* **haystacks** A large stack of hay stored outdoors.

haz·ard | hăz′ərd | —*noun, plural* **hazards** Something that can harm or injure; a source of danger: *These piles of newspapers are a fire hazard.*

haze | hāz | —*noun, plural* **hazes** A light fog or a small amount of smoke, dust, or mist in the air: *There was a haze on the meadow early in the morning.*

ha·zel | hā′zəl | —*noun, plural* **hazels** **1.** A small tree or shrub that has nuts with a smooth brown shell. The nuts are good to eat. **2.** A light or yellowish brown color.

—*adjective* Light or yellowish brown: *Margaret has hazel eyes.*

ha·zel·nut | hā′zəl nŭt′ | —*noun, plural* **hazelnuts** The nut of a hazel.

haz·y | hā′zē | —*adjective* **hazier, haziest** **1.** Covered with haze; foggy: *a hazy day; a hazy sun.* **2.** Not clear; vague or confused: *My memory of that day is hazy.*

he | hē | —*pronoun* **1.** The male person or animal last mentioned: *Tom was here, but now he is gone.* **2.** Any person whose sex is not specified; that person; one: *Each of us is sure he is right.*

—*noun, plural* **hes** A male: *Is the puppy a he or a she?*

head | hĕd | —*noun, plural* **heads** **1.** The top part of the body, containing the brain, eyes, ears, nose, and mouth. **2.** The brain; mind: *Can you add the figures in your head?* **3.** Mental ability or aptitude: *He has a good head for mathematics.* **4.** A person who is in charge; a leader; director: *a head of state.* **5.** The leading position; front: *He marched at the head of the parade.* **6.** The upper part; the top: *Place a number at the head of each column.* **7.** A rounded part that looks like a head: *a head of cabbage; the head of a pin.* **8.** *plural* **head** A single animal or person: *He has seven head of cattle.* **9.** Often **heads** The side of a coin having the main design and usually the date.

—*adjective* Principal; leading; chief: *the head coach.*

—*verb* **headed, heading** **1.** To set out in a certain direction; proceed: *Let's head for home.* **2.** To aim; point: *He headed the boat for shore.* **3.** To be in the first or foremost position of; lead: *John heads the candidates for student president.* **4.** To be in charge of: *Mary heads the club's social committee.*

Idioms **come to a head** **1.** To fill with pus, as a boil or abscess. **2.** To reach a critical point: *The situation came to a head when we all said what we thought of each other.* **keep (one's) head** To remain calm; not lose control of oneself: *I tried to keep my head in the midst of the confusion.* **lose (one's) head** To lose one's composure or calm: *You may drown if you lose your head in deep water.* **over (one's) head** Beyond one's ability to understand: *His speech on nuclear energy was over my head.*

head·ache | hĕd′āk′ | —*noun, plural* **headaches** A pain in the head.

head·dress | hĕd′drĕs′ | —*noun, plural* **headdresses** A fancy covering or ornament worn on the head.

ă	pat	ĕ	pet	î	fierce
ā	pay	ē	be	ŏ	pot
â	care	ĭ	pit	ō	go
ä	father	ī	pie	ô	paw, for
oi	oil	ŭ	cut	zh	vision
ŏŏ	book	û	fur	ə	ago, item,
ōō	boot	*th*	the		pencil, atom,
yōō	abuse	th	thin		circus
ou	out	hw	which	ər	butter

head·first | hĕd′fûrst′ | —*adverb* With the head leading; headlong: *Ronald jumped headfirst into the pile of cushions.*

head·ing | hĕd′ĭng | —*noun, plural* **headings** A word or words at the top of a page, chapter, or letter.

head·light | hĕd′līt′ | —*noun, plural* **headlights** A light mounted on the front of an automobile, bicycle, or other vehicle.

head·line | hĕd′līn′ | —*noun, plural* **headlines** A group of words printed in large type at the top of a newspaper article. A headline tells what the article is about.

head·long | hĕd′lông′ | or | hĕd′lŏng′ | —*adverb* **1.** With the head leading; headfirst: *She slipped on a stone and fell headlong into the water.* **2.** At reckless speed: *He rode headlong down the steep hill.*
—*adjective* | hĕd′lông′ | or | hĕd′lŏng′ | **1.** Done with the head leading: *a headlong fall.* **2.** Recklessly fast: *a headlong race.*

head·on | hĕd′ŏn′ | or | hĕd′ôn′ | —*adjective* With the front end getting hit squarely: *The trains met in a head-on crash.*
—*adverb* | hĕd′ŏn′ | or | hĕd′ôn′ | With the front end directed toward something: *The truck crashed head-on into the building.*

head·quar·ters | hĕd′kwôr′tərz | —*noun* (Used with a singular or plural verb.) **1.** The offices of the commander of a military unit, or a police force: *The soldiers waited for orders from headquarters.* **2.** A center of operations; main office: *Our company is moving their headquarters to Arizona.*

head·stand | hĕd′stănd′ | —*noun, plural* **headstands** An upside-down position in which a person's weight is resting on the arms and the top of the head.

head·way | hĕd′wā′ | —*noun* Forward movement; progress: *We rowed and rowed, but we couldn't make headway against the strong current. Medical science has made headway against diseases.*

heal | hēl | —*verb* **healed, healing** To make or become healthy and sound: *A doctor is trained to heal the sick. My skinned knee healed quickly.*
♦ *These sound alike* **heal, heel, he'll.**

health | hĕlth | —*noun* **1.** The general condition of the body or mind: *Are you in good health?* **2.** Normal or sound condition; freedom from sickness: *We hope you soon return to health.*

health·ful | hĕlth′fəl | —*adjective* Good for one's health: *People come to this resort to drink the healthful mineral water.*

health·y | hĕl′thē | —*adjective* **healthier, healthiest 1.** In good health: *Janet had the flu, but was healthy again after six days.* **2.** Giving good health: *a healthy climate; healthy food.* **3.** Showing good health in mind or body: *a healthy attitude.* **4.** Full; ample: *a healthy portion of dessert.*

heap | hēp | —*noun, plural* **heaps** A collection of things lying or thrown together; pile: *a rubbish heap.*
—*verb* **heaped, heaping 1.** To place in a heap; pile up: *We heaped wood by the fireplace.* **2.** To fill to overflowing; pile high: *We heaped the truck with old newspapers.*

hear | hîr | —*verb* **heard, hearing 1.** To be aware of a sound with one's ears: *I heard a dog barking. She doesn't hear well.* **2.** To get as information; learn: *I heard the news from a friend.* **3.** To receive communication, as by letter or telephone: *Have you heard from Helen lately?* **4.** To listen to so as to judge: *The judge will hear the case tomorrow.*
♦ *These sound alike* **hear, here.**

headline
Newspaper headlines about historic events

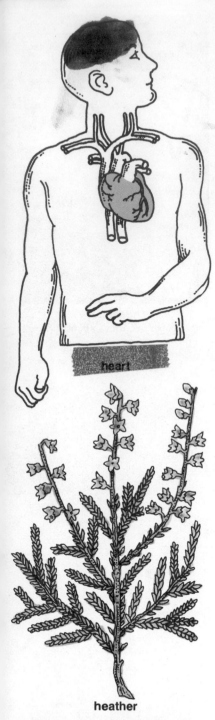

heart

heather

heard |hûrd| The past tense and past participle of the verb **hear**: *She heard the news on the radio. He had heard that Jimmy was sick.*

♦ *These sound alike* **heard, herd.**

hear·ing |hîr′ĭng| —*noun, plural* **hearings 1.** The sense by which one detects sound; ability to hear: *The doctor tested my hearing.* **2.** The area within which sounds can be heard: *They plotted their scheme to rob the bank within my hearing.* **3.** An official meeting, as in a court of law, to listen to arguments or to people giving information.

hear·say |hîr′sā′| —*noun* Information heard from someone else; gossip.

hearse |hûrs| —*noun, plural* **hearses** A car for carrying a dead person to a church or cemetery.

heart |härt| —*noun, plural* **hearts 1.** The organ that pumps blood throughout the body. In human beings the heart is in the middle of the chest. **2.** The central or main part: *the heart of the country.* **3.** The center of a person's feelings: *I thank you from the bottom of my heart.* **4.** Enthusiasm, energy, or courage: *I didn't have the heart to tell him the dog had died.* **5.** One's hopes or wishes: *She had her heart set on going to the big game.* **6.** A red figure shaped like a heart: *The valentine was decorated with hearts.* **7. a.** A red figure that looks like a heart found on a playing card. **b.** A playing card marked with this figure. **c. hearts** The suit of cards that has this figure: *ace of hearts.*

Idiom **by heart** Entirely by memory: *Do you know the poem by heart?*

heart·beat |härt′bēt| —*noun, plural* **heartbeats** A single pumping movement of the heart.

heart·bro·ken |härt′brō′kən| —*adjective* Suffering great sorrow; very sad: *The woman was heartbroken after her husband died.*

hearth |härth| —*noun, plural* **hearths** The floor of a fireplace and the area around it.

heart·y |här′tē| —*adjective* **heartier, heartiest 1.** Showing warm, friendly feeling; strong and cheerful: *a hearty laugh; a hearty slap on the back.* **2.** Giving or needing much nourishment; substantial: *a hearty soup; a hearty appetite.*

heat |hēt| —*noun* **1.** The condition of being hot; warmth: *We could feel the heat of the sun.* **2.** Very warm weather: *the summer heat.*

—*verb* **heated, heating** To make or become warmer: *The fire in the fireplace heated the room. The soup heated up slowly.*

heat·er |hē′tər| —*noun, plural* **heaters** A device for supplying heat, as to the inside of a house or car.

heath·er |hĕth′ər| —*noun* A low shrub with many small purplish flowers. Heather often grows in dense masses. It is common in Scotland and England.

heave |hēv| —*verb* **heaved, heaving 1.** To raise, lift, or throw with effort or force; hoist: *He heaved the bundle up onto the shelf.* **2.** To utter with a long, deep breath: *She heaved a great sigh.*

heav·en |hĕv′ən| —*noun, plural* **heavens 1.** Often **heavens** The sky or universe as seen from the earth. **2.** The place where God lives, according to many religions.

heav·en·ly |hĕv′ən lē| —*adjective* **1.** Of or in the heavens: *The planets are among the heavenly bodies.* **2.** Of or like heaven: *They*

ă	pat	ĕ	pet	î	fierce
ā	pay	ē	be	ŏ	pot
â	care	ĭ	pit	ō	go
ä	father	ī	pie	ô	paw, for
oi	oil	ŭ	cut	zh	vision
ŏŏ	book	û	fur	ə	ago, item,
ōō	boot	*th*	the		pencil, atom,
yōō	abuse	th	thin		circus
ou	out	hw	which	ər	butter

lived in heavenly peace. **3.** Pleasing in every way; delightful: *Isn't this a heavenly day?*

heav·i·ly |hĕv′ə lē| —*adverb* To a great degree; extremely; intensely: *The neighborhood is heavily populated.*

heav·y |hĕv′ē| —*adjective* **heavier, heaviest** **1.** Having great weight; hard to pick up: *a heavy rock.* **2.** Large in amount or output: *a heavy rain; heavy traffic.* **3.** Sturdy or thick: *heavy clothing; heavy thread.* **4.** Very dense: *a heavy fog; a heavy growth of weeds.* **5.** Requiring much effort: *heavy work.*

He·brew |hē′brōo| —*noun, plural* **Hebrews** **1.** A member of one of the Jewish peoples of ancient times. **2.** The language of the ancient Jews.

hec·tare |hĕk′târ′| —*noun, plural* **hectares** A unit of area in the metric system equal to 10,000 square meters or 2.471 acres.

hec·tic |hĕk′tĭk| —*adjective* Busy and confused; rushed and excited: *The first day of school is usually hectic.*

hecto- A prefix that means "hundred": *hectometer.*

hec·to·me·ter |hĕk′tə mē′tər| —*noun, plural* **hectometers** A unit of length in the metric system equal to 100 meters.

he'd |hēd| A contraction of "he had" or "he would".
♦ *These sound alike* **he'd, heed.**

hedge |hĕj| —*noun, plural* **hedges** A row of closely planted shrubs or small trees. Hedges form fences.
—*verb* **hedged, hedging** **1.** To enclose with a hedge. **2.** To avoid giving a direct answer: *She always hedges when we ask her opinions.*

hedge

hedge·hog |hĕj′hôg′| or |hĕj′hŏg′| —*noun, plural* **hedgehogs** A small animal whose back is covered with short, stiff spines. It rolls itself into a spiny ball to protect itself.

heed |hēd| —*verb* **heeded, heeding** To pay attention to; listen to and consider: *Why didn't they heed the warning?*
—*noun* **1.** Close attention or consideration: *He gave no heed to her greeting.* **2.** Care; caution: *Take heed while crossing the street.*
♦ *These sound alike* **heed, he'd.**

hedgehog

heel |hēl| —*noun, plural* **heels** **1.** The rounded back part of the foot. **2.** The part of a sock, shoe, or stocking that covers the heel. **3.** The part of a shoe or boot under the heel of the foot.
—*verb* **heeled, heeling** **1.** To put a heel or heels on. **2.** To follow closely behind: *She can't train her dog to heel.*
♦ *These sound alike* **heel, heal, he'll.**

heft·y |hĕf′tē| —*adjective* **heftier, heftiest** **1.** Heavy: *a hefty calf.* **2.** Of a powerful build; strong: *a hefty sailor.*

heif·er |hĕf′ər| —*noun, plural* **heifers** A young cow.

height |hīt| —*noun, plural* **heights** **1.** How high something is; distance from bottom to top: *The height of the mountain is 27,000 feet above sea level.* **2.** How tall someone is; distance from foot to head: *Your height has increased two inches this year.* **3.** Often **heights** A high place: *Are you afraid of heights?* **4.** The highest point; peak: *We went to Florida at the height of the tourist season.*

height·en |hīt′n| —*verb* **heightened, heightening** To make or become higher; raise or rise; increase: *The farmer heightened the fence to keep out animals. The excitement in our home heightened as the holidays approached.*

heir |âr| —*noun, plural* **heirs** Someone who gets the money, property, or title of another person after that person dies.
♦ *These sound alike* **heir, air.**

heir·ess | âr′ ĭs | —*noun, plural* **heiresses** A female heir.

heir·loom | âr′ lōōm′ | —*noun, plural* **heirlooms** A possession valued by members of a family and passed down from one generation to the next: *This old clock is an heirloom from my grandfather.*

held | hĕld | The past tense and past participle of the verb **hold:** *He held the racket in his hand. She has held the package for two hours now.*

Hel·e·na | hĕl′ ə nə | The capital of Montana.

hel·i·cop·ter | hĕl′ ĭ kŏp′tər | or | hē′ lĭ kŏp′tər | —*noun, plural* **helicopters** An aircraft without wings that is kept in the air by rotating blades mounted above the craft.

helicopter

hel·i·port | hĕl′ ə pôrt′ | or | hĕl′ ə pōrt′ | —*noun, plural* **heliports** An airport or landing place for helicopters.

he·li·um | hē′ lē əm | —*noun* A very light gas used to fill balloons and dirigibles. Helium is a chemical element.

hell | hĕl | —*noun, plural* **hells** 1. Often **Hell** In many religions, a place of punishment where the souls of wicked people go after death. 2. Any place or condition of great suffering or misery: *War is hell.*

he'll | hēl | A contraction of "he will" or "he shall."
♦ *These sound alike* **he'll, heal, heel.**

hel·lo | hĕ lō′ | or | hə lō′ | or | hĕl′ ō | —*interjection* A word used to greet someone, answer the telephone, or attract attention: *Hello! Is anyone at home?*
—*noun, plural* **helloes** A call or greeting of "hello": *We exchanged helloes and that was all.*

helm | hĕlm | —*noun, plural* **helms** The steering wheel or tiller of a ship.

helmet

hel·met | hĕl′ mĭt | —*noun, plural* **helmets** A head covering of metal or other hard material to protect the head in battle, work, or sports: *Football players are required to wear helmets.*

help | hĕlp | —*verb* **helped, helping** 1. To give or do things useful to; assist; aid: *She helped her mother clean the house.* 2. To give relief to; ease: *This medicine will help your cold.* 3. To prevent or change: *We couldn't help what happened.* 4. To refrain from; avoid: *She couldn't help laughing.* 5. To wait on, as in a store or restaurant: *The manager found someone to help me.*
—*noun* 1. The act or an example of helping: *Thanks so much for your help.* 2. Someone or something that helps: *A good dictionary is a great help when studying.*
Idiom **help (oneself) to** To serve oneself: *Help yourself to the food.*

help·ful | hĕlp′ fəl | —*adjective* Providing help; useful: *a helpful person; helpful advice.*

help·ing | hĕl′ pĭng | —*noun, plural* **helpings** A portion of food for one person: *Have another helping of mashed potatoes.*

help·less | hĕlp′ lĭs | —*adjective* Not capable of taking care of oneself; dependent upon others: *She's as helpless as a baby.*

hem | hĕm | —*noun, plural* **hems** The edge of a garment or cloth, especially the lower edge of a dress. Hems are made by folding under the raw edge and sewing it down.
—*verb* **hemmed, hemming** To fold back and sew down the edge of: *She hemmed her skirt.*
Phrasal verb **hem in** To surround and shut in; enclose: *The mountains hemmed in the little village.*

hem·i·sphere | hĕm′ ĭ sfîr′ | —*noun, plural* **hemispheres**

ă	pat	ĕ	pet	î	fierce
ā	pay	ē	be	ŏ	pot
â	care	ĭ	pit	ō	go
ä	father	ī	pie	ô	paw, for

oi	oil	ŭ	cut	zh	vision
ŏŏ	book	û	fur	ə	ago, item,
ōō	boot	*th*	the		pencil, atom,
yōō	abuse	th	thin		circus
ou	out	hw	which	ər	butter

1. Either of the two halves into which a sphere is divided.
2. Often **Hemisphere** One half of the earth's surface. The earth is divided by the equator into the Northern and Southern Hemispheres. The earth can also be divided into the Eastern and Western Hemispheres. North and South America are in the Western Hemisphere.

hem·lock |hĕm′lŏk′| —*noun, plural* **hemlocks 1.** An evergreen tree with short, flat needles and small cones. **2.** A poisonous plant with feathery leaves and clusters of small whitish flowers. **3.** Poison made from this plant.

hemp |hĕmp| —*noun* A tall plant with stems that yield a tough, strong fiber. The fiber is used to make rope and cord.

hen |hĕn| —*noun, plural* **hens 1.** A fully grown female chicken. **2.** The female of some other birds, like the peacock and turkey.

hence |hĕns| —*adverb* **1.** For this reason; therefore: *The children ate candy all afternoon and hence had no appetite for dinner.* **2.** From now: *Ten years hence the town will have changed.*

her |hûr| —*pronoun* **1.** The pronoun **her** is the objective case of **she.** It is used: **a.** As the direct object of a verb: *I saw her on the street.* **b.** As the indirect object of a verb: *He told her the news.* **c.** As the object of a preposition: *We left the keys with her.* **2.** The pronoun **her** is a possessive form of **she.** It means: **a.** Of or belonging to a female person or animal: *her hat.* **b.** Done or performed by a female person or animal: *her first job. The ballerina finished her third solo of the evening.* The pronoun **her** as a possessive form of **she** belongs to a class of words called **determiners.** They signal that a noun is coming.

herb |ûrb| or |hûrb| —*noun, plural* **herbs** A plant with leaves, roots, or other parts used to flavor food or as medicine. Parsley, dill, and thyme are herbs.

her·biv·o·rous |hər bĭv′ər əs| —*adjective* Feeding entirely on plants or plant parts: *Cattle, deer, and rabbits are herbivorous animals.*

herd |hûrd| —*noun, plural* **herds 1.** A group of animals, such as cattle or elephants, that live or are kept together. **2.** A large group of people; a throng: *A herd of customers pushed through the doors of the store.*
—*verb* **herded, herding** To gather, keep, or drive together: *The cowboys herded the cattle.*
♦ *These sound alike* **herd, heard.**

here |hîr| —*adverb* At or to this place: *You go and I'll stay here. Come here, please.*
—*noun* This place: *The nearest town is four miles from here.*
—*interjection* A word used in calling an animal, getting someone's attention, or answering to one's name in a roll call.
♦ *These sound alike* **here, hear.**

here·by |hîr bī′| or |hîr′bī′| —*adverb* By this means: *The boys gave Jimmy a paper that said "You are hereby declared a member of our club."*

he·red·i·tar·y |hə rĕd′ĭ tĕr′ē| —*adjective* Passing or capable of passing from a parent to offspring: *Red hair is hereditary. The duke got his hereditary title from his father.*

he·red·i·ty |hə rĕd′ĭ tē| —*noun, plural* **heredities 1.** The passing of characteristics from parents to offspring: *Wilma got her height by heredity from her very tall parents.* **2.** The characteristics that a child gets from birth from its parents: *Being very tall must*

hemlock
Tree (*above*) and needles and cone (*below*)

be part of Jackson's heredity, because all his brothers and sisters are very tall too.

here's |hîrz| A contraction of "here is."

her·i·tage |hĕr′ĭ tĭj| —*noun, plural* **heritages** The customs, achievements, and other things handed down from earlier generations; tradition: *Celebrating Thanksgiving Day is part of our heritage.*

her·mit |hûr′mĭt| —*noun, plural* **hermits** A person who lives alone and far away from other people.

he·ro |hîr′ō| —*noun, plural* **heroes** 1. A person admired for bravery or outstanding accomplishment: *a war hero; a sports hero.* 2. The main male character in a story, poem, play, or movie.

he·ro·ic |hĭ rō′ĭk| —*adjective* 1. Of or having to do with heroes: *heroic legends.* 2. Very brave; noble and daring: *a heroic rescue.*

her·o·in |hĕr′ō ĭn| —*noun, plural* **heroins** A very strong, dangerous drug. Heroin is habit-forming and can cause death.

♦ *These sound alike* **heroin, heroine.**

her·o·ine |hĕr′ō ĭn| —*noun, plural* **heroines** 1. A woman or girl admired for bravery or outstanding accomplishment. 2. The main female character in a story, poem, play, or movie.

♦ *These sound alike* **heroine, heroin.**

her·o·ism |hĕr′ō ĭz′əm| —*noun, plural* **heroisms** Great bravery; courage: *They all received medals for heroism in battle.*

her·on |hĕr′ən| —*noun, plural* **herons** A bird with a long neck, long legs, and a long, pointed bill.

her·ring |hĕr′ĭng| —*noun, plural* **herring** or **herrings** A fish of the North Atlantic Ocean. It is caught in large numbers for food. Herring are usually canned, pickled, or smoked.

hers |hûrz| —*pronoun* The pronoun **hers** is a possessive form of **she.** It is used to show that something or someone belongs to a female person or animal: *This book is hers. If his desk is occupied, use hers. He is no friend of hers.*

her·self |hər sĕlf| —*pronoun* The pronoun **herself** is a special form of the pronoun **her.** 1. It means: **a.** Her own self: *She cut herself with the scissors. Mary is proud of herself.* **b.** Her normal self: *Josie is not herself today.* 2. It is used to call special attention to someone or something: *Mother herself is going. She herself saw the accident.*

he's |hēz| A contraction of "he is" or "he has."

hes·i·tant |hĕz′ĭ tənt| —*adjective* Stopping or waiting because one is not sure; doubtful: *The boy with short legs was hesitant about jumping the wide gap.*

hes·i·tate |hĕz′ĭ tāt′| —*verb* **hesitated, hesitating** 1. To stop or wait because one is not sure: *If you hesitate too long your chance to go will be lost.* 2. To pause in speaking or acting: *The dancers hesitated for a moment and then continued their dance.*

hes·i·ta·tion |hĕz′ĭ tā′shən| —*noun, plural* **hesitations** 1. The act of hesitating; a pause or delay: *A slight hesitation showed that the actor had forgotten his lines.* 2. The condition of being hesitant; lack of assurance: *We feel a certain hesitation about accepting the promise of a boy who lies.*

hey |hā| —*interjection* A word used to show surprise or attract attention: *Hey, I won! Hey, watch out!*

♦ *These sound alike* **hey, hay.**

hi |hī| —*interjection* A word used as a greeting, like "hello."

♦ *These sound alike* **hi, high.**

heron

ă	pat	ĕ	pet	î	fierce
ā	pay	ē	be	ŏ	pot
â	care	ĭ	pit	ō	go
ä	father	ī	pie	ô	paw, for
oi	oil	ŭ	cut	zh	vision
ŏŏ	book	û	fur	ə	ago, item,
ōō	boot	th	the		pencil, atom,
yōō	abuse	th	thin		circus
ou	out	hw	which	ər	butter

hi·ber·nate |hī′bər nāt′| —*verb* **hibernated, hibernating** To spend the winter asleep in a protected place, as certain animals do: *Woodchucks and some bears hibernate.*

hi·bis·cus |hī bĭs′kəs| or |hĭ bĭs′kəs| —*noun, plural* **hibiscuses** The large, showy flower of a shrub that grows in warm places.

hic·cup |hĭk′ŭp| —*noun, plural* **hiccups** **1.** A sudden catching of the breath in the throat. **2. the hiccups** An attack in which a person has one hiccup after another.
—*verb* **hiccupped, hiccupping** To have the hiccups.

hick·o·ry |hĭk′ə rē| —*noun, plural* **hickories** A North American tree that has hard wood and nuts with a hard shell. The nuts are good to eat.

hid |hĭd| The past tense and a past participle of the verb **hide:** *He hid the book behind the desk. He had hid himself behind the barn many times.*

hid·den |hĭd′n| A past participle of the verb **hide:** *Mary has hidden the money.*

hide¹ |hīd| —*verb* **hid, hidden** or **hid, hiding** **1.** To put or keep out of sight: *Let's hide the presents where no one can find them.* **2.** To keep from being known; conceal: *The boy could not hide his embarrassment, and blushed.*

hide² |hīd| —*noun, plural* **hides** The skin of an animal: *Leather is made from hides.*

hide-and-seek |hīd′n sēk′| —*noun* A children's game in which one player at a time tries to find and catch the other players who are hiding.

hide·a·way |hīd′ə wā′| —*noun, plural* **hideaways** A place that is a secret from or hard to find by other people: *People are still trying to discover the hideaway where the pirates buried their treasure.*

hid·e·ous |hĭd′ē əs| —*adjective* Very bad to look at or think about; ugly; horrible: *a hideous car accident; a hideous plan to cut down forests and destroy the homes of birds and animals.*

hide·out |hīd′out′| —*noun, plural* **hideouts** A place where one can safely hide: *The club members made a hideout in a cave in the mountainside.*

hi-fi |hī′fī′| —*noun, plural* **hi-fi's** A radio or phonograph that reproduces sound very accurately.

high |hī| —*adjective* **higher, highest** **1.** Having great height; tall: *a high mountain; a tower 400 feet high.* **2.** At a great distance above the ground: *The balloon was high in the air. That's a high ceiling.* **3.** Above others in rank or importance: *high government officials.* **4.** Greater than usual: *a high temperature; high prices.* **5.** Sharp; shrill: *a soprano's high voice.* **6.** Very favorable: *He has a high opinion of himself.*
—*adverb* At, in, or to a high position or level: *Hawks can fly high in the sky.*
—*noun, plural* **highs** A high level or position: *Prices for food are at a new high.*
♦ *These sound alike* **high, hi.**

high jump A contest in which a person tries to jump over a bar without knocking it down. The bar is set as high as possible between two posts.

high·land |hī′lənd| —*noun, plural* **highlands** A country or area that is higher or more hilly than the region around it.

high·light |hī′līt′| —*noun, plural* **highlights** An outstanding event, part, or place: *Swimming and tennis were the highlights of our*

hickory
Above: Tree
Center: Leaves
Below: Nut

hide¹, hide²
Both words spelled **hide** appeared long ago in English. **Hide¹** goes back to an old Germanic root meaning "to cover over, to conceal." **Hide²** came from the same Germanic root in the sense "a covering, a skin or pelt."

hilt

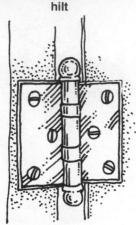

vacation. *The royal palace is a highlight of the European tour.*

high·ly | **hī′lē** | —*adverb* **1.** To a great degree; very: *Dogs have a highly developed sense of smell. Mr. Boggs told some highly amusing stories.* **2.** In a good or favorable way: *All his friends think highly of him.* **3.** At a high price: *a highly paid worker.*

High·ness | **hī′nĭs** | —*noun, plural* **Highnesses** A title of honor for a member of a royal family: *Their Highnesses the King and Queen have returned to the palace.*

high school A school attended by students who have finished elementary school. High school usually includes grades nine through twelve.

high tide The time when the ocean reaches its highest level on the shore.

high·way | **hī′wā′** | —*noun, plural* **highways** A main public road.

hi·jack | **hī′jăk′** | —*verb* **hijacked, hijacking** To take over by force; seize control of: *Two men hijacked the airplane and forced the pilot to fly them to a secret destination.*

hike | **hīk** | —*verb* **hiked, hiking** To go on a long walk: *We hiked for ten miles through the forest.*
—*noun, plural* **hikes** A long walk.

hik·er | **hī′kər** | —*noun, plural* **hikers** A person who hikes.

hi·lar·i·ous | **hĭ lâr′ē əs** | or | **hĭ lăr′ē əs** | —*adjective* Very funny in a noisy way; noisily merry: *The clowns at the circus were hilarious.*

hill | **hĭl** | —*noun, plural* **hills** **1.** A raised part of the earth's surface that is not as high as a mountain. **2.** A small mound of earth or sand: *Ants could be seen running back and forth from their hills.*

hill·side | **hĭl′sīd′** | —*noun, plural* **hillsides** The side of a hill.

hill·top | **hĭl′tŏp′** | —*noun, plural* **hilltops** The top of a hill.

hill·y | **hĭl′ē** | —*adjective* **hillier, hilliest** Having many hills: *The countryside beyond the river is very hilly.*

hilt | **hĭlt** | —*noun, plural* **hilts** The handle of a sword or dagger.

him | **hĭm** | —*pronoun* The pronoun **him** is the objective case of **he.** It is used: **1.** As the direct object of a verb: *I saw him on the street.* **2.** As the indirect object of a verb: *Mary gave him the wallet.* **3.** As the object of a preposition: *We left the keys with him.*
♦ *These sound alike* **him, hymn.**

him·self | **hĭm sĕlf′** | —*pronoun* The pronoun **himself** is a special form of the pronoun **him. 1.** It means: **a.** His own self: *He cut himself with the knife. James is angry with himself.* **b.** His normal self: *Bill is not himself today.* **2.** It is used to call special attention to someone or something: *Father himself is driving the car. He himself scored the goal.*

hind | **hīnd** | —*adjective* Back; rear: *The dog stood on its hind legs and begged for food.*

hind·er | **hĭn′dər** | —*verb* **hindered, hindering** To get in the way of; make difficult: *Thick underbrush hindered our walk through the woods.*

hin·drance | **hĭn′drəns** | —*noun, plural* **hindrances** Something that hinders; obstacle: *Strong winds are a hindrance to small sailboats.*

hinge | **hĭnj** | —*noun, plural* **hinges** A jointed device on which a door, gate, or cover turns or swings back and forth.
—*verb* **hinged, hinging 1.** To attach by means of a hinge. **2.** To depend: *Getting a good grade hinges on your studying hard.*

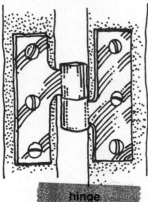
hinge
Two kinds of hinge

ă	pat	ĕ	pet	î	fierce
ā	pay	ē	be	ŏ	pot
â	care	ĭ	pit	ō	go
ä	father	ī	pie	ô	paw, for
oi	oil	ŭ	cut	zh	vision
ŏŏ	book	û	fur	ə	ago, item,
ōō	boot	*th*	the		pencil, atom,
yōō	abuse	th	thin		circus
ou	out	hw	which	ər	butter

hint | hĭnt | —*noun, plural* **hints** **1.** A slight sign or suggestion: *My mother's tight mouth was a hint that she was getting angry.* **2.** A bit of useful information: *The book offered hints on how to make good cookies.*
—*verb* **hinted, hinting** To show by hints; tell indirectly; suggest: *We kept hinting that we would like new bicycles for Christmas.*

hip¹ | hĭp | —*noun, plural* **hips** The bony part that sticks out on each side of the body between the waist and the thigh.

hip² | hĭp | —*noun, plural* **hips** The seed case of a rose. It looks like a bright red berry.

hip·po | hĭp′ō | —*noun, plural* **hippos** A hippopotamus.

hip·po·pot·a·mus | hĭp′ə pŏt′ə məs | —*noun, plural* **hippopotamuses** A large African animal that lives in or near water. It has short legs, a broad snout, and a wide mouth.

hire | hīr | —*verb* **hired, hiring** **1.** To pay a person for working or performing a service; employ: *We hired a plumber to fix the pipes. The couple hired a cook and a nurse.* **2.** To rent for a limited time: *The traveler hired a car to drive to the airport.*
—*noun, plural* **hires** The act of hiring; employment: *With the hire of two new workers the job became easier.*

his | hĭz | —*pronoun* The pronoun **his** is the possessive form of **he.** **1.** It means: **a.** Of or belonging to a male person or animal: *his hat.* **b.** Done or performed by a male person or animal: *his first job. The quarterback completed his third pass of the game.* The pronoun **his** as the possessive form of **he** belongs to a class of words called **determiners.** They signal that a noun is coming. **2.** It is used to show that something or someone belongs to a male person or animal: *This book is his. If her desk is occupied, use his. I am no friend of his.*

hiss | hĭs | —*noun, plural* **hisses** A sound like a long *s*: *The air made a hiss as it escaped from the tire.*
—*verb* **hissed, hissing** **1.** To make a hiss: *The angry snake hissed.* **2.** To show dislike for by making a hiss: *The audience hissed the villain when he came on the stage.*

his·to·ri·an | hĭ stôr′ē ən | or | hĭ stŏr′ē ən | —*noun, plural* **historians** A person who writes about or studies history.

his·tor·ic | hĭ stôr′ĭk | or | hĭ stŏr′ĭk | —*adjective* Important or famous in history: *The town's church is historic because it is the oldest building in the area. In a historic meeting the treaty was signed.*

his·tor·i·cal | hĭ stôr′ĭ kəl | or | hĭ stŏr′ĭ kəl | —*adjective* Of or having to do with history: *historical events; historical documents; a historical novel.*

his·to·ry | hĭs′tə rē | —*noun, plural* **histories** A record or story of past events: *I'm reading a history of the United States. The history of popular music is full of famous singers.*

hit | hĭt | —*verb* **hit, hitting** **1.** To give a blow to; strike: *I hit the nail hard, but it wouldn't go in. The boy hit back hard in defense. The tennis players hit the ball back and forth across the net.* **2.** To knock or knock against: *He fell and hit his elbow. The ball hit the wall and bounced.* **3.** To get to; reach: *The ride was smooth until we hit a country road.* **4.** To affect as if by a blow: *The bad news hit them hard.*
—*noun, plural* **hits** **1.** A blow or shot that hits something: *a direct hit on the target; a hit on the head.* **2.** A great success: *The movie is the hit of the season.* **3.** A baseball that is hit so that the batter can at least reach first base safely.

hip¹, hip²
Hip¹ and hip² come from words used long ago in English; they are not related.

hippopotamus

Above: Ice hockey
Below: Field hockey

hockey

hoe

hold¹, hold²
Hold¹ and **hold²** have both always had their current meanings. **Hold²** was originally **hole**, but the meaning of **hold¹** no doubt influenced the change to its current spelling.

ă	pat	ĕ	pet	î	fierce
ā	pay	ē	be	ŏ	pot
â	care	ĭ	pit	ō	go
ä	father	ī	pie	ô	paw, for
oi	oil	ŭ	cut	zh	vision
ŏŏ	book	û	fur	ə	ago, item,
ōō	boot	*th*	the		pencil, atom,
yōō	abuse	th	thin		circus
ou	out	hw	which	ər	butter

hitch |hĭch| —*verb* **hitched, hitching 1.** To tie or fasten with a rope, strap, loop, or ring: *The farmer hitched a horse to his wagon.* **2.** To raise or pull with a tug: *The soldiers hitched their knapsacks higher on their shoulders and marched off.*
—*noun, plural* **hitches 1.** A short pull or jerk; tug: *He put his thumbs in his belt and gave his pants a hitch.* **2.** A delay or difficulty: *Heavy traffic put a hitch in our plans to get an early start.* **3.** A knot used to fasten a rope to another object.

hitch·hike |hĭch′hīk′| —*verb* **hitchhiked, hitchhiking** To travel by standing by the sides of roads and getting free rides from passing cars.

hive |hīv| —*noun, plural* **hives 1.** The home of a swarm of bees. It can be a hollow tree or a man-made shelter. **2.** A swarm of bees that lives in such a place.

hives |hīvz| —*plural noun* A red rash on the skin.

hoard |hôrd| or |hōrd| —*noun, plural* **hoards** A supply of something that is stored away or kept hidden: *The squirrel kept a hoard of nuts for the winter.*
—*verb* **hoarded, hoarding** To save and store away: *People hoarded canned food when they heard that prices would rise.*
♦ *These sound alike* **hoard, horde.**

hoarse |hôrs| or |hōrs| —*adjective* **hoarser, hoarsest** Low and rough in sound or voice: *After the game our voices were hoarse from shouting. A bad cough can make you hoarse.*
♦ *These sound alike* **hoarse, horse.**

hoax |hōks| —*noun, plural* **hoaxes** A false story or report made up to fool people into believing it: *The story that there was a dinosaur on the loose turned out to be a hoax.*

hob·ble |hŏb′əl| —*verb* **hobbled, hobbling 1.** To walk with jerks or awkwardly; limp: *I've had to hobble around since I broke my leg skiing.* **2.** To tie the legs of an animal to prevent free movement.
—*noun, plural* **hobbles 1.** A jerky or awkward walk; limp. **2.** A rope or strap used to hobble an animal.

hob·by |hŏb′ē| —*noun, plural* **hobbies** Something that a person does or studies for fun in his spare time; a pastime: *Gardening and stamp collecting are his hobbies.*

hock·ey |hŏk′ē| —*noun, plural* **hockeys** A game played with long, curved sticks by two teams on ice or a field. In ice hockey, the players wear skates and try to hit a hard rubber disk, or puck, into the other team's goal. In field hockey, the players run on foot and use a ball instead of a puck.

hoe |hō| —*noun, plural* **hoes** A gardening tool with a flat blade set at the end of a long handle. Hoes are used for loosening soil and weeding.
—*verb* **hoed, hoeing** To loosen, cut, or dig with a hoe.

hog |hôg| or |hŏg| —*noun, plural* **hogs 1.** A pig, especially a fully grown pig raised for meat. **2.** A very greedy person.
—*verb* **hogged, hogging** To take more than one's fair share of: *My big brother always hogs the pancakes.*

hoist |hoist| —*verb* **hoisted, hoisting** To raise up or lift, often with the help of a machine: *The sailors hoisted the sails. The workers hoisted the steel beams with a crane.*
—*noun, plural* **hoists 1.** A device used to lift heavy objects. **2.** A lift; pull: *One boy gave his friend a hoist over the wall.*

hold¹ |hōld| —*verb* **held, holding 1.** To take and keep in the hands or arms; clasp; grasp: *The Statue of Liberty is holding a torch.*

The mother held her baby to her breast. Hold tightly to that rope while you are in the pool. **2.** To keep confined; restrain: *The police are holding him prisoner.* **3.** To keep in a certain place or position: *She held her head high as she entered the room.* **4.** To contain: *This box will hold four dozen cookies.* **5.** To bear or support: *Will this cable hold such a heavy load? These props hold up the roof.* **6.** To have, be in, or occupy: *Thomas Jefferson held the office of President of the United States for two terms.* **7.** To cause to take place; conduct: *hold an election; hold a meeting in the teachers' lounge.* **8.** To believe; think; consider: *"We hold these truths to be self-evident, that all men are created equal. . ."* (The Declaration of Independence). **9.** To put off; postpone: *Please hold dinner until I get home. Kindly hold your applause until the end of the concert.*

   Phrasal verbs **hold on** **1.** To keep a grip; cling: *When you take my hand, hold on.* **2.** To wait; stop: *Hold on a minute while I wrap this package.* **3.** To keep on; continue: *The losing team held on until they had no strength left.* **hold out** To last: *How long do you think our water supply will hold out?* **hold over** To keep longer than planned: *The movie has been held over for another week.* **hold up** To stop and rob: *Outlaws held up the train.*

—*noun, plural* **holds** **1.** An act or way of holding; grip: *keep a firm hold; a wrestling hold.* **2.** Something used for support: *A small ledge provided a hold on the cliff side.* **3.** A strong influence: *The evil wizard had a hold over the creatures of the forest.*

hold² | hōld | —*noun, plural* **holds** A space inside a ship or airplane where cargo is carried.

hold·up | hōld′ŭp′ | —*noun, plural* **holdups** **1.** A robbery by someone having or pretending to have a weapon. **2.** A delay: *We are sorry for the holdup in the delivery of your order.*

hole | hōl | —*noun, plural* **holes** **1.** An opening: *Ellen tore a hole in her stocking. There is a hole in the paper where the pen poked through.* **2.** An empty or hollow place: *The tunnel forms a hole right through the mountain.* **3.** A small hollow place on a golf course into which the ball must be hit with a club.

  ♦ *These sound alike* **hole, whole.**

hol·i·day | hŏl′ĭ dā′ | —*noun, plural* **holidays** A special day when, instead of working, people celebrate an important date or honor someone. Columbus Day and Christmas are holidays.

Hol·land | hŏl′ənd | A country in western Europe. Another name for this country is **the Netherlands.**

hol·low | hŏl′ō | —*adjective* **hollower, hollowest** **1.** Having an empty space or hole inside: *a hollow log; a hollow rubber ball.* **2.** Curved in like a bowl: *Rain formed pools in the hollow spaces on the rocks.* **3.** Sunken: *His cheeks were hollow from days without food.* **4.** Insincere; shallow: *hollow promises.*

—*noun, plural* **hollows** **1.** An empty space; gap or cavity: *There is a hollow behind this wall.* **2.** A sunken area; depression: *There were hollows in the sick man's cheeks.* **3.** A small valley.

—*verb* **hollowed, hollowing** To make or become hollow.

hol·ly | hŏl′ē | —*noun, plural* **hollies** A shrub or tree that has evergreen leaves with prickly edges. Holly has bright-red berries.

hol·ly·hock | hŏl′ē hŏk′ | —*noun, plural* **hollyhocks** A tall garden plant with a long cluster of large, colorful flowers.

hol·ster | hōl′stər | —*noun, plural* **holsters** A leather case for holding a pistol, usually worn on a belt.

ho·ly | hō′lē | —*adjective* **holier, holiest** **1.** Of or having to do

holly

hollyhock

holster

with God; sacred: *The Bible is a holy book.* **2.** Deeply religious; saintly: *a holy man; a holy life.*

♦ *These sound alike* **holy, wholly.**

home |hōm| —*noun, plural* **homes** **1.** A place where a person or animal lives: *My home is in an apartment building. The squirrel's home is a nest high in a tree.* **2.** A place where a person feels natural or comfortable: *My real home is the seashore. I already feel at home even though I just met your family.* **3.** A place for caring for those who cannot care for themselves: *My grandmother lives in a nursing home.* **4.** A goal in some games and sports.
—*adverb* **1.** To or at one's home: *The kids raced home from school.* **2.** To the place aimed at: *The arrow struck home, right in the center of the target.*
—*verb* **homed, homing** To return home: *After being released in the country the pigeons homed to their nests in the city.*

home·land |hōm′lǎnd′| —*noun, plural* **homelands** The country where a person was born or feels most at home.

home·ly |hōm′lē| —*adjective* **homelier, homeliest** **1.** Typical of home life; everyday; simple: *a homely meal.* **2.** Not good-looking; plain: *His long nose and small chin gave him a homely face.*

home·made |hōm′mād′| —*adjective* Made at home: *homemade cookies.*

home·maker |hōm′mā′kər| —*noun, plural* **homemakers** A person who runs a household: *In some marriages, the husband and wife take turns being the homemaker.*

home plate In baseball, the base at which the batter stands. Home plate must be touched by a runner after touching the other three bases to score a run.

hom·er |hō′mər| —*noun, plural* **homers** A hit in baseball, a home run.

home·room |hōm′rōōm′| or |hōm′rŏŏm′| —*noun, plural* **homerooms** A school classroom where all the pupils in a class report in the morning.

home run A hit in baseball that allows the batter to touch all bases and score a run.

home·sick |hōm′sĭk| —*adjective* Sad and lonely because of being away from home.

home·spun |hōm′spŭn′| —*adjective* **1.** Woven at home: *beautiful homespun cloth.* **2.** Simple and comfortable: *I love homespun pleasures like having snacks and watching television with my shoes off.*

home·stead |hōm′stĕd′| —*noun, plural* **homesteads** **1.** A house, especially the main house on a farm, with the land and buildings belonging to it. **2.** A piece of land given by a government to a family settling on it.

home·ward |hōm′wərd| —*adverb* Toward home: *In the evening the fishing boats begin to sail homeward. The teacher walked homeward from school.* Another form of this word is **homewards.**
—*adjective* Going in the direction of home: *a homeward journey.*

home·wards |hōm′wərdz| A form of the adverb **homeward.**

home·work |hōm′wûrk′| —*noun, plural* **homeworks** School lessons to be done at home or outside the classroom.

hom·i·ny |hŏm′ə nē| —*noun, plural* **hominies** Kernels of corn hulled and boiled as a food. Sometimes hominy is ground into a coarse white meal called hominy grits.

ho·mog·e·nize |hə mŏj′ə nīz′| —*verb* **homogenized,**

homestead

ă	pat	ĕ	pet	î	fierce
ā	pay	ē	be	ŏ	pot
â	care	ĭ	pit	ō	go
ä	father	ī	pie	ô	paw, for

oi	oil	ŭ	cut	zh	vision
ōō	book	û	fur	ə	ago, item,
ōō	boot	*th*	the		pencil, atom,
yōō	abuse	th	thin		circus
ou	out	hw	which	ər	butter

homogenizing To mix the cream in milk evenly so that the cream does not rise to the top.

hon·est |ŏn′ĭst| —*adjective* **1.** Not lying, stealing, or cheating; trustworthy: *If an honest person finds your lost wallet, he will return it.* **2.** Obtained in a fair and decent way: *They make an honest living selling fresh fruits and vegetables.* **3.** Not hiding anything; frank; sincere: *If you want my honest opinion, I think your orange hat looks silly.*

hon·es·ty |ŏn′ĭ stē| —*noun* The quality of being honest.

hon·ey |hŭn′ē| —*noun, plural* **honeys 1.** A thick, sweet, yellowish substance made by bees. It is made from nectar that the bees gather from flowers. Honey is good to eat. **2.** A person who is loved; darling.

hon·ey·bee |hŭn′ē bē′| —*noun, plural* **honeybees** A bee that makes honey.

hon·ey·comb |hŭn′ē kōm′| —*noun, plural* **honeycombs** A container made by honeybees to hold honey. It is made of wax and has many small openings with six sides.
—*verb* **honeycombed, honeycombing** To fill with spaces like those of a honeycomb: *The cliff was honeycombed with small caves made by birds and little animals.*

hon·ey·moon |hŭn′ē mōōn′| —*noun, plural* **honeymoons** A trip or vacation taken by two people who have just been married.
—*verb* **honeymooned, honeymooning** To spend a honeymoon: *They honeymooned on a beautiful island.*

hon·ey·suck·le |hŭn′ē sŭk′əl| —*noun* A vine or shrub with yellowish, white, or pink flowers shaped like a tube. The flowers often have a very sweet smell.

honk |hôngk| or |hŏngk| —*noun, plural* **honks** A loud, harsh sound, such as that made by a goose or by a car horn.
—*verb* **honked, honking** To make or cause to make a honk: *The geese honked in fright at the barking dog. Honk your horn to let them know we're here.*

Hon·o·lu·lu |hŏn′ə lōō′lōō| The capital of Hawaii.

hon·or |ŏn′ər| —*noun, plural* **honors 1.** Special respect: *We display the flag to show honor to the United States.* **2.** A sign of someone's excellence or worth; a mark of respect: *Election to baseball's Hall of Fame is an honor paid to very few players.* **3.** Someone or something that brings special distinction; credit: *The heroic nurse is an honor to her profession.* **4.** Good name; reputation: *To protect his honor, he had to answer the charges of treason made against him.* **5.** A sense of what is right; honesty; self-respect: *He felt bound by honor to tell the truth no matter what.* **6. honors** Special recognition for doing well in one's work at school.
—*verb* **honored, honoring** To show special respect for: *The city honored the foreign guest by giving him a parade.*

hon·or·a·ble |ŏn′ər ə bəl| —*adjective* **1.** Deserving honor or respect: *Medicine and law are two of many honorable professions.* **2.** Doing what is right; honest; decent: *It is not honorable to take the credit for someone else's work.*

hood |hŏŏd| —*noun, plural* **hoods 1.** A soft, loose covering for the head and neck, often attached to a coat. **2.** Something that is like a hood in shape or use: *The old stove had a hood over it to trap smoke and steam from things cooking.* **3.** A hinged, metal covering for the engine of a car.

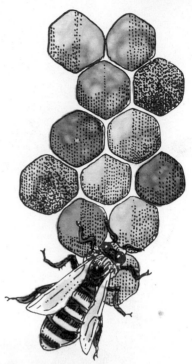

honeybee and honeycomb

honeysuckle

hood·lum | hŏŏd′ləm | or | hood′ləm | —*noun, plural* **hoodlums** A rough, mean person who causes trouble.

hoof | hŏŏf | or | hŏŏf | —*noun, plural* **hoofs** or **hooves** The tough, horny covering on the foot of some animals. Horses, cattle, deer, and pigs have hoofs.

hook | hŏŏk | —*noun, plural* **hooks** A curved or bent piece of metal, wood, or other material that is used to hold, fasten, or catch something: *a hook for catching fish; a hook in the cloakroom for hanging a coat; a hook on a dress.*
—*verb* **hooked, hooking** To hold, fasten, or catch with a hook: *He hooked a fish. She hooked up her dress.*
   Phrasal verb **hook up** To put together or connect: *He hooked up the TV to the antenna.*

hoop | hŏŏp | or | hŏŏp | —*noun, plural* **hoops** A large circular band or ring made of wood, metal, or other material. Plastic hoops are used as toys that can be spun around the body. Metal hoops are used to keep barrels from coming apart.
♦ *These sound alike* **hoop, whoop.**

hoot | hŏŏt | —*noun, plural* **hoots** 1. The cry of an owl or a similar sound. 2. A shout indicating lack of approval or ridicule.
—*verb* **hooted, hooting** 1. To make a hoot or a similar sound: *Owls hooted in the woods at night.* 2. To shout sounds indicating lack of approval or ridicule: *The audience hooted when the villain appeared on stage.*

hooves | hŏŏvz | or | hŏŏvz | A plural of the noun **hoof.**

hop | hŏp | —*verb* **hopped, hopping** 1. To move with light jumping leaps or skips: *The rabbit hopped across the lawn. The frog hopped from one lily pad to another.* 2. To jump on one foot: *You must hop from one square to another when you play hopscotch.* 3. To jump over: *We had to hop a lot of puddles as we crossed the wet school yard.*
—*noun, plural* **hops** An act of hopping; a short jump: *She gave three short hops to catch the ball.*

hope | hōp | —*verb* **hoped, hoping** To wish for something possible; want with some confidence: *I hope I get a new bike for my birthday.*
—*noun, plural* **hopes** 1. A strong wish for something that a person thinks could happen: *Young people are full of hope and energy.* 2. Something that is wished for: *Her hope is that she will be elected class president.* 3. Chance; possibility: *There is no hope of finding a seat on the subway during the rush hour. The weather forecast for rain is not definite, so there is still hope for a nice day.*

hope·ful | hōp′fəl | —*adjective* 1. Feeling or showing hope: *The players arrived hopeful of a victory.* 2. Giving hope: *There were hopeful signs of peace.*

hope·less | hōp′lĭs | —*adjective* Having or offering no chance of success: *He ran to the station, but it was hopeless because the train had already left.*

hops | hŏps | —*plural noun* Fruits that grow on a climbing vine and that look like small, yellowish pine cones. Hops are used in making beer.

hop·scotch | hŏp′skŏch′ | —*noun, plural* **hopscotches** A children's game played on numbered squares drawn on the ground. Players take turns hopping through the squares in order.

horde | hôrd | or | hōrd | —*noun, plural* **hordes** A large group

hoop

crowded together: *A horde of locusts ate the crops. Hordes of customers came for the big sale.*

♦ *These sound alike* **horde, hoard.**

ho·ri·zon |hə **rī′**zən| —*noun, plural* **horizons** **1.** The line where the sky and the land or water seem to meet. **2.** The range of a person's experience, knowledge, and interests: *People with narrow horizons can be very dull and boring.*

hor·i·zon·tal |hôr′ĭ **zŏn′**tl| or |hŏr′ĭ **zŏn′**tl| —*adjective* Parallel to the ground; straight across: *Floors are horizontal and walls are vertical.*

hor·mone |**hôr′**mōn′| —*noun, plural* **hormones** A substance that is made in one of the glands of the body and released into the bloodstream. Hormones control growth. They also regulate such body functions as breathing, sweating, and digestion.

horn |hôrn| —*noun, plural* **horns** **1.** One of the hard, pointed growths on the head of some animals. Cattle, sheep, and goats have horns. Horns and antlers are not the same. Horns do not fall off and grow back again, as antlers do. **2.** A part that sticks out from the head like a horn: *the horns of a snail.* **3.** A container made from an animal's horn: *In pioneer days, horns were used to carry gunpowder.* **4.** A musical instrument played by blowing into the narrow end. Horns used to be made of animal horns, but now they are usually made of brass. Trumpets, trombones, and tubas are horns. **5.** A device on a car or other vehicle that makes a loud warning noise: *The driver honked his horn at the stopped car in front of him.*

horned toad |hôrnd| A lizard of southwestern North America. It has a short tail, a broad, spiny body, and sharp spines on its head. Also called *horned lizard.*

hor·net |**hôr′**nĭt| —*noun, plural* **hornets** A large wasp that can give a painful sting. Hornets often build large nests.

horn·y |**hôr′**nē| —*adjective* **hornier, horniest** Like or made of horn: *a horny growth; a tough, horny patch of skin.*

hor·ri·ble |**hôr′**ə bəl| or |**hŏr′**ə bəl| —*adjective* **1.** Causing horror; terrible: *The Chinese do not think of a dragon as a horrible monster.* **2.** Very unpleasant: *a horrible smell; horrible weather.*

hor·rid |**hôr′**ĭd| or |**hŏr′**ĭd| —*adjective* **1.** Causing horror or disgust; horrible: *a horrid crime.* **2.** Very unpleasant: *a noisy, horrid little child.*

hor·ri·fy |**hôr′**ə fī′| or |**hŏr′**ə fī′| —*verb* **horrified, horrifying, horrifies** **1.** To cause horror in; terrify; frighten: *The sight of the escaped lion horrified us.* **2.** To surprise unpleasantly; shock: *The news that police officers were guilty of a crime horrified the people.*

hor·ror |**hôr′**ər| or |**hŏr′**ər| —*noun, plural* **horrors** **1.** A strong feeling of surprise, sorrow, and fear; terror: *Imagine his horror at the sight of the accident.* **2.** A terrible or disgusting thing: *Cruelty to children is indeed a horror.* **3.** A strong feeling of dislike; hatred: *He had a horror of dirt.*

horse |hôrs| —*noun, plural* **horses** **1.** A large animal that has hoofs and a long mane and tail. Horses are used for riding and for pulling or carrying heavy loads. **2.** A supporting frame with legs: *The work table was made of an old door laid on two wooden horses.* **3.** A padded frame on four legs, used in gyms for gymnastics and other exercises.

♦ *These sound alike* **horse, hoarse.**

horse·back |**hôrs′**băk′| —*noun, plural* **horsebacks** The back of

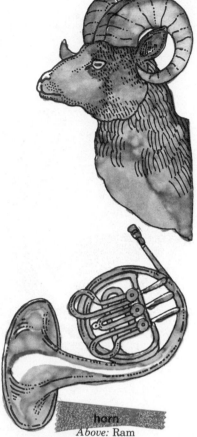

horn
Above: Ram
Below: French horn

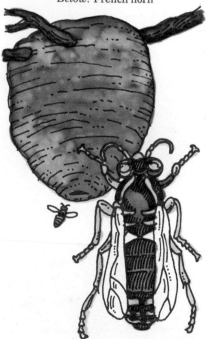

hornet
Nest *(above)* and hornet *(below)*

a horse: *a soldier on horseback.*

—*adverb* On the back of a horse: *She rode horseback.*

horse chestnut A tree that has large, pointed clusters of white flowers and shiny brown nuts. The nuts grow in a spiny bur.

horse·fly |**hôrs′flī′**| —*noun, plural* **horseflies** A large fly that bites and sucks blood from horses and other animals.

horse·play |**hôrs′plā′**| —*noun* Play that is rough and mischievous: *Stop that horseplay before someone gets hurt!*

horse·pow·er |**hôrs′pou′ər**| —*noun, plural* **horsepowers** A unit used for measuring the power of an engine.

horse·rad·ish |**hôrs′răd′ĭsh**| —*noun* The large, whitish root of a tall plant. It has a sharp taste. Grated horseradish is mixed with vinegar and eaten as a relish.

horse·shoe |**hôrs′shōo′**| or |**hôrsh′shōo′**| —*noun, plural* **horseshoes** **1.** A U-shaped piece of iron fitted and nailed to a horse's hoof. **2.** **horseshoes** (Used with a singular verb.) A game in which players try to throw horseshoes so that they land around a post set in the ground.

horseshoe crab A sea animal with a large, oval shell and a stiff, pointed tail.

hose |**hōz**| —*noun* **1.** *plural* **hoses** A long rubber tube used to carry liquids or air: *We used a hose to water the garden.* **2.** *plural* **hose** Stockings.

—*verb* **hosed, hosing** To wash or spray with water from a hose: *The boys hosed down the monkeys' cage.*

hos·pi·ta·ble |**hŏs′pĭ tə bəl**| or |**hŏ spĭt′ə bəl**| —*adjective* Welcoming guests with warm generosity; friendly to visitors: *Ted's mother was very hospitable, even though she didn't expect me for dinner.*

hos·pi·tal |**hŏs′pĭ təl**| or |**hŏs′pĭt′l**| —*noun, plural* **hospitals** A building where doctors and nurses take care of people who are sick or hurt.

hos·pi·tal·i·ty |**hŏs′pĭ tăl′ĭ tē**| —*noun* Friendly treatment of visitors and guests.

hos·pi·tal·ize |**hŏs′pĭ tə līz′**| —*verb* **hospitalized, hospitalizing** To put in a hospital for medical treatment: *When the man's cough and fever did not go away, his doctor decided to hospitalize him.*

host[1] |**hōst**| —*noun, plural* **hosts** A person or group that invites guests and entertains them: *We were the hosts for a group of foreign students visiting our town.*

host[2] |**hōst**| —*noun, plural* **hosts** A large number; multitude: *A host of little islands dot the coast.*

hos·tage |**hŏs′tĭj**| —*noun, plural* **hostages** A person who is held as a prisoner until certain conditions are met: *The bank manager was held hostage until a ransom was paid.*

host·ess |**hō′stĭs**| —*noun, plural* **hostesses** **1.** A woman who acts as host. **2.** A woman who welcomes passengers or customers, as on an airplane or in a restaurant.

hos·tile |**hŏs′təl**| or |**hŏs′tīl**| —*adjective* Feeling or showing hatred; openly unfriendly: *When my neighbor refused to keep his dog quiet, I stopped being polite and sent him a hostile letter.*

hos·til·i·ty |**hŏ stĭl′ĭ tē**| —*noun, plural* **hostilities** **1.** Hatred; ill will: *The tiger looked at us with hostility.* **2.** **hostilities** Open warfare: *The hostilities between the two countries have been going on for years.*

hot |**hŏt**| —*adjective* **hotter, hottest** **1.** Having a lot of heat; very

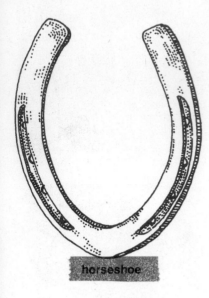

horseshoe

---

host¹, host²
Both of these words traveled from Latin through French into English. **Host¹** meant both "host" and "guest" in the original Latin; **host²** had the meaning of "stranger" or "enemy."

ă	pat	ĕ	pet	î	fierce
ā	pay	ē	be	ŏ	pot
â	care	ĭ	pit	ō	go
ä	father	ī	pie	ô	paw, for
oi	oil	ŭ	cut	zh	vision
ōo	book	û	fur	ə	ago, item,
ōo	boot	*th*	the		pencil, atom,
yōo	abuse	th	thin		circus
ou	out	hw	which	ər	butter

warm: *Don't touch the hot stove. This room is too hot for comfort.*
2. Burning to the taste; sharp or spicy: *hot pepper; hot sauce.*
3. Violent: *Jim had a hot temper.* **4.** Close: *In hot pursuit.*

hot dog A long, thin sausage, usually served on a long roll;
frankfurter.

ho·tel | hō tĕl′ | —*noun, plural* **hotels** A business establishment
that consists of a building with many rooms that people pay to
sleep in. Some hotels serve food and offer many services.

hot·house | hŏt′ hous′ | —*noun, plural* **hot·hous·es** | hŏt′ hou′zĭz |
A heated house, usually with a glass roof and sides, for growing
plants that need an even, warm temperature; greenhouse.

hound | hound | —*noun, plural* **hounds** One of several kinds of
dogs originally bred and trained for hunting. Hounds usually
have drooping ears and a good sense of smell.
—*verb* **hounded, hounding** To ask or remind over and over;
pester; nag: *The boy kept hounding the baseball star for an
autograph until he gave in.*

hour | our | —*noun, plural* **hours** **1.** A unit of time that is equal
to sixty minutes: *There are twenty-four hours in one day.* **2.** A
particular time of day: *At what hour shall we be leaving?* **3.** Often
hours The time for something: *My working hours are from 9 to 5.*
♦ *These sound alike* **hour, our.**

hour·glass | our′ glăs′ | or | our′ glăs′ | —*noun, plural* **hourglasses**
An instrument for measuring time. It is made of two glass
chambers with a narrow neck connecting them. A quantity of
sand in the top chamber takes one hour to pass down to the
bottom chamber.

hour·ly | our′ lē | —*adjective* **1.** Done every hour: *hourly
temperature readings.* **2.** By the hour: *I get an hourly wage for
mowing lawns.*
—*adverb* Every hour: *The news is broadcast hourly on this radio
station.*

house | hous | —*noun, plural* **hous·es** | hou′zĭz | **1.** A building
people live in. **2.** A building used for a certain purpose: *An opera
house.* **3.** A business firm: *a banking house; a publishing house.*
4. The people who live in one building or home; household: *The
whole house was awakened by the thunder storm.* **5.** An audience:
There was a full house on the opening night of the play. **6.** A group
of people who make laws; a law-making body. The House of
Representatives and the Senate are the two houses of the United
States Congress.
—*verb* | houz | **housed, housing** To provide living quarters for: *We
can house ten people overnight.*

house·boat | hous′ bōt′ | —*noun, plural* **houseboats** A large flat-
bottomed boat that people can live on.

house·fly | hous′ flī′ | —*noun, plural* **houseflies** A common fly
that is found in or near homes. It carries and spreads the germs
of many diseases.

house·hold | hous′ hōld′ | —*noun, plural* **households** **1.** The
people who live in a house: *Our household all came down with colds
at the same time.* **2.** A home and its management.

house·keeper | hous′ kē′pər | —*noun, plural* **housekeepers**
Someone who takes care of a house and does such things as
cleaning and cooking.

House of Commons The lower house of Parliament in a
British or Canadian government.

hothouse

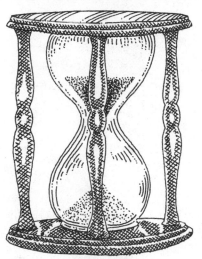

hourglass

House of Representatives

House of Lords The upper house of Parliament in a British government.

House of Representatives The lower branch of the United States Congress. Members are elected every two years.

house sparrow A small bird with brown and gray feathers. It is common everywhere.

house·wife | **hous'**wīf' | —*noun, plural* **house·wives** | **hous'**wīvz' | A married woman who takes care of her family's household.

house·work | **hous'**wûrk' | —*noun* The jobs involved in taking care of a house, such as cooking, cleaning, and washing.

hous·ing | **hou'**zĭng | —*noun, plural* **housings** 1. Buildings in which people live: *The government is helping to pay for new housing in our city.* 2. Something that covers, contains, or protects a machine or part of a machine: *The housing on an electric drill prevents the user from getting an electric shock.*

hov·er | **hŭv'**ər | or | **hŏv'**ər | —*verb* **hovered, hovering** 1. To stay in one place in the air; float or fly without moving much: *The bee hovered over the flower looking for a spot to land.* 2. To stay or wait nearby; linger: *Mother put the frosting on the cake while we children hovered around her.*

how | hou | —*adverb* 1. In what way; by what means: *How can you prove that you're right about this? How do you do that trick?* 2. In what condition: *How does she look now that she's lost weight?* 3. To what degree or amount: *How much do we have to contribute? How do you like your new bike?* 4. At what cost or price: *How much was that dress?*

how·ev·er | hou ĕv'ər | —*adverb* 1. By whatever way: *However you get there, be there on time.* 2. To whatever degree or amount: *However I tried, I couldn't reach the top shelf.*
—*conjunction* Nevertheless; yet: *It grew very dark; however, we had a flashlight with us.*

howl | houl | —*noun, plural* **howls** A long; wailing cry, as of a dog or someone in pain.
—*verb* **howled, howling** To make a long, wailing cry: *Your dog howled all night from hunger and cold. The wind howled through the trees.*

hub | hŭb | —*noun, plural* **hubs** 1. The center part of a wheel. The spokes come out of the hub and are attached to the rim. 2. A center of activity: *Our town is the business hub of the surrounding area.*

huck·le·ber·ry | **hŭk'**əl bĕr'ē | —*noun, plural* **huckleberries** A shiny, blackish berry that looks like a blueberry.

hud·dle | **hŭd'**l | —*noun, plural* **huddles** A closely packed group or crowd: *The football team formed a huddle to discuss the next play. A huddle of small tents could be seen in the clearing.*
—*verb* **huddled, huddling** To crowd together: *The sheep huddled against the storm. The boy scouts huddled around the bonfire. The football players huddled.*

hue | hyōō | —*noun, plural* **hues** A color; shade: *We enjoyed the orange and reddish hues of the sunset.*

hug | hŭg | —*verb* **hugged, hugging** To put the arms around and hold tightly; embrace, especially with affection: *The little girl hugged the puppy. The old friends hugged when they met.*
—*noun, plural* **hugs** A tight clasp in the arms; an embrace: *The mother gave her child a hug.*

huckleberry

ă	pat	ĕ	pet	î	fierce
ā	pay	ē	be	ŏ	pot
â	care	ĭ	pit	ō	go
ä	father	ī	pie	ô	paw, for
oi	oil	ŭ	cut	zh	vision
ōō	book	û	fur	ə	ago, item,
ōō	boot	*th*	the		pencil, atom,
yōō	abuse	th	thin		circus
ou	out	hw	which	ər	butter

huge |hyōoj| —*adjective* **huger, hugest** Of great size; very big; enormous: *a huge iceberg; a huge building.*

hu·la |hōō′lə| —*noun, plural* **hulas** A Hawaiian dance that tells a story with movements of the arms, hands, and body.

hull |hŭl| —*noun, plural* **hulls** **1.** The body of a ship, including its sides and bottom. **2.** The cluster of small leaves near the stem of a strawberry and some other fruits. **3.** The outer covering of some nuts and seeds.
—*verb* **hulled, hulling** To remove the hulls from fruit, nuts, or seeds.

hum |hŭm| —*verb* **hummed, humming** **1.** To make a low, soft sound like a long *m*: *When you sing with your lips closed you are humming. I like to hum while I work. The bees are humming. The radio hums for a minute after we turn it on.* **2.** To be full of busy activity: *The factories hum each working day.*
—*noun, plural* **hums** **1.** The act or sound of humming. **2.** The confused sound of busy activity: *the hum of a room full of people.*

hu·man |hyōō′mən| —*adjective* Of or characteristic of people: *the human body; human needs; human nature.*
—*noun, plural* **humans** A person.

hu·mane |hyōō mān′| —*adjective* Not cruel; kind: *the humane treatment of injured animals.*

hu·man·i·ty |hyōō măn′ĭ tē| —*noun, plural* **humanities** **1.** Human beings as a group; people: *Humanity has made great progress since the days when men lived in caves.* **2.** The condition or quality of being human: *When strangers get together and talk, they often discover their common humanity.* **3.** The quality of being humane; kindness: *The judge's humanity kept him from giving out harsh sentences.*

hum·ble |hŭm′bəl| —*adjective* **humbler, humblest** **1.** Not proud; modest: *She remained a humble person even after she became famous.* **2.** Of low rank or importance; lowly: *a humble servant.*
—*verb* **humbled, humbling** To make humble: *The great paintings in the museum humbled the young artist when he went to see them.*

hu·mid |hyōō′mĭd| —*adjective* Damp; moist: *humid summer air; a humid day.*

hu·mid·i·ty |hyōō mĭd′ĭ tē| —*noun* Water vapor in the air; air moisture.

hu·mil·i·ate |hyōō mĭl′ē āt′| —*verb* **humiliated, humiliating** To hurt the pride or self-respect of; make ashamed: *John was humiliated when his father treated him like a baby.*

hum·ming·bird |hŭm′ĭng bûrd′| —*noun, plural* **hummingbirds** A very small, brightly colored bird with a long, slender bill. The wings of a hummingbird move so fast that they make a humming sound.

hu·mor |hyōō′mər| —*noun, plural* **humors** **1.** The quality of being funny: *I could find no humor in his dull jokes.* **2.** The ability to see and enjoy what is funny: *Since you have a good sense of humor, you might like this cartoon.* **3.** A state of mind; mood: *He's been in bad humor ever since he got that big homework assignment.*
—*verb* **humored, humoring** To go along with the wishes of: *He may be boring but try to humor him just for now.*

hu·mor·ous |hyōō′mər əs| —*adjective* Funny; amusing: *a humorous story.*

hump |hŭmp| —*noun, plural* **humps** A rounded lump, as on the back of a camel.

hull
Above: Boat
Below: Strawberry

hummingbird

hu·mus |**hyōō′**məs| —*noun* Dark soil formed from dead leaves and other plant parts that have decayed. Humus contains substances that help plants grow.

hunch |hŭnch| —*noun, plural* **hunches** A belief without any reason for it; a guess or suspicion: *I have a hunch their house may be right around this corner.*
—*verb* **hunched, hunching** To make rounded by drawing up or in: *The cold air made us cross our arms and hunch up our shoulders.*

hunch·back |**hŭnch′**băk′| —*noun, plural* **hunchbacks 1.** An unusually curved back resulting from a defect in the spinal column. **2.** A person having such a back.

hun·dred |**hŭn′**drĭd| —*noun, plural* **hundreds** A number, written 100, that is equal to the product of 10 × 10.
—*adjective* Being ten more than ninety in number: *a hundred pencils.* The adjective **hundred** belongs to a class of words called **determiners.** They signal that a noun is coming.

hun·dredth |**hŭn′**drĭdth| —*noun, plural* **hundredths 1.** In a group of people or things that are in numbered order, the one that matches the number 100. **2.** One of a hundred equal parts, written 1/100.
—*adjective: the hundredth airplane landing today.*

hung |hŭng| A past tense and a past participle of the verb **hang:** *She hung new curtains in the room. Jerry had hung several posters on the wall.*

hun·ger |**hŭng′**gər| —*noun, plural* **hungers 1.** A strong desire for food: *After school, we satisfied our hunger by eating snacks.* **2.** Lack of food: *People still die of hunger in some parts of the world.* **3.** A strong desire; craving: *a hunger for learning.*
—*verb* **hungered, hungering** To have a strong desire or craving: *After three straight losses, the team hungered for victory.*

hun·gry |**hŭng′**grē| —*adjective* **hungrier, hungriest 1.** Wanting food: *We were all hungry, so we stopped for pizza.* **2.** Having a strong desire; eager: *The lonely child was hungry for attention.*

hunk |hŭngk| —*noun, plural* **hunks** A large piece; a chunk: *I pulled off a hunk of fresh bread.*

hunt |hŭnt| —*verb* **hunted, hunting 1.** To look for so as to capture or kill: *The Indians hunted buffalo.* **2.** To make a careful search; look: *Help me hunt for my eyeglasses.*
—*noun, plural* **hunts 1.** The act or activity of hunting. **2.** A careful search.

hunt·er |**hŭn′**tər| —*noun, plural* **hunters** A person or animal who hunts.

hur·dle |**hûr′**dl| —*noun, plural* **hurdles 1.** A barrier that must be jumped over in a race. **2. hurdles** (Used with a singular verb.) A race in which runners must jump over barriers. **3.** A problem that must be overcome; obstacle.
—*verb* **hurdled, hurdling 1.** To jump over: *The dog escaped by hurdling the fence.* **2.** To overcome: *We'll hurdle that problem when we come to it.*

hurl |hûrl| —*verb* **hurled, hurling** To throw with force: *Tim hurled the ball against the wall.*

hur·rah |hŏŏ **rä′**| or |hŏŏ **rô′**| —*interjection* A word used as a shout of joy or praise: *"Hurrah!" cried the crowd when the ball went into the goal.*
—*noun, plural* **hurrahs** A shout of joy or praise; cheer.

hur·ri·cane |**hûr′**ĭ kān′| or |**hŭr′**ĭ kān| —*noun, plural*

hurdle

hurricanes A powerful storm with very strong winds and heavy rains.

hur·ried |hûr′ ēd| or |hŭr′ ĕd| —*adjective* Done in a hurry; hasty; rushed: *I just had time for a hurried lunch before getting back to class.*

hur·ry |hûr′ ē| or |hŭr′ ē| —*verb* **hurried, hurrying** To act or urge to act quickly; to rush: *Hurry or we will miss the train. Don't hurry me when I am eating.*
—*noun, plural* **hurries 1.** The act of hurrying; rush: *In his hurry this morning, he forgot his keys.* **2.** The need or wish to go quickly: *We walked fast, because we were in a hurry to get there.*

hurt |hûrt| —*verb* **hurt, hurting 1.** To cause pain or injury to: *The child fell and hurt his wrist.* **2.** To have a feeling of pain: *Do your legs hurt?* **3.** To upset; offend: *It hurt me that I wasn't invited to the party.* **4.** To have a bad effect on; harm: *His weak serve will hurt his chances of winning the tennis match.*
—*noun, plural* **hurts** Something that hurts; injury.

hus·band |hŭz′ bənd| —*noun, plural* **husbands** A man who is married.

hush |hŭsh| —*verb* **hushed, hushing** To make or become quiet: *She hushed the crying baby by rocking it. The dog finally hushed.*
—*noun, plural* **hushes** A stillness; quiet: *A sudden hush fell on the crowd.*

husk |hŭsk| —*noun, plural* **husks** The dry outer covering of an ear of corn and of some other seeds and fruits.
—*verb* **husked, husking** To remove the husk from: *We husked the fresh corn and boiled it for dinner.*

husk·y¹ |hŭs′ kē| —*adjective* **huskier, huskiest 1.** Big and strong: *a husky man.* **2.** Rough; hoarse: *a husky voice.*

husk·y² |hŭs′ kē| —*noun, plural* **huskies** A dog with a thick, furry coat. Huskies are used for pulling sleds in the far north.

hus·tle |hŭs′ əl| —*verb* **hustled, hustling** To hurry; rush: *We can get there in time if we hustle. Guards hustled the loud students out of the meeting hall.*

hut |hŭt| —*noun, plural* **huts** A small, simple house or shed; shack.

hy·a·cinth |hī′ ə sĭnth| —*noun, plural* **hyacinths** A plant that grows from a bulb. It has a thick cluster of fragrant flowers.

hy·brid |hī′ brĭd| —*noun, plural* **hybrids** A plant or animal that has parents of different kinds. A mule is a hybrid that has a horse for its mother and a donkey for its father. A rose with white flowers and a rose with red flowers may produce a hybrid with pink flowers.
—*adjective* Being a hybrid; from mixed sources: *hybrid corn; a hybrid language.*

hy·drant |hī′ drənt| —*noun, plural* **hydrants** An outlet from a water pipe that sticks out of the ground. Fire hoses are connected to hydrants to get water for putting out fires.

hy·dro·gen |hī′ drə jən| —*noun* A gas that is very light and that burns easily. Hydrogen combines with oxygen to form water. Hydrogen is one of the chemical elements.

hydrogen bomb A very powerful bomb that can destroy an entire large city. When a hydrogen bomb is set off, hydrogen atoms combine to form helium atoms, and energy is released in a tremendous explosion.

hy·e·na |hī ē′ nə| —*noun, plural* **hyenas** An Asian or African

husky¹, husky²
Husky¹ originally meant "tough like a husk." Husky² used to refer to an Eskimo; later it came to refer to an Eskimo dog.

husky²

hyacinth

animal that looks rather like a large dog. It has thick, coarse hair and powerful jaws. Hyenas often feed on the flesh of dead animals.

hy·giene |**hī′** jĕn′| —*noun* The rules of cleanliness and good health.

hymn |hĭm| —*noun, plural* **hymns** A song of joy, praise, or thanksgiving, especially when sung to God.

♦ *These sound alike* **hymn, him.**

hy·phen |**hī′** fən| —*noun, plural* **hyphens** A mark (-) used to connect words, parts of a compound word, or parts of a word divided between two lines. The word **baby-sit** has a hyphen in it. So does the phrase **life-science class.**

hy·phen·ate |**hī′** fə nāt′| —*verb* **hyphenated, hyphenating** To put a hyphen in: *When a word doesn't fit on a line, hyphenate it and finish it on the next line.*

hyp·no·tize |**hĭp′** nə tīz′| —*verb* **hypnotized, hypnotizing** To put into a special, very relaxed but alert state. A person who has been hypnotized is likely to do just what he is told to do by the person who is hypnotizing him.

hy·poc·ri·sy |hĭ **pŏk′** rĭ sē| —*noun, plural* **hypocrisies** The act or fact of pretending what one is not or feeling what one does not feel; lack of sincere feelings.

hyp·o·crite |**hĭp′** ə krĭt| —*noun, plural* **hypocrites** A person who puts on a false appearance of being good, kind, honest, or religious.

hyp·o·crit·i·cal |hĭp′ə **krĭt′** ĭ kəl| —*adjective* Of or like a hypocrite; insincere; false: *Mr. Smith was a poor player, and hypocritical when he congratulated the winner of the game.*

hys·ter·i·cal |hĭ **stĕr′** ĭ kəl| —*adjective* Excited or frightened; beyond control: *The people trapped in the elevator became hysterical and cried and pounded on the walls.*

ă	pat	ĕ	pet	î	fierce
ā	pay	ē	be	ŏ	pot
â	care	ĭ	pit	ō	go
ä	father	ī	pie	ô	paw, for
oi	oil	ŭ	cut	zh	vision
ŏŏ	book	û	fur	ə	ago, item,
ōō	boot	*th*	the		pencil, atom,
yōō	abuse	th	thin		circus
ou	out	hw	which	ər	butter

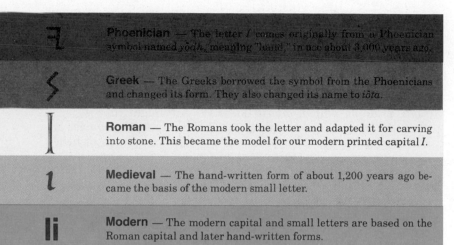

Phoenician — The letter *I* comes originally from a Phoenician symbol named *yôdh*, meaning "hand," in use about 3,000 years ago.

Greek — The Greeks borrowed the symbol from the Phoenicians and changed its form. They also changed its name to *iōta*.

Roman — The Romans took the letter and adapted it for carving into stone. This became the model for our modern printed capital *I*.

Medieval — The hand-written form of about 1,200 years ago became the basis of the modern small letter.

Modern — The modern capital and small letters are based on the Roman capital and later hand-written forms.

i or **I** |ī| —*noun, plural* **i's** or **I's** The ninth letter of the English alphabet.

I |ī| —*pronoun* The person who is speaking or writing: *I went to the movies last night.*

♦ *These sound alike* **I, aye, eye.**

i·bis |ī′bĭs| —*noun, plural* **ibises** A large bird with long legs and a long bill that curves downward. Ibises are found in or near water.

ice |īs| —*noun, plural* **ices** **1.** Water that has been frozen solid. **2.** A frozen dessert made of crushed ice flavored with sweet fruit juice or syrup.

—*verb* **iced, icing** **1.** To make cold or keep cold with ice; chill: *We iced the cans of soda so they would stay cold all day.* **2.** To decorate with icing: *Sam was icing the cake.* **3.** To cover with ice; turn into ice; freeze: *The streets ice over in the winter.*

ice·berg |īs′bûrg′| —*noun, plural* **icebergs** A very large mass of floating ice in the ocean. An iceberg is a piece of a glacier that has broken off, and can be very dangerous to ships.

ice·box |īs′bŏks′| —*noun, plural* **iceboxes** **1.** A heavy box into which ice is put to store and cool food. **2.** A refrigerator.

ice·break·er |īs′brā′kər| —*noun, plural* **icebreakers** A strong ship used to break or cut a path or channel through water covered by ice. Icebreakers are most often used in places such as the Arctic.

ice cap A sheet of ice and snow that covers an area of land all year round.

ice cream A smooth, sweet frozen food made of ice, milk or cream, eggs, and sweeteners. It comes in many flavors.

ice skate A boot or shoe with a metal blade attached to the bottom, worn for skating on ice.

ice-skate |īs′skāt′| —*verb* **ice-skated, ice-skating** To skate on ice.

i·ci·cle |ī′sĭ kəl| —*noun, plural* **icicles** A thin, pointed, hanging piece or stick of ice. An icicle is formed by water freezing as it drips.

ic·ing |ī′sĭng| —*noun, plural* **icings** A smooth, sweet mixture of sugar, butter, and eggs; frosting. Icing is made in many flavors and is used to cover cakes, cookies, and other pastries.

ibis

icebreaker

ice-skate

icy

Idaho

Idaho probably comes from a combination of Indian words meaning either "light on the mountains" or "gem of the mountains."

ic·y |ī′sē| —*adjective* **icier, iciest** **1.** Covered with ice; frozen or slippery: *Herb slipped on the icy sidewalk.* **2.** Feeling like ice; very cold: *icy feet. That was the iciest water I ever went swimming in.* **3.** Cold and unfriendly: *an icy stare.*

I'd |īd| A contraction of "I had," "I would," or "I should."

I·da·ho |ī′də hō′| A state in the northwestern United States. The capital of Idaho is Boise.

i·de·a |ī dē′ə| —*noun, plural* **ideas** **1.** A thought that is carefully or completely worked out in the mind: *Do you have an idea of what is meant by pollution control?* **2.** An opinion or belief: *My teacher has strong ideas about how much time a homework assignment should take.*

i·de·al |ī dē′əl| or |ī dēl′| —*noun, plural* **ideals** A person or thing that is perfect or thought of as being perfect; a model to be imitated: *Peggy says that her aunt is her ideal of the perfect lawyer. Honesty is an ideal that everyone should aim for.*
—*adjective* Perfect or best possible: *It's an ideal day for swimming.*

i·den·ti·cal |ī dĕn′tĭ kəl| —*adjective* **1.** Exactly alike; equal: *We bought identical shirts.* **2.** The very same: *Those are the identical words the man on television used.*

i·den·ti·fi·ca·tion |ī dĕn′tə fĭ kā′shən| —*noun, plural* **identifications** **1.** The act of identifying: *Three customers agreed with the clerk's identification of the man who had held up the store.* **2.** Something that is used to prove who a person is or what something is; proof: *My mother uses her driver's license as identification.*

i·den·ti·fy |ī dĕn′tə fī′| —*verb* **identified, identifying, identifies** **1.** To recognize a particular person or thing; give an accurate description of: *Fingerprints are used to identify persons. She identified her pocketbook by telling what was in it.* **2.** To think of two or more things as the same or as being connected in some way: *Many people identify success with having a good job.*

i·den·ti·ty |ī dĕn′tĭ tē| —*noun, plural* **identities** **1.** Who a person is or what a thing is: *Many famous people try to hide their identities by wearing sunglasses. The tourist proved his identity by showing his passport.* **2.** The condition of being exactly the same as something else: *The identity of the two pictures was clear to anyone who looked at them.*

id·i·om |ĭd′ē əm| —*noun, plural* **idioms** A phrase or expression that has a special meaning that cannot be understood from the normal or regular meaning of the words in it. For example, *up in the air* is an idiom that means "not settled or decided."

id·i·ot |ĭd′ē ət| —*noun, plural* **idiots** **1.** A person who is mentally retarded in the most severe way. Idiots are not able to learn how to read or write or how to take care of themselves. **2.** A very foolish or stupid person: *I was an idiot to lose my mother's birthday present.*

i·dle |īd′l| —*adjective* **idler, idlest** **1.** Not working or busy; doing nothing: *The idle children couldn't find anything to do.* **2.** Not in use; not being operated: *idle machines.* **3.** Avoiding work; lazy: *They're just idle boys who don't want to do anything but play.* **4.** Worthless or useless: *His story about running away from home was only idle talk.*
—*verb* **idled, idling** **1.** To spend time by not working or avoiding work: *We idled away our vacation lying in the sun and going*

ă	pat	ĕ	pet	î	fierce
ā	pay	ē	be	ŏ	pot
â	care	ĭ	pit	ō	go
ä	father	ī	pie	ô	paw, for
oi	oil	ŭ	cut	zh	vision
ŏŏ	book	û	fur	ə	ago, item,
ōō	boot	*th*	the		pencil, atom,
yōō	abuse	th	thin		circus
ou	out	hw	which	ər	butter

swimming. **2.** To run a motor or machine at a low speed or while it is not in gear: *The truck's engine idled smoothly.*

♦ *These sound alike* **idle, idol.**

i·dol |īd′l| —*noun, plural* **idols 1.** A statue, picture, or other object that is worshiped as a god. **2.** A person who is admired or loved very much: *The famous athlete is an idol to millions of people all over the world.*

♦ *These sound alike* **idol, idle.**

if |if| —*conjunction* **1.** On the condition that: *I will come only if you do.* **2.** Supposing that; in case that: *Even if his story is true, what can we do about it?* **3.** Whether: *I wonder if she is coming.* **4.** Even though: *This is a useless if interesting gadget.*

ig·loo |ĭg′loō| —*noun, plural* **igloos** An Eskimo hut or house shaped like a dome. An igloo is often made from blocks of ice or hard snow.

ig·ne·ous |ĭg′nē əs| —*adjective* Formed or made from molten rock. Lava is an igneous rock formed by volcanoes. Granite is an igneous rock formed from minerals that were once a very hot liquid deep inside the earth.

ig·nite |ĭg nīt′| —*verb* **ignited, igniting** To set fire to or catch fire; begin or cause to begin to burn: *Robert ignited the campfire. The pile of gasoline-soaked rags ignited.*

ig·ni·tion |ĭg nĭsh′ən| —*noun, plural* **ignitions 1.** The act or process of igniting: *The ignition of the fireworks is supposed to begin at eight o'clock.* **2.** An electrical system that starts and controls the explosion of gasoline in a gasoline engine. The ignition produces a very hot spark at just the right time.

ig·no·rance |ĭg′nər əns| —*noun* The condition of being ignorant; a lack of knowledge: *Prejudice against people who are different comes from ignorance. Kirby couldn't fix the car because of his ignorance of how the engine is supposed to work.*

ig·no·rant |ĭg′nər ənt| —*adjective* **1.** Not having education or knowledge: *He's ignorant but not stupid, and will learn rapidly.* **2.** Having the wrong information or not enough information: *Many people are ignorant about how difficult it is to ski.*

ig·nore |ĭg nôr′| or |ĭg nōr′| —*verb* **ignored, ignoring** To pay no attention to; disregard: *Whenever I try to talk to her, she ignores me.*

i·gua·na |ĭ gwä′nə| —*noun, plural* **iguanas** A large tropical American lizard with a ridge of spines along the back.

ill |ĭl| —*adjective* **worse, worst 1.** Not healthy; sick: *She has been ill with a cold.* **2.** Not normal; not strong: *ill health.* **3.** Not favorable; bad: *suffering ill luck; the ill effects of not eating well.*
—*adverb* **worse, worst** Not kindly; badly or cruelly: *You shouldn't speak ill of someone you don't know.*
—*noun, plural* **ills 1.** Evil; sin: *for good or for ill.* **2.** Something that causes suffering; harm; disaster: *People who lived in those times faced many ills.*

I'll |īl| A contraction of "I shall" or "I will."

♦ *These sound alike* **I'll, aisle, isle.**

il·le·gal |ĭ lē′gəl| —*adjective* Against the law or against the rules: *It is illegal to drive a car without a license.*

Il·li·nois |ĭl′ə noi′| or |ĭl′ə noiz′| A state in the central United States. The capital of Illinois is Springfield.

il·lit·er·ate |ĭ lĭt′ər ĭt| —*adjective* Not knowing how to read and write: *an illiterate person.*

igloo

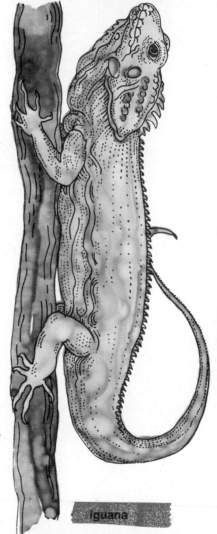

iguana

Illinois

The name **Illinois** comes from the name of an Indian tribe that lived in the region that is today the state. French explorers spelled the Indian word "Illinois." The original Indian word meant "perfect men."

illuminate
Skyscraper and city lights

ill·ness |ĭl′nĭs| —*noun, plural* **illnesses** **1.** Sickness of body or mind: *Her illness lasted many weeks.* **2.** A particular sickness or disease: *Pneumonia is a more serious illness than whooping cough.*

il·lu·mi·nate |ĭ lōō′mə nāt′| —*verb* **illuminated, illuminating** To light up; shine light on: *The hills and fields were illuminated by the moonlight. Street lamps illuminate the city at night.*

il·lu·sion |ĭ lōō′zhən| —*noun, plural* **illusions** **1.** Something that fools the eye, ear, or any of the other senses: *The artist created an illusion of depth in that painting. The banging of a shutter in the wind gave us the illusion that there were ghosts in the house.* **2.** An idea or belief that is mixed up or mistaken: *Tom had the illusion that he would be happier if only he were taller.*

il·lus·trate |ĭl′ə strāt′| or |ĭ lŭs′trāt′| —*verb* **illustrated, illustrating** **1.** To explain something by using examples, stories, pictures, or comparisons: *The teacher dropped a ball and a piece of paper to the floor to illustrate how gravity works.* **2.** To add pictures or diagrams that explain or decorate to a book, magazine, or other type of printed matter: *This book about the United States has been illustrated with pictures of all different parts of the country.*

il·lus·tra·tion |ĭl′ə strā′shən| —*noun, plural* **illustrations** **1.** A picture, diagram, chart, or other device used to explain or decorate: *The illustration of all the planets showed which ones were closest to the sun.* **2.** Something serving as an example, explanation, or proof: *A rock falling to the ground is an illustration of gravity.*

ill will An unfriendly feeling; dislike or hatred: *He feels ill will toward the person who ran over his bicycle.*

I'm |īm| A contraction of "I am."

im·age |ĭm′ĭj| —*noun, plural* **images** **1.** The picture formed by light shining through lenses or mirrors: *I can see the image of myself in the mirror. The image on the movie screen was not bright enough.* **2.** A picture of something in the mind: *The smell of onions brings to my mind images of hamburgers.* **3.** A reproduction or copy of a person or thing, such as a statue or a figure in a painting: *Whose image is on a dollar bill?* **4.** Something or someone who looks very much like another: *She is the image of her grandmother.* **5.** Public opinion about someone: *The mayor was worried more about his image than about solving the city's problems.*

i·mag·i·nar·y |ĭ măj′ə nĕr′ē| —*adjective* Existing only in the imagination; made-up; not real: *Ghosts and goblins are imaginary creatures.*

i·mag·i·na·tion |ĭ măj′ə nā′shən| —*noun, plural* **imaginations** **1.** The ability of the mind to form pictures or images of things that are not there: *In her imagination she could picture the old house where she used to live.* **2.** The ability to create or make up things that are not real or events that did not really happen: *That writer must have a good imagination to think up all the things that happen in his story.*

i·mag·i·na·tive |ĭ măj′ə nə tĭv| or |ĭ măj′ə nā′tĭv| —*adjective* **1.** Having a strong imagination: *The imaginative child is always making up stories and drawing pictures to go with them.* **2.** Showing or having to do with imagination: *an imaginative story.*

i·mag·ine |ĭ măj′ĭn| —*verb* **imagined, imagining** **1.** To form a picture of a person or thing in the mind; have an idea of: *Can you imagine a blue horse with a yellow tail?* **2.** To make a guess; think: *How many people do you imagine will be at the party?*

ă	pat	ē	pet	î	fierce
ā	pay	ē	be	ŏ	pot
â	care	ĭ	pit	ō	go
ä	father	ī	pie	ô	paw, for
oi	oil	ŭ	cut	zh	vision
ōō	book	û	fur	ə	ago, item,
ōō	boot	th	the		pencil, atom,
yōō	abuse	th	thin		circus
ou	out	hw	which	ər	butter

im·i·tate |ĭm′ĭ tāt′| —*verb* **imitated, imitating** **1.** To copy the actions, appearance, or sounds of someone or something else: *He was imitating his father by walking and talking slowly.* **2.** To look like; resemble: *The wallpaper is designed to imitate wood.*

im·i·ta·tion |ĭm′ĭ tā′shən| —*noun, plural* **imitations** **1.** The act of imitating: *He does a funny imitation of a monkey.* **2.** A copy of something else: *These aren't real diamonds, they're imitations.*

im·ma·ture |ĭm′ə tŏŏr′| or |ĭm′ə tyŏŏr′| or |ĭm′ə chŏŏr′| —*adjective* **1.** Not fully grown, developed, or ripe; not mature: *an immature ear of corn.* **2.** Not acting one's age; behaving childishly: *Crying when you don't get what you want is immature.*

im·me·di·ate |ĭ mē′dē ĭt| —*adjective* **1.** Taking place at once or very soon; happening without delay: *I want an immediate answer.* **2.** Coming next or very soon: *the immediate future.* **3.** Close; nearby: *There are no food stores in the immediate area.*

im·me·di·ate·ly |ĭ mē′dē ĭt lē| —*adverb* **1.** Right away; at once; without delay: *Do your homework immediately.* **2.** Right after; next: *Come home immediately after your piano lesson.*

im·mense |ĭ mĕns′| —*adjective* Of great size, extent, or degree: *China is an immense country. She gets immense satisfaction from the simple things in life.*

im·mi·grant |ĭm′ĭ grənt| —*noun, plural* **immigrants** A person who leaves the country in which he or she was born to live in another country: *My grandparents were immigrants to the United States from Germany.*

im·mi·grate |ĭm′ĭ grāt′| —*verb* **immigrated, immigrating** To move to or go live in a country in which one was not born.

im·mor·al |ĭ môr′əl| or |ĭ mŏr′əl| —*adjective* Not moral; not just; evil; wicked: *He was found guilty of immoral conduct.*

im·mor·tal |ĭ môr′tl| —*adjective* **1.** Living or lasting forever; never dying: *No one on earth is immortal.* **2.** Never to be forgotten; having fame that will last forever: *an immortal poet.*

im·mune |ĭ myōōn′| —*adjective* Protected from disease: *Vaccinations can make people immune to smallpox.*

im·pact |ĭm′păkt′| —*noun, plural* **impacts** The action of one object striking against another; collision: *Neither car had been moving very fast at impact, so nobody was hurt.*

im·pair |ĭm pâr′| —*verb* **impaired, impairing** To reduce the strength or quality of; weaken: *The lack of vitamins can impair a person's health. Her hearing had been impaired by the accident.*

im·pa·la |ĭm pä′lə| or |ĭm păl′ə| —*noun, plural* **impalas** An African antelope with curved, spreading horns. It can make long, high leaps.

im·par·tial |ĭm pär′shəl| —*adjective* Not favoring one person or side more than another; fair; just: *an impartial judge; an impartial opinion.*

im·pa·tience |ĭm pā′shəns| —*noun* **1.** The condition of being impatient; the fact of not being able or willing to wait patiently: *my brother's impatience with the crying baby.* **2.** The condition of being very eager: *The whole family noticed my brother's impatience for his new car to arrive.*

im·pa·tiens |ĭm pā′shəns| or |ĭm pā′shənz| —*noun* A garden plant with white, pink, red, or orange flowers.

im·pa·tient |ĭm pā′shənt| —*adjective* **1.** Not able or willing to wait calmly or put up with opposition or annoyance: *I get*

immigrant
Family arriving in the United States by ship

impala

impatiens

impatient with Larry because he always keeps me waiting. **2.** Very eager: *Pamela was impatient for the game to begin.*

im·peach |ĭm pēch'| —*verb* **impeached, impeaching** To accuse a public official with wrong or illegal behavior before a special type of court. If he or she is found guilty, an official may be removed from office, made to pay a fine, or be sent to jail.

im·per·fect |ĭm pûr'fĭkt| —*adjective* Not perfect; having faults, errors, or gaps: *imperfect speech; an imperfect memory.*

im·pe·ri·al |ĭm pîr'ē əl| —*adjective* **1.** Having to do with an empire or an empress or emperor: *the imperial palace; the imperial court of Japan.* **2.** Having to do with one country's rule, control, or authority over another country or a colony: *Egypt was once under the imperial control of the Roman Empire.*

im·ple·ment |ĭm'plə mənt| —*noun, plural* **implements** A tool or piece of equipment used to do a particular job or task: *Tractors and plows are farming implements.*

im·ply |ĭm plī'| —*verb* **implied, implying, implies** To say or mean something without saying it directly; suggest without stating; to hint: *Mom wouldn't let us go to the movie, but she implied that she might change her mind if we were good.*

im·po·lite |ĭm'pə līt'| —*adjective* Not polite or having good manners; rude: *I didn't like your impolite behavior at your aunt's house.*

im·port |ĭm pôrt'| or |ĭm pōrt'| or |ĭm'pôrt'| or |ĭm'pōrt'| —*verb* **imported, importing** To bring in goods or products from a foreign country for sale or use: *The United States imports much oil.* —*noun* |ĭm'pôrt'| or |ĭm'pōrt'|, *plural* **imports** Something imported: *Are you buying an import or a car that was built here?*

im·por·tance |ĭm pôr'tns| —*noun* The condition or quality of being important; value or significance: *Don't ever forget the importance of a good education.*

im·por·tant |ĭm pôr'tnt| —*adjective* Having great value, meaning, or influence; significant: *an important message; an important person. Eating well is important for your health.*

im·pose |ĭm pōz'| —*verb* **imposed, imposing** To put on or assign to a person something that is a burden, such as a tax, punishment, or task: *The judge imposed a sixty-day jail sentence on the robber.*

im·pos·si·ble |ĭm pŏs'ə bəl| —*adjective* **1.** Not able to happen or exist: *It is impossible for a person to be in two different places at the same time.* **2.** Not able to be done: *It will be impossible to get there without taking the train.* **3.** Difficult to tolerate or put up with: *He's an impossible child when he's sick.*

im·press |ĭm prĕs'| —*verb* **impressed, impressing** **1.** To have a strong effect on the feelings or mind: *He impressed us by being so friendly and generous.* **2.** To put firmly into someone's mind: *They impressed on their children that they should treat everyone fairly.*

im·pres·sion |ĭm prĕsh'ən| —*noun, plural* **impressions** **1.** An effect, image, or feeling that stays in the mind: *My sister's new friend made a good impression on my parents.* **2.** An idea, notion, or belief: *I had the impression I'd met him before.* **3.** A mark, pattern, or design made on a surface by pressing or being pressed into it: *We made impressions of our feet in the snow.* **4.** A funny imitation of someone's speech, actions, or behavior: *She did an impression of the clown at the circus.*

im·pres·sive |ĭm prĕs'ĭv| —*adjective* Making an impression

implement
Farm implements

ă	pat	ĕ	pet	î	fierce
ā	pay	ē	be	ŏ	pot
â	care	ĭ	pit	ō	go
ä	father	ī	pie	ô	paw, for

oi	oil	ŭ	cut	zh	vision
ŏŏ	book	û	fur	ə	ago, item,
ōō	boot	*th*	the		pencil, atom,
yŏŏ	abuse	th	thin		circus
ou	out	hw	which	ər	butter

that is strong or that lasts a long time: *an impressive speech; an impressive view from the top of the building.*

im·print |ĭm′prĭnt′| —*noun, plural* **imprints** **1.** A mark, pattern, or design made by pressing something on a surface: *an imprint of dog's tracks in the sand.* **2.** An influence or effect that is easy to notice: *The style of buildings in the Southwest shows the imprint of Indian culture.*
—*verb* |ĭm prĭnt′| **imprinted, imprinting** To make a mark, pattern, or design on a surface by stamping or pressing: *He imprinted his name on the card.*

im·pris·on |ĭm prĭz′ən| —*verb* **imprisoned, imprisoning** To put in jail or prison; lock up: *The criminal was imprisoned for ten years.*

im·prop·er |ĭm prŏp′ər| —*adjective* **1.** Not proper; incorrect; wrong: *To eat nothing but cookies and soda is an improper diet.* **2.** Showing or having bad manners: *Laughing and joking is improper behavior in a church.*

improper fraction A fraction that is equal to or greater than 1. $\frac{4}{3}$ and $\frac{3}{3}$ are improper fractions.

im·prove |ĭm proōv′| —*verb* **improved, improving** To make or become better: *Dominique improved her tennis serve by practicing. He was very sick but his health is improving.*

im·prove·ment |ĭm proōv′mənt| —*noun, plural* **improvements** **1.** A change or addition that improves something: *Dad made improvements on the house by building two more rooms.* **2.** A person or thing that is better than another or what it replaces: *The new gym teacher is an improvement over the one last year.* **3.** The act or process of improving: *His swimming shows a lot of improvement since last summer.*

im·pro·vise |ĭm′prə vīz′| —*verb* **improvised, improvising** **1.** To make up and perform without preparing or rehearsing beforehand: *improvise a song; improvise a speech.* **2.** To build or make from whatever things or materials are around: *She improvised a picnic table from some long boards.*

im·pu·dent |ĭm′pyə dənt| —*adjective* Showing a bold lack of respect; rude: *The impudent child yelled at his parents.*

im·pulse |ĭm′pŭls′| —*noun, plural* **impulses** **1.** A sudden urge or desire; a whim: *I had an impulse to buy that red shirt, but I'm glad I didn't.* **2.** A sudden force; thrust; push: *The quick impulse of the wind knocked over the garbage can.*

im·pure |ĭm pyoōr′| —*adjective* **1.** Not pure or clean; dirty: *The water in the river is impure because of pollution.* **2.** Mixed with other substances: *Coal is an impure form of carbon.*

in |ĭn| —*preposition* **1.** Inside: *Put your books in the drawer. She lives in a house.* **2.** To or at the condition or situation of: *I am in pain. She is in trouble.* **3.** Into a certain space: *I could not get in the house.* **4.** During: *Don't call in the evening.* **5.** By the end of: *Your glasses will be ready in a few minutes.* **6.** At the time of: *We bought the car in the spring.* **7.** With the use of: *drawings done in chalk.* **8.** Out of: *She said that in anger.* **9.** According to: *the latest thing in fashion. In my opinion she's not telling the truth.* **10.** By means of: *She paid for her hat in cash.* **11.** Covered with; having on: *I saw a man in a blue raincoat.* **12.** Placed so as to make: *They built several houses in a row.* **13.** For the purpose of: *These pots are used in cooking.* **14.** In respect to; regarding: *These books are different in color.*
—*adverb* **1.** Toward the inside; indoors: *Come in out of the rain.*

inauguration
The inauguration of President
John F. Kennedy, 1961

---

incense¹, incense²
Even though **incense¹** and **incense²** are pronounced differently, they are related. **Incense¹** is from a Latin verb meaning "to set on fire" and "to make someone angry." This same verb formed a noun meaning "substance for burning"; this noun was the source of **incense²**. Both words traveled through French before arriving in English.

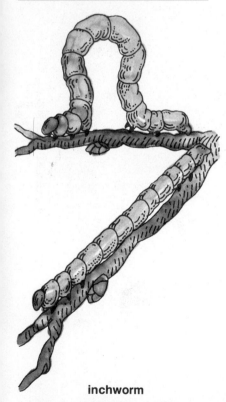

inchworm

ă	pat	ĕ	pet	î	fierce
ā	pay	ē	be	ŏ	pot
â	care	ĭ	pit	ō	go
ä	father	ī	pie	ô	paw, for
oi	oil	ŭ	cut	zh	vision
ŏŏ	book	û	fur	ə	ago, item,
ōō	boot	th	the		pencil, atom,
yōō	abuse	th	thin		circus
ou	out	hw	which	ər	butter

---

2. Inside a place; at home or at work: *Mother is not in today. Is the doctor in?*
♦ *These sound alike* **in, inn.**

in-¹ A prefix that means "without, not": *informal; insane.*

in-² A prefix that means "in, within, or into": *inland; indoors.*

in·au·gu·rate |ĭ nô′gyə rāt′| —*verb* **inaugurated, inaugurating**
1. To place or install a person in office with a formal ceremony: *Every four years a President and Vice President of the United States are inaugurated.* **2.** To open for public use with a formal ceremony; dedicate: *The mayor is going to make a speech when the city inaugurates the new library.*

in·au·gu·ra·tion |ĭ nô′gyə rā′shən| —*noun, plural* **inaugurations**
1. The formal ceremony of placing or installing a person in office: *It rained during the inauguration of the governor.* **2.** A formal beginning or opening; dedication: *The city held a big picnic as part of the inauguration of the new park.*

in·born |ĭn′bôrn′| —*adjective* Present in a person or animal from birth: *Some people have an inborn ability to run fast.*

in·cense¹ |ĭn sĕns′| —*verb* **incensed, incensing** To make very angry; infuriate: *The old man's cruelty to his dog incenses me.*

in·cense² |ĭn′sĕns′| —*noun, plural* **incenses** A substance that gives off a sweet smell when burned. Incense is burned as a part of some religious ceremonies.

in·cen·tive |ĭn sĕn′tĭv| —*noun, plural* **incentives** Something that urges a person to act or make an effort: *Beth's desire to help people was her incentive to become a lawyer.*

inch |ĭnch| —*noun, plural* **inches** A unit of length that equals ¹⁄₁₂ of a foot. Twelve inches equal one foot. In the metric system, an inch equals 2.54 centimeters.
—*verb* **inched, inching** To move or cause to move very slowly: *He inched down the corridor hoping no one would see him. She inched the boulder across the yard.*

inch·worm |ĭnch′wûrm′| —*noun, plural* **inchworms** A caterpillar that moves by looping up its body and then stretching it out.

in·ci·dent |ĭn′sĭ dənt| —*noun, plural* **incidents 1.** Something that happens; an event: *We saw two interesting incidents on our way to the zoo.* **2.** A minor event that can cause trouble or annoyance: *The plane took off without incident.*

in·ci·den·tal·ly |ĭn′sĭ dĕn′tl ē| —*adverb* In addition to something else; by the way: *Incidentally, did you go to see Sarah last weekend?*

in·cin·er·a·tor |ĭn sĭn′ə rā′tər| —*noun, plural* **incinerators** A furnace for burning trash or garbage.

in·cli·na·tion |ĭn′klə nā′shən| —*noun, plural* **inclinations 1.** A tendency to act in a certain way: *He has an inclination to stoop and has to force himself to stand up straight.* **2.** A natural preference; a liking: *She has an inclination for roller skating.*

in·cline |ĭn klīn′| —*verb* **inclined, inclining** To lean, slant, or slope: *The road inclines sharply upward. He inclined the ladder against the house.*
—*noun* |ĭn′klīn′|, *plural* **inclines** A surface that inclines; a slope or slant: *I lost speed running up the incline.*

in·clude |ĭn klōōd′| —*verb* **included, including 1.** To be made up of, either completely or in part; contain: *The art show includes* *some of my mother's paintings.* **2.** To put into a group, a class, or a total: *Please include your name and address on the form.*

in·come |**ĭn′** kŭm′ | —*noun, plural* **incomes** The amount of money that a person or business receives from work, goods, services, property, or other things that are owned.

income tax A tax on a person's income. The income tax is based on how much a person earns in a year.

in·com·plete | ĭn′kəm **plēt′** | —*adjective* Not complete: *an incomplete set of dishes.*

in·cor·rect | ĭn′kə **rĕkt′** | —*adjective* Not correct; wrong; not proper: *That answer is incorrect.*

in·crease | ĭn **krēs′** | —*verb* **increased, increasing** To make or become greater or larger: *He increased his income by taking a second job. The population increased rapidly.*
—*noun* | **ĭn′** krēs′ |, *plural* **increases** **1.** The act of increasing; growth: *an increase in homework.* **2.** The amount or rate by which something is increased: *an increase in price of two dollars.*

in·creas·ing·ly | ĭn **krē′** sĭng lē | —*adverb* More and more: *The sky became increasingly pink as the sun went down.*

in·cred·i·ble | ĭn **krĕd′** ə bəl | —*adjective* **1.** Hard to believe: *an incredible excuse.* **2.** Astonishing; amazing: *The bird flew to an incredible height.*

in·cu·bate | **ĭn′** kyə bāt′ | or | **ĭng′** kyə bāt′ | —*verb* **incubated, incubating** To keep eggs warm until they hatch. The heat for incubating may come from a mother bird's body, from the sun, or from a special machine.

in·cu·ba·tor | **ĭn′** kyə bā′tər | or | **ĭng′** kyə bā′tər | —*noun, plural* **incubators** **1.** A machine or box that provides heat at just the right temperature for incubating and hatching eggs. **2.** A device that provides the right temperature, humidity, and oxygen for a baby that has been born earlier than usual.

in·deed | ĭn **dēd′** | —*adverb* In fact; in reality: *Her parents were indeed pleased with her grades.*

in·def·i·nite | ĭn **dĕf′** ə nĭt | —*adjective* **1.** Not fixed; likely to change: *an indefinite period of time.* **2.** Not clear; vague: *In the fog, we could see only the indefinite outline of the house.* **3.** Not decided; not sure: *Our plans will be indefinite until we hear from Aunt May.*

indefinite article Either of the articles **a** or **an.** The indefinite articles belong to a class of words called **determiners.** They signal that a noun is coming.

in·dent | ĭn **dĕnt′** | —*verb* **indented, indenting** To begin a line of writing or printing farther in from the margin than the other lines. The first line of a paragraph is often indented.

in·de·pen·dence | ĭn′dĭ **pĕn′** dəns | —*noun* The condition or quality of being independent and not controlled by or dependent on others.

Independence Day Another name for the **Fourth of July.**

in·de·pen·dent | ĭn′dĭ **pĕn′** dənt | —*adjective* **1.** Not under the control of a foreign government: *an independent country.* **2.** Not influenced or controlled by other people; able to make decisions for oneself: *an independent mind.* **3.** Not depending on other people for food and shelter; earning one's own living: *My older brother has moved away from home and is now independent.*

in·dex | **ĭn′** dĕks′ | —*noun, plural* **indexes** An alphabetical list that is used for finding information. An index may contain

incubator
For a baby

names, dates, places, subjects, or titles of books or articles.
—*verb* **indexed, indexing** **1.** To make or write an index for. **2.** To arrange in an index.

index finger The finger next to the thumb.

In·di·a |ĭn′dē ə| A country in southern Asia.

In·di·an |ĭn′dē ən| —*noun, plural* **Indians** **1.** A person who was born in or is a citizen of India. **2.** An American Indian.
—*adjective* **1.** Of India or its people. **2.** Of the American Indians or their languages and culture.

In·di·an·a |ĭn′dē ăn′ə| A state in the central United States. The capital of Indiana is Indianapolis.

In·di·an·ap·o·lis |ĭn′dē ə năp′ə lĭs| The capital of Indiana.

Indian Ocean An ocean lying between Africa, Asia, Australia, and Antarctica.

Indian pipe A waxy plant with a single nodding flower. Indian pipes grow in the woods.

in·di·cate |ĭn′dĭ kāt′| —*verb* **indicated, indicating** **1.** To show or point out exactly: *Please indicate on this map how to get to your house.* **2.** To serve as a sign of: *The dark sky indicated that we would have rain.*

in·di·ca·tion |ĭn′dĭ kā′shən| —*noun, plural* **indications** Something that indicates; a sign or symptom: *The look on her face was an indication of great anger.*

in·dict |ĭn dīt′| —*verb* **indicted, indicting** To accuse a person of committing a crime; to charge.

in·dif·fer·ence |ĭn dĭf′ər əns| —*noun* A lack of concern or interest: *The party was called off because of our indifference.*

in·dif·fer·ent |ĭn dĭf′ər ənt| —*adjective* Having or showing no interest; not caring one way or the other: *She is indifferent to other people's opinion of her.*

in·dig·nant |ĭn dĭg′nənt| —*adjective* Feeling or showing anger about something that is unfair, mean, or bad: *We were indignant over her nasty remarks.*

in·dig·na·tion |ĭn′dĭg nā′shən| —*noun* Anger that is caused by something that is unfair, mean, or bad.

in·di·go |ĭn′dĭ gō′| —*noun, plural* **indigos** or **indigoes** **1.** A plant from which a blue dye is made. **2.** A dark-blue dye. It can be made from the indigo plant or man-made.
—*adjective* Dark blue.

in·di·rect |ĭn′də rĕkt′| —*adjective* **1.** Not going in a direct path; roundabout: *He took an indirect route home in order to avoid an unfriendly dog.* **2.** Not getting to the main point: *Her comment about color was an indirect way of telling me she didn't like my shirt.* **3.** Not directly planned for; secondary: *An indirect result of all that exercise is that his clothes don't fit anymore.*

in·di·vid·u·al |ĭn′də vĭj′o̅o̅ əl| —*adjective* **1.** Single; separate: *for each individual child; individual words.* **2.** Of, by, or for one person: *individual servings of sugar.* **3.** Having a special quality; unique; distinct: *the individual aroma of cloves.*
—*noun, plural* **individuals** **1.** A single person considered separately from a group: *An individual has rights that no group can take away.* **2.** Someone who is independent or has some remarkable quality: *She is a real individual, never just going along with the crowd. He is a grouchy individual, always shouting at us to stay off his lawn.*

in·di·vid·u·al·i·ty |ĭn′də vĭj′o̅o̅ ăl′ĭ tē| —*noun, plural*

Indiana
Indiana means "land of the Indians." The word was created by giving a Latin ending to the word "Indian."

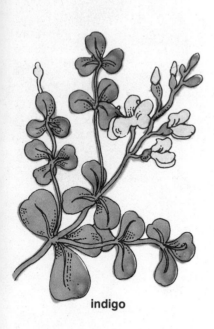

indigo

ă	pat	ĕ	pet	î	fierce
ā	pay	ē	be	ŏ	pot
â	care	ĭ	pit	ō	go
ä	father	ī	pie	ô	paw, for

oi	oil	ŭ	cut	zh	vision
o̅o̅	book	û	fur	ə	ago, item,
o̅o̅	boot	*th*	the		pencil, atom,
yo̅o̅	abuse	th	thin		circus
ou	out	hw	which	ər	butter

individualities The qualities that make a person or thing different from others: *Some people express their individuality through art, some through sports.*

in·di·vid·u·al·ly |ĭn′də vĭj′ o͞o ə lē| —*adverb* As individuals; separately: *The principal knew all the students individually.*

in·di·vis·i·ble |ĭn′də vĭz′ə bəl| —*adjective* Not capable of being divided evenly so that there is no remainder in the quotient. For example, 7 is indivisible by 3.

in·door |ĭn′dôr′| or |ĭn′dōr′| —*adjective* Of, in, or taking place within a house or other building: *an indoor pool; an indoor party.*

in·doors |ĭn dôrz′| or |ĭn dōrz′| —*adverb* In or into a house or other building: *Why are you staying indoors on such a beautiful day? Please come indoors out of the rain.*

in·dus·tri·al |ĭn dŭs′trē əl| —*adjective* **1.** Of or having to do with industry: *industrial products.* **2.** Having highly developed industries: *an industrial nation.* **3.** Used in industry: *industrial diamonds.*

in·dus·tri·al·ize |ĭn dŭs′trē ə līz′| —*verb* **industrialized, industrializing** To make or become industrial rather than agricultural; develop industries in: *The new government wanted to industrialize the country.*

in·dus·tri·ous |ĭn dŭs′trē əs| —*adjective* Working hard; diligent: *an industrious student.*

in·dus·try |ĭn′də strē| —*noun, plural* **industries** **1. a.** The making or producing of things by businesses and factories: *That city is the center of much industry.* **b.** A specific branch of business: *the textbook industry; the recreation industry.* **2.** Hard work; steady effort: *We admired the industry with which the beavers built their home.*

in·ed·i·ble |ĭn ĕd′ə bəl| —*adjective* Not edible; not suitable as food: *Some mushrooms are inedible because they are poisonous.*

in·e·qual·i·ty |ĭn′ĭ kwŏl′ĭ tē| —*noun, plural* **inequalities** The condition of being not equal: *Inequalities sometimes exist in the chance for good jobs and housing.*

in·ert |ĭ nûrt′| —*adjective* **1.** Not able to move or act: *rocks, boulders, and other inert objects.* **2.** Slow to move, act, or respond: *Animals are inert while they are hibernating.*

in·ev·i·ta·ble |ĭn ĕv′ĭ tə bəl| —*adjective* Not capable of being avoided or prevented: *An inevitable result of rain is that things get wet.*

in·ex·pen·sive |ĭn′ĭk spĕn′sĭv| —*adjective* Not expensive; of low price; cheap: *an inexpensive watch.*

in·fant |ĭn′fənt| —*noun, plural* **infants** A child from birth to about two years of age; a baby.

in·fan·tile paralysis |ĭn′fən tīl′| or |ĭn′fən tĭl| A disease that is caused by a virus and affects mostly children. It can affect muscles and nerves and cause paralysis. Other names for this disease are **poliomyelitis** and **polio.**

in·fan·try |ĭn′fən trē| —*noun, plural* **infantries** The part of an army that fights on foot.

in·fect |ĭn fĕkt′| —*verb* **infected, infecting** To give or transfer a disease to: *One child with measles infected ten of his friends.*

in·fec·tion |ĭn fĕk′shən| —*noun, plural* **infections** A disease in the body or part of the body: *I have an infection in my foot because I stepped on a rusty nail.*

in·fec·tious |ĭn fĕk′shəs| —*adjective* **1.** Caused by or spread by

industry
Above: Pouring molten steel
Below: Inside a steel mill

infantry
U.S. soldiers in France during World War I

infection: *infectious diseases such as chicken pox and measles.*
2. Spreading easily: *infectious laughter.*

in·fe·ri·or |ĭn fîr′ē ər| —*adjective* **1.** Low or lower in rank or position: *He started in an inferior position in the company and rose to become president.* **2.** Low or lower in quality: *inferior merchandise that falls apart easily.* **3.** Of low or lower intelligence or ability: *She is so smart she makes the rest of us feel inferior.*

in·field |ĭn′fēld′| —*noun, plural* **infields** **1.** The playing area of a baseball field inside the diamond, including the bases and the area inside them. **2.** The members of the baseball team that play in the infield.

in·fi·nite |ĭn′fə nĭt| —*adjective* **1.** Having no limit in space, time, extent, or number; endless: *We may assume that the universe is infinite.* **2.** Greater in value than any number, no matter how large it is: *an infinite number.* **3.** Seeming to have no limit; very great: *She took infinite care in putting the model airplane together.*

in·fin·i·tive |ĭn fĭn′ĭ tĭv| —*noun, plural* **infinitives** A simple form of a verb that is often preceded by the word "to." In the sentence *They like to walk, to walk* is an infinitive.

in·flame |ĭn flām′| —*verb* **inflamed, inflaming** **1.** To become or cause to become sore, red, swollen, and warm to the touch because of injury or disease: *Our eyes inflamed in the smog. A bad cold had inflamed her throat.* **2.** To make very upset or angry: *Their bad behavior inflamed the whole neighborhood.*

in·flam·ma·tion |ĭn′flə mā′shən| —*noun, plural* **inflammations** The condition of being inflamed: *He stayed home from school with an inflammation in his throat.*

in·flate |ĭn flāt′| —*verb* **inflated, inflating** **1.** To make bigger and more firm by filling with air or another gas: *We inflated all four tires on the car. You have to blow very hard to make this balloon inflate.* **2.** To become or cause to become greater: *A demand from customers may cause food prices to inflate.*

in·fla·tion |ĭn flā′shən| —*noun, plural* **inflations** **1.** The act or process of inflating: *The inflation of the huge balloon took almost an hour.* **2.** The condition or degree of being inflated: *These tires require an inflation of fifty pounds.* **3.** A fast rise in the cost of living.

in·flu·ence |ĭn′floo əns| —*noun, plural* **influences** **1.** The ability or power to change or have an effect on things: *a person with a great influence in government.* **2.** A change or effect produced by such an ability or power: *The book of fairy tales had a big influence on me.* **3.** Someone or something that can cause a change or have an effect: *Everyone thought Uncle Henry was a bad influence on me.*

—*verb* **influenced, influencing** To make a change in or have an effect on: *Parents can influence their children by the way they behave themselves.*

in·flu·en·za |ĭn′floo ĕn′zə| —*noun, plural* **influenzas** A disease caused by a virus. The disease causes fever, coughing, and pains in the muscles and chest; flu.

in·form |ĭn fôrm′| —*verb* **informed, informing** To give information to; advise: *We will inform you when the bicycle you ordered has arrived.*

in·for·mal |ĭn fôr′məl| —*adjective* Done in a simple way; without ceremony; casual: *an informal party.*

in·for·ma·tion |ĭn′fər mā′shən| —*noun* Facts about a certain

ă	pat	ĕ	pet	î	fierce
ā	pay	ē	be	ŏ	pot
â	care	ĭ	pit	ō	go
ä	father	ī	pie	ô	paw, for
oi	oil	ŭ	cut	zh	vision
oo	book	û	fur	ə	ago, item,
oo	boot	*th*	the		pencil, atom,
yoo	abuse	th	thin		circus
ou	out	hw	which	ər	butter

event or subject: *The neighbors gave us information on the best places to eat while we were traveling.*

in·fu·ri·ate |ĭn **fyŏŏr′**ē āt′| —*verb* **infuriated, infuriating** To make very angry; enrage: *His behavior infuriated his friends.*

-ing A suffix that forms the present participle of verbs: *guiding; moving; trying.*

in·ge·nu·i·ty |ĭn′jə **nōō′**ĭ tē| or |ĭn′jə **nyōō′**ĭ tē| —*noun, plural* **ingenuities** Skill in inventing things; imagination: *The way you make animals out of clay shows great ingenuity.*

in·gre·di·ent |ĭn **grē′**dē ənt| —*noun, plural* **ingredients**
1. Something added to or required in a mixture or compound: *Eggs and milk are ingredients for scrambled eggs.* **2.** A necessary part of something: *Good sense is an ingredient in making any plan.*

in·hab·it |ĭn **hăb′**ĭt| —*verb* **inhabited, inhabiting** To live in or have as a home: *In winter squirrels and rabbits inhabit protected places in the forest.*

in·hab·i·tant |ĭn **hăb′**ĭ tənt| —*noun, plural* **inhabitants** A person or animal that lives in a particular place.

in·hale |ĭn **hāl′**| —*verb* **inhaled, inhaling** To pull into the lungs; breathe in: *He inhaled the fresh, cool air that was left behind by the storm. When you breathe, first you inhale, then you exhale.*

in·her·it |ĭn **hĕr′**ĭt| —*verb* **inherited, inheriting 1.** To receive something from someone after he or she has died: *The family inherited a farm from their grandfather.* **2.** To receive from one's parents or ancestors: *She inherited her mother's gift for music.*

in·her·i·tance |ĭn **hĕr′**ĭ təns| —*noun, plural* **inheritances** Something that is inherited: *A house and some money were the inheritance she received from her aunt.*

in·hu·man |ĭn **hyōō′**mən| —*adjective* Lacking kindness or pity; cruel; brutal: *Beating the dog was an inhuman thing to do.*

in·i·tial |ĭ **nĭsh′**əl| —*adjective* Of or happening at the beginning; first: *The initial step in our plan will be to make a chart.*
—*noun, plural* **initials** The first letter of a word or name: *The initials "U.S." stand for "United States."*
—*verb* **initialed, initialing** To mark or sign with the initials of one's name: *The governor initialed the new law and gave the papers to her assistant.*

in·i·ti·ate |ĭ **nĭsh′**ē āt′| —*verb* **initiated, initiating 1.** To begin; start: *The new committee initiated the practice of ending meetings on time.* **2.** To bring into a club or other organization as a new member. Often there is a special test or ceremony: *We initiated ten new members this year.*

in·i·ti·a·tive |ĭ **nĭsh′**ē ə tĭv| or |ĭ **nĭsh′**ə tĭv| —*noun, plural* **initiatives 1.** The ability to begin or carry out a plan or task: *With enough initiative you can teach yourself a great deal about the world.* **2.** The first step or action in beginning something: *If you will take the initiative, we will begin plans for the party at once.*

in·jec·tion |ĭn **jĕk′**shən| —*noun, plural* **injections 1.** The act of putting a liquid medicine or other substance into the body by using a hollow needle; a shot. **2.** The dose of medicine that is used for this: *an injection of penicillin.*

in·jure |**ĭn′**jər| —*verb* **Injured, injuring** To harm or damage; hurt: *He fell and injured his foot.*

in·ju·ry |**ĭn′**jə rē| —*noun, plural* **injuries 1.** Damage to a person or thing; harm: *Luckily he escaped injury when he fell off his bike.* **2.** A wound or other damage to the body: *a leg injury.*

initial
Fancy initials used in books

in·jus·tice | ĭn jŭs′tĭs | —*noun, plural* **injustices** **1.** Lack of justice; an unfair condition: *We became angry at the injustice of the mayor's decision.* **2.** An act that is not just: *Sentencing an innocent person to prison was an injustice.*

ink | ĭngk | —*noun, plural* **inks** A colored liquid or paste used especially for writing or printing.
—*verb* **inked, inking** To cover with ink; spread ink on: *We inked the rubber stamp pad with black ink.*

ink·well | ĭngk′wĕl′ | —*noun, plural* **inkwells** A small container for ink, usually kept on the top of a desk.

ink·y | ĭng′kē | —*adjective* **inkier, inkiest** **1.** Stained with ink: *inky fingers.* **2.** Dark: *inky shadows in the night.*

in·land | ĭn′lənd | —*adjective* Located away from the coast or border; of or located in the interior of a land or country: *an inland waterway.*
—*adverb* In, toward, or to the interior of a land or country: *The storm moved inland, doing great damage.*

in·lay | ĭn′lā′ | —*noun, plural* **inlays** Pieces of wood, ivory, metal, or other material that is set into a surface to form a pattern or decoration.

in·let | ĭn′lĕt′ | or | ĭn′lĭt | —*noun, plural* **inlets** A bay or other recess along the coast: *There were several small boats tied up on the inlet.*

in·most | ĭn′mōst′ | —*adjective* **1.** Farthest or deepest in: *the inmost part of the forest.* **2.** Most secret: *my inmost wish.*

inn | ĭn | —*noun, plural* **inns** **1.** A hotel: *We stayed overnight at an inn.* **2.** A tavern or restaurant: *We had an excellent meal at the inn.*
♦ *These sound alike* **inn, in.**

in·ner | ĭn′ər | —*adjective* **1.** Located farther inside: *the inner core of the earth.* **2.** Of the spirit or mind: *inner thoughts; inner feelings.*

inner ear The innermost part of the ear in animals that have backbones. The inner ear has nerves that go to the brain so that sounds can be understood. It is also important for the sense of balance.

in·ner·most | ĭn′ər mōst′ | —*adjective* **1.** Located farthest in: *the innermost parts of an automobile engine.* **2.** Most personal and private: *His innermost desires and hopes were something he never talked about.*

in·ning | ĭn′ĭng | —*noun, plural* **innings** A part of a baseball game during which each team comes to bat. A baseball game usually has nine innings.

inn·keep·er | ĭn′kē′pər | —*noun, plural* **innkeepers** A person who owns or manages an inn.

in·no·cence | ĭn′ə səns | —*noun, plural* **innocences** The condition or quality of being innocent and free from evil.

in·no·cent | ĭn′ə sənt | —*adjective* **1.** Not guilty of a crime or fault: *The jury found him innocent.* **2.** Not experienced: *an innocent child.* **3.** Not intended to cause harm: *an innocent remark.*
—*noun, plural* **innocents** A person, especially a child, who is free of evil.

in·no·va·tion | ĭn′ə vā′shən | —*noun, plural* **innovations** **1.** The act or process of creating or discovering new things and ideas: *This is a time of innovation, when every day something new is discovered.* **2.** Something newly introduced; a change: *innovations in methods of teaching.*

inlay

ă	pat	ĕ	pet	î	fierce
ā	pay	ē	be	ŏ	pot
â	care	ĭ	pit	ō	go
ä	father	ī	pie	ô	paw, for
oi	oil	ŭ	cut	zh	vision
ŏŏ	book	û	fur	ə	ago, item,
ōō	boot	th	the		pencil, atom,
yōō	abuse	th	thin		circus
ou	out	hw	which	ər	butter

in·oc·u·late |ĭ **nŏk′**yə lāt′| —*verb* **inoculated, inoculating** To put a special form of the germs of a disease into a person's or animal's body. This causes the body to develop protection against the disease. People can be inoculated against smallpox, measles, mumps, and many other diseases.

in·quire |ĭn **kwīr′**| —*verb* **inquired, inquiring** To try to find out about by asking questions: *We inquired the way to the station.*

in·quir·y |ĭn **kwīr′**ē| or |**ĭn′**kwə rē| —*noun, plural* **inquiries**
1. The act or process of inquiring: *We have started our inquiry about a nice place to go for our vacation.* **2.** A request for information: *There have been many inquiries about the new mail rates.* **3.** A detailed examination; an investigation: *The police have started an inquiry into the robbery.*

in·quis·i·tive |ĭn **kwĭz′**ĭ tĭv| —*adjective* Eager to learn: *an inquisitive child.*

in·sane |ĭn **sān′**| —*adjective* **1.** Of, showing, or affected by a serious mental illness; crazy; mad: *an insane person.* **2.** Very foolish; wild: *an insane idea.*

in·scribe |ĭn **skrīb′**| —*verb* **inscribed, inscribing** To write, print, carve, engrave, or mark words or letters on something: *They inscribed a metal plate with the names of the winners.*

in·scrip·tion |ĭn **skrĭp′**shən| —*noun, plural* **inscriptions 1.** The act or an example of inscribing: *the inscription of names on the trophy. Can you read the inscription?* **2.** Something inscribed: *a wall covered with inscriptions.*

in·sect |**ĭn′**sĕkt′| —*noun, plural* **insects** A small animal with six legs and a body divided into three main parts. Most insects have wings. There are thousands of different kinds of insects. Among them are ants, bees, flies, grasshoppers, and butterflies.

in·sec·ti·cide |ĭn **sĕk′**tĭ sīd′| —*noun, plural* **insecticides** A poison or other substance used to kill insects.

in·se·cure |ĭn′sĭ **kyoͻr′**| —*adjective* **1.** Not safe: *an insecure fort.* **2.** Not firm or steady: *an insecure hold on the slippery rock.* **3.** Lacking confidence: *I feel very insecure.*

in·sert |ĭn **sûrt′**| —*verb* **inserted, inserting** To put or set in: *She inserted the key in the lock.*
—*noun* |**ĭn′**sûrt′|, *plural* **inserts** Something that is inserted: *The newspaper had an insert this week advertising all the summer sales.*

in·side |**ĭn′**sīd′| or |ĭn **sīd′**| —*noun, plural* **insides** The inner part: *the inside of a house.*
—*adjective* **1.** Inner; interior: *an inside pocket.* **2.** Of or coming from someone who has special knowledge: *inside information on who stole the necklace.*
—*adverb* |ĭn **sīd′**| Into, toward, or in the inner part of; within: *Let's go inside. The children were playing inside.*
—*preposition* |ĭn **sīd′**| **1.** On the inner side or part of: *inside the cave.* **2.** Into: *Go inside the house if it rains.*

in·sig·ni·a |ĭn **sĭg′**nē ə| —*noun, plural* **insignias** A medal or badge that is worn or carried to show a person's office, rank, membership, or a position of some honor; an emblem: *He wore the insignia of captain of the police force.*

in·sig·nif·i·cant |ĭn′sĭg **nĭf′**ĭ kənt| —*adjective* **1.** Having little or no meaning; not important: *an insignificant detail; insignificant information.* **2.** Small in size, power, or value: *an insignificant reward; an insignificant official.*

in·sin·cere |ĭn′sĭn **sîr′**| —*adjective* Not sincere; dishonest: *Don't*

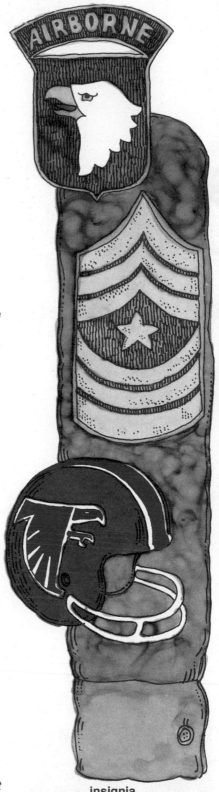

insignia
On uniforms (*above*) and on a helmet (*below*)

bother with insincere apologies.

in·sist | ĭn sĭst′ | —*verb* **insisted, insisting** **1.** To be firm in making a demand; take a strong stand: *I insist on watching the ball game today.* **2.** To say strongly: *I insist that you wash your hair tonight.*

in·spect | ĭn spĕkt′ | —*verb* **inspected, inspecting** To look at or examine carefully: *We inspected the house before we decided to buy it. Government officials inspected the factory to make sure it was safe.*

in·spec·tion | ĭn spĕk′shən | —*noun, plural* **inspections** **1.** The act or an example of inspecting: *An inspection of the electrical wiring showed the cause of the fire.* **2.** An official examination or review: *Airplanes undergo inspections after they have been flown a certain number of hours.*

in·spec·tor | ĭn spĕk′tər | —*noun, plural* **inspectors** **1.** A person whose job is to inspect: *a fire inspector.* **2.** A police officer of high rank.

in·spi·ra·tion | ĭn′spə rā′shən | —*noun, plural* **inspirations** **1.** A feeling of being inspired; the act or process of causing the mind or the emotions to react: *His cheerful manner, in spite of his illness, was an inspiration to the rest of us.* **2.** Someone or something that inspires: *Nature was an inspiration to many composers.* **3.** Something that is inspired; a sudden, original idea: *Painting this dark hallway bright yellow was pure inspiration.*

in·spire | ĭn spīr′ | —*verb* **inspired, inspiring** **1.** To fill with noble emotion: *hymns that inspire the people at church.* **2.** To move someone to action: *The children's needs inspired their parents to work very hard.* **3.** To cause others to think or feel a certain way: *The sergeant tried to inspire courage in his men.*

in·stall | ĭn stôl′ | —*verb* **installed, installing** **1.** To put in place and set up for use: *The company is installing a telephone in every office.* **2.** To place a person in office with ceremony: *My father was installed as chairman of the board.*

in·stall·ment | ĭn stôl′mənt | —*noun, plural* **installments** **1.** One of a series of payments: *The loan may be paid back in installments of ten dollars per week.* **2.** A portion or part of something issued at intervals, such as a story in a newspaper or magazine.

in·stance | ĭn′stəns | —*noun, plural* **instances** A case; example: *There have been many instances of people failing this test.*

Idiom **for instance** For example: *She plays many instruments, for instance, piano, flute, and trumpet.*

in·stant | ĭn′stənt | —*noun, plural* **instants** A period of time almost too short to notice; a moment: *We saw the sun for an instant before the clouds hid it again.*

—*adjective* **1.** Immediate: *My instant reaction to the noise was to jump.* **2.** Processed to be prepared quickly: *instant coffee.*

in·stant·ly | ĭn′stənt lē | —*adverb* At once; right away; immediately: *She recognized him instantly.*

in·stead | ĭn stĕd′ | —*adverb* In place of another; as a substitute: *They didn't have pears for dessert, so I ordered peaches instead.*

Idiom **instead of** In place of; rather than: *You should be laughing instead of crying.*

in·step | ĭn′stĕp′ | —*noun, plural* **insteps** **1.** The middle part of the top of the human foot, between the toes and the ankle. **2.** The part of a shoe or stocking covering this part of the foot.

in·stinct | ĭn′stĭngkt′ | —*noun, plural* **instincts** **1.** An inner feeling or way of behaving that is present at birth and is not

ă	pat	ĕ	pet	î	fierce
ā	pay	ē	be	ŏ	pot
â	care	ĭ	pit	ō	go
ä	father	ī	pie	ô	paw, for
oi	oil	ŭ	cut	zh	vision
ōō	book	û	fur	ə	ago, item,
ōō	boot	*th*	the		pencil, atom,
yōō	abuse	th	thin		circus
ou	out	hw	which	ər	butter

learned: *Squirrels store nuts for the winter by instinct.* **2.** A natural talent or ability: *He has an instinct for saying and doing the right thing at the right time.*

in·sti·tute |ĭn′stĭ tōōt′| or |ĭn′stĭ tyōōt′| —*noun, plural* **institutes 1.** An organization set up for some special purpose: *a research institute; an art institute.* **2.** The building or buildings of such an organization.

in·sti·tu·tion |ĭn′stĭ tōō′shən| or |ĭn′stĭ tyōō′shən| —*noun, plural* **institutions 1.** A custom or practice that is important to a group of people: *the institution of marriage.* **2. a.** An organization, especially one that has been set up for public service: *learning institutions.* **b.** The building or buildings of such an organization.

in·struct |ĭn strŭkt′| —*verb* **instructed, instructing 1.** To give knowledge or skill to; teach: *We are being instructed in reading, writing, and math at school.* **2.** To give orders to; direct: *The teacher instructed us to line up in single file.*

in·struc·tion |ĭn strŭk′shən| —*noun, plural* **instructions 1.** Something that is taught; a lesson or series of lessons: *I received musical instruction for many years.* **2.** The act or process of teaching; education: *The instruction of young people can be very rewarding.* **3. instructions** Directions; orders: *Read the instructions on the package before starting to make the cake.*

in·struc·tor |ĭn strŭk′tər| —*noun, plural* **instructors** Someone who teaches; a teacher.

in·stru·ment |ĭn′strə mənt| —*noun, plural* **instruments 1.** A device used to measure, indicate, or record information: *The copilot checked the instruments as the pilot prepared for landing.* **2.** A device used for a certain kind of work; tool; implement: *A dentist needs many different instruments for working on teeth.* **3.** A device for producing music: *My sister plays the piano, flute, guitar, and other instruments.*

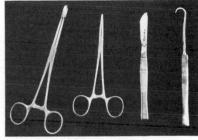
instrument
Doctors' instruments

in·su·late |ĭn′sə lāt′| or |ĭns′yə lāt′| —*verb* **insulated, insulating** To cover, surround, or line with a material that slows or stops the passage of electricity, sound, or heat: *We insulated our house so it would be warmer in the winter.*

in·su·la·tion |ĭn′sə lā′shən| or |ĭns′yə lā′shən| —*noun, plural* **insulations 1.** The process of insulating or the condition of being insulated: *insulation of homes.* **2.** The material used for insulating: *He wrapped insulation around the wire.*

in·sult |ĭn sŭlt′| —*verb* **insulted, insulting** To speak to or treat in a way that is rude or not polite; offend: *You insulted me when you refused to answer my letters.*
—*noun* |ĭn′sŭlt′|, *plural* **insults** An action or remark that is meant to insult.

in·sur·ance |ĭn shōōr′əns| —*noun, plural* **insurances 1.** A business that guarantees to pay for certain losses or damages if they happen, in exchange for small amounts of money paid on a regular schedule. **2.** A contract that makes such guarantees. Insurance can be bought to cover accidents, illness, theft, death, and many other things. **3.** The amount of money for which someone or something is insured.

in·sure |ĭn shōōr′| —*verb* **insured, insuring** To make arrangements for payment of money in case of loss or damage.

in·take |ĭn′tāk′| —*noun, plural* **intakes 1.** An opening in a container or pipe by which liquid or gas enters. **2.** The act of taking in: *Breathing requires the intake of air.* **3.** The amount of

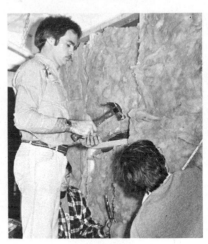
insulate
Insulating a house

something taken in: *Running requires an increase in the intake of air.*

in·te·grate |ĭn′tĭ grāt′| —*verb* **integrated, integrating 1.** To make into a whole; combine; unite: *We will try to integrate all the ideas into one plan.* **2.** To take away or get rid of restrictions based on ethnic group or family background.

in·te·gra·tion |ĭn′tĭ grā′shən| —*noun* The act or process of making something open to people of all ethnic groups: *the integration of public schools.*

in·tel·lect |ĭn′tl ĕkt′| —*noun, plural* **intellects 1.** The ability of the mind to think, reason, and learn. **2.** Someone of high mental ability: *Only a real intellect could figure out these instructions!*

in·tel·lec·tu·al |ĭn′tl ĕk′chōō əl| —*adjective* **1.** Using or requiring the intellect: *a subject for intellectual discussion.* **2.** Having or seeming to have very high intelligence: *an intellectual student who is always on the honor roll.*
—*noun, plural* **intellectuals** A person of high mental ability, training, and interests.

in·tel·li·gence |ĭn tĕl′ə jəns| —*noun* **1.** The ability to learn, think, understand, and know; mental ability. **2.** Information; news, especially secret information: *The captain read us the latest intelligence on the enemy's movements.*

in·tel·li·gent |ĭn tĕl′ə jənt| —*adjective* **1.** Having intelligence: *an intelligent child who learns quickly.* **2.** Showing intelligence; wise; thoughtful: *an intelligent decision; an intelligent plan.*

in·tend |ĭn tĕnd′| —*verb* **intended, intending 1.** To have as a purpose; have in mind; plan: *We intended to get an early start, but we were delayed.* **2.** To design for a special purpose or use: *This building is intended to hold no more than two hundred people. That hammer is not intended for driving nails that big.* **3.** To be for a particular person: *This gift is intended for my uncle.*

in·tense |ĭn tĕns′| —*adjective* Very deep, strong, or concentrated: *intense feeling; intense color; intense sunlight.*

in·ten·si·ty |ĭn tĕn′sĭ tē| —*noun, plural* **intensities 1.** The condition or quality of being intense; great strength: *intensity of feelings; the storm's intensity.* **2.** Degree or amount of strength or force: *the intensity of the sun's rays.*

in·tent |ĭn tĕnt′| —*adjective* **1.** Showing concentration; intense: *The judge listened with an intent expression on his face.* **2.** Having one's mind set on; determined: *I am intent on getting good grades.*
—*noun, plural* **intents** Purpose; meaning: *What is the intent of your letter to the governor?*

in·ten·tion |ĭn tĕn′shən| —*noun, plural* **intentions** Something intended; a purpose or plan: *It is my firm intention to do my grocery shopping early this week.*

in·ten·tion·al |ĭn tĕn′shə nəl| —*adjective* Done on purpose; intended: *Was that an intentional error?*

inter- A prefix that means "between" or "among": *international.*

in·ter·cept |ĭn′tər sĕpt′| —*verb* **intercepted, intercepting** To meet, stop, or interrupt something or someone on the way from one person or place to another: *We intercepted him on his way home from the store. Mom intercepted the package from Aunt June so my birthday surprise wouldn't be spoiled.*

in·ter·com |ĭn′tər kŏm′| —*noun, plural* **intercoms** A device used for talking between one part of a building, office, ship, or aircraft and another.

ă	pat	ĕ	pet	î	fierce
ā	pay	ē	be	ŏ	pot
â	care	ĭ	pit	ō	go
ä	father	ī	pie	ô	paw, for
oi	oil	ŭ	cut	zh	vision
ōō	book	û	fur	ə	ago, item,
ōō	boot	*th*	the		pencil, atom,
yōō	abuse	th	thin		circus
ou	out	hw	which	ər	butter

in·ter·est | ĭn′trĭst | or | ĭn′tər ĭst | —*noun, plural* **interests 1. a.** A desire to give special attention to something; curiosity: *This book captures the reader's interest from the first page.* **b.** The quality of causing this desire: *a speech that lacked interest for me.* **c.** A subject that causes such a desire: *Music is Leonard's chief interest in life.* **2.** Advantage; benefit: *That decision was not in my best interest.* **3.** A right or legal share in something: *The family has large interests in the oil refining industry.* **4.** Money paid or charged for the use of someone else's money. Banks pay interest on money that is put into them for saving. Banks charge interest for money that is borrowed from them.
—*verb* **interested, interesting 1.** To cause interest in: *The teacher interested her pupils in ecology.* **2.** To cause to become involved or concerned: *Can I interest you in coming to work for me?*

in·ter·est·ed | ĭn′trĭ stĭd | or | ĭn′tər ĭ stĭd | or | ĭn′tə rĕs′tĭd | —*adjective* **1.** Having or showing interest: *She is interested in the study of languages.* **2.** Having a right, claim, or share: *The interested parties in the argument met to discuss a compromise.*

in·ter·est·ing | ĭn′trĭ stĭng | or | ĭn′tər ĭ stĭng | —*adjective* Causing or holding interest or attention: *an interesting story; an interesting person.*

in·ter·fere | ĭn′tər fîr′ | —*verb* **interfered, interfering 1.** To get in the way of; interrupt; hinder: *Noise interferes with my studying.* **2.** To meddle in the business of others: *A true friend doesn't always interfere in everyone's life.*

in·te·ri·or | ĭn tîr′ē ər | —*noun, plural* **interiors 1.** The inner part of something; the inside: *The outside of the house is shabby, but the interior is warm and cozy.* **2.** The area farthest inland; remote part: *People in the interior of Alaska travel by dog sled.*
—*adjective* **1.** Of or located on the inside; inner: *the interior walls of the cave.* **2.** Located away from a coast or border: *Interior Canada has a small population.*

in·ter·jec·tion | ĭn′tər jĕk′shən | —*noun, plural* **interjections** A word or phrase that expresses a strong emotion or feeling. The words *ouch* and *oh* are interjections.

in·ter·me·di·ate | ĭn′tər mē′dē ĭt | —*adjective* In between; in the middle: *I don't need such a small shoe; show me some of the intermediate sizes.*

in·ter·mis·sion | ĭn′tər mĭsh′ən | —*noun, plural* **intermissions** An interruption or recess in an activity; a break: *We went outside for a breath of fresh air during the intermission of the play.*

in·tern | ĭn′tûrn′ | —*noun, plural* **interns** Someone who has recently graduated from medical school and is receiving further training under the supervision of other doctors.

in·ter·nal | ĭn tûr′nəl | —*adjective* **1.** Of or located on the inside; inner; interior: *The driver received internal injuries from the accident.* **2.** Of or relating to the political or social matters within a country: *Internal problems in the nation led to civil war.*

in·ter·na·tion·al | ĭn′tər năsh′ə nəl | —*adjective* Of or between two or more nations or their people: *international trade.*

in·ter·plan·e·tar·y | ĭn′tər plăn′ĭ tĕr′ē | —*adjective* Between planets of the solar system: *interplanetary travel.*

in·ter·pret | ĭn tûr′prĭt | —*verb* **interpreted, interpreting 1.** To explain the meaning or importance of: *Can you interpret these numbers?* **2.** To understand or see in a certain way: *He interpreted the letter to mean that there would be further trouble.*

interior
Of a museum in New York City

3. To perform or present according to one's understanding of: *The actor interpreted the character well.* **4.** To translate from one language to another: *Who will interpret for us when we meet our German guests?*

in·ter·pre·ta·tion |ĭn tûr′prĭ **tā′**shən| —*noun, plural* **interpretations 1.** The act or process of interpreting: *The judge's interpretation of the law was fair.* **2.** An explanation of the meaning of something: *an interesting interpretation of a bad dream.* **3.** An artistic performance that shows the artist's understanding of a work: *an unusual interpretation of the role.*

in·ter·rog·a·tive |ĭn′tə **rŏg′**ə tĭv| —*adjective* **1.** Having the form or the function of a question: *an interrogative sentence; an interrogative look.* **2.** Used in asking a question: *"How" is an interrogative pronoun.*

—*noun, plural* **interrogatives** A word or form used in asking a question: *A question does not always have to begin with an interrogative.*

in·ter·rupt |ĭn′tə **rŭpt′**| —*verb* **interrupted, interrupting 1.** To break in upon: *interrupt a class; interrupt a conversation.* **2.** To keep something from continuing; to put a temporary stop to: *Illness in the family interrupted the children's education.*

in·ter·rup·tion |ĭn′tə **rŭp′**shən| —*noun, plural* **interruptions** A break in something that keeps it from continuing: *There was an interruption in the television program when the President made an important announcement.*

in·ter·sect |ĭn′tər **sĕkt′**| —*verb* **intersected, intersecting** To come together or cross: *Two major streets intersect one block from here.*

in·ter·sec·tion |ĭn′tər **sĕk′**shən| —*noun, plural* **intersections** The point where two or more things intersect: *This is a busy intersection, so wait for the green light before crossing.*

in·ter·val |ĭn′tər vəl| —*noun, plural* **intervals 1.** A period of time between two events: *an interval of rest before starting work again.* **2.** A space between two points or objects: *Draw a series of dots at one-inch intervals. There is an interval of one mile between traffic lights.*

in·ter·view |ĭn′tər vyoo′| —*noun, plural* **interviews 1.** A face-to-face meeting: *an interview for a job.* **2.** A conversation to obtain information and facts for a report: *The reporter tried to arrange an interview with the senator.*

—*verb* **interviewed, interviewing** To have an interview with: *We interviewed the principal for the school newspaper.*

in·tes·tine |ĭn **tĕs′**tĭn| —*noun, plural* **intestines** The part of the digestive system that extends below the stomach. The intestine is a long tube in which food is digested completely and water is absorbed. The intestine is divided into the large intestine and the small intestine.

in·ti·mate |ĭn′tə mĭt| —*adjective* **1.** Showing complete knowledge; very familiar: *an intimate understanding of children.* **2.** Innermost: *one's intimate thoughts.* **3.** Very personal; close: *an intimate friend.*

in·to |ĭn′too| —*preposition* **1.** To the inside of: *She was going into the house.* **2.** So as to be in or within: *The two partners entered into an agreement.* **3.** To the occupation or action of: *She wants to go into banking after she graduates.* **4.** To a time in: *It's getting well into the week.* **5.** In the direction of; toward: *He was*

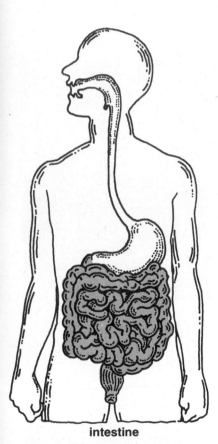

intestine

ă	pat	ĕ	pet	î	fierce
ā	pay	ē	be	ŏ	pot
â	care	ĭ	pit	ō	go
ä	father	ī	pie	ô	paw, for
oi	oil	ŭ	cut	zh	vision
oo	book	û	fur	ə	ago, item,
oo	boot	*th*	the		pencil, atom,
yoo	abuse	th	thin		circus
ou	out	hw	which	ər	butter

looking into the distance. **6.** Against: *The car ran into a tree.* **7.** To the form or state of: *The water changed into ice.*

in·tol·er·ant |ĭn tŏl′ər ənt| —*adjective* **1.** Not respecting what other people think or do: *He was so intolerant that he hated everyone who was the least bit different from himself.* **2.** Unable to endure: *He had to stay inside because his illness had made him intolerant to sunlight.*

in·tox·i·cate |ĭn tŏk′sĭ kāt′| —*verb* **intoxicated, intoxicating** **1.** To make drunk. **2.** To fill with great excitement, enthusiasm, or delight: *The idea intoxicated me.*

in·tri·cate |ĭn′trĭ kĭt| —*adjective* **1.** Having a complicated structure or pattern; complex: *an intricate design.* **2.** Hard to understand: *intricate instructions.*

in·trigue |ĭn trēg′| —*verb* **intrigued, intriguing** **1.** To catch the interest or increase the curiosity of; fascinate: *Dolphins intrigue people because of their high intelligence.* **2.** To plot or scheme secretly: *The enemies intrigued against one another.*
—*noun* |ĭn′trēg′| or |ĭn trēg′|, *plural* **intrigues** Plots or schemes carried on in secret.

in·tro·duce |ĭn′trə dōos′| or |ĭn′trə dyōos′| —*verb* **introduced, introducing** **1.** To present a person by name to others: *Mary, I'd like to introduce you to Carol.* **2.** To provide with a first experience of something: *He introduced me to classical music.* **3.** To open or begin: *She wrote a new chapter to introduce her book.* **4.** To bring or put in; add: *Introduce excitement to your story.* **5.** To propose, create, or bring into use for the first time: *She introduced new and safer methods of work in her factory.*

in·tro·duc·tion |ĭn′trə dŭk′shən| —*noun, plural* **introductions** **1.** A short section at the beginning of something, such as a book or play, that prepares the way for what will follow. **2.** The act of introducing: *the introduction of the printing press. John made the introductions at the party.* **3.** Anything that introduces: *Books on this subject will be your introduction to this class.*

in·vade |ĭn vād′| —*verb* **invaded, invading** **1.** To enter with force; attack: *The Romans invaded Britain.* **2.** To enter in great numbers: *In summer, tourists invade our quiet, pretty, tiny village.* **3.** To trespass or intrude on; interfere with: *Would you invade someone's privacy by asking such personal questions?*

in·va·lid |ĭn′və lĭd| —*noun, plural* **invalids** A sick, weak, or disabled person, especially someone who has been in poor health for a long time.

in·vent |ĭn vĕnt′| —*verb* **invented, inventing** **1.** To think up and make, create, or put together something that did not exist before: *Who invented the electric light bulb?* **2.** To make up: *He's always inventing excuses for not doing his homework.*

in·ven·tion |ĭn vĕn′shən| —*noun, plural* **inventions** **1.** Something invented: *The cotton gin was an important invention.* **2.** The act of inventing: *No one person can take credit for the invention of the printing press.* **3.** The power or ability to invent: *a writer of great invention.* **4.** Something made up or not true: *His story is an obvious invention.*

in·ven·tor |ĭn vĕn′tər| —*noun, plural* **inventors** A person who thinks up new ideas and creates new things or methods.

in·ven·to·ry |ĭn′vən tôr′ē| or |ĭn′vən tōr′ē| —*noun, plural* **inventories** **1.** A detailed list of goods, supplies, possessions, or other things. **2.** The process of making such a list. **3.** The

invention
A camera that develops pictures in seconds

Inventor
Thomas A. Edison

supply of goods on hand: *The store's inventory of bicycles is low.*

in·vert |ĭn vûrt′| —*verb* **inverted, inverting** **1.** To turn upside down: *If you invert the jar, the jam will spill out.* **2.** To reverse the order, position, or arrangement of: *You can invert a sentence by putting a predicate first.*

in·ver·te·brate |ĭn vûr′tə brĭt| or |ĭn vûr′tə brāt′| —*noun, plural* **invertebrates** An animal that has no backbone. Worms, jellyfish, clams, lobsters, and insects are invertebrates.
—*adjective* Having no backbone: *A starfish is an invertebrate animal.*

in·vest |ĭn věst′| —*verb* **invested, investing** **1.** To put money into something that will earn interest or make a profit: *She invested her money in stocks.* **2.** To spend or use for future advantage: *They invested time and energy in the election campaign.*

in·ves·ti·gate |ĭn věs′tĭ gāt′| —*verb* **investigated, investigating** To examine carefully in a search for facts, knowledge, or information: *The cat investigated the whole living room before deciding to sleep on the new sofa.*

in·ves·ti·ga·tion |ĭn věs′tĭ gā′shən| —*noun, plural* **investigations** A careful examination, study, search, or inquiry to get facts or information.

in·vest·ment |ĭn věst′mənt| —*noun, plural* **investments** **1.** The act of investing: *Investment in oil wells can bring in a lot of money or it can cost you a fortune.* **2.** A sum of money invested: *He made an investment of one hundred dollars in his sister's store.* **3.** Something in which money, time, or some other valuable thing is invested: *A house is almost always a good investment.*

in·ves·tor |ĭn věs′tər| —*noun, plural* **investors** A person or group of people that invests money in the hope of making a profit.

in·vis·i·ble |ĭn vĭz′ə bəl| —*adjective* Not capable of being seen; not visible: *Air is invisible.*

in·vi·ta·tion |ĭn′vĭ tā′shən| —*noun, plural* **invitations** A spoken or written request for someone to come somewhere or do something: *I received an invitation to Martha and Joe's wedding.*

in·vite |ĭn vīt′| —*verb* **invited, inviting** **1.** To ask someone to come somewhere or do something; give an invitation: *Did they invite you to the party?* **2.** To ask in a formal way: *The children invited the mayor to talk to their class.* **3.** To be likely to cause; bring on: *You're inviting trouble if you aren't more careful.* **4.** To tempt; attract: *The sun invites a person to be out in the open air.*

in·vol·un·tar·y |ĭn vŏl′ən tĕr′ē| —*adjective* Not subject to the control of the will: *The muscle in my face gave an involuntary twitch.*

in·volve |ĭn vŏlv′| —*verb* **involved, involving** **1.** To call for; require: *Housework involves a lot of energy and time.* **2.** To have to do with; include: *The plot of the play involves kings, queens, and a magic elf.* **3.** To draw in; mix up: *His friends involved him in an illegal scheme.* **4.** To give all one's attention to: *She is involved in her work.*

in·volved |ĭn vŏlvd′| —*adjective* Complicated: *a long, involved story.*

in·ward |ĭn′wərd| —*adverb* Toward the inside or center: *The door swung inward. There is a passage leading inward.* Another form of this adverb is **inwards.**
—*adjective* Directed toward or located on the inside or interior: *inward thoughts; an inward pull on the door.*

invitation

ă	pat	ĕ	pet	î	fierce	
ā	pay	ē	be	ŏ	pot	
â	care	ĭ	pit	ō	go	
ä	father	ī	pie	ô	paw, for	
oi	oil	ŭ	cut	zh	vision	
ōŏ	book	û	fur	ə	ago, item,	
ōō	boot	th	the		pencil, atom,	
yōō	abuse	th	thin		circus	
ou	out	hw	which	ər	butter	

in·ward·ly |ĭn′wərd lē| —*adverb* **1.** On the inside; internally: *bleeding inwardly.* **2.** In the mind; within oneself: *Inwardly the boy was afraid.* **3.** Privately: *chuckling inwardly to himself.*

in·wards |ĭn′wərdz| A form of the adverb **inward.**

i·o·dine |ī′ə dēn′| or |ī′ə dīn′| —*noun, plural* **iodines 1.** A poisonous gray solid. Iodine is one of the chemical elements. **2.** A liquid mixture that contains iodine and is used to treat skin wounds.

IOU |ī′ō yōō′| An abbreviation for "I owe you"; a written promise to pay a debt.

I·o·wa |ī′ə wə| A state in the central United States. The capital of Iowa is Des Moines.

Ire·land |īr′lənd| A large island in the Atlantic Ocean west of Great Britain. It is divided into two sections, the Republic of Ireland, an independent country, and Northern Ireland, united with Great Britain.

i·ris |ī′rĭs| —*noun, plural* **irises 1.** The colored part of the eye around the pupil. The iris controls the amount of light that gets through the lens by making the pupil appear larger or smaller. **2.** A plant that has large flowers in various colors and long, pointed leaves.

I·rish |ī′rĭsh| —*noun* **1. the Irish** (Used with a plural verb.) **a.** People who were born in or are citizens of Ireland. **b.** People whose ancestors were from Ireland. **2.** A language of Ireland. —*adjective* Of Ireland, the Irish, or their language and culture.

Irish setter A rather large dog with a silky reddish coat.

i·ron |ī′ərn| —*noun, plural* **irons 1.** A hard, gray, brittle metal. It is an important metal and is used to make steel. Iron is one of the chemical elements. **2.** A metal appliance that has a handle and a flat bottom. It is heated and used for pressing wrinkles out of clothing or other materials. —*adjective* Strong and hard: *She has an iron will.* —*verb* **ironed, ironing** To press fabric with a heated iron.

i·ro·ny |ī′rə nē| —*noun, plural* **ironies 1.** A mocking way of using words so that they suggest a meaning that is the opposite of their usual meaning: *I'm sure he was using irony when he said, on that dreary, rainy Tuesday, "What shall we do with the rest of this lovely day?"* **2.** An event or result that is the opposite of what is expected: *The biggest irony of all was that the child started acting just like the bully he hated the most.*

ir·reg·u·lar |ĭ rĕg′yə lər| —*adjective* **1.** Not regular or standard in shape, size, arrangement, or in some other way: *an irregular ocean shore; irregular splashes of color.* **2.** Not following a regular schedule: *He works irregular hours.* **3.** Unusual or improper: *a highly irregular decision.*

ir·re·sist·i·ble |ĭr′ĭ zĭs′tə bəl| —*adjective* **1.** Too powerful to be resisted: *an irresistible desire for hamburgers.* **2.** Having appeal that is too strong to resist or deny: *irresistible beauty.*

ir·re·spon·si·ble |ĭr′ĭ spŏn′sə bəl| —*adjective* Not concerned about the effects of one's actions; not reliable; not to be trusted: *It was irresponsible of me to leave my bicycle out in the rain.*

ir·ri·gate |ĭr′ĭ gāt′| —*verb* **irrigated, irrigating** To supply land or crops with water by a system of streams and pipes: *If it doesn't rain soon, we'll have to irrigate our garden.*

ir·ri·ga·tion |ĭr′ĭ gā′shən| —*noun* The act or process of supplying water to land or crops.

Iowa

The name **Iowa** comes from an Indian word that is believed to mean "the sleepy ones." It is the name by which one Indian tribe called another. French settlers in the region took the name for a major river, and the state name came from the name of the river.

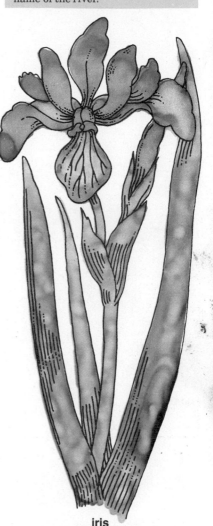

iris

Irish setter

ir·ri·ta·ble | ĭr′ ĭ tə bəl | —*adjective* **1.** Easily annoyed or angered; cross: *Lack of sleep made him nervous and irritable.* **2.** Too sensitive: *red, irritable skin.*

ir·ri·tate | ĭr′ ĭ tāt′ | —*verb* **irritated, irritating** **1.** To make angry or impatient; annoy or bother: *Your bragging irritates me.* **2.** To cause to become sore: *The smoke in the room irritated her eyes.*

is | ĭz | The third person singular present tense of the verb **be:** *He is tall. She is bright.*

-ish A suffix that forms adjectives and means "looking like; somewhat; very much like": *brownish; reddish; childish.*

Is·lam | ĭs′ ləm | or | ĭz′ ləm | or | ĭs läm′ | —*noun* A religion based on the teachings of the prophet Mohammed.

is·land | ī′ lənd | —*noun, plural* **islands** **1.** A piece of land that is surrounded by water. **2.** Anything that is like an island because it is completely separated or different in character from what surrounds it: *We floated an island of sherbet in the punch bowl.*

is·land·er | ī′ lən dər | —*noun, plural* **islanders** A person who lives on or was born on an island.

isle | īl | —*noun, plural* **isles** An island, especially a small one.
♦ *These sound alike* **isle, aisle, I'll.**

is·let | ī′ lĭt | —*noun, plural* **islets** A very small island.
♦ *These sound alike* **islet, eyelet.**

-ism A suffix that forms nouns and means: **1.** An act or practice: *terrorism.* **2.** A set of beliefs or principles; a system: *socialism.*

is·n't | ĭz′ ənt | A contraction of "is not": *She isn't here today.*

i·so·late | ī′ sə lāt′ | —*verb* **isolated, isolating** To set apart; separate from others: *We will isolate the sick animal from the others.*

Is·ra·el | ĭz′ rē əl | A country in southwestern Asia.

is·sue | ĭsh′ ōō | —*noun, plural* **issues** **1.** The act of sending out or releasing: *the government's issue of a new stamp.* **2.** Something that is put into circulation: *a new issue of silver dollars.* **3.** A single copy of a newspaper or magazine: *the July issue.* **4.** A subject being discussed or argued about: *The use of nuclear power is an important issue.*
—*verb* **issued, issuing** **1.** To send out; announce: *The principal issued a new set of cafeteria rules.* **2.** To put into circulation: *The government has issued a new postage stamp.* **3.** To give out; distribute: *The company issues uniforms to its workers.* **4.** To come out; flow out: *Water issued from the broken pipe.*

-ist A suffix that forms nouns and means: **1.** Someone who has a certain job or profession: *violinist; cartoonist.* **2.** Someone who has a certain set of beliefs or principles: *socialist.* **3.** Someone who performs certain acts: *humorist.*

isth·mus | ĭs′ məs | —*noun, plural* **isthmuses** A narrow strip of land connecting two larger masses of land.

it | ĭt | —*pronoun* **1.** The animal or thing last mentioned: *He grabbed the snake and flung it into the bush. This is my ball. Give it to me!* **2.** The pronoun **it** is used before a verb in the position that is usually occupied by the subject: **a.** To indicate a condition or fact: *It is very dark outside. It is nearly noon.* The pronoun **it** is not the subject of these sentences. They have no subject. **b.** To introduce a sentence. For example, in the sentences *It was my father on the phone* and *It is always easy to blame someone else,* the pronoun **it** only introduces the sentences. The subjects of these sentences are *my father* and *to blame someone else.*

I·tal·ian | ĭ tăl′ yən | —*noun, plural* **Italians** **1.** A person who was

ă	pat	ĕ	pet	î	fierce
ā	pay	ē	be	ŏ	pot
â	care	ĭ	pit	ō	go
ä	father	ī	pie	ô	paw, for

oi	oil	ŭ	cut	zh	vision
ōō	book	û	fur	ə	ago, item,
ōō	boot	th	the		pencil, atom,
yōō	abuse	th	thin		circus
ou	out	hw	which	ər	butter

born in or is a citizen of Italy. **2.** The Romance language of Italy.
—*adjective* Of Italy, the Italians, or their language.

i·tal·ic |ĭ tăl′ĭk| or |ī tăl′ĭk| —*adjective* Of a style of printing with the letters slanting to the right: *This is italic print.*
—*noun* Often **italics** Italic print or type: *This sentence is in italics.*

It·a·ly |ĭt′l ē| A country in southern Europe.

itch |ĭch| —*noun, plural* **itches 1.** A tickling feeling of the skin that causes one to want to scratch: *the itch of a mosquito bite; the itch from poison ivy.* **2.** A strong, restless desire: *an itch to travel.*
—*verb* **itched, itching 1.** To feel, have, or cause an itch: *I itch all over when I wear wool. This sweater is itching me.* **2.** To have a strong, restless desire: *She was just itching to show him what she had done.*

i·tem |ī′təm| —*noun, plural* **items 1.** A single article or unit: *an item of clothing.* **2.** A piece of news: *an interesting item in today's newspaper.*

it'll |ĭt′l| A contraction for "it will" or "it shall."

its |ĭts| —*pronoun* The pronoun **its** is the possessive form of **it.** It means: **1.** Of or belonging to a thing or animal: *The book was in its place. The dog licked its paw.* **2.** Done or performed by a thing or animal: *The book is not just pretty; its function is to teach. He has a large dog; its job is to hunt for squirrels and rabbits.*
♦ *These sound alike* **its, it's.**

it's |ĭts| A contraction for "it is" or "it has."
♦ *These sound alike* **it's, its.**

it·self |ĭt sĕlf′| —*pronoun* The pronoun **itself** is a special form of the pronoun **it. 1.** It is used: **a.** As the direct object of a verb: *The team surprised itself.* **b.** As the indirect object of a verb: *The board of directors voted itself a salary increase.* **c.** As the object of a preposition: *The new law is not important in itself.* **d.** To call special attention to something: *The Constitution itself defines treason very clearly.* **2.** The pronoun **itself** is used to mean "its normal self": *A traditional Fourth of July would not be itself without parades and fireworks.*

-ity A suffix that forms nouns and means "a quality or condition": *austerity; capability; equality.*

-ive¹ A suffix that forms adjectives and means: **1.** Tending to perform or achieve something: *constructive; destructive.* **2.** Of or having to do with: *instinctive.*

-ive² A suffix that forms nouns and means "something that performs or achieves something": *sedative.*

I've |īv| A contraction for "I have."

i·vo·ry |ī′və rē| —*noun, plural* **ivories 1.** The smooth, hard, yellowish-white material forming the tusks of elephants and certain other animals: *Ivory is used for making piano keys.* **2.** A yellowish-white color. ◊ The noun **ivory** can be used like an adjective for things made of ivory: *an ivory bracelet.*
—*adjective* Yellowish white: *an ivory blouse.*

i·vy |ī′vē| —*noun, plural* **ivies 1.** A leafy plant with long stems that can climb up walls. **2.** A plant that is like ivy. Poison ivy is one of these plants.

-ize A suffix that forms verbs and means: **1.** To become or cause to become: *Americanize; personalize.* **2.** To treat with or cause to become affected by: *magnetize.*

ivory
A carved ivory bracelet

ivy
Two kinds of ivy

Jj

j or **J** |jā| —*noun, plural* **j's** or **J's** The tenth letter of the English alphabet.

jab |jăb| —*verb* **jabbed, jabbing** To poke or hit, especially with something pointed: *The doctor jabbed the needle into my arm. She jabbed his arm with her elbow.*
—*noun, plural* **jabs** A poke or hit with something pointed: *I gave the button a jab and the doorbell rang.*

jab·ber |jăb′ər| —*verb* **jabbered, jabbering** To talk fast and in a confusing way; chatter; babble: *Those two are always jabbering about silly things.*

jack |jăk| —*noun, plural* **jacks** **1.** A tool or device that is used to lift something heavy a short distance. A jack is used to raise one end of a car in order to change a tire or to work underneath the car. **2.** A playing card that has the picture of a young man on it. A jack ranks above a ten and below a queen. **3. jacks** (Used with a singular verb.) A game that is played with a set of small, six-pointed metal pieces and a small ball. The object of the game is to pick up the metal pieces as the ball bounces.
—*verb* **jacked, jacking** To lift with a jack: *He is jacking the car up so I can look at the bottom of it.*

jack·al |jăk′əl| or |jăk′ôl| —*noun, plural* **jackals** An African or Asian animal that looks like a dog. It often feeds on what is left of animals that lions or leopards have killed as prey.

jack·et |jăk′ĭt| —*noun, plural* **jackets** **1.** A short coat: *a sport jacket; a winter jacket.* **2.** An outer, protective cover for a book or record album.

jack-in-the-box |jăk′ĭn *thə* bŏks′| —*noun, plural* **jack-in-the-boxes** A toy that is made of a box with a doll or puppet inside that pops out when the box lid is opened.

jack-in-the-pul·pit |jăk′ĭn *thə* pŏŏl′pĭt| or |jăk′ĭn *thə* pŭl′pĭt| —*noun, plural* **jack-in-the-pulpits** A plant that has a green or brownish flower. A part that looks like a leaf curves over a stalk shaped like a club.

jack·knife |jăk′nīf′| —*noun, plural* **jackknives** A large pocketknife. It usually has two blades that can be folded into the handle.

jack-o'-lan·tern |jăk′ə lăn′tərn| —*noun, plural* **jack-o'-lanterns** A pumpkin hollowed out and with holes cut to look like eyes.

jack-o'-lantern

ă	pat	ĕ	pet	î	fierce
ā	pay	ē	be	ŏ	pot
â	care	ĭ	pit	ō	go
ä	father	ī	pie	ô	paw, for

oi	oil	ŭ	cut	zh	vision
ŏŏ	book	û	fur	ə	ago, item,
ōō	boot	*th*	the		pencil, atom,
yōō	abuse	th	thin		circus
ou	out	hw	which	ər	butter

nose, and mouth. The top is cut out like a lid and a candle is set inside. Jack-o'-lanterns are made for Halloween.

jack·pot |jăk′ pŏt′| —*noun, plural* **jackpots** The largest prize or amount of money that can be won in a game or contest.

jack rabbit A hare of western North America. It has long ears and long, strong legs.

Jack·son |jăk′sən| The capital of Mississippi.

jade |jād| —*noun, plural* **jades** A hard green or white stone. Jade is used for jewelry and ornaments.

jag·ged |jăg′ĭd| —*adjective* Having notches or points; sharp, rough, and uneven: *jagged edges.*

jag·uar |jăg′wär′| —*noun, plural* **jaguars** A large, spotted wild cat of tropical America. The jaguar looks very much like a leopard.

jail |jāl| —*noun, plural* **jails** A place where persons who are waiting for a trial or serving a prison sentence are locked up; prison.
—*verb* **jailed, jailing** To put into jail; lock up.

jam¹ |jăm| —*verb* **jammed, jamming** 1. To squeeze or become squeezed into a tight space; wedge: *He jammed all the toys into the small box. That rug always jams under the front door.* 2. To crowd tightly: *Two hundred people jammed the auditorium.* 3. To become or cause to become stuck so as not to be able to work: *My bicycle pedals jammed and won't move. You deliberately jammed the film in the camera.* 4. To thrust or push hard: *Rick jammed on the brakes.* 5. To bruise or crush by squeezing: *I jammed my finger when I fell down.*
—*noun, plural* **jams** 1. A large group or mass of people or things crowded together so that it is hard or impossible to move: *a traffic jam.* 2. A difficult situation: *Herb got into a real jam when his mother found out he'd skipped his piano lesson.*

jam² |jăm| —*noun, plural* **jams** A thick, sweet food. Jam is made by boiling fruit and sugar until the mixture is thick.

jan·i·tor |jăn′ĭ tər| —*noun, plural* **janitors** A person whose job it is to clean and take care of a building.

Jan·u·ar·y |jăn′yōo ĕr′ē| —*noun, plural* **Januarys** The first month of the year, after December and before February. January has 31 days.

Ja·pan |jə păn′| A country of four main islands in the Pacific Ocean. Japan is off the eastern coast of Asia.

Jap·a·nese |jăp′ə nēz′| or |jăp′ə nēs′| —*adjective* Of Japan, its people, or their language.
—*noun* 1. A person who was born in or is a citizen of Japan. 2. The language of these people.

jar¹ |jär| —*noun, plural* **jars** 1. A container with a wide mouth. Jars usually do not have handles and are made of glass or pottery. 2.a. A jar with something in it: *a jar of jam.* b. The amount that a jar holds: *I ate a jar of pickles.*

jar² |jär| —*verb* **jarred, jarring** 1. To cause to shake violently; rock; rattle: *The earthquake jarred buildings up to fifty miles away.* 2. To come as an upsetting surprise; to shock: *The news of his death jarred her.*
—*noun, plural* **jars** A violent shaking movement; jolt or shock: *The car was so old we felt all the jars and bumps from the road.*

jas·mine |jăz′mĭn| —*noun* A vine with fragrant yellow or white flowers. Jasmine grows in warm places.

jaguar

jam¹, jam²
Both of these words first appeared in the eighteenth century. **Jam¹** is said to be a word that was formed to sound like the action it describes. **Jam²** is probably from **jam¹**, since fruit is pounded or "jammed together" to make preserves.

jar¹, jar²
Jar¹ traveled through Arabic and then French before arriving in English. It originally meant "a large pot." Like a number of other words, **jar²** was probably first used in imitation of the sound it describes.

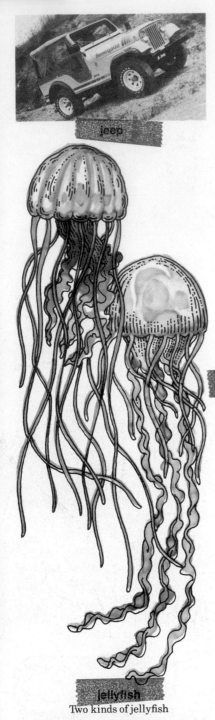

jeep

jellyfish

Two kinds of jellyfish

jaw |jô| —*noun, plural* **jaws** **1.** Either of a pair of hard structures of the mouth. The jaws are made of bone and cartilage. They form the framework and shape of the mouth and hold the teeth. **2.** One of two parts of a tool that can be closed and are used to grasp or hold something. A pair of pliers has jaws.

jay |jā| —*noun, plural* **jays** A bird with a loud, harsh voice and feathers that are often brightly colored. Some jays have a crest.

jay·walk |jā′wôk′| —*verb* **jaywalked, jaywalking** To cross a street without paying attention to traffic laws: *You are jaywalking if you cross the street when the sign says "Don't walk."*

jazz |jăz| —*noun* A kind of American music that was first played by blacks in the southern United States. Jazz has strong rhythms and accented notes or beats that come at unusual places. Jazz has changed a lot and today there are many different forms of it.

jeal·ous |jĕl′əs| —*adjective* **1.** Having a feeling that someone you love may or could love someone else more than you: *The child was jealous of the new baby. Her husband was always jealous.* **2.** Resenting what another person has, can do, or has achieved; envious: *She was jealous of her older sister, who could stay up late. You're just jealous because I got a better mark.*

jeal·ous·y |jĕl′ə sē| —*noun, plural* **jealousies** A jealous feeling; envy: *Since you can play the clarinet as well as he can, there's no reason for jealousy. Your jealousy is silly; you know I love you.*

jeans |jēnz| —*plural noun* Strong pants made of heavy cotton cloth.

jeep |jēp| —*noun, plural* **jeeps** A small, powerful, rugged automobile. Jeeps are most often used for driving in places where there are no good roads.

Jef·fer·son City |jĕf′ər sən| The capital of Missouri.

jel·ly |jĕl′ē| —*noun, plural* **jellies** A food that is soft but also firm and springy. Jelly is made by boiling fruit juice with sugar, and sometimes adding a substance to the liquid to make it set or harden. Another type of jelly is made by boiling meat juice and bones.
—*verb* **jellied, jellying, jellies** To turn into or make jelly: *A lot of liquids jelly when they get cold.*

jel·ly·fish |jĕl′ē fĭsh′| —*noun, plural* **jellyfish** or **jellyfishes** A sea animal with a soft, rounded body that looks and feels like jelly. Jellyfish have tentacles that can give an unpleasant sting.

jerk |jûrk| —*verb* **jerked, jerking** **1.** To give something a quick pull, push, or twist: *The window was stuck and I had to jerk it open.* **2.** To move with or make a sudden, sharp movement: *The fisherman felt his line suddenly jerk. The old streetcar jerked down the hill.*
—*noun, plural* **jerks** A sudden, sharp movement: *The fish gave a jerk to the line.*

jerk·in |jûr′kən| —*noun, plural* **jerkins** A short jacket worn by men during the fifteenth and sixteenth centuries. Jerkins were usually fit closely, had no sleeves, and were often made of leather.

jerk·y |jûr′kē| —*adjective* **jerkier, jerkiest** Making sudden stops and starts: *The bus ride was very jerky. I didn't like the dancer because of her jerky movements.*

jer·sey |jûr′zē| —*noun, plural* **jerseys** **1.** A soft, knitted fabric or cloth made of wool, cotton, or other materials. **2.** A garment

made of this material, especially a sweater or shirt made to be
pulled down over the head.

jest |jĕst| —*noun, plural* **jests** Something said or done for fun;
joke; prank: *We hid his glasses as a jest but he got angry.*
—*verb* **jested, jesting** To joke or play a prank; fool around: *Stop
jesting and start working.*

jes·ter |jĕs′tər| —*noun, plural* **jesters** **1.** A person who makes
jokes. **2.** In the Middle Ages, a person kept by kings, queens,
and other nobles to entertain or amuse them.

Je·sus |jē′zəs| The founder of the Christian religion. Christians
believe Jesus is the Son of God. Jesus is also known as **Jesus
Christ** and **Christ.**

jet |jĕt| —*noun, plural* **jets** **1.** A very fast stream of liquid or
gas that is forced out of a small hole or opening by great
pressure: *A fountain and a garden hose send out jets of water.* **2.** A
jet-propelled aircraft or other vehicle.
—*verb* **jetted, jetting** To gush forth; squirt: *Smoke jetted from the
chimney.*

jet engine An engine that develops power by forcing out a jet
from a small hole in the back. The jet is usually made of gases
from material burned inside the engine.

jet-pro·pelled |jĕt′prə pĕld′| —*adjective* Powered or propelled
by one or more jet engines: *a jet-propelled airplane.*

jet·ty |jĕt′ē| —*noun, plural* **jetties** A wall or dam that is built
out into a body of water, such as a harbor or river. A jetty is
usually made of rocks and wood. It protects the land or coast
from strong waves.

jetty

Jew |jōō| —*noun, plural* **Jews** **1.** A person whose religion is
Judaism. **2.** A person who is descended from the Hebrew people
described in the Bible or Old Testament.

jew·el |jōō′əl| —*noun, plural* **jewels** **1.** A precious stone; gem.
Jewels are valued because of their beauty and are often used in
jewelry. Because jewels are among the hardest substances on
earth, they are also often used in the moving parts of watches
and other machines. **2.** A valuable piece of jewelry made with
precious stones, such as a ring or necklace.

jew·el·er |jōō′ə lər| —*noun, plural* **jewelers** A person who
makes, repairs, or sells jewelry.

jew·el·ry |jōō′əl rē| —*noun* Ornaments that are made to be
worn, such as a bracelet, necklace, or ring. Jewelry is usually
made of gold or silver, with precious stones set into the metal.

Jew·ish |jōō′ĭsh| —*adjective* Of the Jews, their religion, or their
customs: *a Jewish holiday; a Jewish service.*

jewelry

jig |jĭg| —*noun, plural* **jigs** **1.** A fast, lively dance. **2.** The
music for such a dance.

jig·saw |jĭg′sô′| —*noun, plural* **jigsaws** A saw with a narrow
blade that is set straight up and down in a frame. A jigsaw is
used for cutting curved or wavy lines.

jigsaw puzzle A puzzle that is made of differently shaped pieces
of wood or cardboard. When they are fitted together, they make a
picture.

jin·gle |jĭng′gəl| —*verb* **jingled, jingling** To make or cause to
make a tinkling or ringing sound: *He jingled his keys. The breeze
jingled the bells hanging on the door.*
—*noun, plural* **jingles** **1.** A tinkling or ringing sound made by
small metal objects striking one another: *I could hear the jingle of*

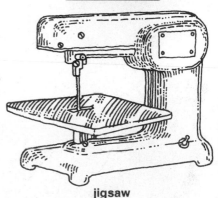
jigsaw

jockey

jonquil

coins in his pocket as he walked. **2.** A simple tune that is easy to remember. A jingle often has rhyming words or verses.

job | jŏb | —*noun, plural* **jobs 1.** A piece of work that needs to be done; task: *Cleaning your room is a job well done.* **2.** A position of employment: *I got a job at the grocery store.*

jock·ey | jŏk′ē | —*noun, plural* **jockeys** A person who rides horses in races.

jog | jŏg | —*verb* **jogged, jogging** To run at a slow, steady pace: *We jogged five miles this morning.*
—*noun, plural* **jogs** A slow, steady pace.

join | join | —*verb* **joined, joining 1.** To come or put together so as to become a group or one: *The children joined in a circle.* **2.** To connect with; link: *This road joins the main highway.* **3.** To fasten together or attach: *Solder is used to join two metal parts together.* **4.** To become a member of: *join the navy; join the club.* **5.** To enter into the company of: *Will you join us for lunch?*

joint | joint | —*noun, plural* **joints 1.** The place where two or more bones meet or come together. There are joints at the elbows and knees. **2.** Any place where two or more things come together: *a joint in a metal pipe.*
—*adjective* Done or shared by two or more people: *a joint effort; a joint bank account.*

joint·ed | join′tĭd | —*adjective* Having a joint or joints: *the jointed legs of an insect.*

joke | jōk | —*noun, plural* **jokes** Something that is said or done to make people laugh.
—*verb* **joked, joking** To say or do something as a joke; speak in fun.

jok·er | jō′kər | —*noun, plural* **jokers 1.** A person who tells or plays jokes. **2.** An extra playing card in a deck of cards that has a figure of a jester on it.

jol·ly | jŏl′ē | —*adjective* **jollier, jolliest** Full of fun and good spirits; cheerful; merry: *He laughs a lot and is a jolly man.*

jolt | jōlt | —*verb* **jolted, jolting** To move with sudden, rough bumps or jerks: *The bus jolted along the country road.*
—*noun, plural* **jolts 1.** A sudden bump or jerk: *The car stopped with a jolt.* **2.** Something or someone that causes a sudden shock or surprise: *The news of his death gave me a jolt.*

jon·quil | jŏng′kwĭl | or | jŏn′kwĭl | —*noun, plural* **jonquils** A garden plant with yellow flowers that look very much like daffodils.

Josh·u·a tree | jŏsh′ōō ə | A plant that grows in deserts of the southwestern United States. It looks like a tree with stiff, pointed leaves at the ends of the branches.

jos·tle | jŏs′əl | —*verb* **jostled, jostling** To push or bump: *People jostled one another trying to get out of the bus.*

jot | jŏt | —*verb* **jotted, jotting** To write down quickly and usually in a short form: *I jotted down a few notes on a piece of paper.*

jour·nal | jûr′nəl | —*noun, plural* **journals 1.** A daily record of events: *We kept a journal when we were in Europe. The druggist keeps a journal of his sales.* **2.** A magazine or newspaper containing articles about a particular subject: *a medical journal.*

jour·nal·ism | jûr′nə lĭz′əm | —*noun, plural* **journalisms** The gathering and presentation of news, especially by newspapers and magazines: *I took courses in journalism when I was in college.*

jour·nal·ist | jûr′nə lĭst | —*noun, plural* **journalists** A person who gathers and presents news, especially a reporter or editor for a newspaper or magazine.

jour·ney |jûr′nē| —*noun, plural* **journeys** **1.** A trip, especially over a great distance: *We journeyed to Europe and then to Asia.* **2.** The distance traveled on a journey or the time required for such a trip: *a journey of 3,000 miles; a journey of three days.* —*verb* **journeyed, journeying** To travel a great distance; make a long trip: *We journeyed around the world.*

joust |joust| —*noun, plural* **jousts** A combat between two knights on horses. The knights wore armor and carried lances to fight with. —*verb* **jousted, jousting** To take part in a joust.

jo·vi·al |jō′vē əl| —*adjective* Full of fun and good cheer; jolly: *a jovial person. Dad was jovial at my birthday party and we had a good time.*

jowl |joul| —*noun, plural* **jowls** The flesh under the lower jaw, especially when plump or hanging loosely.

joy |joi| —*noun, plural* **joys** **1.** A feeling of great happiness or delight: *shouts of joy.* **2.** A cause of or reason for great happiness: *My family is a joy to me.*

joy·ful |joi′fəl| —*adjective* Full of joy or showing joy: *a joyful occasion; a joyful song.*

joy·ous |joi′əs| —*adjective* Full of joy; joyful: *a joyous occasion; a joyous look.*

Ju·da·ism |jōō′dē ĭz′əm| —*noun* The religion of the Jewish people, as set forth in the Old Testament. Judaism is based on the belief in one God.

judge |jŭj| —*noun, plural* **judges** **1.** A public official who hears and decides cases in a court of law: *The judge sentenced him to prison after he heard the evidence presented.* **2.** A person who decides the winner of a contest or race: *judge of a beauty contest; judges at the horse race.* **3.** A person who gives an opinion about the value or quality of something: *a good judge of houses; a reliable judge of people.* —*verb* **judged, judging** **1.** To hear and pass judgment on someone or something in a court of law. **2.** To decide the winner of: *He was asked to judge the contest.* **3.** To form an opinion of: *You should judge a book by reading it yourself, and not by what other people say about it.*

judge
U.S. Supreme Court judges

judg·ment |jŭj′mənt| —*noun, plural* **judgments** **1.** A decision reached after hearing all sides of a question or complaint in a court of law: *It was the judgment of the court that the man was innocent.* **2.** The ability to choose or decide wisely; good sense: *I trust his judgment.* **3.** An opinion after thinking about someone or something carefully: *In my judgment he would be excellent as the villain in the play.*

ju·di·cial |jōō dĭsh′əl| —*adjective* Of or ordered by judges or courts of law: *the judicial branch of the government; a judicial decision.*

ju·do |jōō′dō| —*noun* A way of fighting and defending oneself by making one's opponents use their weight and strength against themselves. It is studied as a way of mental and physical control and is also played as a sport.

jug |jŭg| —*noun, plural* **jugs** **1.** A large container for storing, holding, and carrying liquids. A jug usually has a narrow mouth and a small handle. **2.a.** A jug with something in it: *I bought a* jug of cider. **b.** The amount that a jug holds: *I drank half a jug of cider.*

jug·gle |jŭg′əl| —*verb* **juggled, juggling** To keep two or more objects in the air at one time by skillful tossing and catching: *The children loved to watch him juggle the balls.*

jug·gler |jŭg′lər| —*noun, plural* **jugglers** An entertainer who juggles balls or other objects.

juice |jōōs| —*noun, plural* **juices** **1.** A liquid contained in the fruit, stem, or roots of plants: *tomato juice; carrot juice.* **2.** A fluid made inside an organ of the body: *digestive juices.*

juic·y |jōō′sē| —*adjective* **juicier, juiciest** Full of juice: *These peaches are juicy and delicious.*

Ju·ly |jōō lī′| —*noun, plural* **Julys** The seventh month of the year, after June and before August. July has 31 days.

jum·ble |jŭm′bəl| —*verb* **jumbled, jumbling** To mix or throw together without order: *All the clothes were jumbled in the middle of the floor.*
—*noun, plural* **jumbles** A confused, crowded grouping: *a jumble of modern automobiles and old-fashioned ox carts.*

jump |jŭmp| —*verb* **jumped, jumping** **1.** To rise up off the ground by using the legs: *Some grasshoppers can jump very high.* **2.** To leap into the air: *Bobby jumped off the high diving board.* **3.** To move suddenly and in one motion: *The students jumped from their seats when they heard the fire alarm.* **4.** To leap over: *He jumped over a mud puddle. He jumped the hurdle and won the race.*
—*noun, plural* **jumps** **1.** A leap off the ground: *It takes a high jump to get over that fence.* **2.** The distance or height reached by a leap: *a jump of 16 feet.* **3.** A sudden movement: *I gave a jump because you surprised me.* **4.** A sudden rise: *a jump in temperature; a jump in the price of milk.*

jump·er¹ |jŭm′pər| —*noun, plural* **jumpers** Someone or something that jumps: *Joe is the best jumper on the basketball team. Grasshoppers are jumpers.*

jump·er² |jŭm′pər| —*noun, plural* **jumpers** A dress without sleeves, worn over a blouse or sweater.

jun·co |jŭng′kō| —*noun, plural* **juncos** A small bird with mostly gray feathers.

junc·tion |jŭngk′shən| —*noun, plural* **junctions** **1.** The act of joining or the condition of being joined: *the exact junction of the beams.* **2.** The place at which two things join, meet, or cross: *the junction of the two rivers; a railroad junction.*

June |jōōn| —*noun, plural* **Junes** The sixth month of the year, after May and before July. June has 30 days.

Ju·neau |jōō′nō| The capital of Alaska.

jun·gle |jŭng′gəl| —*noun, plural* **jungles** A very thick growth of tropical trees and plants that covers a large area.

jun·ior |jōōn′yər| —*adjective* **1.** Of or for younger or smaller persons: *a junior skating championship; junior dress sizes.* **2. Junior** A term used with the name of a son named after his father: *William, Junior, was the eldest boy in the family.* **3.** Of lower rank or shorter length of service: *a junior partner.* **4.** Of the third year of high school or college: *the junior class dance.*
—*noun, plural* **juniors** **1.** A person who is younger than another. **2.** A student in the third year of a four-year high school or college.

ju·ni·per |jōō′nə pər| —*noun, plural* **junipers** An evergreen tree

---

jumper¹, jumper²
Jumper¹ is formed from **jump** by the addition of the ending **-er**. This ending is used to show that someone or something does the action of the verb to which the ending is attached. **Jumper¹** is someone or something that jumps. It is likely that **jumper²** originally comes from an Arabic word. That word traveled through French, where it meant "skirt," and into English, where it referred to a man's loose jacket.

juniper
Tree (*above*) and needles and berries (*below*)

ă	pat	ĕ	pet	î	fierce
ā	pay	ē	be	ŏ	pot
â	care	ĭ	pit	ō	go
ä	father	ī	pie	ô	paw, for
oi	oil	ŭ	cut	zh	vision
ōō	book	û	fur	ə	ago, item,
ōō	boot	*th*	**the**		pencil, atom,
yōō	abuse	th	thin		circus
ou	out	hw	which	ər	butter

or shrub with very small prickly needles. It has bluish berries with a strong, spicy smell.

junk¹ |jŭngk| —*noun, plural* **junks** Something that no longer can be used and is ready to be thrown away; waste materials; trash.

junk² |jŭngk| —*noun, plural* **junks** A Chinese sailing ship with a flat bottom.

Ju·pi·ter |jōō′pĭ tər| A planet of our solar system. It is the largest planet and the fifth in distance from the sun.

ju·ry |jŏŏr′ē| —*noun, plural* **juries** A group of citizens sworn to hear the facts and evidence on cases presented in a court of law. The jury makes decisions or offers recommendations based on the law and on the facts and evidence presented.

just |jŭst| —*adjective* Honest and fair: *His boss was a just man.* —*adverb* **1.** Exactly: *Everything happened just the way you said it would.* **2.** At that instant: *Just then a flash of lightning lit up the room.* **3.** Quite recently: *We just ran out of milk. We just finished painting our house.* **4.** Shortly; barely: *Carl set out just after midnight.* **5.** Simply; merely: *You can't become an expert in tennis just by reading about it.*

jus·tice |jŭs′tĭs| —*noun, plural* **justices** **1.** Fair treatment according to law or honor: *Justice is everyone's right.* **2.** A judge: *The Supreme Court is made up of a Chief Justice and as many associate justices as Congress determines.*

jus·ti·fy |jŭs′tə fī′| —*verb* **justified, justifying** **1.** To show or prove to be just, fair, and right: *He justified his reasons for wanting a raise.* **2.** To prove and declare innocent; clear of blame: *He was sure that the court would justify him.*

jut |jŭt| —*verb* **jutted, jutting** To stick out or project sharply upward or outward: *Those tall buildings seem to jut up as high as the sky.*

jute |jōōt| —*noun* A strong fiber used to make rope, cord, and coarse cloth. Jute comes from a plant that grows in tropical Asia.

ju·ve·nile |jōō′və nəl| or |jōō′və nīl′| —*adjective* **1.** Young; childish; immature: *juvenile behavior.* **2.** Of or for young people: *a juvenile section of the library; a juvenile law court.* —*noun, plural* **juveniles** A young person: *athletic and social programs to keep our juveniles busy.*

junk¹, junk²

Junk¹ comes from a word used by sailors long ago to refer to old, worn-out pieces of rope. It can be traced back to the fifteenth century, but its original source is not known. **Junk²** comes from Dutch *jonk* and Portuguese *junco.* Both of these words are borrowed from *jong,* a word used in a language spoken in parts of Southeast Asia to mean "a seagoing ship."

junk²

Kk

Phoenician — The letter K comes from a Phoenician symbol named *kaph*, meaning "hollow of the hand."		
Greek — The Greeks borrowed the symbol from the Phoenicians and changed its form. They also changed its name to *kappa*.		
Roman — The Romans took the letter and adapted it for carving into stone. This became the model for our modern printed capital *K*.		
Medieval — The hand-written form of about 1,200 years ago became the basis of the modern small letter.		
Modern — The modern capital and small letters are based on the Roman capital and later hand-written forms.		

kangaroo

Kansas

Kansas comes from an Indian word that means "people of the south wind."

ă	pat	ĕ	pet	î	fierce
ā	pay	ē	be	ŏ	pot
â	care	ĭ	pit	ō	go
ä	father	ī	pie	ô	paw, for
oi	oil	ŭ	cut	zh	vision
ōo	book	û	fur	ə	ago, item,
ōo	boot	*th*	the		pencil, atom,
yōo	abuse	th	thin		circus
ou	out	hw	which	ər	butter

k or **K** |kā| —*noun, plural* **k's** or **K's** The eleventh letter of the English alphabet.

kale |kāl| —*noun* A kind of cabbage with crinkled leaves that are not in a tight head.

ka·lei·do·scope |kə lī′də skōp′| —*noun, plural* **kaleidoscopes** A tube that contains small bits or pieces of colored glass at one end and a small hole at the other end. When a person looks through the hole and turns the tube, mirrors inside show continually changing patterns formed by the moving pieces of glass.

kan·ga·roo |kăng′gə rōo′| —*noun, plural* **kangaroos** An animal of Australia with long, strong hind legs and a long tail. It can take very long leaps. The female kangaroo carries her newborn young in a pouch on the outside of her body.

Kan·sas |kăn′səs| A state in the central United States. The capital of Kansas is Topeka.

kar·at |kăr′ət| —*noun, plural* **karats** A unit of measure that shows how much gold is in a mixture. Most jewelry is made of 14-karat gold, but 24-karat gold is the purest. Another form of this word is **carat.**

♦ *These sound alike* **karat, carat, carrot.**

ka·ra·te |kə rä′tē| —*noun* A kind of fighting in which the fighters do not use weapons. Karate fighters try to strike blows with the hands or feet. Karate was invented in Japan.

ka·ty·did |kā′tē dĭd| —*noun, plural* **katydids** An insect that looks like a large green grasshopper. The males rub their front wings together to make a hoarse sound that is like the name "katydid."

kay·ak |kī′ăk′| —*noun, plural* **kayaks** An Eskimo canoe made of animal skins stretched over a light wooden frame. The top or deck of a kayak is closed, and there is a hole or opening in the middle in which one person can sit.

keel |kēl| —*noun, plural* **keels** **1.** A strong piece or beam of wood or metal that runs down the center of the bottom of a ship or boat. The keel is the main support of a ship, and the whole frame or hull is attached to it. **2.** A fin or flat-shaped piece that is attached lengthwise to the bottom of a sailboat and hangs down into the water. The keel keeps the sailboat upright so it will not tip over.

—*verb* **keeled, keeling** **1.** To turn upside-down; capsize: *The sailboat keeled over in the strong wind.* **2.** To fall down: *He felt so dizzy he thought he might keel over.*

keen | kĕn | —*adjective* **keener, keenest** **1.** Having a sharp edge or point: *a keen knife cutting through cloth.* **2.** Able to think or understand quickly and well; very bright: *Gail has a keen mind and learns fast.* **3.** Very quick or sensitive, especially in seeing, hearing, tasting, or smelling: *Dogs have a keener sense of smell than people.* **4.** Full of enthusiasm; eager: *She is a keen sports fan.*

keep | kēp | —*verb* **kept, keeping** **1.** To have and hold on to; have and not give up: *You may keep the puppy.* **2.** To continue or cause to continue in a particular condition, position, or place; to stay: *keeping warm; keep quiet; keep in line.* **3.** To stay fresh: *Milk won't keep long.* **4.** To continue doing something: *keep guessing.* **5.** To put something in a place where it is safe or easy to get to; store or put away: *Are you keeping your money in the bank?* **6.** To take care of; tend: *He helps his mother keep house.* **7.** To carry out or fulfill, as a promise: *keep your word.* **8.** To prevent; stop: *She kept the wagon from overturning.* **9.** To make someone stay late; detain or delay: *The teacher kept him after school.*

Phrasal verbs **keep back** To refuse to give or tell; withhold: *Tell me all about it; don't keep back anything.* **keep on** To continue; go on: *He kept on trying until he passed his swimming test.* **keep up** **1.** To stay or continue at the same speed or pace as others: *He was keeping up with the leader in the race.* **2.** To maintain in good condition: *She keeps up the garden.*

—*noun, plural* **keeps** **1.** Food, clothing, and a place to live: *He earns his keep by doing chores.* **2.** The main tower or safest and strongest part of a castle.

keep·ing | kē′ pǐng | —*noun* **1.** Care or custody; charge: *I left my dog Tillie in my cousin's keeping.* **2.** The condition of agreeing with or matching; harmony: *The suit and tie he wore were in keeping with the serious nature of a funeral.*

keg | kĕg | —*noun, plural* **kegs** **1.** A small barrel. **2.a.** A keg with something in it: *a keg of pickles.* **b.** The amount that a keg holds: *drank a keg of beer.*

kelp | kĕlp | —*noun* A brown seaweed. Some kinds of kelp grow to a very large size.

ken·nel | kĕn′ əl | —*noun, plural* **kennels** **1.** Often **kennels** A place or business in which dogs are bred, trained, or left by their owners to be cared for. **2.** A small shelter for one or more dogs.

Ken·tuck·y | kən tŭk′ ē | A state in the central United States. The capital of Kentucky is Frankfort.

kept | kĕpt | The past tense and past participle of the verb **keep**: *She kept the stray dog she found. She threw out the baked beans he had kept for too long.*

ker·chief | kûr′ chĭf | —*noun, plural* **kerchiefs** **1.** A square scarf or piece of cloth worn over the head or around the neck. **2.** A handkerchief.

ker·nel | kûr′ nəl | —*noun, plural* **kernels** **1.a.** A grain or seed of corn, wheat, or rice. **b.** The part inside the shell of a nut or the hard pit of some fruit. **2.** The most important or central part of something; the heart; core: *The kernel of the President's speech was that the country must learn to use less energy.*

♦ *These sound alike* **kernel, colonel.**

keg
Kegs at the bottom of a delivery cart

kennel

Kentucky
Some people believe that the name **Kentucky** comes from an Indian name meaning "land of tomorrow." Others think it means "meadow land" or "flat land."

key¹, key²

Key¹ comes from an old English word that meant the same as it does today. Its earlier source is still a mystery. **Key²** comes from a Spanish word that means "a small island" and "a sandbar."

key¹

Above: Antique keys
Below: Modern key

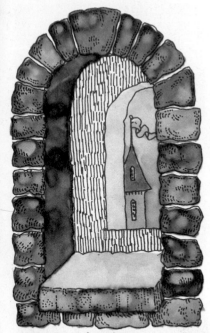

keystone

ă	pat	ĕ	pet	î	fierce
ā	pay	ē	be	ŏ	pot
â	care	ĭ	pit	ō	go
ä	father	ī	pie	ô	paw, for

oi	oil	ŭ	cut	zh	vision
ŏŏ	book	û	fur	ə	ago, item,
ōō	boot	*th*	the		pencil, atom,
yŏŏ	abuse	th	thin		circus
ou	out	hw	which	ər	butter

ker·o·sene | kĕr′ə sēn′ | or | kăr′ə sēn′ | or | kĕr′ə **sēn′** | or | kăr′ə **sēn′** | —*noun* A thin, light-colored oil that is made from petroleum. Kerosene is used as a fuel in such things as lamps, stoves, and jet engines.

ketch·up | kĕch′əp | or | kăch′əp | —*noun, plural* **ketchups** A thick, spicy red sauce made with tomatoes. Ketchup is used to add flavor to hamburgers, steak, potatoes, and other foods. Another form of this word is **catsup.**

ket·tle | kĕt′l | —*noun, plural* **kettles** **1.** A metal pot for boiling liquids or cooking food. A kettle usually has a lid. **2. a.** A kettle with something in it: *She's boiling a kettle of water for tea.* **b.** The amount that a kettle will hold: *The guests ate a kettle of chowder.*

ket·tle·drum | kĕt′l drŭm′ | —*noun, plural* **kettledrums** A large drum with a bowl-shaped body and a top made of parchment. A kettledrum is tuned by making the parchment tighter or looser.

key¹ | kē | —*noun, plural* **keys** **1. a.** A small piece of shaped metal that is used to open or close a lock on such things as a door, a car, or a chest. **b.** Anything shaped or used like a key, as to wind the spring in a clock or a toy. **2.** Anything that solves a problem or explains a question or puzzle; a solution: *The missing gun is the key to the mystery.* **3.** The most important element or part: *Hard work is the key to success.* **4.** A list or chart that explains the symbols, colors, or abbreviations used in such things as a map or a dictionary. There is a pronunciation key on every left-hand page of this dictionary. **5.** One of a set of buttons or levers that is pressed down to operate a machine or certain musical instruments: *a typewriter key. How many keys are there on a piano?* **6.** A group or scale of musical tones in which all the tones are related. There is one basic tone or note in every key, and all the other tones are built around it: *the key of D.*

♦ *These sound alike* **key, quay.**

key² | kē | —*noun, plural* **keys** A low island or reef along a coast. Many keys off the coast of Florida are connected by bridges.

♦ *These sound alike* **key, quay.**

key·board | kē′bôrd′ | or | kē′bōrd′ | —*noun, plural* **keyboards** A set of keys on a piano, organ, or typewriter.

key·hole | kē′hōl′ | —*noun, plural* **keyholes** The hole in a lock into which a key is put.

key·stone | kē′stōn′ | —*noun, plural* **keystones** The middle stone at the top of the curve of an arch. The keystone is often shaped like a wedge. It holds or locks the other stones of the arch in place.

khak·i | kăk′ē | or | kä′kē | —*noun, plural* **khakis** **1.** A dull, yellowish-brown color. **2. a.** A strong, heavy khaki-colored cloth, used for army uniforms. **b. khakis** A uniform made of this cloth. —*adjective* Yellowish brown.

kick | kĭk | —*verb* **kicked, kicking** **1.** To strike with the foot: *He kicked the table leg so hard that he hurt his big toe. Zebras kick as hard as mules.* **2.** To make repeated motions with the feet or legs, as in swimming: *Water birds have to paddle and kick for a long time before they can take off and fly.* **3.** To hit, produce, or move by striking with the foot: *kick up dust. They kicked off their shoes to dance. He kicked a fifty-yard field goal.* **4.** To spring back suddenly when fired: *He staggered when the rifle kicked.*
—*noun, plural* **kicks** **1.** A blow with the foot. **2.** Any of the different motions of the legs used in swimming: *a flutter kick.*

3. a. The act of kicking a ball, as in soccer or football. **b.** The kicked ball: *Block that kick!* **c.** The distance a kicked ball travels or covers. **4.** The backward spring of a gun or cannon when fired: *The kick of the rifle was so strong it knocked him over backward.* **5.** A quick feeling of pleasure; a thrill: *You'll get a kick out of this joke.* **6.** A temporary or short interest in something; a fad: *A lot of people are on a jogging kick.*

kick·off |kĭk′ôf′| or |kĭk′ŏf′| —*noun, plural* **kickoffs** A kick in football or soccer that puts the ball in play at the beginning of the game or after a touchdown or goal is scored.

kid |kĭd| —*noun, plural* **kids** **1. a.** A young goat. **b.** Soft leather made from the skin of a young goat. **2.** A child or young person.
—*adjective* Younger: *my kid brother.*
—*verb* **kidded, kidding** To make fun of playfully; tease or fool: *The boys were kidding him about his hat.*

kid·nap |kĭd′năp′| —*verb* **kidnaped** or **kidnapped, kidnaping** or **kidnapping** To carry off and hold or keep someone by force. The people who kidnap someone usually demand a ransom or large sum of money before they will set the person free.

kid·ney |kĭd′nē| —*noun, plural* **kidneys** One of two body organs located in the abdomen. The kidneys separate waste matter from the blood and pass it through the bladder in the form of urine.

kidney bean The reddish seed of the string bean when its pods are completely ripe.

kill |kĭl| —*verb* **killed, killing** **1.** To cause the death of; put to death; slay: *In eighteen months Buffalo Bill killed 4,280 buffaloes. Most wild animals kill for food, not for fun.* **2.** To put an end to; eliminate: *Dropping the ball three times killed his chance of making the team.* **3.** To cause pain to; hurt: *These shoes are killing me.* **4.** To use up or pass time: *I killed two hours watching television.*
—*noun, plural* **kills** **1.** An act of killing: *The hunter made six kills today.* **2.** Something that has just been killed: *The lions ate their kill immediately.*

kill·deer |kĭl′dîr′| —*noun, plural* **killdeers** or **killdeer** A North American bird that has two dark bands across the breast. It has a call that sounds like its name.

kill·er |kĭl′ər| —*noun, plural* **killers** Someone or something that kills, especially a murderer or a predatory animal.

kiln |kĭl| or |kĭln| —*noun, plural* **kilns** An oven or furnace used for hardening, drying, or burning such things as grain and lumber. A special kiln that can heat up to very high temperatures is used to fire or bake pottery and bricks.

ki·lo |kē′lō| or |kĭl′ō| —*noun, plural* **kilos** **1.** A kilogram. **2.** A kilometer.

kilo- A prefix that means "a thousand": *kilogram.*

kil·o·gram |kĭl′ə grăm′| —*noun, plural* **kilograms** The basic unit of mass in the metric system. A kilogram is equal to 1,000 grams or about 2⅕ pounds.

kil·o·me·ter |kĭl′ə mē′tər| or |kĭ lŏm′ĭ tər| —*noun, plural* **kilometers** A unit of length in the metric system. A kilometer is equal to 1,000 meters, or 0.6214 mile.

kil·o·watt |kĭl′ə wŏt′| —*noun, plural* **kilowatts** A unit of electric power. A kilowatt is equal to 1,000 watts.

kilt |kĭlt| —*noun, plural* **kilts** A pleated plaid skirt that reaches down to the knees. Kilts are worn by men in Scotland.

kickoff
In football

killdeer

kilt

kimono

ă	pat	ĕ	pet	î	fierce
ā	pay	ē	be	ŏ	pot
â	care	ĭ	pit	ō	go
ä	father	ī	pie	ô	paw, for
oi	oil	ŭ	cut	zh	vision
ōō	book	û	fur	ə	ago, item,
ōō	boot	*th*	the		pencil, atom,
yōō	abuse	th	thin		circus
ou	out	hw	which	ər	butter

ki·mo·no | kĭ mō′ nə | or | kĭ mō′ nō | —*noun, plural* **kimonos** A long, loose robe that has wide sleeves and is tied with a wide sash. Kimonos are worn as outer garments by both women and men in Japan.

kin | kĭn | —*noun* A person's relatives; family: *Most of my kin were at the Thanksgiving dinner.*

kind¹ | kīnd | —*adjective* **kinder, kindest 1.** Helpful and considerate: *He is always kind to little children and old people.* **2.** Gentle, thoughtful, or courteous: *It was kind of you to write to us.*

kind² | kīnd | —*noun, plural* **kinds 1.** A group of the same or similar things; a type or category: *Swans are a kind of water bird. The store sells all different kinds of tents.* **2.** A living or natural group; a species: *Many wild animals live in small groups of their own kind.*

kin·der·gar·ten | kĭn′ dər gär′tn | —*noun, plural* **kindergartens** A school class for children from the ages of four to six. Kindergarten prepares children for elementary school.

kin·dle | kĭn′dl | —*verb* **kindled, kindling 1. a.** To build and start a fire: *kindle a fire with matches.* **b.** To begin to burn; catch fire: *The paper kindled quickly.* **2.** To stir up or arouse; excite: *The teacher showed slides of Greece that kindled my interest.*

kin·dling | kĭnd′lĭng | —*noun* Material, such as twigs, dry wood, and paper, used for starting a fire.

kind·ly | kīnd′lē | —*adjective* **kindlier, kindliest** Considerate and friendly; kind: *a warm, kindly person.*
—*adverb* **1.** In a friendly or kind way; warmly: *She greeted us kindly.* **2.** Out of kindness: *He kindly offered to give us a ride.* **3.** As a kind act; please: *Kindly read the letter aloud.*

kind·ness | kīnd′nĭs | —*noun, plural* **kindnesses 1.** The condition or quality of being kind; generosity: *The old man's kindness to animals made him popular with all the children.* **2.** A kind act; a favor: *In addition to planting trees, Johnny Appleseed did many kindnesses for the pioneers.*

king | kĭng | —*noun, plural* **kings 1.** A man who alone rules a country. **2.** A person or thing that is the best, the most important, or the most powerful of its type: *When Hank Aaron broke Babe Ruth's record, he became the king of home runs. The lion is the king of the jungle.* **3.** An important piece in the games of chess and checkers. **4.** A playing card having the picture of a king. It ranks above a queen and below an ace.

king·dom | kĭng′dəm | —*noun, plural* **kingdoms 1.** A country that is ruled by a king or queen. **2.** One of the three groups into which all living things and natural substances are divided. These groups are the animal kingdom, the plant kingdom, and the mineral kingdom.

king·fish·er | kĭng′fĭsh′ər | —*noun, plural* **kingfishers** A bird with a large bill and a crest on its head. Kingfishers feed on fish.

king-size | kĭng′sīz′ | —*adjective* Extra large: *a king-size container.*

kink | kĭngk | —*noun, plural* **kinks 1.** A tight curl or sharp twist of hair, wire, or rope. **2.** A pain or stiff feeling in a muscle; a cramp: *I have a kink in my shoulder from sleeping on it.*
—*verb* **kinked, kinking** To form or cause to form a kink; curl or twist sharply: *My hair kinked after I washed it. She was kinking yarn around the knitting needle.*

kin·ship | kĭn′shĭp′ | —*noun* **1.** The condition of being related, as in a family, or of having the same origin or beginning: *Did you know there is a kinship between your pet beagle and the wild coyotes that live in the desert?* **2.** A strong connection or similarity between persons or things: *As a baseball player he felt a kinship with other athletes.*

ki·osk | kē′ŏsk′ | or | kē ŏsk′ | —*noun, plural* **kiosks** A small building or shed. A kiosk is usually used as a place to sell such things as newspapers, candy, or refreshments.

kiss | kĭs | —*verb* **kissed, kissing** To touch and press with lips as a sign of love, affection, friendship, greeting, or respect.
—*noun, plural* **kisses** **1.** A touch with the lips: *She gave him a kiss.* **2.** A small piece of chocolate candy.

kit | kĭt | —*noun, plural* **kits** **1.** A set of parts or pieces of something that have to be assembled or put together: *a model airplane kit.* **2.** A small set of tools or equipment for a special purpose: *a first-aid kit; a sewing kit.*

kitch·en | kĭch′ən | —*noun, plural* **kitchens** A room where food is cooked or prepared.

kitch·en·ette | kĭch′ə nĕt′ | —*noun, plural* **kitchenettes** A very small kitchen.

kite | kīt | —*noun, plural* **kites** **1.** A bird with a long, often forked tail. Kites hunt and kill other animals for food. **2.** A light wooden frame covered with cloth, paper, or plastic. A kite is flown in the wind at the end of a long string.

kit·ten | kĭt′n | —*noun, plural* **kittens** A young cat.

knack | năk | —*noun, plural* **knacks** A special talent or skill: *He has a knack for getting along with people.*

knap·sack | năp′săk′ | —*noun, plural* **knapsacks** A canvas or leather bag made to be worn on the back. A knapsack is used to carry clothing, equipment, or supplies on a hike or march.

knead | nēd | —*verb* **kneaded, kneading** **1.** To mix and work a substance, such as dough or clay, by folding, pressing, or stretching it with the hands: *The children watched the pizza man kneading the dough.* **2.** To squeeze, press, or roll with the hands, as in massaging or rubbing a sore muscle: *Lilly has to knead her leg muscles when she jogs too much.*
♦ *These sound alike* **knead, need.**

knee | nē | —*noun, plural* **knees** **1.** The joint at which the thigh and the lower leg come together. **2.** The region of the leg around this joint.

knee·cap | nē′kăp′ | —*noun, plural* **kneecaps** A small, movable bone at the front of the knee.

kneel | nēl | —*verb* **knelt** or **kneeled, kneeling** To go down, rest, or fall on a bent knee or knees: *The doctor kneeled beside the patient's bed. The monks were kneeling in prayer.*

knelt | nĕlt | A past tense and a past participle of the verb **kneel:** *He knelt down to look for the coins he had dropped. She had knelt by the fire.*

knew | nōō | or | nyōō | The past tense of the verb **know:** *She knew my bus was arriving this morning.*
♦ *These sound alike* **knew, gnu, new.**

knick·ers | nĭk′ərz | —*plural noun* Loose trousers with short legs that are gathered in just below the knee. Boys often wore knickers instead of long pants in the 1920's and 1930's; men wore them while playing golf.

knife | nīf | —*noun, plural* **knives** **1.** A tool or device used for

kite
Four kinds of kite

kitten

cutting and made of a sharp blade attached to a handle. **2.** A similar tool used as a weapon.

—*verb* **knifed, knifing** To cut or stab with a knife.

knight |nīt| —*noun, plural* **knights** **1.** A soldier in the Middle Ages who served and pledged loyalty to a king or lord. A knight swore to obey the rules of chivalry and to do good deeds for people in need or in danger. Before a man could become a knight, he learned warfare and chivalry by serving as a page and a squire. **2.** In Great Britain, a man who is given the title "knight" for service to his country or for his personal achievements. A knight uses "Sir" before his name. **3.** One of two pieces in the game of chess.

—*verb* **knighted, knighting** To make someone a knight: *The queen knighted him for his courage in battle.*

♦ *These sound alike* **knight, night.**

knit |nĭt| —*verb* **knit** or **knitted, knitting** **1.** To make cloth or a garment by interlocking or looping together yarn or thread, either by hand with special needles or by machine: *She was knitting a sweater. Can you knit?* **2.** To join or grow closely together: *A common background helped to knit the original thirteen colonies into a country. Her broken leg failed to knit correctly.*

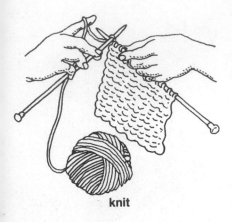

knit

knives |nīvz| The plural of the noun **knife.**

knob |nŏb| —*noun, plural* **knobs** **1.a.** A rounded handle for opening such things as a door or drawer. **b.** A rounded dial for operating such things as a radio or television. **2.** A rounded lump or mass, as on the trunk of a tree.

knock |nŏk| —*verb* **knocked, knocking** **1.** To strike with a hard blow or blows; to hit: *knock someone on the head. He knocked his elbow against the desk.* **2.** To make a loud noise by hitting a hard surface; to rap; bang: *knock on wood for luck. He knocked and knocked, but nobody answered the door.* **3.** To bump or cause to bump; collide: *The tree branches were knocking together in the wind. He grabbed the two robbers and knocked their heads together.* **4.** To make a pounding or clanking noise: *Dad took the car to the garage when the engine started to knock.* **5.** To hit and cause to fall: *knocked the vase off the table.*

Phrasal verbs **knock down** To take apart; demolish: *We watched them knock down the building.* **knock out** To hit so hard as to make unconscious: *The fighter was knocked out by the champion's last punch.*

—*noun, plural* **knocks** **1.** A hard or sharp blow: *She got a knock on the head when she fell.* **2.** A rap, as on a door: *We waited for our guest's knock before cutting the cake.* **3.** A pounding or clanking noise, as of an engine that needs to be fixed.

knocker

knock·er |nŏk′ər| —*noun, plural* **knockers** A small metal ring, knob, or hammer that is attached to a door by a hinge. A knocker is used for knocking on a door to let someone inside know that you want to come in.

knoll |nōl| —*noun, plural* **knolls** A small, rounded hill.

knot |nŏt| —*noun, plural* **knots** **1.** A fastening made by tying together one or more pieces of string, rope, or twine: *There is a knot in your shoelace.* **2.** A tightly twisted roll or clump of hair; a tangle: *The dog's fur is full of knots.* **3.** A tight group or cluster of persons or things: *a knot of people standing in the corridor.* **4.** A hard, dark spot in wood or in a board. **5.** A unit of measurement of speed, used by ships and aircraft. A knot is equal to one

ă	pat	ĕ	pet	î	fierce
ā	pay	ē	be	ŏ	pot
â	care	ĭ	pit	ō	go
ä	father	ī	pie	ô	paw, for
oi	oil	ŭ	cut	zh	vision
ōō	book	û	fur	ə	ago, item,
ōō	boot	*th*	the		pencil, atom,
yōō	abuse	th	thin		circus
ou	out	hw	which	ər	butter

nautical mile, or about 6,076 feet, per hour.

—*verb* **knotted, knotting** To tie or fasten in or with a knot: *She wrapped the scarf over her forehead and knotted it in the back. He knotted his shoelaces tighter.*

♦ *These sound alike* **knot, not.**

knot·ty |nŏt′ē| —*adjective* **knottier, knottiest 1.** Tied or tangled in knots: *knotty rope.* **2.** Having many knots: *knotty lumber.* **3.** Hard or difficult: *a knotty math problem.*

know |nō| —*verb* **knew, known, knowing 1.** To be certain of the facts or truth of; understand clearly: *We all know how the war started. Do you know what causes thunder?* **2.** To be sure: *I know that I'm right.* **3.** To be acquainted or familiar with: *I've known him for years. He knows the roads around the lake because he spent five summer vacations here.* **4.** To have skill in or experience with: *She wished she knew how to make friends. Both of them know three languages.* **5.** To find out; learn: *How did you know I was here?* **6.** To recognize or be able to tell apart from others: *I know his dog because she's wearing a bandanna around her neck.*

♦ *These sound alike* **know, no.**

knowl·edge |nŏl′ĭj| —*noun* **1.** What can be learned from study or experience; facts and ideas; information: *Jim has a very good knowledge of plants. She has enough knowledge about car engines to be able to fix most things that go wrong.* **2.** Awareness; understanding: *Every year scientists add to our knowledge of the universe.* **3.** The fact of knowing or being aware: *The knowledge that the knife was sharp made him handle it with care.*

known |nōn| The past participle of the verb **know:** *I've known for a long time that the bridge was going to fall down.*

—*adjective* **1.** Familiar to or accepted by most people: *It's known that she's the best swimmer in the group.* **2.** Proven to be true: *It's a known fact that the world is round.*

knuck·le |nŭk′əl| —*noun, plural* **knuckles** A joint of a finger, especially one of the joints connecting a finger to the rest of the hand.

ko·a·la |kō ä′lə| —*noun, plural* **koalas** An animal of Australia that looks something like a small, furry teddy bear. It lives in eucalyptus trees and feeds on their leaves.

ko·sher |kō′shər| —*adjective* **1.** Prepared according to Jewish laws: *kosher meat.* **2.** Preparing or selling kosher food: *a kosher restaurant.*

kum·quat |kŭm′kwŏt′| —*noun, plural* **kumquats** A fruit that looks like a small orange. Kumquats have thin skin and are eaten whole.

koala

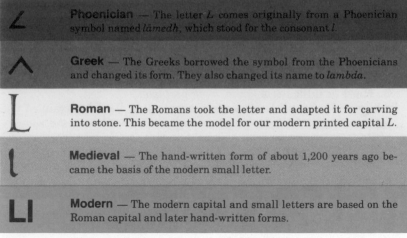

Phoenician — The letter *L* comes originally from a Phoenician symbol named *lāmedh*, which stood for the consonant *l*.

Greek — The Greeks borrowed the symbol from the Phoenicians and changed its form. They also changed its name to *lambda*.

Roman — The Romans took the letter and adapted it for carving into stone. This became the model for our modern printed capital *L*.

Medieval — The hand-written form of about 1,200 years ago became the basis of the modern small letter.

Modern — The modern capital and small letters are based on the Roman capital and later hand-written forms.

lace

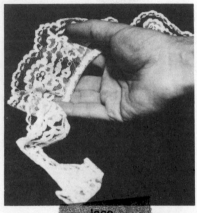

lacrosse

ă	pat	ĕ	pet	î	fierce
ā	pay	ē	be	ŏ	pot
â	care	ĭ	pit	ō	go
ä	father	ī	pie	ô	paw, for
oi	oil	ŭ	cut	zh	vision
ōō	book	û	fur	ə	ago, item,
ōō	boot	*th*	the		pencil, atom,
yōō	abuse	th	thin		circus
ou	out	hw	which	ər	butter

l or **L** | ĕl | —*noun, plural* **l's** or **L's** The twelfth letter of the English alphabet.

lab | lăb | —*noun, plural* **labs** A laboratory.

la·bel | lā′bəl | —*noun, plural* **labels** **1.** A tag or sticker put on something to give useful information about it: *The label on the inside of a shirt tells how the shirt should be cleaned.* **2.** A word, letter, number, or abbreviation used to identify: *a part-of-speech label.*
—*verb* **labeled, labeling** To put a label on: *Eileen labeled the packages for mailing. Label the parts of speech used in that sentence.*

la·bor | lā′bər | —*noun, plural* **labors** **1.** Work; toil: *It took many months of labor to build the house.* **2.** The group of people who work for a living; workers: *Labor wanted a 35-hour work week.*
—*verb* **labored, laboring** **1.** To work; to toil: *He labored at the task. She labored to make the painting just right.* **2.** To move slowly and with effort: *His car labored to the top of the hill.*

lab·o·ra·to·ry | lăb′rə tôr′ē | or | lăb′rə tōr′ē | —*noun, plural* **laboratories** A room or building with special tools and machines for doing scientific research, experiments, and testing.

Labor Day A holiday on the first Monday in September, in honor of working people.

la·bor·er | lā′bər ər | —*noun, plural* **laborers** A worker, especially one who does hard physical labor.

lace | lās | —*noun, plural* **laces** **1.** A delicate fabric of fine threads woven in an open pattern like a web with fancy designs. **2.** A cord or string drawn through holes or around hooks to pull and tie opposite edges together.
—*verb* **laced, lacing** To fasten or tie with a lace or laces: *Lace up your shoes.*

lack | lăk | —*noun, plural* **lacks** **1.** A total absence: *Lack of food made us very hungry.* **2.** Something that is needed: *Water is a serious lack in some desert areas.*
—*verb* **lacked, lacking** **1.** To be totally without: *The empty room lacked furniture.* **2.** To be in need of: *He lacked a pair of boots.*

lac·quer | lăk′ər | —*noun, plural* **lacquers** A liquid coating that is put on metal or wood to give it a glossy finish.

la·crosse | lə krôs′ | or | lə krŏs′ | —*noun* A game that is played on a field with two teams of ten players. Each player uses a stick with a net on the end to catch or throw a ball. The object of the game is to throw the ball into the opponents' goal.

lac·y |lā′sē| —*adjective* **lacier, laciest** Of or like lace: *A lacy white cloth covered the table.*

lad |lăd| —*noun, plural* **lads** A boy or young man.

lad·der |lăd′ər| —*noun, plural* **ladders** A piece of equipment used for climbing up and down. It has two side pieces connected by evenly spaced rungs.

lad·en |lād′n| —*adjective* Loaded or filled with something: *The ship was laden with fruits from the tropics.*

la·dle |lād′l| —*noun, plural* **ladles** A spoon having a long handle with a bowl shaped like a cup at the end. A ladle is used for dipping out liquids.

la·dy |lā′dē| —*noun, plural* **ladies** **1.** A woman of culture, high social position, or wealth. **2.** A woman or young girl who has good manners. **3.** Any woman: *the lady who lives next door.* **4. Lady** A woman of noble rank in Great Britain.

la·dy·bird |lā′dē bûrd′| —*noun, plural* **ladybirds** An insect, the ladybug.

la·dy·bug |lā′dē bŭg′| —*noun, plural* **ladybugs** A small, round, reddish or yellowish beetle with black spots. Ladybugs eat and destroy insects that are harmful to plants and trees.

lag |lăg| —*verb* **lagged, lagging** To fall behind: *The little child lagged behind the rest of the group.*
—*noun, plural* **lags** **1.** The act or condition of lagging: *Sometimes the guide has to wait for the lag of one child behind the group.* **2.** A gap or space: *There is a lag between the end of the music and the beginning of the applause.*

la·goon |lə gōōn′| —*noun, plural* **lagoons** A shallow body of water that is usually connected to a larger body of water, such as an ocean. A lagoon is often surrounded by coral reefs.

laid |lād| The past tense and past participle of the verb **lay:** *I laid the boxes on the chair. We have laid tiles in two rooms.*

lain |lān| The past participle of the verb **lie** (to recline or rest): *Mother had lain down for a nap.*
♦ *These sound alike* **lain, lane.**

lair |lâr| —*noun, plural* **lairs** The den or home of a wild animal: *The bear slept in its lair.*

lake |lāk| —*noun, plural* **lakes** A large inland body of fresh or salt water.

lamb |lăm| —*noun, plural* **lambs** **1.** A young sheep. **2.** Meat from a lamb.

lame |lām| —*adjective* **lamer, lamest** **1.** Not able to walk well; limping: *She was lame from walking so far.* **2.** Crippled in a leg or foot: *Polio made her lame.* **3.** Weak; not satisfactory: *That's a lame excuse for missing school.*
—*verb* **lamed, laming** To make lame; to cripple: *Too much exercise lamed him.*

lamp |lămp| —*noun, plural* **lamps** A device that gives off light. Most lamps work by using electricity. Some lamps burn oil, kerosene, or gas to give light.

lance |lăns| or |läns| —*noun, plural* **lances** **1.** A weapon made of a long spear with a sharp metal head. Knights and warriors on horseback used them for fighting. **2.** A tool or utensil that looks like this weapon. Small lances are used by doctors for operating.
—*verb* **lanced, lancing** To cut into with a lance: *lance a boil.*

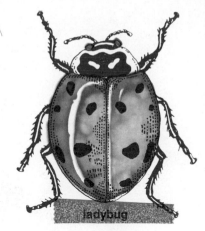
ladybug

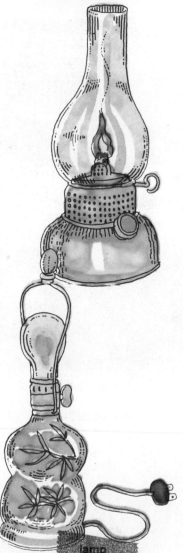
Above: Kerosene lamp
Below: Electric lamp

land |lănd| —*noun, plural* **lands 1.** The part of the earth's surface not covered by water. **2.** A region or area: *Michigan is a land of many rivers.* **3.** A country; a nation: *Washington, D.C., is the capital of our land.* **4.** Earth; ground: *We cleared the land to build houses.* **5.** Property: *They bought some land in Vermont.*
—*verb* **landed, landing 1.** To come or bring to shore: *We landed safely on the island. They landed the cargo on the dock.* **2.** To come or cause to come down and stop: *The helicopter landed on the roof of the skyscraper. He landed the airplane.* **3.** To arrive or cause to arrive in a place: *He landed in prison after robbing the bank.*

land·ing |lăn′dĭng| —*noun, plural* **landings 1.** The act of coming to a stop and settling after a voyage or flight: *a landing on the moon.* **2.** A place where boats can stop and unload; a wharf or pier. **3.** A level area at the top or bottom of a set of stairs.

land·la·dy |lănd′lā′dē| —*noun, plural* **landladies** A woman who owns a house or apartment building. She rents out rooms or living space to other people.

land·lord |lănd′lôrd′| —*noun, plural* **landlords** A man who owns a house or apartment building. He rents out rooms or living space to other people.

land·mark |lănd′märk′| —*noun, plural* **landmarks 1.** A familiar or easily seen object or feature of the landscape. A landmark can be used as a guide: *The State House is one of Boston's landmarks.* **2.** An event, discovery, or work that is important in the history of something: *The invention of the x-ray machine was a landmark in medicine.*

land·own·er |lănd′ō′nər| —*noun, plural* **landowners** A person who owns land.

land·scape |lănd′skāp′| —*noun, plural* **landscapes 1.** A piece of land or countryside that has its own special appearance: *The snow-covered mountains make a pretty landscape.* **2.** A painting or photograph showing such a scene.
—*verb* **landscaped, landscaping** To make a piece of ground pretty by planting trees, bushes, or flowers: *Parks are often landscaped.*

land·slide |lănd′slīd′| —*noun, plural* **landslides 1. a.** The sliding down a hill or mountain of a large amount of earth and rock. **b.** The earth and rock that moves in this way. **2.** A very large number of votes that causes a candidate or political party to win.

lane |lān| —*noun, plural* **lanes 1.** A narrow path or road, often having grass, trees, hedges, or fences along its sides. **2.** A division along the length of a road for a single line of vehicles: *a four-lane highway.* **3.** The part of a bowling alley down which the ball is rolled.
♦ *These sound alike* **lane, lain.**

lan·guage |lăng′gwĭj| —*noun, plural* **languages 1. a.** Spoken or written human speech. Language is used to communicate thoughts and feelings. **b.** A particular system of human speech that is shared by the people of a country or another group of people: *the English language; the Chinese language.* **2.** Any system of signs, symbols, or gestures used for giving information: *a computer language; sign language.*

lank·y |lăng′kē| —*adjective* **lankier, lankiest** Tall, thin, and clumsy: *Alan is a long, lanky boy.*

Lan·sing |lăn′sĭng| The capital of Michigan.

lan·tern |lăn′tərn| —*noun, plural* **lanterns** A container for

lantern

Two kinds of lantern

ă	pat	ĕ	pet	î	fierce
ā	pay	ē	be	ŏ	pot
â	care	ĭ	pit	ō	go
ä	father	ī	pie	ô	paw, for
oi	oil	ŭ	cut	zh	vision
ōō	book	û	fur	ə	ago, item,
ōō	boot	th	the		pencil, atom,
yōō	abuse	th	thin		circus
ou	out	hw	which	ər	butter

holding a light, with sides or an opening through which the light can shine.

lap¹ |lăp| —*noun, plural* **laps** The part of the body from the knees to the waist of a person who is sitting: *Hold these books on your lap.*

lap² |lăp| —*verb* **lapped, lapping** To lie or place partly over something; overlap: *Lap the shingles over one another.*
—*noun, plural* **laps** The act of going over the entire length of something: *Mark dived into the pool and swam three laps. Louise ran two laps around the track.*

lap³ |lăp| —*verb* **lapped, lapping** **1.** To drink by taking up with the tongue: *The kitten lapped up the milk.* **2.** To splash with a light, slapping sound: *The sea lapped the shore. Little waves lapped against the boat.*

la·pel |lə pĕl′| —*noun, plural* **lapels** Either of the two flaps that go down from the collar of a coat or jacket and fold back against the chest.

lard |lärd| —*noun, plural* **lards** The white, greasy substance made from the melted-down fat of pigs or hogs. Lard is used for cooking.

large |lärj| —*adjective* **larger, largest** **1.** Big in size, amount, or number; not small: *The chair came in a large box.* **2.** Broad or great; considerable: *An actress of large experience was chosen for the part.*

large intestine The lower part of the intestine. It absorbs water from the waste matter left after food is digested.

large·ly |lärj′lē| —*adverb* **1.** For the most part; mainly: *The accident was largely Nancy's fault.* **2.** On a large scale; generously: *Bill gave largely to the poor.*

lar·i·at |lăr′ē ət| —*noun, plural* **lariats** A long rope with a sliding noose at one end, used especially to catch horses or cattle; a lasso.

lark¹ |lärk| —*noun, plural* **larks** A songbird that sings as it flies high in the air.

lark² |lärk| —*noun, plural* **larks** A merry adventure; a frolic: *Ginger went to New York on a lark.*

lark·spur |lärk′spûr′| —*noun, plural* **larkspurs** A plant with a long cluster of flowers that are usually blue. The flowers have a long, narrow, pointed part.

lar·va |lär′və| —*noun, plural* **larvae** or **larvas** An insect in an early form, when it has just hatched from an egg. A larva has a soft body and looks like a worm. Caterpillars and grubs are larvae.

lar·vae |lär′vē| A plural of the noun **larva.**

lar·ynx |lăr′ĭngks| —*noun, plural* **larynxes** The upper part of the passage between the nose and mouth and the lungs. The vocal cords are located in the larynx.

la·ser |lā′zər| —*noun, plural* **lasers** A device that uses atoms or molecules to make a very strong beam of light. Lasers are used in medicine and industry.

lash¹ |lăsh| —*noun, plural* **lashes** **1.a.** A whip. **b.** A blow given with a whip. **2.** An eyelash.
—*verb* **lashed, lashing** **1.** To hit with or as if with a whip: *The tree lashed the side of the house during the storm.* **2.** To beat back and forth; wave or strike with a motion like that of a whip: *The cat crouched low and lashed her tail from side to side.*

larkspur

lasso

last¹, last²

The source of **last¹** was a word used by English-speaking people of long ago. **Last²** comes from an old English word that meant "to continue" or "to go on." Earlier still it came from a prehistoric Germanic word that meant "to follow a trail."

lash² |lăsh| —*verb* **lashed, lashing** To hold firmly in place with ropes, chains, or straps: *They lashed the cargo to the boat so it wouldn't fall off in the stormy seas.*

lass |lăs| —*noun, plural* **lasses** A girl or young woman.

las·so |lăs′ō| or |lă sōō′| —*noun, plural* **lassos** or **lassoes** A long rope with a sliding noose at one end, used especially for catching horses and cattle; a lariat.
—*verb* **lassoed, lassoing, lassoes** To catch with a lasso: *The cowboys lassoed the runaway calf.*

last¹ |lăst| or |läst| —*adjective* **1.** Coming at the end; final: *the last day of camp.* **2.** Being the only one or ones left: *the last cooky in the box.* **3.** Just past: *last night.* **4.** The least likely: *Ray was the last person we expected to see.*
—*adverb* **1.** After all others: *Dale came last.* **2.** At the end; finally: *Put on your sweater, then your coat, and last of all your gloves.* **3.** Most recently: *When Juan last called, I was away.*
—*noun* **1.** Someone or something that is last: *She ate all the chocolates but the last. That bus was the last to run this evening.* **2.** The end: *He held out to the last.*

last² |lăst| or |läst| —*verb* **lasted, lasting** **1.** To continue for a period of time: *Our talk lasted two hours.* **2.** To be in good condition: *That car has lasted for ten years.*

last·ing |lăs′tĭng| or |lä′stĭng| —*adjective* Going on or remaining for a long time: *Their fathers had formed a lasting friendship in the Navy.*

latch |lăch| —*noun, plural* **latches** A lock or catch to fasten a door, window, or gate. A latch is a movable bar that fits into a notch or slot.
—*verb* **latched, latching** To close or lock with a latch.

late |lāt| —*adjective* **later, latest** **1.** Coming after the usual or expected time: *We had a late supper.* **2.** Near or toward the end: *It was late in the evening.* **3.** Of a time just past; recent: *This car is a late model.* **4.** Not long dead: *the late Mr. Luckenbill.*
—*adverb* **later, latest** **1.** After or beyond the usual or expected time: *The bus left late.* **2.** Near or toward the end: *Jack batted late in the inning.* **3.** Recently: *as late as yesterday.*

late·ly |lāt′lē| —*adverb* Not long ago; recently: *Have you been to the movies lately?*

lat·er·al |lăt′ər əl| —*adjective* On, of, toward, or from the side: *a lateral pass in football.*

lathe |lāth| —*noun, plural* **lathes** A machine for holding a long piece of wood or metal while turning it against a cutting tool. The cutting part of the lathe gives the desired shape to the piece of wood or metal.

lath·er |lăth′ər| —*noun, plural* **lathers** **1.** A thick foam formed by soap mixed with water. **2.** Froth formed by heavy sweating, especially on a horse.
—*verb* **lathered, lathering** **1.** To cover with lather: *He lathered his chin before shaving.* **2.** To produce or form lather: *The horse lathered at the end of the race.*

Lat·in |lăt′n| or |lăt′ĭn| —*adjective* **1.** Of or in the language of the ancient Romans. **2.** Of those peoples or countries that use the Romance languages that come from Latin. Italy, France, Spain, and Portugal are Latin countries.
—*noun, plural* **Latins** **1.** The language of the ancient Romans. **2.** A member of a people who speak a Romance language.

ă	pat	ĕ	pet	î	fierce
ā	pay	ē	be	ŏ	pot
â	care	ĭ	pit	ō	go
ä	father	ī	pie	ô	paw, for
oi	oil	ŭ	cut	zh	vision
ŏŏ	book	û	fur	ə	ago, item,
ōō	boot	*th*	the		pencil, atom,
yōō	abuse	th	thin		circus
ou	out	hw	which	ər	butter

Latin America The countries of the Western Hemisphere south of the United States, having Spanish or Portuguese as their official language.

Lat·in-A·mer·i·can | lăt′n ə měr′ĭ kən | or | lăt′ĭn ə měr′ĭ kən | —*adjective* Of Latin America.

lat·i·tude | lăt′ĭ tōōd′ | or | lăt′ĭ tyōōd′ | —*noun, plural* **latitudes** Distance north or south of the equator, expressed in degrees. On a map or globe, latitude lines are drawn running east and west.

lat·ter | lăt′ər | —*adjective* **1.** The second or second mentioned of two: *I have a dictionary and an atlas; I use the latter book as often as the former.* **2.** Closer to the end: *the latter part of the program.*

lat·tice | lăt′ĭs | —*noun, plural* **lattices** A framework made of strips of wood or metal crossed with open spaces between them.

laugh | lăf | or | läf | —*verb* **laughed, laughing 1.** To make sounds and often movements of the face and body to express happiness or amusement: *He laughed when he saw the clown.* **2.** To express or show happiness or amusement: *The girl's eyes laughed as she spoke.*
—*noun, plural* **laughs** The act of laughing or a sound made in laughing.

laugh·ter | lăf′tər | or | läf′tər | —*noun* **1.** The act or sound of laughing. **2.** Happiness or amusement expressed by or as if by laughing: *There was laughter in her eyes.*

launch¹ | lônch | or | länch | —*verb* **launched, launching 1.** To move or set in motion with force; send off: *The space center will launch a rocket.* **2.** To put a boat or ship into the water: *The workers at the shipyard will launch a new submarine.* **3.** To begin or start something: *The two friends will launch a new magazine.*

launch² | lônch | or | länch | —*noun, plural* **launches** An open or partly open motorboat.

launch pad The platform or base from which a spacecraft is launched. Another form of this phrase is **launching pad.**

launch·ing pad | lônch′ĭng | or | länch′ĭng | A form of the phrase **launch pad.**

laun·der | lôn′dər | or | län′dər | —*verb* **laundered, laundering 1.** To wash or wash and iron clothes and linens. **2.** To be capable of being washed: *This dress launders well.*

laun·dry | lôn′drē | or | län′drē | —*noun, plural* **laundries 1.** A place or business where clothes and linens are washed and sometimes ironed. **2.** Clothes and linens that need to be washed or have been washed: *Sort the laundry by color.*

lau·rel | lôr′əl | or | lŏr′əl | —*noun, plural* **laurels 1.** A shrub or tree with shiny evergreen leaves that have a spicy smell. A laurel wreath was a sign of victory or great achievement in ancient times. **2.** A shrub or tree like a laurel, the **mountain laurel.**

la·va | lä′və | or | lăv′ə | —*noun* **1.** Hot melted rock that flows from a volcano. **2.** The rock formed when this substance cools and hardens.

lav·en·der | lăv′ən dər | —*noun* **1.** A plant with small, fragrant purplish flowers. Oil from these flowers is used to make perfume. The dried flowers are sometimes used to give clothing and linens a pleasant smell. **2.** A pale or light purple color.
—*adjective* Pale or light purple.

law | lô | —*noun, plural* **laws 1.** A rule made by a government for the people living in a country, state, city, or town: *There is a law against smoking in elevators.* **2.** A set of such rules: *French law*

lattice

launch¹, launch²
Launch¹ comes from an old French word that meant "to throw." The source of **launch²** is the Portuguese word *lancha,* meaning "small, fast boat." The Portuguese word came from *lancharan,* a word used to refer to a kind of boat in Malay, a language spoken in parts of Southeast Asia.

laurel

differs from U.S. law. **3.** The study or knowledge of such rules; the profession of a lawyer: *Mandy wants to practice law.* **4.** Any rule, principle, or practice: *the laws of grammar.*

law·ful |lô′fəl| —*adjective* **1.** Allowed by law: *It is lawful to park there.* **2.** Recognized by law: *a lawful marriage.*

law·less |lô′lĭs| —*adjective* **1.** Not controlled by law: *Once the West was wild and lawless.* **2.** Not obeying the law: *a lawless mob.*

law·mak·er |lô′mā′kər| —*noun, plural* **lawmakers** A person who helps write or pass laws; a legislator.

lawn |lôn| —*noun, plural* **lawns** An area of ground planted with grass that is usually mowed regularly.

lawn·mow·er |lôn′mō′ər| —*noun, plural* **lawnmowers** A machine for cutting grass.

law·suit |lô′sōot′| —*noun, plural* **lawsuits** A question or claim that is brought before a court of law for settlement.

law·yer |lô′yər| or |loi′ər| —*noun, plural* **lawyers** A person who is trained and qualified to give legal advice to people and to represent them in a court of law.

lay¹ |lā| —*verb* **laid, laying** **1.** To put or place: *He laid the baby in the cradle. Lay down your pencil and visit for a while.* **2.** To put down in place; install: *Mr. Jones will lay the tiles for flooring.* **3.** To produce an egg or eggs: *Our hen has stopped laying.*

   Phrasal verbs **lay down** To establish: *lay down rules for the club.*

lay off **1.** To dismiss from a job. **2.** To stop bothering someone.

♦ *These sound alike* **lay, lei.**

lay² |lā| The past tense of **lie** (to rest): *I lay on the beach for an hour.*

♦ *These sound alike* **lay, lei.**

lay·er |lā′ər| —*noun, plural* **layers** A single coating or thickness of something: *We used only one layer of paint on the walls.*

lay·off |lā′ôf′| or |lā′ŏf′| —*noun, plural* **layoffs** A temporary dismissal of employees.

la·zi·ness |lā′zē nĭs| —*noun* The condition of being lazy: *Sheer laziness kept him from having a neat room.*

la·zy |lā′zē| —*adjective* **lazier, laziest** **1.** Not willing to work: *a lazy person.* **2.** Moving slowly: *lazy clouds floating overhead.*

lead¹ |lēd| —*verb* **led, leading** **1.** To show or guide along the way: *He led me to his office.* **2.** To be first or ahead of others in: *Mary leads the class in science. The flag carriers will lead the parade.* **3.** To be or form a way, route, or passage: *The trail leads to the pond. This hallway leads to the office.* **4.** To direct; conduct: *The music teacher leads the student orchestra.* **5.** To live; experience: *Mr. Jones led an interesting life.*

—*noun, plural* **leads** **1.a.** The front or winning position: *Our team took the lead in the game.* **b.** The amount by which one is ahead: *We had a five-point lead.* **2.** Leadership: *They followed his lead and joined in prayer.* **3.** A clue or hint: *He had many leads that helped solve the mystery.* **4.** The main part in a performance: *the lead in a play.*

lead² |lĕd| —*noun, plural* **leads** **1.** A soft, heavy, dull-gray metal. Lead is used to make pipes, fuses, and solder. It is a chemical element. **2.** A material used in pencils as the writing substance.

♦ *These sound alike* **lead², led.**

lead·er |lē′dər| —*noun, plural* **leaders** Someone who leads: *Jerry is the leader of the debating team.*

---

lead¹, lead²
Lead¹ and **lead²** can be traced back to different old English words. **Lead²** was probably borrowed from a European language called Celtic.

ă	pat	ĕ	pet	î	fierce
ā	pay	ē	be	ŏ	pot
â	care	ĭ	pit	ō	go
ä	father	ī	pie	ô	paw, for

oi	oil	ŭ	cut	zh	vision
ŏŏ	book	û	fur	ə	ago, item,
ōō	boot	*th*	the		pencil, atom,
yōō	abuse	th	thin		circus
ou	out	hw	which	ər	butter

lead·er·ship | lē′dər shĭp′ | —*noun, plural* **leaderships** **1.** The position of a leader: *He was offered the leadership of the Democratic Party.* **2.** The ability to act as a leader: *He has shown strong leadership.* **3.** The guidance of a leader or leaders: *He worked under the leadership of skillful engineers.*

leaf | lēf | —*noun, plural* **leaves** **1.** A thin, flat, green part that grows from the stem of a plant. **2.** One of the sheets of paper forming the pages of a book, magazine, or notebook. **3.** A very thin sheet of metal: *gold leaf.*
—*verb* **leafed, leafing** **1.** To produce or put forth leaves. **2.** To turn or glance at pages: *Jeff leafed through a book.*

leaf·let | lēf′lĭt | —*noun, plural* **leaflets** **1.** A small leaf: *A clover leaf has three leaflets.* **2.** A small pamphlet or booklet.

leaf·y | lē′fē | —*adjective* **leafier, leafiest** **1.** Having many leaves; covered with leaves: *leafy branches.* **2.** Made up of leaves: *a leafy vegetable salad.*

league¹ | lēg | —*noun, plural* **leagues** **1.** A group of nations, people, or organizations working together for a common purpose. **2.** An association of sports teams that compete mainly among themselves: *a baseball league; a football league.*

league² | lēg | —*noun, plural* **leagues** An old unit of distance equal to three miles.

leak | lēk | —*noun, plural* **leaks** A hole, crack, or other opening that lets something pass through by accident: *They discovered a dangerous leak in the dam. The roof of the tool shed had many bad leaks.*
—*verb* **leaked, leaking** **1.** To pass through by accident: *Water leaked from the rusty pail.* **2.** To allow something to escape or pass through an opening or openings: *The boat struck a rock and began to leak.* **3.** To become or allow to be known by accident or by a deliberate break in secrecy: *The information leaked out that I was moving away. He leaked the information to the newspapers.*
♦ *These sound alike* **leak, leek.**

leak·y | lē′kē | —*adjective* **leakier, leakiest** Having or allowing a leak or leaks: *a leaky container; a leaky valve.*

lean¹ | lēn | —*verb* **leaned** or **leant, leaning** **1.** To bend or slant: *She leaned her head forward to hear better. The walls of the old house leaned out.* **2.** To rest on a person or thing for support: *Lean on my shoulder.* **3.** To put something in a slanted position: *He leaned his skis against the wall.* **4.** To rely, as for help; depend: *He leans on his friends when he is in trouble.*

lean² | lēn | —*adjective* **leaner, leanest** **1.** Having little or no fat: *a lean piece of meat; a lean cat.* **2.** Not productive or plentiful; poor: *a lean crop; a lean year for oranges.*

leant | lēnt | A past tense and past participle of the verb **lean** (to bend): *Jack leant over and picked up his hat from the floor. That tree has leant in the wind.*

leap | lēp | —*verb* **leaped** or **leapt, leaping** **1.** To move with a sudden springing motion; to jump: *The horse leaped over the fence.* **2.** To move or seem to move with a similar sudden motion: *My heart leaped with joy.*
—*noun, plural* **leaps** **1.** The act of leaping; a jump: *The frog made a leap onto the rock.* **2.** The distance covered by a leap: *a leap of ten feet.*

leap·frog | lēp′frôg′ | or | lēp′frŏg′ | —*noun, plural* **leapfrogs** A game in which players take turns leaping over each other. One

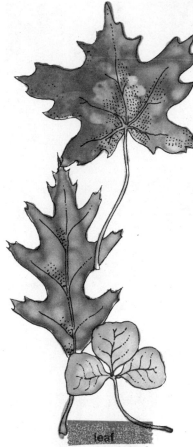
leaf
Above: Maple leaf
Center: Oak leaf
Below: Clover leaf

league¹, league²
League¹ comes from a Latin word that meant "to bind." Traveling through Italian, the word came to mean "a group that is tied together by promises." Before arriving in English it appeared in French. **League²** comes from a different and later Latin word that stood for a measure of distance.

lean¹, lean²
Lean¹ has always had the same meaning. Before arriving in English it came from prehistoric Germanic, where it still meant "to bend." **Lean²** can definitely be traced to an old English word, but it is not related to **lean¹**.

leash

leather
Above: Animal skin
Below: Leather boots

---

leave[1], leave[2]
Even though **leave[1]** and **leave[2]** may seem similar, they come from completely unrelated words used by English-speaking people of long ago.

ă	pat	ĕ	pet	î	fierce
ā	pay	ē	be	ŏ	pot
â	care	ĭ	pit	ō	go
ä	father	ī	pie	ô	paw, for
oi	oil	ŭ	cut	zh	vision
ŏŏ	book	û	fur	ə	ago, item,
ōō	boot	*th*	the		pencil, atom,
yōō	abuse	th	thin		circus
ou	out	hw	which	ər	butter

player crouches down and the one behind leaps over him.

leapt | lĕpt | or | lēpt | A past tense and past participle of the verb **leap:** *The fire leapt into flame. The salmon had leapt over the dam.*

leap year A year having 366 days and occurring every fourth year. The extra day is February 29.

learn | lûrn | —*verb* **learned** or **learnt, learning 1.** To gain knowledge or skill through study or experience: *He learned to play the piano. She learned both English and French.* **2.** To become informed; find out: *We learned that there will be a parade next week.* **3.** To fix in the mind; memorize: *Joe learned the lines for the school play.*

learn·ed | lûr′nĭd | —*adjective* Having or showing great knowledge: *The professor was a very learned man.*

learn·ing | lûr′nĭng | —*noun, plural* **learnings 1.** Education; instruction: *He has a real wish for learning.* **2.** Knowledge gained by study: *scientists, philosophers, and other men of learning.*

learnt | lûrnt | A past tense and past participle of the verb **learn:** *Midge learnt the multiplication tables. We have learnt to be careful with matches.*

lease | lēs | —*noun, plural* **leases** A written agreement between the owner of a piece of property and the person who rents it. The lease states how much rent is to be paid for the use of the property. It also states the length of time the agreement is in effect: *We signed a lease on the apartment.*
—*verb* **leased, leasing** To rent: *He leased his house to us. We leased the house for a year.*

leash | lēsh | —*noun, plural* **leashes** A cord, chain, or strap attached to a collar and used to hold or lead an animal: *We bought a leash for our dog.*
—*verb* **leashed, leashing** To hold, lead, or hold back with a leash: *Leash your dog.*

least | lēst | —*adjective* A superlative of the adjective **little.**
1. Smallest: *The least criticism made her cry.* **2.** Lowest in importance: *Painting the house is my least worry.*
—*adverb* The superlative of the adverb **little.** To the smallest degree: *He always saves the least important news in the paper to read on the train. We all liked vanilla ice cream best and strawberry least.*
—*noun* **1.** The smallest in size or importance: *The job of painting the house is the least of my worries.* **2.** The smallest correct thing: *The least you could do would be to apologize.*

leath·er | lĕth′ər | —*noun, plural* **leathers** A material made from animal skin or hide that has been cleaned and tanned. Belts, boots, shoes, and gloves are usually made of leather.

leave[1] | lēv | —*verb* **left, leaving 1.** To depart; go away from: *I'm leaving on Thursday. He left town in a hurry.* **2.** To go without taking; forget: *She left her umbrella.* **3.** To let stay in a certain condition or place: *She left her bed all made for the night. Jack left his books on the table.* **4.** To quit; withdraw from: *He left his job.* **5.** To give to someone else to do or use: *You must leave the cleaning to me.* **6.** To give after one's death, as in a will: *He left his house to us.* **7.** To have as a result: *The hurricane left a million dollars' worth of damage.* **8.** To cause to remain after a loss or reduction: *Ten minus two leaves eight.*

Phrasal verbs **leave alone** To stop bothering or annoying. **leave out** To fail to include: *You left out the comma in the sentence.*

leave² |lēv| —*noun, plural* **leaves 1.** Permission: *She has her father's leave to stay out until midnight.* **2. a.** Permission to be absent from duty: *The soldier got a leave so he could see his new baby.* **b.** The length of an absence of this kind: *a leave of ten days*

leaves |lēvz| The plural of the noun **leaf.**

lec·ture |lĕk′chər| —*noun, plural* **lectures 1.** A speech or talk given to an audience: *The writer gave a lecture on his travels.* **2.** A serious, long warning: *My mother gave me a lecture after I went out into the rain without an umbrella.*
—*verb* **lectured, lecturing 1.** To give a lecture or lectures: *Jim's father lectures on electricity at the college.* **2.** To scold or warn at length: *Dad lectured me about being rude to guests.*

led |lĕd| The past tense and past participle of the verb **lead** (to show or guide): *Paul led his horse to the stable. Mary has led the school band for two years.*
♦ *These sound alike* **led, lead².**

ledge |lĕj| —*noun, plural* **ledges 1.** A flat space like a shelf on the side of a cliff or rock wall: *We rested on the ledge of the mountain.* **2.** A narrow shelf that juts out from a wall: *a window ledge.*

leech |lēch| —*noun, plural* **leeches** A worm that lives in water. Leeches suck blood from other animals.

leek |lēk| —*noun, plural* **leeks** A vegetable related to the onion. It has long, dark-green leaves and a narrow white bulb.
♦ *These sound alike* **leek, leak.**

left¹ |lĕft| —*noun, plural* **lefts** The side from which one begins to read a line of English: *The number 9 is on the left of a clock face.*
—*adjective* **1.** Located on the left: *the left hand.* **2.** Done to the left: *a left turn.*
—*adverb* On or to the left: *Turn left at the next corner.*

left² |lĕft| The past tense and past participle of the verb **leave** (to go away): *We left the house before dawn. Perry was in trouble because he had left the dirty dishes in the sink.*

left-hand |lĕft′hănd′| —*adjective* **1.** Located on the left: *the left-hand corner of the picture.* **2.** Of or for the left hand: *left-hand scissors.*

left-hand·ed |lĕft′hăn′dĭd| —*adjective* **1.** Using the left hand more easily and naturally than the right hand: *Both my parents are left-handed, and so am I.* **2.** Designed for use by the left hand: *a left-handed wrench.* **3.** Done with the left hand: *a left-handed toss of the ball.*

left·o·ver or **left-o·ver** |lĕft′ō′vər| —*noun, plural* **leftovers** or **left-overs** Something that has not been used or eaten and is left: *We had yesterday's leftovers for dinner tonight.*
—*adjective* Remaining not used or not eaten: *With the leftover material we can make a scarf.*

leg |lĕg| —*noun, plural* **legs 1.** One of the parts of the body that a human being or animal uses in standing or moving about. **2.** One of the parts of a pair of trousers or stockings that fits around the leg. **3.** A part of an object that juts out and supports the object: *a table leg.* **4.** A stage of a journey or course: *the first leg of a relay race.*

le·gal |lē′gəl| —*adjective* **1.** Of law or lawyers: *legal help; legal training.* **2.** Permitted by law; lawful: *legal activities.*

leg·end |lĕj′ənd| —*noun, plural* **legends 1.** A story that has been handed down from earlier times. It is usually not certain

ledge
On a cliff

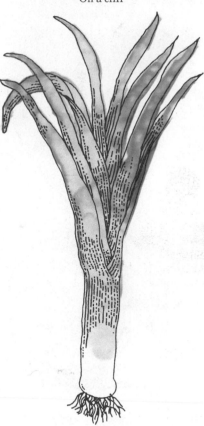

leek

whether a legend is true or not. **2.** A group of such stories: *Norse legend.*

leg·en·dar·y | lĕj′ən dĕr′ē | —*adjective* **1.** Told of in legends: *legendary heroes.* **2.** Talked about often; famous: *a legendary artist.*

leg·gings | lĕg′ĭngz | —*plural noun* Leg coverings of cloth or leather stretching from the waist or knee to the ankle.

leg·i·ble | lĕj′ə bəl | —*adjective* Capable of being read; easily read; clear: *He has a very legible handwriting.*

le·gion | lē′jən | —*noun, plural* **legions** **1.** A unit of the ancient Roman army. A legion was made up of at least 3,000 foot soldiers and 100 soldiers on horseback. **2.** Any of several large groups of soldiers in modern times; an army. **3.** A large group or number of persons or things: *legions of insects.*

leg·is·late | lĕj′ĭs lāt′ | —*verb* **legislated, legislating** To make or pass a law or laws.

leg·is·la·tion | lĕj′ĭs lā′shən | —*noun, plural* **legislations** **1.** The process of making or passing laws: *Legislation is a main concern of Congress.* **2.** The law or laws that are made: *The people want legislation to lower property taxes.*

leg·is·la·tive | lĕj′ĭs lā′tĭv | —*adjective* **1.** Having to do with making or passing laws: *Congressmen have legislative powers.* **2.** Of a group of people who make or pass laws: *They had very high legislative goals at the beginning of the year.* **3.** Having power to make or pass laws: *Congress is the legislative branch of government.*

leg·is·la·tor | lĕj′ĭs lā′tər | —*noun, plural* **legislators** A person who is a member of a group that makes or passes laws: *our legislators in Congress.*

leg·is·la·ture | lĕj′ĭs lā′chər | —*noun, plural* **legislatures** A group of persons given the power to make and pass the laws of a nation or state: *The tax bill was voted by the state legislature.*

le·git·i·mate | lĕ jĭt′ə mĭt | —*adjective* **1.** Being or acting in agreement with the law; lawful: *He was the legitimate owner of the house.* **2.** Supported by logic or common sense; reasonable: *She had a legitimate reason for being absent.* **3.** Genuine; real: *Their document listed many legitimate complaints.*

lei | lā | or | lā′ē | —*noun, plural* **leis** A wreath or chain of flowers worn around the neck, especially in Hawaii: *a lei of orchids.*
♦ *These sound alike* **lei, lay.**

lei·sure | lē′zhər | or | lĕzh′ər | —*noun* Freedom from work or other duties; time in which to do what one wants or likes: *Mike spends his leisure collecting stamps.*

lei·sure·ly | lē′zhər lē | or | lĕzh′ər lē | —*adjective* Without haste; not hurried: *She had a leisurely lunch.*
—*adverb* At a slow or not fast rate of speed; slowly: *He drove leisurely toward town.*

lem·on | lĕm′ən | —*noun, plural* **lemons** **1.** A juicy yellow fruit that is shaped like an egg and has a sour taste. Lemons grow on trees in warm parts of the world. They are related to limes, oranges, and grapefruit. **2.** A bright, clear yellow color.
—*adjective* Bright, clear yellow.

lem·on·ade | lĕm′ə nād′ | —*noun, plural* **lemonades** A drink made of lemon juice, water, and sugar.

lend | lĕnd | —*verb* **lent, lending** **1.** To let someone use something with the understanding that it is to be returned: *Mother lent me her pink shawl for the party.* **2.** To give someone money that is to

lei

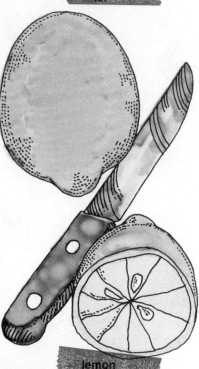

lemon
Whole (*above*) and cut in half (*below*)

ă	pat	ĕ	pet	î	fierce
ā	pay	ē	be	ŏ	pot
â	care	ĭ	pit	ō	go
ä	father	ī	pie	ô	paw, for
oi	oil	ŭ	cut	zh	vision
ŏŏ	book	û	fur	ə	ago, item,
ōō	boot	*th*	the		pencil, atom,
yōō	abuse	th	thin		circus
ou	out	hw	which	ər	butter

be returned after an agreed period of time, usually at a certain rate of interest. **3.** To give; add: *The holiday decorations lend a festive air to the ballroom.*

length |lĕngkth| or |lĕngth| —*noun, plural* **lengths** **1.** The distance of a thing measured from one end to the other: *the length of a boat.* **2.** The full extent of something long or stretched out: *The explorers traveled the length of the river.* **3.** A piece cut from a larger piece: *a length of wire; a length of silk.* **4.** The amount of time something lasts: *The movie was two hours in length.*

length·en |lĕngk′thən| or |lĕng′thən| —*verb* **lengthened, lengthening** To make or become longer: *The seamstress will lengthen the dress.*

length·wise |lĕngkth′wīz′| or |lĕngth′wīz′| —*adverb* and *adjective* Along the direction of the length: *She folded a sheet of paper lengthwise. His shirt has lengthwise pleats.*

length·y |lĕngk′thē| or |lĕng′thē| —*adjective* **lengthier, lengthiest** **1.** Lasting a long time: *a lengthy speech.* **2.** Extending for a long distance: *a lengthy road.*

lens |lĕnz| —*noun, plural* **lenses** **1. a.** A piece of glass or other clear material that has been shaped to cause light rays that pass through it to meet or to spread out. **b.** A combination of two or more lenses used to make things look larger or seem nearer. Cameras, telescopes, and eyeglasses have lenses. **2.** A clear part of the eye behind the iris that focuses light onto the retina.

lent |lĕnt| The past tense and past participle of the verb **lend**: *Pat lent his class notes to Jane. She had lent him hers many times.*

Lent |lĕnt| —*noun* A time when some Christians fast and ask that their sins be forgiven. Lent begins on Ash Wednesday and ends at Easter.

len·til |lĕn′təl| or |lĕn′tl| —*noun, plural* **lentils** A flat, round seed of a plant related to the beans and peas.

leop·ard |lĕp′ərd| —*noun, plural* **leopards** A large wild cat of Africa and Asia. Most leopards have a yellowish coat with black spots. Some leopards are all black.

le·o·tard |lē′ə tärd′| —*noun, plural* **leotards** Often **leotards** A tight-fitting piece of clothing, first worn by dancers and acrobats.

less |lĕs| —*adjective* A comparative of the adjective **little.** **1.** Not as great in amount: *She has less work to do than her sister.* **2.** Fewer: *The more police on the highways, the less accidents.* **3.** Lower in rank or importance: *The guest of honor was no less a person than the mayor.*
—*adverb* The comparative of the adverb **little.** To a smaller extent or degree: *He was less scared than his friend.*
—*preposition* **1.** Minus; subtracting: *Six less 1 is 5.* **2.** Except for; leaving out: *The shipment arrived in good condition, less a couple of broken pots.*
—*noun* A smaller amount or part: *He got less than he asked for.*
—*pronoun* Fewer things or persons: *Many things begin badly; less end well.*

–less A suffix that forms adjectives. The suffix"-less" means "without, free of": *motherless; nameless; childless.*

less·en |lĕs′ən| —*verb* **lessened, lessening** To make or become less: *He took a drug to lessen the pain. The pain lessened immediately.*
♦ *These sound alike* **lessen, lesson.**

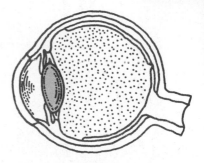

lens
Of the human eye

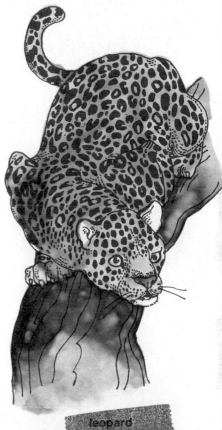

leopard

leotard

less·er | lĕs′ər | —*adjective* **1.** Smaller in size or importance: *a lesser evil; lesser gods.* **2.** Of inferior quality: *a lesser athlete than others.*

les·son | lĕs′ən | —*noun, plural* **lessons** **1.** Something to be learned: *The first lesson for your dog is to learn the meaning of the word "come."* **2.** An assignment or exercise that is to be learned: *The math textbook is divided into 40 lessons.* **3.** A period of time for teaching or learning a certain subject; a class: *three piano lessons a week.*

♦ *These sound alike* **lesson, lessen.**

lest | lĕst | —*conjunction* **1.** For fear that: *Hold on tightly lest you fall off.* **2.** That: *Friends tried to warn her about driving too fast, fearing lest she be hurt.*

let | lĕt | —*verb* **let, letting** **1.** To permit; allow: *She let him talk.* **2.** To make; cause: *Let me know what happened.* **3.** To permit to move in a certain way: *Let me in. Let the cat out.* **4.** To permit to escape; to release: *Jim let the air out of the balloon.* **5.** To rent or lease: *He lets his extra rooms to students.*

—*helping,* or *auxiliary, verb* As a helping verb **let** is used in the imperative to show: **1.** Request or command: *Let's get going.* **2.** Warning or threat: *Just let him try to lay his hands on me!*

Phrasal verbs let down 1. To slow down; ease up: *We've almost finished, so don't let down now.* **2.** To fail to support or satisfy; disappoint: *My friends let me down by not coming to the party.* **let off 1.** To excuse from work or duty: *let the students off early.* **2.** To release with little or no punishment: *The principal let us off with a warning.* **let up** To become slower or less strong; diminish: *By evening the rain had let up a little.*

let's | lĕts | A contraction of "let us."

let·ter | lĕt′ər | —*noun, plural* **letters** **1.** A written or printed mark that stands for a speech sound and is used to spell words; one of the signs of an alphabet: *a capital letter.* **2.** A written message addressed to someone and usually sent by mail in an envelope: *a fan letter.*

—*verb* **lettered, lettering** To mark or write with letters: *The painter lettered the title. Letter the poster neatly.*

letter carrier A person who delivers mail to homes and businesses; a mailman.

let·tuce | lĕt′ĭs | —*noun, plural* **lettuces** Any of several plants with light-green leaves that are eaten as salad.

lev·el | lĕv′əl | —*adjective* **1.** Having a flat, smooth surface: *a level driveway. The pencils keep falling off the table because it isn't level.* **2.** Being at the same height or position; even: *The night table is level with the bed.*

—*noun, plural* **levels** **1.** A particular height: *The highest beach dunes rose to a level of fifteen feet.* **2.** A stage in a process: *Although she's in the third grade, she's already reading at a fourth-grade level.* **3.** A flat, smooth piece or stretch of land. **4.** A device or tool that is used to show whether or not a surface is flat. Carpenters use levels when they build such things as tables and bookcases.

—*verb* **leveled, leveling** **1.** To make smooth or flat: *They had to level the field before they could build the tennis court.* **2.** To knock or tear down completely: *The bulldozer leveled the whole building in five minutes.* **3.** To be frank and open: *Tell me what's bothering you; you can level with me.*

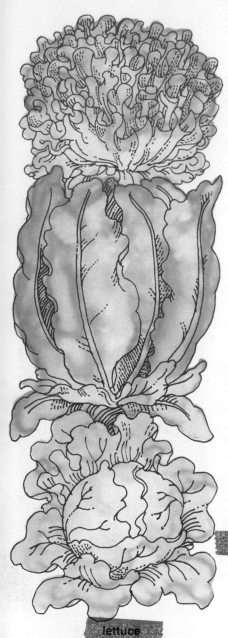

lettuce
Different kinds of lettuce

ă	pat	ĕ	pet	î	fierce
ā	pay	ē	be	ŏ	pot
â	care	ĭ	pit	ō	go
ä	father	ī	pie	ô	paw, for
oi	oil	ŭ	cut	zh	vision
ŏŏ	book	û	fur	ə	ago, item,
ōō	boot	*th*	the		pencil, atom,
yōō	abuse	th	thin		circus
ou	out	hw	which	ər	butter

lev·er |lĕv′ər| or |lē′vər| —*noun, plural* **levers** **1.** A simple machine made up of a strong, stiff bar that rests on a fixed point on which it turns. It is used to lift heavy things. **2.** A handle that juts out and is used to control or operate a machine.

lev·y |lĕv′ē| —*verb* **levied, levying, levies** To impose or collect a tax, tariff, or other fee: *The government levied a tax on the sale of clothing.*

li·a·ble |lī′ə bəl| —*adjective* **1.** Responsible under the law; legally obligated: *We are liable for any damage we do to other people's property.* **2.** Likely: *He is liable to make mistakes.*

li·ar |lī′ər| —*noun, plural* **liars** A person who tells lies.

lib·er·al |lĭb′ər əl| or |lĭb′rəl| —*adjective* **1.** Giving freely; generous: *Teddy was a liberal boy who shared his allowance with his poor friend Jimmy.* **2.** Generous in amount; ample; abundant: *Dad left the waiter a liberal tip.* **3.** Having respect for different people and different ideas; tolerant. **4.** Wanting or supporting political reform and social progress.

—*noun, plural* **liberals** A person who has liberal political or social opinions.

lib·er·ate |lĭb′ə rāt′| —*verb* **liberated, liberating** To set free: *Moses liberated his people from slavery in ancient Egypt.*

lib·er·ty |lĭb′ər tē| —*noun, plural* **liberties** **1.** Freedom from the control or rule of another or others; independence: *The American colonies won their liberty from England in 1781.* **2.** Freedom to act, speak, think, or believe as one chooses: *Our forefathers came to America seeking liberty.* **3.** Often **liberties** A bold or rude statement or action: *He took liberties when he called my parents by their first names.*

li·brar·i·an |lī brâr′ē ən| —*noun, plural* **librarians** A person who works in or is in charge of a library.

li·brar·y |lī′brĕr′ē| —*noun, plural* **libraries** **1.** A large, permanent collection of books, magazines, films, or records. **2.** A room or building where such a collection is kept.

lice |līs| The plural of the noun **louse.**

li·cense |lī′səns| —*noun, plural* **licenses** **1.** Legal permission to do or own something: *He has the license to open a bakery.* **2.** A document, card, or other object showing that such permission has been given: *You must always carry your driver's license when operating a car.*

—*verb* **licensed, licensing** To grant a license to or for: *Is he licensed to teach school in this state?*

li·chee |lē′chē| —*noun, plural* **lichees** A form of the word **litchi.**

li·chen |lī′kən| —*noun, plural* **lichens** A small plant that has no flowers. Lichens form a covering on rocks and tree trunks.

lick |lĭk| —*verb* **licked, licking** **1.** To pass the tongue over: *He licked his lips.* **2.** To move or flicker like a tongue: *We watched the flames lick around the logs in the fireplace.* **3.** To defeat; overcome: *Our players licked their team in the game.*

—*noun, plural* **licks** **1.** A movement of the tongue over something: *She gave the stamp a lick.* **2.** A natural deposit of salt that is licked by passing animals.

lic·o·rice |lĭk′ə rĭs| or |lĭk′ər ĭsh| —*noun* **1.** A flavoring with a blackish color and a sweet, strong taste. It is made from the root of a plant. **2.** Candy flavored with licorice.

lid |lĭd| —*noun, plural* **lids** **1.** A cover for a container; a top: *the lid of a jar; the lid on a box.* **2.** An eyelid.

library
Above: In a school
Below: In a mansion

lie¹, lie²
Lie¹ comes through old English and Germanic from the prehistoric language from which many languages spoken today descend. Its root in that language meant "to stretch oneself out on the ground, to recline." (**Lay¹** is from the same root, which also meant "to place something on the ground, to put." Thus these two words are closely related.) **Lie²** comes from an old English word that was originally used as a verb.

life preserver
Jacket and ring

ă	pat	ĕ	pet	î	fierce
ā	pay	ē	be	ŏ	pot
â	care	ĭ	pit	ō	go
ä	father	ī	pie	ô	paw, for

oi	oil	ŭ	cut	zh	vision
ōō	book	û	fur	ə	ago, item,
ōō	boot	th	the		pencil, atom,
yōō	abuse	th	thin		circus
ou	out	hw	which	ər	butter

lie¹ | lī | —*verb* **lay, lain, lying, lies** **1.** To be in or take a flat or resting position: *He lies asleep under that elm tree. She likes to lie on the floor to watch TV.* **2.** To be or rest on a horizontal surface: *The newspaper is lying on the floor.* **3.** To be located: *East of here lie many tiny islands.* **4.** To remain in a certain condition or position: *We let the land lie barren.* **5.** To be; exist: *The answer lies in further research. Love lies in the heart, not the head.* **6.** To be buried: *His father lies on that shady hill in back of their farm.*
♦ *These sound alike* **lie, lye.**
 Idioms **lie down on the job** To do less than one can or should. **lie low** To keep out of sight; hide.

lie² | lī | —*noun, plural* **lies** A statement that is not true made by someone who knows that it is not true.
—*verb* **lied, lying, lies** To tell a lie or lies.
♦ *These sound alike* **lie, lye.**

lieu·ten·ant | lōō tĕn′ənt | —*noun, plural* **lieutenants** **1.** An officer in the Army, Air Force, or Marine Corps ranking below a captain. A **first lieutenant** ranks above a **second lieutenant. 2.** An officer in the Navy ranking above an ensign and below a lieutenant commander. **3.** An officer in a police or fire department ranking below a captain. **4.** Someone who acts for another person higher in authority; a chief assistant; deputy: *He talks to his employees only through his lieutenant, the plant manager.*

life | līf | —*noun, plural* **lives** **1.** The property or quality that distinguishes people, plants, and animals from rocks, metals, and other objects that cannot grow and reproduce. **2.** The condition of being or remaining alive: *He risked his life.* **3.** The period of time between birth and death; lifetime: *He lived there for the rest of his life.* **4.** The period during which something is useful, working, or in existence: *the life of a car; the life of a contract.* **5.** Living things in general: *plant life; marine life.* **6.** A living being: *The earthquake claimed hundreds of lives.* **7.** Human existence or activity in general: *the problems we face in real life. Life is like that.* **8.** A way of living: *I prefer the outdoor life to life in the city.*

life belt A life preserver worn like a belt.

life·boat | līf′bōt′ | —*noun, plural* **lifeboats** An open boat carried on a large ship for use if the ship must be abandoned.

life·guard | līf′gärd′ | —*noun, plural* **lifeguards** A person whose job is to look out for the safety of people who swim.

life·less | līf′lĭs | —*adjective* **1.** No longer alive; dead: *the soldier's lifeless body.* **2.** Not supporting life; without living things: *a lifeless planet.*

life·like | līf′līk′ | —*adjective* **1.** Resembling a living person or thing: *a lifelike statue of Lincoln.* **2.** Closely imitating real life: *The author wrote a lifelike description of a country fair.*

life·long | līf′lông′ | or | līf′lŏng′ | —*adjective* Lasting over a lifetime: *a lifelong friend; a lifelong ambition.*

life preserver A ring, jacket, belt, or other device designed to keep a person from sinking in water. It is either filled with air or made of cork or another material that floats.

life-size | līf′sīz′ | —*adjective* Of the same size as the person or thing represented: *a life-size portrait of the President.*

life·time | līf′tīm′ | —*noun, plural* **lifetimes** The period of time during which someone or something remains alive, exists, or functions: *in one man's lifetime; the lifetime of a car.*

lift |lĭft| —*verb* **lifted, lifting 1.** To raise into the air from a resting position; pick up: *She lifted the telephone receiver to her ear. The suitcase is too heavy to lift.* **2.** To move or direct upward; raise: *She lifted her eyes from the book.* **3.** To rise and disappear: *We are waiting for the fog to lift.*
    Phrasal verb **lift off** To begin flight, as a rocket or spacecraft.
—*noun, plural* **lifts 1.** The act or process of lifting or being lifted: *With a graceful lift of her hand, she dismissed him. He gave her a lift into the saddle.* **2.** The distance or height something rises or is raised: *the lift of a kite; a lift of 15 feet per second.* **3.** A short ride in a car or other vehicle: *My neighbor gave me a lift home from the office in town.* **4.** A better and happier feeling; a rise in spirits: *The news from home gave us all a lift.* **5.** A moving cable to which seats are attached. It is used to carry people up a hill or mountain: *a ski lift; a chair lift.*

lift·off |lĭft′ôf′| or |lĭft′ŏf′| —*noun, plural* **liftoffs 1.** The takeoff of a rocket or spacecraft. **2.** The point in time at which this happens.

light¹ |līt| —*noun, plural* **lights 1.** A natural or man-made bright form of energy that makes it possible for human beings to see: *the bright light of a sunny day; light from a thousand candles.* **2.** Anything that gives off any of these forms of energy. An electric lamp, a candle, or a star are lights: *Leave a light burning in the hallway. A million lights shone in the clear night sky.* **3.** A means of setting something on fire: *Give me a light for the campfire.* **4.** A way of looking at or thinking about a certain matter: *This puts the whole problem in a different light.*
—*adjective* **lighter, lightest 1.** Bright; not dark: *a light, airy room. It gets light about 6 o'clock in the morning.* **2.** Pale in color: *light gray; light hair; a light complexion.*
—*verb* **lighted** or **lit, lighting 1.** To begin to burn or set burning: *The oven won't light. He lighted a fire in the stove.* **2.** To cause to give off light; turn on: *Will you light the lamp?* **3.** To provide with light: *We lit the room with candles.* **4.** To guide or show with a light: *Here is a lantern to light your way.* **5.** To make lively: *A smile lighted her face.*

light² |līt| —*adjective* **lighter, lightest 1.** Having little weight; not heavy: *a light suitcase; a light jacket.* **2.** Small in amount, force, intensity, or impact: *a light lunch; a light breeze; light breathing; a light blow.* **3.** Not serious; requiring little thought; entertaining: *light reading.* **4.** Moving easily and gracefully; nimble; agile: *Acrobats and dancers are light on their feet.* **5.** Requiring little effort; easy to do or to deal with: *light housework; light typing; a light teaching job.* **6.** Slightly unsteady or faint; dizzy: *Standing up too quickly makes me feel light in the head.*
—*adverb* With little or no luggage: *He travels light.*
—*verb* **lighted** or **lit, lighting 1.** To come to rest; to land; to perch: *The bird lit on my shoulder.* **2.** To get down; alight: *The truck stopped and six soldiers lighted from the back of it.*

light·en¹ |līt′n| —*verb* **lightened, lightening** To make or become brighter or less dark: *Adding white to colors lightens them.*

light·en² |līt′n| —*verb* **lightened, lightening 1.** To make less heavy; reduce the weight of: *He lightened his suitcase by removing some books.* **2.** To make less difficult to do or hard to bear: *Many appliances lighten housework.* **3.** To make happier; to cheer: *A merry song lightens everyone's heart.*

liftoff

light¹, light²
Light¹ and **light²** have always had their present meanings. Each had its source in the prehistoric language that is the basis for many languages spoken today. Each traveled through Germanic and arrived in English with its separate meaning.

lighten¹, lighten²
Lighten¹ is formed from **light¹**, and **lighten²** is from **light²**.

lighthouse

lightning

like¹, like²

Like¹ came from an old English word meaning "to please, to have a pleasing appearance." **Like²** came from another old English word, one that meant "similar" or "having the same form or appearance." Both words came from the same root in prehistoric Germanic; it meant "form" or "appearance."

light·er | lī′tər | —*noun, plural* **lighters** **1.** A person who lights or ignites something: *a lighter of fires.* **2.** A mechanical device used to light or ignite a cigarette, cigar, or pipe for smoking.

light·heart·ed | līt′här′tĭd | —*adjective* Carefree and gay: *a lighthearted song; a lighthearted greeting.*

light·house | līt′hous′ | —*noun, plural* **light·hous·es** | līt′hou′zĭz | A tower with a powerful light at the top for guiding ships.

light·ly | līt′lē | —*adverb* **1.** With little weight, force, pressure, or intensity; gently: *She ran her fingers lightly over the piano keys. He sat on the floor lightly petting the puppy.* **2.** To a small amount or degree; slightly: *lightly tarnished metal. He was lightly punished for such a bad crime.* **3.** In an easy and graceful way: *She waltzed lightly around the room.*

light·ning | līt′nĭng | —*noun* A big flash of light that appears in the sky from natural causes. Lightning is a form of electricity.

lik·a·ble | lī′kə bəl | —*adjective* Easy to like; having a pleasing personality: *a likable fellow.* Another form of this word is **likeable.**

like¹ | līk | —*verb* **liked, liking** **1.** To be fond of; regard favorably: *She likes Jim a lot. Which dress do you like best?* **2.** To find pleasant; enjoy: *He liked the ranch so much he decided to stay an extra week.* **3.** To wish or want: *Take as much as you like.*
—*plural noun* **likes** The things a person enjoys or favors; preferences: *a list of his likes and dislikes.*

like² | līk | —*preposition* **1.** Similar to; much the same as: *His bicycle is like mine. The town is like a picture from a book.* **2.** In character with; typical of: *It's not like him to let his friends down.* **3.** In the same manner as: *He acts like a grown-up person.* **4.** Such as: *They bought many vegetables like cucumbers, spinach, mushrooms, and lettuce for the salad.* **5.** In the mood for: *I feel like taking a nap.* **6.** As if something is happening or will happen: *It looks like rain.*
—*adjective* Exactly or nearly the same; similar: *My uncle gave five dollars to me and a like sum to my cousins.*
—*noun* The equal of a person, animal, or thing: *What a great football player! I have never seen his like before.*

–like A suffix that forms adjectives. The suffix "-like" means: **1.** Similar to: *lifelike.* **2.** Having the nature of; resembling: *ladylike; catlike; childlike.*

like·a·ble | lī′kə bəl | A form of the word **likable.**

like·li·hood | līk′lē hŏŏd′ | —*noun, plural* **likelihoods** The chance of something happening; probability: *There is a strong likelihood that our team will win the game.*

like·ly | līk′lē | —*adjective* **likelier, likeliest** **1.** Having or showing a good chance of happening; more or less certain; probable: *It's likely to rain at any moment. Mr. Jones is a likely choice for the job.* **2.** Seeming to be true; such as can be believed: *They had a likely excuse for being late.* **3.** Suitable; fitting; appropriate: *June 25 seems a likely date for the party.*
—*adverb* Probably: *Most likely it's just a passing fad.*

like·ness | līk′nĭs | —*noun, plural* **likenesses** **1.** Similarity or resemblance: *There is an amazing likeness between Edward and his father.* **2.** A copy or picture of someone or something: *That portrait is a perfect likeness of you.*

like·wise | līk′wīz′ | —*adverb* **1.** In the same way; similarly: *The students watched him swim in the lake and did likewise.* **2.** Moreover; also; too: *He is likewise the captain of our football team.*

ă	pat	ĕ	pet	î	fierce
ā	pay	ē	be	ŏ	pot
â	care	ĭ	pit	ō	go
ä	father	ī	pie	ô	paw, for
oi	oil	ŭ	cut	zh	vision
ŏŏ	book	û	fur	ə	ago, item,
ōō	boot	*th*	the		pencil, atom,
yōō	abuse	th	thin		circus
ou	out	hw	which	ər	butter

lik·ing |lī′kĭng| —*noun, plural* **likings** **1.** A kindly feeling; a special feeling of affection: *She has a special liking for young children and small dogs.* **2.** Preference or taste: *He has a liking for chocolate ice cream. I'll try to choose a name more to your liking.*

li·lac |lī′lək| or |lī′lŏk′| or |lī′lăk| —*noun, plural* **lilacs** **1.** A garden shrub with clusters of fragrant purplish or white flowers. **2.** A pale purple color.
—*adjective* Pale purple: *a lilac dress.*

lil·y |lĭl′ē| —*noun, plural* **lilies** A plant with white or brightly colored flowers shaped like trumpets. There are several kinds of lilies.

lily of the valley —*plural* **lilies of the valley** A plant with small, fragrant white flowers that are shaped like bells. The flowers grow in a row along the plant stem.

li·ma bean |lī′mə| A large light-green bean that is eaten as a vegetable.

limb |lĭm| —*noun, plural* **limbs** **1.** A leg, arm, wing, or flipper. **2.** One of the larger branches of a tree.

lim·ber |lĭm′bər| —*adjective* **limberer, limberest** Bending or moving easily; supple; flexible: *limber muscles; a limber athlete.*
—*verb* **limbered, limbering** To make or become limber: *The dancer did some exercises to limber up her muscles. The runners took a few minutes to limber up before the race.*

lime¹ |lĭm| —*noun, plural* **limes** A juicy green fruit with a sour taste. Limes are related to lemons and oranges.

lime² |lĭm| —*noun* A white powder made up of calcium and oxygen. Lime is used in making steel, glass, cement, and insect poisons.

lim·er·ick |lĭm′ər ĭk| —*noun, plural* **limericks** A funny poem having five lines. The first and second lines rhyme with the last line. The third and fourth lines are shorter and rhyme with each other.

lime·stone |lĭm′stōn′| —*noun, plural* **limestones** A rock that is used for building. It is also used in making lime and cement.

lim·it |lĭm′ĭt| —*noun, plural* **limits** **1.** A point or line beyond which one cannot go; a final boundary at which something stops or must stop: *the limit of his view from the hilltop; a limit to my patience; limits as to how much one can do in a lifetime.* **2.** Often **limits** The boundary around a certain area; boundary line: *within the city limits.* **3.** The greatest amount or number allowed or possible: *a speed limit; a limit on what we can spend for a car.*
—*verb* **limited, limiting** To place a limit on; restrict; confine: *Try to limit your talk to ten minutes. I am limiting myself to one candy bar a week.*

limp |lĭmp| —*verb* **limped, limping** **1.** To walk with an uneven or awkward movement, placing the body's weight mostly on one leg. **2.** To move or proceed slowly or with difficulty: *The damaged ship limped back to port.*
—*noun, plural* **limps** An uneven or awkward way of walking: *The accident left him with a limp.*

Lin·coln |lĭng′kən| The capital of Nebraska.

line¹ |līn| —*noun, plural* **lines** **1.** A path taken by a point that is free to move: *a straight line; a curved line.* **2.** A long, thin mark. A line can be made by a pen, pencil, or tool: *She drew a line on the paper.* **3.** A border or boundary: *a property line; the county line.* **4.** Something that separates two things: *He has to learn to draw*

lilac

lime¹, lime²
Lime¹ comes from an Arabic word that traveled through French before appearing in English. **Lime²** is from an old English word that originally meant "slimy substance."

limerick
There was a young fellow named Paul
Who attended a fancy dress ball.
  They say, just for fun,
  He dressed up as a bun,
And a dog ate him up in the hall.

line¹, line²

Line¹ and **line²** have a common source in a Latin word that referred to flax, a plant from which fiber is obtained to make cloth. This Latin word had an additional form meaning "a thread of flax," which was borrowed into old English in the sense "cord, rope" and "long, thin mark." This is **line¹** in modern English. The word also came into English in the meaning "to reinforce fabric with flax cloth," which is the source of **line²** in modern English.

link

lion and lioness

ă	pat	ĕ	pet	î	fierce
ā	pay	ē	be	ŏ	pot
â	care	ĭ	pit	ō	go
ä	father	ī	pie	ô	paw, for

oi	oil	ŭ	cut	zh	vision
ŏŏ	book	û	fur	ə	ago, item,
ōō	boot	th	the		pencil, atom,
yōō	abuse	th	thin		circus
ou	out	hw	which	ər	butter

the line between good and bad. **5.** A group of people or things in a row: *The band marched in a line.* **6.** Often **lines** The outline or style of something: *She doesn't like the lines of his new suit.* **7.** A row of words on a page or column: *This story has 30 lines.* **8. lines** The words said by an actor in a play: *Memorize your lines.* **9.** A wrinkle or crease on the skin: *The old man's face had many lines.* **10.** A rope, string, cord, or wire: *a fishing line.* **11.** A certain point of view or course of action: *Follow the party line.* **12.** A system of transportation: *a bus line; a railroad line.* **13.** A system of wires used to connect electricity: *a power line; a telegraph line.* **14.** A range or kind of goods having several styles and sizes: *a new line of china.* **15.** A person's job or trade: *Her line of work is banking.* **16.** A short letter: *I'll drop you a line from California.* —*verb* **lined, lining** **1.** To mark with lines: *Line this paper.* **2.** To form a line along: *People lined the sidewalk.* **3.** To fill or cover: *The hall was lined with mirrors.*

Phrasal verb **line up** **1.** To arrange in or form a line: *The cars must line up to get on the ferry.* **2.** To win over; gain: *Jerry lined up some votes at the meeting.*

line² |līn| —*verb* **lined, lining** **1.** To cover the inside of something with a layer of material: *Line the box with tissue.* **2.** To serve as a lining for: *Fur lined her coat.*

lin·e·ar |lĭn′ē ər| —*adjective* **1.** Of or using a line or lines: *a linear design.* **2.** Of length: *A meter is a linear measurement.*

lin·en |lĭn′ən| —*noun, plural* **linens** **1.** A strong cloth made from flax fibers. **2.** Often **linens** Cloth things such as tablecloths, sheets, and napkins that are made of linen.

lin·er |lī′nər| —*noun, plural* **liners** A ship or airplane that carries passengers on a regular route: *The liner set sail for South America.*

lin·ger |lĭng′gər| —*verb* **lingered, lingering** To stay on longer than usual, as if not willing to leave: *The guests lingered in the dining room long after dinner was over.*

lin·ing |lī′nĭng| —*noun, plural* **linings** A layer of material used on the inside surface of something: *the lining of a coat.*

link |lĭngk| —*noun, plural* **links** **1.** A ring or loop that is part of a chain: *A chain is only as strong as its weakest link.* **2.** Anything that joins or connects: *a link with the past. The new road is a link between two cities.* —*verb* **linked, linking** To join or connect: *The bridge links the two sides of the river.*

link·ing verb |lĭng′kĭng| A verb that does not express an action but functions only as a bridge between the subject of a sentence and a word or phrase that tells something about the subject. In the sentences "She was very happy," "Then she became a truck driver," and "I got sleepy," the verbs, "was," "became," and "got," are linking verbs.

li·no·le·um |lĭ nō′lē əm| —*noun, plural* **linoleums** A covering for floors and counters. Linoleum is a material made by pressing a mixture of ground cork and hot linseed oil onto a cloth backing.

lin·seed oil |lĭn′sēd′| A yellowish oil from the seeds of the flax plant. Linseed oil is used in paints and varnishes.

lint |lĭnt| —*noun* Bits of fiber and fluff from yarn or cloth.

li·on |lī′ən| —*noun, plural* **lions** A large, powerful wild cat of Africa and India. Lions have a smooth, light-brown coat. The males have a shaggy mane around the neck and shoulders.

li·on·ess |lī′ə nĭs| —*noun, plural* **lionesses** A female lion.

lip |lĭp| —*noun, plural* **lips** **1.** One of the two muscular folds of tissue that form the outside edge of the mouth. **2.** The rim or edge of a container: *the lip of a cup.*

lip·stick |lĭp′stĭk′| —*noun, plural* **lipsticks** A stick of material like wax, used to color the lips.

liq·uid |lĭk′wĭd| —*noun, plural* **liquids** A form of matter that is not a gas or a solid. A liquid flows readily and it can take the shape of its container. Unlike a gas the liquid will not necessarily fill its container. Water, milk, and juice are liquids.
—*adjective* In the state of a liquid: *liquid fuel.*

liq·uor |lĭk′ər| —*noun, plural* **liquors** An alcoholic beverage. Whiskey is a liquor.

lisp |lĭsp| —*noun, plural* **lisps** A speech problem in which the letters *s* and *z* are said as *th.*
—*verb* **lisped, lisping** To speak with a lisp.

list¹ |lĭst| —*noun, plural* **lists** A series of names of people or things written one after the other: *a list of guests; a shopping list.*
—*verb* **listed, listing** **1.** To make a list of: *She listed her grades in a notebook.* **2.** To include in a list: *Dr. Stroll is listed in the book.*

list² |lĭst| —*noun, plural* **lists** A tilt or slant to one side.
—*verb* **listed, listing** To tilt to one side: *The ship listed as the waves beat the hull.*

lis·ten |lĭs′ən| —*verb* **listened, listening** To try to hear something: *They listened carefully.*
  Phrasal verb **listen in** **1.** To tune in and listen to a radio broadcast. **2.** To listen to what other people are saying without taking part in the conversation. **3.** To eavesdrop.

lis·ten·er |lĭs′ə nər| —*noun, plural* **listeners** A person who listens or pays attention.

lit¹ |lĭt| A past tense and past participle of the verb **light** (to begin to burn): *The oven lit easily. We had lit the lamps by the time darkness came.*

lit² |lĭt| A past tense and past participle of the verb **light** (to come to rest): *The robin lit on the lawn.*

lit·chi |lē′chē| —*noun, plural* **litchis** The sweet fruit of a Chinese tree. It has a thin shell and a hard seed. Another form of this word is **lichee.**

li·ter |lē′tər| —*noun, plural* **liters** A unit of liquid measure in the metric system. A liter is equal to about 1.056 liquid quarts.

lit·er·al·ly |lĭt′ər ə lē| —*adverb* **1.** Word for word: *He translated the Spanish poem into English literally.* **2.** Really; actually: *He literally fell to his knees in shock.*

lit·er·ar·y |lĭt′ə rĕr′ē| —*adjective* Of literature: *a literary critic.*

lit·er·a·ture |lĭt′ər ə chər| —*noun, plural* **literatures** **1.** A body of writing, especially writing that has lasting value because it shows beauty of expression, nobility of thought, or great imagination. Literature includes plays, poetry, and stories. **2.** Printed material of any kind: *campaign literature.*

lit·mus |lĭt′məs| —*noun* A powder that changes from blue to red in an acid solution and from red to blue in a base solution.

litmus paper Paper treated with litmus.

lit·ter |lĭt′ər| —*noun, plural* **litters** **1.** A couch on poles on which a person is carried. **2.** A stretcher for carrying sick or wounded people. **3.** Young animals born at one time: *a litter of kittens.* **4.** Scraps of paper and other waste material left lying around:

list¹, list²
List¹ comes from an old French word meaning "edge, strip of paper." We don't know the origin of **list²**.

litter
Of puppies

live¹, live²
Live¹ comes from an old English word that originally meant "to continue." Live² is a shortened form of **alive**.

livery
Servants in livery

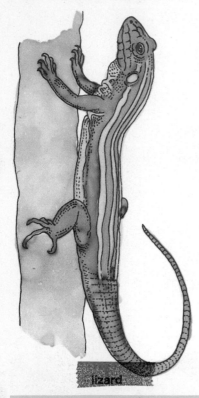

lizard

Our class picked up all the litter on the school playground.
—verb littered, littering To make a place messy by leaving litter around: *Do not litter this picnic area.*

lit·tle |lĭt′l| —*adjective* **littler, littlest** or **least 1.** Small in size or quantity; not big: *a little table.* **2.** Young: *The little children didn't go on the trip.* **3.** Also *comparative* **less,** *superlative* **least.**
a. Short in time or distance; brief: *Walk down the road a little way.*
b. Unimportant: *Jack spent a lot of time worrying about a little problem.* **4.** Without much force; weak: *a little sob.*
—adverb less, least Not much: *She eats little.*
—noun 1. A small amount: *What little they have is broken.* **2.** A short time or distance: *a little past four o'clock; a little down the road.*

Little Rock The capital of Arkansas.

live¹ |lĭv| —*verb* **lived, living 1.** To have life; exist: *Fish cannot live long out of water.* **2.** To continue to stay alive: *Long live the king!* **3.** To support oneself; maintain life: *They live on what she earns.* **4.** To make one's home; dwell: *Judy lives in New Hampshire.* **5.** To lead one's life in a certain way: *They married and lived happily ever after.*

live² |lĭv| —*adjective* **1.** Having life; alive: *a real live monkey.* **2.** Glowing or burning: *live coals.* **3.** Carrying electric current: *a live wire.* **4.** Not exploded; able to be fired: *live ammunition.* **5.** Broadcast while actually being performed; not taped: *a program coming live from New York.*

live·li·hood |lĭv′lē hŏŏd′| —*noun, plural* **livelihoods** The way a person earns a living: *Her livelihood is fishing. Jackson practiced medicine as a livelihood.*

live·ly |lĭv′lē| —*adjective* **livelier, liveliest 1.** Full of life; active: *a lively baby.* **2.** Bright; vivid: *lively colors.* **3.** Brisk; alert: *lively talk; a lively mind.*
—adverb In a lively manner; briskly or vigorously: *Step lively!*

liv·er |lĭv′ər| —*noun, plural* **livers 1.** A large organ in the abdomen of people and animals. The liver makes bile and helps the body process food. **2.** The liver of an animal used as food.

liv·er·y |lĭv′ə rē| or |lĭv′rē| —*noun, plural* **liveries 1.** A uniform worn by the male servants of a household. **2.** The care and shelter of horses for money.

lives |lĭvz| The plural of the noun **life.**

live·stock |lĭv′stŏk′| —*noun* Animals raised on a farm: *Mr. Johnson's livestock included pigs, cows, horses, and sheep.*

liv·id |lĭv′ĭd| —*adjective* **1.** Changed in color because of a bruise. **2.** Very pale or white, as from anger or some other strong feeling: *She was livid with anger after fighting with her sister.*

liv·ing |lĭv′ĭng| —*adjective* **1.** Having life; alive: *living trees.* **2.** In present use: *English is a living language.* **3.** True to life: *He is the living picture of his brother.* **4.** Of or for a certain way of life: *Living conditions in the building improved greatly after the plumbing was repaired.*
—noun, plural livings 1. The condition of being alive: *Living is painful for this sick cat.* **2.** A manner or style of life: *fancy living.* **3.** A way of maintaining life; a livelihood: *I earn my living as a carpenter.* **4. the living** Those who are alive.

living room A room in a home for general use.

liz·ard |lĭz′ərd| —*noun, plural* **lizards** An animal that has a scaly body, four legs, and a long tail. There are many kinds of lizards. Most of them live in warm parts of the world.

lla·ma |lä′mə| —*noun, plural* **llamas** A South American animal with a soft coat. The llama is raised for its wool. It is also used for carrying loads. The llama is related to the alpaca.

load |lōd| —*noun, plural* **loads** **1.** Something that is carried: *Phil took two loads of books downstairs.* **2.** The amount of work or number of duties to be done by a person or machine: *The typists have a heavy work load.* **3.** One charge of ammunition for a gun. **4.** Often **loads** A great number or amount: *loads of fun.*
—*verb* **loaded, loading** **1.a.** To put something to be carried in or on a vehicle or structure: *The workers were loading grain onto a train.* **b.** To place something to be carried in or on: *The movers loaded the truck with furniture.* **2.** To provide or fill nearly to overflowing: *At Halloween people loaded our sacks with candy.* **3.** To weigh down: *His father was loaded with problems.* **4.** To charge with ammunition: *The soldiers loaded the gun.* **5.** To put needed materials into a machine: *Load film into the camera before taking any pictures.*
♦ *These sound alike* **load, lode.**

loaf¹ |lōf| —*noun, plural* **loaves** **1.** Bread that is baked in one piece. **2.** Any kind of food that is shaped like a loaf: *a meat loaf.*

loaf² |lōf| —*verb* **loafed, loafing** To spend time in a lazy manner or without purpose: *We loafed all morning.*

loaf·er |lō′fər| —*noun, plural* **loafers** **1.** A person who loafs. **2.** A shoe shaped like a moccasin.

loan |lōn| —*noun, plural* **loans** **1.** The act of lending: *the loan of a raincoat to a friend.* **2.a.** Something borrowed: *That lamp is a loan from my neighbor.* **b.** A sum of money lent: *Jennifer asked for a loan at the bank.*
—*verb* **loaned, loaning** To lend: *Phil loaned money to a friend.*
♦ *These sound alike* **loan, lone.**

loaves |lōvz| The plural of the noun **loaf.**

lob·by |lŏb′ē| —*noun, plural* **lobbies** **1.** A hall or waiting room in a hotel, apartment house, or theater. **2.** A group of private people who try to influence lawmakers: *the farmers' lobby.*
—*verb* **lobbied, lobbying, lobbies** To try to influence lawmakers: *Many were lobbying in favor of the equal rights bill.*

lob·ster |lŏb′stər| —*noun, plural* **lobsters** A sea animal that has a long body covered with a hard shell. The two front legs have large, heavy claws. Lobsters are often eaten as food.

lo·cal |lō′kəl| —*adjective* **1.** Of a certain area or place: *local governments; a local storm.* **2.** Making many stops; not express: *a local train.* **3.** Of one part of the body rather than the entire system: *a local infection.*
—*noun, plural* **locals** A local train or bus: *The local runs every fifteen minutes.*

lo·cal·i·ty |lō kăl′ĭ tē| —*noun, plural* **localities** A certain neighborhood, place, or area: *The people of this locality need a new park.*

lo·cate |lō′kāt′| or |lō kāt′| —*verb* **located, locating** **1.** To find and show the position of: *Show Sally how to locate Alabama on the map.* **2.** To find by searching or asking: *Scouts are trained to locate food in the woods. The reporter located valuable information.* **3.** To place or put in a certain spot: *Try to locate your vegetable garden in a sunny area.* **4.** To go and live somewhere: *The family has located in Iowa.*

loaf¹, loaf²
Loaf¹ comes from an old English word that meant "loaf, bread." It came from a prehistoric Germanic word. **Loaf²** probably comes from **loafer**, whose source is not known.

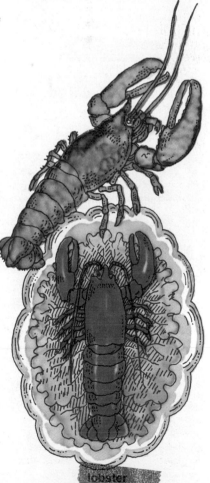

lobster
Live (*above*) and cooked (*below*)

lock¹, lock²
Lock¹ and **lock²** were originally from different but very similar old English words, and they are probably related. It is likely that **lock¹** meant "turning, twisting device," while **lock²** referred to a twist of hair.

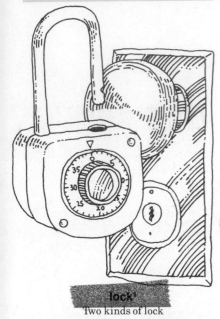

lock¹
Two kinds of lock

locomotive
Above: Steam locomotive
Below: Diesel locomotive

ă	pat	ě	pet	î	fierce
ā	pay	ē	be	ŏ	pot
â	care	ĭ	pit	ō	go
ä	father	ī	pie	ô	paw, for

oi	oil	ŭ	cut	zh	vision
ŏŏ	book	û	fur	ə	ago, item,
ōō	boot	*th*	the		pencil, atom,
yōō	abuse	th	thin		circus
ou	out	hw	which	ər	butter

lo·ca·tion | lō kā′shən | —*noun, plural* **locations** **1.** A place where something is located or found; a position: *Ask the driver for the location of the hospital.* **2.** The act of locating: *The geologists spent a lot of time in the location of water.* **3.** An area away from a motion-picture studio where a scene is filmed: *made a movie on location in Spain.*

lock¹ | lŏk | —*noun, plural* **locks** **1.** A fastener worked by a key or a combination that holds something shut. Doors, windows, drawers, lids, and many other things are fastened with locks. **2.** A part of a canal, closed off with gates, in which a ship can be raised or lowered by pumping water in or out. **3.** A part in a gun for exploding the charge.
—*verb* **locked, locking** **1.** To fasten with a lock or locks: *lock the door.* **2.** To hold, fasten, or bind tightly in place: *The brakes locked the wheels. Energy is locked up in the atom.* **3.** To become tightly held, fastened, or firm: *This valve locks automatically under pressure.* **4.** To link together: *They locked arms and walked off.*

lock² | lŏk | —*noun, plural* **locks** **1.** A curl of hair; a ringlet: *a lock of the baby's first hair.* **2.** **locks** The hair of the head.

lock·er | lŏk′ər | —*noun, plural* **lockers** A small closet in a gymnasium or public place in which clothes and valuables can be locked up.

lock·et | lŏk′ĭt | —*noun, plural* **lockets** A small, ornamental metal case for a picture, lock of hair, or something else that one wants to keep. Lockets are usually worn on a chain.

lock·smith | lŏk′smĭth′ | —*noun, plural* **locksmiths** A person who makes or repairs locks.

lo·co·mo·tive | lō′kə mō′tĭv | —*noun, plural* **locomotives** An engine used to pull or push railroad cars along a track.

lo·cust | lō′kəst | —*noun, plural* **locusts** **1.** A kind of grasshopper that travels in huge swarms. Locusts often do great damage to growing crops. **2.** A tree that has feathery leaves and clusters of fragrant white flowers.

lode | lōd | —*noun, plural* **lodes** A deposit of an ore that bears metal: *a lode of silver.*
♦ *These sound alike* **lode, load.**

lodge | lŏj | —*noun, plural* **lodges** **1.** A cottage or cabin, especially a small one used as a temporary shelter: *a ski lodge; a fishing lodge.* **2.** A small branch of a large organization, as a club.
—*verb* **lodged, lodging** **1.** To provide with a place for sleeping: *We lodged six guests in the basement.* **2.** To live in a place: *We have lodged in Washington for years.* **3.** To live in a rented room or rooms: *John lodged with the Murphys.* **4.** To be or become stuck or caught: *A splinter lodged in his heel.* **5.** To present a charge or complaint to the proper official: *The neighbors lodged a protest with the mayor about speeding trucks.*

lodg·er | lŏj′ər | —*noun, plural* **lodgers** A person who rents a room or rooms in another person's house.

lodg·ing | lŏj′ĭng | —*noun, plural* **lodgings** **1.** A temporary place to sleep. **2.** **lodgings** A rented room or rooms in another person's house.

loft | lôft | or | lŏft | —*noun, plural* **lofts** **1.** A large, often open floor in a business building. Lofts are usually used as storage areas, work areas, or artists' studios. **2.** An open space under a roof; an attic: *a loft full of old furniture.* **3.** A balcony in a church or large hall: *a choir loft.*

loft·y |lôf′tē| or |lŏf′tē| —*adjective* **loftier, loftiest** **1.** Of great height; very tall: *lofty mountains.* **2.** On a high moral level; noble: *lofty thoughts; lofty ideals.* **3.** Arrogant; haughty: *a lofty treatment of others.*

log |lôg| or |lŏg| —*noun, plural* **logs** **1. a.** A large trunk of a tree that has fallen or been cut down. **b.** A cut length of such wood used for building, firewood, or lumber. **2. a.** An official record of speed, progress, and important events, kept on a ship or aircraft. **b.** Any written report or record: *The secretary keeps a log of the meetings.*
—*verb* **logged, logging** **1.** To cut down trees, trim them, and carry the logs away from a forest area. **2.** To enter something in a log or other record: *The coach logged the number of errors for each player.*

lo·gan·ber·ry |lō′gən bĕr′ē| —*noun, plural* **loganberries** A large, dark-red berry that is related to the raspberry and the blackberry.

log·ger |lô′gər| or |lŏg′ər| —*noun, plural* **loggers** A person whose work is cutting down trees and trimming them into logs; a lumberjack.

log·ic |lŏj′ĭk| —*noun, plural* **logics** **1.** Clear thinking or reasoning: *Your explanation shows a lack of logic.* **2.** A way of thinking or reasoning: *the simple logic of mountain people.*

log·i·cal |lŏj′ĭ kəl| —*adjective* **1.** Able to think clearly and sensibly: *a logical mind.* **2.** Reasonable: *a logical choice.*

loin |loin| —*noun, plural* **loins** **1.** Often **loins** The part of the sides and back of the body between the ribs and hip. **2.** A cut of meat taken from this part of an animal.

loi·ter |loi′tər| —*verb* **loitered, loitering** **1.** To stand about in an idle manner; linger: *My friends and I used to loiter on the corner after school.* **2.** To go slowly, stopping often: *She loitered on the way to the dentist.*

lol·li·pop or **lol·ly·pop** |lŏl′ē pŏp′| —*noun, plural* **lollipops** or **lollypops** A piece of hard candy on the end of a stick.

lone |lōn| —*adjective* **1.** Not with another person or persons; alone; single: *a lone man on horseback.* **2.** Located at a place far away; remote: *the lone prairie.*
♦ *These sound alike* **lone, loan.**

lone·ly |lōn′lē| —*adjective* **lonelier, loneliest** **1.** Sad at being alone: *a lonely little boy with no friends.* **2.** Not with another person or persons; alone: *a lonely traveler.* **3.** Far away and not visited by many people; remote or deserted: *a lonely road.*

lone·some |lōn′səm| —*adjective* **1.** Sad and upset at feeling alone: *When no one will play with me, I get lonesome.* **2.** Causing a feeling of sadness at being alone: *a lonesome voyage.* **3.** Far away and not visited by many people; remote: *a lonesome mountain trail.*

long¹ |lông| or |lŏng| —*adjective* **longer, longest** **1.** Having great length; not short: *a long river; a long novel.* **2.** Of great duration or extent: *a long time; a long journey.* **3.** Of a certain extent or duration: *The snake was 30 feet long. His speech was an hour long.* **4.** Having a sound that is drawn out; for example, the *a* in *pane* is a long vowel, while the *a* in *pan* is short.
—*adverb* **longer, longest** **1.** During or for a great amount of time: *Stay as long as you like.* **2.** For or throughout a certain period: *all night long.* **3.** At a very distant time: *long ago.*

long² |lông| or |lŏng| —*verb* **longed, longing** To have a strong

loganberry

long¹, long²
When we **long²** for something, the time seems **long¹**. This explains the basic difference between the two old English words from which **long¹** and **long²** come. **Long¹** has always had its current meaning. **Long²** originally meant "to grow longer."

desire; wish for very much: *She longed to go back home.*

long·hand |lông′ hănd′| or |lŏng′ hănd′| —*noun, plural*
longhands Writing in which the letters in each word are joined
together; ordinary handwriting.

long·horn |lông′ hôrn′| or |lŏng′ hôrn′| —*noun, plural*
longhorns One of a breed of cattle with long, spreading horns.

long·ing |lông′ ĭng| or |lŏng′ ĭng| —*noun, plural* **longings** A
deep wish; a strong desire: *I have a longing to own a boat.*
—*adjective* Showing a deep wish or strong desire: *a longing look.*

lon·gi·tude |lŏn′ jĭ tōōd′| or |lŏn′ jĭ tyōōd′| —*noun, plural*
longitudes Distance east or west of the meridian line at
Greenwich, England, expressed in degrees. On a map or globe,
longitude lines are drawn running north and south.

look |lŏŏk| —*verb* **looked, looking 1.** To use the eyes to see: *Sue
looked everywhere, but couldn't find her friend.* **2.** To fix one's gaze
or attention: *She looked toward the river.* **3. a.** To seem: *These
bananas look ripe.* **b.** To seem to be: *He does not look his age.*
4. To face in a certain direction: *The house looks on the sea.*

Phrasal verbs **look after** To take care of: *Look after the baby.* **look
at 1.** To regard; consider: *a good way to look at the problem.*
2. To examine: *Look at the tires of my car.* **look down on** (or **upon**)
To regard with contempt: *That fool looks down on women.* **look for**
To search for: *On the prairie he saw animals looking for food.* **look
forward to** To wait for, usually with pleasure: *I'm looking forward
to my trip to Florida.* **look into** To inquire into; investigate: *I'll look
into the price of tickets for you.* **look out (for)** To be on guard: *Look
out for snakes in the woods.* **look over** To examine, often in a
casual manner: *He looked over my book report.* **look up 1.** To
search for: *look up a word in the dictionary.* **2.** To locate and call
on; to visit: *Look us up when you are in town.* **3.** To improve:
Things are beginning to look up around here. **look up to** To admire
and respect: *He looks up to the baseball coach.*
—*noun, plural* **looks 1.** The action of looking; a gaze or glance:
a quick look at the map. **2.** An expression or appearance: *a look of
pain in her eyes.* **3. looks** Personal appearance: *He is famous for
his good looks.*

looking glass A mirror.

look·out |lŏŏk′ out′| —*noun, plural* **lookouts 1.** A person whose
job it is to watch carefully for something: *The ship's lookout
spotted the island in the distance.* **2.** The action of watching and
waiting: *He kept a sharp lookout for the enemy.* **3.** A place from
which a careful watch can be kept: *From the lookout high in the
trees the ranger could see even small forest fires.*

loom¹ |lōōm| —*verb* **loomed, looming 1.** To come into view as
large and dangerous: *Clouds loomed behind the mountains.* **2.** To
seem close at hand; be about to happen: *The day of his final exams
loomed before him.*

loom² |lōōm| —*noun, plural* **looms** A machine or frame for
weaving threads to make cloth.

loon |lōōn| —*noun, plural* **loons** A diving bird with a back with
small whitish spots and a pointed bill. The cry of the loon sounds
like a wild laugh.

loop |lōōp| —*noun, plural* **loops 1.** A circular or oval piece of
rope, thread, wire, or other material that is folded over or joined
at the ends. **2.** A pattern or path that closes or almost closes on
itself and looks like a loop: *The car made a loop around the town.*

loom¹, loom²
Although we can't be sure, **loom¹** is
probably borrowed from a word used
a very long time ago in a form of
German. This is similar to a word
meaning "to move slowly" used by
people living long ago in a northern
part of the Netherlands. The source
of **loom²** is an old English word
meaning "a tool, a device."

loom²

loon

ă	pat	ĕ	pet	î	fierce
ā	pay	ē	be	ŏ	pot
â	care	ĭ	pit	ō	go
ä	father	ī	pie	ô	paw, for

oi	oil	ŭ	cut	zh	vision
ŏŏ	book	û	fur	ə	ago, item,
ōō	boot	th	the		pencil, atom,
yōō	abuse	th	thin		circus
ou	out	hw	which	ər	butter

—*verb* **looped, looping** **1.** To make or form into a loop or loops: *The brook looped around the farm.* **2.** To fasten or join with a loop or loops: *looped the yarn around the knitting needle.*

loose |lŏos| —*adjective* **looser, loosest** **1.** Not attached or fastened tightly: *a loose shoelace.* **2.** Not confined; free: *The dog is loose in the yard.* **3.** Not tight-fitting: *a loose sweater.* **4.** Not bound, tied, or joined together: *I carry loose change in my pocket. The string holding the balloons broke, and now they are loose and floating in the air.* **5.** Not tightly packed: *Loose gravel was put on the driveway.* **6.** Not strict or exact: *a loose style of writing; a loose count of the people at the ball park.*
—*verb* **loosed, loosing** **1.** To set free; release: *I loosed the bird from its cage.* **2.** To make less tight; loosen: *She loosed the laces of her sneakers.*

loos·en |lŏo′sən| —*verb* **loosened, loosening** **1.** To make or become loose or looser: *Joe loosened his belt. When my shoelaces loosened, I made them tighter.* **2.** To free, untie, or release: *He loosened the rabbit from the trap.*

loot |lŏot| —*noun* Valuable things that have been stolen: *The soldiers hid the loot in a cave.*
—*verb* **looted, looting** To rob of valuable things; steal: *The thief looted Dad's library.*
♦ *These sound alike* **loot, lute.**

lord |lôrd| —*noun, plural* **lords** **1.** A person, like a king or an owner of an estate, who has great authority or power. **2. Lord** A man of noble rank in Great Britain. **3. Lord a.** God: *People of many religions pray to the Lord for help.* **b.** Christ.
—*verb* **lorded, lording** To behave in a haughty, stuffy, or conceited way: *She lorded over other members of the club.*

lose |lŏoz| —*verb* **lost, losing** **1.** To fail to find; to no longer have: *I lost my gloves.* **2.** To be unable to keep or maintain: *He lost his temper. The acrobat lost her balance while performing.* **3.** To fail to win: *They lost the game.* **4.** To fail to take advantage of; to waste: *We'll lose too much time if we stop to eat.* **5.** To be deprived of, as by accident: *He lost an arm in a car crash. Sheila lost her job.* **6.** To fail to see, understand, or hear; to miss: *The river patrol lost the rowboat in the fog.* **7.** To cause the loss of: *Paul's behavior lost him some friends.*

loss |lôs| or |lŏs| —*noun, plural* **losses** **1.** The fact or act of losing something: *a loss of memory; the loss of a game.* **2.** Someone or something that is lost.

lost |lôst| or |lŏst| The past tense and past participle of the verb **lose:** *Jean lost her scarf. Pat has lost his hat.*
—*adjective* **1.** Misplaced; missing: *a lost ring.* **2.** Not won: *a lost game.* **3.** Gone or passed away: *lost youth.* **4.** Occupied with: *lost in daydreams.* **5.** Puzzled; uncertain: *She felt lost in the new school.* **6.** Not used; wasted: *a lost opportunity.*

lot |lŏt| —*noun, plural* **lots** **1.** A large amount or number: *I have a lot of work to do. There were a lot of cars on the street.* **2.** A number of people or things of a kind: *This tomato is the ripest of the lot.* **3.** A kind, type, or sort: *Thieves are a bad lot of people.* **4. a.** A piece of land: *We bought a lot and then built a house on it.* **b.** A piece of land used for a special purpose: *a parking lot.* **5. a.** An object used to decide or choose something by chance: *We drew lots to see who would go first.* **b.** The use of such an object to decide or choose something: *We selected our leader by lot.*

lotus

Louisiana

Louisiana comes from the name of King Louis XIV of France. The name was given to a huge area of the Mississippi Valley by a French explorer. Later Louisiana became the name of one of the states created by the division of the area.

6. One's fortune in life; fate: *It was my lot to be unhappy.*
—*adverb* Very much; a great deal: *He knows a lot about baseball.*

lo·tion |**lō′**shən| —*noun, plural* **lotions** A liquid used on the skin. Some lotions contain medicine and are used to heal the skin or to relieve pain. Others cleanse or soften the skin.

lot·ter·y |**lŏt′**ə rē| —*noun, plural* **lotteries** A contest in which the winner is chosen by drawing lots.

lo·tus |**lō′**təs| —*noun, plural* **lotuses** A water plant with large, colorful flowers and broad leaves.

loud |loud| —*adjective* **louder, loudest 1.** Having a high volume or strong sound: *loud music.* **2.** Producing or able to produce strong sounds: *a loud instrument.* **3.** Not in good taste; gaudy: *a loud shirt.*
—*adverb* **louder, loudest** In a loud manner: *She screamed loud when she saw the mouse.*

loud·speak·er or **loud-speak·er** |**loud′**spē′kər| —*noun, plural* **loudspeakers** or **loud-speakers** A device that converts an electrical signal into sound and makes the sound louder.

Lou·i·si·an·a |lōō ē′zē ăn′ə| A state in the southern United States. The capital of Louisiana is Baton Rouge.

lounge |lounj| —*verb* **lounged, lounging** To stand, sit, or lie in a lazy or relaxed way: *She lounged in a comfortable chair.*
—*noun, plural* **lounges** A room where a person may relax or lounge: *We'll wait for you in the lounge of the hotel.*

louse |lous| —*noun, plural* **lice** A small insect with no wings. Lice bite and suck blood from the skin of animals. Some kinds of lice live on the bodies of human beings. Lice can spread serious diseases.

lous·y |**lou′**zē| —*adjective* **lousier, lousiest** Not nice; mean; nasty: *a lousy personality; a lousy day.*

lov·a·ble |**lŭv′**ə bəl| —*adjective* Having qualities that attract affection: *a lovable kitten; a lovable child.*

love |lŭv| —*noun, plural* **loves 1.** Strong affection and warm feeling for another. **2.** Affectionate regards: *Give her my love.* **3.** A strong liking for something: *his love of sports.* **4.** A beloved person.
—*verb* **loved, loving 1.** To feel love or strong affection for: *All his classmates loved him because he was such a nice person.* **2.** To have a strong liking for; delight in: *I just love to play tennis.*

love·ly |**lŭv′**lē| —*adjective* **lovelier, loveliest 1.** Having pleasing and attractive qualities; beautiful: *a lovely woman; a lovely house.* **2.** Inspiring love and affection: *a lovely, sweet person.* **3.** Giving pleasure; delightful: *We had a lovely time at the party.*

lov·er |**lŭv′**ər| —*noun, plural* **lovers 1.** Someone who loves another person. **2.** Someone who has a strong liking for something: *a music lover; a lover of good books.*

low |lō| —*adjective* **lower, lowest 1.** Having little height; not high or tall: *a low stool.* **2.** Of less than usual depth; shallow: *a low river.* **3.** At or near the horizon: *The moon was low in the sky.* **4.** Below average, as in amount, degree, or intensity: *low pay; a low cost; low temperature.* **5.** Not loud: *She speaks in a low voice.* **6.** Not sufficient; not adequate in amount: *Our supplies are low.* **7.** Depressed: *I feel very low today.* **8.** Of small value or quality; not favorable; bad: *She has a low opinion of her brother's friend.*
—*adverb* **lower, lowest 1.** At or to a low position or level: *an airplane flying low.* **2.** Not loudly; softly: *speaking low.*

ă	pat	ĕ	pet	î	fierce
ā	pay	ē	be	ŏ	pot
â	care	ĭ	pit	ō	go
ä	father	ī	pie	ô	paw, for
oi	oil	ŭ	cut	zh	vision
ōō	book	û	fur	ə	ago, item,
ōō	boot	*th*	the		pencil, atom,
yōō	abuse	th	thin		circus
ou	out	hw	which	ər	butter

—*noun, plural* **lows** A low level, position, or degree: *The temperature dropped to a new low today.*

low·er |lō′ər| The comparative of the adjective and adverb **low.**
—*verb* **lowered, lowering** **1.** To let, bring, or move something down to a lower level: *lower the flag. Jack lowered his head because he was ashamed.* **2.** To make or become less in value, degree, or quality: *lower the prices. Prices lowered during the summer.* **3.** To make less loud: *Lower your voice when you are in the library.*

low·land |lō′lənd| —*noun, plural* **lowlands** An area of land that is lower than the surrounding country.

low tide The time when the tide is at its lowest point.

loy·al |loi′əl| —*adjective* Faithful to a person, country, idea, or thing: *He is a loyal friend.*

loy·al·ty |loi′əl tē| —*noun, plural* **loyalties** The condition of being loyal; faithful and loyal behavior.

lu·bri·cant |lo͞o′brĭ kənt| —*noun, plural* **lubricants** A slippery substance, such as oil or grease, used as a coating on moving parts to allow them to move easily and to reduce wear.

lu·bri·cate |lo͞o′brĭ kāt′| —*verb* **lubricated, lubricating** To apply oil or grease to the moving parts of a machine so they will move easily.

luck |lŭk| —*noun* **1.** The chance happening of good or bad events; fate: *Losing that game was just our luck!* **2.** Good fortune; success: *beginner's luck. I wish you luck in your new job.*

luck·i·ly |lŭk′ə lē| —*adverb* Fortunately; by good luck.

luck·y |lŭk′ē| —*adjective* **luckier, luckiest** **1.** Having good luck: *Joe was lucky and won the lottery.* **2.** Bringing good luck: *a lucky penny.*

lug |lŭg| —*verb* **lugged, lugging** To drag, haul, or carry with great difficulty: *They lugged supplies up the trail to the cabin. He lugged the heavy books home from school.*

lug·gage |lŭg′ĭj| —*noun* The bags, suitcases, boxes, and trunks taken on a trip; baggage.

luke·warm |lo͞ok′wôrm′| —*adjective* **1.** Slightly or mildly warm: *Wash wool sweaters in lukewarm water.* **2.** Showing little interest; lacking enthusiasm; indifferent: *a lukewarm greeting; lukewarm applause.*

lull |lŭl| —*verb* **lulled, lulling** **1.** To cause to sleep or rest; soothe: *The mother sang a song to lull the child to sleep.* **2.** To make or become quiet; calm: *His soothing words lulled my fears.*
—*noun, plural* **lulls** A brief period of quiet or calm: *a lull in the storm; a lull in sales.*

lull·a·by |lŭl′ə bī′| —*noun, plural* **lullabies** A soothing song used to lull a child to sleep.

lum·ber¹ |lŭm′bər| —*noun* Timber that has been sawed into boards and planks.
—*verb* **lumbered, lumbering** To cut down and prepare timber for market: *They are lumbering in the north woods.*

lum·ber² |lŭm′bər| —*verb* **lumbered, lumbering** To move or walk in a clumsy and often noisy manner: *Twenty elephants lumbered slowly into the circus arena. The big truck lumbered up the hill.*

lum·ber·jack |lŭm′bər jăk′| —*noun, plural* **lumberjacks** A person whose work is to chop down trees and get the logs to a sawmill.

lu·mi·nous |lo͞o′mə nəs| —*adjective* Giving off light; shining: *a luminous glow of candles; luminous paint; a luminous sign.*

luggage

lumber¹, lumber²
Lumber¹ earlier meant "rough bits of wood" and originally meant "bits and pieces, odds and ends." The origin of **lumber²** is not clear; the word may be related to a Swedish word meaning "to move heavily."

lumberjack

lunar module

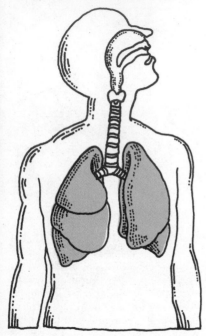
lung

lute

ă	pat	ĕ	pet	î	fierce
ā	pay	ē	be	ŏ	pot
â	care	ĭ	pit	ō	go
ä	father	ī	pie	ô	paw, for
oi	oil	ŭ	cut	zh	vision
o͞o	book	û	fur	ə	ago, item,
o͞o	boot	th	the		pencil, atom,
yo͞o	abuse	th	thin		circus
ou	out	hw	which	ər	butter

lump |lŭmp| —*noun, plural* **lumps** **1.** An irregularly shaped piece of something; a hunk: *a lump of rock; a lump of dough.* **2.** A small cube of sugar: *She takes two lumps in her coffee.* **3.** A swelling or bump that is not usual or normal in a part of the body: *That blow on the head raised quite a lump. The lump on his back was a boil.*
—*adjective* **1.** Formed into lumps: *lump sugar.* **2.** Not divided into parts; whole: *a lump sum.*
—*verb* **lumped, lumping** **1.** To make or become full of lumps: *Melted chocolate lumps when a cold liquid is added to it. Don't lump the pudding by letting it cool too fast.* **2.** To put or consider together in one group or pile: *In a one-room country school the teacher lumps children of all ages in one class.*

lu·nar |lo͞o′nər| —*adjective* **1.** Of, like, or having to do with the moon: *a lunar orbit; a lunar landing.* **2.** Measured by the motions of the moon: *a lunar year.*

lunar module A small space vehicle designed to take astronauts from a spacecraft flying around the moon to the moon's surface and back.

lunch |lŭnch| —*noun, plural* **lunches** **1.** A meal eaten at midday. **2.** The food for this meal.
—*verb* **lunched, lunching** To eat lunch: *We lunched with John and Mary.*

lunch·eon |lŭn′chən| —*noun, plural* **luncheons** A midday meal; lunch.

lunch·room |lŭnch′ro͞om′| or |lŭnch′ro͝om′| —*noun, plural* **lunchrooms** A cafeteria or room in a building, such as a school, where lunch is eaten.

lung |lŭng| —*noun, plural* **lungs** One of two organs for breathing found in the chest of man and most animals. The lungs take in oxygen from the atmosphere and give out carbon dioxide into the atmosphere.

lunge |lŭnj| —*noun, plural* **lunges** A sudden, forceful movement forward: *The fielder made a lunge for the ball.*
—*verb* **lunged, lunging** To make a sudden, forceful movement forward: *The pirate lunged at his foe with his sword. The tackle lunged for the quarterback.*

lure |lo͝or| —*noun, plural* **lures** **1.** Something that attracts: *Candy is a powerful lure for most children. The hope of finding gold was the lure that brought people to California in 1849.* **2.** The power of attracting; appeal: *The explorer couldn't resist the lure of foreign lands. The sea's lure has made many young men decide to become sailors.* **3.** Anything used as bait to attract and catch animals, especially an artificial device used to catch fish.
—*verb* **lured, luring** To attract; tempt: *The bright sun and beautiful weather lured the children outside to play. We used every trick we knew to lure the kitten from its hiding place.*

lush |lŭsh| —*adjective* **lusher, lushest** Thick and plentiful: *lush green lawns; lush grass.*

lus·ter |lŭs′tər| —*noun, plural* **lusters** The brightness of a surface that reflects light; gloss; shine: *the luster of pearls; the luster of well-polished wood.*

lute |lo͞ot| —*noun, plural* **lutes** A stringed musical instrument with a body shaped like half a pear and a long, bent neck. It is played by plucking the strings.
♦ *These sound alike* **lute, loot.**

lux·u·ri·ous | lŭg **zhŏor′** ē əs | or | lŭk **shŏor′** ē əs | —*adjective*
Very rich, comfortable, splendid, or costly: *a luxurious apartment; a luxurious fur coat.*

lux·u·ry | lŭg′ zhə rē | or | lŭk′ shə rē | —*noun, plural* **luxuries**
1. Something that is not considered necessary but that gives great pleasure, enjoyment, or comfort. A luxury is usually something expensive or hard to get: *Diamonds are a luxury that few people can afford.* **2.** A very rich, costly, or comfortable way of living: *They live in luxury. Having been born into wealth, he was used to luxury.*

–ly¹ A suffix that forms adjectives. The suffix "-ly" means:
1. Having the nature of; characteristic of: *sisterly; soldierly.*
2. Appearing or happening at certain intervals: *weekly; hourly; monthly.*

–ly² A suffix that forms adverbs. The suffix "-ly" means: **1.** In a given manner: *weakly; loudly.* **2.** At certain intervals: *weekly; hourly.*

lye | lī | —*noun* A very strong solution used in making soaps, detergents, and cleaning fluids. Lye is made by allowing water to wash through wood ashes.
♦ *These sound alike* **lye, lie.**

ly·ing¹ | lī′ ĭng | The present participle of the verb **lie** (to be in a resting position): *Pat is lying on her side near the fireplace.*

ly·ing² | lī′ ĭng | The present participle of the verb **lie** (to tell a lie or lies): *Jim is lying when he says he doesn't know who ate the cake.*

lymph | lĭmf | —*noun* A clear liquid in the tissues of the body. Lymph brings nourishment to the tissues and returns waste matter to the bloodstream.

lynx | lĭngks | —*noun, plural* **lynxes** A wild cat with thick, soft fur. The lynx has a short tail and tufts of hair on its ears.

lynx

lyre | līr | —*noun, plural* **lyres** An ancient stringed instrument like a small harp.

lyr·ic | lĭr′ ĭk | —*adjective* Expressing deep feelings; very emotional: *lyric descriptions of the simple country life; a lyric outburst of song.* Another form of this word is **lyrical.**
—*noun, plural* **lyrics 1.** A short poem expressing the poet's personal feelings and thoughts. **2. lyrics** The words of a song.

lyr·i·cal | lĭr′ ĭ kəl | A form of the adjective **lyric.**

lyre

Mm

ʍ	**Phoenician** — The letter *M* comes originally from a Phoenician symbol named *mēm*, meaning "water," in use about 3,000 years ago.
M	**Greek** — The Greeks borrowed the symbol from the Phoenicians and changed its form. They also changed its name to *mu*.
M	**Roman** — The Romans took the letter and adapted it for carving into stone. This became the model for our modern printed capital *M*.
m	**Medieval** — The hand-written form of about 1,200 years ago became the basis of the modern small letter.
Mm	**Modern** — The modern capital and small letters are based on the Roman capital and later hand-written forms.

macaw

m or **M** |ĕm| —*noun, plural* **m's** or **M's** The thirteenth letter of the English alphabet.

Ma'am |măm| A contraction of "Madam." *Ma'am* is used when speaking to a woman: *Good morning, Ma'am.*

mac·a·ro·ni |măk′ə rō′nē| —*noun* A food made of dried flour paste and shaped into hollow tubes. Macaroni is boiled and is usually served with a sauce of cheese or tomatoes.
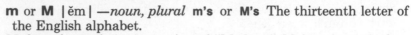

ma·caw |mə kô′| —*noun, plural* **macaws** A large, brightly colored tropical American parrot with a long tail.

ma·chine |mə shēn′| —*noun, plural* **machines** **1.** A device that uses energy to do a job. A machine is made of wheels, gears, blades, or other parts put together in a particular way. Some common machines are an automobile, a bicycle, a vacuum cleaner, and a washing machine. **2.** A simple device that helps make work easier. Some simple machines are a wheel, a pulley, a lever, a screw, and an inclined plane.

machine gun A rifle that fires fast and keeps firing as long as the trigger is pressed.

ma·chin·er·y |mə shē′nə rē| —*noun* **1.** Machines: *The company ordered new machinery for the factory.* **2.** The parts of a machine: *He repaired and cleaned the clock's machinery.*

mack·er·el |măk′ər əl| or |măk′rəl| —*noun, plural* **mackerel** or **mackerels** An ocean fish that is often used as food.

ma·cron |mā′krŏn′| or |mā′krən| —*noun, plural* **macrons** A mark (ˉ) placed over a vowel in a pronunciation to show that the vowel is long. In the pronunciation of the word "make" (māk), the macron is placed over the "a."

mad |măd| —*adjective* **madder, maddest** **1.** Having a sick mind; insane; crazy: *The poor mad woman wandered about talking to herself.* **2.** Very annoyed; angry: *He is mad at us for not inviting him.* **3.** Very foolish; not sensible: *They have a mad plan to sneak aboard a rocket to the moon.* **4.** Very interested and enthusiastic: *He is mad about basketball.* **5.** Very confused and excited: *There was a mad scramble for ice cream.* **6.** Having rabies: *The mad dog had to be killed.*

Mad·am |măd′əm| —*noun, plural* **Madams** A word used as a polite way of addressing a woman in writing or speech.

made |mād| The past tense and past participle of the verb

ă	pat	ĕ	pet	î	fierce
ā	pay	ē	be	ŏ	pot
â	care	ĭ	pit	ō	go
ä	father	ī	pie	ô	paw, for
oi	oil	ŭ	cut	zh	vision
o͝o	book	û	fur	ə	ago, item,
o͞o	boot	*th*	the		pencil, atom,
yo͞o	abuse	th	thin		circus
ou	out	hw	which	ər	butter

make: *She made a dress for herself. He has made many drawings of his house.*

♦ *These sound alike* **made, maid.**

made-up |mād′ ŭp′| —*adjective* Not real; invented; imaginary: *She told a made-up story about a talking giraffe.*

Mad·i·son |măd′ĭ sən| The capital of Wisconsin.

mag·a·zine |măg′ə zēn′| or |măg′ə zēn′| —*noun, plural* **magazines** A printed publication that comes out regularly and has articles, stories, and often pictures. A magazine usually has paper covers and pages that are fastened together.

mag·got |măg′ət| —*noun, plural* **maggots** The larva of a fly. It has a soft, thick body and looks something like a worm.

mag·ic |măj′ĭk| —*noun* **1.** The art of using spells, charms, and special powers to make changes in nature or in people and in their lives; witchcraft: *The fairy godmother used magic to turn the pumpkin into a coach.* **2.** The art of entertaining people with tricks that make it seem that impossible things are happening: *Through magic, he made the coins disappear.*
—*adjective* Of, done by, or using magic: *a magic wand; a magic show; a magic disappearance.*

mag·i·cal |măj′ĭ kəl| —*adjective* Of or made by magic: *The wizard cast a magical spell that changed the mice into horses.*

ma·gi·cian |mə jĭsh′ən| —*noun, plural* **magicians** **1.** An entertainer who does magic tricks. **2.** Someone who is supposed to have real magic powers; wizard.

magician

mag·ne·si·um |măg nē′zē əm| or |măg nē′zhəm| —*noun* A metal that is light, silver-white, and fairly hard. Magnesium is used in many alloys and in fireworks. Magnesium is one of the chemical elements.

mag·net |măg′nĭt| —*noun, plural* **magnets** **1.** A piece of metal or rock that attracts iron, steel, and some other substances. Magnets are used in machines and compasses. They also make interesting toys. **2.** Someone or something that attracts: *The amusement park was a magnet for the young people.*

mag·net·ic |măg nĕt′ĭk| —*adjective* **1.** Having the power to draw iron and steel to it: *a magnetic rock; a magnetic board.* **2.** Of or having to do with the earth's magnetic pole: *magnetic north.*

magnetic field The area around a magnet in which its power of attraction can be felt.

magnetic pole **1.** Either of the two points or areas at the ends of a magnet where the magnetic field is strongest. **2.** Often **Magnetic Pole** Either of two points on the surface of the earth where the earth's magnetic field is strongest. The magnetic poles are near the geographical poles, but not in the exact same spots. A compass needle anywhere on earth points to the North Magnetic Pole.

mag·net·ism |măg′nĭ tĭz′əm| —*noun* **1.** The power to attract iron, steel, and some other substances and to produce a magnetic field. Some metals and all electric currents show magnetism. The earth itself also has magnetism. **2.** An unusual power to attract or charm: *the magnetism of the actor's personality.*

mag·ne·tize |măg′nĭ tīz′| —*verb* **magnetized, magnetizing** To cause to be magnetic: *The magnet magnetized the pins that it held.*

mag·nif·i·cence |măg nĭf′ĭ səns| —*noun* Great beauty or excellence; splendor: *The magnificence of the great hall amazed us.*

mag·nif·i·cent |măg nĭf′ĭ sənt| —*adjective* **1.** Very grand and

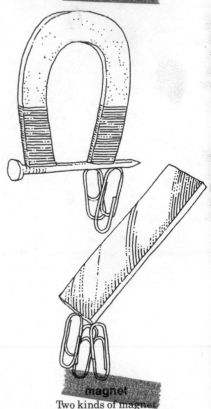
magnet
Two kinds of magnet

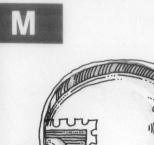

magnifying glass

magpie

fine; large and beautiful; splendid: *a magnificent palace.*
2. Outstanding; excellent: *She has a magnificent voice.*

mag·ni·fy |mǎg′nə fī′| —*verb* **magnified, magnifying, magnifies**
1. To make seem greater or more important; exaggerate: *She likes to magnify her problems.* **2.** To make an object appear larger than it really is; enlarge: *The microscope magnified the bacteria so that they could be seen clearly.*

mag·ni·fy·ing glass |mǎg′nə fī′ĭng| A lens that makes things look bigger.

mag·ni·tude |mǎg′nǐ tōōd′| or |mǎg′nǐ tyōōd′| —*noun* **1.** The condition of being great in size or extent: *Scientists have devices that can measure the magnitude of an earthquake.* **2.** Importance; significance: *Newspapers use big headlines for stories of great magnitude.*

mag·no·lia |mǎg nōl′yə| or |mǎg nō′lē ə| —*noun, plural* **magnolias** A tree or shrub with large, showy flowers that are usually white or pink.

mag·pie |mǎg′pī′| —*noun, plural* **magpies** A noisy black and white bird with a long tail. Magpies are related to the crows and jays.

ma·hog·a·ny |mə hǒg′ə nē| —*noun* **1.** The hard, reddish-brown wood of a tropical American tree. Mahogany is often used to make furniture. **2.** The tree from which this wood comes. **3.** A dark reddish-brown color. ◊ The noun **mahogany** can be used as an adjective for things made of mahogany: *a mahogany table.*
—*adjective* Reddish brown: *a mahogany stain for the pine shelves.*

maid |mād| —*noun, plural* **maids** **1.** A girl or woman who has not married; maiden. **2.** A female servant.
♦ *These sound alike* **maid, made.**

maid·en |mād′n| —*noun, plural* **maidens** A girl or woman who has not married.
—*adjective* **1.** Of or suited to a maiden: *Her maiden shyness charmed him.* **2.** Never having married: *an elderly maiden aunt.*
3. First; earliest: *a ship's maiden voyage; a horse's maiden race.*

maiden name The family name that a woman had before she married: *Mrs. Miller still uses her maiden name, Smith, in business.*

maid of honor —*plural* **maids of honor** A woman friend that is not married, chosen by a bride to walk and stand by her side before and after a wedding ceremony.

mail¹ |māl| —*noun, plural* **mails** **1.** Letters, packages, and other items sent and received through a postal system: *Today's mail included two letters and a magazine.* **2.** The system by which letters and packages are sent: *We will answer your questions by mail, not by telephone.*
—*verb* **mailed, mailing** To send by a postal system: *I mailed the letter yesterday.*
♦ *These sound alike* **mail, male.**

mail² |māl| —*noun* Armor made of connected metal rings, chain loops, or scales. Mail was worn in battle for protection against spears and arrows.
♦ *These sound alike* **mail, male.**

mail·box |māl′bǒks′| —*noun, plural* **mailboxes** **1.** A public container in which to place letters being sent by mail. **2.** A private container for mail delivered to a home or business.

mail·man |māl′mǎn′| —*noun, plural* **mailmen** A person who carries and delivers mail; postman.

---

mail¹, mail²

Mail¹ originally meant "a bag for carrying letters." It came from an old French word meaning "bag, pouch." **Mail²** comes from a Latin word that meant "spot, mesh." The word traveled through French, in which it meant "mesh, network," before it appeared in English.

ǎ	pat	ě	pet	î	fierce
ā	pay	ē	be	ŏ	pot
â	care	ĭ	pit	ō	go
ä	father	ī	pie	ô	paw, for
oi	oil	ŭ	cut	zh	vision
ōō	book	û	fur	ə	ago, item,
ōō	boot	th	the		pencil, atom,
yōō	abuse	th	thin		circus
ou	out	hw	which	ər	butter

main |mān| —*adjective* Most important; chief; principal: *Can you summarize the main points of the chapter? Steak was the main course served at the dinner.*
—*noun, plural* **mains** A large pipe or cable. Mains carry water, oil, gas, or electricity to smaller pipes or cables.
♦ *These sound alike* **main, mane.**
  Idiom **in the main** For the most part; on the whole: *We had some problems, but in the main all went well.*

Maine |mān| A state in the northeastern United States. The capital of Maine is Augusta.

main·land |mān′lănd′| or |mān′lənd| —*noun, plural* **mainlands** The main part of a country, territory, or continent, not including islands off the coast: *Hawaii is not connected to the mainland of the United States.*

main·ly |mān′lē| —*adverb* For the most part; chiefly: *His paintings are mainly of city scenes.*

main·tain |mān tān′| —*verb* **maintained, maintaining** **1.** To keep up; continue with: *It is hard to maintain speed going up a hill on a bicycle.* **2.** To keep in good condition: *The road crew maintains the highways.* **3.** To take care of; pay the expenses of; support: *He maintains a large family. They maintain a house in the city and one in the country.* **4.** To say firmly; declare; insist: *The prisoner maintained that he did not commit the crime.*

main·te·nance |mān′tə nəns| —*noun* **1.** The act of maintaining or taking care of: *the maintenance of roads; the maintenance of a family.* **2.** A means of support; a bare living: *The shop provides a small maintenance for its owner.*

maize |māz| —*noun* The corn plant, or its ears or kernels.
♦ *These sound alike* **maize, maze.**

ma·jes·tic |mə jĕs′tĭk| —*adjective* Full of majesty; dignified and noble: *The queen gave a majestic wave of her hand. A majestic oak grew in the yard.*

maj·es·ty |măj′ĭ stē| —*noun, plural* **majesties** **1.** The power and dignity of a king or queen. **2.** A stately, grand appearance; splendor: *the majesty of the mountains.* **3.** **Majesty** A title of honor used when speaking or writing to or about a king, queen, or other monarch: *His Majesty, the King; Your Majesty.*

ma·jor |mā′jər| —*adjective* **1.** Large and important: *Speeding is a major cause of car accidents. His cold got worse and became a major illness.* **2.** Larger or largest; most important: *The major part of his vacation was spent in Texas.*
—*noun, plural* **majors** An officer in the Army, Air Force, or Marine Corps who ranks above a captain.

ma·jor·i·ty |mə jôr′ĭ tē| or |mə jŏr′ĭ tē| —*noun, plural* **majorities** **1.** More than half; the greater number: *The majority of the class liked the new teacher.* **2.** The difference between a larger number and a smaller number of votes cast: *The Senator got 200,000 votes and his opponent got 180,000, so the Senator won with a majority of 20,000 votes.*

make |māk| —*verb* **made, making** **1.** To bring into being; put together; create: *She made a new dress. He made a table out of a barrel. Let's make some cookies.* **2.** To bring about; cause to exist or appear: *Please don't make a fuss. The children are making a lot of noise.* **3.** To cause to be or feel a certain way: *That song makes me sad. Slicing onions makes me cry. The beard makes him look older.* **4.** To force; compel: *Don't make me take that medicine.*

maize

Maine
The name **Maine** has two possible origins. The more likely is that it is named after the province of Maine in France. The other is that it comes from an older English phrase that meant "mainland."

5. To perform; carry out: *He made an attempt to save the drowning man. They want to make war.* **6.** To serve as; be useful for: *The fancy jar will make a good bank for my little sister. He makes a fine baseball coach.* **7.** To get for oneself; gain; earn: *He made ten dollars on the sale of lemonade.* **8.** To count for the same as; amount to; equal: *Two halves make a whole. Five pennies make a nickel.* **9.** To put into good order; prepare for use: *He made his bed.* **10.** To manage to achieve; get to be on: *Will she make the tennis team this year?* **11.** To get to; reach: *Do we have time to make the train?* **12.** To allow for; provide: *Can you make room for one more person?* **13.** To think: *What do you make of his letter?* **14.** To be responsible for the success of: *The scenery makes that movie.*

Phrasal verbs **make away with 1.** To carry off; steal: *The thieves made away with all the silver.* **2.** To kill; destroy: *The tyrant made away with his enemies.* **make out 1.** To see or hear clearly; recognize: *Can you make out the sign ahead? I cannot make out the lyrics of the song.* **2.** To write out; fill in: *Make out a list of the people you want to invite.* **3.** To get along; succeed: *How did you make out in your new class?* **make up 1.** To create out of one's imagination; invent: *He made up a story about meeting a gorilla in his back yard.* **2.** To supply in exchange for a fault, lack, or error: *I'll make up the difference between what it costs and the money you have.* **3.** To settle a quarrel: *Let's shake hands and make up.* **4.** To put make-up on: *The actor begins to make up an hour before the show starts.* **5.** To settle; decide: *Can you make up your mind what to eat?* **6.** To compose; form: *It is mostly students who make up the orchestra.*

—noun, plural **makes 1.** A style or manner in which something is designed: *a machine of a very simple make.* **2.** A particular kind; brand: *A famous make of shirt is on sale.*

Idiom **make do** To manage with less than is needed: *He made do with bread and tea for breakfast.*

make-be·lieve | māk′ bĭ lēv′ | *—noun* Imagination; fiction: *Toys come to life in the world of make-believe.*

—adjective Not existing in reality; imaginary; pretended: *She likes to invite her make-believe playmate to a make-believe party.*

make-up or **make·up** | māk′ ŭp′ | *—noun, plural* **make-ups** or **makeups 1.** The way something is put together or arranged; composition: *The make-up of this year's ball team has changed, since there are more girls on it.* **2.** Lipstick, rouge, and other cosmetics: *The girls like to put on their mother's make-up.*

ma·lar·i·a | mə lâr′ē ə | *—noun* An infectious disease that causes spells of chills, fever, and sweating. Malaria is carried from person to person by a certain kind of mosquito.

male | māl | *—adjective* **1.** Of or belonging to the sex that can fertilize eggs and become fathers: *A rooster is a male chicken.* **2.** Of or being a man or boy: *a male voice; a male student.*

—noun, plural **males** A male person or animal: *Boys and men are males. Bulls and roosters are males.*

♦ *These sound alike* **male, mail.**

mal·ice | măl′ ĭs | *—noun* The desire to hurt others or see them suffer; ill will; spite: *She tried to bear no malice toward the girl who beat her in the race.*

ma·li·cious | mə lĭsh′ əs | *—adjective* **1.** Wanting to hurt others or see them suffer; full of spite: *The malicious boy would get his*

ă	pat	ĕ	pet	î	fierce
ā	pay	ē	be	ŏ	pot
â	care	ĭ	pit	ō	go
ä	father	ī	pie	ô	paw, for

oi	oil	ŭ	cut	zh	vision
ŏŏ	book	û	fur	ə	ago, item,
ōō	boot	*th*	the		pencil, atom,
yōō	abuse	th	thin		circus
ou	out	hw	which	ər	butter

brother into trouble and then pretend to be innocent. **2.** Causing harm or suffering to others: *a malicious lie.*

mal·lard |**măl′**ərd| —*noun, plural* **mallards** A wild duck. The male has a shiny green head and neck.

mal·let |**măl′**ĭt| —*noun, plural* **mallets** **1.** A hammer with a wooden head and a short handle. **2.** A sports tool with a wooden head and a long handle. Mallets are used in the game of croquet.

mal·nu·tri·tion |măl′nōō **trĭsh′**ən| or |măl′nyōō **trĭsh′**ən| —*noun* A weakened condition that comes from eating too little food or the wrong kinds of food.

malt |môlt| —*noun, plural* **malts** Barley or other grain that has been soaked until it sprouts and then dried. Malt is used in making beer, ale, and other drinks.

malt·ed milk |môl′tĭd| A drink made of milk, a powder containing malt, flavoring, and sometimes ice cream.

ma·ma or **mam·ma** |**mä′**mə| or |mə **mä′**| —*noun, plural* **mamas** or **mammas** Mother: *She tells her mama everything.*

mam·mal |**măm′**əl| —*noun, plural* **mammals** Any of a group of animals that have hair or fur on their bodies. Female mammals have special glands that produce milk to feed their young. Cats, dogs, cows, elephants, mice, bats, whales, and human beings are all mammals.

mam·moth |**măm′**əth| —*noun, plural* **mammoths** An elephant that lived thousands of years ago. It had long tusks and thick, shaggy hair.
—*adjective* Very large; huge; gigantic: *Cleaning up after the party was a mammoth job.*

man |măn| —*noun, plural* **men** **1.** A fully grown male human being: *A boy grows up to be a man.* **2.** Human beings in general: *Man has built great civilizations.* **3.** Any human being; person; individual: *A man must eat to live.* **4.** A male worker or servant: *a crew of ten men.* **5.** A piece used in chess, checkers, or other board games.
—*verb* **manned, manning** **1.** To take one's post at; operate or run: *She is supposed to man the telephones.* **2.** To supply with people to do work: *The captain manned his ship with a new crew.*

man·age |**măn′**ĭj| —*verb* **managed, managing** **1.** To control; run; direct: *Who will manage the store when you are away? That horse is hard to manage.* **2.** To succeed with a special effort; be able with difficulty: *We managed to get along on less money.*

man·age·ment |**măn′**ĭj mənt| —*noun, plural* **managements** **1.** The act of managing; control: *Careful management of his allowance left him money for a baseball bat.* **2.** The people in charge of a business or organization; supervisors: *The company's management decided to build a new factory.*

man·a·ger |**măn′**ĭ jər| —*noun, plural* **managers** A person who manages a business, a department of a business, or a sports team: *a sales manager; a baseball manager.*

man·a·tee |**măn′**ə tē′| —*noun, plural* **manatees** A water animal that lives in rivers and bays along the tropical Atlantic Ocean coast. It has two front flippers and a broad tail that looks like a paddle.

man·do·lin |**măn′**dl ĭn′| or |măn′dl **ĭn′**| —*noun, plural* **mandolins** A stringed musical instrument that has a pear-shaped body and a long neck. Most mandolins have four pairs of metal strings.

mallard

mammoth

mandolin

mane
Of a horse (*above*) and a lion (*below*)

mane | mān | —*noun, plural* **manes** The long hair that grows from the neck and head of certain animals. Horses and male lions have manes.
♦ *These sound alike* **mane, main.**

ma·neu·ver | mə nōo′ vər | or | mə nyōo′ vər | —*noun, plural* **maneuvers** **1.** A planned movement carried out by soldiers, ships, or aircraft: *The general ordered his troops to surround the enemy, and this maneuver proved successful.* **2.** A clever act; skillful trick: *The lawyer's maneuvers helped his client win his freedom.*
—*verb* **maneuvered, maneuvering** **1.** To move or guide in a clever, planned way: *The ship maneuvered to avoid the icebergs. He maneuvered his car along the steep road.* **2.** To use clever tricks: *He maneuvered to get himself elected chairman.*

man·ga·nese | măng′ gə nēz′ | or | măng′ gə nēs′ | —*noun* A gray, brittle metal used in steel alloys to improve their strength. Manganese is a chemical element.

man·ger | mān′ jər | —*noun, plural* **mangers** An open box or trough to hold food for horses or cattle.

man·go | măng′ gō | —*noun, plural* **mangoes** or **mangos** A tropical fruit with a smooth rind and sweet, juicy, yellow-orange flesh.

man·grove | măn′ grōv′ | or | măng′ grōv′ | —*noun, plural* **mangroves** A tropical tree or shrub that has many roots growing above the ground. Mangroves form dense thickets in marshes and along shores.

man·gy | mān′ jē | —*adjective* **mangier, mangiest** Having bare or dirty spots; shabby: *a mangy old blanket.*

man·hole | măn′ hōl′ | —*noun, plural* **manholes** A hole in the street with a cover that can be removed. Workmen go down manholes to repair and inspect sewers, pipes, electrical lines, and other equipment.

man·hood | măn′ hŏod′ | —*noun* **1.** The time or condition of being a grown man: *He plans to do many things when he reaches manhood.* **2.** The qualities that are expected of an adult man; courage and strength: *The young Indian braves had to prove their manhood by bringing home deer for food.*

ma·ni·ac | mā′ nē ăk′ | —*noun, plural* **maniacs** An insane or violent person.

man·i·cure | măn′ ĭ kyŏor′ | —*noun, plural* **manicures** A cleaning and shaping of the fingernails. Often, a manicure also includes polishing the nails.
—*verb* **manicured, manicuring** To groom the fingernails by cleaning and shaping: *She manicures her own nails.*

ma·nip·u·late | mə nĭp′ yə lāt′ | —*verb* **manipulated, manipulating** **1.** To use the hands on something so as to achieve some purpose; handle: *He manipulated the dials on the air conditioner, and soon the room became cooler.* **2.** To influence or persuade without seeming to do so; get what one wants out of someone cleverly: *By pretending to be angry, Ann manipulated us into feeling sorry for her and taking her to the movies.*

Man·i·to·ba | măn′ ĭ tō′ bə | A province in south-central Canada. The capital of Manitoba is Winnipeg.

man·kind | măn′ kīnd′ | or | măn′ kīnd′ | —*noun* Human beings as a group: *All mankind would enjoy peace.*

man-made | măn′ mād′ | —*adjective* Created by people, not by nature; artificial: *Nylon is a man-made fiber.*

Manitoba
The origin of the name **Manitoba** is not known for certain. It probably comes from an Indian word that means "the strait of the spirit."

ă	pat	ĕ	pet	î	fierce		
ā	pay	ē	be	ŏ	pot		
â	care	ĭ	pit	ō	go		
ä	father	ī	pie	ô	paw, for		
oi	oil	ŭ	cut	zh	vision		
ōo	book	û	fur	ə	ago, item,		
ōo	boot	*th*	the		pencil, atom,		
yōo	abuse	th	thin		circus		
ou	out	hw	which	ər	butter		

man·ner | măn′ər | —*noun, plural* **manners 1.** A way or style of doing things: *He washed his hands in the usual manner, but he could not remove the ink. He dresses in a sloppy manner.* **2.** A way of behaving; style of acting: *Her pleasant manner made us like her at once.* **3. manners** Behavior that is considered proper; social conduct: *He is careful of his manners when he visits his aunt.*
♦ *These sound alike* **manner, manor.**

man-of-war | măn′ə wôr′ | or | măn′əv wôr′ | —*noun, plural* **men-of-war 1.** A sea creature, the **Portuguese man-of-war. 2.** A warship used in former times.

man·or | măn′ər | —*noun, plural* **manors 1.** The land and buildings belonging to a lord in the Middle Ages. Peasants worked on small farms on a manor and paid the lord by doing jobs for him and giving him part of their crops. The lord lived in a house called a *manor house.* **2.** Any large estate. **3.** The large main house of an estate.
♦ *These sound alike* **manor, manner.**

manor

man·sion | măn′shən | —*noun, plural* **mansions** A large, fine house.

man·slaugh·ter | măn′slô′tər | —*noun, plural* **manslaughters** The killing of a person, especially when it is accidental but still unlawful.

man·tel | măn′tl | —*noun, plural* **mantels** The shelf above a fireplace.

man·tel·piece | măn′tl pēs′ | —*noun, plural* **mantelpieces** The shelf above a fireplace.

man·tid | măn′tĭd | —*noun, plural* **mantids** An insect, the **mantis.**

mansion

man·tis | măn′tĭs | —*noun, plural* **mantises** A large insect that looks something like a grasshopper. It seizes and feeds on other insects. The mantis holds its front legs folded up as if praying. For that reason, it is often called a *praying mantis.*

man·u·al | măn′yōō əl | —*adjective* **1.** Of, by, or using the hands: *The airplane has both automatic and manual controls. Laying bricks is manual labor.* **2.** Not run by electricity: *a manual typewriter.*
—*noun, plural* **manuals** A small book of instructions; handbook: *a Boy Scout manual; a manual on repairing furniture.*

man·u·fac·ture | măn′yə făk′chər | —*verb* **manufactured, manufacturing 1.** To make a product in large quantities, usually by using machinery: *The company manufactures cars and trucks. The plant manufactures iron ore into steel.* **2.** To make up; think up; invent: *He manufactured clues to throw the police off his trail.*
—*noun, plural* **manufactures 1.** The making of goods in large quantities: *Their business is the manufacture of toys.* **2.** A product made in a factory: *Bricks and automobiles are the principal manufactures of the area.*

ma·nure | mə nŏŏr′ | or | mə nyŏŏr′ | —*noun, plural* **manures** Animal wastes used to enrich the soil so that plants will grow well.

man·u·script | măn′yə skrĭpt′ | —*noun, plural* **manuscripts** A book written by hand or by typewriter. Often a writer sends a manuscript to a publisher, who makes it into a printed book. In earlier days, before printing, all books were manuscripts.

man·y | měn′ē | —*adjective* **more, most** A large number of; a lot of: *Many children like ice cream.*

—noun (Used with a plural verb.) A large number: *Many of us were at the party.*

—pronoun A large number of people or things: *Many were invited, but few came.*

map | map | —*noun, plural* **maps** A drawing or chart that shows where things are. A map of the earth's surface shows countries, cities, oceans, lakes, rivers, mountains, and other features. A map may show a large country or a small neighborhood. Maps are also made of the moon, of planets, and of the sky.
—verb **mapped, mapping** **1.** To make a map or maps of: *The explorers mapped the new places they had seen. They are trying to map the ocean floor.* **2.** To figure out in detail: *The boys mapped out a plan to start a physical education center.*

ma·ple | mā′ pəl | —*noun, plural* **maples** **1.** A tree that has broad leaves with deep notches. The seeds grow in pairs and have narrow, thin parts that look like wings. There are several kinds of maples. The sweet sap of one kind is boiled to make syrup and sugar. **2.** The hard wood of a maple. It is often used to make furniture.

maple
Above: Tree
Below: Leaf and seeds

mar·a·thon | măr′ ə thŏn′ | —*noun, plural* **marathons** **1.** A race for runners over a distance of 26 miles, 385 yards, which equals about 42 kilometers. **2.** Any very long contest, performance, or show: *a dance marathon; a fund-raising marathon on public television.*

mar·ble | mär′ bəl | —*noun, plural* **marbles** **1.** A kind of hard stone that is often white with streaks of color through it. It can be carved into beautiful shapes and is used for statues, buildings, and table tops. **2.** A little glass ball, often brightly colored, used in games. **3.** **marbles** (Used with a singular verb.) Any of several games played with these balls. In the most common game, players shoot their marbles with a flick of the finger to try to knock other marbles out of a circle.

march | märch | —*verb* **marched, marching** **1.** To walk with regular steps in an orderly group, as soldiers do: *The police officers joined the parade and marched down the street to the beat of drums. He marched his soldiers across the field and back again.* **2.** To walk in a steady, determined way: *He marched up to the blackboard and wrote what he hoped was the right answer.* **3.** To move or advance in a steady way: *The days marched on.*
—noun, plural **marches** **1.** The act of marching: *The army's march was stopped by an enemy attack.* **2.** Forward movement: *the march of time.* **3.** A piece of music with a strong beat that people can march to.

March | märch | —*noun, plural* **Marches** The third month of the year, after February and before April. March has 31 days.

mare | mâr | —*noun, plural* **mares** A female horse, zebra, or related animal.

mar·ga·rine | mär′ jər ĭn | or | mär′ jə rēn′ | —*noun, plural* **margarines** A food used as a substitute for butter. Margarine is made of vegetable oils and colorings. Another name for margarine is **oleomargarine.**

mar·gin | mär′ jĭn | —*noun, plural* **margins** **1.** The space between the edge of a paper and the printing on the page. This dictionary has illustrations in the margins. **2.** An extra amount beyond what is needed: *We allowed ourselves a margin of an hour to catch the plane in case the roads were crowded.*

mar·i·gold | măr′ ĭ gōld′ | or | mâr′ ĭ gōld′ | —*noun, plural*

marigold

ă	pat	ĕ	pet	î	fierce
ā	pay	ē	be	ŏ	pot
â	care	ĭ	pit	ō	go
ä	father	ī	pie	ô	paw, for
oi	oil	ŭ	cut	zh	vision
ōō	book	û	fur	ə	ago, item,
ōō	boot	*th*	the		pencil, atom,
yōō	abuse	th	thin		circus
ou	out	hw	which	ər	butter

marigolds A garden plant that has orange, yellow, or reddish flowers.

ma·rine |mə rēn′| —*adjective* **1.** Of or living in the sea: *He studies lobsters, starfish, and other marine animals.* **2.** Of ships and shipping: *The store sells ropes, compasses, sails, and other marine supplies.*
—*noun, plural* **marines** Often **Marine** A member of the U.S. Marine Corps.

Marine Corps A branch of the U.S. armed forces whose troops are specially trained and equipped to be sent into battle by ship or aircraft. Marines are trained to take part in landing operations.

mar·i·o·nette |măr′ē ə nĕt′| —*noun, plural* **marionettes** A puppet or doll that has strings that someone can work to make it move and seem alive.

Mar·i·time Provinces |măr′ĭ tīm′| Three provinces on the Atlantic coast of Canada. The Maritime Provinces are Nova Scotia, New Brunswick, and Prince Edward Island.

mar·jo·ram |măr′jər əm| —*noun* A plant with leaves that have a spicy smell and taste. They are used as flavoring.

mark |märk| —*noun, plural* **marks** **1.** A scratch, stain, dent, ring, or other flaw that changes a surface's appearance: *The wet glass left a mark on the table top.* **2.** A line, dot, check, or symbol made to show something: *Make a mark next to the names of those who have paid their dues. Commas, periods, and apostrophes are punctuation marks.* **3.** Anything used to show a position or point reached: *We used our shirts as marks at the boundaries of the playing field.* **4.** A sign; indication: *His questions were a mark of intelligence.* **5.** Something that is aimed at; target or goal: *The arrow found its mark. Her work falls short of the mark.* **6.** A letter or number that shows how well one has done on a test or in a class: *Her marks for the year were all A's and B's.*
—*verb* **marked, marking** **1.** To make a mark on: *He marked the trees with his knife.* **2.** To show by making or being a mark: *She marked the path with colored pebbles. The fence marks the border of our property.* **3.** To put grades on: *The teacher spent the evening marking papers.* **4.** To be a feature of; show; indicate: *The falling leaves mark the beginning of autumn.*

Phrasal verbs **mark down** To lower in price: *The store marked down the dresses from $50.00 to $35.00.* **mark off** To show the limits or boundaries of: *He marked off the playing field with chalk.*

Idiom **make (one's) mark** To become famous; be a success: *He wants to make his mark in acting.*

mark·er |mär′kər| —*noun, plural* **markers** A pen or other device used to put marks on things: *We wrote our names on our lockers with green markers.*

mar·ket |mär′kĭt| —*noun, plural* **markets** **1.** A public place for buying and selling goods: *The farmers bring their fruits and vegetables to market.* **2.** A store: *a fish market.* **3.** A particular type or group of buyers: *Many records are designed mainly for the teen-age market.*
—*verb* **marketed, marketing** **1.** To sell or offer to sell: *She markets her pottery through two stores. The stores market her pottery.* **2.** To go shopping for food: *The whole family markets on Saturdays.*

mark·ing |mär′kĭng| —*noun, plural* **markings** A mark or marks: *He left markings along the trail for others to follow. The bird had red markings on its wings.*

marionette

mar·ma·lade | mär′mə lād′ | —*noun, plural* **marmalades** A jam made from sugar and the pulp and rind of fruits.

mar·mot | mär′mət | —*noun, plural* **marmots** A burrowing animal with short legs and brownish fur. The woodchuck is a kind of marmot.

ma·roon¹ | mə rōōn′ | —*verb* **marooned, marooning** To leave a person helpless and alone on a deserted shore or island; strand: *The shipwreck marooned him on a rocky coast.*

ma·roon² | mə rōōn′ | —*noun, plural* **maroons** A dark purplish red.
—*adjective* Dark purplish red: *a maroon velvet skirt.*

mar·quis | mär′kwĭs | or | mär kē′ | —*noun, plural* **marquis** or **marquises** A nobleman above the rank of earl or count and below the rank of duke.

mar·riage | măr′ĭj | —*noun, plural* **marriages** 1. The condition of being united as husband and wife: *They have a happy marriage.* 2. The act or ceremony that unites people as husband and wife; wedding: *The minister will perform two marriages today.*

mar·ried | măr′ēd | —*adjective* 1. Having a husband or wife: *a married woman; a married man.* 2. United by marriage: *a married couple.* 3. Of or from marriage: *her married name.*

mar·row | măr′ō | —*noun, plural* **marrows** The soft material inside of bones.

mar·ry | măr′ē | —*verb* **married, marrying, marries** 1. To take as husband or wife: *Susan married John. They will marry next month.* 2. To unite as husband and wife: *The rabbi married them at home.*

Mars | märz | A planet of our solar system. It is the fourth in distance from the sun. Mars has two small moons.

marsh | märsh | —*noun, plural* **marshes** An area of low, wet land; swamp.

mar·shal | mär′shəl | —*noun, plural* **marshals** 1. A kind of police officer who works for the federal government. 2. The head of a police or fire department. 3. A person in charge of a parade or a ceremony.
—*verb* **marshaled, marshaling** To place in proper order; organize; arrange: *We marshaled our best brains to put a man on the moon.*
♦ *These sound alike* **marshal, martial.**

marsh·mal·low | märsh′mĕl′ō | or | märsh′măl′ō | —*noun, plural* **marshmallows** A soft, white candy.

mar·su·pi·al | mär sōō′pē əl | —*noun, plural* **marsupials** One of a group of animals that live mostly in Australia. The females have a pouch on the outside of the body. The newborn young are carried and nursed in this pouch. Kangaroos and opossums are marsupials.

mar·tial | mär′shəl | —*adjective* Of or for war; warlike: *martial arts; martial music.*
♦ *These sound alike* **martial, marshal.**

Mar·tian | mär′shən | —*adjective* Of the planet Mars: *the Martian landscape.*
—*noun, plural* **Martians** A creature that is supposed to live on Mars.

mar·tin | mär′tn | —*noun, plural* **martins** A bird related to the swallows. It has dark feathers and a forked tail.

mar·tyr | mär′tər | —*noun, plural* **martyrs** A person who chooses to die or be tortured rather than give up a religion or belief.

mar·vel | mär′vəl | —*noun, plural* **marvels** Someone or

---

maroon¹, maroon²

Maroon¹ comes from a Spanish word meaning "wild." The word came to mean "to escape into the wilds" and later "to put someone in the wilds" before it took on its current meaning. **Maroon²** simply comes from a French word meaning "chestnut."

ă	pat	ĕ	pet	î	fierce
ā	pay	ē	be	ŏ	pot
â	care	ĭ	pit	ō	go
ä	father	ī	pie	ô	paw, for

oi	oil	ŭ	cut	zh	vision
ōō	book	û	fur	ə	ago, item,
ōō	boot	*th*	the		pencil, atom,
yōō	abuse	th	thin		circus
ou	out	hw	which	ər	butter

something that is wonderful, surprising, or astonishing: *That player can't hit well, but he's a marvel in the field. Space capsules are marvels of modern science.*
—*verb* **marveled, marveling** To be filled with wonder or admiration: *We marveled at the beauty of the snow-topped mountains.*

mar·vel·ous |**mär′**və ləs| —*adjective* **1.** Causing wonder or great admiration; amazing: *a marvelous cure for a disease; a marvelous journey to Mars.* **2.** Of the best quality; very fine; excellent: *She gave a marvelous party.*

Mar·y·land |**mâr′**ə lənd| or |**měr′**ə lənd| A state in the eastern United States. The capital of Maryland is Annapolis.

mas·cot |**măs′**kŏt| or |**măs′**kət| —*noun, plural* **mascots** An animal or person believed to bring good luck: *The team's mascot is a donkey.*

mas·cu·line |**măs′**kyə lĭn| —*adjective* Of or belonging to men or boys rather than women: *Robert and Peter are masculine names.*

mash |măsh| —*verb* **mashed, mashing** To crush or grind into a soft mixture: *She mashed the cooked potatoes and carrots together.*
—*noun, plural* **mashes** A soft mixture of grain and warm water, used for feeding horses and other animals.

mask |măsk| or |mäsk| —*noun, plural* **masks** **1.** Something that covers and hides the face or part of the face. Masks are worn as part of costumes and disguises. **2.** Something worn as protection for all or part of the face: *a gas mask; a catcher's mask.* **3.** Anything that hides or disguises: *Her high spirits served as a mask for her shyness.*
—*verb* **masked, masking** **1.** To hide or cover: *He masked his real feelings with sweet words. The thick sauce masks the taste of the fish.* **2.** To put a mask on: *They masked their faces for the party.*

ma·son |**mā′**sən| —*noun, plural* **masons** A person who builds things of stone or brick.

ma·son·ry |**mā′**sən rē| —*noun, plural* **masonries** **1.** The trade or work of a mason. **2.** A wall, fireplace, or other structure made of stone or brick.

mas·que·rade |măs′kə **rād′**| —*noun, plural* **masquerades** A party or dance where people wear masks and fancy costumes.

mass |măs| —*noun, plural* **masses** **1.** A thing or body of things with no particular shape; a pile or lump: *a mass of clay; a mass of leaves on the lawn.* **2.** A large amount or quantity: *A mass of letters poured in asking about the actor's health.* **3.** The largest part of something: *The great mass of his wealth is in jewels.* **4.** Bulk; size: *The sheer mass of the whale was overpowering.* **5.** The amount of matter in a body. Objects that have the same mass have the same weight in a particular place.
—*verb* **massed, massing** To gather or group into a mass: *The general massed his troops at the frontier. The people massed downtown to watch the parade.*
—*adjective* **1.** Of or including many people: *There was a mass meeting to oppose the highway through town.* **2.** On a large scale; making or involving many: *the mass production of cars.*

Mass |măs| —*noun, plural* **Masses** The main religious service in Roman Catholic and some Protestant churches.

Mas·sa·chu·setts |măs′ə **chōō′**sĭts| or |măs′ə **chōō′**zĭts| A state in the northeastern United States. The capital of Massachusetts is Boston.

mask
Above: Costume mask
Below: Diving mask

massacre
Soldiers fire on people
in what became known as the
Boston Massacre, 1770.

mastiff

match¹, match²
Match¹ comes from an old English
word meaning "companion" or "one
of a pair." **Match²** originally meant
"lamp wick" and was borrowed from
French.

ă	pat	ĕ	pet	î	fierce
ā	pay	ē	be	ŏ	pot
â	care	ĭ	pit	ō	go
ä	father	ī	pie	ô	paw, for
oi	oil	ŭ	cut	zh	vision
oo	book	û	fur	ə	ago, item,
oo	boot	*th*	the		pencil, atom,
yoo	abuse	th	thin		circus
ou	out	hw	which	ər	butter

mas·sa·cre |măs′ə kər| —*noun, plural* **massacres** A cruel and brutal killing of many people or animals.
—*verb* **massacred, massacring** To kill many people or animals in a cruel and brutal way.

mas·sage |mə säzh′| or |mə säj′| —*noun, plural* **massages** A rubbing of the body to relax the muscles and improve the circulation of the blood.
—*verb* **massaged, massaging** To give a massage to: *He massaged his leg to ease the cramp.*

mas·sive |măs′ĭv| —*adjective* Very large and heavy; huge: *a massive elephant; a massive dose of medicine; a massive battle.*

mast |măst| or |mäst| —*noun, plural* **masts** A tall pole for the sails and rigging of a sailing ship or sailboat.

mas·ter |măs′tər| or |mä′stər| —*noun, plural* **masters** **1.** A person who has power over others; ruler or owner: *He thinks he is the master of the house. The dog ran to its master.* **2.** A man who teaches: *a dancing master; a master in a private school.* **3.** A person who is very good at something; an expert: *a master at water-color painting; a master of clever remarks.* **4. Master** A word used in speaking of or to a boy who is not old enough to be called "Mister."
—*adjective* **1.** Very skilled; expert: *a master composer; a master plumber.* **2.** Most important or largest; main: *the master bedroom. With a master switch, you can turn off all the electricity in a building.*
—*verb* **mastered, mastering** **1.** To bring under control; overcome: *She mastered her fear of heights and climbed the tower.* **2.** To become very skilled in: *He mastered photography after a few lessons.*

mas·ter·piece |măs′tər pēs′| or |mä′stər pēs′| —*noun, plural* **masterpieces** An outstanding work of art or craft, especially an artist's greatest work: *The painting is a masterpiece. That novel is the writer's masterpiece.*

mas·tiff |măs′tĭf| —*noun, plural* **mastiffs** A large dog with a short brownish coat and short, square jaws.

mas·to·don |măs′tə dŏn′| —*noun, plural* **mastodons** An animal that looked very much like an elephant. It lived thousands of years ago.

mat |măt| —*noun, plural* **mats** **1.** A small rug used to cover a part of a floor: *a fluffy bath mat; a straw welcome mat.* **2.** A small piece of material that can be put under dishes, vases, and other things to protect a surface: *We used place mats under each table setting.* **3.** A thick pad used on the floor for activities like wrestling and boxing. **4.** A thick, tangled or twisted mass: *His mat of hair had not been combed.*
—*verb* **matted, matting** To tangle into a thick mass: *The rain matted the cat's fur.*

match¹ |măch| —*noun, plural* **matches** **1.** Someone or something that is very much like another: *This thread is a good match for the cloth. The smaller dog was no match for the big one.* **2.** Someone or something that goes well with another: *The tan sweater is a good match for the plaid slacks.* **3.** A contest; game or bout: *a wrestling match; a chess match.*
—*verb* **matched, matching** **1.** To be or look alike: *The two colors match exactly.* **2.** To do as well as; equal: *Can you match his score at darts?* **3.** To go well with: *His polka dot shirt does not match his plaid trousers.* **4.** To put or fit together: *The stripes match at the*

seams of the skirt. **5.** To put two similar things together; pair: *Match up your socks.*

match² | măch | —*noun, plural* **matches** A small stick of wood or cardboard coated at one end so that it catches fire when it is rubbed on a rough surface.

mate | māt | —*noun, plural* **mates** **1.** One of a pair: *Find the mate to this glove.* **2.** A husband or wife. **3.** An officer on a ship. **4.** The male or female of a pair of animals or birds.
—*verb* **mated, mating** To join together to have offspring: *Many animals mate in the spring.*

ma·te·ri·al | mə tîr′ē əl | —*noun, plural* **materials** **1.** Anything that can be used to make something else: *a store that sells painting materials.* **2.** Cloth or fabric: *She bought material and thread in the sewing department.*
—*adjective* **1.** Of or in the form of matter; physical: *Chairs and tables are material things; ideas are not.* **2.** Of or for the well-being of the body: *She likes soft sheets, warm baths, and other material comforts.*

ma·ter·nal | mə tûr′nəl | —*adjective* **1.** Of or like a mother: *The teacher had a maternal feeling for the children.* **2.** Related through one's mother: *Her maternal grandmother lives next door.*

math | măth | —*noun* Mathematics.

math·e·mat·i·cal | măth′ə măt′ĭ kəl | —*adjective* Of or using mathematics: *He does mathematical problems quickly in his head.*

math·e·ma·ti·cian | măth′ə mə tĭsh′ən | —*noun, plural* **mathematicians** A person who is good at mathematics or who specializes in it.

math·e·mat·ics | măth′ə măt′ĭks | —*noun* (Used with a singular verb.) The study of numbers, shapes, and measurements. Arithmetic, algebra, and geometry are branches of mathematics.

mat·i·nee | măt′n ā′ | —*noun, plural* **matinees** An afternoon performance in a theater.

mat·ter | măt′ər | —*noun, plural* **matters** **1.** Anything that takes up space and has weight; the stuff that makes up all things. Matter can be solid, liquid, or gas. **2.** Material; contents; substance: *The fire provided matter for several newspaper stories.* **3.** A subject of interest; affair: *We talked about costs, salaries, and other business matters.* **4.** Trouble; problem: *What's the matter with your foot?* **5.** Something written or printed: *These books are good reading matter.*
—*verb* **mattered, mattering** To be important: *He tried to pretend that it didn't matter if he did not make the team.*

   Idioms **as a matter of fact** In fact; actually; really: *As a matter of fact, we visited them on Monday, not Tuesday.* **for that matter** So far as that is concerned; as for that: *I invited him to the party, and for that matter I even called to see if he was coming.* **no matter** Regardless of: *He does what he wants no matter how hard we try to stop him.*

mat·tress | măt′rĭs | —*noun, plural* **mattresses** A large cloth pad stuffed with soft material, used as a bed or on a bed.

ma·ture | mə tŏŏr′ | or | mə tyŏŏr′ | or | mə chŏŏr′ | —*adjective* **maturer, maturest** **1.** Having reached full growth or development: *Pick the mature fruits, not the green ones.* **2.** Of or like an adult; grown-up: *She is very mature for her age.*
—*verb* **matured, maturing** To reach full growth or development; ripen: *The crops matured early this year.*

meadowlark

---

meal¹, meal²

Meal¹ and **meal²** come from totally unrelated old English words. **Meal¹** originally meant "flour" or "ground grain." **Meal²** came from a word meaning "fixed time," "measure," and finally "mealtime."

---

mean¹, mean², mean³

Mean¹ comes from a word used long ago by English-speaking people to mean "to intend, to tell." **Mean²** comes from a different old English word that first meant "common, shared by all" but later came to mean "ordinary" and then "inferior." The source of **mean³** was a Latin word meaning "middle, median." It traveled through French before arriving in English.

ă	pat	ĕ	pet	î	fierce
ā	pay	ē	be	ŏ	pot
â	care	ĭ	pit	ō	go
ä	father	ī	pie	ô	paw, for

oi	oil	ŭ	cut	zh	vision
ŏŏ	book	û	fur	ə	ago, item,
ōō	boot	*th*	the		pencil, atom,
yōō	abuse	th	thin		circus
ou	out	hw	which	ər	butter

max·i·mum |măk′sə məm| —*noun, plural* **maximums** The highest or greatest possible number or degree: *This table seats a maximum of ten people.*
—*adjective* Highest or greatest possible: *He reached his maximum height at age seventeen.*

may |mā| —*helping,* or *auxiliary, verb* Past tense **might** As a helping verb **may** is used to show: **1.** That something will possibly happen: *It may rain this weekend.* **2.** A request for permission or the giving of it: *May I take a swim? Yes, you may.* **3.** The hope or the wish for something: *May all your days be happy ones. May he live to regret this day.*

May |mā| —*noun, plural* **Mays** The fifth month of the year, after April and before June. May has 31 days.

may·be |mā′bē| —*adverb* Possibly; perhaps: *Maybe our teacher will be absent today, but I doubt it.*

may·flow·er |mā′flou′ər| —*noun, plural* **mayflowers** Any of several plants that bloom in spring.

may·on·naise |mā′ə nāz′| or |mā′ə nāz′| —*noun, plural* **mayonnaises** A thick dressing for salads and other foods. It is made of beaten egg yolks, oil, lemon juice or vinegar, and seasonings.

may·or |mā′ər| or |mâr| —*noun, plural* **mayors** The highest government official of a city or town.

maze |māz| —*noun, plural* **mazes** A complicated, winding arrangement of paths through which it is hard to find one's way.
♦ *These sound alike* **maze, maize.**

me |mē| —*pronoun* The pronoun **me** is the objective case of **I.** It is used: **1.** As the direct object of a verb: *They blamed me.* **2.** As the indirect object of a verb: *Give me the letter.* **3.** As the object of a preposition: *She sent the letter to me.*

mead·ow |měd′ō| —*noun, plural* **meadows** An area of grassy ground.

mead·ow·lark |měd′ō lärk′| —*noun, plural* **meadowlarks** A North American songbird. It has a brownish back and a yellow breast with a black marking shaped like a V.

mea·ger |mē′gər| —*adjective* Lacking in quantity; poor: *a meager diet. He earned a meager living from his little shop.*

meal¹ |mēl| —*noun, plural* **meals** Grain that has been ground until it is coarse. Meal is not as fine as flour.

meal² |mēl| —*noun, plural* **meals** **1.** The food served and eaten in one sitting: *He had a good meal of meat, vegetables, bread, and dessert.* **2.** The regular time for eating: *Don't eat between meals.*

mean¹ |mēn| —*verb* **meant, meaning** **1.** To have the sense of; be defined as: *Your dictionary tells you what words mean.* **2.** To be a sign or symbol of; show: *The green light means that we can go.* **3.** To try to say: *What do you think this poem means?* **4.** To have in mind; intend: *He means no harm. What do you mean by that look?* **5.** To be important; matter: *His friendship means a lot to me.*

mean² |mēn| —*adjective* **meaner, meanest** **1.** Not kind or good; cruel; nasty: *Hiding the boy's lunch was a mean thing to do.* **2.** Hard to handle; troublesome: *a mean old bull; a mean car to drive.*

mean³ |mēn| —*noun, plural* **means** **1.** Something that is in the middle between two extremes; a middle point: *a pleasant mean between wealth and poverty. The mean between 1 and 9 is 5.* **2. means** Something that is used to help reach a goal; method:

We need a practical means of using the sun's energy. He won the election by unfair means. **3. means** Money; wealth: *She is a woman of means.*

—*adjective* In the middle between two extremes; average: *The mean temperature for the day was 22° Fahrenheit.*

   Idioms **by all means** Of course; certainly: *The visitors are welcome by all means.* **by no means** Not at all; certainly not: *I shall by no means apologize if I think I am right.*

mean·ing |mē′nĭng| —*noun, plural* **meanings** The way something can be understood; the way something is intended or stands for; thing signified: *What is the meaning of the word "fabulous"? I did not understand the meaning of that paragraph.*

mean·ing·ful |mē′nĭng fəl| —*adjective* Full of meaning; significant: *A meaningful glance from my mother told me that it was time to go to bed.*

mean·ing·less |mē′nĭng lĭs| —*adjective* Having no meaning; without sense: *He mumbled some meaningless words in his sleep.*

meant |mĕnt| The past tense and past participle of the verb **mean:** *She meant no harm. What do you think his friendship has meant to her?*

mean·time |mēn′tīm′| —*noun* The time between one thing and another: *We'll leave tomorrow; in the meantime, please start packing.*

mean·while |mēn′hwīl′| or |mēn′wīl′| —*adverb* **1.** During the time in between: *I'll leave in ten minutes; meanwhile I'll polish my shoes.* **2.** At the same time: *I'll cook supper; meanwhile you set the table.*

mea·sles |mē′zəlz| —*noun* (Used with a singular verb.) A contagious disease caused by a virus. People with measles cough, have a fever, and break out in red spots.

meas·ure |mĕzh′ər| —*noun, plural* **measures** **1.** The size, amount, weight, or volume of something: *I took the measure of her waist with a piece of string.* **2.** A unit for figuring out size, amount, or volume: *Liters and quarts are measures of volume.* **3.** An instrument or device for figuring out size, amount, weight, or volume: *A scale is a measure for weight. Use the cup as a measure for the flour.* **4.** Amount, extent, or degree: *He has a large measure of good sense.* **5.** An action taken for a purpose: *The teacher took measures to stop noise in the class.* **6.** A bill or act that may become law: *The Senate passed a measure to lower taxes.* **7.** The music between two bars on a staff; a bar: *Sing a few measures of the song.*

—*verb* **measured, measuring** **1.** To find the size, amount, weight, or volume of: *He measured the room. How would you measure the water in the tank?* **2.** To be a unit of size, amount, weight, or volume for: *Meters and yards measure length. Degrees measure temperatures.* **3.** To have as size, amount, weight, or volume: *The paper measures 8 by 12 inches. The bag of flour measures one kilogram.*

meas·ure·ment |mĕzh′ər mənt| —*noun, plural* **measurements** **1.** The act of measuring: *We used a yardstick for the measurement of the room.* **2.** A system of measuring: *The United States is slowly accepting metric measurement.* **3.** A dimension or number found by measuring: *The tailor wrote down the measurements of the man's waist and chest.*

meat |mēt| —*noun, plural* **meats** **1.** The flesh of an animal that can be eaten as food. Beef, pork, and lamb are kinds of meat.

2. The part of a nut or fruit that can be eaten. **3.** The main or most important part: *the meat of the story.*

♦ *These sound alike* **meat, meet.**

me·chan·ic |mə kăn′ĭk| —*noun, plural* **mechanics** A person who is skilled in making, using, or repairing machines.

me·chan·i·cal |mə kăn′ĭ kəl| —*adjective* Of or using machines or tools: *She has great mechanical skill. With mechanical help, land can be plowed quickly.*

mech·a·nism |mĕk′ə nĭz′əm| —*noun, plural* **mechanisms** The parts that make a machine work: *The mechanism of our record player broke.*

med·al |mĕd′l| —*noun, plural* **medals** A flat, round piece of metal with a design or writing on it. Medals are awarded to honor outstanding achievements. Some medals have religious figures.

♦ *These sound alike* **medal, meddle.**

med·dle |mĕd′l| —*verb* **meddled, meddling** To interfere in other people's things or business without being asked: *That nosy woman is always meddling in our affairs.*

♦ *These sound alike* **meddle, medal.**

me·di·a |mē′dē ə| —*noun* **1.** A plural of the noun **medium. 2.** (Used with a plural verb.) Newspapers, television, and other means of public communication: *The media sent people to cover the moon launch.*

med·i·cal |mĕd′ĭ kəl| —*adjective* Of the study or treatment of diseases: *She went to medical school to become a doctor. That wound needs medical attention.*

med·i·cine |mĕd′ĭ sĭn| —*noun, plural* **medicines 1.** Any substance used to treat or prevent disease and relieve pain. Many medicines are taken through the mouth. **2.** The scientific study of diseases and of methods to discover, treat, and prevent them.

medicine man —*plural* **medicine men** A person believed to have magic powers for healing the sick and dealing with spirits. Medicine men have been important among North American Indians and other peoples.

me·di·e·val |mē′dē ē′vəl| or |mĕd′ē ē′vəl| —*adjective* Of, from, or like the Middle Ages, or the period of European history from about A.D. 500 to about 1400.

Med·i·ter·ra·ne·an Sea |mĕd′ĭ tə rā′nē ən| or |mĕd′ĭ tə rān′yən| A sea between Europe and Africa.

me·di·um |mē′dē əm| —*noun* **1.** *plural* **mediums** Something that is in the middle between two extremes: *He needs to find a happy medium between all work and all play.* **2.** *plural* **media** or **mediums** Anything in which something lives, is carried, or is done: *Rich soil is a good medium for those plants. Sound waves travel through the medium of air.* **3.** *plural* **media** Any of the means used to transfer information in a society: *Radio is a medium. Magazines, newspapers, television, and films are other media.*
—*adjective* In the middle between two extremes: *She rode her bike at a medium speed.*

meet |mēt| —*verb* **met, meeting 1.** To join; touch; connect: *The walls meet at the corner.* **2.** To come face to face with; encounter: *Penguins bow when they meet. I met an old friend by chance in the store.* **3.** To come together with by appointment: *I'll meet you at the restaurant in ten minutes.* **4.** To be introduced to: *I'd like you to meet my brother.* **5.** To pay; pay for: *She met her expenses.*

medal

ă	pat	ĕ	pet	î	fierce
ā	pay	ē	be	ŏ	pot
â	care	ĭ	pit	ō	go
ä	father	ī	pie	ô	paw, for
oi	oil	ŭ	cut	zh	vision
o͝o	book	û	fur	ə	ago, item,
o͞o	boot	*th*	the		pencil, atom,
yo͞o	abuse	th	thin		circus
ou	out	hw	which	ər	butter

—*noun, plural* **meets** A gathering of people or teams for a sports competition: *a track meet.*
♦ *These sound alike* **meet, meat.**

meet·ing |mē′tĭng| —*noun, plural* **meetings** **1.** The act of coming together: *We had a chance meeting with our cousins at the circus.* **2.** A gathering of people: *the Sunday club meeting; a business meeting.*

meg·a·phone |mĕg′ə fōn′| —*noun, plural* **megaphones** A device shaped like a funnel for increasing and directing the sound of the voice.

megaphone

mel·an·chol·y |mĕl′ən kŏl′ē| —*noun* Low spirits; sad feeling; sorrow: *Their melancholy remained for many weeks after she died.* —*adjective* **1.** Sad; gloomy: *There was a melancholy expression on the lonely boy's face.* **2.** Making one feel sad: *a dark, rainy, melancholy day.*

mel·low |mĕl′ō| —*adjective* **mellower, mellowest** **1.** Soft and sweet; rich and full: *a mellow peach; mellow tones.* **2.** Grown wiser and gentler with age: *a mellow gentleman with a twinkle in his eye.*

mel·o·dy |mĕl′ə dē| —*noun, plural* **melodies** **1.** A group of musical tones in a pleasing order; a tune: *He hummed some old melodies.* **2.** The main part of a piece of music: *You play the melody; we'll play the accompaniment.*

mel·on |mĕl′ən| —*noun, plural* **melons** A large fruit with a hard rind and juicy flesh. Melons grow on vines. Cantaloupes and watermelons are melons.

melt |mĕlt| —*verb* **melted, melting** **1.** To change a solid into a liquid by adding heat: *The workers melted iron in a huge furnace. The icicles melted as the day grew warm.* **2.** To dissolve: *Sugar melts faster in hot water than in cold.* **3.** To fade, blend, or disappear: *The sunset's reds and golds melted into purples.* **4.** To make or become gentler or milder; soften: *The look on her face melted my heart.*

mem·ber |mĕm′bər| —*noun, plural* **members** **1.** A person or thing that belongs to a group or organization: *A zebra is a member of the horse family. She is a member of the Senate.* **2.** A body part that sticks out; limb.

mem·ber·ship |mĕm′bər shĭp′| —*noun, plural* **memberships** **1.** The condition of being a member: *He renewed his membership in the nature club.* **2.** The people who are members: *The membership of the society voted for a new president.*

mem·brane |mĕm′brān′| —*noun, plural* **membranes** A thin layer of tissue in the body of an animal or plant. Membranes cover surfaces and act as boundaries between certain parts of the body.

me·mo·ri·al |mə môr′ē əl| or |mə mōr′ē əl| —*noun, plural* **memorials** Anything built, kept, or done in memory of a person, people, or event: *The monument was a memorial to those who died.*

Memorial Day A holiday to remember people who died for their country. Memorial Day is the last Monday in May.

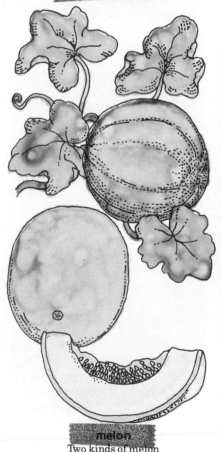

melon
Two kinds of melon

mem·o·rize |mĕm′ə rīz′| —*verb* **memorized, memorizing** To learn by heart; commit to memory: *She memorized all the words to the song.*

mem·o·ry |mĕm′ə rē| —*noun, plural* **memories** **1.** The power of storing things in the mind and bringing them back when needed; the ability to remember: *He has a good memory for telephone numbers.* **2.** Something that is remembered; a thought of someone or something out of the past: *Her earliest memory is of her third birthday party.*

men |mĕn| The plural of the noun **man**.

men·ace |mĕn′əs| —*noun, plural* **menaces** A threat; danger: *The falling rocks were a menace to cars on the road. The giant's voice was full of menace.*
—*verb* **menaced, menacing** To threaten with harm; endanger: *An oil spill menaced the lives of birds, fish, and plants.*

mend |mĕnd| —*verb* **mended, mending 1.** To put back in good condition; repair; fix: *Can you mend the rip in my jacket?* **2.** To get better; heal: *Children's bones usually mend quickly.*
—*noun, plural* **mends** A place that has been mended; a repaired part: *Can you find the mend in the plate?*
Idiom **on the mend** Getting better; improving: *He is on the mend.*

men-of-war |mĕn′ə wôr′| or |mĕn′əv wôr′| The plural of the noun **man-of-war**.

–ment A suffix that forms nouns. The suffix "-ment" means: **1.** An act or process: *attachment; government.* **2.** A condition: *amazement.* **3.** The product or result of an action: *improvement.*

men·tal |mĕn′tl| —*adjective* **1.** Of, in, or done by the mind: *Tom showed his quick mental ability by adding the figures in his head. I have never met your brother, but I have a mental image of him.* **2.** Of, for, or suffering from a disease of the mind: *a mental patient.*

men·tal·ly re·tard·ed |mĕn′tl ē rĭ tär′dĭd| Of a person who suffers from or has a condition of mental retardation.

mental re·tar·da·tion |rē′tär dā′shən| The condition of having mental ability that is lower than normal. A person can be born with this condition or it can be caused by an injury or disease that damages the brain.

men·tion |mĕn′shən| —*verb* **mentioned, mentioning** To speak or write about in a brief way; refer to: *He forgot to mention that he was going on vacation next week.*
—*noun, plural* **mentions** A brief statement; remark; note: *The very mention of rats makes me shiver.*

men·u |mĕn′yōō| or |mā′nyōō| —*noun, plural* **menus** A list of the foods and drinks available in a restaurant or other place where one eats.

me·ow |mē ou′| or |myou| —*noun, plural* **meows** The high, whining sound a cat makes.
—*verb* **meowed, meowing** To make this sound: *The cats meowed in the alley.*

mer·chan·dise |mûr′chən dīz′| or |mûr′chən dīs′| —*noun* Things bought and sold; goods: *The store carries a great variety of merchandise.*

mer·chant |mûr′chənt| —*noun, plural* **merchants 1.** A person who makes money by buying and selling goods: *The tea merchant imports tea from Asia and sells it in America.* **2.** A person who operates a retail store; storekeeper.
—*adjective* Having to do with business or trade: *a merchant ship.*

mer·cu·ry |mûr′kyə rē| —*noun* A shiny, silver-white metal that is a liquid at normal temperatures. It is used in thermometers, barometers, some electric switches, and some batteries. Mercury is a chemical element.

Mer·cu·ry |mûr′kyə rē| The planet that is closest to the sun in our solar system. Mercury is the smallest known planet.

mer·cy |mûr′sē| —*noun, plural* **mercies 1.** Kind or soft

merchandise
In an old-fashioned store

ă	pat	ĕ	pet	î	fierce
ā	pay	ē	be	ŏ	pot
â	care	ĭ	pit	ō	go
ä	father	ī	pie	ô	paw, for

oi	oil	ŭ	cut	zh	vision
ōō	book	û	fur	ə	ago, item,
ōō	boot	*th*	the		pencil, atom,
yōō	abuse	th	thin		circus
ou	out	hw	which	ər	butter

treatment to a person who is in one's power: *The warriors showed no mercy to their captives.* **2.** Something to be grateful for; a blessing: *It's a mercy that nobody was hurt.*

mere | mîr | —*adjective* Being nothing more than what is stated; only: *He is a mere child. A mere fifty cents cannot buy much.*

mere·ly | mîr′lē | —*adverb* Nothing more than; only; simply: *Don't be afraid—that strange noise is merely the sound of our footsteps.*

merge | mûrj | —*verb* **merged, merging** To bring or come together; combine; unite: *The presidents merged their companies. The rivers merged.*

me·rid·i·an | mə rĭd′ē ən | —*noun, plural* **meridians** A half circle along the earth's surface that goes from north pole to south pole; a line of longitude.

mer·it | mĕr′ĭt | —*noun, plural* **merits** **1.** Quality that deserves praise or reward; value; worth: *a painting of great merit. Pay raises here are given according to merit, not length of time on the job.* **2. merits** The actual facts of a matter: *He won the lawsuit on its merits, not because the judge liked him.*
—*verb* **merited, meriting** To be worthy of; deserve: *Your idea merits further discussion.*

mer·maid | mûr′mād′ | —*noun, plural* **mermaids** An imaginary sea creature with the head and upper body of a woman and a fish's tail.

mer·ri·ment | mĕr′ĭ mənt | —*noun* Laughter and fun; gaiety; amusement: *They enjoyed the merriment of the holiday season.*

mer·ry | mĕr′ē | —*adjective* **merrier, merriest** Full of fun, laughter, and gaiety; jolly: *He whistled a merry tune.*

mer·ry-go-round | mĕr′ē gō round′ | —*noun, plural* **merry-go-rounds** A round platform with seats shaped like horses and other animals. People ride while the merry-go-round turns.

mesh | mĕsh | —*noun, plural* **meshes** A structure or material with many small open spaces in it; network: *I need a strainer with a fine mesh.*

mes·quite | mĕ skēt′ | or | mĕs′kēt′ | —*noun, plural* **mesquites** A thorny shrub or tree of southwestern North America. It has feathery leaves and long, narrow pods.

mess | mĕs | —*noun, plural* **messes** **1.** A cluttered or untidy condition of something: *His drawers are in such a mess that he can't find anything.* **2.** Someone or something that is dirty, sloppy, or untidy: *The dog was a mess after he rolled in the mud.* **3.** A situation that is confused, complicated, and unpleasant: *Who got us into this mess?* **4.** A group of soldiers, sailors, or campers who eat together.
—*verb* **messed, messing** **1.** To make sloppy, dirty, or untidy: *She messed up my closet looking for a dress to borrow.* **2.** To handle in a bad way; ruin: *He messed up his chance for first prize.*

mes·sage | mĕs′ĭj | —*noun, plural* **messages** **1.** Words sent from one person or group to another: *Please leave a message for her to call me back.* **2.** A statement or speech to a certain audience: *The President broadcast his message on energy.*

mes·sen·ger | mĕs′ən jər | —*noun, plural* **messengers** A person who carries messages or other things from one place to another.

mess·y | mĕs′ē | —*adjective* **messier, messiest** **1.** Sloppy or cluttered; untidy: *This is the messiest house I've ever seen.* **2.** Likely to cause a mess: *Squeezing lemons is a messy job.*

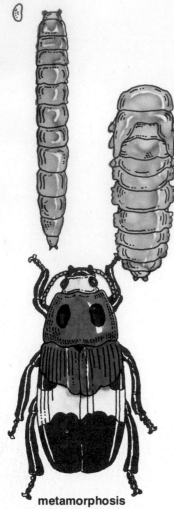

metamorphosis
Above: Egg (*left*), larva (*center*), and
pupa (*right*)
Below: Adult beetle

meter¹, meter², meter³
These three words all come from the
same Greek word, *metron*. This word
meant, among other things, "the
measure of rhythm in poetry,"
meter¹. **Meter²** is from a French word
that was taken directly from *metron*
in its basic sense of "measure."
Meter³ is also directly related to
metron.

ă	pat	ĕ	pet	î	fierce
ā	pay	ē	be	ŏ	pot
â	care	ĭ	pit	ō	go
ä	father	ī	pie	ô	paw, for

oi	oil	ŭ	cut	zh	vision
ŏŏ	book	û	fur	ə	ago, item,
ōō	boot	*th*	the		pencil, atom,
yōō	abuse	th	thin		circus
ou	out	hw	which	ər	butter

met |mĕt| The past tense and past participle of the verb **meet**:
They met at the theater's entrance. She had met him before.

me·tab·o·lism |mə tăb′ə lĭz′əm| —*noun* The chemical and
physical processes that living things carry on to stay alive.
Metabolism includes the changing of food molecules into forms
that the body can use to make cells and tissues.

met·al |mĕt′l| —*noun, plural* **metals** A substance that is shiny
and conducts heat and electricity. Most metals can be melted and
can be hammered into shapes. Some metals are elements, like
iron, tin, silver, and gold. Others are alloys, like bronze, brass,
and steel.

me·tal·lic |mə tăl′ĭk| —*adjective* Of or like metal: *shiny metallic
coins; a metallic clank of chains.*

met·a·mor·pho·ses |mĕt′ə môr′fə sēz′| The plural of the noun
metamorphosis.

met·a·mor·pho·sis |mĕt′ə môr′fə sĭs| —*noun, plural*
metamorphoses Changes that some animals go through during
their natural development. In one kind of metamorphosis, a
caterpillar hatches from an egg, becomes a pupa, and then turns
into a butterfly. A tadpole becomes a frog by metamorphosis.

me·te·or |mē′tē ər| or |mē′tē ôr′| —*noun, plural* **meteors** A
streak of light that appears in the sky when a chunk of matter
from outer space enters the earth's atmosphere and burns up.

me·te·or·ite |mē′tē ə rīt′| —*noun, plural* **meteorites** A chunk of
matter from outer space that lands on earth.

me·ter¹ |mē′tər| —*noun, plural* **meters** The basic unit of length
in the metric system. There are 100 centimeters in a meter. A
meter is equal to about 39.37 inches, or a little more than a yard.

me·ter² |mē′tər| —*noun, plural* **meters** An instrument that
measures something. Meters are used to measure and show such
things as the amount of gas, water, and electricity used in a
house.

me·ter³ |mē′tər| —*noun, plural* **meters** A pattern of rhythm in
music or poetry.

meth·od |mĕth′əd| —*noun, plural* **methods** **1.** A way of doing
something: *Two methods of cooking a steak are broiling and frying.*
2. Definite order or purpose; system: *Since the arrangement of
things in his notebook lacked method, Joseph couldn't find the math
problem.*

met·ric |mĕt′rĭk| —*adjective* Of or using the metric system: *a
metric scale; a metric ruler.*

metric system A system of weights and measures based on the
number 10. In the metric system, the meter is the basic unit of
length; the kilogram is the basic unit of weight or mass; and the
liter is the basic unit of volume.

me·trop·o·lis |mə trŏp′ə lĭs| —*noun, plural* **metropolises** The
largest or most important city of an area.

met·ro·pol·i·tan |mĕt′rə pŏl′ĭ tən| —*adjective* Of or like a big
city with its suburbs: *metropolitan newspapers; a metropolitan area.*

Mex·i·can |mĕk′sĭ kən| —*noun, plural* **Mexicans** A person who
was born in or is a citizen of Mexico.
—*adjective* Of Mexico, the Mexicans, or their language: *a
Mexican volcano; a Mexican dinner.*

Mex·i·co |mĕk′sĭ kō′| A country just south of the United
States.

mice |mīs| The plural of the noun **mouse**.

A Guide to the Metric System

Long ago people had a hard time explaining how tall or how far away something was, how much a basket could hold, or what an object weighed. The Greeks and Egyptians began to use a person's foot to describe height and distance, but people's feet differed in size. Should the standard measure be a king's foot, or a queen's foot, or a child's foot? No one could decide, and when they tried, someone else would come up with a new way to measure. One king declared that a yard would be the distance from the tip of his nose to the end of his thumb. There were other problems in describing volume and weight. A man might say that he needed three baskets of corn to feed his animals, but his baskets might be bigger or smaller than the baskets belonging to the farmer who was selling the corn. Or he might say that he needed a bag of corn that was as heavy as a big rock, but his idea of how much a big rock weighed might be very different from the farmer's. The way people described weights and measures changed so much between countries and over the years that it was impossible to communicate.

In 1790 the French Academy of Sciences solved these differences by creating a simple system of weights and measures based on proven scientific principles that all countries understood. The system's basic unit was named *meter* after the Greek word *metron*, meaning "measure." The whole system was called the *metric system*.

The metric system is easy to use because length, weight, and capacity are all related to the scientific standard and because the metric system is based on the number ten, just as our money system is. Our money system is easy to use because ten pennies make a dime, ten dimes make a dollar, and so on. In our old system of measuring it was difficult to add and subtract — ten inches did not make a foot, ten ounces did not make a pound, and ten liquid ounces did not make a pint. In the metric system prefixes are used to tell how many tens are in each unit. These are the prefixes and what they mean:

> **kilo-** means 1,000, or 100 tens
> **hecto-** means 100, or 10 tens
> **deka-** means 10, or 1 ten
> **deci-** means 1/10, or ten divided by 100
> **centi-** means 1/100, or ten divided by 1,000
> **milli-** means 1/1000, or ten divided by 10,000

In length the basic unit is the *meter*, in weight the basic unit is the *gram*, and in capacity the basic unit is the *liter*. These units all mean *one* of something; when a prefix is added, it tells you how many more have been added or subtracted. So if you see *kilometer*, *kilogram*, and *kiloliter*, you know that the words mean 1,000 meters, 1,000 grams, and 1,000 liters.

Many of the prefixes are not used very often. In measurement *kilometer*, *meter*, *centimeter*, and *millimeter* are used most often; in weight *kilogram*, *gram*, and *milligram* are used most often; and in volume *liter* and *milliliter* are used most often.

0°C

30°C

2 centimeters

1 meter

400 meters

A paper clip = 1 gram

A 12-year-old boy = 36 kilograms

A soda bottle = 2 liters

A measuring cup = 500 milliliters

ă	pat	ĕ	pet	î	fierce
ā	pay	ē	be	ŏ	pot
â	care	ĭ	pit	ō	go
ä	father	ī	pie	ô	paw, for

oi	oil	ŭ	cut	zh	vision
ŏŏ	book	û	fur	ə	ago, item,
ōō	boot	th	the		pencil, atom,
yōō	abuse	th	thin		circus
ou	out	hw	which	ər	butter

Temperature

Temperature in the metric system is measured on the *Celsius scale*. This scale was invented in 1742 by a Swedish astronomer named Anders Celsius. Today all scientists use this scale, and most countries in the world measure daily temperature in degrees Celsius. The United States generally uses the Fahrenheit scale to measure daily temperature, but in most weather reports the temperature is given in both Celsius and Fahrenheit.

Anders Celsius based his temperature system on the temperature at which water will freeze or boil. On the Celsius scale water freezes at 0°C and boils at 100°C, so the scale is divided into 100 equal degrees between these points. The following examples will help you to remember different temperatures in degrees Celsius.

0°C	Water freezes	**37°C**	Normal body temperature
10°C	A warm winter day	**40°C**	A heat wave
20°C	A mild spring day	**100°C**	Water boils
30°C	A hot day		

Length

A *meter* is the basic unit of length in the metric system. A baseball bat and a guitar are both about 1 meter long. Larger objects or distances are measured in *kilometers*. A football field is 120 yards, or about 109 meters, long. A suspension bridge, like the Golden Gate Bridge in San Francisco, is 1 kilometer and 280 meters long. The Sears Tower in Chicago is about ½ kilometer tall.

In measuring smaller lengths *centimeters* and *millimeters* are used. A penny is 2 centimeters in diameter. A dime is about 1 millimeter thick.

The units of length that are used most often are *kilometer*, *meter*, *centimeter*, and *millimeter*.

Weight

The basic unit of weight in the metric system is the *gram*. Grams and *kilograms* are the units of weight used most often. A paper clip weighs about 1 gram; a penny weighs 2.8 grams. A tennis ball weighs about 10 grams, and a basketball weighs 560 grams, or about ½ kilogram. Most foods—meat and bags of sugar, for example—are measured in kilograms. People's weight is also measured in kilograms. A heavyweight boxer weighs about 90 to 100 kilograms. An average sixth-grade student weighs between 35 and 40 kilograms.

Capacity

A *liter* is the basic unit of capacity in the metric system. Capacity is how much something holds. Liter and *milliliter* are the units of capacity that are used most often. Measuring cups are marked in milliliters. Smaller bottles of liquid, like medicine, are also measured in milliliters. Larger quantities, like gasoline, bottles of milk, soft drinks, and liquid foods, are measured in liters.

Mich·i·gan |mĭsh´ĭ gən| A state in the north-central United States. The capital of Michigan is Lansing.

mi·crobe |mī´krōb´| —*noun, plural* **microbes** A living thing so small that it can be seen only through a microscope. The germs that cause disease are often called microbes.

mi·cro·phone |mī´krə fōn´| —*noun, plural* **microphones** An instrument used to send sound over a distance or to make sound louder. A microphone works by changing sound waves into electrical signals.

mi·cro·scope |mī´krə skōp´| —*noun, plural* **microscopes** An instrument that makes a very small thing look larger so that a person can see and study it. Microscopes enlarge the image of an object, by using a combination of lenses.

mi·cro·scop·ic |mī´krə skŏp´ĭk| —*adjective* Too small to be seen by the eye alone, but large enough to be seen through a microscope: *a microscopic plant.*

mid |mĭd| —*adjective* Middle; central: *It was mid afternoon when we got out of school.*

mid·air |mĭd âr´| —*noun* A point in the middle of the air.

mid·day |mĭd´dā´| —*noun, plural* **middays** The middle of the day; noon: *The sun is high at midday.*

mid·dle |mĭd´l| —*noun, plural* **middles** 1. A point that is about equal in distance or time from both ends or from all sides; center: *Fold the paper in the middle. Kansas is in the middle of the country.* 2. A person's waist: *He hugged his mother around the middle.* —*adjective* 1. At or in the middle: *the middle finger.* 2. Medium; average: *a dog of middle size.*

mid·dle-aged |mĭd´l ājd´| —*adjective* Between youth and old age: *a middle-aged woman.*

Middle Ages The period in European history from about A.D. 500 to about 1400.

middle ear The part of the ear between the eardrum and the inner ear. The middle ear has three small bones that carry sound vibrations from the eardrum to the inner ear.

Middle East A region including the countries of southwestern Asia and northeastern Africa.

Middle West A region of the United States that includes Ohio, Indiana, Michigan, Illinois, Wisconsin, Missouri, Iowa, and Minnesota. Another name for this region is **Midwest.**

mid·get |mĭj´ĭt| —*noun, plural* **midgets** A person who is unusually small but whose body has normal proportions.

mid·night |mĭd´nīt´| —*noun, plural* **midnights** Twelve o'clock at night.

midst |mĭdst| —*noun* 1. The middle part; center: *They came to a clearing in the midst of the forest.* 2. A group of people: *A new classmate came into our midst.*

mid·way |mĭd´wā´| —*adverb* In the middle; halfway: *New Hampshire is located midway between Maine and Vermont.* —*adjective* Occurring in the middle; intermediate: *We took a break at the midway point of our work period.* —*noun, plural* **midways** A place at a fair, carnival, or circus for games and sideshows.

Mid·west |mĭd´wĕst´| —*noun* A region of the central United States, the **Middle West.**

might[1] |mīt| —*noun* 1. Great power or force: *The whole might of the storm seemed to be aimed at the little village.* 2. Physical

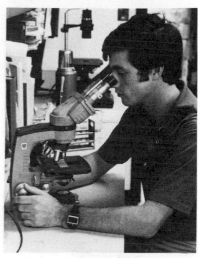

microscope

strength: *He pushed the heavy cart with all his might.*

♦ *These sound alike* **might, mite.**

might² |mīt| —*helping,* or *auxiliary, verb* The past tense of **may** As a helping verb **might** is used to show: **1.** That something will possibly happen: *Do as you are told, and we might let you go to the movies.* **2.** That something could possibly but not certainly have happened: *If she had rushed, she might have caught the plane.* **3.** A request for permission: *Might I trouble you for another cup of tea?* **4.** Any request or polite order: *You might pay attention when I speak to you.* **5.** A complaint that someone is not acting properly or not being polite: *He might at least call. You might at least say "Thank you."*

♦ *These sound alike* **might, mite.**

might·y |mī′tē| —*adjective* **mightier, mightiest 1.** Having or showing great strength or power: *a mighty queen; a mighty hunter.* **2.** Great; immense: *the mighty ocean.*

mi·grate |mī′grāt′| —*verb* **migrated, migrating 1.** To move from one country or region and settle in another: *Many people migrated to the West.* **2.** To move regularly to a different place at a certain time of the year: *Birds migrate to the South for the winter.*

mi·gra·tion |mī grā′shən| —*noun, plural* **migrations** The act of migrating; movement to another place to live or stay.

mild |mīld| —*adjective* **milder, mildest 1.** Gentle and kind in manner or behavior: *a mild woman.* **2.** Not harsh or severe; moderate; slight: *a mild complaint; a mild soap; a mild breeze.* **3.** Not extreme in temperature; neither very hot nor very cold: *California has a mild climate.* **4.** Not sharp, bitter, or strong in taste or smell: *a mild cheese; a mild tobacco.*

mil·dew |mĭl′dōō′| or |mĭl′dyōō′| —*noun* A fungus that forms a grayish coating on plant leaves, cloth, leather, and other things in damp weather.

—*verb* **mildewed, mildewing** To become covered with this coating.

mile |mīl| —*noun, plural* **miles 1.** A unit of length equal to 5,280 feet, 1,760 yards, or 1,609.34 meters. **2.** A unit of length used in air or sea travel, equal to 1,852 meters or about 6,076 feet. Another name for this unit is **nautical mile.**

mile·age |mī′lĭj| —*noun* **1.** The measure of a length or distance in miles. **2.** The number of miles traveled, driven, or used: *We put a lot of mileage on our car during that trip.*

mil·i·tar·y |mĭl′ĭ tĕr′ē| —*adjective* Of or having to do with soldiers or war: *a military base; military uniforms; a military victory.*

—*noun* **the military** The armed forces.

mi·li·tia |mĭ lĭsh′ə| —*noun, plural* **militias** A group of citizens who are trained to fight or keep public order in times of emergency.

milk |mĭlk| —*noun* **1.** A white liquid produced by glands of female mammals for feeding their young. **2.** The milk of cows. It is used as food by human beings. **3.** A liquid like milk: *coconut milk.*

—*verb* **milked, milking** To press milk from the udder of a cow or other animal.

milk shake A drink made of milk, flavoring, and usually ice cream, shaken together until thick and full of froth.

milk·weed |mĭlk′wēd′| —*noun* A plant with milky juice and large seed pods. The pods split open to release seeds that look like down.

migration

milkweed

ă	pat	ĕ	pet	î	fierce
ā	pay	ē	be	ŏ	pot
â	care	ĭ	pit	ō	go
ä	father	ī	pie	ô	paw, for
oi	oil	ŭ	cut	zh	vision
ōō	book	û	fur	ə	ago, item,
ōō	boot	*th*	the		pencil, atom,
yōō	abuse	th	thin		circus
ou	out	hw	which	ər	butter

milk·y |mǐl′kē| —*adjective* **milkier, milkiest 1.** Like milk in appearance: *a milky tree cap.* **2.** Having milk in it: *a milky pudding.*

Milky Way The large group of stars that our sun and its planets belong to. The Milky Way can be seen on clear nights as a band of hazy light stretching across the sky.

mill |mǐl| —*noun, plural* **mills 1.** A machine that grinds or crushes something into very small pieces: *a coffee mill; a pepper mill.* **2.** A building with machines for grinding corn, wheat, or other grains into meal or flour. **3.** A building with machines for making things: *a steel mill; a paper mill.*
—*verb* **milled, milling 1.** To grind or crush into powder or very small pieces: *He milled the wheat for the farmers. Coffee is milled at that store.* **2.** To move around in a confused way: *A crowd of people milled around outside.*

milli– A prefix that means "one thousandth": *millimeter; milligram.*

mil·li·gram |mǐl′ə grăm′| —*noun, plural* **milligrams** A unit of mass or weight in the metric system equal to ¹⁄₁₀₀₀ gram.

mil·li·li·ter |mǐl′ə lē′tər| —*noun, plural* **milliliters** A unit of fluid volume or capacity in the metric system equal to ¹⁄₁₀₀₀ liter.

mil·li·me·ter |mǐl′ə mē′tər| —*noun, plural* **millimeters** A unit of length in the metric system equal to ¹⁄₁₀₀₀ meter.

mil·lion |mǐl′yən| —*noun, plural* **million** or **millions 1.** A number, written 1,000,000, that is equal to the product of 1,000 × 1,000. **2.** Often **millions** A very large number: *As for mosquitoes there were millions of them in the woods.*
—*adjective* **1.** Being equal to one thousand thousands. **2.** A great many: *He always has a million jokes.* The adjective **million** belongs to a class of words called **determiners.** They signal that a noun is coming.

mil·lion·aire |mǐl′yə nâr′| —*noun, plural* **millionaires** A person who has at least a million dollars.

mil·lionth |mǐl′yənth| —*noun, plural* **millionths 1.** In a group of people or things that are in numbered order, the one that matches the number 1,000,000. **2.** One of a million equal parts, written ¹⁄₁₀₀₀₀₀₀.
—*adjective:* *the millionth book produced that year.*

mill·stone |mǐl′stōn′| —*noun, plural* **millstones** One of two large, round, flat stones used to grind grain.

mim·e·o·graph |mǐm′ē ə grăf′| or |mǐm′ē ə gräf′| —*noun, plural* **mimeographs 1.** A machine that makes copies of material that is written, drawn, or typed on a stencil. The stencil is fitted around a cylinder that is covered with ink. When the cylinder turns around, the image on the stencil is printed on the paper passing beneath it. **2.** A copy made by such a machine.
—*verb* **mimeographed, mimeographing** To copy with a mimeograph.

mim·ic |mǐm′ĭk| —*verb* **mimicked, mimicking, mimics 1.** To copy; imitate: *Judy mimicked the bird's song.* **2.** To make fun of by imitating; mock: *Justin mimicked the way the old man walked.*
—*noun, plural* **mimics** A person or animal that mimics.

mince |mǐns| —*verb* **minced, mincing** To cut or chop into very small pieces: *She minced an onion for the stew.*

mince·meat |mǐns′mēt′| —*noun* A mixture of finely chopped fruit, spices, suet, and sometimes meat, used as a pie filling.

mind |mīnd| —*noun, plural* **minds 1.** The part of a human

mill
Above: Pepper mill
Below: Steel mill

being that thinks, feels, learns, remembers, wishes, imagines, and dreams. **2.** Mental ability; intelligence: *Use your mind to solve this problem.* **3.** Attention: *Sometimes it's hard to keep your mind on your homework.* **4.** Opinion; view: *Did you change your mind about going to the movies?* **5.** Mental health; sanity: *She lost her mind after the accident.*

—*verb* **minded, minding 1.** To dislike; object to: *He really minds this rainy weather.* **2.** To obey: *Mind your teachers.* **3.** To take care of; look after: *She minded the store while her mother was away.* **4.** To attend to: *Mind your own business.* **5.** To be careful about: *Mind your manners.*

Idioms make up (one's) mind To decide. **never mind** It doesn't matter. **on (one's) mind** In one's thoughts.

mine¹ |mīn| —*noun, plural* **mines 1.** A hole or tunnel dug in the earth to take out metals, coal, salt, or other minerals. **2.** A great amount or source of something valuable: *a mine of information.* **3.** A bomb placed underwater or just under the ground, designed to go off when something touches or comes near it.

—*verb* **mined, mining 1.** To take ore or minerals from the earth: *People mine iron ore in Minnesota.* **2.** To place bombs in or under: *mine the harbor; mine the field.*

mine² |mīn| —*pronoun* The pronoun **mine** is a possessive form of **I.** It is used to show that something or someone belongs to me; my own: *This book is mine. If his desk is occupied, use mine. He is no friend of mine.*

min·er |mī′nər| —*noun, plural* **miners** Someone who works in a mine and takes minerals out of the earth.

♦ *These sound alike* **miner, minor.**

min·er·al |mĭn′ər əl| —*noun, plural* **minerals 1.** A useful substance that is taken from the earth. Gold, copper, coal, oil, and chalk are all minerals. **2.** Any natural substance that is not an animal or plant.

min·i·a·ture |mĭn′ē ə chər| or |mĭn′ə chər| —*adjective* Much smaller than the usual size: *Jimmy has a miniature train.*

—*noun, plural* **miniatures 1.** A small model or copy of something: *Tom bought a miniature of the White House when he was in Washington, D.C.* **2.** A very small painting, especially of a person's head and face.

min·i·mum |mĭn′ə məm| —*noun, plural* **minimums 1.** The smallest amount possible or allowed: *She spoke with a minimum of words. The bank requires people to keep a minimum of five dollars in their accounts.* **2.** The lowest amount or number: *Today's temperature reached a minimum of sixty degrees.*

—*adjective* Lowest possible or allowed: *Sixteen is the minimum age for getting a driver's license in that state.*

min·ing |mī′nĭng| —*noun* **1.** The work or business of taking minerals from the earth. **2.** The process of putting bombs underground or underwater.

min·is·ter |mĭn′ĭ stər| —*noun, plural* **ministers 1.** Someone who leads religious services in a church. **2.** Someone who is in charge of a government department; secretary: *the minister of education.*

mink |mĭngk| —*noun, plural* **minks** or **mink 1.** An animal with a slender body and thick, soft brown fur. **2.** The fur of this animal. It is often used to make or trim clothing.

---

mine¹, mine²
Mine¹ is from the old French word *mine,* which is from a word meaning "ore" in a language spoken in western Europe. **Mine²** simply comes from an old English word. It is closely related to **my.**

miner

mink

ă	pat	ĕ	pet	î	fierce
ā	pay	ē	be	ŏ	pot
â	care	ĭ	pit	ō	go
ä	father	ī	pie	ô	paw, for
oi	oil	ŭ	cut	zh	vision
ōō	book	û	fur	ə	ago, item,
ōō	boot	*th*	the		pencil, atom,
yōō	abuse	th	thin		circus
ou	out	hw	which	ər	butter

Min·ne·so·ta |mĭn'ĭ sō'tə| A state in the north-central United States. The capital of Minnesota is St. Paul.

min·now |mĭn'ō| —*noun, plural* **minnows** A very small fish. Minnows are often used as bait.

mi·nor |mī'nər| —*adjective* Small in size, amount, or importance; lesser: *a minor change; a minor cost; a minor planet; a minor official.*
—*noun, plural* **minors** Someone who has not yet reached the legal adult age: *Minors are not allowed to vote.*
♦ *These sound alike* **minor, miner.**

mi·nor·i·ty |mĭ nôr'ĭ tē| or |mĭ nŏr'ĭ tē| or |mī nôr'ĭ tē| or |mī nŏr'ĭ tē| —*noun, plural* **minorities** **1.** The smaller in number of two groups forming a whole: *A majority of the class voted in favor of keeping hamsters, but a large minority opposed it.* **2.** A group of people thought of as different from the rest of society because of their race, religion, or nationality.

mint¹ |mĭnt| —*noun, plural* **mints** **1.** A plant with leaves that have a strong, pleasant smell and taste. Some kinds of mint are used to flavor candy, chewing gum, and other things. **2.** A candy flavored with mint.

mint² |mĭnt| —*noun, plural* **mints** **1.** A place where the coins of a country are made by the government. **2.** A large amount or supply: *That car must have cost a mint of money.*
—*verb* **minted, minting** To make by stamping metal: *The government mints many coins each year. This coin was minted in 1970.*
—*adjective* Freshly made; unused: *This postage stamp is in mint condition.*

min·u·end |mĭn'yōō ĕnd'| —*noun, plural* **minuends** A number from which another number is to be subtracted. In the example 8 − 5 = 3, 8 is the minuend and 5 is the subtrahend.

mi·nus |mī'nəs| —*preposition* Made less by the subtraction of; decreased by: *Seven minus four equals three.*
—*adjective* **1.** Less than zero; negative: *The temperature fell to minus eight degrees last night.* **2.** A little lower or less than: *a grade of B minus.*
—*noun, plural* **minuses** The sign (−), used to show that the number following is to be subtracted or that the number following has a negative value.

min·ute¹ |mĭn'ĭt| —*noun, plural* **minutes** **1.** A unit of time equal to 1/60 of an hour or sixty seconds. **2.** Any short amount of time; a moment: *Wait a minute.* **3.** A definite point in time: *We are leaving this minute.* **4.** **minutes** An official record of what happens at a meeting of an organization: *The secretary of the student council takes minutes at each meeting.*

mi·nute² |mī nōōt'| or |mī nyōōt'| or |mĭ nōōt'| or |mĭ nyōōt'| —*adjective* **1.** Very, very small; tiny: *The wind blew a minute speck of dirt into her eye.* **2.** Careful and detailed; thorough: *a minute inspection.*

mir·a·cle |mĭr'ə kəl| —*noun, plural* **miracles** **1.** An event that seems impossible because it can't be explained by the laws of nature: *It would be a miracle if it snowed when the temperature was ninety degrees.* **2.** An amazing and unlikely person, thing, or feat; a wonder: *The moon landings were miracles of modern technology. It will be a miracle if you can sleep through all this noise.*

mi·rac·u·lous |mĭ răk'yə ləs| —*adjective* **1.** Like a miracle: *She*

Minnesota
The name **Minnesota** comes from an Indian word meaning "white water." The name of the river came before the name of the state.

mint¹, mint²
Mint¹ comes from a Greek word that referred to the mint plant. **Mint²** comes from a Latin word that meant both "the mint" and "money."

mint¹

minute¹, minute²
Minute¹ and **minute²** both come from the same source word in Latin. That word meant both "small part" and "small."

mirror

Above: Antique mirror
Below: A castle mirrored in water

made a miraculous recovery from a fatal disease. **2.** Having the power to work miracles: *a miraculous drug.*

mir·ror | mĭr′ər | —*noun, plural* **mirrors 1.** Any smooth surface that reflects the image of an object placed in front of it. Most mirrors are made of glass with a sheet of metal behind it. **2.** Anything that gives an accurate picture of something else: *That book is a mirror of life in the Middle Ages.*
—*verb* **mirrored, mirroring** To reflect in or as if in a mirror: *The lake mirrored the sky and the clouds. Her happy laughter mirrored her enjoyment.*

mis- A prefix that means: **1.** In error; wrong: *misspell.* **2.** Bad or badly: *misdeed; misbehave.*

mis·be·have | mĭs′bĭ hāv′ | —*verb* **misbehaved, misbehaving** To behave badly: *Don't misbehave at school.*

mis·be·hav·ior | mĭs′bĭ hāv′yər | —*noun* Bad behavior.

mis·cel·la·ne·ous | mĭs′ə lā′nē əs | —*adjective* Made up of a number of different kinds of things; diverse: *a miscellaneous assortment of candies.*

mis·chief | mĭs′chĭf | —*noun* **1.a.** Naughty behavior: *The boys were playing baseball in the living room until Mother came home and stopped their mischief.* **b.** Trouble resulting from such behavior: *Those children are always getting into mischief.* **2.** Harm or damage: *I hope you're proud of the mischief you've done!*

mis·chie·vous | mĭs′chə vəs | —*adjective* **1.** Full of mischief; naughty: *a mischievous puppy.* **2.** Causing harm or damage: *a mischievous trick.*

mis·con·duct | mĭs kŏn′dŭkt | —*noun, plural* **misconducts** Bad or unlawful behavior: *The judge was accused of misconduct in office.*

mis·count | mĭs kount′ | —*verb* **miscounted, miscounting** To make a mistake in counting: *The clerk miscounted the number of packages.*
—*noun* | mĭs′kount′ |, *plural* **miscounts** A wrong count.

mis·deed | mĭs dēd′ | —*noun, plural* **misdeeds** A bad deed; a mistaken or wicked act: *The boy who broke the window was taken to explain his misdeed before the principal.*

mi·ser | mī′zər | —*noun, plural* **misers** A stingy person who likes to save money. A miser may live like a poor person to save as much money as possible.

mis·er·a·ble | mĭz′ər ə bəl | or | mĭz′rə bəl | —*adjective* **1.** Very unhappy: *It was a lonely, rainy weekend and Kim sat inside feeling miserable.* **2.** Very bad; awful: *a miserable cold; miserable weather.* **3.** Poor; mean; wretched: *They live in a miserable shack.*

mis·er·y | mĭz′ə rē | —*noun, plural* **miseries 1.** Great pain or suffering: *The injured dog was in great misery, but the doctor knew she could cure him.* **2.** Poor conditions of life; poverty: *Millions of people still live in misery.*

mis·fit | mĭs fĭt′ | or | mĭs′fĭt′ | —*noun, plural* **misfits** Someone or something that does not fit properly into a place or group: *Jane, who loved books and knitting, felt like a misfit among her more active friends.*

mis·for·tune | mĭs fôr′chən | —*noun, plural* **misfortunes 1.** Bad luck: *Jim had the misfortune to lose his wallet.* **2.** An unlucky event: *The hurricane was a great misfortune for the fishermen.*

mis·giv·ing | mĭs gĭv′ĭng | —*noun, plural* **misgivings** A feeling that one might be doing the wrong thing; doubt: *I lent Mario my* *pen with some misgivings, because I knew he might lose it.*

mis·hap |mĭs′hăp′| or |mĭs hăp′| —*noun, plural* **mishaps** An unlucky accident: *Alan scraped his elbow in a gym-class mishap.*

mis·laid |mĭs lād′| The past tense and past participle of the verb **mislay:** *Yesterday I mislaid the car keys. I have mislaid my notebook.*

mis·lay |mĭs lā′| —*verb* **mislaid, mislaying** To put in a place that is later forgotten: *I must have mislaid my math book somewhere in the study hall.*

mis·lead |mĭs lēd′| —*verb* **misled, misleading 1.** To send in the wrong direction: *Follow the road signs and don't let that out-of-date map mislead you.* **2.** To give the wrong idea to; deceive: *The crook lied to mislead the police.*

mis·lead·ing |mĭs lēd′ĭng| —*adjective* Causing a mistake: *An old guidebook gave us misleading information, so we never found the entrance to the park.*

mis·led |mĭs lĕd′| The past tense and past participle of the verb **mislead:** *The sign by the road misled us. The report has misled many people with its false statements.*

mis·place |mĭs plās′| —*verb* **misplaced, misplacing 1.** To put in the wrong place: *The secretary misplaced the folder in the file cabinet.* **2.** To lose; mislay: *I misplaced the keys.*

mis·print |mĭs′prĭnt′| or |mĭs prĭnt′| —*noun, plural* **misprints** A mistake in printing.

mis·pro·nounce |mĭs′prə nouns′| —*verb* **mispronounced, mispronouncing** To pronounce in a bad or incorrect way: *It is easy to mispronounce foreign words.*

miss¹ |mĭs| —*verb* **missed, missing 1.** To fail to hit, reach, or touch: *The batter swung and missed the ball. We missed the train. The two friends missed each other in the dark. The arrow missed the target.* **2.** To fail to see, hear, or understand: *They missed the whole point of the story.* **3.** To fall short of: *Nancy missed getting an "A" on the test by one point.* **4.** To fail to be present at: *Jim was sick and missed three weeks of school.* **5.** To leave out or let slip by: *You missed your chance to go. The teacher missed my name in reading the list.* **6.** To get away from; escape or avoid: *The hikers just missed being hurt in an accident.* **7.** To notice or feel the loss of: *I missed my wallet after we left the crowded subway. I miss my family when I go to camp.*

—*noun, plural* **misses** A failure to hit, reach, or touch something: *The archer hit the bull's eye twice without a miss.*

miss² |mĭs| —*noun, plural* **misses 1.** A woman or girl who is not married: *a pretty young miss.* **2. Miss** A title used for a woman or girl who is not married: *May I help you, Miss? My teacher is Miss White.*

mis·sile |mĭs′əl| or |mĭs′īl′| —*noun, plural* **missiles** Any object that is thrown, fired, or dropped at a target. A spear, a rocket, or a stone can be missiles.

miss·ing |mĭs′ĭng| —*adjective* **1.** Lost: *The missing ring was found the next day.* **2.** Absent: *Who is missing from class today?* **3.** Not in place or available; lacking: *This checkers set has some missing pieces.*

mis·sion |mĭsh′ən| —*noun, plural* **missions 1.** A special job that someone is sent to carry out; task: *a rescue mission. Ronald was sent on a mission to buy fruit juice for his Cub Scout troop.* **2.** A place where missionaries do their work: *The city started as a small*

miss¹, miss²

Miss¹ comes from the old English word *missan*, which basically meant "to go wrong." **Miss²** is shortened from **mistress**.

mission
A Spanish mission in California

Spanish mission. **3.** A purpose; goal: *Her mission in life is helping the poor.*

mis·sion·ar·y |mĭsh′ə nĕr′ē| —*noun, plural* **missionaries** Someone sent by a church to a foreign country or land. A missionary teaches the church's religion and often helps to set up schools and hospitals.

Mis·sis·sip·pi |mĭs′ĭ sĭp′ē| A state in the southern United States. The capital of Mississippi is Jackson.

Mis·sou·ri |mĭ zŏor′ē| or |mĭ zŏor′ə| A state in the central United States. The capital of Missouri is Jefferson City.

mis·spell |mĭs spĕl′| —*verb* **misspelled, misspelling** To spell incorrectly: *He misspelled four words on his spelling test.*

mist |mĭst| —*noun, plural* **mists** A mass of tiny drops of water or other liquid in the air; fog: *Mist hovered over the pond all morning.*
—*verb* **misted, misting** To rain in a fine shower: *It began to mist at four o'clock.*

mis·take |mĭ stāk′| —*noun, plural* **mistakes** Something that is done, thought, or figured in an incorrect way; error: *a mistake in arithmetic; a mistake in judgment.*
—*verb* **mistook, mistaken, mistaking** **1.** To understand in a wrong way: *I mistook her tears to mean sadness, not joy.* **2.** To recognize in a wrong way: *I mistook your notebook for mine. When I first saw Bill come in, I mistook him for his brother.*

mis·tak·en |mĭ stā′kən| The past participle of the verb **mistake**: *She has mistaken a high-flying bird for a plane.*
—*adjective* Wrong; in error: *If I am not mistaken, you were here about two years ago.*

mis·ter |mĭs′tər| —*noun, plural* **misters** **1.** A word used in speaking to a man, used without his name: *You left your hat on the seat, mister.* **2.** **Mister** A title used for a man. It is written **Mr.** and is used before a man's last name: *Mr. Anderson.*

mis·tle·toe |mĭs′əl tō′| —*noun* A plant with light-green leaves and white berries. It is a parasite that lives and grows on trees. Mistletoe is often used as a Christmas decoration.

mis·took |mĭ stŏok′| The past tense of the verb **mistake**: *He mistook Jill for her twin sister.*

mis·treat |mĭs trēt′| —*verb* **mistreated, mistreating** To treat in a bad or unkind way: *The boy mistreated the bird by throwing stones at it.*

mis·tress |mĭs′trĭs| —*noun, plural* **mistresses** **1.** A woman who is the head of a household: *The mistress of the house planned the meals with her cook.* **2.** The female owner of a dog, horse, or other animal: *The dog ran to its mistress.*

mis·trust |mĭs trŭst′| —*noun* Lack of trust; suspicion.
—*verb* **mistrusted, mistrusting** To have no trust in: *Our dog mistrusts strangers and barks at them.*

mist·y |mĭs′tē| —*adjective* **mistier, mistiest** **1.** Clouded or covered with mist: *a misty morning.* **2.** Not clear; vague; dim: *She had only misty memories of her dead father.*

mis·un·der·stand |mĭs′ŭn dər stănd′| —*verb* **misunderstood, misunderstanding** To understand incorrectly: *Did you misunderstand the question?*

mis·un·der·stand·ing |mĭs′ŭn dər stăn′dĭng| —*noun, plural* **misunderstandings** **1.** A failure to understand or agree about instructions or directions: *Because of a misunderstanding, Jerry and*

mistletoe

ă	pat	ĕ	pet	î	fierce
ā	pay	ē	be	ŏ	pot
â	care	ĭ	pit	ō	go
ä	father	ī	pie	ô	paw, for
oi	oil	ŭ	cut	zh	vision
ŏŏ	book	û	fur	ə	ago, item,
ōō	boot	*th*	the		pencil, atom,
yōō	abuse	th	thin		circus
ou	out	hw	which	ər	butter

I waited for each other on different corners. **2.** An argument or quarrel: *They did not speak to each other after their misunderstanding.*

mis·un·der·stood |mĭs′ŭn dər **stŏŏd′** | The past tense of the verb **misunderstand:** *She misunderstood the directions and got lost.*

mis·use |mĭs yōōz′ | —*verb* **misused, misusing** To use incorrectly or badly; abuse: *The senator misused his power by placing his friends in government jobs.*
—*noun* |mĭs yōōs′ |, *plural* **misuses** Wrong or improper use: *the misuse of language.*

mite |mīt| —*noun, plural* **mites** A very small animal related to the spiders. Mites often live on plants or other animals.
♦ *These sound alike* **mite, might.**

mitt |mĭt| —*noun, plural* **mitts** **1.** A large, well-padded glove worn by a baseball player. **2.** A mitten.

mit·ten |mĭt′n| —*noun, plural* **mittens** A warm covering for the hand. A mitten has one wide part to cover all four fingers, and a separate part to cover the thumb.

mix |mĭks| —*verb* **mixed, mixing** **1.** To put together and combine; blend: *Mix the flour, water, and eggs to form a dough.* **2.** To be able to blend together: *Oil does not mix with water.* **3.** To make by putting different ingredients together: *mix a cake; mix a pitcher of lemonade.* **4.** To get along together; be friendly: *The boys and girls mixed well at the dance.*
   Phrasal verb **mix up** To confuse: *You mixed up the instructions so much we didn't know what to do first.*
—*noun, plural* **mixes** **1.** A food in which the ingredients are mixed: *We bought a cake mix.* **2.** A combination; mixture.

mixed |mĭkst| —*adjective* **1.** Made of different things or kinds: *a mixed salad; mixed emotions.* **2.** With or for both men and women: *a mixed audience; a mixed chorus.*

mixed number A number made up of a whole number and a fraction. The number 7⅜ is a mixed number.

mix·er |mĭk′sər| —*noun, plural* **mixers** A machine that mixes or blends things together: *a cement mixer.*

mix·ture |mĭks′chər| —*noun, plural* **mixtures** **1.** Anything that is made up of different ingredients, things, or kinds; combination: *A mixture of sleet and rain was falling. For paste we used a mixture of flour and water.* **2.** The act of mixing: *The mixture of red and yellow will make orange.*

moan |mōn| —*noun, plural* **moans** A long, low sound, usually of pain or sadness: *He let out a moan and rubbed his sore shoulder.*
—*verb* **moaned, moaning** **1.** To make a moan or moans: *He was moaning in his sleep.* **2.** To make a sound like a moan: *The wind moaned through the trees.* **3.** To say with a moan or moans; complain: *She's been moaning all morning that she doesn't want to go to the dentist.*
♦ *These sound alike* **moan, mown.**

moat |mōt| —*noun, plural* **moats** A wide, deep ditch, usually filled with water. In the Middle Ages a moat was dug around castles and towns to protect them from enemies. A bridge could be lowered over the moat so people could cross over.

mob |mŏb| —*noun, plural* **mobs** **1.** A large group of people; a crowd: *There was a mob at the airport waiting for the baseball players.* **2.** A large, angry crowd, especially one that acts violently and breaks the law.

mitt
A baseball mitt

moat

—*verb* **mobbed, mobbing** To crowd around in anger or excitement: *The singer was mobbed by teen-agers.*

mo·bile |mō′bəl| or |mō′bēl′| or |mō′bīl′| —*adjective* Able to move or be moved from place to place: *a mobile home.*

moc·ca·sin |mŏk′ə sĭn| —*noun, plural* **moccasins** **1.** A soft leather shoe, slipper, or low boot that does not have a heel. Moccasins were first worn by North American Indians. **2.** A poisonous snake, the **water moccasin.**

moccasin

mock |mŏk| —*verb* **mocked, mocking** To make fun of in a cruel way, often by imitating: *The teacher was angry at Fred for mocking the new student's accent. My friends mocked me for staying inside and doing my homework.*
—*adjective* False or imitation: *a mock diamond.*

mock·ing·bird |mŏk′ĭng bûrd′| —*noun, plural* **mockingbirds** A gray and white American songbird. It often imitates the songs of other birds.

mode |mōd| —*noun, plural* **modes** A way or style of doing something: *Airplanes are a modern mode of transportation.*

mo·del |mŏd′l| —*noun, plural* **models** **1.** A small copy of something: *I built a model of a pirate ship.* **2.** A style or kind of thing: *This car is last year's model.* **3.** A person or thing that is a good example of something: *Mark is a model of good cheer.* **4.** A person whose job is to wear new clothes in order to show them to people who might buy them. Models also pose for pictures in magazines and newspapers and work in stores and fashion shows. **5.** A person who poses for an artist or photographer.
—*verb* **modeled, modeling** **1.** To make or build out of clay, wax, or other material: *Sam models animals in clay. Those figures are modeled from animals I saw on my uncle's farm.* **2.** To copy or imitate someone or something: *The library is modeled after a famous building in France. Jimmy wants to model himself after his older brother.* **3.** To show or display clothing by wearing it; work as a model: *May modeled her new dress for her father. My sister models for a living.*

mockingbird

mod·er·ate |mŏd′ər ĭt| —*adjective* **1.** Not too much or too little; not extreme or excessive: *moderate prices. My father always drives at a moderate speed.* **2.** Not severe; mild: *We moved to Arizona because it has a moderate climate.*
—*verb* |mŏd′ə rāt′| **moderated, moderating** To make or become less extreme: *This terrible hot weather should moderate by Tuesday.*

mod·ern |mŏd′ərn| —*adjective* Having to do with the present time or the recent past: *The transistor radio is a modern invention.*

mo·der·nize |mŏd′ər nīz′| —*verb* **modernized, modernizing** To make modern; to change in order to meet present or new needs: *The school was modernized last year.*

mod·est |mŏd′ĭst| —*adjective* **1.** Not bragging or thinking too highly about one's own talents, abilities, or accomplishments: *We were all surprised by how modest the famous artist was.* **2.** Average or less than average; not extreme: *a modest salary; modest prices.*

mod·i·fi·er |mŏd′ə fī′ər| —*noun, plural* **modifiers** A word or group of words that limits the meaning of another word or group of words. A modifier can be an adjective, an adverb, or a noun. In the sentences "He saw the red barn," "Drive slowly," and "We had a family reunion," the words "red," "slowly," and "family" are modifiers.

mod·i·fy |mŏd′ə fī′| —*verb* **modified, modifying, modifies** **1.** To

ă	pat	ĕ	pet	î	fierce
ā	pay	ē	be	ŏ	pot
â	care	ĭ	pit	ō	go
ä	father	ī	pie	ô	paw, for
oi	oil	ŭ	cut	zh	vision
ŏŏ	book	û	fur	ə	ago, item,
ōō	boot	th	the		pencil, atom,
yōō	abuse	th	thin		circus
ou	out	hw	which	ər	butter

change; alter: *Plans for the new school were modified so three extra classrooms could be added.* **2.** In grammar, to limit the meaning of a word or group of words. In the sentence "He bought a blue car," the word "blue" modifies the word "car."

mod·ule |mŏj′ool| or |mŏd′yool| —*noun, plural* **modules** The separate parts of a spacecraft, each being used for a special job or jobs: *the command module; a lunar module.*

Mo·ham·med |mō hăm′ĭd| or |mō hä′mĭd| The founder of Islam, the Moslem religion.

moist |moist| —*adjective* Slightly wet; damp: *a moist towel.*

mois·ten |moi′sən| —*verb* **moistened, moistening** To make slightly wet or damp: *Will you moisten the sponge and wipe the table?*

mois·ture |mois′chər| —*noun* Water or other liquid that is in the air or in the ground or that forms tiny drops on a surface: *The roots of a plant get moisture from the ground. When I take a shower, moisture forms on the bathroom mirror.*

mo·lar |mō′lər| —*noun, plural* **molars** Any of the large teeth in the back of the mouth. They have wide, flat tops for grinding food. Human beings have twelve molars.

mo·las·ses |mə lăs′ĭz| —*noun* A thick, sweet syrup that is produced when sugar cane is made into sugar.

mold¹ |mōld| —*noun, plural* **molds** A hollow container that is made in a particular shape. A liquid or soft material, such as wax, gelatin, or plaster, is put into a mold. When the material hardens, it takes the shape of the mold.
—*verb* **molded, molding** **1.** To make or form into a shape: *Use your hands to mold the clay.* **2.** To influence and form the personality and character of; to shape: *The job of the boss is to mold the workers into an effective team.*

mold² |mōld| —*noun, plural* **molds** A tiny plant that is a kind of fungus. Molds often form a fuzzy coating on food or other substances with a damp surface.
—*verb* **molded, molding** To become covered with mold.

mold·y |mōl′dē| —*adjective* **moldier, moldiest** **1.** Covered with mold: *The old loaf of bread is moldy.* **2.** Having a damp, stale smell: *The cabin in the woods is always moldy after the winter.*

mole¹ |mōl| —*noun, plural* **moles** A small brown growth or spot on the skin.

mole² |mōl| —*noun, plural* **moles** A small animal that digs burrows under the ground. Moles have very small eyes and short, silky fur.

mol·e·cule |mŏl′ə kyool′| —*noun, plural* **molecules** The smallest and most basic particle into which a substance can be divided and still be the same substance. A molecule is made up of atoms.

mol·lusk |mŏl′əsk| —*noun, plural* **mollusks** One of a large group of animals that have a soft body and usually live in water. Most mollusks have a hard outer shell. Snails, clams, and oysters are mollusks with shells. Octopuses, squids, and slugs are mollusks with no outer shell.

molt |mōlt| —*verb* **molted, molting** To shed an outer covering such as skin, feathers, or hair. The outer covering is replaced by a new growth: *Some snakes molt in the spring.*

molt·en |mōl′tən| —*adjective* Made into liquid or melted by heat: *We poured molten lead into molds to make toy circus animals.*

mold¹, mold²
Mold¹ comes from an old French word that meant "small measure" or "model." People who lived in Scandinavia a long time ago used **mold²** to mean "growth of mold."

mole¹, mole²
Mole¹ comes from a word used long ago by English-speaking people to mean "spot, blemish." **Mole²** comes from an old Germanic name for the animal.

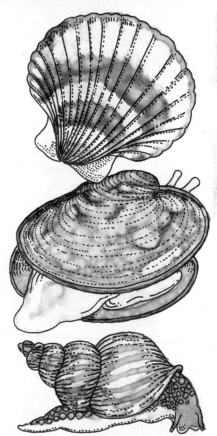

mollusk
Above: Scallop
Center: Clam
Below: Snail

monarch
A monarch butterfly

monkey
Two kinds of monkey

ă	pat	ĕ	pet	î	fierce
ā	pay	ē	be	ŏ	pot
â	care	ĭ	pit	ō	go
ä	father	ī	pie	ô	paw, for

oi	oil	ŭ	cut	zh	vision
ŏŏ	book	û	fur	ə	ago, item,
ōō	boot	th	the		pencil, atom,
yōō	abuse	th	thin		circus
ou	out	hw	which	ər	butter

mom |mŏm| —*noun, plural* **moms** A shortened form of "mother."

mo·ment |mō′mənt| —*noun, plural* **moments** **1.** A very short period of time; an instant: *Wait a moment while I wash my hands.* **2.** A certain point in time: *This is the happiest moment of my life.*

mo·men·tar·y |mō′mən ter′ē| —*adjective* Lasting only for a short time or a moment: *I caught only a momentary glance of him as he ran by.*

mo·men·tous |mō mĕn′təs| —*adjective* Very important or significant: *The landing of the first spacecraft on the moon was a momentous event.*

mo·men·tum |mō mĕn′təm| —*noun, plural* **momentums** The force or speed that an object has when it moves: *The sled gained momentum as it raced down the hill.*

mon·arch |mŏn′ərk| —*noun, plural* **monarchs** **1.** A king, queen, or emperor. **2.** A large orange and black butterfly.

mon·ar·chy |mŏn′ər kē| —*noun, plural* **monarchies** **1.** Government by a monarch. **2.** A country ruled by a monarch.

mon·as·ter·y |mŏn′ə ster′ē| —*noun, plural* **monasteries** A building or set of buildings where monks live and work in a group.

Mon·day |mŭn′dē| or |mŭn′dā′| —*noun, plural* **Mondays** The second day of the week, after Sunday and before Tuesday.

mon·ey |mŭn′ē| —*noun, plural* **moneys** **1.** The different coins and paper bills printed by the government of a country; currency. It is used to buy or pay for things or services. Pennies, nickels, dimes, quarters, and dollar bills are United States money. **2.** Anything of value that is in a form that can be exchanged for goods or services. Checks are used for money. Seashells, pieces of iron, gold, and silver have also all been used for money. **3.** The amount of money needed for a particular purpose: *Do we have enough money for the movies tonight?*

mon·goose |mŏng′gōōs′| or |mŏn′gōōs′| —*noun, plural* **mongooses** An animal with a long, narrow body and a long tail. Mongooses live in warm regions. They are good at killing poisonous snakes. They also kill rats and small birds.

mon·grel |mŭng′grəl| or |mŏng′grəl| or |mŏn′grəl| —*noun, plural* **mongrels** A dog that is a mixture of different breeds: *That puppy is a mongrel; its father is a beagle and its mother is a poodle.*

mon·i·tor |mŏn′ĭ tər| —*noun, plural* **monitors** **1.** A student who does a special job to help the teacher: *a blackboard monitor; an attendance monitor.* **2.** Someone or something that keeps watch or warns of trouble: *Monitors were appointed to watch for stolen goods.*
—*verb* **monitored, monitoring** To keep watch over; keep track of: *He monitors the production in the factory. The machines monitor the patient's condition.*

monk |mŭngk| —*noun, plural* **monks** A member of a men's religious order who lives in a monastery and observes the rules of that order.

mon·key |mŭng′kē| —*noun, plural* **monkeys** An animal that has hands with thumbs and a long tail. There are many kinds of monkeys. They belong to the same group as apes and human beings.
—*verb* **monkeyed, monkeying** To fool around; play or meddle: *He monkeyed with the radio, but couldn't make it work. Mom said, "Do your homework and don't monkey around."*

monkey wrench —*plural* **monkey wrenches** A tool with a jaw that adjusts to fit different sizes of nuts and bolts.

mon·o·gram |**mŏn′**ə grăm′| —*noun, plural* **monograms** A design made by combining a person's initials. Monograms are used to identify and decorate clothing, jewelry, and other possessions.

mo·nop·o·ly |mə **nŏp′**ə lē| —*noun, plural* **monopolies**
1. Complete control over selling or making a product or service: *The electric company has a monopoly in supplying electric power to the area.* **2.** A company that has complete control over selling or making a product or service: *In some countries, the airline is a monopoly owned by the government.*

mo·not·o·nous |mə **nŏt′**n əs| —*adjective* Always the same; never changing; dull: *a monotonous voice; a monotonous job.*

mon·soon |mŏn **soon′**| —*noun, plural* **monsoons** **1.** A wind in southern Asia that changes with the seasons. It blows from the ocean toward the land in summer months and brings lots of rain. It blows from the land toward the ocean in winter months and brings hot, dry weather. **2.** The wet, rainy summer season brought by this wind.

mon·ster |**mŏn′**stər| —*noun, plural* **monsters** **1.** A huge, frightening, imaginary creature: *The knight had slain fire-breathing dragons and other monsters.* **2.** A very large animal, person, or thing: *A monster of a wave struck the beach.* **3.** An animal or plant that is rare and not normal in form: *A hen with four legs is a monster.* **4.** A very evil or cruel person or animal: *That monster has no regard for other people's lives.*
—*adjective* Very large: *a monster turtle.*

mon·stros·i·ty |mŏn **strŏs′**ĭ tē| —*noun, plural* **monstrosities** Anything that is extremely large, ugly, or evil: *That painting is a monstrosity!*

mon·strous |**mŏn′**strəs| —*adjective* **1.** Of or like a monster or monsters: *There are legends of monstrous birds attacking human beings.* **2.** Very ugly in shape or form: *The villain had a monstrous scar on his face.* **3.** Very large; enormous; huge: *a monstrous iceberg.* **4.** Evil, cruel, or shocking: *That was a monstrous thing to say!*

Mon·tan·a |mŏn **tăn′**ə| A state in the northwestern United States. The capital of Montana is Helena.

Mont·gom·er·y |mŏnt **gŭm′**ə rē| The capital of Alabama.

month |mŭnth| —*noun, plural* **months** One of the twelve divisions of the year. On our calendar, most of the months have 31 days. April, June, September, and November have 30 days. February has 28 days, except in leap years, when it has 29.

month·ly |**mŭnth′**lē| —*adjective* **1.** Happening, appearing, or to be paid once every month: *Our club has monthly meetings. The monthly rent is due today.* **2.** For a period of one month: *the monthly rainfall for June; the monthly sales of cars.*
—*adverb* Every month; once a month: *He writes to me monthly.*
—*noun, plural* **monthlies** A magazine that is issued once a month.

Mont·pe·lier |mŏnt **pēl′**yər| The capital of Vermont.

mon·u·ment |**mŏn′**yə mənt| —*noun, plural* **monuments** **1.** A statue, sculpture, or other structure built to honor a person, group, or event: *They built a monument to those who died in the Civil War.* **2.** Anything that is kept or admired for its importance or

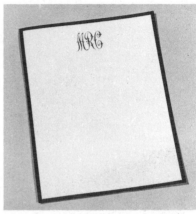

monkey wrench

monogram

Montana
Montana comes from the Latin word that means "mountainous regions."

monument

beauty: *The plantation is kept as a monument to the old days. His book was a monument of scientific thought.*

moo | mōō | —*noun, plural* **moos** The deep sound a cow makes. —*verb* **mooed, mooing, moos** To make such a sound: *The cows mooed in the barn.*

mood | mōōd | —*noun, plural* **moods** The way someone feels at a certain time; a person's spirits or attitude: *She was in a good mood after she won the tennis match.*

mood·y | mōō′dē | —*adjective* **moodier, moodiest** Changing moods often: *The moody boy was happy this morning but sad and thoughtful this afternoon.*

moon | mōōn | —*noun, plural* **moons** **1.** Earth's natural satellite. The moon orbits the earth and reflects the sun's light. **2.** The natural satellite of any other planet: *Two moons orbit Mars.* **3.** A month: *I haven't seen you in many moons.*

moon·beam | mōōn′bēm′ | —*noun, plural* **moonbeams** A ray of moonlight.

moon·light | mōōn′līt′ | —*noun* The light that comes from the moon. —*adjective* Of or happening by the light of the moon: *a moonlight boat ride.* —*verb* **moonlighted, moonlighting** To work at a second job in addition to a regular job: *The police officer moonlights as a taxi driver.*

moon·lit | mōōn′lĭt′ | —*adjective* Having light from the moon: *a clear, moonlit night.*

moor¹ | mŏŏr | —*verb* **moored, mooring** To tie up or anchor: *We moored the rowboat to the dock. The ship moored in the bay. They moored the blimp with ropes and rocks.*

moor² | mŏŏr | —*noun, plural* **moors** A broad stretch of open land with weeds and marshes.

moose | mōōs | —*noun, plural* **moose** A large animal related to the deer. The male has large, broad antlers. Moose live in northern regions. The European moose is called an *elk.*

mop | mŏp | —*noun, plural* **mops** **1.** A tool for washing and wiping floors. A mop has a sponge, yarn, or rags attached to a long handle. **2.** A thick, tangled head of hair. —*verb* **mopped, mopping** To wash, scrub, or wipe with a mop or other material that absorbs moisture: *She mopped the floor and then waxed it. He mopped up the spill with a sponge.*

mope | mōp | —*verb* **moped, moping** **1.** To be gloomy and silent; be dejected. **2.** To move in an aimless way: *He moped around the house with nothing to do.*

mor·al | môr′əl | or | mŏr′əl | —*adjective* **1.** Good and just; virtuous: *A moral person does not lie, cheat, or steal.* **2.** Concerned with what is right and wrong: *The father was forced to make a moral decision on whether to steal food or let his family starve.* **3.** Teaching what is right, good, or just: *a moral lesson; a moral book.* **4.** Mental rather than physical; psychological: *They offered him moral support in his fight against the foe.* —*noun, plural* **morals** **1.** The lesson taught by a fable, story, or event; basic message: *The moral was "Don't count your chickens before they hatch."* **2.** **morals** Rules and practice of good and right behavior: *He has no morals, so you can't trust him.*

mo·rale | mə răl′ | —*noun* The spirit or enthusiasm shown by a person or group working toward a goal: *The team's morale was high after it won a series of games.*

---

moor¹, moor²

Moor¹ comes from a form of German spoken about the thirteenth through fifteenth centuries. **Moor²** is an old English word.

moose

ă	pat	ĕ	pet	î	fierce
ā	pay	ē	be	ŏ	pot
â	care	ĭ	pit	ō	go
ä	father	ī	pie	ô	paw, for

oi	oil	ŭ	cut	zh	vision
ŏŏ	book	û	fur	ə	ago, item,
ōō	boot	th	the		pencil, atom,
yōō	abuse	th	thin		circus
ou	out	hw	which	ər	butter

more |môr| or |mōr| —*adjective* The comparative of the adjectives **many** and **much. 1.** Greater in number: *Many people came yesterday, but more people came today.* **2.** Greater in size, amount, or degree: *She did much work, but he did more work.* **3.** Additional; extra: *We brought more food along, just in case.* The adjective **more** belongs to a class of words called **determiners.** They signal that a noun is coming.
—*noun* A greater or additional amount, number, or degree: *More of the flowers have been ordered. More of them are coming than we expected.*
—*adverb* **1.** To a greater extent or degree. The word **more** forms the comparative of many adjectives and adverbs that do not form comparatives by adding "-er": *This is more difficult than I had expected. She dressed more simply than her sister.* **2.** In addition; again: *I'll call her once more.*
   Idiom more or less About; roughly: *The trip takes six hours more or less.*

more·o·ver |môr ō′vər| or |mōr ō′vər| or |**môr**′ō′vər| or |**mōr**′ō′vər| —*adverb* Beyond what has been said; also; besides: *I don't want to go fishing, and moreover I don't have the right clothes.*

morn·ing |**môr**′nĭng| —*noun, plural* **mornings** The early part of the day. Morning is from sunrise to noon or from midnight to noon.
—*adjective* Of or during the early part of the day: *the morning sun; a morning walk.*
   ♦ *These sound alike* **morning, mourning.**

mor·ning-glo·ry |**môr**′nĭng glôr′ē| or |**mōr**′nĭng glôr′ē| —*noun, plural* **morning-glories** A climbing vine with showy flowers that are shaped like a funnel. The flowers usually close in the afternoon.

mor·sel |**môr**′səl| —*noun, plural* **morsels** A small piece of food; a bit: *I cannot eat another morsel.*

mor·tal |**môr**′tl| —*adjective* **1.** Certain to die someday: *All human beings are mortal.* **2.** Causing death of the body or soul: *a mortal wound; a mortal sin.* **3.** Lasting until death: *a mortal enemy; a mortal battle.*
—*noun, plural* **mortals** A human being: *No mortal can fly to the sun.*

mor·tar |**môr**′tər| —*noun, plural* **mortars 1.** A bowl in which spices or other things are crushed or ground with a pestle. **2.** A building material made of sand, water, lime, and sometimes cement. Mortar is used to hold bricks or stones together. **3.** A short cannon that fires shells in a high arc.

mo·sa·ic |mō zā′ĭk| —*noun, plural* **mosaics** A picture or design made by fitting together and cementing small pieces of colored tile, glass, stone, or other material.

Mos·lem |**mŏz**′ləm| or |**mŏs**′ləm| —*noun, plural* **Moslems** A person who believes in the religion of Islam.
—*adjective* Of or for the religion of Islam: *a Moslem prayer; a Moslem temple.* Another form of this word is **Muslim.**

mosque |mŏsk| —*noun, plural* **mosques** A Moslem house of worship.

mos·qui·to |mə **skē**′tō| —*noun, plural* **mosquitoes** or **mosquitos** A small flying insect. Female mosquitoes bite and suck blood from animals and human beings. Some kinds of mosquitoes spread the diseases malaria and yellow fever.

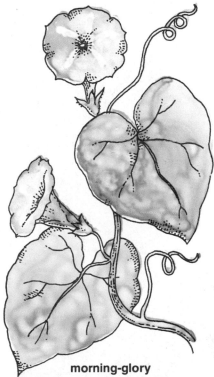

morning-glory

mosaic

moss |môs| or |mŏs| —*noun, plural* **mosses** One of a group of small green plants that do not have flowers. Moss often forms a covering on damp ground, rocks, or tree trunks.

moss·y |mô′sē| or |mŏs′ē| —*adjective* **mossier, mossiest** Like or covered with moss: *a mossy green; mossy rocks.*

most |mōst| —*adjective* **1.** The superlative of the adjectives **many** and **much.** Greatest in number: *I won many prizes; he won more prizes; she won the most prizes. Our school has the most students of any school in town.* **2.** The superlative of the adjective **much.** Largest in amount, size, or degree: *She has much luck; I had more luck; he had the most luck.* **3.** In the greatest number of cases: *Most fish have fins.* The adjective **most** belongs to a class of words called **determiners.** They signal that a noun is coming. —*noun* **1.** The greatest amount, quantity, or degree; the largest part: *Most of this land is good for farming.* **2.** The largest number; the majority: *Most of these boys play baseball.* —*adverb* **1.** In the highest degree, quantity, or extent. The word **most** forms the superlative of many adjectives and adverbs that do not form superlatives by adding "-est": *This is the most difficult job I have ever done. He ran most quickly of all.* **2.** Very: *That is a most beautiful painting.*

Idioms **at (the) most** At the top limit: *She is 12 or 13, or at most 15. I'll spend $20 to $25, at most $30.* **make the most of** To do the best possible with: *He made the most of his little farm.*

most·ly |mōst′lē| —*adverb* For the greater part; mainly; chiefly: *The dog is mostly black with a few tan patches.*

mo·tel |mō tĕl′| —*noun, plural* **motels** A hotel with a parking lot where guests can park their cars.

moth |môth| or |mŏth| —*noun, plural* **moths** |mô*th*z| or |mŏ*th*z| or |môths| or |mŏths| An insect that is very much like a butterfly. Moths usually fly at night. Some kinds of moths cause serious harm to trees. Another kind damages things made of wool or fur.

moth·er |mŭ*th*′ər| —*noun, plural* **mothers** The female parent of a child.

moth·er·hood |mŭ*th*′ər hŏŏd′| —*noun* The condition of being a mother.

moth·er-in-law |mŭ*th*′ər ĭn lô′| —*noun, plural* **mothers-in-law** The mother of a person's wife or husband.

moth·er·ly |mŭ*th*′ər lē| —*adjective* Of or like a mother; loving and protective: *She gave him a motherly hug.*

Mother's Day A holiday celebrated on the second Sunday in May, in honor of mothers.

mo·tion |mō′shən| —*noun, plural* **motions** **1.** The process of moving; change of position; movement: *The sea is always in motion.* **2.** A movement of a hand, arm, or other part of the body; a gesture: *the graceful motions of the dancer.* **3.** Operation; action: *We set our plan in motion. He put the machine in motion.* **4.** A formal request or proposal made during a meeting or trial. —*verb* **motioned, motioning** To tell or signal with a motion; gesture: *The police officer motioned us to cross the street.*

mo·tion·less |mō′shən lĭs| —*adjective* Not moving: *The motionless leaves showed that there was no wind.*

motion picture A series of pictures projected so quickly on a screen that the objects in the pictures seem to be moving; moving picture.

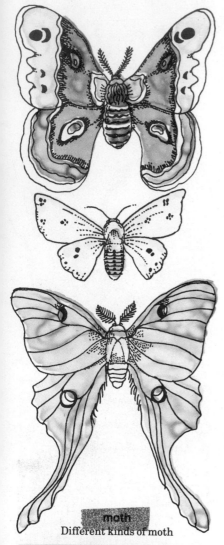
moth
Different kinds of moth

ă	pat	ĕ	pet	î	fierce
ā	pay	ē	be	ŏ	pot
â	care	ĭ	pit	ō	go
ä	father	ī	pie	ô	paw, for
oi	oil	ŭ	cut	zh	vision
ŏŏ	book	û	fur	ə	ago, item,
ōō	boot	*th*	the		pencil, atom,
yōō	abuse	th	thin		circus
ou	out	hw	which	ər	butter

mo·tive |mō′tĭv| —*noun, plural* **motives** A reason for doing something: *Her motive for inviting us is to ask for our help.*

mo·tor |mō′tər| —*noun, plural* **motors** A device or machine that provides the power to make something go; engine: *The car's motor broke, and the car won't go. The fan has an electric motor.*
—*adjective* **1.** Driven by a motor or engine: *a motor vehicle.* **2.** Of vehicles that are driven by engines: *a motor accident; a motor race.* **3.** Of or for motors: *motor oil; a motor part.* **4.** Of nerves or muscles that control movements: *She has poor motor control.*
—*verb* **motored, motoring** To drive or travel in a motor vehicle: *They motored across country.*

mo·tor·boat |mō′tər bōt′| —*noun, plural* **motorboats** A boat that moves by the power of a motor.

mo·tor·cy·cle |mō′tər sī′kəl| —*noun, plural* **motorcycles** A vehicle with two wheels and a motor to drive it. A motorcycle is larger and heavier than a bicycle.

mot·to |mŏt′ō| —*noun, plural* **mottoes** or **mottos** A saying that expresses what is important to a state, nation, family, group, person, or organization: *Their motto was "All for one and one for all."*

mound |mound| —*noun, plural* **mounds** **1.** An area of earth that is raised above the surrounding area; small hill. **2.** A heap or pile: *a mound of leaves; mounds of mashed potatoes.* **3.** The raised area for the pitcher in the middle of a baseball diamond.

mount¹ |mount| —*verb* **mounted, mounting** **1.** To go up; climb; rise: *We mounted the stairs. The balloon mounted into the sky.* **2.** To get up on a horse or other animal: *She mounted the pony for a short trot. The knights mounted and rode off to battle.* **3.** To put in a suitable place for use or display; set: *Let's mount the antenna on the roof. He mounted the diamond in a gold ring.*
—*noun, plural* **mounts** **1.** A horse or other animal for riding. **2.** A frame, background, or structure for holding something: *a glass mount for a microscope slide; a mount for a precious gem.*

mount² |mount| —*noun, plural* **mounts** A mountain.

moun·tain |moun′tən| —*noun, plural* **mountains** **1.** An area of land that rises high above its surroundings; a high, steep hill. **2.** A large heap or amount: *He has mountains of homework.*

mountain goat An animal that lives in the mountains of northwestern North America. Mountain goats have short black horns and thick white hair.

mountain laurel A shrub with evergreen leaves and clusters of pink or white flowers. Mountain laurel leaves are poisonous.

mountain lion A large light-brown wild cat of western North America and South America. Also called *cougar* and *puma*.

moun·tain·ous |moun′tə nəs| —*adjective* **1.** Having many mountains: *a mountainous region.* **2.** Very large; massive: *a mountainous pile of garbage.*

mountain range A series of mountains that are connected.

mourn |môrn| or |mōrn| —*verb* **mourned, mourning** To feel or show sorrow or grief for a death or a loss: *She is mourning for her mother. The nation mourned its dead President.*

mourn·ing |môr′nĭng| or |mōr′nĭng| —*noun* **1.** Grief for a person who has died. **2.** An outward sign of grief for a death. Some signs of mourning are wearing black clothing and flying a flag at half-mast. **3.** A period of time during which a dead person

motorboat

mount¹, mount²
Both **mount¹** and **mount²** can be traced back to the same Latin word, one that was used to mean "mountain." **Mount²** comes directly from this word. **Mount¹** comes from a related Latin word that meant "to climb a mountain." Both of these words appeared in French before appearing in English.

mountain goat

mountain lion

mouse

is mourned: *He will not attend parties during mourning.*

♦ *These sound alike* **mourning, morning.**

mouse |mous| —*noun, plural* **mice** A small animal with a long, thin, almost hairless tail. Some kinds of mice live in or near the houses of human beings.

mouse·trap |mous′trăp′| —*noun, plural* **mousetraps** A trap for catching mice.

mous·tache |mŭs′tăsh′| or |mə stăsh′| —*noun, plural* **moustaches** A form of the word **mustache.**

mouth |mouth| —*noun, plural* **mouths** |mou*th*z| **1.** The part of the body through which an animal takes in food. A human mouth includes the tongue, teeth, and lips. **2.** The part of a river that empties into a larger body of water. **3.** An opening: *the mouth of a bottle; the mouth of a canyon.*

mouth·ful |mouth′fŏol′| —*noun, plural* **mouthfuls** An amount taken into the mouth at one time.

mouth·piece |mouth′pēs′| —*noun, plural* **mouthpieces** The part of a musical instrument or other device that goes in or near the mouth or lips: *He blew into the mouthpiece of the trumpet. Please speak into the mouthpiece of the telephone.*

mov·a·ble |mōo′və bəl| —*adjective* **1.** Capable of being moved or carried: *a movable platform; movable park benches.* **2.** Changing its date from year to year: *Palm Sunday is a movable festival.* Another form of this word is **moveable.**

move |mōov| —*verb* **moved, moving 1.** To change or cause to change position or place: *Move your chair closer to the fire. Don't move or the bee will sting you.* **2.** To change the place where one lives or does business: *My grandfather moved to Florida.* **3.** To go ahead; advance; progress: *The story is not moving fast enough.* **4.** To arouse strong feelings in: *Her sad story moved us to tears.* **5.** To cause to act; persuade: *The attack moved the king to declare war.* **6.** To shift a piece to a different position in a board game: *He moved his checker. You move!* **7.** To suggest or propose in a formal way: *The lawyer moved to transfer the trial to another city.* —*noun, plural* **moves 1.** The act of moving: *He made a move to defend himself. It's time for our move back to the city.* **2.** An action taken to achieve a goal: *Our surprise move upset the enemy's plan.* **3.** A shifting of or a turn to shift pieces in a board game: *He won the chess game in fifteen moves. It's your move!*

move·a·ble |mōo′və bəl| A form of the word **movable.**

move·ment |mōov′mənt| —*noun, plural* **movements 1.** The act or process of changing place or position: *A slight movement of her chest showed she was still alive.* **2.** Action; activity: *The police watched the criminal's movements.* **3.** The work, membership, or cause of a group of people who are trying to achieve a social or political goal: *She is a member of the strike movement.* **4.** The working parts of a device; mechanism: *the movement of a watch.*

mov·er |mōo′vər| —*noun, plural* **movers** A person or company that is hired to move furniture and other belongings from one place to another.

mov·ie |mōo′vē| —*noun, plural* **movies 1.** A motion picture: *We stood in line to see the new movie.* **2.** A theater that shows motion pictures: *Have you seen the picture at the local movie?* **3. movies** The industry that produces motion pictures: *He is a star in the movies and on television.*

mow |mō| —*verb* **mowed, mowed** or **mown, mowing 1.** To cut

ă	pat	ĕ	pet	î	fierce
ā	pay	ē	be	ŏ	pot
â	care	ĭ	pit	ō	go
ä	father	ī	pie	ô	paw, for

oi	oil	ŭ	cut	zh	vision
ŏŏ	book	û	fur	ə	ago, item,
ōō	boot	*th*	the		pencil, atom,
yōō	abuse	th	thin		circus
ou	out	hw	which	ər	butter

grass or grain: *Mow the grass before it gets too high.* **2.** To cut grass or grain from: *Please mow the lawn. The peasants mowed the field.*

mow·er |**mō′**ər| —*noun, plural* **mowers** **1.** A person who mows grass or grain. **2.** A machine that cuts grass or grain.

mown |mōn| A past participle of the verb **mow:** *He had mown the lawn before the thunderstorm hit.*

♦ *These sound alike* **mown, moan.**

Mr. |**mĭs′**tər| An abbreviation used as a title before a man's last name or full name: *Mr. Miller; Mr. John B. Miller.*

Mrs. |**mĭs′**ĭz| An abbreviation used as a title before a woman's married name: *Mrs. Fuller used to be Miss Johnson.*

Ms. or **Ms** |mĭz| An abbreviation used as a title before a woman's last name or full name, whether she is married or not married: *Ms. Ethel Jones; Ms. Wilson.*

much |mŭch| —*adjective* **more, most** Great in amount, degree, or extent; a lot of: *Is there much work to do? He doesn't have much sense. How much money will it cost?*
—*noun* **1.** A large amount: *Did you get much done?*
2. Something important: *He'll never amount to much.*
—*adverb* **1.** To a large extent; by far; greatly: *It is much harder than I thought. She doesn't laugh much.* **2.** Just about; almost: *Life there was much the same as it had always been.*

  Idioms **make much of** To pay a lot of attention to: *We made much of the baby when he started to walk.* **much as** Even though: *Much as I like ice cream, I can't eat more.* **think much of** To think well of; like: *He doesn't think much of your idea.*

mu·cus |**myōo′**kəs| —*noun* The moist material that lines and protects the insides of the mouth, the throat, and other body parts. Mucus is discharged from the nose and throat when a person has a head cold.

mud |mŭd| —*noun* Earth that is wet, soft, and sticky.

muff |mŭf| —*noun, plural* **muffs** A tube of fur or cloth into which one can put one's hands to keep them warm.

muf·fin |**mŭf′**ĭn| —*noun, plural* **muffins** A small cup-shaped bread that is often sweetened and usually served hot with butter.

muf·fle |**mŭf′**əl| —*verb* **muffled, muffling** **1.** To wrap up: *Mother muffled me in a warm coat and wool cap.* **2.** To soften or absorb the sound of: *The rugs muffled the sound of footsteps.*

muf·fler |**mŭf′**lər| —*noun, plural* **mufflers** **1.** A long scarf worn around the neck. **2.** A device to soften the noise of an automobile engine.

mug |mŭg| —*noun, plural* **mugs** A large, heavy, thick cup, usually with a handle.

mug·gy |**mŭg′**ē| —*adjective* **muggier, muggiest** Very warm and humid: *a muggy day in August.*

mul·ber·ry |**mŭl′**bĕr′ē| —*noun, plural* **mulberries** **1.** A tree with sweet, purplish or white fruit shaped like blackberries. **2.** The fruit of this tree.

mule |myōol| —*noun, plural* **mules** An animal that looks like a horse but has longer ears and a tail like a donkey's. The parents of a mule are a male donkey and a female horse. Mules are used as work animals.

mul·ti·ple |**mŭl′**tə pəl| —*noun, plural* **multiples** A number that contains another number an exact number of times: *6, 9, and 12 are multiples of 3.*

mulberry

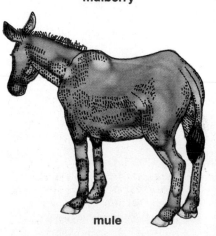

mule

—adjective Many; numerous: *The accident left him with multiple bruises.*

mul·ti·pli·cand | mŭl′tə plĭ **kănd′** | *—noun, plural* **multiplicand** A number that is multiplied by another number. In the example 324 × 8, the multiplicand is 324.

mul·ti·pli·ca·tion | mŭl′tə plĭ **kā′**shən | *—noun, plural* **multiplications** A mathematical operation that is like adding a certain number to itself a particular number of times. For example, 3 × 4 is the same as adding 3 four times (3 + 3 + 3 + 3). The answer is 12.

mul·ti·pli·er | mŭl′tə plī′ər | *—noun, plural* **multipliers** A number that tells how many times a multiplicand is to be multiplied. For example, in 324 × 8, the multiplier is 8.

mul·ti·ply | mŭl′tə plī′ | *—verb* **multiplied, multiplying, multiplies** **1.** To increase in number; grow fast: *The tribe prospered and multiplied.* **2.** To perform the mathematical operation of multiplication on a pair of numbers: *Can you multiply 222 by 12? She just learned how to multiply.*

mul·ti·tude | mŭl′tĭ tōōd′ | or | mŭl′tĭ tyōōd′ | *—noun, plural* **multitudes** A great number; a large amount: *They had a multitude of problems to solve.*

mum | mŭm | *—noun, plural* **mums** A name for a chrysanthemum.

mum·ble | mŭm′bəl | *—verb* **mumbled, mumbling** To speak in a low voice that is not clear and is hard to understand: *She mumbled a quick apology and ran off.*

mum·my | mŭm′ē | *—noun, plural* **mummies** The body of a person or animal that has been preserved and kept from decaying. Ancient Egyptian mummies were wrapped in specially treated cloth, placed in cases, and sealed in tombs.

mumps | mŭmps | *—noun* (Used with a singular verb.) A contagious disease that causes the glands around the jaw and lower cheeks to be swollen.

munch | mŭnch | *—verb* **munched, munching** To chew in a noisy, steady way: *She munched some carrots and celery.*

mu·nic·i·pal | myōō nĭs′ə pəl | *—adjective* Of or having to do with a city or its government: *The municipal building has records of the history of our city.*

mu·ral | myŏŏr′əl | *—noun, plural* **murals** A large painting on or for a wall or ceiling.

mur·der | mûr′dər | *—noun, plural* **murders** The unlawful and deliberate killing of a person by another.
—verb **murdered, murdering** To kill on purpose and against the law: *The bandit murdered the sheriff. He has robbed and murdered all over the country.*

mur·der·er | mûr′dər ər | *—noun, plural* **murderers** A person who murders someone; killer.

murk·y | mûr′kē | *—adjective* **murkier, murkiest** Dark and gloomy: *a murky night; murky caves.*

mur·mur | mûr′mər | *—noun, plural* **murmurs** A low, soft, continuing sound: *the murmur of the sea; the murmur of the crowd.*
—verb **murmured, murmuring** **1.** To make a low, soft, continuing sound: *The leaves murmured in the breeze.* **2.** To say in a low, soft voice: *The shy pupil murmured his answer.*

mus·cle | mŭs′əl | *—noun, plural* **muscles** **1.** A kind of tissue in the body that can be tightened or relaxed to make body parts

mummy

mural
View of a mural in a building

ă	pat	ĕ	pet	î	fierce
ā	pay	ē	be	ŏ	pot
â	care	ĭ	pit	ō	go
ä	father	ī	pie	ô	paw, for
oi	oil	ŭ	cut	zh	vision
ōō	book	û	fur	ə	ago, item,
ōō	boot	*th*	the		pencil, atom,
yōō	abuse	th	thin		circus
ou	out	hw	which	ər	butter

move. **2.** Any particular mass of such tissue: *He has good muscles in his upper arms.* **3.** Strength: *Moving those crates requires lots of muscle.*
♦ *These sound alike* **muscle, mussel.**

mus·cu·lar |**mŭs′**kyə lər| —*adjective* **1.** Of or in muscles: *The heart is a muscular organ. She had muscular pains from too much exercise.* **2.** Having strong, well-developed muscles: *a muscular wrestler.*

mu·se·um |myōō zē′əm| —*noun, plural* **museums** A building for keeping and exhibiting interesting and valuable things. Most museums contain works of art, historical objects and documents, or displays of scientific information.

mush |mŭsh| —*noun, plural* **mushes** Corn meal or other meal boiled in water or milk.

mush·room |**mŭsh′**rōom′| or |**mŭsh′**rŏŏm′| —*noun, plural* **mushrooms** A plant that has a stalk topped by a cap shaped like an umbrella. A mushroom is a type of fungus. Some mushrooms are used as food, but many kinds are poisonous.
—*verb* **mushroomed, mushrooming** To grow, multiply, or spread quickly: *Factories mushroomed all over town.*

mu·sic |**myōō′**zĭk| —*noun* **1.** The art of making pleasing combinations of sounds. **2.** Sounds for voices to sing or instruments to play: *She wrote the words and he wrote the music to the opera.* **3.** Notes written on paper to be played or sung: *He plays the piano well but can't read music.*

mu·si·cal |**myōō′**zĭ kəl| —*adjective* **1.** Of, with, or for making music: *a musical instrument; a musical education; a musical play.* **2.** Pleasing to the ear: *a musical speaking voice.*
—*noun, plural* **musicals** A play that has songs and dances as well as spoken lines.

mu·si·cian |myōō zĭsh′ən| —*noun, plural* **musicians** Someone who is skilled in playing or composing music.

mus·ket |**mŭs′**kĭt| —*noun, plural* **muskets** An old gun with a long barrel. Muskets were used before the invention of the rifle.

musk·mel·on |**mŭsk′**mĕl′ən| —*noun, plural* **muskmelons** A cantaloupe, or a melon like a cantaloupe.

musk ox A large animal of northern North America. Musk oxen have dark, shaggy hair and curved horns.

musk·rat |**mŭs′**krăt′| —*noun, plural* **muskrats** **1.** A North American animal that lives in or near water. The muskrat has thick brown fur and a narrow, flat, scaly tail. **2.** The fur of this animal.

Mus·lim |**mŭz′**ləm| or |**mŏŏs′**ləm| or |**mŏŏz′**ləm| A form of the word **Moslem.**

mus·lin |**mŭz′**lĭn| —*noun, plural* **muslins** A cotton cloth with a plain weave. Muslin may be delicate and sheer or coarse and thick. It is used for sheets, curtains, and clothing.

muss |mŭs| —*verb* **mussed, mussing** To make untidy or messy: *Can you take off the sweater without mussing your hair?*

mus·sel |**mŭs′**əl| —*noun, plural* **mussels** A water animal with a soft body and a pair of narrow dark-blue shells. Some mussels are used as food.
♦ *These sound alike* **mussel, muscle.**

must |mŭst| —*helping,* or *auxiliary, verb* As a helping verb **must** is used to show that the subject: **1.** Is required or obliged to; has to: *Citizens must obey the laws. I must leave now.* **2.** Ought

mushroom
Different kinds of mushroom

to; should: *You must try to see her more often.* **3.** Is almost certain to: *This must be what Mrs. Jones means. His car isn't here, so he must have gone.*

—*noun, plural* **musts** Something that is essential, required, or necessary: *Catch that new movie; it's a must.*

mus·tache |mŭs′tăsh′| or |mə stăsh′| —*noun, plural* **mustaches** The hair growing on a man's upper lip. Another form of this word is **moustache.**

mus·tang |mŭs′tăng′| —*noun, plural* **mustangs** A small, wild horse of the plains of western North America.

mus·tard |mŭs′tərd| —*noun, plural* **mustards** **1.** A plant with yellow flowers and small, sharp-tasting seeds. **2.** A sharp-tasting yellow powder made from the ground seeds of this plant and used to flavor food. **3.** A yellow paste made by mixing the ground seeds with vinegar, wine, or water. Mustard is used as a relish on food.

mus·ter |mŭs′tər| —*verb* **mustered, mustering** **1.** To bring or come together; assemble: *He mustered the troops for inspection. The soldiers mustered for roll call.* **2.** To call forth with difficulty: *He mustered the courage to ask for a raise in his allowance.*

Idiom **pass muster** To be considered good enough: *His work couldn't pass muster.*

must·n't |mŭs′ənt| A contraction of "must not."

mute |myōot| —*adjective* **1.** Not having the power to speak or make sounds: *The accident left him mute. Are giraffes mute?* **2.** Choosing not to speak: *He remained mute under questioning.* **3.** Not spoken; silent: *Her mute agreement was shown by a nod. The "n" in "hymn" is mute.*

—*noun, plural* **mutes** **1.** A person who is not able to speak. **2.** A device used to soften or change the tone of a musical instrument.

—*verb* **muted, muting** To muffle or soften the sound of: *He muted his trumpet. They muted their voices.*

mu·ti·late |myōot′l āt′| —*verb* **mutilated, mutilating** **1.** To injure by cutting off an arm, leg, or other part: *The explosion killed two people and mutilated three others.* **2.** To damage badly by tearing or breaking: *Someone mutilated this library book by ripping out the illustrations.*

mu·ti·ny |myōot′n ē| —*noun, plural* **mutinies** Open rebellion against people in charge, especially by sailors or soldiers against their officers.

—*verb* **mutinied, mutinying, mutinies** To rebel against one's superiors; commit mutiny: *The sailors mutinied against their captain.*

mut·ter |mŭt′ər| —*verb* **muttered, muttering** To speak or say in a low voice that is not clear; mumble: *She muttered to herself as she walked down the street.*

—*noun, plural* **mutters** A low voice or sound that is not clear: *a mutter of complaint.*

mut·ton |mŭt′n| —*noun* The meat of a fully grown sheep.

mu·tu·al |myōo′chōo əl| —*adjective* **1.** Felt or given by each; each for the other: *Their mutual suspicion keeps them from being friends.* **2.** Shared in common: *The two boys discovered they have a mutual friend in Jack.*

muz·zle |mŭz′əl| —*noun, plural* **muzzles** **1.** The projecting part of an animal's face that includes the nose and mouth; snout: *She rubbed the horse's muzzle to calm him.* **2.** A set of straps or

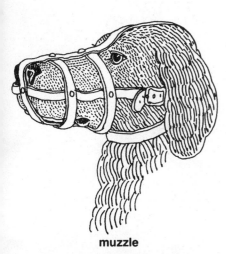

muzzle

ă	pat	ĕ	pet	î	fierce
ā	pay	ē	be	ŏ	pot
â	care	ĭ	pit	ō	go
ä	father	ī	pie	ô	paw, for
oi	oil	ŭ	cut	zh	vision
ōo	book	û	fur	ə	ago, item,
ōo	boot	*th*	the		pencil, atom,
yōo	abuse	th	thin		circus
ou	out	hw	which	ər	butter

wires that fits over an animal's snout to keep the animal from biting or eating. **3.** The open front end of the barrel of a gun.
—*verb* **muzzled, muzzling** To put a muzzle on: *They muzzled the dog to keep it from biting people.*

my |mī| —*pronoun* The pronoun **my** is a possessive form of **I**. It means: **1.** Of or belonging to me: *my hat.* **2.** Done or performed by me: *my first job. I completed my homework on time.* The pronoun **my** as a possessive form of **I** belongs to a class of words called **determiners.** They signal that a noun is coming.

myr·tle |mûr′tl| —*noun* **1.** A trailing vine with shiny evergreen leaves and blue flowers. Also called *periwinkle.* **2.** A shrub with evergreen leaves, white or pinkish flowers, and blackish berries.

my·self |mī sĕlf′| —*pronoun* The pronoun **myself** is a special form of **me**. **1.** It means: **a.** My own self: *I cut myself with the knife.* **b.** My own normal self: *I am not myself today.* **2.** It is used to call attention to me: *I myself had to laugh. I found it amusing myself.*

mys·te·ri·ous |mĭ stîr′ē əs| —*adjective* Hard to explain, know, or understand; strange: *A mysterious light came from the deserted house. Her mysterious smile puzzles everyone.*

mys·te·ry |mĭs′tə rē| —*noun, plural* **mysteries** **1.** Anything that is not known or understood; a secret: *Someone donated the money, but his or her identity is a mystery. The spacecraft will explore the mysteries of the surface of Mars.* **2.** A strange, hidden quality; secrecy: *Those remote caves, never before explored, are full of mystery.* **3.** A story, play, or motion picture in which there is a crime or puzzling matter to solve: *She loves to read mysteries.*

myth |mĭth| —*noun, plural* **myths** **1.** A legend or traditional story that expresses what a people believes and values. Myths often deal with ancestors, heroes, or gods. Some myths try to explain natural events like the seasons and the weather, and others are about how people, plants, and animals were created. **2.** A body of such stories: *We read about dragons in myth and legend.* **3.** A story or idea that is not true: *There is a myth that elephants are afraid of mice.*

myth·i·cal |mĭth′ĭ kəl| —*adjective* **1.** Of or existing only in myths: *A mermaid is a mythical being.* **2.** Imaginary; made-up: *He wrote a mythical tale of a voyage through the center of the earth.*

my·thol·o·gy |mĭ thŏl′ə jē| —*noun, plural* **mythologies** A collection of myths: *American Indian mythology.*

myrtle

Nn

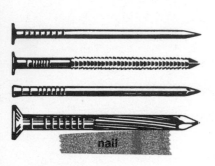

nail

nap¹, nap²
Nap¹ comes from an old English word that meant "to doze." **Nap²** appeared in Dutch before arriving in English as it was spoken about 1100 – 1500.

ă	pat	ĕ	pet	î	fierce
ā	pay	ē	be	ŏ	pot
â	care	ĭ	pit	ō	go
ä	father	ī	pie	ô	paw, for
oi	oil	ŭ	cut	zh	vision
ōŏ	book	û	fur	ə	ago, item,
ōō	boot	*th*	the		pencil, atom,
yōō	abuse	th	thin		circus
ou	out	hw	which	ər	butter

n or **N** |ĕn| —*noun, plural* **n's** or **N's** The fourteenth letter of the English alphabet.

nag |năg| —*verb* **nagged, nagging** To pester or annoy by complaining, scolding, or finding fault all the time: *His mother nags him about doing his chores. Mary nagged at Sandy all morning.*

nail |nāl| —*noun, plural* **nails** 1. A slim, pointed piece of metal with a flat or round head. Nails are hammered into pieces of wood or other material in order to hold them together. 2. The thin, hard covering at the end of a finger or toe.
—*verb* **nailed, nailing** 1. To join or attach with or as if with a nail or nails: *I nailed the boards together. Fear nailed him to his seat.* 2. To seize; catch: *The police nailed the thief.*

na·ked |nā′kĭd| —*adjective* 1. Not wearing clothing or other covering on the body or a part of the body: *a naked boy; naked feet.* 2. Stripped or bare: *trees with naked branches.* 3. Not concealed or disguised: *the naked truth.*

name |nām| —*noun, plural* **names** 1. A word or words by which a person, place, animal, or thing is called or known: *Her son's name is Simon. Iris is the name of a kind of flower. "The Hub" is a name for Boston.* 2. a. Reputation in general: *Jesse James had a bad name.* b. An outstanding reputation; fame: *That young man has made quite a name for himself in politics.*
—*verb* **named, naming** 1. To give a name to: *We named the baby Mary.* 2. To call or mention by name; identify: *Did he name the person whom he suspected of the crime? Name the 50 states and their capitals.* 3. To specify, fix, or set: *Have they named the date for the wedding? Name your price.* 4. To appoint or nominate, as to a certain duty, office, or honor: *He was named coach of the team.*

name·less |nām′lĭs| —*adjective* 1. Having no name: *a nameless puppy; a new invention as yet nameless.* 2. Unknown by name; obscure: *the nameless dead of World War I.* 3. Not identified by name; anonymous: *The owner shall remain nameless.*

name·ly |nām′lē| —*adverb* That is to say: *The lawyer questioned two people, namely Bill Smith and John Roe.*

nap¹ |năp| —*noun, plural* **naps** A short sleep, usually during a period of time other than one's regular sleeping hours.
—*verb* **napped, napping** To sleep for a short time; to doze: *The old man napped in front of the television.*

nap² | năp | —*noun, plural* **naps** A soft or fuzzy surface on
certain kinds of cloth or leather.

nap·kin | năp′kĭn | —*noun, plural* **napkins** A piece of cloth or
soft paper used while eating to protect the clothes or to wipe the
mouth and fingers.

nar·cis·sus | när sĭs′əs | —*noun, plural* **narcissuses** A garden
plant that is related to the daffodil. The narcissus has yellow or
white flowers with a central part that is shaped like a cup or
trumpet.

nar·cot·ic | när kŏt′ĭk | —*noun, plural* **narcotics** Any drug that
dulls the senses, causes sleep, and can cause a person to be
dependent on it when it is used regularly. Heroin and opium are
narcotics.

nar·rate | năr′āt′ | or | nă rāt′ | —*verb* **narrated, narrating** To give
an account or tell the story of in speech or writing; relate:
Bobby's English theme narrated his experiences at summer camp.

nar·row | năr′ō | —*adjective* **narrower, narrowest 1.** Small in
width as compared to length; not wide: *a narrow face; a narrow
ribbon.* **2.** Having little room or space: *The sailors slept in narrow
quarters below the ship's deck.* **3.** Small or limited in size, variety,
or extent: *a narrow circle of friends; a narrow range of knowledge; a
narrow majority of votes.* **4.** Limited in outlook; not liberal; rigid: *a
man of narrow ideas.* **5.** Barely successful: *a narrow escape.*
—*verb* **narrowed, narrowing** To make or become narrow or
narrower: *He narrowed his eyes. The river narrows at this point.*
—*noun, plural* **narrows 1.** A narrow part of a road, valley, or
mountain pass: *The entrance to the farm is located at the narrow in
the road.* **2. narrows** A narrow body of water connecting two
wider ones.

na·sal | nā′zəl | —*adjective* Of or in the nose: *a nasal irritation.*

Nash·ville | năsh′vĭl′ | The capital of Tennessee.

na·stur·tium | nə stûr′shəm | or | nă stûr′shəm | —*noun, plural*
nasturtiums A garden plant with orange, yellow, or red flowers.
The leaves are rounded and have a strong taste.

nast·y | năs′tē | —*adjective* **nastier, nastiest 1.** Mean; malicious:
a nasty old man. **2.** Dirty, disgusting, or offensive; filthy: *the nasty
gutter; a nasty word.* **3.** Very unpleasant or troublesome: *a nasty
temper; nasty weather.* **4.** Very harmful or dangerous; serious: *a
nasty accident; a nasty cough; a nasty cut.*

na·tion | nā′shən | —*noun, plural* **nations 1.** A group of people
organized under a single government; a country: *the new nations
of Africa.* **2.** The territory occupied by a country: *All across the
nation new industries are developing.*

na·tion·al | năsh′ə nəl | —*adjective* Of or involving a nation as a
whole: *a national symbol; the national parks; a national election.*

na·tion·al·ism | năsh′ə nə lĭz′əm | —*noun* Devotion or loyalty to
one's country.

na·tion·al·i·ty | năsh′ə năl′ĭ tē | —*noun, plural* **nationalities
1.** The condition of belonging to a particular nation: *Children
born in the United States have American nationality.* **2.** A people
sharing the same origins or traditions: *Many nationalities have
settled in America.*

na·tive | nā′tĭv | —*adjective* **1.** Belonging to a person by nature;
inborn; natural: *native ability; a native talent for sports.* **2.** Born in
a particular country or place: *a native American.* **3.** Belonging to a
person because of nationality or place of birth: *our native land;*

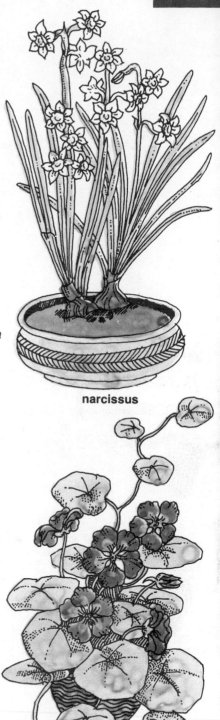

narcissus

nasturtium

one's native language. **4.** Originally living, growing, or produced in a particular place: *a plant native to Europe; the native handicrafts of Mexico.* **5.** Of the original, sometimes primitive, inhabitants of a region: *We had native guides on our trip up the river.*

—*noun, plural* **natives 1.** Someone born in a particular country or place: *a native of Boston; a native of France.* **2.** One of the original inhabitants of a region or place, especially as distinguished from immigrants, colonizers, or visitors: *The natives of the small village were happy to see the summer tourists leave.* **3.** An animal or plant originally living or growing in a particular place: *The kangaroo is a native of Australia.*

nat·u·ral |năch′ər əl| *or* |năch′rəl| —*adjective* **1.** Present in or produced by nature; not artificial: *The moon is a natural satellite of the earth. We crossed the gorge over a natural bridge in the rock.* **2.** Of or having to do with nature and all objects, living things, and events that are part of it: *natural laws.* **3.** Expected or occurring in the normal course of things: *a natural death; natural enemies.* **4.** Present from birth; inborn: *a natural curiosity; a natural talent for acting.* **5.** Not artificial, learned, or affected: *a natural way of speaking.*

—*noun, plural* **naturals** A person who is particularly able at some activity because of inborn qualities or talents: *She is a natural for the presidency.*

nat·u·ral·ly |năch′ər ə lē| *or* |năch′rə lē| —*adverb* **1.** In a natural manner: *It is best to behave naturally and be yourself with people.* **2.** By nature: *His hair is naturally blond.* **3.** Without a doubt: *Naturally, the faster you grow, the more food you need.*

natural resource Anything that grows or exists in nature and is the source of something necessary or useful to human beings. Forests, mineral deposits, and water are natural resources.

na·ture |nā′chər| —*noun, plural* **natures 1.** The world and all life, objects, or events in it apart from things made by man. **2.** Living things and the outdoors not touched by man; wildlife and natural scenery: *enjoying the beauties of nature.* **3.** The basic characteristics and qualities of a person, animal, or thing: *a person with a kind nature; understanding the nature of the problem.* **4.** Kind; type: *a story of a mysterious nature.*

naught |nôt| —*pronoun* Nothing: *After the nuclear explosion there were no trees, no shrubs, no animals, naught but a terrible desert.*

—*noun* Zero; the digit 0. Another form of this word is **nought.**

naugh·ty |nô′tē| —*adjective* **naughtier, naughtiest** Disobedient; mischievous: *Naughty boys broke the window of the store.*

nau·se·a |nô′zē ə| *or* |nô′zhə| *or* |nô′sē ə| *or* |nô′shə| —*noun* A feeling of sickness in the stomach and a need to vomit.

nau·ti·cal |nô′tĭ kəl| —*adjective* Of ships, sailors, or navigation: *a nautical story; a man with nautical experience.*

na·val |nā′vəl| —*adjective* **1.** Of, belonging to, or having to do with a navy or ships: *naval battles; naval officers; naval law.* **2.** Having a navy: *For three centuries England was the greatest naval power in the world.*

♦ *These sound alike* **naval, navel.**

na·vel |nā′vəl| —*noun, plural* **navels** A mark left on the abdomen of mammals. It shows where the cord that connects a newborn infant with its mother was attached.

♦ *These sound alike* **navel, naval.**

ă	pat	ĕ	pet	î	fierce
ā	pay	ē	be	ŏ	pot
â	care	ĭ	pit	ō	go
ä	father	ī	pie	ô	paw, for

oi	oil	ŭ	cut	zh	vision
ōō	book	û	fur	ə	ago, item,
ōō	boot	*th*	the		pencil, atom,
yōō	abuse	th	thin		circus
ou	out	hw	which	ər	butter

nav·i·gate |năv′ĭ gāt′| —*verb* **navigated, navigating** **1.** To plan, guide, and control the course of a ship or aircraft: *The sailor navigated his small boat across the Pacific Ocean to Japan. The ancient Hawaiians navigated by the stars.* **2.** To travel or voyage over or across: *He navigated the rapids in the river successfully.*

nav·i·ga·tion |năv′ĭ gā′shən| —*noun* **1.** The act or practice of navigating: *Heavy winds and rough seas made navigation of the ship very difficult.* **2.** The science of locating the position or planning the course of a ship or aircraft: *All graduates of the naval academy have studied navigation.*

nav·i·ga·tor |năv′ĭ gā′tər| —*noun, plural* **navigators** **1.** A crew member who plans and directs the course of a ship or aircraft. **2.** A person who leads voyages of exploration: *The island was discovered by a Norse navigator.* **3.** A mechanical instrument that directs the course of an aircraft or missile.

na·vy |nā′vē| —*noun, plural* **navies** **1.** All of a nation's warships. **2.** Often **Navy** A nation's whole organization for war at sea, including ships, men and officers, and shore bases. **3.** A very dark blue.
—*adjective* Of the color navy.

navigator

nay |nā| —*adverb* No: *Four Democrats voted nay to the treaty.*
—*noun, plural* **nays** **1.** A vote of "no." **2.** **the nays** Those who vote no: *The nays carried it, and the treaty was defeated.*
♦ *These sound alike* **nay, neigh.**

near |nîr| —*adverb* **nearer, nearest** **1.** To, at, or within a short distance or interval in space or time: *The days grow shorter as winter draws near.* **2.** Almost; nearly: *We were near exhausted from the heat.*
—*adjective* **nearer, nearest** **1.** Close in space, time, position, or degree: *near neighbors; near equals.* **2.** Closely related or connected, as by kinship or association: *near relatives; those near and dear friends.* **3.** Achieved or missed by a small margin; close; narrow: *a near escape; a near tragedy; near perfection.* **4.** Closer of two or more: *the near side of the house.* **5.** Short and direct: *Could you tell me the nearest route to the airport?*
—*preposition* Close to, as in time, space, or degree: *We stayed at a small inn near Boston.*
—*verb* **neared, nearing** To draw near or nearer; to approach: *The holiday season nears. The bus slowed as it neared the corner.*

near·by |nîr′bī′| —*adverb* Not far away; near at hand; close by: *A little brook ran nearby.*
—*adjective* Located a short distance away: *All the neighborhood children play in a nearby park.*

near·ly |nîr′lē| —*adverb* Almost but not quite; close to: *That house cost nearly $100,000.*

near·ness |nîr′nĭs| —*noun* The state or condition of being near: *We were excited by the nearness of the holidays.*

near·sight·ed |nîr′sī′tĭd| —*adjective* Unable to see objects that are far away as clearly as objects that are close by.

neat |nēt| —*adjective* **neater, neatest** **1.** In clean condition, appearance, or habits; not careless or messy; tidy: *a neat room; a neat handwriting; a neat person.* **2.** Performed with precision and skill: *a neat, graceful takeoff; a neat job of acting.* **3.** Very fine; wonderful: *They give neat prizes at the fair.*

Ne·bras·ka |nə brăs′kə| A state in the central United States. The capital of Nebraska is Lincoln.

Nebraska
The name **Nebraska** comes from an Indian word that means "flat water."

nec·es·sar·i·ly |nĕs′ĭ **sâr′ə** lē| —*adverb* **1.** By or because of need or necessity: *You don't necessarily have to complete this assignment today.* **2.** As a sure result: *A new quarterback doesn't necessarily mean the other team will win the game.*

nec·es·sar·y |nĕs′ĭ sĕr′ē| —*adjective* **1.** Impossible to do without; essential: *We don't have the necessary tool to fix the car. Food is necessary for life.* **2.** Happening or following as a certain result; inevitable: *An upset stomach is the necessary consequence of eating too much.*
—*noun, plural* **necessaries** Something that is needed or required; an essential: *Two of the necessaries of life are food and water.*

ne·ces·si·ty |nə sĕs′ĭ tē| —*noun, plural* **necessities** **1.** Something impossible to get along without; an essential: *The sun is a necessity to life on Earth.* **2.** The fact of being necessary: *I felt the necessity of sleep when I was working hard.* **3.** Great need; poverty; want: *Many families were living in great necessity.*

neck |nĕk| —*noun, plural* **necks** **1.** The part of the body that joins the head to the shoulders. **2.** The part of a garment that fits around the neck. **3.** Any relatively narrow or connecting part: *the neck of a bottle; the neck of a violin.*

neck·er·chief |nĕk′ər chĭf| —*noun, plural* **neckerchiefs** A scarf or cloth worn around the neck.

neck·lace |nĕk′ləs| —*noun, plural* **necklaces** An ornament, such as a string of beads or a gold chain, worn around the neck.

neck·tie |nĕk′tī′| —*noun, plural* **neckties** A narrow band of cloth worn around the neck. It is placed under the shirt collar and tied in front, either in a knot with hanging ends or in a bow.

nec·tar |nĕk′tər| —*noun* A sweet liquid in many flowers. Bees make honey from nectar.

need |nēd| —*noun, plural* **needs** **1.** A condition or situation in which something is required or wanted: *The crops were in need of water. That boy is in need of a good haircut.* **2.** A wish for something that is missing or desired: *She has a constant need for attention.* **3.** Something that is required or wanted: *That man's needs are few.* **4.** Necessity or obligation: *There wasn't any need for you to pay me back.* **5.** Extreme poverty or misfortune: *The sick old man lived in great need.*
—*verb* **needed, needing** **1.** To must have: *Tina needs a new dress. His father needs rest.* **2.** To be obliged to; have to: *You don't need to return the book until tomorrow. Need I come to your house to help you? No, you need not.* **3.** To require; have need of: *Let's collect everything that needs repairing.*
♦ *These sound alike* **need, knead.**

nee·dle |nēd′l| —*noun, plural* **needles** **1.** A small, thin tool for sewing, usually made of polished steel. A needle has a sharp point at one end and a hole at the other through which a length of thread is passed and held. **2.** A slender, pointed rod used in knitting. **3.** A slender rod with a hook at one end, used in crocheting. **4.** The pointer or indicator of a compass or gauge. **5.** A thin tube with a sharp point used to pierce the skin and force liquid medicine into the body. **6.** Any sharp, pointed instrument like a needle: *a phonograph needle.* **7.** A narrow, stiff leaf, such as that found on a pine tree or fir tree: *The forest floor was covered with a carpet of pine needles.*
—*verb* **needled, needling** To tease, annoy, or provoke: *He constantly needles me about being short.*

neckerchief

ă	pat	ĕ	pet	î	fierce
ā	pay	ē	be	ŏ	pot
â	care	ĭ	pit	ō	go
ä	father	ī	pie	ô	paw, for
oi	oil	ŭ	cut	zh	vision
ōō	book	û	fur	ə	ago, item,
ōō	boot	*th*	the		pencil, atom,
yōō	abuse	th	thin		circus
ou	out	hw	which	ər	butter

need·less |nĕd′lĭs| —*adjective* Not needed; not necessary: *If you put your books on the shelf, you will avoid needless disorder on your desk.*

need·n't |nĕd′nt| A contraction of "need not."

need·y |nē′dē| —*adjective* **needier, neediest** Being in need; very poor: *In our town there are many needy families.*

neg·a·tive |nĕg′ə tĭv| —*adjective* **1.** Expressing a refusal or denial; saying "no": *When I asked if I could go to the ball game, Dad gave me a negative answer.* **2.** Not positive or helpful: *A negative feeling about a problem often makes it difficult to solve.* **3.** Showing that a particular disease or germ is not present: *The result of the blood test was negative.* **4.** Less than zero: *−20 is a negative number.* **5.** Having one of two opposite electrical charges. One of the ends of a magnet has a negative charge; the opposite end has a positive charge.
—*noun, plural* **negatives 1.** In grammar, a word or part of a word that expresses denial or refusal. *No, not,* and *un-* are negatives. **2.** In photography, an image on film in which the areas that are normally light and those that are normally dark are reversed.

ne·glect |nĭ glĕkt′| —*verb* **neglected, neglecting 1.** To fail to care for or give proper attention to: *He never neglects his pets. He neglects his clothing. If you neglect your school work, you will get poor marks.* **2.** To fail to do: *He neglected to tell his friend that he had tickets to the play.*
—*noun* **1.** The act or an example of neglecting: *His neglect of his work cost him his job.* **2.** The condition of being neglected: *The garden has fallen into neglect.*

ne·go·ti·ate |nĭ gō′shē āt′| —*verb* **negotiated, negotiating** To discuss or talk over in order to reach an agreement or settlement: *The three leaders negotiated a peace treaty. The two sides negotiated for ten days without success.*

ne·go·ti·a·tion |nĭ gō′shē ā′shən| —*noun, plural* **negotiations** The act or process of negotiating: *Negotiation of a contract between the union and the company is going to be difficult. Months of secret negotiations between the two nations produced a peace treaty.*

Ne·gro |nē′grō| —*noun, plural* **Negroes** A Negroid person.
—*adjective* Of Negroid persons.

Ne·groid |nē′groid′| —*adjective* Of a major division of the human species whose members have brown to black skin color and often tightly curled hair. This division includes the native peoples of central and southern Africa and their descendants in other parts of the world.
—*noun, plural* **Negroids** A Negroid person.

neigh |nā| —*noun, plural* **neighs** The long, high-pitched sound made by a horse.
—*verb* **neighed, neighing** To make such a sound.
♦ *These sound alike* **neigh, nay.**

neigh·bor |nā′bər| —*noun, plural* **neighbors 1.** A person who lives next door to or near another: *Yesterday we called on our new neighbors across the street.* **2.** A person or thing placed or located next to or near another: *Earth's nearest neighbor is the moon.* **3.** A fellow human being: *We should always remember to love our neighbors.*

neigh·bor·hood |nā′bər hŏod′| —*noun, plural* **neighborhoods 1.** A district or area, especially of a city or town: *Several*

neighborhoods in the north end of town were without electricity.
2. The people who live in the same area or district: *The noise disturbed the whole neighborhood.*

nei·ther |nē′ thər| or |nī′ thər| —*adjective* Not one nor the other; not either: *Neither shoe fits comfortably.* The adjective **neither** belongs to a class of words called **determiners.** They signal that a noun is coming.
—*pronoun* Not the one nor the other; not either one: *Neither of them fits comfortably.*
—*conjunction* **1.** The conjunction **neither** is used with **nor** to present two negative alternatives: *They had neither seen nor heard of us. I have neither time nor money.* **2.** Nor: *You don't want to go? Neither do I.*

ne·on |nē′ ŏn′| —*noun* A gas that has no color and no odor and is found in very small amounts in the earth's atmosphere. Neon is one of the chemical elements. It is commonly used in certain electric signs.

neph·ew |nĕf′ yōō| —*noun, plural* **nephews 1.** A son of a person's brother or sister. **2.** A son of the brother or sister of a husband or wife.

Nep·tune |nĕp′ tōōn′| or |nĕp′ tyōōn′| —*noun* A planet of our solar system. It is the fourth largest planet and the eighth in distance from the sun.

nerve |nûrv| —*noun, plural* **nerves 1.** Any of the bundles of fibers that link the brain and spinal cord with the other parts of the body. Nerves carry messages that make the muscles and organs work. **2.** Strong will; courage: *It took nerve to stand up to that bully.*

nerv·ous |nûr′ vəs| —*adjective* **1.** Of or affecting the nerves or the nervous system: *a nervous disorder; nervous exhaustion.*
2. Easily excited or upset; tense: *a nervous person.* **3.** Uneasy; anxious: *He is nervous about taking the test.*

nervous system The system in the body that controls all of its actions. The nervous system includes the brain, the spinal cord, and the nerves.

–ness A suffix that forms nouns. The suffix "-ness" means "a state, condition, or quality": *kindness; politeness; rudeness.*

nest |nĕst| —*noun, plural* **nests 1.** A container or shelter made by birds for holding their eggs and young. A bird's nest is often shaped like a cup or bowl. It may be made of grass, mud, twigs, or other things. **2.** A similar shelter made by insects, fish, mice, or other animals. **3.** A snug, warm, cozy place.
—*verb* **nested, nesting** To build or stay in a nest: *Robins nested in the willow tree.*

net¹ |nĕt| —*noun, plural* **nets 1.** An open fabric made of threads, cords, or ropes that are woven or knotted together so as to leave holes at regular intervals. Some nets are fine and delicate, as those used for veils or to hold a person's hair in place. Other nets are heavy and strong, as those used to catch fish or as a barrier dividing the halves of a tennis or volleyball court. **2.** A trap or snare made of or resembling a net: *a butterfly net; a net of a thousand policemen covering a ten-block area.*
—*verb* **netted, netting** To catch in or as if in a net: *He netted a rare butterfly. The search of the police finally netted the speeder.*

net² |nĕt| —*adjective* **1.** Remaining after all necessary additions, subtractions, or adjustments have been made: *What was your net*

nest

Different kinds of nest

net¹, net²
Net¹ had the same meaning to English-speaking people of long ago. **Net²** originally meant "clear, plain." It is borrowed from the old French word *net,* "plain, simple, neat."

ă	pat	ĕ	pet	î	fierce
ā	pay	ē	be	ŏ	pot
â	care	ĭ	pit	ō	go
ä	father	ī	pie	ô	paw, for
oi	oil	ŭ	cut	zh	vision
ōō	book	û	fur	ə	ago, item,
ōō	boot	*th*	the		pencil, atom,
yōō	abuse	th	thin		circus
ou	out	hw	which	ər	butter

income after expenses? **2.** Final; ultimate: *What was the net result of your discussion?*

—*verb* **netted, netting** To bring in or gain as profit: *The store netted about $58,000 from $100,000 in sales.*

Neth·er·lands, the |nĕ*th*′ər ləndz| A country in western Europe. Another name for this country is **Holland.**

net·work |nĕt′wûrk′| —*noun, plural* **networks 1.** A system or pattern of lines, routes, passages, or parts that cross: *a network of roads and railways; a network of veins.* **2.** A group of radio or television stations that are linked together and that share many or most of the same programs.

neu·tral |nōō′trəl| or |nyōō′trəl| —*adjective* **1.** Not supporting, favoring, or belonging to any side in a war, dispute, or fight: *a neutral nation.* **2.** Lacking color or hue; having no tint: *Gray, black, and white are neutral colors.* **3.** In chemistry, neither an acid nor a base: *a neutral solution; a neutral salt.*

—*noun* The arrangement of a set of gears in an engine in which no motion or power can be transmitted.

neu·tron |nōō′trŏn′| or |nyōō′trŏn′| —*noun, plural* **neutrons** A small particle found in the nucleus of any atom except one of hydrogen. A neutron has no electrical charge and is slightly larger than a proton.

Ne·vad·a |nə văd′ə| or |nə vä′də| A state in the western United States. The capital of Nevada is Carson City.

nev·er |nĕv′ər| —*adverb* **1.** At no time; not ever: *I have never been here before.* **2.** Absolutely not; under no circumstances; not at all: *Would I steal? Never! Never fear.*

nev·er·the·less |nĕv′ər *th*ə lĕs′| —*adverb* All the same; anyway: *The plan may fail, but we must try it nevertheless.*

—*conjunction* In spite of that; still; however; but: *He ate a great deal; nevertheless, he felt hungry.*

new |nōō| or |nyōō| —*adjective* **newer, newest 1.** Recently made, built, formed, or grown: *a new skyscraper; a new nation; a new leaf.* **2.** Just found, discovered, learned about, or obtained; not known or possessed before now: *new information; new political power; new friends.* **3.** Never used or worn; not old or secondhand: *a new bicycle; new furniture.* **4.** Taking the place of what is old; modern; up-to-date: *a new style; a new edition of a book; a new technique in teaching math.* **5.** Starting over again: *a new moon; a new year; a new life.* **6.** Not familiar; strange: *words that are new to you.* **7.** Recently settled or arrived in a new position or place: *a new teacher; new neighbors.* **8.** Not trained or experienced: *He is new at his work.*

—*adverb* Freshly; newly; recently: *new-cut grass.*

♦ *These sound alike* **new, gnu, knew.**

new·born |nōō′bôrn′| or |nyōō′bôrn′| —*adjective* **1.** Just born: *newborn babies.* **2.** Born again; renewed: *newborn courage.*

New Bruns·wick |brŭnz′wĭk| A province on the Atlantic coast of Canada. The capital of New Brunswick is Fredericton.

new·com·er |nōō′kŭm′ər| or |nyōō′kŭm′ər| —*noun, plural* **newcomers** A person that has only recently arrived or appeared in a place or situation: *His parents are newcomers in town.*

New Eng·land |ĭng′glənd| The northeastern part of the United States. New England consists of the states of Maine, New Hampshire, Vermont, Massachusetts, Connecticut, and Rhode Island.

Nevada
The name **Nevada** comes from a shortening of *Sierra Nevada,* Spanish words that mean "snow-covered mountain range."

New Brunswick
The province of **New Brunswick** was named for King George III of Britain. One of the king's titles was Duke of Brunswick. Brunswick is the name of a former state in Germany.

Newfoundland
The name **Newfoundland** comes from a combination of words originally used to describe any new place along a coast beyond the Atlantic Ocean that was visited by European fishermen.

New Hampshire
The state of **New Hampshire** was named after Hampshire, a county in England.

New Jersey
New Jersey was named after Jersey, an island in the English Channel. A native of Jersey became one of the first settlers of the American colony.

New Mexico
The state of **New Mexico** was named after the country Mexico by a Spanish explorer who had traveled there. The name Mexico means "place of the war god."

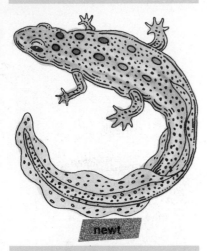

newt

New York
New York was named after the Duke of York and Albany. The duke (later King James II of England) was granted the colony of New York by his brother, King Charles II.

ă	pat	ĕ	pet	î	fierce
ā	pay	ē	be	ŏ	pot
â	care	ĭ	pit	ō	go
ä	father	ī	pie	ô	paw, for
oi	oil	ŭ	cut	zh	vision
ōō	book	û	fur	ə	ago, item,
ōō	boot	*th*	the		pencil, atom,
yōō	abuse	th	thin		circus
ou	out	hw	which	ər	butter

New·found·land |nōō′fən lənd| or |nōō′fən lănd′| or |nyōō′fən lənd| or |nyōō′fən lănd′| or |nōō **found′**lənd| or |nyōō **found′**lənd| **1.** An island off the southeastern coast of Canada. **2.** A province of Canada, consisting of this island and nearby territories. The capital of Newfoundland is St. John's.

New Hamp·shire |hămp′shər| or |hăm′shər| or |hămp′shîr′| or |hăm′shîr| A state in the northeastern United States. The capital of New Hampshire is Concord.

New Jer·sey |jûr′zē| A state in the eastern United States. The capital of New Jersey is Trenton.

new·ly |nōō′lē| or |nyōō′lē| —*adverb* Recently; lately; just: *a newly discovered chemical product; a newly mown lawn.*

New Mex·i·co |měk′sĭ kō′| A state in the southwestern United States. The capital of New Mexico is Santa Fe.

news |nōōz| or |nyōōz| —*noun* (Used with a singular verb.) Information about one or more events that have recently happened. News may be passed on from person to person or reported by newspapers, news magazines, radio, or television.

news·cast |nōōz′kăst′| or |nōōz′käst′| or |nyōōz′kăst′| or |nyōōz′käst′| —*noun, plural* **newscasts** A radio or television program that gives news reports.

news·pa·per |nōōz′pā′pər| or |nyōōz′pā′pər| —*noun, plural* **newspapers** Sheets of paper printed daily or weekly and containing news, articles, pictures, and advertisements.

newt |nōōt| or |nyōōt| —*noun, plural* **newts** A small animal with soft, smooth skin, short legs, and a long tail. Newts live both on land and in the water. A newt is a kind of salamander.

New Testament The second part of the Bible. It contains the life and teachings of Christ and his followers.

New World The Western Hemisphere; North America and South America.

New Year's Day The first day of the year, January 1.

New Year's Eve December 31, the last day of the year.

New York |yôrk| A state in the eastern United States. The capital of New York is Albany.

New Zea·land |zē′lənd| A country that consists of two islands in the Pacific Ocean southeast of Australia.

next |někst| —*adjective* **1.** Coming right after the present or previous one: *Next year we are going to Europe. The next day was sunny.* **2.** Closest or nearest in position: *the next town.* —*adverb* **1.** Following right after the present or previous one: *What comes next? Who came next?* **2.** On the first occasion after the present or previous occasion: *When will you visit us next? First he went shopping; next he went to the library.* —*preposition* Close to; nearest: *I keep your picture next to my chair.*

next-door |někst′dôr′| or |někst′dōr′| —*adjective* In, to, or at the nearest house, building, apartment, or office: *His next-door neighbors are taking care of his dog.*

next door **1.** In, to, or at the nearest house, building, apartment, or office: *She called to the woman next door. Mike has just moved next door to Tom.* **2.** The nearest house, building, apartment, or office: *Someone from next door came to visit.*

nib·ble |nĭb′əl| —*verb* **nibbled, nibbling** **1.** To take small, quick bites: *It's better to nibble on raisins than on cake. The rabbit's nose wiggled when he nibbled.* **2.** To eat with small, quick bites: *The*

mouse is nibbling the cheese. Jack nibbles while he watches TV.
—*noun, plural* **nibbles** **1.** A small bite, such as a fish might take
at bait. **2.** A small bite or piece of food.

nice | nīs | —*adjective* **nicer, nicest** **1.** Good; pleasant: *a nice
smell; a nice place for a picnic.* **2.** Very pleasing: *Have a nice day at
the zoo.* **3.** Of good quality: *a nice shirt; a nice pair of shoes.*
4. Pretty: *You look nice in your new dress.* **5.** Kind and good;
thoughtful: *It's nice of you to help me.* **6.** Showing skill; very fine:
That table you made is a nice bit of workmanship. **7.** Very good;
well done: *a nice job.*

nick | nĭk | —*noun, plural* **nicks** A small cut or chip in a surface
or edge: *There was a nick in the plate.*
—*verb* **nicked, nicking** To make a small cut or chip in: *Dad nicked
his face while he was shaving.*

   Idiom **in the nick of time** Just at the last moment: *I stopped
Patsy from stepping off the curb in the nick of time.*

nick·el | nĭk′ əl | —*noun, plural* **nickels** **1.** A hard, silvery metal.
Nickel is one of the chemical elements. **2.** A United States or
Canadian coin worth five cents and made from nickel and copper.

nick·name | nĭk′ nām′ | —*noun, plural* **nicknames** **1.** A name
used instead of the real name of a person, place, or thing: *The tall
boy's nickname was "Legs."* **2.** A shortened form of a proper
name: *"Beth" is a nickname for Elizabeth.*
—*verb* **nicknamed, nicknaming** To call by a nickname: *Denis
nicknamed his little brother "Baby face."*

nic·o·tine | nĭk′ ə tēn′ | —*noun* A poison that is found in tobacco.
It is used in medicine and as an insect poison.

niece | nēs | —*noun, plural* **nieces** **1.** A daughter of a person's
brother or sister. **2.** A daughter of the brother or sister of a
husband or wife.

night | nīt | —*noun, plural* **nights** **1.** The time between sunset
and sunrise, especially the hours of darkness. **2.** The part of the
night when people sleep or rest: *He tossed and turned all night.*
♦ *These sound alike* **night, knight.**

night·gown | nīt′ goun′ | —*noun, plural* **nightgowns** A loose gown
worn to sleep in by a woman or child.

night·in·gale | nīt′ n gāl′ | or | nī′ tĭng gāl′ | —*noun, plural*
nightingales A brownish bird of Europe and Asia. The nightingale
has a sweet song and often sings at night.

night·ly | nīt′ lē | —*adjective* Taking place, done, or used at night
or every night: *secret nightly meetings; a nightly bath.*
—*adverb* Every night: *The family watches the TV news nightly.*

night·mare | nīt′ mâr′ | —*noun, plural* **nightmares** **1.** A bad
dream that is very frightening. **2.** A frightening experience that
is like a bad dream: *The accident was a nightmare.*

night·time | nīt′ tīm′ | —*noun* The time between sunset and
sunrise; night.

nim·ble | nĭm′ bəl | —*adjective* **nimbler, nimblest** Moving or able
to move quickly, lightly, and easily: *nimble mountain goats; nimble
fingers.*

nine | nīn | —*noun, plural* **nines** A number, written 9, that is
equal to the sum of 8 + 1.
—*adjective* Being one more than eight in number: *nine cars.* The
adjective **nine** belongs to a class of words called **determiners.**
They signal that a noun is coming.

nine·teen | nīn′ tēn′ | —*noun, plural* **nineteens** A number,

nightingale

written 19, that is equal to the sum of 10 + 9.

—*adjective* Being one more than eighteen in number: *nineteen bees.* The adjective **nineteen** belongs to a class of words called **determiners.** They signal that a noun is coming.

nine·teenth | nīn′tēnth′ | —*noun, plural* **nineteenths 1.** In a group of people or things that are in numbered order, the one that matches the number nineteen. **2.** One of nineteen equal parts, written ¹⁄₁₉.

—*adjective: the nineteenth name on the list.*

nine·ti·eth | nīn′tē ĭth | —*noun, plural* **ninetieths 1.** In a group of people or things that are in numbered order, the one that matches the number ninety. **2.** One of ninety equal parts, written ¹⁄₉₀.

—*adjective: the ninetieth day of the year.*

nine·ty | nīn′tē | —*noun, plural* **nineties** A number, written 90, that is equal to the product of 9 × 10.

—*adjective* Being ten more than eighty: *ninety pieces of paper.* The adjective **ninety** belongs to a class of words called **determiners.** They signal that a noun is coming.

ninth | nīnth | —*noun, plural* **ninths 1.** In a group of people or things that are in numbered order, the one that matches the number nine. **2.** One of nine equal parts, written ¹⁄₉.

—*adjective: the ninth chapter of the book.*

nip | nĭp | —*verb* **nipped, nipping 1. a.** To give a small, sharp bite or bites to: *The puppy nipped my leg.* **b.** To pinch or squeeze: *The lobster nipped my toe with its claw.* **2.** To remove by biting or pinching: *The rabbit nipped off the plant leaf.* **3.** To sting or chill, as sharp, biting cold does: *The icy wind nipped our ears and noses.*

—*noun, plural* **nips 1.** A small, sharp bite or pinch. **2.** Sharp, biting cold: *There's a nip in the air on November mornings.*

nip·ple | nĭp′əl | —*noun, plural* **nipples 1.** The small tip at the center of a breast or udder. An infant or a baby animal can get milk from its mother by sucking on a nipple. **2.** A soft rubber cap on a baby's bottle from which the baby drinks.

ni·tro·gen | nī′trə jən | —*noun* A gas that has no color or smell. Nitrogen is one of the chemical elements. It makes up about four fifths of the air.

no | nō | —*adverb* The adverb **no** is used: **1.** To express refusal, denial, or disagreement: *Let's go! No, I'm not going. She said, "No, you are wrong."* **2.** With the comparative of adjectives or adverbs: *He is no better today than he was yesterday. Harry is no more serious than his friends. Be at the station no later than three o'clock.*

—*adjective* **1.** Not any: *There are no cookies left in the jar.* **2.** Not at all: *He is no fool.* The adjective **no** belongs to a class of words called **determiners.** They signal that a noun is coming.

—*noun, plural* **noes 1.** A negative response; a denial or refusal: *Her suggestion met with a chorus of noes.* **2.** A negative vote or voter: *There were more noes than yeses, and the bill did not pass. The chairman asked the noes to raise their hands.*

—*interjection* A word used to express surprise, doubt, or disbelief: *No, that's impossible.*

♦ *These sound alike* **no, know.**

no·bil·i·ty | nō bĭl′ĭ tē | —*noun, plural* **nobilities 1.** A social class having titles of rank and often wealth and power. Queens, kings, princes, and princesses are all part of the nobility. **2.** Noble rank

ă	pat	ĕ	pet	î	fierce
ā	pay	ē	be	ŏ	pot
â	care	ĭ	pit	ō	go
ä	father	ī	pie	ô	paw, for
oi	oil	ŭ	cut	zh	vision
ōō	book	û	fur	ə	ago, item,
ōō	boot	th	the		pencil, atom,
yōō	abuse	th	thin		circus
ou	out	hw	which	ər	butter

or status: *Congress may not grant titles of nobility.*

no·ble |nō′bəl| —*adjective* **nobler, noblest 1.** Of or belonging to the nobility: *a noble family; a lady of noble birth.* **2.** Having or showing qualities of high character, as courage or generosity: *a noble spirit.*
—*noun, plural* **nobles** A person of noble birth, position, or title.

no·ble·man |nō′bəl mən| —*noun, plural* **noblemen** A man of noble birth, position, or title.

no·ble·wom·an |nō′bəl wo͝om′ən| —*noun, plural* **noblewomen** A woman of noble birth, position, or title.

no·bod·y |nō′bŏd′ē| or |nō′bə dē| —*pronoun* No person; no one; not anybody: *Nobody was looking. Nobody came out to play.*
—*noun, plural* **nobodies** A person of no importance or position.

noc·tur·nal |nŏk tûr′nəl| —*adjective* **1.** Of the night or happening at night: *nocturnal stillness; a nocturnal breeze.* **2.** Active at night rather than during the day: *nocturnal birds.*

nod |nŏd| —*verb* **nodded, nodding 1. a.** To move the head down and then up in a quick motion. This shows agreement or approval and is a way of saying yes or of greeting someone. **b.** To show agreement, approval, or a greeting by moving the head in this way: *He nodded his approval when I asked if I should help.* **2.** To let the head droop and fall forward, as when one is sleepy or dozing: *The old woman nodded in her chair.*
—*noun, plural* **nods** A nodding motion: *a nod of his head.*

noise |noiz| —*noun, plural* **noises 1.** Sound or a sound that is loud, unpleasant, or unexpected: *You're making too much noise. I couldn't sleep because of the noise of the trucks.* **2.** Sound or a sound of any kind: *The only noise was the wind in the trees.*

nois·y |noi′zē| —*adjective* **noisier, noisiest 1.** Making a lot of noise: *a noisy crowd; a noisy car.* **2.** Full of noise: *noisy streets.*

nom·i·nate |nŏm′ə nāt′| —*verb* **nominated, nominating 1.** To choose as a candidate in an election to fill an office: *The class nominated Marion for the presidency.* **2.** To appoint to a position, office, or honor: *The President nominated a new chief justice.*

nom·i·na·tion |nŏm′ə nā′shən| —*noun, plural* **nominations 1.** The act or process of choosing a candidate for election: *the nomination of a vice president.* **2.** Appointment to a position, office, or honor: *the President's nomination of a chief justice.*

nom·i·nee |nŏm′ə nē′| —*noun, plural* **nominees** A person chosen as a candidate for an office or award: *the Democrats' nominee for President.*

non– A prefix that means "not, absence of, or the avoiding of": *nonviolence.* When "non-" is followed by a capital letter, it appears with a hyphen: *non-American.*

none |nŭn| —*pronoun* **1. a.** Not any: *I went through all the pictures, but there were none of her.* **b.** No part or quantity: *Sheila has done none of her homework.* **2.** Not one: *None dare to call him a coward.*
—*adverb* Not at all: *Crops were none too good this year.*
♦ *These sound alike* **none, nun.**

non·poi·son·ous |nŏn poi′zə nəs| —*adjective* **1.** Having no poison that can harm or kill: *a nonpoisonous snake.* **2.** Containing no poison: *a nonpoisonous liquid.*

non·sense |nŏn′sĕns′| or |nŏn′səns| —*noun* Foolish or silly talk or behavior: *Steve's story of the flying cow was nonsense.*

noo·dle |noōd′l| —*noun, plural* **noodles** A long, thin strip of

nobleman
Noblemen in robes and crowns
at a coronation

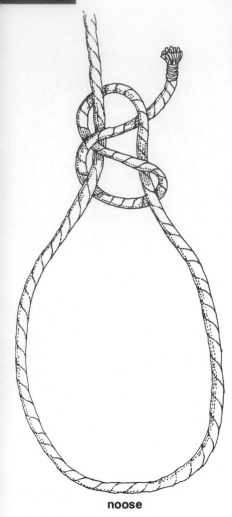

noose

North Carolina

The state of **North Carolina** was named for King Charles I of England. It was at first called *Carolana,* but King Charles II changed the name officially to Carolina in 1663. Later the area was split into North Carolina and South Carolina.

North Dakota

North Dakota was named after the Dakota Indian tribe. Dakota means "allies."

ă	pat	ĕ	pet	î	fierce
ā	pay	ē	be	ŏ	pot
â	care	ĭ	pit	ō	go
ä	father	ī	pie	ô	paw, for
oi	oil	ŭ	cut	zh	vision
ŏŏ	book	û	fur	ə	ago, item,
ōō	boot	*th*	the		pencil, atom,
yŏŏ	abuse	th	thin		circus
ou	out	hw	which	ər	butter

dried dough. Noodles are made of eggs, flour, and water.

noon |nō͞on| —*noun, plural* **noons** The middle of the day; twelve o'clock in the daytime.

no one No person; nobody: *No one is going skating today.*

noose |nō͞os| —*noun, plural* **nooses** A loop formed in a rope with a kind of knot that lets the loop tighten as the rope is pulled.

nor |nôr| or |nər| —*conjunction* **1.** The conjunction **nor** is used with **neither** to present two negative alternatives: *They had neither seen nor heard of us.* **2.** The conjunction **nor** is used in place of "and . . . not" to introduce a second negative statement: *He has no experience, nor does he want any.*

nor·mal |nôr′məl| —*adjective* **1.** Usual or ordinary: *Her weight is normal for her height. Sixty-eight degrees is a normal room temperature.* **2.** Happening in a natural, healthy way: *a normal heartbeat; normal growth.*
—*noun* The normal condition, level, measure, or degree: *Her temperature was above normal.*

Norse |nôrs| —*adjective* Of ancient Scandinavia, its people, or their language.
—*noun* **the Norse** (Used with a plural verb.) The people of ancient Scandinavia.

north |nôrth| —*noun* **1.** The direction to the right of a person who faces the sunset. **2.** Often **North** A region in this direction. **3. the North a.** The Arctic region. **b.** The northern part of the United States, especially the states north of Maryland, West Virginia, Kentucky, and Missouri. **c.** The states that supported the Union during the Civil War.
—*adjective* **1.** Of, in, or toward the north: *the north shore of the island.* **2.** Coming from the north: *a chill north wind.*
—*adverb* Toward the north: *We drove north.*

North America The northern continent of the western hemisphere. North America includes Canada, the United States, Mexico, and Central America.

North American 1. A person who was born in or lives in North America. **2.** Of North America: *a North American animal.*

North Car·o·li·na |kăr′ə lī′nə| A state in the southern United States. The capital of North Carolina is Raleigh.

North Da·ko·ta |də kō′tə| A state in the north-central United States. The capital of North Dakota is Bismarck.

north·east |nôrth ēst′| —*noun* **1.** The direction that is halfway between north and east. **2.** Often **Northeast** A region in this direction. **3. the Northeast** The part of the United States that includes New England and usually New York, Pennsylvania, and New Jersey.
—*adjective* **1.** Of, in, or toward the northeast: *the northeast section of the state.* **2.** Coming from the northeast: *a northeast wind.*
—*adverb* Toward the northeast: *They walked northeast.*

north·east·er·ly |nôrth ē′stər lē| —*adjective* **1.** In or toward the northeast: *The plane flew on a northeasterly route.* **2.** From the northeast: *a northeasterly breeze.*
—*adverb* **1.** In or toward the northeast: *Paul drove his car northeasterly.* **2.** From the northeast: *breezes blowing northeasterly.*

north·east·ern |nôrth ē′stərn| —*adjective* **1.** Of, in, or toward the northeast: *a northeastern college; a northeastern state.* **2.** From the northeast: *a northeastern gale.*

north·er·ly |nôr′ thər lē| —*adjective* **1.** In or toward the north: *The compass needle points in a northerly direction.* **2.** From the north: *a northerly breeze.*
—*adverb* **1.** In or toward the north: *The army advanced northerly.* **2.** From the north: *The winds blew northerly.*

north·ern |nôr′ thərn| —*adjective* **1.** Of, in, or toward the north: *the northern border.* **2.** From the north: *a northern wind.* **3.** Like what is found in the north: *a northern climate; northern speech.* **4. Northern** Of the states that supported the Union during the Civil War: *the Northern army; a Northern general.*

north·ern·er |nôr′ thər nər| —*noun, plural* **northerners** Often **Northerner 1.** A person who lives in or comes from the north: *Many northerners take winter vacations in the south.* **2.** A person from the North of the United States, especially during or before the Civil War.

north·ern·most |nôr′ thərn mōst′| —*adjective* Farthest north: *Alaska is the northernmost state of the United States.*

North Pole The northern end of the axis around which the earth rotates. The North Pole is the point on the surface of the earth that is farthest north.

north·ward |nôrth′ wərd| —*adverb* To or toward the north: *He turned the ship northward.* Another form of this word is **northwards.**
—*adjective* Moving to or toward the north: *They began their northward journey.*

north·wards |nôrth′ wərdz| A form of the adverb **northward.**

north·west |nôrth wĕst′| —*noun* **1.** The direction that is halfway between north and west. **2.** Often **Northwest** A region in this direction. **3. the Northwest** The northwestern part of the United States, especially the region that includes the states of Washington, Oregon, Idaho, and Montana.
—*adjective* **1.** Of, in, or toward the northwest: *the northwest region of the country.* **2.** Coming from the northwest: *a northwest wind.*
—*adverb* Toward the northwest: *We drove northwest.*

north·west·er·ly |nôrth wĕs′ tər lē| —*adjective* **1.** In or toward the northwest: *The birds migrated in a northwesterly direction.* **2.** From the northwest: *a northwesterly gust of air.*
—*adverb* **1.** In or toward the northwest: *Jack aimed his bow and arrow northwesterly.* **2.** From the northwest: *gales blowing northwesterly.*

north·west·ern |nôrth wĕs′ tərn| —*adjective* **1.** Of, in, or toward the northwest: *a northwestern plant; a northwestern state.* **2.** From the northwest: *a northwestern breeze.*

nose |nōz| —*noun, plural* **noses 1.** The part of the face or head through which people and animals breathe and usually smell. **2.** The sense of smell: *The dog's nose told him dinner was ready.* **3.** The ability to find things, as if by smell: *That reporter has a nose for news.* **4.** The narrow front end of an airplane, rocket, submarine, or other structure.
—*verb* **nosed, nosing 1.** To smell: *The deer nosed the wind and caught a scent of danger.* **2.** To touch, push, or examine with the nose: *The cats nosed about the garbage cans.*
Idioms **by a nose** By a very small difference: *He won by a nose.*

on the nose Exactly: *He guessed my weight right on the nose.* **under (one's) nose** In plain view; just where it should or could be seen: *The books he couldn't find were right under his nose.*

nose cone The front end of a rocket or missile. A nose cone is narrower at the front than at the back. Many nose cones are made to separate from the rocket or missile at some time in the flight.

nos·tril | nŏs′trəl | —*noun, plural* **nostrils** Either of the two outer openings of the nose.

nos·y | nō′zē | —*adjective* **nosier, nosiest** Curious about other people's business: *That nosy girl asked how much my dress cost.*

not | nŏt | —*adverb* In no way; to no degree: *I will not go. You may not have any candy. It is not raining.* The adverb **not** is used to make negative statements.

♦ *These sound alike* **not, knot.**

no·ta·ble | nō′tə bəl | —*adjective* Worth noticing; remarkable: *The meeting was a notable success.*

—*noun, plural* **notables** A well-known person; an important figure: *All the town's notables were invited to the dinner.*

no·ta·tion | nō tā′shən | —*noun, plural* **notations** **1.** A short note: *He made a notation on the calendar about the time and place of the meeting.* **2.** A system of figures or symbols used to stand for numbers, words, notes, or other things: *mathematical notation.*

notch | nŏch | —*noun, plural* **notches** A V-shaped cut. —*verb* **notched, notching** To cut a notch or notches in.

note | nōt | —*noun, plural* **notes** **1.** A short letter or message: *Send me a note when you arrive.* **2.** A short written record to help the memory; a reminder: *He made some notes of what he planned to say in his speech.* **3.** An explanation for a word, paragraph, or section of a book: *This dictionary has notes in the margins.* **4.** A piece of paper money issued by a government: *Can you change a $10 note?* **5.** Importance: *Many people of note attended the ball.* **6.** Notice; attention: *Take note of how she moves her fingers.* **7. a.** A symbol that represents a musical tone. **b.** A musical tone. **8.** A sign; hint: *There was a note of hope in his voice.* —*verb* **noted, noting** **1.** To pay attention to; observe; notice: *Note how his tie matches his handkerchief.* **2.** To make a short record of; write down: *He noted what had happened in his diary.*

note
Musical notes

note·book | nōt′bŏŏk′ | —*noun, plural* **notebooks** A book with blank pages to write on.

not·ed | nō′tĭd | —*adjective* Well known; famous: *a noted actor.*

noth·ing | nŭth′ĭng | —*pronoun* **1.** Not anything: *I have nothing more to say. Nothing is that important!* **2.** Zero: *We won, five to nothing. Nothing plus nothing equals nothing.* **3.** A person or thing that is not important: *He's just a nothing, you know.* —*adverb* Not at all; not a bit: *He looks nothing like me.*

no·tice | nō′tĭs | —*verb* **noticed, noticing** **1.** To become aware of; perceive: *He noticed a dark cloud in the sky.* **2.** To pay attention to: *He sat in the back and hoped that nobody would notice him.* —*noun, plural* **notices** **1.** A condition of being perceived; observation; attention: *She escaped notice by hiding behind a door.* **2.** An announcement in a public place or publication: *The newspaper had a notice about their marriage.* **3.** An announcement or warning: *The maid left without notice.*

no·ti·fy | nō′tə fī′ | —*verb* **notified, notifying, notifies** To let know; inform: *Please notify me when you will return.*

no·tion |nō′shən| —*noun, plural* **notions** **1.** A picture in the mind of what something is or how it works; a general idea: *He has a notion of what the house should look like. Do you have any notion of what makes this machine run?* **2.** A sudden idea or desire; a whim: *She had a notion to sing.* **3.** **notions** Small, useful items, such as needles, thread, and other things for sewing.

no·to·ri·ous |nō tôr′ē əs| or |nō tōr′ē əs| —*adjective* Well known for something, especially for something bad or unpleasant: *a notorious bank robber. Dick is notorious for telling dull stories.*

nought |nôt| A form of the word **naught.**

noun |noun| —*noun, plural* **nouns** A word used to name a person, place, thing, quality, or action. For example, in the sentence "The children found many shells on the beach this morning," *children, shells, beach,* and *morning* are nouns. Nouns can be singular (*beach, morning*) or plural (*children, shells*). A common noun, the kind given in the example above, names one or all of a whole group of persons or things. A proper noun, like *William* or *Boston,* names only one person or thing. A proper noun begins with a capital letter.

nour·ish |nûr′ĭsh| or |nŭr′ĭsh| —*verb* **nourished, nourishing** To provide with what is needed to grow and develop; to feed: *Meat, milk, and vegetables nourished their bodies.*

nour·ish·ment |nûr′ĭsh mənt| —*noun* Something needed for life and growth; food.

No·va Sco·tia |nō′və skō′shə| A province of Canada. Nova Scotia consists of a peninsula that extends into the Atlantic Ocean, together with nearby islands. The capital of Nova Scotia is Halifax.

nov·el[1] |nŏv′əl| —*noun, plural* **novels** A story, long enough to fill a book, about invented people and events.

nov·el[2] |nŏv′əl| —*adjective* Very new or different: *He found a novel way to lace his sneakers.*

nov·el·ist |nŏv′ə lĭst| —*noun, plural* **novelists** A person who writes novels.

nov·el·ty |nŏv′əl tē| —*noun, plural* **novelties** **1.** The condition of being new or different: *She enjoyed the novelty of swimming in the ocean instead of a pool.* **2.** A thing that is new and unusual: *At first the light bulb was just an interesting novelty.* **3.** **novelties** Small items for sale, as toys and cheap jewelry: *key chains, rubber toys, pennants, and other novelties for tourists.*

No·vem·ber |nō vĕm′bər| —*noun, plural* **Novembers** The eleventh month of the year, after October and before December. November has 30 days.

nov·ice |nŏv′ĭs| —*noun, plural* **novices** **1.** A person who is new to a field or activity; a beginner: *He is a novice at tennis.* **2.** A person who is studying to become a nun or monk but has not taken final vows.

now |nou| —*adverb* **1.** At the present time: *Now he is writing a book.* **2.** At once; immediately: *We'd better start now.* **3.** Nowadays: *You hardly ever see plowing with horses now.* —*conjunction* Since; seeing that: *Now we're done eating, let's get out of here.* —*noun* The present: *Now is the time to go.*

now·a·days |nou′ə dāz′| —*adverb* In the present times; in these days: *Many girls wear slacks to school nowadays.*

no·where |nō′hwâr′| or |nō′wâr′| —*adverb* In or to no place;

notions

Nova Scotia
The name **Nova Scotia** comes from a Latin phrase that means "New Scotland."

---

novel[1], **novel**[2]
When short stories became popular, in about the fourteenth to sixteenth century, they were called in Italian *storie novelle,* "new stories." This was borrowed into English as **novel**[1]. **Novel**[2] is from the Latin word meaning "new."

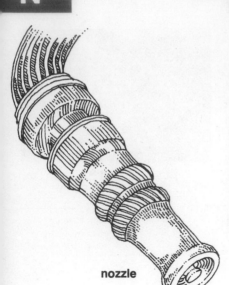

nozzle

not anywhere: *The dog was nowhere to be found.*
—*noun* A place that is not known or not important: *a cabin in the middle of nowhere.*

noz·zle |**nŏz′**əl| —*noun, plural* **nozzles** A metal spout at the end of a hose or pipe through which a liquid or a gas is forced out: *the nozzle of a garden hose; the nozzle on a bicycle pump.*

nu·cle·ar |**nōo′**klē ər| or |**nyōo′**klē ər| —*adjective* **1.** Of or forming a nucleus or nuclei: *the nuclear material in a cell.* **2.** Of or using energy from the nuclei of atoms: *a nuclear power plant; a nuclear submarine.* **3.** Having or using bombs that explode by the energy from the nuclei of atoms: *a nuclear power; a nuclear attack.*

nu·cle·i |**nōo′**klē ī′| or |**nyōo′**klē ī′| The plural of the noun **nucleus.**

nu·cle·us |**nōo′**klē əs| or |**nyōo′**klē əs| —*noun, plural* **nuclei** **1.** A central or most important part around which other parts are grouped; a core: *The three boys were the nucleus of the team.* **2.** A structure in a living cell that controls the cell's important activities, such as growth, development, and reproduction. **3.** The central part of an atom. Protons and neutrons make up the nucleus.

nudge |nŭj| —*verb* **nudged, nudging** To poke or push in a gentle way: *He nudged her to get her to stop talking.*
—*noun, plural* **nudges** A gentle poke or push.

nug·get |**nŭg′**ĭt| —*noun, plural* **nuggets** A hard lump of matter, especially of a precious metal: *a nugget of gold.*

nui·sance |**nōo′**səns| or |**nyōo′**səns| —*noun, plural* **nuisances** Someone or something that annoys or is not convenient; a bother: *He made a nuisance of himself by complaining.*

numb |nŭm| —*adjective* **number, numbest** Having no ability to feel or move in a normal way: *My toes are numb with cold.*
—*verb* **numbed, numbing** To lose or cause to lose the ability to feel or move in a normal way; to deaden: *Her fingers numbed with cold. The dentist numbed her jaw before pulling the tooth.*

num·ber |**nŭm′**bər| —*noun, plural* **numbers** **1.** A unit of counting: *One, six, and three hundred are numbers.* **2.** A numeral: *1, 6, and 300 are numbers.* **3.** One of a series in order: *What number are you in this line?* **4.** A numeral or series of numerals assigned to a person or thing: *What is your telephone number? The football player's number is 12.* **5.** An amount or quantity that is the sum of the units; a total: *the number of centimeters in a meter.* **6.** Quantity; amount: *Great numbers of people marched in the parade. The crowd was small in number.* **7. numbers** Arithmetic: *He is good at numbers.* **8. a.** In grammar, the indication of whether a word refers to one (singular) or more than one (plural): *The verb agrees in number with the subject.* **b.** The form that shows this. For example, "train" and "mouse" are singular in number, while "trains" and "mice" are plural.
—*verb* **numbered, numbering** **1.** To count: *Can you number from one to ten in French?* **2.** To add up to: *The crowd numbered more than two thousand.* **3.** To give a number or numbers to: *Please number the pages.* **4.** To include in a certain group: *I number her among the school's best students.* **5.** To limit in number: *The days were numbered before cold weather would set in.*

num·ber·less |**nŭm′**bər lĭs| —*adjective* Too many to count: *Numberless grasshoppers attacked the crops.*

nu·mer·al |**nōo′**mər əl| or |**nyōo′**mər əl| —*noun, plural*

ă	pat	ĕ	pet	î	fierce
ā	pay	ē	be	ŏ	pot
â	care	ĭ	pit	ō	go
ä	father	ī	pie	ô	paw, for

oi	oil	ŭ	cut	zh	vision
ŏŏ	book	û	fur	ə	ago, item,
ōō	boot	*th*	the		pencil, atom,
yōō	abuse	th	thin		circus
ou	out	hw	which	ər	butter

numerals A symbol or group of symbols that represents a
number. Some examples of numerals are 6, 39, 201, and VI.

nu·mer·a·tor |nōō′mə rā′tər| or |nyōō′mə rā′tər| —*noun,*
plural **numerators** The number above or to the left of the line in
a fraction. For example, in the fraction ²/₇ the numerator is 2.

nu·mer·i·cal |nōō **mĕr′**ĭ kəl| or |nyōō **mĕr′**ĭ kəl| —*adjective* Of
a number or series of numbers: *numerical order.*

nu·mer·ous |nōō′mər əs| or |nyōō′mər əs| —*adjective* Large
in number; many: *The store has numerous items to sell.*

nun |nŭn| —*noun, plural* **nuns** A woman who has devoted
herself to a religious life and has become a member of a church
order.

♦ *These sound alike* **nun, none.**

nurse |nûrs| —*noun, plural* **nurses 1.** Someone trained to take
care of people who are sick or not able to move about. Nurses
usually carry out the instructions of doctors. **2.** A woman who is
hired to take care of someone else's child or children.
—*verb* **nursed, nursing 1.** To take care of sick people; do the
work of a nurse: *She nursed her mother back to health. After nursing
all day she was tired.* **2.** To try to cure or treat: *She nursed her
cough with tea and honey.* **3.** To feed an infant or young animal
at the breast or a milk gland: *The dog nursed her puppies.*

nurs·er·y |nûr′sə rē| or |nûrs′rē| —*noun, plural* **nurseries**
1. A room for babies or young children. **2.** A place where young
plants are raised, often to be sold.

nursery school A school for children who are not old enough to
go to kindergarten.

nut |nŭt| —*noun, plural* **nuts 1.** A seed or dry fruit with a hard
outer shell and usually one kernel inside the shell. The kernels of
many kinds of nuts are good to eat. **2.** A small metal, wood, or
plastic block having a hole with spiral grooves called threads in
the center. A nut screws onto a bolt, screw, or threaded rod and
holds it in place. **3.** A person who is silly or crazy.

nut·crack·er |nŭt′krăk′ər| —*noun, plural* **nutcrackers 1.** A tool
for cracking nuts. **2.** A gray and white bird with a sharp bill.

nut·meg |nŭt′mĕg′| —*noun* The hard seed of a tropical tree.
The seed is shaped like an egg and has a pleasant smell. Nutmeg
is used as a spice when ground or grated.

nu·tri·ent |nōō′trē ənt| or |nyōō′trē ənt| —*noun, plural*
nutrients Something that nourishes: *Fruits and vegetables give us
many nutrients.*

nu·tri·tion |nōō trĭsh′ən| or |nyōō trĭsh′ən| —*noun* **1.** The use
of food that nourishes: *Good nutrition helps us stay healthy.* **2.** The
processes by which a living thing takes in and uses food.

nu·tri·tious |nōō trĭsh′əs| or |nyōō trĭsh′əs| —*adjective*
Capable of helping growth and development; nourishing: *He ate a
nutritious breakfast of juice, toast, eggs, and milk.*

nuz·zle |nŭz′əl| —*verb* **nuzzled, nuzzling** To rub or push in a
gentle way with the nose or snout: *The calf nuzzled the cow.*

ny·lon |nī′lŏn′| —*noun, plural* **nylons** A strong, elastic synthetic
material that can be produced in the form of cloth, thread, yarn,
bristles, or plastic. Nylon is used for making such things as
clothing, parachutes, rugs, brushes, and rope.

nymph |nĭmf| —*noun, plural* **nymphs 1.** A graceful female
spirit that is thought to live in woods and water. **2.** A young
insect that has not yet developed into its adult state.

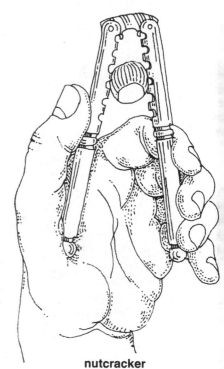

nutcracker

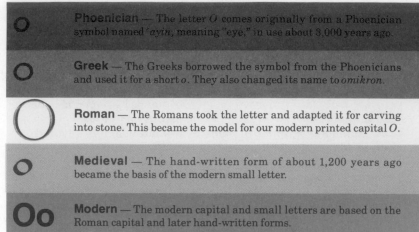

Phoenician — The letter *O* comes originally from a Phoenician symbol named *'ayin*, meaning "eye," in use about 3,000 years ago.

Greek — The Greeks borrowed the symbol from the Phoenicians and used it for a short *o*. They also changed its name to *omikron*.

Roman — The Romans took the letter and adapted it for carving into stone. This became the model for our modern printed capital *O*.

Medieval — The hand-written form of about 1,200 years ago became the basis of the modern small letter.

Modern — The modern capital and small letters are based on the Roman capital and later hand-written forms.

Oo

oak
Acorns and leaf (*above*)
and tree (*below*)

o or **O** |ō| —*noun, plural* **o's** or **O's** The fifteenth letter of the English alphabet.

oak |ōk| —*noun, plural* **oaks** **1.** Any of several trees that bear acorns. The leaves of oaks often have uneven notches along the edges. **2.** The hard, strong wood of an oak tree.

oar |ôr| or |ōr| —*noun, plural* **oars** **1.** A long, thin pole with a flat blade at one end. Oars are used to row or steer boats. **2.** Someone who rows a boat.

♦ *These sound alike* **oar, or, ore.**

o·a·ses |ō ā'sēz'| The plural of the noun **oasis.**

o·a·sis |ō ā'sĭs| —*noun, plural* **oases** An area in a desert where there is water. Usually there are also trees and plants at an oasis.

oats |ōts| —*plural noun* The seeds of a grain plant. Oats are used as food for human beings and horses.

oath |ōth| —*noun, plural* **oaths** |ōthz| or |ōthz| **1.** A promise to tell the truth or act in a particular way, with God or some sacred object as witness: *The man took an oath on the Bible to tell the truth.* **2.** A word or phrase that shows lack of respect for something sacred or that offends people's idea of what is decent or proper; a curse.

oat·meal |ōt'mēl'| or |ōt'mēl'| —*noun, plural* **oatmeals** **1.** Seeds of oats that have been ground or pressed flat. **2.** A cooked cereal made from this.

o·be·di·ence |ō bē'dē əns| —*noun* The practice of obeying rules, laws, or requests: *a dog trained in obedience.*

o·be·di·ent |ō bē'dē ənt| —*adjective* Doing what is asked, ordered, or required; willing to obey: *an obedient horse.*

o·bey |ō bā'| —*verb* **obeyed, obeying** **1.** To carry out or follow a law, order, or request: *She did not obey the instructions.* **2.** To do what is commanded: *The sailors obeyed the captain and lowered the sails.*

o·bi |ō'bē| —*noun, plural* **obis** A wide sash worn with a kimono by Japanese women.

ob·ject |ŏb'jĭkt| or |ŏb'jĕkt'| —*noun, plural* **objects** **1.** Something that has shape and can be seen or felt; a thing: *There were some strange objects on the table.* **2.** Someone or something toward which attention is directed; target: *He was the object of many angry cartoons. The puppy is the object of her affection.* **3.** A purpose; goal: *The object of the game is to get the*

ă	pat	ĕ	pet	î	fierce
ā	pay	ē	be	ŏ	pot
â	care	ĭ	pit	ō	go
ä	father	ī	pie	ô	paw, for
oi	oil	ŭ	cut	zh	vision
ŏŏ	book	û	fur	ə	ago, item,
ōō	boot	*th*	the		pencil, atom,
yōō	abuse	th	thin		circus
ou	out	hw	which	ər	butter

ball through the hoop. **4.** In grammar, a word that receives the action of a verb or follows a preposition. For example, in the sentence "He flew a kite," "kite" is the object of the verb "flew." In the phrase "against the tide," "the tide" is the object of the preposition "against."

—*verb* | əb **jĕkt′** | **objected, objecting 1.** To express an opposite opinion or argument: *They objected to the loud radios in the streets.* **2.** To say in protest: *"Now see here," he objected.*

ob·jec·tion | əb **jĕk′**shən | —*noun, plural* **objections 1.** A feeling of being against; an opposing view or argument: *She has a strong objection to smoking.* **2.** A reason or cause for being against: *Her main objection to the trip is the cost.*

ob·jec·tive | əb **jĕk′**tĭv | —*adjective* Not influenced by one's own feelings or prejudices; fair; impartial: *A referee must be objective.*
—*noun, plural* **objectives** Something that one tries to achieve or reach; goal; purpose: *The objective was to control the bridge.*

ob·li·gate | **ŏb′**lĭ gāt′ | —*verb* **obligated, obligating** To bind by a sense of duty or law: *The contract obligated him to work for them.*

ob·li·ga·tion | ŏb′lĭ **gā′**shən | —*noun, plural* **obligations 1.** A duty that one feels bound to by law or by a sense of what is right or proper: *He felt an obligation to help the man who had once helped him.* **2.** Something owed in money or behavior: *She took care of her dead brother's obligations.*

o·blige | ə **blīj′** | —*verb* **obliged, obliging 1.** To force to act in a certain way: *The weather obliged him to cancel his trip.* **2.** To make grateful or thankful: *I am obliged to you for helping me.* **3.** To satisfy the wishes of; do a favor for: *The singer obliged her audience with another number.*

ob·long | **ŏb′**lông′ | or | **ŏb′**lŏng′ | —*adjective* Greater in length than in width: *an oblong table.*

o·boe | **ō′**bō | —*noun, plural* **oboes** A musical instrument of the woodwind family. An oboe has a high, smooth, piercing sound. The oboe is played by blowing into a mouthpiece made of two thin pieces of reed.

ob·scure | əb **skyŏor′** | —*adjective* **obscurer, obscurest 1.** Difficult to understand: *an obscure paragraph in a book.* **2.** Not well known; not noticed by many: *an obscure part of the world; an obscure professor.* **3.** Not easy to figure out; not distinct: *obscure marks on an ancient stone wall.*
—*verb* **obscured, obscuring** To hide from view; make difficult to see or understand; conceal: *Clouds obscured the stars.*

ob·ser·va·tion | ŏb′zûr **vā′**shən | —*noun, plural* **observations 1.** The act of watching or noticing: *a tower for observation of the forest.* **2.** The ability to pay attention and notice: *his great powers of observation in studying insects.* **3.** The fact of being noticed: *The heavy fog helped the detective avoid observation.* **4.** Something that has been seen and noticed: *The doctor wrote his observations on the patient's chart.* **5.** A comment or remark: *She made a few observations about the weather.*

ob·ser·va·to·ry | əb **zûr′**və tôr′ē | or | əb **zûr′**və tōr′ē | —*noun, plural* **observatories** A place with telescopes and other instruments for studying the stars and planets, the heavens, the weather, or other natural occurrences.

ob·serve | əb **zûrv′** | —*verb* **observed, observing 1.** To watch in a close and careful way; see and pay attention to; notice: *She observed some birds on the branch. Did you observe how he*

oboe

observatory

scratches his ear when he is nervous? **2.** To make a remark; to comment: *"It will soon be time for vacation," she observed.* **3.** To abide by a law, duty, or custom: *He observed the speed limit.* **4.** To keep or celebrate a holiday, religious festival, or other special day: *They observed their anniversary by giving a party.*

ob·so·lete | ŏb′sə **lēt**′ | or | **ŏb**′sə lēt′ | —*adjective* No longer used; out of date: *an obsolete word; obsolete airplanes.*

ob·sta·cle | **ŏb**′stə kəl | —*noun, plural* **obstacles** Something that blocks the way: *Fallen rocks and other obstacles made it impossible to drive up the road.*

ob·struct | əb **strŭkt**′ | —*verb* **obstructed, obstructing 1.** To block with obstacles; cause difficulty for something to pass through: *Fallen leaves obstructed the drain pipes.* **2.** To get in the way of: *The new building obstructs our view of the river.*

ob·tain | əb **tān**′ | —*verb* **obtained, obtaining** To get by means of planning or effort; acquire; gain: *His skill at carving wood helped him obtain a good job.*

ob·tuse angle | əb **tōos**′ | or | əb **tyōos**′ | An angle that is wider than a right angle. An obtuse angle measures between 90 and 180 degrees.

ob·vi·ous | **ŏb**′vē əs | —*adjective* Easy to notice or understand; very clear: *He made an obvious error in addition.*

oc·ca·sion | ə **kā**′ zhən | —*noun, plural* **occasions 1.** The time when something takes place: *We met at the occasion of my last visit to my aunt.* **2.** An important event: *The Thanksgiving dinner was a big occasion.* **3.** A chance; opportunity: *He never missed an occasion to visit the observatory.*

oc·ca·sion·al | ə **kā**′zhə nəl | —*adjective* Happening from time to time; not steady or regular; occurring now and then: *Except for an occasional sore throat, he has been well this year.*

oc·ca·sion·al·ly | ə **kā**′zhə nə lē | —*adverb* From time to time; not in a steady or regular way; now and then: *They occasionally go out to dinner but usually dine at home.*

Oc·ci·dent | **ŏk**′sĭ dənt | —*noun* **1. occident** The west; western lands. **2.** The countries of Europe, Africa, and the Americas.

Oc·ci·den·tal | ŏk′sĭ **dĕn**′tl | —*adjective* **1. occidental** Western. **2.** Of the Occident or any of its people.
—*noun, plural* **Occidentals 1.** A person born in the Occident. **2.** A person whose ancestors are from the Occident.

oc·cu·pant | **ŏk**′yə pənt | —*noun, plural* **occupants** Someone or something that is in a place or position: *Squirrels and mice were the only occupants of the old barn.*

oc·cu·pa·tion | ŏk′yə **pā**′shən | —*noun, plural* **occupations 1.** The work a person does to earn a living; job or profession: *He left his occupation as a waiter and became an actor.* **2.** An activity one does to keep busy: *Her main occupation has been gardening since she retired.* **3.** The act of taking possession of and holding or using: *the occupation of a small cabin by a large family. The army's occupation of the conquered country lasted 25 years.*

oc·cu·py | **ŏk**′yə pī′ | —*verb* **occupied, occupying, occupies 1.** To live in; inhabit: *The family occupies a two-bedroom house.* **2.** To fill; take up: *Reading occupies most of his spare time. Old furniture occupied most of the attic.* **3.** To keep busy: *She occupied herself with many small tasks.* **4.** To take possession of and control by force: *The troops invaded and occupied the city.* **5.** To have, hold, or control: *He occupies the office of treasurer.*

ă	pat	ĕ	pet	î	fierce
ā	pay	ē	be	ŏ	pot
â	care	ĭ	pit	ō	go
ä	father	ī	pie	ô	paw, for
oi	oil	ŭ	cut	zh	vision
ōo	book	û	fur	ə	ago, item,
ōo	boot	*th*	the		pencil, atom,
yōo	abuse	th	thin		circus
ou	out	hw	which	ər	butter

oc·cur |ə kûr′| —*verb* **occurred, occurring 1.** To take place; happen: *Many accidents occur at home.* **2.** To be found; appear or live; exist: *Many errors occurred in his story.*

    Phrasal verb occur to To come to the mind of; suggest itself to: *It didn't occur to her that her mother might object.*

oc·cur·rence |ə kûr′əns| —*noun, plural* **occurrences 1.** The act of taking place or appearing: *the occurrence of an accident; the occurrence of dead fish in the river.* **2.** Something that takes place; an event: *There were many strange occurrences that summer.*

o·cean |ō′shən| —*noun, plural* **oceans 1.** The great mass of salt water that covers almost three quarters of the earth's surface. **2.** Any of the four main divisions of this mass of salt water; the Atlantic, Pacific, Indian, or Arctic Ocean.

oc·e·lot |ŏs′ə lŏt′| or |ō′sə lŏt′| —*noun, plural* **ocelots** A wild cat of Mexico, Central America, and South America. The ocelot has a yellowish coat spotted with black.

o'clock |ə klŏk′| —*adverb* Of or according to the clock: *It is now ten o'clock.*

oc·tave |ŏk′tĭv| or |ŏk′tāv′| —*noun, plural* **octaves 1.** The musical interval between a musical tone and the next tone of the same name just above it or just below it. **2.** Either of two tones that are separated by this interval. **3.** A series of tones that are included in this interval: *the lowest octave of a flute.*

Oc·to·ber |ŏk tō′bər| —*noun, plural* **Octobers** The tenth month of the year, after September and before November. October has 31 days.

oc·to·pus |ŏk′tə pəs| —*noun, plural* **octopuses** A sea animal that has a soft body with eight parts that look like arms. The undersides of the arms have small parts that help the octopus cling and hold by suction.

odd |ŏd| —*adjective* **odder, oddest 1.** Not ordinary or usual; strange; peculiar: *an odd noise in the closet; an odd name.* **2.** Leaving a remainder of 1 when divided by two; not even: *5, 7, 9, and 11 are odd numbers.* **3.** Forming one of a pair with the other one missing: *She had a pair of gloves and an odd mitten.* **4.** Remaining after others are placed into groups or sets; extra; left over: *a few odd saucers from an old set of china.* **5.** Available or happening now and then; occasional: *He does odd jobs.*

odds |ŏdz| —*plural noun* **1.** The likely chance that a particular thing will happen; probability: *The odds are that it will rain tomorrow.* **2.** A number that tells how likely it is that something will happen: *"The odds are 2 to 1 that John will win over Sam"* means that John is twice as likely to win as Sam. **3.** Advantage in a game or contest: *The odds are with the champion.*

o·dor |ō′dər| —*noun, plural* **odors** A smell; scent: *An odor of fish came from the kitchen.*

o·dor·less |ō′dər lĭs| —*adjective* Having no odor: *It is hard to find an odorless soap.*

of |ŭv| or |ŏv| —*preposition* **1.** Made with or from: *a wall of stone; tables and chairs of fine wood; shoes of black leather.* **2.** Containing or carrying: *a box of chocolate; a bag of groceries.* **3.** Belonging or connected to: *the rungs of a ladder; the roof of the barn; the color of roses.* **4.** From: *Boston is east of Albany. We sell the fruits of our orchards.* **5.** Named or called: *the city of Boston.* **6.** About; concerning: *We watched a movie of his trip.* **7.** By: *Have you read the sonnets of Shakespeare?* **8.** Having; with: *a man of*

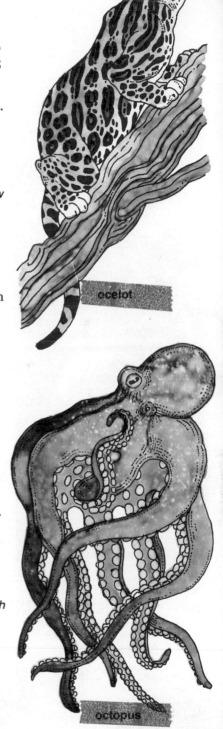

ocelot

octopus

honor. **9.** Coming from: *men and women of the West.* **10.** Before; until: *five minutes of six.* **11.** Because of: *He died of pneumonia.* **12.** So as to be freed or relieved from: *She was cured of cancer.* **13.** Set aside for: *a day of rest.*

off |ôf| or |ŏf| —*adverb* **1.** Away from the present place or time: *The house is about a mile off. The holidays are a week off.* **2.** So as to be no longer on or connected: *Turn off the radio. She turned the gas off before she left.* **3.** Away from work or duty: *He is taking the day off.* **4.** So as to be smaller, fewer, or less: *Car sales are dropping off these days.*
—*adjective* **1.** More distant or removed: *The horses moved to the off side of the barn.* **2.** Not on: *His shoes were off. The lights are off.* **3.** Not in use or operation: *The stove is off.* **4.** Canceled: *The wedding is off.* **5.** Less or smaller: *Car production is off this year.* **6.** Below the usual standard: *His performance in the game today was off.* **7.** In error; wrong: *She was off in her estimate by fifty dollars.* **8.** Away from work or duty: *I'm off tonight.*
—*preposition* **1.** So as to be removed or away from: *Lily took the papers off the table. Marie dived off the cliff.* **2.** Away or relieved from: *He is off duty tonight.* **3.** With the aid or use of: *He's retired and lives off his pension.* **4.** Extending from: *The car turned into a narrow street off the avenue.* **5.** Not consuming; not using: *She has been off cigarettes for weeks now.* **6.** Less than or below the usual level or standard of: *The store was selling books at 20 per cent off regular prices.*

of·fend |ə fĕnd′| —*verb* **offended, offending** To cause bad feelings, pain, annoyance, or anger: *His rude remarks offended our guest. That wallpaper offends my sense of good taste.*

of·fense |ə fĕns′| —*noun, plural* **offenses 1.** Anything that causes bad feelings, anger, or annoyance: *His insults were an offense to everyone in the room.* **2.** An act that breaks a law or rule; a crime or sin: *Driving through a red light is a traffic offense.* **3.** |ô′fĕns′| or |ŏf′ĕns′| The person or team who is leading an attack against the other side: *The offense is on the field.*

of·fen·sive |ə fĕn′sĭv| —*adjective* **1.** Unpleasant to the senses: *an offensive odor of garbage.* **2.** Causing bad feelings, anger, or annoyance: *his offensive language.* **3.** |ô′fĕn′sĭv| or |ŏf′ĕn′sĭv| Of attack; making an attack: *an offensive play in football.*
—*noun, plural* **offensives 1.** An attack: *their third major offensive of the war.* **2.** An attitude of attack: *If you take the offensive, you may scare him into backing down.*

of·fer |ô′fər| or |ŏf′ər| —*verb* **offered, offering 1.** To put forward to be accepted or refused: *She offered the child some candy. He offered his help.* **2.** To suggest; propose: *She offered a plan to win the game.* **3.** To show a wish to do; attempt: *Will the enemy offer any resistance?*
—*noun, plural* **offers 1.** Something put forward to be accepted or refused; suggestion or proposal: *an offer to do the dishes.* **2.** Something suggested as a price: *an offer of $250 for the piano.*

of·fice |ô′fĭs| or |ŏf′ĭs| —*noun, plural* **offices 1.** A building or part of a building for people who do professional work or keep business records: *a doctor's office. The office is across the street from the factory.* **2.** All the people who work in such a place: *The office gave the boss a surprise party.* **3.** A position of trust or responsibility: *She was elected to the office of judge.*

of·fi·cer |ô′fĭ sər| or |ŏf′ĭ sər| —*noun, plural* **officers 1.** A

officer
Above: Police officer
Below: Navy officer

ă	pat	ĕ	pet	î	fierce
ā	pay	ē	be	ŏ	pot
â	care	ĭ	pit	ō	go
ä	father	ī	pie	ô	paw, for
oi	oil	ŭ	cut	zh	vision
ōō	book	û	fur	ə	ago, item,
ōō	boot	*th*	the		pencil, atom,
yōō	abuse	th	thin		circus
ou	out	hw	which	ər	butter

person who has a position of trust or responsibility: *The vice president and the treasurer are officers of the company.* **2.** A person who is in a position to command others, as in military service or on a ship: *The officers eat in a room apart from the men.* **3.** A member of a police force: *The officer helped the child across the street.*

of·fi·cial |ə físh′əl| —*noun, plural* **officials** A person who is in a position of command or authority: *city officials.*
—*adjective* **1.** Of or connected with a position of trust or command: *One of his official duties is to greet important visitors.*
2. Coming from the proper authority: *an official report.*

off·set |ôf′sĕt′| or |ŏf′sĕt′| —*verb* **offset, offsetting** To balance against something else; make up for: *The winning games at the end of the season offset the losses at the beginning.*

off·shoot |ôf′shōōt′| or |ŏf′shōōt′| —*noun, plural* **offshoots**
1. A shoot that branches out from the main stem of a plant.
2. Something that branches out or comes from a main source: *Her recent novel was an offshoot of her trip to China.*

off·shore |ôf′shôr′| or |ôf′shōr′| or |ŏf′shôr′| or |ŏf′shōr′|
—*adjective* **1.** Away from the shore: *offshore rocks; offshore oil wells.* **2.** Moving away from the shore: *an offshore breeze.*
—*adverb* **1.** In a direction away from shore: *The breeze was blowing offshore.* **2.** At a distance from shore: *The sea lion was swimming a half mile offshore.*

off·spring |ôf′sprĭng′| or |ŏf′sprĭng′| —*noun, plural* **offspring**
One or more young living things produced by people, animals, or plants: *The boy was their only offspring. Rabbits produce many offspring. The entire orchard was the offspring of one tree.*

of·ten |ô′fən| or |ŏf′ən| or |ôf′tən| or |ŏf′tən| —*adverb* Many times; again and again; in a repeated way: *He often reads before going to bed. Did you visit them often?*

oh |ō| —*interjection* A word used to express surprise, anger, pain, happiness, and other feelings: *"Oh! How horrible!"*
♦ *These sound alike* **oh, owe.**

O·hi·o |ō hī′ō| A state in the central United States. The capital of Ohio is Columbus.

oil |oil| —*noun, plural* **oils** **1.** A thick, slippery, greasy liquid, or a fat that easily becomes liquid. Oils may be mineral, vegetable, or animal. All oils float on water, do not mix with water, and burn easily. **2.** Petroleum or any mineral oil that comes from petroleum. **3.** A paint made by mixing coloring materials in an oil, especially in linseed oil. **4.** A painting done in such paints.
—*verb* **oiled, oiling** To cover with, polish, or put oil in or on: *They oiled the tools to keep them from rusting.*

oil·y |oi′lē| —*adjective* **oilier, oiliest** **1.** Of or like oil: *an oily liquid.* **2.** Covered with or containing much oil: *old oily rags; an oily spaghetti sauce; oily skin.*

oint·ment |oint′mənt| —*noun, plural* **ointments** A thick substance made to be rubbed on to heal or soothe the skin.

O.K. or **OK** |ō′kā′| or |ō kā′| —*adverb* Well; fine: *He's doing O.K.*
—*adjective* All right; fine: *The plan is O.K. with me.*
—*interjection* All right; very well: *O.K., fellows, let's go.*
—*noun, plural* **O.K.'s** or **OK's** An approval; agreement; a yes: *Get your dad's O.K. before you start the trip.*
—*verb* **O.K.'d** or **OK'd, O.K.'ing** or **OK'ing, O.K.'s** or **OK's** To

offspring
Mother and baby hippopotamus

Ohio
The name **Ohio** comes from an Indian word that probably meant "beautiful" or "beautiful river." The Indians used the word for the river that flowed through their land. The state was named for the river.

Oklahoma
The name **Oklahoma** comes from Indian words that mean "red people."

okra

approve; agree to: *The teacher O.K.'d the plans for the class play.*

O·kla·ho·ma |ō′klə hō′mə| A state in the south-central United States. The capital of Oklahoma is Oklahoma City.

Oklahoma City The capital of Oklahoma.

ok·ra |ō′krə| —*noun* The narrow, sticky seed pods of a tall plant. Okra is usually used in soups or stews.

old |ōld| —*adjective* **older** or **elder, oldest** or **eldest** **1.** Having lived or existed for many years; not young: *an old man with white hair; a huge old pine tree; an old part of the city.* **2.** Of a certain age: *She is four years old.* **3.** Worn and showing signs of age and use; not new: *a box of old toys; old clothing.* **4.** Belonging to an earlier time; of the past: *He went to visit his old neighborhood.* **5.** Well known and liked; familiar; dear: *By kindergarten, the two girls were old friends.* **6.** Skilled through long experience: *He is an old hand at sailing.* **7.** Former: *Yesterday I saw her old teacher.* —*noun* **1.** Times of the past; former days: *In days of old, people believed in dragons and goblins.* **2. the old** Old people.

old·en |ōl′dən| —*adjective* Of an earlier time when things were very different from the way they are now: *In olden days, there were no electric lights.*

old-fash·ioned |ōld′ făsh′ ənd| —*adjective* **1.** Of the style of an earlier time and no longer in fashion; out-of-date: *The children found some old-fashioned shoes and hats in the attic.* **2.** Preferring the ways, customs, or ideas of an earlier time: *an old-fashioned family that still does many things together.*

Old Testament The collection of sacred writings that make up the whole of the Jewish Bible and the first of the two main divisions of the Christian Bible.

Old World Europe, Asia, and Africa; the portion of the world that was known before the discovery of America.

o·le·o·mar·ga·rine |ō′lē ō mär′ jər ĭn| or |ō′lē ō mär′ jə rēn′| —*noun, plural* **oleomargarines** A food made as a substitute for butter; margarine.

ol·ive |ŏl′ĭv| —*noun, plural* **olives** **1.** The small, oval greenish or blackish fruit of a tree that grows in warm regions. Olives are often eaten as relish. **2.** A tree that bears olives. **3.** A dull yellowish green. —*adjective* Dull yellowish green: *an olive uniform.*

olive oil A yellowish oil pressed from olives. Olive oil is used for cooking, in salad dressings, and for making soap.

O·lym·pi·a |ō lĭm′pē ə| The capital of the state of Washington.

O·lym·pic games |ō lĭm′pĭk| **1.** An ancient Greek series of competitions and contests in athletics, poetry, and dancing. It was held once every four years in honor of the Greeks' chief god. **2.** A modern series of competitions in athletics, held every four years in different parts of the world. Many countries send athletes to compete in these contests.

O·lym·pics |ō lĭm′pĭks| —*noun* **1.** Modern Olympic games. **2. olympics** Any series of contests in athletics.

om·e·let |ŏm′ə lĭt| or |ŏm′lĭt| —*noun, plural* **omelets** A dish of eggs that have been beaten, sometimes with milk and seasonings, and then cooked quickly in a pan. Omelets are often folded around a filling of cheese, jelly, mushrooms, or meat.

o·men |ō′mən| —*noun, plural* **omens** Something thought to be a sign of good or bad luck to come: *He considered the sunny weather to be an omen of success.*

ă	pat	ĕ	pet	î	fierce
ā	pay	ē	be	ŏ	pot
â	care	ĭ	pit	ō	go
ä	father	ī	pie	ô	paw, for

oi	oil	ŭ	cut	zh	vision
ŏŏ	book	û	fur	ə	ago, item,
ōō	boot	*th*	the		pencil, atom,
yōō	abuse	th	thin		circus
ou	out	hw	which	ər	butter

om·i·nous | ŏm′ə nəs | —*adjective* Seeming to be a sign of trouble, danger, disaster, or bad fortune; threatening: *an ominous rumble beneath the earth.*

o·mit | ō mĭt′ | —*verb* **omitted, omitting** To leave out; not include: *He omitted sweets from his meals in order to lose weight.*

on | ŏn | or | ôn | —*preposition* **1.** Supported by and touching; upon: *Place the dishes on the table. Don't hang pictures on the wall.* **2.** Located upon: *a house on the beach.* **3.** Near; along: *a city on the border.* **4.** Against: *She hit her head on the roof of the car.* **5.** For the purpose of: *He travels a great deal on business.* **6.** Covering: *I have shoes on my feet.* **7.** Concerning; about: *a book on history.* **8.** In the course of; during: *We will leave on Tuesday.* **9.** Taking part in; as a member of: *He is on the basketball team.* **10.** With the help or use of: *She lives on very little money.* **11.** Supported or justified by: *On principal, we should forget their mistakes.* **12.** In the possession of: *I don't have a cent on me.* **13.** At the expense of: *Lunch is on me today.* **14.** Not behind or ahead of: *He will arrive on time.*
—*adverb* **1.** In or into a position of covering or being attached to something: *She pulled her coat on.* **2.** In the direction of something: *He was looking on when the ship came in.* **3.** Forward; ahead: *They are moving on to the next town.* **4.** In or into action or operation: *Don't forget to turn the radio on.* **5.** In or at the present place or position: *We are staying on until later.*
—*adjective* **1.** Attached to or covering something: *His shoes are on.* **2.** In use or operation: *The stove is on. The lights are on.* **3.** In progress or taking place: *The game was on when she arrived.*

once | wŭns | —*adverb* **1.** One time only: *Take your medicine once a day.* **2.** At some time in the past; formerly: *I was a baby once, too.* **3.** At some time in the future; some day: *I would like to ride an elephant once before I am too old.*
—*noun* One single time: *Please let me go out, just this once.*
—*conjunction* As soon as; if ever; when: *I'll show you what to do once we get started.*

one | wŭn | —*noun, plural* **ones 1.** A number, written 1, that leaves the same any number multiplied with it: *1×8=8.* **2.** A single person or thing: *I'd like a dozen apples, but please don't give me any green ones.*
—*pronoun* **1.** A particular person or thing: *One of my friends is ill.* **2.** Any person; a person: *From here one can see the ocean.*
—*adjective* **1.** Being a single person or thing: *one boy and four girls.* **2.** Some: *One day you'll be going to college.* The adjective **one** belongs to a class of words called **determiners.** They signal that a noun is coming.
♦ *These sound alike* **one, won.**

one·self | wŭn sĕlf′ | —*pronoun* The pronoun **oneself** is a special form of the third person singular pronoun **one.** It is used: **1.** As the direct object of a verb: *It is very easy to fool oneself when it comes to dieting.* **2.** As the indirect object of a verb: *One must buy oneself whatever is needed for the trip.* **3.** As the object of a preposition: *One soon finds out that there are many people different from oneself.*

one-way | wŭn′ wā′ | —*adjective* Moving or allowing movement, travel, or use in one direction only: *a one-way street.*

on·ion | ŭn′ yən | —*noun, plural* **onions** The rounded bulb of a plant widely grown as a vegetable. Onions have a strong smell.

onion
Whole (*above*) and sliced (*below*)

on·ly |ōn′lē| —*adjective* **1.** One and no more; by itself; sole: *our only reason for going; an only child; our only chance.* **2.** The best and most suitable: *the only way to do it.*
—*adverb* **1.** Without anyone or anything else: *Only three people survived the fire.* **2.** Just; merely: *I only followed orders.*
—*conjunction* But: *Go ahead and quit school, only don't come complaining when you can't get a job.*

on·set |ŏn′sĕt′| or |ôn′sĕt′| —*noun, plural* **onsets** A beginning or start: *the onset of a disease; the onset of a blizzard.*

On·tar·i·o |ŏn târ′ē ō| A province of Canada. The capital of Ontario is Toronto.

on·to |ŏn′tōō′| or |ôn′tōō′| or |ŏn′tə| or |ôn′tə| —*preposition* To a position on or upon: *onto the train.*

on·ward |ŏn′wərd| or |ôn′wərd| —*adverb* In a direction or toward a position that is ahead in space or time; forward: *The hunters were plodding onward through the storm.* Another form of this adverb is **onwards.**
—*adjective* Moving to or toward a position that is ahead in space or time: *The pioneers continued their onward march.*

on·wards |ŏn′wərdz| or |ôn′wərdz| A form of the adverb **onward.**

ooze |ōōz| —*verb* **oozed, oozing** **1.** To flow slowly out or through; seep, drip, or leak slowly: *Blood oozed from the cut in his finger. Mud oozed between his fingers.* **2.** To give out little by little through a small opening or openings: *Sap oozed from the trees.*

o·paque |ō pāk′| —*adjective* **1.** Not capable of letting light through: *A metal door is opaque.* **2.** Not reflecting light; not shiny; dull: *We used an opaque paint on the chair.*

o·pen |ō′pən| —*adjective* **1.a.** Providing entrance and exit: *an open door.* **b.** Not shut, fastened, closed, or sealed: *an open lock; an open book; an open envelope.* **2.** Allowing free passage or view; not enclosed: *open country; the open seas.* **3.** Having no cover or protection; exposed: *an open wound; an open jar; cooking over an open fire.* **4.** Not filled or engaged: *The job is still open.* **5.** Ready for business: *The store is open now.* **6.** Frank; honest: *She is a warm, open, friendly person.* **7.** Not prejudiced; able to take in new ideas: *keeping an open mind.* **8.** Not secret or hidden: *They have an open dislike of one another.*
—*verb* **opened, opening** **1.** To make or become no longer shut, fastened, sealed, or closed: *The door opened slowly. He opened a can of peas. Open the letter.* **2.** To spread out or apart: *He opened the map on the table. The buds will open soon into lovely flowers.* **3.** To begin: *Read the sentence that opens the chapter.* **4.** To start business: *We're opening a restaurant soon.* **5.** To allow free passage or view: *These two doors open onto the hallway.*
—*noun* **the open** An area of land or water that is not covered or hidden: *The deer walked cautiously into the open.*

o·pen·er |ō′pə nər| —*noun, plural* **openers** **1.** Something that is used to open closed or sealed containers: *Get the can opener and open the beans. We need an opener for this bottle of soda.* **2.** The first in a series: *the opener of the football season.*

o·pen·ing |ō′pə nĭng| —*noun, plural* **openings** **1.** The act of becoming open or being made to open: *Many Indians suffered with the opening of the West.* **2.** An open space or clearing: *an opening in the woods.* **3.** The first period or stage of something: *The author sets the opening of his novel in Japan.* **4.** The first time of

---

Ontario
The name **Ontario** comes from an Indian word meaning "beautiful waters."

ă	pat	ĕ	pet	î	fierce
ā	pay	ē	be	ŏ	pot
â	care	ĭ	pit	ō	go
ä	father	ī	pie	ô	paw, for

oi	oil	ŭ	cut	zh	vision
ōō	book	û	fur	ə	ago, item,
ōō	boot	*th*	the		pencil, atom,
yōō	abuse	th	thin		circus
ou	out	hw	which	ər	butter

something: *Tomorrow is the opening of the play.* **5.** A job that is not filled: *There are two openings on the teaching staff.*

op·er·a | ŏp′ər ə | or | ŏp′rə | —*noun, plural* **operas** A musical play that has most of its words sung to music, and an orchestra to accompany the singing.

op·er·ate | ŏp′ə rāt′ | —*verb* **operated, operating 1.** To work: *The machine operates well.* **2.** To control the running of something: *A pilot operates an airplane. She operates a dress shop in New York.* **3.** To perform surgery: *The doctor operated on him.*

op·er·a·tion | ŏp′ə rā′shən | —*noun, plural* **operations 1.** The act or process of operating: *You must teach him about the operation of a printing press. The operation of his business was very rewarding to him.* **2.** The condition of being able to operate or function: *a machine no longer in operation.* **3.** A process of treatment for diseases and disorders of the living body by using surgery: *He had an operation to remove his appendix.*

op·er·a·tor | ŏp′ə rā′tər | —*noun, plural* **operators** Someone who operates a machine or device: *a computer operator.*

op·er·et·ta | ŏp′ə rĕt′ə | —*noun, plural* **operettas** A short, funny opera that has some spoken parts.

o·pin·ion | ō pĭn′yən | —*noun, plural* **opinions 1.** A belief that is not supported by actual knowledge or proof: *It is my opinion that it will snow today.* **2.** A judgment based on special knowledge and given by an expert: *I wanted my lawyer's opinion before I bought the house.* **3.** A judgment or estimate of the value of a person or thing: *The teacher had a high opinion of the child's ability.*

o·pi·um | ō′pē əm | —*noun* A bitter, powerful drug prepared from a poppy plant: *Opium is a narcotic drug.*

o·pos·sum | ə pŏs′əm | —*noun, plural* **opossums** A furry animal that lives mostly in trees. The female opossum carries her young in a pouch. This animal is also called *possum.*

op·po·nent | ə pō′nənt | —*noun, plural* **opponents** A person who is against another person in a fight or contest: *My opponent is taller and heavier than I am.*

op·por·tu·ni·ty | ŏp′ər tōō′nĭ tē | or | ŏp′ər tyōō′nĭ tē | —*noun, plural* **opportunities** Time or situation that is good for a purpose; a good chance: *We have an opportunity to travel to Europe this summer.*

op·pose | ə pōz′ | —*verb* **opposed, opposing 1.** To be against: *We opposed the idea of going to the zoo on Sunday.* **2.** To place in contrast; set against: *Mrs. Burns opposed sunlight and shadow in her painting of the lake.*

op·po·site | ŏp′ə zĭt | or | ŏp′ə sĭt | —*adjective* **1.** Placed or located directly across from something else or from each other: *We sat on opposite sides of the room.* **2.** Moving away from each other: *They went off in opposite directions.* **3.** Completely different: *The two sisters have opposite personalities.*
—*noun, plural* **opposites** Someone or something that is completely different from another: *Darkness and daylight are opposites.*

op·po·si·tion | ŏp′ə zĭsh′ən | —*noun, plural* **oppositions 1.** The act or condition of opposing or being against; resistance: *His opposition to the idea surprised us.* **2.** Something that is an opposing obstacle: *Their offense met with strong opposition from our team.* **3.** A political party that is opposed to the party of the government in power.

operator
Telephone operators

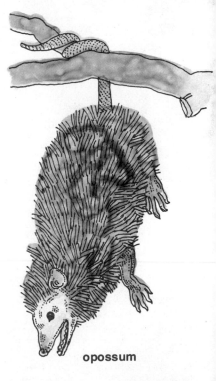

opossum

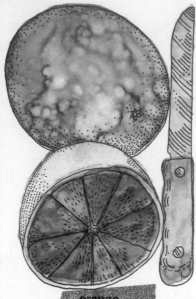

orange

Whole (*above*) and cut in half (*below*)

orangutan

ă	pat	ĕ	pet	î	fierce
ā	pay	ē	be	ŏ	pot
â	care	ĭ	pit	ō	go
ä	father	ī	pie	ô	paw, for

oi	oil	ŭ	cut	zh	vision
ŏŏ	book	û	fur	ə	ago, item,
ōō	boot	*th*	the		pencil, atom,
yōō	abuse	th	thin		circus
ou	out	hw	which	ər	butter

op·press | ə **prĕs'** | —*verb* **oppressed, oppressing 1.** To control or rule with a heavy hand; treat in a harsh and unjust way: *The people waged war on their king because he had oppressed them for years.* **2.** To weigh heavily upon the mind; trouble; depress: *Grief oppressed her after the death of her husband.*

op·ti·cal | ŏp'tĭ kəl | —*adjective* **1.** Of or having to do with sight: *Being far-sighted is an optical defect. He saw an optical illusion at the science museum.* **2.** Made to assist sight; helping to see: *Telescopes and microscopes are optical instruments.*

op·ti·mis·tic | ŏp'tə **mĭs'**tĭk | —*adjective* Tending to take an encouraging or cheerful view of a situation; seeing the bright side of things: *I'm optimistic that our team will win the championship.*

op·tion·al | ŏp'shə nəl | —*adjective* Not required; left to choice: *A radio is optional equipment for a car.*

or | ôr | or | ər | —*conjunction* **1.** The conjunction **or** is used to show: **a.** The second of two, and only two, alternatives, the first being preceded by *either* or *whether*: *I want either vanilla or strawberry ice cream. I don't know whether to laugh or cry.* **b.** Any number of alternatives: *Will you have coffee or tea? Do you want your soup hot or lukewarm or cold?* **2.** In other words; namely: *The Netherlands, or Holland, exports large quantities of tulips.* **3.** And maybe; and possibly: *I have called his office three or four times already.* **4.** Otherwise: *Get out of here or I'll never get my work done.*

♦ *These sound alike* **or, oar, ore.**

–or[1] A suffix that forms nouns from verbs: *operator.*

–or[2] A suffix that forms nouns and means "condition or activity": *behavior.*

or·a·cle | ôr'ə kəl | or | ŏr'ə kəl | —*noun, plural* **oracles** In ancient Greece, a shrine for the worship of a god who told the future.

♦ *These sound alike* **oracle, auricle.**

o·ral | ôr'əl | or | ōr'əl | —*adjective* **1.** Spoken; not written: *An oral examination is a test in which the instructor asks you questions and you tell him the answers.* **2.** Used in or taken through the mouth: *an oral thermometer.*

or·ange | ôr'ĭnj | or | ŏr'ĭnj | —*noun, plural* **oranges 1.** A round fruit with a reddish-yellow rind and juicy pulp. Orange trees grow in warm regions. They have evergreen leaves and fragrant white flowers. **2.** The reddish-yellow color of an orange.

—*adjective* Of the color of an orange; reddish yellow.

o·rang·u·tan | ō **răng'**ə tăn' | or | ə **răng'**ə tăn' | —*noun, plural* **orangutans** A large ape that lives on islands south of Asia. Orangutans have long arms and shaggy reddish-brown hair.

or·bit | ôr'bĭt | —*noun, plural* **orbits 1.** The path in which a heavenly body moves around another. The earth and the planets in our solar system move around the sun. **2.** The path a man-made satellite or spacecraft takes around the earth.

—*verb* **orbited, orbiting 1.** To put into orbit: *The United States orbited an artificial satellite around the earth.* **2.** To move in an orbit around: *The moon orbits the earth.*

or·chard | ôr'chərd | —*noun, plural* **orchards** A piece of land where fruit trees are grown: *an apple orchard; a peach orchard.*

or·ches·tra | ôr'kĭ strə | —*noun, plural* **orchestras 1.** A group of musicians who play together on various instruments. **2.** The instruments played by such a group of musicians. **3.** The main floor of a theater.

or·chid | ôr′kĭd | —*noun, plural* **orchids** Any of many related plants with flowers that have unusual shapes. The flowers are often large and brightly colored.

or·dain | ôr dān′ | —*verb* **ordained, ordaining** **1.** To decide or establish by law: *The governor ordained that next Monday will be a holiday.* **2.** To install as a minister, priest, or rabbi by means of a formal ceremony.

or·deal | ôr dēl′ | —*noun, plural* **ordeals** A very difficult or painful experience or test: *It is always an ordeal for me to go to the dentist.*

or·der | ôr′dər | —*noun, plural* **orders** **1.** An arrangement of things in which everything is in its correct place: *Put your room in order.* **2.** The arrangement or placing of things one after another: *the team's batting order. Place these names in alphabetical order.* **3.** A condition in which rules, laws, or customs are obeyed: *Gun fights stopped when law and order came to the frontier.* **4.** A command: *I expect you to obey my orders.* **5.** Something requested, bought, sold, or supplied: *They will not mail your order unless you pay for the merchandise in advance.* **6.** A portion of food in a restaurant: *an order of fried potatoes.* **7.** A group of people who belong to the same organization or live under the same rules: *He joined an order of monks. He joined the order of the Elks.* —*verb* **ordered, ordering** **1.** To give an order to; command: *I order you to wash the car.* **2.** To ask for; place a request for: *I'd like to order one dozen roses.* **3.** To arrange things one after another: *The librarian ordered the books on his shelves according to title.*

   Idioms **in order to** For the purpose of; so that: *I lay in the sun in order to get a tan.* **out of order** Not working properly.

or·der·ly | ôr′dər lē | —*adjective* **1.** Arranged in neat order: *an orderly kitchen.* **2.** Without making trouble or noise: *The children walked out of the room in an orderly manner.*

or·di·nal number | ôr′dn əl | A number that shows position in a series: *First, second, and tenth are ordinal numbers.*

or·di·nar·i·ly | ôr′dn âr′ə lē | or | ôr′dn ĕr′ə lē | —*adverb* As a general rule; usually: *Ordinarily I get home before six o'clock.*

or·di·nar·y | ôr′dn ĕr′ē | —*adjective* **1.** Usual; normal: *After the flood the creek goes back to its ordinary size.* **2.** Of no special quality; average: *an ordinary dress. We lived in an ordinary house.*

ore | ôr | or | ōr | —*noun, plural* **ores** A mineral or rock that contains a valuable substance such as iron.

   ♦ *These sound alike* **ore, oar, or.**

Or·e·gon | ôr′ə gən | or | ôr′ə gŏn′ | or | ŏr′ə gən | or | ŏr′ə gŏn′ | A state in the northwestern United States. The capital of Oregon is Salem.

or·gan | ôr′gən | —*noun, plural* **organs** **1.** A musical instrument that has pipes of different sizes, through which air is blown to produce different tones. An organ has one or more keyboards that regulate the mechanism that controls the flow of air to the pipes. **2.** A part of a living thing that is used to do a particular job. The eyes, stomach, liver, and lungs are just a few of the organs in the human body.

or·gan·ic | ôr găn′ĭk | —*adjective* **1.** Of or coming from living things: *Decaying leaves, grass, and animal manure are organic fertilizers.* **2.** Grown by using decaying plant and animal matter instead of artificial fertilizers: *organic farming.*

orchid
Different kinds of orchid

Oregon
The origin of the name **Oregon** is not at all certain. We do know, however, that Oregon was formerly the name for the Columbia River, a river that flows along part of the border between Oregon and the state of Washington.

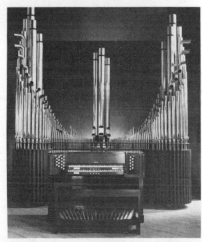

organ

oriole

ostrich

or·gan·ism | ôr′gə nĭz′əm | —*noun, plural* **organisms** Any living thing; a plant or animal.

or·gan·i·za·tion | ôr′gə nĭ zā′shən | —*noun, plural* **organizations** **1.** The act of organizing: *Planning the organization of the convention takes a lot of time.* **2.** The way of being organized: *The organization of books in our library is by title.* **3.** A group of people joined together for a common purpose: *Political parties, churches, and clubs are organizations.*

or·gan·ize | ôr′gə nĭz′ | —*verb* **organized, organizing 1.** To put together or arrange in an orderly way: *I like the way you organized your kitchen. He organized the campaign so well that his party's candidate won.* **2.** To form a group in order to work together for a common purpose: *They organized a club to raise money for different charities.* **3.** To cause employees to form or join a labor union: *There were several attempts to organize the factory workers.*

O·ri·ent | ôr′ē ənt | or | ôr′ē ĕnt′ | or | ōr′ē ənt | or | ōr′ē ĕnt′ | —*noun* **1. orient** The east; eastern lands. **2.** The countries of Asia. China and Japan are part of the Orient.

O·ri·en·tal | ôr′ē ĕn′tl | or | ōr′ē ĕn′tl | —*adjective* **1. oriental** Eastern. **2.** Of the Orient or any of its peoples. —*noun, plural* **Orientals 1.** A person born in the Orient. **2.** A person whose ancestors are from the Orient.

or·i·gin | ôr′ə jĭn | or | ŏr′ə jĭn | —*noun, plural* **origins 1.** The cause or beginning of something: *the origin of life.* **2.** Line of descent; parents: *She is of Italian origin.*

o·rig·i·nal | ə rĭj′ə nəl | —*adjective* **1.** Existing from the beginning; first: *the original thirteen states of the Union. This dress was marked down from the original price.* **2.** Newly created; not copied: *That dress is an original design.* —*noun, plural* **originals** The first from which varieties and copies were later made: *The later movie kept many features of the original.*

o·rig·i·nal·ly | ə rĭj′ə nə lē | —*adverb* **1.** At first; in the beginning: *This dress was originally priced at $40.00.* **2.** By origin: *He was originally from Ireland.*

o·rig·i·nate | ə rĭj′ə nāt′ | —*verb* **originated, originating** To bring or come into being: *The idea of mass production and the assembly line originated in America.*

o·ri·ole | ôr′ē ōl′ | or | ōr′ē ōl′ | —*noun, plural* **orioles** A songbird with feathers that are usually black and orange. Orioles often build nests that hang from the branches of trees.

or·na·ment | ôr′nə mənt | —*noun, plural* **ornaments** Decorations that make something more attractive: *Christmas tree ornaments.* —*verb* **ornamented, ornamenting** To supply with ornaments: *The room was ornamented with flowers and posters.*

or·nate | ôr nāt′ | —*adjective* Made with much decoration; fancy; elaborate: *an ornate palace; ornate furniture.*

or·phan | ôr′fən | —*noun, plural* **orphans** A child whose parents are dead.

or·phan·age | ôr′fə nĭj | —*noun, plural* **orphanages** A home for the care of orphans.

or·tho·dox | ôr′thə dŏks′ | —*adjective* **1.** Something generally accepted by most people; conventional: *His parents have very orthodox political ideas.* **2.** Sticking to officially approved religious beliefs.

os·trich | ŏs′trĭch | or | ô′strĭch | —*noun, plural* **ostriches** A very large African bird with long legs and a long neck. The ostrich

ă	pat	ĕ	pet	î	fierce
ā	pay	ē	be	ŏ	pot
â	care	ĭ	pit	ō	go
ä	father	ī	pie	ô	paw, for
oi	oil	ŭ	cut	zh	vision
ŏŏ	book	û	fur	ə	ago, item,
ōō	boot	*th*	the		pencil, atom,
yōō	abuse	th	thin		circus
ou	out	hw	which	ər	butter

cannot fly, but it can run very fast. The long, soft feathers of the ostrich are used to make fans and other things.

oth·er | ŭ*th*′ər | —*adjective* **1. a.** Being the remaining one of two or more: *Let me look at the other shoe.* **b.** Being the remaining ones of several: *My other friends are away on vacation.* **2.** Different: *Call me some other time. Any other kid would have run away.* **3.** Just recent or past: *The other day I saw Louise at the theater.* **4.** Additional; extra: *I have no other clothes than what I'm wearing. She has other sisters.* **5.** Opposite: *the other side of the street.* **6.** Reverse: *Write your name on the other side of the paper.* **7.** Alternate; second: *We play tennis every other day.*
—*pronoun* A different or additional person or thing: *The reporters were at the airport trying to interview some movie star or other.*
—*adverb* Otherwise: *She soon found out that she would never succeed other than by work.*
—*noun, plural* **others 1. a.** The remaining one of two or more: *One girl took a taxi, a second took the subway, and the other walked home.* **b.** The remaining ones of several: *How are the others doing now that I'm gone?* **2.** A different person or thing: *We were hit by one hurricane after the other.* **3.** An additional person or thing: *A few of the guests have arrived; how many others are you expecting?*

oth·er·wise | ŭ*th*′ər wīz′ | —*adverb* **1.** In another way; differently: *With no help how could he not have done otherwise?* **2.** Under other circumstances: *Explanations tend to clear up things that you might not be able to understand otherwise.* **3.** In other ways: *It was windy, but otherwise a beautiful day.*
—*adjective* Other than supposed; different: *The truth of the matter was otherwise.*
—*conjunction* Else: *She asked me not to tell anyone, otherwise I would tell you.*

Ot·ta·wa | ŏt′ə wə | or | ŏt′ə wä′ | or | ŏt′ə wô′ | The capital of Canada.

ot·ter | ŏt′ər | —*noun, plural* **otters 1.** An animal that has webbed feet and thick dark-brown fur. Otters live in or near water. **2.** The fur of this animal.

ouch | ouch | —*interjection* A word used to express sudden pain: *Ouch! Don't step on my foot!*

ought | ôt | —*helping,* or *auxiliary, verb* As a helping verb **ought** is used to show: **1.** What is a duty or obligation: *You ought to be polite to your parents.* **2.** What is almost certain or expected: *The piano ought to sound better when it's tuned. Tonight ought to be a good night for looking at the stars. Dinner ought to be ready by now.* **3.** What is almost an obligation; what is needed: *She ought to leave now if she is not going to be late. We ought to have new clothes for the trip.* **4.** What is wise: *The doctor said we ought to get plenty of rest.*

ounce | ouns | —*noun, plural* **ounces** A unit of weight equal to 1/16 of a pound. In the metric system, an ounce equals 28.350 grams.

our | our | —*pronoun* The pronoun **our** is a possessive form of **we.** It means: **1.** Of or belonging to us: *our books.* **2.** Done or performed by us: *our first job.* The pronoun **our** belongs to a class of words called **determiners.** They signal that a noun is coming.
♦ *These sound alike* **our, hour.**

otter

ours | ourz | —*pronoun* The pronoun **ours** is a possessive form of **we**. It is used to show that something or someone belongs to us: *These books are ours. If his car is not working, use ours. They are no friends of ours.*

our·selves | our **sĕlvz'** | or | är **sĕlvz'** | —*pronoun* The pronoun **ourselves** is a special form of **us**. **1.** It means: **a.** Our own selves: *We injured ourselves when the car hit the tree.* **b.** Our normal selves: *We are not ourselves today.* **2.** It is used to call special attention to us: *We ourselves are going to the party.*

-ous A suffix that forms adjectives and means "full of or having": *dangerous; joyous.*

out | out | —*adverb* **1.** Away from the inside: *He was going out of the house.* **2.** Away from the middle: *The posse spread out.* **3.** Away from a usual place: *The doctor stepped out for a minute.* **4.** To or at an end: *Time ran out.* **5.** Into being or view: *The moon came out.* **6.** Without shyness; boldly; plainly: *Speak out.* **7.** Away from current fashion: *Ostrich plumes on hats went out a long time ago.* **8.** So as to lose the right to continue batting or to run bases: *He was struck out.*
—*adjective* **1.** Not available; not a choice: *Going to the movies is out because we're broke.* **2.** In baseball, no longer at bat or on base: *Three strikes and you're out.*
—*preposition* Through; toward the outside: *The cat was falling out the window.*
—*noun, plural* **outs 1.** A way to escape from something: *The window was his only out from the burning room.* **2.** Any play in which a batter or base runner is retired in baseball.

out·board motor | **out'**bôrd' | or | **out'**bôrd' | A small motor attached to the stern of a boat.

out·break | **out'**brāk' | —*noun, plural* **outbreaks** A sudden breaking out: *an outbreak of flu; an outbreak of violence.*

out·burst | **out'**bûrst' | —*noun, plural* **outbursts** A bursting forth of activity or emotion: *an outburst of laughter.*

out·come | **out'**kŭm' | —*noun, plural* **outcomes** A final result; end: *the outcome of an election.*

out·cry | **out'**krī' | —*noun, plural* **outcries 1.** A loud cry or scream. **2.** A strong protest: *a loud public outcry.*

out·door | **out'**dôr' | or | **out'**dōr' | —*adjective* Placed, used, or done in the outdoors: *outdoor clothing. Football is an outdoor sport.*

out·doors | out **dôrz'** | or | out **dōrz'** | —*adverb* In or into the open air; outside a house or building: *eat outdoors.*
—*noun* (Used with a singular verb.) Any area outside a house or building in the open air: *The ranger enjoys protecting the great outdoors.*

out·er | **out'**ər | —*adjective* On the outside; farther out: *The outer petals of the flower have withered.*

outer space The space beyond the earth's atmosphere: *Astronauts travel through outer space in spaceships.*

out·field | **out'**fēld' | —*noun, plural* **outfields 1.** The grassy playing area of a baseball field outside the baseball diamond. The outfield is divided into right field, center field, and left field. **2.** The members of the baseball team that play in the outfield.

out·fit | **out'**fĭt' | —*noun, plural* **outfits 1.** A set of equipment needed for doing something: *a diving outfit.* **2.** A set of clothes: *She wore a pretty blue outfit.* **3.** A group of people who work together: *The team is a pretty tough outfit.*

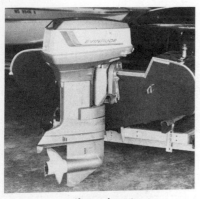

outboard motor

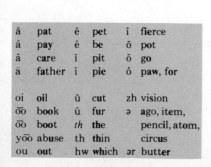

ă	pat	ĕ	pet	î	fierce
ā	pay	ē	be	ŏ	pot
â	care	ĭ	pit	ō	go
ä	father	ī	pie	ô	paw, for
oi	oil	ŭ	cut	zh	vision
ŏŏ	book	û	fur	ə	ago, item,
ōō	boot	th	the		pencil, atom,
yōō	abuse	th	thin		circus
ou	out	hw	which	ər	butter

—*verb* **outfitted, outfitting** To give the necessary equipment or clothing: *Mrs. Roberts outfitted her son for school.*

out·go·ing |out′gō′ĭng| —*adjective* **1.** Leaving; departing: *an outgoing steamer.* **2.** Friendly; sociable: *an outgoing person.*

out·ing |ou′tĭng| —*noun, plural* **outings** A trip or walk outdoors for pleasure: *We went on an outing to the beach.*

out·law |out′lô′| —*noun, plural* **outlaws** A person who breaks the law; a criminal.
—*verb* **outlawed, outlawing** To make illegal: *The governor outlawed the sale of firearms.*

out·let |out′lĕt′| or |out′lĭt| —*noun, plural* **outlets** **1.** A place or way to get out; an exit. **2.** A means of releasing something: *Music is a good outlet for her talent and energy.* **3.** A place in the wall for plugging in anything run by electricity.

out·line |out′līn′| —*noun, plural* **outlines** **1.** A line marking the outer edge or boundary of something: *The outline of Lower Michigan looks like a mitten.* **2.** A drawing that shows only the outer edge of an object: *Trace an outline of California from the map.* **3.** A summary or description, usually given point by point: *an outline for a report.*
—*verb* **outlined, outlining** To give the main points of: *You must outline your plans for the senior prom at the class meeting.*

out·look |out′lŏŏk′| —*noun, plural* **outlooks** **1.** A place from which something can be seen: *a photograph taken from an outlook high in the mountains.* **2.** A way of looking at or feeling about something: *a happy outlook on life.* **3.** The way things are expected to happen; the probable situation or result: *the weather outlook for tomorrow.*

out·ly·ing |out′lī′ĭng| —*adjective* Located at a distance from the center or the main part; far away: *the outlying suburbs.*

out·num·ber |out nŭm′bər| —*verb* **outnumbered, outnumbering** To be more in number than: *The soldiers outnumbered the Indians during the attack.*

out-of-date |out′əv dāt′| —*adjective* No longer in style; old-fashioned: *Short dresses are out-of-date.*

out·post |out′pōst′| —*noun, plural* **outposts** **1.** A small group of soldiers placed away from the main army camp. An outpost is set up to watch for or stop a surprise attack against the main camp. **2.** The post where the soldiers are placed. **3.** A settlement on the frontier or in a distant place.

out·put |out′pŏŏt′| —*noun, plural* **outputs** **1.** The amount of something produced: *the output of a mine.* **2.** The energy or work produced by something: *the output of an engine.*

out·rage |out′rāj′| —*noun, plural* **outrages** **1.** A violent or wicked act: *Many outrages were committed during the war.* **2.** Great anger caused by such an act: *There was great public outrage over the kidnaping.*
—*verb* **outraged, outraging** To make very angry or insult: *Everyone was outraged by his behavior.*

out·ra·geous |out rā′jəs| —*adjective* Far from what is right or proper; shocking; terrible: *an outrageous crime; outrageous prices.*

out·rig·ger |out′rĭg′ər| —*noun, plural* **outriggers** A long, thin float attached lengthwise to the outside of a canoe by a frame. The outrigger keeps the canoe from turning over.

out·right |out′rīt′| —*adjective* Complete; absolute: *an outright gift; an outright lie.*

outrigger

—*adverb* |**out′rīt′**| or |**out′**rīt′| **1.** Completely; absolutely: *We accepted his offer outright.* **2.** Openly; straight to someone's face: *We decided to tell him the news outright.*

out·side |out sīd′| or |**out′**sīd′| —*noun, plural* **outsides** **1.** The outer side or surface: *the outside of the house.* **2.** The surface appearance; the way something appears: *On the outside, the offer seems very attractive.*
—*adjective* **1.** Coming from another place: *We need outside help.* **2.** Very small; slight: *I'll wait here on the outside chance that something will happen.*
—*adverb* On or to the outside: *He is going outside to play.*
—*preposition* To the other side of: *Don't go outside the fence.*

out·skirts |**out′**skûrts′| —*plural noun* The areas away from a central part: *He lives on the outskirts of town.*

out·spo·ken |out spō′kən| —*adjective* Honest and bold: *an outspoken congressman; outspoken remarks.*

out·stand·ing |out stăn′dĭng| or |**out′**stăn′dĭng| —*adjective* **1.** Standing out from others; better than others: *an outstanding book.* **2.** Not paid or settled: *outstanding debts.*

out·ward |**out′**wərd| —*adverb* Away from the center: *The door opens outward.* Another form of this adverb is **outwards.**
—*adjective* **1.** Toward the outside: *an outward bound train.* **2.** Seen on the surface: *an outward look of calm.*

out·wards |**out′**wərdz| A form of the adverb **outward.**

out·weigh |out wā′| —*verb* **outweighed, outweighing** **1.** To weigh more than: *He outweighs everyone on the team.* **2.** To be more important than: *The good outweighs the bad.*

o·val |ō′vəl| —*adjective* Shaped like an egg or an ellipse: *an oval dish; an oval face.*
—*noun, plural* **ovals** Something shaped like an egg or an ellipse.

o·va·ry |ō′və rē| —*noun, plural* **ovaries** **1.** A part of a female animal in which egg cells are produced. **2.** A plant part in which seeds are formed.

ov·en |ŭv′ən| —*noun, plural* **ovens** An enclosed space used for baking, heating, or drying food. An oven is usually in a stove.

o·ver |ō′vər| —*preposition* **1.** Above or higher than: *There is a sign over the door. A major is over a lieutenant.* **2.** From one side to the other side of; across: *The horse jumped over the fence.* **3.** On the other side of: *They live in a town over the border.* **4.** Across or along the surface of; upon: *Jean spilled milk all over the floor. We drove over a new road.* **5.** On top of; upon: *Apply a coat of varnish over the woodwork.* **6.** Through the period of; during: *The stores will be closed over the weekend.* **7.** In excess of; more than: *I spent over fifteen dollars for the tickets.* **8.** Throughout; here and there in: *She has traveled over most of Europe.* **9.** On account of; because of: *She cried over her lost money.*
—*adverb* **1.** Above: *Several planes flew over this morning.* **2. a.** Across to another or an opposite side: *When are you flying over to California?* **b.** Across the edge or brim: *The coffee in the pot boiled over.* **3.** To a different opinion, belief, or loyalty: *The preacher won over many converts. Several troops went over to the enemy.* **4.** To a different place or person from another: *Billy and Joel came over for dinner tonight. I'll be over shortly.* **5.** To a different person or ownership: *Before he died, he signed all his land over to his sisters.* **6.** So as to be completely covered: *The river froze over.* **7.** From beginning to end; through: *Read this over and*

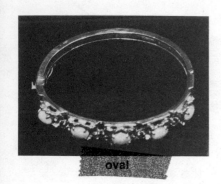
oval

ă	pat	ĕ	pet	î	fierce
ā	pay	ē	be	ŏ	pot
â	care	ĭ	pit	ō	go
ä	father	ī	pie	ô	paw, for
oi	oil	ŭ	cut	zh	vision
ŏŏ	book	û	fur	ə	ago, item,
ōō	boot	*th*	the		pencil, atom,
yōō	abuse	th	thin		circus
ou	out	hw	which	ər	butter

let's talk. Let me think it over. **8.a.** From an upright position: *The cat toppled the chair over.* **b.** So that the underside will be up: *Flip the coin over. Turn the bowl over.* **9.a.** Again: *Alice had to do her homework over.* **b.** Again and again: *He played the same tune ten times over.* **10.** In addition; beyond what was planned: *He stayed a week over. I have a dollar left over.*
—*adjective* Finished; ended: *The movie is over.*

over– A prefix that means: **1.** To excess; too much: *overdo.* **2.** Beyond the normal; extra: *overtime.* **3.** Above or across: *overcoat; overseas.* **4.** To a lower or inferior position: *overthrow; overturn.*

o·ver·alls |ō′vər ôlz′| —*plural noun* Loose-fitting trousers with a top part that covers the chest. Overalls are often worn over regular clothes to protect them from dirt.

o·ver·board |ō′vər bôrd′| or |ō′vər bōrd′| —*adverb* Over the side of a boat: *He fell overboard.*

o·ver·came |ō′vər kām′| The past tense of the verb **overcome**: *He overcame his fear of flying.*

o·ver·cast |ō′vər kăst′| or |ō′vər käst′| or |ō′vər **kăst′**| or |ō′vər **käst′**| —*adjective* Covered over with clouds or mist; gloomy; dark: *an overcast sky.*

o·ver·coat |ō′vər kōt′| —*noun, plural* **overcoats** A long, heavy outdoor coat worn over a suit or other clothing for warmth.

o·ver·come |ō′vər kŭm′| —*verb* **overcame, overcome, overcoming** **1.** To get the better of; conquer: *He had overcome his fear of flying.* **2.** To make weak or tired: *Fear overcame him.*

o·ver·did |ō′vər dĭd′| The past tense of the verb **overdo**: *We overdid the cheering and became hoarse.*

o·ver·do |ō′vər dōō′| —*verb* **overdid, overdone, overdoing 1.** To do or use too much; to tire oneself with: *Don't overdo the exercise or you'll get sore.* **2.** To cook too long or too much: *Dad won't overdo the steak.*
♦ *These sound alike* **overdo, overdue.**

o·ver·done |ō′vər dŭn′| The past participle of the verb **overdo**: *We have overdone the vegetables.*

o·ver·due |ō′vər dōō′| or |ō′vər dyōō′| —*adjective* **1.** Not paid on time: *The payment is overdue.* **2.** Later than usual: *an overdue train.*
♦ *These sound alike* **overdue, overdo.**

o·ver·flow |ō′vər flō′| —*verb* **overflowed, overflowing 1.** To flow over the top, brim, or banks: *The river overflows its banks every year. The heavy rains caused the river to overflow.* **2.** To fill until full and continue to fill and spread: *The people overflowed from the stands onto the playing field.*
—*noun* |ō′vər flō′|, *plural* **overflows** Something that flows over: *The overflow of the reservoir goes into the river.*

o·ver·hand |ō′vər hănd′| —*adjective* With the hand moving above the shoulder: *an overhand pitch.*
—*adverb* With the hand raised above the shoulder: *He throws overhand.*

o·ver·haul |ō′vər hôl′| or |ō′vər hôl′| —*verb* **overhauled, overhauling 1.** To examine in order to repair or make changes: *The mechanic will overhaul the car.* **2.** To gain upon in a chase; overtake: *The police car quickly overhauled the bank robbers' car.*
—*noun* |ō′vər hôl′|, *plural* **overhauls** The act of overhauling: *The boat's motor needs a thorough overhaul.*

overalls

o·ver·head | ō′vər hĕd′ | —*adverb* Above the head: *Birds flew overhead.*
—*adjective* | ō′vər hĕd′ | Placed higher than the head: *an overhead light.*
—*noun* | ō′vər hĕd′ |, *plural* **overheads** Money spent for rent, insurance, taxes, lighting, heating, and repairs by a business.

o·ver·hear | ō′vər hîr′ | —*verb* **overheard, overhearing** To hear something not meant to be heard by others; hear accidentally: *Jim overheard Bill talking to Nancy.*

o·ver·heard | ō′vər hûrd′ | The past tense and past participle of the verb **overhear:** *We overheard her remarks to the teacher. He had overheard her remarks.*

o·ver·joyed | ō′vər joid′ | —*adjective* Very happy or delighted: *We were overjoyed to meet him at last.*

o·ver·lap | ō′vər lăp′ | —*verb* **overlapped, overlapping 1.** To rest over and cover part of another thing: *The scales of a fish overlap.* **2.** To occur partly at the same time: *Our vacations overlap.*

o·ver·look | ō′vər lŏŏk′ | —*verb* **overlooked, overlooking 1.** To look over from a higher place; have or give a view over: *The porch overlooks the sea.* **2.** To fail to see: *We overlooked an important detail.* **3.** To ignore: *I will overlook your mistakes this time.*

o·ver·night | ō′vər nīt′ | —*adjective* **1.** Happening or lasting for a night: *an overnight trip.* **2.** For use over one night: *an overnight bag.*
—*adverb* | ō′vər nīt′ | **1.** During or through the night: *Soak the beans overnight.* **2.** Very quickly; suddenly: *He was a star overnight.*

o·ver·pass | ō′vər păs′ | or | ō′vər päs′ | —*noun, plural* **overpasses** A road or bridge that crosses above another road.

o·ver·pow·er | ō′vər pou′ər | —*verb* **overpowered, overpowering 1.** To get the better of; conquer by superior force: *The Red Sox overpowered the Yankees.* **2.** To affect strongly; overcome: *The heat overpowered everyone and they had to leave the beach.*

o·ver·seas | ō′vər sēz′ | or | ō′vər sēz′ | —*adverb* Across the sea; abroad: *He was sent overseas.*
—*adjective* Of, from, or located across the sea: *an overseas flight.*

o·ver·shoe | ō′vər shōō′ | —*noun, plural* **overshoes** A shoe or boot worn over another shoe to keep the foot warm and dry. Overshoes are often made of rubber or plastic.

o·ver·sight | ō′vər sīt′ | —*noun, plural* **oversights** A mistake that is not made on purpose: *Forgetting to call her name was an oversight.*

o·ver·take | ō′vər tāk′ | —*verb* **overtook, overtaken, overtaking 1.** To catch up with: *The green car overtook the red one on the curve.* **2.** To come upon suddenly: *A storm overtook him while he was hiking in the mountains.*

o·ver·tak·en | ō′vər tā′kən | The past participle of the verb **overtake:** *The flu has overtaken them, and they are all in bed.*

o·ver·time | ō′vər tīm′ | —*noun, plural* **overtimes** Time beyond the regular limit: *The game went into overtime.*
—*adverb* Beyond the regular hours: *She has to work overtime.*
—*adjective* Of or for overtime: *overtime pay.*

o·ver·took | ō′vər tŏŏk′ | The past tense of the verb **overtake:** *The brown horse overtook the gray to win the race.*

o·ver·ture | ō′vər chər | —*noun, plural* **overtures 1.** A musical composition played by an orchestra as an introduction to a larger

overpass

ă	pat	ĕ	pet	î	fierce
ā	pay	ē	be	ŏ	pot
â	care	ĭ	pit	ō	go
ä	father	ī	pie	ô	paw, for
oi	oil	ŭ	cut	zh	vision
ŏŏ	book	û	fur	ə	ago, item,
ōō	boot	th	the		pencil, atom,
yōō	abuse	th	thin		circus
ou	out	hw	which	ər	butter

musical work. Overtures often come before ballets and operas.
2. An offer or proposal to begin something: *The enemy was making peace overtures.*

o·ver·turn |ō′vər tûrn′| —*verb* **overturned, overturning 1.** To turn over; upset: *overturn a glass of water.* **2.** To defeat: *The soldiers overturned the enemy attack.*

o·ver·weight |ō′vər wāt′| —*adjective* Weighing more than usual or necessary: *an overweight person.*

o·ver·whelm |ō′vər hwĕlm′| or |ō′vər wĕlm′| —*verb* **overwhelmed, overwhelming 1.** To pour over and cover completely: *Grief overwhelmed her.* **2.** To overcome completely; overpower: *The enemy soldiers overwhelmed the remaining troops.*

o·ver·work |ō′vər wûrk′| —*verb* **overworked, overworking** To work or make someone work too hard: *She overworks terribly. The manager overworks the staff.*
—*noun* |ō′vər wûrk′| Too much work: *The horse died from overwork.*

owe |ō| —*verb* **owed, owing 1.** To have to pay: *He owes the store $10.* **2.** To have to give: *We owe him an apology.* **3.** To be obligated for: *The Pilgrims owed much to the Indians for their help and friendship.*
♦ *These sound alike* **owe, oh.**

owl |oul| —*noun, plural* **owls** Any of several birds that usually fly at night. Owls have a large head, large eyes, and a short, hooked bill. They catch and eat small animals and birds.

own |ōn| —*adjective* Of or belonging to oneself or itself: *Jim's own book; my own home.*
—*verb* **owned, owning 1.** To have or possess: *Do you own a car?* **2.** To confess or admit: *I own that I've made a mistake.*
Phrasal verb **own up** To admit completely and openly: *He owned up to the crime under questioning.*

own·er |ō′nər| —*noun, plural* **owners** Someone who owns something: *the owner of a house.*

ow·ner·ship |ō′nər shĭp′| —*noun, plural* **ownerships** The fact or condition of being an owner: *The ownership of the land was decided in court.*

ox |ŏks| —*noun, plural* **oxen 1.** A fully grown male of cattle, used as a work animal. **2.** Any of several animals related to cattle, such as the musk ox.

ox·en |ŏk′sən| The plural of the noun **ox.**

ox·ide |ŏk′sīd′| —*noun, plural* **oxides** A compound of oxygen and another chemical element: *zinc oxide.*

ox·i·dize |ŏk′sĭ dīz′| —*verb* **oxidized, oxidizing** To combine with oxygen: *Copper turns green when it oxidizes.*

ox·y·gen |ŏk′sĭ jən| —*noun* A gas without color or smell. Oxygen is one of the chemical elements. It makes up one fifth of the air. People, animals, and plants need oxygen to live.

oy·ster |oi′stər| —*noun, plural* **oysters** A sea animal that has a soft body and a rough, uneven shell with two parts. Many kinds of oysters are used as food. Some kinds produce pearls inside their shells.

owl
Three kinds of owl

Pp

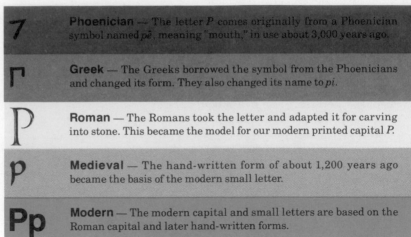

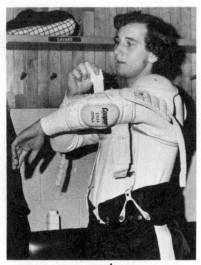

pad
Hockey pads

ă	pat	ĕ	pet	î	fierce
ā	pay	ē	be	ŏ	pot
â	care	ĭ	pit	ō	go
ä	father	ī	pie	ô	paw, for
oi	oil	ŭ	cut	zh	vision
ŏŏ	book	û	fur	ə	ago, item,
ōō	boot	*th*	the		pencil, atom,
yōō	abuse	th	thin		circus
ou	out	hw	which	ər	butter

p or **P** |pē| —*noun, plural* **p's** or **P's** The sixteenth letter of the English alphabet.

pace |pās| —*noun, plural* **paces** **1.** A step made in walking. **2.** The length of a step in walking, usually 30 inches. **3.** The speed at which something moves or happens: *He ran at a steady pace.* **4.** A step of a horse in walking or running.
—*verb* **paced, pacing** **1.** To walk back and forth: *The tiger paced nervously in his cage. He paced the floor impatiently.* **2.** To measure length by counting paces: *He paced the distance between the trees.*

Pa·cif·ic Ocean |pə sĭf′ĭk| The largest of the oceans. It extends from the Arctic to the Antarctic and from the Americas to Asia and Australia.

pack |păk| —*noun, plural* **packs** **1.** A group of things tied or wrapped together; a bundle. **2.** A group of like or similar items, animals, or people: *a pack of matches; a pack of cards; a pack of wolves; a pack of thieves.* **3.** A large amount: *a pack of trouble.*
—*verb* **packed, packing** **1.** To put in a bag, box, or other container: *pack groceries; pack clothes.* **2.** To fill with things: *pack a suitcase.* **3.** To press closely together: *Workmen packed ten sardines into each tiny can.* **4.** To fill up tight: *The crowd packed the movie theater.*

pack·age |păk′ĭj| —*noun, plural* **packages** **1.** A wrapped or boxed parcel holding one or more things: *a package of cookies.* **2.** A container used to store or send something.
—*verb* **packaged, packaging** To put or make into a package: *The clerk will package the oranges.*

pack rat A rat that carries small things away and collects them in its nesting place.

pact |păkt| —*noun, plural* **pacts** An agreement made between countries, groups, or persons to act a certain way or do certain things; treaty.

pad |păd| —*noun, plural* **pads** **1.** A cushion or mass of soft, firmly packed material. Pads are used for comfort, stuffing, or protection: *chair pads; shoulder pads for football players.* **2.** An ink-soaked cushion in a container used with a marking stamp. **3.** A number of sheets of paper glued together at one end: *a yellow pad for notes.* **4.** The part that is like a small cushion on the bottom of the feet of dogs, cats, and other animals.

—*verb* **padded, padding** To line, stuff, or cover with soft, firmly packed material: *We padded the baby's bed.*

pad·dle |păd′l| —*noun, plural* **paddles 1.** A short oar with a flat blade used to move and steer a boat through water. **2.** A tool with a flat blade used for stirring, mixing, or beating. **3.** A small, flat board with a short handle used in some games: *a Ping-Pong paddle.*

—*verb* **paddled, paddling 1.** To move and steer a boat through the water with a paddle: *We paddled the canoe upstream.* **2.** To spank or beat with or as if with a paddle: *The man paddled the child with his hand.*

paddle wheel A large wheel with boards or paddles around its edge. Paddle wheels are powered by steam and used to move a ship.

pad·dock |păd′ək| —*noun, plural* **paddocks** A fenced field or area where horses graze and exercise. Horses are saddled and paraded in the paddock of a race track.

pad·dy |păd′ē| —*noun, plural* **paddies** A flooded field where rice is grown.

pad·lock |păd′lŏk′| —*noun, plural* **padlocks** A lock that can be put on and taken off. Padlocks have a bar on the top shaped like the letter U that is hinged at one end. The other end may be put through a ring or link and then snapped shut.

—*verb* **padlocked, padlocking** To lock with a padlock: *Sam padlocked the gate.*

pa·gan |pā′gən| —*noun, plural* **pagans** Someone who is not a Christian, Moslem, or Jew. A pagan may worship many gods or no god.

page¹ |pāj| —*noun, plural* **pages 1.** One side of a sheet of paper in a book, newspaper, letter, or magazine. **2.** An important time or event: *The Space Age is a recent page in world history.*

page² |pāj| —*noun, plural* **pages 1.** In the Middle Ages, a boy who served a knight. Being a page was the first step in training to become a knight. **2.** Someone who runs errands, carries messages, or acts as a guide. Pages are used in many hotels, clubs, and in Congress.

—*verb* **paged, paging** To call or summon someone by name in a public place: *The nurse paged Dr. Jones on the hospital loudspeaker.*

pag·eant |păj′ənt| —*noun, plural* **pageants 1.** A play or dramatic program usually about an event in history: *an Easter pageant; a Thanksgiving pageant.* **2.** A parade, procession, or celebration for a special event: *the pageant of the queen's wedding; a beauty pageant.*

pa·go·da |pə gō′də| —*noun, plural* **pagodas** A Buddhist tower that has many stories. Pagodas are usually built as shrines or memorials in Eastern countries like China and Japan.

paid |pād| The past tense and past participle of the verb **pay:** *He paid his bills last week. He has always paid his bills on time.*

pail |pāl| —*noun, plural* **pails 1.** A round, open container with a handle, used for carrying water, sand, and other things; a bucket. **2. a.** A pail with something in it: *I have a pail of berries.* **b.** The amount that a pail can hold: *The horse drank two pails of water each night.*

♦ *These sound alike* **pail, pale.**

pain |pān| —*noun, plural* **pains 1.** A sharp ache or sore place in some part of the body that is caused by an injury or sickness.

paddle

paddle wheel

page¹, page²
The original source of **page¹** is a Latin word that meant "a sheet of writing." It was used by French-speaking people before appearing in English. **Page²** can be traced back to a Greek word meaning "child" or "boy." **Page²** traveled through both Italian and French before arriving in English.

pagoda

painter
A house painter

palace

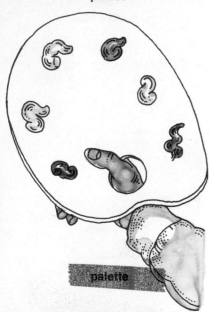

palette

2. Mental or emotional suffering; distress: *Her daughter's death caused her great pain.* **3. pains** Trouble, care, or effort: *Take great pains to do this job right.*
—*verb* **pained, paining** To cause to suffer; hurt: *His broken wrist pained him greatly. The criticism pained the shy girl.*
♦ *These sound alike* **pain, pane.**

pain·ful |pān′fəl| —*adjective* **1.** Causing or full of pain: *a painful injury.* **2.** Causing worry or suffering: *a painful decision.*

pains·tak·ing |pānz′tā′kĭng| —*adjective* Needing or showing great care; careful: *Putting that jigsaw together was painstaking work that took several days.*

paint |pānt| —*noun, plural* **paints** A mixture of coloring matter and a liquid. Paint is put on surfaces as a coating to protect or decorate them.
—*verb* **painted, painting** **1.** To cover or decorate with paint: *We painted the house.* **2.** To draw a picture using paint: *Her father painted a portrait of the president's wife.* **3.** To describe clearly with words: *His story painted a dark picture of the victims of the hurricane.*

paint·er |pān′tər| —*noun, plural* **painters** **1.** A person who paints as an artist. **2.** A person who paints as a worker: *The painter charged us by the room.*

paint·ing |pān′tĭng| —*noun, plural* **paintings** **1.** The art, process, or work of one who paints. **2.** A picture or design done with paint: *Several of her paintings were bought by the museum.*

pair |pâr| —*noun, plural* **pairs** **1.** A set of two things that are exactly the same or matched, usually used together: *a pair of shoes; a pair of earrings.* **2.** One thing that is made of two parts joined together: *a pair of scissors; a pair of pants; a pair of binoculars.* **3.** Two persons or animals that are alike or go together: *a pair of dancers; a pair of oxen.*
—*verb* **paired, pairing** **1.** To arrange in sets of two: *Pair the socks after you've washed them.* **2.** To provide a partner for: *At the dinner they paired Alice with John.*
♦ *These sound alike* **pair, pare, pear.**

pa·ja·mas |pə jä′məz| *or* |pə jăm′əz| —*plural noun* An outfit of jacket and trousers that are worn to sleep in or for lounging.

pal |păl| —*noun, plural* **pals** A close friend or chum.

pal·ace |păl′ĭs| —*noun, plural* **palaces** The official residence of a king, queen, or other ruler. A palace is usually large and splendid.

pal·ate |păl′ĭt| —*noun, plural* **palates** The roof of the mouth in man and other animals with a backbone. The bony front part is the hard palate and the movable part that hangs from the palate at the back is the soft palate. The palate forms a separation between the inside of the mouth and the passages of the nose.
♦ *These sound alike* **palate, palette.**

pale |pāl| —*adjective* **paler, palest** **1.** Having skin that is whitish or lighter than usual, often because of illness. **2.** Containing a large amount of white; light in color: *a pale blue.*
—*verb* **paled, paling** To turn or become pale: *She paled when I told her the bad news.*
♦ *These sound alike* **pale, pail.**

pal·ette |păl′ĭt| —*noun, plural* **palettes** A thin board upon which an artist mixes colors. It is held with the hand and often has a hole for the thumb.
♦ *These sound alike* **palette, palate.**

ă	pat	ĕ	pet	î	fierce
ā	pay	ē	be	ŏ	pot
â	care	ĭ	pit	ō	go
ä	father	ī	pie	ô	paw, for

oi	oil	ŭ	cut	zh	vision
ŏŏ	book	û	fur	ə	ago, item,
ōō	boot	*th*	the		pencil, atom,
yōō	abuse	th	thin		circus
ou	out	hw	which	ər	butter

pal·i·sades | păl′ĭ **sādz′** | —*plural noun* A line of high cliffs, usually along a river: *the New Jersey Palisades.*

palm¹ | päm | —*noun, plural* **palms** The inside of a person's hand from the wrist to the fingers.
—*verb* **palmed, palming** To hide something in the palm of the hand: *The magician palmed the coin after he had picked it out of Sam's ear.*

palm² | päm | —*noun, plural* **palms** One of many related trees that grow in warm parts of the world. Palm trees have leaves that look like feathers or fans. They often grow at the top of a tall trunk with no branches.

pal·met·to | păl **mĕt′**ō | or | păl **mĕt′**ō | —*noun, plural* **palmettos** or **palmettoes** A palm tree with leaves shaped like fans. Palmettos grow in the southeastern United States.

pal·o·mi·no | păl′ə **mē′**nō | —*noun, plural* **palominos** A horse with a light tan coat and a whitish mane and tail.

pam·per | **păm′**pər | —*verb* **pampered, pampering** To give in to the wishes of someone; baby: *She pampers the child so much he's spoiled rotten.*

pam·phlet | **păm′**flĭt | —*noun, plural* **pamphlets** A short book with a paper cover; booklet.

pan | păn | —*noun, plural* **pans** A wide, shallow, open metal container. It is used for holding liquids, for cooking, or for other household tasks: *Which pan shall we use to roast the turkey?*
—*verb* **panned, panning** To wash dirt or gravel in a pan in search of gold.

pan·cake | **păn′**kāk′ | —*noun, plural* **pancakes** A thin, flat cake of batter, cooked on a griddle or in a skillet.

pan·cre·as | **păn′**krē əs | —*noun, plural* **pancreases** A gland that is behind the stomach. The pancreas helps to digest food.

pan·da | **păn′**də | —*noun, plural* **pandas** An animal that looks like a bear and lives in the mountains of China. It has long, thick fur with black and white markings. This kind of panda is often called the *giant panda.*

pane | pān | —*noun, plural* **panes** A sheet of glass in a window or door.
♦ *These sound alike* **pane, pain.**

pan·el | **păn′**əl | —*noun, plural* **panels** **1.** A flat part or section of a wall, ceiling, or door that is framed by a border or by the surrounding parts: *The door has several panels that were painted by hand.* **2.** A board with instruments or controls for a vehicle or machine: *the instrument panel of an airplane.* **3.** A group of persons brought together to discuss or decide something: *a panel of experts on a television show.*
—*verb* **paneled, paneling** To cover or decorate with panels: *The altar was paneled with scenes from the Bible.*

panel truck A small delivery truck with a closed top and back.

pang | păng | —*noun, plural* **pangs** A short, sharp pain or feeling: *hunger pangs. I had a pang of sorrow when we moved away.*

pan·ic | **păn′**ĭk | —*noun, plural* **panics** A sudden feeling of great fear: *I felt panic when I realized I had lost my wallet.*
—*verb* **panicked, panicking, panics** **1.** To feel panic: *A swimmer may drown if he panics.* **2.** To cause panic in: *Thunder and lightning panicked the cattle.*

pan·o·ram·a | păn′ə **răm′**ə | or | păn′ə **rä′**mə | —*noun, plural* **panoramas** A view or picture of everything that can be seen over

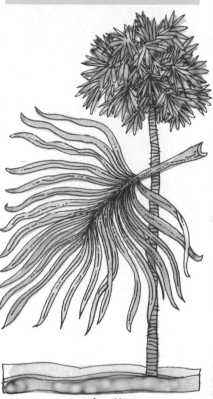

palmetto
Tree and leaf

panda

panther

papaya
Fruit *(left)* and tree *(right)*

parachute

ă	pat	ĕ	pet	î	fierce
ā	pay	ē	be	ŏ	pot
â	care	ĭ	pit	ō	go
ä	father	ī	pie	ô	paw, for

oi	oil	ŭ	cut	zh	vision
ŏŏ	book	û	fur	ə	ago, item,
ōō	boot	*th*	the		pencil, atom,
yōō	abuse	th	thin		circus
ou	out	hw	which	ər	butter

a wide area: *a vast panorama of the canyon.*

pan·sy |păn′zē| —*noun, plural* **pansies** A garden flower with rounded petals that look like velvet and are often purple and yellow.

pant |pănt| —*verb* **panted, panting** To breathe in short, quick gasps: *The dog panted after running to his master.*

pan·ther |păn′thər| —*noun, plural* **panthers** 1. A leopard, especially a black leopard. 2. A mountain lion or other large wild cat.

pan·to·mime |păn′tə mīm′| —*noun, plural* **pantomimes** 1. Acting by body movements and gestures without speaking. 2. A play or other entertainment acted in this way. 3. Movements of the face and body used instead of words to express a meaning: *We had to act out the book titles in pantomime.* —*verb* **pantomimed, pantomiming** To perform or represent by pantomime.

pan·try |păn′trē| —*noun, plural* **pantries** A small room or closet, usually next to a kitchen. Food, dishes, and utensils are kept in a pantry.

pants |pănts| —*plural noun* Trousers or slacks.

pa·pal |pā′pəl| —*adjective* Of the pope: *papal robes; papal authority.*

pa·pa·ya |pə pä′yə| —*noun, plural* **papayas** The large, sweet yellow fruit of a tropical American tree. The papaya looks like a melon.

pa·per |pā′pər| —*noun, plural* **papers** 1. A material made from wood pulp, rags, and other things and usually produced in thin sheets. Paper is used for writing, printing, drawing, wrapping, and covering walls. 2. A single sheet of this material. 3. A sheet of this material with writing or printing on it; a document: *The attorney took several papers out of his desk drawer.* 4. **papers** Documents that establish a person's identity: *In some countries you do not dare go out without your papers.* 5. A report or essay assigned in school: *I have to write a paper on the Civil War.* 6. A newspaper: *Father always reads the paper at breakfast.* —*verb* **papered, papering** To cover with wallpaper: *She wants to paper her room in blue.*

pa·per·back |pā′pər băk′| —*noun, plural* **paperbacks** A book with a soft paper cover: *Ann has a shelf full of paperbacks that she hasn't read yet.*

paper clip A bent piece of wire that is used to hold loose papers together.

pa·poose |pă pōōs′| —*noun, plural* **papooses** A North American Indian baby: *The Indian mother traveled with the papoose on her back.*

pap·ri·ka |pă prē′kə| or |păp′rĭ kə| —*noun* A red spice with a mild taste. It is made from powdered sweet red peppers.

pa·py·rus |pə pī′rəs| —*noun* A tall water plant of northern Africa. The ancient Egyptians made a kind of paper from the stems of this plant.

par·a·chute |păr′ə shōōt′| —*noun, plural* **parachutes** A large cloth device shaped like an umbrella. A parachute opens in midair and slows the fall of a person or object from great heights. —*verb* **parachuted, parachuting** 1. To come down by means of a parachute: *The pilot of the disabled plane parachuted to safety.*

2. To drop supplies by parachute: *The Red Cross parachuted food to the victims of the earthquake.*

pa·rade |pə rād′| —*noun, plural* **parades** A public event, usually festive and colorful, in which bands, people, and vehicles pass before crowds of spectators: *the Independence Day parade.*
—*verb* **paraded, parading 1.** To take part in a parade: *The Marines paraded in their colorful uniforms.* **2.** To show oneself or one's things too proudly: *She parades her wealth.*

par·a·dise |păr′ə dīs′| or |păr′ə dīz′| —*noun* **1.** Heaven. **2.** A place or condition of perfect happiness or beauty: *We found our paradise in Arizona. That river is a paradise for fishermen.*

par·af·fin |păr′ə fĭn| —*noun* A substance, usually white or colorless, that is like wax. It is used in making candles and wax paper, and in sealing jars of jelly.

par·a·graph |păr′ə grăf′| or |păr′ə gräf| —*noun, plural* **paragraphs** A division of a piece of writing that begins on a new line and is usually indented. A paragraph consists of one or more sentences on a single subject or idea.

par·a·keet |păr′ə kēt′| —*noun, plural* **parakeets** A small parrot with a long, pointed tail.

par·al·lel |păr′ə lĕl′| —*adjective* **1.** Lying in the same plane but not touching at any point: *parallel lines.* **2.** Matching feature for feature; alike or corresponding: *I have two friends with parallel likes and dislikes.*
—*adverb* In a parallel course or direction: *The reef runs parallel to the shore.*
—*noun, plural* **parallels 1.** Any of a set of parallel geometric lines or other figures. **2.** Something that closely resembles something else; a corresponding case: *He showed the parallel between last spring's rainfall and the amount of this summer's crops.* **3.** Any of the lines considered to go around the earth in the same direction as the equator. These lines are used to mark off latitude.
—*verb* **paralleled, paralleling 1.** To be or extend in a parallel way to: *The waves parallel the shore.* **2.** To be like; resemble: *His career paralleled that of his father.*

par·a·ly·sis |pə răl′ĭ sĭs| —*noun* Complete or partial loss of being able to feel anything in a part of the body or to move a part of the body. Paralysis is caused by disease or injury that damages nerves going to and from that part.

par·a·lyze |păr′ə līz′| —*verb* **paralyzed, paralyzing 1.** To make a person unable to feel or move; cause paralysis in: *The accident paralyzed him from the waist down.* **2.** To make unable to do anything; make unable to function: *The fright paralyzed her. A blizzard paralyzed the city.*

par·a·me·ci·a |păr′ə mē′shē ə| or |păr′ə mē′sē ə| A plural of the noun **paramecium.**

par·a·me·ci·um |păr′ə mē′shē əm| or |păr′ə mē′sē əm| —*noun, plural* **paramecia** or **parameciums** A very small water animal that has only one cell. It is shaped like an oval or a slipper. Paramecia can be seen only with a microscope.

par·a·site |păr′ə sīt′| —*noun, plural* **parasites** A plant or animal that lives in or on a different kind of plant or animal. The parasite gets its food from the other plant or animal. Parasites are often harmful.

par·a·sol |păr′ə sôl′| or |păr′ə sŏl′| —*noun, plural* **parasols** A

parakeet

parasol

paratrooper

parchment

small, light umbrella, often of fine material, used to protect a person from the sun.

par·a·troop·er | păr′ə trōo′pər | —*noun, plural* **paratroopers** A member of an army unit that is trained to parachute from airplanes and engage in battle after reaching the ground.

par·cel | pär′səl | —*noun, plural* **parcels 1.** Something wrapped up in a bundle; a package: *The woman dropped several parcels getting on the elevator.* **2.** A section or piece of land; a plot: *We have two parcels of the farm for sale.*
—*verb* **parceled, parceling** To divide into parts and give out or distribute: *The foreman parceled out the work to the workers who were present.*

parch | pärch | —*verb* **parched, parching 1.** To make or become very dry: *Hot winds parched the crops. The skin wrinkles and parches from age.* **2.** To make or become very thirsty: *Climbing to the top of the mountain parched us.*

parch·ment | pärch′mənt | —*noun, plural* **parchments** The skin of a sheep or goat, prepared as a material to write on. Diplomas are often written on parchment.

par·don | pär′dn | —*verb* **pardoned, pardoning 1.** To free or release a person from punishment: *The king pardoned the duke and allowed him to return to court.* **2.** To excuse or overlook a mistake or fault: *Please pardon my being late.*
—*noun, plural* **pardons 1.** A polite excuse of a mistake or fault: *to beg one's pardon.* **2.** The act of releasing from punishment by an official, such as a president or governor.

pare | pâr | —*verb* **pared, paring** To remove the skin or rind of something with a knife or other device; peel: *We pared the potatoes for the stew.*
♦ *These sound alike* **pare, pair, pear.**

par·ent | pâr′ənt | or | păr′ənt | —*noun, plural* **parents 1.** A father or mother. **2.** A plant or animal that produces another of its own kind.

pa·ren·tal | pə rĕn′tl | —*adjective* **1.** Of a parent: *A child needs parental teaching.* **2.** Like a parent; fatherly or motherly: *He takes a parental interest in his nephew's progress at school.*

pa·ren·the·sis | pə rĕn′thĭ sĭs | —*noun, plural* **parentheses** Either of two upright curved lines ( ), used in writing or printing. Parentheses are used to set off an additional phrase or explanation.

par·ish | păr′ĭsh | —*noun, plural* **parishes 1.** A district with its own church and clergymen. **2.** The people who belong to such a district: *The priest asked the parish to support the new program.*

park | pärk | —*noun, plural* **parks 1.** An area of public land used for amusement and recreation by the people of a town or city. **2.** An area of land set apart by the government to be kept in its natural state. Wild animals and birds are protected in national parks.
—*verb* **parked, parking** To leave a vehicle in a certain place when it is not in use: *I'll get the tickets for the game while you park the car.*

par·ka | pär′kə | —*noun, plural* **parkas** A warm jacket with a hood. Parkas are often lined with fur.

park·way | pärk′wā′ | —*noun, plural* **parkways** A wide road or highway that is planted with grass, bushes, and trees along the sides.

ă	pat	ĕ	pet	î	fierce
ā	pay	ē	be	ŏ	pot
â	care	ĭ	pit	ō	go
ä	father	ī	pie	ô	paw, for
oi	oil	ŭ	cut	zh	vision
ŏŏ	book	û	fur	ə	ago, item,
ōō	boot	*th*	the		pencil, atom,
yōō	abuse	th	thin		circus
ou	out	hw	which	ər	butter

par·lia·ment |**pär′**lə mənt| —*noun, plural* **parliaments** An assembly of persons that makes the laws for some nations; a legislative body.

par·lia·men·ta·ry |pär′lə **měn′**tə rē| or |pär′lə **měn′**trē| —*adjective* **1.** Of a parliament: *parliamentary laws.* **2.** Carried out according to the rules of procedure of a parliament: *parliamentary debate.* **3.** Having a parliament: *a nation with a parliamentary government.*

par·lor |**pär′**lər| —*noun, plural* **parlors 1.** A room for entertaining visitors. **2.** A room or building designed for some special use or business: *a beauty parlor; a funeral parlor.*

pa·ro·chi·al |pə **rō′**kē əl| —*adjective* Of a church parish: *a parochial school; a parochial priest.*

pa·role |pə **rōl**| —*noun, plural* **paroles** The release, for good behavior, of a person from prison before he or she has finished his or her full sentence. People on parole must follow certain rules and they are under supervision of a parole officer.
—*verb* **paroled, paroling** To release a person on parole.

par·rot |**pär′**ət| —*noun, plural* **parrots** Any of several tropical birds with a short, hooked bill and brightly colored feathers. Some kinds of parrots are kept as pets. They can often be taught to imitate spoken words.
—*verb* **parroted, parroting** To repeat or imitate another person's words or actions without understanding their meaning: *On our first day in French class, we could only parrot what our teacher was saying.*

pars·ley |**pär′**slē| —*noun* A plant with feathery or curly leaves that are used to flavor or decorate food.

pars·nip |**pär′**snĭp| —*noun, plural* **parsnips** A long, whitish plant root with a rather strong taste. Parsnips are eaten as a vegetable.

par·son |**pär′**sən| —*noun, plural* **parsons** A clergyman in charge of a parish; a minister.

part |pärt| —*noun, plural* **parts 1.** Something that along with other things makes a whole; a division or portion of a larger thing: *Would you like part of my dessert? We were late and missed part of the movie.* **2.** One portion of a whole: *I mixed one part of vinegar with three parts of oil for the salad dressing.* **3.** Something or someone thought of as an equal or necessary feature or element: *Our nurse was always treated as part of the family.* **4.** A piece in a machine or mechanism that can be taken out and replaced: *I need a new part for my radio.* **5.** A role or character in a play or movie: *Amy has a part in the school play.* **6.** A side in an argument or dispute: *She didn't completely agree with me, but she took my part.* **7.** A dividing line formed across the scalp when the hair is combed to one side or the other.
—*verb* **parted, parting 1.** To divide into two or more parts; split: *He parted the log with his ax. The tree trunk parts into branches higher up.* **2.** To leave one another: *We parted at the bottom of the hill.* **3.** To put or keep apart; come between: *A silly argument parted them. After angry words they parted.*
Phrasal verb **part with** To give up; let go of: *The old miser hated to part with a penny.*
—*adjective* Not full; partial: *He is part owner of a bowling alley.*
—*adverb* In part; partially: *Her dog is part collie, part German shepherd.*

parrot

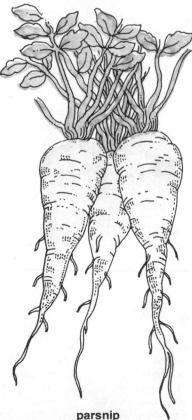

parsnip

Idioms **for the most part** In most cases; chiefly: *For the most part his books were too hard for me.* **take part** To be active; join; participate: *You should take part in community programs.*

par·tial |pär'shəl| —*adjective* **1.** Being only a part; not total; incomplete: *Her poems enjoyed a partial success.* **2.** Favoring one side; prejudiced; biased: *A judge should not be partial.* **3.** Especially attracted or inclined: *She's partial to tall boys.*

par·tic·i·pate |pär tĭs'ə pāt'| —*verb* **participated, participating** To join with others in being active; take part: *She participated in the class play.*

par·ti·ci·ple |pär'tĭ sĭp'əl| —*noun, plural* **participles** Either of two verb forms that are used with helping verbs to indicate certain tenses. Participles can also function in some cases as adjectives or nouns. Present participles often end in *-ing: doing; seeing; taking.* Past participles often end in *-n, -en, -ed, -d,* or *-t,* as in the words *spoken, fallen, boiled, baked,* and *dreamt.*

par·ti·cle |pär'tĭ kəl| —*noun, plural* **particles** A very small piece or amount of something solid; speck: *Particles of dust floated in the air.*

par·tic·u·lar |pər tĭk'yə lər| —*adjective* **1.** Of or for a single person, group, or thing: *My particular interest is sailing.* **2.** Distinct from any other; certain; specific: *This particular vase was made by hand.* **3.** Special or exceptional; unusual: *I want you to pay particular attention to this lesson.* **4.** Showing or demanding close attention to details; fussy: *She's very particular about how her meat is cooked.*

—*noun, plural* **particulars** A single item or fact; a detail: *The report is correct in every particular.*

par·ti·tion |pär tĭsh'ən| —*noun, plural* **partitions** A wall, panel, or screen that divides up a room or space.

—*verb* **partitioned, partitioning** **1.** To divide into separate spaces or sections: *We partitioned the room with a curtain.* **2.** To make into a separate space by means of a partition: *We used a screen to partition off the dining area from the kitchen.*

part·ly |pärt'lē| —*adverb* To some extent or degree; in part: *The sun is partly hidden by a cloud.*

part·ner |pärt'nər| —*noun, plural* **partners** **1.** One of two or more persons joined in an activity, especially a business: *The law firm has four partners.* **2.** A person with whom one dances: *It's a dance in which you keep changing partners.* **3.** Either of two persons playing together in a game: *a tennis partner.*

part·ner·ship |pärt'nər shĭp'| —*noun, plural* **partnerships** The condition of being partners: *I started a lemonade stand in partnership with two friends.*

part of speech One of several classes in which words are placed according to the way they are used in a phrase or sentence. English words are usually classified as *noun, pronoun, verb, adjective, adverb, preposition, conjunction,* and *interjection.* Sometimes *article* is considered a separate part of speech.

par·tridge |pär'trĭj| —*noun, plural* **partridges** or **partridge** A bird with a plump body and brownish feathers. The partridge is often hunted as game.

part-time |pärt'tīm'| —*adjective* For or during only part of the usual working time: *a part-time job; a part-time clerk.*

—*adverb* |pärt'tīm'| On a part-time basis: *He works part-time as a waiter.*

partridge

ă	pat	ĕ	pet	î	fierce
ā	pay	ē	be	ŏ	pot
â	care	ĭ	pit	ō	go
ä	father	ī	pie	ô	paw, for

oi	oil	ŭ	cut	zh	vision
ŏŏ	book	û	fur	ə	ago, item,
ōō	boot	*th*	the		pencil, atom,
yōō	abuse	th	thin		circus
ou	out	hw	which	ər	butter

par·ty |pär′tē| —*noun, plural* **parties** **1.** A group of persons who join together in some activity: *There is a search party looking for the lost child.* **2.** A gathering of people for fun or pleasure: *a birthday party.* **3.** A group of people who are organized for political activity. They nominate and support their candidates for public office: *the Republican Party.* **4.** A person or group who takes part in some action: *She refused to be a party to the argument.*

pass |păs| or |päs| —*verb* **passed, passing** **1.** To go from one place to another: *The delivery boy passed from house to house.* **2.** To go by without stopping: *Many people pass my house on their way to work.* **3.** To catch up with and go by: *He passed us going about eighty miles an hour.* **4.** To go by in time; spend time: *The fishermen sang to make the hours pass faster. He passed his vacation in Colorado.* **5.** To come to an end: *We waited for the storm to pass.* **6.** To hand or throw from one person to another: *Pass your plate for more turkey. They passed the ball back and forth.* **7.** To complete with satisfactory results: *I passed my history test. My car passed the inspection.* **8.** To make into a law; become a law: *The senate passed the bill for the new dam. The other bill did not pass.*

Phrasal verbs **pass away** To die. **pass out** **1.** To hand out; give: *The theater passed out free tickets.* **2.** To faint: *It's so hot in here I'm about to pass out.*

—*noun, plural* **passes** **1.** A motion with the hand or something held in the hand: *He made a few passes with the sponge to clean the table.* **2.** A way or opening that is hard to get through: *We had to ride in a single line through the mountain pass.* **3.** A written or printed permission: *The soldier had a pass for twenty-four hours from the camp.* **4.** A ticket that gives free admission: *He gave me two passes to the circus.* **5.** In sports, the act of passing a ball or puck to someone on the same team: *a pass of thirty yards for a touchdown.*

pas·sage |păs′ĭj| —*noun, plural* **passages** **1.** The act or process of passing; movement: *It was so hot we opened the windows to allow the passage of air into the room.* **2.** A narrow way between two places or points: *an underground passage from the cellar to the barn out back.* **3.** A journey or trip, especially on a ship: *Our passage across the ocean took five days.* **4.** A channel or tube in the body through which something may pass: *nasal passages.* **5.** The act of making a law by a legislative body: *the passage of a bill in Congress.* **6.** A part of a written work or a piece of music: *He read a passage from the story out loud. Play that violin passage again.*

pas·sage·way |păs′ĭj wā′| —*noun, plural* **passageways** A way or route along which someone or something can pass; passage.

pas·sen·ger |păs′ən jər| —*noun, plural* **passengers** A person riding in a train, airplane, bus, ship, car, or other vehicle.

passenger pigeon A pigeon that used to be common in North America. Passenger pigeons have been extinct since the late 1800s.

pass·ing |păs′ĭng| or |pä′sĭng| —*adjective* **1.** Going by; moving by: *a passing car.* **2.** Not lasting long; brief: *She had a passing interest in being a nurse.* **3.** Said or done quickly; casual: *a passing remark. She took a passing look in the store window.* **4.** Allowing one to pass a test; satisfactory: *a passing grade.*

—*noun, plural* **passings** The act of going by: *The passing of winter went quickly because we were busy.*

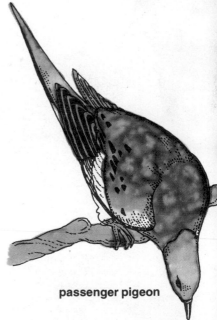

passenger pigeon

pas·sion |păsh′ən| —*noun, plural* **passions 1.** A powerful or very strong feeling. Love, joy, anger, or hatred are passions. **2.** A strong liking for something: *Charlene has a passion for reading.*

pas·sion·flow·er |păsh′ən flou′ər| —*noun, plural* **passionflowers** The large, brightly colored flower of a vine that grows in warm regions.

pas·sive |păs′ĭv| —*adjective* **1.** Not joining or taking part; not active: *a passive role; a passive interest in games.* **2.** Giving in to another or others; not resisting: *He listened in passive silence.*

passive voice A form of a verb or phrasal verb that shows that the subject of the sentence is the object or the receiver of the action expressed by the verb. In the sentence "The money was stolen," the verb form "was stolen," is in the passive voice.

Pass·o·ver |păs′ō′vər| or |päs′ō′vər| —*noun, plural* **Passovers** A Jewish festival that lasts eight days. It celebrates the escape of the Jews from ancient Egypt, where they had been slaves for a long time. Passover comes in the spring.

pass·port |păs′pôrt′| or |păs′pōrt′| or |päs′pôrt′| or |päs′pōrt′| —*noun, plural* **passports** A document given out by the government of a country. A passport identifies a person as a citizen and gives official permission to travel in foreign countries.

pass·word |păs′wûrd′| or |päs′wûrd′| —*noun, plural* **passwords** A secret word or phrase spoken to a guard that identifies a person and allows him or her to enter a special place.

past |păst| or |päst| —*adjective* **1.** Gone by; over: *Winter is past. Her illness is past.* **2.** Just ended; just over: *I went to the movies twice in the past week.* **3.** Having existed or taken place at an earlier time; former: *a past president.*
—*noun, plural* **pasts 1.** All the time gone by before the present: *America's past is one of steady growth. In the past many children worked in factories.* **2.** A person's history and background: *In his past he worked on a ranch.*
—*preposition* **1.** Alongside and beyond: *The river flows past my house.* **2.** Beyond in time; later or older: *She is three months past nine years old. It is ten past three.* **3.** Beyond in position: *How did you get past the guard?*
—*adverb* To and beyond a point near at hand; by: *He tooted the horn as he drove past.*

paste |pāst| —*noun, plural* **pastes 1.** A smooth, sticky substance that is used to fasten things together. Paste is often made of a mixture of flour and water. **2.** A food that has been made soft by pounding or grinding: *tomato paste.*
—*verb* **pasted, pasting 1.** To fasten or stick together with paste: *She pasted the broken pieces of the plate together.* **2.** To cover with something to which paste has been applied: *It took him all day to paste the wall with posters.*

paste·board |pāst′bôrd′| or |pāst′bōrd′| —*noun* A thin, stiff board made of many sheets of paper pasted together or of wood pulp that is wet, formed into a special shape, and then dried till it is hard.

pas·tel |pă stĕl′| —*noun, plural* **pastels 1.** A crayon that is like chalk. It is used in drawing. **2.** A picture drawn or painted with such crayons. **3.** A soft, pale color.

pas·teur·ize |păs′chə rīz′| —*verb* **pasteurized, pasteurizing** To heat milk or other liquids hot enough so that certain germs are killed. Pasteurizing milk makes it safer to drink.

passionflower

passport

ă	pat	ĕ	pet	î	fierce
ā	pay	ē	be	ŏ	pot
â	care	ĭ	pit	ō	go
ä	father	ī	pie	ô	paw, for
oi	oil	ŭ	cut	zh	vision
ōō	book	û	fur	ə	ago, item,
ōō	boot	*th*	the		pencil, atom,
yōō	abuse	th	thin		circus
ou	out	hw	which	ər	butter

pas·time |păs′tīm′| —*noun, plural* **pastimes** An activity, such as a game or hobby, that uses one's time in a pleasant way: *Fishing and camping are two of Diana's favorite pastimes.*

pas·tor |păs′tər| —*noun, plural* **pastors** A minister who is in charge of a church.

past participle A form of a verb that shows an action, a condition, or a state that happened or existed in or during the past. The past participle can be used as an adjective. In the phrase *given name* the past participle *given* is used as an adjective. The past participle is also used to form the passive voice.

pas·try |pā′strē| —*noun, plural* **pastries** **1.** Baked foods, such as pies and tarts. **2.** Dough used to make the crusts of such foods.

past tense A verb tense that shows an action that happened or a condition that existed in or during the past. In the sentence *I picked the winner,* the verb *picked* is in the past tense.

pas·ture |păs′chər| or |päs′chər| —*noun, plural* **pastures** **1.** A piece of land covered with grass and other plants that are eaten by horses, cattle, sheep, or other animals that graze. **2.** The grass and other plants eaten by animals that graze.
—*verb* **pastured, pasturing** To put animals in a pasture to graze: *Robin pastures the sheep every morning.*

pat |păt| —*verb* **patted, patting** **1.** To touch or stroke gently with the open hand: *Don't be afraid to pat the dog.* **2.** To flatten or shape by patting: *After filling in the hole he patted the dirt down so it would be flat.*
—*noun, plural* **pats** **1.** A gentle stroke or tap: *a light pat on the head.* **2.** A small piece or lump: *Have a pat of butter with your bread.*

patch |păch| —*noun, plural* **patches** **1.** A small piece of material. A patch is used to cover a hole, a tear, or a worn place. **2.** A bandage or pad worn over a wound or an injured eye to protect it. **3.** A small piece of land with plants growing on it: *We have a strawberry patch in our back yard.* **4.** A small area that is different from what is around it: *Even though it's cloudy I can see a patch of blue in the sky.*
—*verb* **patched, patching** **1.** To cover or fix with a patch; put a patch on: *Lisa patched the hole in her skirt. I patched the hole in the tire.* **2.** To make by sewing pieces of material or cloth together: *She's patching a quilt.*

patch·work |păch′wûrk′| —*noun* Pieces of cloth of different colors, shapes, and sizes that are sewn together. A patchwork is used to make coverings, such as quilts for beds.

pat·ent |păt′nt| —*noun, plural* **patents** A document given by the government to an inventor or company. A patent gives a person or company the right to be the only one to make, use, or sell an invention for a certain number of years.
—*verb* **patented, patenting** To get a patent for: *The doctor patented his new medicine.*

patent leather Leather with a smooth, hard, shiny surface, used to make shoes, belts, and pocketbooks.

pa·ter·nal |pə tûr′nəl| —*adjective* **1.** Of or like a father; fatherly: *Sam has paternal feelings for his niece and nephew.* **2.** Related to through one's father: *Jimmy's paternal grandparents live in Florida.*

pasture

patchwork

path | păth | or | päth | —*noun, plural* **paths** | pă*thz* | or | pä*thz* | or | păths | or | päths | **1.** A way or trail made by footsteps: *a path in the woods.* **2.** A way made for walking: *Would you shovel a path through the snow?* **3.** The line or route along which something or someone moves: *The path of the hurricane moved all the way up the coast from Florida to Maine.*

pa·thet·ic | pə thĕt′ĭk | —*adjective* Causing or making one feel pity or sorrow; sad; pitiful: *The frightened people whose homes were destroyed in the war are pathetic.*

pa·tience | pā′shəns | —*noun* The condition or quality of being patient: *Father showed great patience when the children refused to go to bed.*

pa·tient | pā′shənt | —*adjective* Putting up with or enduring trouble, hardship, delay, and pain without complaining or getting angry: *If you want to see the movie, you'll have to stand in line and be patient.*

—*noun, plural* **patients** A person who is under the treatment or care of a doctor.

pat·i·o | păt′ē ō′ | —*noun, plural* **patios** **1.** An inside yard or court that is not covered by a roof but is open to the sky. In Spain and Mexico, many large, old houses and public buildings were built around patios. **2.** A space or part of a yard next to a house or apartment that is used for outdoor eating and recreation. A patio is usually paved with stones or tiles.

pa·tri·ot | pā′trē ət | or | pā′trē ŏt′ | —*noun, plural* **patriots** A person who loves, supports, and defends his or her country: *You can learn a lot about the United States by studying the lives of our country's patriots.*

pa·tri·ot·ic | pā′trē ŏt′ĭk | —*adjective* Feeling or showing love and support for one's country: *a patriotic song; a patriotic holiday.*

pa·tri·ot·ism | pā′trē ə tĭz′əm | —*noun* Love of and loyalty to one's country.

pa·trol | pə trōl′ | —*verb* **patrolled, patrolling** To go or walk through an area to guard it and make sure that there is no trouble: *The police car patrols the neighborhood every hour during the night.*

—*noun, plural* **patrols** **1.** The act of patrolling: *The soldiers are out on patrol.* **2.** A person or group of persons who do such a job: *the highway patrol.*

pa·tron | pā′trən | —*noun, plural* **patrons** **1.** A person who helps or supports a person, group, or institution by giving money: *Museums and libraries need patrons.* **2.** A regular customer of a store or restaurant: *One patron has been buying our fruits and vegetables for twenty years.*

pat·tern | păt′ərn | —*noun, plural* **patterns** **1.** The way in which shapes and colors are arranged; a design: *Margery's skirt has a pattern of black and white squares.* **2.** A guide or model for something to be made: *a dress pattern.* **3.** A combination of events or qualities that always happen the same way or in the same order: *Many birds follow a pattern of flying south in the winter.*

—*verb* **patterned, patterning** To make or follow according to a special pattern or model: *That country's constitution is patterned after the United States Constitution.*

pause | pôz | —*verb* **paused, pausing** To stop for a short time in the middle of doing or saying something: *The teacher paused for a second and then began reading the lesson again.*

patio

ă	pat	ĕ	pet	î	fierce
ā	pay	ē	be	ŏ	pot
â	care	ĭ	pit	ō	go
ä	father	ī	pie	ô	paw, for
oi	oil	ŭ	cut	zh	vision
ōō	book	û	fur	ə	ago, item,
ōō	boot	*th*	the		pencil, atom,
yōō	abuse	th	thin		circus
ou	out	hw	which	ər	butter

P

—*noun, plural* **pauses** A short stop or rest: *a pause to get a breath.*

pave |pāv| —*verb* **paved, paving** To cover a road, sidewalk, driveway, or other area with pavement: *The men are paving the dirt road that goes to the lake.*

pave·ment |pāv′mənt| —*noun, plural* **pavements** A hard covering or surface used on roads, streets, sidewalks, and driveways. Pavement may be made from concrete, tar, asphalt, or crushed rocks.

pa·vil·ion |pə vĭl′yən| —*noun, plural* **pavilions** **1.** A fancy or elaborate tent. **2.** An open structure with a roof. A pavilion often has a raised wooden floor and is used at parks and fairs for amusement or shelter. **3.** One of a group of buildings that are part of a hospital.

paw |pô| —*noun, plural* **paws** The foot of an animal that has four feet and claws or nails.

—*verb* **pawed, pawing** **1.a.** To touch or strike with a paw: *The cat pawed the toy mouse and jumped back when it squeaked.* **b.** To scrape with a front foot: *The bull pawed the ground before charging.* **2.** To handle in a clumsy or rude way: *Bill was pawing through his toy chest, trying to find his marbles.*

pawn¹ |pôn| —*verb* **pawned, pawning** To give or leave something valuable with someone temporarily in exchange for a loan: *I pawned my watch, but I'm going to get it back next week when I pay back the money.*

pawn² |pôn| —*noun, plural* **pawns** **1.** The least valuable piece in the game of chess. **2.** A person that is used or controlled by another person in order to get something: *He used his friends as pawns to reach his goals.*

pay |pā| —*verb* **paid, paying** **1.** To give money to someone in exchange for goods or for work done: *How much did you pay for the basketball? The job pays a hundred dollars a week.* **2.** To give a particular amount of money that is owed or due; give the required amount: *We have to pay taxes and rent.* **3.** To be worthwhile or helpful; be worth the effort: *It pays to be nice to people.* **4.** To give, do, or make: *Pay attention in class. I am going to pay a visit to you soon.*

Phrasal verbs **pay back** To get even with; revenge: *I paid him back for his insults.* **pay for** To suffer because of something: *You'll pay for your mistakes.*

—*noun* Money given in return for work done; salary: *I got a raise in pay.*

pay·ment |pā′mənt| —*noun, plural* **payments** **1.** The act of paying: *Full payment had to be made before we could get the new car.* **2.** Something that is paid: *His rent payments are ninety dollars a month.*

pay·roll |pā′rōl′| —*noun, plural* **payrolls** **1.** A list of all workers or employees and the amount of money or salary that each one is to be paid: *His company has forty people on the payroll.* **2.** The total amount of money or salaries paid to employees at one time: *His payroll keeps getting bigger as his business grows, and he plans to hire ten more people.*

pea |pē| —*noun, plural* **peas** One of the round green seeds of a plant that has long green pods. Peas are eaten as a vegetable.

peace |pēs| —*noun* **1.** Freedom from war or fighting: *All nations must work together if there is to be peace in the world.* **2.** A

pawn¹, pawn²
Both words spelled **pawn** can be traced from Latin through French into English. **Pawn¹** originally meant "a piece of cloth, a garment"; it came to mean "a pledge." **Pawn²** meant "one who has wide feet" or "foot soldier" in late Latin; in French it meant "chess pawn."

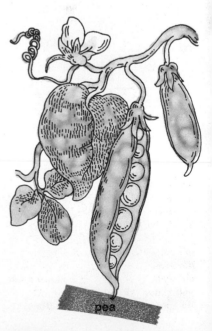

pea

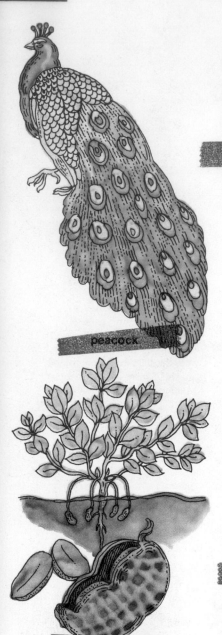

peacock

peanut
Above: Plant
Below: Nut *(left)* and
nuts in pod *(right)*

ă	pat	ĕ	pet	î	fierce
ā	pay	ē	be	ŏ	pot
â	care	ĭ	pit	ō	go
ä	father	ī	pie	ô	paw, for
oi	oil	ŭ	cut	zh	vision
ŏŏ	book	û	fur	ə	ago, item,
ōō	boot	*th*	the		pencil, atom,
yōō	abuse	th	thin		circus
ou	out	hw	which	ər	butter

condition of calm, order, and good feelings between people: *Stop arguing and let me have some peace and quiet.*

♦ *These sound alike* **peace, piece.**

peace·ful |pēs′fəl| —*adjective* **1.** Against war or fighting; liking to live in peace: *Their country has been peaceful for a long time.* **2.** Calm and quiet; serene: *It's so peaceful in the mountains.*

peace pipe A long pipe for smoking. Peace pipes were used by North American Indians in ceremonies and festivals as a sign of friendship.

peach |pēch| —*noun, plural* **peaches 1.** A sweet, round, juicy fruit. It has smooth yellow or reddish skin that feels fuzzy, and a pit with a hard shell. **2.** A light yellowish-pink color.
—*adjective* Light yellowish pink.

pea·cock |pē′kŏk′| —*noun, plural* **peacocks** The male of the peafowl. The peacock has brilliant blue or green feathers. Its long tail feathers have spots that look like eyes. These feathers can be spread out like a large fan.

pea·fowl |pē′foul′| —*noun, plural* **peafowls** or **peafowl** A large bird related to the pheasants; a peacock or a peahen.

pea·hen |pē′hĕn′| —*noun, plural* **peahens** The female of the peafowl. The peahen does not have the bright colors of the peacock.

peak |pēk| —*noun, plural* **peaks 1.** The pointed or narrow top of a mountain: *The peaks of very high mountains are usually covered with snow all year round.* **2.** The mountain itself. **3.** Any pointed top or end: *A pyramid ends in a peak.* **4.** The highest point of development or value: *The team reached its peak in June when it won fifteen games in a row.* **5.** The round brim of a cap that sticks out in front: *A peak helps keep the sun out of a person's eyes.*

♦ *These sound alike* **peak, peek.**

peal |pēl| —*noun, plural* **peals 1.** A loud ringing of a set of bells. **2.** A long, loud noise or series of noises: *a peal of laughter.*
—*verb* **pealed, pealing** To ring out in a peal or shout loudly: *The bells peal every day at noon.*

♦ *These sound alike* **peal, peel.**

pea·nut |pē′nŭt′| or |pē′nət| —*noun, plural* **peanuts** A plant seed that looks and tastes like a nut. Peanuts grow in pods that ripen underground. Oil from peanuts is used for cooking.

peanut butter A soft food made by grinding roasted peanuts. Peanut butter is used to make sandwiches and as a spread.

pear |pâr| —*noun, plural* **pears** A sweet, juicy fruit with smooth yellowish or brown skin. A pear is rounded at one end and tapers to a point at the other end.

♦ *These sound alike* **pear, pair, pare.**

pearl |pûrl| —*noun, plural* **pearls 1.** A smooth whitish or grayish gem with a soft shine. Pearls are formed inside the shells of some kinds of oysters. **2.** Something that looks like a pearl: *pearls of dew.*

peas·ant |pĕz′ənt| —*noun, plural* **peasants** A person who belongs to the group or class of small farmers and farm workers in Europe.

peat |pēt| —*noun* A kind of soil found in bogs and marshes. Peat is a rich soil because it is made up of decaying plants. It is used as a fertilizer and can also be dried and burned as fuel.

peb·ble |pĕb′əl| —*noun, plural* **pebbles** A small stone that has been made smooth and round by wind and water.

pe·can |pĭ **kän′**| or |pĭ **kăn′**| or |pē′kăn′| —*noun, plural* **pecans** A nut that grows on a tall tree and has a smooth, oval shell. Pecans are good to eat.

pec·ca·ry |pĕk′ə rē| —*noun, plural* **peccaries** A tropical American animal that is rather like a pig. The peccary has long, dark bristles.

peck[1] |pĕk| —*verb* **pecked, pecking** **1.** To strike something with a beak or an instrument with a sharp point: *The parakeet pecked me on the arm.* **2.** To make a hole in by striking over and over with a beak: *The woodpeckers were pecking the tree outside my window all morning.* **3.** To pick up grain or other food with the beak: *The pigeons pecked at the bread crumbs on the ground.* —*noun, plural* **pecks** **1.** A short strike or blow with the beak: *The bird gave me a peck on the hand.* **2.** A light, quick kiss: *a peck on the cheek.*

peck[2] |pĕk| —*noun, plural* **pecks** **1.** A unit of measure for grain, vegetables, fruit, and other dry things. **2.** A container holding just this amount used as a measure.

pe·cu·liar |pĭ **kyōol′**yər| —*adjective* **1.** Unusual or odd; not normal; strange: *It was peculiar that all the lights in the house were on but nobody was home. She had a peculiar expression on her face.* **2.** Belonging to a special or particular person, group, place, or thing: *Palm trees are peculiar to tropical areas.*

pe·cu·li·ar·i·ty |pĭ kyōo′lē ăr′ĭ tē| —*noun, plural* **peculiarities** **1.** Something that is peculiar or odd: *He has a peculiarity of not looking at people when he talks to them. One peculiarity of the house is that three sides are painted white and the fourth is painted blue.* **2.** The condition or quality of being peculiar: *In a large city peculiarity attracts less notice.*

ped·al |pĕd′l| —*noun, plural* **pedals** A lever that is worked or operated by the foot. Pedals are used on many machines and instruments to control some of the things they do. Pedals are used to start and stop a car. —*verb* **pedaled, pedaling** To use or operate the pedals of something: *Irving pedaled his bike to work.*
♦ *These sound alike* **pedal, peddle.**

ped·dle |pĕd′l| —*verb* **peddled, peddling** To travel or go from place to place selling goods: *The boy peddled boxes of candy door to door.*
♦ *These sound alike* **peddle, pedal.**

ped·dler |pĕd′lər| —*noun, plural* **peddlers** A person who travels from place to place selling goods.

ped·es·tal |pĕd′ĭ stəl| —*noun, plural* **pedestals** **1.** The base on which a statue or column stands. **2.** The base or other part on which something stands or by which it is held up. Tall vases, lamps, and candlesticks often have pedestals.

pe·des·tri·an |pə **dĕs′**trē ən| —*noun, plural* **pedestrians** A person who travels on foot: *People who drive cars must always be careful of pedestrians.*

pe·di·a·tri·cian |pē′dē ə **trĭsh′**ən| —*noun, plural* **pediatricians** A doctor who takes care of children and babies and treats their diseases.

ped·i·gree |pĕd′ĭ grē′| —*noun, plural* **pedigrees** The whole line of ancestors or family of a person or animal.

peek |pēk| —*verb* **peeked, peeking** To look or glance quickly or secretly: *I peeked into the den to see what my sister was doing.*

pecan
Above: Leaves
Center: Tree
Below: Nuts

peck[1], **peck**[2]
Peck[1] comes from an English word used about 1100–1500. **Peck**[2] comes from French.

pedestal
Statue on a pedestal

Pekingese

pelican

ă	pat	ĕ	pet	î	fierce
ā	pay	ē	be	ŏ	pot
â	care	ĭ	pit	ō	go
ä	father	ī	pie	ô	paw, for

oi	oil	ŭ	cut	zh	vision
ŏŏ	book	û	fur	ə	ago, item,
ōō	boot	th	the		pencil, atom,
yōō	abuse	th	thin		circus
ou	out	hw	which	ər	butter

—*noun, plural* **peeks** A quick or secret look or glance: *Take a peek at the stove and see if everything is cooking.*
♦ *These sound alike* **peek, peak.**

peel | pēl | —*noun, plural* **peels** The skin or rind of certain fruits, such as an orange or banana.
—*verb* **peeled, peeling 1.** To remove the skin or outer covering from: *peel a banana.* **2.** To strip away; pull off: *She peeled the label from the jar.* **3.** To come off in thin strips or layers: *The paint was peeling from the walls.* **4.** To lose or shed skin or other covering: *We peeled after a day in the sun.*
♦ *These sound alike* **peel, peal.**

peep¹ | pēp | —*noun, plural* **peeps** A weak, high sound, like that made by a young bird; chirp: *We heard peeps coming from the robin's nest.*
—*verb* **peeped, peeping** To make such a sound: *The baby birds are peeping because they are hungry.*

peep² | pēp | —*verb* **peeped, peeping 1.** To look quickly or secretly, especially through a small hole or from a hiding place; peek: *I peeped at the people next door through the fence.* **2.** To be able to be seen; become visible: *The sun peeped out from behind the clouds.*
—*noun, plural* **peeps** A quick look; a peek.

peep·er | pē′pər | —*noun, plural* **peepers** A small tree frog with a high, chirping call. Peepers are heard in early spring.

peer¹ | pîr | —*verb* **peered, peering 1.** To look closely in order to see something clearly; stare: *They were peering at us through the window.* **2.** To come into view or peep out; show: *The moon peered from behind a cloud.*
♦ *These sound alike* **peer, pier.**

peer² | pîr | —*noun, plural* **peers 1.** Someone who is equal to another in age, ability, or rank: *All the students in the fourth grade are your peers. As a singer she has no peers.* **2.** Someone who has a title; nobleman. Dukes, duchesses, and princes are all peers.
♦ *These sound alike* **peer, pier.**

peg | pĕg | —*noun, plural* **pegs** A piece of wood or metal that is used to fasten things together, to plug a hole, or to hang things on. Pegs come in many different sizes and are usually shaped like a pin or pencil.
—*verb* **pegged, pegging** To fasten or plug with pegs: *We will peg down the tent. They pegged the barrel so that nothing would spill out.*

Pe·king·ese | pē′kĭ nēz′ | or | pē′kĭ nēs′ | or | pē′kĭng ēz′ | or | pē′kĭng ēs′ | —*noun* A small dog with short legs, long hair, and a flat nose. The Pekingese was originally from China.

pel·i·can | pĕl′ĭ kən | —*noun, plural* **pelicans** A large bird with a long bill and webbed feet. Under its lower bill the pelican has a large pouch used for holding the fish it has caught.

pel·let | pĕl′ĭt | —*noun, plural* **pellets 1.** A very small, hard ball made of different substances. Medicine, food, and paper can all be formed into pellets. **2.** A kind of bullet for certain kinds of guns.

pelt¹ | pĕlt | —*noun, plural* **pelts** An animal skin with the hair or fur still on it.

pelt² | pĕlt | —*verb* **pelted, pelting 1.** To hit or strike with something over and over; throw things at: *The children were pelting each other with snow. The angry crowd pelted the team with popcorn and candy wrappers.* **2.** To beat down on over and over: *Rain pelted down all night.*

pen¹ |pĕn| —*noun, plural* **pens** An instrument for writing with ink. Some pens have ink inside them and others are dipped in ink.

pen² |pĕn| —*noun, plural* **pens** A small, fenced area in which animals are kept.
—*verb* **penned, penning** To keep in or as if in a pen: *The farmer penned his sheep.*

pe·nal·ize |pē'nə līz'| —*verb* **penalized, penalizing** To give a punishment to: *The law penalizes people who drive too fast. The referee penalized the basketball player for pushing another player.*

pen·al·ty |pĕn'əl tē| —*noun, plural* **penalties** **1.** A punishment set by law for a crime: *The judge ordered a penalty of five years in jail.* **2.** Something that must be given up for an offense. In sports, a penalty can be a sum of money that must be paid or a giving up of a position.

pence |pĕns| A plural of **penny.**

pen·cil |pĕn'səl| —*noun, plural* **pencils** **1.** A thin stick of a hard material inside a covering of wood, used for writing. **2.** Something shaped or used like a pencil: *an eyebrow pencil.*
—*verb* **penciled, penciling** To write or draw with a pencil: *She penciled a picture of the house.*

pen·du·lum |pĕn'jə ləm| or |pĕn'dyə ləm| —*noun, plural* **pendulums** A weight hung by a light cord, chain, or bar so that it can easily swing back and forth. Some clocks have pendulums to help them run properly.

pen·e·trate |pĕn'ĭ trāt'| —*verb* **penetrated, penetrating** **1.** To go into or through: *Rain penetrated the top of our tent. This forest is too thick to penetrate.* **2.** To study and understand: *With space travel we can penetrate the mysteries of outer space.*

pen·guin |pĕng'gwĭn| —*noun, plural* **penguins** A sea bird with webbed feet and narrow wings that look like flippers. Penguins cannot fly, but use their wings for swimming. Many penguins live in or near Antarctica.

pen·i·cil·lin |pĕn'ĭ sĭl'ən| —*noun* An antibiotic drug that is made from a mold. Penicillin is used to kill bacteria that cause certain diseases and infections.

pen·in·su·la |pə nĭn'sə lə| or |pə nĭns'yə lə| —*noun, plural* **peninsulas** A piece of land that is almost surrounded by water and connected to a larger body of land. Florida is a peninsula.

pen·i·ten·tia·ry |pĕn'ĭ tĕn'shə rē| —*noun, plural* **penitentiaries** A prison for people who are found guilty of serious crimes.

pen·man·ship |pĕn'mən shĭp'| —*noun* The art, skill, style, or manner of handwriting.

pen·nant |pĕn'ənt| —*noun, plural* **pennants** **1.** A long, narrow flag, shaped like a triangle. It is used by ships for giving signals. **2.** In sports, a flag that is the emblem of the winning team.

Penn·syl·va·nia |pĕn'səl vān'yə| or |pĕn'səl vā'nē ə| A state in the eastern United States. The capital of Pennsylvania is Harrisburg.

pen·ny |pĕn'ē| —*noun, plural* **pennies** **1.** A United States or Canadian coin worth ¹⁄₁₀₀ of a dollar; a cent. **2.** *plural* **pence** or **pennies** A British coin worth ¹⁄₁₀₀ of a pound.

pen·sion |pĕn'shən| —*noun, plural* **pensions** A sum of money paid regularly to a person who has retired from work. Pensions are also paid when a person cannot work because of a long illness or an injury.

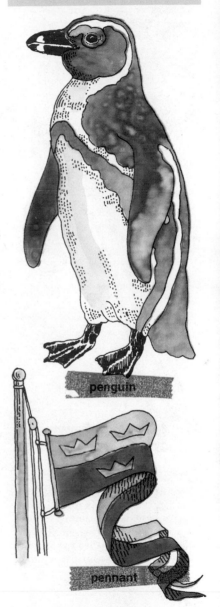

penguin

pennant

pen¹, pen²
Pen¹ comes from an old French word meaning "feather, pen." The word meant "feather" in its older Latin source. **Pen²** meant "enclosure for animals" to the English-speaking people who first used it long ago.

Pennsylvania
The name **Pennsylvania** is formed from a combination of the name Penn and a Latin word that means "wood" or "forest." The place was named for Sir William Penn. He was the father of William Penn, the founder of the colony that became the state of Pennsylvania.

peony

peppermint
Peppermint candy cane

---

perch¹, perch²
Perch¹ comes from an old French word, *perche,* which in turn came from a Latin word meaning "a pole or stick." **Perch²** came from another old French word spelled *perche,* which also had its source in a Latin word. But the Latin word can be traced further still to a Greek word.

ă	pat	ĕ	pet	î	fierce
ā	pay	ē	be	ŏ	pot
â	care	ĭ	pit	ō	go
ä	father	ī	pie	ô	paw, for

oi	oil	ŭ	cut	zh	vision
ōŏ	book	û	fur	ə	ago, item,
ōō	boot	*th*	the		pencil, atom,
yōō	abuse	th	thin		circus
ou	out	hw	which	ər	butter

—*verb* **pensioned, pensioning** To give a pension to: *The company pensioned the woman after her accident on the job.*

pen·ta·gon | pĕn′tə gŏn′ | —*noun, plural* **pentagons** A geometric shape that has five sides and five angles.

pent·house | pĕnt′hous′ | —*noun, plural* **pent·hous·es** | pĕnt′hou′zĭz | An apartment, usually with a terrace, located on the roof of a building.

pe·o·ny | pē′ə nē | —*noun, plural* **peonies** The large pink, red, or white flower of a garden plant.

peo·ple | pē′pəl | —*noun, plural* **people** 1. Human beings. 2. A group of people living in the same country under one national government: *the American people.* 3. *plural* **peoples** A group of people sharing the same religion, culture, and language: *primitive peoples.* 4. **the people** The large group of ordinary people: *the rights of the people.* 5. Family, relatives, or ancestors: *Her people are farmers.*

—*verb* **peopled, peopling** To give a population to: *Thousands of Spaniards peopled the New World.*

pep | pĕp | —*noun* High spirits or energy.

pep·per | pĕp′ər | —*noun, plural* **peppers** 1. A seasoning made from the dried, blackish berries of a vine. Pepper has a very sharp taste. 2. The hollow green or red fruit of a bushy plant. This kind of pepper is eaten as a vegetable or used as a spice. Some kinds have a mild taste, and some have a very sharp taste. —*verb* **peppered, peppering** 1. To season with pepper. 2. To sprinkle or hit with many small things: *They peppered us with pellets of snow.*

pep·per·corn | pĕp′ər kôrn′ | —*noun, plural* **peppercorns** A dried, blackish berry of the pepper vine.

pep·per·mint | pĕp′ər mĭnt′ | —*noun, plural* **peppermints** 1. A plant with a strong, pleasant taste and smell. 2. Oil from this plant, used to flavor candy, chewing gum, and other things. 3. A candy flavored with peppermint.

per | pûr | —*preposition* 1. For every: *forty cents per gallon.* 2. According to: *per your instructions.* 3. By means of; through: *The teacher sent the note per his student.*

per·ceive | pər sēv′ | —*verb* **perceived, perceiving** 1. To become aware of by seeing, hearing, tasting, smelling, or touching: *He perceived the change of color in the sky before the storm.* 2. To get an understanding of: *Try to perceive the meaning of these sentences.*

per cent For or out of each hundred; per hundred: *Twenty-five per cent of the members voted.* Another form of this phrase is **percent.**

per·cent | pər sĕnt′ | —*noun* A form of the phrase **per cent.**

per·cent·age | pər sĕn′tĭj | —*noun, plural* **percentages** 1. A fraction that is understood to have 100 as its denominator; a fraction written or spoken by using the phrase *per cent.* 2. A part of a whole: *A certain percentage of his wages goes for taxes.*

perch¹ | pûrch | —*noun, plural* **perches** 1. A branch or rod that a bird holds with its claws while it is resting. 2. Any resting place, especially one that is up high: *Jed slid down from his perch on the haystack.*

—*verb* **perched, perching** 1. To land or rest on or as if on a perch: *The tiny bird perched on my finger.* 2. To be in a high position: *The village was perched on the top of the hill.*

perch² | pûrch | —*noun, plural* **perch** or **perches** A fish that is much used for food. Some kinds of perch live in fresh water, and others live in salt water.

per·cus·sion instrument | pər kŭsh'ən | A musical instrument, such as a drum, xylophone, or piano, in which sound is made by striking one thing against another.

per·fect | pûr'fĭkt | —*adjective* **1.** Completely free from mistakes; exact: *a perfect copy.* **2.** Without faults or defects: *a perfect piece of marble.* **3.** Completely skilled in a certain job: *She's the perfect carpenter to build this house.* **4.** Excellent and delightful in every way: *perfect weather.*
—*verb* | pər fĕkt' | **perfected, perfecting** To make perfect or complete: *They perfected their plans for the trip.*

per·fec·tion | pər fĕk'shən | —*noun* **1.** The act or process of perfecting: *The perfection of his diving took much practice.* **2.** The condition of being perfect: *The perfection of this weather is all we could have wished for.*

per·fo·rate | pûr'fə rāt' | —*verb* **perforated, perforating** **1.** To punch a hole or holes in: *Perforate the top of the pie to let the steam out.* **2.** To punch rows of holes in something to make it easy to pull apart: *The edges of postage stamps are perforated so that they can be used one at a time.*

per·form | pər fôrm' | —*verb* **performed, performing** **1.** To begin and carry through to the end; do: *Scientists perform experiments. He performed his job perfectly.* **2.** To sing, dance, act, play a musical instrument, or do tricks in front of people; entertain an audience: *They performed a play for their parents. The orchestra performed the symphony.*

per·form·ance | pər fôr'məns | —*noun, plural* **performances** **1.** The act or process of performing: *The race was a fine performance.* **2.** The way in which something or someone works: *Look for good performance when buying a car. Is his job performance good?* **3.** A public entertainment, such as acting, singing, dancing, or playing a musical instrument.

per·form·er | pər fôr'mər | —*noun, plural* **performers** Someone who acts, sings, dances, plays a musical instrument, or entertains an audience in some way.

per·fume | pûr'fyo͞om' | or | pər fyo͞om' | —*noun, plural* **perfumes** **1.** A pleasant-smelling liquid made from flowers. **2.** A pleasant smell.
—*verb* **perfumed, perfuming** To put on or fill with perfume: *She perfumed her wrists.*

per·haps | pər hăps' | —*adverb* Maybe; possibly: *Perhaps he'll come with us.*

per·il | pĕr'əl | —*noun, plural* **perils** **1.** The chance of harm or loss: *His life will be in peril if his parachute doesn't open.* **2.** Something dangerous; a big risk: *The perils of a trip by covered wagon were many.*

pe·rim·e·ter | pə rĭm'ə tər | —*noun, plural* **perimeters** The sum of the lengths of the sides of an area or geometric shape: *That square has a perimeter of sixteen inches.*

pe·ri·od | pîr'ē əd | —*noun, plural* **periods** **1.** A portion of time: *the Civil War period. A period of twelve months is a year. A football game has four periods of play.* **2.** The punctuation mark (.) used at the end of certain sentences and after many abbreviations.

pe·ri·od·ic | pîr'ē ŏd'ĭk | —*adjective* **1.** Happening at regular

percussion instrument
The percussion section of
an orchestra

periods of time: *A pendulum has a periodic motion.* **2.** Taking place from time to time: *There has always been periodic fighting between the two countries.*

pe·ri·od·i·cal | pîr'ē ŏd'ĭ kəl | —*noun, plural* **periodicals** A publication, especially a magazine, that is printed regularly, but less than daily.

per·i·scope | pěr'ĭ skōp' | —*noun, plural* **periscopes** An instrument with mirrors or prisms that allows a view of something that a person cannot see directly. Periscopes are used in submarines.

per·ish | pěr'ĭsh | —*verb* **perished, perishing 1.** To die in a violent way: *Ten people perished in the accident.* **2.** To disappear over a length of time; pass from existence: *The dinosaur perished from the earth.*

per·ish·a·ble | pěr'ĭ shə bəl | —*adjective* Likely to decay or spoil easily: *perishable fruits and vegetables.*

per·i·win·kle¹ | pěr'ĭ wĭng'kəl | —*noun, plural* **periwinkles** A small sea snail that is sometimes eaten as food.

per·i·win·kle² | pěr'ĭ wĭng'kəl | —*noun, plural* **periwinkles** A trailing vine with shiny evergreen leaves and blue flowers.

per·ju·ry | pûr'jə rē | —*noun, plural* **perjuries** In law, the telling of a lie when one has promised to tell the truth.

perk | pûrk | —*verb* **perked, perking** To raise in a smart or brisk way: *The dog perked his ears at the sound of footsteps.*

Phrasal verb **perk up 1.** To become or cause to become lively or bright again: *She perked up at the good news. The hot soup perked him up.* **2.** To make prettier or more attractive: *She perked up the blouse with a new necklace.*

per·ma·nent | pûr'mə nənt | —*adjective* Lasting or meant to last for a long time: *They had a permanent arrangement to walk to school together.*

per·mis·sion | pər mĭsh'ən | —*noun, plural* **permissions** Agreement to let someone do or have something: *The teacher gave Judy permission to leave the room.*

per·mit | pər mĭt' | —*verb* **permitted, permitting 1.** To give permission to; allow: *Smoking is not permitted in the theater. Will you permit me to leave?* **2.** To make possible: *The heavy snow permitted sledding.*

—*noun* | pûr'mĭt | or | pər mĭt' |, *plural* **permits** A written order or license that allows a person to do something: *You need a permit to hunt in these woods.*

per·pen·dic·u·lar | pûr'pən dĭk'yə lər | —*adjective* **1.** Crossing at or making a right angle or angles: *perpendicular lines.* **2.** At right angles to the horizon; vertical: *A skyscraper is perpendicular to the ground.*

—*noun, plural* **perpendiculars** A line or surface that crosses another at right angles.

per·pet·u·al | pər pěch'ōō əl | —*adjective* **1.** Lasting forever: *promises of perpetual friendship; the perpetual ice and snow of the North Pole.* **2.** Repeated again and again or going on without stopping: *perpetual complaining.*

per·plex | pər plěks' | —*verb* **perplexed, perplexing** To confuse or puzzle: *Parts of his story perplexed me.*

per·se·cute | pûr'sĭ kyōot' | —*verb* **persecuted, persecuting** To cause to suffer, especially because of political or religious beliefs: *The Romans persecuted the Christians.*

---

periwinkle¹, periwinkle²
Periwinkle¹ probably comes from an old English word that is made up of a Latin word and an old English form. Periwinkle² came to English through French from Latin.

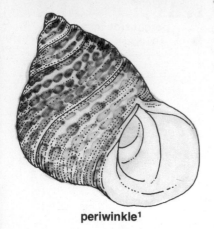

periwinkle¹

perpendicular

ă	pat	ē	pet	î	fierce
ā	pay	ē	be	ŏ	pot
â	care	ĭ	pit	ō	go
ä	father	ī	pie	ô	paw, for
oi	oil	ŭ	cut	zh	vision
ōō	book	û	fur	ə	ago, item,
ōō	boot	th	the		pencil, atom,
yōō	abuse	th	thin		circus
ou	out	hw	which	ər	butter

per·se·cu·tion | pûr′sĭ kyōō′shən | —*noun, plural* **persecutions**
The act of persecuting: *The Romans' persecution of the Christians led to many deaths.*

Per·sian cat | pûr′zhən | A cat with long silky fur, often kept as a pet.

per·sim·mon | pər sĭm′ən | —*noun, plural* **persimmons** An orange-red fruit. Its juicy pulp becomes sweet and good to eat only when it is fully ripe.

per·sist | pər sĭst′ | —*verb* **persisted, persisting** To repeat again and again; insist: *She persisted in saying she was innocent.*

per·sist·ent | pər sĭs′tənt | —*adjective* **1.** Refusing to give up or let go: *A persistent salesman finally sold me the broom.* **2.** Lasting for a long time: *a persistent cold.*

per·son | pûr′sən | —*noun, plural* **persons** **1.** A living human being. **2.** The body of a living human being: *He had only two dollars on his person.* **3.** In grammar, any of the pronouns or verb forms that refer to the speaker (first person), the one or ones spoken to (second person), and someone or something spoken of (third person). For example, in the sentence *I told you about her, I* is in the first person, *you* is in the second person, and *her* is in the third person.

per·son·al | pûr′sə nəl | —*adjective* **1.** Of a certain person; private; one's own: *That was a personal experience and I don't want to talk about it yet.* **2.** Likely to make remarks about another person, often in an unfriendly way: *He always becomes personal in an argument.* **3.** Done or made in person: *She made a personal appearance at the ball.* **4.** Of the body: *personal cleanliness.*

per·son·al·i·ty | pûr′sə năl′ĭ tē | —*noun, plural* **personalities**
1. All the kinds of behavior and feelings that one person has that make that person different from everyone else: *Martin has a pleasing personality.* **2.** A person of fame or importance: *Television personalities were at the opening of the new play.*

per·son·al·ly | pûr′sə nə lē | —*adverb* **1.** In person or by oneself; without the help of others: *I thanked her personally.* **2.** As far as oneself is concerned: *Personally, I can't stand chocolate.* **3.** As a person: *I don't know him personally.* **4.** In a personal way: *Don't take it personally.*

personal pronoun In grammar, a pronoun that indicates the person speaking *(I, me, we, us),* the person spoken to *(you),* or the person or thing spoken of *(he, she, it, they, him, her, them).*

per·son·nel | pûr′sə nĕl′ | —*noun* **1.** The people who work for a company, business, or organization: *Only personnel of the firm can park their cars there.* **2.** The division of a company or organization that hires, trains, and places people to work for the company: *The manager in personnel called a meeting.*

per·spec·tive | pər spĕk′tĭv | —*noun, plural* **perspectives**
1. The way things are drawn on a flat surface so that they appear to be the same as when seen by the eye. **2.** A way of looking at things; point of view: *Try to get another perspective on this problem.*

per·spi·ra·tion | pûr′spə rā′shən | —*noun* **1.** The salty moisture given off through the skin by the sweat glands; sweat: *The perspiration rolled down her face in the hot sun.* **2.** The act or process of perspiring: *One way the body gives off waste material is by perspiration.*

per·spire | pər spīr′ | —*verb* **perspired, perspiring** To give off perspiration; to sweat.

persimmon

perspective

pestle
A pestle in a mortar

petunia

pewter
A pewter mug with a lid

ă	pat	ĕ	pet	î	fierce
ā	pay	ē	be	ŏ	pot
â	care	ĭ	pit	ō	go
ä	father	ī	pie	ô	paw, for

oi	oil	ŭ	cut	zh	vision
ŏŏ	book	û	fur	ə	ago, item,
		th	the		pencil, atom,
		th	thin		circus
		hw	which	ər	butter

per·suade | pər swād′ | —*verb* **persuaded, persuading** To cause someone to do or believe something by arguing, begging, or reasoning; convince: *Heather persuaded us to go to the dance with her.*

per·tain | pər tān′ | —*verb* **pertained, pertaining** To belong to or have to do with; be related to; be connected with: *His answer did not pertain to the question.*

pes·si·mis·tic | pĕs′ə mĭs′tĭk | —*adjective* Likely to take the gloomiest view of one's situation or the world: *He is pessimistic about cleaning the town up after the flood.*

pest | pĕst | —*noun, plural* **pests** **1.** A harmful or troublesome animal or plant. Mosquitoes are pests. Dandelions are pests when they grow in lawns. **2.** An annoying or troublesome person.

pes·ter | pĕs′tər | —*verb* **pestered, pestering** To annoy or bother: *That dog pesters the children on their bicycles.*

pes·tle | pĕs′əl | or | pĕs′təl | —*noun, plural* **pestles** A tool with a rounded end used for crushing or mashing things. A pestle is usually used with a bowl called a mortar.

pet | pĕt | —*noun, plural* **pets** **1.** An animal that a person likes and takes care of. Dogs and cats are often kept as pets. Mice, birds, and even snakes are sometimes kept as pets. **2.** Someone or something that is a favorite: *mother's pet. That project is the scientist's pet.*
—*verb* **petted, petting** To stroke or pat gently: *pet a dog.*

pet·al | pĕt′l | —*noun, plural* **petals** One of the parts of a flower that give it the color and shape by which we know it. Some petals are brightly colored. Others are small and very hard to notice.

pe·ti·tion | pə tĭsh′ən | —*noun, plural* **petitions** **1.** A special request to someone in charge: *a petition for an interview.* **2.** A written request for a right or benefit from someone in charge: *The boys drew up a petition for all the students to sign.*
—*verb* **petitioned, petitioning** To make a formal request: *The parents petitioned for a new stop sign.*

pet·rel | pĕt′rəl | —*noun, plural* **petrels** A small sea bird that flies over the open ocean far from land.

pet·ri·fy | pĕt′rə fī′ | —*verb* **petrified, petrifying, petrifies** **1.** To turn wood or other material into stone. **2.** To daze with fear or surprise: *The thunder rolled and petrified Beth.*

pe·tro·le·um | pə trō′lē əm | —*noun* A kind of dark yellowish-black oil that is found below the ground. Petroleum is easy to set on fire and can burn very quickly. Gasoline, kerosene, and paraffin are made from petroleum.

pet·ti·coat | pĕt′ē kōt′ | —*noun, plural* **petticoats** A skirt or slip worn by girls and women as an undergarment.

pe·tu·nia | pə tōō′nyə | or | pə tyōō′nyə | —*noun, plural* **petunias** A garden plant with white, reddish, or purple flowers shaped like funnels.

pew | pyōō | —*noun, plural* **pews** A bench for people to sit on in a church.

pe·wee | pē′wē | —*noun, plural* **pewees** A small, brownish North American bird. The call of the pewee sounds like its name.

pew·ter | pyōō′tər | —*noun* A kind of metal made from tin, copper, and lead. Pewter is used to make dishes, candlesticks, plates, and other utensils.

Phar·aoh or **phar·aoh** | fâr′ō | or | fā′rō | —*noun, plural*

Pharaohs or **pharaohs** The title of the rulers of ancient Egypt.

phar·ma·cist | fär′mə sĭst | —*noun, plural* **pharmacists** A person who is trained to prepare drugs and medicines; druggist.

phar·ma·cy | fär′mə sē | —*noun, plural* **pharmacies** A place where drugs are prepared and sold; a drugstore.

phase | fāz | —*noun, plural* **phases** 1. A clear or distinct stage of development: *the next phase of our building program.* 2. A part or side: *Look at every phase of this plan.* 3. Any of the forms in which the moon or the planets appear at any given time: *My favorite phase of the moon is when it is full.*

pheas·ant | fĕz′ənt | —*noun, plural* **pheasants** A large, brightly colored bird with a long tail. Pheasants are often hunted as game.

phe·nom·e·na | fĭ nŏm′ə nə | A plural of the noun **phenomenon**.

phe·nom·e·non | fĭ nŏm′ə nŏn′ | —*noun, plural* **phenomena** or **phenomenons** 1. A fact or event that can be seen, heard, or otherwise known: *An earthquake is a natural phenomenon.* 2. Someone or something that is unusual or extraordinary: *Steve is a phenomenon at cards.*

phil·o·den·dron | fĭl′ə dĕn′drən | —*noun, plural* **philodendrons** A climbing plant with glossy evergreen leaves. The philodendron is often grown as a house plant.

phi·los·o·pher | fĭ lŏs′ə fər | —*noun, plural* **philosophers** A person who studies philosophy and seeks wisdom.

phil·o·soph·i·cal | fĭl′ə sŏf′ĭ kəl | —*adjective* 1. Of philosophy: *philosophical textbooks.* 2. Calm, reasonable, and wise: *He has a philosophical way of looking at things.*

phi·los·o·phy | fĭ lŏs′ə fē | —*noun, plural* **philosophies** 1. The study of the truths and laws that rule life and nature. 2. A system of ideas based on this kind of study. 3. A person's own beliefs and opinions about life and the world.

phlox | flŏks | —*noun* A plant with clusters of reddish, purple, or white flowers.

phoe·be | fē′bē | —*noun, plural* **phoebes** A small, grayish North American bird. The call of the phoebe sounds like its name.

Phoe·ni·cia | fə nē′shə | or | fə nĭsh′ə | An ancient country at the eastern end of the Mediterranean Sea.

Phoe·ni·cian | fə nē′shən | or | fə nĭsh′ən | —*noun, plural* **Phoenicians** 1. A person who lived in ancient Phoenicia. 2. The language of the people who lived in Phoenicia.

Phoe·nix | fē′nĭks | The capital of Arizona.

phone | fōn | —*noun, plural* **phones** A telephone.
—*verb* **phoned, phoning** To call by telephone: *Warren phoned to say he wasn't coming to the party.*

pho·net·ic | fə nĕt′ĭk | —*adjective* Of, having to do with, or standing for speech sounds. Phonetic symbols are marks and letters that are used to show how to pronounce words. In the pronunciation of the first syllable of this word, "f" stands for "ph" and "ə" stands for "o."

pho·no·graph | fō′nə grăf′ | or | fō′nə gräf′ | —*noun, plural* **phonographs** A machine that reproduces sound from a groove cut into a record. As the record turns, a special needle set in the arm of the machine picks up the recorded sounds. The phonograph then plays these sounds through loudspeakers.

phos·pho·rus | fŏs′fər əs | —*noun* A substance that is found in white, yellow, red, and black forms. Phosphorus shines in the dark and is poisonous. It is one of the chemical elements and is

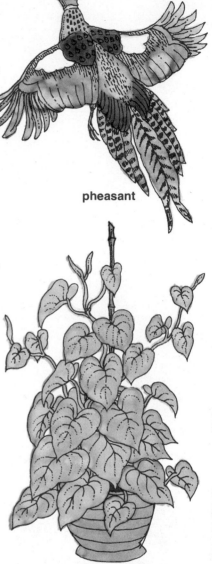

pheasant

philodendron

phlox

used to make matches, fireworks, and smoke bombs. Phosphorus is also widely used for detergents and fertilizers.

pho·to |fō′tō| —*noun, plural* **photos** A photograph.

pho·to·graph |fō′tə grăf′| or |fō′tə gräf′| —*noun, plural* **photographs** A picture formed on a surface that is sensitive to light by a camera. This surface is developed by chemicals to give a positive proof.

—*verb* **photographed, photographing 1.** To make a photograph of; take a picture of: *Alix photographed the house.* **2.** To be a subject for a photograph: *Some models photograph better than others.*

pho·tog·ra·pher |fə tŏg′rə fər| —*noun, plural* **photographers** Someone who takes photographs, especially as a job.

pho·to·graph·ic |fō′tə grăf′ĭk| —*adjective* Of or used in photography or a photograph: *a photographic lens.*

pho·tog·ra·phy |fə tŏg′rə fē| —*noun* The art or job of taking and making photographs.

phras·al verb |frā′zəl| A verb phrase in which the first word is the main-entry word used as a verb. The second word of the phrase is usually a preposition but may also be a conjunction or an adverb. For example, *pass out, set aside, make up,* and *pick up* are phrasal verbs.

phrase |frāz| —*noun, plural* **phrases 1.** A group of words that means something but is not a complete sentence. For example, *on the table* is a phrase. **2.** A short saying. For example, *from the frying pan into the fire* is a phrase.

—*verb* **phrased, phrasing** To express something by speaking or writing: *Dad phrased his answer carefully.*

phys·i·cal |fĭz′ĭ kəl| —*adjective* **1.** Of the body rather than the mind or feelings: *physical comfort.* **2.** Solid or material: *That rock is a physical object.* **3.** Of matter that is not living or of energy rather than living matter: *the physical sciences.* **4.** Of or having to do with the natural features of the earth's surface: *A physical map shows the mountains, rivers, and other natural features but does not show roads or anything made by man.*

phy·si·cian |fĭ zĭsh′ən| —*noun, plural* **physicians** A person who has a license to treat and care for people who are sick or hurt; a medical doctor.

phy·sics |fĭz′ĭks| —*noun* The science of matter and energy and the laws that rule them. Physics deals with light, motion, sound, heat, electricity, and force.

pi |pī| —*noun, plural* **pis** A number that equals the quotient of the circumference of a circle divided by its diameter. Pi is equal to about 3.1416. Its symbol is π.

♦ *These sound alike* **pi, pie.**

pi·an·ist |pē ăn′ĭst| or |pē′ə nĭst| —*noun, plural* **pianists** Someone who plays the piano.

pi·an·o |pē ăn′ō| —*noun, plural* **pianos** A large musical instrument with a keyboard and wire strings of different lengths and thicknesses. When a key on the keyboard is struck by the player's finger, the movement makes a hammer that is covered with felt hit a metal string. This produces a tone.

pic·co·lo |pĭk′ə lō′| —*noun, plural* **piccolos** A small flute. It produces sounds about an octave higher than an ordinary flute.

pick¹ |pĭk| —*verb* **picked, picking 1.** To choose or select: *She picked the right person for the job.* **2.** To gather with the fingers; pluck: *She went to pick flowers. We must pick the apples when they*

piano

pick¹, pick²
Pick¹ is probably from an old French word that meant "to prick or pierce." **Pick²** comes from an old English word that was used to mean "sharp object."

ă	pat	ĕ	pet	î	fierce
ā	pay	ē	be	ŏ	pot
â	care	ĭ	pit	ō	go
ä	father	ī	pie	ô	paw, for
oi	oil	ŭ	cut	zh	vision
ōō	book	û	fur	ə	ago, item,
ōō	boot	th	the		pencil, atom,
yōō	abuse	th	thin		circus
ou	out	hw	which	ər	butter

are ripe. **3.** To dig at with something pointed: *He used a toothpick to pick his teeth. It is hard to pick the ground in winter.* **4.** To cause on purpose; provoke: *Are you trying to pick a fight with me?* **5.** To open without using a key: *He picked the lock with a piece of wire.* **6.** To steal the contents of: *He picked my pocket.* **7.** To pluck the strings of a musical instrument in order to play a tune: *He picked a lively song on his guitar.*

   Phrasal verbs **pick at 1.** To eat in small bites, without much appetite. **2.** To criticize someone for small, unimportant things. **pick on** To tease or bully: *Stop picking on me.* **pick out** To choose or select: *I helped her pick out wallpaper for her living room.* **pick up 1.** To lift up or take up: *He picked up his suitcase and walked toward the train.* **2.** To take on: *We will not pick up a person walking along the road.* **3.** To go faster: *The truck picked up speed as it went down the hill.* **4.** To receive: *He picked up radio signals from a ship in trouble.* **5.** To put things back in order; clean up: *He finally picked up his room because he had no place left to sit down.* —*noun, plural* **picks 1.** A choice: *She took her pick of the tomatoes.* **2.** The best one: *This puppy is the pick of the litter.*

   Idiom **pick and choose** To choose or select with care.

pick² | pĭk | —*noun, plural* **picks 1.** A tool for loosening or breaking up soil or other hard material. It is made up of a slightly curved bar pointed at both ends and fitted onto a long wooden handle **2.** A toothpick or any pointed tool for breaking, piercing, or picking. **3.** A small, flat piece of plastic or bone that is used to pluck the strings of an instrument: *He used a pick when he played the guitar.*

pick·er·el | pĭk′ər əl | —*noun, plural* **pickerel** or **pickerels** A freshwater fish that looks like the pike but is smaller.

pick·et | pĭk′ĭt | —*noun, plural* **pickets 1.** A pointed stake or spike. A picket is driven into the ground to hold up a fence, fasten down a tent, or hold an animal in place. **2.** Someone who walks in front of a place of work to protest something during a strike: *The pickets were quiet, but tried to keep people from going into the store.*

   —*verb* **picketed, picketing** To protest against during a strike: *We picketed the factory to ask for better working conditions and more pay.*

pick·le | pĭk′əl | —*noun, plural* **pickles** Any food that has been preserved and flavored in vinegar or salt water. Some pickles are made of cucumbers, cooked beets, and other vegetables, with different spices added.

pick·pock·et | pĭk′pŏk′ĭt | —*noun, plural* **pickpockets** Someone who steals from a person's pocket or purse.

pick·up | pĭk′ŭp′ | —*noun, plural* **pickups 1.** The act of picking up packages, mail, freight, or passengers for delivery to another place: *The truck made a pickup at 2:00.* **2.** The ability to increase speed quickly: *a car with a good pickup.* **3.** A pickup truck.

pickup truck A small, light truck with an open body and low sides, used for carrying small loads.

pic·nic | pĭk′nĭk | —*noun, plural* **picnics** A meal eaten outdoors.

   —*verb* **picnicked, picnicking, picnics** To have a picnic: *We picnicked at the beach.*

pic·ture | pĭk′chər | —*noun, plural* **pictures 1.** A painting, drawing, or photograph that represents someone or something: *This book has beautiful color pictures of animals.* **2.** The image on a

picket
Above: Pickets marching in protest
Below: A picket fence

television screen: *We need to get the TV repaired because the picture is dim.* **3.** A clear description given in words: *The way you picture him makes him seem very interesting.* **4.** A good likeness or example: *Bob is the picture of his father. She is a picture of happiness.* **5.** A motion picture or movie: *What picture is playing downtown?*

—*verb* **pictured, picturing 1.** To make a picture of: *The painter pictured sea gulls against the setting sun.* **2.** To imagine: *I picture her as being short and fat.* **3.** To describe clearly and in detail: *I pictured the house to them as well as I could.*

pic·tur·esque | pĭk′chə rĕsk′ | —*adjective* Like or making one think of a picture; interesting or very attractive: *a picturesque cottage; the picturesque country in spring.*

pie | pī | —*noun, plural* **pies** A food that has a filling such as fruit, meat, or custard held in pastry and baked. A pie is often covered with a crust or some other topping.

♦ *These sound alike* **pie, pi.**

piece | pēs | —*noun, plural* **pieces 1.** A part that has been cut or separated from a whole: *a piece of pie.* **2.** A part of a set: *There are sixty pieces in this set of china.* **3.** Something that is part of a larger quantity or group: *a piece of wood; a piece of land.* **4.** An artistic, musical, or literary work: *He played a piece on the piano. She is going to say a piece in front of the class.* **5.** An example; an instance: *What a fine piece of work.* **6.** A coin: *a gold piece.*

—*verb* **pieced, piecing** To join the parts of: *We had fun trying to piece the puzzle together.*

♦ *These sound alike* **piece, peace.**

pier | pîr | —*noun, plural* **piers 1.** A platform built over water from a shore. It is used as a landing place or protection for boats or ships. **2.** A pillar or other supporting structure that holds up a bridge.

♦ *These sound alike* **pier, peer.**

pierce | pîrs | —*verb* **pierced, piercing** To run through or into; puncture; penetrate: *Arrows pierced the target. A nail pierced the tire. A cry pierced the still night.*

Pierre | pîr | The capital of South Dakota.

pig | pĭg | —*noun, plural* **pigs** An animal with short legs, hoofs, and bristles. The pig has a blunt snout used for digging. Pigs are often raised for meat and other products.

pi·geon | pĭj′ĭn | —*noun, plural* **pigeons** A bird with short legs, a plump body, and a small head. Pigeons are common everywhere, even in cities. They can be raised for food or trained to carry messages.

pig·gy·back | pĭg′ē băk′ | —*adverb* On the shoulders or back of another: *The baby likes to ride piggyback.*

pig·let | pĭg′lĭt | —*noun, plural* **piglets** A young, small pig.

pig·ment | pĭg′mənt | —*noun, plural* **pigments** A material or substance used to give color to something: *We mixed different pigments to get the paint the exact color we wanted.*

pig·pen | pĭg′pĕn′ | —*noun, plural* **pigpens** A fenced area where pigs are kept.

pig·tail | pĭg′tāl′ | —*noun, plural* **pigtails** A braid of hair at the back of the head.

pike | pīk | —*noun, plural* **pike** or **pikes** A large freshwater fish with a narrow body and long jaws. The pike is often caught for sport.

pier

pig

pigeon

ă	pat	ĕ	pet	î	fierce
ā	pay	ē	be	ŏ	pot
â	care	ĭ	pit	ō	go
ä	father	ī	pie	ô	paw, for
oi	oil	ŭ	cut	zh	vision
ōō	book	û	fur	ə	ago, item,
ōō	boot	*th*	the		pencil, atom,
yōō	abuse	th	thin		circus
ou	out	hw	which	ər	butter

pile¹ | pīl | —*noun, plural* **piles 1.** A lot of things heaped or stacked together, one on top of another; a heap: *a pile of firewood; a pile of sawdust; a pile of newspapers.* **2.** A large amount: *I've got a pile of homework to do tonight.*
—*verb* **piled, piling 1.** To place or stack in a heap: *They piled the dishes in the sink.* **2.** To cover or load with a pile: *I piled a tray with apples. I piled papers on my desk.*

pile² | pīl | —*noun, plural* **piles** A heavy beam of wood, concrete, or steel that is driven into the ground as a support or foundation for a structure: *They used hundreds of piles as a foundation for the bridge.*

pile³ | pīl | —*noun, plural* **piles** The soft, thick fibers of yarn that make the surface of a carpet or of materials like velvet.

pil·grim | pĭl′grĭm | —*noun, plural* **pilgrims 1.** Someone who travels to a religious shrine or some other sacred place: *Pilgrims still go to see where Christ lived.* **2. Pilgrim** One of the English settlers who founded a colony in Massachusetts in 1620. The Pilgrims established the first permanent settlement in New England.

pill | pĭl | —*noun, plural* **pills** A small ball or tablet of medicine to be taken by mouth.

pil·lar | pĭl′ər | —*noun, plural* **pillars 1.** A column that is used to hold up or decorate a building or that stands alone: *Pillars supported the roof of the house. There is a monument in town that looks like a pillar.* **2.** Something like a pillar in size or shape: *A pillar of flame rose from the volcano.*

pil·lo·ry | pĭl′ə rē | —*noun, plural* **pillories** A wooden framework on a post with holes for the head and hands. People who had done something wrong used to be locked into pillories in the public square as a punishment.

pil·low | pĭl′ō | —*noun, plural* **pillows** A cloth case stuffed with feathers, foam rubber, or other soft material. A pillow is used to support a person's head while resting or sleeping.

pil·low·case | pĭl′ō kās′ | —*noun, plural* **pillowcases** A cloth cover with an open end, used to fit over a pillow.

pi·lot | pī′lət | —*noun, plural* **pilots 1.** Someone who operates an aircraft or spacecraft. **2.** An experienced person who steers large ships in and out of a harbor or through dangerous waters.
—*verb* **piloted, piloting** To operate and set the course of a plane, ship, or other vehicle.

pi·men·to | pĭ mĕn′tō | —*noun, plural* **pimentos** A form of the word **pimiento.**

pi·mien·to | pĭ mĕn′tō | —*noun, plural* **pimientos** A red pepper with a mild taste. It is often used to stuff olives or to give color and flavor to foods. Another form of this word is **pimento.**

pim·ple | pĭm′pəl | —*noun, plural* **pimples** A small swelling on the skin, sometimes red and sore, and often filled with pus.

pin | pĭn | —*noun, plural* **pins 1.** A short, straight, stiff piece of wire with a round head and a sharp point. A pin is used to fasten one thing to another. **2.** Anything like a pin in shape or use: *safety pins; pins to hold hair in place.* **3.** An ornament fastened to clothing by a pin or clasp: *I wore a diamond pin on the collar of my dress.* **4.** A bar or rod made of wood, plastic, or metal that fastens or supports things, especially by passing through or into holes: *We need pins for those hinges.* **5.** One of the ten wooden clubs shaped like a bottle at which a ball is rolled in bowling.

pile¹, pile², pile³
Pile¹ comes originally from a Latin word meaning "pillar." It traveled through French, in which it meant "heap, heap of stone," before arriving in English. **Pile²** meant "pointed stake of wood" to English-speaking people of long ago. It came from a Latin word referring to a kind of spear. **Pile³** comes from the Latin word for "hair."

pilgrim
Pilgrims in Massachusetts

pillar

—*verb* **pinned, pinning** **1.** To fasten or attach with a pin: *She pinned the flower to her coat.* **2.** To cause to be unable to move: *The tree pinned Jim to the ground.*

Idiom **on pins and needles** Anxious or nervous: *I'm on pins and needles about the big exam next week.*

pin·a·fore | pĭn′ə fôr′ | or | pĭn′ə fōr′ | —*noun, plural* **pinafores** A garment without sleeves that looks like an apron.

pi·ña·ta | pĭn yä′tə | —*noun, plural* **piñatas** A colorfully decorated container filled with candy and toys and hung from the ceiling. In some countries it is a Christmas tradition for a child to be blindfolded and given a stick to try and hit the piñata and break it open.

pinch | pĭnch | —*verb* **pinched, pinching** **1.** To squeeze between the thumb and fingers or between edges: *The cat's tail got pinched between the door and the frame when I closed the door.* **2.** To squeeze so hard as to cause pain: *The shoes pinched her feet.* **3.** To make wrinkled: *She had a face pinched by fear and the cold.* —*noun, plural* **pinches** **1.** A squeeze or other pressure caused by pressing between the thumb and a finger or between edges: *The crab gave him a pinch on the toe with his claw.* **2.** The amount that can be held between the thumb and a finger: *a pinch of salt.* **3.** A time of trouble; an emergency: *He knew his parents would help him out in a pinch.*

pinch-hit | pĭnch′hĭt′ | —*verb* **pinch-hit, pinch-hitting** In baseball, to bat for another player.

pin·cush·ion | pĭn′koŏsh′ən | —*noun, plural* **pincushions** A small, firm cushion or ball in which pins and needles are stuck when they are not being used.

pine | pīn | —*noun, plural* **pines** **1.** An evergreen tree that has cones and clusters of leaves shaped like needles. There are many kinds of pines. **2.** The wood of a pine tree.

pine·ap·ple | pīn′ăp′əl | —*noun, plural* **pineapples** A large, juicy tropical fruit. Pineapples have a rough, thorny skin and a tuft of narrow, prickly leaves at the top.

Ping-Pong | pĭng′pông′ | or | pĭng′pŏng′ | —*noun* The trademark for the equipment used in the game of table tennis. The name Ping-Pong is often used to refer to the game of table tennis itself.

pink | pĭngk | —*noun, plural* **pinks** **1.** A light or pale red. **2.** A garden plant that has white or reddish flowers with a pleasant, spicy smell. —*adjective* **pinker, pinkest** Light red or pale red.

pink·ish | pĭng′kĭsh | —*adjective* Somewhat pink.

pi·ñon | pĭn′yən | or | pĭn′yŏn′ | —*noun, plural* **piñons** A pine tree of western North America. The seeds of the piñon are like small nuts and are good to eat. Another form of this word is **pinyon.**

pint | pīnt | —*noun, plural* **pints** A unit of measurement equal to sixteen fluid ounces, or one-half quart. In the metric system, a pint equals 0.47 liters.

pin·to | pĭn′tō | —*noun, plural* **pintos** A horse with spots or other markings that are not regular. —*adjective* Having spots or markings that are not regular: *a pinto pony.*

pin·yon | pĭn′yən | or | pĭn′yŏn′ | —*noun, plural* **pinyons** A form of the word **piñon.**

pineapple
Plant *(above)* and fruit cut in half *(below)*

pink

ă	pat	ĕ	pet	î	fierce
ā	pay	ē	be	ŏ	pot
â	care	ĭ	pit	ō	go
ä	father	ī	pie	ô	paw, for
oi	oil	ŭ	cut	zh	vision
oŏ	book	û	fur	ə	ago, item,
ōō	boot	th	the		pencil, atom,
yōō	abuse	th	thin		circus
ou	out	hw	which	ər	butter

pi·o·neer | pī′ə **nîr′** | —*noun, plural* **pioneers** **1.** A person who is the first to enter and settle a region and open it up for others. **2.** A person who leads the way or is first in a field of science or research: *a pioneer in the development of a polio vaccine.*
—*verb* **pioneered, pioneering** **1.** To explore, open up, or settle a region: *Her father pioneered those mountains. His family pioneered North Dakota.* **2.** To take part in developing something new: *They pioneered the flight of a spacecraft to Mars.*

pipe | pīp | —*noun, plural* **pipes** **1.** A tube or hollow cylinder through which a liquid or gas flows. **2.** An object used for smoking. A pipe has a hollow tube with a mouthpiece at one end and at the other a small bowl to hold tobacco. **3.** A musical instrument shaped like a tube that is played by blowing air into one end. Flutes and clarinets are pipes.
—*verb* **piped, piping** **1.** To carry or send by means of a pipe: *He piped water into his fields from the river.* **2.** To play music on a pipe: *He piped a lively tune and everyone danced.*

pipe·line | **pīp′**līn′ | —*noun, plural* **pipelines** A channel of pipe used to carry water, oil, natural gas, and other substances over long distances.

pi·ra·nha | pĭ **rän′**yə | —*noun, plural* **piranhas** A small freshwater fish of tropical South America. Piranhas have sharp teeth and are very fierce. A group of piranhas can destroy a large animal very quickly.

pi·rate | **pī′**rĭt | —*noun, plural* **pirates** A person who robs ships at sea.

pis·ta·chi·o | pĭ **stăsh′**ē ō′ | —*noun, plural* **pistachios** A small nut with a hard shell and a sweet green kernel. Also called *pistachio nut.*

pis·til | **pĭs′**təl | —*noun, plural* **pistils** The female part of a flower. The pistil has a part that receives pollen and a part in which seeds develop.
♦ *These sound alike* **pistil, pistol.**

pis·tol | **pĭs′**təl | —*noun, plural* **pistols** A small firearm that can be held and fired with one hand.
♦ *These sound alike* **pistol, pistil.**

pis·ton | **pĭs′**tən | —*noun, plural* **pistons** A circular block or disk that fits snugly into a hollow cylinder and moves back and forth. In many engines, a piston moves back and forth by the pressure of a fluid such as oil. In a pump, a piston moves or compresses a fluid.

pit¹ | pĭt | —*noun, plural* **pits** **1.** A hole in the ground that is either natural or man-made: *a barbecue pit. We had a pit dug for a swimming pool.* **2.** Any hollow place on the surface of something: *She has pits on her face because she had smallpox.*
—*verb* **pitted, pitting** **1.** To make holes or depressions in: *Bullets have pitted the castle's walls.* **2.** To mark with small scars: *Smallpox pitted his face during his childhood.* **3.** To set in competition; match: *This tournament pits one school against another.*

pit² | pĭt | —*noun, plural* **pits** The single hard seed of some fruits, such as a peach or cherry.
—*verb* **pitted, pitting** To remove the pits from.

pitch¹ | pĭch | —*noun* A sticky, dark, thick substance made from tar or petroleum. Pitch is used to make roofs waterproof and also to pave streets.

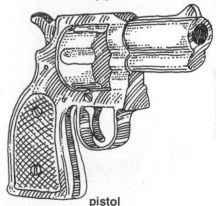

pipeline
Above: Oil pipeline in Alaska
Below: A closer view of an oil pipeline

pistol

---

pit¹, pit²
Pit¹ comes from a Latin word meaning "a well, a pit." **Pit²** was taken from the word used in Dutch about the twelfth through fifteenth centuries to refer to a pit in fruit.

pitch¹, pitch²
Pitch¹ came from a Latin word that meant "pitch" before appearing long ago in English. **Pitch²** comes from the word used in English about 1100–1500 to mean "to fix or set."

pitcher¹, pitcher²
Pitcher¹ was formed from **pitch²**. Pitcher² can be traced back much further than most other words. We think it may have come from a very old Egyptian word that meant "a container to hold oil." Traveling through Greek and Latin, it came to mean "goblet," which is a kind of drinking glass. Finally it appeared in French and then in English.

pitcher¹

pitcher²

pitch² | pĭch | —*verb* **pitched, pitching** **1.** To throw; hurl; toss: *We like to pitch horseshoes. He pitched the ball to the batter.* **2.** To put up: *I pitched a tent. We pitched camp by the river.* **3.** To fall forward: *He missed his footing and pitched headfirst down the lawn.* **4.** To plunge back and forth: *Heavy storms made the ship pitch.* —*noun, plural* **pitches** **1.** An act of pitching; a toss: *My pitch missed the wastebasket.* **2.** A throw of the ball in baseball. **3.** A degree or level: *The New Year's Eve party reached the highest pitch of excitement just before midnight.* **4.** A slope downward; slant: *the steep pitch of the roof.* **5.** In music, the high or low quality of a sound.

pitch·er¹ | pĭch′ ər | —*noun, plural* **pitchers** The baseball player who pitches the ball to the batter.

pitch·er² | pĭch′ ər | —*noun, plural* **pitchers** **1.** A container used to hold and pour out liquids. A pitcher has a handle on one side and a spout on the other. **2. a.** A pitcher with something in it: *A pitcher of milk is on the table.* **b.** The amount that a pitcher holds: *He drank the whole pitcher of lemonade.*

pitcher plant A plant with leaves that are shaped like pitchers. The leaves contain a liquid in which insects are trapped.

pitch·fork | pĭch′fôrk′ | —*noun, plural* **pitchforks** A large fork with sharp prongs that are far apart. A pitchfork is used to move hay or straw.

pith | pĭth | —*noun* The soft substance in the center of the stems of many plants.

pit·i·ful | pĭt′ĭ fəl | —*adjective* Arousing pity, sorrow, and sympathy: *The cold, hungry, shaking child was a pitiful sight.*

pi·ty | pĭt′ē | —*noun, plural* **pities** **1.** A feeling of sorrow for another's suffering: *We felt pity for the orphaned children.* **2.** A cause for regret or sorrow: *It's a pity that she cut her hair so short.*

piv·ot | pĭv′ət | —*noun, plural* **pivots** A short rod or shaft about which something turns or swings: *The hands of a clock turn on a pivot.* —*verb* **pivoted, pivoting** To swing or turn on or as if on a pivot: *The admiral ordered that the cannons be pivoted to get a better shot at the enemy ship. He pivoted under the basket and was ready for a shot.*

piz·za | pēt′zə | —*noun, plural* **pizzas** A baked food, originally Italian, made up of a crust like a pie covered with tomatoes, cheese, and other mixtures, and seasonings.

place | plās | —*noun, plural* **places** **1.** A particular area or spot: *That is the place on my foot that hurts.* **2.** A city or other locality: *What place were you born in?* **3.** A dwelling or residence: *Come over to my place for dinner.* **4.** An area or building used for a special purpose: *A university is a place of learning.* **5.** A space for one person to sit or stand: *Set an extra place at the table. Keep my place in line.* **6.** A duty or right: *It's not my place to tell him what to do.* **7.** Position or rank: *Mother's pie won first place at the fair.* **8.** The point to which one has read in a book: *Mark your place with a piece of paper.* —*verb* **placed, placing** **1.** To put in a particular spot, position, or order: *The United States placed a spaceship on the moon. Please place the dishes on the table. Place these words in alphabetical order.* **2.** To remember where or how something or someone was first seen or met: *His face looks familiar, but I can't place him.* **3.** To finish a contest in a certain order: *He placed third in the race.*

ă	pat	ĕ	pet	î	fierce
ā	pay	ē	be	ŏ	pot
â	care	ĭ	pit	ō	go
ä	father	ī	pie	ô	paw, for
oi	oil	ŭ	cut	zh	vision
ŏŏ	book	û	fur	ə	ago, item,
ōō	boot	*th*	the		pencil, atom,
yōō	abuse	th	thin		circus
ou	out	hw	which	ər	butter

***Idioms* in place of** Instead of. **take place 1.** To happen: *Sometimes changes take place very slowly.* **2.** To be set in a particular time or region: *This story takes place in England during the Middle Ages.* **take the place of** To be a substitute for.

plac·id | **plăs′ĭd** | —*adjective* Calm or peaceful: *She has a placid personality. The sea is placid today.*

plague | plāg | —*noun, plural* **plagues 1.** A very serious disease that spreads rapidly from person to person. **2.** Something that causes great trouble or misery: *A plague of locusts devoured the farmer's crops.* **3.** A cause of annoyance; bother; nuisance: *Stop being a plague with your silly questions.*
—*verb* **plagued, plaguing** To bother, pester, or annoy: *He plagues me with his constant complaining.*

plaid | plăd | —*noun, plural* **plaids 1.** A pattern of squares formed by stripes of different widths and colors that cross one another; a tartan. **2.** A fabric that has such a pattern. Plaid is used for making scarfs, skirts, and other articles of clothing.

plain | plān | —*adjective* **plainer, plainest 1.** Easy to understand: *Her meaning was very plain.* **2.** Open to view; clear; distinct: *The mountain stood out plain against the sky.* **3.** Not fancy; simple: *We are used to eating plain food.* **4.** Ordinary or average: *Her car is a plain old model.* **5.** Not beautiful or handsome: *She is a plain girl.* **6.** Without anything added; pure; natural: *Please give me a glass of plain water.* **7.** Frank; direct; outspoken: *plain talk.* **8.a.** Without a pattern or design; all of one color: *plain wallpaper; a plain fabric.* **b.** Not elaborate; without ornaments: *She had on a plain silk dress.*
—*noun, plural* **plains** A large, flat area of land without any trees.
♦ *These sound alike* **plain, plane.**

plan | plăn | —*noun, plural* **plans 1.** An idea of what to do or how to do it that has been thought out ahead of time: *What are your plans for Saturday?* **2.** A drawing that shows how to make or build something: *plans for our new house; plans for a nuclear submarine.*
—*verb* **planned, planning 1.** To think out what to do or how to do it ahead of time: *We like to plan our summer vacation during the winter.* **2.** To make a drawing of something to be built or made: *The architect is now planning five different kinds of houses for the land.*

plane¹ | plān | —*noun, plural* **planes 1.** A smooth, flat surface, usually level. **2.** A stage of development: *He reached a high plane of success.* **3.** An airplane.
—*adjective* **1.** Lying in a plane: *a plane curve; a plane figure.* **2.** Level; flat: *a plane surface.*
♦ *These sound alike* **plane, plain.**

plane² | plān | —*noun, plural* **planes** A hand tool with a blade that can be adjusted. The blade of a plane sticks out from the bottom. A plane is used to shave down rough spots in wood: *We used the plane to smooth the edge of the door where it was sticking.*
—*verb* **planed, planing** To smooth or shave with a plane.
♦ *These sound alike* **plane, plain.**

plane³ | plān | —*noun, plural* **planes** A tree with leaves shaped like maple leaves and seed clusters shaped like a ball. Plane trees are often used as shade trees in cities.
♦ *These sound alike* **plane, plain.**

plan·et | **plăn′ĭt** | —*noun, plural* **planets** A heavenly body that

plaid
A plaid shirt

plane¹, plane², plane³
The Latin adjective meaning "flat, smooth" formed two nouns. One meant "a flat surface" and was borrowed into English as **plane¹**. The other, meaning "a smoothing tool," was borrowed as **plane²**. **Plane³** came through French from Latin. The Latin word came from a Greek word meaning "broad," from the broad leaves of the tree.

planet
The planet Jupiter

moves in an orbit around the sun. There are nine planets that orbit the sun in our solar system. One of the planets is Earth.

plan·e·tar·i·um | plăn′ĭ târ′ē əm | —*noun, plural* **planetariums** A building that has special equipment to show the movements of the sun, moon, planets, and stars. In a planetarium the heavens are shown by projecting lights on the inside of a ceiling shaped like a dome.

plank | plăngk | —*noun, plural* **planks** A thick, wide, long piece of wood that has been sawed: *He needs planks for the floor.*

plank·ton | plăngk′tən | —*noun* Tiny plants and animals that float or drift in great numbers in salt or fresh water. Many water animals feed on plankton.

plant | plănt | or | plänt | —*noun, plural* **plants** **1.** A living thing that is not an animal. Most plants are able to make their own food, and they cannot move from place to place as animals do. Flowers, trees, vegetables, grasses, ferns, mushrooms, and algae are plants. **2.** A plant that does not have a woody stem; a plant that is not a tree or a shrub. **3.** A factory where something is made: *My father works at the electric power plant.*
—*verb* **planted, planting** **1.** To put in the ground or in earth to grow: *We planted marigold seeds in pots. The class planted a tree in the yard at school.* **2.** To fix or set firmly: *I planted my feet on the ground and wouldn't move.* **3.** To cause to take hold or develop; introduce: *The teacher planted new ideas in their minds.*

plan·tain¹ | plăn′tən | —*noun* A plant like a weed with narrow clusters of small green or whitish flowers.

plan·tain² | plăn′tən | —*noun, plural* **plantains** A fruit that is very much like a banana but not as sweet.

plan·ta·tion | plăn tā′shən | —*noun, plural* **plantations** A large farm or estate on which crops are grown and cared for by workers who also live on the farm. Cotton, sugar, tobacco, and rubber are among things grown on plantations.

plant·er | plăn′tər | or | plän′tər | —*noun, plural* **planters** **1.** Someone or something that plants, especially a tool or machine for planting seed. **2.** The owner of a plantation. **3.** A decorative container for growing plants.

plas·ma | plăz′mə | —*noun* The clear, yellowish liquid part of the blood in which cells are suspended.

plas·ter | plăs′tər | or | plä′stər | —*noun, plural* **plasters** A mixture of sand, lime, and water that hardens when dry. Plaster forms a smooth surface and is used to cover ceilings and walls.
—*verb* **plastered, plastering** **1.** To cover with plaster: *We plastered the walls and ceilings of our new house.* **2.** To cover as if with plaster: *He plastered posters all over the walls of his room.*

plas·tic | plăs′tĭk | —*noun, plural* **plastics** Any of a large number of materials made from chemicals and used for making things. When it is hot, plastic can be formed into films and objects of almost any shape or drawn into fibers for making nylon and other similar materials.
—*adjective* **1.** Able to be shaped or molded: *Clay is a plastic material.* **2.** Made of plastic: *a plastic cup; a plastic toy.*

plate | plāt | —*noun, plural* **plates** **1.** A dish that is round, but not deep, from which food is eaten. **2.** The food on such a dish: *Finish your plate and then you may leave the table.* **3.** A thin, flat sheet or piece of metal or other material: *a plate of armor; a plate of glass.* **4.** A piece of flat metal on which something is stamped,

---

plantain¹, plantain²
Plantain¹ comes from the Latin word for "sole of the foot," because of the broad leaves of the plant. The word traveled through French before arriving in English. **Plantain²** came from a different form of the Latin word for **plane³**, the tree, and appeared in Spanish before appearing in English.

plantation
A coffee plantation in South America

ă	pat	ĕ	pet	î	fierce
ā	pay	ē	be	ŏ	pot
â	care	ĭ	pit	ō	go
ä	father	ī	pie	ô	paw, for
oi	oil	ŭ	cut	zh	vision
ōo	book	û	fur	ə	ago, item,
ōō	boot	*th*	the		pencil, atom,
yōo	abuse	th	thin		circus
ou	out	hw	which	ər	butter

printed, or engraved: *a license plate; a name plate.* **5. the plate** In baseball, home plate.

—verb **plated, plating** To cover or coat with a thin layer of metal: *The jeweler plated the coffee pot with silver.*

pla·teau |plă tō′| *—noun, plural* **plateaus** A flat area that is higher than the land around it.

plat·form |plăt′fôrm′| *—noun, plural* **platforms 1.** A floor or flat surface higher than a connecting area: *a speakers' platform; the platform of a railroad station.* **2.** A formal statement of principles or beliefs, as by a political party or candidate.

plat·i·num |plăt′n əm| *—noun* A valuable, silver-white metal that does not tarnish. Platinum is used for jewelry and in dental work. It is one of the chemical elements.

plat·ter |plăt′ər| *—noun, plural* **platters 1.** A large, shallow dish or plate for serving food. **2.** The amount held by such a dish or plate: *a platter of fried fish.*

plat·y |plăt′ē| *—noun, plural* **platies** or **platys** A small, brightly colored tropical fish. Platies are often kept in home aquariums.

plat·y·pus |plăt′ə pəs| *—noun, plural* **platypuses** A furry water animal of Australia. The platypus has webbed feet and a bill like a duck's. It is one of the few mammals that lay eggs.

play |plā| *—verb* **played, playing 1.** To have fun; amuse oneself: *The children went outdoors to play. Susan likes to play with dolls.* **2.** To take part in a game or another amusement: *We want to play baseball. Our team plays next week. The children are playing house.* **3.** To act the part or role of on or as if on a stage: *He played the good guy.* **4.** To act in a certain way: *You're not playing fair.* **5.** To give forth or make music: *He found a station on his radio that played popular music. The band will play next.*

—noun, plural **plays 1.** A story that is written to be acted on the stage: *a play by Shakespeare. We went to the opening of a new play last night.* **2.** An activity taken part in for fun or enjoyment: *All work and no play make Jack a dull boy.* **3.** A move, turn, or act in a game: *Beth gets the first play this time. Play begins with the kickoff.* **4.** Action or use: *fair or foul play.*

play·er |plā′ər| *—noun, plural* **players 1.** A person who takes part in a game or sport: *There are nine players on a baseball team.* **2.** An actor: *The players performed on a stage without scenery.* **3.** A person who plays a musical instrument: *He is the tuba player in our band.* **4.** A machine that reproduces sound: *a record player.*

play·ful |plā′fəl| *—adjective* **1.** Full of fun and high spirits: *a playful cat.* **2.** Said or done in fun; not serious: *a playful remark.*

play·ground |plā′ground′| *—noun, plural* **playgrounds** An outdoor area for play, sports, and games.

play·mate |plā′māt′| *—noun, plural* **playmates** A person who plays with another.

play·off |plā′ôf′| or |plā′ŏf′| *—noun, plural* **play-offs** A final game or series of games played to decide a winner or championship.

play·pen |plā′pĕn′| *—noun, plural* **playpens** A small pen in which a baby or young child can be left to play. Playpens can be folded up and moved.

play·thing |plā′thĭng′| *—noun, plural* **playthings** Something to play with; a toy.

play·wright |plā′rīt′| *—noun, plural* **playwrights** A person who writes plays.

platform
A subway platform

platypus

playpen

plaza

pla·za |plăz′ə| or |plä′zə| —*noun, plural* **plazas** A public square or open area in a town or city.

plea |plē| —*noun, plural* **pleas** **1.** A request for something right away: *After the storm there were many pleas for food and shelter.* **2.** In law, the answer of an accused person to the charges against him or her: *a plea of guilty.*

plead |plēd| —*verb* **pleaded** or **pled, pleading** **1.** To ask for again and again; beg: *They were pleading with him to return.* **2.** To give an answer or a plea in a court of law: *He pleaded guilty to the charges.* **3.** To defend a case in a court of law: *The lawyer pleaded the poor man's case.* **4.** To give as an excuse: *He pleaded poverty to escape punishment for stealing food.*

pleas·ant |plĕz′ənt| —*adjective* **pleasanter, pleasantest** **1.** Pleasing, agreeable, or delightful: *pleasant weather; a pleasant smell.* **2.** Pleasing in manner; friendly: *a pleasant person; a pleasant disposition.*

please |plēz| —*verb* **pleased, pleasing** **1.** To give someone or something pleasure or satisfaction: *The island pleased the settlers. John is eager to please.* **2.** To be willing to; be so kind as to. The word *please* is used to begin a request or as an exclamation showing a desire: *Please tell us a story. Attention, please!* **3.** To wish; prefer: *They can do exactly as they please during their vacation on the beach.*

pleas·ing |plē′zĭng| —*adjective* Giving pleasure or satisfaction; agreeable: *a pleasing way of doing things; a pleasing smell.*

pleas·ure |plĕzh′ər| —*noun, plural* **pleasures** **1.** A pleasant feeling or happening; a delight: *She smiled with pleasure.* **2.** Something that gives enjoyment, satisfaction, or happiness: *Reading is his main pleasure.*

pleat |plēt| —*noun, plural* **pleats** A flat fold in cloth or other material that is made by doubling the material on itself and pressing or sewing it in place.
—*verb* **pleated, pleating** To make pleats in; arrange in pleats: *The tailor pleated the trousers in the new style.*

pled |plĕd| A past tense and past participle of the verb **plead:** *I pled with him not to drive in the snow. He had pled his cause for a safe railroad crossing for many months.*

pledge |plĕj| —*noun, plural* **pledges** **1.** A formal promise; a vow: *They made a pledge to do their duty.* **2.** Something valuable that is kept to make sure that a loan is paid back: *She left a necklace as a pledge for a loan of one hundred dollars.*
—*verb* **pledged, pledging** **1.** To make a formal promise or vow: *They pledged to support their country.* **2.** To leave something valuable as a promise that a loan will be paid back; pawn: *She pledged her necklace for a loan of one hundred dollars.*

plen·ti·ful |plĕn′tĭ fəl| —*adjective* In full supply or in a great amount; ample; abundant: *plentiful food; plentiful rainfall.*

plen·ty |plĕn′tē| —*noun* A full amount or supply; as much of something as is needed: *Growing children need plenty of exercise. I have plenty of time for my homework.*

pli·ers |plī′ərz| —*noun* (Used with a plural verb.) A tool with two parts attached together as in a pair of scissors. Pliers are used for holding, bending, or cutting things.

plod |plŏd| —*verb* **plodded, plodding** **1.** To walk heavily or with great effort: *They plodded through the forest.* **2.** To work or act slowly and with effort: *She plodded through her lessons.*

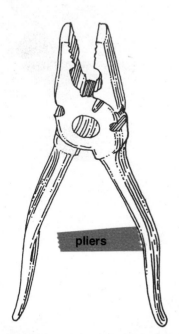

pliers

ă	pat	ĕ	pet	î	fierce
ā	pay	ē	be	ŏ	pot
â	care	ĭ	pit	ō	go
ä	father	ī	pie	ô	paw, for
oi	oil	ŭ	cut	zh	vision
ōo	book	û	fur	ə	ago, item,
ōo	boot	*th*	the		pencil, atom,
yōo	abuse	th	thin		circus
ou	out	hw	which	ər	butter

plop |plŏp| —*verb* **plopped, plopping** To fall or let fall with a sound like that of something that drops into water: *He let the dough plop down into the sink. She plopped the tomatoes onto the plate.*
—*noun, plural* **plops** A dull sound of something plopping: *The pebble fell with a plop into the pool.*
—*adverb* With the sound of a plop: *He heard the frog jump plop into the creek.*

plot |plŏt| —*noun, plural* **plots** **1.** A small piece of ground: *a plot of good land for a garden.* **2.** The different action or events in a story or play. **3.** A secret plan to do something, often against the law: *They have a plot against the sheriff.*
—*verb* **plotted, plotting** **1.** To mark, note, or stand for, as on a map or chart: *We plotted our drive to California on the map.* **2.** To plan secretly or in a tricky way: *We must plot a way to make the party a surprise.*

plov·er |plŭv′ər| or |plō′vər| —*noun, plural* **plovers** A bird with a short bill and a short tail. Plovers live on shores or open fields.

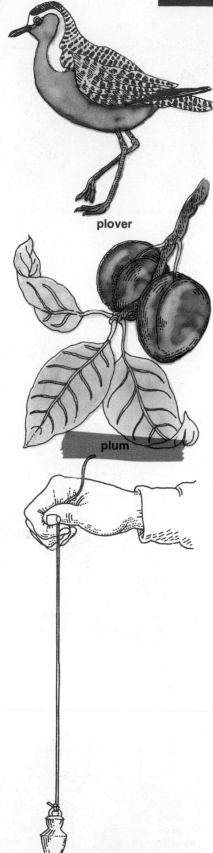

plover

plum

plumb

plow |plou| —*noun, plural* **plows** **1.** A farm tool pulled by an animal or tractor. A plow is used for breaking up soil and cutting rows to get ready for planting seeds. **2.** Some other machine or device that is used to do a job like this. One kind of plow is used to remove snow.
—*verb* **plowed, plowing** **1.** To break or turn over soil with a plow: *He plowed the field and then plowed around the hill.* **2.** To get ahead at a steady rate and with effort: *He plowed his way through the deep snow.* **3.** To remove snow from with a plow: *He plowed the driveway after the blizzard.*

pluck |plŭk| —*verb* **plucked, plucking** **1.** To separate by pulling with the fingers; pick: *She plucked a lily flower from the plant.* **2.** To pull out the feathers or hair of: *The butcher plucked the turkey.* **3.** To pull or tug: *She plucked at her brother's sleeve to try to catch him. He plucked the strings of the banjo softly.*
—*noun, plural* **plucks** **1.** A tug or pull. **2.** Courage and daring: *A child with pluck is not afraid of the dark.*

plug |plŭg| —*noun, plural* **plugs** **1.** A piece of wood, cork, or other material, used to stop a hole or leak: *a plug in a sink.* **2.** An electrical device connected to the end of a wire or cable. A plug has prongs and fits into a matching socket to make an electrical connection.
—*verb* **plugged, plugging** **1.** To fill a hole or leak with or as with a plug; stop up: *He plugged the hole in the wall with plaster. Grease plugged up the kitchen sink.* **2.** To make an electrical connection by putting a plug into a socket or outlet: *He plugged in a lamp.*

plum |plŭm| —*noun, plural* **plums** **1.** A juicy fruit with smooth skin and a hard pit. **2.** A raisin in a pudding or pie. **3.** A dark reddish purple.
—*adjective* Dark reddish purple.
♦ *These sound alike* **plum, plumb.**

plum·age |plōō′mĭj| —*noun* The feathers of a bird.

plumb |plŭm| —*noun, plural* **plumbs** A weight that is hung from the end of a cord. It is used to measure how deep something is or how straight up and down.
—*verb* **plumbed, plumbing** To test with a plumb.
♦ *These sound alike* **plumb, plum.**

plume
Cadets holding hats with plumes

plumb·er |plŭm′ər| —*noun, plural* **plumbers** A person whose work is putting in pipes and plumbing or repairing them.

plumb·ing |plŭm′ĭng| —*noun* **1.** The work or job of a plumber. **2.** A set of pipes, fixtures, and other equipment used in a system through which a liquid or gas flows: *The old building had poor plumbing.*

plume |plōōm| —*noun, plural* **plumes** **1.** A large or showy feather. Plumes are often used for decoration. **2.** Something that looks like a large feather: *A plume of smoke rose from the chimney.*

plump |plŭmp| —*adjective* **plumper, plumpest** Rounded and full in shape: *a plump figure; a plump peach.*
—*verb* **plumped, plumping** To make or become rounded and full: *She plumped up the pillow. The child plumped out as he grew.*

plun·der |plŭn′dər| —*verb* **plundered, plundering** To take goods or valuable things from; rob: *Pirates plundered the city on the coast.*
—*noun* **1.** Property stolen by force or by trickery: *The pirates dug a hole to hide their plunder.* **2.** The act of taking property by force: *The pirate's treasure had all been gotten by plunder.*

plunge |plŭnj| —*verb* **plunged, plunging** **1.** To throw oneself suddenly into water, a place, or an activity: *He plunged into the sea. She plunged into her work.* **2.** To come down steeply or sharply; fall: *The river plunged over the falls.*
—*noun, plural* **plunges** The act of plunging: *a plunge into the sea to cool off; a plunge into work.*

plu·ral |plōōr′əl| —*adjective* In grammar, of the form of a word that tells you that there is more than one person or thing.
—*noun, plural* **plurals** The form of a word that tells you that there is more than one person or thing. For example, *birds* is the plural of *bird,* and *children* is the plural of *child.*

plus |plŭs| —*preposition* **1.** Added to: *Two plus three equals five.* **2.** Increased by; along with: *two weeks' vacation plus holidays.*
—*adjective* **1.** Of addition: *a plus sign.* **2.** Just a little more than: *a grade of B plus.*
—*noun, plural* **pluses** The sign (+), used to show addition. Also called *plus sign.*

Plu·to |plōō′tō| The planet that is farthest from the sun in our solar system.

plu·to·ni·um |plōō tō′nē əm| —*noun* A radioactive silver-white metal. Plutonium is one of the chemical elements. It is man-made and used to produce atomic energy.

ply·wood |plī′wŏŏd′| —*noun* A building material made of layers of wood laid on top of one another and glued together.

p.m. or **P.M.** After noon or between noon and midnight: *Bedtime is at 8:00 p.m.* P.M. is an abbreviation for the Latin words *post meridiem,* meaning "after noon."

pneu·mo·nia |nŏŏ mōn′yə| or |nyŏŏ mōn′yə| —*noun* A serious disease of the lungs. Different kinds of pneumonia are caused by bacteria, viruses, or chemicals.

poach |pōch| —*verb* **poached, poaching** To cook eggs, fish, or other food in a liquid that is gently boiling: *poach eggs.*

pock·et |pŏk′ĭt| —*noun, plural* **pockets** A small bag, open at the top, that is sewn into or onto clothing and used to hold things: *I carry my wallet in the pocket of my pants.*
—*adjective* **1.** Meant to be carried in a pocket: *a pocket watch; a pocket handkerchief.* **2.** Small enough to be carried in a pocket: *a pocket dictionary; a pocket copy of a book.*

ă	pat	ĕ	pet	î	fierce
ā	pay	ē	be	ŏ	pot
â	care	ĭ	pit	ō	go
ä	father	ī	pie	ô	paw, for
oi	oil	ŭ	cut	zh	vision
ŏŏ	book	û	fur	ə	ago, item,
ōō	boot	*th*	the		pencil, atom,
yōō	abuse	th	thin		circus
ou	out	hw	which	ər	butter

—*verb* **pocketed, pocketing** To place in a pocket: *He pocketed his money.*

pock·et·book | pŏk′ ĭt book′ | —*noun, plural* **pocketbooks** A bag used to hold money, papers, make-up, and other small things; handbag.

pock·et·knife | pŏk′ ĭt nīf′ | —*noun, plural* **pocketknives** A small knife with a blade or blades that fold into the handle.

pod | pŏd | —*noun, plural* **pods** A plant part in which seeds grow. The pod splits open when the seeds are ripe. Peas and beans have pods.

po·em | pō′ əm | —*noun, plural* **poems** A kind of writing, usually in verses. In poems, words are chosen for their sounds and beauty. Poems are often about strong feelings, such as love and sorrow.

po·et | pō′ ĭt | —*noun, plural* **poets** A writer of poems.

po·et·ic | pō ĕt′ ĭk | —*adjective* Of or like poetry: *poetic works; poetic language.*

po·et·ry | pō′ ĭ trē | —*noun* **1.** The art or work of a poet: *Her poetry shows great thought.* **2.** Poems thought of as part of literature: *Our class will be studying poetry next week.*

poin·set·ti·a | poin sĕt′ ē ə | —*noun, plural* **poinsettias** A tropical plant with showy, bright-red leaves that look like petals. The flowers are small and yellowish. Poinsettias are often used for Christmas decoration.

point | point | —*noun, plural* **points** **1.** The sharp, thin end of something: *the point of a pencil.* **2.** A thin piece of land that extends into a body of water: *Our house is out on the point near the lighthouse.* **3.** A dot or period: *6.4 is read six point four.* **4.** A place or position: *the highest point in the country.* **5.** An exact degree or condition: *The water was at the boiling point.* **6.** An exact moment in time: *At that point he noticed someone running away.* **7.** An important or necessary part of an idea: *She missed the point of the story.* **8.** A purpose, goal, or reason: *He came to the point of his visit.* **9.** A special quality or characteristic: *That smart girl has made the most of her good points.* **10.** A score of 1 in a game or test: *Our team is three points ahead.* **11.** A direction shown on a compass.

—*verb* **pointed, pointing** **1.** To guide someone or something to or toward; direct; aim: *He pointed the flashlight down the road. He pointed the gun at the target.* **2.** To call attention to something with or as if with the finger: *He pointed to the tree in bloom.*

Phrasal verb **point out** To make known by showing: *Please point out the good ideas in this book.*

Idioms **beside the point** Having nothing to do with what is happening; unimportant: *Your excuse is beside the point.* **make a point of** To stick to a plan of action or rule: *make a point of being on time.*

point·er | poin′ tər | —*noun, plural* **pointers** **1.** Something that points or shows: *The pointer on the wall tells you that the doctor's office is upstairs.* **2.** A long stick that is used to point out something on a map or blackboard. **3.** Information about how to do something; advice: *Let me give you some pointers on cooking.* **4.** A dog with a short, smooth coat. Pointers are often trained to help hunters find game.

point·less | point′ lĭs | —*adjective* Not having a meaning or purpose: *a pointless question.*

point of view The way someone thinks about something;

pocketknife

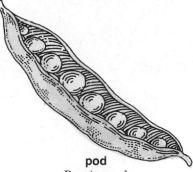

pod
Peas in a pod

poinsettia

pointer

attitude: *From my point of view movies are more fun to go to than baseball games.*

poise | poiz | —*verb* **poised, poising** To balance or be balanced: *He poised the flashlight on the edge of the table. The dog poised on its back legs.*
—*noun* **1.** Balance: *He walked on the top of the fence with perfect poise.* **2.** Confidence in the way one behaves; dignity: *She showed poise when she had to sing in front of the whole school.*

poi·son | poi′ zən | —*noun, plural* **poisons** A substance that can cause injury, sickness, or death when eaten or breathed. Lye, lead, and arsenic are poisons.
—*verb* **poisoned, poisoning** **1.** To kill or harm with poison; give poison to: *The men poisoned the rats that lived in the basement.* **2.** To put poison in or on: *Pollution can poison the air and water. The Indians poisoned their arrows.* **3.** To have a bad influence or effect on; harm: *Brian's envy of Tom's new car poisoned their friendship.*

poison ivy A plant with leaves that have three leaflets. Poison ivy can cause an itching skin rash if it is touched.

poi·son·ous | poi′ zə nəs | —*adjective* Causing harm or death by poison; containing poison: *Certain snakes and plants are poisonous.*

poke | pōk | —*verb* **poked, poking** **1.** To give someone a sudden sharp jab, as with a finger or elbow: *She poked me in the stomach.* **2.** To push forward; thrust: *Don't poke your head out the window.* **3.** To move slowly: *We were just poking around the neighborhood.*
—*noun, plural* **pokes** A sudden sharp jab: *She gave me a poke in the ribs.*
Idiom **poke fun at** To make fun of; kid: *Why are you always poking fun at your sister?*

pok·er¹ | pō′ kər | —*noun, plural* **pokers** A metal rod used to stir a fire.

pok·er² | pō′ kər | —*noun* A card game for two or more players. In poker the players bet if they think their cards have a higher value than everyone else's. The winning player gets what everyone has bet.

po·lar | pō′ lər | —*adjective* Of or near the North Pole or South Pole: *polar regions; polar animals; polar expeditions.*

polar bear A large white bear that lives in far northern regions.

pole¹ | pōl | —*noun, plural* **poles** **1.** Either end of the earth's axis where it meets the earth's surface; the North Pole or the South Pole. **2.** Either end of a battery or magnet where the force is strongest.
♦ *These sound alike* **pole, poll.**

pole² | pōl | —*noun, plural* **poles** **1.** A long, thin rod made of wood or metal: *a fishing pole.* **2.** A post made of wood or metal, especially one that is put into the ground and stands upright: *a telephone pole; a totem pole.*
♦ *These sound alike* **pole, poll.**

pole·cat | pōl′ kăt′ | —*noun, plural* **polecats** **1.** A European animal that looks like a weasel. Polecats can spray a liquid with an unpleasant smell. **2.** A skunk.

pole vault | vôlt | A sport or contest in which a person tries to jump over a high bar with the help of a long pole.

po·lice | pə lēs′ | —*noun, plural* **police** (Used with a plural verb.) A group of people who are given the power by government to keep order and to make sure that the laws are obeyed.

poison ivy

poker¹, poker²
Poker¹ was formed from **poke** and basically means "one that pokes." The source of **poker²** is not known.

polar bear

pole¹, pole²
Pole¹ comes from the Greek word that meant "turning point, pivot." The source of **pole²** was a Latin word meaning "pointed stick."

ă	pat	ĕ	pet	î	fierce
â	pay	ē	be	ŏ	pot
â	care	ĭ	pit	ō	go
ä	father	ī	pie	ô	paw, for
oi	oil	ŭ	cut	zh	vision
ōō	book	û	fur	ə	ago, item,
ōō	boot	*th*	the		pencil, atom,
yōō	abuse	th	thin		circus
ou	out	hw	which	ər	butter

—*verb* **policed, policing 1.** To guard in order to keep or maintain order: *Special guards policed the streets when the President came to visit the city.* **2.** To clean or tidy up: *Jack and I policed the beach, picking up paper and trash.*

po·lice·man |pə lēs′mən| —*noun, plural* **policemen** A man who is a member of the police.

po·lice·wom·an |pə lēs′wŏom′ən| —*noun, plural* **policewomen** A woman who is a member of the police.

pol·i·cy¹ |pŏl′ĭ sē| —*noun, plural* **policies** A belief or plan of action for doing something that is followed by a government, organization, group, or person: *The government's policy is to try to stop pollution. It's my mother's policy never to serve dinner until everyone is home.*

pol·i·cy² |pŏl′ĭ sē| —*noun, plural* **policies** A written agreement or contract between an insurance company and the person who is being insured.

po·li·o |pō′lē ō′| —*noun* Poliomyelitis.

po·li·o·my·e·li·tis |pō′lē ō mī′ə lī′tĭs| —*noun* A disease that can cause paralysis, damage to the muscles, and sometimes death. Poliomyelitis affects mainly children and young people, but now there is a vaccine that can prevent it. Other names for this disease are **polio** and **infantile paralysis.**

pol·ish |pŏl′ĭsh| —*verb* **polished, polishing** To make or become smooth and shiny, especially by rubbing with a special substance: *Polish your shoes. The new car polishes easily.*

　Phrasal verb polish off To finish or use up something quickly: *We polished off our dinner in ten minutes.*

—*noun, plural* **polishes 1.** A substance that is rubbed on the surface of something to make it smooth and shiny: *shoe polish; silver polish.* **2.** A smooth and shiny surface; a shine: *The kitchen floor has a bright polish.*

po·lite |pə līt′| —*adjective* **politer, politest** Having or showing good manners; courteous: *He is always polite to people who visit his parents.*

po·lit·i·cal |pə lĭt′ĭ kəl| —*adjective* **1.** Of the affairs or activities of government: *Democracy is a political system.* **2.** Of politics or politicians: *a political party.*

pol·i·ti·cian |pŏl′ĭ tĭsh′ən| —*noun, plural* **politicians** A person who runs for or holds a political office or position.

pol·i·tics |pŏl′ĭ tĭks| —*noun* **1.** (Used with a singular verb.) The work or activities of government or of the people who work in the government: *When I grow up I want to go into politics and run for governor. Politics is hard work.* **2.** (Used with a plural verb.) A person's attitudes or opinions about government or political subjects: *His father's politics are very conservative.*

pol·ka |pōl′kə| or |pō′kə| —*noun, plural* **polkas** A kind of lively dance, performed by couples.

polka dot One of many colored round dots that are printed on various materials to form a pattern. Polka dots are used on clothing, such as shirts, dresses, and scarves.

poll |pōl| —*noun, plural* **polls 1.** The casting and counting of votes in an election. **2. polls** The place where votes are cast: *During elections, many schools are used as polls.* **3.** A survey in which people are asked to answer questions in order to find out what they think about a particular question or subject.

—*verb* **polled, polling 1.** To receive votes in an election: *Mr.*

policy¹, policy²
Both **policy¹** and **policy²** come from Greek words. **Policy¹** comes from a word that meant "government" or "constitution." The source of **policy²** was a word that meant "demonstration" or "proof." The word was borrowed into Italian, where it meant "proof, document."

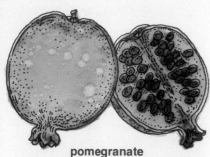

pomegranate
Whole fruit *(left)* and fruit cut in half
(right)

pond

poodle

pool¹, pool²
Pool¹ comes from an old English word used to refer to a pond. **Pool²** comes from the French word for "hen." It seems the word comes from an old game in which the prize was a chicken.

ă	pat	ĕ	pet	î	fierce
ā	pay	ē	be	ŏ	pot
â	care	ĭ	pit	ō	go
ä	father	ī	pie	ô	paw, for
oi	oil	ŭ	cut	zh	vision
ŏŏ	book	û	fur	ə	ago, item,
ōō	boot	th	the		pencil, atom,
yōō	abuse	th	thin		circus
ou	out	hw	which	ər	butter

McCarthy was elected senator because he polled more votes than Mr. Nelson. **2.** To take a poll: *Newspaper reporters were polling people to see if they agreed with the Governor's decision to build a new airport.*
♦ *These sound alike* **poll, pole.**

pol·len |pŏl′ən| —*noun* A fine powder produced by the male parts of a flower. The grains of pollen unite with female cells of a plant to produce seeds.

pol·li·wog |pŏl′ē wŏg′| or |pŏl′ē wôg′| —*noun, plural* **polliwogs** A tadpole. Another form of this word is **pollywog.**

pol·lu·tant |pə lōōt′nt| —*noun, plural* **pollutants** Anything that pollutes, such as smoke, garbage, or other waste materials.

pol·lute |pə lōōt′| —*verb* **polluted, polluting** To make harmful to living things: *Garbage pollutes rivers. The air is polluted by gasoline exhaust from cars.*

pol·lu·tion |pə lōō′shən| —*noun* The process of making air, water, food, and other substances harmful to living things. Pollution is often caused by factories that dump waste materials into rivers and streams and by the smoke that goes into the air by burning waste.

pol·ly·wog |pŏl′ē wŏg′| or |pŏl′ē wôg′| —*noun, plural* **pollywogs** A form of the word **polliwog.**

po·lo |pō′lō| —*noun* A sport or game played by two teams of horseback riders who hit a wooden ball with mallets with long handles. One team tries to hit the ball into the other team's goal.

pol·y·gon |pŏl′ē gŏn′| —*noun, plural* **polygons** A flat, closed figure that has three or more sides. Squares are polygons.

pol·yp |pŏl′ĭp| —*noun, plural* **polyps** A small water animal with a body shaped like a tube. Its mouth is an opening surrounded by tentacles. Coral is formed by colonies of polyps.

pome·gran·ate |pŏm′grăn′ĭt| or |pŭm′grăn′ĭt| —*noun, plural* **pomegranates** A fruit with a tough, reddish rind and many small seeds. Each seed is enclosed in juicy red flesh that has a pleasant, slightly sour taste.

pon·cho |pŏn′chō| —*noun, plural* **ponchos** A cloak or garment like a blanket. A poncho has a hole in the center for the head. Plastic or waterproof ponchos are worn like raincoats. Wool or cloth ponchos are worn like coats or jackets.

pond |pŏnd| —*noun, plural* **ponds** A small, still body of water. Ponds are smaller than lakes.

pon·der |pŏn′dər| —*verb* **pondered, pondering** To think about something carefully; consider: *She pondered the teacher's question. He pondered over the decision.*

po·ny |pō′nē| —*noun, plural* **ponies** A horse that is small in size when fully grown.

pony express A former system of carrying mail in the western United States. Riders used fast horses that went only a part of the way. Then fresh horses were used, and in this way the mail was delivered quickly.

poo·dle |pōō′dl| —*noun, plural* **poodles** A dog with thick, curly hair. Some types of poodle are quite large. Others are very small.

pool¹ |pōōl| —*noun, plural* **pools** **1.** A still, small body of water. **2.** A tank of water, especially one for people to swim in or to keep fish in: *a swimming pool; a lobster pool.* **3.** A small amount of a liquid; puddle: *There is a pool of oil on the garage floor.*

pool² |pōōl| —*noun, plural* **pools** **1.** A game played on a table

that has six pockets, one on each corner and one in the middle of each of the long sides. The object of the game is to hit or knock balls into the pockets with a long stick called a cue. **2.** A system in which a group of people share something or take turns doing something for one another: *Today is my dad's turn to drive the people in the car pool to work.*
—*verb* **pooled, pooling** To put together for common use; share in common: *We pooled our money and bought a baseball.*

poor |pŏor| —*adjective* **poorer, poorest 1.** Having little or no money: *He was too poor to buy new clothes for school.* **2.** Not good enough; not as good as it should be; inferior: *This homework assignment is the poorest one you've done.* **3.** Deserving or needing pity; unfortunate: *The poor lost dog is hungry.*

pop |pŏp| —*noun, plural* **pops 1.** A sudden sharp, exploding sound: *The balloon broke with a pop.* **2.** A soft drink with bubbles in it; soda: *a bottle of pop.*
—*verb* **popped, popping 1.** To make or cause to make a sound like a pop: *The children were popping corn. The firecracker popped.* **2.** To burst or cause to burst with a pop; break: *Don't pop the balloon. The soda bottle popped open.* **3.** To come or appear suddenly: *I just popped in to say hello.* **4.** To stick out suddenly: *He popped his head out the window.*

pop·corn |pŏp′kôrn′| —*noun* Corn kernels that pop open and become white and puffed up when heated. Warm buttered popcorn is a popular food.

pope |pōp| —*noun, plural* **popes** Often **Pope** The head of the Roman Catholic Church.

pop·lar |pŏp′lər| —*noun, plural* **poplars** A tree with leaves shaped like a triangle and soft wood. There are several kinds of poplar.

pop·py |pŏp′ē| —*noun, plural* **poppies** A plant with showy flowers that are often a bright red. The small, dark seeds of some poppies are used in cooking and baking. The drug opium comes from one kind of poppy.

pop·u·lar |pŏp′yə lər| —*adjective* **1.** Well liked in general; having many friends: *a popular teacher.* **2.** Enjoyed or liked by many people: *Movies are a popular form of entertainment.* **3.** Of, for, or by the people; having to do with most people: *Governors are elected by popular vote.* **4.** Accepted or believed by many people: *It is a popular belief that thirteen is an unlucky number.*

pop·u·lar·i·ty |pŏp′yə lăr′ĭ tē| —*noun* The condition of being popular or being liked by many people: *We saw the athlete's popularity by the long line of people who waited for his autograph.*

pop·u·late |pŏp′yə lāt′| —*verb* **populated, populating 1.** To supply with inhabitants: *People came from many different countries to populate the United States.* **2.** To live in; inhabit: *That island is populated with fishermen. The small town is thinly populated.*

pop·u·la·tion |pŏp′yə lā′shən| —*noun, plural* **populations 1.a.** All of the people who live in a certain place; people: *The whole population of the town turned out for the parade.* **b.** The number of people who live in a certain place: *The population of the city is 30,000.* **2.** All the plants or animals of the same kind that live in a particular place: *There is a large deer population in these woods.*

pop·u·lous |pŏp′yə ləs| —*adjective* Full of people; having many inhabitants: *a populous city.*

poppy

porcelain
Antique figures made of porcelain

porcupine

---

pore¹, pore²
Pore¹ came to English through French from Latin. The Latin word came from a Greek source word meaning "passage." **Pore²** comes from a verb used in English as it was spoken about 1100–1500; we do not know its earlier history.

porpoise
Porpoise performing at an aquarium

ă	pat	ĕ	pet	î	fierce
ā	pay	ē	be	ŏ	pot
â	care	ĭ	pit	ō	go
ä	father	ī	pie	ô	paw, for
oi	oil	ŭ	cut	zh	vision
ŏŏ	book	û	fur	ə	ago, item,
ōō	boot	th	the		pencil, atom,
yōō	abuse	th	thin		circus
ou	out	hw	which	ər	butter

por·ce·lain | pôr′sə lĭn | or | pōr′sə lĭn | —*noun, plural* **porcelains** A hard, white kind of china made by baking fine clay at a high temperature. Porcelain allows light to pass through.

porch | pôrch | or | pōrch | —*noun, plural* **porches** A section with a roof that is attached to the outside of a house. Some porches are open at the sides. Others have large glass windows or wire screens.

por·cu·pine | pôr′kyə pīn′ | —*noun, plural* **porcupines** An animal covered with long, sharp spines called quills.

pore¹ | pôr | or | pōr | —*noun, plural* **pores** A tiny opening in skin or an outer covering. There are pores in an animal's skin and on the surface of a leaf.
♦ *These sound alike* **pore, pour.**

pore² | pôr | or | pōr | —*verb* **pored, poring** To look at or examine with great care and attention: *He pored through some old stamp catalogs.*
♦ *These sound alike* **pore, pour.**

pork | pôrk | or | pōrk | —*noun* The meat of a pig or hog used as food.

por·poise | pôr′pəs | —*noun, plural* **porpoises** A sea animal related to the whales but smaller. Porpoises usually have a short, blunt snout.

por·ridge | pôr′ĭj | or | pōr′ĭj | —*noun, plural* **porridges** A thick cereal or soup made by boiling oatmeal, other grains, or beans or peas in water or milk.

port | pôrt | or | pōrt | —*noun, plural* **ports** **1.** A place along a river, lake, ocean, or other body of water where ships may dock or anchor; harbor. **2.** A city or town with a harbor: *Boston has been an important port since colonial days.*

port·a·ble | pôr′tə bəl | or | pōr′tə bəl | —*adjective* Easy to carry about: *a portable radio.*

por·ter | pôr′tər | or | pōr′tər | —*noun, plural* **porters** **1.** A person hired to carry or move luggage at a station, airport, or hotel. **2.** A person who waits on passengers in a railroad car.

port·hole | pôrt′hōl′ | or | pōrt′hōl′ | —*noun, plural* **portholes** A small, round window in the side of a ship.

por·ti·co | pôr′tĭ kō′ | or | pōr′tĭ kō′ | —*noun, plural* **porticos** A porch or walk with a roof held up by columns.

por·tion | pôr′shən | or | pōr′shən | —*noun, plural* **portions** **1.** A part of a larger thing: *He finished his portion of the wall painting early and then helped others.* **2.** One helping of food for one person: *If you like this stew, you may have a second portion.*
—*verb* **portioned, portioning** To give out in portions: *He portioned the cake among the four boys.*

port·ly | pôrt′lē | or | pōrt′lē | —*adjective* **portlier, portliest** Fat or stout in a dignified way: *His father is a portly gentleman with a white mustache.*

por·trait | pôr′trĭt′ | or | pôr′trāt′ | or | pōr′trĭt′ | or | pōr′trāt′ | —*noun, plural* **portraits** A painting or photograph of someone's face, or sometimes of the whole person: *Portraits of all the Presidents hang on the walls of the White House.*

por·tray | pôr trā′ | or | pōr trā′ | —*verb* **portrayed, portraying** **1.** To make a picture of: *The artist portrayed the queen with a gold crown.* **2.** To describe in words: *The book portrays a young boy's life in the wilderness.* **3.** To play the part of: *The actress portrayed an old woman.*

Por·tu·gal | pôr′chə gəl | or | pōr′chə gəl | A country in southwestern Europe.

Por·tu·guese | pôr′chə gēz′ | or | pôr′chə gēs′ | or | pōr′chə gēz′ | or | pōr′chə gēs′ | —*adjective* Of Portugal, the Portuguese, or their language.
—*noun* **1. the Portuguese** (Used with a plural verb.) A person who was born in or is a citizen of Portugal. **2.** The Romance language of Portugal and other countries.

Portuguese man-of-war A sea animal with a blue floating part that looks like a balloon. It has long tentacles that can give a painful sting.

pose | pōz | —*verb* **posed, posing 1.** To take a special position for a picture: *The family posed in front of the fireplace.* **2.** To pretend to be someone or something: *He posed as a policeman to get into the house.*
—*noun, plural* **poses 1.** A special way of holding the body: *That is a good pose of the horse and rider.* **2.** A false way of acting; a pretense: *Her cheerful manner is just a pose.*

po·si·tion | pə zĭsh′ən | —*noun, plural* **positions 1.** The place where someone or something is to be found: *the position of the sun in the sky at noon.* **2.** The way a person or thing is placed or arranged: *His neck was stiff from sleeping in an awkward position.* **3.** Good standing or rank: *People of high position were invited.* **4.** A way of thinking; point of view: *What is your position on selling candy in school cafeterias?* **5.** A job: *He has an important position in the government.*

pos·i·tive | pŏz′ĭ tĭv | —*adjective* **1.** Absolutely certain; sure: *He is positive that we have met before.* **2.** Expressing consent or approval; favorable: *An up-and-down nod is a positive answer.* **3.** Helping by saying what is good and what is bad; helpful; constructive: *The teacher's positive criticism helped him improve his public speaking.* **4.** Greater than zero: *We usually multiply positive numbers in arithmetic.* **5.** Having one of two opposite electrical charges. One of the ends of a magnet has a positive charge; the opposite end has a negative charge. **6.** Showing that a particular disease or germ is present: *a positive blood test for anemia.*
—*noun, plural* **positives** In photography, an image on film in which the dark areas and light areas appear as they normally would.

pos·i·tive·ly | pŏz′ĭ tĭv lē | —*adverb* **1.** In a positive manner: *Please criticize the work positively, not negatively.* **2.** Absolutely; certainly: *It's positively driving me crazy!*

pos·se | pŏs′ē | —*noun, plural* **posses** A group of men called together by a sheriff to help catch an outlaw or to keep law and order.

pos·sess | pə zĕs′ | —*verb* **possessed, possessing 1.** To have or own: *You possess the ability to do great things. The family possesses a great deal of land in the West.* **2.** To influence strongly: *What possesses Harry to behave like this?*

pos·ses·sion | pə zĕsh′ən | —*noun, plural* **possessions 1.** The condition of having or owning something: *Both teams fought for possession of the ball. She tried to gain possession of the stolen jewels.* **2.** Something that is owned; a belonging: *They escaped, leaving all their possessions behind.* **3.** A territory ruled by an outside power: *Alaska was once a United States possession; now it is a state.*

pos·ses·sive | pǝ zĕs′ ĭv | —*adjective* **1.** Of or showing ownership: *"Our" is the possessive form of the pronoun "we."* **2.** Having a strong desire to own or control things or people: *Little children are often very possessive with their toys.*
—*noun, plural* **possessives** A word that shows ownership: *"Tom's," "his," and "my" are possessives.*

pos·si·bil·i·ty | pŏs′ǝ bĭl′ ĭ tē | —*noun, plural* **possibilities 1.** The fact or condition of being possible; likelihood: *the possibility of life on Mars; no possibility of rain tomorrow.* **2.** Something that may exist, happen, or come true: *His return to health is a possibility.*

pos·si·ble | pŏs′ǝ bǝl | —*adjective* **1.** Capable of existing, happening, or being done: *Is life possible on Mars? I'll phone you as soon as possible. It is possible to make the trip in one day.* **2.** Capable of happening or of not happening; likely to be either true or not true: *Snow is possible at Thanksgiving. His story is possible, but not probable.* **3.** Capable of fitting a special purpose: *a possible site for a new school; two possible wedding dates.*

pos·si·bly | pŏs′ǝ blē | —*adverb* **1.** Perhaps; maybe: *This is possibly the last time we shall meet here. He is possibly the best soccer player in the world.* **2.** Under any circumstances; at all: *I can't possibly do it.*

pos·sum | pŏs′ǝm | —*noun, plural* **possums** An opossum.

post¹ | pōst | —*noun, plural* **posts 1.** A straight piece of wood or metal set up in the ground to mark something or hold something up: *A sign nailed to the post said "Keep Out."* **2.** Any straight rod: *These earrings have gold posts instead of hooks.*
—*verb* **posted, posting** To put up in a place or in several places for everyone to see: *They posted notices about the lost dog all over the neighborhood.*

post² | pōst | —*noun, plural* **posts 1.** A military base where troops are stationed: *Soldiers from the army post sometimes come into town.* **2.** A position or station assigned to a guard, sentry, or other person: *The ranger has a lookout post in the forest.* **3.** A position or job, especially a job to which one is appointed: *a high post in the government.* **4.** A store or station where goods may be bought or traded; trading post.
—*verb* **posted, posting** To assign to a post or station: *The police captain posted guards at all the exits. The ambassador was posted to a new nation.*

post³ | pōst | —*noun, plural* **posts 1.** The carrying and delivering of mail: *letters sent by post.* **2.** The mail that is delivered: *The letter came in this morning's post.*
—*verb* **posted, posting 1.** To mail a letter or package: *He posted the letter two weeks ago, and she received it today.* **2.** To inform of the latest news: *Please keep me posted on how your work is coming along.*

post- A prefix that means: **1.** After in time; later: *postdate.* **2.** After in position; behind: *postscript.*

post·age | pō′stĭj | —*noun* The charge for sending something by mail.

postage stamp A small piece of paper issued by the government for the amount shown on the front. Stamps are attached to mail to pay the charge for mailing.

post·al | pō′stǝl | —*adjective* Of the post office or mail service: *postal rates; a postal clerk.*

post·card | pōst′ kärd′ | —*noun, plural* **postcards** A card for

---

post¹, post², post³

All three words spelled **post** have different sources in Latin. **Post¹** came from a word meaning "post, door post." **Post²** had the meaning "station, position." **Post³** originally meant "relay station for mail."

postage stamp

ă	pat	ĕ	pet	î	fierce	
ā	pay	ē	be	ŏ	pot	
â	care	ĭ	pit	ō	go	
ä	father	ī	pie	ô	paw, for	

oi	oil	ŭ	cut	zh	vision
ŏŏ	book	û	fur	ǝ	ago, item,
ōō	boot	*th*	the		pencil, atom,
yōō	abuse	th	thin		circus
ou	out	hw	which	ǝr	butter

sending short messages through the mail. A postcard usually has a picture on one side and room for the address and a message on the other side.

post·date | pōst dāt′ | —*verb* **postdated, postdating** To put a date on a letter, check, or document that is later than the actual date.

post·er | pō′stər | —*noun, plural* **posters** A large printed sign with a public notice or advertisement.

post·man | pōst′mən | —*noun, plural* **postmen** A male letter carrier.

post·mark | pōst′märk′ | —*noun, plural* **postmarks** An official mark stamped on mail. It serves to cancel the stamp and to show the date and the place of mailing.

post·mas·ter | pōst′măs′tər | —*noun, plural* **postmasters** A person in charge of a post office.

post office A place for receiving, sorting, and delivering mail and for selling stamps.

post·pone | pōst pōn′ | —*verb* **postponed, postponing** To put off until a later time: *If you are not well, please postpone your visit.*

post·script | pōst′skrĭpt′ | —*noun, plural* **postscripts** A message added at the end of a letter, below the writer's signature.

pos·ture | pŏs′chər | —*noun, plural* **postures** The way a person holds or carries the body; carriage: *His poor posture makes him look sloppy and heavy.*

po·sy | pō′zē | —*noun, plural* **posies** A flower or bunch of flowers.

pot | pŏt | —*noun, plural* **pots** **1.** A deep, round container. Some pots have lids, handles, or spouts. Pots may be used for cooking, growing plants, or many other purposes. **2.** A pot and its contents: *a pot of soup on the stove; a pot of ferns in the parlor.* **3.** The amount a pot holds: *They served six pots of chili to the hungry crowd.* **4.** A trap for catching lobsters, fish, or other sea creatures.
—*verb* **potted, potting** To plant or put in a pot: *She potted the tulip bulbs.*

po·tas·si·um | pə tăs′ē əm | —*noun* A soft, silver-white, lightweight metal that is found in compounds. Potassium compounds are used to make soaps, fertilizers, and explosives. Potassium is one of the chemical elements.

po·ta·to | pə tā′tō | —*noun, plural* **potatoes** **1.** A vegetable with brown or reddish skin and an uneven shape. The potato is a type of plant stem that grows underground. **2.** A sweet potato.

po·ten·tial | pə tĕn′shəl | —*adjective* Not yet real or definite, but possible in the future: *a potential skating star; potential buyers.*
—*noun, plural* **potentials** The capacity for developing well in a special way: *He has good potential as a pitcher.*

pot·ter | pŏt′ər | —*noun, plural* **potters** A person who makes pots, dishes, or other things from clay.

pot·ter·y | pŏt′ə rē | —*noun* Pots, dishes, vases, and other things shaped from damp clay and hardened by baking.

pouch | pouch | —*noun, plural* **pouches** **1.** A bag or sack of leather, cloth, plastic, or other soft material: *a mail pouch; a tobacco pouch.* **2.** A part of an animal's body that is like a bag or a pocket. Female kangaroos have pouches for holding their developing babies. A pelican has a pouch in the lower bill for holding fish.

postmark

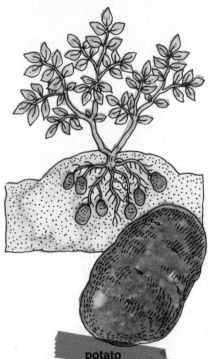
potato
Plant *(above)* and vegetable *(below)*

potter

poultry
Young chickens

---

pound¹, pound², pound³
All three words spelled **pound**
appeared in English a very long
time ago. **Pound¹** meant "weight,"
pound² meant "to crush," and
pound³ was "an enclosure." **Pound¹**
can be traced back to a Latin source
also meaning "weight."

---

poul·try |pōl′trē| —*noun* Chickens, turkeys, ducks, geese, or
other birds raised for their meat or eggs.

pounce |pouns| —*verb* **pounced, pouncing** To leap or swoop
suddenly in order to catch something: *The lion pounced on the
antelope.*
—*noun, plural* **pounces** A sudden leap or swoop to catch
something: *With a pounce, the hawk seized the mouse and flew off.*

pound¹ |pound| —*noun, plural* **pounds** or **pound** **1.** A unit of
weight that equals 16 ounces. In the metric system, a pound
equals 453.59 grams. **2.** The basic unit of money in Great Britain
and some other countries.

pound² |pound| —*verb* **pounded, pounding** **1.** To hit hard and
often: *He pounded the nail into the board with a hammer. The surf
pounded against the rocks.* **2.** To beat with excitement; throb: *Her
heart pounded with fear.* **3.** To crush to a powder or pulp: *She
pounded the corn into meal.*

pound³ |pound| —*noun, plural* **pounds** An enclosed place for
keeping stray dogs or other animals.

pour |pôr| or |pōr| —*verb* **poured, pouring** **1.** To flow or cause
to flow in a steady stream: *Salt poured out on the table. Please pour
the milk slowly. Mother pours when we have tea.* **2.** To rain hard:
Take your umbrella; it's pouring outside.
♦ *These sound alike* **pour, pore.**

pout |pout| —*verb* **pouted, pouting** To push out the lips to show
that one is annoyed or unhappy: *She pouted when her father said
she couldn't go to the movies.*

pov·er·ty |pŏv′ər tē| —*noun* **1.** The condition of being poor and
having little money or other necessities: *They lived in poverty,
sleeping in the streets and begging for bread.* **2.** The condition of
being of very poor quality: *The poverty of the rocky soil made it
impossible to grow any crops.*

pow·der |pou′dər| —*noun, plural* **powders** **1.** Solid material
that has been made into very fine particles; dust: *The rocks
crumbled to powder in his hands.* **2.** Fine particles used for a
particular purpose: *bath powder; soap powder.* **3.** Gunpowder: *He
tried to keep his powder dry when he crossed the river.*
—*verb* **powdered, powdering** **1.** To turn into powder by crushing,
crumbling, or drying: *They powdered the milk by evaporating its
moisture. Chalk powders easily.* **2.** To cover or sprinkle with a
powder: *She powdered herself after the bath. They powdered the
cookies with sugar.*

powder horn A container for gunpowder. A powder horn is
made of an animal's horn with a cap or stopper at the open end.

pow·er |pou′ər| —*noun, plural* **powers** **1.** The ability to do or
accomplish something: *He is gaining the power to move the leg he
hurt. It is in our power to clean up the environment.* **2.** Strength or
force: *a man of amazing power; the power of his argument.* **3.** The
right to decide or command; authority: *The President has the
power to veto bills passed by Congress.* **4.** A nation or state that
has great influence in the world: *Small nations are sometimes
caught in the middle of quarrels between great powers.* **5.** A person,
group, or thing that is the source of authority: *He was king, but his
mother was the real power behind the throne.* **6.** Energy that can
be used to do work: *Water power can be changed to electric power.*
7. Electricity: *During the storm, the power failed and the lights went
out.*

ă	pat	ĕ	pet	î	fierce	
ā	pay	ē	be	ŏ	pot	
â	care	ĭ	pit	ō	go	
ä	father	ī	pie	ô	paw, for	

oi	oil	ŭ	cut	zh	vision
ŏŏ	book	û	fur	ə	ago, item,
ōō	boot	*th*	the		pencil, atom,
yōō	abuse	th	thin		circus
ou	out	hw	which	ər	butter

—*verb* **powered, powering** To supply with power: *A gasoline engine powers the truck.*

pow·er·ful |pou′ər fəl| —*adjective* Having or using great power; strong: *a powerful nation; powerful muscles; a powerful push; a powerful medicine.*

pow·er·less |pou′ər lĭs| —*adjective* Without strength or power; not able to resist or help; helpless: *The people with their sticks and knives were powerless against guns and tanks.*

prac·ti·cal |prăk′tĭ kəl| —*adjective* **1.** Having or serving a useful purpose: *practical presents like socks and mittens. The parachute was invented hundreds of years before anyone found a practical use for it.* **2.** Coming from experience, practice, or use instead of study: *She studied business in school and took a summer job to get some practical training.* **3.** Concerned with useful matters, not with ideas or imagination: *a practical man whose main interest is making a living.* **4.** Having or showing good judgment; sensible: *It is not practical to wear fancy shoes on a hike.*

practical joke A mischievous trick or prank that is played to make a person look or feel foolish: *He put frogs in his friend's bed as a practical joke.*

prac·ti·cal·ly |prăk′tĭk lē| —*adverb* **1.** Almost, but not quite; nearly: *He is practically ten years old; next week is his birthday.* **2.** In a practical, useful, or sensible way: *They dressed practically for skiing.*

prac·tice |prăk′tĭs| —*verb* **practiced, practicing** **1.** To do an activity over and over again in order to learn to do it well: *She practices the piano every day. The team practices every day.* **2.** To make a habit of; do in a regular way: *He practices what he preaches.* **3.** To follow; carry out: *They do not practice their religion.* **4.** To work at a profession: *He has practiced medicine here for twenty-five years. The lawyer used to practice in a different state.*

—*noun, plural* **practices** **1.** The experience that comes from doing something over and over to develop, maintain, or improve it: *Being a good dancer takes lots of practice. He was a good skater but is now out of practice.* **2.** A period or a session for exercise and drill in an activity: *football practice; violin practice.* **3.** A usual way of doing things; custom; habit: *the practice of reading from left to right.* **4.** Actual action; performance: *She couldn't wait for a chance to put her ideas into practice.* **5.** The work of a profession: *the practice of law.* **6.** The group of people who use the services of a doctor or lawyer; patients or clients: *The young doctor has a small but growing practice.*

prai·rie |prâr′ē| —*noun, plural* **prairies** A wide area of flat or gently sloping country with tall grass and not many trees.

prairie dog A furry, brownish animal related to the woodchuck. Prairie dogs dig underground tunnels and live in large colonies.

prairie schooner A large wagon covered by a curved canvas top; covered wagon. Prairie schooners were used by pioneers traveling across the North American prairies.

praise |prāz| —*noun, plural* **praises** Words or thoughts that show admiration or approval: *The passengers had great praise for the pilot who made a safe landing in the storm.*

—*verb* **praised, praising** **1.** To express approval or admiration for; speak well of: *The teacher praised her work.* **2.** To give glory to; honor: *They praised the Lord with trumpets and harps.*

prairie dog

prank

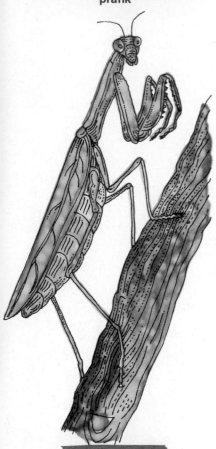

praying mantis

prance | prăns | —*verb* **pranced, prancing** **1.** To rise on the hind legs and spring forward: *The horses pranced in the circus ring.* **2.** To run, leap, or move in a playful or proud way: *Children pranced on the lawn. She pranced about the room in her new clothes.*

prank | prăngk | —*noun, plural* **pranks** A playful or mischievous trick or joke.

prawn | prôn | —*noun, plural* **prawns** A water animal that looks like a shrimp. Prawns are eaten as food.

pray | prā | —*verb* **prayed, praying** **1. a.** To say a prayer to God: *They knelt and prayed.* **b.** To ask for something from God: *The farmers prayed for rain.* **2.** To ask in a serious way; want seriously: *I pray you to let me go. I hope and pray that the teacher won't call on me.* **3.** To be so good as to; please: *Pray tell me your name.*

♦ *These sound alike* **pray, prey.**

prayer | prâr | —*noun, plural* **prayers** **1.** Words spoken to God: *They said a prayer for a safe voyage.* **2.** The act of praying: *He clasped his hands in prayer.* **3.** A serious request or appeal; plea: *a prayer for mercy.*

pray·ing mantis | prā′ĭng | An insect, the mantis.

pre- A prefix that means "before": *prehistoric.*

preach | prēch | —*verb* **preached, preaching** **1.** To give a talk on religious matters: *The minister preached the morning sermon. He preaches on television Sundays.* **2.** To teach or urge: *The leaders preached honesty and hard work. Practice what you preach.*

preach·er | prē′chər | —*noun, plural* **preachers** A person who preaches.

pre·cau·tion | prĭ kô′shən | —*noun, plural* **precautions** An action taken to avoid possible danger, error, or accident: *She uses a pad when she cooks as a precaution against burning herself.*

pre·cede | prĭ sēd′ | —*verb* **preceded, preceding** To come or go before: *February precedes March in the year.*

pre·ced·ing | prĭ sēd′ĭng | —*adjective* Coming or going just before: *She had bought a container of milk on the preceding day.*

pre·cinct | prē′sĭngkt | —*noun, plural* **precincts** A section or district of a city or town: *There are forty-three police precincts in our city.*

pre·cious | prĕsh′əs | —*adjective* **1.** Of high price or value: *Diamonds and rubies are precious gems.* **2.** Dear; beloved: *She kissed her precious baby.*

pre·cip·i·tate | prĭ sĭp′ĭ tāt′ | —*verb* **precipitated, precipitating** **1.** To cause to happen; bring on: *Drought and famine precipitated a large migration from the land.* **2.** To change from vapor into water and fall to earth as rain, snow, sleet, or hail.

pre·cip·i·ta·tion | prĭ sĭp′ĭ tā′shən | —*noun* **1.** Any form of water that falls from the sky and reaches the ground as rain, snow, sleet, or hail: *Deserts have little or no precipitation.* **2.** The amount of water that falls from the sky and reaches the ground: *Precipitation is measured in centimeters or inches.*

pre·cise | prĭ sīs′ | —*adjective* **1.** Clearly expressed; definite; exact: *Please make your instructions precise so that we can understand them.* **2.** Clear and correct; accurate: *He has a precise way of pronouncing his words.*

pre·ci·sion | prĭ sĭzh′ən | —*noun* The condition of being precise or exact; accuracy: *A moon launch requires great precision.*

pred·a·tor | prĕd′ə tər | or | prĕd′ə tôr′ | —*noun, plural* **predators**

ă	pat	ĕ	pet	î	fierce
ā	pay	ē	be	ŏ	pot
â	care	ĭ	pit	ō	go
ä	father	ī	pie	ô	paw, for

oi	oil	ŭ	cut	zh	vision
ŏŏ	book	û	fur	ə	ago, item,
ōō	boot	*th*	the		pencil, atom,
yōō	abuse	th	thin		circus
ou	out	hw	which	ər	butter

An animal that lives by catching and eating other animals.

pred·a·to·ry |**prĕd′**ə tôr′ē| or |**prĕd′**ə tōr′ē| —*adjective* Living by preying on other animals. Tigers are predatory animals. Eagles are predatory birds.

pred·e·ces·sor |**prĕd′**ĭ sĕs′ər| —*noun, plural* **predecessors** Someone or something that had a job, office, or function before another: *The President continued the policies of his predecessor. A round stone was the predecessor of the wheel.*

pred·i·cate |**prĕd′**ĭ kĭt| —*noun, plural* **predicates** The part of a sentence that tells something about the subject. In the sentences *Buttermilk tastes good, Jack is small,* and *Mary went to the market early,* the predicates are *tastes good, is small,* and *went to the market early.*

pre·dict |prĭ **dĭkt′**| —*verb* **predicted, predicting** To tell what will happen before it happens; foretell: *The radio report predicts snow tomorrow. The prophet predicted seven years of drought.*

pre·dic·tion |prĭ **dĭk′**shən| —*noun, plural* **predictions** **1.** Something that is predicted; a prophecy: *Her worst predictions came true.* **2.** The act of predicting: *Prediction of weather is now a science.*

pref·ace |**prĕf′**ĭs| —*noun, plural* **prefaces** Words that go before the main part of a book or speech; introduction.

pre·fer |prĭ **fûr′**| —*verb* **preferred, preferring** To like better: *I prefer to stay home tonight. Do you prefer the red jacket or the blue?*

pref·er·ence |**prĕf′**ər əns| —*noun, plural* **preferences** **1.** A liking for one thing or person over others or another: *She has a preference for the color blue.* **2.** Someone or something that is liked better than others: *Salads are always his preference for lunch.*

pre·fix |**prē′**fĭks′| —*noun, plural* **prefixes** A syllable or syllables placed at the beginning of a word. A prefix changes the meaning of the word. For example, *un-* in *unable* and *non-* in *nonstop* are prefixes.

preg·nant |**prĕg′**nənt| —*adjective* Having a baby or babies growing inside the body: *Elephants are pregnant for almost two years before they have baby elephants.*

pre·his·tor·ic |prē′hĭ **stôr′**ĭk| or |prē′hĭ **stōr′**ĭk| —*adjective* Of a time before events from history were written down: *the ruins of a prehistoric community; dinosaurs, mammoths, and other prehistoric animals.*

prej·u·dice |**prĕj′**ə dĭs| —*noun, plural* **prejudices** **1.** A strong feeling or judgment made about something or someone without knowing much about the thing or person; a bias: *a prejudice against foreign foods; a prejudice for things from his home town.* **2.** A feeling against people of races, religions, or backgrounds other than one's own.
—*verb* **prejudiced, prejudicing** To fill with prejudice; to bias: *His one visit to a city prejudiced him against all city people.*

pre·lim·i·nar·y |prĭ **lĭm′**ə nĕr′ē| —*adjective* Preparing for or leading to the main part: *He made some preliminary sketches for costumes.*

pre·mier |prĭ **mîr′**| —*noun, plural* **premiers** The chief minister of a government; prime minister.

prem·ise |**prĕm′**ĭs| —*noun, plural* **premises** **1.** A sentence that is used as the starting point of an argument or from which a conclusion is made. **2.** **premises** Someone's land or building: *The*

prehistoric
Two kinds of dinosaur

playground is part of the school premises.

prep·a·ra·tion |prĕp′ə **rā**′shən| —*noun, plural* **preparations** **1.** The action of preparing or getting ready: *The preparation of dinner for six persons takes time.* **2.** An action necessary in getting ready for something: *They are making final preparations for the rocket launch.* **3.** A mixture prepared for a certain use: *a preparation of medicines for her illness.*

pre·pare |prĭ **pâr**′| —*verb* **prepared, preparing** **1.** To get ready for some task or event: *Prepare yourself for a surprise. The children prepared for dinner.* **2.** To plan and make: *prepare a book report.* **3.** To put together and make from various things: *meals that are easy to prepare.*

prep·o·si·tion |prĕp′ə **zĭsh**′ən| —*noun, plural* **prepositions** A word that shows the relation between a noun or pronoun and another word or words (called the object of the preposition). For example, in the phrase *a store on the next corner* the preposition *on* shows the relation between the noun *store* and the words *next corner*. Other common prepositions are *at, by, from, out, to,* and *with*.

prep·o·si·tion·al |prĕp′ə **zĭsh**′ən əl| —*adjective* Having a preposition; functioning as a preposition. The phrases *instead of* and *in regard to* are prepositional phrases.

pre·school |prē′**skōōl**′| —*adjective* Of or for a child before he or she enters elementary school.

pre·scribe |prĭ **skrīb**′| —*verb* **prescribed, prescribing** To order or advise the use of a drug, diet, or remedy: *The doctor prescribed rest in bed and lots of liquids for my illness.*

pre·scrip·tion |prĭ **skrĭp**′shən| —*noun, plural* **prescriptions** A written instruction from a doctor telling what treatment or medicine a patient is to receive.

pres·ence |**prĕz**′əns| —*noun* **1.** The fact or condition of being present: *My parents require my presence at the table during dinner.* **2.** The company of someone or something: *She ordered the car in the presence of the sales manager.*

pres·ent[1] |**prĕz**′ənt| —*noun* A moment or period of time between the past and future; now.
—*adjective* **1.** Happening now: *present research into space; his present problems.* **2.** In the same place as someone or something: *The people present began clapping.*
   Idioms **at present** At the present time; right now. **for the present** For the time being; lasting for a certain time.

pre·sent[2] |prĭ **zĕnt**′| —*verb* · **presented, presenting** **1.** To make a gift of; give: *She presented the pennant to the winners. They presented the sheriff with two horses.* **2.** To introduce a person to another or others: *He presented the guests to his father.* **3.** To put oneself before a person or at a place: *She presented herself to the club members.* **4.** To bring before the public; display: *The children presented a play for their parents.*
—*noun* |**prĕz**′ənt |, *plural* **presents** Something presented; a gift.

pres·en·ta·tion |prĕz′ən **tā**′shən| or |prē′zĕn **tā**′shən| —*noun, plural* **presentations** The act of presenting: *the presentation of diplomas to the graduating students.*

pres·ent·ly |**prĕz**′ənt lē| —*adverb* **1.** In a short time; soon: *She will be here presently.* **2.** At this time; now: *They are presently exploring the jungle.*

present participle A form of a verb that shows an action or

---

present¹, present²
Present¹ comes, through French, from a form of the Latin verb meaning "to be before one, to be present." **Present²** also comes from Latin, also through French. The two Latin source words are related.

ă	pat	ĕ	pet	î	fierce
ā	pay	ē	be	ŏ	pot
â	care	ĭ	pit	ō	go
ä	father	ī	pie	ô	paw, for

oi	oil	ŭ	cut	zh	vision
ōō	book	û	fur	ə	ago, item,
ōō	boot	*th*	the		pencil, atom,
yōō	abuse	th	thin		circus
ou	out	hw	which	ər	butter

condition that is happening or exists now. The present participle can be used as an adjective. In the phrase *a guiding light,* the present participle *guiding* is used as an adjective.

present tense A verb tense that shows an action that is happening or a condition that exists now. In the sentence *They are in a hurry,* the verb *are* is in the present tense.

pre·serv·a·tive | prĭ **zûr'** və tĭv | —*noun, plural* **preservatives** Something that is used to preserve. Preservatives are added to foods to keep them from spoiling.

pre·serve | prĭ **zûrv'** | —*verb* **preserved, preserving 1.** To protect; keep in safety: *The explorer was worried about preserving his life in the wilderness.* **2.** To keep in perfect or the same form: *A tape recorder can preserve sound on tape.* **3.** To protect food from spoiling by freezing, smoking, pickling, or canning it.
—*noun, plural* **preserves 1.** Often **preserves** Fruit cooked with sugar to keep it from spoiling. **2.** A place where wild animals, plants, and fish can live safely.

pres·i·den·cy | **prĕz'** ĭ dən sē | —*noun, plural* **presidencies** Often **Presidency 1.** The office of president: *She hopes to be elected to the presidency.* **2.** The period of time during which a president is in office: *During his presidency many changes took place.*

pres·i·dent | **prĕz'** ĭ dənt | —*noun, plural* **presidents 1. President** The chief executive of the United States. **2.** The chief officer of a club, company, or university.

pres·i·den·tial | prĕz'ĭ **dĕn'** shəl | —*adjective* Often **Presidential** Of a president or presidency: *a presidential election.*

press | prĕs | —*verb* **pressed, pressing 1.** To put force or pressure against; bear down on: *Press the button.* **2.** To flatten or form into a desired shape by using force: *Giant machines press useless cars into small blocks.* **3. a.** To squeeze the juice from: *We press grapes to make wine.* **b.** To remove by squeezing: *press juice from oranges.* **4.** To smooth by using heat and pressure; to iron: *The dry cleaner pressed the shirt.* **5.** To take hold of or embrace: *Michael pressed her hand in friendship.* **6.** To try hard to convince; ask again and again: *Joy pressed her aunt to stay.*
—*noun, plural* **presses 1.** Any machine or device used to squeeze or put pressure on something. **2.** A printing press. **3.** Printed matter, especially newspapers and magazines.

press

pres·sure | **prĕsh'** ər | —*noun, plural* **pressures 1.** The force of one thing pressing on another thing that is touching it: *The tires are made to take a very high pressure of air in them. The pressure of the straps made the backpack seem heavier.* **2.** A burden that causes distress: *The tests were putting great pressure on the students.*
—*verb* **pressured, pressuring** To force by using influence or arguments: *Her agent pressured her into singing tonight.*

pres·tige | prĕ **stēzh'** | or | prĕ **stēj'** | —*noun* Great respect in the eyes of others that is gotten through success, fame, or wealth.

pre·tend | prĭ **tĕnd'** | —*verb* **pretended, pretending 1.** To put on a false show of: *He pretended illness.* **2.** To make believe: *Pretend you are a sponge soaking up all the liquid around you.* **3.** To make a claim that is not true: *He pretended to have done his homework.*

pret·ty | **prĭt'** ē | —*adjective* **prettier, prettiest** Pleasing, attractive, or appealing: *a pretty shell; a pretty sunset.*
—*adverb* Somewhat; rather: *He is pretty tired.*

pret·zel | **prĕt'** səl | —*noun, plural* **pretzels** A thin roll of dough, baked in the form of a crisp knot or stick.

pre·vail | prĭ vāl′ | —*verb* **prevailed, prevailing** **1.** To be greater in strength and influence; triumph: *We hope that good will prevail over evil.* **2.** To be most common or happen most often: *Cold winds and snow prevail high in the mountains.*

pre·vent | prĭ vĕnt′ | —*verb* **prevented, preventing** **1.** To keep from happening: *Good eating habits help to prevent illness.* **2.** To keep someone from doing something; hinder: *My brother's snoring prevents me from sleeping.*

pre·ven·tion | prĭ vĕn′shən | —*noun* **1.** The act of preventing: *We must all work at the prevention of illness.* **2.** Something that prevents; a hindrance: *Keeping dry is a prevention against colds.*

pre·view | prē′vyōō′ | —*noun, plural* **previews** A showing of a motion picture, art exhibit, or play to some people before it is shown to everyone.

pre·vi·ous | prē′vē əs | —*adjective* Coming before something else; earlier: *In the previous chapter we met the hero.*

prey | prā | —*noun* **1.** An animal hunted or caught by another animal for food: *Mice are the prey of owls.* **2.** Someone or something that is helpless against attack or trouble: *The little boy was the prey of the neighborhood bully.*

—*verb* **preyed, preying** —**prey on** (or **upon**) **1.** To hunt for food: *Owls prey on mice.* **2.** To take unfair advantage of: *The bully preyed on the smaller children.* **3.** To trouble; bother: *Worry preyed on his mind.*

♦ *These sound alike* **prey, pray.**

Idiom **of prey** Living by taking other animals as prey: *Owls are birds of prey.*

price | prīs | —*noun, plural* **prices** **1.** The amount of money asked or given for something: *The price of the book is $5.99.* **2.** The cost at which something is gotten: *The price of her success was years of hard work.* **3.** An amount of money offered as a reward for capturing someone: *There is a price on the thief's head.*

—*verb* **priced, pricing** **1.** To put a price on: *The grocer priced squash at 29 cents a pound.* **2.** To find out the price of: *Let's price the dress in the shop window.*

price·less | prīs′lĭs | —*adjective* Having great worth; valuable: *priceless treasures.*

prick | prĭk | —*noun, plural* **pricks** A small hole or mark left by piercing.

—*verb* **pricked, pricking** To make a small hole or mark with a pointed object: *The straw poked out of the mattress and pricked her arm.*

prick·ly | prĭk′lē | —*adjective* **pricklier, prickliest** **1.** Having small, sharp thorns or points: *a prickly cactus.* **2.** Tingling: *a prickly feeling.*

prickly pear **1.** A cactus with flat, thorny stems and showy yellow or reddish flowers. **2.** The reddish fruit of this cactus. Prickly pears are sometimes eaten as food.

pride | prīd | —*noun* **1.** A feeling of one's own worth or dignity. **2.** Pleasure or satisfaction in what one has done or in the things one owns: *My aunt takes great pride in her furniture.* **3.** Someone or something that is a source of pride: *That painting is the pride of his collection.* **4.** A too high opinion of oneself; conceit: *Pride is one of the seven deadly sins.*

—*verb* **prided, priding** —**pride oneself on** To be proud of: *She prided herself on her good manners.*

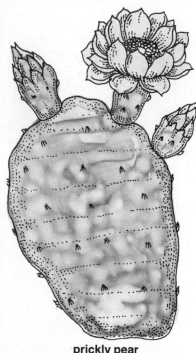

prickly pear

ă	pat	ĕ	pet	î	fierce
ā	pay	ē	be	ŏ	pot
â	care	ĭ	pit	ō	go
ä	father	ī	pie	ô	paw, for
oi	oil	ŭ	cut	zh	vision
ōō	book	û	fur	ə	ago, item,
ōō	boot	*th*	the		pencil, atom,
yōō	abuse	th	thin		circus
ou	out	hw	which	ər	butter

priest | prēst | —*noun, plural* **priests** A clergyman in the Roman Catholic Church and certain other Christian churches.

pri·mar·i·ly | prī **měr′**ĭ lē | or | prī **mâr′**ĭ lē | —*adverb* In the first place; mainly: *The United States was settled primarily by Europeans.*

pri·mar·y | **prī′**měr′ē | or | **prī′**mə rē | —*adjective* **1.** First in time or in order; original: *Our primary problem was to find a new place to live.* **2.** First in importance, order, or value; chief: *The primary reason for exercising is to keep your body in good condition.*
—*noun, plural* **primaries** An election in which members of the same political party run against one another. The winner becomes the party's candidate for office in the regular election.

primary accent 1. The strongest amount of stress placed on that syllable of a word that is spoken loudest. **2.** The mark (′) used to show which syllable of a word receives the strongest amount of stress. In this sense also called *primary stress.*

primary color Any of the three colors, red, yellow, and blue, from which all other colors can be made. For example, purple is made by mixing red and blue.

pri·mate | **prī′**māt′ | —*noun, plural* **primates** Any member of the group of mammals that includes human beings, monkeys, and apes. Primates have a very highly developed brain. Their hands have thumbs with which they can hold and grasp things.

prime | prīm | —*adjective* **1.** First in importance or value; greatest: *Her prime concern was to get home before her parents started to worry.* **2.** Of the highest quality; excellent: *She buys only prime beef.*
—*noun* The best or highest stage or condition: *The star athlete is in his prime.*

prime minister The chief minister and head of the cabinet in certain governments. Canada and Japan have prime ministers.

prim·er | **prĭm′**ər | —*noun, plural* **primers 1.** A beginning reading book. **2.** A book that covers the basic points of any subject: *a mathematics primer.*

prim·i·tive | **prĭm′**ĭ tĭv | —*adjective* **1.** Of or in an early stage of growth or development: *Amebas are a primitive form of life.* **2.** Simple or crude: *The primitive table we built out of old planks collapsed.*

prim·rose | **prĭm′**rōz′ | —*noun, plural* **primroses** A garden plant with clusters of colorful flowers.

prince | prĭns | —*noun, plural* **princes 1.** The son of a king or queen. **2.** A male member of a royal family other than the king. **3.** A nobleman of high rank in some countries.

Prince Ed·ward Island | **ĕd′**wərd | A province of Canada. The capital of Prince Edward Island is Charlottetown.

prin·cess | **prĭn′**sĭs | or | **prĭn′**sĕs′ | or | prĭn **sĕs′** | —*noun, plural* **princesses 1.** The daughter of a king or queen. **2.** The wife of a prince. **3.** A female member of a royal family other than the queen.

prin·ci·pal | **prĭn′**sə pəl | —*adjective* First in order or importance; prime: *The principal reason for our trip is to go to Donna's wedding.*
—*noun, plural* **principals 1.** The head of a school. **2.** A person who is an important member of something: *He is one of the principals of the group that is building the new department store.*
♦ *These sound alike* **principal, principle.**

primary color

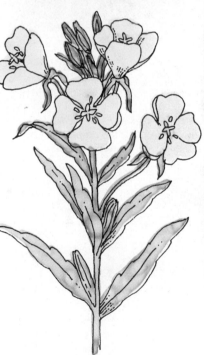
primrose

Prince Edward Island
The province of **Prince Edward Island** was named after Prince Edward Augustus of England, the father of Queen Victoria.

print
Above: A fingerprint
Below: A child examining prints
made in cement

prin·ci·ple |prĭn′sə pəl| —*noun, plural* **principles** **1.** A basic truth or law: *One of the principles of our government is that every person has the right to vote.* **2.** A rule of conduct or behavior: *She makes it a principle to be courteous to everyone.* **3.** Honesty or goodness: *The senator is a man of high principles.*
♦ *These sound alike* **principle, principal.**

print |prĭnt| —*verb* **printed, printing** **1.** To write something in individual letters, like those in books and newspapers: *Print your name clearly.* **2.** To use type to stamp or put words on paper: *That big building is where they print the newspaper.* **3.** To offer in printed form: *The magazine wouldn't print my father's letter.* **4.** To press or imprint a mark or design on a surface, such as paper or cloth: *Do you know whose face is printed on a penny?*
—*noun, plural* **prints** **1.** Letters that are made by printing: *The print in this book is so small it's hard to read.* **2.** A mark or design made in a surface by pressure: *We made prints of our hands in the wet cement.* **3.** Cloth with a pattern or design on it: *Mom made me a dress out of the blue and green print.* **4.** A photograph that is made from a negative: *We sent prints of the new baby to all our relatives.*

print·er |prĭn′tər| —*noun, plural* **printers** A person or company whose job is printing.

print·ing |prĭn′tĭng| —*noun, plural* **printings** **1.** The act, process, or business of making printed material, such as books, magazines, and newspapers, on a printing press. **2.** Letters written like those used in print: *My printing is not messy.*

printing press A machine that prints letters, words, or designs onto sheets of paper.

prism |prĭz′əm| —*noun, plural* **prisms** A transparent solid object with three long sides in the shape of rectangles and two ends in the shape of triangles. When a ray of light hits and passes through one side of it, the prism breaks the ray up into the colors of the rainbow. The separate colors come out on the other side of the prism.

pris·on |prĭz′ən| —*noun, plural* **prisons** A place where persons convicted or accused of crimes are kept.

pris·on·er |prĭz′ə nər| *or* |prĭz′nər| —*noun, plural* **prisoners** **1.** A person who is under arrest or being kept in a prison. **2.** A person who is captured or held by force by someone else: *The soldiers took two enemy prisoners during the battle. She was held as a prisoner by soldiers.*

pri·va·cy |prī′və sē| —*noun, plural* **privacies** **1.** The condition of being alone or away from others: *I need quiet and privacy if I'm going to finish my homework.* **2.** Secrecy or isolation: *I closed the door because I wanted a little privacy.*

pri·vate |prī′vĭt| —*adjective* **1.** Of or owned by one person or group; not for the public: *We can't swim here, it's a private beach.* **2.** Not meant to be shared with or known by others; personal: *Don't read that letter, it's private.* **3.** Not known publicly; secret: *The two men made a private agreement.* **4.** Not holding public office: *The defeated governor is now a private citizen.*
—*noun, plural* **privates** A soldier of the lowest rank in the U.S. Army or Marine Corps.

priv·et |prĭv′ĭt| —*noun* A shrub with small, dark-green leaves and clusters of small white flowers. It is often used for hedges.

priv·i·lege |prĭv′ə lĭj| —*noun, plural* **privileges** A special right

ă	pat	ĕ	pet	î	fierce
ā	pay	ē	be	ŏ	pot
â	care	ĭ	pit	ō	go
ä	father	ī	pie	ô	paw, for
oi	oil	ŭ	cut	zh	vision
ŏŏ	book	û	fur	ə	ago, item,
ōō	boot	*th*	the		pencil, atom,
yōō	abuse	th	thin		circus
ou	out	hw	which	ər	butter

or permission given to a person or group: *My sister and I have the privilege of staying up late on weekends.*

priv·i·leged | **prĭv′**ə lĭjd | —*adjective* Having special rights or privileges: *Famous people are often treated like a privileged class.*

prize | prīz | —*noun, plural* **prizes** Something won as an award for winning or doing well in a game or contest: *My prize for coming in second at the science fair was a red ribbon.*
—*adjective* **1.** Given as a prize: *She won prize money on the television show.* **2.** Worthy of or good enough to win a prize: *a prize cow.*
—*verb* **prized, prizing** To value highly: *I prize my father's advice.*

pro | prō | —*noun, plural* **pros** A person who is a professional, especially in sports: *Watch him, he's a golf pro.*

prob·a·bil·i·ty | prŏb′ə **bĭl′**ĭ tē | —*noun, plural* **probabilities**
1. The fact or condition of being likely to happen; likelihood: *If you study hard, the probability increases that you'll do well on the test.*
2. Something that is likely to happen: *Since she's sick, there's a strong probability she won't go to the dance tonight.*

prob·a·ble | **prŏb′**ə bəl | —*adjective* Likely to happen or be true: *Dad says it's probable that we'll go to California for a vacation.*

pro·ba·tion | prō **bā′**shən | —*noun, plural* **probations** A period of time for testing a person's ability, behavior, or qualifications: *Ellen was given six months' probation at work to see if she could learn the new job. The man was released from prison and put on probation for a year to prove he could stay out of trouble.*

probe | prōb | —*noun, plural* **probes** **1.** A complete or thorough investigation; an examination: *The police are working on a probe to find the causes of the fire that destroyed three stores.* **2.** A long, thin tool used to reach into or touch something in order to examine it. It is used by doctors to see how bad or deep a wound or injury is. **3.** A spaceship or satellite that has scientific equipment. It is sent into space to study and collect information on planets and other heavenly bodies.
—*verb* **probed, probing** To investigate or explore: *The explorers spent all day probing the cave. The doctor probed the cut on my leg.*

prob·lem | **prŏb′**ləm | —*noun, plural* **problems** **1.** A question or situation that causes difficulty or confusion: *Scientists are trying to find solutions to the growing pollution problem.* **2.** Someone who is difficult to deal with: *My sister is a real problem.* **3.** A question that is solved by using mathematics: *There are ten arithmetic problems on the test.*

pro·ce·dure | prə **sē′**jər | —*noun, plural* **procedures** A correct way or method of doing something. It has a series of steps that are done in a particular order: *The first step in the procedure for making a kite is to build the frame.*

pro·ceed | prə **sēd′** | —*verb* **proceeded, proceeding** **1.** To move on or go forward, especially after having stopped: *After waiting for the red light, the bus proceeded down the street.* **2.** To do or carry on an action or activity: *The whole family proceeded to get ready for bed after dinner. My aunt proceeded to tell us about her trip.*

pro·ceeds | **prō′**sēdz′ | —*plural noun* The amount of money collected for a particular purpose by having a special sale or contest: *The proceeds from the charity ball will be used to buy new equipment for the hospital.*

proc·ess | **prŏs′**ĕs′ | or | **prō′**sĕs′ | —*noun, plural* **processes** A series of steps or actions followed in doing or making something:

prize
A prize awarded at a county fair

probe
Satellites in outer space

We learned the process of making paper from wood. We're in the process of moving to a new house.
—*verb* **processed, processing** To prepare or treat something by following a process: *Machines process milk to kill germs.*

pro·ces·sion |prə sĕsh′ən| —*noun, plural* **processions** **1.** The act of going forward in an orderly way: *All the Girl Scout troops walked in procession down to the lake.* **2.** A group of persons walking or riding along in an orderly line: *a graduation procession.*

pro·claim |prō klām′| or |prə klām′| —*verb* **proclaimed, proclaiming** To announce officially and publicly: *The mayor proclaimed Monday as a city holiday.*

proc·la·ma·tion |prŏk′lə mā′shən| —*noun, plural* **proclamations** An official public announcement: *The President issued a proclamation praising the astronauts who landed on the moon.*

prod |prŏd| —*verb* **prodded, prodding** **1.** To poke or jab with something pointed: *She prodded the horse with her toe.* **2.** To urge to do something; stir up: *She constantly prodded him to do his homework.*

pro·duce |prə dōōs′| or |prə dyōōs′| —*verb* **produced, producing** **1.** To make or build something; manufacture: *The factory produces tractors.* **2.** To bring forth something; yield: *These seeds will produce plants.* **3.** To bring forward; show or exhibit: *The little boy produced a frog from his pocket. The fourth grade is producing a play.*
—*noun* |**prŏd′**ōōs| or |**prŏd′**yōōs| or |**prō′**dōōs| or |**prō′**dyōōs| Fruits, vegetables, and other farm products that are raised for selling: *There's a stand on the side of the road where she buys fresh produce.*

produce

pro·duc·er |prə dōō′sər| or |prə dyōō′sər| —*noun, plural* **producers** **1.** A person, company, or thing that produces something: *South America is the world's biggest producer of coffee.* **2.** A person who manages the making and presentation of a movie, play, or other form of entertainment.

prod·uct |**prŏd′**əkt| —*noun, plural* **products** **1.** Something that is made or created: *The market sells food products. I think that tale is a product of your imagination.* **2.** The number or result gotten from multiplying two or more numbers: *The product of 3 times 2 is 6.*

pro·duc·tion |prə dŭk′shən| —*noun, plural* **productions** **1.** The act or process of making or producing something: *Automobile production is a large industry in the United States.* **2.** Something that is produced: *This is the theater company's best production so far.*

pro·duc·tive |prə dŭk′tĭv| —*adjective* **1.** Producing or capable of producing large amounts of something: *The Middle West is productive farm land. Jerry is the company's most productive worker.* **2.** Producing or getting favorable or useful results: *Your work at school has not been very productive.*

pro·fes·sion |prə fĕsh′ən| —*noun, plural* **professions** **1.** A kind of regular work, especially work that calls for special study: *the profession of law.* **2.** The group of persons doing such work: *the teaching profession.*

pro·fes·sion·al |prə fĕsh′ə nəl| —*adjective* **1.** Of, working in, or trained for a profession: *Teachers and doctors are professional people. Your paintings have a professional look.* **2.** Making money or getting paid for doing something that other people do for

ă	pat	ĕ	pet	î	fierce
ā	pay	ē	be	ŏ	pot
â	care	ĭ	pit	ō	go
ä	father	ī	pie	ô	paw, for

oi	oil	ŭ	cut	zh	vision
ōō	book	û	fur	ə	ago, item,
ōō	boot	*th*	the		pencil, atom,
yōō	abuse	th	thin		circus
ou	out	hw	which	ər	butter

pleasure or as a hobby: *a professional writer. After college Ted wants to play professional football.*
—*noun, plural* **professionals 1.** A person who works at a profession: *Dentists are professionals.* **2.** A person who gets paid for doing something that other people do for pleasure or as a hobby: *That tennis player has just become a professional.*

pro·fes·sor |prə fĕs′ər| —*noun, plural* **professors** A teacher of the highest rank in a college or university.

pro·file |prō′fīl′| —*noun, plural* **profiles 1.** A view of something from the side, especially of a person's head or face: *Take a picture of my profile. Whose profile is on the penny?* **2.** A short description or outline of something: *He wrote a profile of President Kennedy.*

prof·it |prŏf′ĭt| —*noun, plural* **profits 1.** Money made in a business. It is the amount of money left after the costs of operating a business and of goods have been subtracted from all the money taken in: *Dick made a profit of five cents on every newspaper he sold.* **2.** A gain from doing something; a benefit: *He saw there was no profit in crying about it.*
—*verb* **profited, profiting 1.** To gain an advantage or benefit: *You should profit from watching how he does it.* **2.** To be a help to; help improve: *It would profit you to pay closer attention.*
♦ *These sound alike* **profit, prophet.**

prof·it·a·ble |prŏf′ĭ tə bəl| —*adjective* **1.** Giving a profit; making money: *Selling ice cream on a hot day can be profitable.* **2.** Giving benefits; useful: *He learned a lot in school that was profitable to him when he grew up.*

pro·found |prə found′| —*adjective* **profounder, profoundest 1.** Having or showing great knowledge and understanding of something; wise: *This book is a profound examination of how government works. That scientist is a profound man.* **2.** Felt very deeply; great; strong: *I felt a profound sadness when she died.*

pro·gram |prō′grăm| or |prō′grəm| —*noun, plural* **programs 1.** A list of the order of events along with the people performing or taking part in them at a show, concert, or meeting: *The program tells you the music the orchestra will play.* **2.** Such a show, presentation, or performance: *The class planned a program of folk music.* **3.** A radio or television show. **4.** A plan or list of things to be done: *Our school has a good athletic program. Landing a spaceship on the moon was one goal of the space program.*

prog·ress |prŏg′rĕs′| or |prŏg′rĭs| —*noun* **1.** Forward movement: *He made slow progress pulling the cart up the hill.* **2.** Steady improvement; development: *The baby was making fast progress learning how to talk.*
—*verb* **pro·gress** |prə grĕs′| **progressed, progressing 1.** To move forward; advance: *The building of the barn is progressing quickly.* **2.** To get better; improve: *Her broken leg has progressed so far she no longer needs to use crutches.*

pro·gres·sive |prə grĕs′ĭv| —*adjective* **1.** Moving on or advancing step by step: *You could hardly see the progressive rising of the water in the lake.* **2.** Working for improvement or reform: *The governor has progressive ideas for fighting poverty.*
—*noun, plural* **progressives** A person who works for improvement or reform.

pro·hib·it |prō hĭb′ĭt| —*verb* **prohibited, prohibiting 1.** To forbid by law; make unlawful: *The city rules prohibit bicycles.* **2.** To prevent; stop: *Rain prohibited us from going to the beach.*

profile

program

projectile

pro·hi·bi·tion |prō′ə bĭsh′ən| —*noun, plural* **prohibitions** The act of prohibiting something: *There is a prohibition on smoking in the school.*

proj·ect |**prŏj′**ĕkt′| or |**prŏj′**ĭkt| —*noun, plural* **projects 1.** A plan, especially one requiring a lot of work: *The town has a project to build three new libraries.* **2.** A special study or experiment done by a student or group of students: *For her science project she built a copy of an ant colony.* **3.** A group of houses or apartment buildings built and operated as a unit.
—*verb* **pro·ject** |prə **jĕkt′**| **projected, projecting 1.** To extend forward; stick out: *Two long horns projected from the bull's head.* **2.** To shoot or throw forward; hurl: *The fountain projected a stream of water.* **3.** To cause light to throw an image or shadow on a surface: *The color slides were projected on a wall.*

pro·jec·tile |prə **jĕk′**təl| or |prə **jĕk′**tīl′| —*noun, plural* **projectiles** Any object that can be thrown or shot through the air or through space. Bullets and rockets are projectiles.

pro·jec·tor |prə **jĕk′**tər| —*noun, plural* **projectors** A machine that uses lenses and light to project a picture or shadow onto a screen or surface: *Movies and slides are shown by a projector.*

prom |prŏm| —*noun, plural* **proms** A formal dance held for a school class: *She wore a long dress to the prom.*

prom·e·nade |prŏm′ə **nād′**| or |prŏm′ə **näd′**| —*noun, plural* **promenades 1.** A slow, easy walk for pleasure or recreation: *We took a promenade around the park.* **2.** A place for taking such a walk: *Go to the promenade along the beach.*
—*verb* **promenaded, promenading** To go on a stroll: *We promenaded down the street.*

prom·i·nent |**prŏm′**ə nənt| —*adjective* **1.** Standing or sticking out: *He has a long, prominent nose.* **2.** Easy to see or spot: *The new skyscraper is prominent.* **3.** Important or well-known; famous: *The scientist is one of the most prominent men in his field.*

prom·ise |**prŏm′**ĭs| —*noun, plural* **promises 1.** A statement in which a person swears to do or not to do something: *I promised my grandmother I'd write her a letter.* **2.** A sign or indication that gives a reason to hope for success in the future: *The young dancer shows promise.* **3.** A sign or clue that something might happen: *Mom's bad mood is a promise of trouble.*
—*verb* **promised, promising 1.** To make a promise; give one's word; swear: *I promised her I'd be home early.* **2.** To give a reason to hope or believe that something might happen: *The clear sky promises a beautiful day.*

pro·mon·to·ry |**prŏm′**ən tôr′ē| or |**prŏm′**ən tō′rē| —*noun, plural* **promontories** A high piece of land or rock that juts or extends out into a body of water.

pro·mote |prə **mōt′**| —*verb* **promoted, promoting 1.** To raise or be raised to a higher rank; make more important: *The Army promoted him to general. I was promoted to the fourth grade.* **2.** To help the development or growth of; contribute to: *The President is promoting a plan to give food to poor countries.* **3.** To try to sell: *They're giving free samples to promote a new kind of peanut butter.*

pro·mo·tion |prə **mō′**shən| —*noun, plural* **promotions 1.** A raise or advance in rank: *Carole got a promotion at work.* **2.** The act of encouraging the development or growth of something: *The group was working for the promotion of cleaner streets and parks.*

prompt |prŏmpt| —*adjective* **prompter, promptest 1.** On time;

ă	pat	ĕ	pet	î	fierce
ā	pay	ē	be	ŏ	pot
â	care	ĭ	pit	ō	go
ä	father	ī	pie	ô	paw, for
oi	oil	ŭ	cut	zh	vision
ŏŏ	book	û	fur	ə	ago, item,
ōō	boot	*th*	the		pencil, atom,
yōō	abuse	th	thin		circus
ou	out	hw	which	ər	butter

not late: *She was always prompt for dinner.* **2.** Done at once or
without delay; quick: *She sent a prompt answer to my letter.*
—*verb* **prompted, prompting 1.** To cause someone to act: *The
news of his mother's illness prompted him to phone her.* **2.** To
remind a speaker or actor what to do or say if he or she forgets:
I'll prompt you if you forget part of your speech.

prompt·ly |**prŏmpt′**lē| —*adverb* Without delay; at once: *Return
overdue library books promptly.*

prompt·ness |**prŏmpt′**nĭs| —*noun* Lack of delay: *Promptness in
closing the screen door helps keep out flies.*

prone |prōn| —*adjective* **1.** Lying with the front or face
downward: *He was napping prone on the sofa.* **2.** Having a
tendency to act or feel in a certain way: *He is prone to be late for
work.*

prong |prông| or |prŏng| —*noun, plural* **prongs** One of the
pointed ends of a fork or other tool.

prong·horn |**prông′**hôrn′| or |**prŏng′**hôrn′| —*noun, plural*
pronghorns An animal that has short, forked horns and can run
very fast. Pronghorns live in western North America. Also called
pronghorn antelope or *antelope.*

pro·noun |**prō′**noun′| In grammar, a word that refers to or is
used in place of a noun or name. *I, you, they, who,* and *which* are
pronouns. In the sentence *Who owns that house across the street
from hers? Who* and *hers* are pronouns.

pro·nounce |prə **nouns′**| —*verb* **pronounced, pronouncing 1.** To
speak or make the sound of a letter, a word, or words: *Pronounce
your words clearly.* **2.** To say or declare something to be so: *The
mayor pronounced the meeting over. The judge pronounced
sentence.*

pro·nounced |prə **nounst′**| —*adjective* Strongly or clearly
marked; easy to notice: *Since her accident she walks with a
pronounced limp.*

pro·nun·ci·a·tion |prə nŭn′sē **ā′**shən| —*noun, plural*
pronunciations 1. The act of pronouncing or the correct way a
letter or word should be spoken: *An actor must have clear
pronunciation.* **2.** The symbols or letters used to show how to
pronounce a letter or word: *This dictionary gives pronunciations
after each word.*

proof |prŏof| —*noun, plural* **proofs** Evidence or facts that show
that something is true: *The police had no proof that the man robbed
the bank. Can you show proof of your age?*

proof·read |**prŏof′**rēd′| —*verb* **proof·read** |**prŏof′**rĕd′|,
proofreading To read over and correct mistakes in printed or
written material: *I proofread my book report before handing it in to
the teacher.*

prop |prŏp| —*verb* **propped, propping 1.** To keep from falling by
putting a support under or against: *I propped up the sagging shelf
with a board.* **2.** To put in a leaning or resting position: *She
propped her chin in her hands.*
—*noun, plural* **props** Something used to keep another thing in
position; a support: *She used a stack of books as a prop for the
mirror.*

prop·a·gan·da |prŏp′ə **găn′**də| —*noun* The attempt or effort to
influence or change the way people think about something by
spreading ideas, opinions, or information. Propaganda may often
give information about only one side of an issue or question, so it

pronghorn

propeller
Airplane propellers

may not be completely true or fair: *She is always giving out propaganda on how good her club is, but she doesn't say that it costs ten dollars to join.*

pro·pel | prə pĕl' | —*verb* **propelled, propelling** To make something move forward or keep moving: *The boat was propelled by oars. The hunter leaned back and propelled the spear.*

pro·pel·ler | prə pĕl'ər | —*noun, plural* **propellers** A device that is made up of blades that are attached to or stick out from a hub. When the blades spin around, they move air or water and produce force to propel or move an aircraft or boat. Propellers are driven by an engine or motor.

prop·er | prŏp'ər | —*adjective* **1.** Suitable for a certain purpose or occasion; appropriate: *A hammer is the proper tool for banging a nail. Being quiet and still is proper behavior in church.* **2.** Of or belonging to a certain person, place, or thing: *If you squeeze a sponge, it will pop back into its proper shape. John is a proper name.* **3.** In the strict or most real sense of the word: *Even though he owns the swamp, it is not part of his farm proper.*

prop·er·ly | prŏp'ər lē | —*adverb* **1.** Done in a proper or correct way: *Clean your room again and do it properly this time.* **2.** In a strict or actual sense: *Properly speaking, silver coins are not made of silver.*

proper noun A noun that is the name of a particular person, place, or thing. *John, Florida,* and *Golden Gate Bridge* are proper nouns.

prop·er·ty | prŏp'ər tē | —*noun, plural* **properties** **1.** A thing or things owned by someone: *That bicycle is my property.* **2.** Land owned by someone: *There is a stream on the border of our property.* **3.** A characteristic or quality of something: *Being slippery and cold are two properties of ice.*

proph·e·cy | prŏf'ĭ sē | —*noun, plural* **prophecies** Something said that tells or warns about what will happen in the future: *The stranger made a prophecy that in one year the whole city would be destroyed by a fire.*

proph·et | prŏf'ĭt | —*noun, plural* **prophets** **1.** A religious leader who gives messages or orders that he or she believes were told to him or her by God. **2.** A person who can tell the future and give advice.

♦ *These sound alike* **prophet, profit.**

pro·por·tion | prə pôr'shən | or | prə pōr'shən | —*noun* **1.** A part or amount of something: *There is a high proportion of sugar in this cereal.* **2.** **proportions** The size or amount of one thing when compared to the size or amount of another thing; relation: *I make chocolate milk by mixing syrup and milk in the proportions of two tablespoons of syrup to every glass of regular milk.* **3.** A correct or pleasing relation between things: *That table is so small it's out of proportion with the other furniture in the room.* **4.** Often **proportions** Size or extent: *That puppy will grow to big proportions.*

pro·pos·al | prə pō'zəl | —*noun, plural* **proposals** **1.** The act of proposing; an offer: *a proposal of friendship.* **2.** A plan or scheme; suggestion: *a proposal for a new shopping center.* **3.** An offer of marriage.

pro·pose | prə pōz' | —*verb* **proposed, proposing** **1.** To bring up something or someone for consideration; suggest: *He proposed a new law to the town council.* **2.** To intend to do something: *Susan proposes to be the first girl on the football team.* **3.** To make an offer of marriage: *He proposed to her last night.*

pro·pri·e·tor | prə **prī′** ĭ tər | —*noun, plural* **proprietors** A person who owns property or a business: *the proprietor of a house. Who is the proprietor of this store?*

pro·pul·sion | prə **pŭl′** shən | —*noun* **1.** The act or process of moving something forward: *the propulsion of the ship by steam engines.* **2.** Anything that propels: *A rocket engine furnishes propulsion for the spacecraft.*

prose | prōz | —*noun* Ordinary writing or speech that is not verse or poetry.

pros·e·cute | **prŏs′** ĭ kyōōt′ | —*verb* **prosecuted, prosecuting** To bring before a court of law for punishment or settlement: *They prosecuted the police officer for taking a bribe.*

pros·pect | **prŏs′** pĕkt′ | —*noun, plural* **prospects** **1.** Something that is looked forward to or expected: *the prospect of a good dinner.* **2.** A possible customer or candidate: *The car salesman talked to several prospects.*

—*verb* **prospected, prospecting** To search or explore: *The old man prospected for gold in the stream.*

pros·pec·tor | **prŏs′** pĕk′tər | —*noun, plural* **prospectors** Someone who searches or explores an area for gold or other valuable minerals.

pros·per | **prŏs′** pər | —*verb* **prospered, prospering** To be successful; do well; thrive: *We hope the business will prosper.*

pros·per·i·ty | prŏ **spĕr′** ĭ tē | —*noun, plural* **prosperities** A prosperous condition; success, especially in money matters: *The factory has not had a period of prosperity in many years.*

pros·per·ous | **prŏs′** pər əs | —*adjective* Doing well, having success, and usually making a profit: *prosperous cities; a prosperous business.*

prospector
A prospector panning for gold

pro·tect | prə **tĕkt′** | —*verb* **protected, protecting** To keep from harm; guard; preserve: *She wore sunglasses to protect her eyes from the glare.*

pro·tec·tion | prə **tĕk′** shən | —*noun, plural* **protections** **1.** The condition of being kept from harm: *We grew a hedge for protection from the wind.* **2.** Someone or something that protects: *Keeping a dog can provide protection against being robbed.*

pro·tec·tive | prə **tĕk′** tĭv | —*adjective* Helping to protect: *a protective coat of paint on the wall.*

pro·tec·tor | prə **tĕk′** tər | —*noun, plural* **protectors** Someone or something that protects; a guard: *The catcher wore a padded chest protector.*

pro·tein | **prō′** tēn′ | —*noun, plural* **proteins** A substance that contains nitrogen and occurs in all plants and animals. Protein is necessary to life. Meat, milk, cheese, eggs, fish, and beans contain much protein.

pro·test | **prō′** tĕst′ | —*noun, plural* **protests** **1.** A statement that shows that one dislikes or objects to something or someone: *I will send a protest to the principal's office.* **2.** A gathering to show dislike or objection: *a student protest against the war.*

—*verb* | prə **tĕst′** | **protested, protesting** To make strong objections: *He protested to the principal.*

Prot·es·tant | **prŏt′** ĭ stənt | —*noun, plural* **Protestants** Any Christian belonging to a church that broke away from the Roman Catholic Church.

—*adjective* Of Protestants or their religions: *the Protestant Bible.*

pro·ton | **prō′** tŏn′ | —*noun, plural* **protons** A tiny particle of an atom. A proton has a positive charge of energy that is equal to the negative charge of an electron in the atom.

pro·to·plasm | prō′tə plăz′əm | —*noun, plural* **protoplasms** A substance that is like jelly. Protoplasm is the living matter in all plant and animal cells.

pro·to·zo·an | prō′tə zō′ən | —*noun, plural* **protozoans** One of a large group of tiny animals made up of only one cell. Protozoans are too small to be seen without a microscope. Amebas and paramecia are protozoans.

pro·trude | prō trood′ | —*verb* **protruded, protruding** To stick out: *His ears protruded from the side of his head.*

proud | proud | —*adjective* **prouder, proudest 1.** Feeling pleased over something done, made, or owned: *proud of his black skin; proud to be named to the Olympic team.* **2.** Thought highly of; honored: *a proud name; a proud tradition.* **3.** Full of self-respect; dignified: *He is poor but is too proud to ask for help.*

prove | proov | —*verb* **proved, proved** or **proven, proving 1.** To show something is true: *He proved that he could lift 400 pounds.* **2.** To test; try out: *Mechanics were proving a new car on the open road.* **3.** To turn out: *The story proved to be true.*

prov·en | proo′vən | A past participle of the verb **prove:** *He has proven that he can run faster than Joe.*

prov·erb | prŏv′ərb | —*noun, plural* **proverbs** A short, often used saying that shows a truth. "No news is good news" is a proverb.

pro·vide | prə vīd′ | —*verb* **provided, providing 1.** To give what is needed or useful: *The motors provided power for the pump.* **2.** To take care of; maintain: *He worked hard to provide for his family.* **3.** To make ready; prepare: *We provided for an emergency by taking our first-aid kit.* **4.** To set down instructions or rules: *The constitution provides for protection of a person's civil rights.*

pro·vid·ed | prə vī′dĭd | —*conjunction* On the condition; if: *You may go out provided your bed is made.*

Prov·i·dence | prŏv′ĭ dəns | or | prŏv′ĭ děns′ | The capital of Rhode Island.

prov·ince | prŏv′ĭns | —*noun, plural* **provinces 1.** A big division of a country: *Ontario and Quebec are large provinces of Canada.* **2.** The total of someone's job or knowledge: *Surgery is not within the provinces of nursing.*

pro·vi·sion | prə vĭzh′ən | —*noun, plural* **provisions 1.** The act of giving what is needed or useful: *He is in charge of the provision of food for the camping trip.* **2. provisions** Supplies of food and other necessary items: *He packed the provisions for the hike.* **3.** Steps taken to get ready: *She is making provisions for her wedding.* **4.** A condition or requirement that deals with a certain subject: *a provision in a peace treaty for arms control.*

pro·voke | prə vōk′ | —*verb* **provoked, provoking 1.** To bring on; arouse: *The movie provoked much laughter.* **2.** To stir into action; excite: *The speech provoked him to join in the protest march.* **3.** To make angry: *The boy provoked the bear to attack.*

prow | prou | —*noun, plural* **prows** The pointed front part of a ship or boat; bow.

prowl | proul | —*verb* **prowled, prowling** To move about slowly and quietly, as if in search of prey: *City cats prowl through alleys at night.*

pru·dence | prood′ns | —*noun* Caution in everyday or practical

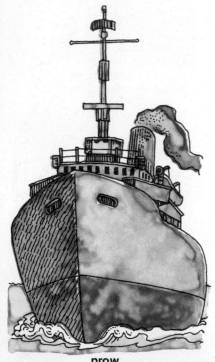

prow

ă	pat	ĕ	pet	î	fierce
ā	pay	ē	be	ŏ	pot
â	care	ĭ	pit	ō	go
ä	father	ī	pie	ô	paw, for

oi	oil	ŭ	cut	zh	vision
ōō	book	û	fur	ə	ago, item,
ōō	boot	th	the		pencil, atom,
yōō	abuse	th	thin		circus
ou	out	hw	which	ər	butter

matters, especially one's own affairs; good sense: *Her prudence kept her from taking chances.*

prune¹ |prōon| —*noun, plural* **prunes** A dried plum, used as food.

prune² |prōon| —*verb* **pruned, pruning** To cut or trim branches and stems on a plant to improve the plant's growth or shape: *The gardener pruned the rose bushes.*

pry¹ |prī| —*verb* **pried, prying, pries** 1. To raise or move by force: *Lily attempted to pry the lid off the box.* 2. To find out with difficulty: *She pried answers from the child.*
—*noun, plural* **pries** Something used as a lever.

pry² |prī| —*verb* **pried, prying, pries** To look closely or curiously: *The old woman pried into something that was not her business.*

psalm |säm| —*noun, plural* **psalms** A sacred song or poem.

psy·chi·a·trist |sĭ kī′ə trĭst| or |sī kī′ə trĭst| —*noun, plural* **psychiatrists** A doctor who treats mental illness.

psy·cho·log·i·cal |sī′kə lŏj′ĭ kəl| —*adjective* Dealing with the mind and how people behave: *psychological testing of the disturbed patient.*

psy·chol·o·gy |sī kŏl′ə jē| —*noun, plural* **psychologies** The science of the mind and how people behave.

ptar·mi·gan |tär′mĭ gən| —*noun, plural* **ptarmigans** A bird of northern regions. Its feathers are white in winter and brownish in summer.

pter·o·dac·tyl |tĕr′ə dăk′təl| —*noun, plural* **pterodactyls** A flying lizard that lived millions of years ago. Some pterodactyls were large and had very long wings.

pub·lic |pŭb′lĭk| —*adjective* 1. Of or relating to the people or the community: *public opinion; public safety.* 2. Intended for use by the community; not private: *a public library; a public telephone; a public school.* 3. Serving or acting for the people or community: *public officials; public servants.* 4. Presented in the presence of the public: *a public announcement.*
—*noun* All of the people: *The museum is open to the public.*

pub·lic-ad·dress system |pŭb′lĭk ə drĕs′| An electronic system that uses loudspeakers and other equipment to send sound throughout a large area. They are used in such places as arenas, stadiums, schools, and hospitals.

pub·li·ca·tion |pŭb′lĭ kā′shən| —*noun, plural* **publications** A book, magazine, newspaper, or other printed material that is published: *This new publication about science comes out monthly.*

pub·lic·i·ty |pŭ blĭs′ĭ tē| —*noun* 1. Information that is given out so that the public will know about or be aware of a person, object, or event: *These newspaper and television advertisements are publicity for a new automobile.* 2. The act or job of giving out such information: *We're working on the publicity for the school play.*

public school A school that all people can attend for free. It is paid for by public taxes.

pub·lish |pŭb′lĭsh| —*verb* **published, publishing** To print a book, magazine, or any printed material and offer it for sale to the public: *The newspaper published my article.*

pub·lish·er |pŭb′lĭ shər| —*noun, plural* **publishers** A person or company that produces or sells printed material, such as books, magazines, or newspapers.

puck |pŭk| —*noun, plural* **pucks** A hard rubber disk used in playing ice hockey.

prune¹, prune²
Prune¹ comes from a Latin word that meant "a plum." **Prune²** comes from a different Latin word — one that has not been found in written documents — meaning "to cut around." Both **prune¹** and **prune²** traveled through French before arriving in English.

pry¹, pry²
Pry¹ was formed from *prize*, a word meaning "to force open"; *prize* comes from French. **Pry²** appeared in English in the fourteenth century; its origin is not clear.

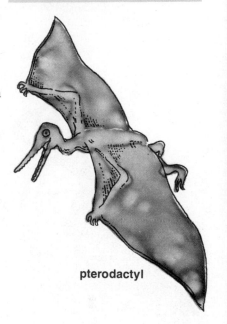

pterodactyl

puck·er |pŭk′ər| —*verb* **puckered, puckering** To gather into small folds or wrinkles: *She puckered the skirt before sewing it. She puckered her lips and kissed the baby.*

pud·ding |po͝od′ĭng| —*noun, plural* **puddings** A sweet, soft, cooked dessert that is like custard.

pud·dle |pŭd′l| —*noun, plural* **puddles** A small pool of water or other liquid: *We splashed through the mud puddles.*

pud·gy |pŭj′ē| —*adjective* **pudgier, pudgiest** Short and chubby: *a pudgy baby.*

pueb·lo |pwĕb′lō| —*noun, plural* **pueblos** An American Indian village of the southwest made up of stone and adobe buildings built very close together. The buildings were often on the side of a mountain.

Puer·to Ri·co |pwĕr′tō rē′kō| or |pôr′tō rē′kō| or |pōr′tō rē′kō| An island associated with the United States.

Puerto Ri·can |rē′kən| **1.** A person who was born in Puerto Rico. Puerto Ricans are United States citizens. **2.** Of Puerto Rico and its people.

puff |pŭf| —*noun, plural* **puffs 1.** A short, sudden gust, as of air, smoke, or steam: *A puff of wind blew the letter off the table.* **2.** Something that is or looks light and fluffy: *a powder puff; little puffs of white clouds.* **3.** A light pastry. It is often filled with whipped cream or custard.
—*verb* **puffed, puffing 1.** To blow in short, sudden gusts: *The breeze puffed the pile of leaves.* **2.** To send out or move with puffs: *The steamboat puffed smoke. The train puffed down the tracks.* **3.** To swell up: *His face puffed up from the blow.*

puff·ball |pŭf′bôl′| —*noun, plural* **puffballs 1.** A fungus that is shaped like a ball. When it is broken open, its spores come out like a puff of dust. **2.** The fluffy head of a dandelion that has gone to seed.

puf·fin |pŭf′ĭn| —*noun, plural* **puffins** A sea bird of northern regions. The puffin has a plump body, black and white feathers, and a heavy, brightly colored bill.

pug |pŭg| —*noun, plural* **pugs** A small dog with short hair, a flat nose, and a curled tail.

pull |po͝ol| —*verb* **pulled, pulling 1.** To grasp something and cause it to move forward or toward oneself: *pull a wagon; pull on a rope.* **2.** To take from or draw out of a firm position: *pull weeds. The dentist pulled the tooth.* **3.** To move: *The car pulled off the road. Pull your bicycle up to the fence.* **4.** To tug at; jerk: *I pulled her hair.*

Phrasal verbs **pull through** To get through a dangerous or difficult situation: *He was very sick, but the doctor said he'd pull through.* **pull up** To come to a stop: *The truck pulled up in front of the building.*
—*noun, plural* **pulls 1.** The act of pulling; a tug or jerk: *Give the door a pull if it sticks.* **2.** The amount of force or strength used in pulling something: *We tried to move the boulder but the pull broke the rope. The pull of a magnet attracts many metal objects.* **3.** The effort of pulling something or of doing something: *It was a hard pull to climb to the top of the mountain before dark.*

Idiom **pull oneself together** To get control of one's emotions and feelings: *Stop crying and pull yourself together.*

pul·let |po͝ol′ĭt| —*noun, plural* **pullets** A young hen, especially one less than a year old.

puffin

ă	pat	ĕ	pet	î	fierce
ā	pay	ē	be	ŏ	pot
â	care	ĭ	pit	ō	go
ä	father	ī	pie	ô	paw, for
oi	oil	ŭ	cut	zh	vision
o͝o	book	û	fur	ə	ago, item,
o͞o	boot	*th*	the		pencil, atom,
yo͞o	abuse	th	thin		circus
ou	out	hw	which	ər	butter

pul·ley |pŏŏl′ē| —*noun, plural* **pulleys** A wheel with a groove in the outside edge through which a rope, chain, or belt moves as the wheel turns. Pulleys are used to lift or lower heavy weights.

pulp |pŭlp| —*noun, plural* **pulps** **1.** The soft, juicy part of fruits and certain vegetables. **2.** A damp mixture of ground-up wood or rags. It is used for making paper.

pul·pit |pŏŏl′pĭt| or |pŭl′pĭt| —*noun, plural* **pulpits** A platform in a church from which a clergyman speaks to the congregation.

pulse |pŭls| —*noun, plural* **pulses** **1.** The rhythmic movement of the arteries as blood is pumped through them by the beating of the heart. **2.** Any regular or rhythmic beat: *We could hear the pulse of the warriors' drums in the distance.*

pu·ma |pyŏŏ′mə| —*noun, plural* **pumas** An animal, the mountain lion.

pump |pŭmp| —*noun, plural* **pumps** A device used to move a liquid or gas from one place or container to another: *a gasoline pump.*
—*verb* **pumped, pumping** **1.** To raise or move a liquid or gas with a pump: *We pumped the water out of the boat.* **2.** To fill with air or gas using a pump: *pump a flat tire.* **3.** To move up and down or back and forth: *He said hello and pumped my hand heartily.* **4.** To question carefully: *We pumped her for further news.*

pump·kin |pŭmp′kĭn| or |pŭm′kĭn| or |pŭng′kĭn| —*noun, plural* **pumpkins** A large fruit with a thick orange rind. The pulp of the pumpkin is often used for making pies.

pun |pŭn| —*noun, plural* **puns** A funny or clever use of a word that has more than one meaning or a word that sounds like another word but has a different meaning. For example, "I spend most of my time with my mom because my dad is farther away" is a pun on the different meanings of "father" and "farther."
—*verb* **punned, punning** To make a pun.

punch¹ |pŭnch| —*verb* **punched, punching** To make a hole, mark, or design by piercing: *I punched a hole in the paper with a pencil. The bus driver punched our tickets.*
—*noun, plural* **punches** A tool for making holes in something: *I used a punch to make a new hole in my belt.*

punch² |pŭnch| —*verb* **punched, punching** **1.** To hit with the fists: *She punched me in the shoulder.* **2.** To herd or move cattle: *All the cowboys learned to punch cows.*
—*noun, plural* **punches** A blow with or as if with the fist: *a punch in the stomach.*

punch³ |pŭnch| —*noun, plural* **punches** A sweet drink that is made by mixing fruit juices, soda, or other ingredients.

punc·tu·al |pŭngk′chŏŏ əl| —*adjective* Acting or arriving on time; prompt: *She is always punctual for school.*

punc·tu·ate |pŭngk′chŏŏ āt′| —*verb* **punctuated, punctuating** To mark written material with punctuation, such as periods and commas, in order to make the meaning clear.

punc·tu·a·tion |pŭngk′chŏŏ ā′shən| —*noun* The use of periods, commas, and other marks to make the meaning of written or printed material clear.

punctuation mark Any of the marks, as a comma (,), semicolon (;), hyphen (-), period (.), question mark (?), or exclamation point (!), used to make the meaning of written or printed material clear to the reader.

punc·ture |pŭngk′chər| —*verb* **punctured, puncturing** To pierce

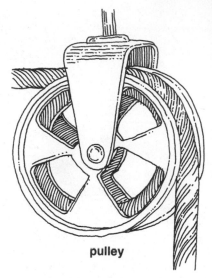
pulley

pumpkin

punch¹, punch², punch³
Punch¹ is a shortened form of a word meaning "punching tool." **Punch²** is a different form of a word meaning "to puncture." **Punch³** is said to have come from a word used by people living in India. That word means "five" and refers to the five ingredients that make up this kind of drink. But this is only a possibility.

or make a hole in with something sharp: *A nail punctured the car's tire. The dog didn't bite me hard enough to puncture the skin.*
—*noun, plural* **punctures** A hole made by something sharp: *The mechanic said there were three punctures in the tire.*

pun·ish |pŭn′ĭsh| —*verb* **punished, punishing** To make someone suffer or pay a penalty for a crime, fault, or misbehavior: *She punished the students for cheating. He was punished severely.*

pun·ish·ment |pŭn′ĭsh mənt| —*noun, plural* **punishments**
1. The act of punishing: *Courts decide the punishment of criminals.*
2. A penalty for a crime or error: *Your punishment for being late will be to stay after school.*

punt |pŭnt| —*noun, plural* **punts** In football, to drop a football and kick it before it hits the ground.
—*verb* **punted, punting** To kick a football before it hits the ground.

pu·ny |pyōō′nē| —*adjective* **punier, puniest** Small or unimportant in size, strength, or value; weak: *What a puny horse. Saying that you're tired is a puny excuse for not cleaning the yard.*

pup |pŭp| —*noun, plural* **pups** **1.** A young dog; a puppy.
2. The young of some other animals, such as a seal, wolf, or fox.

pu·pa |pyōō′pə| —*noun, plural* **pupas** An insect during a resting stage while it is changing from a larva into an adult. A pupa is protected by an outer covering such as a cocoon.

pu·pil¹ |pyōō′pəl| —*noun, plural* **pupils** A student who is studying in school or with a private teacher.

pu·pil² |pyōō′pəl| —*noun, plural* **pupils** The opening in the center of the iris through which light enters the eye. It looks like a black dot and gets bigger in darkness and smaller in bright light.

pup·pet |pŭp′ĭt| —*noun, plural* **puppets** A small figure or doll made to look like a person or animal. Some fit over the hand and others have strings that are moved from above.

pup·py |pŭp′ē| —*noun, plural* **puppies** A young dog.

pur·chase |pûr′chĭs| —*verb* **purchased, purchasing** To get something by paying money; buy: *We purchased a new house.*
—*noun, plural* **purchases** Something that is bought: *She carried her purchases home from the store.*

pure |pyŏŏr| —*adjective* **purer, purest** **1.** Not mixed with anything; perfectly clean: *pure drinking water. This necklace is pure silver.* **2.** Nothing else but; complete; total: *It was pure luck that I found the keys in the street.*

pure·bred |pyŏŏr′brĕd′| —*adjective* Having ancestors that are all of the same breed or kind: *purebred dogs and horses.*

pu·ri·fy |pyŏŏr′ə fī′| —*verb* **purified, purifying, purifies** To make pure or clean: *Machines purify water to make it safe to drink.*

Pu·ri·tan |pyŏŏr′ĭ tən| —*noun, plural* **Puritans** A member of a group of Protestants in England and the American Colonies in the 16th and 17th centuries. The Puritans wanted simpler forms of religious worship and very strict moral behavior.

pu·ri·ty |pyŏŏr′ĭ tē| —*noun* The condition of being pure or clean: *The city is always checking the purity of the drinking water.*

pur·ple |pûr′pəl| —*noun, plural* **purples** A color that is a mixture of red and blue.
—*adjective* Of the color purple: *purple grapes.*

pur·plish |pûr′plĭsh| —*adjective* Somewhat purple: *After the storm the sky was a purplish color.*

---

pupil¹, pupil²
Pupil¹ and **pupil²** come from Latin words meaning "little boy" and "little girl," respectively. **Pupil¹** traveled through French and arrived in English with the meaning "orphan, ward" and thus "student." The meaning for **pupil²** comes from the fact that it is possible to see a tiny reflection of oneself by looking into the pupil of another person's eye.

puppet

puppy

ă	pat	ĕ	pet	î	fierce
ā	pay	ē	be	ŏ	pot
â	care	ĭ	pit	ō	go
ä	father	ī	pie	ô	paw, for
oi	oil	ŭ	cut	zh	vision
ŏŏ	book	û	fur	ə	ago, item,
ōō	boot	*th*	the		pencil, atom,
yōō	abuse	th	thin		circus
ou	out	hw	which	ər	butter

pur·pose |pûr′pəs| —*noun, plural* **purposes** The result one hopes for in doing or making something; goal; aim; intention: *What is the purpose of that knob on the television set? The purpose of the cake sale is to raise money for the library.*

pur·pose·ly |pûr′pəs lē| —*adverb* Done with a special purpose; deliberately: *She purposely came over to ask me if she could borrow my sweater.*

purr |pûr| —*noun, plural* **purrs** The low, murmuring sound made by a cat when it's happy.
—*verb* **purred, purring** To make a purr.

purse |pûrs| —*noun, plural* **purses** A woman's handbag or pocketbook.
—*verb* **pursed, pursing** To fold together; pucker or wrinkle: *purse one's lips.*

pur·sue |pər soo′| —*verb* **pursued, pursuing** **1.** To chase in order to capture or kill: *The police pursued the robbers. Lions pursue other animals for food.* **2.** To carry on an activity; keep on doing something: *He's pursuing his medical studies.*

pur·suit |pər soot′| —*noun, plural* **pursuits** **1.** The act of pursuing: *The sheriff rode off in pursuit of the horse thieves.* **2.** A hobby or job; an interest a person has: *Hiking is his favorite pursuit.*

pus |pŭs| —*noun* A thick, yellowish-white liquid that forms in an infected sore or wound.

push |poosh| —*verb* **pushed, pushing** **1.** To press against something in order to move it: *He pushed the rock but it wouldn't budge. They pushed hard.* **2.** To exert force on an object by using something to press against it: *The police officer pushed his shoulder against the door.* **3.** To move forward by using force: *He pushed through the crowd.* **4.** To urge or try to force someone to do something: *The family pushed him to try out for the football team.* **5.** To make a strong effort; work hard: *He pushed to finish his homework on time.* **6.** To press with one's finger: *push a button.* **7.** To try to sell; promote: *advertisers pushing a new brand of toothpaste.*
—*noun, plural* **pushes** **1.** The act of pushing; a shove: *The car needs a push to get started. The push of the wind knocked the fence over.* **2.** A strong effort: *It took a big push to get the project finished on time.*

push·cart |poosh′kärt′| —*noun, plural* **pushcarts** A light cart that is pushed by hand: *The peddler was selling hot dogs and soda from a pushcart.*

push·up |poosh′ŭp′| —*noun, plural* **pushups** An exercise in which a person lies face down and holds the body up with the hands and toes. The body is then raised and lowered by bending the arms while keeping the back straight.

puss |poos| —*noun, plural* **pusses** A cat.

puss·y |poos′ē| —*noun, plural* **pussies** A cat.

pussy willow A shrub that has small, silky gray flower clusters in early spring.

put |poot| —*verb* **put, putting** **1.** To set or cause to be in a certain place or condition; to place: *Put your pencils in the desk. I'm putting on my shoes. Put everything back where it belongs.* **2.** To cause to undergo something: *You put us to a lot of trouble for nothing.* **3.** To assign; attribute: *The teacher puts a lot of importance on honesty.* **4.** To impose; levy: *put a tax on tobacco.* **5.** To say or state; express: *She didn't put her question clearly.*

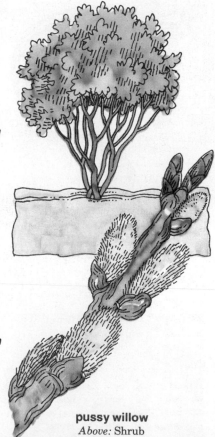

pussy willow
Above: Shrub
Below: Branch with flower clusters

6. To apply: *You can succeed if you put your mind to it.*
　Phrasal verbs **put away** To kill: *The sick horse had to be put away.* **put down** **1.** To put an end to; block: *The soldiers put down the uprising.* **2.** To criticize: *My sister puts me down every time I ask a question.* **put in** **1.** To use time doing: *He's putting in five hours a day practicing the piano.* **2.** To say: *Put in a good word for me with the boss.* **put off** **1.** To avoid: *My boss keeps putting me off whenever I ask for a raise.* **2.** To postpone: *Don't put off until tomorrow what you can do today.* **put on** **1.** To cause to operate: *put on the brakes.* **2.** To present on a stage: *The drama club is putting on three plays this year.* **3.** To gain or add to: *She's putting on weight.* **put out** **1.** To extinguish: *put out a campfire; put out a cigarette.* **2.** To cause to undergo trouble for another: *Please don't put yourself out for me.* **put through** **1.** To connect by telephone: *The operator put me through to the hospital.* **2.** To do or complete successfully: *My father has just put through a big business deal.* **put up** **1.** To lift or raise: *Put up your hand if you wish to speak.* **2.** To build: *We're putting up a new barn.* **3.** To provide food or a place to sleep: *Can you put us up just for the night?* **put up with** To bear or endure; tolerate: *Your bad behavior is more than I can put up with today.*

putt | pŭt | —*verb* **putted, putting** In golf, to hit a ball gently when it is on the green so that it will roll into the hole or cup.
—*noun, plural* **putts** Such a hit or stroke.

put·ty | pŭt′ē | —*noun, plural* **putties** A soft cement that looks like dough, used to fill holes in woodwork and hold panes of glass in place.

puz·zle | pŭz′əl | —*noun, plural* **puzzles** Something that is difficult to solve or understand: *a jigsaw puzzle. It's a puzzle to me how she can finish her homework so quickly.*
—*verb* **puzzled, puzzling** **1.** To confuse: *Mary's rude behavior puzzled the teacher.* **2.** To work hard trying to do or understand something; be confused: *Sally puzzled over her arithmetic assignment for two hours.*

pyg·my | pĭg′mē | —*noun, plural* **pygmies** **1.** **Pygmy** A member of an African or Asian people. Pygmies are usually between four and five feet tall. **2.** An unusually small person or thing.

pyr·a·mid | pĭr′ə mĭd | —*noun, plural* **pyramids** **1.** A solid object with a flat base and four sides shaped like triangles that meet in a point at the top. **2.** A very large stone structure in the shape of a pyramid. The pyramids of ancient Egypt were built as tombs and as structures to study the movement of stars.

py·thon | pī′thŏn′ | —*noun, plural* **pythons** A very large, nonpoisonous snake of Africa, Asia, and Australia. Pythons coil around and crush the animals they eat.

python

ă	pat	ĕ	pet	î	fierce
ā	pay	ē	be	ŏ	pot
â	care	ĭ	pit	ō	go
ä	father	ī	pie	ô	paw, for

oi	oil	ŭ	cut	zh	vision
ŏŏ	book	û	fur	ə	ago, item,
ōō	boot	th	the		pencil, atom,
yōō	abuse	th	thin		circus
ou	out	hw	which	ər	butter

Phoenician — The letter *Q* comes originally from a Phoenician symbol named *qoph*, meaning "monkey."

Greek — The Greeks borrowed the symbol from the Phoenicians and changed its form. They also changed its name to *qoppa*.

Roman — The Romans took the letter and adapted it for carving into stone. This became the model for our modern printed capital *Q*.

Medieval — The hand-written form of about 1,200 years ago became the basis of the modern small letter.

Modern — The modern capital and small letters are based on the Roman capital and later hand-written forms.

q or **Q** | kyōō | —*noun, plural* **q's** or **Q's** The seventeenth letter of the English alphabet.

quack | kwăk | —*noun, plural* **quacks** The hoarse sound made by a duck.
—*verb* **quacked, quacking** To make such a sound.

quad·ri·lat·er·al | kwŏd′rĭ lăt′ ər əl | —*noun, plural* **quadrilaterals** Any figure that has four sides. A rectangle is a quadrilateral.

quad·ru·ped | kwŏd′rōō pĕd′ | —*noun, plural* **quadrupeds** Any animal that has four feet or four paws or hoofs. Dogs, cats, and horses are quadrupeds; chickens and human beings are not.

qua·hog | kwô′hôg′ | or | kwô′hŏg′ | or | kwō′hôg′ | or | kwō′hŏg′ | —*noun, plural* **quahogs** A clam of the Atlantic coast of North America. Quahogs are used as food. The hard, rounded shell of the quahog was used by Indians to make wampum.

quail | kwāl | —*noun, plural* **quail** or **quails** A rather small, plump bird with a short tail and brownish feathers.

quaint | kwānt | —*adjective* **quainter, quaintest** Old-fashioned, especially in a pleasing way: *a quaint village.*

quake | kwāk | —*verb* **quaked, quaking** To shake, tremble, or shiver: *The poor dog quaked with cold. The ground quaked when the heavy freight train passed.*
—*noun, plural* **quakes** An earthquake.

qual·i·fi·ca·tion | kwŏl′ə fĭ kā′shən | —*noun, plural* **qualifications** **1.** A skill or other quality that makes a person able to do a certain kind of work: *What are the qualifications for an airline pilot?* **2.** Something that limits or restricts: *The group accepted her plan without qualification.*

qual·i·fy | kwŏl′ə fī′ | —*verb* **qualified, qualifying, qualifies** **1.** To make or become fit for a certain kind of work or position: *That college will qualify you to be a teacher. She qualified as a surgeon after many years of studying.* **2.** To make less harsh or extreme: *He qualified his remarks to avoid making anyone angry.*

qual·i·ty | kwŏl′ĭ tē | —*noun, plural* **qualities** **1.** The nature or character of something that makes it what it is: *the sour quality of vinegar.* **2.** A part of a person's looks, character, or personality: *She has many good qualities.* **3.** The degree or grade of how good something is: *Cloth of poor quality tears easily.*

qualm | kwäm | or | kwôm | —*noun, plural* **qualms** **1.** A feeling

quail

of doubt: *I had some qualms about riding on the roller coaster.* **2.** A sudden feeling of conscience: *He had no qualms about telling lies.*

quan·ti·ty |**kwŏn′**tĭ tē| —*noun, plural* **quantities 1.** An amount or number of a thing or things: *Fresh fruits and vegetables contain vitamins in various quantities.* **2.** A large amount or number: *The school cafeteria buys milk in quantity.*

quar·an·tine |**kwôr′**ən tēn′| or |**kwŏr′**ən tēn′| —*noun, plural* **quarantines 1.** A period of time during which a person, an animal, or a plant is kept apart from others to stop the spread of disease. **2.** Any act of keeping someone or something apart from others, especially to keep from spreading disease.
—*verb* **quarantined, quarantining** To keep or place someone or something in quarantine.

quar·rel |**kwôr′**əl| or |**kwŏr′**əl| —*noun, plural* **quarrels** An angry argument: *The twins had a quarrel over the new toy.*
—*verb* **quarreled, quarreling 1.** To have a quarrel; argue angrily: *The boys quarreled over the use of the tennis court.* **2.** To find fault: *I won't quarrel with what you say.*

quar·ry |**kwôr′**ē| or |**kwŏr′**ē| —*noun, plural* **quarries** An open place where stone is taken out by cutting or blasting. Some quarries are very deep.

quart |kwôrt| —*noun, plural* **quarts 1.** A unit of measure equal to two pints: *You use almost a quart of milk to make that custard.* **2. a.** A container that holds one quart. **b.** A quart with something in it: *Please pick up a quart of milk at the store.*

quar·ter |**kwôr′**tər| —*noun, plural* **quarters 1.** Any of four equal parts of something: *Cut the orange into quarters.* **2.** One fourth of the time it takes for the moon to travel around the earth. **3.** A United States or Canadian coin worth twenty-five cents. **4.** In football, basketball, and some other sports, any of the four time periods that make up a game. **5.** A district or section: *the French quarter of the city.* **6. quarters** A place to sleep or live: *the officers' quarters on a ship; the family quarters in the White House.*
—*verb* **quartered, quartering** To cut or divide into four equal parts: *Dad quartered the orange for us.*

quar·ter·back |**kwôr′**tər băk′| —*noun, plural* **quarterbacks** In football, the player who directs the offense and usually passes the ball.

quartz |kwôrts| —*noun, plural* **quartzes** A clear, hard kind of rock. Quartz is often seen as tiny, sparkling bits in rock such as granite. Larger crystals may be used in jewelry, especially the colored types such as amethyst.

qua·sar |**kwā′**zär′| or |**kwā′**sär′| —*noun, plural* **quasars** An object like a star. Quasars give off radio waves or very bright light and are at great distances from the earth.

quay |kē| —*noun, plural* **quays** A stone wharf or strong bank where ships are loaded or unloaded.
♦ *These sound alike* **quay, key.**

Que·bec |kwĭ **bĕk′**| **1.** A province of eastern Canada. **2.** The capital of this province.

queen |kwēn| —*noun, plural* **queens 1.** A woman who is the ruler of a country. **2.** The wife of a king. **3.** A woman or girl who is chosen or considered as the most outstanding in some way: *a beauty queen.* **4.** A playing card on which there is a picture of a queen. Its value is above jack and below king. **5.** In

Quebec
The name **Quebec** comes from an Indian word meaning "where the river narrows."

queen
The queen of England on a visit to the United States

ă	pat	ĕ	pet	î	fierce
ā	pay	ē	be	ŏ	pot
â	care	ĭ	pit	ō	go
ä	father	ī	pie	ô	paw, for
oi	oil	ŭ	cut	zh	vision
ŏŏ	book	û	fur	ə	ago, item,
ōō	boot	*th*	the		pencil, atom,
yōō	abuse	th	thin		circus
ou	out	hw	which	ər	butter

chess, a player's most powerful piece. **6.** In a colony of bees, ants, or termites, a large female that lays eggs. The queen is usually the only one of this kind in the colony.

Queen Anne's lace | ănz | A plant with feathery leaves and flat clusters of small white flowers. It is a wild form of the carrot.

queer | kwîr | —*adjective,* **queerer, queerest** Unusual; odd; strange: *He had a queer expression on his face when we told him we had lost the game.*

quench | kwĕnch | —*verb* **quenched, quenching 1.** To put out a fire: *We quenched the flames with a bucket of water.* **2.** To satisfy, especially thirst: *A glass of cider will quench your thirst.*

que·ry | kwîr′ē | —*noun, plural* **queries** A question; an inquiry: *He has a good answer to your query.*

—*verb* **queried, querying, queries 1.** To ask questions of: *Our friends queried us about our vacation trip.* **2.** To show doubt about; to question: *The principal queried my decision to leave before the exam.*

quest | kwĕst | —*noun, plural* **quests** A search, especially for something valuable: *The pirates were on a quest for gold.*

ques·tion | kwĕs′chən | —*noun, plural* **questions 1.** Something that is asked in order to get an answer. **2.** A subject that is being argued about: *The chairperson called for a vote on the question of building a new library.* **3.** A problem: *It's not a question of money.* **4.** A point that is not certain; doubt: *There is no question that she is a good student.*

—*verb* **questioned, questioning 1.** To ask questions of: *Dad questioned me about the party.* **2.** To have or show doubt about: *No one questions her orders.*

Idiom **out of the question** Not to be considered or even thought about: *Brad wanted a car of his own, but Dad said it was out of the question.*

question mark A punctuation mark (?) written at the end of a sentence or phrase. It shows that a question is being asked.

quet·zal | kĕt säl′ | —*noun, plural* **quetzals** A bird of Central America with bright green and red feathers. The tail feathers of the male are very long.

quick | kwĭk | —*adjective* **quicker, quickest 1.** Moving or acting with speed; fast: *quick on his feet.* **2.** Done in a short amount of time: *a quick trip; a quick recovery.* **3.** Fast to understand, think, or learn; bright; alert: *a quick mind.* **4.** Easily stirred up: *a quick temper.*

—*adverb* Rapidly; promptly: *Come quick! He'll find out quick enough.*

—*noun, plural* **quicks** The sensitive, tender skin under the fingernails.

quick·en | kwĭk′ən | —*verb* **quickened, quickening 1.** To make or become more rapid: *She quickened her steps. His pulse quickened.* **2.** To make or become livelier or more intense: *Such stories quicken the imagination. Interest in the election quickened.*

quick·sand | kwĭk′sănd′ | —*noun* A mixture of sand and water that is too thick to float on and too soft to stand on. Quicksand sucks down anything that rests or is on its surface.

qui·et | kwī′ĭt | —*adjective* **quieter, quietest 1.** Making little or no noise; silent or almost silent: *quiet children; a quiet engine.* **2.** Free of noise; hushed: *a quiet street.* **3.** Not loud: *He spoke in a quiet voice.* **4.** Not moving; still; calm: *The sea was quiet after the*

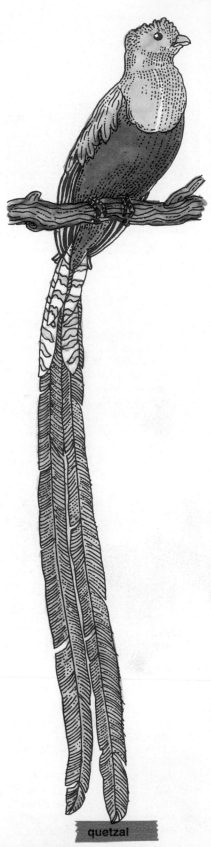

quetzal

storm. **5.** Peaceful: *a quiet evening at home.*
—*noun* **1.** Freedom from noise; silence: *The speaker asked for quiet.* **2.** Peace: *She retired to the quiet of her country home.*
—*verb* **quieted, quieting** To make or become quiet: *The teacher quieted the class. The audience quieted down.*

quill | kwĭl | —*noun, plural* **quills** **1. a.** A long, stiff feather, usually from the tail or wing of a bird. **b.** The hollow, hard central part of a feather. **2.** A writing pen that is made from a long, stiff feather. Also called *quill pen.* **3.** One of the sharp, hollow spines of a porcupine.

quilt | kwĭlt | —*noun, plural* **quilts** A covering for a bed. A quilt is made of two layers of cloth sewn together with a padding of cotton, feathers, or other material in between.
—*verb* **quilted, quilting** To work on or make a quilt or quilts: *They quilted together once a week.*

quince | kwĭns | —*noun, plural* **quinces** A hard fruit that looks like an apple and has a pleasant smell. Quinces are used mostly for making jam or jelly.

qui·nine | kwī′nīn′ | —*noun* A bitter, colorless drug used to treat malaria.

quit | kwĭt | —*verb* **quit, quitting** **1.** To stop: *He quit smoking. Quit bothering me!* **2.** To give up; resign: *I quit my job.* **3.** To depart from; leave: *They quit the city to move to the country.*

quite | kwīt | —*adverb* **1.** Completely; altogether: *I am not quite finished with my homework.* **2.** Somewhat; rather: *Our own group of planets is quite small.* **3.** Really; truly: *a quite large number of mistakes.*

Idioms **quite a** Unusual; remarkable: *quite a large crowd; quite a baseball player.* **quite a few** A large number; many: *Quite a few people came to the party.*

quiv·er¹ | kwĭv′ər | —*verb* **quivered, quivering** To shake with a slight vibrating motion; tremble: *His lips quivered with excitement.*
—*noun* A slight vibrating motion.

quiv·er² | kwĭv′ər | —*noun, plural* **quivers** A case for holding and carrying arrows.

quiz | kwĭz | —*noun, plural* **quizzes** A short test.
—*verb* **quizzed, quizzing** **1.** To question: *He quizzed the thief about the robbery.* **2.** To test someone's knowledge by asking questions: *The teacher quizzed us about state capitals.*

quo·ta | kwō′tə | —*noun, plural* **quotas** **1.** An amount of something to be done, made, or sold: *Dad gave each of us a quota of chores.* **2.** The greatest number of people or things that may be let into a country, group, or institution: *a quota of immigrants.*

quo·ta·tion | kwō tā′shən | —*noun, plural* **quotations** **1.** The act of one person repeating another person's words: *These remarks are not for quotation.* **2.** The words that are repeated: *a quotation from the President; a quotation from the Bible.*

quotation mark Either of a pair of punctuation marks (" ") used to mark the beginning (") and the end (") of a quotation.

quote | kwōt | —*verb* **quoted, quoting** To repeat the words of another person: *She quoted a famous poet. The newspaper quoted the mayor.*
—*noun, plural* **quotes** **1.** A quotation. **2.** A quotation mark.

quo·tient | kwō′shənt | —*noun, plural* **quotients** The number that is gotten by dividing one number by another. If 10 is divided by 5, the quotient is 2.

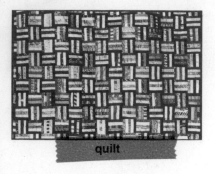

quilt

quiver¹, quiver²
Quiver¹ comes from an old English root that meant "nimble," which is probably related to **quick**. **Quiver²** appeared in old French, but it probably had an even older source in a language spoken by people living in Asia.

quiver²

ă	pat	ĕ	pet	î	fierce
ā	pay	ē	be	ŏ	pot
â	care	ĭ	pit	ō	go
ä	father	ī	pie	ô	paw, for
oi	oil	ŭ	cut	zh	vision
ŏŏ	book	û	fur	ə	ago, item,
ōō	boot	*th*	the		pencil, atom,
yōō	abuse	th	thin		circus
ou	out	hw	which	ər	butter

Phoenician — The letter *R* comes originally from a Phoenician symbol named *resh*, meaning "head," in use about 3,000 years ago.

Greek — The Greeks borrowed the symbol from the Phoenicians and changed its form. They also changed its name to *rhō*.

Roman — The Romans took the letter and added a tail to distinguish it from *P*. This became the model for our modern capital *R*.

Medieval — The hand-written form of about 1,200 years ago became the basis of the modern small letter.

Modern — The modern capital and small letters are based on the Roman capital and later hand-written forms.

r or **R** |är| —*noun, plural* **r's** or **R's** The eighteenth letter of the English alphabet.

rab·bi |răb′ī′| —*noun, plural* **rabbis** **1.** The leader of a Jewish congregation. **2.** A teacher of Jewish laws and customs.

rab·bit |răb′ĭt| —*noun, plural* **rabbits** A burrowing animal with long ears, soft fur, and a short, furry tail.

ra·bies |rā′bēz′| —*noun* A disease that can affect people and other warm-blooded animals such as dogs, cats, and wolves. Rabies is caused by a virus and almost always causes death unless it is treated quickly.

rac·coon |ră kōon′| —*noun, plural* **raccoons** A North American animal with black face markings that look like a mask, grayish-brown fur, and a bushy tail with black rings.

race¹ |rās| —*noun, plural* **races** A contest of speed, as in running, riding, or swimming: *a horse race; a sailboat race.*
—*verb* **raced, racing** **1.** To take part in a race: *I'll race you to the house.* **2.** To move or rush very fast: *She raced home.*

race² |rās| —*noun, plural* **races** A large group of people with certain physical characteristics that are passed on from one generation to another. The population of the world is made up of many different races.

ra·cial |rā′shəl| —*adjective* Of or having to do with race: *racial features; racial characteristics.*

rack |răk| —*noun, plural* **racks** **1.** A pole with pegs or a frame with pegs or shelves. Racks are used for storing, hanging, or displaying things: *a hat rack; a coat rack; a magazine rack.* **2.** An old instrument of torture on which a person's body was stretched.
—*verb* **racked, racking** To cause great suffering; torture.

rack·et¹ |răk′ĭt| —*noun, plural* **rackets** A round wooden or metal frame with tightly laced strings and a handle. Rackets are used in games like tennis and badminton.

rack·et² |răk′ĭt| —*noun, plural* **rackets** A loud, continuous, unpleasant noise: *The trucks driving down the street make a racket day and night.*

ra·dar |rā′där′| —*noun* A device used to find out the location and speed of objects, such as airplanes and rockets, that are not seen or are distant. Radar works by sending out radio waves that bounce off distant objects.

raccoon

race¹, race²
Race¹ appeared long ago in the language of people living in Scandinavia. It meant "a running, a fast current of water." **Race²** is from an old French word meaning "a group of people." Its earlier origin is not clear.

racket¹, racket²
Racket¹ comes from a word used long ago by French-speaking people to mean "palm of the hand" and also "snowshoe" and "tennis racket." We are not sure about the source of **racket²**.

ra·di·ant |rā′dē ənt| —*adjective* **1.** Shining or beaming brightly: *radiant sunshine.* **2.** Filled with happiness; glowing: *a radiant smile. His face was radiant after he won the race.* **3.** Made up of or given off as waves: *The sun produces radiant heat.*

radiant energy Energy that is sent or given off as rays or waves. Heat, light, and x-rays are kinds of radiant energy.

ra·di·ate |rā′dē āt′| —*verb* **radiated, radiating** **1.** To give off energy as rays or waves: *The sun radiates heat.* **2.** To be given off as rays or waves: *Light radiated from the lamp in the corner.* **3.** To spread out from a center: *Trails radiate from the lake in many directions.*

ra·di·a·tion |rā′dē ā′shən| —*noun* The act or process of sending out rays of heat, light, or other energy that travel through the air.

ra·di·a·tor |rā′dē ā′tər| —*noun, plural* **radiators** **1.** A device for heating a room. A radiator is made up of a series of pipes through which steam or hot water passes. **2.** A device for cooling something, as an automobile engine. A radiator gives off heat that cools the water inside it.

rad·i·cal |răd′ĭ kəl| —*adjective* **1.** Having to do with or affecting the most important or basic part of something; fundamental: *Leaving school and getting a job was a radical change in his plans.* **2.** Wanting or favoring extreme changes or reforms: *a man of radical political opinions.*

ra·di·i |rā′dē ī| A plural of the noun **radius.**

ra·di·o |rā′dē ō′| —*noun, plural* **radios** **1.** A way of sending sounds through the air by electric waves. **2.** The equipment used to send and receive sounds by electric waves.
—*verb* **radioed, radioing** To signal or send a message by radio.

ra·di·o·ac·tive |rā′dē ō ăk′tĭv| —*adjective* Of, having, or caused by radioactivity: *Radium is a radioactive element.*

ra·di·o·ac·tiv·i·ty |rā′dē ō ăk tĭv′ĭ tē| —*noun* The property or capability of certain metals to give off energy in the form of certain types of rays.

rad·ish |răd′ĭsh| —*noun, plural* **radishes** A plant with a white root that has a strong, sharp taste. The skin of the root may be red or white.

ra·di·um |rā′dē əm| —*noun* A white, highly radioactive metal that is used in treating cancer. Radium is one of the chemical elements.

ra·di·us |rā′dē əs| —*noun, plural* **radii** or **radiuses** **1.** Any line that goes straight from the center to the outside of a circle or sphere. **2.** A circular area or region that is measured by the length of its radius: *no buildings within a radius of fifty miles.*

raft |răft| or |räft| —*noun, plural* **rafts** A floating platform made of logs or other material that floats.

rag |răg| —*noun, plural* **rags** **1.** A piece or scrap of old, torn, or leftover cloth. **2.** **rags** Shabby, torn, or worn-out clothing.

rage |rāj| —*noun, plural* **rages** Violent anger.
—*verb* **raged, raging** **1.** To show violent anger: *He raged at the driver who crashed into his car.* **2.** To act in a violent way: *The forest fire raged for three days.*

rag·ged |răg′ĭd| —*adjective* **1.** Torn into rags; worn-out: *The old shirt was ragged and dirty.* **2.** Dressed in torn or shabby clothes: *The ragged old lady begged people for food.* **3.** Rough or jagged; uneven: *Be careful, that bench has a ragged edge.*

raid |rād| —*noun, plural* **raids** A sudden or surprise attack: *The*

raft
Above: Wooden raft
Below: Rubber raft

ă	pat	ĕ	pet	î	fierce
ā	pay	ē	be	ŏ	pot
â	care	ĭ	pit	ō	go
ä	father	ī	pie	ô	paw, for
oi	oil	ŭ	cut	zh	vision
ŏŏ	book	û	fur	ə	ago, item,
ōō	boot	*th*	the		pencil, atom,
yōō	abuse	th	thin		circus
ou	out	hw	which	ər	butter

army planned a raid on the enemy fort.
—*verb* **raided, raiding** To carry out or make a raid on.

rail |rāl| —*noun, plural* **rails 1.** A narrow bar of wood or metal. Rails are often placed lengthwise and held up by upright posts or pieces, as in a fence. Rails are laid along the ground in pairs to form a path or track for railroad cars. **2.** A railroad.

rail·ing |rā′lĭng| —*noun, plural* **railings 1.** A fence made of rails. **2.** A rail or banister.

rail·road |rāl′rōd′| —*noun, plural* **railroads 1.** A path or track made of a pair of parallel metal rails on which a train rides. **2.** A system of transportation, including all the trains, tracks, stations, land, and other equipment that is needed to operate it.

railroad
A railroad yard

rain |rān| —*noun, plural* **rains 1.** Water that falls from the clouds to the earth in drops: *Plants and flowers need lots of rain.* **2.** A fall of rain; a shower: *The rain spoiled our picnic.*
—*verb* **rained, raining 1.** To fall in drops of water from the clouds: *I hope it doesn't rain tomorrow.* **2.** To fall or pour or cause to fall or pour like rain: *Leaves rained from the trees.*
♦ *These sound alike* **rain, reign, rein.**

rain·bow |rān′bō′| —*noun, plural* **rainbows** An arc of colored light seen in the sky opposite the sun, especially after it rains. A rainbow is caused when the sun's rays are seen through small drops of water in the sky. A rainbow has seven colors: red, orange, yellow, blue, green, violet, and indigo.

rain·coat |rān′kōt′| —*noun, plural* **raincoats** A waterproof coat to keep a person dry when it is raining.

rain·fall |rān′fôl′| —*noun, plural* **rainfalls** The total amount of water in the form of rain, sleet, and snow that falls on an area or region during a certain length of time.

rain·y |rā′nē| —*adjective* **rainier, rainiest** Having a lot of rain.

raise |rāz| —*verb* **raised, raising 1.** To move or cause to move to a higher position; lift: *Would you raise the window a little?* **2.** To increase in amount, size, or value: *It is time to raise prices.* **3.** To build; erect: *We expect to raise the new building in a month.* **4.** To bring up and take care of: *raise a family. He raises horses.* **5.** To make louder: *Don't raise your voice.* **6.** To gather together; collect: *We must raise money for charity.* **7.** To bring up; ask: *I want to raise a question.*
—*noun, plural* **raises** An increase in price or pay.

rai·sin |rā′zən| —*noun, plural* **raisins** A sweet dried grape.

rake |rāk| —*noun, plural* **rakes** A tool with a long handle and teeth or prongs at one end. A rake is used to gather such things as leaves and grass or to loosen or smooth dirt.
—*verb* **raked, raking** To gather or smooth with a rake.

rake

Ra·leigh |rô′lē| or |răl′ē| The capital of North Carolina.

ral·ly |răl′ē| —*verb* **rallied, rallying, rallies 1.** To assemble again; bring back together: *The general rallied his tired soldiers for the next battle. The team rallied and won the game in the last minute.* **2.** To come to help: *You have to rally behind your friends when they're in trouble.* **3.** To improve suddenly in strength and health: *The patient rallied after being very sick for a week.*
—*noun, plural* **rallies** A meeting of many people for some purpose: *a political rally.*

ram |răm| —*noun, plural* **rams 1.** A male sheep. **2.** A battering ram.
—*verb* **rammed, ramming 1.** To force into a small or tight space;

ram

ramrod

rank¹, rank²
Rank¹ comes from an old French word that meant "line, row, rank." **Rank²** can be traced back to an old English word meaning "full-grown, overbearing."

rare¹, rare²
Rare¹ comes from a Latin word that meant "thin, scarce." **Rare²** comes from an old English word that originally meant "undercooked"; it also applied to eggs and meant "soft-boiled."

ă	pat	ĕ	pet	î	fierce
ā	pay	ē	be	ŏ	pot
â	care	ĭ	pit	ō	go
ä	father	ī	pie	ô	paw, for
oi	oil	ŭ	cut	zh	vision
ŏŏ	book	û	fur	ə	ago, item,
ōō	boot	th	the		pencil, atom,
yōō	abuse	th	thin		circus
ou	out	hw	which	ər	butter

drive or force down or in: *He rammed the stick in the ground.*
2. To crash or smash into: *An iceberg rammed the ship and sank it.*

ramp | rămp | —*noun, plural* **ramps** A sloping passage or road that leads from one level to another.

ram·rod | răm′rŏd′ | —*noun, plural* **ramrods** A metal rod used to push or ram the ammunition into the barrel of a gun that is loaded from the muzzle.

ran | răn | The past tense of the verb **run:** *She ran home.*

ranch | rănch | —*noun, plural* **ranches** A large farm on which cattle, sheep, or horses are raised.

ran·dom | răn′dəm | —*adjective* Having no plan, pattern, or purpose; by chance: *a random selection of books.*

rang | răng | The past tense of the verb **ring:** *I rang the bell.*

range | rānj | —*noun, plural* **ranges** **1.** The distance or extent between certain limits: *This shirt comes in a range of different colors. There is a wide price range for cars.* **2.** The longest distance at which something can work or travel: *The car will go up to a range of two hundred miles on a tank of gas.* **3.** A place for shooting at targets. **4.** A large area of open land on which livestock graze freely. **5.** A stove with an oven, broiler, and burners. **6.** A group or series of mountains.
—*verb* **ranged, ranging** **1.** To move between certain limits: *Their children range in age from three to ten.* **2.** To roam or wander.

rang·er | rān′jər | —*noun, plural* **rangers** **1.** A person whose job is to guard and patrol a forest or park owned by the government. **2.** A member of a group of a certain kind of police that keeps order in a particular region.

rank¹ | răngk | —*noun, plural* **ranks** **1.** A position or grade within a group or class: *My brother graduated with the highest rank in his class. He has a rank of colonel in the army.* **2.** A row or line, especially of people or things side by side: *The soldiers formed ranks for the parade.* **3. ranks** All soldiers who are not officers.
—*verb* **ranked, ranking** **1.** To have a rank: *She ranked fourth in a class of thirty.* **2.** To give a rank to; judge someone or something compared with others like it: *The judges ranked Marlene the best in the singing contest.* **3.** To arrange in a row or rows: *She ranked the children according to height.*

rank² | răngk | —*adjective* **ranker, rankest** **1.** Having a strong, unpleasant smell or taste: *a rank cigar. That's the rankest cheese I ever tasted.* **2.** Complete or extreme; total: *a rank coward.*

ran·som | răn′səm | —*noun, plural* **ransoms** **1.** The release of someone who is being held prisoner in exchange for money: *The criminals were holding three people for ransom.* **2.** The amount of money demanded or paid so that a person being held prisoner may be set free: *a ransom of fifty thousand dollars.*
—*verb* **ransomed, ransoming** To free a person being held prisoner by paying a demanded price: *The parents ransomed their son.*

rap | răp | —*verb* **rapped, rapping** To hit or knock a surface sharply; strike: *He rapped on the window. Don't rap the table.*
—*noun, plural* **raps** A quick, sharp knock or blow.
♦ *These sound alike* **rap, wrap.**

rap·id | răp′ĭd | —*adjective* Very fast or quick; swift: *a rapid walk through the park. We did a rapid job cleaning up the house.*
—*noun* **rapids** A particular place in a river where the water flows very quickly: *a canoe trip through the rapids.*

rare¹ | râr | —*adjective* **rarer, rarest** **1.** Not found, seen, or

happening very often: *a few rare patches of green in the desert.*
2. Unusually valuable or good; special: *rare books.*

rare² |râr| —*adjective* **rarer, rarest** Cooked for a short time.

rash¹ |răsh| —*adjective* **rasher, rashest** Too hasty; not careful; reckless: *a rash decision.*

rash² |răsh| —*noun, plural* **rashes** An outbreak of little red spots on the skin. A rash usually itches.

rasp·ber·ry |răz′bĕr′ē| or |răz′bĕr′ē| —*noun, plural* **raspberries** A sweet berry that has many seeds. The raspberry grows on a prickly bush with long, woody stems.

rat |răt| —*noun, plural* **rats** A gnawing animal with a long tail, related to the mouse.

rate |rāt| —*noun, plural* **rates** **1.** An amount, number, or pace that is measured against the measured amount, number, or pace of something else: *The airplane could fly at a rate of one hundred miles an hour.* **2.** The cost or price of something: *The rate at the bowling alley is two dollars a game.* **3.** A level of quality; class: *His school work is always of the first rate.*
—*verb* **rated, rating** **1.** To judge or decide how good or valuable something is: *I would rate this book as good.* **2.** To put in a certain rank or level: *They rated Paula third in her class.*

rath·er |răth′ər| or |rä′thər| —*adverb* **1.** To a certain extent; somewhat: *I'm feeling rather sleepy.* **2.** More willingly: *I'd rather stay home tonight.* **3.** More exactly; more accurately: *The shoes cost about ten dollars, or, rather, ten dollars and sixty cents.*

ra·tio |rā′shō| or |rā′shē ō′| —*noun, plural* **ratios** The relation or comparison of the number or size between two different things. Ratio means the number of times the second thing can be divided into the first. If there are nine men and three women who work in a store, the ratio of men to women is three to one, or three times as many men as women.

ra·tion |răsh′ən| or |rā′shən| —*noun, plural* **rations** A fixed amount or portion of food for a person or animal: *The dog's daily ration of food is one can.*
—*verb* **rationed, rationing** **1.** To give out in a portion or share: *My mother rationed the ice cream to the children because there wasn't much left.* **2.** To limit the amount of something each person can use or have: *The government was rationing water during the drought.*

ra·tion·al |răsh′ə nəl| —*adjective* **1.** Able to think clearly: *Humans are the only rational animals.* **2.** Based on reason; sensible; thought out: *a rational decision.*

rat·tle |răt′l| —*verb* **rattled, rattling** **1.** To make or cause a quick series of short, sharp sounds: *The coins rattled in my pocket as I walked. The wind rattled the windows.* **2.** To talk quickly and without stopping: *rattle off a list of names. He rattled on about his family.* **3.** To confuse or upset: *She forgot the words to the song because she was rattled by the big audience.*
—*noun, plural* **rattles** **1.** A quick series of short, sharp sounds: *I heard the rattle of the rain on the roof.* **2.** A baby's toy or other device that rattles when shaken.

rat·tle·snake |răt′l snāk′| —*noun, plural* **rattlesnakes** Any of several poisonous American snakes. The rattlesnake has several dry, hard rings at the end of its tail. When it shakes the rings rapidly, a rattling or buzzing sound is made.

rav·el |răv′əl| —*verb* **raveled, raveling** To separate into single, loose threads; fray: *She raveled her sweater.*

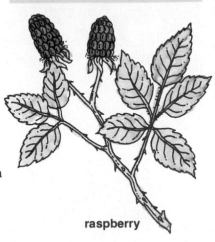

raspberry

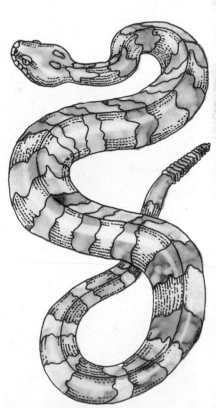

rattlesnake

raven

reactor
Above: An outside view of a reactor plant
Below: A nuclear reactor

ă	pat	ě	pet	î	fierce
ā	pay	ē	be	ŏ	pot
â	care	ĭ	pit	ō	go
ä	father	ī	pie	ô	paw, for

oi	oil	ŭ	cut	zh	vision
ŏŏ	book	û	fur	ə	ago, item,
ōō	boot	*th*	the		pencil, atom,
yōō	abuse	th	thin		circus
ou	out	hw	which	ər	butter

ra·ven | rā′vən | —*noun, plural* **ravens** A large black bird that resembles the crow. The raven has a croaking cry.

raw | rô | —*adjective* **rawer, rawest** **1.** Not cooked: *raw meat.* **2.** In a natural condition; not treated or processed: *Petroleum, metal ores, coal, and wood are raw materials.* **3.** Not trained; without experience: *She can be a good dancer, but her raw skills must be developed by practice.* **4.** Having the skin scraped off; sore: *My knee is raw from falling on the sidewalk.* **5.** Cold and damp: *The weather is raw even though it stopped raining.*

ray | rā | —*noun, plural* **rays** **1.** A thin line or narrow beam of light or other radiation: *the sun's rays; sound rays.* **2.** A small amount; a trace; hint: *There isn't a ray of hope left that we can still win the game.* **3.** One of many lines or parts going out from a center. The spokes on a wagon wheel are rays.

ray·on | rā′ŏn′ | —*noun, plural* **rayons** A cloth or fiber made from cellulose.

ra·zor | rā′zər | —*noun, plural* **razors** An instrument with a sharp blade that is used to shave hair, especially on the face.

re- A prefix that means: **1.** Again; *reelect.* **2.** Back: *recall.*

reach | rēch | —*verb* **reached, reaching** **1.** To go as far as; arrive at; come to: *The United States was the first to reach the moon. We reached the house before it rained.* **2.** To stretch out; extend: *The river reaches from one end of the state to the other.* **3.** To stretch or hold out an arm or hand: *reach out for an apple. He reached out and grabbed the ball.* **4.** To touch or grasp: *I couldn't reach the bread from where I was sitting.* **5.** To try to get something: *She reached in her pocketbook for a handkerchief.* **6.** To communicate or get in touch with someone: *I couldn't reach her on the telephone.* —*noun, plural* **reaches** **1.** An act of reaching: *The frog grabbed the butterfly with a quick reach of its tongue.* **2.** The distance to which a person can stretch an arm: *My reach isn't long enough to get to the cookie jar.* **3.** All or as much as a person can understand or do: *Swimming twenty laps is beyond my reach.*

re·act | rē ăkt′ | —*verb* **reacted, reacting** To act in response to or because something else has happened; respond: *The dog reacted to the knock on the door by barking.*

re·ac·tion | rē ăk′shən | —*noun, plural* **reactions** An action or effect in response to something that has happened: *Her first reaction was to cry.*

re·ac·tor | rē ăk′tər | —*noun, plural* **reactors** A device in which atoms are split under controlled conditions. This results in the production of heat, which is used to generate electricity and many radioactive substances.

read | rēd | —*verb* **read** | rĕd |, **reading** **1.** To look at and understand the meaning of something that is printed or written: *reading books. It's nine o'clock and I've read the mail.* **2.** To speak out loud something that is printed or written: *She read the poem to the class.* **3.** To learn about something by reading: *We read about native Americans in our history class.* **4.** To understand the meaning of something: *My mother says she can read my mind.* **5.** To indicate or show: *The scale read one hundred degrees.*
♦ *These sound alike* **read, reed.**

read·er | rē′dər | —*noun, plural* **readers** **1.** A person who reads. **2.** A book for learning and practicing reading.

read·i·ly | rĕd′l ē | —*adverb* **1.** Willingly and quickly: *Lisa readily obeyed.* **2.** Without difficulty; easily: *readily available at any store.*

read·ing | rē′dĭng | —*noun, plural* **readings 1.** The act of looking at and understanding something that is printed or written. **2.** Books and other things to be read. **3.** The act of speaking out loud something printed or written: *The poet gave a reading of his most famous poems on television.*

read·y | rĕd′ē | —*adjective* **readier, readiest 1.** Prepared for action or use: *Are you ready to go? Dinner is ready.* **2.** Willing: *I'm ready to listen to your idea.* **3.** About to do something; likely: *She looked like she was ready to cry.* **4.** Quick; prompt and alert: *She has a ready answer for everything.* **5.** Easy to get at; close at hand: *You should always have some ready money.*

re·al | rē′əl | or | rēl | —*adjective* **1.** Actual or true; not made up; not imaginary: *This is a story about real people.* **2.** Genuine or authentic; not artificial: *These are real diamonds.* **3.** Serious or important: *You're in real trouble.*

real estate Land and everything on it, such as buildings, trees, or roads: *Dad bought some real estate out in the country.*

re·al·is·tic | rē′ə lĭs′tĭk | —*adjective* **1.** Resembling real people or things; lifelike: *a realistic story; a realistic painting.* **2.** Practical or reasonable: *He's very realistic about money.*

re·al·i·ty | rē ăl′ĭ tē | —*noun, plural* **realities 1.** The condition or quality of being real; actual existence: *After seeing the pictures on television, you have to believe the reality of men walking on the moon.* **2.** Someone or something that is real: *His dream of owning a car became a reality.*

re·al·ize | rē′ə līz′ | —*verb* **realized, realizing 1.** To be aware of; understand completely: *I never realized how hard it is to build a boat.* **2.** To make real; achieve: *She worked hard to realize her goal of becoming a veterinarian.*

re·al·ly | rē′ə lē | or | rē′lē | —*adverb* **1.** In fact; actually: *Although they live in the ocean, whales are really mammals and not fish.* **2.** Truly; very: *It's a really beautiful day, isn't it?*

realm | rĕlm | —*noun, plural* **realms 1.** A kingdom: *The king's family had ruled the realm for the last five hundred years.* **2.** Any particular field of interest or activity: *the realm of music.*

reap | rēp | —*verb* **reaped, reaping 1.** To cut down wheat or a similar crop and gather: *Farmers reap grain in early fall.* **2.** To gather the crop of a plot of land: *We must reap a field of oats.*

reap·er | rē′pər | —*noun, plural* **reapers 1.** A person who reaps grain or a similar crop. **2.** A machine used in harvesting.

rear¹ | rîr | —*noun, plural* **rears** The back part of something: *Deliveries are made at the rear of the house.*
—*adjective* Of or at the rear: *a rear entrance.*

rear² | rîr | —*verb* **reared, rearing 1.** To care for during the early years; bring up: *My parents reared three children.* **2.** To rise on the hind legs: *The horse reared, and I almost fell off.*

rea·son | rē′zən | —*noun, plural* **reasons 1.** A cause or explanation: *What were her reasons for being late?* **2.** The ability to think clearly: *Humans have reason, animals do not.*
—*verb* **reasoned, reasoning 1.** To have an opinion; conclude: *He reasoned that we were headed north.* **2.** To argue in a sensible way; try to change someone's mind: *The mayor tried to reason with the angry mob.*

rea·son·a·ble | rē′zə nə bəl | —*adjective* **1.** Using sound judgment or good sense to settle problems: *a reasonable man.* **2.** Fair or sensible; sound: *a reasonable solution to a dispute.*

reaper
Above: A reaper worked by hand and used about 1800
Below: A reaper pulled by a horse and used about 1850

rear¹, rear²
Rear¹ is a shortened form of *arrear*, a word that means "the state of being behind in paying debts." *Arrear* came from an old French word that in turn came from a Latin word meaning "backward." **Rear²** comes from a word used very long ago by English-speaking people to mean "to lift up, to raise."

3. Not extreme; fair; moderate: *a reasonable price.*

rea·son·ing | rē′zə nǐng | or | rēz′nǐng | —*noun* The process of thinking with logic and common sense to reach an answer, form a judgment, or come to conclusions: *Sheila solved the problem after long reasoning.*

re·bel | rǐ běl′ | —*verb* **rebelled, rebelling** **1.** To resist or oppose any authority: *The American colonists rebelled against British rule.* **2.** To show strong dislike or resentment: *I always rebel when I'm told to wear a necktie.*
—*noun* **reb·el** | rěb′əl |, *plural* **rebels** A person who rejects authority or fights against it.

re·bel·lion | rǐ běl′yən | —*noun, plural* **rebellions** **1.** A revolt intended to overthrow a government by force. **2.** An open defiance of any authority: *a rebellion against unfair working hours.*

re·call | rǐ kôl′ | —*verb* **recalled, recalling** **1.** To call back; ask or order to return: *The government recalled the ambassador from a foreign country. The audience recalled the conductor for another bow.* **2.** To bring back to memory: *Father recalled his days in the army.*

re·ceipt | rǐ sēt′ | —*noun, plural* **receipts** **1.** A written acknowledgment that money or merchandise has been received: *The store gave me a receipt for my radio.* **2.** **receipts** The quantity or amount received: *Ticket receipts hit an all-time record.*

re·ceive | rǐ sēv′ | —*verb* **received, receiving** **1.** To get or acquire something given or offered: *I received a gift.* **2.** To greet or welcome: *They received us as though we were family.*

re·ceiv·er | rǐ sē′vər | —*noun, plural* **receivers** **1.** Someone or something that receives. **2.** The unit of a telephone, radio, television, or other communications system that receives electrical signals and converts them into sound or pictures.

re·cent | rē′sənt | —*adjective* Of a time just before the present: *Do you have a recent photo of yourself?*

re·cep·tion | rǐ sěp′shən | —*noun, plural* **receptions** **1.** The act of receiving someone or something: *We got a warm reception at her house.* **2.** A social gathering in honor of someone: *a wedding reception.* **3.** The quality of electrical signals received by a radio or television set: *We got poor reception due to the storm.*

re·cess | rǐ sěs′ | or | rē′sěs′ | —*noun, plural* **recesses** **1.** A temporary halt in an activity: *We played baseball during recess at school.* **2.** A small hollow place; an alcove: *The toad lived in a recess in the wall.*
—*verb* **recessed, recessing** To stop an activity for a time; suspend or adjourn: *The chairperson recessed the meeting.*

rec·i·pe | rěs′ə pē | —*noun, plural* **recipes** A set of directions for preparing food: *a recipe for banana bread.*

re·cite | rǐ sīt′ | —*verb* **recited, reciting** **1.** To repeat something memorized in front of an audience: *She will recite a poem to the class.* **2.** To tell in detail: *Jack recited his trip home.*

reck·less | rěk′lǐs | —*adjective* Without care or caution; careless: *He was arrested for reckless driving.*

reck·on | rěk′ən | —*verb* **reckoned, reckoning** **1.** To count; figure; add up: *The cashier reckoned her bill.* **2.** To think or assume; suppose: *I reckon the train will be here soon.*

rec·og·ni·tion | rěk′əg nǐsh′ən | —*noun* **1.** The act of recognizing or the condition of being recognized: *She gave no sign of recognition of the old friend.* **2.** Favorable notice of one's efforts;

rebellion
A farmers' rebellion that took place
in Massachusetts in 1786

ă	pat	ĕ	pet	î	fierce
ā	pay	ē	be	ŏ	pot
â	care	ĭ	pit	ō	go
ä	father	ī	pie	ô	paw, for
oi	oil	ŭ	cut	zh	vision
ŏŏ	book	û	fur	ə	ago, item,
ōō	boot	*th*	the		pencil, atom,
yōō	abuse	th	thin		circus
ou	out	hw	which	ər	butter

approval; praise: *Recognition of the artist came late in life.*

rec·og·nize |rĕk′əg nīz′| —*verb* **recognized, recognizing** **1.** To know or identify from past experience: *I recognized him by his deep voice.* **2.** To realize or understand: *He recognizes the value of education.* **3.** To acknowledge; accept: *We recognized his right to defend himself.*

rec·om·mend |rĕk′ə mĕnd′| —*verb* **recommended, recommending** **1.** To praise or speak highly of a person to another; mention favorably: *I recommended him for the job.* **2.** To advise a course of action: *The doctor recommended a strict diet.*

rec·ord |rĕk′ərd| —*noun, plural* **records** **1.** Facts or other information set down in writing to be preserved: *We looked up some records in the county courthouse.* **2.** The history of a person's performance or achievements: *The college will want to see your high school record.* **3.** The best performance known: *He holds the record for the broad jump.* **4.** The highest or lowest mark: *Yesterday we reached an all-time record for daily rainfall.* **5.** A disk designed to reproduce sound when it is played on a phonograph: *He bought several new records for his collection.*
—*verb* **re·cord** |rĭ kôrd′| **recorded, recording** **1.** To preserve in writing or other permanent form: *Record the number of hours you worked.* **2.** To register or indicate: *A thermometer records the temperature.* **3.** To register sound on a disk or magnetic tape: *He will record the concert.*

re·cord·er |rĭ kôr′dər| —*noun, plural* **recorders** **1.** Someone or something that records: *a tape recorder.* **2.** A wooden flute with eight finger holes and a mouthpiece resembling a whistle.

re·cord·ing |rĭ kôr′dĭng| —*noun, plural* **recordings** Something on which sound is recorded; a phonograph record or a magnetic tape: *He bought all the latest recordings.*

re·cov·er |rĭ kŭv′ər| —*verb* **recovered, recovering** **1.** To get back; regain: *She is recovering her health.* **2.** To return to a normal condition: *Fred has recovered after a long illness.*

re·cov·er·y |rĭ kŭv′ə rē| —*noun, plural* **recoveries** **1.** A return to a normal condition: *We wish the patients a fast recovery.* **2.** The act of getting back: *the recovery of the lost jewelry.*

rec·re·a·tion |rĕk′rē ā′shən| —*noun, plural* **recreations** Something done for amusement or for the relaxation of one's mind or body after a period of work: *My favorite recreation is swimming. Bob's favorite recreation is reading.*

re·cruit |rĭ krōōt′| —*verb* **recruited, recruiting** To get a person to join: *They must recruit men and women for the navy.*
—*noun, plural* **recruits** A newly enlisted member of the armed forces: *The recruits arrived in camp to begin their training.*

rec·tan·gle |rĕk′tăng′gəl| —*noun, plural* **rectangles** A geometric figure that has four sides and four right angles. Two of the sides are longer than the other two.

red |rĕd| —*noun, plural* **reds** The color of blood or of a ripe strawberry.
—*adjective* **redder, reddest** Of the color red: *a red necktie.*

red blood cell Any of the cells in the blood that give the blood its red color. These cells carry oxygen to the cells and tissues of the body.

red·dish |rĕd′ĭsh| —*adjective* Somewhat red.

re·duce |rĭ dōōs′| or |rĭ dyōōs′| —*verb* **reduced, reducing**

recorder

recruit
A poster to recruit men in 1776

1. To make or become less in amount or size: *Evaporation reduced the water in the pond.* **2.** To bring to a specified condition: *The powerful machine reduced marble to dust.* **3.** To lose body weight by diet or exercise: *I have to reduce till I've lost ten pounds.*

re·duc·tion | rĭ dŭk′shən | —*noun, plural* **reductions 1.** The action or process of reducing: *a reduction in the size of classes from ten to five students.* **2.** The amount by which something is reduced: *a one per cent reduction in the sales tax.*

red·wood | rĕd′wŏod′ | —*noun, plural* **redwoods** A very tall evergreen tree of northwestern California. Redwoods are the world's tallest trees. They sometimes grow to a height of more than 300 feet (91 meters).

reed | rēd | —*noun, plural* **reeds 1.** Any of several tall grasses or similar plants that have hollow stems. Reeds grow in wet places. **2.** A thin strip of cane or metal used in the mouthpiece of certain wind instruments. The reed vibrates when air passes over it and produces a musical tone in the instrument. **3.** A woodwind instrument played with a reed. Oboes and clarinets are played with a reed.

♦ *These sound alike* **reed, read.**

reef | rēf | —*noun, plural* **reefs** A strip or ridge of rock, sand, or coral at or near the surface of a body of water: *The ship was grounded on a reef.*

reel¹ | rēl | —*noun, plural* **reels 1.** A device similar to a large spool, used for winding a hose, rope, tape, film, or wire. **2.** The amount held by a reel: *A reel of the movie is missing.*

reel² | rēl | —*verb* **reeled, reeling 1.** To stagger: *We all reeled as we stepped off the roller coaster.* **2.** To go round and round; whirl: *All those TV shows reeled in my head.*

re·e·lect | rē′ĭ lĕkt′ | —*verb* **reelected, reelecting** To elect again: *The mayor was reelected to serve another two years.*

re·en·try or **re·en·try** | rē ĕn′trē | —*noun, plural* **re-entries** or **reentries 1.** The act of entering again. **2.** The return of a missile or spacecraft to the earth's atmosphere.

re·fer | rĭ fûr′ | —*verb* **referred, referring 1.** To direct a person elsewhere for help or information: *The doctor referred his patient to a heart specialist.* **2.** To turn to for information or authority: *Refer to the map on the next page.* **3.** To submit something to a person or group for action: *The legislature referred the bill to a committee.* **4.** To call or direct attention to: *He referred to my work in his remarks to the students.*

ref·e·ree | rĕf′ə rē′ | —*noun, plural* **referees** An official in certain sports who enforces the rules during play.

ref·er·ence | rĕf′ər əns | or | rĕf′rəns | —*noun, plural* **references 1.** Relation, regard, or respect: *a reply in reference to your last letter.* **2.** A note in a book that directs the reader to another page for additional information. **3.** A statement about a person's qualifications for something: *My last boss gave me a good reference.* **4.** A mention: *His book on history contains many references to George Washington.*

re·fill | rē fĭl′ | —*verb* **refilled, refilling** To fill again: *Get some ice cubes, and don't forget to refill the trays.*
—*noun* | rē′fĭl′ |, *plural* **refills 1.** A second or later filling: *Give me your glass for a refill.* **2.** A replacement for something used up: *I must buy a refill for my pen.*

re·fine | rĭ fīn′ | —*verb* **refined, refining 1.** To bring to a pure

---

reel¹, reel²

Both words spelled **reel** may ultimately be related because of their origin in the same old English word. **Reel¹** meant "spool." A word that meant "to whirl around, stagger" (**reel²**) is thought to have come from **reel¹**.

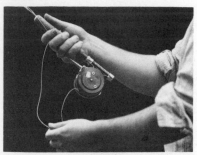

reel¹
A fishing reel

referee
In a football game

ă	pat	ĕ	pet	î	fierce
ā	pay	ē	be	ŏ	pot
â	care	ĭ	pit	ō	go
ä	father	ī	pie	ô	paw, for
oi	oil	ŭ	cut	zh	vision
ŏŏ	book	û	fur	ə	ago, item,
ōō	boot	*th*	the		pencil, atom,
yōō	abuse	th	thin		circus
ou	out	hw	which	ər	butter

state: *equipment to refine oil.* **2.** To make polished or elegant.

re·fin·er·y | rĭ fī′nə rē | —*noun, plural* **refineries** A factory where raw materials are purified and processed: *an oil refinery.*

re·flect | rĭ flĕkt′ | —*verb* **reflected, reflecting 1.** To throw back light rays, heat, or sounds that strike a surface: *The mirror reflects the light back into the room.* **2.** To give back an image as does a mirror or clear water: *The pond reflected the statues along its banks.* **3.** To give back as a result: *His bravery reflects honor upon him.* **4.** To give serious thought to: *The wise old man reflected about his youth.*

re·form | rĭ fôrm′ | —*verb* **reformed, reforming 1.** To make better or more just: *He spent years trying to reform the world.* **2.** To improve the form or method of something: *He joined the movement to reform English spelling.* **3.** To cause to give up or give up evil ways: *He was sent to an institution organized to reform criminals. Sammy promised his father that he would reform.*
—*noun, plural* **reforms** A change for the better; an improvement: *The principal promised a reform in school rules.*

re·form·a·to·ry | rĭ fôr′mə tôr′ē | or | rĭ fôr′mə tōr′ē | —*noun, plural* **reformatories** An institution for young people who have broken the law. A reformatory is partly a prison and partly a school.

re·frain | rĭ frān′ | —*noun, plural* **refrains** A phrase repeated several times in a poem or song.

re·fresh | rĭ frĕsh′ | —*verb* **refreshed, refreshing 1.** To make or become fresh again: *The rain refreshed the grass. A short nap always refreshes me.* **2.** To rouse or stimulate; quicken: *Give me a hint to refresh my memory.*

re·fresh·ment | rĭ frĕsh′mənt | —*noun, plural* **refreshments 1.** Something that refreshes: *Would you care for the refreshment of a good shower?* **2. refreshments** Food and drink.

re·frig·er·ate | rĭ frĭj′ə rāt′ | —*verb* **refrigerated, refrigerating 1.** To make or keep cool or cold: *We refrigerate the soft drinks.* **2.** To keep food by storing at a low temperature: *Tom always refrigerates all fish and meat.*

re·frig·er·a·tor | rĭ frĭj′ə rā′tər | —*noun, plural* **refrigerators** A box, cabinet, or room in which food, chemicals, or other items are stored at low temperatures.

ref·uge | rĕf′yōoj | —*noun* Protection or shelter from danger: *The knights sought refuge in the castle.*

ref·u·gee | rĕf′yōo jē′ | —*noun, plural* **refugees** A person who flees from his or her own country to find protection or safety.

re·fund | rĭ fŭnd′ | —*verb* **refunded, refunding** To give back: *The store refunded the purchase price of my radio.*
—*noun* | rē′fŭnd′ |, *plural* **refunds** The return of money paid: *She demanded a refund for the damaged chair.*

re·fus·al | rĭ fyōo′zəl | —*noun, plural* **refusals** The act of refusing: *I was shocked by her refusal to go with us.*

re·fuse¹ | rĭ fyōoz′ | —*verb* **refused, refusing 1.** To be not willing to do something: *She refuses to tell her age.* **2.** To decline to accept; turn down; reject: *He refused my very generous offer.* **3.** To decline to give: *The club refused permission to use their pool.*

ref·use² | rĕf′yōos | —*noun* Something useless or worthless; trash; rubbish: *to haul refuse to the city dump.*

re·gard | rĭ gärd′ | —*verb* **regarded, regarding 1.** To look at; observe: *She regards people with interest.* **2.** To consider in a

refinery
An oil refinery

reflect
A dog's image reflected in water

refuse¹, refuse²
Refuse¹ comes from an old French word that in turn came from a Latin stem meaning "to pour back, to get rid of." **Refuse²** comes from a related old French word used to mean "refusal, something refused or rejected."

register

Above: An antique cash register
Below: A modern cash register

rehearsal
Of a dance

ă	pat	ĕ	pet	î	fierce
ā	pay	ē	be	ŏ	pot
â	care	ĭ	pit	ō	go
ä	father	ī	pie	ô	paw, for
oi	oil	ŭ	cut	zh	vision
o͞o	book	û	fur	ə	ago, item,
o͞o	boot	*th*	the		pencil, atom,
yo͞o	abuse	th	thin		circus
ou	out	hw	which	ər	butter

particular way: *She regarded her sister as a good friend.* **3.** To hold in affection or esteem; value: *I regard my parents highly.*
—*noun, plural* **regards 1.** A look or gaze: *His cold regard made me shiver.* **2.** Affection or esteem: *He shows regard for his parents.* **3. regards** Good wishes; greetings: *Please give Ed my regards.*

re·gard·less |rĭ gärd′lĭs| —*adjective* With no thought for; without consideration for: *I'm going to go, regardless of the risk.*

re·gime |rĭ zhēm′| or |rā zhēm′| —*noun, plural* **regimes** A system of government: *a democratic regime.*

reg·i·ment |rĕj′ə mənt| —*noun, plural* **regiments** A unit of soldiers made up of two or more battalions.

Re·gi·na |rĭ jī′nə| The capital of Saskatchewan.

re·gion |rē′jən| —*noun, plural* **regions 1.** Any large area of the earth's surface: *the polar regions.* **2.** A section or area of the body: *the chest region.*

re·gion·al |rē′jə nəl| —*adjective* Of a region: *The team made it to the regional play-offs. She has a regional accent.*

reg·is·ter |rĕj′ĭ stər| —*noun, plural* **registers 1.** An official written list or record: *a register of births for the year.* **2.** A machine that records and counts automatically: *a cash register.* **3.** A device that can be adjusted to control a flow of air.
—*verb* **registered, registering 1.** To enter officially in a written list or record: *Her lawyers will register the deed. People register births and marriages.* **2.** To make known for the record; file: *I want to register a complaint.* **3.** To indicate or be indicated on a scale or device: *The thermomenter registered 106° Fahrenheit.* **4.** To enroll a student in a school or class. **5.** To reveal or show: *Her face never registers any emotion.* **6.** To cause mail to be officially recorded by the post office: *Don't forget to register the letters.*

re·gret |rĭ grĕt′| —*verb* **regretted, regretting** To feel sorry about: *I regret my mistake.*
—*noun, plural* **regrets 1.** A sense of distress over a past event or deed: *He must feel regret for his behavior.* **2.** Sadness or disappointment: *deep regret for lost friends.*

reg·u·lar |rĕg′yə lər| —*adjective* **1.** Usual or normal; standard: *The clerk took five dollars off the regular price.* **2.** Appearing again and again; habitual: *a regular customer.* **3.** Happening always at the same time: *regular meals.* **4.** Evenly spaced: *The tides occur at regular intervals.* **5.** Being a permanent member of a staff or organization: *She is one of our regular clerks.*

reg·u·late |rĕg′yə lāt′| —*verb* **regulated, regulating 1.** To control or direct according to certain rules: *The President wants power to regulate business.* **2.** To adjust a machine or device so that it works properly: *You must regulate a clock that runs slow.*

reg·u·la·tion |rĕg′yə lā′shən| —*noun, plural* **regulations 1.** The act or process of regulating: *the regulation of a spring mechanism.* **2.** A law or set of rules by which something is regulated: *new traffic regulations.*

re·hears·al |rĭ hûr′səl| —*noun, plural* **rehearsals** A session devoted to practicing in order to prepare for a performance.

re·hearse |rĭ hûrs′| —*verb* **rehearsed, rehearsing** To practice all or part of a program in order to prepare for a performance: *We rehearsed the Columbus Day program all afternoon.*

reign |rān| —*noun, plural* **reigns** The period of time that a monarch rules: *The American Revolution took place during the reign of George III.*

—*verb* **reigned, reigning** **1.** To have or hold the power of a monarch: *Queen Victoria reigned in England in the 19th century.* **2.** To prevail; be widespread: *Stillness reigned in the forest.*
♦ *These sound alike* **reign, rain, rein.**

rein |rān| —*noun, plural* **reins** Often **reins** **1.** A long leather strap attached to the bit in a horse's mouth and held by the rider or driver to control the horse. **2.** Any means of guidance: *to give up the reins of government.*
♦ *These sound alike* **rein, rain, reign.**

rein·deer |rān′dîr′| —*noun, plural* **reindeer** A deer found in the Arctic regions. Both male and female reindeer have large, spreading antlers.

reindeer

re·in·force |rē′ĭn fôrs′| or |rē′ĭn fôrs′| —*verb* **reinforced, reinforcing** To make stronger by adding extra support to: *The tailor reinforced the pockets with heavy cloth.*

re·ject |rĭ jĕkt′| —*verb* **rejected, rejecting** **1.** To refuse to accept, use, or consider: *They rejected my idea for a school newspaper.* **2.** To fail to give love or affection to: *The dog rejected her ailing puppy and refused to nurse it.*

re·joice |rĭ jois′| —*verb* **rejoiced, rejoicing** To feel or show joy: *The people rejoiced when the new prince was born.*

re·lapse |rĭ lăps′| —*verb* **relapsed, relapsing** To fall back into a previous condition or way of behaving: *Willie has relapsed into bad habits.*
—*noun, plural* **relapses** The action or result of relapsing: *a patient's sudden relapse.*

re·late |rĭ lāt′| —*verb* **related, relating** To tell or narrate: *He related the story of his life.*

re·lat·ed |rĭ lā′tĭd| —*adjective* Connected by blood or marriage: *She is related to me on my mother's side.*

re·la·tion |rĭ lā′shən| —*noun, plural* **relations** **1.** A connection or association between two or more things: *the relation between good grades and hard work.* **2.** A person who belongs to the same family as someone else; a relative: *We saw many of our relations at the annual picnic.* **3. relations** Relationships with other persons or groups: *good relations with all countries.*

re·la·tion·ship |rĭ lā′shən shĭp′| —*noun, plural* **relationships** **1.** A connection between objects, facts, or ideas: *the relationship between the earth's tides and the moon.* **2.** A connection or tie between persons: *The two partners had a business relationship.*

rel·a·tive |rĕl′ə tĭv| —*adjective* **1.** Related or relating; having to do with: *The teacher made comments relative to my work.* **2.** Considered in comparison with something else: *the relative value of gold and silver.*
—*noun, plural* **relatives** A person related by blood or marriage; a person who belongs to the same family as another.

re·lax |rĭ lăks′| —*verb* **relaxed, relaxing** **1.** To make or become less tight or tense: *Try to relax your muscles.* **2.** To make or become less severe or strict: *The teacher relaxed discipline.*

re·lay |rē′lā′| —*noun, plural* **relays** **1.** A crew, group, or team that relieves another; a shift: *They worked in relays to restore electric service.* **2.** A race between two groups of runners or swimmers in which each member goes only part of the total distance.
—*verb* **relayed, relaying** To pass or send along: *Please relay my message to your brother.*

relay
A relay race

relic
An urn from ancient Greece

relief

re·lease | rĭ lēs' | —*verb* **released, releasing** **1.** To set free; liberate: *When will they release the soldiers from the army?* **2.** To let fly or fall: *The archers released their arrows.* **3.** To make available to the public: *The company released the film right after Christmas.* —*noun, plural* **releases** **1.** The act of releasing: *the release of a lion from its cage.* **2.** A document or order granting freedom: *The prisoner's release was signed by the governor.*

rel·e·vant | rĕl' ə vənt | —*adjective* Having some bearing on; having to do with; related: *evidence relevant to the trial.*

re·li·a·ble | rĭ lī' ə bəl | —*adjective* Able to be relied or depended upon: *a reliable person.*

rel·ic | rĕl' ĭk | —*noun, plural* **relics** Something that survives from the distant past: *relics of an ancient civilization.*

re·lief | rĭ lēf' | —*noun, plural* **reliefs** **1.** A lessening of pain or anxiety: *He took medicine for relief from his cold.* **2.** Help or assistance given to the needy, aged, or disaster victims: *The Army brought relief to the flood victims.* **3.a.** A release from a job or duty: *The divers worked in two-hour shifts with one hour's relief.* **b.** A person who takes over the duties of another: *The sentry waited anxiously for his relief.* **4.** A sculptured figure that stands out from a flat background.

re·lieve | rĭ lēv' | —*verb* **relieved, relieving** **1.** To lessen or reduce pain or anxiety; ease: *Did the aspirin relieve your headache?* **2.** To release from a duty or position by being or providing a substitute: *He relieved the sentry at midnight.*

re·lig·ion | rĭ lĭj' ən | —*noun, plural* **religions** **1.** Belief in a supreme being or beings; the worship of God or gods. **2.** A particular system of such belief: *Christianity and Islam are two of the world's religions.*

re·lig·ious | rĭ lĭj' əs | —*adjective* **1.** Of religion: *religious services; religious freedom.* **2.** Following the beliefs of a religion: *He comes from a very religious family.*

rel·ish | rĕl' ĭsh | —*noun, plural* **relishes** A mixture of chopped vegetables, olives, chopped pickles, and other spicy foods. It is used to flavor foods or as a side dish.

re·luc·tant | rĭ lŭk' tənt | —*adjective* Lacking inclination; not willing: *We were reluctant to leave before the game was over.*

re·ly | rĭ lī' | —*verb* **relied, relying, relies** —**rely on** or **upon** To depend on; have confidence in: *I'm relying on your help.*

re·main | rĭ mān' | —*verb* **remained, remaining** **1.** To continue to be; go on being: *She remained my friend.* **2.** To stay in the same place: *Please remain in your seats.* **3.** To be left: *Much work remains to be done.*

re·main·der | rĭ mān' dər | —*noun, plural* **remainders** **1.** The remaining part; the rest: *We'll spend the remainder of the summer in Maine.* **2.** The number left over when one number is subtracted from another: *17 subtracted from 19 gives a remainder of 2.* **3.** The number left over when one number has been divided by another: *5 divided by 2 gives 2 and a remainder of 1. 8 divided by 4 gives 2 and a remainder of 0.*

re·mains | rĭ mānz' | —*plural noun* **1.** Something that remains; something that is left: *the remains of Thanksgiving dinner.* **2.** A dead body; corpse.

re·mark | rĭ märk' | —*noun, plural* **remarks** A brief comment; a casual statement or opinion: *Her remark about my hair was unkind.* —*verb* **remarked, remarking** To say casually; give as an opinion;

ă	pat	ĕ	pet	î	fierce
ā	pay	ē	be	ŏ	pot
â	care	ĭ	pit	ō	go
ä	father	ī	pie	ô	paw, for
oi	oil	ŭ	cut	zh	vision
ŏŏ	book	û	fur	ə	ago, item,
ōō	boot	*th*	the		pencil, atom,
yōō	abuse	th	thin		circus
ou	out	hw	which	ər	butter

mention: *We remarked about the beauty of the landscape.*

re·mark·a·ble |rĭ **mär′**kə bəl| —*adjective* Worthy of notice; out of the ordinary; not common or usual: *a remarkable book.*

rem·e·dy |**rĕm′**ĭ dē| —*noun, plural* **remedies** Something that cures a disease or relieves pain: *There is no sure remedy for the common cold.*

re·mem·ber |rĭ **mĕm′**bər| —*verb* **remembered, remembering** **1.a.** To bring back to the mind: *For a moment I couldn't remember his name.* **b.** To keep carefully in one's memory: *Remember that you have a date tonight.* **2.** To give someone a present or tip: *My aunt always remembers me on my birthday.*

re·mind |rĭ **mīnd′**| —*verb* **reminded, reminding** To cause someone to remember or think of something: *Please remind Jane to water my plants.*

re·mote |rĭ **mōt′**| —*adjective* **remoter, remotest** **1.** Far away; not near: *a remote island in the Pacific.* **2.** Distant in time or relationship: *the remote past; a remote cousin.* **3.** Extremely small; slight: *I haven't a remote idea what you mean.*

remote control Control of a machine or process from a distance by radio, electricity, or other means. Model airplanes and missiles can be guided by remote control.

re·mov·al |rĭ **mōō′**vəl| —*noun, plural* **removals** **1.** The act of removing: *a special cleaner for the removal of spots.* **2.** The act of moving from one place to another: *the removal of a factory to a nearby state.*

re·move |rĭ **mōōv′**| —*verb* **removed, removing** **1.** To move or take from a position or place: *Remove the pie from the oven in ten minutes.* **2.** To take off or away: *He removed his coat.*

ren·der |**rĕn′**dər| —*verb* **rendered, rendering** **1.** To cause to become; make: *The hail rendered the crop worthless.* **2.** To give or make available: *It's easy to render a service to a friend.* **3.** To perform: *Mrs. Simpson rendered the songs very beautifully.*

re·new |rĭ **nōō′**| or |rĭ **nyōō′**| —*verb* **renewed, renewing** **1.** To make new again; restore: *Fresh paint renewed the old building.* **2.** To begin or take up something again; revive: *They renewed their old friendship.* **3.** To extend the term of; cause to continue or last longer: *Don't forget to renew the magazine subscription.*

rent |rĕnt| —*noun, plural* **rents** A payment made at regular intervals for the use of something: *Our monthly rent for the apartment is $150.*
—*verb* **rented, renting** **1.** To occupy another's property in return for regular payment: *We rented my aunt's house for the summer.* **2.** To grant the use of one's own property to another for regular payment: *Grandmother rented her house to my uncle.* **3.** To be for rent: *Rooms rent for $25 a week here.*

re·paid |rĭ **pād′**| The past tense and past participle of the verb **repay**: *We repaid the loan by October. She had repaid his services.*

re·pair |rĭ **pâr′**| —*verb* **repaired, repairing** To put back into proper or useful condition; fix: *The jeweler repaired my watch.*
—*noun, plural* **repairs** **1.** The act or work of repairing: *The car is in need of repair.* **2.** Operating condition of a machine; working order: *He keeps his truck in good repair.*

re·pay |rĭ **pā′**| —*verb* **repaid, repaying** **1.** To pay back: *She must repay the loan.* **2.** To give payment in return for: *He repaid kindness with kindness.* **3.** To make or do in return: *Geraldine is going to repay their visit.*

re·peat |rĭ pēt′| —*verb* **repeated, repeating 1.** To say, do, or go through again: *Would you repeat your question, please?* **2.** To say in imitation of what another has said: *Repeat the word after me.*

re·pel |rĭ pĕl′| —*verb* **repelled, repelling 1.** To drive off, force back, or keep away: *The army repelled the enemy attack.* **2.** To cause a feeling of dislike; disgust: *His loud manner repels me.* **3.** To keep off or out; resist: *This raincoat repels water.*

rep·e·ti·tion |rĕp′ĭ tĭsh′ən| —*noun, plural* **repetitions** The act or process of repeating: *He learned many new words by repetition.*

re·place |rĭ plās′| —*verb* **replaced, replacing 1.** To take or fill the place of: *Automobiles replaced the horse and buggy.* **2.** To put back in place: *She replaced the dishes in the china cabinet.* **3.** To supply something to take the place of something else: *Who is going to replace the broken windows?*

re·ply |rĭ plī′| —*verb* **replied, replying, replies** To say or give an answer: *He replied that he would be happy to come.*
—*noun, plural* **replies** An answer or response: *I didn't hear his reply to my question.*

re·port |rĭ pôrt′| or |rĭ pōrt′| —*noun, plural* **reports** A spoken or written description of something: *a news report; a weather report.*
—*verb* **reported, reporting 1.** To present an account of: *The sentry reported the presence of enemy gunfire.* **2.** To provide an account for publication or broadcast: *Ms. Walters reports the evening news.* **3.** To present oneself: *The police officers reported for duty.*

report card A report of a student's grades and behavior. It is presented regularly to parents by a school.

re·port·er |rĭ pôr′tər| or |rĭ pōr′tər| —*noun, plural* **reporters** A person who gathers and reports news for a newspaper, or radio and television broadcast.

rep·re·sent |rĕp′rĭ zĕnt′| —*verb* **represented, representing 1.** To stand for; take the place of; be a symbol of: *The Roman numeral X represents 10.* **2.** To act for: *He represents our company in Canada.*

rep·re·sen·ta·tive |rĕp′rĭ zĕn′tə tĭv| —*noun, plural* **representatives 1.** A person chosen to represent others: *There was no representative from the family at the funeral.* **2. Representative** A member of the U.S. House of Representatives or of a state legislature.
—*adjective* **1.** Formed of elected members: *A democracy is a representative government.* **2.** Being a good example; characteristic: *This building is representative of the architect's style.*

re·pro·duce |rē′prə dōōs′| or |rē′prə dyōōs′| —*verb* **reproduced, reproducing 1.** To make a copy of: *a machine to reproduce photographs.* **2.** To produce offspring.

re·pro·duc·tion |rē′prə dŭk′shən| —*noun, plural* **reproductions 1.** The act or process of reproducing. **2.** Something that is reproduced; a copy: *reproductions of a famous painting.*

rep·tile |rĕp′tĭl′| —*noun, plural* **reptiles** Any of a group of animals that are cold-blooded and creep or crawl on the ground. Reptiles have a backbone and are covered with scales or hard plates. Snakes, turtles, and dinosaurs are reptiles.

re·pub·lic |rĭ pŭb′lĭk| —*noun, plural* **republics 1.** A form of government in which the supreme power of government rests with the voters. The voters elect representatives to govern the

reptile
Above: Alligator
Center: Turtle
Below: Snake

ă	pat	ĕ	pet	î	fierce
ā	pay	ē	be	ŏ	pot
â	care	ĭ	pit	ō	go
ä	father	ī	pie	ô	paw, for
oi	oil	ŭ	cut	zh	vision
ōō	book	û	fur	ə	ago, item,
ōō	boot	*th*	the		pencil, atom,
yōō	abuse	th	thin		circus
ou	out	hw	which	ər	butter

country. A republic is headed by a president rather than a monarch. **2.** A country that has such a form of government. The United States is a republic.

re·pub·li·can | rĭ pŭb′lĭ kən | —*adjective* **1.** Of or like a republic: *a republican form of government.* **2. Republican** Of or belonging to the Republican Party.
—*noun, plural* **republicans 1.** A person who believes in or supports a republican form of government. **2. Republican** A member or supporter of the Republican Party.

Republican Party One of the two major political parties of the United States, dating from 1854.

rep·u·ta·tion | rĕp′yə tā′shən | —*noun, plural* **reputations** The general worth or quality of someone or something as judged by others: *a man of good reputation.*

re·quest | rĭ kwĕst′ | —*verb* **requested, requesting** To ask or ask for: *I requested him to leave. She requested a book.*
—*noun, plural* **requests 1.** The act of asking for something: *Other sizes are available on request.* **2.** Something that is asked for: *We have had many requests for that book.*

re·quire | rĭ kwīr′ | —*verb* **required, requiring 1.** To have need of; demand; call for: *Playing the violin requires much practice.* **2.** To impose an obligation or duty upon someone: *The new rule requires all students to take at least one year of mathematics.*

re·quire·ment | rĭ kwīr′mənt | —*noun, plural* **requirements** Something that is needed; a demand: *a person's daily food requirement. The school has several requirements for admission.*

res·cue | rĕs′kyōō | —*verb* **rescued, rescuing** To save from danger or harm: *The lifeguard rescued the boy from drowning.*
—*noun, plural* **rescues** The act of rescuing or saving.

re·search | rĭ sûrch′ | or | rē′sûrch′ | —*noun, plural* **researches** The carefully organized study of a subject or problem: *medical research; scientific research.*
—*verb* **researched, researching** To do research on: *Sally is researching ancient Indian customs for her school paper.*

re·sem·blance | rĭ zĕm′bləns | —*noun, plural* **resemblances** Likeness in appearance: *His resemblance to his father is amazing.*

re·sem·ble | rĭ zĕm′bəl | —*verb* **resembled, resembling** To be similar or like: *This house resembles our last one.*

re·sent | rĭ zĕnt′ | —*verb* **resented, resenting** To feel angry or bitter about: *I resented his nasty remark.*

re·sent·ment | rĭ zĕnt′mənt | —*noun, plural* **resentments** A bitter or angry feeling: *It took me weeks to get over my resentment of his insult.*

res·er·va·tion | rĕz′ər vā′shən | —*noun, plural* **reservations 1.** The act of reserving something in advance, such as a hotel room or a seat on an airplane. **2.** Something that causes doubt, limits, or restricts: *I want to believe him, but I have some reservations about his story.* **3.** An area set aside by the government for a certain purpose: *an Indian reservation.*

re·serve | rĭ zûrv′ | —*verb* **reserved, reserving 1.** To set aside for some special use: *Mother reserved her silver for special occasions.* **2.** To arrange the use of something in advance: *Father reserved a car for Memorial Day weekend.* **3.** To keep for oneself: *I reserve the right to reply at a later time.*
—*noun, plural* **reserves 1.** A supply of something for later use: *a fuel reserve.* **2.** A tendency to talk little and keep one's feelings

Republican Party
Symbol of the party

reservoir
A reservoir and dam in Idaho

resort
Above: Ocean resort
Below: Ski resort

ă	pat	ĕ	pet	î	fierce
ā	pay	ē	be	ŏ	pot
â	care	ĭ	pit	ō	go
ä	father	ī	pie	ô	paw, for

oi	oil	ŭ	cut	zh	vision
ōō	book	û	fur	ə	ago, item,
ōō	boot	*th*	the		pencil, atom,
yōō	abuse	th	thin		circus
ou	out	hw	which	ər	butter

to oneself: *a person of great reserve.* **3. reserves** Armed forces not on active duty but ready to be called up in an emergency.

res·er·voir |rĕz′ər vwär′| —*noun, plural* **reservoirs** A body of water that has been collected and stored for use.

re·side |rĭ zīd′| —*verb* **resided, residing** To make one's home in a certain place; live: *He resides in Boston.*

res·i·dence |rĕz′ĭ dəns| —*noun, plural* **residences 1.** The house or building that a person lives in. **2.** The act or fact of living somewhere: *We enjoyed our residence in Mexico.*

res·i·dent |rĕz′ĭ dənt| —*noun, plural* **residents** A person who lives in a particular place: *all residents of the neighborhood.*

res·i·den·tial |rĕz′ĭ dĕn′shəl| —*adjective* Containing homes; suitable for residences: *a residential neighborhood.*

re·sign |rĭ zīn′| —*verb* **resigned, resigning** To give up or quit a position: *He resigned the job after twenty years.*

res·ig·na·tion |rĕz′ĭg nā′shən| —*noun, plural* **resignations** The act of giving up or quitting a position: *The company president announced his resignation.*

res·in |rĕz′ĭn| —*noun, plural* **resins** Any of several yellowish or brownish sticky substances that ooze from pine, balsam, and certain other trees and plants. Resin is used in making varnishes, lacquers, plastics, and many other products.

re·sist |rĭ zĭst′| —*verb* **resisted, resisting 1.** To work or fight against; oppose: *The soldiers resisted the enemy attack.* **2.** To withstand the effect of: *a plastic that resists heat.* **3.** To keep from giving in to: *She could not resist the temptation of eating chocolate.*

re·sis·tance |rĭ zĭs′təns| —*noun* **1.** The act or ability to resist: *The enemy offered little resistance. He catches colds frequently because his resistance is low.* **2.** Any force that tends to hinder motion: *The automobile body is shaped to lessen wind resistance.*

res·o·lu·tion |rĕz′ə lōō′shən| —*noun, plural* **resolutions 1.** The quality of having strong will and determination: *The knights began their quest with great courage and resolution.* **2.** A vow or promise to do something or to keep from doing it: *My New Year's resolution was to give up candy.*

re·solve |rĭ zŏlv′| —*verb* **resolved, resolving** To make a firm decision: *You'd better resolve to work harder.*

res·o·nant |rĕz′ə nənt| —*adjective* Having a full, pleasing sound: *John has a deep, resonant voice.*

re·sort |rĭ zôrt′| —*verb* **resorted, resorting** To go or turn for help or as a means of achieving something: *He often resorts to humor in order to get his way.*
—*noun, plural* **resorts 1.** A place where people go for rest or recreation: *a ski resort.* **2.** A person or thing that one turns to for help: *I asked my mother as a last resort.*

re·sound |rĭ zound′| —*verb* **resounded, resounding 1.** To be filled with sound: *The stadium resounded with cheers.* **2.** To make a loud sound: *The music resounded throughout the auditorium.*

re·source |rĭ sôrs′| or |rĭ sōrs′| or |rē′sôrs′| or |rē′sōrs′| —*noun, plural* **resources 1.** Something that a person can turn to for help: *Faith is a great resource in time of trouble.* **2. resources** Money available or on hand; one's assets: *It took all our resources to buy her a present.* **3.** Something that is a source of wealth to a country: *Forests are a great natural resource.*

re·spect |rĭ spĕkt′| —*noun, plural* **respects 1.** A favorable

opinion; honor; admiration: *Children should be taught to have respect for their elders.* **2.** Regard or esteem: *A good citizen has respect for the law.* **3. respects** Expressions of friendship, sympathy, or consideration; greetings: *to pay one's respects to the dead man's family.* **4.** A particular feature or detail: *In one respect the two brothers are exactly alike.*
—*verb* **respected, respecting** To have respect for.

re·spect·a·ble |rĭ spĕk′tə bəl| —*adjective* **1.** Proper in behavior or appearance: *a very respectable family.* **2.** Worthy of respect: *Our team made a respectable showing.*

re·spec·tive·ly |rĭ spĕk′tĭv lē| —*adverb* Each in the order given: *Albany and Atlanta are, respectively, the capitals of New York and Georgia.*

res·pi·ra·tion |rĕs′pə rā′shən| —*noun* The act or process of inhaling and exhaling; breathing.

res·pi·ra·to·ry system |rĕs′pər ə tôr′ē| or |rĕs′pər ə tōr′ē| The air passages through which a living thing breathes. In man and land animals with backbones, these passages connect the nose and mouth with the lungs.

re·spond |rĭ spŏnd′| —*verb* **responded, responding** **1.** To make a reply; answer: *The class responded to the roll call.* **2.** To react, especially in a favorable or desired way: *The patient has begun to respond to treatment.*

re·sponse |rĭ spŏns′| —*noun, plural* **responses** An answer or reply: *a good response to an appeal for donations.*

re·spon·si·bil·i·ty |rĭ spŏn′sə bĭl′ĭ tē| —*noun, plural* **responsibilities** **1.** The quality or condition of being responsible: *Mark refuses to accept any responsibility for his pets.* **2.** Something that a person is responsible for: *What are her responsibilities?*

re·spon·si·ble |rĭ spŏn′sə bəl| —*adjective* **1.** Having a certain duty or obligation: *You are responsible for cleaning your room.* **2.** Being the cause of something: *Germs are responsible for many diseases.* **3.** Being dependable or reliable; trustworthy: *a responsible person.* **4.** Requiring many duties or obligations: *a responsible job.*

rest¹ |rĕst| —*noun, plural* **rests** **1.** A period when one is relaxed, asleep, or not active: *We stopped work for a brief rest.* **2.** Sleep, ease, or relaxation resulting from this: *I need plenty of rest.* **3.** The end of life; death: *eternal rest.* **4.** Lack or ending of motion: *The car slowed down and came to a rest.*
—*verb* **rested, resting** **1.** To stop working, relax, or sleep so as to regain one's strength: *I like to rest after dinner.* **2.** To allow to relax: *Take off your shoes and rest your feet.* **3.** To place on or against something for support: *Rest your suitcase on the ground.*

rest² |rĕst| —*noun* **1.** The part that is left over after something has been fulfilled or removed; the remainder: *Pay the rest when you can.* **2.** (Used with a plural verb.) Those who remain; the others: *The rest are coming later.*

res·tau·rant |rĕs′tər ənt| or |rĕs′tə ränt′| —*noun, plural* **restaurants** A place where meals are served to the public.

rest·less |rĕst′lĭs| —*adjective* **1.** Without rest or sleep: *a restless night.* **2.** Unable to relax or be still: *a restless child.*

re·store |rĭ stôr′| or |rĭ stōr′| —*verb* **restored, restoring** **1.** To bring back into existence: *Her kindness restored my faith in people.* **2.** To bring back to an original condition: *They want to restore their parents' home.*

---

rest¹, rest²
Rest¹ comes from an old English word meaning "relaxation by sleep or quiet." **Rest²** comes from a noun used long ago by French-speaking people to mean "remainder." This came from a verb that meant "to remain" whose earlier Latin source was a word meaning "to stay back, remain."

re·strain |rĭ strān′| —*verb* **restrained, restraining** **1.** To hold back by physical force: *The police restrained the crowds at the parade.* **2.** To hold back: *I restrained the urge to eat too much.*

re·strict |rĭ strĭkt′| —*verb* **restricted, restricting** To keep within limits; confine: *They restrict the children to the yard.*

re·stric·tion |rĭ strĭk′shən| —*noun, plural* **restrictions** **1.** The act of limiting or restricting: *They told us to enjoy ourselves without restriction.* **2.** Something, as a law or rule, that limits or restricts: *There are no restrictions on the use of your membership.*

re·sult |rĭ zŭlt′| —*noun, plural* **results** Something that happens or follows a cause; outcome: *The result of his bad judgment was a black eye. All this damage is the result of the hurricane.*
—*verb* **resulted, resulting** **1.** To come about as the result of something: *A job resulted from his phone call.* **2.** To end in a certain way: *Her hard work resulted in success.*

re·sume |rĭ zōōm′| —*verb* **resumed, resuming** To begin again after a break; continue: *The play resumed when the laughter had died down.*

re·tail |rē′tāl′| —*noun* The sale of goods to the general public.
—*verb* **retailed, retailing** To sell at a retail price: *The store retails foreign radios at a big profit.*
—*adjective* Of or having to do with the selling of goods at retail: *a retail store; retail prices.*

re·tain |rĭ tān′| —*verb* **retained, retaining** **1.** To continue to have; keep possession of: *He retained his job as factory foreman.* **2.** To keep or hold in a particular place or condition: *Some plants are able to retain moisture for long periods.* **3.** To hire by paying a fee; engage: *Our firm has retained Mr. Jones as its lawyer.*

ret·i·na |rĕt′n ə| or |rĕt′nə| —*noun, plural* **retinas** A lining on the inside of the eyeball that is sensitive to light. The retina is connected to the brain by means of a nerve that carries images of things seen to the brain.

re·tire |rĭ tīr′| —*verb* **retired, retiring** **1.** To give up one's work, usually on reaching a certain age: *The player retired from baseball after twenty years.* **2.** To go to bed: *Let's retire early.*

re·tire·ment |rĭ tīr′mənt| —*noun, plural* **retirements** The period of life when one has stopped working: *He's spending his retirement in Florida.*

re·tir·ing |rĭ tī′rĭng| —*adjective* Shy and reserved; bashful: *She's so retiring she always avoids strangers.*

re·treat |rĭ trēt′| —*verb* **retreated, retreating** To fall back before an enemy attack; withdraw: *The troops retreated under heavy enemy fire.*
—*noun, plural* **retreats** **1.** The act of withdrawing under enemy attack: *a hasty retreat when bombs began falling.* **2.** The signal for such an act: *The bugler sounded retreat.* **3.** A quiet and private place: *a retreat by the lake.*

re·trieve |rĭ trēv′| —*verb* **retrieved, retrieving** **1.** To get back; recover: *The player retrieved a ball from the outfield.* **2.** To find and bring back game that has been shot.

re·triev·er |rĭ trē′vər| —*noun, plural* **retrievers** Any of several kinds of dog that can be trained to find and bring back birds or animals that have been shot.

re·turn |rĭ tûrn′| —*verb* **returned, returning** **1.** To go or come back: *We returned home after two weeks in Canada.* **2.** To bring, send, carry, put, or give back: *She returned my wallet to me.* **3.** To

retriever

ă	pat	ĕ	pet	î	fierce
ā	pay	ē	be	ŏ	pot
â	care	ĭ	pit	ō	go
ä	father	ī	pie	ô	paw, for

oi	oil	ŭ	cut	zh	vision
ŏŏ	book	û	fur	ə	ago, item,
ōō	boot	th	the		pencil, atom,
yōō	abuse	th	thin		circus
ou	out	hw	which	ər	butter

give back in exchange for something: *Mother returned the blanket for a refund.* **4.** To appear or happen again: *Summer returns every year.*
—*noun, plural* **returns 1.** The act of returning: *The return home was dull. We look forward to the return of winter.* **2.** A profit: *He received a poor return on his investments.*

re·un·ion | rē yōōn′yən | —*noun, plural* **reunions** A gathering of friends, relatives, or classmates after a separation.

re·veal | rĭ vēl′ | —*verb* **revealed, revealing 1.** To make known; disclose: *Please don't reveal the secret.* **2.** To show; display: *The fog lifted and revealed the gleaming shore.*

re·venge | rĭ věnj′ | —*verb* **revenged, revenging** To do something to get satisfaction for an injury or insult: *The brothers vowed to revenge the injustice they had suffered.*
—*noun* The act or an example of revenging.

rev·e·nue | rěv′ə nōō′ | or | rěv′ə nyōō′ | —*noun, plural* **revenues 1.** The money that a government collects from taxes and other sources in order to pay its expenses: *Income tax is one source of revenue.* **2.** Income from property or investments: *She has a nice revenue from the house she rents out.*

rev·er·ence | rěv′ər əns | —*noun* A feeling of deep respect: *We were taught to have reverence for learning. The pilgrims showed great reverence in the holy places.*

rev·er·ent | rěv′ər ənt | —*adjective* Feeling or showing reverence: *One should be reverent when attending religious services.*

re·verse | rĭ vûrs′ | —*adjective* **1.** Turned backward or over: *The cloth is blue on the reverse side. See the reverse side of the page.* **2.** Causing backward movement: *a reverse gear.*
—*noun, plural* **reverses 1.** The opposite or contrary of something: *That's the reverse of what I told you to do.* **2.** The back or rear of something: *The reverse of the tablecloth is white flannel.* **3.** A gear or other mechanism in an automobile that allows it to move backward. **4.** A change for the worse: *Her life has been full of reverses.*
—*verb* **reversed, reversing 1.** To move in the opposite direction: *The band marched down the field, then reversed and marched back.* **2.** To turn inside out or upside-down: *The seamstress reversed the fabric.* **3.** To exchange the positions of: *The players reversed the order of batting.*

re·view | rĭ vyōō′ | —*verb* **reviewed, reviewing 1.** To look over; examine: *Review chapter five before the exam tomorrow.* **2.** To write or give a critical report on a book, play, or other work: *He reviews new books for the local newspaper.*
—*noun, plural* **reviews 1.** The act of going over or examining something again: *a review of material studied during the year.* **2.** A report on something that attempts to determine its worth: *a book review; a review of a concert.*

re·vise | rĭ vīz′ | —*verb* **revised, revising 1.** To change in order to improve or bring up-to-date: *Some textbooks are revised every two years.* **2.** To change something because of different circumstances: *We had to revise our vacation plans.*

re·vive | rĭ vīv′ | —*verb* **revived, reviving 1.** To bring back or return to life or consciousness: *The lifeguard revived the drowning boy.* **2.** To bring back or make vigorous again: *The brief nap revived my spirits.*

re·volt | rĭ vōlt′ | —*verb* **revolted, revolting 1.** To take part in a rebellion against a government or other authority: *The American*

reunion
A college reunion

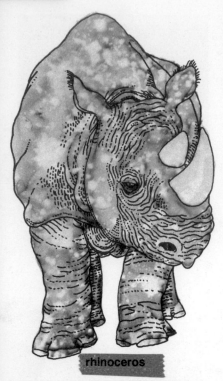

rhinoceros

Rhode Island
There are two theories about the origin of the name **Rhode Island**. One is that an early Italian explorer thought it looked like Rhodes, an island near Greece and Turkey. The other is that a Dutch explorer gave it the name *Rood Eiland,* which means "red island."

rhododendron

ă	pat	ĕ	pet	î	fierce
ā	pay	ē	be	ŏ	pot
â	care	ĭ	pit	ō	go
ä	father	ī	pie	ô	paw, for
oi	oil	ŭ	cut	zh	vision
ōŏ	book	û	fur	ə	ago, item,
ōō	boot	*th*	the		pencil, atom,
yōō	abuse	th	thin		circus
ou	out	hw	which	ər	butter

colonies revolted against British rule. **2.** To fill with disgust; repel: *His behavior really revolted me.*
—noun, plural **revolts** An act of rebellion against authority; an uprising: *a revolt of convicts against prison regulations.*

rev·o·lu·tion | rĕv′ə lōō′shən | *—noun, plural* **revolutions 1.** An uprising or rebellion against a government: *The revolution was quickly put down by the king's troops.* **2.** Any sudden or extensive change: *The industrial revolution changed people's lives forever.* **3.** Movement of an object around another object: *the revolution of the earth around the sun.* **4.** A spinning or rotation about an axis: *The motor makes 3,000 revolutions a minute.*

rev·o·lu·tion·ar·y | rĕv′ə lōō′shə nĕr′ē | *—adjective* **1.** Taking part in, bringing about, or encouraging revolution: *The college forbids revolutionary groups on its campus.* **2.** Of or causing a complete change: *Nuclear power was a revolutionary discovery.*

re·volve | rĭ vŏlv′ | *—verb* **revolved, revolving 1.** To move in orbit: *The planets revolve around the sun.* **2.** To turn or cause to turn: *A small motor revolves the wheels of the machine.*

re·volv·er | rĭ vŏl′vər | *—noun, plural* **revolvers** A pistol with a revolving cylinder that places the bullets one at a time in a position to be fired. A revolver can be fired many times without having to be loaded again.

re·ward | rĭ wôrd′ | *—noun, plural* **rewards 1.** Something given or received in return for an act, service, or accomplishment: *He received a title as a reward for his loyalty.* **2.** Money offered for the capture of a criminal or the return of something lost.
—verb **rewarded, rewarding** To give a reward to or for.

rheu·ma·tism | rōō′mə tĭz′əm | *—noun, plural* **rheumatisms** A disease that causes swelling of the muscles, tendons, bones, joints, or nerves. It also makes them stiff and causes pain.

rhi·noc·er·os | rī nŏs′ər əs | *—noun, plural* **rhinoceros** A large African or Asian animal with short legs, thick skin, and one or two upright horns on the snout.

Rhode Island | rōd | A state in the northeastern United States. The capital of Rhode Island is Providence.

rho·do·den·dron | rō′də dĕn′drən | *—noun, plural* **rhododendrons** A shrub with evergreen leaves and clusters of white, pinkish, or purplish flowers.

rhu·barb | rōō′bärb′ | *—noun* **1.** A plant having large, poisonous leaves and long, fleshy stalks. The stalks are reddish or green. **2.** The stalks of this plant.

rhyme | rīm | *—noun, plural* **rhymes 1.** A repeating of sounds of two or more words, syllables, or the ends of lines of verse. For example, *day* and *May, ever* and *never* are rhymes. **2.** A poem having a regular repetition of sounds at the ends of lines.
—verb **rhymed, rhyming** To correspond in sound: *"Hour" rhymes with "power."*

rhythm | rĭth′əm | *—noun, plural* **rhythms** A regular repeating of a movement, action, or sounds: *the rhythm of the drums.*

rhyth·mic | rĭth′mĭk | *—adjective* Of or having rhythm: *a rhythmic dance.*

rib | rĭb | *—noun, plural* **ribs 1.** Any of the long, curved bones that extend from the backbone toward the breastbone and enclose the chest cavity. **2.** A curved part resembling a rib: *the rib of an umbrella.*

rib·bon | rĭb′ən | *—noun, plural* **ribbons 1.** A narrow strip used for decorating or tying things. Ribbons are made from silk, satin, velvet, paper, or other materials. **2.** A strip of cloth that is like a ribbon: *a typewriter ribbon; a towel torn to ribbons by the cat's claws.*

rice | rīs | —*noun* **1.** A grass that bears grains used as food. Rice is grown in warm regions. **2.** The grains of such a plant.

rich | rĭch | —*adjective* **richer, richest** **1.** Having great wealth: *a rich man; a rich nation.* **2.** Having much of something; well supplied: *Milk and eggs are rich in protein.* **3.** Producing well; fertile: *a rich soil for a vegetable garden.* **4.** Containing a large amount of fat or sugar: *Chocolate is richer than cocoa.* **5.** Full and deep: *a rich bass voice.*

rich·es | rĭch′ ĭz | —*plural noun* Great wealth in the form of money, land, or other valuable things.

Rich·mond | rĭch′ mənd | The capital of Virginia.

rid | rĭd | —*verb* **rid** or **ridded, ridding** To free from something that is bad or not wanted: *What can we do to rid the kitchen of flies? Billy has to rid himself of his lazy habits.*

rid·den | rĭd′ n | The past participle of the verb **ride**: *She has already ridden on the new train.*

rid·dle | rĭd′ l | —*noun, plural* **riddles** A question or problem that is hard to answer or figure out. "What is black and white and read all over? A newspaper" is an example of a riddle.

ride | rīd | —*verb* **rode, ridden, riding** **1.** To sit on and cause to move: *She rides her bicycle every day. He is afraid to ride horses.* **2.** To sit on a horse and cause it to move: *She rides well.* **3.** To be carried in or on a car, train, or other vehicle: *Tom rode in the car as Mary drove.* **4.** To cover a distance of: *He has to ride sixty miles every morning to go to work.* **5.** To be supported or carried along on: *The swimmers were riding the waves into shore.*
—*noun, plural* **rides** **1.** A short trip on an animal or in a car, train, or other vehicle: *It's a quick ride from here to your house.* **2.** Any of the various machines or devices on or in which people ride for pleasure at an amusement park: *We tried the merry-go-round and all the other rides at the park.*

rid·er | rī′ dər | —*noun, plural* **riders** A person who rides.

ridge | rĭj | —*noun, plural* **ridges** **1.** A long, narrow peak or crest of something: *the ridge of a hill; the ridge of a roof.* **2.** A long, narrow chain of hills or mountains. **3.** Any narrow raised strip: *the ridges of a plowed field; the ridges in corduroy.*

rid·i·cule | rĭd′ ĭ kyōol′ | —*noun* Words or actions that make fun of something or someone.
—*verb* **ridiculed, ridiculing** To make fun of; laugh at; mock.

ri·dic·u·lous | rĭ dĭk′ yə ləs | —*adjective* Deserving ridicule; foolish; silly: *a ridiculous idea; a ridiculous paper hat.*

ri·fle | rī′ fəl | —*noun, plural* **rifles** A gun with a long barrel that is fired from the shoulder. The barrel of a rifle has special grooves inside to give the bullet spin as it is fired. This gives the gun greater accuracy.

rig | rĭg | —*verb* **rigged, rigging** **1.** To fit out; equip; prepare: *The farmers rigged out the barn for the storm.* **2.** To fit a boat with masts, sails, lines, and other equipment.
—*noun, plural* **rigs** **1.** The arrangement of masts, sails, lines, and other equipment on a boat. **2.** Any special equipment: *an oil-drilling rig.*

right | rīt | —*noun, plural* **rights** **1.** The side opposite the left: *The number 3 is on the right of the face of a clock.* **2.** Something

rice
A rice paddy

rider
A rider in a rodeo

rifle

that is correct, just, moral, or honorable: *People must be taught the difference between right and wrong.* **3.** A moral or legal claim: *property rights; human rights; women's rights.* **4.** A turn to the right: *Take a right at the next stop light.*

—*adjective* **1.** Located on the side opposite the left: *your right hand; a parking space on the right side of the street.* **2.** Done to the right: *a right turn.* **3.** Intended to be worn facing outward: *the right side of a sweater.* **4.** Correct; accurate; true: *the right answer.* **5.** Morally correct; just: *the right thing to do.* **6.** Suitable; proper: *He is just right to play the prince in the play.*

—*adverb* **1.** On or to the right: *Remember to turn right at the post office.* **2.** In a straight line; directly: *She came right up to us and introduced herself.* **3.** In a correct manner; properly: *My watch isn't working right. You're not doing that right.* **4.** Exactly; just: *The ball landed right where he was standing.* **5.** Immediately: *We will leave right after breakfast.*

—*verb* **righted, righting** **1.** To put back into an upright, proper, or normal position: *They righted their canoe. The car rolled over twice and then righted itself.* **2.** To make amends for: *We must right these wrongs.*

♦ *These sound alike* **right, write.**

right angle An angle formed by two perpendicular lines; an angle of 90 degrees.

right-hand |rīt′ hănd′| —*adjective* **1.** Located on the right: *the right-hand margin of the page.* **2.** Of or for the right hand: *She lost her right-hand glove.* **3.** Most helpful; useful; reliable: *My son is my right-hand man around the house.*

right-hand·ed |rīt′ hăn′ dĭd| —*adjective* **1.** Using the right hand more easily and naturally than the left hand: *a right-handed pitcher in baseball.* **2.** Designed for use by the right hand: *a right-handed wrench.* **3.** Done with the right hand: *a right-handed pitch.*

rig·id |rĭj′ ĭd| —*adjective* **1.** Not changing shape or bending; stiff; not flexible: *a rigid iron frame for a bed.* **2.** Not changing; strict; fixed: *rigid rules.*

rim |rĭm| —*noun, plural* **rims** **1.** The border, edge, or margin of something: *the rim of a coffee cup.* **2.** The outer part of a wheel around which the tire is fitted.

rind |rīnd| —*noun, plural* **rinds** A tough outer covering or skin. Melons, lemons, and some cheeses have rinds.

ring¹ |rĭng| —*noun, plural* **rings** **1.** A circle with an empty center: *a ring of fire; a smoke ring. Hold hands and form a ring.* **2.** A small circular band, often of precious metal, worn on a finger. **3.** An enclosed area in which exhibitions, sports, or contests take place: *a circus ring; a boxing ring.*

—*verb* **ringed, ringing** To form a ring around; encircle: *Beautiful wheat fields ringed the little town.*

♦ *These sound alike* **ring, wring.**

ring² |rĭng| —*verb* **rang, rung, ringing** **1.** To make or cause to make a clear piercing sound like that of a bell when struck: *The doorbell rang. Ring the buzzer.* **2.** To sound a bell or buzzer to summon someone: *Ring if you wish service at this counter.* **3.** To hear a steady buzzing or humming: *My ears are ringing from the sound of the blast.* **4.** To be full of sounds; echo: *The hallways rang with angry shouting.* **5.** To call by telephone: *Ring home as soon as you get to school.*

—*noun, plural* **rings** **1.** The sound made by a bell or other

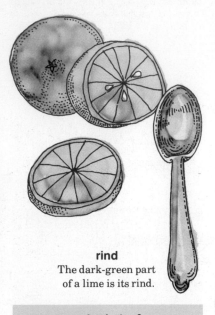

rind
The dark-green part
of a lime is its rind.

ring¹, ring²
Ring¹ and ring² come from two different old English words. They are not related.

ring¹
A napkin ring

ă	pat	ĕ	pet	î	fierce
ā	pay	ē	be	ŏ	pot
â	care	ĭ	pit	ō	go
ä	father	ī	pie	ô	paw, for
oi	oil	ŭ	cut	zh	vision
ŏŏ	book	û	fur	ə	ago, item,
ōō	boot	*th*	the		pencil, atom,
yōō	abuse	th	thin		circus
ou	out	hw	which	ər	butter

metallic object when struck. **2.** A telephone call: *Give your parents a ring to tell them where you are staying.*

♦ *These sound alike* **ring, wring.**

rink |rĭngk| —*noun, plural* **rinks** An area with a smooth surface for ice-skating or roller-skating.

rinse |rĭns| —*verb* **rinsed, rinsing 1.** To wash lightly with water: *Rinse the dishes before putting them in the dishwasher.* **2.** To clean with clear water or other solution: *Rinse your mouth after brushing your teeth.*

—*noun, plural* **rinses** The act of rinsing: *Since his shirt wasn't very dirty, it just needed a rinse.*

ri·ot |rī′ət| —*noun, plural* **riots** A wild, violent disturbance caused by a large number of people: *a prison riot; student riots.*

—*verb* **rioted, rioting** To take part in a wild, violent disturbance: *The prisoners rioted as a protest against conditions in the prison.*

rip |rĭp| —*verb* **ripped, ripping 1.** To tear open or split apart: *The cat's claws ripped the curtain. The sleeve ripped along the seam.* **2.** To remove by pulling or tearing roughly: *She ripped out the seams in the dress. He ripped the envelope open.*

—*noun, plural* **rips** A torn or split place: *The tailor has to sew up the rip in his trousers.*

ripe |rīp| —*adjective* **riper, ripest** Fully grown and ready to be used as food: *The apples are ripe enough to be picked.*

rip·en |rī′pən| —*verb* **ripened, ripening** To make or become ripe: *Grapes must ripen on the vine.*

rip·ple |rĭp′əl| —*noun, plural* **ripples 1.** A small wave: *A trout jumped up and made ripples on the surface of the lake.* **2.** Something like a wave on the surface of any soft material: *The curtains hung in soft ripples.* **3.** A sound like that of small waves: *A ripple of laughter went through the room.*

—*verb* **rippled, rippling** To form or cause to form ripples: *The curtain rippled in the breeze. A trout rippled the surface of the water.*

rise |rīz| —*verb* **rose, risen, rising 1.** To move from a lower to a higher position; go up; ascend: *Hot air rises. The kite rose quickly on the strong wind.* **2.** To get up from a sitting or lying position; stand up: *We all rose when the principal entered the room.* **3.** To get out of bed: *At camp we rose every day at six in the morning.* **4.** To increase in size; swell: *Dough rises. The river rises every spring as the snows melt.* **5.** To increase in number, amount, price, or value: *The temperature today rose to 80 degrees. Membership in our club is rising. The cost of living is rising every month.* **6.** To increase in intensity, force, or speed: *The wind has risen and the windows are rattling.* **7.** To go upward in rank, position, or importance: *Education will help you rise in the world.* **8.** To reach or extend upward: *The mountain rose hundreds of feet above them.* **9.** To come into existence; start; begin: *Many streams rise far up in the mountains.* **10.** To revolt; rebel: *The slaves rose against their masters.*

—*noun, plural* **rises 1.** The act or an example of going up from a lower to a higher position; a climb; ascent: *His sudden rise to power surprised his enemies. Don't stop the rise of the balloon.* **2.** An increase: *a rise in prices.* **3.** An origin; beginning: *The revolution meant the rise of a new nation.* **4.** A gentle slope: *They climbed easily up the rise of the hill.*

ris·en |rĭz′ən| The past participle of the verb **rise**: *The sun has risen.*

rink
An ice-skating rink

ripe
Ripe peaches on a branch *(above)* and cut in half *(below)*

risk | rĭsk | —*noun, plural* **risks** The chance of suffering harm or loss; danger: *Don't run the risk of catching cold.*
—*verb* **risked, risking** 1. To take a chance of harm or loss: *She risked her life by diving into the icy water to save the drowning dog.* 2. To leave oneself open to the chance of: *You are risking an accident by driving a car with bad brakes.*

risk·y | rĭs′kē | —*adjective* **riskier, riskiest** Involving a risk.

ri·val | rī′vəl | —*noun, plural* **rivals** Someone who tries to do as well or better than another; competitor: *The two boys are friendly rivals in every sport they enter.*
—*verb* **rivaled, rivaling** To try to do as well as or better than another; compete with: *Three candidates rivaled for the office of treasurer.*

riv·er | rĭv′ər | —*noun, plural* **rivers** A large natural stream of water that flows into an ocean, lake, or other large body of water.

riv·et | rĭv′ĭt | —*noun, plural* **rivets** A metal bolt or pin that is used to join metal plates or other objects. A rivet has a head on one end and is set through a hole in each piece. The end without a head is then hammered or compressed to form another head.
—*verb* **riveted, riveting** To fasten with a rivet or rivets: *The workers riveted the two steel plates together.*

roach | rōch | —*noun, plural* **roaches** A cockroach.

road | rōd | —*noun, plural* **roads** 1. An open way for the passage of vehicles, persons, and animals. 2. Any path or course: *There is no simple road to success.*
♦ *These sound alike* **road, rode.**

road·run·ner | rōd′rŭn′ər | —*noun, plural* **roadrunners** A bird of southwestern North America that runs very fast. The roadrunner has a long tail, brownish, streaked feathers, and a crest.

roam | rōm | —*verb* **roamed, roaming** To travel over or through an area without a goal or purpose; wander: *At night the coyotes roam the prairie, howling to one another.*

roar | rôr | or | rōr | —*noun, plural* **roars** 1. A loud, deep sound like that made by a lion or some other large animals. 2. Any loud, deep sound or noise: *Can you hear the roar of the jet plane?*
—*verb* **roared, roaring** 1. To make a loud, deep sound: *The lion roared. The huge engines roared. The train roared into the station.* 2. To laugh loudly: *The audience roared at the comic.*

roast | rōst | —*verb* **roasted, roasting** 1. To cook with dry heat in an oven or over an open fire, hot coals, or hot ashes: *We will roast a turkey for Thanksgiving. I like to roast marshmallows on the fireplace.* 2. To dry and brown by heating: *Roast the coffee beans lightly.* 3. To be uncomfortably hot: *I'm roasting in this coat.*
—*noun, plural* **roasts** A cut of meat that is suitable for roasting or that has been roasted.

rob | rŏb | —*verb* **robbed, robbing** To take property or valuables from a person or place unlawfully and especially by force: *Three men robbed the bank.*

rob·ber | rŏb′ər | —*noun, plural* **robbers** A person who robs; thief.

rob·ber·y | rŏb′ə rē | —*noun, plural* **robberies** The act or crime of unlawfully taking the property of someone by force.

robe | rōb | —*noun, plural* **robes** 1. A long, loose garment that is worn as a covering: *Bob put on his robe over his pajamas. She always wears a robe after taking a shower.* 2. Often **robes** A long, loose garment worn over clothing or on official or special

roadrunner

robe
A king's robe

ă	pat	ĕ	pet	î	fierce
ā	pay	ē	be	ŏ	pot
â	care	ĭ	pit	ō	go
ä	father	ī	pie	ô	paw, for
oi	oil	ŭ	cut	zh	vision
ŏŏ	book	û	fur	ə	ago, item,
ōō	boot	th	the		pencil, atom,
yōō	abuse	th	thin		circus
ou	out	hw	which	ər	butter

occasions as a mark of office or rank: *a king's robe; a judge's robes.*
—*verb* **robed, robing** To dress in a robe: *The judge robed herself before entering the courtroom.*

rob·in |rŏb′ĭn| —*noun, plural* **robins** A North American songbird. The robin has a reddish breast and a dark gray back.

ro·bot |rō′bət| or |rō′bŏt′| —*noun, plural* **robots** A machine that looks like a person and can perform some human tasks or imitate some of the things a person can do.

ro·bust |rō bŭst′| or |rō′bŭst′| —*adjective* Full of health and strength: *His parents are robust people who love the outdoors.*

rock¹ |rŏk| —*noun, plural* **rocks** **1.** A hard material that is formed naturally and is of mineral origin. The earth's crust is made up of different kinds of rock. **2.** A fairly small piece of such material; a stone: *The mountain trail was covered with rocks.* **3.** A large mass of rock: *The ship was smashed against the rocks by huge waves.* **4.** Someone or something that is very strong and dependable: *My family has been a rock for me in bad times.*

rock² |rŏk| —*verb* **rocked, rocking** **1.** To move back and forth or from side to side: *The breeze rocked the hammock. The boat rocked in the waves.* **2.** To cause to shake violently: *The earthquake rocked nearby villages.*

rock·er |rŏk′ər| —*noun, plural* **rockers** **1.** A rocking chair. **2.** Either of the two curved pieces on which a rocking chair rocks back and forth or a cradle rocks from side to side.

rock·et |rŏk′ĭt| —*noun, plural* **rockets** Any device that is driven forward or upward by a force provided by the release of gases from burning fuel. Small rockets are used as fireworks, while large ones are used as weapons and to propel spacecraft.

rock 'n' roll |rŏk′ən rōl′| A form of popular music with a very strong, steady beat. Very simple words are set to this music. It is also popular as dance music.

rock·y¹ |rŏk′ē| —*adjective* **rockier, rockiest** Full of or covered with rocks: *a rocky beach.*

rock·y² |rŏk′ē| —*adjective* **rockier, rockiest** Not firm; tending to shake or wobble: *a rocky old chair.*

rod |rŏd| —*noun, plural* **rods** **1.** A thin, stiff, straight piece of wood, metal, or other material: *a steel curtain rod; a fishing rod.* **2.** A branch or stick used to punish people by whipping or thrashing. **3.** A unit of length equal to 16½ feet.

rode |rōd| The past tense of the verb **ride**: *The cowboys rode home from the prairie.*
♦ *These sound alike* **rode, road.**

ro·dent |rōd′nt| —*noun, plural* **rodents** Any of several related animals, such as a mouse, rat, squirrel, or beaver. Rodents have large front teeth used for gnawing.

ro·de·o |rō′dē ō′| or |rō dā′ō| —*noun, plural* **rodeos** A public show in which cowboys display their skills in horseback riding and compete in riding broncos or steers, roping cattle, and similar events.

roe |rō| —*noun, plural* **roes** The eggs of a fish.
♦ *These sound alike* **roe, row¹, row².**

role |rōl| —*noun, plural* **roles** **1.** A part or character played by an actor: *Tom and Sarah are going to play the leading roles in the school play.* **2.** A proper or usual part played by someone or something: *Mothers have important roles in children's lives.*
♦ *These sound alike* **role, roll.**

robin

robot

rock¹, rock²
Rock¹ comes from a word used long ago in French to mean "stone." Rock² comes from an old English word that meant "to sway to and fro."

rocky¹, rocky²
Rocky¹ was formed from **rock¹**, and rocky² from **rock².**

roll |rōl| —*verb* **rolled, rolling** **1.** To move along a surface while turning over and over: *The ball rolled across the lawn and dropped into the hole.* **2.** To cause to keep turning over and over: *Dick found a huge truck tire and rolled it home.* **3.** To move along on wheels or rollers or in a vehicle with wheels: *Roll the wheelbarrow into the tool shed.* **4.** To turn over and over: *Pigs like to roll in mud to keep cool.* **5.** To turn around or upward: *She rolls her eyes to express impatience.* **6.** To wrap or wind round and round: *She rolled her hair around her finger.* **7.** To make flat or even by or as if by passing a roller over it: *The cook is rolling dough for a pie crust.* **8.** To move with steady or increasing speed: *A thick fog was rolling in from the sea.* **9.** To pass steadily: *The years rolled by.* **10.** To move or cause to move from side to side: *The little sailboat rolled and pitched in the storm.* **11.** To make a deep, loud sound: *Thunder rolled across the sky.* **12.** To beat a drum with a rapid series of strokes. **13.** To pronounce with a fluttering sound: *Scottish people roll their "r's."*
—*noun, plural* **rolls** **1.** A rolling or swaying movement: *He watched the roll of the golf ball toward the hole. The roll of the boat was making her sick.* **2.** A rise and fall in a surface: *the gentle roll of the hills of the countryside.* **3.** Something rolled up in the form of a cylinder or tube: *a roll of fabric; a roll of paper towels.* **4.** A list of the names of members of a group: *the roll of the officers of the bank.* **5.** The persons present: *The teacher called the roll at the beginning of each class period.* **6.** A small, rounded portion of bread: *a hamburger roll.* **7.** A deep rumble: *a roll of thunder.* **8.** A continuous sound made by beating a drum rapidly.
♦ *These sound alike* **roll, role.**

roll·er |rō′lər| —*noun, plural* **rollers** **1.** A small wheel. Roller skates have rollers. **2.** A cylinder or tube around which something is wound up: *a roller for a window shade; rollers for setting one's hair.* **3.** A cylinder for flattening, crushing, or squeezing things. **4.** A cylinder for applying paint or ink onto a surface. **5.** A large, heavy wave breaking along a shore.

roller coaster A small railroad in an amusement park. A roller coaster moves very fast on a track with sudden, steep descents and sharp turns.

roller skate A skate with four small wheels. It is worn for skating on pavement and other hard surfaces.

rol·ler-skate |rō′lər skāt′| —*verb* **roller-skated, roller-skating** To skate on roller skates.

ro·man |rō′mən| —*noun* The most common style of type. Roman type has upright letters. This definition is printed in roman.

Ro·man |rō′mən| —*adjective* Of ancient or modern Rome, its people, or their culture.
—*noun, plural* **Romans** **1.** A person who was born in or was a citizen of ancient Rome. **2.** A person who was born in or is a citizen of modern Rome.

Roman Catholic **1.** A member of the Roman Catholic Church. **2.** Of the Roman Catholic Church.

Roman Catholic Church The Christian church that recognizes the pope in Rome as its supreme head.

ro·mance |rō măns′| or |rō′măns′| —*noun, plural* **romances** **1.** A long story or poem about the adventures of heroes: *the romance of King Arthur and his knights.* **2.** Exciting adventure: *a*

roller coaster

roller-skate

ă	pat	ĕ	pet	î	fierce	
ā	pay	ē	be	ŏ	pot	
â	care	ĭ	pit	ō	go	
ä	father	ī	pie	ô	paw, for	
oi	oil	ŭ	cut	zh	vision	
ŏŏ	book	û	fur	ə	ago, item,	
ōō	boot	th	the		pencil, atom,	
yōō	abuse	th	thin		circus	
ou	out	hw	which	ər	butter	

soldier's life full of romance and brave deeds. **3.** A quality of warmth, love, and mystery: *Soft lights add romance to a quiet dinner for two.*

Romance languages The languages that developed from Latin, especially French, Italian, Portuguese, and Spanish.

Roman Empire The empire of the ancient Romans. It included most of Europe, northern Africa, and parts of Asia.

Roman numeral Any of the numerals used in a numbering system based on that of the ancient Romans. In this system letters stand for numbers: I = 1, V = 5, X = 10, L = 50, C = 100, D = 500, and M = 1,000.

ro·man·tic | rō **măn**′tĭk | —*adjective* **1.** Of or having to do with the stories of romance: *a romantic hero whose adventures we loved to read about.* **2.** Full of adventure or heroism: *the romantic lives of sailors who sail to distant places.* **3.** Suitable or proper for love and romance: *the soft, romantic light of candles.* **4.** Full of ideas of romance and adventure; not practical: *His sister has a very romantic view of life.*

Rome | rōm | **1.** The capital of Italy. **2.** The ancient Roman kingdom, republic, or empire.

roof | rŏof | or | rōof | —*noun, plural* **roofs** **1.** The outside top covering of a building. **2.** The top covering of anything: *the roof of a car.* **3.** The upper part of the mouth.
—*verb* **roofed, roofing** To cover with a roof: *roof a house.*

rook | rŏok | —*noun, plural* **rooks** One of the pieces used in the game of chess. It can move any number of squares across or up and down the board.

rook·ie | **rŏok**′ē | —*noun, plural* **rookies** **1.** A first-year player in the major leagues. **2.** A person with no experience.

room | rŏom | or | rōom | —*noun, plural* **rooms** **1.** Space; area: *This desk takes up too much room.* **2.** An area of a building set off by walls or partitions: *How many rooms are there in your house?* **3.** The people occupying a room: *The whole room laughed.* **4.** Opportunity; chance: *There is no room for error in our plan.*
—*verb* **roomed, rooming** To live in a room.

room·mate | **rŏom**′māt′ | or | **rōom**′māt′ | —*noun, plural* **roommates** A person with whom one shares a room or apartment.

room·y | **rŏo**′mē | or | **rōom**′ē | —*adjective* **roomier, roomiest** Having or giving plenty of room: *roomy closets.*

roost | rŏost | —*noun, plural* **roosts** **1.** A branch or other perch on which a bird settles for rest. **2.** A place to which birds regularly go to sleep for the night.
—*verb* **roosted, roosting** To rest or sleep on or in a roost.

roost·er | **rŏo**′stər | —*noun, plural* **roosters** A male chicken when it is fully grown.

root¹ | rŏot | or | rōot | —*noun, plural* **roots** **1. a.** The part of a plant that grows usually down into the ground. A root absorbs water and minerals from the soil, stores food, and keeps the plant firmly in place. **b.** The part of a plant that is usually underground and looks like a root; a bulb or tuber. **2.** A part that looks like a root in use or position. Hair and teeth have roots. **3.** A beginning; source; origin: *The root of our problem is a lack of money.* **4. roots** Strong feelings of belonging to a place or group: *We have lived all over the world but our roots are right here in this small village.* **5.** A word from which other words are formed. The word "hope" is the root of "hopeful" and "hopeless."

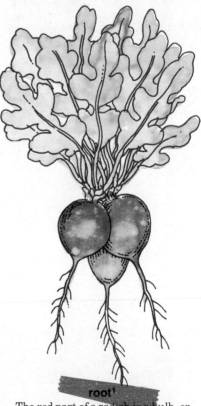

root¹, root², root³
Root¹ and **root²** come from old English words. The two are not related. The origin of **root³** is not clear.

root¹
The red part of a radish is a bulb, or root, that we eat. The long part growing down from the bulb is also a root.

—*verb* **rooted, rooting 1.** To develop or begin to grow a root or roots: *Carrot tops will root in water.* **2.** To be fixed in place by or as if by roots: *We felt rooted to the spot by fear.* **3.** To remove completely: *Use the tractor to root out the tree stumps.*

♦ *These sound alike* **root, route.**

root² | rŏot | or | rŏŏt | —*verb* **rooted, rooting 1.** To dig or dig up with the snout: *She saw two pigs rooting in the mud.* **2.** To search around; rummage.

♦ *These sound alike* **root, route.**

root³ | rŏot | or | rŏŏt | —*verb* **rooted, rooting** To give support to or cheer for a team or contestant.

♦ *These sound alike* **root, route.**

rope | rōp | —*noun, plural* **ropes 1.** A heavy cord made of twisted strands of fiber or other material. **2.** A string of things attached together: *a rope of onions.*

—*verb* **roped, roping 1.** To tie or fasten with a rope: *Don't forget to rope the packages together.* **2.** To catch with a throw of a lasso: *John roped a calf.* **3.** To enclose or mark an area with ropes: *The guards roped the playing field off to keep back the crowds.*

rose¹ | rōz | —*noun, plural* **roses 1. a.** Any of several shrubs or vines with usually prickly stems and showy flowers that have a very pleasant smell. **b.** The flower of such a plant. Roses are usually red or pink, but they can also be white or yellow. **2.** A deep pink color.

—*adjective* Deep pink.

rose² | rōz | The past tense of the verb **rise:** *He rose early.*

Rosh Ha·sha·nah or **Rosh Ha·sha·na** | rŏsh′ hə shä′ nə | or | rōsh′ hə shä′ nə | The Jewish New Year. It falls in September or October.

ros·y | rō′ zē | —*adjective* **rosier, rosiest 1.** Having a reddish or deep pink color: *rosy cheeks from the cold air; rosy clouds at sunset.* **2.** Bright and cheerful; promising: *The future looks rosy.*

rot | rŏt | —*verb* **rotted, rotting** To become rotten; spoil; decay: *Meat will rot if it is not refrigerated.*

—*noun, plural* **rots 1.** The process of rotting; decay: *Rot ruined the roof and the attic of the old house.* **2.** A destructive disease of plants caused by certain fungi or bacteria.

ro·ta·ry | rō′ tə rē | —*adjective* Of, causing, or having rotation: *rotary motion; a rotary water sprinkler.*

ro·tate | rō′ tāt′ | —*verb* **rotated, rotating 1.** To turn or spin around a center point or line: *The earth rotates on its axis.* **2.** To pass from one task or position to another in a regular order: *After every inning each player rotates to a new position.* **3.** To vary crops so that a different one is planted in a field each year: *The farmer rotates corn and wheat on his fields.*

ro·ta·tion | rō tā′ shən | —*noun, plural* **rotations** The action or process of turning around on a center point or line: *One rotation of the earth takes twenty-four hours.*

rot·ten | rŏt′ n | —*adjective* **rottener, rottenest 1.** Decayed; spoiled: *rotten wood; rotten meat.* **2.** Very bad: *rotten weather.*

rough | rŭf | —*adjective* **rougher, roughest 1.** Having a surface that is not even or smooth: *Rough country roads can be hard on a car.* **2.** Coarse or harsh to the touch: *That animal has rough fur.* **3.** Not finely or carefully made or fitted: *rough, homespun clothing.* **4.** Not gentle or careful: *a rough push.* **5.** Ready to fight or use force: *a rough cowboy.* **6.** Rude; impolite: *rough*

rose¹

ă	pat	ĕ	pet	î	fierce
ā	pay	ē	be	ŏ	pot
â	care	ĭ	pit	ō	go
ä	father	ī	pie	ô	paw, for
oi	oil	ŭ	cut	zh	vision
ŏŏ	book	û	fur	ə	ago, item,
ōō	boot	th	the		pencil, atom,
yōō	abuse	th	thin		circus
ou	out	hw	which	ər	butter

manners. **7.** Marked by physical exertion and rugged action: *a rough sport.* **8.** Stormy: *There is rough weather ahead.* **9.** Not precise; approximate: *At a rough guess, this house is 100 years old.*
—*verb* **roughed, roughing 1.** To make rough: *Try roughing the soles of your new shoes with sandpaper.* **2.** To make or sketch in a simple way: *Mother roughed out a plan.*

   Phrasal verb rough up To do physical harm to; beat up: *The boys were roughed up by their new neighbors.*
♦ *These sound alike* **rough, ruff.**

round │round│ —*adjective* **rounder, roundest 1.** Having a shape that is like a ball or circle. **2.** Having a cross section that is circular: *A tree trunk is round.* **3.** Having a curved surface or outline: *The old man has a rounded back. Sue has round shoulders.* **4.** Full; complete: *She added one cooky to make a round dozen.* **5.** Not exact; approximate: *It is enough to give the answers to the math questions in round numbers.*
—*noun, plural* **rounds 1.** Something round in shape: *Cut the cooky dough into rounds.* **2.** Often **rounds** A usual course of places visited or duties performed: *a watchman on his rounds.* **3.** A series of similar events: *a round of parties over Thanksgiving.* **4.** A single shot or series of shots from a firearm or firearms: *They heard a round of cannon shots.* **5.** Ammunition for a single shot: *How many rounds do the soldiers have left?* **6.** A period of struggle, discussion, or competition: *In the next round the workers hope to win their demands from the company.* **7.** A song for two or more voices in which each voice enters at a different time with the same melody at the same pitch: *"Three Blind Mice" and "Row, Row, Row Your Boat" are rounds.*
—*verb* **rounded, rounding 1.** To make or become round: *She rounded her lips to put on the makeup. The carpenter rounded the corners of the planks.* **2.** To make a turn to or on the other side of: *The car rounded a bend in the road.*

   Phrasal verb round up 1. To herd grazing animals together. **2.** To seek out and bring together: *The teacher was rounding up the children for lunch.*
—*adverb* Around: *a wheel spinning round and round.*
—*preposition* Around: *She flung her arms round his neck.*

round·up │round'ŭp'│ —*noun, plural* **roundups 1.** The act of herding cattle or other animals together. **2.** Any similar gathering of persons or things: *a roundup of suspects.*

rouse │rouz│ —*verb* **roused, rousing 1.** To wake up; awaken: *Nothing could rouse him early.* **2.** To cause to become active or alert; excite: *The news of their victory roused the fans.*

rout │rout│ —*noun, plural* **routs** A complete defeat followed by a retreat that lacks discipline and order: *Our attack turned the enemy's resistance into a rout.*
—*verb* **routed, routing 1.** To defeat completely: *We routed the opposing team.* **2.** To put to flight; scatter: *Our ships and planes routed the enemy's naval force.*

route │rōōt│ or │rout│ —*noun, plural* **routes 1.** A road or course for traveling from one place to another. **2.** A highway: *Take route 66.* **3.** A series of places or customers visited regularly: *Dianne and Tommy have a newspaper route and an egg route.*
—*verb* **routed, routing** To send or pass on by a certain route: *The clerk routes the mail through the secretaries to the manager's office.*
♦ *These sound alike* **route, root.**

route
A highway

rou·tine | rōō tēn′ | —*noun, plural* **routines** The usual or regular way of doing things: *He has a daily routine of walking to school.*
—*adjective* According to the usual or regular way of doing things; ordinary: *Take the car for a routine checkup. Today was a routine day, with nothing exciting happening.*

row¹ | rō | —*noun, plural* **rows** **1.** A series of persons or things placed next to one another in a straight line: *Plant the flower seeds in neat rows.* **2.** A series without a break in time: *Our team won first place three years in a row.*
♦ *These sound alike* **row¹, roe, row².**

row² | rō | —*verb* **rowed, rowing** **1.** To move a boat with oars: *We rowed our canoe across the river.* **2.** To carry in a boat moved by oars: *Get in and I'll row you across the lake.*
♦ *These sound alike* **row², roe, row¹.**

row³ | rou | —*noun, plural* **rows** A noisy quarrel or fight.

row·boat | rō′bōt′ | —*noun, plural* **rowboats** A small boat moved with oars.

row·dy | rou′dē | —*adjective* **rowdier, rowdiest** Noisy and rough: *a rowdy group of children.*
—*noun, plural* **rowdies** A noisy, rough person.

roy·al | roi′əl | —*adjective* **1.** Of a king or queen: *the royal family.* **2.** Like or fit for a king or queen: *a royal banquet.* **3.** Belonging to or serving a king or queen: *a royal palace; the royal household.*

roy·al·ty | roi′əl tē | —*noun, plural* **royalties** **1.** A king, queen, or other member of a royal family. **2.** Kings, queens, and their relatives in general: *The ball was a great occasion, when all royalty were present.*

rub | rŭb | —*verb* **rubbed, rubbing** **1.** To press something against a surface and move it back and forth: *Bob rubbed the table with a piece of damp cloth.* **2.** To press and move back and forth: *Rub the sandpaper against the wood.* **3.** To clean, polish, or remove by rubbing: *You must rub the silverware until it shines.* **4.** To apply by rubbing: *Joan rubbed cream on her dry hands.*
—*noun, plural* **rubs** An act or gesture of rubbing: *Give yourself a good rub with the towel.*

rub·ber | rŭb′ər | —*noun, plural* **rubbers** **1.** An elastic or plastic substance prepared from the milky sap of certain tropical trees. Rubber is waterproof and airtight and is used in making many products. **2. rubbers** Low overshoes made of rubber.

rub·bish | rŭb′ĭsh | —*noun, plural* **rubbishes** **1.** Useless material; garbage; trash. **2.** Silly talk or ideas; nonsense.

rub·ble | rŭb′əl | —*noun, plural* **rubbles** Pieces of stone, rock, or other solid material: *the rubble from the plane crash.*

ru·by | rōō′bē | —*noun, plural* **rubies** **1.** A deep-red, hard, clear precious stone. **2.** A deep-red color.
—*adjective* Deep red.

rud·dy | rŭd′ē | —*adjective* **ruddier, ruddiest** Having a healthy pink or reddish color: *a ruddy complexion.*

rude | rōōd | —*adjective* **ruder, rudest** **1.** Having or showing bad manners; impolite: *Don't be rude to the guests.* **2.** Not finely made; crude: *a rude cabin of logs and branches.*

ruff | rŭf | —*noun, plural* **ruffs** A growth of fur or feathers that looks like a collar around the neck of an animal or bird.
♦ *These sound alike* **ruff, rough.**

ruf·fle | rŭf′əl | —*noun, plural* **ruffles** A strip of gathered or pleated cloth, lace, or ribbon attached to fabric by one edge.

row¹, row², row³
Row¹ comes from an old English word meaning "line." **Row²** came from a different English word of long ago meaning "to row with an oar." We don't know the source of **row³**.

row¹

ruff
A bird with a ruff of feathers

ă	pat	ĕ	pet	î	fierce
ā	pay	ē	be	ŏ	pot
â	care	ĭ	pit	ō	go
ä	father	ī	pie	ô	paw, for

oi	oil	ŭ	cut		zh	vision
ŏŏ	book	û	fur		ə	ago, item,
ōō	boot	*th*	the			pencil, atom,
yōō	abuse	th	thin			circus
ou	out	hw	which		ər	butter

—*verb* **ruffled, ruffling** To disturb the smooth or even appearance of: *The father ruffled the boy's hair affectionately. The bird ruffled its feathers at the sight of the cat.*

rug |rŭg| —*noun, plural* **rugs** A piece of thick, heavy fabric that is used to cover part or all of a floor.

rug·ged |rŭg′ĭd| —*adjective* **1.** Having a rough, uneven surface or jagged outline: *This hilly land is too rugged for farming.* **2.** Able to endure a lot; strong and sturdy; durable: *Only rugged people could live in these mountains.* **3.** Hard to put up with; harsh or severe: *I hope this winter won't be as rugged as last year's.*

ru·in |rōō′ĭn| —*noun, plural* **ruins** **1.** Very great destruction or damage: *The flood caused the ruin of all the houses and land along the river.* **2.** The complete loss of a person's money, position, or reputation: *He said his enemies were trying to cause his ruin by spreading lies about him.* **3.** The cause of such destruction or loss: *He seemed like a good person but gambling was his ruin.* **4.** Often **ruins** The remains of a building or other structure or group of structures that has been destroyed or fallen into pieces from age: *I saw American Indian ruins in Colorado and Arizona.*
—*verb* **ruined, ruining** To destroy or damage; make useless or worthless: *The fire ruined the police station.*

rule |rōōl| —*noun, plural* **rules** **1.** A statement that tells how to do something or what may or may not be done: *Baseball and other games have rules. If you want to join the club, you have to obey the rules.* **2.** A regular or approved way of behaving or doing something: *One of the rules of good manners is to say "please" when you ask for something.* **3.** The act or power of governing or controlling: *a country under the rule of a queen.*
—*verb* **ruled, ruling** To have power or authority over; govern: *At sea, a captain rules his ship.*

rul·er |rōō′lər| —*noun, plural* **rulers** **1.** A person who governs a country. A king, a queen, and an emperor are rulers. **2.** A strip of wood, metal, or other material with a straight edge. It is marked off in units of measurement and is used to measure and draw straight lines.

rum·ble |rŭm′bəl| —*verb* **rumbled, rumbling** To make a deep, long rolling sound: *During the storm lightning lit up the sky and thunder rumbled. The old truck rumbled down the road.*
—*noun, plural* **rumbles** A deep, long rolling sound: *the rumble of thunder. Dad thought he heard a rumble in the car engine.*

rum·mage |rŭm′ĭj| —*verb* **rummaged, rummaging** To search thoroughly by moving things around or turning them over: *He rummaged through the attic looking for his old coat.*
—*noun, plural* **rummages** A thorough search.

ru·mor |rōō′mər| —*noun, plural* **rumors** **1.** A statement or story that is spread from one person to another and believed to be true even though there is nothing to prove it: *I heard a rumor that school is going to let out early tomorrow.* **2.** Information that is passed from person to person; general talk: *Rumor is saying that the band will get their new uniforms next week.*
—*verb* **rumored, rumoring** To spread or report by rumor: *It is rumored that the big shoe factory is going to go out of business.*

rump |rŭmp| —*noun, plural* **rumps** **1.** The fleshy part of an animal's body where the legs meet the back. **2.** A piece or cut of meat from this part: *a rump roast.*

run |rŭn| —*verb* **ran, run, running** **1.** To move quickly on foot; go

ruin
A city in ruins after a war

at a pace faster than a walk: *He runs faster than I do. We had run for a mile.* **2.** To cause to move at this pace: *He ran the horse for an hour this morning.* **3.** To move or travel quickly on foot or in a vehicle: *Run down to the store for me on your bicycle.* **4.** To move about freely; roam: *We let the chickens run in the yard.* **5.** To leave quickly or escape: *We have time only to eat and run. Run for your life.* **6.** To go from stop to stop on a regular route: *The trains are running late today.* **7.** To get, become, or pass into a certain condition: *Call me if you run into trouble. She ran up a big telephone bill.* **8.** To take part or cause to take part in a race or contest: *I'm running in the fifty-yard dash. Is he going to run his horse in the big race?* **9.** To compete or be a candidate for elected office: *She's running for President.* **10.** To move or pass quickly: *The thought ran through my mind.* **11.** To pass smoothly through or over a surface: *I ran my hand down her cheek.* **12.** To thrust, drive, or chase: *The sheriff ran the outlaws out of town.* **13.** To do by moving quickly: *run errands.* **14.** To flow or cause to flow in a steady stream: *The spilled milk ran over the edge of the table.* **15.** To spread beyond the intended limits: *The ink ran when the paper got wet.* **16.** To send out a fluid: *Your nose is running.* **17.** To have or suffer: *She's running a fever.* **18.** To extend or stretch: *This road runs down to the lake.* **19.** To last or continue: *A President's term runs four years.* **20.** To work or operate or cause to work or operate: *The car doesn't run well in cold weather.* **21.** To manage or direct; control: *Who runs this store?* **22.** To tear or ravel stitches: *My stockings ran.* **23.** To pass or get through a dangerous situation: *The car ran through the police blockade.*

   Phrasal verbs **run across** To meet or find by chance: *I ran across Uncle Fred in the bakery today.* **run into** **1.** To meet or find by chance: *You'll never guess who I ran into at the movies.* **2.** To collide with: *The bicycle ran into the fence.* **run out** To be used up; come to an end: *My money ran out.*
   —*noun, plural* **runs** **1.** The act of running: *We went for a run in the park. The horse came at a run.* **2.** A trip or journey: *I'm going to take a run into town. The bus makes the run to New York twice a day.* **3.** Freedom to move about: *The children were given the run of the back yard.* **4.** A continuous series of something: *The team has a run of nine victories. We had a run of great weather during our vacation.* **5.** A place or line of torn stitches in a fabric: *a run in your stocking.* **6.** In baseball, a score made by moving or advancing around the bases and reaching home plate safely: *We scored four runs in the last inning to win the game.*

rung¹ |rŭng| —*noun, plural* **rungs** **1.** A rod or bar that forms a step of a ladder. **2.** A crossing piece that connects and supports the legs or back of a chair.
   ♦ *These sound alike* **rung, wrung.**

rung² |rŭng| The past participle of the verb **ring:** *The telephone has rung all day.*
   ♦ *These sound alike* **rung, wrung.**

run·ner |rŭn′ər| —*noun, plural* **runners** **1.** Someone or something that runs: *Only two runners finished the fifty-mile race.* **2.** One of the blades on which a sled, sleigh, or ice skate moves. **3.** The narrow stem of certain plants that runs or lies along the ground and puts down new roots and so grows more plants. **4.** A long, narrow rug. It is used in a hall or on a flight of stairs.

runner
On a plant *(above)*, in a race *(center)*, and on a sled *(below)*

ă	pat	ĕ	pet	î	fierce
ā	pay	ē	be	ŏ	pot
â	care	ĭ	pit	ō	go
ä	father	ī	pie	ô	paw, for
oi	oil	ŭ	cut	zh	vision
ŏŏ	book	û	fur	ə	ago, item,
ōō	boot	*th*	the		pencil, atom,
yōō	abuse	th	thin		circus
ou	out	hw	which	ər	butter

run·ning |rŭn′ĭng| —*noun, plural* **runnings** **1.** The act of a person or thing that runs: *The running of the race will begin at two o'clock.* **2.** A competition or contest: *Three students are in the running for class president.*
—*adjective* **1.** Carried on or performed while running: *He took a running jump off the diving board.* **2.** Without interruption; continuous: *The actress had to face a running fire of questions from the reporters.* **3.** With a liquid coming out; discharging: *He has a running nose.*

runt |rŭnt| —*noun, plural* **runts** A plant, animal, or person that is smaller than the usual size.

rup·ture |rŭp′chər| —*noun, plural* **ruptures** The act of bursting or breaking open; a crack: *a rupture in the wall of the dam.*
—*verb* **ruptured, rupturing** To break; burst.

ru·ral |rŏŏr′əl| —*adjective* In, like, or having to do with the country: *She wants to leave the city and move to a rural area.*

rush |rŭsh| —*verb* **rushed, rushing** **1.** To move or act quickly; hurry: *Fire engines rushed past us. He rushed for help.* **2.** To act or force to act too quickly: *He's always rushing into new projects without knowing what he's doing. Don't rush me.* **3.** To move or flow quickly with great force and noise: *Tons of water rushed over the falls.* **4.** To attack suddenly; charge.
—*noun, plural* **rushes** **1.** The act of rushing; a swift movement: *Bill can hear the rush of the river from his bedroom.* **2.** The movement of many people to or from a place: *There was a great rush to California when gold was found there.* **3.** Hasty or hurried activity; a great hurry: *What's the rush?*

rust |rŭst| —*noun* **1.** A reddish-brown or orange coating that forms on iron and certain other metals when they are exposed to air or moisture. **2.** A plant disease that causes red or brown spots on leaves and stems. **3.** A reddish-brown color.
—*verb* **rusted, rusting** To make or become covered with rust: *Rain rusted the iron gate. The saw and screwdriver rusted.*
—*adjective* Reddish brown: *a rust shirt.*

rus·tle |rŭs′əl| —*verb* **rustled, rustling** **1.** To make or cause to make a soft, fluttering or crackling sound: *The leaves rustled in the wind. A breeze rustled the pages of the calendar on the wall.* **2.** To steal cattle.
—*noun, plural* **rustles** A soft, fluttering or crackling sound: *I looked up when I heard the rustle of the newspaper.*

rust·y |rŭs′tē| —*adjective* **rustier, rustiest** **1.** Covered or coated with rust: *a rusty nail; a rusty knife.* **2.** Made by rust: *a rusty spot on the car.* **3.** Not working or not being done as well as one should because of lack of use or practice: *My arm is a little rusty because I have not thrown a baseball in years.*

rut |rŭt| —*noun, plural* **ruts** **1.** A track or groove made in the ground by the passage of a wheel or foot: *I kept slipping into the ruts left by the truck on the dirt road.* **2.** A fixed way of acting, living, or doing something; routine: *Marlene didn't like her job and felt that she was stuck in a rut.*
—*verb* **rutted, rutting** To make ruts in: *The tractor rutted the fields.*

ruth·less |rŏŏth′lĭs| —*adjective* Having or showing no pity; cruel: *a ruthless person.*

rye |rī| —*noun* **1.** A grass that bears grain. Rye seeds are used for making flour and whiskey. **2.** The seeds of this plant.
♦ *These sound alike* **rye, wry.**

rural
A rural scene

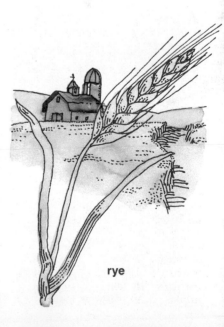

rye

Ss

W Phoenician — The letter *S* comes originally from a Phoenician symbol named *shin*, meaning "tooth," in use about 3,000 years ago.

Ƨ Greek — The Greeks borrowed the symbol from the Phoenicians and changed its form. They also changed its name to *sigma*.

S Roman — The Romans took the letter and adapted it for carving into stone. This became the model for our modern printed capital *S*.

ſ Medieval — The hand-written form of about 1,200 years ago became the basis of the modern small letter.

Ss Modern — The modern capital and small letters are based on the Roman capital and later hand-written forms.

sable

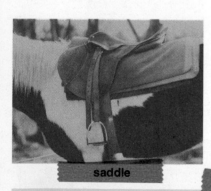

saddle

ă	pat	ĕ	pet	î	fierce		
ā	pay	ē	be	ŏ	pot		
â	care	ĭ	pit	ō	go		
ä	father	ī	pie	ô	paw, for		
oi	oil	ŭ	cut		zh	vision	
ōō	book	û	fur		ə	ago, item,
ōō	boot	*th*	the			pencil, atom,
yōō	abuse	th	thin			circus
ou	out	hw	which		ər	butter

s or **S** |ĕs| —*noun, plural* **s's** or **S's** The nineteenth letter of the English alphabet.

Sab·bath |săb′əth| —*noun, plural* **Sabbaths** The day of the week that is used for rest and worship. Saturday is the Sabbath for Jews, Sunday for Christians.

sa·ber |sā′bər| —*noun, plural* **sabers** A heavy sword with a curved blade. It is used mainly by cavalry.

sa·ble |sā′bəl| —*noun, plural* **sables** 1. An animal of northern Europe and Asia that is related to the mink and weasel. Sables have soft, dark fur that is very valuable. 2. The fur of a sable.

sack |săk| —*noun, plural* **sacks** 1. A large bag made of strong, coarse material. Sacks are used to hold things such as grain, potatoes, and mail. **2.a.** A sack with something in it: *a sack of mail.* **b.** The amount that a sack holds: *Buy two sacks of sugar.*

Sac·ra·men·to |săk′rə **měn**′tō| The capital of California.

sa·cred |sā′krĭd| —*adjective* Of something that is thought of or treated with special respect because it has to do with religion; holy: *a sacred place. The Bible is a sacred book.*

sac·ri·fice |săk′rə fīs′| —*noun, plural* **sacrifices** **1.a.** The act of offering something to a god in order to show love or worship, to ask to be forgiven, or to ask for a favor or blessing. In the past, many peoples killed animals and sometimes people on an altar as a sacrifice. **b.** Something offered as a sacrifice. **2.** The act of giving up something valuable or desired for the sake of something or someone: *They had to make many sacrifices so their children could go to college.*
—*verb* **sacrificed, sacrificing** **1.** To offer something as a sacrifice to a god. **2.** To give up something for the sake of something or someone: *Rick sacrificed a chance to go to the football game to spend the evening with his friend who was sick in bed.*

sad |săd| —*adjective* **sadder, saddest** **1.** Unhappy or filled with sorrow: *a long, sad face. He's sadder today than he was yesterday.* **2.** Causing sorrow: *The defeat of their football team was a sad event.* **3.** In a bad or poor condition: *Your room is in sad shape.*

sad·den |săd′n| —*verb* **saddened, saddening** To make or become sad: *It saddened me that she forgot my birthday.*

sad·dle |săd′l| —*noun, plural* **saddles** A seat for a rider on the back of a horse or other animal, or on a bicycle, tricycle, or

motorcycle. A saddle is usually made out of leather.
—*verb* **saddled, saddling** To put a saddle on: *The sheriff quickly saddled his horse and rode off.*

sad·ness |săd′nĭs| —*noun* The quality or condition of being sad: *There was much sadness in the country when the king died.*

safe |sāf| —*adjective* **safer, safest 1.** Free from danger or harm: *It's not safe to cross the street without looking. Is that the safest place you can find for your money?* **2.** Not likely to cause harm; not dangerous: *Is it safe for the baby to play with those keys?* **3.** Careful or cautious: *a safe driver.* **4.** With no chance of breaking down or going wrong; reliable: *a safe car.* **5.** With no chance of being wrong; certain to be true: *It's safe to say that we'll never see a live dinosaur.* **6.** In baseball, having reached a base without being put out: *He was safe on third base.*
—*noun, plural* **safes** A strong metal container in which money, jewels, or other valuable objects are kept for protection.

safe·guard |sāf′gärd′| —*verb* **safeguarded, safeguarding** To protect from danger or attack; keep safe; guard: *The sheriff safeguarded the town against the cattle robbers.*
—*noun, plural* **safeguards** A device that is used as a means of protection: *A lock is a good safeguard.*

safe·ty |sāf′tē| —*noun* Freedom from danger or harm: *The job of the police is to protect the safety of people and their property.*

safety pin A pin that is bent or curved at one end so as to form a spring. At the other end is a guard that covers the point of the pin and keeps it closed.

sag |săg| —*verb* **sagged, sagging 1.** To sink or hang down: *The roof on the old barn sagged.* **2.** To droop or hang down because of weight or pressure: *The apple trees sagged from all the ripe fruit.*

sage·brush |sāj′brŭsh| —*noun* A shrub that grows in dry areas of western North America. Sagebrush leaves are silver-green and have a strong smell.

sa·gua·ro |sə gwär′ō| or |sə wär′ō| —*noun, plural* **saguaros** A very large cactus that grows in the southwestern United States and Mexico. It has branches that curve upward.

said |sĕd| The past tense and past participle of the verb **say:** *She said hello. He had said that he would be back today.*

sail |sāl| —*noun, plural* **sails 1.** A piece of strong material that is attached to a mast or upright pole on a ship or boat. A sail is stretched out so that it catches the wind that causes the boat to move. **2.** Something that looks like a sail or that catches the wind like a sail, such as the blade of a windmill. **3.** A trip in a ship or boat, especially in a sailboat: *We went for a sail.*
—*verb* **sailed, sailing 1.** To travel on or across water: *The pirate ship sailed the ocean.* **2.** To operate or steer a boat, especially a sailboat: *I'm going to learn how to sail.* **3.** To start out on a trip across water: *The ship will sail tomorrow.* **4.** To move smoothly and easily: *The skaters were sailing along the ice.*
♦ *These sound alike* **sail, sale.**

sail·boat |sāl′bōt′| —*noun, plural* **sailboats** A boat that has a sail or sails so that it can be moved by the wind.

sail·or |sā′lər| —*noun, plural* **sailors 1.** Someone who is a member of a ship's crew or who sails or steers a ship or boat. **2.** A member of a navy who is not an officer.

saint |sānt| —*noun, plural* **saints 1.** Often **Saint** A very good and holy person. The Roman Catholic Church officially calls such

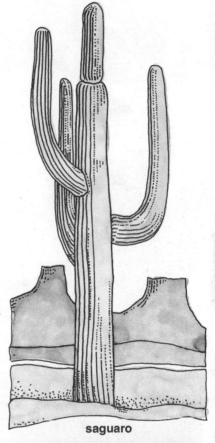

saguaro

sailboat

holy people saints after their death because they deserve special respect. **2.** A person who is very good, kind, and patient: *Everyone thinks my grandmother is a saint.*

sake |sāk| —*noun, plural* **sakes** **1.** Reason or purpose: *Don't go to the picnic just for the sake of having something to do.* **2.** Benefit or good; advantage: *He drove slowly for our sake.*

sal·ad |săl′əd| —*noun, plural* **salads** A dish made up of lettuce, tomatoes, cucumbers, and other raw vegetables. A salad is often served with a dressing. Meat, cheese, fish, eggs, or fruit are sometimes used with or in place of the raw vegetables.

sal·a·man·der |săl′ə măn′dər| —*noun, plural* **salamanders** An animal that looks like a lizard.

sal·a·ry |săl′ə rē| —*noun, plural* **salaries** A fixed sum of money that is paid to someone for doing a job. It is paid on a regular schedule, such as every week or every month.

sale |sāl| —*noun, plural* **sales** **1.** The act of selling; the exchange of goods for money: *the sale of tickets; the sale of a house.* **2.** The special selling of goods for less than they usually cost: *There's a half-price sale at the store.*
♦ *These sound alike* **sale, sail.**

Sa·lem |sā′ləm| The capital of Oregon.

sales·man |sālz′mən| —*noun, plural* **salesmen** A man whose work is selling goods or services.

sales·per·son |sālz′pûr′sən| —*noun, plural* **salespersons** A salesman or saleswoman.

sales·wom·an |sālz′wŏom′ən| —*noun, plural* **saleswomen** A woman whose job is selling goods or services.

sa·li·va |sə lī′və| —*noun* The watery liquid produced in the mouth by certain glands. It has no taste, helps in chewing by keeping the mouth wet, and starts digestion.

sal·mon |săm′ən| —*noun, plural* **salmon** **1.** Any of several large fish that live in northern waters. Its pinkish flesh is used for food. **2.** A yellowish-pink or pinkish-orange color.
—*adjective* Yellowish pink or pinkish orange.

sa·loon |sə lōon′| —*noun, plural* **saloons** A place where alcoholic drinks are served and drunk; a bar.

salt |sôlt| —*noun, plural* **salts** **1.** A white substance that is found in deposits in the earth and in sea water. Human beings and many other animals need salt. It is used to season and preserve food. **2.** A chemical substance or compound that is formed when acids come into contact with a base.
—*verb* **salted, salting** **1.** To season or sprinkle with salt: *Salt the stew on the stove and stir it.* **2.** To preserve food by treating with salt.

Salt Lake City The capital of Utah.

salt·wa·ter |sôlt′wô′tər| or |sôlt′wŏt′ər| —*adjective* Having to do with or living in the sea: *a salt-water pond; salt-water fish.*

salt·y |sôl′tē| —*adjective* **saltier, saltiest** Containing or tasting of salt: *salty tears. The soup is saltier than I like it.*

sa·lute |sə lōot′| —*verb* **saluted, saluting** **1.** To show respect in a formal manner by raising the right hand to the forehead or by shooting guns or cannons: *salute the flag. The President was saluted by the firing of rifles.* **2.** To greet with polite or friendly words or gestures: *John waved his hand to salute his friend.*
—*noun, plural* **salutes** **1.** The act of saluting: *a twenty-one gun salute. He waved in salute.* **2.** The position of the right hand held

salamander

salute

ă	pat	ĕ	pet	î	fierce
ā	pay	ē	be	ŏ	pot
â	care	ĭ	pit	ō	go
ä	father	ī	pie	ô	paw, for
oi	oil	ŭ	cut	zh	vision
ŏŏ	book	û	fur	ə	ago, item,
ōō	boot	*th*	the		pencil, atom,
yōō	abuse	th	thin		circus
ou	out	hw	which	ər	butter

up to the forehead in a formal gesture of respect.

sal·vage |săl′ vĭj| —*verb* **salvaged, salvaging** To save something from being damaged or destroyed: *We salvaged the radio before the boat sank.*
—*noun* The rescue of a damaged or sunken ship or its cargo.

sal·va·tion |săl vā′shən| —*noun* **1.** The act or condition of saving from danger, loss, or destruction; rescue: *Controlling pollution is the only salvation for our rivers and streams.* **2.** Someone or something that saves or rescues: *The extra food we packed was our salvation when we got lost in the forest.*

salve |săv| or |säv| —*noun, plural* **salves** A soft substance or ointment that is spread on wounds and sores to heal or soothe them: *You must rub salve on your elbow where you scraped it.*

same |sām| —*adjective* **1.** Being exactly like something else; identical: *These two books are the same size. That's the same jacket as I have.* **2.** Being the very one as before and not another or different one: *This is the same seat I had yesterday. Isn't that the same book you read last week?* **3.** Not changed in any way: *He's not the same friendly person he used to be.*
—*pronoun* The identical person or thing: *He asked the waiter to bring him more of the same.*

sam·ple |săm′ pəl| or |säm′ pəl| —*noun, plural* **samples** A small part of something that shows what the whole thing is like: *Choose which color you like from these paint samples. The astronaut brought samples of rocks and soil back from the moon.*
—*verb* **sampled, sampling** To test or decide by trying a little of: *Sample these two cakes and tell me which you like better.*

sanc·tu·ar·y |săngk′ chōō ĕr′ē| —*noun, plural* **sanctuaries 1.** A holy place, such as a church or synagogue. **2.** Protection or safety: *We found sanctuary from the blizzard in an old barn.* **3.** An area where animals and birds live and are protected.

sand |sănd| —*noun, plural* **sands** Very small, loose grains of worn or crushed rock. Some sand, such as that on beaches, is very smooth, while other sand, such as that on mountains or in the woods, can be rough and coarse.
—*verb* **sanded, sanding 1.** To sprinkle or cover with sand: *Sand the sidewalk so nobody slips on the ice.* **2.** To rub with sand or sandpaper in order to smooth a surface: *He sanded the table he built before he painted it.*

san·dal |săn′ dl| —*noun, plural* **sandals** A kind of shoe that is made of a sole that is held or fastened to the foot by straps.

sand·box |sănd′ bŏks′| —*noun, plural* **sandboxes** A closed-in area or low box filled with sand for children to play in.

sand·pa·per |sănd′ pā′pər| —*noun* Heavy paper that is coated on one side with sand or other rough material. It is used for cleaning and smoothing wood or other surfaces.
—*verb* **sandpapered, sandpapering** To smooth, polish, or clean by rubbing with sandpaper: *He's busy sandpapering the picnic table.*

sand·pi·per |sănd′ pī′pər| —*noun, plural* **sandpipers** A small bird that lives on the seashore and has a thin, pointed bill.

sand·stone |sănd′ stōn′| —*noun* A kind of rock that is made of grains of sand held together by various materials. It is used mainly in building.

sand·wich |sănd′ wĭch| or |săn′ wĭch| —*noun, plural* **sandwiches** Two or more slices of bread with meat, cheese, peanut butter and jelly, or some other filling between them.

sandal

sandpiper

—*verb* **sandwiched, sandwiching** To squeeze or fit in tightly between two other things: *I was sandwiched between my aunt and my fat uncle on the sofa.*

sand·y | sănʹdē | —*adjective* **sandier, sandiest** **1.** Full of, covered with, or like sand: *a sandy beach; a sandy road.* **2.** Yellowish red in color: *sandy hair.*

sane | sān | —*adjective* **saner, sanest** **1.** Having a normal and healthy mind; not crazy. Not being sane is a sickness and is treated by doctors. **2.** Having or showing good sense or common sense; sensible: *sane advice. That's the sanest approach to the problem anyone has thought of.*
♦ *These sound alike* **sane, seine.**

sang | săng | A past tense of the verb **sing:** *The crowd sang the national anthem.*

san·i·ta·tion | sănʹĭ tāʹshən | —*noun* The different ways used to protect the health of people by keeping the places they live and work clean. It includes removing garbage, cleaning streets, keeping the drinking water clean and pure, and many other things.

san·i·ty | sănʹĭ tē | —*noun* The condition of being sane; mental health.

sank | săngk | A past tense of the verb **sink:** *The rowboat sank during the storm.*

San·ta Fe | sănʹtə fāʹ | The capital of New Mexico.

sap | săp | —*noun, plural* **saps** A liquid that flows through a plant and carries food to its different parts.

sap·phire | săfʹīr′ | —*noun, plural* **sapphires** A hard, deep-blue stone used as a gemstone.

sar·cas·tic | sär kăsʹtĭk | —*adjective* Using nasty, bitter remarks to make fun of someone or something or to hurt a person's feelings: *When she couldn't answer the question, another student made a sarcastic comment and made her cry.*

sar·dine | sär dēnʹ | —*noun, plural* **sardines** A small herring or similar small fish that is canned for use as food.

sash¹ | săsh | —*noun, plural* **sashes** A wide ribbon or piece of cloth that is worn around the waist or over the shoulder. A sash can be worn with a woman's dress and with certain military uniforms.

sash² | săsh | —*noun, plural* **sashes** A frame for the glass in a window or door.

Sas·katch·e·wan | săs kăchʹə wän′ | A province in western Canada. The capital of Saskatchewan is Regina.

sat | săt | The past tense and past participle of the verb **sit:** *We sat in the car. We had sat down in our seats when the movie started.*

Sa·tan | sātʹn | —*noun* The evil spirit; the devil.

sat·el·lite | sătʹl īt′ | —*noun, plural* **satellites** **1.** A heavenly body, such as a star or planet, that moves in an orbit or circle around another, larger heavenly body. The moon is a satellite of the earth, and the earth is a satellite of the sun. **2.** A man-made object that is shot into space by a rocket and then orbits the earth or another heavenly body. It can be used to send television and radio signals all around the world and to collect information about the weather and other scientific subjects.

sat·in | sătʹn | —*noun, plural* **satins** A smooth fabric that is shiny on one side. It is made of silk or other materials.

sat·is·fac·tion | sătʹĭs făkʹshən | —*noun* The condition of being

---

sash¹, sash²
Sash¹ comes from Arabic *shāsh,* meaning "muslin." **Sash²** comes from a French word meaning "frame."

sash¹
On a uniform

Saskatchewan
The name **Saskatchewan** comes from an Indian phrase that means "rapid current." The word was first used for the river that flows through this region.

ă	pat	ĕ	pet	î	fierce
ā	pay	ē	be	ŏ	pot
â	care	ĭ	pit	ō	go
ä	father	ī	pie	ô	paw, for
oi	oil	ŭ	cut	zh	vision
ŏŏ	book	û	fur	ə	ago, item,
ōō	boot	*th*	the		pencil, atom,
yōō	abuse	th	thin		circus
ou	out	hw	which	ər	butter

satisfied or fulfilled: *The whole team got satisfaction from winning the championship game.*

sat·is·fac·to·ry | săt′ĭs făk′tə rē | —*adjective* Good enough to satisfy or fill a need or requirement; adequate but not excellent: *Your test was satisfactory. This apple pie is satisfactory.*

sat·is·fy | săt′ĭs fī′ | —*verb* **satisfied, satisfying 1.** To give or get enough to fill the needs or desires of: *The hamburger satisfied my hunger.* **2.** To set free from doubt; answer or convince: *The firefighters were satisfied that the fire was out.*

sat·u·rate | săch′ə rāt′ | —*verb* **saturated, saturating** To soak or become soaked; fill completely: *Saturate the sponge.*

Sat·ur·day | săt′ər dē | or | săt′ər dā′ | —*noun, plural* **Saturdays** The seventh day of the week. It comes after Friday and before Sunday.

Sat·urn | săt′ərn | A planet of our solar system. It is the sixth in distance from the sun. Saturn is surrounded by rings.

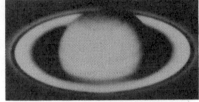

Saturn

sauce | sôs | —*noun, plural* **sauces** A soft or liquid dressing that is served with food to make it taste better.

sauc·er | sô′sər | —*noun, plural* **saucers** A small, shallow dish for holding a cup.

sau·sage | sô′sĭj | —*noun, plural* **sausages** Chopped pork or other meats that are mixed with spices and stuffed into a thin case that is shaped like a tube.

sav·age | săv′ĭj | —*adjective* **1.** Not tamed; wild: *a savage animal. The ice and freezing cold make the Arctic a savage area.* **2.** Cruel and fierce; ferocious; frightening: *the savage roar of a lion.*

save | sāv | —*verb* **saved, saving 1.** To rescue from harm or danger; make safe: *The cowboy saved the helpless woman from the cruel outlaws.* **2.** To keep or set aside money or something else for use in the future; store up: *My sister is saving for a new dress. I'm saving the old lawnmower in case the new one breaks.* **3.** To keep safe from harm, danger, or loss; protect: *save your reputation.* **4.** To keep from or avoid wasting or spending: *save time.*

sav·ing | sā′vĭng | —*noun* **1.** An amount saved: *If we take an airplane instead of driving the car, it'll be a saving of four hours. Nan bought the shoes at a saving of ten dollars.* **2. savings** An amount of money saved: *I keep my savings in the bank.*

saw[1] | sô | —*noun, plural* **saws** A tool or machine with a thin metal blade that has sharp teeth on one edge. It is used for cutting wood, metal, or other hard materials.
—*verb* **sawed, sawed** or **sawn, sawing** To cut or be cut with a saw: *saw off a tree branch. This wood saws easily.*

saw[1]

saw[2] | sô | The past tense of the verb **see:** *We saw George at the dance last night.*

sawn | sôn | A past participle of the verb **saw:** *Have you sawn the boards for the bench yet?*

sax·o·phone | săk′sə fōn′ | —*noun, plural* **saxophones** A musical wind instrument that has a sharply curved metal body, a reed fitted into the mouthpiece, and keys going up and down the body. It is played by blowing into the mouthpiece while pushing down on the different keys with the fingers.

say | sā | —*verb* **said, saying 1.** To speak out loud; talk: *She said no.* **2.** To put into or express in words: *He says he enjoyed the party. If there is something on your mind, say it.*

say·ing | sā′ĭng | —*noun, plural* **sayings** A short statement or proverb. It is usually well known and contains some wisdom.

saxophone

scaffold

scale³

scallop
A plate with scallops around the edge

ă	pat	ĕ	pet	î	fierce
ā	pay	ē	be	ŏ	pot
â	care	ĭ	pit	ō	go
ä	father	ī	pie	ô	paw, for
oi	oil	ŭ	cut	zh	vision
ŏŏ	book	û	fur	ə	ago, item,
ōō	boot	th	the		pencil, atom,
yōō	abuse	th	thin		circus
ou	out	hw	which	ər	butter

scab |skăb| —*noun, plural* **scabs** A crust that forms over a wound or sore to protect it while it heals.

scaf·fold |skăf′əld| or |skăf′ōld′| —*noun, plural* **scaffolds** A platform that is used to support people who are constructing or repairing a building.

scale¹ |skāl| —*noun, plural* **scales** 1. One of the small, thin parts that form the skin of fish and reptiles. 2. A dry, thin flake or crust of paint, rust, dandruff, or other material.
—*verb* **scaled, scaling** To remove the scales from: *I will scale the fish before I cook it.*

scale² |skāl| —*noun, plural* **scales** 1. A series of marks placed at equally spaced distances along a line. It is used on different measuring devices: *This ruler has two scales, inches on one side and centimeters on the other.* 2. The size of a model, drawing, or map compared with the actual size of what it represents: *This map of the United States is drawn to a scale in which every inch stands for fifty miles.* 3. A series of steps, degrees, or stages: *the scale of grades in a class. The wage scale for this job goes from two hundred dollars a week to three hundred dollars a week.* 4. The different or relative size or extent on which many things can be done: *Last week my parents threw a party on a large scale for fifty people, but next week they're having one on a smaller scale for only ten people.* 5. In music, a series of tones that go up or down in pitch. Most of them are made up of the eight notes in an octave.
—*verb* **scaled, scaling** 1. To climb up to the top of or climb over: *We scaled the mountain.* 2. To adjust or change by a certain amount: *The library announced that this year it would buy fewer new books than last year because it has to scale down its spending.*

scale³ |skāl| —*noun, plural* **scales** An instrument or machine for weighing. It works by measuring or balancing the weight of an object against the force of a spring.

scal·lop |skŏl′əp| or |skăl′əp| —*noun, plural* **scallops** 1. A sea animal with a soft body and a double shell that is shaped like a fan. The muscle of the scallop is used as food. 2. One of a series of curves that form a fancy border: *a collar with scallops.*

scalp |skălp| —*noun, plural* **scalps** The skin that covers the top of the head. It is usually covered with hair.

scal·y |skā′lē| —*adjective* **scalier, scaliest** Covered with scales: *A snake is a scaly reptile.*

scam·per |skăm′pər| —*verb* **scampered, scampering** To run quickly: *The dogs scampered around the yard.*

scan |skăn| —*verb* **scanned, scanning** To look at or examine something closely: *She scanned his face with worry.*

scan·dal |skăn′dl| —*noun, plural* **scandals** 1. A wrong or immoral action that shocks people and disgraces those persons who did it: *There was a scandal when it was discovered that the councilor was stealing town money.* 2. Gossip or talk that harms a person's reputation: *My father told us not to mention the scandal about the people who live next door.*

scant |skănt| —*adjective* **scanter, scantest** 1. Not enough in quantity or size: *scant food left for dinner.* 2. Just being short of; not quite: *We're a scant three miles from home.*

scar |skär| —*noun, plural* **scars** 1. A mark left on the skin after a cut or wound has healed: *George showed everyone the scar from his operation.* 2. Any mark like this: *There's a scar on the wall where I banged it with the chair.*

—*verb* **scarred, scarring** To mark with or form a scar: *He scarred the table with a rock.*

scarce |skârs| —*adjective* **scarcer, scarcest** Hard to get or find; not enough: *Food is scarce in some countries.*

scarce·ly |skârs'lē| —*adverb* **1.** Almost not at all; barely: *I could scarcely find my way in the fog.* **2.** Certainly not: *Alvin would scarcely do anything like that.*

scare |skâr| —*verb* **scared, scaring** **1.** To frighten or become frightened or afraid: *The dog scared my brother. She doesn't scare easily.* **2.** To frighten or drive away: *The raccoons were scared off by the barking dogs.*
—*noun, plural* **scares** **1.** A sudden feeling of fear: *Susan got a scare when all the lights in the house went out at once.* **2.** A condition of widespread fear or panic: *a bomb scare.*

scare·crow |skâr'krō'| —*noun, plural* **scarecrows** A figure of a person that is dressed in old clothes. It is set up in a field to scare crows and other birds away from crops.

scarf |skärf| —*noun, plural* **scarfs** or **scarves** A piece of cloth worn around the neck or head for warmth or decoration.

scar·let |skär'lĭt| —*noun, plural* **scarlets** A bright red color.
—*adjective* Bright red: *a scarlet shirt.*

scarves |skärvz| A plural of the noun **scarf.**

scar·y |skâr'ē| —*adjective* **scarier, scariest** Causing fear or alarm; frightening: *That was the scariest movie I ever saw. No it wasn't. I remember one that was scarier.*

scat·ter |skăt'ər| —*verb* **scattered, scattering** **1.** To separate and go or cause to separate and go in different directions: *At the bell, the class scattered into the hallways. The wind scattered the pile of leaves all over the yard.* **2.** To spread or throw about: *The child is always scattering his toys all over.*

scene |sēn| —*noun, plural* **scenes** **1.** A view of a place or area; sight: *The farm and pasture are a beautiful scene when you look at it from the top of the mountain.* **2.** The place where something happens: *the scene of the accident.* **3.** A part or section of an act in a play or of a movie: *Since we were late, we missed the first two scenes of the play.* **4.** A showing or display of strong feelings, such as a temper tantrum, in front of other people: *My sister made a scene in the restaurant because she couldn't have ice cream.*
♦ *These sound alike* **scene, seen.**

scen·er·y |sē'nə rē| —*noun, plural* **sceneries** **1.** The general appearance of a place; landscape: *Every autumn when the leaves change, we drive to the country to look at the scenery.* **2.** The painted structures or curtains on a stage during a play. The scenery is supposed to represent where the action is happening.

scent |sĕnt| —*noun, plural* **scents** **1.** A particular smell: *the scent of roses. Dogs recognize people by their scents.* **2.** The means or trail by which someone or something can be found: *The police were on the scent of the robbers.* **3.** The sense of smell: *Many different types of animals have a sharper scent than people do.*
♦ *These sound alike* **scent, cent, sent.**

scep·ter |sĕp'tər| —*noun, plural* **scepters** A rod or staff that is held by a queen or king. It is a symbol of authority.

sched·ule |skĕj'ōōl| or |skĕj'ōō əl| or |skĕj'əl| —*noun, plural* **schedules** **1.** A listing of events, things to do, or the times something should be finished by: *a television or movie schedule; a schedule of classes. The schedule for our trip says we'll spend three*

scarecrow

school¹, school²

A Greek word that meant "leisure, free time" and came to mean "leisure time devoted to learning, a scientific discussion, a lecture" and thus "a school" was the original source of **school¹**. **School¹** also appeared in Latin, from which it was borrowed into English. **School²** comes from an old Dutch word meaning "troop, group."

school¹

schooner

ă	pat	ĕ	pet	î	fierce
ā	pay	ē	be	ŏ	pot
â	care	ĭ	pit	ō	go
ä	father	ī	pie	ô	paw, for
oi	oil	ŭ	cut	zh	vision
ŏŏ	book	û	fur	ə	ago, item,
ōō	boot	*th*	the		pencil, atom,
yōō	abuse	th	thin		circus
ou	out	hw	which	ər	butter

days in New York. **2.** The times when airplanes, trains, or other types of transportation are supposed to arrive or depart: *According to the schedule the bus will be here at three o'clock.*
—*verb* **scheduled, scheduling** To put in or plan a schedule: *I'm scheduling a doctor's appointment on Monday.*

scheme |skēm| —*noun, plural* **schemes 1.** A plan for doing something: *My uncle says his new business scheme will make him rich. The robbers had a scheme to steal the famous painting from the museum.* **2.** An orderly arrangement or combination: *Do you like the new color scheme in the living room?*
—*verb* **schemed, scheming** To plan or plot: *We were scheming a way to go to the park without being seen by my little brother.*

schol·ar |skŏl'ər| —*noun, plural* **scholars 1.** A person who has a great deal of knowledge: *He is a literature scholar.* **2.** A pupil or student.

schol·ar·ship |skŏl'ər shĭp'| —*noun, plural* **scholarships 1.** Money given to students so that they can continue their education. Scholarships are usually given out on the basis of personal achievement or need. **2.** Knowledge or learning in a particular field: *his scholarship in American history.*

school¹ |skōol| —*noun, plural* **schools 1.** A place for teaching and learning. **2.** A division or department for teaching or studying a particular field within a college or university: *a law school; a medical school.* **3.** The process of being educated at a school; attendance at a school: *She finds school harder this year.*
—*verb* **schooled, schooling** To teach or train: *He's been schooled in diving from a high platform.*

school² |skōol| —*noun, plural* **schools** A large group of fish or other water animals swimming together: *a school of whales.*

schoo·ner |skōo'nər| —*noun, plural* **schooners** A ship with two or more masts and sails that are set across the length of the ship.

schwa |shwä| or |shvä| —*noun, plural* **schwas** A symbol (ə) used in English for certain vowel sounds that are spoken in syllables with no stress. For example, the sounds of *a* in *alone* and *e* in *linen* are represented by a schwa.

sci·ence |sī'əns| —*noun, plural* **sciences 1.** Knowledge about nature and the universe. Science seeks explanations of how animals and things live and work. This knowledge comes through experiments and from careful observation of the world. **2.** Any particular branch or area of knowledge in which observation, experiments, and study are used. Biology, chemistry, physics, economics, and agriculture are all sciences.

sci·en·tif·ic |sī'ən tĭf'ĭk| —*adjective* **1.** Having to do with or used in science: *scientific books; scientific equipment.* **2.** Having or using the facts, laws, or methods of science: *a scientific experiment; a scientific theory.*

sci·en·tist |sī'ən tĭst| —*noun, plural* **scientists** Someone who has a great knowledge of a particular branch of science.

scis·sors |sĭz'ərz| —*plural noun* A cutting tool that has two sharp blades, each with a ring-shaped handle for a finger. The blades are fastened in the middle by a pivot so that they cut when they close against each other.

scold |skōld| —*verb* **scolded, scolding 1.** To find fault with: *She scolded me for leaving the refrigerator open.* **2.** To yell at or speak angrily to: *He's always scolding his younger brother.*

scoop |skōop| —*noun, plural* **scoops 1.** A small tool that is shaped like a shovel and has a short handle. It is used to take up such things as sugar and flour. **2.** A small tool with a round bowl and a thick handle. It is used to take up or give out such things as ice cream. **3. a.** A scoop with something in it: *Give everyone a scoop of mashed potatoes.* **b.** The amount that a scoop holds: *I ate three scoops of ice cream.* **4.** The large bucket of a steam shovel. It is used for removing dirt, refuse, and other materials. —*verb* **scooped, scooping 1.** To lift up or out with a scoop or as if with a scoop: *She scooped a teaspoon of sugar for her cereal.* **2.** To hollow out by digging: *scoop out a hole.*

scoop

scope |skōp| —*noun, plural* **scopes** The range of a person's ideas, actions, understanding, or ability: *You can enlarge the scope of your knowledge by reading.*

scorch |skôrch| —*verb* **scorched, scorching 1.** To burn on the surface: *Tony scorched the table with his cigar. The cookies scorched and didn't taste good.* **2.** To wither or dry up because of heat: *The sun scorched the grass.* —*noun, plural* **scorches** A slight burn: *There's a scorch on your shirt because you left the iron on it when you answered the phone.*

score |skôr| or |skōr| —*noun, plural* **scores 1.** A record of the points made in a game, contest, or test: *We lost the baseball game by a score of three to one. She got a score of ninety on the science test.* **2.** A set or group of something that has twenty items: *a score of people.* **3.** The written or printed form of music. It contains all the parts for instruments and voices. **4.** A wrong that a person must revenge: *I'll settle the score with him.* —*verb* **scored, scoring 1.** To make points in a game, contest, or test: *I scored the winning points.* **2.** To keep a record of the points made: *The teacher scored the test. The umpire is scoring the game.*

score
A sign showing the score at a game

scorn |skôrn| —*verb* **scorned, scorning** To treat someone or something as worthless or bad; look down on: *Most people scorn liars and cowards.* —*noun* A feeling that someone or something is worthless, bad, or inferior: *He only has scorn for lazy people.*

scor·pi·on |skôr′ pē ən| —*noun, plural* **scorpions** An animal related to the spiders. A scorpion has a narrow body and a long tail with a stinger that carries poison.

Scot·land |skŏt′lənd| A part of the island of Great Britain north of England.

Scot·tish |skŏt′ĭsh| —*noun* **1. the Scottish** (Used with a plural verb.) The people of Scotland. **2.** The dialect of English spoken in Scotland. —*adjective* Of Scotland, its people, or their language.

scorpion

scout |skout| —*noun, plural* **scouts 1.** Someone who is sent out from a group to gather and bring back information: *The scout reported to the general that the road was clear and safe.* **2. Scout** A member of the Boy Scouts or Girl Scouts. —*verb* **scouted, scouting** To look at and observe carefully in order to gather and bring back information: *We scouted the hills to see if there were bears there.*

scout·mas·ter |skout′măs′tər| or |skout′mä′stər| —*noun, plural* **scoutmasters** An adult who leads a troop of Boy Scouts.

scowl |skoul| —*verb* **scowled, scowling** To look angry or disapproving by tightening the eyebrows and forehead; frown: *My mother scowled at us for making noise.*

—*noun, plural* **scowls** An angry frown.

scram·ble |skrăm′bəl| —*verb* **scrambled, scrambling** **1.** To move quickly, especially by climbing or crawling: *She scrambled over the wall.* **2.** To struggle or compete with others for something: *The dogs scrambled after the bone.* **3.** To mix together in a confused way: *She scrambled the letters of the word.* **4.** To cook eggs by mixing the yolks and the whites together and frying the mixture.
—*noun, plural* **scrambles** **1.** A difficult climb or hike: *It was a scramble to reach the top of the mountain.* **2.** A struggle or competition for something: *There was a scramble for the football.*

scrap |skrăp| —*noun, plural* **scraps** **1.** A tiny piece; a little bit: *She wrote my address on a scrap of paper.* **2.** **scraps** Leftover bits of food: *We fed the scraps to the cats.* **3.** Material that is left over or thrown out, especially metal that can be used for something else: *Tom sold his old car for scrap.*
—*verb* **scrapped, scrapping** To throw out as useless: *We had to scrap our plan to go to the movies.*

scrape |skrāp| —*verb* **scraped, scraping** **1.** To rub a surface with something in order to clean, smooth, or shape it: *He scraped the carrot with a knife.* **2.** To remove material from a surface by rubbing: *Will you scrape the ice off the car window?* **3.** To hurt or scratch the skin or other surface by rubbing against something rough or sharp: *He tripped and scraped his knee. She scraped the side of the car on the garage.* **4.** To make a harsh, grating sound by rubbing something on a surface: *She scraped the chalk on the blackboard.*
—*noun, plural* **scrapes** **1.** An injury, mark, or scratch made by scraping: *How did you get that scrape on your chin?* **2.** A harsh grating sound: *We heard the scrape of the shovel on the sidewalk.* **3.** A difficult situation or a fight: *Dick got in a scrape when he broke the teacher's ruler.*

scratch |skrăch| —*verb* **scratched, scratching** **1.** To make a thin, shallow cut or mark on a surface with something sharp: *She scratched the table with her knife.* **2.** To rub or scrape to stop itching: *He scratched his back with a stick. Stop scratching the mosquito bite.* **3.** To dig, scrape, or hurt someone or something with fingernails, claws, or anything sharp: *The cat scratched me.* **4.** To make a harsh sound by rubbing something on a surface: *The dog scratched at the door.* **5.** To write, draw, or mark with something pointed: *She scratched her name on the rock.* **6.** To strike out by drawing a line through: *Scratch out the words on your list.*
—*noun, plural* **scratches** **1.** A thin, shallow cut or mark made by scratching: *She put a scratch on the new car.* **2.** A harsh, scraping sound: *Did you hear a scratch at the window?*
Idiom **from scratch** From the beginning or from nothing: *The teacher told me to do my book report over from scratch.*

scream |skrēm| —*verb* **screamed, screaming** To make a loud, sharp, piercing cry or sound. People scream when they are in pain and when they are frightened, excited, or happy: *He screamed for help when the lion ran at him.*
—*noun, plural* **screams** A loud, piercing cry or sound: *There were happy screams when the roller coaster started down.*

screech |skrēch| —*verb* **screeched, screeching** To make a shrill, harsh cry or sound: *She screeched for help from the burning house.*

ă	pat	ĕ	pet	î	fierce
ā	pay	ē	be	ŏ	pot
â	care	ĭ	pit	ō	go
ä	father	ī	pie	ô	paw, for
oi	oil	ŭ	cut	zh	vision
ōo	book	û	fur	ə	ago, item,
ōo	boot	th	the		pencil, atom,
yōo	abuse	th	thin		circus
ou	out	hw	which	ər	butter

He slammed on the brakes and the car screeched to a stop.
—*noun, plural* **screeches** A shrill, harsh cry or sound: *I was awakened by the screech of sea gulls.*

screen |skrēn| —*noun, plural* **screens** **1.** A frame covered with wire mesh. It is used in windows and doors to keep out insects. **2.** A covered, movable frame that is used to separate, hide, or protect: *Dad divided the basement with a screen to make a workshop.* **3.** Anything that separates or hides like a screen: *The soldiers ran up the hill behind a smoke screen.* **4.** A large, flat, white surface on which slides or movies are shown.
—*verb* **screened, screening** **1.** To hide or protect: *Two large trees screened the house. She screened her eyes from the sun with her hand.* **2.** To separate with a screen: *He screened off half the room.*

screw |skrōō| —*noun, plural* **screws** A kind of nail having one long ridge winding around its length. It has a slot in the head so that it can be turned by a screwdriver. It is used to fasten things.
—*verb* **screwed, screwing** **1.** To fasten, attach, or tighten with a screw or screws: *He screwed the hooks on the wall.* **2.** To attach by twisting into place: *Would you screw a new bulb in the lamp?*

screw·driv·er |skrōō'drī'vər| —*noun, plural* **screwdrivers** A tool used to turn screws.

scrib·ble |skrĭb'əl| —*verb* **scribbled, scribbling** To write or draw carelessly or quickly: *I scribbled my name on the test.*
—*noun, plural* **scribbles** Writing or drawing that is done carelessly or quickly: *I can't read her scribbles.*

scribe |skrīb| —*noun, plural* **scribes** A person who copied books, letters, and other kinds of written material before printing was invented.

script |skrĭpt| —*noun, plural* **scripts** **1.** Letters or symbols written by hand; handwriting. **2.** A kind of print that looks like handwriting. **3.** The written text of a play, movie, or television or radio show; manuscript. It contains the lines and speeches of all the actors and actresses.

scroll |skrōl| —*noun, plural* **scrolls** **1.** A roll of paper, parchment, or other material that has writing on it. Each end of it is rolled around a rod or cylinder. **2.** A design that looks like a scroll or spiral curve.

scrub |skrŭb| —*verb* **scrubbed, scrubbing** To clean by rubbing hard: *Scrub your face and hands.*
—*noun, plural* **scrubs** The act of scrubbing: *He gave the pots and pans a good scrub.*

scuff |skŭf| —*verb* **scuffed, scuffing** **1.** To scrape or drag the feet in walking: *Arthur scuffed along the sidewalk.* **2.** To scrape or scratch the surface of: *Joey scuffed up his new shoes.*

scuf·fle |skŭf'əl| —*verb* **scuffled, scuffling** To fight or struggle in a confused way: *The police scuffled with the thieves.*
—*noun, plural* **scuffles** A confused fight or struggle: *The children had a scuffle in the yard.*

sculp·tor |skŭlp'tər| —*noun, plural* **sculptors** A person who carves, molds, or makes sculptures.

sculp·ture |skŭlp'chər| —*noun, plural* **sculptures** **1.** The art of making or modeling figures, such as a statue. It is done by shaping clay, carving or chiseling blocks of wood or stone, or casting or pouring liquid metal into a mold. **2.** A piece of art made this way: *a famous sculpture of Abraham Lincoln.*

scur·ry |skûr'ē| —*verb* **scurried, scurrying** To run or move

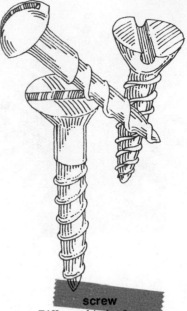

screw
Different kinds of screws

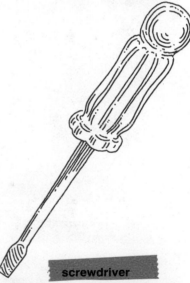

screwdriver

scroll
An ancient scroll

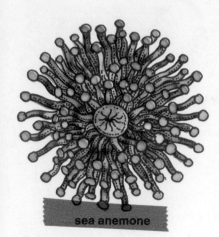

sea anemone

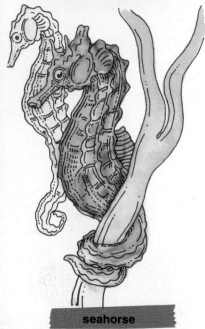

seahorse

---

seal¹, seal²

Seal¹ comes from a word used long ago by French-speaking people. That word came in turn from a Latin word that meant "sign" or "little mark." **Seal²** comes from an old English word that had the same meaning.

ă	pat	ĕ	pet	î	fierce
ā	pay	ē	be	ŏ	pot
â	care	ĭ	pit	ō	go
ä	father	ī	pie	ô	paw, for

oi	oil	ŭ	cut	zh	vision
ŏŏ	book	û	fur	ə	ago, item,
ōō	boot	th	the		pencil, atom,
yōō	abuse	th	thin		circus
ou	out	hw	which	ər	butter

---

about quickly: *Scurry down to the store and buy some milk.*

scur·vy | skûr′vē | —*noun* A disease that is caused by lack of vitamin C in the diet. People with scurvy have bleeding gums, feel weak, and get spots on the skin. Scurvy can be easily prevented by eating fruits with vitamin C or by taking vitamin pills.

scythe | sīth | —*noun, plural* **scythes** A tool with a long, curved blade attached to a long, bent handle. It is used for mowing and reaping.

sea | sē | —*noun, plural* **seas** **1.** The large body of salt water that covers about three fourths of the earth's surface; ocean. **2. a.** A large area of an ocean that has land on some of its sides, such as the Mediterranean Sea. **b.** A very large lake having either salt or fresh water. **3.** Often **seas** The movement of the ocean's waters, especially its current or the swell of waves: *a high sea; churning seas.* **4.** A very large number or amount of something: *I looked at the crowd and saw a sea of faces.*
♦ *These sound alike* **sea, see.**

sea a·nem·o·ne | ə nĕm′ə nē | A sea animal with a flexible body shaped like a tube. The sea anemone can fasten its body to a surface. All around its mouth are tentacles that look like petals.

sea·board | sē′bôrd′ | or | sē′bōrd′ | —*noun* Land near the sea: *the Pacific Ocean seaboard.*

sea·food | sē′fōōd′ | —*noun* Any fish or shellfish eaten as food.

sea gull A gull, especially one that lives along the seaboard.

sea·horse or **sea horse** | sē′hôrs′ | —*noun, plural* **seahorses** A small ocean fish with a head that looks like the head of a horse. The body of a seahorse is covered with bony plates. Its tail can be curled around objects to support itself.

seal¹ | sēl | —*noun, plural* **seals** **1.** A design that is stamped or imprinted on wax or other soft material. It is used as an official mark of identification or ownership: *The President signed the treaty and put the seal of the United States on the bottom.* **2.** An instrument or device used to stamp or imprint such a design. **3.** A small piece of wax, metal, or paper that has such a design stamped on it. **4.** Something that fastens firmly or closes completely: *Don't break the seal on the jar of preserves.* **5.** A small paper sticker or stamp used to close or decorate an envelope: *I put Christmas seals on all the gifts I give to my family.*
—*verb* **sealed, sealing** **1.** To put a seal on: *The agreement was signed and sealed by Mexico, Canada, and the United States.* **2.** To close tightly; fasten: *She sealed the envelope. We sealed the hole in the wall with plaster. He sealed his lips.* **3.** To decide or settle; make a sign that something has been agreed or decided: *The two men sealed the sale by shaking hands.*

seal² | sēl | —*noun, plural* **seals** or **seal** **1.** A sea mammal whose body is streamlined and covered with thick fur. Seals have flippers that can be used as paddles. **2.** The fur of a seal.

sea lion Any of several kinds of seal that are found in the Pacific Ocean. The sea lion has a sleek body and brownish hair.

seam | sēm | —*noun, plural* **seams** **1.** A line formed by sewing together two pieces of leather, cloth, or other soft material at their edges: *The seam on my shirt sleeve is splitting.* **2.** Any line across a surface, such as a crack or wrinkle: *The frozen pond had many seams in the ice.*
—*verb* **seamed, seaming** To join together with a seam: *Mary*

Louise has seamed up the blouse and the skirt into a dress.
♦ *These sound alike* **seam, seem.**

sea·man | sē′mən | —*noun, plural* **seamen** **1.** A sailor. **2.** A sailor of the lowest rank in the navy.

seam·stress | sĕm′strĭs | —*noun, plural* **seamstresses** A woman whose job is sewing.

sea·port | sē′pôrt′ | or | sē′pōrt′ | —*noun, plural* **seaports** **1.** A harbor or port that is used by large ships. **2.** A city or town having a harbor or port.

search | sûrch | —*verb* **searched, searching** To look for carefully; try to find something; seek out: *The firefighters searched for people trapped in the burning building. I've searched everywhere.*
—*noun, plural* **searches** The act of searching or seeking; examination: *The search took three days.*

search·light | sûrch′līt′ | —*noun, plural* **searchlights** **1.** A powerful light that throws a bright beam: *The police used searchlights to look in the forest for the lost campers.* **2.** The beam thrown by such a light: *The searchlight lit up the runway.*

sea·shell or **sea shell** | sē′shĕl′ | —*noun, plural* **seashells** The hard shell of a snail, clam, oyster, or other sea animal.

sea·shore | sē′shôr′ | or | sē′shōr′ | —*noun, plural* **seashores** The land at the edge of or near the ocean; beach.

sea·sick | sē′sĭk′ | —*adjective* Feeling dizzy and sick in the stomach because of the side-to-side motion of a ship or boat.

sea·son | sē′zən | —*noun, plural* **seasons** **1.** One of the four parts of the year; spring, summer, autumn, or winter. **2.** A part of the year when a certain event or activity happens: *the football season; the rainy season.*
—*verb* **seasoned, seasoning** To give food extra flavor by adding seasonings: *I seasoned the stew with salt, pepper, and garlic.*

sea·son·ing | sē′zə nĭng | —*noun, plural* **seasonings** Anything that is added to food to bring out its flavor or to give it extra flavor. Herbs and spices are seasonings.

seat | sēt | —*noun, plural* **seats** **1.** Something to sit on, such as a chair, sofa, or bench. **2.** A place in which someone may sit: *She gave up her seat on the bus to an old man.* **3.** The part of a chair, bench, or other object on which one sits: *I spilled milk on my seat.* **4.** That part of the body on which one sits or the clothes covering it: *He slipped and fell on the seat of his pants.* **5.** A capital or center of something: *A college is a seat of learning. Washington, D.C., is the seat of the federal government.* **6.** Membership in an organization: *She's running for a seat on the School Committee.*
—*verb* **seated, seating** **1.** To place in or on a seat: *Father seated everyone at the table.* **2.** To have seats for: *The ball park seats fifty thousand people.*

seat belt A belt or strap made to hold a person safely in the seat of an automobile or airplane in case of a bump, jolt, or accident.

sea·weed | sē′wēd | —*noun, plural* **seaweeds** Any of the many plants that live in the ocean. Kelp and other large algae are kinds of seaweed.

sec·ond¹ | sĕk′ənd | —*noun, plural* **seconds** One of the sixty parts of a minute; a unit of time equal to ¹⁄₆₀ of a minute: *You have ten seconds to answer each question.*

sec·ond² | sĕk′ənd | —*adjective* **1.** The next after the first in place or time: *His office is on the second floor.* **2.** Another or other: *I failed the test but the teacher is giving me a second chance.*

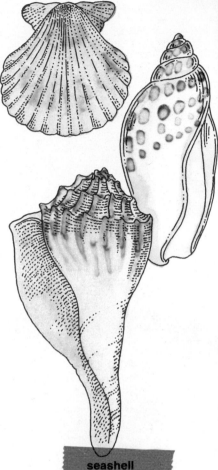

seashell
Different kinds of seashells

seat belt

second¹, second²
When the hour was first divided into sixty parts, the first units were called "small parts," or **minutes.** The smaller subdivisions of minutes were called "second parts" in Latin as it was spoken in the Middle Ages; this was borrowed into English as **second¹. Second²** came from a related Latin word meaning "following, coming next, coming immediately after."

—*adverb* Right after the first and before the third: *He won the race and I came in second.*

—*noun, plural* **seconds** 1. In a group of people or things that are in numbered order, the one that matches the number two. 2. **seconds** More or extra: *If there's any cake left, I'll have seconds.*

sec·on·dar·y |sĕk′ ən dĕr′ē| —*adjective* After the first or most important thing; less important: *I hope you make the team, but that's secondary to doing well in school.*

secondary accent 1. In a word having more than one accented syllable, the accent or stress that is weaker than the primary one. 2. The mark (′) used to indicate this accent. In this sense, also called *secondary stress.*

secondary school A school that is attended after elementary school.

sec·ond·hand |sĕk′ ənd **hănd**′| —*adjective* 1. Having had a former owner; not new: *a secondhand car; secondhand books.* 2. Not learned or told in person: *a secondhand piece of news.*

se·cre·cy |sē′krĭ sē| —*noun, plural* **secrecies** 1. The condition of being secret or being kept secret: *We planned the party in secrecy.* 2. The ability to keep secrets: *Everyone who joins our club is sworn to secrecy.*

se·cret |sē′krĭt| —*adjective* 1. Known only to one person or a small group; kept hidden: *The secret plans were kept in a safe.* 2. Working in a hidden or private way: *a secret agent.*

—*noun, plural* **secrets** 1. Something kept hidden or private: *She told me a big secret.* 2. A special method or way of doing something: *I wish I knew the secret of making friends.*

sec·re·tar·y |sĕk′rĭ tĕr′ē| —*noun, plural* **secretaries** 1. A person whose job is to write letters and keep records for a person, company, or organization: *I ran for secretary of the Girls' Club. The secretary said the doctor would see me in a minute.* 2. The head of a department in the government: *the Secretary of Defense.* 3. A writing desk. It has drawers and often also has shelves for books.

sec·tion |sĕk′shən| —*noun, plural* **sections** 1. A part that is taken from a whole; a portion or share: *She cut the pineapple into five sections.* 2. One of several different parts that make up something; a division: *I always read the sports section of the newspaper first. This chapter is in three sections.*

—*verb* **sectioned, sectioning** To cut or separate into parts: *She sectioned the orange into four parts.*

se·cure |sĭ **kyŏŏr**′| —*adjective* **securer, securest** 1. Free from danger or the chance of loss; safe: *The bank is a secure place to keep money. The soldiers built the fort in the securest place they could find.* 2. Strongly fastened; not likely to fall or break: *Make sure that the ropes holding up the tent are secure.* 3. Free from fear or worry: *I always feel safe and secure at home.*

—*verb* **secured, securing** 1. To guard from danger or the chance of loss; make safe: *We secured the glasses against breaking by wrapping them in paper.* 2. To fasten tightly: *We secured all the doors and windows before the hurricane started.* 3. To get or acquire: *The workers went on strike to secure higher wages.*

se·cu·ri·ty |sĭ kyŏŏr′ĭ tē| —*noun, plural* **securities** 1. Freedom from risk or danger; safety: *There were extra police at the airport for the security of the President. Having a good job gives a person a feeling of security.* 2. Anything that protects: *Locks on doors and windows are security against robbers.*

secretary
An antique secretary

ă	pat	ĕ	pet	î	fierce
ā	pay	ē	be	ŏ	pot
â	care	ĭ	pit	ō	go
ä	father	ī	pie	ô	paw, for

oi	oil	ŭ	cut	zh	vision
ŏŏ	book	û	fur	ə	ago, item,
ōō	boot	*th*	the		pencil, atom,
yōō	abuse	th	thin		circus
ou	out	hw	which	ər	butter

se·dan |sĭ dăn′ | —*noun, plural* **sedans** An automobile with a hard top, four doors, and a front and back seat.

sed·a·tive |sĕd′ə tĭv | —*adjective* Having a soothing or calming effect: *We took a sedative walk around the lake.*
—*noun, plural* **sedatives** A medicine or drug that relaxes or causes one to sleep.

sed·i·ment |sĕd′ə mənt | —*noun, plural* **sediments** **1.** Small pieces of matter that settle at or sink to the bottom of a liquid. The sediment in a lake or river is made up of such things as stones, earth, and twigs. **2.** Very tiny pieces of matter that are suspended or float in a liquid: *sediment in a glass of water.*

see |sē | —*verb* **saw, seen, seeing** **1.** To look at with the eyes: *I could see the whole city from the top of the building.* **2.** To have the power or ability to look at things with the eyes: *Blind people cannot see.* **3.** To understand: *I don't see why I'm the only one who has to go to sleep early.* **4.** To find out: *I'm busy; would you see what your father wants?* **5.** To visit or receive a visitor: *We saw my grandparents yesterday. The doctor wouldn't see her because she didn't have an appointment.* **6.** To go with: *I'll see you to the corner where you can get the bus.* **7.** To make sure; take care: *See that you don't spill paint on the rug.*
♦ *These sound alike* **see, sea.**

seed |sēd | —*noun, plural* **seeds** or **seed** The part of a flowering plant that can grow into a new plant. A seed contains food to get the new plant started and information so that the seed can grow into just one particular kind of plant.
—*verb* **seeded, seeding** **1.** To plant seeds in; sow: *They seeded four acres of land before the end of the day.* **2.** To remove the seeds from fruit: *Dad seeded my grapefruit for me.*

seed·ling |sēd′lĭng | —*noun, plural* **seedlings** A young plant that has grown from a seed.

seek |sēk | —*verb* **sought, seeking** **1.** To try to find; search for; hunt: *We're seeking homes for the kittens.* **2.** To make an attempt; try: *The President is seeking a way to end the war.* **3.** To ask for; request: *We sought help when our car broke down.*

seem |sēm | —*verb* **seemed, seeming** **1.** To appear to be; look like: *She seems worried about something. He seems to like his new bicycle.* **2.** To appear to be true, real, or obvious: *If she's not here yet, then it seems she isn't coming.*
♦ *These sound alike* **seem, seam.**

seen |sēn | The past participle of the verb **see**: *I haven't seen him since last week.*
♦ *These sound alike* **seen, scene.**

seep |sēp | —*verb* **seeped, seeping** To spread or pass through slowly; ooze: *The cold air seeped in through the crack in the window.*

see·saw |sē′sô′ | —*noun, plural* **seesaws** An outdoor device or piece of equipment used by children for play. It is made of a long plank with a support in the middle. With a person sitting on each end, one end goes up in the air as the other goes down.
—*verb* **seesawed, seesawing** To ride on a seesaw.

seg·ment |sĕg′mənt | —*noun, plural* **segments** A part into which a whole is or can be divided; a section or division: *Oranges and grapefruit can be separated into segments.*

seg·re·gate |sĕg′rĭ gāt′ | —*verb* **segregated, segregating** **1.** To separate or keep apart from others or from the main part of a group: *All the students who are sick with the flu will be segregated*

seesaw

from the rest of the class. **2.** To separate or keep apart one racial group from a larger group or from the rest of the society.

seg·re·ga·tion |sĕg'rĭ gā'shən| —*noun* **1.** The act of segregating or the condition of being segregated. **2.** The separation of one racial group from a larger group or from the rest of society. It is done by not allowing a racial group to go to the same schools, restaurants, theaters, and other public places as the rest of the people. Segregation is against the law.

seine |sān| —*noun, plural* **seines** A large fishing net. It has floats attached to the top edge and weights at the bottom to pull it straight down.

♦ *These sound alike* **seine, sane.**

seis·mo·graph |sīz'mə grăf'| *or* |sīz'mə gräf'| —*noun, plural* **seismographs** An instrument that shows or records when and where an earthquake happens and how strong it is.

seize |sēz| —*verb* **seized, seizing** **1.** To take hold of suddenly and quickly; grab: *She seized my arm as she slipped.* **2.** To take possession of by force; capture: *The navy seized the enemy ship.*

sel·dom |sĕl'dəm| —*adverb* Not often; rarely: *He seldom goes to sleep before nine o'clock.*

se·lect |sĭ lĕkt'| —*verb* **selected, selecting** To choose; pick out: *I selected the movie I wanted to see.*

se·lec·tion |sĭ lĕk'shən| —*noun, plural* **selections** **1.** The act of selecting or choosing: *The coach will announce his selection of a quarterback tomorrow.* **2.** Someone or something chosen; a choice: *That color paint is a good selection for your bedroom.*

self |sĕlf| —*noun, plural* **selves** **1.** One's own person apart or thought of as different from all other persons: *I know my own self better than you know me.* **2.** The character of a person; personality: *Ed is being his old nasty self again.*

self- A prefix that forms another word and means: **1.** Oneself or itself: *self-evident.* **2.** Of, to, or by itself or oneself: *self-conscious.* **3.** In an automatic way: *self-winding.*

self-con·scious |sĕlf'kŏn'shəs| —*adjective* Shy and embarrassed around other people: *Betsy was so self-conscious when she got her long hair cut short that she wouldn't go to the party.*

self-de·fense |sĕlf'dĭ fĕns'| —*noun* The protection of one's body, property, or reputation against attack: *He didn't start the fight but hit back in self-defense.*

self·ish |sĕl'fĭsh| —*adjective* Thinking or caring only about oneself; not thinking of others: *The selfish child ate all the cookies.*

self-re·spect |sĕlf'rĭ spĕkt'| —*noun* Regard for oneself, one's character, and one's behavior; pride: *She had too much self-respect to join in their foolish pranks.*

self-ser·vice |sĕlf'sûr'vĭs| —*adjective* Of a store or business in which the customers help themselves: *a self-service restaurant.*

sell |sĕl| —*verb* **sold, selling** **1.** To provide or give goods, property, or services in exchange for money: *He sold his watch for $50.* **2.** To deal in: *The store sells used books and magazines.* **3.** To be available for sale; be sold: *That blouse sells for ten dollars.*

♦ *These sound alike* **sell, cell.**

sell·er |sĕl'ər| —*noun, plural* **sellers** **1.** A person who sells goods or services: *a seller of magazines.* **2.** An item that is sold in a particular manner: *That dress has been a very good seller.*

♦ *These sound alike* **seller, cellar.**

selves |sĕlvz| The plural of the noun **self.**

seismograph

ă	pat	ĕ	pet	î	fierce
ā	pay	ē	be	ŏ	pot
â	care	ĭ	pit	ō	go
ä	father	ī	pie	ô	paw, for
oi	oil	ŭ	cut	zh	vision
ōō	book	û	fur	ə	ago, item,
ōō	boot	*th*	the		pencil, atom,
yōō	abuse	th	thin		circus
ou	out	hw	which	ər	butter

sem·a·phore | sĕm′ə fôr′ | or | sĕm′ə fōr′ | —*noun, plural*
semaphores A device for signaling. A railroad semaphore is a post
with arms that have flashing lights. Another kind of semaphore
uses flags with different patterns that are held and moved by
hand.

semi- A prefix that means: **1.** Half of: *semicircle.* **2.** Happening
twice within a period of time: *semimonthly.*

sem·i·cir·cle | sĕm′ĭ sûr′kəl | —*noun, plural* **semicircles** Half a
circle: *The children sat in a semicircle on the floor around the
teacher.*

sem·i·co·lon | sĕm′ĭ kō′lən | —*noun, plural* **semicolons** A
punctuation mark (;). A semicolon shows a greater separation of
the parts of a sentence than that shown by a comma.

sem·i·nar·y | sĕm′ə nĕr′ē | —*noun, plural* **seminaries** A school
that trains people to become priests, ministers, or rabbis.

sen·ate | sĕn′ĭt | —*noun, plural* **senates** Often **Senate** The
upper and smaller house of a law-making assembly. The Congress
of the United States is made up of the Senate and the House of
Representatives. Many legislatures in states of the United States
also have senates.

sen·a·tor | sĕn′ə tər | —*noun, plural* **senators** A member of a
senate.

send | sĕnd | —*verb* **sent, sending** **1.** To cause to go from one
place to another: *She sent him to the store. The army is sending
supplies to the soldiers by helicopter.* **2.** To cause something to go
by mail, telegraph, radio, or other means; transmit: *We sent the
package air mail. The operator sent the message. I'll send him the
information by telegram.* **3.** To have someone carry a message to
someone else: *He sends you his love.* **4.** To drive or throw; give
off: *The batter sent the ball over the fence. The fire sent smoke into
the sky.* **5.** To cause or force into a certain condition or kind of
behavior: *Don't let his insults send you into a rage.*

sen·ior | sēn′yər | —*adjective* **1.** Older or oldest: *The senior
brother is president of the family business, and the younger brothers
are vice presidents.* **2.** Of or for older persons: *a senior scout troop;
a senior tennis championship.* **3.** A term used with the
name of a father who has a son with the same name: *James
senior is the father of James junior.* **4.** Of higher rank or longer
length of service: *a senior partner; the senior member of his state's
congressmen.* **5.** Of the fourth and last year of high school or
college: *the senior prom.* **6.** Elderly or old: *a senior citizen.*
—*noun, plural* **seniors** **1.** A person who is older or has a higher
rank than another: *My brother is my senior by four years. I'm going
to ask my seniors at work for a raise.* **2.** A student in the fourth
and last year of high school or college.

se·ñor | sān yôr′ | —*noun, plural* **señores** | sān yôr′ās | **1.** The
Spanish word for "sir" or "mister." **2.** The Spanish word for
gentleman.

se·ño·ra | sān yôr′ä | —*noun, plural* **señoras** | sān yôr′äs |
1. The Spanish word for "Mrs." or "Madam." **2.** The Spanish
word for a married lady.

se·ño·ri·ta | sān′yō rē′tä | —*noun, plural* **señoritas**
| sān′yō rē′täs | **1.** The Spanish word for "Miss." **2.** The
Spanish word for a young lady or a girl not yet married.

sen·sa·tion | sĕn sā′shən | —*noun, plural* **sensations** **1.** The
ability to feel through one or more of the five senses; the power

semaphore
Above: An electric semaphore
Below: A flag semaphore

senate
The U.S. Senate

to see, hear, smell, taste, or touch: *The cold made him lose all sensation in his fingers.* **2.** Something felt through a sense or senses; feeling: *The sun gave me a sensation of heat. I felt a dizzy sensation riding in the elevator.* **3.** Great feeling or excitement: *Landing a spaceship on the moon caused a sensation.*

sen·sa·tion·al |sĕn sā′shə nəl| —*adjective* **1.** Attracting great interest, excitement, or admiration: *She gives a sensational performance in the new play.* **2.** Designed to shock or thrill people: *That newspaper carries more sensational stories than serious news.*

sense |sĕns| —*noun, plural* **senses** **1.** Any of the powers through which a living thing can be or become aware of what is around. People have the five senses of sight, hearing, smell, touch, and taste. **2.** A quality of being aware; an ability to notice: *a sense of danger. I have no sense of how cold it is.* **3.** Appreciation; understanding: *She has a good sense of humor.* **4.** Good, sound judgment; practical intelligence: *There is no sense in wearing a heavy coat on a warm day.* **5.** A healthy condition of the mind: *Have you lost all sense, running around in the freezing rain?* **6.** A meaning: *Can you use the word "go" in three different senses?* —*verb* **sensed, sensing** To become aware of without knowing just why: *She sensed that there was something wrong in the room.*

sense·less |sĕns′lĭs| —*adjective* **1.** Without feeling or the power to feel: *He lay senseless after the blow on the head.* **2.** Without meaning or good judgment; foolish: *He muttered a senseless story in his sleep.*

sen·si·ble |sĕn′sə bəl| —*adjective* In agreement with sound judgment and good sense; practical; reasonable: *They wore sensible shoes for the hike.*

sen·si·tive |sĕn′sĭ tĭv| —*adjective* **1.** Able to respond to light, sound, smell, touch, or taste: *Bats are sensitive to sounds that humans cannot hear. Photographic film is sensitive to light.* **2.** Easily hurt, damaged, or irritated: *Her sensitive skin cannot take much sun. His sensitive feelings were upset when the boys left him out.*

sent |sĕnt| The past tense and past participle of the verb **send:** *I sent a letter to California today. He had already sent the packages by mail when she called him.*

♦ *These sound alike* **sent, cent, scent.**

sen·tence |sĕn′təns| —*noun, plural* **sentences** **1.** A group of words, or sometimes one word, that tells or expresses a complete thought. A sentence can be used to make a statement, ask a question, or give a command. For example, *It's almost midnight, Is it raining?* and *Stop!* are sentences. **2.** The punishment given to a person who has been found guilty: *After he served his sentence, he decided to live an honest life.* —*verb* **sentenced, sentencing** To give a legal punishment to: *The judge sentenced him to three years in jail.*

sen·ti·ment |sĕn′tə mənt| —*noun, plural* **sentiments** Feeling or emotion: *The march music stirred up their patriotic sentiments. The speaker swayed the sentiments of the crowd.*

sen·ti·men·tal |sĕn′tə mĕn′tl| —*adjective* **1.** Of the feelings; emotional; tender: *a man with sentimental ties to the country of his birth.* **2.** Easily moved by feelings and emotions: *a sentimental person who cries at sad movies.*

sen·try |sĕn′trē| —*noun, plural* **sentries** A soldier or other person who is posted to watch for attacks and to check people coming and going; guard.

sentry

ă	pat	ĕ	pet	î	fierce
ā	pay	ē	be	ŏ	pot
â	care	ĭ	pit	ō	go
ä	father	ī	pie	ô	paw, for
oi	oil	ŭ	cut	zh	vision
ŏŏ	book	û	fur	ə	ago, item,
ōō	boot	*th*	the		pencil, atom,
yōō	abuse	th	thin		circus
ou	out	hw	which	ər	butter

se·pal |sē′pəl| —*noun, plural* **sepals** One of the parts forming the outer covering of a flower. Sepals are usually green and look like leaves. Sometimes they are brightly colored and look more like the petals.

sep·a·rate |sĕp′ə rāt′| —*verb* **separated, separating** **1.** To divide into parts or distinct sections: *She separated the candies into four piles. The road separates at the traffic light.* **2.** To put or keep apart; be placed between: *A river separates the two states.* **3.** To go in different directions; come or go apart: *The group separated and went off to look for the missing calves.* **4.** To break a marriage, friendship, or other union: *The couple separated after four years of marriage.* **5.** To remove or become removed from a mixture: *The machine separates the milk from the cream.*
—*adjective* |sĕp′ər ĭt| or |sĕp′rĭt| **1.** Apart from others; not connected: *Libraries have a separate section for children's books.* **2.** Not part of a group; individual or independent: *She gave the children separate presents this year. The guests eat at separate tables.*

sep·a·ra·tion |sĕp′ə rā′shən| —*noun, plural* **separations** **1.** The act of separating: *the separation of cream from milk; the separation of boys from girls.* **2.** The condition of being apart: *He missed her during their long separation.* **3.** A space or object that separates or divides: *There is a separation between his front teeth.*

Sep·tem·ber |sĕp tĕm′bər| —*noun, plural* **Septembers** The ninth month of the year, after August and before October. September has 30 days.

se·quence |sē′kwəns| —*noun, plural* **sequences** **1.** The following of one thing after another in a regular or fixed order: *The sequence of even numbers begins 2, 4, 6, 8, . . .* **2.** A group of things in a particular order: *A sequence of many drawings is needed to make an animated picture.*

se·quoi·a |sĭ kwoi′ə| —*noun, plural* **sequoias** A very large evergreen tree that bears cones. Two kinds of sequoias are the giant sequoia and the redwood, both found in California.

se·rene |sə rēn′| —*adjective* **serener, serenest** Peaceful and calm; without trouble, noise, clouds, or other disturbances: *a serene look on the face of the sleeping child; serene lake waters.*

serf |sûrf| —*noun, plural* **serfs** In the Middle Ages, a person who had to live and work on the land that was owned by a lord.
♦ *These sound alike* **serf, surf.**

ser·geant |sär′jənt| —*noun, plural* **sergeants** An officer in the U.S. Army or Marine Corps who ranks just above a corporal.

se·ries |sîr′ēz| —*noun, plural* **series** **1.** A number of similar things that occur in a row or follow one another: *a series of traffic lights along the road; a series of strange happenings.* **2.** A group of related shows or sports events that come one after the other or at regular intervals: *a series of concerts; two series of baseball games.*

se·ri·ous |sîr′ē əs| —*adjective* **1.** Not smiling or happy; grave; solemn: *He had a serious expression on his face when he told us the bad news.* **2.** Not joking or fooling; in earnest: *Is she serious about leaving school?* **3.** Not slight or trivial; important: *Getting married is a serious matter.* **4.** Dangerous: *Smoking can lead to some serious health problems.*

ser·mon |sûr′mən| —*noun, plural* **sermons** **1.** A talk on a religious or moral subject or text. A sermon is delivered as part of a religious service. **2.** Any long serious talk: *He gave his children a sermon about getting home in time for dinner.*

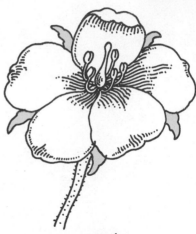

sepal

sequoia
Above: A sequoia tree
Below: A car can drive through this tunnel cut in a giant sequoia.

ser·pent | sûr′pənt | —*noun, plural* **serpents** A snake.

se·rum | sîr′əm | —*noun, plural* **serums** **1.** The clear, yellowish liquid part of the blood that separates from the rest of the blood when it clots. **2.** A liquid taken from the blood of an animal that has been given a certain disease. This liquid is used to fight the same disease in human beings.

ser·vant | sûr′vənt | —*noun, plural* **servants** **1.** A person, such as a cook, maid, or butler, who works for wages in someone else's household. **2.** A person who is employed to perform services for others: *police officers, firefighters, and other public servants.*

serve | sûrv | —*verb* **served, serving** **1.** To do work for; be a servant to: *The butler served the family for a month and then left.* **2.** To act for the interests of; work to help: *Our leaders are supposed to serve the people.* **3.** To spend time fulfilling an obligation or sentence: *He served three years in the army.* **4.** To fill the job of; act as: *He served as chairman for two years.* **5.** To wait on people at a table or in a store: *The waiter often serves famous actors and actresses.* **6.** To provide food: *The restaurant serves all day.* **7.** To be enough to feed: *This can of peaches serves four.* **8.** To be of use: *An old box served as a bed for the cat.* **9.** To hit a ball or other piece of sports equipment and put it into play: *You serve first at badminton.*

—*noun, plural* **serves** The right to serve in a game.

ser·vice | sûr′vĭs | —*noun, plural* **services** **1.** The act or work of helping or assisting others: *She spent her life in service to the poor.* **2.** Work or employment for someone else: *He spent many years in service to the knight.* **3.** The act or manner of serving food or filling customers' demands: *The service in that restaurant is very slow.* **4.** A set of dishes or other objects used for serving and eating food: *a china service for eight; a silver tea service.* **5.** A branch of the government and the people who work for it: *the civil service; the foreign service.* **6.** The armed forces or a branch of the armed forces: *He was drafted into the service.* **7.** A means of supplying the needs of the public: *electricity service; bus service; a messenger service.* **8.** A religious ceremony: *a church service; a marriage service.*

—*verb* **serviced, servicing** To do the work needed to keep a machine or appliance operating: *After the men serviced our washing machine, it worked better than ever.*

ses·a·me | sĕs′ə mē | —*noun* The small, flat seeds of a tropical Asian plant. Sesame seeds are a source of oil.

ses·sion | sĕsh′ən | —*noun, plural* **sessions** **1.** A meeting or series of meetings: *a session of Congress. The committee held a session to study the new rules.* **2.** A meeting of a class, club, or other group: *Our class had a session to make a tape recording.* **3.** A period of time during the day or year when meetings take place: *a morning session; a summer session.*

set¹ | sĕt | —*verb* **set, setting** **1.** To put; place: *Please set the package on the table.* **2.** To become hard, firm, or less liquid: *Allow 24 hours for the glue to set.* **3.** To put in a particular condition: *Please set us free. He set the wagon in motion. The book set me thinking.* **4.** To place in position or condition for proper use: *He set a trap for the mouse. Let's set the table for dinner. The doctor set his broken arm.* **5.** To establish; create: *They set a date for the party. Our team set a new record.* **6.** To fix; assign: *She set her heart on winning the prize. I set some tasks for you to do.* **7.** To

service
A silver tea service

set¹, set²

Set¹ comes from a word used long ago by English-speaking people to mean "to cause something to sit," "to put." A related word meant simply "to sit." Set² came from an old French word meaning "group, division" that in turn came from a Latin word meaning "sect." Set¹ and set² are sometimes confused, but they are not related.

ă	pat	ĕ	pet	î	fierce
ā	pay	ē	be	ŏ	pot
â	care	ĭ	pit	ō	go
ä	father	ī	pie	ô	paw, for
oi	oil	ŭ	cut	zh	vision
ōō	book	û	fur	ə	ago, item,
ōō	boot	*th*	the		pencil, atom,
yōō	abuse	th	thin		circus
ou	out	hw	which	ər	butter

start: *Let's set to work. They set out on a long trip.* **8.** To provide music for words: *He set poems to music.* **9.** To disappear beyond the horizon: *The sun sets later each spring day.*

Phrasal verbs **set about** To begin in a serious way: *They set about to solve the mystery.* **set aside** To keep for a special purpose: *She sets aside some money each month to save for a coat.* **set off** **1.** To cause: *Her story set off some wild laughter.* **2.** To cause to explode: *Who set off the fireworks?* **3.** To show up as being worth noticing: *Quotation marks set off words that are spoken.*

—*adjective* **1.** Not changing or moving: *a set position.* **2.** Fixed by custom or agreement: *a set order of the letters of the alphabet; a set time for lunch.* **3.** Ready: *Are you set for the race?*

set² |sĕt| —*noun, plural* **sets** **1.** A group of things that match or are connected in some way: *a set of china; a chess set.* **2.** A group of people with a similar age or interest: *the kindergarten set; the golf set.* **3.** The parts that make up a radio, television receiver, or another electronic device: *a TV set; a stereo set.* **4.** The scenery, furniture, and other objects on the stage for a play, show, or movie.

set·ter |sĕt′ər| —*noun, plural* **setters** A dog that is often trained and used for hunting.

set·tle |sĕt′l| —*verb* **settled, settling** **1.** To arrange or fix by agreement; put into order: *Let's settle the date and place of the next meeting. They have to settle their problems themselves.* **2.** To come to rest or cause to come to rest: *The butterfly settled on a flower. She settled herself in a comfortable chair.* **3.** To make a home or place to live in: *Pioneers settled in the West. The family settled on an island.* **4.** To move people to a new place to live: *The Spanish began to settle South America in the 1500's.* **5.** To come to rest at the bottom; sink: *Mud settles fast in calm rivers.* **6.** To make or become calm: *Soft music settled his nerves.*

set·tle·ment |sĕt′l mənt| —*noun, plural* **settlements** **1.** The act or process of settling: *a settlement of differences; new land open to settlement; the settlement of dust on furniture.* **2.a.** A small, rather new community: *a fishing settlement along the coast.* **b.** A location in a new country; a colony: *the former British settlements in Asia.*

set·tler |sĕt′lər| —*noun, plural* **settlers** A person who settles in a new region; colonist.

sev·en |sĕv′ən| —*noun, plural* **sevens** A number, written 7, that is equal to the sum of 6 + 1.

—*adjective* Being one more than six in number: *seven dwarfs.* The adjective **seven** belongs to a class of words called **determiners.** They signal that a noun is coming.

sev·en·teen |sĕv′ən tēn′| —*noun, plural* **seventeens** A number, written 17, that is equal to the sum of 10 + 7.

—*adjective* Being one more than sixteen in number: *seventeen pencils.* The adjective **seventeen** belongs to a class of words called **determiners.** They signal that a noun is coming.

sev·en·teenth |sĕv′ən tēnth′| —*noun, plural* **seventeenths** **1.** In a group of people or things that are in numbered order, the one that matches the number seventeen. **2.** One of seventeen equal parts, written $\frac{1}{17}$.

—*adjective: her seventeenth birthday.*

sev·enth |sĕv′ənth| —*noun, plural* **sevenths** **1.** In a group of people or things that are in numbered order, the one that matches the number seven. **2.** One of seven equal parts, written $\frac{1}{7}$.

—*adjective: the seventh dwarf.*

setter

settlement
An early settlement in
Pennsylvania

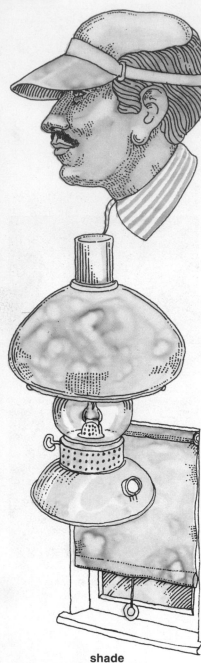

shade

An eye shade *(above)*, a lamp shade *(center)*, and a window shade *(below)*

ă	pat	ĕ	pet	î	fierce
ā	pay	ē	be	ŏ	pot
â	care	ĭ	pit	ō	go
ä	father	ī	pie	ô	paw, for

oi	oil	ŭ	cut		zh	vision
ŏŏ	book	û	fur		ə	ago, item,
ōō	boot	*th*	the			pencil, atom,
yŏŏ	abuse	th	thin			circus
ou	out	hw	which		ər	butter

sev·en·ti·eth | sĕv′ən tē ĭth | —*noun, plural* **seventieths** **1.** In a group of people or things that are in numbered order, the one that matches the number seventy. **2.** One of seventy equal parts, written 1/70.
—*adjective: our seventieth year in business.*

sev·en·ty | sĕv′ən tē | —*noun, plural* **seventies** A number, written 70, that is equal to the product of 7 × 10.
—*adjective* Being ten more than sixty in number: *seventy years.*
The adjective **seventy** belongs to a class of words called **determiners.** They signal that a noun is coming.

sev·er·al | sĕv′ər əl | —*adjective* More than two or three, but not many: *He lives several miles away.*
—*noun* More than two or three people or things: *I have several of these books at home.*

se·vere | sə vîr′ | —*adjective* **severer, severest** **1.** Strict and harsh; stern: *a severe law that punishes people for small offenses.*
2. Causing great pain or distress: *a severe injury; a severe insult.*
3. Very serious; not slight: *severe damage.*

sew | sō | —*verb* **sewed, sewn** or **sewed, sewing** To use a needle and thread or a sewing machine to attach things or make things with stitches: *She likes to sew and knit. She sewed a dress.*
♦ *These sound alike* **sew, so, sow**[1].

sew·age | sōo′ĭj | —*noun* Waste matter from homes or towns that is carried off in drains or sewers.

sew·er | sōo′ər | —*noun, plural* **sewers** A pipe or channel, usually underground, for carrying off waste matter and water.

sew·ing machine | sō′ĭng | A machine that is used for sewing or making stitches.

sewn | sōn | A past participle of the verb **sew:** *He has sewn three buttons back on his shirt.*

sex | sĕks | —*noun, plural* **sexes** **1.** Either of the two groups, male and female, into which many living things are divided: *What is the sex of the new baby, male or female?* **2.** The condition of being male or female: *They hire people according to ability, not by age or sex.*

shab·by | shăb′ē | —*adjective* **shabbier, shabbiest** Very worn and looking old: *a shabby old coat.*

shack | shăk | —*noun, plural* **shacks** A small, roughly built hut or cabin.

shad | shăd | —*noun, plural* **shad** A food fish that swims from ocean waters up rivers and streams to lay eggs.

shade | shād | —*noun, plural* **shades** **1.** An area that is partly dark because light has been blocked off: *Let's sit in the shade of the house.* **2.** Any device that blocks off part of the light or heat from the sun or a lamp: *a shade on the window; a green plastic shade above his eyes.* **3.** A small difference of light or dark in a color: *Pink is a shade of red. The garden has many shades of green.*
4. A tiny bit; small amount: *The sweater is a shade too short.*
—*verb* **shaded, shading** **1.** To keep light or heat from: *Trees shaded the street.* **2.** To give or have different degrees of dark and light: *The artist shaded the picture of the apple to make it look round. The colors shade from yellow to green.*

shad·ow | shăd′ō | —*noun, plural* **shadows** **1.** A dark area where some or all of the light is blocked by someone or something: *When I walk away from the sun, my shadow is in front of me.* **2.** Often **shadows** An area of partial dark; shade: *in the*

shadows of the corner of the room. **3.** A slight trace; small amount: *I'll tell you he is innocent beyond a shadow of a doubt.*
—*verb* **shadowed, shadowing** To follow after, usually in secret: *He shadowed the outlaw to a secret cave.*

shad·y |shā′dē| —*adjective* **shadier, shadiest 1.** Full of shade: *a shady street.* **2.** Providing shade; *large shady trees.* **3.** Not honest, but not easy to prove dishonest: *a shady deal.*

shaft |shăft| —*noun, plural* **shafts 1.** The long, narrow rod of a spear or arrow. **2.** A spear or an arrow: *The archer aimed the shaft straight at the target.* **3.** The handle of a hammer, ax, golf club, or other tool or playing piece. **4.** A long bar that is part of a machine. One or more wheels may turn on a shaft, or the shaft may transfer power from one spot to another. **5.** A ray or beam of light: *Shafts of moonlight appeared through the trees.* **6.** The main section of a chimney, column, or other structure. **7.** A long, narrow passage that goes up and down, not sideways: *An elevator travels up and down inside a shaft.*

shag·gy |shăg′ē| —*adjective* **shaggier, shaggiest 1.** Having long, rough hair, wool, or fibers: *a shaggy dog; a shaggy coat.* **2.** Thick, rough, and uneven; bushy: *his shaggy hair.*

shake |shāk| —*verb* **shook, shaken, shaking 1.** To move or make move up and down or back and forth in short, quick movements: *The flowers shook in the wind. Please shake the bottle carefully.* **2.** To tremble or cause to tremble; vibrate; rock: *He was shaking with cold. The earthquake shook the ground.* **3.** To remove or scatter by making short, jerky movements: *She shook the snow from her boots.* **4.** To make uncomfortable in one's mind or feelings; disturb: *The accident had shaken her badly.* **5.** To cause to change one's mind: *Nothing can shake him from his beliefs.*
—*noun, plural* **shakes** An act of shaking: *a shake of her head.*

shak·en |shā′kən| The past participle of the verb **shake:** *The earthquake had shaken the whole city.*

shak·y |shā′kē| —*adjective* **shakier, shakiest 1.** Trembling or shaking: *the old woman's shaky voice; a shaky hand.* **2.** Not sturdy or firm: *a shaky old building.* **3.** Not reliable; not capable of being trusted: *a shaky promise; a shaky friendship.*

shale |shāl| —*noun* Any of several kinds of rock that come in thin layers and split easily. Shale was formed from mud or clay deposited by rivers thousands of years ago.

shall |shăl| —*helping,* or *auxiliary, verb* Past tense **should** As a helping verb **shall** is used followed by another verb in the infinitive to show: **1.** An action or state that will take place or exist in the future: *He shall arrive tomorrow. She shall be twenty on Friday.* **2.** An order: *You shall leave now.* **3.** The will to do something: *I shall return if I feel like it.*

shal·low |shăl′ō| —*adjective* **shallower, shallowest** Not deep: *a shallow lake; a shallow pan; a shallow friendship.*

shame |shām| —*noun* **1.** A painful or uncomfortable feeling created by the sense of having done something wrong or stupid: *He felt shame because he had lied to his parents.* **2.** Disgrace, dishonor, or embarrassment: *The news stories about his thefts brought shame to him and his family. It is a shame that nobody helped the woman when she fell.* **3.** Something that one regrets or would regret; a pity: *It's a shame to miss the circus because of your cold.*
—*verb* **shamed, shaming** To fill with feelings of shame: *He lies because the truth shames him.*

shaggy
A shaggy dog named Tillie

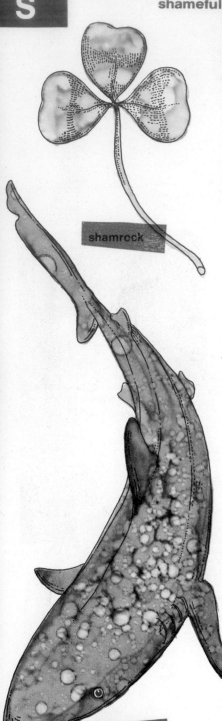

shamrock

shark

shame·ful | shām′fəl | —*adjective* Causing or deserving shame; disgraceful: *He was punished for his shameful behavior in church.*

sham·poo | shăm poō′ | —*noun, plural* **shampoos** A soap or detergent used to wash the hair and scalp.
—*verb* **shampooed, shampooing** To wash with a shampoo: *Can you shampoo your own hair?*

sham·rock | shăm′rŏk′ | —*noun, plural* **shamrocks** A kind of plant that has leaves with three small leaflets. Clover is a kind of shamrock.

shan't | shănt | A contraction of "shall not."

shape | shāp | —*noun, plural* **shapes** **1.** The outer form of an object; outline: *circles, triangles, and other shapes; dark shapes beneath the water.* **2.** A form in which something may appear: *a bowl in the shape of a swan; a demon in the shape of a dragon.* **3.** Good or proper condition: *Athletes must stay in shape.*
—*verb* **shaped, shaping** To give a particular form to: *They shaped the clay into bowls and vases.*
Phrasal verb **shape up** **1.** To develop; turn out: *How is the game shaping up?* **2.** To improve one's behavior or performance: *She had to shape up quickly in the new school.*

share | shâr | —*verb* **shared, sharing** **1.** To have, do, or use with others or another: *He shares a room with his brother. They shared the job of cleaning up.* **2.** To divide something so that more than one can have or use it: *He shared his apple with his friends.* **3.** To present or discuss for the benefit of others: *Will you share your thoughts with us?*
—*noun, plural* **shares** **1.** A part of something that has been divided among two or more; a portion: *His share of the work is greater than hers.* **2.** A fair or full portion: *She did her share to make the party a success.* **3.** One of many equal parts of the ownership of a business. Shares are bought, sold, and kept by people who want to own parts of a business and receive some of the profits and are willing to take some of the risks of losses.

shark | shärk | —*noun, plural* **sharks** Any of several large ocean fish with sharp teeth and tough skin.

sharp | shärp | —*adjective* **sharper, sharpest** **1.** Having a thin edge that cuts or a fine point that pierces: *a sharp razor blade; a sharp needle.* **2.** Not rounded or blunt; pointed: *a sharp pencil; a sharp edge of a desk.* **3.** Abrupt or sudden; not gradual: *a road with sharp turns; a sharp drop at the edge of the cliff.* **4.** Clear; distinct: *a design with sharp outlines; a lens in sharp focus.* **5.** High in pitch; piercing; shrill: *the sharp cry of an unknown bird.* **6.** Harsh and biting; severe: *his sharp words; a sharp pain in his side.* **7.** Alert to see, hear, notice, or think: *a girl with sharp eyes; a dog's sharp hearing; a sharp mind.*
—*adverb* **1.** In a prompt or punctual way; exactly: *Meet me at three o'clock sharp.* **2.** In an alert or keen manner: *Look sharp!*

sharp·en | shär′pən | —*verb* **sharpened, sharpening** To make or become sharp or sharper: *Please sharpen the scissors. His thinking sharpened.*

shat·ter | shăt′ər | —*verb* **shattered, shattering** **1.** To break into many pieces: *He shattered the mirror with a rock.* **2.** To destroy or disturb: *Illness shattered his hopes of running in the race.*

shave | shāv | —*verb* **shaved, shaved** or **shaven, shaving** **1.** To remove the beard or hair from with a razor: *My father shaves his face every morning.* **2.** To cut thin slices or layers from: *The*

ă	pat	ĕ	pet	î	fierce
ā	pay	ē	be	ŏ	pot
â	care	ĭ	pit	ō	go
ä	father	ī	pie	ô	paw, for
oi	oil	ŭ	cut	zh	vision
ōō	book	û	fur	ə	ago, item,
ōō	boot	th	the		pencil, atom,
yōō	abuse	th	thin		circus
ou	out	hw	which	ər	butter

carpenter shaved the edge of the door so it would close.
—*noun, plural* **shaves** The act of removing hair with a razor.

shav·en |shā′vən| A past participle of the verb **shave**: *His face had been smoothly shaven.*

shav·ing |shā′vĭng| —*noun, plural* **shavings** A thin strip of wood, metal, or other material that has been removed in shaping something else: *wood shavings.*

shawl |shôl| —*noun, plural* **shawls** A large piece of cloth worn around the shoulders, head, or neck for warmth or decoration.

she |shē| —*pronoun* The female person or animal last mentioned: *Sally was here, but now she is gone.*
—*noun, plural* **shes** A female: *Is the puppy a he or a she?*

shear |shîr| —*verb* **sheared, sheared** or **shorn, shearing** To remove wool or hair with scissors, shears, or another sharp tool: *He sheared the wool from the sheep. It is hard work to shear sheep.*
♦ *These sound alike* **shear, sheer.**

shears |shîrz| —*plural noun* A tool for cutting. Shears are like scissors, but larger.

sheath |shēth| —*noun, plural* **sheaths** |shē*th*z| or |shēths| A case that fits tightly over the blade of a knife, sword, or other sharp object.

shed¹ |shĕd| —*verb* **shed, shedding** **1.** To take off; remove: *He shed his clothing and jumped into the pool.* **2.** To lose in a natural way; drop: *Some trees shed their leaves in autumn. A snake sheds its skin each year.* **3.** To let fall: *She sheds tears easily.* **4.** To send forth; give off; cast: *The moon shed a pale light.*

shed² |shĕd| —*noun, plural* **sheds** A small, simple building for storage or shelter: *a tool shed; a work shed.*

she'd |shĕd| A contraction of "she had" or "she would."

sheep |shēp| —*noun, plural* **sheep** An animal with hoofs and a thick coat of wool. Sheep are raised for their wool and their meat.

sheep dog A dog trained to guard and herd sheep, or a dog of a breed that was originally raised and trained for herding sheep.

sheer |shîr| —*adjective* **sheerer, sheerest** **1.** Thin and fine enough to see through: *windows with sheer white curtains; sheer nylon stockings.* **2.** Not mixed in any way; pure; complete: *The feast was sheer delight. He fainted from sheer exhaustion.* **3.** Almost straight up or down; very steep: *a sheer cliff right next to the road.*
♦ *These sound alike* **sheer, shear.**

sheet |shēt| —*noun, plural* **sheets** **1.** A large piece of cloth used on a bed to sleep over or under. **2.** A broad, thin piece of paper, metal, glass, or other material: *a sheet of plastic.* **3.** A broad covering on a surface; an expanse: *a sheet of ice on the sidewalk.*

shelf |shĕlf| —*noun, plural* **shelves** **1.** A flat piece of wood, metal, glass, or other material attached to a wall or built into furniture for holding and storing dishes, books, toys, and other things. **2.** Something that looks like or is used as a shelf, such as a flat rock ledge or a balcony.

shell |shĕl| —*noun, plural* **shells** **1. a.** The hard outer covering of some water animals that have soft bodies. Clams, oysters, scallops, and snails are among the animals having a shell. **b.** A similar hard outer covering of certain animals or plants. Crabs, lobsters, turtles, eggs, and nuts have shells. **2.** Something like a shell: *a pastry shell for a pie.* **3.** A long boat used in rowing races. **4.** A bullet or other piece of ammunition that is shot from a gun or cannon.

shawl

shed¹, shed²
Shed¹ can be traced back to a word used long ago in English to mean "to cast off." Earlier it meant "to divide, to separate." Shed² also came from an old English word and may be a different form of **shade** in the sense "a shelter."

sheep dog

shell
Different kinds of bullets

—*verb* **shelled, shelling** **1.** To remove the outer covering from: *You shell the walnuts, and I'll shell the peas.* **2.** To attack with shells; bombard: *Airplanes shelled the village all day.*

she'll |shĕl| A contraction for "she will" or "she shall."

shel·lac |shə lăk′| —*noun, plural* **shellacs** A liquid used as a varnish to form a hard coat on wood, plaster, and other surfaces. —*verb* **shellacked, shellacking** To apply shellac to.

shell·fish |shĕl′fĭsh′| —*noun, plural* **shellfish** or **shellfishes** A water animal that has a shell or an outer covering that is like a shell. Clams, lobsters, and shrimp are shellfish.

shel·ter |shĕl′tər| —*noun, plural* **shelters** **1.** Something that protects or covers; a safe place: *The old barn was their shelter that night.* **2.** Protection: *They looked for shelter from the storm.* **3.** An institution for people or animals that have no homes: *a children's shelter; a dog shelter.*
—*verb* **sheltered, sheltering** To provide a shelter for: *The umbrella sheltered us from the rain.*

shelve |shĕlv| —*verb* **shelved, shelving** **1.** To place on a shelf or shelves: *They shelved the groceries.* **2.** To put aside to consider later: *They shelved the discussion for another meeting.* **3.** To cancel; dismiss: *He shelved his plans.*

shelves |shĕlvz| The plural of the noun **shelf.**

shep·herd |shĕp′ərd| —*noun, plural* **shepherds** A person who takes care of a flock of sheep.

sher·bet |shûr′bĭt| —*noun, plural* **sherbets** A sweet, frozen dessert containing water, milk, sugar, egg whites or gelatin, and flavoring. Many sherbets are flavored with fruits.

sher·iff |shĕr′ĭf| —*noun, plural* **sheriffs** A county official who is in charge of enforcing the law.

she's |shēz| A contraction of "she is" or "she has."

shield |shēld| —*noun, plural* **shields** **1.** A piece of armor carried in olden times by a knight or warrior to protect against an enemy's blows. **2.** An emblem or badge in the shape of a shield: *a police officer's shield.* **3.** Anything used as a protection: *She raised her arm as a shield against the glare.*
—*verb* **shielded, shielding** To protect with or as if with a shield: *She shielded her head from the rain.*

shi·er |shī′ər| A comparative of the adjective **shy.**

shi·est |shī′ĭst| A superlative of the adjective **shy.**

shift |shĭft| —*verb* **shifted, shifting** **1.** To move from one place or position to another; transfer: *He shifted his package to his other arm. Don't shift the blame to me!* **2.** To change: *He shifted to another argument.*
—*noun, plural* **shifts** **1.** A change in place, position, or direction; a transfer: *the shift of people from farms to cities; a shift in the wind from west to north.* **2.** A group of workers who work in one place during the same hours: *The afternoon shift at the factory comes in at four o'clock.* **3.** The period of time that a group of workers work: *The nurse is on the night shift at the hospital.*

shil·ling |shĭl′ĭng| —*noun, plural* **shillings** A British coin worth one twentieth of a pound. It is no longer in official use.

shim·mer |shĭm′ər| —*verb* **shimmered, shimmering** To shine with a flickering or faint light: *Her blond hair shimmered in the moonlight.*

shin |shĭn| —*noun, plural* **shins** The front part of a leg between the knee and the ankle.

shield
Two kinds of shield

ă	pat	ĕ	pet	î	fierce
ā	pay	ē	be	ŏ	pot
â	care	ĭ	pit	ō	go
ä	father	ī	pie	ô	paw, for
oi	oil	ŭ	cut	zh	vision
ŏŏ	book	û	fur	ə	ago, item,
ōō	boot	*th*	the		pencil, atom,
yōō	abuse	th	thin		circus
ou	out	hw	which	ər	butter

—*verb* **shinned, shinning** To climb by holding and pulling with hands and legs: *He shinned up the pole to rescue the flag.*

shine |shīn| —*verb* **shone** or **shined, shining 1.** To give off light or reflect light; be very bright: *The lamp shone in the little room. The silver and crystal shone on the table.* **2.** *Past tense* and *past participle* **shined** To make bright or glossy; polish: *He shined his shoes with a new polish.* **3.** To do very well; be excellent: *She shines at math and science.*
—*noun, plural* **shines 1.** A strong light or reflected light: *the shine from the headlights; the shine of gold coins.* **2.** Fair weather: *We'll go camping rain or shine.* **3.** A polish: *She gave the shoes a quick shine.*

shin·gle |shĭng′gəl| —*noun, plural* **shingles** One of many thin pieces of wood or other material laid in rows that overlap. Shingles are used to cover roofs or the outsides of houses.
—*verb* **shingled, shingling** To put shingles on a roof or wall.

shin·y |shī′nē| —*adjective* **shinier, shiniest** Reflecting light; shining; bright: *a shiny red apple; shiny silver coins.*

ship |shĭp| —*noun, plural* **ships 1.** A large vessel that can sail in deep water; a very big boat. **2.** An airplane, airship, or spacecraft.
—*verb* **shipped, shipping 1.** To send or carry: *The factory ships its goods by truck. The freighter shipped a cargo of grains.* **2.** To take a job on a ship; become part of a ship's crew: *He shipped to Africa as an ordinary sailor.*

-ship A suffix that forms nouns and means "the condition or quality of": *friendship; membership.*

ship·ment |shĭp′mənt| —*noun, plural* **shipments 1.** The act or process of shipping goods: *The iron ore is ready for shipment.* **2.** A group of goods shipped at one time: *The new shipment of workbooks just arrived.*

ship·ping |shĭp′ĭng| —*noun* **1.** The act or business of sending goods by ship, truck, train, or air. **2.** The ships that belong to one country, port, or industry: *The navy attacked enemy shipping.*

ship·wreck |shĭp′rĕk′| —*noun, plural* **shipwrecks** The destruction of a ship by storm, collision, or other disaster: *Several small boats rescued people from the shipwreck.*
—*verb* **shipwrecked, shipwrecking** To cause to suffer a shipwreck: *The iceberg shipwrecked the new liner.*

ship·yard |shĭp′yärd′| —*noun, plural* **shipyards** A place where ships are built, repaired, and made ready for sailing.

shirt |shûrt| —*noun, plural* **shirts** A piece of clothing for the upper part of the body. Shirts usually have collars, sleeves, and an opening in front.

shiv·er |shĭv′ər| —*verb* **shivered, shivering** To shake or tremble from cold, fear, or excitement in a way one cannot control.
—*noun, plural* **shivers** A tremble from cold, fear, or excitement: *A shiver ran down the horse's neck.*

shoal |shōl| —*noun, plural* **shoals** A shallow place in a body of water.

shock[1] |shŏk| —*noun, plural* **shocks 1.** A heavy blow, collision, or impact: *Her leg broke from the shock of her fall. The shock of the explosion could be felt for miles.* **2.** Something sudden that disturbs or upsets the mind or feelings: *Her friend's disappearance was a shock.* **3.** The feeling in the muscles and nerves caused by an electrical current passing through the body or a part of the

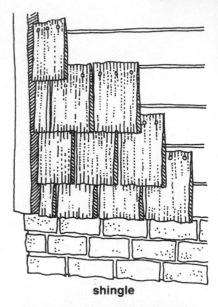
shingle

ship

shock[1], shock[2]
Shock[1] comes from a word that appeared long ago in French and meant "to strike with fear." We are less certain of the origin of **shock[2]**, but we think it probably came from an old Dutch word meaning "stack of grain sheaves."

body: *You'll get a shock if you touch the switch with wet hands.* **4.** A great weakening of the body caused by severe injury, loss of blood, sudden pain, or strong emotion. A person in shock is weak, very pale, and cold, and the heart pumps blood more slowly than usual.

—*verb* **shocked, shocking** To create a feeling of surprise, horror, or disturbance: *The news of the accident shocked us all.*

shock² |shŏk| —*noun, plural* **shocks** **1.** A pile of grain sheaves stacked on end in a field and left to dry. **2.** A thick mass of something: *A shock of red hair hung over his forehead.*

shock·ing |shŏk'ĭng| —*adjective* **1.** Creating great surprise and disturbance: *a shocking train crash; the prisoner's gaunt and shocking appearance.* **2.** Very offensive to good taste; not decent: *his shocking manners and language.*

shoe |shoo| —*noun, plural* **shoes** An outer covering for the foot.

shoe·horn |shoo'hôrn'| —*noun, plural* **shoehorns** A small device that is slipped under the heel to help put on a shoe.

shoe·lace |shoo'lās'| —*noun, plural* **shoelaces** A string or cord for fastening or tying up a shoe.

shoe·mak·er |shoo'mā'kər| —*noun, plural* **shoemakers** Someone who makes or repairs shoes.

shone |shōn| A past tense and past participle of the verb **shine**: *The flashlight shone in the dark. The sun hasn't shone in three days.*
♦ *These sound alike* **shone, shown.**

shook |shŏok| The past tense of the verb **shake**: *We shook the tree and the apples fell.*

shoot |shoot| —*verb* **shot, shooting** **1.** To hit, wound, or kill with a bullet, arrow, or something else fired from a weapon: *Kit shot the bear with his rifle.* **2.** To fire a weapon: *We shot at the target. Something's wrong; this gun won't shoot.* **3.** To fire a bullet, arrow, or other object from a weapon: *He's shooting arrows at the tree.* **4.** To set off or explode: *Don't shoot those firecrackers here.* **5.** To hunt with guns: *He went to shoot with his uncle in the country.* **6.** To send forth or be sent forth quickly or with great force: *We shot a rocket to the moon. The volcano shot lava.* **7.** To move quickly: *The car shot past us.* **8.** To begin to grow: *The tomato plants shot up.* **9.** To take a photograph or make a movie: *They're shooting a movie in our town.*

—*noun, plural* **shoots** A plant or part of a plant that has just begun to grow. Stems, leaves, or buds may be shoots.
♦ *These sound alike* **shoot, chute.**

shop |shŏp| —*noun, plural* **shops** **1.** A place where goods are sold; store: *a clothing shop.* **2.** A place where things are made or repaired: *We took the television to the repair shop.* **3.** A place where a certain kind of work is done: *a barber shop.* **4.** A room in a school where students are taught to use machines and tools or a course in which such skills are taught: *Charlie is taking shop this year.*

—*verb* **shopped, shopping** To go to stores to look at or buy things: *My parents are shopping for a new car.*

shore |shôr| —*noun, plural* **shores** **1.** Land along the edge of an ocean, lake, or large river: *We had a picnic on the shore.* **2.** Land: *I had such a good time on the boat I didn't want to be back on shore.*

shorn |shôrn| or |shōrn| A past participle of the verb **shear**: *We watched while the sheep were shorn.*

shore

ă	pat	ĕ	pet	î	fierce
ā	pay	ē	be	ŏ	pot
â	care	ĭ	pit	ō	go
ä	father	ī	pie	ô	paw, for
oi	oil	ŭ	cut	zh	vision
oo	book	û	fur	ə	ago, item,
oo	boot	*th*	the		pencil, atom,
yoo	abuse	th	thin		circus
ou	out	hw	which	ər	butter

short |shôrt| —*adjective* **shorter, shortest 1.** Not long: *a short skirt. You had your hair cut shorter.* **2.** Not tall: *a short girl.* **3.** Covering a small distance or taking a small amount of time: *a short walk; a short trip. This will take only a short time.* **4.** Not coming up to the right amount; not having enough: *The rope is too short. I couldn't buy the book because I was short of money.* **5.** Being so brief or quick as to be rude: *She was short with me on the phone.* **6.** Angered easily: *a short temper.* **7.** Having a sound that is brief; for example, the *i* in *pin* is a short vowel, while the *i* in *pine* is long.
—*adverb* In a short way; suddenly: *The truck stopped short.*

short·age |shôr′tĭj| —*noun, plural* **shortages** A lack in the amount needed; a supply not big enough: *Many poor countries have a food shortage every year.*

short circuit A path of electricity that allows too much current to flow through it. A short circuit usually forms when the insulation wears off wires that touch each other. It can cause a fire or blow a fuse.

short·en |shôr′tn| —*verb* **shortened, shortening** To make or become shorter: *shorten a skirt. The days shorten in the winter.*

short·en·ing |shôr′tn ĭng| —*noun* Fat used in baking to make cakes and pastry rich or crisp. Butter, vegetable oil, and lard are shortening.

short·hand |shôrt′hănd′| —*noun* A method of quick or rapid writing that uses symbols or letters to take the place of words. It is used by people such as secretaries to write down what someone says while they are saying it.

short·ly |shôrt′lē| —*adverb* In a short time; soon: *The train will arrive shortly.*

shorts |shôrtz| —*plural noun* **1.** Pants worn above the knees. **2.** Men's underpants.

short·stop |shôrt′stŏp′| —*noun, plural* **shortstops 1.** In baseball, the position between second and third base. **2.** The person who plays this position.

shot[1] |shŏt| —*noun, plural* **shots 1.** The firing of a gun, cannon, or other weapon: *Everybody heard three shots.* **2.** *plural* **shot a.** A ball of lead, a bullet, or other object fired from a weapon. **b.** A group of tiny balls or pellets of lead fired from a shotgun. **3.** The launching or sending forth of a rocket or other spacecraft: *a moon shot.* **4.** The distance over which something is or can be shot: *He waited until the boar was within rifle shot before firing.* **5.** A throw, drive, or stroke toward a goal or hole with a ball or puck: *He took three shots before he scored.* **6.** A person who shoots a weapon or a ball or puck accurately or on target: *He's a good shot with a bow and arrow. She's the best shot on the field hockey team.* **7.** A turn or opportunity to shoot: *It's your shot. He had a good shot at the goal but missed.* **8.** A chance or opportunity: *I have a shot at being elected class president.* **9.** A dose of medicine that is injected into the body with a needle: *I get an allergy shot every week.*

shot[2] |shŏt| The past tense and past participle of the verb **shoot:** *He shot the gun five times and didn't hit the target. He had shot and hit the target many times.*

shot·gun |shŏt′gŭn′| —*noun, plural* **shotguns** A kind of gun with no grooves in its barrel. It is used for firing cartridges filled with shot.

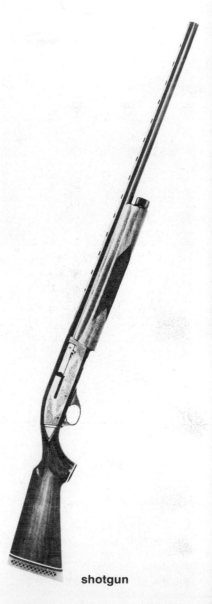

shotgun

should |sho͝od| —*helping*, or *auxiliary, verb* The past tense of **shall**. As a helping verb **should** is used followed by another verb in the infinitive to show: **1.** Duty or obligation: *You should write her a note.* **2.** Expectation: *They should arrive at noon.* **3.** The possibility that something may or may not happen: *If she should call while I'm out, tell her that I'll be right back.*

shoul·der |shōl′dər| —*noun, plural* **shoulders 1.** The part of the human body between the neck and the arm. **2.** A similar part on animals. **3.** The part of a coat, shirt, dress, or other clothing that covers the shoulder. **4.** An edge or border along a road: *The car stopped on the shoulder of the highway.*
—*verb* **shouldered, shouldering 1.** To bear the responsibility or blame for something: *He said that if I wanted a car, I'd have to shoulder the cost of it myself.* **2.** To push with shoulders: *We shouldered our way through the crowd.*

shoulder blade One of the two large, flat bones that form the rear of the shoulder.

should·n't |sho͝od′nt| A contraction of "should not."

shout |shout| —*verb* **shouted, shouting** To say something in a loud voice; cry out; yell: *The coach shouted at the players. Please stop shouting.*
—*noun, plural* **shouts** A loud cry or yell: *I heard a shout.*

shove |shŭv| —*verb* **shoved, shoving** To push forward from behind with force; push or thrust roughly or rudely against: *We shoved the sofa to the other side of the room.*
—*noun, plural* **shoves** A rough push: *That bully gave me a shove.*

shov·el |shŭv′əl| —*noun, plural* **shovels** A tool used for digging or lifting and moving dirt, snow, or loose matter. It has a long handle with a flattened scoop on the end.
—*verb* **shoveled, shoveling 1.** To dig up and throw or clear with a shovel: *Dick shoveled a path through the snow.* **2.** To move or throw in a hasty or careless way: *Don't shovel food into your mouth.*

show |shō| —*verb* **showed, showed** or **shown, showing 1.** To put in sight; allow to be seen: *Show me your new coat. The dog showed his teeth.* **2.** To display for the public; present: *She's showing her paintings at the art fair. The movie is showing only for two weeks.* **3.** To be in sight; be able to be seen: *The scratch on the table shows in the light.* **4.** To reveal or become revealed; be made known: *Her eyes showed curiosity. His anger showed.* **5.** To point out; direct: *Will you show her where the bathroom is?* **6.** To explain; make clear to: *Annette showed me how to skate.* **7.** To grant or give: *The judge showed no mercy to the murderer.*

Phrasal verb **show off** To display something or behave in a way that calls attention to oneself: *He showed off the autographed baseball to his friends. He always shows off to people.*
—*noun, plural* **shows 1.** A public exhibition or display: *My parents went to the flower show.* **2.** Any entertainment event, such as a play, movie, or television or radio program. **3.** A false or pretended display that is designed to trick or fool: *Even though he was scared, the soldier put on a show of courage.*

show·er |shou′ər| —*noun, plural* **showers 1.** A short fall of rain: *The shower stopped the game for thirty minutes.* **2.** Anything that falls like a shower: *A shower of confetti fell on the parade.* **3.** A bath in which water is sprayed down on a person from a nozzle above. **4.** The nozzle used to spray such water: *The shower is broken.*

shovel

ă	pat	ĕ	pet	î	fierce
ā	pay	ē	be	ŏ	pot
â	care	ĭ	pit	ō	go
ä	father	ī	pie	ô	paw, for
oi	oil	ŭ	cut	zh	vision
o͝o	book	û	fur	ə	ago, item,
o͞o	boot	*th*	the		pencil, atom,
yo͞o	abuse	th	thin		circus
ou	out	hw	which	ər	butter

—*verb* **showered, showering 1.** To fall or cause to fall in a shower; spray or sprinkle: *It showered all weekend. The campers showered the wolf with rocks.* **2.** To give generously or in large amounts: *My aunt showered my sisters and me with presents.* **3.** To take a shower bath: *I shower every day.*

shown |shōn| A past participle of the verb **show:** *They have shown me all around the city.*
♦ *These sound alike* **shown, shone.**

show·y |shō′ē| —*adjective* **showier, showiest** Attracting attention because of bright color, size, or some other quality: *a showy uniform; a plant with bright, showy flowers.*

shrank |shrăngk| A past tense of the verb **shrink:** *My pants shrank after washing.*

shred |shrĕd| —*noun, plural* **shreds 1.** A narrow strip or small piece torn or cut off from something: *The dogs ripped the towel to shreds.* **2.** A small amount; fragment; bit: *The police don't think there is a shred of truth in his story.*
—*verb* **shredded, shredding** To cut or tear into strips or pieces.

shrewd |shrood| —*adjective* **shrewder, shrewdest** Clever and sharp; keen: *Hazel is a shrewd lawyer.*

shriek |shrēk| —*noun, plural* **shrieks** A loud, shrill sound or yell: *We heard shrieks of laughter from the children in the park.*
—*verb* **shrieked, shrieking** To make a loud, shrill sound or yell.

shrill |shrĭl| —*adjective* **shriller, shrillest** Having a high, sharp sound: *The coach uses a shrill whistle in practice.*

shrimp |shrĭmp| —*noun, plural* **shrimp** or **shrimps** A small animal that lives in salt water and is related to the lobster. Shrimps are often used for food.

shrine |shrīn| —*noun, plural* **shrines** A holy place. It may be the tomb of a saint, the place where something important happened, or a place where holy objects are kept.

shrink |shrĭngk| —*verb* **shrank** or **shrunk, shrunk** or **shrunken, shrinking 1.** To make or become smaller in size or amount: *She used hot water to shrink my jeans because they were too big. This shirt won't shrink.* **2.** To draw back; retreat: *The boy shrank from the growling dog. Jane shrank at the sight of my messy room.*

shriv·el |shrĭv′əl| —*verb* **shriveled, shriveling** To dry up; shrink and wrinkle: *The hot sun shriveled the flowers.*

shrub |shrŭb| —*noun, plural* **shrubs** A woody plant that is smaller than a tree. Shrubs usually have several separate stems rather than a single trunk.

shrub·ber·y |shrŭb′ə rē| —*noun* **1.** A group of shrubs growing together. **2.** *plural* **shrubberies** An area planted with shrubs.

shrug |shrŭg| —*verb* **shrugged, shrugging** To raise the shoulders to show doubt, dislike, or lack of interest: *I asked him if he knew where Sarah was, and he just shrugged.*
—*noun, plural* **shrugs** The act of raising the shoulders to show doubt, dislike, or lack of interest.

shrunk |shrŭngk| A past tense and a past participle of the verb **shrink:** *The sweater shrunk. It has not shrunk; you are fatter.*

shrunk·en |shrŭng′kən| A past participle of the verb **shrink:** *The sweater has shrunken since you washed it.*

shud·der |shŭd′ər| —*verb* **shuddered, shuddering** To shiver suddenly from fear or cold: *Don shuddered at the sight of the bear.*
—*noun, plural* **shudders** A tremble or shiver: *I felt a shudder of cold as the wind blew in my face.*

shrimp

shrubbery

shuf·fle |shŭf′əl| —*verb* **shuffled, shuffling 1.** To walk by dragging the feet along the ground: *The little boy shuffled down the sidewalk.* **2.** To mix playing cards so as to change the order. **3.** To move things from one place to another; push about: *She shuffled the papers and pencils on the desk.*
—*noun, plural* **shuffles** The act of dragging the feet along the ground: *Nana walked with a shuffle.*

shut |shŭt| —*verb* **shut, shutting 1.** To move something into a closed position: *Shut the window.* **2.** To become moved into a closed position: *The wind shut the door. Her eyes shut.* **3.** To block an opening or entrance: *He shut the hole in the wall with a piece of wood. Dad shut the beach house for the winter.*

Phrasal verb **shut up** To be or become quiet; stop talking: *He told me to shut up. I shut up because I had nothing to say.*

shut·ter |shŭt′ər| —*noun, plural* **shutters 1.** A movable cover for a window or door: *Our house has blue shutters.* **2.** A movable cover over a camera lens that lets in light when a picture is taken.

shut·tle |shŭt′l| —*noun, plural* **shuttles 1.** A device on a loom and a sewing machine. It carries a thread that runs lengthwise over and under threads that run from top to bottom. **2.** A train, bus, or airplane that makes short trips between two places.

shy |shī| —*adjective* **shier** or **shyer, shiest** or **shyest 1.** Feeling uncomfortable around people: *The shy boy sat by himself in a corner during the party.* **2.** Easily frightened; timid: *The shy lamb ran away from the little girl.*
—*verb* **shied, shying, shies** To move back suddenly as if startled or frightened: *I shied away from the horse when it kicked.*

shy·ness |shī′nĭs| —*noun* The quality or condition of being shy: *She shows her shyness when she meets new people.*

sick |sĭk| —*adjective* **sicker, sickest 1.** Suffering from a disease or illness; not well or healthy: *She must be sicker than I was because she is still in bed.* **2.** Feeling like one has to vomit; feeling nausea: *The elevator went up so fast it made me sick.* **3.** Very upset: *I'm sick about losing my watch.* **4.** Having had enough of something; tired: *I'm sick of watching football games on television.*

sick·en |sĭk′ən| —*verb* **sickened, sickening** To make or become sick or disgusted: *The accident sickened her. He sickened at the thought of killing animals.*

sick·le |sĭk′əl| —*noun, plural* **sickles** A tool for cutting grain or tall grass. It has a large curved blade attached to a short handle.

sick·ly |sĭk′lē| —*adjective* **sicklier, sickliest 1.** Often sick; not healthy or strong: *The sickly kitten needed much care.* **2.** Of or caused by sickness: *Her face has a sickly color.*

sick·ness |sĭk′nĭs| —*noun, plural* **sicknesses** Illness or disease.

side |sīd| —*noun, plural* **sides 1.** A line or surface that forms the boundary of or encloses something: *A square has four sides.* **2.** One of the surfaces of an object that connects the top and bottom: *the side of a house.* **3.** One of the two surfaces of a flat object, such as a piece of paper or cloth: *Is there something written on the other side of the letter?* **4.** Either the right or left half of a human or animal body: *The cow has a scar on her left side.* **5.** Either the right or left half of something: *That chair goes on the other side of the room.* **6.** The space next to someone or something: *She sat at my side. I stopped on the side of the road.*

shutter
Window shutters

ă	pat	ĕ	pet	î	fierce
ā	pay	ē	be	ŏ	pot
â	care	ĭ	pit	ō	go
ä	father	ī	pie	ô	paw, for
oi	oil	ŭ	cut	zh	vision
ŏŏ	book	û	fur	ə	ago, item,
ōō	boot	*th*	the		pencil, atom,
yōō	abuse	th	thin		circus
ou	out	hw	which	ər	butter

7. a. One of two or more people, teams, or groups that have different views, ideas, or opinions: *Whose side are you on?* **b.** The different views, ideas, or opinions themselves: *Now tell me your side of the story. I want to hear all sides of the argument before I decide.*
—*verb* **sided, siding** To take sides; put oneself on one side: *He's always siding with his brother and against his sister.*
—*adjective* **1.** At, near, or to the side: *a side door. He took a side look in each direction.* **2.** Not as important; secondary: *When we visited Washington, D.C., we took a side trip to Virginia.* **3.** In addition to the main part: *a side order of French fries.*

side·walk |sīd′wôk′| —*noun, plural* **sidewalks** A path along the side of a road where people can walk. It is usually paved.

side·ways |sīd′wāz′| —*adverb* **1.** To or from one side: *turn sideways.* **2.** With one side forward: *Crabs can move sideways.*
—*adjective* Toward or from one side: *He gave me a sideways look.*

siege |sēj| —*noun, plural* **sieges** The act of surrounding an enemy fort, city, or position for a long time by an army trying to capture it. During a siege food and supplies are cut off from those enclosed to force them to surrender.

si·er·ra |sē ĕr′ə| —*noun, plural* **sierras** A chain or series of mountains whose peaks look like the teeth of a saw.

si·es·ta |sē ĕs′tə| —*noun, plural* **siestas** A rest or nap taken in the afternoon. Siestas are popular in Spain, Mexico, and other countries where it is too hot to work in the afternoon.

sieve |sĭv| —*noun, plural* **sieves** A utensil that has many tiny holes in the bottom. The holes let water and very small pieces of material pass through, but not large pieces. It is used for draining water or liquid or for getting rid of lumps in such foods as flour.

sift |sĭft| —*verb* **sifted, sifting** **1.** To separate large pieces from small pieces by shaking or pushing them through a sieve: *We sifted the dirt to remove the rocks.* **2.** To put through a sieve: *She sifted the flour to break up lumps.* **3.** To fall slowly or loosely as if passing through a sieve; drift: *The snow sifted down into the cracks between the bricks.* **4.** To look at or examine closely and carefully: *We sifted through the rubble of the burned house.*

sigh |sī| —*verb* **sighed, sighing** **1.** To let out a long, deep breathing sound because one is sad, tired, or relieved: *I sighed when the test was over.* **2.** To long or wish for: *The old man sighed for the good old days.*
—*noun, plural* **sighs** The act or sound of sighing: *He gave a sigh of relief when the doctor said he didn't need an operation.*

sight |sīt| —*noun, plural* **sights** **1.** The ability or power to see: *Eileen wears glasses to improve her sight.* **2.** The act of seeing: *The sight of the ocean made us want to go swimming.* **3.** The range or distance that can be seen: *Keep his birthday presents out of sight.* **4.** Something seen: *The sunset was a beautiful sight.* **5.** Something worth seeing: *There are many beautiful sights in Italy.* **6.** A view or glimpse; a quick look: *He caught sight of her in the crowd.* **7.** Something that looks unpleasant or odd: *What a sight she was in her Halloween costume.* **8.** A device on a gun or other object that helps in seeing or aiming: *Line up the target through the sight and pull the trigger.*
—*verb* **sighted, sighting** To see or observe with the eyes: *After four months the sailors sighted land.*
♦ *These sound alike* **sight, cite, site.**

sieve

silhouette

silkworm
Different stages of the silkworm
include the moth *(above)*, silk cocoon
(center), and caterpillar *(below)*.

ă	pat	ĕ	pet	î	fierce
ā	pay	ē	be	ŏ	pot
â	care	ĭ	pit	ō	go
ä	father	ī	pie	ô	paw, for

oi	oil	ŭ	cut	zh	vision
ŏŏ	book	û	fur	ə	ago, item,
ōō	boot	*th*	the		pencil, atom,
yōō	abuse	th	thin		circus
ou	out	hw	which	ər	butter

sign | sīn | —*noun, plural* **signs** **1.** A mark or symbol that stands for a word, process, or something else. For example, the signs for addition, subtraction, and multiplication are +, −, and ×. **2.** A board or poster that gives information or points out something: *The sign says, "Don't pick the flowers."* **3.** Something that suggests or indicates something that is happening that a person may not be aware of or something that may happen in the future: *A high temperature is a sign of illness. A cloudy sky is a sign of rain.* **4.** An action or gesture that is used to express a desire, command, or information: *The police officer held up her hand as a sign for the cars to stop.* **5.** Evidence or proof; a trace: *There was no sign that anybody was home.* **6.** An event or action that is believed to be proof that something will happen: *He believes that walking under a ladder is a sign of bad luck.*
—*verb* **signed, signing** To write one's name: *Did you sign the letter? Sign here, please.*

sig·nal | sĭg′nəl | —*noun, plural* **signals** **1.** A sign, gesture, or device that gives information: *The flashing yellow light was a signal for cars to slow down.* **2.** A sign or action that causes something to happen: *When I give the signal, we'll turn on the lights and shout "Surprise!"*
—*verb* **signaled, signaling** **1.** To make a signal to: *The conductor signaled the orchestra to begin playing.* **2.** To tell or make known with signals: *The bell signals that the class is over.*

sig·na·ture | sĭg′nə chər | —*noun, plural* **signatures** The name of a person as written in his or her own handwriting.

sig·nif·i·cance | sĭg nĭf′ĭ kəns | —*noun, plural* **significances** **1.** Importance: *What's the significance of the battle?* **2.** Special meaning: *He did not understand the significance of the sign.*

sig·nif·i·cant | sĭg nĭf′ĭ kənt | —*adjective* **1.** Having a special meaning: *a significant date in our history.* **2.** Full of meaning: *a significant look.* **3.** Important: *a significant historical event.*

si·lence | sī′ləns | —*noun, plural* **silences** **1.** The absence of sound or noise; total quiet: *There was complete silence in the room.* **2.** Failure to speak out: *The prisoner maintained his silence.*
—*verb* **silenced, silencing** To make silent; quiet: *The speaker silenced the crowd by raising his hands.*
—*interjection* Be silent; keep quiet.

si·lent | sī′lənt | —*adjective* **1.** Making or having no sound; quiet: *the silent night.* **2.** Saying nothing: *He remained silent in class.* **3.** Not said: *There is a silent "w" in the word "write."*

sil·hou·ette | sĭl′ōō ĕt′ | —*noun, plural* **silhouettes** **1.** A drawing of something or someone cut out of or filled in with a dark color. **2.** A dark outline of something against a light background.
—*verb* **silhouetted, silhouetting** To show as a dark outline: *Her profile was silhouetted on the wall by the bright light.*

silk | sĭlk | —*noun, plural* **silks** **1. a.** The fine, shiny fiber that a silkworm produces. **b.** A similar fine, strong fiber produced by spiders for their webs. **2.** Thread or cloth made from the fiber produced by silkworms. **3.** Any fine, soft strands, such as those that grow on the end of an ear of corn.

silk·worm | sĭlk′wûrm′ | —*noun, plural* **silkworms** The caterpillar that spins a cocoon of fine, shiny fiber that is used to make silk thread and cloth.

silk·y | sĭl′kē | —*adjective* **silkier, silkiest** As soft, smooth, and shiny as silk: *Mink is the silkiest fur I've ever felt.*

sill | sĭl | —*noun, plural* **sills** The piece of wood or stone across the bottom of a door or window.

sil·ly | sĭl′ē | —*adjective* **sillier, silliest** Without good sense or reason; stupid; foolish: *silly mistakes.*

si·lo | sī′lō | —*noun, plural* **silos** A tall, round building in which food for farm animals is stored.

silt | sĭlt | —*noun, plural* **silts** Very fine particles of earth, often found at the bottom of lakes and rivers.

silo

sil·ver | sĭl′vər | —*noun, plural* **silvers** **1.** A soft, shiny white metal. Silver is used to make money and jewelry. Silver is one of the chemical elements. **2.** Coins made from silver: *The pirates hid a chest full of silver.* **3.** Spoons, forks, knives, or other things for the table made of silver: *Set the table with the good silver.* **4.** A light, shiny gray color. ◊ The noun **silver** can be used like an adjective for things made of silver: *a silver bell; a silver platter.*
—*verb* **silvered, silvering** To cover or coat with silver or something that looks like silver: *The mirror was silvered again to give a better image.*
—*adjective* Having a light-gray color: *silver hair.*

sil·ver·smith | sĭl′vər smĭth′ | —*noun, plural* **silversmiths** Someone who makes or fixes articles of silver.

sil·ver·ware | sĭl′vər wâr′ | —*noun* Articles made or covered with silver that are used for eating and serving food. Silver forks, knives, and spoons are silverware.

silver
A silver basket

sil·ver·y | sĭl′və rē | —*adjective* **silverier, silveriest** Having the color or glittering appearance of silver; like silver: *a silvery moonlight; a school of silvery fish.*

sim·i·lar | sĭm′ə lər | —*adjective* Alike but not the same: *A wildcat is similar to but smaller than a lion.*

sim·i·lar·i·ty | sĭm′ə lăr′ĭ tē | —*noun, plural* **similarities** A way in which things are alike; likeness: *There is a similarity between bees and wasps.*

sim·mer | sĭm′ər | —*verb* **simmered, simmering** To cook below or just at the boiling point: *She simmered the sauce.*

sim·ple | sĭm′pəl | —*adjective* **simpler, simplest** **1.** Not difficult; easy: *a simple answer.* **2.** Not showy or fancy; plain: *a simple wedding dress. She likes simple, everyday food.* **3.** Open; honest: *He was simple and direct in the way he spoke.*

sim·pli·fy | sĭm′plə fī′ | —*verb* **simplified, simplifying, simplifies** To make or become simple or easier: *Spreading salt and sand on the icy road will simplify driving problems here.*

sim·ply | sĭm′plē | —*adverb* **1.** In a simple manner; plainly: *Explain it simply.* **2.** Merely; only; just: *We knew him simply as Joe.* **3.** Really: *His behavior was simply awful.*

si·mul·ta·ne·ous | sī′məl tā′nē əs | or | sĭm′əl tā′nē əs | —*adjective* Happening, existing, or done at the same time: *The two football games were shown on simultaneous television programs.*

sin | sĭn | —*noun, plural* **sins** **1.** The act of breaking a religious law on purpose: *It is a sin to steal.* **2.** Any serious mistake or wrong action: *The way he treats his son is a sin.*
—*verb* **sinned, sinning** To break a religious law: *The man told the minister that he had sinned.*

since | sĭns | —*adverb* **1.** From then until now: *He left town and hasn't been here since.* **2.** Before now; ago: *long since forgotten.*
—*preposition* From then until now: *Since last month he has been getting all A's in math.*

silversmith
Paul Revere

—*conjunction* **1.** After the time when: *since he graduated.* **2.** From the time when: *He hasn't spoken since he sat down.* **3.** Because: *Since you're not interested, I won't tell you about it.*

sin·cere |sĭn sîr′| —*adjective* **sincerer, sincerest** Without lies; real; honest: *sincere friends; a sincere apology.*

sin·ew |sĭn′yōō| —*noun, plural* **sinews** A strong cord made of tissue that joins a muscle to a bone; tendon. It allows the muscles to move arms, legs, and other parts of the body.

sing |sĭng| —*verb* **sang** or **sung, sung, singing** **1.** To say a series of words with or make sounds in musical tones: *Let's have everyone sing together.* **2.** To make or produce a musical sound: *The birds in the trees are singing.*

sing·er |sĭng′ər| —*noun, plural* **singers** A person or bird that sings: *That parrot's no singer. My sister wants to be an opera singer.*

sin·gle |sĭng′gəl| —*adjective* **1.** Not with another or others; only one: *There was a single tree on the front lawn.* **2.** Designed to be used by one person or one family: *a single bed; a single house; a single portion.* **3.** Not married: *I have two single sisters.* —*noun, plural* **singles** In baseball, a hit that allows the batter to reach first base. —*verb* **singled, singling** **1.** To pick out or choose from others: *She singled out two students for praise.* **2.** In baseball, to hit a single: *He singled three times in the inning.*

sin·gu·lar |sĭng′gyə lər| —*adjective* Of a word that shows or stands for a single person or thing or a group that is thought of as one unit or item. For example, *he* is a singular pronoun, and *table* and *army* are singular nouns. —*noun, plural* **singulars** The form of a word that shows or stands for a single person or thing. For example, *army* is the singular of *armies.*

sin·is·ter |sĭn′ĭ stər| —*adjective* Evil or suggesting evil: *a sinister smile. The dirt road in the forest looks sinister at night.*

sink |sĭngk| —*verb* **sank** or **sunk, sunk** or **sunken, sinking** **1.** To go down or cause to go down below the surface or to the bottom of a liquid or soft substance: *The sled sank into the deep snow. Heavy storms can sink ships.* **2.** To appear to move downward: *The sun sank in the sky.* **3.** To dig or drill: *The men sank a hole for the swimming pool.* **4.** To force or drive into the ground: *We're sinking pegs for the tent.* **5.** To fall or move into a different state or condition: *She sank into a deep sleep.* **6.** To become less or weaker; diminish: *His voice sank to a whisper. Prices are sinking.* **7.** To seep or go completely into: *The rain could hardly sink into the hard dirt.* **8.** To become understood: *Doesn't anything I say ever sink into that head of yours?* —*noun, plural* **sinks** A basin with a drain and faucets for supplying water. It is used for washing.

sip |sĭp| —*verb* **sipped, sipping** To drink little by little: *We sipped the tea. Sip it because it's hot.* —*noun, plural* **sips** A little drink: *He took two sips.*

si·phon |sī′fən| —*noun, plural* **siphons** A tube or pipe that is bent in the shape of an upside-down U. It is used to move liquid from one container to another. When both ends are in a liquid with one container higher than the other, air pressure forces the liquid to move from the higher to the lower container. —*verb* **siphoned, siphoning** To move or transfer a liquid with a siphon: *We had to siphon some gas from another car.*

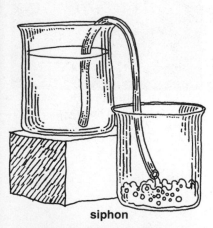

siphon

ă	pat	ĕ	pet	î	fierce
ā	pay	ē	be	ŏ	pot
â	care	ĭ	pit	ō	go
ä	father	ī	pie	ô	paw, for
oi	oil	ŭ	cut	zh	vision
ōō	book	û	fur	ə	ago, item,
ōō	boot	*th*	the		pencil, atom,
yōō	abuse	th	thin		circus
ou	out	hw	which	ər	butter

sir |sîr| —*noun, plural* **sirs** **1.** A title or form of address used in place of a man's name: *I said to the principal, "You wanted to see me, sir?"* **2. Sir** A title used before the name of a knight: *Sir Lancelot.*

Sire |sîr| —*noun, plural* **Sires** A title used when speaking to a king or emperor: *Kneeling before the throne, he said, "What is your command, Sire?"*

si·ren |sī′rən| —*noun, plural* **sirens** A device that makes a loud whistling sound or noise. It is used as a signal or warning: *The fire truck sped past, its siren ringing.*

sis·ter |sĭs′tər| —*noun, plural* **sisters** **1.** A girl or woman who has the same parents as another person. **2. a.** A fellow woman. **b.** A female member of the same group, club, profession, or religion. **3. Sister** A nun.

sis·ter·hood |sĭs′tər hŏŏd′| —*noun, plural* **sisterhoods** **1.** The close feeling or friendship between sisters or other women. **2.** A group of women who are united in an organization or club.

sis·ter-in-law |sĭs′tər ĭn lô′| —*noun, plural* **sisters-in-law** **1.** The sister of one's husband or wife. **2.** The wife of one's brother. **3.** The wife of the brother of one's husband or wife.

sis·ter·ly |sĭs′tər lē| —*adjective* Of or appropriate to a sister; warm and friendly: *She gave me a sisterly kiss.*

sit |sĭt| —*verb* **sat, sitting** **1.** To rest or be in a position with the back being upright and the weight of the body supported by the buttocks and not the feet: *He sat in a chair.* **2.** To cause to sit; seat: *They sat him at the head of the table.* **3.** To rest on a perch, as a bird does: *The bird was sitting on a branch.* **4.** To cover eggs so that they will hatch, as a chicken or hen does. **5.** To stay in one place and not be active or used: *That car has just been sitting in your garage since you bought it.*

site |sīt| —*noun, plural* **sites** The position or location of something: *My father is looking for a site to open a new store.*
♦ *These sound alike* **site, cite, sight.**

sit·u·ate |sĭch′ŏŏ āt′| —*verb* **situated, situating** To put in a certain spot or position; locate: *We situated the house next to the meadow.*

sit·u·a·tion |sĭch′ŏŏ ā′shən| —*noun, plural* **situations** A condition or combination of circumstances; the way events or things are at a certain time: *It was a bad situation because we had to wait for the bus and didn't have money to buy dinner.*

six |sĭks| —*noun, plural* **sixes** A number, written 6, that is equal to the sum of 5 + 1.
—*adjective* Being one more than five in number: *six cars.* The adjective **six** belongs to a class of words called **determiners.** They signal that a noun is coming.

six·teen |sĭks′tēn′| —*noun, plural* **sixteens** A number, written 16, that is equal to the sum of 10 + 6.
—*adjective* Being one more than fifteen in number: *sixteen apples.* The adjective **sixteen** belongs to a class of words called **determiners.** They signal that a noun is coming.

six·teenth |sĭks′tēnth′| —*noun, plural* **sixteenths** **1.** In a group of people or things that are numbered in order, the one that matches the number sixteen. **2.** One of sixteen equal parts, written ¹⁄₁₆.
—*adjective:* *the sixteenth boy in line.*

sixth |sĭksth| —*noun, plural* **sixths** **1.** In a group of people or

sister
A religious sister

things that are in numbered order, the one that matches the number six. **2.** One of six equal parts, written ⅙.
—*adjective:* the sixth bus in a row.

six·ti·eth | sĭks′tē ĭth | —*noun, plural* **sixtieths 1.** In a group of people or things that are in numbered order, the one that matches the number sixty. **2.** One of sixty equal parts, written ¹⁄₆₀.
—*adjective:* the sixtieth runner to cross the finish line.

six·ty | sĭks′tē | —*noun, plural* **sixties** A number, written 60, that is equal to the product of 10 × 6.
—*adjective* Being ten more than fifty in number: *sixty days.* The adjective **sixty** belongs to a class of words called **determiners.** They signal that a noun is coming.

size | sīz | —*noun, plural* **sizes 1.** The height, width, or length of something: *The size of our new car is much smaller than the old one.* **2.** Any of a series of measurements according to which many things are made: *What size shoes do you wear? Those nails are the wrong size, you need smaller ones.* **3.** Number or amount: *The size of our homework assignments is getting bigger.*

siz·zle | sĭz′əl | —*verb* **sizzled, sizzling** To make a hissing or crackling sound: *The steak sizzled on the grill.*

skate | skāt | —*noun, plural* **skates 1.** A boot or shoe that has a piece of metal shaped like a blade attached lengthwise to the sole; an ice skate. It is used for gliding over ice. **2.** A boot or shoe that has a set of four small wheels mounted under the sole; a roller skate. It is used for moving over a hard surface, such as pavement.
—*verb* **skated, skating** To glide or move over on skates.

skate·board | skāt′bôrd′ | or | skāt′bōrd′ | —*noun, plural* **skateboards** A short, narrow board that has a set of four roller-skate wheels mounted under it.

skat·er | skā′tər | —*noun, plural* **skaters** A person who skates.

skel·e·ton | skĕl′ĭ tən | —*noun, plural* **skeletons 1. a.** The internal framework of bones and cartilage that supports the body of all animals with backbones. Birds, fish, snakes, and human beings all have skeletons. **b.** The hard, outer covering of many animals without a backbone, such as a turtle. **2.** Any structure or framework that is used as a support. A tall building has a skeleton made of steel.

sketch | skĕch | —*noun, plural* **sketches 1.** A quick, rough drawing: *My father showed the architect a sketch of the type of house he wanted.* **2.** A short description, story, or play: *Give me a brief sketch of your background.*
—*verb* **sketched, sketching 1.** To make a sketch of: *He went to the park to sketch the trees.* **2.** To make a sketch or sketches: *We sat outside and sketched all afternoon.*

ski | skē | —*noun, plural* **skis** or **ski** One of a pair of long, narrow, flat runners that are attached to a boot or shoe. It is made out of wood, metal, or plastic and is used for gliding or traveling over snow.
—*verb* **skied, skiing, skis 1.** To glide or move on skis: *They've been skiing for three hours.* **2.** To travel over on skis: *I want to ski down the tallest mountain in the state.*

skid | skĭd | —*noun, plural* **skids** The act of slipping or sliding on a surface: *The car went into a skid on the icy road.*
—*verb* **skidded, skidding** To slip or slide over a slippery surface and lose control: *The sled skidded on a patch of ice.*

ski

ă	pat	ĕ	pet	î	fierce
ā	pay	ē	be	ŏ	pot
â	care	ĭ	pit	ō	go
ä	father	ī	pie	ô	paw, for

oi	oil	ŭ	cut	zh	vision
ŏŏ	book	û	fur	ə	ago, item,
ōō	boot	*th*	the		pencil, atom,
yōō	abuse	th	thin		circus
ou	out	hw	which	ər	butter

ski·er |skē′ər| —*noun, plural* **skiers** A person who skis.

skill |skĭl| —*noun, plural* **skills** **1.** The ability to do something well: *She has the skill of always giving good advice.* **2.** The ability or technique to do well in an art, sport, or trade. Such skill comes from study, practice, and experience: *music skills; tennis skills.*

skilled |skĭld| —*adjective* **1.** Having or using skill: *a skilled fisherman.* **2.** Requiring special ability or training: *a skilled job.*

skil·let |skĭl′ĭt| —*noun, plural* **skillets** A shallow frying pan with a long handle.

skill·ful |skĭl′fəl| —*adjective* **1.** Having or using skill: *a skillful carpenter.* **2.** Showing or requiring skill: *a skillful craft.*

skim |skĭm| —*verb* **skimmed, skimming** **1.** To remove floating matter from the surface of a liquid: *skim the cream off the top of the milk.* **2.** To move or glide lightly and quickly over: *The sailboat skimmed the lake.* **3.** To read or glance at quickly: *I'm skimming the book because I don't have time to read the whole thing.*

skim milk Milk from which the cream has been removed.

skin |skĭn| —*noun, plural* **skins** **1.** The tissue that forms the outer covering of the body of a person or animal. **2.** A hide or pelt removed from the body of an animal. A skin covered with hair is used to make fur coats. **3.** Any outer covering that is like skin: *the skin of an apple.*
—*verb* **skinned, skinning** **1.** To remove the skin from: *skin a sheep.* **2.** To hurt or injure by scraping the skin: *He fell and skinned his elbow.*

skin div·ing |dī′vĭng| Swimming underwater for long periods of time with the use of flippers, a mask, and equipment that allows a person to breathe, such as a snorkel or oxygen tank.

skin·ny |skĭn′ē| —*adjective* **skinnier, skinniest** Very thin: *a skinny child. Look at that dog's skinny legs.*

skip |skĭp| —*verb* **skipped, skipping** **1.** To move by springing or hopping on one foot and then the other: *children skipping around the park.* **2.** To jump over: *skip rope.* **3.** To pass quickly over or leave out: *They were skipping television channels, looking for the right program. The teacher skipped my name.* **4.** To be promoted in school beyond the next grade or level: *I skipped the fourth grade.*
—*noun, plural* **skips** A springing or hopping step.

skirt |skûrt| —*noun, plural* **skirts** **1.** A piece of woman's clothing that hangs down from the waist and is not divided between the legs. It is worn with a shirt, blouse, or sweater. **2.** That part of a dress, coat, or other piece of clothing that hangs from the waist down.
—*verb* **skirted, skirting** **1.** To form the border of; lie along or around: *The road skirts the lake.* **2.** To move or go around rather than across or through: *We skirted the playground on our way home.*

skull |skŭl| —*noun, plural* **skulls** The hard, bony framework of the head in animals with a backbone. It protects the brain and the bones of the face.

skunk |skŭnk| —*noun, plural* **skunks** An animal with black and white fur and a bushy tail. The skunk can spray a liquid that smells very bad.

sky |skī| —*noun, plural* **skies** The space or air above and around the earth that seems to cover it.

sky div·ing |dī′vĭng| The act or sport of jumping from an airplane and falling for a great distance before opening a parachute.

skin diving

skunk

sky diving

skyline

skyscraper

sky·light |skī′lĭt′| —*noun, plural* **skylights** A window in a ceiling or roof that lets in daylight.

sky·line |skī′līn′| —*noun, plural* **skylines** 1. The outline of mountains, a group of buildings, or other large objects as seen against the sky: *From the other side of the river we got a good view of the city's skyline.* 2. The line along which the earth and sky seem to meet; horizon: *We watched the sun sink below the skyline in the west.*

sky·scrap·er |skī′skrā′pər| —*noun, plural* **skyscrapers** A very tall building.

slab |slăb| —*noun, plural* **slabs** A broad, flat, thick piece of something: *a slab of cheese. The patio was made of slabs of rock.*

slack |slăk| —*adjective* **slacker, slackest** 1. Not lively; slow: *We were walking at a slack pace.* 2. Not tight; loose: *The tent tipped over because the ropes that tied it down were slack.*
—*noun, plural* **slacks** A loose or slack part: *Pick up the slack in the lamp cord and put it under the rug.*

slacks |slăks| —*plural noun* Long trousers or pants, worn by women and men.

slain |slān| The past participle of the verb **slay**: *When the battle was over, more than half the soldiers had been slain.*

slam |slăm| —*verb* **slammed, slamming** 1. To shut with force and a loud noise: *Don't slam the door.* 2. To throw, strike, or put down with force and a loud noise: *Eileen slammed the book on the table.* 3. To hit or crash into with force: *Rocks are always rolling down the hill and slamming into the fence.*
—*noun, plural* **slams** A hard and noisy striking or closing: *He shut the door with a slam.*

slang |slăng| —*noun* An informal or casual kind of language. It consists of new words and giving new or different meanings to old words. Slang changes continually. Years ago a policeman was called a "flatfoot." Two recent examples of slang are "to rap" for "to talk" and "groovy" for "exciting." Slang adds new energy and interest to the way people use language. You should use slang only in very casual situations, not in writing or formal speaking.

slant |slănt| or |slänt| —*verb* **slanted, slanting** To slope or lie at an angle away from a horizontal or vertical line: *My handwriting slants to the right.*
—*noun, plural* **slants** A sloping line or direction: *The driveway has a sharp slant so it's good for sledding.*

slap |slăp| —*verb* **slapped, slapping** To strike sharply with the palm of the hand or some other light, flat object: *He slapped his knee and laughed. Slap that mosquito.*
—*noun, plural* **slaps** A quick blow with the palm of the hand or other light, flat object: *a slap on the back.*

slash |slăsh| —*verb* **slashed, slashing** 1. To cut or strike with a forceful, sweeping stroke of a knife or other object: *The explorer slashed at the dense bushes with his knife. The boxer slashed at his opponent with his fists.* 2. To make a cut or cuts in: *Don't slash your feet on the rocks.* 3. To reduce or lower greatly: *Prices have been slashed on everything in the store.*
—*noun, plural* **slashes** 1. A forceful, sweeping stroke: *With a slash of his ax he cut the branch off the tree.* 2. A long cut on the skin or other surface; a gash: *How did you get such a big slash on your car?* 3. A sharp reduction or lowering: *The mayor said he had to make slashes in the city's budget.*

ă	pat	ĕ	pet	î	fierce
ā	pay	ē	be	ŏ	pot
â	care	ĭ	pit	ō	go
ä	father	ī	pie	ô	paw, for

oi	oil	ŭ	cut	zh	vision
ōō	book	û	fur	ə	ago, item,
ōō	boot	*th*	the		pencil, atom,
yōō	abuse	th	thin		circus
ou	out	hw	which	ər	butter

slat | slăt | —*noun, plural* **slats** A narrow strip or piece of wood or metal. They are used to make the backs of some chairs, in shutters, and Venetian blinds.

slate | slāt | —*noun* A kind of bluish-gray rock that splits easily into thin layers with smooth surfaces. It is used to make such things as blackboards and to cover roofs and patios.

slaugh·ter | slô′tər | —*noun, plural* **slaughters** **1.** The killing of animals for food: *The rancher raises cattle for slaughter.* **2.** The cruel and brutal murder of many persons or animals; massacre: *The army's attack resulted in the slaughter of the entire village.*
—*verb* **slaughtered, slaughtering** **1.** To butcher or kill animals for food: *The farmer slaughters cattle.* **2.** To kill brutally or in large numbers: *The soldiers slaughtered all the captured prisoners.*

slave | slāv | —*noun, plural* **slaves** **1.** A person who is owned by and forced to work for another person. **2.** Any person who works very hard and receives a low salary: *Many agricultural workers feel like slaves of the owners.*
—*verb* **slaved, slaving** To work very hard: *I slaved for days studying for this test.*

slav·er·y | slā′və rē | or | slāv′rē | —*noun* **1.** The condition of being a slave: *Before the Civil War most black people in the United States lived in slavery.* **2.** The practice of owning slaves: *Slavery in the United States was officially outlawed during the Civil War.*

slay | slā | —*verb* **slew, slain, slaying** To kill violently: *The king said to the stranger, "Slay the dragon."*
♦ *These sound alike* **slay, sleigh.**

sled | slĕd | —*noun, plural* **sleds** A vehicle mounted on runners. It is used for carrying people or cargo over ice and snow.
—*verb* **sledded, sledding** To carry or ride on a sled.

sledge·ham·mer | slĕj′hăm′ər | —*noun, plural* **sledgehammers** A long, heavy hammer that is held and used with both hands. It is used for driving posts into the ground and other heavy work.

sleek | slēk | —*adjective* **sleeker, sleekest** **1.** Smooth and shiny: *That horse has a sleek coat.* **2.** Looking neat, sharp, and graceful: *Did you see her sleek new racing car?*

sleep | slēp | —*noun* A kind of natural rest that occurs at regular times for human beings and animals. During sleep, the body regains strength and the mind does not respond to the things around it in the usual way. For example, noises may not be heard, or the sleeping person may respond as if they were part of his or her dream.
—*verb* **slept, sleeping** To be in or fall into a condition of sleep: *He was sleeping when the phone rang. That dog sleeps all day.*

sleep·ing bag | slē′pĭng | A large, warmly lined bag in which a person may sleep outdoors.

sleep·y | slē′pē | —*adjective* **sleepier, sleepiest** **1.** Ready for or needing sleep: *He's so sleepy he can't keep his eyes open.* **2.** Quiet or dull: *a sleepy little town.*

sleet | slēt | —*noun* Frozen or partially frozen rain.
—*verb* **sleeted, sleeting** To shower or rain down sleet.

sleeve | slēv | —*noun, plural* **sleeves** The part of a garment that covers all or part of the arm.

sleigh | slā | —*noun, plural* **sleighs** A light vehicle or carriage on metal runners. It is usually drawn by a horse and used for traveling on ice or snow.
♦ *These sound alike* **sleigh, slay.**

sled
A sled pulled by dogs

sledgehammer

sleigh

slen·der |slĕn′dər| —*adjective* **slenderer, slenderest 1.** Having little width; thin; slim: *a slender person; a slender tree.* **2.** Small in size or amount: *After doing poorly on the test she had only slender hopes of getting a good mark in math.*

slept |slĕpt| The past tense and past participle of the verb **sleep:** *I slept till noon. She had slept quietly during the storm.*

slew |slo͞o| The past tense of the verb **slay:** *The cowboy slew the wild coyote.*

slice |slīs| —*noun, plural* **slices** A thin, flat piece cut from something: *a slice of bread; a slice of pie.*
—*verb* **sliced, slicing 1.** To cut into slices; cut a slice of: *She's slicing a loaf of bread. Slice off a piece of ham, please.* **2.** To cut or move through like a knife: *The ship sliced through the water.*

slick |slĭk| —*adjective* **slicker, slickest 1.** Having a smooth, shiny surface: *Seals have slick fur.* **2.** Smooth and slippery: *The road is slick where the big truck leaked oil.*
—*noun, plural* **slicks** A smooth or slippery place: *Oil slicks on the ocean made by sinking tankers are a dangerous cause of pollution.*

slid |slĭd| The past tense and past participle of the verb **slide:** *We slid down the hill. The movers had slid the furniture into the room.*

slide |slīd| —*verb* **slid, sliding 1.** To move or cause to move smoothly over a surface: *Look at the pencil slide off the desk. The movers are sliding the furniture into the living room.* **2.** To move or fall out of position or control; slip: *Don't slide on the ice or you'll fall. The rope slid out of my hand.*
—*noun, plural* **slides 1.** A sliding action or movement: *You want to go for a slide on my new sled?* **2.** A slanted device with a smooth surface on which people or objects can slide: *There's a big and a small slide in the playground.* **3.** In baseball, the act of sliding into a base: *Did you see that slide?* **4.** A photographic picture on a transparent piece of material made to be projected or shown on a screen: *After dinner we looked at slides of our trip.* **5.** A small sheet of glass on which objects are put so they can be looked at under a microscope. **6.** The fall of a mass of snow, ice, or rock down a slope: *a rock slide.*

sli·er |slī′ər| A comparative of the adjective **sly.**

sli·est |slī′ĭst| A superlative of the adjective **sly.**

slight |slīt| —*adjective* **slighter, slightest 1.** Small in amount; not much: *There's been a slight change in temperature. There's a slight chance the sun will come out this afternoon.* **2.** Small in size; slender: *a slight old man.* **3.** Not important; small: *a slight problem; a slight headache.*
—*verb* **slighted, slighting** To insult or hurt someone's feelings: *Your friends will feel that they've been slighted if you don't invite them to the party.*

slim |slĭm| —*adjective* **slimmer, slimmest 1.** Thin or slender: *After his diet Marvin was slimmer than he'd ever been.* **2.** Small in amount; slight: *The senator won the election by a slim margin.*
—*verb* **slimmed, slimming** To make or become thinner: *I'm slimming my waist with exercises. The boxer has slimmed down since his last fight.*

sling |slĭng| —*noun, plural* **slings 1.** A strong looped rope, belt, or chain used to lift and move heavy objects: *The workers used a sling to unload the heavy crates from the ship.* **2.** A band or piece of cloth that is looped around the neck and used to support an injured arm or hand: *The doctor said I had to keep my arm in a sling*

slide

ă	pat	ĕ	pet	î	fierce
ā	pay	ē	be	ŏ	pot
â	care	ĭ	pit	ō	go
ä	father	ī	pie	ô	paw, for
oi	oil	ŭ	cut	zh	vision
o͝o	book	û	fur	ə	ago, item,
o͞o	boot	*th*	the		pencil, atom,
yo͞o	abuse	th	thin		circus
ou	out	hw	which	ər	butter

for a month. **3.** A weapon or device for throwing stones. It is made of a piece of leather with a strong string on each end. A stone is put in the piece of leather and the sling is twirled around by the strings and then let go.
—*verb* **slung, slinging** To put, carry, or hang in a sling: *Sling the sack over your shoulder and let's go.*

sling·shot | slĭng′shŏt′ | —*noun, plural* **slingshots** A Y-shaped stick with an elastic band attached to the ends of the prongs. It is used for shooting small stones.

slip¹ | slĭp | —*verb* **slipped, slipping** **1.** To move smoothly; slide or glide: *The fish slipped out of his hands.* **2.** To move or pass easily, quietly, or without being seen: *years and days slipping away. He slipped out of the room while she was on the phone.* **3.** To give to or put into quickly and easily: *Slip me the note when nobody's looking. Slip the key into the lock.* **4.** To put on or take off quickly and easily: *slip on a sweater; slipped off his shoes.* **5.** To lose one's balance on a slippery surface: *slip on the ice.* **6.** To move out of place or position: *The pole slipped and the tent collapsed.* **7.** To escape or get loose: *The dog is always slipping its leash.* **8.** To make a mistake: *Everyone slipped up on the last question.*
—*noun, plural* **slips** **1.** The act of slipping: *She took a slip in the bathtub.* **2.** A small mistake or error: *a slip of the tongue. If the party is to be a surprise, there must be no slips.*

slip² | slĭp | —*noun, plural* **slips** **1.** A small piece of paper or other material: *a shopping list on a slip of paper.* **2.** A part or shoot of a plant cut or broken off and used to grow a new plant.

slip·per | slĭp′ər | —*noun, plural* **slippers** A light, low shoe that may be slipped on and off easily. They are usually worn indoors.

slip·per·y | slĭp′ə rē | —*adjective* **slipperier, slipperiest** Likely to slip or to cause slipping: *I dropped the slippery bar of soap.*

slit | slĭt | —*noun, plural* **slits** A long, narrow cut, tear, or opening: *a slit between the boards of a fence.*
—*verb* **slit, slitting** To cut a slit or slits in: *She slit open the letter.*

sliv·er | slĭv′ər | —*noun, plural* **slivers** A thin, sharp-pointed piece that has been cut off or broken off from something: *Wear shoes so you won't get slivers of wood in your feet.*

slo·gan | slō′gən | —*noun, plural* **slogans** A phrase by a business, team, organization, or other group to advertise its purpose or aim; motto. A store may use a slogan such as "The customer is always right."

sloop | slōōp | —*noun, plural* **sloops** A sailboat with one mast and two sails, one in front and one in back.

slope | slōp | —*verb* **sloped, sloping** To be or make slanted: *The hills slope down to the edge of the river.*
—*noun, plural* **slopes** **1.** Any line, surface, or area that is not flat: *The children use the big slope for sledding.* **2.** The amount of slope: *The slope on the other side of the mountain is very steep.*

slop·py | slŏp′ē | —*adjective* **sloppier, sloppiest** **1.** Very wet or full of slush or mud: *sloppy ground. The roads are sloppy from all the rain.* **2.** Messy or untidy; not neat: *Why is your room always sloppier than your brother's?* **3.** Carelessly done; full of mistakes: *Your homework is getting very sloppy. He did a sloppy painting job.*

slot | slŏt | —*noun, plural* **slots** A long, narrow opening: *a slot for letters in a mailbox; a slot for money in a soda machine.*

sloth | slŏth | or | slôth | or | slōth | —*noun, plural* **sloths** An American animal of tropical regions. Sloths live in trees and hang

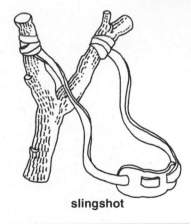

slingshot

sloth

slip¹, slip²
Slip¹ probably comes originally from a form of German. The origin of **slip²** is uncertain.

upside-down from the branches with their claws. They move very slowly.

slouch |slouch| —*verb* **slouched, slouching** To sit, stand, or walk with a bent or drooping posture.

—*noun, plural* **slouches** A bending or hanging down of the head and shoulders: *Don't walk with a slouch.*

slow |slō| —*adjective* **slower, slowest** **1.** Not moving or able to move quickly; going with little speed: *This is the slowest bus I've ever been in.* **2.** Taking or needing a long time or more time than usual: *We ate a slow, relaxing dinner. He's a slower worker than the other men.* **3.** Behind the correct time: *Your watch is slow.* **4.** Late or tardy: *The train is ten minutes slow.* **5.** Not quick to understand or learn; stupid: *I do well in English but I'm slow in science and math.*

—*adverb* **slower, slowest** In a slow manner; not quickly: *Drive slower, please.*

—*verb* **slowed, slowing** To make or become slow or slower: *He slowed the car as they drove past the church.*

slug¹ |slŭg| —*noun, plural* **slugs** **1.** A bullet or other piece of metal fired from a gun. **2.** A small, round piece of metal or fake coin that is illegally used instead of a coin in some machines: *Peter was caught using slugs in the candy machine.*

slug² |slŭg| —*noun, plural* **slugs** A land animal that is related to the snails. It has a soft body, but no shell.

slug³ |slŭg| —*verb* **slugged, slugging** To hit or strike hard: *She slugged him in the stomach. He slugged two home runs.*

—*noun, plural* **slugs** A hard blow, especially with the fist: *Watch it or you'll get a slug in the face.*

sluice |slōōs| —*noun, plural* **sluices** **1.** A man-made channel for water with a gate or valve to control the amount of water that flows through it. **2.** A channel that is used to carry off excess or overflow water. **3.** A slanted channel or trough that is used for such things as floating logs or separating ore from dirt.

slum |slŭm| —*noun, plural* **slums** A poor, run-down, overly crowded area or section of a city. Bad living conditions and bad housing are two serious problems that are found in slums.

slum·ber |slŭm'bər| —*verb* **slumbered, slumbering** To sleep or doze: *He slumbered through the movie.*

—*noun, plural* **slumbers** A sleep or rest: *I awoke from slumber.*

slump |slŭmp| —*verb* **slumped, slumping** To fall or sink suddenly; sag or slouch: *The ice-cream store's business usually slumps in the winter. He slumped in a chair.*

—*noun, plural* **slumps** A sudden fall or decline: *The saleswoman said there was a slump in sales. The team went into a slump and lost eleven games in a row.*

slung |slŭng| The past tense and past participle of the verb **sling:** *He slung the knapsack onto his back. We had slung the knapsacks onto our backs before departing.*

slush |slŭsh| —*noun* Partly melted snow or ice.

sly |slī| —*adjective* **slier** or **slyer, sliest** or **slyest** **1.** Clever or tricky; shrewd: *a sly plan. The sly child took the cookies while his mother wasn't looking.* **2.** Playfully mischievous: *a sly smile.*

smack |smăk| —*verb* **smacked, smacking** **1.** To make a sharp sound by pressing the lips together and opening them quickly: *He smacked his lips watching the waiter make the ice-cream sundae.* **2.** To kiss noisily: *After the dance was over, Steven smacked Paula*

slug¹, slug², slug³

Slug¹ probably came from **slug²**, because of its similarity in shape. **Slug²** comes from an earlier English word for a slow-moving person or animal. Its earlier source was probably a Scandinavian word used long ago. **Slug³** perhaps came from **slug¹**, in the sense "a bullet."

sluice

ă	pat	ĕ	pet	î	fierce
ā	pay	ē	be	ŏ	pot
â	care	ĭ	pit	ō	go
ä	father	ī	pie	ô	paw, for
oi	oil	ŭ	cut	zh	vision
ōō	book	û	fur	ə	ago, item,
ōō	boot	*th*	the		pencil, atom,
yōō	abuse	th	thin		circus
ou	out	hw	which	ər	butter

on the cheek. **3.** To slap or bump with a loud sound: *She smacked the table. He's always smacking into things.*
—noun, plural **smacks 1.** The sound made by smacking the lips. **2.** A noisy kiss. **3.** A sharp blow or loud slap: *The man gave his forehead a smack when he remembered the answer.*
—adverb Directly or squarely; straight into: *She tripped and fell smack in the middle of the mud puddle.*

small |smôl| *—adjective* **smaller, smallest 1.** Not as big in size, number, or amount as other things of the same kind; little: *a small car; a small city.* **2.** Not important: *We had a small problem about who was going to sit next to grandfather.* **3.** Soft or low; weak: *The little girl has such a small voice.* **4.** Mean or selfish: *Not letting your brother play with you was a small thing to do.*
—noun Something that is smaller than the rest: *the small of the back.*

small intestine The part of the digestive system that lies between the stomach and the large intestine. It completes the process of breaking down food, or digestion, and releases the substances needed by the body into the blood.

small letter A letter, such as *a, b,* or *c,* written or printed in a size smaller than the same capital letter, such as *A, B,* or *C.*

small·pox |smôl′pŏks′| *—noun* A serious, very contagious disease that is often fatal. It is characterized by chills, high fever, headaches, and pimples that can leave scars on the skin.

smart |smärt| *—adjective* **smarter, smartest 1.** Intelligent or bright; clever: *Benjy is the smartest student in the class. You have to be pretty smart to answer that question.* **2.** Sharp and quick; brisk; lively: *The parade moved down the street at a smart pace.* **3.** Fashionable or stylish: *My sister bought a smart new dress for the big dance.* **4.** Neat and trim: *smart troops.*
—verb **smarted, smarting 1.** To feel or cause to feel a sharp pain: *My leg smarted from the bee sting. The bruise on my shoulder smarts.* **2.** To feel distress or hurt: *He was smarting from being yelled at.*

smash |smăsh| *—verb* **smashed, smashing 1.** To break or be broken into pieces: *He smashed the glass on the floor. The egg smashed.* **2.** To throw or strike violently or suddenly: *The wind smashed the tree into the house. The car smashed into a truck.*
—noun, plural **smashes 1.** The act or sound of smashing: *Did you see the smash he hit for a home run? What was that smash I just heard?* **2.** A collision; crash: *Two cars had a big smash.*

smear |smîr| *—verb* **smeared, smearing 1.** To spread, cover, or stain with a sticky or greasy substance: *Dirt and soot smeared the windows. This lipstick smears easily.* **2.** To spread something wet or sticky on something else: *She smeared the bread with peanut butter.* **3.** To be or become or cause to be or become dirty, messy, or blurred: *The wet paint will smear if you touch it. Robin smeared the ink before it was dry.* **4.** To harm a person's reputation: *Don't smear him by repeating those lies that he's a thief.*
—noun, plural **smears** A stain or smudge made by smearing: *There are pencil smears on the wall.*

smell |smĕl| *—verb* **smelled** or **smelt, smelling 1.** To recognize or discover the odor of something by using the nose: *I smell smoke.* **2.** To use the nose for smelling; sniff: *Don't smell your food, eat it.* **3. a.** To have or give off an odor: *The roses smell pretty.* **b.** To have or give off a bad or unpleasant odor; stink: *This room smells.*

—*noun, plural* **smells** **1.** The sense by which odors are recognized; the ability to smell: *My dog's sense of smell is a lot better than mine.* **2.** The odor of something; scent: *I love the smell of pine trees.*

smelt¹ | smĕlt | —*verb* **smelted, smelting** To melt ores in order to separate or remove the metal or metals in them.

smelt² | smĕlt | A past tense and a past participle of the verb **smell:** *I thought I smelt something cooking. The dog had smelt smoke and was upset.*

smile | smīl | —*noun, plural* **smiles** An expression on the face that is formed by turning up the corners of the mouth. It shows that a person is happy, pleased, amused, or being friendly.

—*verb* **smiled, smiling** To have, form, or give a smile: *He smiled when she kissed him.*

smock | smŏk | —*noun, plural* **smocks** A garment that is made like a long, loose shirt. It is worn over clothes to protect them: *Put on your smock if you're going to paint.*

smog | smŏg | or | smôg | —*noun* Fog that has become mixed with and polluted by smoke. Smog is produced by such things as factories and automobiles. It looks like a thin, gray cloud.

smoke | smōk | —*noun, plural* **smokes** A mixture of carbon and other gases that is given off by something burning. It contains tiny particles of soot and other substances that make it look like a cloud rising in the air.

—*verb* **smoked, smoking** **1.** To give off or produce smoke: *Is the car engine smoking?* **2.** To draw in and blow out smoke from tobacco: *She's always telling me I smoke too much.* **3.** To preserve meat by exposing it to or treating it with wood smoke: *Did you see him smoking hams?*

smok·er | smō′kər | —*noun, plural* **smokers** **1.** A person who smokes tobacco. **2.** A railroad car in which smoking is permitted.

smoke·stack | smōk′stăk′ | —*noun, plural* **smokestacks** A large chimney or pipe through which smoke escapes or is released. They are used on large ships and factories.

smok·y | smō′kē | —*adjective* **smokier, smokiest** **1.** Producing or giving off a lot of smoke: *a smoky campfire; a smoky furnace.* **2.** Filled, mixed, or polluted with smoke: *smoky air.*

smooth | smo͞oth | —*adjective* **smoother, smoothest** **1.** Having a surface that is not rough; even: *smooth skin; smooth wood.* **2.** Having an even or gentle motion; free from jolts and bumps: *That was the smoothest ride I ever had in an airplane.* **3.** Not having lumps: *smooth ice cream.* **4.** Agreeable and mild; polite: *The dentist has such a smooth manner that I never get scared.*

—*verb* **smoothed, smoothing** **1.** To make level, flat, or even: *I'm smoothing out the wrinkles in my dress.* **2.** To soothe or make calm; make easy: *He smoothed out the problem between his brothers.*

smoth·er | smŭ*th*′ər | —*verb* **smothered, smothering** **1.** To die or cause someone to die from lack of air: *You'll smother the dog if you keep holding that blanket over its head. A lot of miners smothered when they were trapped in the mine.* **2.** To go out or cause a fire to go out from lack of air: *Smother the campfire with dirt.* **3.** To cover thickly: *He smothered the ice cream with fudge sauce.* **4.** To hide or keep back: *When he tripped, I had to smother a laugh.*

smudge | smŭj | —*verb* **smudged, smudging** To make or become dirty; smear or blur: *The cat smudged the floor with dirty paws. The chalk smudges easily.*

smokestack
On a locomotive

ă	pat	ĕ	pet	î	fierce
ā	pay	ē	be	ŏ	pot
â	care	ĭ	pit	ō	go
ä	father	ī	pie	ô	paw, for
oi	oil	ŭ	cut	zh	vision
o͝o	book	û	fur	ə	ago, item,
o͞o	boot	*th*	the		pencil, atom,
yo͞o	abuse	th	thin		circus
ou	out	hw	which	ər	butter

—*noun, plural* **smudges** A dirty mark; a blotch or smear: *Who left all the smudges on the table?*

smug |smŭg| —*adjective* **smugger, smuggest** Believing that one is smarter and can do things better than other people; pleased with oneself: *He didn't look so smug after losing the tennis match.*

smug·gle |smŭg′əl| —*verb* **smuggled, smuggling** **1.** To take, bring, or put secretly: *He tried to smuggle his dog into the movie theater.* **2.** To bring in or take out of a country secretly and illegally: *people smuggling guns across the border.*

snack |snăk| —*noun, plural* **snacks** A small, light meal or a small portion of food or drink eaten between regular meals.

snail |snāl| —*noun, plural* **snails** A land or water animal that has a shell in the shape of a spiral. Snails move slowly. They have soft bodies and often have eyes on stalks that stick out from their heads like horns.

snake |snāk| —*noun, plural* **snakes** A reptile that has a long, narrow body and no legs. Some kinds of snakes can give a poisonous bite.

snap |snăp| —*verb* **snapped, snapping** **1.** To make or cause to make a sharp cracking sound: *The wood in the fireplace snapped as it burned. Snap your fingers.* **2.** To break or cause to break suddenly and sharply: *We snapped the twigs with our feet as we walked. The rope snapped.* **3.** To seize or grab at eagerly or with a snatching motion: *The dog is always snapping at strangers.* **4.** To speak sharply or angrily: *His father snapped at him because he got his good clothes dirty.* **5.** To move or act quickly: *The soldiers snapped to attention.* **6.** To open or close with a click: *The lid snapped shut.* **7.** To take a photograph: *Snap my picture.*
—*noun, plural* **snaps** **1.** A sharp cracking sound: *What was that snap I heard?* **2.** A sudden breaking of something that is under pressure: *the snap of a rope.* **3.** A fastener or clasp that opens and closes with a snapping sound: *You need new snaps on your raincoat.* **4.** A thin, crisp cooky: *ginger snaps.* **5.** A short period of cold weather: *a cold snap.* **6.** A task or job that is easy.
—*adjective* Made or done quickly or suddenly and with little thought: *Don't make snap judgments about people you don't know.*

snap·drag·on |snăp′drăg′ən| —*noun, plural* **snapdragons** A garden plant with bunches of colorful flowers. Each flower has a narrow opening that looks like a mouth. When the side of the flower is pressed, the flower opens and closes like the mouth of a dragon.

snap·shot |snăp′shŏt′| —*noun, plural* **snapshots** An informal photograph taken with a small camera: *snapshots of the baby.*

snare |snâr| —*noun, plural* **snares** A trap for catching birds and small animals. It has a noose that grabs and holds the bird or animal tightly when the trap is set off.
—*verb* **snared, snaring** To trap in or as if in a snare.

snarl[1] |snärl| —*noun, plural* **snarls** An angry growl, often made with bare teeth showing: *The coyote attacked with a fierce snarl.*
—*verb* **snarled, snarling** **1.** To growl, especially while showing teeth: *The dog pulled on the chain and snarled at everyone who passed by.* **2.** To speak in an angry way: *Mr. Smith is always snarling at the children for walking across his lawn.*

snarl[2] |snärl| —*noun, plural* **snarls** **1.** A tangled mass: *How did your hair get full of snarls?* **2.** A confused or complicated situation: *a traffic snarl.*

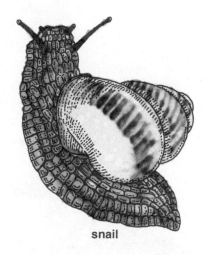

snail

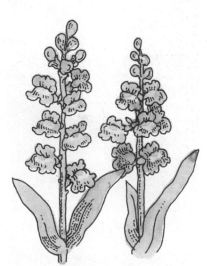

snapdragon

snarl[1], snarl[2]
Snarl[1] comes from *snar*, a word no longer in use, which meant "to snarl." Its earlier source was a word that appeared in a form of German. **Snarl[2]** came from a different English word and is probably related to **snare**.

—*verb* **snarled, snarling** **1.** To tangle or become tangled: *The kitten snarled the ball of yarn. My hair snarls in the wind.* **2.** To make or become confused: *Snow snarled the traffic.*

snatch |snăch| —*verb* **snatched, snatching** **1.** To grab or try to grab suddenly and quickly: *He snatched an apple off the tree.* **2.** To take or steal: *He snatched purses in the park.*
—*noun, plural* **snatches** **1.** The act of snatching: *He made a snatch at the ball as it flew over his head.* **2.** A small amount; a little bit: *I heard snatches of their conversation from the other room.*

sneak |snēk| —*verb* **sneaked, sneaking** To act, move, or take in a quiet, secret way: *He sneaked onto one of the boats. She tried to sneak him into the class.*
—*noun, plural* **sneaks** A tricky, cowardly, or dishonest person: *How did that sneak find out where I hid the present?*

sneak·ers |snē′kərz| —*plural noun* Cloth or leather sport shoes with soft rubber soles.

sneer |snîr| —*noun, plural* **sneers** A look or statement of contempt or scorn: *He raised one corner of his upper lip in a sneer.*
—*verb* **sneered, sneering** To show contempt or say with a sneer: *The boys sneered at Jeff's shabby clothes.*

sneeze |snēz| —*verb* **sneezed, sneezing** To cause air to pass with force from the nose and mouth. A sneeze occurs by itself because of a tickling feeling inside the nose: *The dust made her sneeze.*
—*noun, plural* **sneezes** The act of sneezing.

snick·er |snĭk′ər| —*noun, plural* **snickers** A partly hidden laugh indicating scorn, lack of respect, or amusement at something not funny: *We heard a snicker from the back of the room.*
—*verb* **snickered, snickering** To laugh in this manner: *We knew it was wrong to snicker when Betsy gave the wrong answer.*

sniff |snĭf| —*verb* **sniffed, sniffing** **1.** To breathe air into the nose in short breaths that can be heard: *The boy still sniffed loudly after he stopped crying.* **2.** To smell by sniffing: *Jill sniffed the roses.*
—*noun, plural* **sniffs** The act of sniffing: *The dog took a sniff at his dinner.*

snif·fle |snĭf′əl| —*verb* **sniffled, sniffling** To breathe noisily through the nose, as when suffering from a head cold: *The baby sniffled after he was spanked.*
—*noun* **the sniffles** A head cold that makes someone sniffle: *Jim was out in the rain and now has the sniffles.*

snip |snĭp| —*verb* **snipped, snipping** To cut with short, quick strokes: *The mayor snipped the ribbon and opened the new highway.*
—*noun, plural* **snips** **1.** A small piece cut off: *a snip of hair.* **2.** The act of snipping: *a few snips of the scissors.*

snipe |snīp| —*noun, plural* **snipe** or **snipes** A brownish bird that has a long bill and wades in swamps and marshes.

snob |snŏb| —*noun, plural* **snobs** Someone who feels he or she is better than others and avoids people he or she feels do not have money and social position.

snore |snôr| or |snōr| —*verb* **snored, snoring** To breathe loudly through the mouth and nose while sleeping: *My brother snores.*
—*noun, plural* **snores** A loud breathing noise made while sleeping.

snor·kel |snôr′kəl| —*noun, plural* **snorkels** A plastic breathing tube and mouthpiece used to breathe underwater.

snort |snôrt| —*noun, plural* **snorts** A rough, noisy sound made by a loud breath out of the nose: *The pig gave a snort.*

snipe

snorkel

ă	pat	ĕ	pet	î	fierce
ā	pay	ē	be	ŏ	pot
â	care	ĭ	pit	ō	go
ä	father	ī	pie	ô	paw, for

oi	oil	ŭ	cut	zh	vision
ŏŏ	book	û	fur	ə	ago, item,
ōō	boot	*th*	the		pencil, atom,
yōō	abuse	th	thin		circus
ou	out	hw	which	ər	butter

—*verb* **snorted, snorting** To breathe loudly through the nose: *The frightened horses snorted and ran.*

snout |snout| —*noun, plural* **snouts** The long nose, jaws, or front part of the head of an animal. Pigs and alligators have snouts.

snow |snō| —*noun, plural* **snows** **1.** Soft white crystals of ice that form from water vapor high in the air and fall to the ground. **2.** A falling of snow; a snowstorm. —*verb* **snowed, snowing** **1.** To fall to earth as snow: *It snowed all last night.* **2.** To block or cover with snow: *During the last blizzard we were snowed in for three days and nights.*

snow·flake |snō′flāk′| —*noun, plural* **snowflakes** A single crystal of snow.

snow·man |snō′măn′| —*noun, plural* **snowmen** A figure like that of a person, made from packed and shaped snow.

snow·mo·bile |snō′mō bēl′| —*noun, plural* **snowmobiles** A machine like a sled with a motor, used for traveling over ice and snow.

snow·plow |snō′plou′| —*noun, plural* **snowplows** A machine used to remove snow from roads, sidewalks, and railroad tracks.

snow·shoe |snō′shōō′| —*noun, plural* **snowshoes** A light, racket-shaped frame strung with strips of leather or rawhide. Snowshoes are worn under the shoe and used to keep the feet from sinking into deep snow.

snow·storm |snō′stôrm′| —*noun, plural* **snowstorms** A storm with a heavy fall of snow and strong winds; a blizzard.

snow·y |snō′ē| —*adjective* **snowier, snowiest** **1.** Full of or covered with snow: *snowy roads.* **2.** White like snow: *snowy flowers.*

snug |snŭg| —*adjective* **snugger, snuggest** **1.** Pleasant and comfortable; cozy: *The fireplace made the house snug on cold days.* **2.a.** Fitting closely; tight: *a snug sweater; a snug shoe.* **b.** Close or tight: *a snug fit.*

snug·gle |snŭg′əl| —*verb* **snuggled, snuggling** To press close; nestle: *The children snuggled together under the covers.*

so |sō| —*adverb* **1.** In the way or manner shown, stated, or understood: *He got sick last week and has been so ever since.* **2.** To such a degree: *I'm so happy that I could cry.* **3.** To a great extent: *You're so silly.* **4.** As a result; therefore: *He never studied and so he failed the test.* **5.** Likewise; also; too: *She liked the book and so did I.* **6.** Very much: *My head aches so.* **7.** Very: *You are so nice.*
—*adjective* True: *I wouldn't have told you this if it weren't so.*
—*conjunction* **1.** In order that: *She came early so she could talk to him.* **2.** With the result that; and therefore: *He failed to show up, so we went without him.*
—*interjection* A word used to show surprise or understanding: *So, you finished on time after all.*
♦ *These sound alike* **so, sew, sow**[1].

soak |sōk| —*verb* **soaked, soaking** **1.** To wet thoroughly; make very wet: *I soaked my blouse in a bleach solution in order to get the stains out. The beans soaked overnight.* **2.** To absorb; take in: *Sponges soak up moisture.* **3.** To let lie in water or other liquid: *Louise soaked the beans before cooking them.*

soap |sōp| —*noun, plural* **soaps** A substance used for washing and cleaning things. It is usually made from fat and lye and is

snowmobile

snowshoe

soccer

sock¹, sock²

Sock¹ was *socc* in old English; the word referred to a kind of light shoe. Earlier the word came from Latin; the Latin word probably came from Greek. The origin of **sock²** is obscure.

soda fountain

ă	pat	ĕ	pet	î	fierce
ā	pay	ē	be	ŏ	pot
â	care	ĭ	pit	ō	go
ä	father	ī	pie	ô	paw, for
oi	oil	ŭ	cut	zh	vision
ŏŏ	book	û	fur	ə	ago, item,
ōō	boot	*th*	the		pencil, atom,
yōō	abuse	th	thin		circus
ou	out	hw	which	ər	butter

made in the form of bars, grains, flakes, or liquids.
—*verb* **soaped, soaping** To rub or cover with soap.

soap·y | sō′pē | —*adjective* **soapier, soapiest** Covered or filled with soap: *soapy water.*

soar | sôr | or | sōr | —*verb* **soared, soaring** To fly at great height; fly upward: *The hawk soared by gliding on air currents.*
♦ *These sound alike* **soar, sore.**

sob | sŏb | —*verb* **sobbed, sobbing** To cry aloud with gasping, short breaths: *She sobbed when her dog got hit by a car.*
—*noun, plural* **sobs** The act or sound of sobbing.

so·ber | sō′bər | —*adjective* **soberer, soberest** **1.** Not drunk: *If you are not sober, you should not drive.* **2.** Serious; grave; solemn: *From her sober expression, I knew something was wrong.* **3.** Not gay or frivolous: *The Puritans led a sober life.*

soc·cer | sŏk′ər | —*noun, plural* **soccers** A game played with two teams, on a field, with a ball. The object is to get the ball into the opposing team's goal by kicking it or striking it with any part of the body except the hands or arms.

so·cia·ble | sō′shə bəl | —*adjective* Liking other people; liking company; friendly: *a sociable person.*

so·cial | sō′shəl | —*adjective* **1.** Of or dealing with human beings as a group: *History is a social study.* **2.** Living with others and liking it: *Humans are social beings.* **3.** Of, for, or in the company of others: *a social evening; a social club.* **4.** Liking company; sociable: *He has a social nature.* **5.** Of or occupied with working with people in the community: *a social worker.* **6.** Of or dealing with the activities of rich or famous people: *You will find a description of the wedding in the social pages of the newspaper.*

so·cial·ism | sō′shə lĭz′əm | —*noun, plural* **socialisms** An economic system in which businesses, factories, farms, and other means of producing and distributing goods are owned by the people as a whole and managed by the government.

so·cial·ist | sō′shə lĭst | —*noun, plural* **socialists** A person who believes in socialism.

so·ci·e·ty | sə sī′ĭ tē | —*noun, plural* **societies** **1.** A group of human beings living and working together: *Laws exist to protect society.* **2.** The rich and fashionable people of a particular place. **3.** A group of people sharing mutual goals and interests: *Several people in our town formed a society to preserve its historical sites.*

sock¹ | sŏk | —*noun, plural* **socks** or **sox** A short covering for the foot and the leg reaching no higher than the knee.

sock² | sŏk | —*verb* **socked, socking** To hit forcefully; punch.

sock·et | sŏk′ĭt | —*noun, plural* **sockets** A hollow part for receiving and holding something: *a light bulb socket; a candlestick socket. Her eyes are set deep in their sockets.*

sod | sŏd | —*noun, plural* **sods** **1.** Grass and soil forming the surface of the ground. **2.** A piece of such soil held together by matted roots and removed from the ground: *a roof made of sod.*

so·da | sō′də | —*noun, plural* **sodas** **1.** A soft drink containing carbonated water. **2.** A drink made with carbonated water, flavoring, and sometimes ice cream.

soda fountain A counter equipped for preparing and serving sodas, sandwiches, and other quick dishes.

soda water Carbonated water used in making drinks.

so·di·um | sō′dē əm | —*noun* A soft, silver-white metal that reacts violently with water. Sodium can be found in common salt.

Sodium is one of the chemical elements.

so·fa | sō′fə | —*noun, plural* **sofas** A long, upholstered seat with a back and arms. A sofa can seat two or more people.

soft | sôft | or | sŏft | —*adjective* **softer, softest** **1.** Not hard or firm: *soft snow; a soft pillow.* **2.** Out of condition; weak: *His leg muscles are soft from lack of exercise.* **3.** Smooth, fine, or pleasing to the touch: *the soft fur of the kitten; a soft fabric.* **4.** Not loud: *soft music.* **5.** Not brilliant or glaring: *soft lights; soft colors.*

soft·ball | sôft′bôl′ | or | sŏft′bôl′ | —*noun, plural* **softballs** **1.** A game similar to baseball but played with a slightly larger, softer ball that is thrown by the pitcher with the palm of the hand turned upward. **2.** The ball used in this sport.

soft drink A sweet drink that contains no alcohol and is made with carbonated water.

soft·en | sô′fən | or | sŏf′ən | —*verb* **softened, softening** To make or become soft or softer: *The nurse softened the baby's skin with a lotion. Butter softens in heat.*

sog·gy | sŏg′ē | —*adjective* **soggier, soggiest** Soaked with moisture; wet and heavy: *soggy bread; a soggy sponge.*

soil¹ | soil | —*noun, plural* **soils** **1.** The loose top layer of the earth's surface suitable for growth of plant life. **2.** Land; country: *The soldiers longed to return to their native soil.*

soil² | soil | —*verb* **soiled, soiling** To make or become dirty: *He soiled his hands repairing the car. This fabric soils easily.*

so·lar | sō′lər | —*adjective* **1.** Of or coming from the sun: *a solar eclipse; solar energy.* **2.** Measured with respect to the sun: *solar time.*

solar system The sun and all the planets and their satellites, comets, and other heavenly bodies that orbit around the sun.

sold | sōld | The past tense and past participle of the verb **sell:** *She sold ten books yesterday.*

sol·der | sŏd′ər | —*noun, plural* **solders** A metal that can be melted and used to join two metal pieces together.
—*verb* **soldered, soldering** To mend or fasten with solder.

sol·dier | sōl′jər | —*noun, plural* **soldiers** A person who serves in the army.

sole¹ | sōl | —*noun, plural* **soles** **1.** The bottom surface of the foot. **2.** The bottom surface of a shoe or boot.
—*verb* **soled, soling** To put a sole on a shoe or boot.
♦ *These sound alike* **sole, soul.**

sole² | sōl | —*adjective* **1.** Being the only one; single; only: *her sole purpose in life.* **2.** Belonging only to one person or group: *His sole responsibility was to organize the party. Their sole function was to provide clothes for the needy. He was the dog's sole master.*
♦ *These sound alike* **sole, soul.**

sole³ | sōl | —*noun, plural* **sole** or **soles** A flat fish that is related to the flounder. Sole are good to eat.
♦ *These sound alike* **sole, soul.**

sol·emn | sŏl′əm | —*adjective* **1.** Very serious and grave: *a solemn promise; a solemn occasion.* **2.** Having the impact of a religious ceremony; sacred: *a solemn oath.* **3.** Performed with great ceremony: *a solemn Mass.*

sol·id | sŏl′ĭd | —*adjective* **1.** Having a definite shape; not liquid or gaseous. **2.** Not hollowed out: *a solid chunk of chocolate.* **3.** Being the same material or color throughout: *These are solid silver plates. The fabric is solid black.* **4.** Without breaks;

sofa

soldier

soil¹, soil²
Soil¹ comes through French from a Latin word meaning "seat." Soil² also traveled through French, from a Latin word meaning "little pig."

sole¹, sole², sole³
Sole¹ came to English from the French word *sole.* The French word in turn came from a Latin word meaning "bottom, ground, sole of the foot." Sole² came by the same route from the Latin word meaning "alone, single." Sole³ came from the French word for the fish; sole³ was taken originally from **sole¹** because of the shape of the fish.

continuous: *He talked for a solid hour.* **5.** Very strong and well made: *Their house has a solid foundation.* **6.** Of sound character; reliable; respectable: *a solid citizen.*
—*noun, plural* **solids** A substance that has a definite shape and is not a liquid or a gas.

sol·i·tar·y |sŏl′ ĭ tĕr′ē| —*adjective* **1.** Existing or living alone: *a solitary traveler.* **2.** Happening, done, or passed alone: *a solitary evening.* **3.** Seldom visited; lonely: *a solitary place; a solitary beach.*

so·lo |sō′lō| —*noun, plural* **solos** **1.** A musical composition to be played or sung by a single performer, with or without accompaniment. **2.** Any performance by a single person: *a dance solo.*
—*adjective* Done or performed without accompaniment, a partner, or an instructor: *her first solo flight.*

sol·u·ble |sŏl′yə bəl| —*adjective* Able to be dissolved in a liquid: *a soluble salt.*

so·lu·tion |sə lōō′shən| —*noun, plural* **solutions** **1.** A liquid or mixture formed by dissolving a substance in a liquid: *When you dissolve salt in water, you get a solution.* **2.** The solving of a problem: *It was a difficult problem, but you finally got the correct solution.*

solve |sŏlv| —*verb* **solved, solving** To find an answer or solution to: *She was very good at solving math problems.*

som·ber |sŏm′bər| —*adjective* **1.** Dark; dull: *a somber sky.* **2.** Gloomy; melancholy: *the somber expression in their faces.*

some |sŭm| —*adjective* **1.** Of a number or quantity not known or named; a few; a little: *I saw some people there. Please buy me some sugar.* **2.** A certain or particular, but not known or named: *Some woman called and wanted to speak to you.* The adjective **some** belongs to a class of words called **determiners.** They signal that a noun is coming.
—*adverb* Approximately; about: *some ten people on the bus.*
—*pronoun* A number or quantity not known or named: *There were some who came very late. We have coffee — do you want some?*
♦ *These sound alike* **some, sum.**

some·bod·y |sŭm′bŏd′ē| or |sŭm′bŭd′ē| or |sŭm′bə dē|
—*pronoun* A person who is not known or named; someone: *Somebody has been here, but who?*

some·day |sŭm′dā′| —*adverb* At some time in the future: *We will go to California someday soon.*

some·how |sŭm′hou′| —*adverb* **1.** In a way that is not known or stated; in one way or another: *The early scientists knew that blood and food were somehow related.* **2.** For some reason: *Somehow I can't get mad at him.*

some·one |sŭm′wŭn′| or |sŭm′wən| —*pronoun* A person who is not known or named; somebody: *Someone called you.*

som·er·sault |sŭm′ər sôlt′| —*noun, plural* **somersaults** The act of rolling the body in a complete circle, heels over head.
—*verb* **somersaulted, somersaulting** To perform a somersault.

some·thing |sŭm′thĭng| —*pronoun* **1.** A particular thing or things that are not named: *The child wants something to play with.* **2.** A particular thing that is not known or understood: *Something's wrong with his car.*
—*adverb* To some extent or degree; somewhat; rather: *She looks something like her older sister.*

some·time |sŭm′tīm′| —*adverb* At a time that is not known or

ă	pat	ĕ	pet	î	fierce
ā	pay	ē	be	ŏ	pot
â	care	ĭ	pit	ō	go
ä	father	ī	pie	ô	paw, for
oi	oil	ŭ	cut	zh	vision
ōō	book	û	fur	ə	ago, item,
ōō	boot	*th*	the		pencil, atom,
yōō	abuse	th	thin		circus
ou	out	hw	which	ər	butter

named: *Come and see us sometime. We had a heavy snowstorm sometime last winter.*

some·times |sŭm′tīmz′| —*adverb* Now and then: *I see them sometimes but not often.*

some·what |sŭm′hwät| or |sŭm hwät′| —*adverb* To some extent or degree; rather: *My dress is somewhat like yours.*

some·where |sŭm′hwĕr′| —*adverb* **1.** In, at, or to a place that is not known or named: *I found this turtle somewhere near the edge of the swamp.* **2.** Approximately; about: *His suit cost somewhere around fifty dollars.* **3.** At some time that is not known or named: *It happened somewhere about eighty years ago.*
—*noun* A place that is not known or named: *Find somewhere to sit down.*

son |sŭn| —*noun, plural* **sons** A male child.
♦ *These sound alike* **son, sun.**

so·nar |sō′när′| —*noun, plural* **sonars** A system that uses sound waves to discover underwater objects and find out where they are.

song |sông| or |sŏng| —*noun, plural* **songs** **1.** A musical piece that is meant to be sung by the human voice. **2.** The call like music that is made by a bird.

song·bird |sông′bûrd′| or |sŏng′bûrd′| —*noun, plural* **songbirds** A bird with a musical song or call.

son-in-law |sŭn′ĭn lô′| —*noun, plural* **sons-in-law** The husband of a person's daughter.

son·net |sŏn′ĭt| —*noun, plural* **sonnets** A short poem having fourteen lines that rhyme according to a set pattern.

soon |sōōn| —*adverb* **sooner, soonest** **1.** In the near future: *Soon you'll have to go to sleep.* **2.** Early: *He got there sooner than expected.* **3.** Quickly; fast: *Phone your mother as soon as you get to my house.* **4.** Gladly; willingly: *I'd as soon leave right now.*

soot |sŏŏt| or |sōōt| —*noun, plural* **soots** A fine substance that is like a black powder. It is produced when wood, coal, or oil is burned.

soothe |sōō*th*| —*verb* **soothed, soothing** **1.** To make calm or quiet: *Music soothed the restless baby.* **2.** To ease or relieve pain or distress: *The ointment soothed Eric's burnt finger.*

soph·o·more |sŏf′ə môr′| or |sŏf′ə mōr′| —*noun, plural* **sophomores** A student in the second year of a four-year high school or college.

so·pran·o |sə prăn′ō| or |sə prä′nō| —*noun, plural* **sopranos** **1.** A high singing voice of a woman. A soprano is higher than an alto. **2.** A singer who has such a voice.

sore |sôr| or |sōr| —*adjective* **sorer, sorest** **1.** Painful when touched; tender: *a sore leg.* **2.** Suffering pain; hurting: *He was sore all over.* **3.** Angry or annoyed; offended: *Don't be sore at her because she didn't call you.*
—*noun, plural* **sores** A painful, infected, or bruised place on the body.
♦ *These sound alike* **sore, soar.**

sor·row |sŏr′ō| or |sôr′ō| —*noun, plural* **sorrows** Mental anguish or suffering because of something sad that has happened: *The sons had to bear the sorrow caused by the death of their father.*

sor·row·ful |sŏr′ə fəl| or |sôr′ə fəl| —*adjective* Causing, feeling, or expressing sorrow: *a sorrowful event; a line of sorrowful relatives at the funeral.*

songbird
Two kinds of songbird

soot
A young coal miner with soot on his face

sor·ry | sŏr′ē | or | sôr′ē | —*adjective* **sorrier, sorriest 1.** Feeling or expressing sadness, sympathy, or regret: *Timmy was sorry for his sick brother. I am sorry he turned you down for the job. She is sorry she can't meet you today.* **2.** Not very good; poor: *a sorry excuse.* **3.** Causing sorrow or grief; sad: *sorry news of his death.*

sort | sôrt | —*noun, plural* **sorts** A group of persons or things that are somewhat alike; kind; type: *Mary is the sort who is always on time. This sort of weather is bad for driving.*
—*verb* **sorted, sorting** To arrange according to kind or type: *We sorted the laundry.*
    Idiom out of sorts Not feeling well; in a bad mood: *He is out of sorts in the morning before he has his coffee.*

SOS 1. The letters used by ships and aircraft as a call for help. **2.** Any signal for help.

sought | sôt | The past tense and past participle of **seek**: *She sought help from her doctor. He had always sought peace and quiet.*

soul | sōl | —*noun, plural* **souls 1.** The part of a person that is thought to think, feel, and act. Some religions believe that the soul and body separate at death and that the soul lives forever. **2.** A spirit; a ghost. **3.** A human being: *There wasn't a soul in sight.* **4.** Someone thought of as giving life and spirit to something: *She was the soul of the party.*
♦ *These sound alike* **soul, sole.**

sound¹ | sound | —*noun, plural* **sounds 1.** A type of vibration that travels through the air and is heard by the ear. **2.** A special noise: *the sound of laughter; a hollow sound.* **3.** The distance over which something can be heard: *They sat within sound of the waterfall.* **4.** One of the simple vocal noises that makes up human speech: *the sound of "y" in "try."*
—*verb* **sounded, sounding 1.** To make or cause to make a sound: *The whistle sounded. They sounded the gong.* **2.** To have a certain sound in human speech: *The words "break" and "brake" sound alike.* **3.** To seem to be: *The news sounds good.*

sound² | sound | —*adjective* **sounder, soundest 1.** Free from decay, damage, injury, or sickness: *a sound mind in a sound body. The children are safe and sound.* **2.** Solid and firm: *The house has a sound foundation.* **3.** Sensible and correct: *He always gives sound advice.* **4.** Complete and thorough: *His father gave him a sound scolding.* **5.** Deep and not interrupted: *a sound sleep.*

sound³ | sound | —*noun, plural* **sounds** A long body of water, wider than a strait or channel, connecting two larger bodies of water.

sound⁴ | sound | —*verb* **sounded, sounding 1.** To measure the depth of water, especially with a line having a weight on one end. **2.** To try to learn someone's thoughts or opinions: *I want to sound him out on this before I ask him directly.*

sound·proof | sound′proof′ | —*adjective* Made to let little or no sound pass in or out: *a soundproof wall; a soundproof room.*
—*verb* **soundproofed, soundproofing** To make soundproof: *She soundproofed her office so that she wouldn't be disturbed.*

soup | sōop | —*noun, plural* **soups** A liquid food prepared by boiling meat, vegetables, or fish in water.

sour | sour | —*adjective* **sourer, sourest 1.** Having a sharp and biting taste: *sour lemonade.* **2.** Spoiled: *a sour smell.* **3.** Unpleasant; bad: *He is in a sour temper today. She has a sour look on her face because she lost her keys.*

---

sound¹, sound², sound³, sound⁴

Sound¹ comes from an old French word, which in turn came from a Latin word meaning "sound." **Sound²** comes from a word meaning "healthy" that appeared very long ago in English. It is interesting to see that that word is related to *gesundheit,* the German word we often say when someone sneezes. **Sound³** and **sound⁴** are related. In old English **sound³** was *sund,* which originally meant "the act of swimming, a swim" and later took on the meaning "a body of water narrow enough to swim across." *Sund* was borrowed into French as *sonde,* "a line for measuring the depth of a body of water." From this word was formed a verb meaning "to measure depth," which was borrowed back into English as **sound⁴.**

ă	pat	ĕ	pet	î	fierce
ā	pay	ē	be	ŏ	pot
â	care	ĭ	pit	ō	go
ä	father	ī	pie	ô	paw, for

oi	oil	ŭ	cut	zh	vision
ŏŏ	book	û	fur	ə	ago, item,
ōō	boot	*th*	the		pencil, atom,
yōō	abuse	th	thin		circus
ou	out	hw	which	ər	butter

—verb **soured, souring** To make or become sour: *She soured the milk by adding lemon juice to it. The milk soured when it was left out of the refrigerator.*

source |sôrs| or |sōrs| *—noun, plural* **sources 1.** A place or thing from which something comes: *The sea is a source of food.* **2.** The beginning of a stream or river. **3.** Something or someone that gives information: *A dictionary is a source of knowledge.*

south |south| *—noun* **1.** The direction to the left of a person who faces the sunset. **2.** Often **South** A region in this direction. **3. the South a.** The southern part of the United States, especially the states south of Maryland, the Ohio River, and Missouri. **b.** The states that formed the Confederacy during the Civil War.
—adjective **1.** Of, in, or toward the south: *the south shore of the island.* **2.** Coming from the south: *a warm south wind.*
—adverb Toward the south: *We could not go south.*

South America The southern continent of the western hemisphere.

South American 1. A person who was born in or lives in South America. **2.** Of South America: *a South American animal.*

South Car·o·li·na |kăr´ə lī′nə| A state in the southeastern United States. The capital of South Carolina is Columbia.

South Da·ko·ta |də kō′tə| A state in the north-central United States. The capital of South Dakota is Pierre.

south·east |south ēst′| *—noun* **1.** The direction that is halfway between south and east. **2.** Often **Southeast** A region in this direction. **3. the Southeast** The part of the United States that includes Florida, Georgia, and South Carolina.
—adjective **1.** Of, in, or toward the southeast: *the southeast section of the state.* **2.** Coming from the southeast: *a southeast wind.*
—adverb Toward the southeast: *They walked southeast.*

south·east·er·ly |south ē′stər lē| *—adjective* **1.** In or toward the southeast: *The plane flew on a southeasterly route.* **2.** From the southeast: *a southeasterly breeze.*
—adverb **1.** In or toward the southeast: *Jane drove her car southeasterly.* **2.** From the southeast: *breezes blowing southeasterly.*

south·east·ern |south ē′stərn| *—adjective* **1.** Of, in, or toward the southeast: *a southeastern college; a southeastern state.* **2.** From the southeast: *a southeastern wind.*

south·er·ly |sŭth′ər lē| *—adjective* **1.** In or toward the south: *The ship sailed in a southerly direction.* **2.** From the south: *a southerly breeze.*
—adverb **1.** In or toward the south: *The army advanced southerly.* **2.** From the south: *The winds blew southerly.*

south·ern |sŭth′ərn| *—adjective* **1.** Of, in, or toward the south: *the southern side of the mountain.* **2.** From the south: *a southern breeze.* **3.** Like what is found in the south: *a southern climate.* **4. Southern** Of the states that formed the Confederacy during the Civil War: *the Southern army; a Southern general.*

south·ern·er |sŭth′ər nər| *—noun, plural* **southerners** Often **Southerner 1.** A person who lives in or comes from the south: *Many southerners go to school in the north.* **2.** A person from the South of the United States, especially during or before the Civil War.

South Carolina
South Carolina was named for King Charles I of England. It was at first called *Carolana*, but King Charles II changed the name officially to Carolina in 1663. Later the area was split into North Carolina and South Carolina.

South Dakota
South Dakota was named after the Dakota Indian tribe. Dakota means "allies."

south·ern·most |sŭ*th*′ərn mōst′| —*adjective* Farthest south: *the southernmost point of the United States.*

South Pole The southern end of the axis around which the earth rotates. The South Pole is the point on the surface of the earth that is farthest south.

south·ward |south′wərd| —*adverb* To or toward the south: *He looked southward.* Another form of this adverb is **southwards.** —*adjective* Moving to or toward the south: *They began their southward journey.*

south·wards |south′wərdz| A form of the adverb **southward.**

south·west |south wĕst′| —*noun* **1.** The direction that is halfway between south and west. **2.** Often **Southwest** A region in this direction. **3. the Southwest** The southwestern part of the United States, especially the region that includes the states of Arizona and New Mexico.
—*adjective* **1.** Of, in, or toward the southwest: *the southwest region of the country.* **2.** Coming from the southwest: *a southwest wind.*
—*adverb* Toward the southwest: *We drove southwest.*

south·west·er |south wĕs′tər| or |sou wĕs′tər| —*noun, plural* **southwesters** A waterproof hat with a broad brim in the back to protect the neck.

south·west·er·ly |south wĕs′tər lē| —*adjective* **1.** In or toward the southwest: *The birds migrated in a southwesterly direction.* **2.** From the southwest: *a southwesterly gust of air.*
—*adverb* **1.** In or toward the southwest: *Jane aimed her bow and arrow southwesterly.* **2.** From the southwest: *gales blowing southwesterly.*

south·west·ern |south wĕs′tərn| —*adjective* **1.** Of, in, or toward the southwest: *a southwestern plant; a southwestern state.* **2.** From the southwest: *a southwestern breeze.*

sou·ve·nir |sōō′və nîr′| —*noun, plural* **souvenirs** Something kept to remember a place, person, or event: *Arthur brought many souvenirs from Japan.*

sov·er·eign |sŏv′ə rĭn| or |sŏv′rĭn| —*noun, plural* **sovereigns** A king or queen: *Queen Elizabeth II is the sovereign of Great Britain.*

So·vi·et Union |sō′vē ĕt′| A country in eastern Europe and west-central and northern Asia.

sow[1] |sō| —*verb* **sowed, sown** or **sowed, sowing** **1.** To plant seeds to grow a crop: *The farmer sowed wheat and corn. He sowed in straight, even rows.* **2.** To plant or scatter seeds in or on: *He sowed his fields in the spring.*
♦ *These sound alike* **sow**[1], **sew, so.**

sow[2] |sou| —*noun, plural* **sows** A female pig that is fully grown.

sown |sōn| A past participle of the verb **sow** (to plant): *He had sown the corn too early last year.*

sox |sŏks| A plural of the noun **sock.**

soy·bean |soi′bēn′| —*noun, plural* **soybeans** A bean plant that is native to Asia and is now widely grown as animal food and for its beans. The beans are highly nutritious and are also a source of oil, flour, and chemicals for making plastics.

space |spās| —*noun, plural* **spaces** **1.** The area without limits in which the entire universe exists. **2.** The separation between two things or events: *There was a space of three days between her visits.* **3.** Any blank or empty area: *Leave a space between words. Fill in the blank space.* **4.** An area provided for a certain purpose:

---

sow[1], **sow**[2]
Sow[1] comes from an old English word meaning "to plant seed." It is related to the word **seed. Sow**[2] comes from the word meaning "pig" in the prehistoric language that was the source of many languages spoken today.

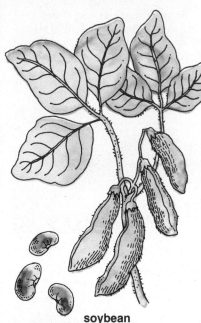

soybean
Soybeans *(left)* and plant *(right)*

ă	pat	ĕ	pet	î	fierce
ā	pay	ē	be	ŏ	pot
â	care	ĭ	pit	ō	go
ä	father	ī	pie	ô	paw, for
oi	oil	ŭ	cut	zh	vision
ŏŏ	book	û	fur	ə	ago, item,
ōō	boot	*th*	the		pencil, atom,
yōō	abuse	th	thin		circus
ou	out	hw	which	ər	butter

a parking space. **5.** A period of time: *He did many chores during the space of the afternoon.*

—verb **spaced, spacing** To arrange with spaces between: *Carefully space the words on the poster.*

space·craft | spās′krăft′ | or | spăs′krăft′ | *—noun, plural* **spacecraft** A vehicle used for travel beyond the earth's atmosphere.

space·ship | spās′shĭp | *—noun, plural* **spaceships** A spacecraft that can carry a crew and passengers.

space walk An excursion by an astronaut outside a spacecraft in space.

spade¹ | spād | *—noun, plural* **spades** A digging tool with a long handle and a flat iron blade that is pressed into the ground with the foot.

—verb **spaded, spading** To dig with a spade.

spade² | spād | *—noun, plural* **spades** **1.** A black figure that looks like an upside-down heart found on a playing card. **2.** A playing card marked with this figure. **3.** **spades** The suit of cards that has this figure: *king of spades.*

Spain | spān | A country in southwestern Europe.

span | spăn | *—noun, plural* **spans** **1.** The distance between two places or objects: *There was a span of one mile between the houses.* **2.** The section of a bridge between the parts that hold it up. **3.** The distance between the tip of the thumb and the tip of the little finger when the hand is spread out. It is about nine inches. This used to be a way of measuring. **4.** A period of time: *a span of four hours.*

—verb **spanned, spanning** To stretch across: *A fallen tree spanned the road. The old man's memories spanned ninety years.*

span·iel | spăn′yəl | *—noun, plural* **spaniels** Any of several breeds of dog that have drooping ears, short legs, and a silky, wavy coat. Spaniels are small to medium in size.

Span·ish | spăn′ĭsh | *—noun* **1.** The Romance language of Spain, Mexico, and many other countries. **2.** **the Spanish** (Used with a plural verb.) The people of Spain.

—adjective Of Spain, the Spanish, or their language.

spank | spăngk | *—verb* **spanked, spanking** To punish by slapping with the open hand or with a flat object.

spare | spâr | *—verb* **spared, sparing** **1. a.** To treat with mercy: *The pirates spared their captives.* **b.** To deal gently with: *Please spare her feelings and don't criticize her.* **2.** To avoid or keep from destroying or harming: *The fire spared the trees beside the house.* **3.** To save or free someone from: *I'll spare myself a trip to the store by ordering by phone.* **4.** To do without; give away or give out: *Can you spare me a dime? They could not spare him from the farm.*

—adjective **sparer, sparest** **1. a.** Ready when needed: *a spare tire.* **b.** Extra: *spare cash.* **c.** Free for other use: *spare time.* **2.** Small in amount: *a spare breakfast.*

—noun, plural **spares** **1.** A replacement, such as a tire, to be used when needed. **2. a.** The act of knocking down all ten pins with two rolls of the bowling ball. **b.** The score for this.

spark | spärk | *—noun, plural* **sparks** **1.** A small, burning bit of material: *The burning logs threw sparks into the air.* **2.** A quick flash of light, especially one made by electricity. **3.** A hint; a trace: *There was a spark of interest in the crowd when the magician walked out on the stage.*

spade¹, spade²
Spade¹ comes from an old word in English meaning "digging tool." Spade² comes from an Italian word meaning "sword."

spade²
A playing card

spaniel

sparrow

spearmint

ă	pat	ĕ	pet	î	fierce
â	pay	ē	be	ŏ	pot
â	care	ĭ	pit	ō	go
ä	father	ī	pie	ô	paw, for
oi	oil	ŭ	cut	zh	vision
oŏ	book	û	fur	ə	ago, item,
ōō	boot	th	the		pencil, atom,
yōō	abuse	th	thin		circus
ou	out	hw	which	ər	butter

—*verb* **sparked, sparking** To make or give off sparks: *The logs in the fireplace sparked and crackled.*

spar·kle |spär′kəl| —*verb* **sparkled, sparkling 1.** To give off sparks of light; glitter: *His eyes sparkled with fun. The diamonds sparkled in the window of the jewelry store.* **2.** To release bubbles of gas: *The soda water sparkled.*
—*noun, plural* **sparkles** A spark of light; a flash; a glitter: *the sparkle of diamonds.*

spar·row |spăr′ō| —*noun, plural* **sparrows** Any of several small brownish or grayish birds that are very common in cities.

sparse |spärs| —*adjective* **sparser, sparsest** Occurring or found here and there; thinly scattered: *an area with sparse vegetation.*

spat¹ |spăt| —*noun, plural* **spats** A short, small quarrel: *I had a spat with my sister.*

spat² |spăt| A past tense and a past participle of the verb **spit**: *He spat out his chewing gum. He had spat out the exciting news without pausing for breath.*

spat·ter |spăt′ər| —*verb* **spattered, spattering** To scatter in drops or small bits: *She spattered paint on her dress.*

spat·u·la |spăch′ə lə| —*noun, plural* **spatulas** A tool with a wide, flat blade. It is used for spreading plaster or paint, for removing food from a pan, for handling or spreading soft foods, and for frosting cakes.

spawn |spôn| —*noun* The eggs of water animals. Fish, oysters, frogs, and other water animals produce spawn.
—*verb* **spawned, spawning** To lay eggs and breed, as fish and certain other water animals do: *Salmon swim up streams to spawn.*

speak |spēk| —*verb* **spoke, spoken, speaking 1.** To say words; talk: *Jane speaks very softly. They spoke about the weather.* **2.** To tell: *She has to speak to her brother before she can leave.* **3.** To give a speech: *The president will speak tonight.* **4.** To make known or express in words: *Do you think she spoke the truth?* **5.** To use or be able to use a language: *He speaks Italian.*

speak·er |spē′kər| —*noun, plural* **speakers 1.** A person who speaks a language: *a speaker of English.* **2.** A person who gives a speech in public: *Mr. Jones is a good speaker.* **3.** A loudspeaker.

spear |spîr| —*noun, plural* **spears 1.** A weapon with a long pole and a sharply pointed head. **2.** A slender stalk or stem: *an asparagus spear.*

spear·mint |spîr′mĭnt| —*noun, plural* **spearmints** A common mint plant whose leaves are used for flavoring.

spe·cial |spĕsh′əl| —*adjective* **1.** Different from what is usual or common; extraordinary or unusual; exceptional: *Christmas is a special holiday. The nurses gave her special care.* **2.** Different from others of a kind: *He ordered a special camera from Japan.*

spe·cial·ist |spĕsh′ə lĭst| —*noun, plural* **specialists** A person whose activity or profession is devoted to a particular branch of study, business, or science.

spe·cial·ize |spĕsh′ə līz′| —*verb* **specialized, specializing** To devote one's activity or profession to a particular branch of study, business, or science: *Peter specialized in French after his graduation. Jane specialized in stocks and bonds when she joined the bank.*

spe·cial·ty |spĕsh′əl tē| —*noun, plural* **specialties 1.** A special study, job, or service: *His specialty is portrait painting.* **2.** A special offer or attraction: *The restaurant's specialty is seafood.*

spe·cies |spē′shēz′| or |spē′sēz′| —*noun, plural* **species 1.** A group of animals or plants that are similar and considered to be of the same kind. Animals of the same species can breed together. **2.** A type, kind, or sort: *There are many species of plants.*

spe·ci·fic | spĭ **sĭf′** ĭk | —*adjective* Clearly stated; particular; definite: *He had specific instructions to meet her at the corner.*

spec·i·fy | **spĕs′** ə fī′ | —*verb* **specified, specifying, specifies** To say in a clear and exact way; make clear: *When you order your ice cream, specify what flavor you want.*

spec·i·men | **spĕs′** ə mən | —*noun, plural* **specimens** One of a group of things that can be taken to stand for the group: *a specimen of soil. He gathered many specimens of butterflies.*

speck | spĕk | —*noun, plural* **specks 1.** A small spot or mark: *brown specks on the paper.* **2.** A small bit or particle: *specks of dust on the table.*

spec·ta·cle | **spĕk′** tə kəl | —*noun, plural* **spectacles 1.** A very unusual or impressive sight or display: *The children were excited by the spectacle of fireworks.* **2.** **spectacles** A pair of eyeglasses.

spec·tac·u·lar | spĕk **tăk′** yə lər | —*adjective* Making a very unusual or impressive sight or display: *The tourists admired the spectacular view of the canyon.*

spec·ta·tor | **spĕk′** tā′tər | —*noun, plural* **spectators** Someone who watches an event but does not take part in it.

spec·trum | **spĕk′** trəm | —*noun, plural* **spectrums** The bands of color seen when white light, especially light from the sun, is broken up into parts, as in a rainbow or when the light passes through a prism.

spectator
Spectators at a baseball game

spec·u·late | **spĕk′** yə lāt′ | —*verb* **speculated, speculating** To guess without having complete knowledge; ponder; wonder: *The boys liked to speculate that life might exist in outer space.*

sped | spĕd | A past tense and a past participle of the verb **speed**: *The car sped past the bicycles. The car had sped by so fast that all I saw was a blur.*

speech | spēch | —*noun, plural* **speeches 1.** The act of speaking: *She burst into rapid speech to disguise her embarrassment.* **2.** The ability to speak: *Speech is a gift to be treasured.* **3.** Something that is spoken: *His speech was full of slang words.* **4.** The way in which a person speaks: *His blurred speech shows that he is very sleepy.* **5.** A talk or address made in public: *The congressman made an interesting speech last night.*

speech·less | **spēch′** lĭs | —*adjective* Not able to speak for a short time through shock, fear, anger, or joy: *She remained speechless throughout the fight between her two brothers.*

speed | spēd | —*noun, plural* **speeds 1.** The condition of acting or moving rapidly: *The road is clear; let's see some speed now.* **2. a.** The rate of moving: *She drove at a speed of forty miles per hour.* **b.** The rate of doing something: *His speed on the spelling test made him finish first.*
—*verb* **sped** or **speeded, speeding 1.** To move rapidly: *The bullet sped through the air. The motorcycles sped down the hill.* **2.** To drive faster than is lawful or safe: *The officer told them that they were speeding.*

spell[1] | spĕl | —*verb* **spelled, spelling 1.** To form a word or part of a word; be the letters of: *Does h, a, t spell "hat"?* **2.** To say or write in proper order the letters of a word: *The teacher asked him to spell "southern."*

spell[1], spell[2], spell[3]
Spell[1] and **spell[2]** had a common origin in a prehistoric Germanic root that meant "to recite, a recitation." The word that became **spell[1]** appeared in old French with the meaning "to read out letter by letter." The word that became **spell[2]** appeared in old English and meant "story, news." **Spell[3]** comes from a different old English word, meaning "to substitute." It later came to mean "to relieve at work."

spider
Two kinds of spider

spike¹, spike²
Spike¹ has always had its present meaning. It is not certain whether it was an original old English word or whether it came from a word used very long ago by people living in Scandinavia. **Spike²** comes from a Latin word meaning "point, ear of grain."

ă	pat	ĕ	pet	î	fierce	
ā	pay	ē	be	ŏ	pot	
â	care	ĭ	pit	ō	go	
ä	father	ī	pie	ô	paw, for	

oi	oil	ŭ	cut	zh	vision
ŏŏ	book	û	fur	ə	ago, item,
ōō	boot	*th*	the		pencil, atom,
yōō	abuse	th	thin		circus
ou	out	hw	which	ər	butter

spell² |spĕl| —*noun, plural* **spells 1.** A word or group of words believed to have the power of magic: *The witch spoke the spell over the princess and she fell asleep.* **2.** Attraction; charm: *The beauty of the tropical islands cast a spell over the tourists.*

spell³ |spĕl| —*noun, plural* **spells** A period of time: *She wants to stay at home for a spell.*
—*verb* **spelled, spelling** To take the place of a person: *I'll spell you now at painting the door.*

spell·er |spĕl'ər| —*noun, plural* **spellers 1.** Someone who spells words: *Joey is a good speller.* **2.** A book used in teaching children how to spell: *a third-grade speller.*

spell·ing |spĕl'ĭng| —*noun, plural* **spellings 1.** The act of forming words with letters by using the proper order: *Your spelling needs improving.* **2.** The way in which a word is spelled: *The spelling of hat is "h," "a," "t."*

spend |spĕnd| —*verb* **spent, spending 1.** To pay out money; make payment: *He spent his last five dollars.* **2.** To use or put out; devote: *She spends an hour each day practicing the piano.* **3.** To pass time in a certain place or doing something: *They will spend their vacation at the beach.*

spent |spĕnt| The past tense and past participle of the verb **spend:** *We spent five dollars on a book. I had spent many hours biking last summer.*

sperm |spûrm| —*noun, plural* **sperms** One of the male cells of reproduction.

sperm whale A whale with a large head and a long, narrow lower jaw with many teeth. The head has several hollow areas that contain a valuable oil and a material like wax, which is used in making candles, ointments, and other things.

sphere |sfîr| —*noun, plural* **spheres 1.** A round object like a ball or globe. All the points on the surface of a sphere are the same distance from a center point. **2. a.** An area of power, control, or influence: *There are many countries within the American sphere.* **b.** A field or area of interest, activity, or knowledge: *Music is outside her sphere.*

sphinx |sfĭngks| —*noun, plural* **sphinxes** An old Egyptian figure with the body of a lion and a human head.

spice |spīs| —*noun, plural* **spices** Material from a plant that smells and tastes strong or pleasant. Cinnamon, nutmeg, pepper, and cloves are spices used to give flavor to food.
—*verb* **spiced, spicing** To flavor with a spice or spices.

spic·y |spī'sē| —*adjective* **spicier, spiciest 1.** Flavored with a spice or spices: *She baked a spicy pumpkin pie.* **2.** Having a sharp or strong taste or smell: *This sausage is so spicy that it burns my mouth. The pine forest always smells spicier after it rains.*

spi·der |spī'dər| —*noun, plural* **spiders** A small animal that has eight legs and a body divided into two parts. Spiders spin webs to catch insects. Spiders are not related to insects. They belong to a different group that includes scorpions and ticks.

spied |spīd| The past tense and past participle of the verb **spy:** *She spied on the enemy and reported to the general. She had spied on the enemy for many years.*

spike¹ |spīk| —*noun, plural* **spikes 1.** A long, heavy nail: *He drove several spikes into the telephone pole.* **2.** A long, thick, sharp-pointed piece of wood or metal: *spikes on a fence.* **3.** One

of the many sharp metal pieces on the soles of shoes worn by
certain athletes. Spikes are used to get a firm footing.

spike² |spīk| —*noun, plural* **spikes 1.** An ear of grain. Corn
ears are spikes. **2.** A bunch of flowers that do not have stalks.

spill |spĭl| —*verb* **spilled** or **spilt, spilling 1.** To cause or allow
something to run or fall out of a container: *Be careful not to spill
water from the bucket.* **2.** To run or fall out: *Milk spilled over the
top of the glass.*

spilt |spĭlt| A past tense and a past participle of the verb **spill:**
He spilt the milk. She has spilt water all over the plants.

spin |spĭn| —*verb* **spun, spinning 1.** To draw out and twist
fibers into thread: *The wizard could spin flax into gold cloth.* **2.** To
form a thread, web, or cocoon from a liquid given off by the
body: *The spiders were busy spinning their webs.* **3.** To tell: *He is
good at spinning tales of the sea.* **4.** To turn about an axis,
especially rapidly; rotate: *The wheels were spinning on the icy
pavement.* **5.** To seem to be whirling from being dizzy; reel: *The
speed of the roller coaster made his head spin.*
—*noun, plural* **spins** A rapid turning or rotating motion: *the spin
of a wheel.*

spin·ach |spĭn′ĭch| —*noun* A plant grown for its dark green
leaves, which are eaten as a vegetable.

spi·nal column |spī′nəl| The backbone.

spinal cord A thick band or cord of nerve tissue that begins at
the brain and goes down through the center of the backbone.
Nerves that go to different parts or regions of the body branch off
from it.

spin·dle |spĭn′dl| —*noun, plural* **spindles 1.** A rod or pin on a
spinning machine that holds and winds thread. **2.** Any thin rod
or pin in a machine that turns around or on which something
turns. The small piece on a phonograph that fits through the
center hole of a record is a spindle.

spine |spīn| —*noun, plural* **spines 1.** The backbone; spinal
column. **2.** A part of a plant or animal that sticks out with a
sharp point. The quills on a porcupine and thorns on a rose are
spines.

spin·ning wheel |spĭn′ĭng| A device that is made of a large
wheel and a spindle. It is used to spin thread.

spin·y |spī′nē| —*adjective* **spinier, spiniest** Full of or covered
with spines; prickly: *A porcupine is a spiny animal.*

spi·ral |spī′rəl| —*noun, plural* **spirals 1.** A curve that gradually
widens as it coils around. **2.** Anything that is shaped like it. The
thread of a screw and many types of springs are spirals.
—*verb* **spiraled, spiraling** To move in or cause to move in the
form of a spiral: *Smoke spiraled up from the chimney.*

spire |spīr| —*noun, plural* **spires** The top part of a steeple or
other structure that tapers upward.

spir·it |spĭr′ĭt| —*noun, plural* **spirits 1.** The part of a human
being that is thought to have control over thinking and feeling,
as distinguished from the physical body; the soul. **2. spirits** A
person's mood or state of mind: *Even though she's very sick, she's
still in good spirits.* **3.** Enthusiasm, courage, or pep: *Our team
showed a lot of spirit.*

spir·i·tu·al |spĭr′ĭ chōō əl| —*adjective* Of or having to do with
the human spirit or with religion: *spiritual matters; spiritual beliefs.*
—*noun, plural* **spirituals** A religious folk song. Spirituals were

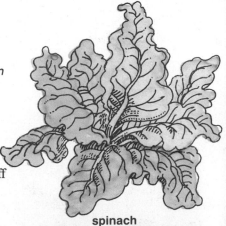

spinach

spinning wheel

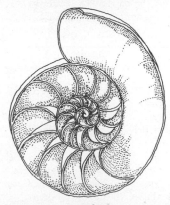

spiral

originally made up and sung by black people in the southern United States.

spit | spĭt | —*verb* **spat** or **spit, spitting** To throw out saliva or something else from the mouth: *Spit out the gum.*

spite | spīt | —*noun* Anger or ill will that causes a person to want to hurt or embarrass another person: *My brother won't talk to me out of spite because I didn't take him with me to the movies.*

—*verb* **spited, spiting** To show spite toward someone: *She's being mean to spite you for forgetting her birthday.*

Idiom **in spite of** Even though; regardless: *We're going to play the football game in spite of the rain.*

splash | splăsh | —*verb* **splashed, splashing** To scatter water or other liquid about: *Rain is splashing on the roof.*

—*noun, plural* **splashes** **1.** The act or sound of splashing: *Did you see the splash I made when I jumped into the pool?* **2.** A mark or spot made by or as if by scattered liquid: *You have a splash of gravy on your shirt. Look at the splashes of lightning in the sky.*

splen·did | splĕn'dĭd | —*adjective* **1.** Very beautiful or striking; brilliant: *a splendid gown; a splendid view; a splendid sunset.* **2.** Excellent or fine; good: *a splendid idea.*

splen·dor | splĕn'dər | —*noun, plural* **splendors** Magnificent or beautiful appearance; glory; great display: *The king was a vision of splendor in his crown and royal robes.*

splint | splĭnt | —*noun, plural* **splints** A strip of wood or other hard material that is used to hold a broken bone in place. It can also be used to support such other things as a thin, young tree while it is growing.

splin·ter | splĭn'tər | —*noun, plural* **splinters** A sharp, thin piece of such things as wood or glass split or broken off from a larger piece or object: *I have a splinter in my finger.*

—*verb* **splintered, splintering** To break into sharp, thin pieces: *Glass splinters easily.*

split | splĭt | —*verb* **split, splitting** **1.** To divide or become divided into parts; to divide lengthwise or from end to end: *We split the logs for firewood. The board split down the middle from the blow.* **2.** To break, burst, or rip apart from force: *I blew too hard and the air split the balloon. He split his pants.* **3.** To separate or cause to separate persons or groups; break off: *My sister and her husband split up. The fight split the club into two sides.*

—*noun, plural* **splits** **1.** The act or result of splitting: *There's a split in your jacket.* **2.** A break or division within a group: *There's a split in the team over who should be captain.*

spoil | spoil | —*verb* **spoiled** or **spoilt, spoiling** **1.** To damage or hurt something so as to make it less valuable or useful; injure: *Stains spoiled the tablecloth. When the car broke down, it spoiled our whole trip.* **2.** To become rotten or damaged so as to be bad to use: *The milk spoiled.* **3.** To praise or give in to the wishes of someone too much so as to harm the character or disposition of: *They spoiled the child by giving her everything she wanted.*

—*noun, plural* **spoils** Goods or property taken by force in a war or battle: *Money and jewels are often spoils of war.*

spoilt | spoilt | A past tense and past participle of the verb **spoil:** *All the food spoilt. He had spoilt the children with all his gifts.*

spoke[1] | spōk | —*noun, plural* **spokes** One of the rods or bars that connect the rim of a wheel to its hub.

spoke[1]
Spokes on antique bicycle wheels

spoke² |spōk| The past tense of the verb **speak:** *I spoke to him yesterday.*

spo·ken |spō′kən| The past participle of the verb **speak:** *But have you spoken to him since then?*
—*adjective* Expressed in speech; said, not written: *The teacher gave us spoken directions.*

sponge |spŭnj| —*noun, plural* **sponges** **1.** A water animal that attaches itself to rocks and other surfaces underwater. It has a soft skeleton with many small holes that absorb water. **2.a.** The soft skeleton of these animals used instead of cloth for such things as bathing and cleaning. **b.** A similar cleaning piece made out of a material that absorbs, such as rubber or plastic.
—*verb* **sponged, sponging** To wash or wipe with a sponge or other material that absorbs: *She sponged his face with her wet handkerchief. Sponge up the spilled orange juice.*

spon·sor |spŏn′sər| —*noun, plural* **sponsors** **1.** A person who is responsible for or supports another person or thing: *My brother got his teacher to be his sponsor for his bid to enter college.* **2.** A business or industry that pays the costs of a radio or television program in return for time during the program to advertise its products or services.
—*verb* **sponsored, sponsoring** To act as a sponsor for: *My uncle's store sponsors a little league team.*

spon·ta·ne·ous |spŏn tā′nē əs| —*adjective* Happening or occurring naturally or by itself; not planned: *Even before the game was over the fans burst into spontaneous cheers.*

spook·y |spōō′kē| —*adjective* **spookier, spookiest** Causing fear; weird; strange: *a spooky old house.*

spool |spōol| —*noun, plural* **spools** **1.** A small cylinder made of wood, metal, or plastic. Thread and wire are wound around spools. **2.a.** A spool with something wound on it: *Buy a spool of white thread.* **b.** The amount a spool holds: *She used a whole spool of thread making those curtains.*

spoon |spōon| —*noun, plural* **spoons** A utensil with a small, shallow bowl at the end of a handle. It is used in preparing, measuring, serving, and eating food.
—*verb* **spooned, spooning** To lift or scoop up with a spoon: *Spoon some more apple sauce on my plate, please.*

spore |spôr| or |spōr| —*noun, plural* **spores** A tiny part of certain plants that have no flowers. Mosses and ferns have spores. Spores are made up of only one cell.

sport |spôrt| or |spōrt| —*noun, plural* **sports** **1.** A game, contest, or recreation that involves some physical exercise. Most sports also require skill and many involve competition. Baseball, basketball, fishing, and jogging are all sports. **2.** A person who behaves or plays according to the rules and loses gracefully: *a good sport; a poor sport.*

sports·man·ship |spôrts′mən shĭp′| —*noun* The conduct and qualities of a good sport; fair play.

spot |spŏt| —*noun, plural* **spots** **1.** A small mark or stain: *grape juice spots on the tablecloth. When I got the measles I had red spots all over my body.* **2.** A small mark or part on a surface that is different from the rest: *a brown dog with white spots.* **3.** A place or location: *This is the spot where the accident happened.*
—*verb* **spotted, spotting** **1.** To mark or cause to become marked with spots or stains: *This tablecloth spots easily. Rain spotted the*

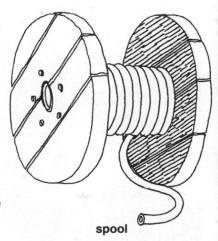

spool

curtains. **2.** To find out or locate; pick out: *I spotted him in the crowd. It's hard to spot his house from here.*

spot·light | spŏt′līt′ | —*noun, plural* **spotlights** A strong lamp that lights up a small area very brightly. A spotlight is often used to draw attention to a performer on a stage.

spout | spout | —*verb* **spouted, spouting** To send forth or force out liquid in a steady stream or in a spurt: *Water is spouting from the broken pipe. Volcanoes spout lava.*

—*noun, plural* **spouts** A narrow tube, pipe, or opening through which liquid is sent or forced out: *the spout of a coffee pot; the spout of a drinking fountain.*

spout
On a silver pot for tea

sprain | sprān | —*noun, plural* **sprains** An injury to a joint or muscle in which it is stretched, twisted, or torn.

—*verb* **sprained, spraining** To cause a sprain: *I sprained my ankle.*

sprang | sprăng | A past tense of the verb **spring**: *The rabbits sprang quickly from their hiding places when they heard the dogs.*

sprawl | sprôl | —*verb* **sprawled, sprawling** **1.** To sit or lie with the body and limbs spread out in an awkward fashion: *He sprawled in the chair to watch television.* **2.** To spread out in a way that is not organized: *The city sprawled over the farms surrounding it.*

spray | sprā | —*noun, plural* **sprays** **1.** Water or other liquid that moves in the form of tiny drops or mist: *the spray of ocean waves.* **2.** A jet of liquid drops that is forced out under pressure from a certain type of container. **3.** A container that forces out such jets. **4.** Any of a lot of different kinds of products that are designed to be applied in the form of a spray. Paint, insect poisons, fertilizers, and cosmetics are often in the form of a spray.

—*verb* **sprayed, spraying** To apply a liquid as a spray: *I'm going to spray paint on the chair. He's spraying the rose bushes.*

spread | sprĕd | —*verb* **spread, spreading** **1.** To open or cause to open wide or wider; open out: *spread a tablecloth; spread your arms. The eagle spread its wings.* **2.** To move or be pushed farther apart: *Spread the chairs. They've been spread all over the room.* **3.** To cover or become covered with a thin layer: *spread bread with jelly. This paint spreads easily.* **4.** To scatter or distribute: *Spread the grass seeds over the yard.* **5.** To make or become widely known: *spread the news. That story spread quickly.*

—*noun, plural* **spreads** **1.** The act of spreading: *The spread of population in the United States has always moved westward. We must stop the spread of this disease.* **2.** The extent to which something can be spread: *That plane has wings with a six-foot spread.* **3.** A cloth cover for a bed or a table. **4.** A soft food that can be spread on bread or crackers. Butter, jelly, and peanut butter are spreads.

spring | sprĭng | —*verb* **sprang** or **sprung, sprung, springing** **1.** To move upward or forward in one quick motion; leap: *Grasshoppers were springing through the field.* **2.** To appear suddenly: *She sprang into view.* **3.** To shift position suddenly: *The door sprang shut.* **4.** To bring out or make happen suddenly: *Let's spring a surprise on Bobby.*

—*noun, plural* **springs** **1.** An elastic device in the shape of a coiled or flat metal bar. A spring will return to its original shape after it is pushed in on itself, pulled out, twisted, or bent. **2.** The act of springing; a leap or jump: *The cat made a spring toward us.* **3.** A natural fountain or flow of water. **4.** The season of the year between winter and summer.

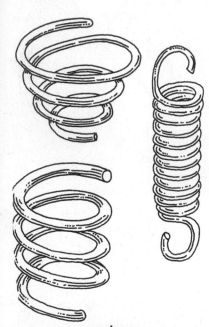

spring
Different kinds of springs

ă	pat	ĕ	pet	î	fierce
ā	pay	ē	be	ŏ	pot
â	care	ĭ	pit	ō	go
ä	father	ī	pie	ô	paw, for
oi	oil	ŭ	cut	zh	vision
ŏŏ	book	û	fur	ə	ago, item,
ōō	boot	*th*	the		pencil, atom,
yōō	abuse	th	thin		circus
ou	out	hw	which	ər	butter

spring·board | sprĭng′bôrd′ | or | sprĭng′bōrd′ | —*noun, plural* **springboards** A board used in diving or gymnastics. It helps a person to jump higher in the air.

Spring·field | sprĭng′fēld′ | The capital of Illinois.

spring·y | sprĭng′ē | —*adjective* **springier, springiest** Able to spring or bounce back: *springy curls; a springy step.*

sprin·kle | sprĭng′kəl | —*verb* **sprinkled, sprinkling 1.** To scatter or let fall in drops or small pieces: *sprinkle salt on the icy steps.* **2.** To scatter drops or small pieces upon: *The gardener sprinkled the lawn.* **3.** To rain or fall in small drops.

sprin·kler | sprĭng′klər | —*noun, plural* **sprinklers** A device put on the end of a water line for watering plants.

sprinkler

sprint | sprĭnt | —*noun, plural* **sprints** A short race run at top speed.
—*verb* **sprinted, sprinting** To run at top speed: *The runners sprinted around the track.*

sprout | sprout | —*verb* **sprouted, sprouting** To begin to grow; produce or appear as a bud, shoot, or new growth: *The newly planted corn sprouted after the rain.*
—*noun, plural* **sprouts** A young plant growth. Buds and shoots are sprouts.

spruce | sprōōs | —*noun, plural* **spruces** An evergreen tree with short needles and soft wood.

sprung | sprŭng | A past tense and the past participle of the verb **spring:** *The door sprung shut. He had sprung to his feet at the sound of the bell.*

spun | spŭn | The past tense and past participle of the verb **spin:** *The toy top spun around and around. After it had spun around many times, it stopped.*

spur | spûr | —*noun, plural* **spurs** A sharp metal piece in the shape of a small wheel with spikes worn on the heel of a person's boot. It is used to make a horse go faster.
—*verb* **spurred, spurring 1.** To make a horse go faster by pricking it with spurs: *The rider spurred the horse to a gallop.* **2.** To move to action; urge on: *The reward spurred us on.*

spruce
Needles and cone *(above)* and tree *(below)*

spurt | spûrt | —*noun, plural* **spurts 1.** A sudden, strong gush of liquid: *When he opened the can, a spurt of soda shot through the air.* **2.** Any sudden outbreak or short burst of energy or activity.
—*verb* **spurted, spurting** To squirt: *oil spurting in the air.*

spy | spī | —*noun, plural* **spies 1.** A secret agent hired to get information about a foreign country. **2.** Someone who secretly watches another or others.
—*verb* **spied, spying, spies** To keep under secret watch: *He spied on the enemy's camp.*

squad | skwŏd | —*noun, plural* **squads 1.** A small group of soldiers brought together for work, drill, or combat. **2.** Any small group brought together for work.

squad·ron | skwŏd′rən | —*noun, plural* **squadrons** A group of soldiers, planes, ships, or other military units.

square | skwâr | —*noun, plural* **squares 1.** A figure having four sides the same length. **2.** Any figure or object having this shape. **3.** The product gotten when a number or quantity is multiplied by itself. **4. a.** An open area where two or more streets cross over one another. **b.** An open space surrounded by streets on all sides.
—*adjective* **squarer, squarest 1.** Having the shape of a square. **2.** Forming a right angle: *a board with square corners.* **3.** Of,

spur

squash¹, squash²
Squash¹ comes from a word used long ago by an American Indian tribe. **Squash²** comes from an old French word that came from a Latin word meaning "to break in pieces."

squash¹
Two kinds of squash

being, or using units that measure the surface of something: *square feet.* **4.** Honest; direct: *a square answer.* **5.** Just and fair: *a square deal.*
—*verb* **squared, squaring 1.** To cut or form into a square: *The carpenter squared the board.* **2.** To multiply a number or quantity by itself. **3.** To agree or conform: *We must square his story with ours. Your story squares with mine.*

squash¹ |skwŏsh| *or* |skwôsh| —*noun, plural* **squashes** A fruit that grows on a vine and is related to the pumpkins and the gourds. Squash is cooked and eaten as a vegetable.

squash² |skwŏsh| *or* |skwôsh| —*verb* **squashed, squashing 1.** To beat or flatten into a soft mass; crush: *He squashed the peach on the pavement.* **2.** To be or become crushed or flattened: *The tomato squashed on the floor.*
—*noun* **1.** The sound of something soft and juicy dropping against a hard surface. **2.** A game played in a room in which players hit a hard rubber ball with a racket.

squat |skwŏt| —*verb* **squatted** *or* **squat, squatting 1.** To sit on one's heels, with the knees drawn close to one's chest: *Kevin squatted down to watch an ant.* **2.** To settle on land without a legal right. **3.** To settle on public land in order to become its owner.
—*adjective* **squatter, squattest** Short and thick; low and broad: *a vase with a squat shape.*

squawk |skwôk| —*noun, plural* **squawks** A loud, harsh, screeching sound, such as a parrot or chicken makes.
—*verb* **squawked, squawking** To make or say with a squawk.

squeak |skwēk| —*noun, plural* **squeaks** A thin, high-pitched cry or sound: *the squeak of chalk on a blackboard.*
—*verb* **squeaked, squeaking** To make a thin, high-pitched cry or sound: *The mouse squeaked when Stephen chased it.*

squeal |skwēl| —*noun, plural* **squeals** A shrill, loud cry or sound: *Bobby gave out a squeal of joy when he saw his Christmas gift.*
—*verb* **squealed, squealing** To make a shrill, loud cry or sound: *The hungry pigs squealed waiting to be fed.*

squeeze |skwēz| —*verb* **squeezed, squeezing 1.** To press hard upon or together: *The baby squeezed the rubber toy. They squeezed the bits of tape together.* **2.** To put pressure on, especially to take liquid out of something: *squeeze an orange.* **3.** To force one's way by pressure: *Sally squeezed through the crowd.* **4.** To crowd; cram: *They squeezed too many people into the room.*
—*noun, plural* **squeezes** An act of squeezing: *He gave my hand a squeeze.*

squid |skwĭd| —*noun, plural* **squids** *or* **squid** A sea animal that is related to the octopus. The squid has a soft, long body and ten arms surrounding the mouth. It has a pair of fins that are triangular or round.

squint |skwĭnt| —*verb* **squinted, squinting** To look with the eyes half open: *Florence squinted at the fine print.*

squire |skwīr| —*noun, plural* **squires 1.** In the Middle Ages, a young man of noble birth who served as an attendant to a knight. **2.** An English country gentleman.

squirm |skwûrm| —*verb* **squirmed, squirming 1.** To twist about in a wriggling motion: *The small child squirmed in her seat.* **2.** To feel or show signs of being ill at ease or embarrassed.

ă	pat	ĕ	pet	î	fierce
ā	pay	ē	be	ŏ	pot
â	care	ĭ	pit	ō	go
ä	father	ī	pie	ô	paw, for
oi	oil	ŭ	cut	zh	vision
ŏŏ	book	û	fur	ə	ago, item,
ōō	boot	*th*	the		pencil, atom,
yōō	abuse	th	thin		circus
ou	out	hw	which	ər	butter

squir·rel | skwûr′əl | or | skwĭr′əl | —*noun, plural* **squirrels** An animal with gray or reddish-brown fur and a bushy tail.

squirt | skwûrt | —*verb* **squirted, squirting** **1.** To push out liquid in a thin, swift stream: *She squirted water on her sister.* **2.** To be pushed out in a thin, swift stream: *The water squirted out of the hose.*
—*noun, plural* **squirts** **1.** Something used to squirt. **2.** The liquid squirted: *Put a squirt of lemon in your tea.*

stab | stăb | —*verb* **stabbed, stabbing** **1.** To cut or hurt with a pointed weapon: *The pirate stabbed the captain with his sword.* **2.** To make a thrust or lunge with something pointed: *The speaker stabbed at the air with her finger.*
—*noun, plural* **stabs** **1.** A thrust made with a pointed object: *He made a stab at the steak with his fork.* **2.** A wound made with a pointed weapon: *a stab in the arm.* **3.** An attempt; a try: *She thought she would take a stab at painting for a living.*

sta·bil·i·ty | stə bĭl′ĭ tē | —*noun, plural* **stabilities** The condition of being stable: *The engineers were testing the stability of the bridge.*

sta·ble¹ | stā′bəl | —*adjective* **stabler, stablest** **1.** Not likely to go through sudden changes in position or condition; fixed; steady; firm: *a stable bridge; a stable economy.* **2.** Tending to return to a condition of balance if moved: *a stable rocking chair.* **3.** Likely to go on or survive: *a stable government.*

sta·ble² | stā′bəl | —*noun, plural* **stables** A building where horses, cattle, and other animals are kept and fed.
—*verb* **stabled, stabling** To put or keep an animal in a stable.

stack | stăk | —*noun, plural* **stacks** **1.** A large pile of straw shaped like a cone. **2.** A pile put in layers: *a stack of pancakes; a stack of magazines.* **3.** A chimney or exhaust pipe.
—*verb* **stacked, stacking** To put in a stack: *stacking hay.*

sta·di·um | stā′dē əm | —*noun, plural* **stadiums** A large building, often without a roof, where athletic events are held.

staff | stăf | or | stäf | —*noun, plural* **staffs** **1.** A long stick carried to help in walking or as a weapon. **2.** A group of assistants who serve a person of authority: *the President and his staff.* **3.** Any organized group of employees working together: *The cafeteria staff makes and serves our lunch at school.* **4.** The set of five lines and the spaces between them on which musical notes are written.

stag | stăg | —*noun, plural* **stags** A male deer that is fully grown.

stage | stāj | —*noun, plural* **stages** **1.** The raised platform in a theater on which actors and other entertainers perform. **2.** The scene or setting of an event or series of events: *Boston was the stage of many demonstrations against the British before the American Revolution.* **3.** A stagecoach. **4.** A level, degree, or period of time in the process of something: *a disease in its early stages.* **5.** Any of a series of rocket sections, each with its own engine and fuel.
—*verb* **staged, staging** **1.** To produce or direct: *Our class will stage a play for the spring pageant.* **2.** To put together and carry out: *The students staged a protest march.*

stage·coach | stāj′kōch′ | —*noun, plural* **stagecoaches** A closed coach with four wheels that was drawn by horses. It was used to carry mail and passengers.

stag·ger | stăg′ər | —*verb* **staggered, staggering** **1.** To move or stand in an unsteady way: *Fred staggered after being hit by the ball.* **2.** To cause to sway or walk in an unsteady way: *The blow staggered the boxer.* **3.** To overwhelm with a severe shock, defeat,

squirrel

stable¹, stable²
Related Latin words were the sources of both words spelled **stable**. **Stable¹** came from a word that meant "standing firm." **Stable²** originated as a word used to mean "a place for animals to stand." Both words traveled through French before arriving in English.

stadium

or misfortune: *He was staggered by the news of the accident.* **4.** To arrange in overlapping time periods: *The terms of U.S. senators are staggered so that only one third are elected every two years.*
—*noun, plural* **staggers** An act of staggering; an unsteady motion or walk: *He walked with a slight stagger.*

stain |stān| —*verb* **stained, staining** **1.** To soil; to spot: *I've stained my fingers with this leaking pen. That cloth stains easily.* **2.** To color wood or a similar material with a dye or tint: *They have stained the table a dark-brown color.*
—*noun, plural* **stains** **1.** A mark or spot: *There's a stain on my shirt.* **2.** A mark of disgrace or dishonor on someone's name, record, or reputation. **3.** A liquid put on wood or similar material to color it.

stair |stâr| —*noun, plural* **stairs** **1.** **stairs** A series or flight of steps; a staircase. Stairs are used to move from one level up or down to another level. **2.** One of a flight of steps.
♦ *These sound alike* **stair, stare.**

stair·case |stâr′kās′| —*noun, plural* **staircases** A flight of steps and its supporting railing and framework.

stake |stāk| —*noun, plural* **stakes** **1.** A stick or post with a sharp end for driving into the ground as a marker, support, or part of a fence. **2.** Often **stakes** Money or something of value risked in a bet, contest, or race: *The stakes are big in such an important boxing match.* **3.** A share or interest in a business or enterprise: *She has a big stake in her husband's store.*
—*verb* **staked, staking** **1.** To mark the place or boundaries of with stakes or other markers; lay claim to: *We staked out a piece of land on which to build our ranch.* **2.** To hold up with or fasten to a stake: *It took two hours to stake all our tomato plants.* **3.** To gamble; risk: *I will stake my reputation on that new theory.*
♦ *These sound alike* **stake, steak.**

sta·lac·tite |stə lăk′tīt′| or |stăl′ək tīt′| —*noun, plural* **stalactites** A round, pointed mineral deposit hanging from the roof of a cave or cavern. It is formed by the dripping of water containing minerals.

sta·lag·mite |stə lăg′mīt′| or |stăl′əg mīt′| —*noun, plural* **stalagmites** A round, pointed mineral deposit pointing upward from the floor of a cave or cavern. It is formed by water containing minerals dripping from above.

stalactite and stalagmite

stale |stāl| —*adjective* **staler, stalest** **1.** Not fresh; having lost flavor: *stale cake.* **2.** Too old or too often used to be interesting or effective: *stale jokes; stale ideas.* **3.** Out of condition; out of practice: *Some athletes practice on their days off for fear of getting stale.*

stalk¹ |stôk| —*noun, plural* **stalks** **1.** The main stem of a plant, or a similar part that supports a leaf or flower. **2.** A similar part that supports or connects. A snail's eyes are on stalks.

stalk² |stôk| —*verb* **stalked, stalking** **1.** To walk in a stiff, dignified, or lofty manner: *I stalked past him in complete silence.* **2.** To move in a quiet, cautious way so as not to be noticed; steal after: *The hungry tiger stalked the herd looking for an easy prey.*

stall |stôl| —*noun, plural* **stalls** **1.** An enclosed space for one animal in a barn or stable. **2.** A small enclosure or covered stand for selling or showing goods; a booth.
—*verb* **stalled, stalling** To come or bring to a sudden stop; stop running: *The plane stalled and went into a dive. I stalled the car.*

---

stalk¹, stalk²

Stalk¹ probably comes from Scandinavian. **Stalk²** is from an old English word meaning "to walk cautiously."

ă	pat	ĕ	pet	î	fierce
ā	pay	ē	be	ŏ	pot
â	care	ĭ	pit	ō	go
ä	father	ī	pie	ô	paw, for
oi	oil	ŭ	cut	zh	vision
ŏŏ	book	û	fur	ə	ago, item,
ōō	boot	*th*	the		pencil, atom,
yōō	abuse	th	thin		circus
ou	out	hw	which	ər	butter

stal·lion |stăl′yən| —*noun, plural* **stallions** A male horse that is fully grown.

sta·men |stā′mən| —*noun, plural* **stamens** The part of a flower that is made up of a thin stalk with pollen at the end of it.

stam·mer |stăm′ər| —*verb* **stammered, stammering 1.** To speak with pauses and sometimes repeated sounds; stutter: *Try not to stammer when you recite in class.* **2.** To say or utter with such pauses or repetitions: *He stammered his words out of fear.*

—*noun, plural* **stammers** An example or habit of stammering: *He takes speech lessons to correct his stammer.*

stamp |stămp| —*verb* **stamped, stamping 1.** To bring or set the foot down heavily or with force: *We stamped our feet at the doorway to shake off the snow. The horse stamped nervously.* **2.** To mark with a tool that leaves a design or message: *The guard stamped our passes and let us into the museum. We stamped "fragile" on the package.* **3.** To put a postage stamp or other sticky paper on: *Don't forget to stamp the letter before mailing it.*

—*noun, plural* **stamps 1.a.** A small piece of paper having a design on its face and glue or sticky gum on its back that is attached to a letter or package to show that a mailing charge has been paid. **b.** A similar piece of paper with a message or design used for various purposes: *a trading stamp; a tax stamp.* **2.** Any of various tools that cut, shape, or leave a mark when pressed against paper, wax, metal, leather, or other surface: *a rubber stamp for marking packages "fragile."*

stamp

stam·pede |stăm pēd′| —*noun, plural* **stampedes 1.** A sudden, violent rush of startled or scared animals, such as horses, cattle, or buffalo. **2.** A similar sudden or headlong rush of people.

—*verb* **stampeded, stampeding** To rush or flee suddenly or wildly: *The frightened horses stampeded through the town.*

stand |stănd| —*verb* **stood, standing 1.** To take or stay in an upright position on the feet: *I had to stand on a chair to change the light bulb. She stood next to the door and listened.* **2.** To rest in an upright position on a base or support: *The rocket stood on its launching pad.* **3.** To occupy a certain position or rank: *An old castle stands on the cliff. Our team stood last at the end of the year.* **4.** To be placed in a certain condition or situation: *The children stood in need of care and attention. My client stands accused of a serious crime.* **5.** To remain in one place without being moved or without moving: *Let the mixture stand for 24 hours before you use it.* **6.** To remain in effect or existence: *Exceptions are made, but the rule still stands.* **7.** To rely on for support: *The Mayor stands on his record.* **8.** To take or have a certain position, policy, attitude, or course: *Which of the candidates stand for peace? I stand ready to help my friends.* **9.** To be likely: *Who stands to gain from this war?* **10.** To put up with; tolerate; endure: *My parents can't stand disco music. We need a metal that can stand high temperatures.*

—*noun, plural* **stands 1.** An act of standing: *a long stand in a line.* **2.** A place where a person or vehicle stands or stops: *The guard took his stand at the entrance to the bank vault. There's a bus stand on the next corner.* **3.** A small, often temporary, structure for the display and sale of goods; a booth, stall, or counter. **4.** A small rack or receptacle for holding something: *an umbrella stand; a plant stand.* **5.** A raised platform on which someone can sit or stand and be clearly seen: *a witness stand.* **6. stands** An outdoor seating area: *We watched the parade from the stands.* **7.** A position or opinion that one is prepared to defend or support: *a strong stand on equal rights for women.* **8.** A group or growth of tall plants or trees: *a stand of pine.*

stan·dard | stăn′dərd | —*noun, plural* **standards 1.** Any accepted measure or model against which other persons, things, or activities may be compared or judged: *This cake isn't up to my usual standard of baking. All canned foods must meet certain standards of quality set by the government.* **2.** A flag or banner used as the emblem of a nation, military unit, school, or other organization or group.
—*adjective* **1.** Used as a basis of measurement, value, or quality: *A yard is a standard measure of distance.* **2.** Widely used or accepted as excellent; accepted or approved by most people: *a standard textbook; standard English.*

stank | stăngk | A past tense of the verb **stink:** *The beach stank of dead fish.*

stan·za | stăn′zə | —*noun, plural* **stanzas** One of the divisions of a poem or song. It is made up of two or more lines.

sta·ple¹ | stā′pəl | —*noun, plural* **staples 1.** A major product grown or produced in a region: *Rice and rubber are the staples of many countries in Asia.* **2.** A basic food or other important product that is always produced and sold because of constant need or demand: *Bread, salt, and sugar are staples.*

sta·ple² | stā′pəl | —*noun, plural* **staples 1.** A metal loop shaped like a U and having pointed ends. It is driven into a surface to hold a hook, bolt, or wire in place. **2.** A similar thin piece of wire, used for fastening papers together.
—*verb* **stapled, stapling** To fasten or attach with a staple or staples: *I stapled the extra pages into the back of my book.*

sta·pler | stā′plər | —*noun, plural* **staplers** A tool for fastening sheets of paper or other materials together with metal staples.

star | stär | —*noun, plural* **stars 1.** A heavenly body that is visible from Earth and appears in the night sky as a fixed point of bright light. **2.** A figure or object, usually with five or more points, that represents such a heavenly body: *a silver star pinned to his jacket.* **3.** An actor or actress who plays a leading part in a movie, television show, or other performance. **4.** An outstanding or famous person in a field or profession: *a baseball star.*
—*adjective* Most outstanding; best: *the star quarterback.*
—*verb* **starred, starring 1.** To decorate or mark with a star or stars: *I starred the words that you spelled incorrectly on your test.* **2.** To play or be presented in a leading role: *She's now starring in a musical show.*

starch | stärch | —*noun, plural* **starches 1.** A white food substance without taste or smell found mostly in the seeds, roots, and other parts of plants. Wheat, corn, rice, and potatoes contain large amounts of starch. **2.** A powdered form of this substance used to make clothes and fabrics stiff.
—*verb* **starched, starching** To make clothes or fabric stiff with starch: *Does your laundry starch your shirts?*

stare | stâr | —*verb* **stared, staring** To look with a long, steady gaze, often with the eyes wide open: *Billy stared at the candy.*
—*noun, plural* **stares** A steady gaze, often with the eyes wide open.
♦ *These sound alike* **stare, stair.**

star·fish | stär′fĭsh′ | —*noun, plural* **starfish** or **starfishes** A sea

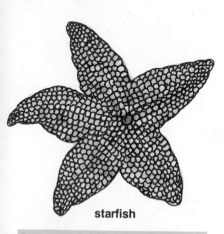
staple¹, staple²
Staple¹ comes from a word used long ago in French to mean "market." Arriving in English, **staple¹** at first meant "market town, trade center" and later came to mean "the major product handled by a particular market." **Staple²** comes from an old English word that originally meant "post, pillar." The meaning of that word changed in time to "iron rod."

starfish

ă	pat	ĕ	pet	î	fierce
ā	pay	ē	be	ŏ	pot
â	care	ĭ	pit	ō	go
ä	father	ī	pie	ô	paw, for
oi	oil	ŭ	cut	zh	vision
ŏŏ	book	û	fur	ə	ago, item,
ōō	boot	*th*	the		pencil, atom,
yōō	abuse	th	thin		circus
ou	out	hw	which	ər	butter

animal with five arms and a body in the shape of a star.

star·ling | stär′lĭng | —*noun, plural* **starlings** A bird with dark, shiny feathers. Starlings often form large flocks.

star·ry | stär′ē | —*adjective* **starrier, starriest** **1.** Shining like stars: *starry eyes.* **2.** Full of stars: *a starry night.*

Stars and Stripes The flag of the United States.

Star-Span·gled Banner, The | stär′spăng′gəld | The national anthem of the United States.

start | stärt | —*verb* **started, starting** **1.** To begin an action or movement; set out: *We started at dawn in order to reach our destination by noon.* **2.** To come into operation; have a beginning; commence: *School starts in September.* **3.** To put into operation or activity; set going: *You start the engine by turning the crank.* **4.** To make a sudden movement of all or a part of the body, as from fear or surprise: *He must have been dozing, because he started when I spoke.*
—*noun, plural* **starts** **1.** A beginning of something; a setting in motion: *This first job is only the start of what is going to be a big career.* **2.** A place or time at which something or someone begins: *We got a late start this morning.* **3.** A sudden movement of the body, as in fear or surprise; a startled reaction: *I awoke from my nightmare with a start.*

starve | stärv | —*verb* **starved, starving** **1.** To suffer or die because of lack of food: *Some of the survivors of the crash starved.* **2.** To be deprived of something necessary: *an orphan starving for love.* **3.** To be very hungry: *When do we eat dinner? I'm starving!*

state | stāt | —*noun, plural* **states** **1.** The condition in which a person or thing exists: *the state of his health; an old house in a state of decay. Ice is water in its solid state.* **2.** A mental or emotional condition; a mood: *a state of joy. Don't speak to him until he's in a calmer state.* **3.** A group of people living within a specified area under a single, independent government; a nation: *the state of Israel.* **4.** Often **States** One of the political units of a federal union such as the United States of America: *Massachusetts is one of fifty states that have joined together to make our nation.*
—*adjective* **1.** Of, belonging to, or involving a government or state: *a state law; a state border; state militia.* **2.** Of or with ceremony; very grand; formal: *a state occasion; a state ball.*
—*verb* **stated, stating** To say or express clearly in words; declare: *State your problem. The child stated that she was tired.*

state·ly | stāt′lē | —*adjective* **statelier, stateliest** Elegant, dignified, or grand in manner or appearance; majestic: *a dance with a slow, stately rhythm; a stately mansion; a stately oak tree.*

state·ment | stāt′mənt | —*noun, plural* **statements** **1.** The act of stating in speech or writing; expression in words; declaration: *the statement of an opinion.* **2.** A sentence or group of sentences that states or asserts something: *After each statement, mark whether you think it is true or false.* **3.** A written summary of a financial account: *a monthly statement from the bank.*

states·man | stāts′mən | —*noun, plural* **statesmen** A person who has experience, wisdom, and skill in dealing with government affairs or important public issues.

stat·ic | stăt′ĭk | —*adjective* Not moving or changing; at rest: *The country's economy has remained static in the last few years.*
—*noun* Noise in a radio or television receiver that results from electrical charges in the air.

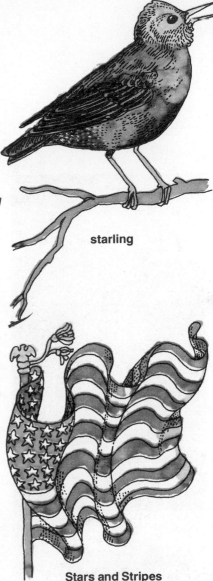

starling

Stars and Stripes

sta·tion |stā′shən| —*noun, plural* **stations** **1.** A place or location where a person or thing stands: *The teacher told us to take our stations for the safety drill.* **2.** A place or special building where certain services or activities are provided or carried on: *a fire station.* **3.** A stopping place along a route for taking on or letting off passengers: *a bus station.* **4.** A place or a channel that sends or receives radio or television signals.
—*verb* **stationed, stationing** To assign to a position or post; place: *We stationed our troops in the nearest town.*

sta·tion·ar·y |stā′shə nĕr′ē| —*adjective* **1.** Not changing position; not moving; remaining still: *Because there wasn't any wind, our sailboat was stationary in the middle of the lake.* **2.** Not capable of being moved; fixed: *a stationary bridge.* **3.** Not changing with time; remaining the same: *For many years the price of gold was stationary at $37.00 an ounce.*
♦ *These sound alike* **stationary, stationery.**

sta·tion·er·y |stā′shə nĕr′ē| —*noun* **1.** Writing paper and envelopes. **2.** Writing or office materials in general, including pens, pencils, paper, typewriter ribbons, and notebooks.
♦ *These sound alike* **stationery, stationary.**

station wagon An automobile with a large interior and one or more rows of rear seats that can be folded down or removed to provide cargo space.

sta·tis·tics |stə tĭs′tĭks| —*plural noun* Facts and figures gathered together and analyzed for information on a particular subject: *Statistics show that women usually live longer than men.*

stat·ue |stăch′ōo| —*noun, plural* **statues** The likeness of a person or thing made by an artist out of stone, clay, metal, or some other solid material.

sta·tus |stā′təs| or |stăt′əs| —*noun, plural* **statuses** **1.** The condition of a person or thing; state: *What is the status of the patient's health?* **2.** Position or rank in a group or a social system: *the high status of doctors in modern society.*

stave |stāv| —*noun, plural* **staves** One of the narrow strips of wood forming the sides of a barrel, tub, or boat.

stay |stā| —*verb* **stayed, staying** **1.** To remain in one place: *We stayed in the house all day.* **2.** To keep on being; continue: *Try to stay awake. We built a fire large enough to stay all night.* **3.** To reside or visit as a guest: *I stayed at a friend's house.*
—*noun, plural* **stays** A short period of residing or visiting: *Did you enjoy your stay in New York?*

St. Ber·nard |sānt′ bər närd′| A very large dog of a breed that was once used to help travelers in the mountains.

stead·y |stĕd′ē| —*adjective* **steadier, steadiest** **1.** Not likely to shift, wobble, or slip; sure; firm: *the steady hands of a surgeon.* **2.** Not changing; constant; even; continuous: *a steady breeze; a steady income; steady progress.* **3.** Not easily excited or disturbed; composed: *steady nerves.* **4.** Reliable; dependable: *steady workers.* **5.** Regular; habitual: *a steady customer.*
—*verb* **steadied, steadying, steadies** To make or become steady: *She raised a hand to steady the bucket on her head. After a time the runner's breathing steadied.*

steak |stāk| —*noun, plural* **steaks** A slice of meat or fish for broiling or frying.
♦ *These sound alike* **steak, stake.**

steal |stēl| —*verb* **stole, stolen, stealing** **1.** To take someone

statue

St. Bernard

ă	pat	ě	pet	î	fierce
ā	pay	ē	be	ŏ	pot
â	care	ĭ	pit	ō	go
ä	father	ī	pie	ô	paw, for
oi	oil	ŭ	cut	zh	vision
ōo	book	û	fur	ə	ago, item,
ōo	boot	*th*	the		pencil, atom,
yōo	abuse	th	thin		circus
ou	out	hw	which	ər	butter

else's property without right or permission: *It's wrong to steal from stores.* **2.** To get or enjoy secretly: *We stole a glimpse of the guests from the top of the stairs.* **3.** To move or pass without making noise or being noticed: *The neighbors' cat stole into our yard. The hours stole by.* **4.** In baseball, to gain another base without the ball being batted, by running to the base as the pitch is thrown: *Mary stole third to set up the winning run.*

♦ *These sound alike* **steal, steel.**

steam |stĕm| —*noun* **1.** Water in the form of an invisible gas or vapor. Water changes into this form by boiling. **2.** A visible mist that forms when hot water vapor cools in the air. **3.** Power or energy: *That boxer ran out of steam and lost the fight.*
—*verb* **steamed, steaming** **1.** To produce or give off steam: *That pot of water on the stove has started to steam.* **2.** To become covered with mist or steam: *The bathroom mirror steams up when the shower is used.* **3.** To move by or as if by steam power: *The ship steamed into the harbor.* **4.** To cook or treat with steam: *I steam vegetables instead of boiling them.*

steam·boat |stĕm′bōt′| —*noun, plural* **steamboats** A boat driven by steam engines.

steam engine An engine driven by hot steam. The steam expands in a closed cylinder and forces a sliding piston to move.

steam·er |stē′mər| —*noun, plural* **steamers** **1.** A steamship. **2.** A container or utensil in which something is cooked or treated with steam: *a rice steamer.*

steam·roll·er |stĕm′rō′lər| —*noun, plural* **steamrollers** A vehicle with a large, heavy roller for crushing down and smoothing road surfaces. The engine of a steamroller is powered by gasoline today, but originally it was powered by steam.

steam·ship |stĕm′shĭp′| —*noun, plural* **steamships** A large ship moved by one or more steam engines.

steel |stēl| —*noun, plural* **steels** Any very hard, strong metal made by combining iron with carbon. Steel is used for making knives, building bridges, and supporting tall buildings.

♦ *These sound alike* **steel, steal.**

steep¹ |stēp| —*adjective* **steeper, steepest** **1.** Having a sharp slope; rising or falling in a nearly straight line: *a steep hill; a steep flight of stairs.* **2.** Very high: *a steep price to pay.*

steep² |stēp| —*verb* **steeped, steeping** To soak in liquid: *The tea steeped for a few minutes.*

steep·le |stē′pəl| —*noun, plural* **steeples** A tall tower rising from the roof of a building.

steer¹ |stîr| —*verb* **steered, steering** **1.** To guide the course of a vessel, vehicle, or aircraft: *He steered his car to avoid the bicycles on the road.* **2.** To be capable of being guided: *This is an automobile that steers easily.*

steer² |stîr| —*noun, plural* **steers** A young bull that is raised for beef.

stem¹ |stĕm| —*noun, plural* **stems** **1.a.** The main supporting part of a plant. Stems are often long or thin and grow above the ground. **b.** A slender plant part that is attached to or supports a leaf, fruit, flower, or other part; a stalk. **2.** Something that connects or supports and resembles such a plant part: *the stem of a pipe; the stem of a glass.*

stem² |stĕm| —*verb* **stemmed, stemming** To plug up; stop: *Quickly, stem the flow of water from the hose.*

steamboat

steep¹, steep²
Steep¹ comes from an old English word meaning "lofty, deep." **Steep²** may have come from a word used very long ago by people who lived in Scandinavia; that word meant "to pour out."

steeple

steer¹, steer²
Steer¹ and **steer²** have always had the same meanings. The old English words from which they come were not related.

stem¹, stem²
Stem¹ is from an old English word that meant "stem, tree trunk." **Stem²** comes from a word used very long ago by people living in Scandinavia.

stepladder

---

stern¹, stern²

Stern¹ comes from a word used very long ago by English-speaking people. It had the same meaning as it does today. **Stern²** can be traced back to a word used by people who lived long ago in Scandinavia. That word meant "steering, rudder."

---

sten·cil |stĕn′səl| —*noun, plural* **stencils** A sheet of paper or other material in which letters or figures have been cut so that when ink is applied to the sheet, the patterns will appear on the surface beneath.
—*verb* **stenciled, stenciling 1.** To mark with a stencil. **2.** To produce by means of a stencil.

step |stĕp| —*noun, plural* **steps 1.** A single movement made by lifting one foot and putting it down in another spot, as in walking. **2.** A short distance: *The park is just a step away from my door.* **3.** The sound of someone walking: *I heard his step in the hall.* **4.** A small platform placed as a rest for the foot in climbing up and down a ladder. **5.** Measures taken to achieve some goal: *We are taking steps to preserve wildlife in our region.* **6.** A degree of progress: *a step forward in learning a language.*
—*verb* **stepped, stepping 1.** To move by taking a step: *Step forward when your name is called.* **2.** To put or press the foot down: *Step on that spider.*

step·fa·ther |stĕp′fä′thər| —*noun, plural* **stepfathers** The husband of one's mother by a later marriage.

step·lad·der |stĕp′lăd′ər| —*noun, plural* **stepladders** A ladder with flat steps instead of round rungs.

step·moth·er |stĕp′mŭth′ər| —*noun, plural* **stepmothers** The wife of one's father by a later marriage.

ste·re·o |stĕr′ē ō′| or |stîr′ē ō′| —*noun, plural* **stereos** A record player that uses more than one speaker, placed in different parts of a room.

ster·e·o·phon·ic |stĕr′ē ə fŏn′ĭk| or |stîr′ē ə fŏn′ĭk| —*adjective* Used in a sound reproduction system that uses two separate channels to give a more natural sound: *stereophonic sound.*

ster·il·ize |stĕr′ə līz′| —*verb* **sterilized, sterilizing** To make free from germs or dirt: *The nurse sterilized the surgeon's instruments.*

stern¹ |stûrn| —*adjective* **sterner, sternest 1.** Grave and severe: *a stern lecture on table manners.* **2.** Strict; firm: *stern discipline.*

stern² |stûrn| —*noun, plural* **sterns** The rear part of a ship or boat.

stew |stoo| or |styoo| —*verb* **stewed, stewing** To cook by simmering or boiling slowly: *The cook stewed the chicken.*
—*noun, plural* **stews** A thick mixture of pieces of meat and vegetables in a liquid.

stew·ard |stoo′ərd| or |styoo′ərd| —*noun, plural* **stewards 1.** A person who manages another's property, household, business, or finances. **2.** A male attendant on a ship or airplane who waits on passengers.

stew·ard·ess |stoo′ər dĭs| or |styoo′ər dĭs| —*noun, plural* **stewardesses** A woman who waits on passengers in an airplane.

stick |stĭk| —*noun, plural* **sticks 1.** A long, slender piece of wood: *a walking stick; a hockey stick.* **2.** Anything having the shape of a stick: *a stick of dynamite; a stick of peppermint candy.*
—*verb* **stuck, sticking 1.** To prick with a pointed object: *She stuck her finger with a thorn.* **2.** To fasten by pushing in a pointed object: *He stuck the pictures to the board with a pin.* **3.** To fasten or attach with glue, tape, or other adhesive material: *The policeman stuck a ticket on the car window.* **4.** To be attached to a surface and not come off easily: *Glue sticks to the fingers.* **5.** To stay in place: *Why won't this stamp stick? The wagon is stuck in the mud.* **6.** To bring to a point where progress stops: *I got stuck on the last*

ă	pat	ĕ	pet	î	fierce
ā	pay	ē	be	ŏ	pot
â	care	ĭ	pit	ō	go
ä	father	ī	pie	ô	paw, for
oi	oil	ŭ	cut	zh	vision
oo	book	û	fur	ə	ago, item,
oo	boot	*th*	the		pencil, atom,
yoo	abuse	th	thin		circus
ou	out	hw	which	ər	butter

question and never finished the test. **7.** To remain in close association with: *Let's stick together or we'll get lost in the crowd.* **8.** To stay with what one starts: *Stick with this project until it is completed.* **9.** To extend: *He stuck out his hand in greeting.*

stick·er |stĭk′ər| —*noun, plural* **stickers** A small seal or piece of paper with glue on the back. It is used to fasten or mark such things as letters or packages: *The sticker on this present says it's for Dad.*

stick·y |stĭk′ē| —*adjective* **stickier, stickiest** **1.** Tending to stick to whatever surface is touched: *sticky paste; sticky candy.* **2.** Hot and humid: *Today is going to be another sticky day.*

stiff |stĭf| —*adjective* **stiffer, stiffest** **1.** Not easily bent or twisted: *a stiff fabric; a stiff new pair of shoes.* **2.** Not moving or operating easily: *a stiff neck; a stiff door handle.* **3.** Not fluid; thick: *a stiff mixture.* **4.** Formal and rigid; not graceful: *a stiff manner.* **5.** Moving with a steady, strong force: *a stiff wind; a stiff current.* **6.** Harsh; mean; severe: *stiff penalties.* **7.** Very high: *stiff prices.*

sti·fle |stī′fəl| —*verb* **stifled, stifling** **1.** To feel uncomfortable because of a lack of air: *This room stifles me.* **2.** To put out: *stifle a flame.* **3.** To hold back: *Stifle your laughter.*

still |stĭl| —*adjective* **stiller, stillest** **1.** Without noise; quiet; silent: *He was still for a moment, then started talking again.* **2.** Without motion: *The lake was still after the storm.*
—*noun, plural* **stills** Quiet; silence: *the still of the night.*
—*adverb* **1.** Not moving: *Sit still!* **2.** Now as before: *Father was still mad at me when I got home.* **3.** In increasing amount or degree: *I've got still more money coming to me.* **4.** Nevertheless; all the same: *a painful but still necessary decision.*
—*conjunction* But: *It was a bad year; still, it had its good moments.*

still·ness |stĭl′nĭs| —*noun* The condition of being still; a lack of movement; quiet or calm: *the dark stillness of the night.*

stilt |stĭlt| —*noun, plural* **stilts** Either of a pair of long, slender poles, each with a foot support part way up. Stilts make it possible for a person to walk way above the ground.

stim·u·late |stĭm′yə lāt′| —*verb* **stimulated, stimulating** To make more active or excited: *Music stimulates her imagination.*

stim·u·li |stĭm′yə lī′| The plural of the noun **stimulus.**

stim·u·lus |stĭm′yə ləs| —*noun, plural* **stimuli** Something that stimulates; incentive: *Praise is a stimulus for better work.*

sting |stĭng| —*verb* **stung, stinging** **1.** To stick with a small, sharp point. **2.** To feel or cause to feel a sharp, smarting pain: *His fingers stung with the freezing cold. Iodine stings.*
—*noun, plural* **stings** **1.** A sharp, piercing part or organ of an insect or animal. It is used for stinging and often injecting a poisonous or irritating substance. **2.** A wound or mark made by such a part. **3.** A sharp, smarting sensation: *the sting of the wind.*

sting·er |stĭng′ər| —*noun, plural* **stingers** An insect or animal part that is used for stinging; a sting.

sting·ray |stĭng′rā′| —*noun, plural* **stingrays** An ocean fish that has a flat body and a long tail that looks like a whip. A long stinger on the tail contains poison.

stin·gy |stĭn′jē| —*adjective* **stingier, stingiest** Giving or spending very little: *He is a very stingy man.*

stink |stĭngk| —*verb* **stank** or **stunk, stunk, stinking** To give off a bad odor: *Dead fish stink.*
—*noun, plural* **stinks** A strong, bad odor.

stilt
In a circus act

stirrup

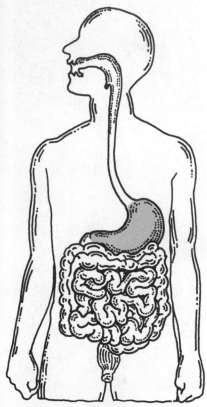

stomach

stir | stûr | —*verb* **stirred, stirring 1.** To mix something by moving it around in a circular motion with a spoon or other similar object: *Stir the cake batter until the milk is mixed thoroughly with the flour. Stir for five minutes.* **2.** To change or cause to change position slightly: *The wind stirred the sand.* **3.** To move vigorously: *The animals began to stir when the sun came up.* **4.** To bring about; urge on: *Don't stir up trouble.* **5.** To excite the emotions of: *The music stirred her imagination.*
—*noun, plural* **stirs 1.** The act of stirring: *Give the batter a stir.* **2.** An excited reaction: *Her appearance caused quite a stir.*

stir·rup | stûr′əp | or | stĭr′əp | —*noun, plural* **stirrups** A loop or ring with a flat bottom, hung by a strap from either side of a horse's saddle. It is used to support the rider's foot.

stitch | stĭch | —*noun, plural* **stitches** A single, complete movement of a threaded needle or similar instrument into and out of material, as in sewing, embroidery, knitting, or crocheting.
—*verb* **stitched, stitching** To fasten, join, or decorate with stitches: *stitch on a pocket; stitch up a seam.*

St. John's | sānt jŏnz′ | The capital of Newfoundland.

stock | stŏk | —*noun, plural* **stocks 1.** A supply of things stored for future use: *a stock of grain; a stock of winter clothing.*
2. Animals like cows, sheep, or pigs; livestock. **3.** Broth made from boiled meat, fish, or poultry: *Meat stock is used as a base for making soups and stews.* **4.** The handle of a firearm. **5.** Shares in a business: *He owns stock in this company.*
—*verb* **stocked, stocking 1.** To provide with stock: *We stocked the store.* **2.** To keep for future use: *The farmer stocked canned goods.*
—*adjective* Kept regularly available for sale or use: *Bread is a stock item.*

stock·ade | stŏ kād′ | —*noun, plural* **stockades 1.** A barrier made of strong, upright posts. It is used for protection in a fort. **2.** The area surrounded by such a barrier.

stock exchange A place where stocks, bonds, or other securities are bought and sold.

stock·ing | stŏk′ĭng | —*noun, plural* **stockings** A close-fitting covering for the foot and leg, especially one reaching higher than the knee.

stock market 1. A stock exchange. **2.** The business that takes place in a stock exchange: *Prices on the stock market went up with the news of the election.*

stock·y | stŏk′ē | —*adjective* **stockier, stockiest** Solidly built; squat and thick: *a stocky boy.*

stock·yard | stŏk′yärd′ | —*noun, plural* **stockyards** A large, enclosed yard in which livestock is kept before being slaughtered or shipped elsewhere.

stole | stōl | The past tense of the verb **steal:** *They stole goods from the store.*

sto·len | stō′lən | The past participle of the verb **steal:** *They had stolen from that store before.*

stom·ach | stŭm′ək | —*noun, plural* **stomachs 1.** The part of the digestive system that receives food that has been swallowed. Food begins to be digested in the stomach. **2.** Any desire or liking: *I don't have the stomach for such adventures.*
—*verb* **stomached, stomaching** To put up with; tolerate: *She had to stomach the teacher's criticism.*

ă	pat	ĕ	pet	î	fierce
ā	pay	ē	be	ŏ	pot
â	care	ĭ	pit	ō	go
ä	father	ī	pie	ô	paw, for

oi	oil	ŭ	cut	zh	vision
ŏŏ	book	û	fur	ə	ago, item,
ōō	boot	th	the		pencil, atom,
yōō	abuse	th	thin		circus
ou	out	hw	which	ər	butter

stomp |stômp| or |stŏmp| —*verb* **stomped, stomping** To step or trample heavily: *stomp on an ant; stomp on the floor.*

stone |stōn| —*noun, plural* **stones** **1.** Hard mineral or material from the earth; rock. **2.** A piece of mineral matter considered to have great beauty and value; a jewel. **3.** A seed with a hard covering, as of a cherry, a plum, or certain other fruits; a pit.
—*verb* **stoned, stoning** To throw stones at: *The angry crowd tried to stone the dictator's car.*

stood |stŏŏd| The past tense and past participle of the verb **stand:** *Helen stood by the door. They had stood there for hours.*

stool |stōōl| —*noun, plural* **stools** **1.** A seat, without arms or a back, supported on legs. **2.** A low support on which to rest the feet while sitting.

stoop¹ |stōōp| —*verb* **stooped, stooping** **1.** To bend from the waist: *She stooped to pick up the child.* **2.** To lower oneself: *He said that he wouldn't stoop to her level.*
—*noun, plural* **stoops** A forward bending, especially when it is a habit: *He walks with a stoop.*

stoop² |stōōp| —*noun, plural* **stoops** A small staircase leading to the entrance of a house or building.

stop |stŏp| —*verb* **stopped, stopping** **1.** To cease moving; come to a halt: *The car stopped suddenly.* **2.** To plug up or block: *You have to stop up the drain.* **3.** To cause to change a course of action or method of behavior: *They tried to stop her from quitting.* **4.** To end or interrupt what one is doing: *He didn't want to stop running.*
—*noun, plural* **stops** **1.** The act or condition of stopping; halt: *The car made a stop at a red light.* **2.** A stay or visit: *We made a stop in Denver.* **3.** A place where a stop is made: *a bus stop.*

stop·per |stŏp'ər| —*noun, plural* **stoppers** Any device put into an opening in order to close it. A cork or plug is a stopper.

stor·age |stôr'ĭj| or |stōr'ĭj| —*noun, plural* **storages** **1.** The act of storing: *She made arrangements for the storage of her furniture in the warehouse.* **2.** A place for storage: *We have storage in the cellar.* **3.** The price charged for storing goods: *How much is storage per month?*

store |stôr| or |stōr| —*noun, plural* **stores** **1.** A place where things are offered for sale; a shop. **2.** A supply of goods reserved for future use: *Do you have a store of wood for the winter?*
—*verb* **stored, storing** To put away for future use: *The squirrels store acorns for the winter.*

store·house |stôr'hous'| or |stōr'hous'| —*noun, plural* **storehouses** A place in which goods are stored.

store·keep·er |stôr'kē'pər| or |stōr'kē'pər| —*noun, plural* **storekeepers** Someone who runs a retail shop or store.

stork |stôrk| or |stōrk| —*noun, plural* **storks** A large bird with long legs for wading and a long, straight bill.

storm |stôrm| —*noun, plural* **storms** **1.** A strong wind with rain, sleet, hail, or snow: *The storm we had last night had a lot of thunder and lightning.* **2.** A sudden, strong outburst, as of emotion: *the girl's storm of anger; storm of tears.* **3.** A sudden, violent attack: *The Indians took the fort by storm.*
—*verb* **stormed, storming** **1.** To blow with a strong wind, rain, snow, lightning, or sleet. **2.** To show a sudden, strong burst of emotion: *The man stormed out of the room in anger.* **3.** To attack violently: *The knights stormed the gates of the castle.*

storm·y |stôr'mē| —*adjective* **stormier, stormiest** **1.** Affected by

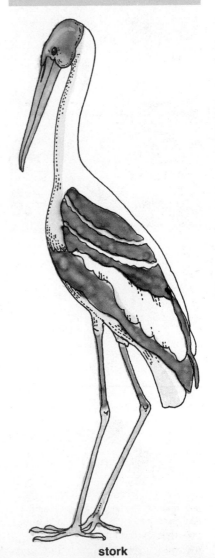

stoop¹, stoop²
Stoop¹ comes from a word used very long ago in English to mean "to bend down." **Stoop²** was borrowed during colonial American times from a Dutch word meaning "small porch."

stork

stove
An old stove

ă	pat	ē	pet	î	fierce
ā	pay	ē	be	ŏ	pot
â	care	ĭ	pit	ō	go
ä	father	ī	pie	ô	paw, for
oi	oil	ŭ	cut	zh	vision
ŏŏ	book	û	fur	ə	ago, item,
ōō	boot	*th*	the		pencil, atom,
yōō	abuse	th	thin		circus
ou	out	hw	which	ər	butter

a storm: *stormy weather.* **2.** Violently emotional: *a stormy temper.*

sto·ry¹ |stôr′ē| or |stōr′ē| —*noun, plural* **stories 1.** An account of something that happened: *a newspaper story.* **2.** An account of something that has been made up or told to entertain somebody: *a story of how America was discovered.* **3.** A lie: *I don't believe that story you just told me.*

sto·ry² |stôr′ē| or |stōr′ē| —*noun, plural* **stories** A floor of a building: *Dad's office is on the ninth story.*

stout |stout| —*adjective* **stouter, stoutest 1.** Not giving in easily; bold; brave: *a stout soldier.* **2.** Strong; firm; sturdy: *The firefighter carried the child to safety in his stout arms.* **3.** Large and fat: *Rita is too stout to wear that coat.*

stove |stōv| —*noun, plural* **stoves** An appliance that is used for cooking or heating. A stove uses fuel or electricity for its power.

stow |stō| —*verb* **stowed, stowing** To put or place; store: *Stow the logs in the shed.*

stow·a·way |stō′ə wā′| —*noun, plural* **stowaways** Someone who hides aboard a ship, plane, or train to get a free ride.

St. Paul |sānt pôl′| The capital of Minnesota.

strag·gle |străg′əl| —*verb* **straggled, straggling 1.** To stray or fall behind: *The children straggled after their teacher.* **2.** To spread out in a scattered way: *Vines straggled along the garden walk.*

straight |strāt| —*adjective* **straighter, straightest 1.** Extending continuously in the same direction; without bend; not curved: *a straight line.* **2.** Direct; honest: *He gave us a straight answer.* **3.** In proper order; neatly: *He keeps his room straight.* **4.** Not interrupted; in a row: *Mary was gone for three straight days.* —*adverb* **1.** In a straight line; directly: *The car came straight at us.* **2.** Without delay; immediately: *She went straight to the phone when the plane landed.* **3.** In an upright way: *Stand straight.*
♦ *These sound alike* **straight, strait.**

straight·en |strāt′n| —*verb* **straightened, straightening** To make or become straight: *Straighten your tie. The road straightened.*

straight·for·ward |strāt fôr′wərd| —*adjective* **1.** Going about things in a direct way: *Let's try a more straightforward course.* **2.** Honest; open: *a straightforward person.*

strain |strān| —*verb* **strained, straining 1.** To pull tight; stretch: *The sled dogs strained at their leashes.* **2.** To try hard; strive: *She strained to understand the foreign language.* **3.** To hurt or injure by overwork: *strain a muscle.* **4.** To force or stretch a point: *Lee strained the truth to impress the new girl.* **5.** To pass through a strainer; sift: *They strained the oranges to make juice.* —*noun, plural* **strains 1.** A pressure; pull; force: *They felt a strain on the lines.* **2.** An injury from too much effort: *a muscle strain.* **3.** A great worry; emotional pressure: *His illness was a strain on the family.*

strain·er |strā′nər| —*noun, plural* **strainers** A tool that strains things.

strait |strāt| —*noun, plural* **straits 1.** A narrow passage that connects two bodies of water. **2. straits** Troubles; difficulties: *He was in bad straits after he lost his money in the stock market.*
♦ *These sound alike* **strait, straight.**

strand¹ |strănd| —*verb* **stranded, stranding 1.** To drive or be driven aground: *The ship was stranded on a reef.* **2.** To leave in a difficult position or place: *They were stranded on the mountain when their car broke down.*

strand² | strănd | —*noun, plural* **strands** **1.** A single wire or fiber from a cord or rope. **2.** A hair or thread. **3.** A string of beads: *a strand of pearls.*

strange | strānj | —*adjective* **stranger, strangest** **1.** Not known before; not familiar: *They came to a strange land.* **2.** Odd; unusual; different: *strange behavior.* **3.** Out of place; not at home: *Marcy felt strange on her first day at camp.*

stran·ger | strān'jər | —*noun, plural* **strangers** **1.** Someone who is not known as a friend or acquaintance. **2.** Someone from another place: *There were many strangers in town for the holidays.*

stran·gle | străng'gəl | —*verb* **strangled, strangling** **1.** To kill or die by squeezing the neck to stop the breath. **2.** To choke: *Rita's scarf was so tight it was strangling her.*

strap | străp | —*noun, plural* **straps** A long, thin piece of leather or other material. A strap may be used to hold things in place or keep them together: *the strap on a dress.*
—*verb* **strapped, strapping** To fasten or hold firmly: *We strapped on our safety belts. John's knapsack was strapped to his back.*

stra·te·gic | strə tē'jĭk | —*adjective* **1.** Of strategy: *He is responsible for all strategic plans of the army.* **2.** Very important to strategy: *The harbor was strategic for the defense of the city.*

strat·e·gy | străt'ə jē | —*noun, plural* **strategies** **1.** The science of planning a series of actions that would be useful in gaining a goal: *In the army they studied military strategy.* **2.** A plan of action arrived at by this science: *Our strategy is to take them by surprise.*

straw | strô | —*noun, plural* **straws** **1.** Stalks of wheat, oats, or other grain from which the seeds have been removed. Straw is used as bedding and food for animals, and for making things. **2.** A narrow tube of paper or plastic through which a person can drink or suck up liquids.

straw·ber·ry | strô'bĕr'ē | —*noun, plural* **strawberries** A sweet red fruit that has many small seeds on the surface.

stray | strā | —*verb* **strayed, straying** To wander about or roam; get lost: *Our cat sometimes strays from home.*
—*noun, plural* **strays** A lost person or animal.
—*adjective* **1.** Wandering; lost: *a stray horse.* **2.** Scattered or separate: *stray pins on the floor.*

streak | strēk | —*noun, plural* **streaks** **1.** A line or mark, usually long and thin: *streaks of dirt on his nose.* **2.** A trace of something: *Randy has a selfish streak.*
—*verb* **streaked, streaking** To mark with or form a streak: *Colors streaked the evening sky.*

stream | strēm | —*noun, plural* **streams** **1.** A body of water that flows along. Streams can be brooks or small rivers. **2.** A steady flow of anything: *a stream of compliments; a stream of sunlight.*
—*verb* **streamed, streaming** **1.** To move along or flow as a stream does; move steadily: *People streamed from the store.* **2.** To float or wave: *Flags streamed in the breeze.*

stream·er | strē'mər | —*noun, plural* **streamers** **1.** A long flag or banner: *Streamers hung on the buildings for the parade.* **2.** Any long, narrow strips: *We decorated the room with paper streamers.*

stream·line | strēm'līn' | —*verb* **streamlined, streamlining** **1.** To design and build something so it has the least possible resistance to water or air; give a streamlined shape to. **2.** To make more efficient or modern; improve: *The new manager streamlined the store to increase profits.*

strawberry
Above: Blossom *(left)* and berry *(right)*
Below: Plant

streetcar

street |strēt| —*noun, plural* **streets** A road or public way in a city or town.

street·car |strēt′kär′| —*noun, plural* **streetcars** A car that runs on rails and carries passengers along a regular route through city streets.

strength |strĕngkth| or |strĕngth| —*noun, plural* **strengths** **1.** The quality of being strong; power; energy: *Bob has great strength and can pick up Molly. The strength of her love kept the family together.* **2.** The power to take much strain or stress: *Maria tested the strength of the ladder.* **3.** The degree of power or force: *This coffee does not have much strength.*

strength·en |strĕngk′thən| or |strĕng′thən| —*verb* **strengthened, strengthening** To make or become strong.

stress |strĕs| —*noun, plural* **stresses** **1.** Special importance or meaning put on something: *Great stress was put on eating at regular hours.* **2.** The stronger tone of voice used when pronouncing a word or syllable; accent: *In the word "maple" the stress is on the first syllable.* **3.** Pressure; force; strain: *The stress of the job was too much for Maryanne.*
—*verb* **stressed, stressing** To give special importance to: *She stressed the good points of the book.*

stretch |strĕch| —*verb* **stretched, stretching** **1. a.** To lengthen or widen by pulling: *Stretch those socks before you put them on.* **b.** To become lengthened or widened: *My sweater stretched out of shape.* **2.** To extend across a certain space; spread: *The road stretched for miles ahead.* **3.** To lie down with arms and legs out: *Stretch out for a nap.* **4.** To reach out: *They stretched out their arms to catch the balls.* **5.** To spread out or flex one's muscles: *It feels good to stretch after a long trip.*
—*noun, plural* **stretches** **1.** The act of stretching: *Milly made a big stretch over the table and took the salt.* **2.** A period of time or area of land that is not interrupted or broken: *After a long stretch they came to the gate.* **3.** A straight section of a course or racetrack leading to the finish line: *the home stretch.*

stretch·er |strĕch′ər| —*noun, plural* **stretchers** A kind of portable bed or cot on which people who are hurt or ill can be carried.

strick·en |strĭk′ən| A past participle of the verb **strike:** *He was stricken by grief.*
—*adjective* Affected or attacked by sickness, troubles, or something else serious: *Food and medicine was sent to the stricken farmers after the earthquake.*

strict |strĭkt| —*adjective* **stricter, strictest** **1.** Demanding a strong discipline; severe; stern: *Aunt Sarah is very strict about bedtime.* **2.** Absolute; complete: *The story was told to me in strict confidence.* **3.** Not changing; carefully enforced: *His parents have a strict rule about bedtime.*

strid·den |strĭd′ən| The past participle of the verb **stride:** *He had stridden across the park before.*

stride |strīd| —*verb* **strode, stridden, striding** To walk with long steps: *Jennifer strode across the plaza.*
—*noun, plural* **strides** **1.** A long step: *The giant took great strides toward Jack.* **2.** A step forward; progress: *We have made new strides in space exploration.*

strike |strīk| —*verb* **struck, struck** or **stricken, striking** **1.** To hit; give a blow to: *He struck the desk in anger.* **2.** To collide or crash

into: *The truck struck a car. Their helmets struck when they fell.*
3. To show by sound: *The clock struck one.* **4.** To impress strongly: *The plan struck her as wise.* **5.** To discover; come upon: *strike oil.* **6.** To stop work in order to get something such as more money or better benefits: *The union struck the city newspapers.*

 Phrasal verb strike out 1. To cross off; get rid of: *Strike out the mistake.* **2. a.** In baseball, to get a batter out with three strikes. **b.** To be put out in such a way: *Jones struck out in the first inning.*
—*noun, plural* **strikes 1.** An act of striking; a hit: *a strike on the head.* **2.** The stopping of work by employees in order to get a better working arrangement: *The strike lasted for 38 days.* **3.** In baseball, a pitched ball that the batter swings at and misses.

string |strĭng| —*noun, plural* **strings 1.** A thin cord made of fibers, used for fastening or tying up. **2.** Anything like a string in appearance: *a string of lights.* **3.** A set of things with a cord running through them: *a string of pearls.* **4. a.** A wire stretched across part of a musical instrument and struck, plucked, or bowed to make tones. **b. strings** Instruments that have strings and are played with a bow: *Violins are strings.*
—*verb* **strung, stringing 1.** To provide with strings: *He asked the store to string his racket.* **2.** To put on a string or run a string through: *The jeweler will string the beads.* **3.** To arrange in a string: *Jessica and Billy were busy stringing lights on the Christmas tree.* **4.** To stretch from one place to another: *We strung the line from pole to pole.*

string bean A long, narrow green bean pod that grows on a bushy plant. String beans are eaten as vegetables.

stringed |strĭngd| —*adjective* Having strings: *The guitar is a stringed instrument.*

strip¹ |strĭp| —*verb* **stripped, stripping 1.** To take off the clothing or covering; make bare: *Jose stripped off his wet shirt.* **2.** To take away; remove the important parts of: *They stripped the garden of all its flowers.*

strip² |strĭp| —*noun, plural* **strips** A long, narrow piece of material or land: *a strip of cloth; a strip of beach.*

stripe |strīp| —*noun, plural* **stripes** A line, strip, or band: *Some animals have stripes on their tails. Joseph's coat had many stripes.*
—*verb* **striped, striping** To mark with stripes: *Dad striped the bicycle with safety stickers.*

strive |strīv| —*verb* **strove, striven** or **strived, striving** To try hard: *Warren strives hard to be a good brother.*

striv·en |strĭv′ən| A past participle of the verb **strive:** *We had striven to reach our goal.*

strode |strōd| The past tense of the verb **stride:** *Jennie strode so quickly that we could not keep up with her.*

stroke |strōk| —*noun, plural* **strokes 1.** A blow or strike: *a stroke of the whip.* **2.** A single complete movement that is repeated often: *a swimming stroke; the stroke of an oar.* **3.** The time shown by the striking of a clock: *at the stroke of midnight.* **4.** A mark made by a brush, pen, or pencil: *She painted with broad strokes.* **5.** An unexpected event with powerful effect: *a stroke of good luck.* **6.** A light pat: *a gentle stroke of her hand.* **7.** A sudden sickness caused by the blocking or breaking of a blood vessel in the brain: *My uncle had a stroke and can't move his arm.*
—*verb* **stroked, stroking** To run the hand over lightly; pat.

string bean
Above: Plant
Below: Pods *(left)* and beans *(right)*

---

strip¹, strip²
Strip¹ comes from an old English word meaning "to plunder." **Strip²** may be a different form of **stripe** ("a long, narrow band"), but this is not certain.

structure
Buildings in New York

stroll │strōl│ —*verb* **strolled, strolling** To walk or wander at a slow and relaxed pace: *They strolled through the park.*
—*noun, plural* **strolls** A slow, relaxed walk.

strong │strông│ or │strŏng│ —*adjective* **stronger, strongest**
1. Having much power, energy, or strength: *The strong lad carried the suitcase. The strong wind blew down a tree.* **2.** Able to resist stress or strain; not easily broken: *A strong wall will last for years.*
3. Having great mental will or force: *a strong belief; a strong argument.* **4.** In good health: *She is stronger after her operation.*

strove │strōv│ The past tense of the verb **strive**: *She strove against the high waves of the sea.*

struck │strŭk│ The past tense and a past participle of the verb **strike**: *Lightning struck the tree. Lightning had struck the tree before.*

struc·ture │strŭk′chər│ —*noun, plural* **structures 1.** Anything made up of a number of parts arranged together: *Our government is a complex structure.* **2.** The way parts are put together to form something: *The structure of the barn was sound.* **3.** A building; something that is built: *This church is a famous structure.*

strug·gle │strŭg′əl│ —*verb* **struggled, struggling 1.** To fight against; work hard at: *Amy struggled through the tall grass.* **2.** To compete: *Our team struggled for second place.*
—*noun, plural* **struggles 1.** A great effort: *a struggle to get home.* **2.** Battle; fighting: *The warriors engaged in a fierce struggle.*

strum │strŭm│ —*verb* **strummed, strumming** To play a stringed instrument by plucking the strings with the fingers: *Billy strummed a tune on the guitar.*

strung │strŭng│ The past tense and past participle of the verb **string**: *She strung the racket. Billy had strung the racket last week.*

stub │stŭb│ —*noun, plural* **stubs 1.** A short end that is left over after something has been used up or broken off: *a pencil stub.*
2. The part of a check or bill kept as a record. **3.** The part of a ticket kept to show payment.
—*verb* **stubbed, stubbing** To bump one's toe or foot against something: *He stubbed his toe on the step of the staircase.*

stub·ble │stŭb′əl│ —*noun* **1.** Short, stiff stalks of grain or other plants that are left after a crop has been cut. **2.** Something that looks like this, especially a short, stiff growth of beard or hair.

stub·born │stŭb′ərn│ —*adjective* **1.** Not willing to change; fixed in purpose; not giving in: *Sam is very stubborn about following safety rules.* **2.** Hard to handle or deal with: *a stubborn cold.*

stuck │stŭk│ The past tense and past participle of the verb **stick**: *The glue stuck to his fingers. The postage stamp had stuck to the back of the envelope and he couldn't find it.*

stu·dent │stood′nt│ or │styood′nt│ —*noun, plural* **students 1.** A person who goes to some kind of school: *Laurie is a student at the university.* **2.** One who makes a study of something: *a student of languages.*

stu·di·o │stoo′dē ō′│ or │styoo′dē ō′│ —*noun, plural* **studios 1.** A room, loft, or building where an artist works. **2.** A place where motion pictures, television shows, or radio programs are made or broadcast.

stud·y │stŭd′ē│ —*noun, plural* **studies 1.** The act or process of learning something; an effort to learn: *Much study went into this program.* **2.** A branch of knowledge; a subject that is studied: *history studies.* **3.** A work on a certain subject; careful examination: *Beth made a study of kitchen design.* **4.** A room used

ă	pat	ĕ	pet	î	fierce
ā	pay	ē	be	ŏ	pot
â	care	ĭ	pit	ō	go
ä	father	ī	pie	ô	paw, for
oi	oil	ŭ	cut	zh	vision
oo	book	û	fur	ə	ago, item,
oo	boot	*th*	the		pencil, atom,
yoo	abuse	th	thin		circus
ou	out	hw	which	ər	butter

for studying, reading, or working: *Dad likes to read in the study.*
—*verb* **studied, studying, studies 1.** To try to learn: *We studied ecology before we took our nature walk.* **2.** To examine closely: *He studied her face before answering.*

stuff | stŭf | —*noun, plural* **stuffs 1.** The material from which something is made: *Juan found some orange stuff for his costume.* **2.** Useless material; junk: *That drawer is full of stuff she doesn't want. Watch out for that old stuff in the garage.* **3.** Things; belongings: *Jamie brought his football stuff to our house.*
—*verb* **stuffed, stuffing 1.** To pack tightly; fill up: *He stuffed his school bag with magazines.* **2.** To stop up; choke; block: *They stuffed up the cracks in the wall. My nose is stuffed up.* **3.** To fill with a stuffing: *stuff a chicken.* **4.** To fill the skin of a dead animal to make it look as it did when alive: *He stuffed the owl for the bird exhibit.* **5.** To eat too much; fill oneself with too much food: *We stuffed ourselves at the picnic.*

stuff·ing | stŭf'ĭng | —*noun, plural* **stuffings 1.** Soft material used to stuff, fill, or pad things made of or covered with cloth: *The stuffing is coming out of my pillow.* **2.** A mixture of bread crumbs, spices, and other foods that is put inside a turkey, chicken, meat, or vegetables.

stuff·y | stŭf'ē | —*adjective* **stuffier, stuffiest 1.** Not having enough fresh air; close: *I opened the window because it was stuffy in here.* **2.** Having blocked or clogged breathing passages: *a stuffy nose.* **3.** Dull and boring; stiff: *This book on manners is stuffy.*

stum·ble | stŭm'bəl | —*verb* **stumbled, stumbling 1.** To trip and almost fall: *I stumbled running around the corner.* **2.** To move in a clumsy way: *She stumbled out of bed.* **3.** To make a mistake; blunder: *Speak slowly and you won't stumble over your words.* **4.** To meet or happen by chance: *You'll never guess who I stumbled into in the store. The police stumbled upon a clue.*

stump | stŭmp | —*noun, plural* **stumps 1.** The part of a tree trunk left in the ground after the tree has fallen or been cut down. **2.** A short or broken piece or part: *the stump of a pencil.*

stun | stŭn | —*verb* **stunned, stunning 1.** To daze or knock unconscious: *The fall from the horse had stunned her.* **2.** To shock or confuse: *Our three home runs stunned the other team.*

stung | stŭng | The past tense and past participle of the verb **sting:** *A bee stung me. I have been stung before.*

stunk | stŭngk | A past tense and the past participle of the verb **stink:** *The dead rabbit stunk. The city air has stunk for days.*

stunt¹ | stŭnt | —*verb* **stunted, stunting** To stop or hinder the growth or development of: *Air pollution may stunt many kinds of plants.*

stunt² | stŭnt | —*noun, plural* **stunts 1.** An act or feat that shows unusual skill or courage: *The circus performer did some amazing stunts on the tightrope.* **2.** An act that is unusual, illegal, or dangerous: *Trying to jump out of the second-floor window was a stupid stunt.*

stu·pid | stōo'pĭd | or | styōo'pĭd | —*adjective* **stupider, stupidest 1.** Not intelligent; slow to understand; dull: *That was a stupid thing to say.* **2.** Not showing common sense: *It's stupid to have a picnic if you know it's going to rain.*

stur·dy | stûr'dē | —*adjective* **sturdier, sturdiest** Strong and durable; hardy: *That sturdy tree is over two hundred years old.*

stur·geon | stûr'jən | —*noun, plural* **sturgeons** or **sturgeon** A

stunt¹, stunt²
Stunt¹ has two sources: an old English word meaning "dull, foolish" and a word meaning "short, like a dwarf" in the language of people who lived long ago in Scandinavia. The origin of **stunt²** is unknown. It was a slang word in American colleges in the 1890's, but no earlier source can be determined.

large fish that lives in fresh or salt water and has bony plates on its body. The flesh of the sturgeon is good to eat.

stut·ter | stŭt′ər | —*verb* **stuttered, stuttering** To repeat the same sound while speaking. A person who stutters will repeat or stumble over certain letters, especially at the beginning of a word. For example, "I d-d-don't r-r-remember the s-s-story."
—*noun, plural* **stutters** The act or habit of stuttering.

style | stīl | —*noun, plural* **styles** **1.** A particular way or manner in which something is done: *The new police station is built in a modern style. I liked the book because its style is simple and easy to understand.* **2.** A way of dressing or behaving; fashion: *Long dresses are in style this year.*
—*verb* **styled, styling** To design or arrange in a special way: *Who styled your hair?*

styl·ish | stī′lĭsh | —*adjective* Following the latest style; fashionable: *His new suit is very stylish.*

sub·ject | sŭb′jĭkt | —*noun, plural* **subjects** **1.** Something that is thought about, discussed, or is the object of an action: *The subject of my report is "A Trip to the Museum." What is the subject of that book? The old barn is the subject of my painting.* **2.** A course or area of study: *What is your favorite subject in school?* **3.** A person or thing that is used as the object of a special study: *Scientists use mice and rabbits as subjects to try to find new cures for diseases.* **4.** Someone who is under the control of or owes allegiance to a government or ruler: *British subjects.* **5.** A word or group of words in a sentence that does or receives the action of the verb. In the sentences *Jimmy threw the ball, Jill and I went to the movies,* and *The cake tastes good,* the subjects are *Jimmy, Jill and I,* and *The cake.*
—*adjective* **1.** Under the control or authority of another: *All citizens are subject to the laws of the country in which they live.* **2.** Likely to have or get; prone: *She is subject to colds.* **3.** Depending on: *The President appoints judges to the Supreme Court subject to the approval of the Senate.*
—*verb* | səb jĕkt′ | **subjected, subjecting** **1.** To bring under some power or control: *At one time England subjected many countries around the world to its rule.* **2.** To cause to undergo: *The doctor subjected the patient to tests to see what was wrong.*

sub·ma·rine | sŭb′mə rēn′ | or | sŭb′mə rēn′ | —*noun, plural* **submarines** A ship that can go underwater. They are used in war to locate and attack enemy ships and to launch missiles at targets on land.
—*adjective* Below the surface of the sea: *submarine life.*

sub·merge | səb mûrj′ | —*verb* **submerged, submerging** **1.** To cover with water: *The flood submerged the island.* **2.** To place or go beneath the surface of water or some other liquid: *The swimmer submerged in the pool.*

sub·mit | səb mĭt′ | —*verb* **submitted, submitting** **1.** To yield to the control, influence, or authority of another: *Even though I didn't want to take oboe lessons, I submitted to my mother's wish.* **2.** To deliver or present: *The teacher wants us to submit our book reports on Friday.* **3.** To offer for the judgment or consideration of another: *Please submit suggestions to the committee.*

sub·or·di·nate | sə bôr′dn ĭt | —*adjective* Belonging to a lower rank; having less importance: *All the people who work in the store are subordinate to the boss.*

submarine

ă	pat	ĕ	pet	î	fierce
ā	pay	ē	be	ŏ	pot
â	care	ĭ	pit	ō	go
ä	father	ī	pie	ô	paw, for
oi	oil	ŭ	cut	zh	vision
ŏŏ	book	û	fur	ə	ago, item,
ōō	boot	*th*	the		pencil, atom,
yōō	abuse	th	thin		circus
ou	out	hw	which	ər	butter

—*noun, plural* **subordinates** Someone or something that is subordinate.

sub·scribe |səb **skrīb**′| —*verb* **subscribed, subscribing 1.** To agree to receive and pay for a certain number of issues of a publication: *My dad subscribes to that magazine.* **2.** To express or give one's agreement or approval: *I don't subscribe to his opinion that foreign cars are better than American cars.*

sub·scrip·tion |səb **skrĭp**′shən| —*noun, plural* **subscriptions 1.** The act of subscribing to something: *I bought a subscription to the new fishing magazine.* **2.** Something subscribed to: *My subscription to the newspaper runs out next week.*

sub·side |səb **sīd**′| —*verb* **subsided, subsiding 1.** To sink to a lower or more normal level: *The flood waters subsided.* **2.** To become less active: *The child's fever subsided.*

sub·stance |**sŭb**′stəns| —*noun, plural* **substances 1.** Anything that has weight and takes up space; matter. **2.** The material that a thing is made of. Wood is the main substance in such things as pencils and paper. **3.** The most important part of something said or written; the meaning: *The substance of the President's speech was that everyone must use less energy.*

sub·stan·tial |səb **stăn**′shəl| —*adjective* **1.** Large in amount; ample; sufficient: *He was paid a substantial salary for that dangerous job. On Thanksgiving we ate a substantial meal.* **2.** Solidly built; strong: *That substantial raft will hold six people without sinking.* **3.** Real or true; not imaginary: *Ghosts and goblins are not substantial creatures.*

sub·sti·tute |**sŭb**′stĭ tōōt′| or |**sŭb**′stĭ tyōōt′| —*noun, plural* **substitutes** Someone or something that takes the place of another: *The coach put in a substitute for the player who was injured.* —*verb* **substituted, substituting 1.** To put in the place of another: *Dad substituted walnuts for pecans in the recipe.* **2.** To take the place of another: *Ellen substituted for her in the play.*

sub·tle |**sŭt**′l| —*adjective* **subtler, subtlest** So slight as to be difficult to detect or recognize: *a subtle flavor. There was a damp, subtle smell in the air after it rained.*

sub·tract |səb **trăkt**′| —*verb* **subtracted, subtracting** To take away from; to find the number left when one number is taken away from another: *If you subtract 4 from 10, you get 6.*

sub·trac·tion |səb **trăk**′shən| —*noun, plural* **subtractions** The process of finding the number left over when one number is taken away from another; $8 - 3 = 5$ is an example of subtraction.

sub·tra·hend |**sŭb**′trə hĕnd′| —*noun, plural* **subtrahends** The number to be subtracted from another number. In $7 - 5 = 2$, 5 is the subtrahend.

sub·urb |**sŭb**′ûrb′| —*noun, plural* **suburbs** An area with homes and stores near or next to a large city. A suburb may be a town or a small city.

sub·ur·ban |sə **bûr**′bən| —*adjective* Of, located in, or having to do with a suburb: *Dad wants to leave the city and move to a suburban area. Mom took us to a suburban shopping center.*

sub·way |**sŭb**′wā′| —*noun, plural* **subways** An underground railroad in a city.

suc·ceed |sək **sēd**′| —*verb* **succeeded, succeeding 1.** To follow or come next in time or order; to replace another in office or position: *He succeeded his mother.* **2.** To carry out something desired or attempted: *He succeeded in fixing the watch.*

subway

suc·cess |sək sĕs′| —*noun, plural* **successes** **1.** The carrying out of something desired or attempted: *the success of the experiment.* **2.** The getting of fame or wealth: *She won success as a skater.* **3.** Someone or something that is successful: *He is a success at his job.*

suc·cess·ful |sək sĕs′fəl| —*adjective* **1.** Having a desired or good result: *a successful try.* **2.** Having gotten fame or wealth: *a successful actress.*

suc·ces·sion |sək sĕsh′ən| —*noun, plural* **successions** **1.** The process of following in order: *the succession of events.* **2.** A group of people or things following in order: *a succession of teachers; a succession of sounds.*

suc·ces·sive |sək sĕs′ĭv| —*adjective* Following one after another: *three successive years.*

such |sŭch| —*adjective* **1.** Of this or that kind: *We never dreamed she could do such work.* **2.** Alike though not the same: *He writes two or three such books a year.* The adjective **such** belongs to a class of words called **determiners**. They signal that a noun is coming.
—*adverb* Very; especially: *I'm having such a hard time doing my homework.*
—*pronoun* **1.** A person or persons or thing or things of that kind: *We've got root beer and fruit juices if you're interested in such.* **2.** Someone or something alike: *roses, violets, and such.*
  Idioms **as such** In itself: *As such the job pays very little.* **such a** In so great a degree; so: *She felt such a terrible pain.* **such as** **1.** For example: *books such as dictionaries.* **2.** Of the same kind: *nice people, such as we always invite.*

suck |sŭk| —*verb* **sucked, sucking** **1.** To draw liquid or gas into the mouth by inhaling or pulling in the cheeks. **2.** To draw in a liquid or gas by lowering the air pressure inside. This can be done with a pump.

suc·tion |sŭk′shən| —*noun, plural* **suctions** A difference in pressure caused by removing part or all of the air in a space. This causes a liquid or a gas to flow into the space.

sud·den |sŭd′n| —*adjective* **1.** Happening without warning: *a sudden burst of anger; a sudden snowstorm.* **2.** Happening quickly; rapid; swift: *sudden changes.*

suds |sŭdz| —*plural noun* **1.** Water with soap. **2.** Foam; lather.

sue |soō| —*verb* **sued, suing** To bring a lawsuit against someone if they have hurt you in some way.

suede |swād| —*noun, plural* **suedes** Leather that is rubbed to make it look and feel soft like velvet.

su·et |soō′ĭt| —*noun* The hard tissue full of fat around the kidneys of cattle and sheep. It is used in cooking and in making soap and candles.

suf·fer |sŭf′ər| —*verb* **suffered, suffering** **1.** To feel pain or distress: *suffer from illness.* **2.** To be or seem to be at a disadvantage: *The film suffers from poor acting.* **3.** To endure or bear; put up with: *suffer pain; suffer the heat.*

suf·fer·ing |sŭf′ər ĭng| —*noun, plural* **sufferings** The feeling of pain or sorrow.

suf·fi·cient |sə fĭsh′ənt| —*adjective* As much as is needed; enough: *These were not sufficient reasons for going.*

suf·fix |sŭf′ĭks| —*noun, plural* **suffixes** An ending added to a

ă	pat	ĕ	pet	î	fierce
ā	pay	ē	be	ŏ	pot
â	care	ĭ	pit	ō	go
ä	father	ī	pie	ô	paw, for
oi	oil	ŭ	cut	zh	vision
ŏŏ	book	û	fur	ə	ago, item,
ōō	boot	th	the		pencil, atom,
yōō	abuse	th	thin		circus
ou	out	hw	which	ər	butter

word to form a new word or show a grammatical function. For example, *-er* in *hunter* and *-est* in *coldest* are suffixes.

suf·fo·cate |sŭf′ə kāt′| —*verb* **suffocated, suffocating 1.** To kill or destroy by cutting off from air: *The men suffocated when the mine caved in.* **2.** To choke; smother: *The kitten may suffocate if you don't let it breathe.*

sug·ar |shŏog′ər| —*noun, plural* **sugars** A sweet substance that comes mainly from sugar cane or sugar beets.

sugar beet A kind of beet from which sugar is obtained. Sugar beets have long whitish roots.

sugar cane A tall grass with thick, juicy stems that are one of the main sources of sugar.

sug·gest |səg jĕst′| or |sə jĕst′| —*verb* **suggested, suggesting 1.** To bring up for consideration: *She suggested that we go to the circus.* **2.** To bring to mind: *The thought of winter suggests cold and snow.* **3.** To show indirectly; hint: *Taking off her hat and coat suggests that she will stay.*

sug·ges·tion |səg jĕs′chən| or |sə jĕs′chən| —*noun, plural* **suggestions 1.** The act of suggesting. **2.** Something suggested: *following her suggestion.* **3.** A trace; a touch: *There's just a suggestion of cinnamon in this cake.*

su·i·cide |sōo′ĭ sīd′| —*noun, plural* **suicides 1.** The act of killing oneself on purpose. **2.** Someone who kills himself or herself on purpose.

suit |sōot| —*noun, plural* **suits 1.** A set of clothes to be worn together. A suit usually has a coat or jacket with matching pants or skirt. **2.** Clothes that are worn for a certain purpose: *a gym suit.* **3.** One of the four sets in a deck of playing cards. The four suits are spades, clubs, hearts, and diamonds. **4.** A case brought to a court of law.

—*verb* **suited, suiting 1.** To meet the requirements of; satisfy: *The house suited the old couple.* **2. a.** To be acceptable for: *The song suited the occasion.* **b.** To make acceptable: *They suited the play to their audience.* **3.** To please: *It suits our friends to play tennis.*

suit·a·ble |sōo′tə bəl| —*adjective* Right for a purpose or occasion: *suitable clothes; a suitable song.*

suit·case |sōot′kās′| —*noun, plural* **suitcases** A piece of luggage that is flat and shaped like a rectangle.

suite |swēt| —*noun, plural* **suites** A series of connected rooms used to live in.

♦ *These sound alike* **suite, sweet.**

suit·or |sōo′tər| —*noun, plural* **suitors 1.** Someone who brings a suit in a court of law. **2.** A man who is dating a woman.

sul·fur |sŭl′fər| —*noun* A pale-yellow substance that has a blue flame and a bad smell when burned. It is used to make gunpowder and matches. Sulfur is a chemical element.

sul·len |sŭl′ən| —*adjective* **1.** Showing bad humor; silent and angry; glum: *Fred was sullen after being scolded.* **2.** Dark; gloomy: *sullen winter skies.*

sul·tan |sŭl′tən| —*noun, plural* **sultans** The ruler of certain Moslem countries.

sul·try |sŭl′trē| —*adjective* **sultrier, sultriest** Very hot and humid: *a sultry summer day.*

sum |sŭm| —*noun, plural* **sums 1.** A number gotten as a result of addition. **2.** The whole amount, number, or quantity: *the sum*

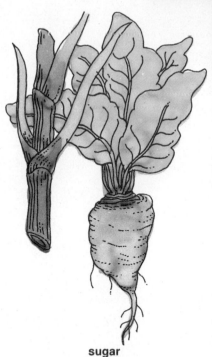

sugar
Sugar cane *(left)* and sugar beet *(right)*

suitcase

of our knowledge. **3.** An amount of money: *the sum of one hundred dollars.*

—*verb* **summed, summing** —**sum up 1.** To state in brief form; make a summary of: *The teacher summed up the talk by asking all students to work harder.* **2.** To add in amount.

♦ *These sound alike* **sum, some.**

sum·ma·rize | sŭm′ə rīz′ | —*verb* **summarized, summarizing** To make a summary of: *We had to summarize the story on our test.*

sum·ma·ry | sŭm′ə rē | —*noun, plural* **summaries** A short statement of the main points of something larger: *the summary of a story; the summary of a chapter.*

sum·mer | sŭm′ər | —*noun, plural* **summers** The season of the year between spring and autumn.

sum·mit | sŭm′ĭt | —*noun, plural* **summits** The highest point or part; the top: *the summit of the mountain.*

sum·mon | sŭm′ən | —*verb* **summoned, summoning 1.** To send for; call for: *He summoned her to the principal's office.* **2.** To call up; stir up: *I will have to summon all my will power to do that.*

sum·mons | sŭm′ənz | —*noun, plural* **summonses 1.** An order for someone, such as a witness to appear in court. **2.** A call or order to appear or do something: *The messenger received a summons from the king to deliver an important paper.*

sun | sŭn | —*noun, plural* **suns 1.** The star around which the earth and the other planets revolve. The sun gives light and heat to the earth. **2.** Any star, especially one that has planets circling it. **3.** The light given off by the sun.

—*verb* **sunned, sunning** To put in the light and heat of the sun: *The cat sunned itself on the porch.*

♦ *These sound alike* **sun, son.**

sun·dae | sŭn′dē | or | sŭn′dā′ | —*noun, plural* **sundaes** Ice cream with syrup, fruit, or nuts on top: *a chocolate sundae.*

♦ *These sound alike* **sundae, Sunday.**

Sun·day | sŭn′dē | or | sŭn′dā′ | —*noun, plural* **Sundays** The first day of the week, after Saturday and before Monday.

♦ *These sound alike* **Sunday, sundae.**

sun·down | sŭn′doun′ | —*noun, plural* **sundowns** The time of sunset: *He returned at sundown.*

sun·flow·er | sŭn′flou′ər | —*noun, plural* **sunflowers** A tall plant whose large flowers have yellow petals and dark centers. Sunflowers bear seeds that are rich in oil.

sung | sŭng | A past tense and the past participle of the verb **sing:** *We sung three tunes yesterday. We have sung this song before.*

sun·glass·es | sŭn′glăs′ĭz | or | sŭn′glä′sĭz | —*plural noun* Eyeglasses with colored lenses, worn to protect the eyes from the sun's glare.

sunk | sŭngk | A past tense and a past participle of the verb **sink:** *The pirates sunk the boat. The lake has sunk for lack of rain.*

sunk·en | sŭng′kən | A past participle of the verb **sink:** *They have sunken the toy boat in the pond.*

—*adjective* **1.** Fallen in; hollow: *sunken eyes.* **2.** Below the surface of the water or ground: *sunken treasure.* **3.** Below the area around it: *a sunken bathtub.*

sun·light | sŭn′līt′ | —*noun* The light of the sun: *The closed curtain kept the sunlight out of the room.*

sun·ny | sŭn′ē | —*adjective* **sunnier, sunniest 1.** Full of sunshine: *a sunny day.* **2.** Cheerful: *a sunny mood.*

sunflower

ă	pat	ĕ	pet	î	fierce
ā	pay	ē	be	ŏ	pot
â	care	ĭ	pit	ō	go
ä	father	ī	pie	ô	paw, for

oi	oil	ŭ	cut	zh	vision
ōō	book	û	fur	ə	ago, item,
ōō	boot	th	the		pencil, atom,
yōō	abuse	th	thin		circus
ou	out	hw	which	ər	butter

sun·rise | sŭn′rīz′ | —*noun, plural* **sunrises** The rising of the sun in the morning: *The Indian faced the sunrise and prayed.*

sun·set | sŭn′sĕt′ | —*noun, plural* **sunsets** The setting of the sun in the evening: *The flag was taken down at sunset.*

sun·shine | sŭn′shīn′ | —*noun* The light of the sun; sunlight.

su·perb | sŏŏ pûrb′ | —*adjective* Of very fine quality; excellent: *a superb meal.*

su·per·in·ten·dent | sŏŏ′pər ĭn tĕn′dənt | —*noun, plural* **superintendents** Someone who is in charge of something: *a superintendent of schools; a superintendent of an apartment building.*

su·pe·ri·or | sə pîr′ē ər | or | sŏŏ pîr′ē ər | —*adjective* **1.** High or higher in position or rank: *a superior officer.* **2.** High or higher in quality: *a superior product.* **3.** High or higher in ability: *a superior student.* **4.** Considering oneself above others: *What makes him feel so superior?*
—*noun, plural* **superiors** Someone who is above others in rank: *The bank president is the teller's superior.*

su·pe·ri·or·i·ty | sə pîr′ē ôr′ĭ tē | or | sə pîr′ē ŏr′ĭ tē | or | sŏŏ pîr′ē ôr′ĭ tē | or | sŏŏ pîr′ē ŏr′ĭ tē | —*noun, plural* **superiorities** The state or quality of being superior: *The girl proved her superiority in spelling by winning the state spelling bee.*

su·per·la·tive | sə pûr′lə tĭv | or | sŏŏ pûr′lə tĭv | —*adjective* Of the highest order, quality, or degree: *a superlative performance.*
—*noun, plural* **superlatives** The form of an adjective or adverb that gives the idea of the greatest quality, quantity, or other relation expressed by the adjective or adverb. Most superlatives are formed by adding the ending *-est* to the adjective or adverb, as in "largest," "greatest," and "earliest." Some, however, are completely different from the original adjective or adverb. For example, the superlatives of the adjectives "good" and "bad" are "best" and "worst," and the superlative of the adverb "well" is "best." Many adjectives do not have a true superlative; the superlatives of such adjectives are formed by placing the word "most" before the adjective, as in the sentence *This seat is the most comfortable on the bus.*

su·per·mar·ket | sŏŏ′pər mär′kĭt | —*noun, plural* **supermarkets** A large store selling food and household goods.

su·per·nat·u·ral | sŏŏ′pər năch′ər əl | or | sŏŏ′pər năch′rəl | —*adjective* Outside the natural world: *Devils and angels are supernatural beings.*

su·per·sti·tion | sŏŏ′pər stĭsh′ən | —*noun, plural* **superstitions** A belief that one action will cause a second action not related to it: *One superstition says that walking under a ladder brings bad luck.*

su·per·sti·tious | sŏŏ′pər stĭsh′əs | —*adjective* Likely to believe in superstition: *a superstitious person.*

su·per·vise | sŏŏ′pər vīz′ | —*verb* **supervised, supervising** To watch over and inspect an action, work, or performance: *He supervises the canning in this factory.*

su·per·vi·sor | sŏŏ′pər vī′zər | —*noun, plural* **supervisors** Someone who supervises.

sup·per | sŭp′ər | —*noun, plural* **suppers** The evening meal; the last meal of the day.

sup·ple·ment | sŭp′lə mənt | —*noun, plural* **supplements** Something added to finish a thing or make up for a missing part: *This geography book has a supplement with maps of new nations.*

—verb **supplemented, supplementing** To give a supplement to: *The teacher supplemented our reading with pictures and films.*

sup·ply | sə **plī′** | *—verb* **supplied, supplying, supplies 1.** To make ready for use; provide: *Large forests supply trees for lumber.* **2.** To furnish with what is needed or missing: *Supply capital letters in the following sentences.*

—noun, plural **supplies 1.** An amount ready for use; stock: *Our supply of chocolate is low.* **2. supplies** Materials kept and passed out when needed: *The medical supplies were low after the battle.*

sup·port | sə **pôrt′** | or | sə **pōrt′** | *—verb* **supported, supporting 1.** To hold in position; to keep from falling: *the towers that support a bridge.* **2.** To be able to bear; withstand: *His prayers supported him in his grief.* **3.** To provide with money or care: *She supports two children.* **4.** To back up or help prove: *The facts seem to support his ideas.*

—noun, plural **supports 1.** The act of supporting: *His support was needed to give Betty courage.* **2.** Someone or something that supports: *The supports on the building are weakening with age.*

sup·port·er | sə **pôr′** tər | or | sə **pōr′** tər | *—noun, plural* **supporters 1.** Someone or something that supports: *The big posts in the barn are supporters for the roof.* **2.** A person who agrees with or supports a person or group.

sup·pose | sə **pōz′** | *—verb* **supposed, supposing 1.** To believe; assume: *I suppose you're right, as usual.* **2.** To imagine to be true; consider: *Suppose his story is right and Bill is in danger.* **3.** To expect; intend: *The rocket lifted off exactly as it was supposed to.*

sup·po·si·tion | sŭp′ə **zĭsh′** ən | *—noun, plural* **suppositions** Something supposed; a statement, idea, or assumption that is accepted but that has not been proved: *Many ancient peoples believed the supposition that the sun revolves around the earth.*

su·preme | sə **prēm′** | *—adjective* **1.** Greatest in rank, power, or authority: *That general is the supreme commander of the army.* **2.** Extreme; utmost: *a supreme effort.*

Supreme Court The highest federal court in the United States. It has nine justices including a chief justice.

sure | shŏor | *—adjective* **surer, surest 1.** Feeling certain about someone or something; having no doubt: *I'm sure he's coming to the party.* **2.** Certain to happen or occur: *His failure to score meant sure defeat for the team.* **3.** Steady or firm: *a sure grip.* **4.** Dependable or reliable: *What is the surest way of getting there?*

sure·ly | shŏor′lē | *—adverb* Certainly; without doubt: *I will surely go to that restaurant again.*

surf | sûrf | *—noun* The waves of the sea as they break upon the shore or the white foam that is on the top of breaking waves.

—verb **surfed, surfing** To ride on a surfboard.

♦ *These sound alike* **surf, serf.**

sur·face | sûr′fəs | *—noun, plural* **surfaces 1. a.** The outermost or top layer of an object: *The surface of the table is smooth.* **b.** The material such a layer is made of: *The surface of a road is concrete.* **2.** The outward appearance of something: *He seems mean on the surface but deep down he's really kind and friendly.*

—verb **surfaced, surfacing 1.** To rise or come to the surface: *The swimmer surfaced after going the length of the pool underwater.* **2.** To cover the surface of: *We surfaced the area around the garden with small stones.* **3.** To appear after being hidden: *The police knew that sooner or later the criminal would surface.*

Supreme Court
The Supreme Court building

ă	pat	ĕ	pet	î	fierce
ā	pay	ē	be	ŏ	pot
â	care	ĭ	pit	ō	go
ä	father	ī	pie	ô	paw, for

oi	oil	ŭ	cut	zh	vision
ŏŏ	book	û	fur	ə	ago, item,
ōō	boot	*th*	the		pencil, atom,
yōō	abuse	th	thin		circus
ou	out	hw	which	ər	butter

surf·board | sûrf′bôrd′ | or | sûrf′bōrd′ | —*noun, plural*
surfboards A long, flat board with rounded ends that is used for
riding the tops of waves into shore.

surf·ing | sûr′fĭng | —*noun* The sport of riding waves into shore
on a surfboard.

surge | sûrj | —*verb* **surged, surging** To rise and move forward
with force, as rolling waves do: *The soldiers surged ahead.*
—*noun, plural* **surges** **1.** A swelling motion or movement like
that of a wave: *the surge of the sea against the rocks.* **2.** A sudden
increase: *a surge of excitement; a surge of electrical power.*

sur·geon | sûr′jən | —*noun, plural* **surgeons** A doctor who
performs surgery.

sur·ger·y | sûr′jə rē | —*noun, plural* **surgeries** The medical
treatment of certain injuries or diseases by physically handling
the parts that have injuries or disease. This usually involves the
cutting open of the body and the repair of damaged parts; an
operation.

sur·name | sûr′nām′ | —*noun, plural* **surnames** A person or
family's last name. Washington is the surname of George
Washington.

sur·pass | sər păs′ | or | sər päs′ | —*verb* **surpassed, surpassing**
To be better, greater, or stronger than; exceed: *The height of the
redwoods surpassed the tallest ship's mast.*

sur·plus | sûr′plŭs | or | sûr′pləs | —*noun, plural* **surpluses** An
amount or quantity that is greater than what is needed or used:
The United States sells its surplus of wheat to other countries.

sur·prise | sər prīz′ | —*verb* **surprised, surprising** **1.** To come
upon suddenly and without warning: *I surprised my mother in the
attic where she was going through old boxes of clothes.* **2.** To cause
to feel astonishment or wonder: *My parents surprised me.*
—*noun, plural* **surprises** **1.** The act of coming upon someone or
something suddenly and without warning: *The angry dog caught
me by surprise.* **2.** Something sudden and unexpected: *The test
was a complete surprise.* **3.** A feeling of astonishment or wonder
caused by something unexpected: *Being elected class president
filled Rachel with surprise.*

sur·ren·der | sə rĕn′dər | —*verb* **surrendered, surrendering** To
give up; give oneself up; yield: *The enemy soldiers surrendered.*
—*noun, plural* **surrenders** The act of surrendering: *The surrender
of the city came after midnight.*

sur·round | sə round′ | —*verb* **surrounded, surrounding** To be on
all sides of; make a circle around: *The soldiers surrounded the city.*

sur·round·ings | sə roun′dĭngz | —*plural noun* The things,
circumstances, and conditions that surround a person: *The
surroundings in the country are peaceful and quiet.*

sur·vey | sər vā′ | or | sûr′vā′ | —*verb* **surveyed, surveying** **1.** To
look over and examine; investigate in detail: *The farmer surveyed
the damage to his crops after the hurricane.* **2.** To measure the size,
shape, and boundaries of a piece or area of land: *The men were
surveying the forest to find the best place to build the new road.*
—*noun* | sûr′vā′ |, *plural* **surveys** **1.** A general view of an area or
subject: *After a quick survey of the town we thought it might be a
good place to live.* **2.** A detailed investigation or study of persons
or things: *A survey of public opinion showed that most people would
not vote for the mayor again.* **3.** The act of surveying land or the
report on land that has been surveyed: *a survey of the ranch.*

surfing

sur·vey·or | sər vā′ər | —*noun, plural* **surveyors** A person whose work is surveying land.

sur·viv·al | sər vī′vəl | —*noun, plural* **survivals** 1. The act or fact of surviving: *the survival of the fittest.* 2. Someone or something that survives: *These traditions are survivals of former days.*

sur·vive | sər vīv′ | —*verb* **survived, surviving** 1. To stay alive or in existence: *The ancient myths and stories will survive forever.* 2. To live through: *Most of the passengers survived the train wreck.* 3. To live longer than: *My grandfather survived my grandmother.*

sur·vi·vor | sər vī′vər | —*noun, plural* **survivors** A person who has survived an accident or disaster that caused the death of others: *survivors from the sunken ship.*

sus·pect | sə spĕkt′ | —*verb* **suspected, suspecting** 1. To think that someone is or may be guilty, without having proof: *The police suspected the two brothers of having robbed the gas station.* 2. To have doubts about: *I suspect that they copied that from you.* 3. To believe something without being sure; imagine that something is true: *I suspect that we'll be there on time.*
—*noun* | sŭs′pĕkt′ |, *plural* **suspects** A person who is suspected of having committed a crime.

sus·pend | sə spĕnd′ | —*verb* **suspended, suspending** 1. To attach something so that it hangs down: *We suspended the punching bag from the ceiling.* 2. To hold or stay in place as if by hanging; to cause to or appear to float: *For a second the acrobat seemed to suspend herself in the air. Sand was suspended in the glass of water.* 3. To stop or cause to stop for a period of time; interrupt or postpone: *He suspended payments on the bank loan.* 4. To temporarily take away a person's position or privileges: *She was suspended from school for a month.*

sus·pen·ders | sə spĕn′dərz | —*noun* (Used with a plural verb.) A pair of straps worn over the shoulders to hold trousers up.

sus·pense | sə spĕns′ | —*noun* The condition of being not certain or worried about what will happen: *Harvey waited in suspense for the dentist to tell him how many cavities he had.*

sus·pen·sion | sə spĕn′shən | —*noun, plural* **suspensions** 1. The act of suspending: *a suspension of the rules; the suspension of the tiny pieces of pulp in the orange juice.* 2. The condition of being suspended: *His suspension from school ends next week.*

suspension bridge A bridge suspended from cables that are stretched between large towers.

sus·pi·cion | sə spĭsh′ən | —*noun, plural* **suspicions** 1. A feeling or belief, without proof or evidence: *I had the suspicion that someone was following me.* 2. The condition of being suspected, especially of committing a crime: *The man was being held under suspicion of robbery.* 3. Lack of trust; doubt: *She looked at the stranger with suspicion.*

sus·pi·cious | sə spĭsh′əs | —*adjective* 1. Causing suspicion: *The men standing by the door of the jewelry store looked suspicious.* 2. Tending to feel suspicion: *Mary was taught to be suspicious of strangers.* 3. Expressing or showing suspicion: *She gave me a suspicious look when I quickly hid the bag behind my back.*

swal·low[1] | swŏl′ō | —*verb* **swallowed, swallowing** 1. To cause food or liquid to pass from the mouth through the throat into the stomach: *Chew your food before you swallow it.* 2. To take in or be covered by: *They were swallowed up by the crowd.* 3. To keep back; hold in: *Cry if you want to; don't swallow your tears.*

suspenders

suspension bridge

swallow[1], swallow[2]
Swallow[1] comes from an old English word. **Swallow[2]** comes from a different old English word. Both words have kept their original meanings.

ă	pat	ĕ	pet	î	fierce
ā	pay	ē	be	ŏ	pot
â	care	ĭ	pit	ō	go
ä	father	ī	pie	ô	paw, for
oi	oil	ŭ	cut	zh	vision
ŏŏ	book	û	fur	ə	ago, item,
ōō	boot	*th*	the		pencil, atom,
yōō	abuse	th	thin		circus
ou	out	hw	which	ər	butter

—*noun, plural* **swallows 1.** An act of swallowing: *I drank the whole glass of milk in one swallow.* **2.** The amount that can be swallowed at one time: *Take three swallows of cough medicine.*

swal·low² |swŏl′ō| —*noun, plural* **swallows** A bird that has narrow, pointed wings and a forked tail. Swallows chase and catch insects in the air.

swam |swăm| The past tense of the verb **swim:** *I swam across the lake.*

swamp |swŏmp| —*noun, plural* **swamps** An area of soft and wet land full of mud.

—*verb* **swamped, swamping** To fill or soak or become filled or soaked with water or other liquid: *The waves swamped the boat and sunk it. The garden was swamped after the storm.*

swan |swŏn| —*noun, plural* **swans** A large water bird that is usually white and has a long, slender neck and webbed feet.

swarm |swôrm| —*noun, plural* **swarms 1.** A large number of insects flying or moving together: *There are swarms of mosquitos in the park.* **2.** A group of bees who fly or move together to find a new hive and start a new colony. **3.** A large group of people all in the same place or moving together: *His friends came in a swarm to congratulate him for winning the election.*

—*verb* **swarmed, swarming 1.** To move in or form a swarm, as bees and other insects do. **2.** To move or gather in large numbers: *The fans swarmed into the stadium to see the game.* **3.** To be filled: *The lake is swarming with fish.*

sway |swā| —*verb* **swayed, swaying 1.** To move or cause to move back and forth or from side to side: *The trees are swaying in the wind. The dancers swayed their hips.* **2.** To influence or cause to change the thinking of: *I did everything I could to sway him from dropping out of school.*

—*noun, plural* **sways 1.** The act of swaying: *The sway of the ship made me seasick.* **2.** Power, influence, or control: *The United States is under the sway of the need to use less oil.*

swear |swâr| —*verb* **swore, sworn, swearing 1.** To make a solemn statement or promise while calling on a sacred person or object to show or prove the honesty or truth of what is said: *I swear to God I didn't steal it. Swear on this Bible that you'll tell the truth.* **2.** To promise with a solemn oath: *He swore his loyalty to the club. They're sworn to secrecy.* **3.** To curse or use language that most people consider bad.

sweat |swĕt| —*noun* **1.** A salty liquid given off through the skin. **2.** Water that forms small drops on a surface. The drops are caused by condensation: *Sweat formed on the outside of the bottle of cold soda.*

—*verb* **sweated, sweating 1.** To give off or cause to give off sweat: *Those exercises made me sweat.* **2.** To condense water in drops on a surface.

sweat·er |swĕt′ər| —*noun, plural* **sweaters** A knitted garment worn on the upper part of the body. It is made of wool or other soft, warm material.

sweep |swēp| —*verb* **swept, sweeping 1.** To clean or clear a surface with a broom or brush: *sweep the floor.* **2.** To clean or clear away with or as if with a broom or brush: *She's sweeping up the dust. He swept the coins off the table with his hand.* **3.** To move or carry with a forceful sweeping motion: *The flood swept away trees and bushes.* **4.** To cover or extend over a large area: *The*

swallow²

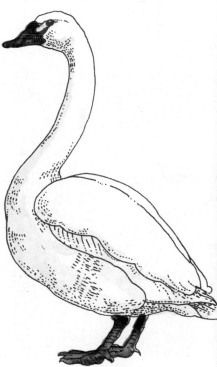

swan

epidemic of measles is sweeping the city. **5.** To win all the parts of a contest or competition: *The team swept all three games.* **6.** To move quickly or steadily: *The eagle swept over the trees.*

—*noun, plural* **sweeps** **1.** The act of sweeping: *I'm going to do a quick sweep in the kitchen.* **2.** Any sweeping motion; a quick, steady movement: *She pushed everything off the table with a sweep of her hand.* **3.** A reach or extent: *There was a sweep of fresh snow on the pasture.*

sweet |swĕt| —*adjective* **sweeter, sweetest** **1.** Having a pleasant taste like that of sugar: *sweet grapes; sweet cake.* **2.** Not salty: *sweet water.* **3.** Not spoiled; fresh: *sweet cream. The milk is still sweet.* **4.** Having a pleasant smell: *The flowers in the garden smell so sweet.* **5.** Having a pleasant disposition; lovable: *They're such sweet children.* **6.** Pleasing or satisfying: *That was the sweetest victory the team won all season.*

—*noun, plural* **sweets** Any food with a lot of sugar: *a box of sweets. We had sweets for dessert.*

♦ *These sound alike* **sweet, suite.**

sweet corn A type of corn with kernels that are sweet and juicy when young. This is the kind of corn we usually eat.

sweet·en |swĕt′n| —*verb* **sweetened, sweetening** To make or become sweeter: *She sweetened her coffee. Fruit sweetens as it grows on the tree.*

sweet·en·er |swĕt′n ər| —*noun, plural* **sweeteners** A substance that is added to a food or beverage to make it sweet.

sweet·heart |swĕt′härt′| —*noun, plural* **sweethearts** A person who is loved by another.

sweet pea A climbing plant whose colorful flowers have a pleasant smell.

sweet potato The thick, sweet root of a tropical vine that is cooked and eaten as a vegetable. The root is usually yellow or reddish.

swell |swĕl| —*verb* **swelled, swelled** or **swollen, swelling** **1.** To increase in size or volume; expand: *My injured ankle swelled and became very sore. The membership of the Girl Scout troop swelled.* **2.** To cause to increase in size or volume: *The flood water swelled the river.* **3.** To be or become filled with emotion: *Alan swelled with pride when he won the game with a home run.*

—*noun, plural* **swells** A long wave or series of waves that moves without breaking or rising to a crest: *The boat floated on the swell of the ocean.*

swell·ing |swĕl′ĭng| —*noun, plural* **swellings** **1.** The act or process of swelling. **2.** Something swollen: *I have a swelling on my arm where the wasp stung me.*

swept |swĕpt| The past tense and past participle of the verb **sweep:** *He swept the crumbs off the table. She had swept the leaves off the lawn.*

swerve |swûrv| —*verb* **swerve, swerving** To turn or cause to turn quickly and sharply: *The car swerved off the road and on to the sidewalk. I swerved the car to avoid hitting the squirrel.*

—*noun, plural* **swerves** The act of swerving: *I had to make a fast swerve to avoid the tree.*

swift |swĭft| —*adjective* **swifter, swiftest** **1.** Moving with great speed; fast: *a swift jet; a swift race; the swiftest horse on the racetrack.* **2.** Coming or happening quickly: *The mayor made a swift response to the charges against him.*

sweet pea

—noun, plural **swifts** A gray or blackish bird that has long, narrow wings and flies fast. The chimney swift is one kind that builds its nest in chimneys and smokestacks.

swim |swĭm| *—verb* **swam, swum, swimming 1. a.** To move oneself through water by moving the arms, legs, or fins: *I'm learning how to swim. The goldfish were swimming around the bowl.* **b.** To move oneself through or across a body of water by swimming: *We swam the lake.* **2.** To float on water or other liquid: *I threw rocks at the leaves swimming in the pond.* **3.** To be covered or flooded with water or other liquid: *The turkey was swimming in gravy.* **4.** To feel dizzy: *I stayed out in the sun too long and my head was swimming.*

—noun, plural **swims 1.** The act of swimming: *We went for a swim.* **2.** The amount of time spent swimming or the distance swum: *a two-hour swim.*

swim·mer |swĭm′ər| *—noun, plural* **swimmers** A person, animal, or fish that swims.

swin·dle |swĭn′dl| *—verb* **swindled, swindling** To get someone's money or property through illegal or dishonest means; cheat: *The store owner swindled the customer.*

—noun, plural **swindles** The act of swindling: *Those men pulled off a big swindle selling people worthless land in the desert.*

swine |swīn| *—noun, plural* **swine** A pig or hog.

swing |swĭng| *—verb* **swung, swinging 1.** To move or cause to move back and forth: *a broken branch swinging from a tree. He swung his keys on a chain.* **2.** To move or turn or cause to move or turn in a curve: *He swung the car around the corner. The player swung the baseball bat.*

—noun, plural **swings 1.** The act of swinging: *She took a big swing at the tennis ball.* **2.** A seat suspended or hanging from above, on which a person may ride back and forth.

swirl |swûrl| *—verb* **swirled, swirling** To move or spin or cause to move or spin round and round: *The wind swirled the snow. The skaters were swirling around the ice.*

—noun, plural **swirls 1.** A spinning or circling motion: *I watched the swirls of the cigar smoke rise in the air.* **2.** Something that is shaped like a curl or twist: *swirls of hair; swirls of fudge in the ice cream.*

swish |swĭsh| *—verb* **swished, swishing** To move or cause to move with a whistling or hissing sound: *The airplane swished by in the sky above us. The cow swished her tail.*

—noun, plural **swishes** A swishing sound or movement: *I heard the swish of the wind through the trees.*

switch |swĭch| *—noun, plural* **switches 1.** A shift or change: *There has been a switch in plans.* **2.** A thin, flexible rod or stick that is used for whipping. **3.** A lashing or swinging motion; stroke: *I got hit in the face with a switch of the horse's tail.* **4.** A device used to open or close an electric circuit: *Turn off the light switch, please.* **5.** A device made of two sections of railroad tracks and certain other movable parts. It is used to move a train from one track to another.

—verb **switched, switching 1.** To shift or change: *We switched the conversation to a different subject.* **2.** To jerk or move suddenly: *The dog's tail switched back and forth.* **3.** To open or close an electric circuit with a switch: *I switched on the radio.* **4.** To transfer trains from one track to another.

swimmer

swing

switchboard

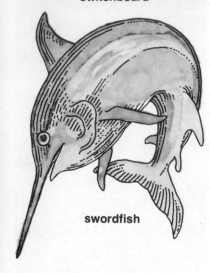
swordfish

symmetry

switch·board | swĭch′bôrd′ | or | swĭch′bōrd′ | —*noun, plural* **switchboards** A panel with switches and plugs that is used for connecting electric circuits. The most common kind is used to connect and disconnect telephone lines.

swol·len | swō′lən | A past participle of the verb **swell:** *Her arm had swollen from the bee sting.*

swoop | swoop | —*verb* **swooped, swooping 1.** To fly or move with a quick, sudden, sweeping motion: *The owl swooped down and caught the mouse. The helicopter flew low over the swamp and then swooped upward.* **2.** To grab or seize with a quick, sweeping motion: *Maria swooped up the kitten before Kate could reach it.* —*noun, plural* **swoops** The act of swooping; a quick, sudden sweeping motion: *With one swoop he picked the football off the ground and ran.*

sword | sôrd | or | sōrd | —*noun, plural* **swords** A hand weapon that is made of a long, pointed blade set in a handle or hilt.

sword·fish | sôrd′fĭsh′ | or | sōrd′fĭsh′ | —*noun, plural* **swordfish** or **swordfishes** A large ocean fish whose upper jaw comes forward in a point like a sword. Swordfish are good to eat.

swore | swôr | or | swōr | The past tense of the verb **swear:** *He swore it wasn't true.*

sworn | swôrn | or | swōrn | The past participle of the verb **swear:** *She had sworn she knew nothing of the crime.*

swum | swŭm | The past participle of the verb **swim:** *I have swum that race four times and never won.*

swung | swŭng | The past tense and past participle of the verb **swing:** *I swung the bat so hard I fell down. He had swung the bat before.*

syc·a·more | sĭk′ə môr′ | or | sĭk′ə mōr′ | —*noun, plural* **sycamores** A North American tree with leaves that look like maple leaves, seed clusters that are shaped like balls, and bark that often comes off in large patches.

syl·lab·i·cate | sĭ lăb′ĭ kāt′ | —*verb* **syllabicated, syllabicating** To divide a word into syllables.

syl·lab·i·fy | sĭ lăb′ə fī′ | —*verb* **syllabified, syllabifying, syllabifies** To divide a word into syllables.

syl·la·ble | sĭl′ə bəl | —*noun, plural* **syllables** A single sound that forms part of a word or an entire word. For example, "ball" has only one syllable and is spoken without a break or pause. "Basketball" has three syllables.

sym·bol | sĭm′bəl | —*noun, plural* **symbols** Something that represents or stands for something else. For example, the lion is a symbol of courage; the dove is a symbol of peace; a red traffic light is a symbol that tells drivers to stop; the marks +, −, and = are symbols for add, subtract, and equals.

♦ *These sound alike* **symbol, cymbal.**

sym·bol·ize | sĭm′bə līz′ | —*verb* **symbolized, symbolizing 1.** To be a symbol of; represent; stand for: *The fox symbolizes cunning.* **2.** To represent by a symbol or symbols: *The Indians and Pilgrims held the first Thanksgiving dinner to symbolize a good harvest.*

sym·me·try | sĭm′ĭ trē | —*noun, plural* **symmetries** An exact matching of the shape and the form or arrangement of parts on opposite sides of a line or around a center. If you drew an imaginary line down a jersey from the neck to the waist, each half would show symmetry. If there was a pocket on only one side, there would not be symmetry.

ă	pat	ĕ	pet	î	fierce
ā	pay	ē	be	ŏ	pot
â	care	ĭ	pit	ō	go
ä	father	ī	pie	ô	paw, for
oi	oil	ŭ	cut	zh	vision
ŏŏ	book	û	fur	ə	ago, item,
ōō	boot	*th*	the		pencil, atom,
yōō	abuse	th	thin		circus
ou	out	hw	which	ər	butter

sym·pa·thet·ic | sĭm′pə thĕt′ĭk | —*adjective* **1.** Showing or feeling understanding, pity, or kindness toward others: *Our sympathetic neighbor made my mother some chicken soup when she was sick. My friends were sympathetic when I broke my arm.* **2.** In favor of; in agreement: *They were sympathetic to our plan and said they would help.*

sym·pa·thize | sĭm′pə thīz′ | —*verb* **sympathized, sympathizing** **1.** To feel or show sympathy for another: *I sympathize with your problem but I don't know what I can do about it.* **2.** To share or understand another's feelings or ideas: *We sympathized with her ambition to go to law school.*

sym·pa·thy | sĭm′pə thē | —*noun, plural* **sympathies 1.** The ability to understand and share another's problems or sorrow; a feeling sorry for another: *We all felt sympathy for Gail when her cat was killed in an accident.* **2.** Agreement or support: *My parents are in sympathy with my plan to get a job.*

sym·pho·ny | sĭm′fə nē | —*noun, plural* **symphonies 1.** A long and elaborate musical composition that is written to be played by an orchestra. **2.** A large orchestra that performs symphonies and other large musical compositions. It is usually made up of string, wind, and percussion instruments.

symp·tom | sĭmp′təm | —*noun, plural* **symptoms** A sign or indication that something is changing or wrong: *A fever and sore throat are usually symptoms of a cold.*

syn·a·gogue | sĭn′ə gŏg′ | or | sĭn′ə gôg′ | —*noun, plural* **synagogues** A building or place used by Jews for worship and religious instruction.

syn·o·nym | sĭn′ə nĭm | —*noun, plural* **synonyms** A word that has the same meaning or almost the same meaning as another. For example, the words *bright* and *smart* are synonyms.

syn·on·y·mous | sĭ nŏn′ə məs | —*adjective* Having the same meaning or almost the same meaning. *Wide* and *broad* are synonymous.

syn·thet·ic | sĭn thĕt′ĭk | —*adjective* Of something that is made by man and not found in nature; artificial. Plastic and nylon are synthetic materials.

syr·up | sĭr′əp | or | sûr′əp | —*noun, plural* **syrups** A thick, sweet liquid. It is usually made by boiling the juice of a fruit or plant with sugar: *maple syrup.*

sys·tem | sĭs′təm | —*noun, plural* **systems 1.** A set of parts or things that form a whole: *The railroad system covers most of the United States.* **2.** An orderly way of doing something: *The coach has a system of exercises for getting everyone on the football team in good condition.* **3.** A form of organization and a set of rules or beliefs: *Our economic system is based on competition. The United States has a democratic system of government.*

synagogue

syrup
Taking sap from a tree

system
A stereo system

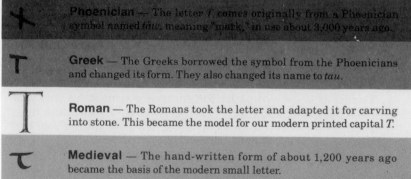

Phoenician — The letter *T* comes originally from a Phoenician symbol named *tāw*, meaning "mark," in use about 3,000 years ago.

Greek — The Greeks borrowed the symbol from the Phoenicians and changed its form. They also changed its name to *tau*.

Roman — The Romans took the letter and adapted it for carving into stone. This became the model for our modern printed capital *T*.

Medieval — The hand-written form of about 1,200 years ago became the basis of the modern small letter.

Modern — The modern capital and small letters are based on the Roman capital and later hand-written forms.

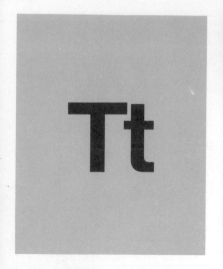

tackle
Fishing tackle

ă	pat	ĕ	pet	î	fierce
ā	pay	ē	be	ŏ	pot
â	care	ĭ	pit	ō	go
ä	father	ī	pie	ô	paw, for
oi	oil	ŭ	cut	zh	vision
ōŏ	book	û	fur	ə	ago, item,
ōō	boot	*th*	the		pencil, atom,
yōō	abuse	th	thin		circus
ou	out	hw	which	ər	butter

t or **T** |tē| —*noun, plural* **t's** or **T's** The twentieth letter of the English alphabet.

tab |tăb| —*noun, plural* **tabs** A small flap or strip that is attached to an object and sticks out from it. Tabs are used for opening cans, to help mark cards used in filing, and sometimes for fastening buttons on some kinds of coats.

ta·ble |tā'bəl| —*noun, plural* **tables** **1.** A piece of furniture with a flat top that is supported by one or more vertical legs. **2.a.** The food served at a table: *My aunt sets a good table.* **b.** The people seated at a table: *The whole table asked for second helpings.* **3.** A brief list of facts and information: *a multiplication table. The table of contents tells you there are ten chapters in the book.*

ta·ble·cloth |tā'bəl klôth'| or |tā'bəl klŏth'| —*noun, plural* **ta·ble·cloths** |tā'bəl klô*thz*'| or |tā'bəl klŏ*thz*'| or |tā'bəl klôths'| or |tā'bəl klŏths'| A piece of cloth for covering a table, especially during a meal.

ta·ble·spoon |tā'bəl spōōn'| —*noun, plural* **tablespoons** **1.** A large spoon used for serving food. **2.a.** A tablespoon with something in it: *a tablespoon of flour.* **b.** The amount that a tablespoon holds: *He sprinkled two tablespoons of sugar on his cereal.* **3.** A unit of measure in cooking. It is equal to three teaspoons.

tab·let |tăb'lĭt| —*noun, plural* **tablets** **1.** A flat slab of wood or stone. Ancient peoples used them to write and draw on before paper was invented. **2.** A pad of writing paper in which the paper sheets are glued together at one end. **3.** A small, flat piece of medicine that is meant to be swallowed.

table tennis A game that is similar to tennis. It is played on a table with a small plastic ball and wooden paddles. The surface of the paddles is covered with a thin sheet of rubber or cork.

tack |tăk| —*noun, plural* **tacks** **1.** A short, thin nail with a wide, round head. **2.** A course of action or an approach: *We'll have to try a new tack to solve this problem.*
—*verb* **tacked, tacking** **1.** To fasten or attach with a tack or tacks: *I tacked the calendar up on the wall over the desk.* **2.** To add: *I tacked a message on at the end of her letter.*

tack·le |tăk'əl| —*noun, plural* **tackles** **1.** The equipment used in a sport, especially in fishing; gear: *I need a new box for my*

fishing tackle. **2.** A system of ropes and pulleys used for lifting and lowering large or heavy objects. It is used on ships for raising and lowering sails and cargo. **3.** The act or an example of knocking someone to the ground, especially in football: *Ralph made four tackles in the game.*
—*verb* **tackled, tackling 1.** To take on and deal with such things as difficulties, opportunities, or problems: *Let's work together and tackle this problem.* **2.** To grab another person and throw him or her to the ground, especially in football.

ta·co |tä′kō| —*noun, plural* **tacos** A tortilla that is folded in half and stuffed with a filling such as meat or cheese.

tact |tăkt| —*noun* The ability to say or do the right thing in a difficult situation so as to avoid offending others: *Even though I didn't like the picture he had drawn, I used tact and said I thought it was interesting.*

tact·ful |tăkt′fəl| —*adjective* Having or showing tact: *You were tactful to tell your aunt you liked that ugly shirt she bought for you.*

tad·pole |tăd′pōl′| —*noun, plural* **tadpoles** A frog or toad when it has just been hatched and lives underwater. In this stage it has gills, a tail, and no legs. The gills and tail disappear as the legs develop and the frog or toad becomes fully grown.

taf·fy |tăf′ē| —*noun, plural* **taffies** A chewy candy made from molasses or brown sugar that is mixed with butter and boiled until it is very thick. It is then pulled into long threads or pieces until it hardens.

tag¹ |tăg| —*noun, plural* **tags** A piece of paper, metal, plastic, or other material that is attached to something or worn by someone. It is used for identifying, labeling, or giving information: *The price tag on the radio says ten dollars.*
—*verb* **tagged, tagging 1.** To label or identify with a tag or tags; attach a tag to: *Tag your coat so nobody else will take it by mistake.* **2.** To follow closely: *My brother is tagging along after me.*

tag² |tăg| —*noun, plural* **tags 1.** A game in which one person chases the others until he or she touches one of them. The person touched must then chase the others. **2.** In baseball, the act of putting a runner out by touching him, her, or the base with the ball.
—*verb* **tagged, tagging 1.** To touch another player, as in the game of tag: *I tagged you, so you're "it."* **2.** In baseball, to put a runner out: *Butch tagged out Jack, who was sliding into the base.*

tail |tāl| —*noun, plural* **tails 1.** The part of an animal's body that is farthest to the rear. A tail usually extends beyond the main part of the body: *All the dogs were wagging their tails.*
2. Anything that looks, hangs, or follows behind like an animal's tail: *Tuck in your shirt tails. The jet left a tail of smoke behind it as it flew.* **3.** The rear, end, or bottom part of anything: *The little girl sat on the tail of the sled.*
—*verb* **tailed, tailing** To follow and watch: *The police are tailing the suspect.*
♦ *These sound alike* **tail, tale.**

tai·lor |tā′lər| —*noun, plural* **tailors** A person who makes, repairs, or alters clothing.
—*verb* **tailored, tailoring** To make, repair, or alter as the work of a tailor: *He tailored Jennie's dress so that it would fit her better.*

take |tāk| —*verb* **took, taken, taking 1.** To capture, seize, or win: *The soldiers took the enemy fort. I hope she takes first prize.* **2.** To grasp with the hand or hands: *Take my arm when we cross the*

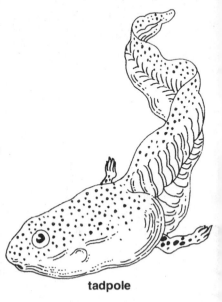

tadpole

tag¹, tag²
Tag¹ probably came from an old word used by people who lived in Scandinavia to mean "prickle, sharp point." **Tag²** comes from a word used long ago in English, meaning "to touch lightly."

street. **3.** To carry to another place: *Take this book back to the library. This train takes you to Oklahoma and Texas.* **4.** To go with; escort: *They're taking her to the airport.* **5.** To move or remove: *She took the glass from the shelf. He's taking out the garbage.* **6.** To get or receive: *I took the present.* **7.** To eat, drink, swallow, or inhale: *She took her medicine. Take a deep breath.* **8.** To perform or do: *Take precautions so you don't get sick again. Let's take a walk.* **9.** To require or need: *It takes time to learn how to play the clarinet.* **10.** To choose or select; pick out: *Take any seat you want.* **11.** To subtract: *Take five away from fifteen.* **12.** To endure or put up with: *I can't take this racket anymore.* **13.** To accept what someone says, either willingly or reluctantly: *Can I take your word on that? Take my advice.* **14.** To react or respond to in a certain way: *Don't take what she said seriously.* **15.** To have a feeling about oneself or something one has done: *She takes pride in her work.* **16.** To undertake; commit oneself to: *I can see that the only way this will get done is for me to take the initiative. You'll have to take the responsibility.* **17.** To use or make use of: *Take the bus. She took the seat near the door.* **18.** To become: *She took sick at the party.* **19.** To come upon suddenly: *Let's take them by surprise.* **20.** To study: *I'm taking French.* **21.** To find out, using a special method: *I have to take your temperature.* **22.** To please; to charm: *The whole family is taken with the new baby.* **23.** To make by photography: *Take my picture.* **24.** To hire, rent, or lease: *He's taking on three new workers. We took a cabin for the summer.* **25.** To buy or subscribe to: *I've taken two new magazines.*

Phrasal verbs **take after** **1.** To chase: *The dog took after the cat.* **2.** To resemble or look like: *He takes after his mother.* **take for** To think or suppose to be: *He took me for his uncle. Don't take me for a fool.* **take over** To assume control of: *When his partner retired, my father took over the whole company.* **take up** **1.** To shorten: *I have to take up my new dress.* **2.** To use up, occupy, or consume: *That table takes up a lot of room.* **3.** To begin again or start to do something: *He took up where he had left off.*

tak·en | tā′kən | The past participle of the verb **take:** *I've taken about as much of your bad behavior as I can put up with.*

take·off | tāk′ôf′ | or | tāk′ŏf′ | —*noun, plural* **takeoffs** The act or process of rising up in flight: *The spaceship's takeoff failed.*

tale | tāl | —*noun, plural* **tales** **1.** A report of facts or events: *The soldier told us the horrible tale of the great battle. Dad told tales about his childhood.* **2.** An imaginary or made-up story; a lie: *The old man tells tales about his days as a sailor.*

♦ *These sound alike* **tale, tail.**

tal·ent | tăl′ənt | —*noun, plural* **talents** **1. a.** A natural ability to do something well. Although talent is something a person is born with, it almost always has to be developed with study and practice: *Judy has a lot of musical talent.* **b.** A person with such ability: *Of all the students in the art class Sara is the biggest talent.* **2.** A knack: *Fred has a talent for getting himself into trouble.*

tal·ent·ed | tăl′ən tĭd | —*adjective* Having or showing talent: *They are both talented actors.*

talk | tôk | —*verb* **talked, talking** **1.** To use human speech; utter words: *The baby can talk.* **2.** To communicate, using something that takes the place of speech: *They're talking in sign language.* **3.** To express ideas, thoughts, or feelings, using speech: *I talked seriously about my plans for the summer.* **4.** To speak of or discuss:

takeoff

ă	pat	ĕ	pet	î	fierce
ā	pay	ē	be	ŏ	pot
â	care	ĭ	pit	ō	go
ä	father	ī	pie	ô	paw, for

oi	oil	ŭ	cut	zh	vision
ŏŏ	book	û	fur	ə	ago, item,
ōō	boot	*th*	the		pencil, atom,
yōō	abuse	th	thin		circus
ou	out	hw	which	ər	butter

We talked sports while they talked politics. **5.** To chatter on and on: *He did nothing but talk.* **6.** To influence by speech: *We talked them into coming to the party with us.*
—*noun, plural* **talks** **1.** An informal speech or conference: *The police chief gave a talk on how to prevent crime. The enemies called a truce and are going to start peace talks.* **2.** The exchange of ideas; conversation: *She came over and we had a nice talk.*

tall | tôl | —*adjective* **taller, tallest** **1.** Having a greater than ordinary or average height: *My brother is a lot taller than all his friends.* **2.** Having a specific height: *The plant is three feet tall.* **3.** Imaginary or made-up; hard to believe: *That's a tall tale.*

Tal·la·has·see | tăl′ə hăs′ē | The capital of Florida.

tal·low | tăl′ō | —*noun* The fat of such animals as cattle, sheep, or horses, melted and mixed together. It is used to make such things as soap and candles.

tal·on | tăl′ən | —*noun, plural* **talons** The claw of an animal or bird that seizes other animals as prey: *The eagle grabbed the squirrel in its talons and flew off.*

tam·bou·rine | tăm′bə rēn′ | —*noun, plural* **tambourines** A small drum that has metal disks attached to the rim. The disks jingle when the tambourine is struck or shaken.

tame | tām | —*adjective* **tamer, tamest** **1.** Taken from a naturally wild state and made obedient or gentle: *There is a tame lion at the game farm.* **2.** Not fierce or dangerous; gentle and not afraid: *The deer in the forest were so tame they let me pet them.*
—*verb* **tamed, taming** To make or become obedient or gentle: *She tames tigers and lions for the circus. Horses tame easily.*

tam·per | tăm′pər | —*verb* **tampered, tampering** To interfere or meddle in a harmful way: *Don't tamper with the lock.*

tan | tăn | —*verb* **tanned, tanning** **1.** To make animal hides into leather by soaking them in certain chemicals or mixtures. **2.** To make or become brown by exposure to the sun: *I spent my whole vacation tanning myself on the beach.*
—*noun, plural* **tans** **1.** A light yellowish-brown color. **2.** The brown color gotten by exposing the skin to the sun.
—*adjective* **tanner, tannest** Of the color tan: *tan gloves; a tan shirt.*

tan·ger·ine | tăn′jə rēn′ | —*noun, plural* **tangerines** **1.** A fruit that is related to the orange, but a little smaller. Tangerines have dark orange skin that peels easily. **2.** A deep reddish-orange color.
—*adjective* Deep reddish orange.

tan·gle | tăng′gəl | —*verb* **tangled, tangling** To mix or become mixed together in a confused or twisted mass; snarl: *Who tangled up the telephone cord? Curly hair tangles easily.*
—*noun, plural* **tangles** A confused, snarled mass: *There's a big tangle of string in the drawer.*

tank | tăngk | —*noun, plural* **tanks** **1.** A large container for holding liquids: *Cars and trucks have gas tanks.* **2. a.** A tank with something in it: *a fish tank filled with water.* **b.** The amount a tank holds: *I bought a tank of gas.* **3.** A heavily armored vehicle that is used in combat. It is enclosed, covered with thick metal plates, and equipped with cannon and guns. A tank moves on two continuous metal belts that have treads.

tank·er | tăng′kər | —*noun, plural* **tankers** A ship, truck, or airplane that is built to carry a large amount of oil or other liquids or gases.

tank
An armored tank

tanker

tan·ner | tăn′ər | —*noun, plural* **tanners** Someone who tans hides to make them into leather.

tan·trum | tăn′trəm | —*noun, plural* **tantrums** A fit or outburst of bad temper: *Sally had a tantrum when her father wouldn't let her stay up late.*

tap¹ | tăp | —*verb* **tapped, tapping** 1. To strike or hit gently with a light blow or blows: *She tapped him on the shoulder. He sat there tapping his pencil on the desk.* 2. To imitate or produce with light blows: *Tap the beat of the song with your hand.*
—*noun, plural* **taps** 1. A light or gentle blow: *Give him a tap; he can't hear you.* 2. The sound made by such a blow: *I heard a tap on the window.*

tap² | tăp | —*noun, plural* **taps** A device at the end of a pipe for turning water or other liquid on and off and for regulating the amount of liquid that flows out; a faucet. Sinks have taps.
—*verb* **tapped, tapping** 1. To pierce or put a hole in something in order to draw liquid out of it. Maple trees are tapped to get syrup. 2. To cut in on and make a connection with: *The police tapped the suspect's telephone.*

tape | tāp | —*noun, plural* **tapes** 1. A long, narrow, flexible piece of material, such as plastic, paper, or metal. Tape has many uses. Some tape has glue on one or both sides and is used for repairing things or sealing packages. Other tape is marked like a ruler and used for measuring. 2. A long, narrow piece of specially treated plastic on which sounds or images can be recorded: *I bought a new tape of my favorite singer.*
—*verb* **taped, taping** 1. To fasten or bind with tape: *She taped a bow on the package. The doctor taped my sprained wrist.* 2. To record sounds or images on tape: *I taped the radio program.*

ta·per | tā′pər | —*verb* **tapered, tapering** 1. To make or become gradually thinner toward one end: *When he built the fence, my father tapered the posts to a point. The steeple on the church tapers toward the top.* 2. To become slowly smaller or less: *When the lights in the movie theater were lowered, the noise in the audience tapered off.*
♦ *These sound alike* **taper, tapir.**

tape recorder A machine that can record sound on specially treated plastic tape and that can also play the sound back.

tap·es·try | tăp′ĭ strē | —*noun, plural* **tapestries** A heavy cloth with designs or pictures in many colors woven in it. It is hung on walls as decoration or used to cover furniture.

tape·worm | tāp′wûrm′ | —*noun, plural* **tapeworms** A long, flat worm that looks like a ribbon. Tapeworms live as parasites in the intestines of human beings and other animals.

ta·pir | tā′pər | —*noun, plural* **tapirs** An animal with a heavy body, short legs, and a long, fleshy snout. Tapirs live in tropical America and Asia.
♦ *These sound alike* **tapir, taper.**

taps | tăps | —*noun* (Used with a singular verb.) A bugle call that is played at night as an order to put out all lights. It is also played at funerals.

tar | tär | —*noun* A thick, sticky, dark substance that is made from wood, coal, or peat. It is used to pave roads and cover roofs.
—*verb* **tarred, tarring** To coat or cover with tar: *Workers are tarring the street behind my house.*

tar·an·tu·la | tə răn′chə lə | —*noun, plural* **tarantulas** A large,

---

tap¹, tap²

Tap¹ comes from a word that appeared in old French and in Germanic before arriving in English long ago. **Tap²** comes from a different old English word. Neither has changed in meaning.

tapir

tarantula

ă	pat	ĕ	pet	î	fierce
ā	pay	ē	be	ŏ	pot
â	care	ĭ	pit	ō	go
ä	father	ī	pie	ô	paw, for

oi	oil	ŭ	cut	zh	vision
ōō	book	û	fur	ə	ago, item,
ōō	boot	th	the		pencil, atom,
yōō	abuse	th	thin		circus
ou	out	hw	which	ər	butter

hairy spider whose bite is painful but not seriously poisonous. Tarantulas are usually found in the tropical parts of the world.

tar·dy | tär′dē | —*adjective* **tardier, tardiest** Happening or coming late; delayed; late: *Why were you tardy for school yesterday?*

tar·get | tär′gĭt | —*noun, plural* **targets** **1.** Something, such as a mark, circle, or object, that is aimed or fired at: *We shot arrows at a target tacked up on a tree. The target of the bombs was the large bridge over the river.* **2.** A person or object that is made fun of, ridiculed, or criticized: *He was the target of the other children's jokes because he was fat.* **3.** A goal or aim: *Our target is to raise two hundred dollars for charity.*

tar·iff | tär′ĭf | —*noun, plural* **tariffs** A tax or duty that a government places on imported or exported goods: *There is a high tariff on foreign cars brought into the United States.*

tar·nish | tär′nĭsh | —*verb* **tarnished, tarnishing** **1.** To dull the color or luster of: *Air and moisture tarnish most metals.* **2.** To become dull; lose color or luster: *The silver plate tarnished.* —*noun* **1.** The condition of being tarnished. **2.** A thin dull coating on the surface of a metal, as on silver. Tarnish can be removed with polish.

tar·pon | tär′pən | —*noun, plural* **tarpon** or **tarpons** A large silvery fish that lives along the coast of the Atlantic Ocean. It is often caught for sport.

tart¹ | tärt | —*adjective* **tarter, tartest** **1.** Having a sharp taste; sour: *a tart apple. This is the tartest lemonade I ever drank.* **2.** Sharp or harsh in tone or meaning: *When I asked her why she was mad, she gave me a tart answer and walked off.*

tart² | tärt | —*noun, plural* **tarts** A small pie with no crust on top.

tar·tan | tär′tn | —*noun, plural* **tartans** **1.** Any one of many plaid fabric patterns having stripes of different colors and widths that cross one another at right angles. Every clan in Scotland has its own tartan pattern. **2.** A woolen fabric having such a pattern.

tar·tar | tär′tər | —*noun* A hard yellowish substance that collects on the teeth. It forms into a hard crust if it is not removed by brushing.

task | tăsk | or | täsk | —*noun, plural* **tasks** A piece of work: *That science project was a hard task.*

tas·sel | tăs′əl | —*noun, plural* **tassels** **1.** A bunch of loose threads or cords that are tied together at one end and hanging free at the other. Tassels are used as ornaments on such things as curtains and clothing. A graduation cap has a tassel. **2.** Anything that looks like this, such as a growth of hair at the end of the tail of certain animals and the silky flower clusters on an ear of corn.

taste | tāst | —*noun, plural* **tastes** **1.** The sensation that is produced by food or some other substance that is placed in the mouth; flavor. The four basic tastes are sweet, sour, salty, and bitter: *These apples have a sweet taste. The eggs left a bad taste in my mouth.* **2.** The sense by which one can notice the flavor or flavors of something placed in the mouth. **3.** A small amount eaten or tasted: *Just try a taste of this before you decide you don't like it.* **4.** A liking or preference for something: *She has a taste for music. His new suit is nice, but it's not to my taste.* **5. a.** The ability to know what is good in a certain situation or to appreciate what is good, beautiful, or of high quality: *She has better taste in clothes than her sister.* **b.** A manner, quality, or style that shows such an ability: *Her new furniture is in good taste.*

tart¹, tart²
Tart¹ comes from a word that meant "sharp, severe" to English-speaking people of long ago. Tart² comes from an old French word meaning "round bread, twisted object."

tartan
Two kinds of tartan

—*verb* **tasted, tasting** **1.** To notice the flavor of by taking into the mouth: *I can't taste the beef because there's so much gravy.* **2.** To have a certain flavor: *This apple cider tastes sweet.* **3.** To sample a small amount of: *Taste the string beans.*

tast·y | tā′stē | —*adjective* **tastier, tastiest** Having a good or pleasing flavor: *a tasty stew.*

tat·tered | tăt′ərd | —*adjective* Torn or worn to shreds; ragged: *tattered clothes. The collar of your shirt is tattered.*

tat·tle | tăt′l | —*verb* **tattled, tattling** **1.** To talk or chatter foolishly: *He tattled on and on about his new bicycle.* **2.** To tell secrets; reveal by talking: *He tattled on his sister.*

tat·tle·tale | tăt′l tāl′ | —*noun, plural* **tattletales** A person who tells the secrets of another or tells private things about another.

tat·too | tă tōo′ | —*noun, plural* **tattoos** A mark or design on the skin made by pricking the skin with needles that have dye or colors on the points.

—*verb* **tattooed, tattooing** To mark the skin with a tattoo.

taught | tôt | The past tense and past participle of the verb **teach:** *My brother taught me how to ski. She has taught English for many years.*

♦ *These sound alike* **taught, taut.**

taut | tôt | —*adjective* **tauter, tautest** **1.** Pulled or drawn tight: *The ropes holding up the circus tent were taut.* **2.** Strained or tense: *His face was taut and angry.*

♦ *These sound alike* **taut, taught.**

tav·ern | tăv′ərn | —*noun, plural* **taverns** **1.** A place where alcoholic beverages are sold and drunk; a bar. **2.** A place where travelers can eat and sleep during a trip; an inn.

tax | tăks | —*noun, plural* **taxes** **1.** Money that people must pay in order to support government. People pay a certain part of the money they earn every year as a tax. They also pay a tax on many objects they buy. **2.** A heavy demand; a strain or burden: *Michael's job puts a heavy tax on his energy.*

—*verb* **taxed, taxing** **1.** To place a tax on: *The state taxes incomes.* **2.** To make a heavy demand upon; to strain or burden: *You're taxing your muscles by carrying all those boulders.*

tax·a·tion | tăk sā′shən | —*noun* The act or system of taxing. The money collected by taxation is used by governments to pay for such things as public schools, police and firemen, and building and paving roads.

tax·i | tăk′sē | —*noun, plural* **taxis** or **taxies** A taxicab.

—*verb* **taxied, taxiing** or **taxying, taxis** or **taxies** **1.** To ride or be transported in a taxicab: *We taxied to the train station.* **2.** To move slowly over the surface of the ground or water before taking off or landing: *The airplane taxied down the runway.*

tax·i·cab | tăk′sē kăb′ | —*noun, plural* **taxicabs** An automobile that can be hired to drive passengers wherever they want to go. It usually has a meter that registers the cost or fare.

tea | tē | —*noun, plural* **teas** **1.** A drink made by soaking or brewing the dried leaves of an Asian shrub in boiling water. **2.** The dried leaves of this shrub. **3.** The shrub these leaves grow on. **4.** A drink resembling tea, made from the leaves or flowers of other plants or from other substances: *My aunt served us herb tea.* **5.** A light meal or small party in the late afternoon at which tea is served: *My mother had a tea for the women she plays cards with.*

taxicab

tea
Shrub *(left)* and leaves *(right)*

ă	pat	ē	pet	î	fierce
ā	pay	ē	be	ŏ	pot
â	care	ĭ	pit	ō	go
ä	father	ī	pie	ô	paw, for
oi	oil	ŭ	cut	zh	vision
ŏŏ	book	û	fur	ə	ago, item,
ōō	boot	*th*	the		pencil, atom,
yōō	abuse	th	thin		circus
ou	out	hw	which	ər	butter

teach | tēch | —*verb* **taught, teaching** **1.** To help someone learn; give knowledge of or lessons in: *I'm teaching him to read. She taught piano for a living.* **2.** To do this regularly as one's job: *He teaches kindergarten.* **3.** To show or learn from experience or example: *Science teaches us how to save our forests.*

teach·er | tē′chər | —*noun, plural* **teachers** A person whose job is teaching.

teach·ing | tē′chĭng | —*noun, plural* **teachings** **1.** The work or occupation of teachers. **2.** Something taught: *Christ's teachings.*

tea·ket·tle | tē′kĕt′l | —*noun, plural* **teakettles** A kettle with a handle and a spout that is used for boiling water.

teal | tēl | —*noun, plural* **teal** or **teals** A small wild duck that often has brightly marked feathers.

team | tēm | —*noun, plural* **teams** **1.** Two or more animals that are harnessed together to do work: *The plow was pulled by a team of oxen.* **2.** A group of players on the same side in a game: *We have a good girls' field hockey team this year.* **3.** Two or more people who work together: *a team of doctors.*
—*verb* **teamed, teaming** To work together as a team; form a team: *The classes teamed up to decorate the hall for the dance.*
♦ *These sound alike* **team, teem.**

tear¹ | târ | —*verb* **tore, torn, tearing** **1.** To pull apart, be pulled apart, divide, or be divided by force; to split: *Tear the paper in half. Some materials tear more easily than others.* **2.** To make an opening or wound in by ripping: *I tore my best jacket on the fence.* **3.** To pull or remove forcefully: *She tore the poster off the wall.* **4.** To upset emotionally: *She was torn over whether to keep or give back the money she had found.* **5.** To move with great speed; to rush: *She went tearing down the road to catch the bus.*
　　Phrasal verb **tear down** To destroy or demolish: *Workmen were tearing down the old building on the corner.*
—*noun, plural* **tears** A cut, hole, or opening made by tearing; a rip: *There's a big tear in the tablecloth.*

tear² | tîr | —*noun, plural* **tears** **1.** A drop of the clear, salty liquid that comes from the eye. It is produced by a certain gland in the eye. **2. tears** The act of weeping: *The whole team broke into tears when they lost the championship game.*
♦ *These sound alike* **tear², tier.**

tease | tēz | —*verb* **teased, teasing** To annoy or bother by making fun of: *I tease my younger brother by telling him he'll never be as tall as Dad. She is only teasing.*
—*noun, plural* **teases** Someone who teases: *Don't pay any attention to him; he's just a tease.*

tea·spoon | tē′spo͞on′ | —*noun, plural* **teaspoons** **1.** A small spoon used for stirring liquids and eating soft foods. **2. a.** A teaspoon with something in it: *a teaspoon of sugar.* **b.** The amount that a teaspoon holds: *I took a teaspoon of cough medicine.* **3.** A unit of measure in cooking. A teaspoon is equal to one third of a tablespoon or a half ounce.

tech·ni·cal | tĕk′nĭ kəl | —*adjective* **1.** Of or having to do with technique: *This painting shows good technical ability.* **2.** Of or having to do with a particular subject or field, such as a science or an art: *The physics book is written in technical language that I don't understand.* **3.** Of or having to do with mechanical or industrial arts: *The engineer is giving technical help to the people.*

tech·nique | tĕk nēk′ | —*noun, plural* **techniques** **1.** A method

teal

team
Above: A baseball team
Below: A team of horses

tear¹, tear²
Tear¹ and **tear²** both came from old English words, but they are not related. **Tear¹** meant "to pull apart"; **tear²** comes from the word for "a teardrop."

telephone
Above: An early telephone
Below: A modern telephone

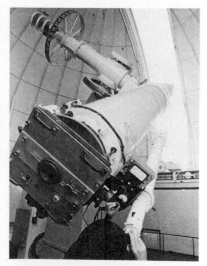

telescope

ă	pat	ĕ	pet	î	fierce	
ā	pay	ē	be	ŏ	pot	
â	care	ĭ	pit	ō	go	
ä	father	ī	pie	ô	paw, for	

oi	oil	ŭ	cut	zh	vision
ŏŏ	book	û	fur	ə	ago, item,
ōō	boot	*th*	the		pencil, atom,
yōō	abuse	th	thin		circus
ou	out	hw	which	ər	butter

or way of doing something difficult or complicated, as in science or art: *My sister is learning all the techniques of ballet dancing. There are many different techniques in basketball.* **2.** The degree to which someone has mastered or can do this: *My dentist has a great technique; I never feel pain.*

tech·nol·o·gy |tĕk nŏl′ə jē| —*noun, plural* **technologies** The use of scientific knowledge in industry, especially in such technical fields as engineering and mechanical arts. *The United States developed a whole new technology in order to send astronauts to the moon. We are also creating new technologies to clean up pollution in water and air.*

ted·dy bear |tĕd′ē| A child's toy bear that is usually stuffed with soft material.

te·di·ous |tē′dē əs| —*adjective* Long and tiring; boring: *Mowing the lawn is a tedious job.*

teem |tēm| —*verb* **teemed, teeming** To be full of; abound or swarm: *The park was teeming with flies and mosquitoes. The county fair teemed with people.*
♦ *These sound alike* **teem, team.**

teen·ag·er |tēn′ā′jər| —*noun, plural* **teen-agers** A person between the ages of thirteen and nineteen.

teens |tēnz| —*plural noun* The years of a person's life between the ages of thirteen and nineteen.

teeth |tēth| The plural of the noun **tooth.**

teethe |tē*th*| —*verb* **teethed, teething** To have teeth develop and start to come through the gums: *The baby teethed for two weeks.*

tel·e·gram |tĕl′ə grăm′| —*noun, plural* **telegrams** A message that is sent by telegraph.

tel·e·graph |tĕl′ə grăf′| or |tĕl′ə gräf′| —*noun, plural* **telegraphs** **1.** A system of sending messages over wire or radio to a special receiving station. **2.** A message sent by such a system; a telegram.
—*verb* **telegraphed, telegraphing** To send a message to someone by telegraph: *We telegraphed our aunt in Wyoming to tell her when we were coming.*

tel·e·phone |tĕl′ə fōn′| —*noun, plural* **telephones** An instrument that sends and receives speech and other sounds over long distances. A telephone sends sounds over wires by means of electricity. It also sends sounds by means of radio waves.
—*verb* **telephoned, telephoning** **1.** To call or talk with someone by telephone: *She telephoned twice yesterday.* **2.** To send a message or other information by telephone: *I'm going to telephone her my apologies for breaking her window.*

tel·e·scope |tĕl′ə skōp′| —*noun, plural* **telescopes** An instrument that makes distant objects appear closer and larger. It uses a series of lenses or mirrors that are arranged inside a long tube. Telescopes are often used to observe stars and planets.

tel·e·vise |tĕl′ə vīz′| —*verb* **televised, televising** To broadcast by television: *Two stations are televising the football game tonight.*

tel·e·vi·sion |tĕl′ə vĭzh′ən| —*noun, plural* **televisions** **1.** A system for sending and receiving pictures of objects and actions with the sounds that go with them. **2.** A device that receives these pictures and sounds and on which they can be seen or heard: *Our color television is broken again.*

tell |tĕl| —*verb* **told, telling** **1.** To express in words; say: *I have to tell her how happy I am.* **2.** To give an account of; relate or describe: *Tell us what happened. I'm going to tell you a story.* **3.** To show or inform; indicate: *The clock tells you what time it is.* **4.** To know or recognize: *Can you tell whose voice this is?* **5.** To order or command: *Why can't you ever do what you're told?*

tell·er |tĕl′ər| —*noun, plural* **tellers 1.** A person who tells something, such as a story or tale. **2.** A person working in a bank who receives and pays out money.

tem·per |tĕm′pər| —*noun, plural* **tempers 1.** One's usual mood or state of mind; disposition: *Michael has such an even temper that it takes a lot to make him angry.* **2.** The condition of being calm in the mind or emotions: *Don't lose your temper just because she spilled the water.* **3.** A tendency to become angry or annoyed: *Tracy has quite a temper when she doesn't get what she wants.* —*verb* **tempered, tempering** To soften or make less harsh: *The principal tempered his punishment because John had never done anything wrong before.*

tem·per·ate |tĕm′pə rĭt| or |tĕm′prĭt| —*adjective* Of or having a climate that is never too hot or too cold.

tem·per·a·ture |tĕm′pər ə chər| or |tĕm′prə chər| —*noun, plural* **temperatures 1.** The relative degree of hot or cold: *The temperature today is too low for us to go swimming.* **2.** A body temperature that has risen above normal because of some disease or disorder. Normal body temperature is 98.6 degrees: *I'm calling the doctor because her temperature is 101 degrees.*

tem·ple¹ |tĕm′pəl| —*noun, plural* **temples 1.** A building or place used to worship a god or gods: *When we went to Europe, we saw the ruins of many ancient Roman temples.* **2.** Any building used for worship, especially a Jewish synagogue.

tem·ple² |tĕm′pəl| —*noun, plural* **temples** The flat part on either side of a person's head.

tem·po·rar·y |tĕm′pə rĕr′ē| —*adjective* Lasting or used for a short time only; not permanent: *He got a temporary job.*

tempt |tĕmpt| —*verb* **tempted, tempting 1.** To persuade or try to persuade someone to do something that is foolish or wrong: *The teacher told us to keep our papers covered during the test so nobody would be tempted to cheat.* **2.** To appeal strongly to; attract: *The swimming pool tempted me so much that I jumped in with my clothes on.* **3.** To take the chance of loss, harm, or injury from: *You're tempting your luck if you skate on the frozen pond.*

temp·ta·tion |tĕmp tā′shən| —*noun, plural* **temptations 1.** The act of tempting or condition of being tempted: *Don't give in to temptation.* **2.** Something that tempts: *The cookies were such a temptation that I ate them all before dinner.*

ten |tĕn| —*noun, plural* **tens** A number, written 10, that is equal to the sum of 9 + 1.
—*adjective* Being one more than nine in number: *ten pencils.* The adjective **ten** belongs to a class of words called **determiners.** They signal that a noun is coming.

ten·ant |tĕn′ənt| —*noun, plural* **tenants** A person who pays rent to use or occupy land, a building, an apartment, a store, or other property owned by another person.

tend¹ |tĕnd| —*verb* **tended, tending 1.** To move or lead in a certain direction: *This route tends toward the south.* **2.** To be likely; incline: *He tends to be lazy.*

tend² |tĕnd| —*verb* **tended, tending** To look after; take care of: *She's tending my canary while I'm in the hospital.*

---

temple¹, temple²

Temple¹ comes from a Latin word meaning "sanctuary, shrine, temple." **Temple²** comes from a different Latin word that means "flat side of the head."

---

tend¹, tend²

Tend¹ comes from a Latin word that meant "to stretch, to extend in a particular direction, to be inclined toward." **Tend²** is shortened from **attend,** which can be traced back to a Latin word meaning "to think about, to stretch toward."

Tennessee

The name **Tennessee** comes from an Indian word whose meaning is not known. It was the name of an important Indian town and river before becoming the name of the state.

tennis

tense¹, tense²

Tense¹ comes from a form of the Latin verb meaning "to stretch out." **Tense²** comes through French from the Latin noun meaning "time."

tentacle
Tentacles on an octopus

tepee

ă	pat	ĕ	pet	î	fierce
ā	pay	ē	be	ŏ	pot
â	care	ĭ	pit	ō	go
ä	father	ī	pie	ô	paw, for
oi	oil	ŭ	cut	zh	vision
ŏŏ	book	û	fur	ə	ago, item,
ōō	boot	*th*	the		pencil, atom,
yōō	abuse	th	thin		circus
ou	out	hw	which	ər	butter

ten·den·cy |tĕn′dən sē| —*noun, plural* **tendencies** An inclination to think, act, or behave in a certain way: *Diana has a tendency to eat too much.*

ten·der |tĕn′dər| —*adjective* **tenderer, tenderest 1.** Not hard or strong; easily crushed or damaged; fragile: *The petals of a rose are very tender.* **2.** Not tough; soft: *The steak is so tender you can cut it with a fork.* **3. a.** Easily hurt; sensitive: *A baby has tender skin.* **b.** Painful or sore: *My arm is very tender where it got hit with the baseball.* **4.** Kind and loving; gentle: *My mother gave me a tender hug. He's very tender with animals.*

ten·don |tĕn′dən| —*noun, plural* **tendons** A strong band or cord of tissue that connects a muscle with a bone.

ten·e·ment |tĕn′ə mənt| —*noun, plural* **tenements** A cheap apartment building that is found in the poorer sections of a city.

Ten·nes·see |tĕn′ĭ sē′| A state in the southern United States. The capital of Tennessee is Nashville.

ten·nis |tĕn′ĭs| —*noun* A sport, played by two or four people on a rectangular court, in which a ball is hit back and forth over a net with a large racket. The object is to hit the ball so that it bounces on the other side of the court in a way that the other player cannot hit it back.

ten·or |tĕn′ər| —*noun, plural* **tenors 1.** A man's singing voice, higher than a baritone and lower than an alto. **2.** A singer who has such a voice.

tense¹ |tĕns| —*adjective* **tenser, tensest 1.** Stretched or pulled tight; strained: *The muscles in his arms were tense as he climbed up the rope.* **2.** Causing or showing suspense, strain, or excitement: *It was a tense moment, waiting to see which of the two cowboys would go for his gun first.*
—*verb* **tensed, tensing** To make or become tense: *I tensed my muscles before jumping. She felt herself tense as she waited before her audition for the director.*

tense² |tĕns| —*noun, plural* **tenses** Any of the forms of a verb that indicate the time when something takes place. *I eat* is in the present tense, *I ate* is in the past tense, and *I shall* (or *will*) *eat* is in the future tense.

tent |tĕnt| —*noun, plural* **tents** A shelter of canvas or nylon that is supported by poles and held in place by ropes and pegs.

ten·ta·cle |tĕn′tə kəl| —*noun, plural* **tentacles** One of the thin, flexible parts that extend from the body of an octopus, jellyfish, or other animal. Tentacles are used for grasping and moving.

tenth |tĕnth| —*noun, plural* **tenths 1.** In a group of people or things that are in numbered order, the one that matches the number ten. **2.** One of ten equal parts, written 1/10.
—*adjective:* the tenth chapter of the book.

te·pee |tē′pē| —*noun, plural* **tepees** A tent in the shape of a cone that is made of animal skins or bark. Tepees were used as dwellings by many North American Indians.

term |tûrm| —*noun, plural* **terms 1.** A period of time: *a school term; a six-year term as senator.* **2.** A word having a precise meaning: *I don't understand the medical terms in my uncle's books.* **3. terms** The conditions under which something can be done or achieved: *What are the terms of the car sale?* **4. terms** The relation between persons or groups: *John and I are on friendly terms.*

—*verb* **termed, terming** To name; to call: *He has been termed a brilliant scientist.*

ter·mi·nal |tûr′mə nəl| —*noun, plural* **terminals** A station at the end of a railroad, bus line, or air line: *a bus terminal.*

ter·mite |tûr′mīt′| —*noun, plural* **termites** An insect that looks like an ant but is not related to it. Termites live in large groups, feeding on and destroying wood.

ter·race |tĕr′əs| —*noun, plural* **terraces** **1.** A porch or balcony: *She lives in a tenth-floor apartment with a small terrace.* **2.** An open, paved area next to a house; patio. **3.** A raised bank of earth having straight or slanting sides and a level top. Terraces are often cut into the sides of a hill to allow more space for crops.

ter·ri·ble |tĕr′ə bəl| —*adjective* **1.** Causing terror or extreme fear: *a terrible accident.* **2.** Not pleasant: *the terrible heat of the tropics. She had a terrible time at the party.* **3.** Extremely bad: *a terrible book.*

ter·ri·er |tĕr′ē ər| —*noun, plural* **terriers** Any of several dogs that are usually small and active. Terriers were once used to hunt small animals that dig burrows in the ground.

ter·rif·ic |tə rĭf′ĭk| —*adjective* **1.** Causing great fear or terror: *a terrific hurricane.* **2.** Very good: *a terrific book.* **3.** Very great or intense: *She has to work under a terrific strain.*

ter·ri·fy |tĕr′ə fī′| —*verb* **terrified, terrifying, terrifies** To fill with terror; frighten greatly: *Heights have always terrified me.*

ter·ri·to·ry |tĕr′ĭ tôr′ē| or |tĕr′ĭ tōr′ē| —*noun, plural* **territories** **1.** An area of land; a region. **2.** The land and waters controlled by a state, nation, or government. **3.** A part of the United States not admitted as a state: *Alaska was a territory until it became the state of Alaska in 1959.*

ter·ror |tĕr′ər| —*noun, plural* **terrors** **1.** Great or intense fear: *The wicked witch filled the children with terror.* **2.** A person or thing that causes such fear: *The boys were the terror of the town.*

test |tĕst| —*noun, plural* **tests** **1.** A way of finding out the nature or quality of something: *A test will show if this is real gold.* **2.** A way of finding out if something is in proper working order: *The state requires a yearly performance test for each automobile.* **3.** A series of questions or tasks to determine a person's knowledge or ability: *a history test; a driver's test.*
—*verb* **tested, testing** To study or examine by means of a test: *The teacher tested the students in spelling.*

Tes·ta·ment |tĕs′tə mənt| —*noun, plural* **Testaments** Either of the two major parts of the Bible, the Old Testament and the New Testament.

tes·ti·fy |tĕs′tə fī′| —*verb* **testified, testifying, testifies** **1.** To state something under oath: *The witness testified against him in court.* **2.** To serve as evidence or proof of: *The increase in sales testifies to his ability as manager.*

tes·ti·mo·ny |tĕs′tə mō′nē| —*noun, plural* **testimonies** **1.** A statement made under oath: *The jury listened to her testimony.* **2.** Any evidence or proof: *The increase in business was testimony to his success as a salesman.*

test tube A long tube of clear glass, open at one end and rounded at the other. Test tubes are used in laboratory tests and experiments.

Tex·as |tĕk′səs| A state in the south-central United States. The capital of Texas is Austin.

terrier

Texas
The name **Texas** comes from an Indian word that means "allies." Spanish explorers heard stories from Indians about "the great kingdom of Texas"; the name was much later taken for the state.

text |tĕkst| —*noun, plural* **texts 1.** The actual words of a piece of writing or of a speech: *We read the text of the President's message in the newspaper.* **2.** The main body of writing in a book: *The text of each lesson is followed by several questions.*

text·book |tĕkst′bŏŏk′| —*noun, plural* **textbooks** A book used by a student for studying a particular subject: *We have a new textbook in American History.*

tex·tile |tĕk′stəl| or |tĕk′stīl′| —*noun, plural* **textiles** Cloth or fabric that is made by weaving or knitting. Wool, silk, and linen are textiles.

tex·ture |tĕks′chər| —*noun, plural* **textures** The look or feel of a fabric. The texture of a fabric results from the way its threads are woven or arranged: *Velvet has a smooth, soft texture.*

than |*th*ăn| —*conjunction* The conjunction **than** is used: **1.** To introduce a comparison: *Pound cake is richer than angel food cake.* **2.** To introduce a choice that has been rejected: *I would rather play tennis than study.*

thank |thăngk| —*verb* **thanked, thanking** To tell a person that one is grateful or pleased: *I thanked him for his help.*

thank·ful |thăngk′fəl| —*adjective* Showing or feeling gratitude; grateful: *We were thankful the storm did no damage.*

thanks |thăngks| —*plural noun* A saying or showing that one is grateful: *We sent our thanks to them for the nice gift.*
—*interjection* A word used to express gratitude: *Thanks, I'm feeling better now.*

Thanks·giv·ing |thăngks gĭv′ĭng| —*noun, plural* **Thanksgivings** A holiday for giving thanks. In the United States, Thanksgiving is the fourth Thursday in November. In Canada, it is the second Monday in October.

that |*th*ăt| or |*th*ət| —*adjective, plural* **those 1.** Being the person or thing at a distance: *This is the car I was talking about, not that one.* **2.** Indicating the person or thing at a distance or already mentioned: *Give the book to that girl over there.* The adjective **that** belongs to a class of words called **determiners.** They signal that a noun is coming.
—*pronoun, plural* **those 1.** Something already pointed out or mentioned: *Ask her to tell you that again.* **2.** The other: *This is a bigger piece of cake than that.* **3.** Something at a distance: *This is a plane, and that's a spacecraft.* **4.** Who, whom, or which: *Mary and Rosalie are some of the girls that I have met. Give me a list of things that have to be done.* **5.** In, on, or for which: *She called the day that she arrived. I was busy the entire time that you stayed out.*
—*adverb* To that extent: *Is it that difficult to do your homework?*
—*conjunction* The conjunction **that** is used to introduce another part of a sentence: *I didn't think that you were coming.*

thatch |thăch| —*noun* Straw, reeds, or palm fronds, used to cover a roof.
—*verb* **thatched, thatching** To cover with thatch: *The workers thatched the roof of the house.*

that's |*th*ăts| A contraction for "that is."

thaw |thô| —*verb* **thawed, thawing 1.** To change from a solid to a liquid by gradual warming; melt: *The ice thawed as I held it in my hand.* **2.** To become warm enough for snow and ice to melt: *It often thaws in late January.* **3.** To become more friendly: *After the excellent dinner the guests began to thaw.*
—*noun, plural* **thaws** A period of warm weather that melts ice

thatch

and snow: *The sudden thaw last week was a taste of spring.*

the¹ | *th*ē | or | *th*ə | —*definite article* **1.** The definite article **the** is used before a noun or phrase that stands for a particular person or thing: *The man we are looking for has a scar. The pencil I need has disappeared.* **2.** Any; every: *The squirrel is an animal with grayish fur.* The definite article **the** belongs to a class of words called **determiners.** They signal that a noun is coming.

the² | *th*ə | or | *th*ē | —*adverb* To that extent; by that much: *the sooner the better. The more I see her, the more I like her.*

the·a·ter or **the·a·tre** | thē′ə tər | —*noun, plural* **theaters** or **theatres 1.** A building or outdoor area where plays or motion pictures are presented. **2.** The work of people who write or act in plays or are employed in putting on plays.

theft | thĕft | —*noun, plural* **thefts** The act or an instance of stealing: *He was arrested for the theft of their car.*

their | *th*âr | or | *th*ər | —*pronoun* The pronoun **their** is a possessive form of **they.** It means: **1.** Of or belonging to them: *their hats.* **2.** Done or performed by them: *The twins had to finish their homework.* The pronoun **their** belongs to a class of words called **determiners.** They signal that a noun is coming.

♦ *These sound alike* **their, there, they're.**

theirs | *th*ârz | —*pronoun* The pronoun **theirs** is a possessive form of **they.** It is used to show that something or someone belongs to them: *The large package is theirs. He is no friend of theirs. If your car is out of order, use theirs.*

♦ *These sound alike* **theirs, there's.**

them | *th*ĕm | —*pronoun* The pronoun **them** is the objective case of **they.** It is used: **1.** As the direct object of a verb: *She touched them on the arm.* **2.** As the indirect object of a verb: *I gave them good advice.* **3.** As the object of a preposition: *Paul gave the car keys to them.*

theme | thĕm | —*noun, plural* **themes 1.** The subject of a talk or a piece of writing: *The theme of the discussion was pet care.* **2.** A melody on which a musical composition is based.

them·selves | *th*ĕm sĕlvz′ | or | *th*əm sĕlvz′ | —*pronoun* The pronoun **themselves** is a special form of **they. 1.** It is used: **a.** As the direct object of a verb: *They blamed themselves.* **b.** As the indirect object of a verb: *Paul and Fred gave themselves enough time to finish their tasks.* **c.** As the object of a preposition: *They saved all the ice cream for themselves.* **d.** To call special attention to certain persons or things: *Her parents themselves are going. They themselves saw the accident.* **2.** The pronoun **themselves** is used to mean "their normal selves": *They have not been themselves since the accident.*

then | *th*ĕn | —*adverb* **1.** At that time: *Rents were lower then.* **2.** After that; next: *One more game, and then we'll go home.* **3.** In that case: *If you want to go, then go.*
—*noun* That time or moment: *From then on, I got to class on time.*

   Idioms **and then some** And much more: *You'll have to do your best and then some to pass that test.* **now and then** From time to time; once in a while: *I don't jog regularly, just now and then.*

the·o·ry | thē′ə rē | or | thîr′ē | —*noun, plural* **theories 1.** An idea or set of ideas made up to explain why something happened or continues to happen: *a theory about the creation of the universe.* **2.** A guess, estimate, or judgment based on limited knowledge or information: *What's your theory about why we lost the game?*

the¹, the²
The¹ and the² both come from old English.

theater
An inside view of a college theater

there | *th*âr | —*adverb* **1.** At or in that place: *Put the groceries there on the table.* **2.** To or toward that place: *How long did it take to get there?*
—*pronoun* **1.** The pronoun **there** is used to introduce a sentence or part of a sentence: *There is no reason to do that. I wondered why there were no towels.* **2.** That place: *Her house is a long way from there.*
—*interjection* A word used to express satisfaction, sympathy, or encouragement: *There, it's done! There, there, I know just how you feel.*
♦ *These sound alike* **there, their, they're.**

there·a·bouts | *th*âr'ə **bouts'** | —*adverb* **1.** Near that time, age, or number: *It's 10:30 or thereabouts.* **2.** In that area or neighborhood: *They live in West Canyon or thereabouts.*

there·af·ter | *th*âr **ăf'** tər | or | *th*âr **äf'** tər | —*adverb* After that or from then on: *Thereafter the kingdom was peaceful for many years.*

there·by | *th*âr **bī'** | or | **thâr'** bī' | —*adverb* By that means; in that way: *The gadget cuts gas consumption, thereby reducing our fuel bills.*

there·fore | **thâr'** fôr' | or | **thâr'** fōr' | —*adverb* For that reason: *The grass wasn't watered and therefore turned brown.*

there's | *th*ârz | A contraction for "there is" and "there has."
♦ *These sound alike* **there's, theirs.**

ther·mom·e·ter | thər **mŏm'** ĭ tər | —*noun, plural* **thermometers** An instrument for measuring and indicating temperature. A thermometer usually consists of a long glass tube with a column of liquid, which has been marked off in a scale to show degrees of temperature.

Ther·mos bottle | **thûr'** məs | A container having a double lining with a vacuum between to slow down any change of temperature. A Thermos bottle is used to carry liquids while keeping them either hot or cold. The phrase Thermos bottle is a trademark.

ther·mo·stat | **thûr'** mə stăt' | —*noun, plural* **thermostats** A device that controls temperature automatically. Thermostats are used to control furnaces, ovens, refrigerators, and many other things.

these | *th*ēz | The plural of the word **this**: *These shoes are too tight. Are these the right keys?*

they | *th*ā | —*pronoun* **1.** The persons, animals, or things last mentioned: *Paula and Dick worked here last summer, but now they are back in school. I bought several books yesterday, but they have not been delivered yet.* **2.** People in general: *Whatever they say, I'll do it. She's as tough as they come.* The pronoun **they** is the plural of **he, she,** and **it.**

they'd | *th*ād | A contraction of "they had" and "they would."

they'll | *th*āl | A contraction of "they will."

they're | *th*âr | A contraction of "they are."
♦ *These sound alike* **they're, their, there.**

they've | *th*āv | A contraction of "they have."

thick | thĭk | —*adjective* **thicker, thickest** **1.** Having much space between opposite sides or surfaces; not thin: *a thick board.* **2.** Measured between surfaces; measured in distance between opposite sides: *I need a board two inches thick.* **3.** Not flowing easily; heavy: *thick chocolate syrup.* **4.** Very dense or heavy: *thick fog; thick hair.*
—*adverb* So as to be thick: *I like my roast beef sliced thick.*

thermometer
Different kinds of thermometers

ă	pat	ĕ	pet	î	fierce
ā	pay	ē	be	ŏ	pot
â	care	ĭ	pit	ō	go
ä	father	ī	pie	ô	paw, for

oi	oil	ŭ	cut	zh	vision
ōō	book	û	fur	ə	ago, item,
ōō	boot	*th*	the		pencil, atom,
yōō	abuse	th	thin		circus
ou	out	hw	which	ər	butter

—noun The center of action or activity; the most intense part of something: *in the thick of the battle.*

thick·en | thĭk′ən | *—verb* **thickened, thickening** To make or become thick or thicker: *Use flour to thicken the gravy.*

thick·et | thĭk′ĭt | *—noun, plural* **thickets** A dense growth of shrubs or small trees.

thick·ness | thĭk′nĭs | *—noun, plural* **thicknesses** **1.** The condition of being thick: *The thickness of the fog made it difficult for him to see the road.* **2.** The distance through or between opposite surfaces: *The thickness of that plank is four inches.*

thief | thēf | *—noun, plural* **thieves** A person who steals, especially in secret when the victim is not present.

thieves | thēvz | The plural of the noun **thief.**

thigh | thī | *—noun, plural* **thighs** The upper part of the leg, between the knee and the hip.

thim·ble | thĭm′bəl | *—noun, plural* **thimbles** A small metal or plastic cap worn to protect the finger that pushes the needle in sewing.

thin | thĭn | *—adjective* **thinner, thinnest** **1.** Having little space between opposite sides or surfaces; not thick: *a thin board.* **2.** Of small diameter; fine: *thin wire.* **3.** Having a lean or slender figure: *a thin man.* **4.** Flowing easily: *a thin oil.* **5.** Not dense or heavy: *thin hair; a thin mist.* **6.** Easy to see through; poor: *a thin excuse.*
—adverb So as to be thin; thinly: *I like my roast beef sliced thin.*
—verb **thinned, thinning** To make or become thin or thinner: *She thinned the tea with hot water. The river thinned to a trickle.*

thing | thĭng | *—noun, plural* **things** **1.** An object or creature that cannot be precisely named: *What's that thing on the table?* **2.** An object that has no life, as distinguished from a living being: *That vase is a beautiful thing.* **3.** A creature or person: *I pity the poor thing. The baby is such a sweet little thing.* **4.** An act or deed: *What a mean thing to do!* **5.** **things** One's personal possessions: *Put your things in the bottom drawer.* **6.** **things** Conditions in general; the state of affairs: *Things are going from bad to worse.*

think | thĭngk | *—verb* **thought, thinking** **1.** To use one's mind to make decisions or judgments: *Think a moment before you speak.* **2.** To have as a thought; imagine: *He thought he would like to be an astronaut.* **3.** To believe or suppose: *I think that she is wrong.* **4.** To remember or recall: *I can't think what his name is.*
   ***Phrasal verb* think about 1.** To consider the possibility of: *We're thinking about going to Europe.* **2.** To remember; reflect: *She was thinking about her childhood.*

third | thûrd | *—noun, plural* **thirds** **1.** In a group of people or things that are in numbered order, the one that matches the number three. **2.** One of three equal parts, written ⅓.
—adjective: the third door to the right.

thirst | thûrst | *—noun, plural* **thirsts** **1.** A feeling that one's mouth is very dry, caused by a desire to drink; a craving for water: *The potato chips gave me a tremendous thirst.* **2.** Any desire or yearning: *He had a thirst for adventure.*

thirst·y | thûr′stē | *—adjective* **thirstier, thirstiest** **1.** Feeling thirst: *Salty foods always make me thirsty.* **2.** Needing moisture; arid; parched: *The fields are thirsty for rain.*

thir·teen | thûr′tēn′ | *—noun, plural* **thirteens** A number, written 13, that is equal to the sum of 10 + 3.
—adjective Being one more than twelve in number: *thirteen cars.*

thimble

The adjective **thirteen** belongs to a class of words called **determiners.** They signal that a noun is coming.

thir·teenth | thûr′tĕnth′ | —*noun, plural* **thirteenths 1.** In a group of people or things that are in numbered order, the one that matches the number thirteen. **2.** One of thirteen equal parts, written 1/13.
—*adjective: the thirteenth car of the train.*

thir·ti·eth | thûr′tē ĭth | —*noun, plural* **thirtieths 1.** In a group of people or things that are in numbered order, the one that matches the number thirty. **2.** One of thirty equal parts, written 1/30.
—*adjective: the thirtieth chapter of the book.*

thir·ty | thûr′tē | —*noun, plural* **thirties** A number, written 30, that is equal to the product of 10 × 3.
—*adjective* Being ten more than twenty in number: *thirty books.* The adjective **thirty** belongs to a class of words called **determiners.** They signal that a noun is coming.

this | *th*ĭs | —*adjective, plural* **these 1.** Being the person or thing present, nearby, or just mentioned: *This book is the one I wanted to buy.* **2.** Indicating the person or thing present, nearby, or just mentioned: *Sheila, I want you to meet this friend of mine.* The adjective **this** belongs to a class of words called **determiners.** They signal that a noun is coming.
—*pronoun, plural* **these 1.** The person or thing present, nearby, or just mentioned: *This is my friend Judy. This is my house right here.* **2.** Something that is about to be said or pointed out: *What she meant was this. This will really make you laugh.* **3.** A person or thing that is nearer than another person or thing or is contrasted to another person or thing: *Everybody agreed that this is a better painting than that. That car accident was nothing compared to this.* **4.** The present time: *Jim's been out later than this.*
—*adverb* To this extent; so: *I never knew Jim to stay out this late.*

this·tle | thĭs′əl | —*noun, plural* **thistles** A prickly plant with purple flowers and seeds that have tufts of silky fluff.

thong | thông | or | thŏng | —*noun, plural* **thongs** A thin strip of leather used to fasten something, such as a sandal.

tho·rax | thôr′ăks′ | or | thōr′ăks′ | —*noun, plural* **thoraxes 1.** The part of the human body that is between the neck and the abdomen; the chest. The thorax is partly surrounded by the ribs. **2.** The middle part in the body of an insect, which is divided into three parts.

thorn | thôrn | —*noun, plural* **thorns 1.** A sharp point that grows from the stem of a plant. **2.** A shrub, tree, or other plant that has such points.

thorn·y | thôr′nē | —*adjective* **thornier, thorniest 1.** Full of or covered with thorns: *the thorny stem of a rose.* **2.** Causing trouble; difficult: *a thorny problem.*

thor·ough | thûr′ō | or | thŭr′ō | —*adjective* **1.** Complete in all respects: *The doctor gave me a thorough examination.* **2.** Very careful: *a thorough search; a thorough worker.*

thor·ough·ly | thûr′ō lē | or | thŭr′ō lē | —*adverb* In a thorough manner; completely, fully, or carefully: *They cleaned the garage thoroughly.*

those | *th*ōz | The plural of the word **that:** *Those are the girls I was telling you about.*

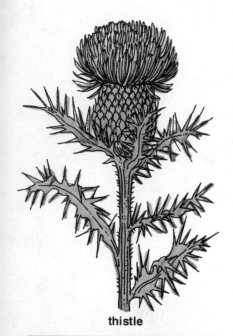

thistle

ă	pat	ĕ	pet	î	fierce
ā	pay	ē	be	ŏ	pot
â	care	ĭ	pit	ō	go
ä	father	ī	pie	ô	paw, for
oi	oil	ŭ	cut	zh	vision
ŏŏ	book	û	fur	ə	ago, item,
ōō	boot	*th*	the		pencil, atom,
yōō	abuse	th	thin		circus
ou	out	hw	which	ər	butter

though |thō| —*adverb* However; nevertheless: *I've a lot of work to do; I'm tired, though, so I'm going to take a short nap.*
—*conjunction* Even if; although: *Though she was sure to lose, she played the match anyway.*

thought |thôt| The past tense and past participle of the verb **think:** *I thought she would leave early. She had thought about going home for the holidays.*
—*noun, plural* **thoughts 1.** The act or process of thinking: *a problem that requires much thought.* **2.** The result of thinking; an idea: *What are your thoughts on the subject?* **3.** Consideration or attention; concern: *Give some serious thought to this matter.*

thought·ful |thôt′fəl| —*adjective* **1.** Occupied with thought; thinking: *She looked thoughtful.* **2.** Showing concern for others; considerate: *He is a thoughtful man.*

thought·less |thôt′lĭs| —*adjective* **1.** Not thinking; careless: *It was thoughtless of you to forget her birthday.* **2.** Not showing concern for others; not considerate; rude: *It was thoughtless of you to say a thing like that.*

thou·sand |thou′zənd| —*noun, plural* **thousands** A number, written 1,000, that is equal to the product of 10 × 100.
—*adjective* Being ten times more than one hundred in number: *a thousand cars.* The adjective **thousand** belongs to a class of words called **determiners.** They signal that a noun is coming.

thou·sandth |thou′zəndth| or |thou′zənth| —*noun, plural* **thousandths 1.** In a group of people or things that are in numbered order, the one that matches the number 1,000. **2.** One of a thousand equal parts, written ⅟₁₀₀₀.
—*adjective: the thousandth car in the parade.*

thrash |thrăsh| —*verb* **thrashed, thrashing 1.** To beat or whip: *He thrashed the boy soundly.* **2.** To move wildly or violently: *The frightened girl thrashed about in the water.*

thread |thrĕd| —*noun, plural* **threads 1.** A fine, thin cord made of two or more strands of fiber twisted together. Thread can be woven into cloth or used in sewing things together. **2.** Anything that resembles a thread: *a thread of smoke rising from the chimney.* **3.** An idea or theme that joins together the parts of a story or speech: *The thread of the story was the hero's attempt to catch a spy.* **4.** The winding ridge on a screw, nut, or bolt.
—*verb* **threaded, threading 1.** To pass one end of a thread through the eye of a needle or through the hooks and holes on a sewing machine. **2.** To join by running a thread through; to string: *Mary was busy threading beads to make a necklace.* **3.** To make one's way cautiously through something: *We threaded our way through the traffic after the baseball game.*

threat |thrĕt| —*noun, plural* **threats 1.** Something said or expressed with the idea of hurting or punishing: *They had heard the old witch's threat to turn the children into frogs.* **2.** A sign of coming danger: *There's a threat of frost in the air.* **3.** A person or thing regarded as dangerous: *Pollution is a threat to all.*

threat·en |thrĕt′n| —*verb* **threatened, threatening 1.** To say a threat against: *The sergeant threatened the soldiers with punishment if they were late.* **2.** To be a threat to; endanger: *The flood threatened the tiny village.* **3.** To give signs or warning of: *Dark skies threatened rain.*

three |thrē| —*noun, plural* **threes** A number, written 3, that is equal to the sum of 2 + 1.

—*adjective* Being one more than two in number: *three pencils.* The adjective **three** belongs to a class of words called **determiners.** They signal that a noun is coming.

thresh |thrĕsh| —*verb* **threshed, threshing** To separate the seeds or grain from a plant by striking or beating: *The farmers threshed the wheat with a giant reaper.*

thresh·old |thrĕsh′ōld| or |thrĕsh′hōld| —*noun, plural* **thresholds 1.** The piece of wood or stone placed beneath a door; a sill. **2.** The place or point of beginning: *Science is on the threshold of new discoveries.*

threw |thrōō| The past tense of the verb **throw:** *She threw the ball well.*

♦ *These sound alike* **threw, through.**

thrift |thrĭft| —*noun* The wise or careful management of one's money or other resources: *You can't raise a large family without thrift.*

thrift·y |thrĭf′tē| —*adjective* **thriftier, thriftiest** Practicing thrift; careful in the use of money; economical: *a thrifty man.*

thrill |thrĭl| —*verb* **thrilled, thrilling** To feel or cause to feel sudden joy, fear, or excitement: *The trapeze artists thrilled the audience.*

—*noun, plural* **thrills** A sudden, intense feeling of joy, fear, or excitement: *The roller coaster always gives me a thrill.*

thrive |thrīv| —*verb* **throve** or **thrived, thrived** or **thriven, thriving 1.** To do well; be or stay in a healthy condition: *The polar bear thrives in a cold climate.* **2.** To be successful; make progress: *His new business is thriving.*

thriv·en |thrĭv′ən| A past participle of the verb **thrive:** *They have thriven in the new business better than they expected.*

throat |thrōt| —*noun, plural* **throats 1.** The passage between the mouth and the esophagus. Food passes through the throat to get to the stomach. **2.** Any narrow part resembling the human throat: *the throat of a bottle.*

throb |thrŏb| —*verb* **throbbed, throbbing** To beat rapidly or violently; pound: *His heart throbbed with excitement.*

—*noun, plural* **throbs** A rapid or violent beating or pounding: *He could feel the throb of his heart after jogging.*

throne |thrōn| —*noun, plural* **thrones 1.** The chair occupied by a king, queen, or other ruler. **2.** The rank or power of a ruler: *The prince succeeded to the throne after the queen died.*

♦ *These sound alike* **throne, thrown.**

throng |thrông| or |thrŏng| —*noun, plural* **throngs** A large group of people or things crowded together: *I elbowed my way through the throng to see the President.*

—*verb* **thronged, thronging** To crowd into; fill: *The spectators thronged the stadium to see the game.*

throt·tle |thrŏt′l| —*noun, plural* **throttles 1.** A valve in an engine that controls the flow of fuel. **2.** A pedal or lever that controls such a valve.

through |thrōō| —*preposition* **1.** In one side and out the other: *We walked through the parking lot.* **2.** Among or between: *She walked through the flowers.* **3.** By means of; with the help of: *We bought our house through an agency.* **4.** At or to the end of: *We stayed up through the night.* **5.** At or to the conclusion of: *We're through the most difficult part of the job.* **6.** Here and there in; around: *We traveled through France.*

throne

ă	pat	ĕ	pet	î	fierce
ā	pay	ē	be	ŏ	pot
â	care	ĭ	pit	ō	go
ä	father	ī	pie	ô	paw, for
oi	oil	ŭ	cut	zh	vision
ōō	book	û	fur	ə	ago, item,
ōō	boot	*th*	the		pencil, atom,
yōō	abuse	th	thin		circus
ou	out	hw	which	ər	butter

—adverb **1.** From one side of to the other: *The door opened and we went through.* **2.** Completely; thoroughly: *We were soaked through.* **3.** From beginning to end: *This is important, so hear me through.* **4.** At or to the conclusion: *Let's see this thing through.* **5.** All the way: *Does the bus go through to Boston?*

—adjective **1.** Allowing passage without stopping: *a through street.* **2.** Going all the way without stopping: *a through flight to Washington.* **3.** Finished with a task or action; done: *When you're through, I'd like a word with you.*

♦ *These sound alike* **through, threw.**

through·out | thrōō out′ | *—preposition* In, through, or during every part of: *We traveled throughout the country.*

—adverb In, during, or through every part: *We searched the house throughout.*

throve | thrōv | A past tense of the verb **thrive:** *The family throve from all the good food at the farm.*

throw | thrō | *—verb* **threw, thrown, throwing** **1.** To send through the air with a swift motion of the arm; fling: *Mike threw the ball to Larry.* **2.** To thrust with great force, as in anger: *The wrestler threw himself at his opponent.* **3.** To cause to fall: *The horse reared and threw the rider.* **4.** To cast; project: *The sun throws a shadow on the wall.* **5.** To put on or take off hurriedly: *She threw on her coat and ran out the door.* **6.** To put in a particular condition or position: *Throw the light switch.*

Phrasal verbs **throw away** To discard as useless: *He threw away a candy wrapper.* **throw out** To discard; cast out; reject: *Don't forget to throw out the scraps after the meal.*

—noun, plural **throws** **1.** The act of throwing: *You get two throws for each dime.* **2.** A scarf, shawl, or cover: *Grandmother knitted a throw for the couch.*

throw·er | thrō′ər | *—noun, plural* **throwers** Someone or something that throws.

thrown | thrōn | The past participle of the verb **throw:** *She had thrown the chestnuts into the fire.*

♦ *These sound alike* **thrown, throne.**

thrush | thrŭsh | *—noun, plural* **thrushes** Any of several songbirds usually having a brownish back and a spotted breast.

thrust | thrŭst | *—verb* **thrust, thrusting** **1.** To push with force; shove: *We thrust our way through the crowd.* **2.** To stab or pierce: *She thrust a fork into the roast.*

—noun, plural **thrusts** A forceful push or shove: *She braced herself for the thrust of the crowd.*

thumb | thŭm | *—noun, plural* **thumbs** **1.** The short, thick first finger of the human hand, next to the forefinger and opposite the little finger. **2.** The part of a glove or mitten that fits over the thumb.

—verb **thumbed, thumbing** To ask or get a ride by pointing one's thumb in the direction one is traveling; hitchhike: *I thumbed a rides as far as Austin.*

Phrasal verb **thumb through** To turn rapidly the pages of a book or other publication while looking at it: *She thumbed through several magazines at the drugstore.*

thumb·tack | thŭm′tăk′ | *—noun, plural* **thumbtacks** A tack with a large, flat head that can be pressed into place with the thumb.

thump | thŭmp | *—noun, plural* **thumps** **1.** A blow with a blunt instrument: *a thump on the back of the head.* **2.** The dull sound

produced by such a blow: *We heard a thump on the back porch.*
—*verb* **thumped, thumping 1.** To strike with a blunt instrument
or with the hand or foot so as to produce a dull sound: *He angrily
thumped the desk with his fist.* **2.** To beat, hit, or fall so as to
produce a thump: *Her heart thumped with fear.*

thun·der | thŭn′dər | —*noun* **1.** The rumbling or crashing noise
that accompanies a bolt of lightning. **2.** Any similar noise: *the
thunder of distant guns.*
—*verb* **thundered, thundering 1.** To produce thunder: *It began to
thunder, so we rushed home.* **2.** To produce sounds like thunder:
You could hear guns thundering in the distance.

thun·der·storm | thŭn′dər stôrm′ | —*noun, plural* **thunderstorms**
A heavy storm accompanied by lightning and thunder.

Thurs·day | thûrz′dē | or | thûrz′dā′ | —*noun, plural* **Thursdays**
The fifth day of the week, after Wednesday and before Friday.

thus | *th*ŭs | —*adverb* **1.** In this way or manner: *Tied thus, the
knot is much easier to undo.* **2.** To this degree or extent; so: *Thus
far I haven't had a chance to look over your work.* **3.** As a consequence;
thereby: *The pole fell, thus cutting off electricity to the area.*

thyme | tīm | —*noun, plural* **thymes** A plant that grows near the
ground and has leaves with a spicy smell. Thyme is used to flavor
cooked food.
♦ *These sound alike* **thyme, time.**

thy·roid gland | thī′roid′ | A gland in the neck of human beings.
It makes a substance that regulates body growth.

tick¹ | tĭk | —*noun, plural* **ticks 1.** One of a series of soft, clicking
sounds made by parts of a mechanism striking together, as in a
clock or watch. **2.** A light mark used to check off an item: *Put a
tick by each item on your list as I call it out.*
—*verb* **ticked, ticking 1.** To produce a series of ticks: *The only
sound was the clock ticking in the corner.* **2.** To function in a
certain way: *I don't know what makes him tick.*

tick² | tĭk | —*noun, plural* **ticks** A small animal that looks like a
spider. Ticks attach themselves to the skin of human beings and
other animals and suck their blood. Ticks often carry diseases.

tick·et | tĭk′ĭt | —*noun, plural* **tickets 1.** A paper slip or card
that gives a person certain rights or services, such as a seat in a
stadium or entrance to a club. **2.** A list of candidates in an
election: *the Republican ticket for 1980.* **3.** A legal summons given
to a person accused of violating a traffic law.
—*verb* **ticketed, ticketing 1.** To attach a label or tag to: *Ticket the
merchandise before putting it on sale.* **2.** To give a legal summons
to: *The policeman ticketed the cars for parking on the hill.*

tick·le | tĭk′əl | —*verb* **tickled, tickling 1.** To touch the body and
cause a tingling sensation or feeling: *He put the feather to my ear,
and it tickled.* **2.** To delight or amuse; please: *It tickled me to see
her win the prize.*
    Idiom tickled pink Delighted; extremely pleased: *John was
tickled pink to get the new bicycle.*

tid·al wave | tīd′l | A large, powerful ocean wave. Tidal waves
are very destructive and may be caused by hurricanes or
earthquakes.

tide | tīd | —*noun, plural* **tides** The regular change in the level of
the oceans, seas, and other large bodies of water of the earth.
Tides usually occur twice a day and are caused by the pull of the
moon and sun on the earth.

---

tick¹, tick²
Tick¹ was probably formed in imitation of the sound it refers to. **Tick²**
came from an old English word
meaning "animal louse."

tide
Above: High tide
Below: Low tide

ă	pat	ĕ	pet	î	fierce
ā	pay	ē	be	ŏ	pot
â	care	ĭ	pit	ō	go
ä	father	ī	pie	ô	paw, for
oi	oil	ŭ	cut	zh	vision
oo	book	û	fur	ə	ago, item,
oo	boot	*th*	the		pencil, atom,
	use	th	thin		circus
		hw	which	ər	butter

—*verb* **tided, tiding** —**tide over** To help someone get through a difficult period; support: *I need some money to tide me over until I get my allowance.*

ti·dy | tī′dē | —*adjective* **tidier, tidiest 1.** Placed or kept in order; neat; orderly: *a tidy room; a tidy closet.* **2.** Large or fairly large; considerable: *She had saved a tidy sum of money.*

—*verb* **tidied, tidying, tidies** To put in order; make neat: *Tidy your room before you go out to play.*

tie | tī | —*verb* **tied, tying 1.** To fasten or bind with a cord or rope: *Wrap the package and then tie it. Tie the dog to the fence.* **2.** To fasten by knotting strings or laces: *He bent over to tie his shoes. Her apron ties at the back.* **3.** To fasten with a knot or bow: *Can you tie your own necktie? She tied a scarf around her head.* **4.** To equal another in score; equal the score of: *He tied the school record for the pole vault. The two teams tied for first place.*

   Phrasal verb tie up 1. To cause to stop; to halt: *The accident tied up traffic for hours.* **2.** To be busy, occupied, or in use: *Father is tied up all afternoon with appointments.*

—*noun, plural* **ties 1. a.** A cord, string, or rope with which something is tied: *We bought fancy ties for decorating the Christmas packages.* **b.** Anything that holds or binds people together: *The two families have strong ties of friendship.* **2.** A necktie: *Wear your striped tie.* **3.** An equal score or vote: *The game ended in a tie.* **4.** A heavy beam laid across a railroad bed to support the tracks.

tier | tîr | —*noun, plural* **tiers** One of a series of rows or layers that are placed one above another: *The theater has four tiers of seats.*

   ♦ *These sound alike* **tier, tear**[2].

ti·ger | tī′gər | —*noun, plural* **tigers** A very large wild cat that lives in Asia. A tiger has light brown fur with black stripes.

tight | tīt | —*adjective* **tighter, tightest 1.** Held, closed, or fastened firmly; secure: *The knot on the package is so tight I can't untie it.* **2.** Made or built so that nothing, such as air or water, can pass through: *a tight roof; a tight boat.* **3.** Fitting close to the body: *a tight shirt; tight shoes.* **4.** Pulled or stretched out to the fullest extent: *We set up the tent and made sure the ropes were tight.* **5.** Having no room or time to spare: *The doctor couldn't give me an appointment for a month because he has a tight schedule.* **6.** Not generous or liberal; stingy: *Her uncle is very tight with money.* **7.** Hard to get: *We couldn't buy the new car because money is tight right now.* **8.** Hard to deal with or get out of: *He didn't hand in his homework and now he's in a tight spot.* **9.** Almost even; close: *That was one of the tightest races I ever saw.*

—*adverb* **1.** Firmly; securely: *Close the door tight.* **2.** Soundly: *Sleep tight.*

tight·en | tīt′n | —*verb* **tightened, tightening** To make or become tight: *She tightened the lid on the jar. The cord tightened as they pulled on it.*

tight·rope | tīt′rōp′ | —*noun, plural* **tightropes** A rope or wire stretched high above the ground. Acrobats and circus artists perform on a tightrope.

ti·gress | tī′grĭs | —*noun, plural* **tigresses** A female tiger.

tile | tīl | —*noun, plural* **tiles** A thin slab or piece of baked clay, plastic, porcelain, or other material. They are laid in rows and used to cover floors, walls, or roofs.

—*verb* **tiled, tiling** To cover with tiles: *Mom tiled the floor.*

tiger

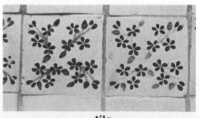

tile

timber

till¹ | tĭl | —*verb* **tilled, tilling** To prepare land for growing crops by plowing and fertilizing. In the United States farmers use machines to till land, but in many parts of the world it is still done by hand or by an animal that pulls a plow.

till² | tĭl | —*preposition* Until: *I won't see you till tomorrow.* —*conjunction* **1.** Before or unless: *I can't help you till you tell me what is wrong.* **2.** Until: *Wait till I call you.*

till³ | tĭl | —*noun, plural* **tills** A drawer for keeping or holding money, especially in a store.

til·ler | tĭl′ər | —*noun, plural* **tillers** A lever or handle used to turn a rudder and steer a boat.

tilt | tĭlt | —*verb* **tilted, tilting** To slope or cause to slope by having one end or side raised higher than the other; tip: *The table tilted and the plates fell on the floor. The children tilted the barrel to empty it.* —*noun, plural* **tilts** A slanting position; a slope: *He left the ladder in a tilt against the house.*

tim·ber | tĭm′bər | —*noun, plural* **timbers 1.** Trees or land covered with trees; forest: *Most of the land out behind the barn is timber.* **2.** Wood used for building; lumber: *The workers delivered the timber for the new porch.* **3.** A long, large, heavy piece of wood shaped like a beam. It is used for such things as building the frame of a house or ship.

time | tīm | —*noun, plural* **times 1.** All the days since the world began; the continuous period including the past, the present, and the future: *The winter was one of the coldest of all time.* **2.** Any period of time that has a beginning and an end, such as the period during which an event or condition takes place or continues: *How much time does it take you to get to school? For a long time people believed the world was flat.* **3.** A period in history: *Thomas Jefferson lived during the time of the American Revolution.* **4.** A specific moment or point in time: *What time does the movie start? It's dinner time.* **5.** A period of time set aside for a special purpose: *I have to be at his house in ten minutes so I don't have the time to help you now.* **6.** An instance or occasion: *I'm going to catch a big fish this time. He sang the song four times before he got it right.* **7.** An experience or feeling during a certain period or event: *We had a good time at the party.* **8.** The meter or beat in music: *Keep time to the song by clapping your hands.* —*verb* **timed, timing 1.** To set the time at which something happens or will happen: *The alarm clock is timed to go off at eight o'clock.* **2.** To record or measure the speed of something: *He was timed as the fastest runner on the team.*

♦ *These sound alike* **time, thyme.**

times | tīmz | —*preposition* Multiplied by: *Eight times three equals twenty-four.*

tim·id | tĭm′ĭd | —*adjective* Lacking in courage; easily scared; shy: *The timid little boy hid from strangers.*

tim·pa·ni | tĭm′pə nē | —*plural noun* A set of kettledrums.

tin | tĭn | —*noun, plural* **tins 1.** A soft silvery metal. Tin is one of the chemical elements. **2.** A container made of tin: *a tin of cookies.*

tin·gle | tĭng′gəl | —*verb* **tingled, tingling** To have a prickly, stinging feeling, often from cold or excitement: *My fingers and toes tingled from the cold.* —*noun, plural* **tingles** A prickly or stinging feeling: *He felt a tingle down his back as he stepped into the dark cave.*

ă	pat	ĕ	pet	î	fierce
ā	pay	ē	be	ŏ	pot
â	care	ĭ	pit	ō	go
ä	father	ī	pie	ô	paw, for
oi	oil	ŭ	cut	zh	vision
ōō	book	û	fur	ə	ago, item,
ōō	boot	*th*	the		pencil, atom,
yōō	abuse	th	thin		circus
ou	out	hw	which	ər	butter

tin·kle | tĭng′kəl | —*verb* **tinkled, tinkling** To make or cause to make light, ringing sounds, like the sound of small bells.
—*noun, plural* **tinkles** A light, clear, ringing sound.

tint | tĭnt | —*noun, plural* **tints** 1. A delicate or pale shade of color. 2. A slight trace of color: *a tint of red in the sky.*
—*verb* **tinted, tinting** To give a tint to; to color: *She tinted the shirt blue.*

ti·ny | tī′nē | —*adjective* **tinier, tiniest** Very, very small.

tip[1] | tĭp | —*noun, plural* **tips** 1. The end or farthest point of something: *a house on the tip of the island; asparagus tips.* 2. A piece that can be fitted on the end of something: *a pen with a plastic tip.*
—*verb* **tipped, tipping** 1. To put a tip on: *tip the chair legs with rubber.* 2. To hit a baseball with the side of the bat so that it goes off sideways.

tip[2] | tĭp | —*verb* **tipped, tipping** 1. To knock over: *The wind tipped over the vase on the table.* 2. To slant; tilt: *The children tipped the table. The boat tipped suddenly.* 3. To touch or raise one's hat in greeting.

tip[3] | tĭp | —*noun, plural* **tips** 1. A sum of money given in return for service: *She left a tip for the waiter.* 2. Useful information; a helpful hint: *a book with tips on gardening.*
—*verb* **tipped, tipping** To give a sum of money to in return for service: *He tipped the waiter. He tips generously.*
　Phrasal verb **tip off** To give secret information to.

tip·toe | tĭp′tō′ | —*verb* **tiptoed, tiptoeing** To walk on the tip of one's toes.

tire[1] | tīr | —*verb* **tired, tiring** 1. To make or become weary: *The long walk tired me. She tires easily.* 2. To make or become bored; lose interest: *His long speech tired the listeners. The audience tired after the first act of the play.*

tire[2] | tīr | —*noun, plural* **tires** 1. A covering for a wheel, usually made of rubber and filled with air. 2. A hoop of metal or rubber fitted around a wheel.

tired | tīrd | —*adjective* 1. Weary: *a tired athlete.* 2. Impatient; bored: *a tired audience.*

tis·sue | tĭsh′ōo | —*noun, plural* **tissues** 1. A group or type of animal or plant cells that are alike in form and in what they do. Often they make up an organ or certain part of the body or plant: *lung tissue; muscle tissue; leaf tissue.* 2. Light, thin paper used for wrapping or packing. 3. A piece of soft, thin paper used as a handkerchief.

ti·tle | tīt′l | —*noun, plural* **titles** 1. A name given to a book, painting, song, or poem. 2. A word or name given to a person to show rank, office, or job. Some titles are *Sir, Judge,* and *Her Majesty.* 3. a. The legal right or claim to ownership or possession: *Has he any title to the throne?* b. The piece of paper proving this ownership or possession: *the title to a house.* 4. A championship in sports.
—*verb* **titled, titling** To give a title to.

to | tōo | or | tə | —*preposition* 1. In a direction toward: *going to town.* 2. In the direction of: *a trip to Washington.* 3. To the point or range of: *starving to death.* 4. In contact with: *back to back; cheek to cheek.* 5. In front of: *face to face.* 6. Through and including; until: *That shop is open from nine to six.* 7. Into: *torn to shreds.* 8. As compared with: *a score of four to three.* 9. Before:

tip¹, tip², tip³

Tip¹ comes from a word used long ago by people who lived in Scandinavia. That word meant "end, extremity" and is related to **top¹**. The origin of **tip²** is not clear. **Tip³** is probably related to **tip¹**. It first meant "to touch lightly"; later it came to mean "to give to, to pass information to."

tiptoe

tire¹, tire²

Tire¹ comes from a word used very long ago in English to mean "to be exhausted, to fail." **Tire²** is from *tire*, a word that is no longer used but that was shortened from **attire**. Its original meaning was "clothing"; in the fifteenth century it came to be used in the sense "covering or clothing for the wheel." (Tires inflated with air were introduced in the late nineteenth century, and this word was extended to apply to them.)

toad

The time is ten to five. **10.** The preposition **to** is used before a verb to show the infinitive: *I'd like to go.* It is also used alone when the infinitive is understood: *Go if you want to.*

—adverb **1.** Into a shut position: *slammed the door to.* **2.** Into awareness: *It was a few minutes before I came to.* **3.** Into a state of working at something: *We sat down to lunch and everyone fell to.*

♦ *These sound alike* **to, too, two.**

toad | tōd | *—noun, plural* **toads** An animal that is very much like a frog, but has rougher, drier skin. Toads live mostly on land when they are fully grown.

toad·stool | tōd'stool' | *—noun, plural* **toadstools** A kind of mushroom that is not considered fit to eat, especially one of the poisonous kinds.

toast¹ | tōst | *—verb* **toasted, toasting 1.** To heat and brown things like bread or marshmallows by placing them close to the heat. **2.** To warm all the way through: *We toasted our feet by the fireplace.*

—noun Sliced bread heated and browned.

toast² | tōst | *—noun, plural* **toasts 1.** The act of drinking in honor of or to the health of a person, place, or thing. **2.** Any person receiving a lot of attention: *The star of the play was the toast of the town.*

—verb **toasted, toasting** To drink in honor of or to the health of: *The guests toasted the bride.*

toast·er | tō'stər | *—noun, plural* **toasters** An electrical device used to toast bread.

to·bac·co | tə băk'ō | *—noun, plural* **tobaccos** or **tobaccoes 1.** A plant whose large leaves are used for smoking and chewing. **2.** The leaves of such a plant. **3.** Cigarettes and cigars that are made from tobacco.

to·bog·gan | tə bŏg'ən | *—noun, plural* **toboggans** A long, narrow sled without runners. It is made of thin boards curved up at the front.

—verb **tobogganed, tobogganing** To ride on a toboggan.

to·day or **to-day** | tə dā' | *—adverb* **1.** During or on the present day: *He will visit today.* **2.** During or at the present time: *Today more cars are sold than ever before.*

—noun The present day, time, or age: *the students of today; the music of today.*

toe | tō | *—noun, plural* **toes 1.** One of the end parts of the foot. **2.** The part of a sock, stocking, shoe, or boot that fits over the toes.

—verb **toed, toeing** To touch or reach with the toes.

♦ *These sound alike* **toe, tow.**

to·geth·er | tə gĕth'ər | or | too gĕth'ər | *—adverb* **1.** In one group or place: *Many people were crowded together.* **2.** With some other person or thing: *getting along together; rubbing hands together.* **3.** Considered as a whole: *He's done more for the school than all of us together.* **4.** At the same time: *The clocks all sounded the hour together.*

toi·let | toi'lət | *—noun, plural* **toilets 1.** A porcelain bowl with a seat and a water tank for flushing the bowl clean. A toilet is used to get rid of waste matter from the body. **2.** A bathroom. **3.** The process of dressing oneself: *The maid helped the lady finish her toilet.*

to·ken | tō'kən | *—noun, plural* **tokens 1.** A sign or symbol of

---

toast¹, toast²

Toast¹ comes from an old French word that in turn came from a Latin word meaning "to dry, parch, scorch." **Toast²** is a special use of **toast¹**. Long ago small pieces of spiced toast were put into drinks to flavor them. In the late seventeenth century it was the custom at drinking parties for each man in turn to name a lady to whom the whole company would drink. The lady named was called the *toast* because her name would add flavor to the drink as a piece of spiced toast would.

ă	pat	ĕ	pet	î	fierce
ā	pay	ē	be	ŏ	pot
â	care	ĭ	pit	ō	go
ä	father	ī	pie	ô	paw, for
oi	oil	ŭ	cut	zh	vision
ŏŏ	book	û	fur	ə	ago, item,
ōō	boot	*th*	the		pencil, atom,
yōō	abuse	th	thin		circus
ou	out	hw	which	ər	butter

something else: *A white flag is a token of surrender.* **2.** A souvenir: *This ring was a token of our wedding anniversary.* **3.** A piece of metal used as a substitute for money: *The man put his token in the box as he got on the bus.*

told | tōld | The past tense and past participle of the verb **tell:** *She told me her name. I have told you to hang up your coat.*

tol·er·ance | tŏl′ər əns | —*noun* The will to allow other people to hold opinions or follow customs that differ from one's own: *The two statesmen showed great tolerance for each other's views.*

tol·er·ant | tŏl′ər ənt | —*adjective* Showing or having tolerance: *a tolerant attitude about religion.*

tol·er·ate | tŏl′ə rāt′ | —*verb* **tolerated, tolerating** To put up with; endure: *I can't tolerate his rude manners.*

toll¹ | tōl | —*noun, plural* **tolls** **1.** A tax for a privilege: *They had to pay a toll to cross the bridge.* **2.** A charge for a service: *He paid a toll to make a telephone call to Atlanta.*

toll² | tōl | —*verb* **tolled, tolling** To sound a bell slowly and regularly: *The man was tolling the church bells.*
—*noun, plural* **tolls** The sound of a tolling bell.

tom·a·hawk | tŏm′ə hôk′ | —*noun, plural* **tomahawks** A light ax used by North American Indians.

to·ma·to | tə mā′tō | or | tə mä′tō | —*noun, plural* **tomatoes** The juicy, usually reddish fruit of a plant that is widely grown. Tomatoes are eaten raw or cooked.

tomb | tōōm | —*noun, plural* **tombs** A grave or vault for a dead body: *We saw the tombs of many soldiers.*

tom·boy | tŏm′boi | —*noun, plural* **tomboys** A lively, athletic girl.

tom·cat | tŏm′kăt′ | —*noun, plural* **tomcats** A male cat.

to·mor·row | tə mŏr′ō | or | tə môr′o | —*noun, plural* **tomorrows** **1.** The day after today. **2.** The near future: *space trips of tomorrow.*
—*adverb* On or for the day after today: *I will return your book tomorrow.*

tom-tom | tŏm′tŏm′ | —*noun, plural* **tom-toms** A small drum that is beaten with the hands.

ton | tŭn | —*noun, plural* **tons** A unit of weight. A ton can be 2,000 pounds or 2,240 pounds. A metric ton equals 1,000 kilograms.

tone | tōn | —*noun, plural* **tones** **1.** A sound with a certain pitch, length, volume, and quality: *angry tones; gentle tones.* **2.** The quality of an instrument or voice: *the mellow tone of a guitar.* **3.** The difference in pitch between two musical notes. **4.** The shade of a color: *the dark tone of the red in the picture.* **5.** A way of talking or writing: *His tone was abrupt and harsh.* **6.** The general quality or mood: *the tone of the discussion.*

tongs | tôngz | or | tŏngz | —*plural noun* A tool for holding or lifting something. Tongs have two arms joined at one end.

tongue | tŭng | —*noun, plural* **tongues** **1.** A muscular piece of flesh in the mouth. The tongue is used in tasting, and helps in chewing and swallowing food. People use their tongues for talking. **2.** The tongue of an animal, used for food: *beef tongue.* **3.** A flap of material under the laces or buckles of a shoe. **4.** A language: *His native tongue is German.* **5.** The power to speak: *"Have you lost your tongue?" the mother asked the child.* **6.** A way of speaking: *She has a very sharp tongue.*

tomato
Whole (*left*) and cut in half (*right*)

tongs

to·night | tə nīt′ | —*adverb* On or during this night: *I'll see you at ten tonight.*
—*noun, plural* **tonights** The night of this day.

ton·sils | tŏn′səlz | —*plural noun* Two small masses of tissue on the sides of the throat in the back of the mouth.

too | tōō | —*adverb* **1.** Also; besides: *I can play the piano too.* **2.** More than enough: *You played too long.* **3.** Very; extremely: *I'm only too happy to help. He's not too smart.*
♦ *These sound alike* **too, to, two.**

took | tŏŏk | The past tense of the verb **take:** *He took his teddy bear to bed with him.*

tool | tōōl | —*noun, plural* **tools** **1.** An instrument used for doing work. Tools are held in the hand. Some tools are a hammer, saw, knife, shovel, and ax. **2.** Someone or something that is used as a tool: *The soldiers were tools to break open the enemy lines.*
—*verb* **tooled, tooling** To use a tool on: *The craftsman tooled the belt with fancy designs.*

toot | tōōt | —*verb* **tooted, tooting** To make a short, loud blast on a horn or whistle: *Dad tooted the car horn when it was time to go.*
—*noun, plural* **toots** A short, loud blast on a horn or whistle.

tooth | tōōth | —*noun, plural* **teeth** **1.** One of the hard, bony parts in the mouth used to chew and bite. Teeth are set in the gums around the jaws. Animals often use their teeth to grasp, or as weapons of attack or defense. **2.** Something that looks like or is used like a tooth: *the teeth of a comb; the teeth of a saw.*

tooth·brush | tōōth′brŭsh′ | —*noun, plural* **toothbrushes** A small brush for cleaning the teeth.

tooth·paste | tōōth′pāst′ | —*noun, plural* **toothpastes** A paste used to clean the teeth.

tooth·pick | tōōth′pĭk′ | —*noun, plural* **toothpicks** A small, thin piece of wood used to remove food from between the teeth.

top¹ | tŏp | —*noun, plural* **tops** **1.** The highest part, point, side, or end: *the top of the page; the top of the tree; the top of the car.* **2.** The highest rank or place: *He is at the top of his class.* **3.** The highest degree or pitch: *shouting at the top of his voice.*
—*adjective* The highest or greatest: *at top speed; the top shelf.*
—*verb* **topped, topping** **1.** To give or use as a top: *top a building with a tower; top a cake with frosting.* **2.** To reach the top of: *We topped the hill and started to climb down.* **3.** To do better than: *He just topped his old hitting record.*

top² | tŏp | —*noun, plural* **tops** A toy that spins on a point.

to·paz | tō′păz′ | —*noun, plural* **topazes** A mineral used as a gemstone. Topazes are usually yellow.

To·pe·ka | tə pē′kə | The capital of Kansas.

top·ic | tŏp′ĭk | —*noun, plural* **topics** The subject of a speech or paper; a theme: *The topic of his report was "North American Indians."*

to·pog·ra·phy | tə pŏg′rə fē | —*noun, plural* **topographies** **1.** A detailed and accurate description of a place or region. **2.** The features of a place or region: *The topography of this area includes wooded mountains.*

top·ple | tŏp′əl | —*verb* **toppled, toppling** **1.** To push over; make fall: *The baby toppled his dish to the floor.* **2.** To sway and fall: *The pile of books toppled over.*

top·soil | tŏp′soil′ | —*noun, plural* **topsoils** The rich layer of soil at the surface of the ground.

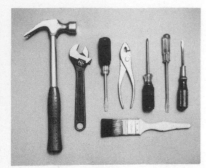

tool
Different kinds of tools

---

top¹, top²
Top¹ comes from an old English word spelled *topp,* "highest point." **Top²** also comes from an old English word of the same spelling; it referred to some kind of child's toy. We think **top¹** and **top²** are from the same word, but we are not sure about the details.

ă	pat	ĕ	pet	î	fierce
ā	pay	ē	be	ŏ	pot
â	care	ĭ	pit	ō	go
ä	father	ī	pie	ô	paw, for
oi	oil	ŭ	cut	zh	vision
ōō	book	û	fur	ə	ago, item,
ōō	boot	*th*	the		pencil, atom,
yōō	abuse	th	thin		circus
ou	out	hw	which	ər	butter

torch | tôrch | —*noun, plural* **torches** **1.** A flaming light to be carried around. Torches have a long wooden handle with flaming material at one end. **2.** A device for producing a flame hot enough for welding, soldering, or cutting metals.

tore | tôr | or | tōr | The past tense of the verb **tear** (to pull apart or split): *He tore a hole in his pants on the wire fence.*

tor·ment | tôr′mĕnt′ | —*noun, plural* **torments** **1.** Great pain: *the torment of a headache; the torments of jealousy.* **2.** A cause of bother or pain: *That child is the torment of his parents.*
—*verb* **tormented, tormenting** **1.** To cause to have pain: *That bad tooth tormented me until I went to the dentist.* **2.** To annoy: *Stop tormenting your sister with that mouse!*

torn | tôrn | or | tōrn | The past participle of the verb **tear** (to pull apart or split): *The page had been torn in half.*

tor·na·do | tôr nā′dō | —*noun, plural* **tornadoes** or **tornados** A violent whirlwind or hurricane. A tornado has an air column shaped like a funnel that spins at a violent speed.

To·ron·to | tə rŏn′tō | The capital of Ontario.

tor·pe·do | tôr pē′dō | —*noun, plural* **torpedos** **1.** A shell shaped like a cigar that explodes when it reaches its target. A torpedo moves underwater by its own power. **2.** A small kind of fireworks that explodes when it hits a hard surface.
—*verb* **torpedoed, torpedoing** To attack or destroy with a torpedo or torpedos: *The enemy torpedoed and sank the destroyer.*

tor·rent | tôr′ənt | or | tŏr′ənt | —*noun, plural* **torrents** **1.** A violent stream of water that moves very fast. **2.** A heavy falling down of something: *rain falling in torrents.* **3.** Any violent or rushing flow: *a torrent of mail; a torrent of tears.*

tor·so | tôr′sō′ | —*noun, plural* **torsos** The human body except for the head and limbs; the trunk.

tor·til·la | tôr tē′yə | —*noun, plural* **tortillas** A round, flat Mexican bread made from cornmeal and water.

tor·toise | tôr′təs | —*noun, plural* **tortoises** A turtle, especially one that lives on land.

tor·ture | tôr′chər | —*noun, plural* **tortures** **1.** The causing of great pain as a means of punishment. Torture is also used to make someone do something against his or her will. **2.** Physical or mental pain: *Waiting to perform was like torture for Sue.*
—*verb* **tortured, torturing** To cause to give great pain: *This awful sunburn is torturing me.*

toss | tôs | or | tŏs | —*verb* **tossed, tossing** **1.** To throw or be thrown to and fro: *Toss the ball to your partner. Heavy seas tossed the ship.* **2.** To move or lift quickly: *She tossed her head and marched out of the room.* **3.** To flip a coin to decide something: *The team lost the toss of the coin and had to kick off.*
—*noun, plural* **tosses** A throw; tossing: *a toss of his head.*

to·tal | tōt′l | —*noun, plural* **totals** **1.** The answer that one gets when adding; a sum: *The total of two and three is five.* **2.** A whole amount: *He paid the total of the bill.*
—*adjective* **1.** Of a whole amount: *the total population of the state.* **2.** Complete; full: *a total eclipse of the moon.*
—*verb* **totaled** or **totalled, totaling** or **totalling** **1.** To find the sum of: *She totaled my grocery bill at the counter.* **2.** To amount to: *Your bill for clothes totals twenty-five dollars.*

to·tal·ly | tōt′l ē | —*adverb* Completely; fully; without reservation: *I am totally on your side in this argument.*

torch

tortoise

totem pole

toucan

ă	pat	ĕ	pet	î	fierce
ā	pay	ē	be	ŏ	pot
â	care	ĭ	pit	ō	go
ä	father	ī	pie	ô	paw, for
oi	oil	ŭ	cut	zh	vision
ŏŏ	book	û	fur	ə	ago, item,
ōō	boot	*th*	the		pencil, atom,
yōō	abuse	th	thin		circus
ou	out	hw	which	ər	butter

to·tem |tō′təm| —*noun, plural* **totems 1.** An animal, plant, or natural object that among some people stands for a clan or family and is thought to be its ancestor: *The totem of one tribe of Indians was the eagle.* **2.** A picture or carving of a totem.

totem pole A post carved and painted with totems and put up in front of one's home. Totem poles are used mostly among the Indians of the northwestern coast of North America.

tou·can |tō′kăn′| or |tōō′kăn′| —*noun, plural* **toucans** A tropical American bird with a very large bill and brightly colored feathers.

touch |tŭch| —*verb* **touched, touching 1.** To come or bring against: *The tree's branches touch the ground. Touch the pencil to the paper.* **2.** To feel with a part of the body, especially with the hand or fingers: *If you touch that flower, its petals will fall off.* **3.** To tap, press, or strike lightly: *The godmother touched her with a magic wand.* **4.** To harm or injure, especially by hitting: *I never touched my little brother.* **5.** To disturb, especially by handling: *Don't touch anything until the police come.* **6.** To eat or drink; taste: *They wouldn't touch the soup because it didn't look good to them.* **7.** To affect or move the emotions: *The whines of the injured puppy touched my heart.*

—*noun, plural* **touches 1.** The sense by which one can find out how things feel; the ability to learn or know by feeling with the hand or some other part of the body: *In the dark I can find my way around by touch.* **2.** An act of touching or way of touching: *a touch of the hand; a light touch.* **3.** The feel of something: *The touch of velvet is smooth, thick, and soft.* **4.** Contact or communication: *I'll be in touch with you about this again later.* **5.** A little bit; a hint or trace: *Use just a touch of garlic in the stew.* **6.** A mild attack of some common disease: *He has a touch of the flu.* **7.** A detail that improves something or makes it perfect: *A bow on the dress made a finishing touch.*

touch·down |tŭch′doun′| —*noun, plural* **touchdowns** In football, a score of six points, usually made by running with the ball or catching a pass thrown by the quarterback across the other team's goal line.

tough |tŭf| —*adjective* **tougher, toughest 1.** Very strong; able to stand a heavy strain or load without tearing or breaking: *Big trucks need tough tires.* **2.** Hard to cut or chew: *a tough piece of meat.* **3.** Able to stand hardships; strong and rugged: *Only a really tough hiker could climb that mountain.* **4.** Difficult: *We got through a tough lesson in math today.* **5.** Stubborn: *The company decided to get tough with the striking workers.* **6.** Mean; rough: *tough robbers.*

tour |tŏŏr| —*noun, plural* **tours 1.** A trip to visit several places of interest: *He made a tour of Europe, stopping in five countries.* **2.** A brief trip to or through a place in order to see it: *a tour of a printing plant.*

—*verb* **toured, touring** To go on a tour or make a tour of: *Last summer we toured France.*

tour·ist |tŏŏr′ĭst| —*noun, plural* **tourists** A person who is traveling for pleasure: *forty tourists on a bus they hired.*

tour·na·ment |tŏŏr′nə mənt| or |tûr′nə mənt| —*noun, plural* **tournaments** A contest among several persons or teams in which they compete until one is declared winner: *a tennis tournament. Our school's baseball team took part in a state tournament.*

tow |tō| —*verb* **towed, towing** To pull along behind with a chain, rope, or cable: *He towed our car to the garage for repairs.*
♦ *These sound alike* **tow, toe.**

to·ward |tôrd| or |tōrd| or |tə **wôrd'**| —*preposition* **1.** In the direction of: *The train was moving toward the coast.* **2.** In a position facing: *a window toward the square.* **3.** Somewhat before in time; close to: *It started raining toward dawn.* **4.** With or in relation to; regarding: *He has a poor attitude toward his bosses. They made many efforts toward peace.* Another form of this preposition is **towards.**

to·wards |tôrdz| or |tōrdz| or |tə **wôrdz'**| A form of the preposition **toward.**

tow·el |tou'əl| —*noun, plural* **towels** A piece of cloth or paper that can soak up moisture and is used for wiping or drying: *Use this towel to dry your hands.*
—*verb* **toweled, toweling** To wipe or rub dry with a towel: *After the dog's bath we toweled him dry.*

tow·er |tou'ər| —*noun, plural* **towers** **1.a.** A very tall building. **b.** A very tall part of a building, often part of a church or castle. **2.** A tall framework or structure high enough to use for a lookout post or to send signals some distance: *the control tower at the airport; the radio station's antenna tower.*
—*verb* **towered, towering** To rise up very high: *Jim towers over his dad. The skyscraper towered over the rest of the city.*

tow·er·ing |tou'ər ĭng| —*adjective* **1.** Very tall: *towering mountains.* **2.** Intense; very great: *in a towering rage.*

town |toun| —*noun, plural* **towns** **1.** A community larger than a village and smaller than a city: *Five miles west of the city is the town where my grandfather lives.* **2.** Any city.

toy |toi| —*noun, plural* **toys** Something for children to play with.
—*verb* **toyed, toying** To play around with something, showing just a little interest in it: *He toyed with his food.*

trace |trās| —*noun, plural* **traces** **1.** A mark of some kind showing that someone or something has been there: *In the forest we found traces of the lost campers.* **2.** A very small amount: *This drinking water has traces of chemicals in it.*
—*verb* **traced, tracing** **1.** To follow the track or trail of: *We will try to trace that lost letter.* **2.** To copy by following lines seen through thin paper: *Trace this circle on your paper.*

tra·che·a |trā'kē ə| —*noun, plural* **tracheas** A tube in the throat that brings air to the lungs; the windpipe.

track |trăk| —*noun, plural* **tracks** **1.** A mark, such as a footprint or wheel rut, left behind by something moving: *We saw rabbit tracks in the snow. Tire tracks covered the driveway.* **2.** A path: *a bicycle track in the park.* **3.** A way of doing something or reaching a goal: *He thought he had a clue to the crime, but he was on the wrong track.* **4.** The rail or rails on which a train or trolley moves: *railroad tracks.* **5.** A racetrack. **6.** A sport that includes running, jumping, and throwing.
—*verb* **tracked, tracking** **1.** To follow the footprints or trail of: *They tracked the bear through the woods.* **2.** To watch and follow: *Radar is used to track weather balloons.* **3.** To carry something on the feet and leave it as tracks: *He tracked mud onto the kitchen floor.*

tract |trăkt| —*noun, plural* **tracts** **1.** An area of land: *He owns*

tower

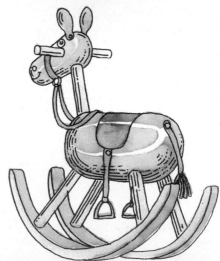

toy

tractor

the tract on the other side of the mountain. **2.** A set of body organs and tissues that work together: *the digestive tract.*

trac·tion |trăk'shən| —*noun* The friction that keeps a wheel from slipping or skidding: *The tires are so worn they can't get enough traction on wet roads.*

trac·tor |trăk'tər| —*noun, plural* **tractors** A vehicle with large tires powered by an engine. Tractors are used for pulling farm machines: *She rode the tractor as it pulled the plow through the field.*

trade |trād| —*noun, plural* **trades** **1.** The business of buying and selling: *Trade has begun between China and the United States.* **2.** An exchange of one thing for another: *Let's make a trade: my wagon for your bike.* **3.** A kind of work, especially one that involves skill with the hands; a craft: *the carpenter's trade.* **4.** The people who work in a business: *the hardware trade.*
—*verb* **traded, trading** **1. a.** To take part in buying, selling, or bartering: *They traded with the Indians.* **b.** To buy, sell, or barter: *They traded their furs all along the river.* **2.** To exchange or swap: *Will you trade your picture of that football player for my ice-cream cone?*

trade·mark |trād'märk'| —*noun, plural* **trademarks** A name, symbol, or other sign that is put on a product to show who makes or owns it. Trademarks are registered with the government so that only their owners can use them.

trad·er |trā'dər| —*noun, plural* **traders** A person who trades or deals: *He is a trader in diamonds.*

trad·ing post |trā'dĭng| A store in a frontier area. A trading post offers food and supplies in exchange for local products.

tra·di·tion |trə dĭsh'ən| —*noun, plural* **traditions** The practice of passing down ideas, customs, and beliefs from one generation to the next, especially by telling about them.

tra·di·tion·al |trə dĭsh'ə nəl| —*adjective* Of or according to tradition: *a traditional costume.*

traf·fic |trăf'ĭk| —*noun* **1.** The movement of vehicles and people along roads and streets, or of ships on the seas, or aircraft in the sky: *the heavy air traffic at major airports.* **2.** The number of vehicles, ships, or aircraft in movement: *Traffic is always heavy on this highway.* **3.** Trade in goods: *laws to stop traffic in drugs.*
—*verb* **trafficked, trafficking, traffics** To carry on trade in: *They trafficked in stolen goods.*

trag·e·dy |trăj'ĭ dē| —*noun, plural* **tragedies** **1.** A serious play that ends badly for the main character or characters. **2.** A terrible event; a disaster: *The loss of many lives in a plane crash is a tragedy.*

trag·ic |trăj'ĭk| —*adjective* Bringing very bad luck, suffering, or sadness: *His night swim was a tragic mistake.*

trail |trāl| —*verb* **trailed, trailing** **1. a.** To drag or allow to drag behind: *The child trailed a toy cart.* **b.** To be dragged along behind: *A red wagon trailed behind Jimmy.* **2.** To follow the traces or scent of; track: *Hounds trailed a fox through the meadow.* **3.** To lag behind: *The home team trailed by two touchdowns at the end of the first half.* **4.** To move or walk wearily: *The tired soldiers trailed past us one by one.* **5.** To be or grow along the ground or over a surface: *The curtains trailed the floor. The ivy you planted now trails all over the wall.*
—*noun, plural* **trails** **1.** A mark, trace, or path left by a moving body: *The stagecoach left a trail of dust.* **2.** The scent of a person

or animal: *The robbers left a trail that the police dogs followed.* **3.** A path or track: *Walk along this trail until you come to a cabin.*

trail·er | trā′lər | —*noun, plural* **trailers 1.** A large vehicle pulled by a truck and used to carry something: *Don's truck has a trailer for hauling logs.* **2.** A large van that can be pulled and when parked can be used as a home or office.

train | trān | —*noun, plural* **trains 1.** A group of connected railroad cars pulled by a locomotive or powered by electricity. Some carry freight and others carry people: *Can we take a train from here to Austin?* **2.** A long line of moving persons, animals, or vehicles: *a wagon train; a mule train.* **3.** The part of a long dress that trails behind the person wearing it: *The train of her wedding gown was two feet long.* **4.** A series of events or thoughts: *The ring of the telephone broke my train of thought.*
—*verb* **trained, training 1.** To coach in a way of performing something: *He trained his children to be polite. They are training young men to be good citizens.* **2. a.** To teach a person some art or skill: *a school that trains drivers.* **b.** To teach an animal to perform: *They are training their dog to do tricks.* **3.** To make or become ready to perform in athletic contests: *Coaches trained the players for the important game. He trains for the contest on a diet of milk, vegetables, and vitamins.* **4.** To make a plant or one's hair grow or lie in a certain way: *Train your hair to stay out of your eyes.*

train·er | trā′nər | —*noun, plural* **trainers** A person who trains a person or animal, especially one who coaches athletes, race horses, or show animals.

train·ing | trā′nĭng | —*noun* **1.** The act or process of being trained; instruction: *You can get training to be a model.* **2. a.** A program of exercise, diet, and practice for an athlete: *A daily run of five miles is part of his training.* **b.** The physical condition of a person or animal that has been trained: *The boxer lost because he was out of training.*

trait | trāt | —*noun, plural* **traits** A special feature or quality, especially of a living thing: *The farmers were looking for certain traits in the animals they bought: good health, resistance to disease, and ability to gain weight rapidly.*

trai·tor | trā′tər | —*noun, plural* **traitors** A person who betrays his or her country, a cause, or an idea.

tramp | trămp | —*verb* **tramped, tramping 1.** To walk with a firm, heavy step: *She tramped loudly up the steps.* **2.** To go on foot: *We tramped the fields, looking for wild berries.* **3.** To flatten with the feet: *Tramp down the snow on the walk.*
—*noun, plural* **tramps 1.** The sound of heavy walking or marching: *From our house we could hear the tramp of hikers on the road.* **2.** A walking trip: *a long tramp through the woods.* **3.** A person who wanders around and usually has no regular job or place to stay: *A tramp camped for a week in our empty lot.*

tram·ple | trăm′pəl | —*verb* **trampled, trampling** To walk heavily on something, hurting or ruining it: *Playing children trampled the daisies in our garden.*

tram·po·line | trăm′pə lēn′ | or | trăm′pə lĭn | —*noun, plural* **trampolines** A sheet of canvas stretched across a metal frame and fastened with springs. Trampolines are used for jumping and other gymnastics.

tran·quil | trăng′kwĭl | or | trăn′kwĭl | —*adjective* Calm; peaceful: *a tranquil lake; leading a tranquil life.*

train

trainer
A seal trainer

trampoline

tran·quil·li·ty or **tran·quil·i·ty** |trăng kwĭl′ĭ tē| or |trăn kwĭl′ĭ tē| —*noun* The condition of being tranquil: *The tranquillity of the wilderness is in great contrast with the bustle of the city.*

trans·fer |trăns fûr′| or |trăns′fər| —*verb* **transferred, transferring** **1.** To move or shift from one place, person, or thing to another: *Bees transfer pollen from one flower to another.* **2.** To change from one way of traveling to another: *They transferred the coal from the ship to railroad cars. Take the downtown subway and transfer to a bus at Third Street.* **3.** To move or be moved from one job, school, or place of work to another: *They transferred him from a branch office to the company headquarters. We transferred from a private school to a public one.*
—*noun* |trăns′fər|, *plural* **transfers 1.** An act or example of transferring or being transferred: *the transfer of land; a transfer of energy.* **2.** A ticket for changing from one bus, plane, or train to another without paying extra: *On the first bus the conductor handed me a transfer to use on the second bus.*

trans·form |trăns fôrm′| —*verb* **transformed, transforming 1.** To change very much in form or appearance: *The wizard transformed the men into mice.* **2.** To change energy from one form to another: *The electric bulb transforms electricity into light.*

trans·for·ma·tion |trăns′fər mā′shən| —*noun, plural* **transformations** The act or process of transforming or condition of being transformed: *Her new hair style made quite a transformation in her appearance.*

trans·fu·sion |trăns fyōō′zhən| —*noun, plural* **transfusions** The putting of blood or a similar fluid directly into a person's body, using a hollow needle. Only specially trained people should do this: *a transfusion to replace the blood she had lost.*

tran·sis·tor |trăn zĭs′tər| or |trăn sĭs′tər| —*noun, plural* **transistors** A small, sometimes very tiny, device that controls the flow of electricity. Transistors are used in radios, televisions, computers, calculators, and many other electronic devices.

tran·si·tion |trăn zĭsh′ən| or |trăn sĭsh′ən| —*noun, plural* **transitions 1.** The process of changing or passing from one form, subject, or place to another: *The transition from child to teen-ager is often difficult.* **2.** An example of this: *Your story is good, but it needs a better transition from the first part to the second.*

trans·late |trăns lāt′| or |trănz lāt′| or |trăns′lāt′| or |trănz′lāt′| —*verb* **translated, translating 1.** To change into or express in another language: *He translated the book from French into English.* **2.** To act as a translator: *He translates for a living.*

trans·la·tion |trăns lā′shən| or |trănz lā′shən| —*noun, plural* **translations 1.** The act or process of translating: *We hired three people for the translation.* **2.** Something translated: *The books are translations from the French.*

trans·lu·cent |trăns lōō′sənt| or |trănz lōō′sənt| —*adjective* Allowing only some light to pass through: *Frosted glass is translucent.*

trans·mis·sion |trăns mĭsh′ən| or |trănz mĭsh′ən| —*noun, plural* **transmissions 1.** The act or process of sending from one person or place to another: *the transmission of news.* **2.** The sending of radio or television waves. **3.** A series of gears in an automobile by which power is carried from the motor to the wheels.

translate
A sign with the same message in two languages

ă	pat	ĕ	pet	î	fierce
ā	pay	ē	be	ŏ	pot
â	care	ĭ	pit	ō	go
ä	father	ī	pie	ô	paw, for
oi	oil	ŭ	cut	zh	vision
ōō	book	û	fur	ə	ago, item,
ōō	boot	*th*	the		pencil, atom,
yōō	abuse	th	thin		circus
ou	out	hw	which	ər	butter

trans·mit | trăns mĭt′ | or | trănz mĭt′ | —*verb* **transmitted,
transmitting 1.** To send from one person, place, or thing to
another: *transmit a message; transmit an infection.* **2.** To send out
signals by wire or radio: *We transmitted the broadcast at 10:00 p.m.*

trans·mit·ter | trăns mĭt′ ər | or | trănz mĭt′ ər | —*noun, plural*
transmitters 1. Someone or something that transmits. **2.** A
device that sends out electrical, radio, or television signals.

trans·par·ent | trăns pâr′ ənt | or | trăns păr′ ənt | —*adjective*
1. Allowing light to pass through so that objects on the other
side can be clearly seen: *transparent lenses for eyeglasses;
transparent tape.* **2.** Easy to see or understand; obvious: *His
excuse was very transparent. That's a transparent lie.*

trans·plant | trăns plănt′ | or | trăns plänt′ | —*verb* **transplanted,
transplanting 1.** To remove a living plant from the place where it
is growing and plant it in another place. **2.** To transfer tissue or
an organ from one body or body part to another.
—*noun, plural* **transplants 1.** Something transplanted, especially
tissue or an organ transplanted by surgery. **2.** The act or
operation of transplanting: *The doctor performed a heart transplant.*

trans·port | trăns pôrt′ | or | trăns pōrt′ | —*verb* **transported,
transporting** To carry from one place to another: *transport cargo.*
—*noun* | **trăns′** pôrt′ | or | **trăns′** pōrt′ |, *plural* **transports 1.** The
act or process of transporting: *goods lost in transport.* **2.** A ship
used to transport troops or military equipment.

trans·por·ta·tion | trăns′pər tā′shən | —*noun, plural*
transportations 1. The act or process of transporting: *the
transportation of mail.* **2.** A means of transport: *Planes are fast
transportation.* **3.** The business of transporting passengers and
freight: *a company engaged in transportation.* **4.** A charge for
transporting; a fare: *He was paying his own transportation.*

trap | trăp | —*noun, plural* **traps 1.** A device for catching
animals. **2.** A way of tricking a person: *Her trap to make me admit
I did it failed.*
—*verb* **trapped, trapping 1.** To catch in a trap: *trap a rabbit.*
2. To trick someone: *She trapped me into admitting I did it.*

trap door A hinged or sliding door in a floor or roof.

tra·peze | tră pēz′ | —*noun, plural* **trapezes** A short bar hung
between two parallel ropes, used to swing from for exercises or
gymnastics.

trap·per | trăp′ ər | —*noun, plural* **trappers** A person who traps
wild animals for their fur.

trash | trăsh | —*noun* Stuff that is thrown away; garbage: *We
took the trash to the dump.*

trav·el | trăv′ əl | —*verb* **traveled, traveling 1.** To go from one
place to another: *She traveled through Europe.* **2.** To move from
one place to another: *Electricity travels by current.*

trav·el·er | trăv′ ə lər | or | trăv′ lər | —*noun, plural* **travelers** A
person who travels.

tray | trā | —*noun, plural* **trays** A flat dish with a raised rim or
edge, used to carry and display articles: *She carried the food into
the dining room on a large tray.*

treach·er·ous | trĕch′ ər əs | —*adjective* **1.** Betraying a trust;
disloyal: *a treacherous friend.* **2.** Not dependable: *a treacherous
memory; treacherous surf. The ice was treacherous.*

tread | trĕd | —*verb* **trod, trodden** or **trod, treading 1.** To walk on,
over, or along: *Someone was seen treading down the sidewalk.*

trapeze

tread
On a tractor

2. To step on heavily; tramp: *He noisily trod up the stairs.*
—*noun, plural* **treads 1.** The act, manner, or sound of treading: *the swift tread of a horse; a familiar tread on the stairs.* **2.** The top part of a step in a staircase. **3.** The part of a wheel or shoe sole that touches the ground. **4.** The pattern of grooves in a tire that enables it to grip the road better.

trea·son |trē′zən| —*noun, plural* **treasons** The betraying of a person's country by helping an enemy: *He was tried for treason during the Civil War.*

treas·ure |trĕzh′ər| —*noun, plural* **treasures** An accumulation of valuables, such as jewels.
—*verb* **treasured, treasuring** To value highly: *I treasured his friendship.*

treas·ur·er |trĕzh′ər ər| —*noun, plural* **treasurers** A person who has charge of money belonging to a club or business.

treas·ur·y |trĕzh′ə rē| —*noun, plural* **treasuries 1.** The place where money belonging to a government or organization is kept. **2.** The money kept in such a place. **3. Treasury** The department of a government that is in charge of collecting and managing the country's money.

treat |trēt| —*verb* **treated, treating 1.** To act or behave toward in a certain way: *We've always treated animals with kindness.* **2.** To deal with or handle: *The author treated the subject honestly.* **3.** To give medical attention to: *The doctor was treating her for an infection on her foot.* **4.** To pay for the entertainment of someone else: *I'd like to treat you to a movie.*
—*noun, plural* **treats 1.** The act of treating. **2.** Anything considered a special pleasure: *Going to a concert is a treat to me.*

treat·ment |trēt′mənt| —*noun, plural* **treatments 1.** The act or manner of treating something: *her kind treatment of the people working for her.* **2.** The use of something to cure an illness: *She gets two treatments a month for her illness.*

trea·ty |trē′tē| —*noun, plural* **treaties** A formal agreement between two or more states or countries: *The peace treaty ended the war.*

treaty
Signing a treaty at the end of a war

tree |trē| —*noun, plural* **trees 1.** A woody plant that is usually tall and has one main stem, or trunk. **2.** Something that looks like a tree, such as a pole with pegs or hooks for hanging clothes.

trel·lis |trĕl′ĭs| —*noun, plural* **trellises** A framework used for training climbing plants.

trem·ble |trĕm′bəl| —*verb* **trembled, trembling** To shake, as from cold or fear; shiver: *I was trembling because I was so cold.*

tre·men·dous |trĭ mĕn′dəs| —*adjective* **1.** Extremely large; enormous: *The clap of thunder made a tremendous noise.* **2.** Wonderful; marvelous: *a tremendous performance.*

tre·mor |trĕm′ər| —*noun, plural* **tremors 1.** A shaking or vibrating movement: *an earth tremor.* **2.** An involuntary twitching of muscles: *a facial tremor.*

trench |trĕnch| —*noun, plural* **trenches** A long, narrow ditch: *Soldiers dug trenches in the battlefield.*

trend |trĕnd| —*noun, plural* **trends** A direction or course that is being followed: *The trend of prices is to keep increasing.*

Tren·ton |trĕn′tən| The capital of New Jersey.

tres·pass |trĕs′pəs| or |trĕs′păs′| —*verb* **trespassed, trespassing** To go onto someone's property without their permission: *Hunters trespassed on our land.*

trellis

ă	pat	ĕ	pet	î	fierce
ā	pay	ē	be	ŏ	pot
â	care	ĭ	pit	ō	go
ä	father	ī	pie	ô	paw, for

oi	oil	ŭ	cut	zh	vision
ōō	book	û	fur	ə	ago, item,
ōō	boot	*th*	the		pencil, atom,
yōō	abuse	th	thin		circus
ou	out	hw	which	ər	butter

—*noun, plural* **trespasses** A sin: *We pray that our trespasses will be forgiven.*

tri·al | trī′əl | or | trīl | —*noun, plural* **trials** **1.** The examination and deciding of a case brought to a court of law. **2.** The act or process of trying or testing anything: *the trial of a new type of gasoline; the trial of a new employee.*

  Idiom **on trial** In the state or process of being tested or tried.

tri·an·gle | trī′ăng′gəl | —*noun, plural* **triangles** **1.** An object or a figure that has three sides and three angles. **2.** A small musical instrument that is struck to produce a clear tone like that of a bell.

tri·an·gu·lar | trī ăng′gyə lər | —*adjective* Shaped or looking like a triangle: *The tent had a triangular shape.*

trib·al | trī′bəl | —*adjective* Having to do with a tribe: *tribal music; tribal customs.*

tribe | trīb | —*noun, plural* **tribes** A group of people united because they have the same social customs, language, ancestors, or other characteristics. There are many tribes of North American Indians.

tri·bute | trĭb′yōōt′ | —*noun, plural* **tributes** Something done or given to show respect: *The memorial was erected as a tribute to the soldiers that fought for our freedom.*

trick | trĭk | —*noun, plural* **tricks** **1.** A special stunt or skillful act: *magic tricks; tricks by acrobats.* **2.** Something done to fool someone else. **3.** A prank or practical joke: *Halloween tricks.* —*verb* **tricked, tricking** **1.** To fool, cheat, or deceive. **2.** To persuade by trickery: *She tricked me into taking my medicine.*

trick·er·y | trĭk′ə rē | —*noun, plural* **trickeries** The use of tricks: *He got the money by trickery.*

trick·le | trĭk′əl | —*verb* **trickled, trickling** **1.** To flow drop by drop or in a thin stream: *a trickle of water from the faucet.* **2.** To move slowly or bit by bit: *The audience trickled in late.* —*noun, plural* **trickles** A small flow; a thin stream: *a trickle of customers; a trickle of perspiration.*

trick·y | trĭk′ē | —*adjective* **trickier, trickiest** **1.** Using tricks; cunning; sly: *a tricky businessman; a tricky politician.* **2.** Requiring caution or skill: *a tricky job.*

tri·cy·cle | trī′sĭ′kəl | —*noun, plural* **tricycles** A vehicle with three wheels, usually propelled by pedals.

tried | trīd | The past tense and past participle of the verb **try:** *I tried to get home before dark. I had tried to fix the faucet before.*

tri·fle | trī′fəl | —*noun, plural* **trifles** **1.** Something of very little value. **2.** A small amount; a little. —*verb* **trifled, trifling** To play with something in a careless way: *She was trifling with a pencil.*

trig·ger | trĭg′ər | —*noun, plural* **triggers** A small lever that is pressed by the finger to shoot a gun.

trim | trĭm | —*verb* **trimmed, trimming** **1.** To make neat and tidy by chopping: *He trimmed his beard. Father trimmed the shrubs.* **2.** To decorate: *Tonight we will trim the Christmas tree.* —*noun, plural* **trims** **1.** Something that decorates or ornaments. **2.** The act of cutting or clipping: *Your beard needs a trim.*

trim·ming | trĭm′ĭng | —*noun, plural* **trimmings** **1.** Something added as a decoration: *fur trimming on a coat.* **2.** **trimmings** Things that usually go with something else: *turkey, gravy, stuffing, and all the trimmings.*

triangle

tricycle

tripod

trolley

trombone

ă	pat	ĕ	pet	î	fierce
ā	pay	ē	be	ŏ	pot
â	care	ĭ	pit	ō	go
ä	father	ī	pie	ô	paw, for
oi	oil	ŭ	cut	zh	vision
ōō	book	û	fur	ə	ago, item,
ōō	boot	th	the		pencil, atom,
yōō	abuse	th	thin		circus
ou	out	hw	which	ər	butter

trin·ket | trĭng′kĭt | —*noun, plural* **trinkets** A small ornament or a piece of jewelry.

tri·o | trē′ō | —*noun, plural* **trios** **1.** A group of three. **2.** A musical piece for three performers.

trip | trĭp | —*noun, plural* **trips** **1.** A journey: *We took a trip to Europe.* **2.** The distance traveled on a journey: *a trip of one thousand miles.*
—*verb* **tripped, tripping** **1.** To stumble or fall. **2.** To make a mistake. **3.** To dance or skip lightly and quickly: *The children tripped home from school.*

trip·le | trĭp′əl | —*adjective* **1.** Made up of three parts. **2.** Three times as many: *She got triple the number of apples that I got.*
—*verb* **tripled, tripling** To make or become three times as much: *She tripled the number of eggs that the recipe called for.*

tri·pod | trī′pŏd | —*noun, plural* **tripods** A stand with three legs, used especially to support a camera.

tri·umph | trī′əmf | —*verb* **triumphed, triumphing** To be victorious or successful: *The team triumphed over great odds and won.*
—*noun, plural* **triumphs** **1.** The act of winning; success: *His performance was a triumph over his physical handicap.* **2.** Joy from winning: *a cry of triumph.*

tri·um·phant | trī ŭm′fənt | —*adjective* **1.** Victorious; successful: *a triumphant campaign.* **2.** Rejoicing over having been successful: *a triumphant return home.*

triv·i·al | trĭv′ē əl | —*adjective* **1.** Of little or no importance: *a trivial mistake.* **2.** Ordinary; usual: *trivial household tasks.*

trod | trŏd | The past tense and a past participle of the verb **tread:** *I hope you haven't trod through the mud puddle. She had trod that path many times before.*

trod·den | trŏd′n | A past participle of the verb **tread:** *We had trodden that path before.*

trol·ley | trŏl′ē | —*noun, plural* **trolleys** **1.** An electrically operated bus that runs on tracks; a streetcar. **2.** A small, grooved wheel that runs along an overhead wire and supplies current to an electrically powered vehicle.

trom·bone | trŏm bōn′ | or | trŏm′bōn′ | —*noun, plural* **trombones** A brass wind musical instrument, like the trumpet but with two long tubes shaped like U's and having a lower pitch.

troop | trōōp | —*noun, plural* **troops** **1.** A group of people or animals: *A troop of third-grade children toured the newspaper offices.* **2.** A group of soldiers: *Troops raided the village.*

troop·er | trōō′pər | —*noun, plural* **troopers** A policeman.

tro·phy | trō′fē | —*noun, plural* **trophies** A prize received as a symbol of victory.

trop·i·cal | trŏp′ĭ kəl | —*adjective* **1.** Of, like, or found in the tropics: *tropical plants; tropical fish.* **2.** Hot and humid: *Southern Florida has a tropical climate.*

trop·ics | trŏp′ĭks | —*plural noun* The very hot regions of the earth that are near the equator.

trot | trŏt | —*noun, plural* **trots** A running gait of a horse that is faster than a walk and slower than a gallop. In a trot, the left, front foot and the right, rear foot are lifted at the same time.
—*verb* **trotted, trotting** **1.** To move or ride or cause to move or ride at a trot: *The horses trotted down the road. She trotted her pony around the yard.* **2.** To run or walk quickly: *He trotted down the street after his sister.*

trou·ble |trŭb′əl| —*noun, plural* **troubles 1.** A difficult or dangerous situation: *The ship was in trouble and signaled for help.* **2.** A problem or difficulty: *I'm having trouble with my homework.* **3.** Extra work or effort: *They went to a lot of trouble to make the party a success.*
—*verb* **troubled, troubling 1.** To disturb or worry; cause distress: *The thought that I might fail the test troubled me.* **2.** To require extra effort or work: *May I trouble you for another glass of milk? Don't trouble yourself for me.*

trou·ble·some |trŭb′əl səm| —*adjective* Causing trouble; annoying: *a troublesome child; a troublesome car.*

trough |trôf| or |trŏf| —*noun, plural* **troughs** A long, narrow box or other container. It is used for holding water or feed for animals.

trou·sers |trou′zərz| —*noun* (Used with a plural verb.) An outer garment worn from the waist down and divided into two sections that fit each leg separately: *Those trousers are too big for you.*

trough

trout |trout| —*noun, plural* **trout** A fish that is related to the salmon and lives in fresh water. The trout has a spotted body and is highly valued for sport and as food.

truce |trōōs| —*noun, plural* **truces** A short or temporary stop in fighting: *A truce was called so the two armies could bury the dead and care for the wounded.*

truck |trŭk| —*noun, plural* **trucks** A kind of motor vehicle designed to carry large or heavy loads. They are made in many different sizes and types. Some are the size of an automobile and have an open area in the back; others are much larger and can have an open or closed area in the back.

trudge |trŭj| —*verb* **trudged, trudging** To walk slowly with effort, as if one is tired or carrying a heavy weight: *With knapsacks on our backs, we trudged up the hill.*

truck

true |trōō| —*adjective* **truer, truest 1.** In agreement with fact or reality; right; accurate; not false: *Is this statement true or false? I don't believe that's a true story.* **2.** Real or genuine: *This bracelet is made of true gold.* **3.** Loyal to someone or something; faithful: *He's the truest friend I ever had.*
—*adverb* In a right or true manner; truthfully: *Her excuse for being late doesn't sound true.*

tru·ly |trōō′lē| —*adverb* **1.** In a sincere, honest, or truthful manner; sincerely or accurately: *I'm truly sorry that I hurt your feelings. Tell me what you truly think of my new dress.* **2.** In fact or indeed: *The view from the top of the mountain is truly magnificent.*

trum·pet |trŭm′pĭt| —*noun, plural* **trumpets 1.** A brass wind instrument that has a strong tone with a high pitch. It is made of a long metal tube that is coiled in a loop, with a mouthpiece at one end and a flared bell at the other. **2.** Something that is shaped like a trumpet, such as the yellow flowers of daffodils.
—*verb* **trumpeted, trumpeting** To make a loud, high sound like a trumpet: *Elephants trumpeted in the jungle.*

trunk |trŭngk| —*noun, plural* **trunks 1.** The tall main stem of a tree. The branches grow out of it. **2.** A large box or case with a lid that locks or clasps shut. It is used for storing and carrying clothes or other objects. **3.** The covered section in the rear of an automobile. It is used for carrying suitcases and other objects. **4.** The main part of a human or animal body, not including the

trumpet

arms, legs, or head. **5.** The long, flexible snout of an elephant, used for grasping and holding. **6. trunks** Short pants worn by men for swimming and for playing certain sports.

trust |trŭst| —*verb* **trusted, trusting 1.** To believe or have confidence in as being honest, fair, or dependable: *You shouldn't have trusted him. Trust my judgment.* **2.** To depend or rely on; count on: *That old ladder is falling apart so you can't trust it to support your weight.*
—*noun* **1.** Confidence or a strong belief in someone or something; faith: *I must live up to his trust.* **2.** The act or condition of keeping or taking care of someone or something for another person; custody: *He left his pet turtle in my trust.*

trust·wor·thy |trŭst′wûr′thē| —*adjective* Able to be relied on; dependable: *The teacher chose a trustworthy student to collect the money for the dance.*

truth |trŏŏth| —*noun, plural* **truths 1.** Something that is true: *He asked me what happened and I told him the truth.* **2.** The quality of being honest, sincere, loyal, or true: *The police did not believe the truth of the suspect's story.*

truth·ful |trŏŏth′fəl| —*adjective* Telling the truth; honest: *a truthful person. He gave us a truthful account of how the fight started.*

try |trī| —*verb* **tried, trying, tries 1.** To attempt to do something; make an effort: *He tried to get the kitchen cleaned up before his mother got home. Please try to be home in time for dinner.* **2.** To taste, sample, or test something: *I want to try the new flavor of ice cream. She's trying my bicycle.* **3.** To examine or investigate in a court of law: *It took over a month to try the case.*
—*noun, plural* **tries** An attempt; an effort: *We each had three tries to guess the right answer.*

try·out |trī′out′| —*noun, plural* **tryouts** A test to find out a person's skill or ability: *I had a tryout for the school's marching band.*

T-shirt |tē′shûrt′| —*noun, plural* **T-shirts** A light shirt with short sleeves and no collar. It is worn in warm weather and while playing sports. Men often wear T-shirts as undershirts.

tub |tŭb| —*noun, plural* **tubs 1.** A round, wide, open container used for packing, storing, or washing. It is usually made of wood. **2.** A small, round container used for keeping food: *a tub of butter.* **3.** A bathtub.

tu·ba |tŏŏ′bə| *or* |tyŏŏ′bə| —*noun, plural* **tubas** A large brass wind instrument that has a deep, mellow tone.

tube |tŏŏb| *or* |tyŏŏb| —*noun, plural* **tubes 1.** A long, hollow piece of metal, glass, rubber, plastic, or other material shaped like a pipe. It is used to carry liquids or gasses. A garden hose and a drinking straw are both tubes. **2.** Anything that is shaped or used like a tube, such as a tunnel or pipe. **3.** A small, flexible container made of metal or plastic that is shaped like a tube. It has a cap on one end that screws on. It is used for holding toothpaste, shampoo, or other materials that can be squeezed out.

tu·ber |tŏŏ′bər| *or* |tyŏŏ′bər| —*noun, plural* **tubers** A swollen, underground stem, such as a potato. A tuber bears buds from which new plants grow.

tu·ber·cu·lo·sis |tŏŏ bûr′kyə lō′sĭs| *or* |tyŏŏ bûr′kyə lō′sĭs| —*noun* A disease caused by bacteria that destroys tissues of the body, especially the lungs. It affects both people and animals. Tuberculosis is very contagious.

tuba

ă	pat	ĕ	pet	î	fierce
ā	pay	ē	be	ŏ	pot
â	care	ĭ	pit	ō	go
ä	father	ī	pie	ô	paw, for
oi	oil	ŭ	cut	zh	vision
ŏŏ	book	û	fur	ə	ago, item,
ōō	boot	*th*	the		pencil, atom,
yōō	abuse	th	thin		circus
ou	out	hw	which	ər	butter

tuck |tŭk| —*verb* **tucked, tucking 1.** To fold or shove the edges or ends of a garment or piece of fabric in place: *He tucked his shirt into his pants. Make your bed and tuck in the blankets.* **2.** To cover or wrap snugly: *Mom is tucking in the baby.* **3.** To put or store in a safe or secret place: *He tucked the letter in a book so he wouldn't lose it.*
—*noun, plural* **tucks** A narrow fold sewed into a garment to decorate it or make it look better: *She put a tuck in the dress because it was too big.*

Tues·day |to̅o̅z′dē| or |to̅o̅z′dā′| or |tyo̅o̅z′dē| or |tyo̅o̅z′dā′| —*noun, plural* **Tuesdays** The third day of the week, after Monday and before Wednesday.

tuft |tŭft| —*noun, plural* **tufts** A bunch of grass, feathers, hair, threads, or other flexible materials that grow or are held tightly together at one end and are loose at the other: *The donkey has a tuft of hair at the end of its tail.*

tug |tŭg| —*verb* **tugged, tugging** To pull hard on something; move something by pulling with force or effort: *Cathy tugged her father's tie. He tugged the chair across the room.*
—*noun, plural* **tugs** A hard pull: *The boys gave a tug on the rope.*

tug·boat |tŭg′bōt′| —*noun, plural* **tugboats** A very powerful small boat that is designed to tow or push larger boats.

tu·i·tion |to̅o̅ ĭsh′ən| or |tyo̅o̅ ĭsh′ən| —*noun, plural* **tuitions** Money paid for lessons or instruction, especially at a college or private school.

tu·lip |to̅o̅′lĭp| or |tyo̅o̅′lĭp| —*noun, plural* **tulips** A garden plant with showy, colorful flowers that are shaped like cups. Tulips grow from bulbs.

tum·ble |tŭm′bəl| —*verb* **tumbled, tumbling 1.** To fall in a helpless way: *He tumbled down the stairs.* **2.** To fall or roll end over end; toss about: *The kittens were tumbling over each other.* **3.** To spill or roll out in a confusing or not orderly way: *Schoolchildren tumbled out of the bus.* **4.** To do somersaults, leaps, or other gymnastics.
—*noun, plural* **tumbles** A fall caused by tumbling: *He took a tumble when he slipped on the banana peel.*

tu·mor |to̅o̅′mər| or |tyo̅o̅′mər| —*noun, plural* **tumors** Any swelling within the body that is not normal.

tu·na |to̅o̅′nə| or |tyo̅o̅′nə| —*noun, plural* **tuna** or **tunas** A large ocean fish that is caught in large numbers for food.

tun·dra |tŭn′drə| —*noun, plural* **tundras** A very large plain without trees in arctic regions. Mosses and small shrubs are the only kind of plant life that grows on it. The ground beneath the surface of a tundra remains frozen all year round.

tune |to̅o̅n| or |tyo̅o̅n| —*noun, plural* **tunes 1.** A melody that is easy to remember: *I forget the name of the song, but I can hum the tune.* **2.** The correct pitch: *The piano is out of tune.* **3.** Agreement or harmony: *Her grandmother's old-fashioned ideas about how to bring up children are out of tune with the times.*
—*verb* **tuned, tuning** To put in the proper pitch; put in tune: *Eric is tuning the violin.*

tu·nic |to̅o̅′nĭk| or |tyo̅o̅′nĭk| —*noun, plural* **tunics 1.** A garment that looks like a shirt and reaches down to the knees. They were worn by men in ancient Greece and Rome and during the Middle Ages. **2.** A short, snug jacket. It is usually worn as part of a uniform by soldiers or police.

tugboat

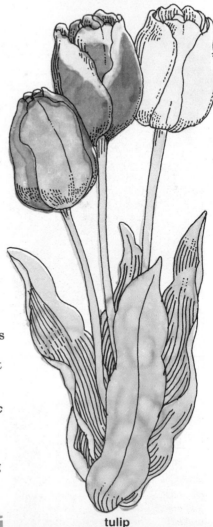
tulip

turban

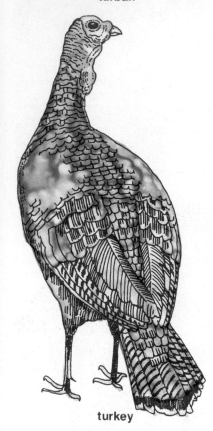

turkey

tun·nel |tŭn′əl| —*noun, plural* **tunnels** A long passage that is built underground or underwater: *You can take the tunnel or the bridge to get from New York to New Jersey.*

—*verb* **tunneled, tunneling** To make a tunnel under or through: *The highway crew tunneled through the mountain and under the river for the new road.*

tur·ban |tûr′bən| —*noun, plural* **turbans** 1. A long scarf that is wound around the head. It is worn like a hat by men in some Oriental countries. 2. Any similar head covering.

tur·bine |tûr′bĭn| or |tûr′bīn′| —*noun, plural* **turbines** A machine or motor in which the force of air, steam, or water is used to turn a wheel by pushing against paddles attached to it.

turf |tûrf| —*noun, plural* **turfs** An upper layer of earth having much grass and roots; sod.

tur·key |tûr′kē| —*noun, plural* **turkeys** 1. A large brownish American bird with a bare head. Skin hangs down in folds from its neck. Once common in its wild form, the turkey is now mostly raised on farms as a source of food. 2. The meat of a turkey.

tur·moil |tûr′moil′| —*noun, plural* **turmoils** A condition of great confusion or disorder: *The zoo was thrown into turmoil when the animals escaped from their cages.*

turn |tûrn| —*verb* **turned, turning** 1. To move or cause to move around a center or in a circle; rotate; revolve: *She turned the hands of a clock. The car wheels turned on the pavement.* 2. To perform or do by rotating or revolving: *The children turned somersaults.* 3. To appear to be revolving, especially when one is dizzy: *The walls turned wildly.* 4. To roll from side to side or back and forth: *The ship was pitching and turning.* 5. To change or cause to change direction: *He turned and waved. She turned the car into a side street.* 6. To move or cause to move in an opposite direction; reverse: *His condition turned for the worse.* 7. To make one's way around or about: *They turned the corner.* 8. To direct one's way in a certain direction: *Turn west here.* 9. To direct in a certain way; point: *She turned the hose at him. He turned his eyes to the ceiling.* 10. To direct one's attention, interest, or mind toward or away from something: *turned his thoughts to home.* 11. To change the position of so that the underside becomes the upper side: *turn the pancakes; turn the pages of a book.* 12. To change: *Many caterpillars turn into butterflies.* 13. To change color or change to a certain color: *Leaves turn in the fall. He felt his face turning red.* 14. To make sour: *The hot weather turned the milk.* 15. To upset or make sick to the stomach: *Greasy food turns my stomach.* 16. To become, reach, or go beyond a certain age, time, or amount: *He will turn twelve on his next birthday.*

Phrasal verbs **turn down** 1. To make less the volume, degree, speed, or flow of: *Turn down the heat.* 2. To reject or refuse a person, request, or suggestion. **turn out** 1. To come out, especially for a public event: *The whole town turned out for the parade.* 2. To produce or make: *She turned out a large amount of work.* 3. To be found to be: *That rumor turned out to be false.* 4. To result; end up: *plans turning out perfectly.*

—*noun, plural* **turns** 1. The act of turning or the condition of being turned; rotation or revolution. 2. A change of direction, motion, or position, or the point of such a change: *a right turn; a turn in the road.* 3. A point of change in time: *the turn of the century.* 4. A movement in the direction of: *a turn for the worse;*

an unusual turn of events. **5.** A chance to do something: *my turn to deal the cards.* **6.** A deed or action having a certain effect on another person: *did him a good turn.*

tur·nip | tûr′nĭp′ | —*noun, plural* **turnips** A plant whose leaves and large, rounded yellowish or white root are eaten as vegetables.

turn·pike | tûrn′pīk′ | —*noun, plural* **turnpikes** A road, especially a wide highway. People have to pay a toll on certain turnpikes.

turn·ta·ble | tûrn′tā′bəl | —*noun, plural* **turntables** **1.** A round platform with a railway track that is able to rotate. It is used for turning locomotives. **2.** The round, rotating platform of a record player, on which the record is placed.

tur·pen·tine | tûr′pən tīn′ | —*noun* **1.** A thin oil distilled from the wood or resin of certain pine trees. It is used to make paint thinner. **2.** The sticky mixture of resin and oil from which this oil is distilled.

tur·quoise | tûr′koiz′ | or | tûr′kwoiz′ | —*noun, plural* **turquoises** **1.** A bluish-green mineral used as a gem in jewelry. **2.** A light bluish-green color.
—*adjective* Light bluish green.

tur·ret | tûr′ĭt | or | tŭr′ĭt | —*noun, plural* **turrets** A small tower on the side of a building.

tur·tle | tûr′tl | —*noun, plural* **turtles** Any of a group of reptiles that live on water or land and have a body covered by a hard shell. The turtle can pull its head, legs, and tail into the shell to protect itself.

tusk | tŭsk | —*noun, plural* **tusks** A long, pointed tooth, usually one of a pair. It extends outside of the mouth of certain animals. The elephant, walrus, and wild boar have tusks.

tu·tor | tōō′tər | or | tyōō′tər | —*noun, plural* **tutors** A person who teaches someone privately.

TV | tē′vē′ | —*noun, plural* **TV's** Television: *We watched the game on TV.*

tweed | twēd | —*noun, plural* **tweeds** A rough, woolen cloth, usually having several colors. Tweed is used to make jackets, slacks, and other clothes.

tweet | twēt | —*noun, plural* **tweets** A high, chirping sound, such as a small bird makes.

tweez·ers | twē′zərz | —*noun* (Used with a plural verb.) A small, V-shaped tool used for plucking or handling small objects.

twelfth | twĕlfth | —*noun, plural* **twelfths** **1.** In a group of people or things that are in numbered order, the one that matches the number twelve. **2.** One of twelve equal parts, written $\frac{1}{12}$.
—*adjective: the twelfth chapter of the book.*

twelve | twĕlv | —*noun, plural* **twelves** A number, written 12, that is equal to the sum of 10 + 2.
—*adjective* Being one more than eleven in number: *twelve pencils.* The adjective **twelve** belongs to a class of words called **determiners.** They signal that a noun is coming.

twen·ti·eth | twĕn′tē ĭth | —*noun, plural* **twentieths** **1.** In a group of people or things that are in numbered order, the one that matches the number twenty. **2.** One of twenty equal parts, written $\frac{1}{20}$.
—*adjective: the twentieth page of the book.*

twen·ty | twĕn′tē | —*noun, plural* **twenties** A number, written 20, that is equal to the sum of 10 + 10.

turnpike

turret
On a castle

turtle

—*adjective* Being one more than nineteen in number: *twenty books*. The adjective **twenty** belongs to a class of words called **determiners**. They signal that a noun is coming.

twice | twīs | —*adverb* **1.** On two occasions; two times: *He saw the movie twice.* **2.** Double the amount or degree: *She works twice as hard as her friend.*

twig | twĭg | —*noun, plural* **twigs** A small branch of a tree or shrub.

twi·light | twī′līt′ | —*noun* The period of time when the sun is below the horizon but there is a little light in the sky.

twin | twĭn | —*noun, plural* **twins** **1.** Either of two children born of the same parents at the same time. **2.** One of two persons, animals, or things that are alike or the same.
—*adjective* **1.** Being one or two of two children from the same birth: *her twin sister; twin brothers.* **2.** Being one or two of two persons, animals, or things that are alike or the same.

twine | twīn | —*noun, plural* **twines** A strong cord or string made of threads twisted together.
—*verb* **twined, twining** **1.** To form by twisting: *twine strings of beads.* **2.** To coil about: *A vine twined over the fence.*

twin·kle | twĭng′kəl | —*verb* **twinkled, twinkling** To shine with slight, winking gleams; sparkle: *stars twinkling in the sky.*
—*noun, plural* **twinkles** A slight, winking gleam of light.

twin·kling | twĭng′klĭng | —*noun* A very short period of time; an instant: *In a twinkling he was gone.*

twirl | twûrl | —*verb* **twirled, twirling** To turn around and around quickly: *She twirled her baton.*

twist | twĭst | —*verb* **twisted, twisting** **1.** To wind together two or more threads to form one strand. **2.** To wind or coil around something: *She twisted cord around the package. Vines twisted around the fence.* **3.** To move or go in a winding course: *A river twisted across the plains.* **4.** To pull sharply or sprain: *She twisted her ankle.* **5.** To change the shape of: *He twisted the paper clip into different shapes.*
—*noun, plural* **twists** **1.** The act of twisting; a spin: *a twist of the wrist.* **2.** A turn or bend: *every twist in the road.*

twist·er | twĭs′tər | —*noun, plural* **twisters** A tornado.

twitch | twĭch | —*verb* **twitched, twitching** To move or cause to move with a quick jerk: *He twitched his nose.*

twit·ter | twĭt′ər | —*verb* **twittered, twittering** To make a series of high, fast, chirping sounds. Birds make this kind of sound.
—*noun, plural* **twitters** **1.** A series of high, fast, chirping sounds. **2.** A condition of nervous excitement: *The children were in a twitter about the next day's party.*

two | tōō | —*noun, plural* **twos** A number, written 2, that is equal to the sum of 1 + 1.
—*adjective* Being one more than one in number: *two pens.* The adjective **two** belongs to a class of words called **determiners.** They signal that a noun is coming.
♦ *These sound alike* **two, to, too.**

type | tīp | —*noun, plural* **types** **1.** A group of persons or things that are alike in certain ways that set them apart from others; group; class: *He grew a certain type of flower in his garden.* **2.a.** In printing, a small block of wood or metal with a letter on it. **b.** A group of such blocks, from which printing is done.
—*verb* **typed, typing** **1.** To put into a certain group or class: *She*

type
Different kinds of type used in printing

ă	pat	ĕ	pet	î	fierce
ā	pay	ē	be	ŏ	pot
â	care	ĭ	pit	ō	go
ä	father	ī	pie	ô	paw, for
oi	oil	ŭ	cut	zh	vision
ōō	book	û	fur	ə	ago, item,
ōō	boot	*th*	the		pencil, atom,
yōō	abuse	th	thin		circus
ou	out	hw	which	ər	butter

typed the rock samples by studying each one. **2.** To write with a typewriter.

type·writ·er |tīp′rī′tər| —*noun, plural* **typewriters** A machine that prints letters and numbers on a piece of inserted paper. It has keys that, when pressed by hand, strike the paper through an inked ribbon.

ty·phoid fever |tī′foid′| A serious disease caused by bacteria found in bad food and water.

ty·phoon |tī foon′| —*noun, plural* **typhoons** A severe hurricane occurring in the western Pacific Ocean.

typ·i·cal |tĭp′ĭ kəl| —*adjective* **1.** Showing the characteristics of a certain kind or group: *a typical college; a typical monster movie.* **2.** Characteristic of someone or something: *his typical manner of speech.*

typ·ist |tī′pĭst| —*noun, plural* **typists** A person who types on a typewriter.

ty·pog·ra·phy |tī pŏg′rə fē| —*noun* **1.** The preparation of printed material by the setting of type on a special machine. **2.** The way printed material looks or is arranged: *The typography of this book is very clear.*

ty·ran·nic |tī răn′ĭk| or |tī răn′ĭk| —*adjective* A form of the word **tyrannical.**

ty·ran·ni·cal |tī răn′ĭ kəl| or |tī răn′ĭ kəl| —*adjective* Of or like a tyrant; cruel or unjust: *The men refused to work because of the tyrannical way their boss was treating them.*

ty·ran·no·saur |tī răn′ə sôr′| or |tī răn′ə sôr′| —*noun, plural* **tyrannosaurs** A dinosaur with small front legs, a large head, and sharp teeth. Tyrannosaurs lived on the land and ate other animals.

tyr·an·ny |tĭr′ə nē| —*noun, plural* **tyrannies** **1.** A government in which one person has all the power. **2.** Absolute power, especially when it is used in a way that is cruel or unjust.

ty·rant |tī′rənt| —*noun, plural* **tyrants** **1.** A ruler who uses power unjustly or cruelly. **2.** Any person who is unjust and cruel.

tyrannosaur

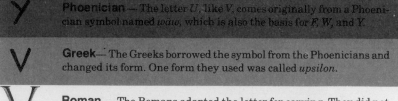

Phoenician — The letter *U*, like *V*, comes originally from a Phoenician symbol named *wāw*, which is also the basis for *F*, *W*, and *Y*.

Greek — The Greeks borrowed the symbol from the Phoenicians and changed its form. One form they used was called *upsilon*.

Roman — The Romans adapted the letter for carving. They did not always distinguish *u*, *v*, and *w*, so *V* was the only symbol used.

Medieval — The hand-written form of about 1,200 years ago became the basis of the modern small letter.

Modern — The modern capital got its rounded form in modern times. The small letter is based on the medieval hand-written form.

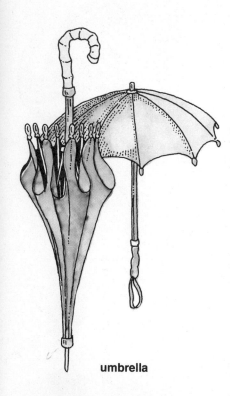

umbrella

ă	pat	ĕ	pet	î	fierce
ā	pay	ē	be	ŏ	pot
â	care	ĭ	pit	ō	go
ä	father	ī	pie	ô	paw, for

oi	oil	ŭ	cut	zh	vision
ŏŏ	book	û	fur	ə	ago, item,
ōō	boot	*th*	the		pencil, atom,
yōō	abuse	th	thin		circus
ou	out	hw	which	ər	butter

u or **U** | yōō | —*noun, plural* **u's** or **U's** The twenty-first letter of the English alphabet.

ug·ly | ŭg′lē | —*adjective* **uglier, ugliest** **1.** Not pleasing to look at: *The monster had an ugly face and a scaly body. That's the ugliest painting I ever saw.* **2.** Not agreeable; unpleasant: *The weather has been ugly all weekend.* **3.** Having a bad temper; mean: *He's been in an ugly mood all day.*

u·ku·le·le | yōō′kə lā′lē | —*noun, plural* **ukuleles** A small guitar with four strings that is played by plucking. It first became a popular instrument in Hawaii.

ul·ti·mate | ŭl′tə mĭt | —*adjective* **1.** Final or last: *The ultimate result of not doing your homework is that you'll fail the test.* **2.** Most basic; fundamental: *Most people think the ultimate element of education is knowing how to read and write.*

um·brel·la | ŭm brĕl′ə | —*noun, plural* **umbrellas** A round piece of cloth or plastic on a frame that is attached to a handle. It is used for protection from the rain or sun and can be collapsed or folded up when it's not being used.

um·pire | ŭm′pīr′ | —*noun, plural* **umpires** A person who rules on the plays in baseball and some other sports.
—*verb* **umpired, umpiring** To act as an umpire: *I umpired the school basketball game.*

un- A prefix that means: **1.** Not; the opposite of: *unable; unbecoming.* **2.** Lack of: *unemployment.* **3.** To do the opposite of: *unlock.*

un·a·ble | ŭn ā′bəl | —*adjective* Not having the ability, knowledge, or power to do something: *Shelly is unable to reach the top shelf. Everyone in the class was unable to solve the math problem.*

u·nan·i·mous | yōō năn′ə məs | —*adjective* Based on or showing complete agreement: *Jill was elected class president by a unanimous vote. The family's decision to go to the circus instead of the baseball game was unanimous.*

un·be·com·ing | ŭn′bĭ kŭm′ĭng | —*adjective* **1.** Not attractive: *an unbecoming dress.* **2.** Not proper or suitable: *I was ashamed of your unbecoming behavior at the wedding.*

un·be·liev·a·ble | ŭn′bĭ lē′və bəl | —*adjective* Not to be believed: *She will never accept that unbelievable excuse.*

un·can·ny | ŭn kăn′ē | —*adjective* **uncannier, uncanniest**

1. Mysterious; strange: *It was uncanny the way Bill showed up right after we were talking about him.* **2.** Not to be explained by reason: *He has an uncanny ability to know what people like.*

un·cer·tain | ŭn sûr′tn | —*adjective* **1.** Not certain; not known for sure; doubtful: *He was uncertain of the answer to the question. It's uncertain whether or not we can drive to Indiana in two days from here.* **2.** Likely to change; not dependable: *We decided not to go to the beach because the weather was uncertain.*

un·cle | ŭng′kəl | —*noun, plural* **uncles** **1.** The brother of one's father or mother. **2.** The husband of one's aunt.

un·com·fort·a·ble | ŭn kŭmf′tə bəl | or | ŭn kŭm′fər tə bəl | —*adjective* **1.** Not comfortable: *He was uncomfortable because his pants were too tight.* **2.** Not making comfortable: *an uncomfortable wooden chair.* **3.** Uneasy; awkward: *There was an uncomfortable silence when he left.*

un·com·mon | ŭn kŏm′ən | —*adjective* Not common; rare or unusual: *There are many uncommon animals in the zoo.*

un·con·scious | ŭn kŏn′shəs | —*adjective* **1.** Not conscious; in a condition that looks like sleep: *He was knocked unconscious when the ball hit him on the head.* **2.** Not aware; not realizing: *He was completely unconscious of having said the wrong thing at the party.* **3.** Not meant or done on purpose: *an unconscious mistake.*

un·con·sti·tu·tion·al | ŭn kŏn′stĭ tōō′shə nəl | or | ŭn kŏn′stĭ tyōō′shə nəl | —*adjective* Not in keeping with the principles of the constitution of a state or country: *The Supreme Court declared the law unconstitutional.*

un·cov·er | ŭn kŭv′ər | —*verb* **uncovered, uncovering** **1.** To remove a cover or top from: *Will you uncover the pot and see if the water's boiling?* **2.** To make known; reveal; expose: *The plot was uncovered by the police.*

un·de·cid·ed | ŭn′dĭ sī′dĭd | —*adjective* **1.** Not yet settled or decided upon: *The question of where to go on our vacation was still undecided.* **2.** Not having reached a decision: *The puppy seemed undecided whether to chase the squirrel or make friends with it.*

un·der | ŭn′dər | —*preposition* **1.** In or into a lower position or place than; below; beneath: *The cat is under the table. The boat is passing under the bridge.* **2.** Concealed or covered by: *She is wearing a red sweater under her coat. There were flowers under the leaves of the tree.* **3.** Less than: *Children under five years of age can go in free. All the gifts should cost under ten dollars.* **4.** Subject to the action or effort of; receiving the effects of: *She is under her mother's influence. He is under the doctor's treatment. The old road is under repair.* **5.** Subject to the authority of: *The country made great progress under the new President.* **6.** Bound by; under the obligation of: *You are under oath; now tell the truth! He will have to pay a fine under the conditions of the contract.*
—*adverb* In or into a place below or beneath: *Lift the rug and put your hand under. The strong current sucked the boat under.*
—*adjective* Lower: *the under parts of a machine.*

under- A prefix that means: **1.** Beneath; below: *underground; underwater.* **2.** Not enough: *underdeveloped.*

un·der·brush | ŭn′dər brŭsh′ | —*noun* Small trees, shrubs, and other plants that grow thickly beneath tall trees in a forest or wooded area.

un·der·clothes | ŭn′dər klōz′ | or | ŭn′dər klōthz′ | —*plural noun* Underwear.

un·der·de·vel·oped | ŭn′dər dĭ **vĕl′**əpt | —*adjective* **1.** Not developed in a full or normal way: *underdeveloped muscles.* **2.** Having a poorly developed industry and economy. There are still many underdeveloped nations in the world in which most people have a low standard of living.

un·der·dog | **ŭn′**dər dôg′ | or | **ŭn′**dər dŏg′ | —*noun, plural* **underdogs** A person or group that is expected to lose a contest or struggle: *Everyone was surprised when Mr. Rubinstein was elected mayor, since he was the underdog.*

un·der·foot | ŭn′dər **fŏŏt′** | —*adjective* **1.** Below or under the foot or feet; on the ground: *We were going to cross the field but it was too full of mud underfoot.* **2.** In the way: *The puppies are running around and always getting underfoot.*

un·der·gar·ment | **ŭn′**dər gär′mənt | —*noun, plural* **undergarments** An article of underwear.

un·der·go | ŭn′dər **gō′** | —*verb* **underwent, undergone, undergoing** To go through or be subjected to; experience: *Many insects undergo three changes during their lives. The pioneers underwent many hardships on their way to the West.*

un·der·gone | ŭn′dər **gôn′** | or | ŭn′dər **gŏn′** | The past participle of the verb **undergo:** *The United States has undergone many changes in the last twenty years.*

un·der·grad·u·ate | ŭn′dər **grăj′**ōō ĭt | —*noun, plural* **undergraduates** A student who is studying at a college or university but has not yet graduated.

un·der·ground | **ŭn′**dər ground′ | —*adjective* **1.** Below the surface of the earth: *There is an underground passage that leads to the forest behind the castle.* **2.** Acting or done in secret; hidden: *an underground political organization.*
—*noun* A secret organization: *The underground was made up of patriots who were fighting the tyrant who ruled their country.*
—*adverb* **1.** Below the surface of the earth: *Miners were digging coal underground.* **2.** In secret: *There are spies living underground all over the country.*

un·der·growth | **ŭn′**dər grōth′ | —*noun* Small trees, plants, and shrubs that grow close to the ground beneath tall trees in a forest or wooded area.

un·der·hand·ed | **ŭn′**dər **hăn′**dĭd | —*adjective* Done in a secret or dishonest way: *It was pretty underhanded of him to borrow my car without asking me first.*

un·der·line | **ŭn′**dər līn′ | —*verb* **underlined, underlining** To draw a line under: *The teacher told us to underline any word we didn't understand.*

un·der·neath | ŭn′dər **nēth′** | —*preposition* Beneath; below; under: *Don't forget to put newspapers underneath the leaky pail.*
—*adverb* Below: *She found a worm underneath.*

un·der·pants | **ŭn′**dər pănts′ | —*plural noun* Short or long pants worn next to the skin under pants, shorts, or a skirt.

un·der·pass | **ŭn′**dər păs′ | or | **ŭn′**dər päs′ | —*noun, plural* **underpasses** A part or section of a road that goes under another road or a railroad.

un·der·priv·i·leged | ŭn′dər **prĭv′**ə lĭjd | —*adjective* Not having the advantages or opportunities that most other people have because one is poor: *There are many underprivileged children in the world who do not have enough food or clothing.*

underpass

ă	pat	ĕ	pet	î	fierce
ā	pay	ē	be	ŏ	pot
â	care	ĭ	pit	ō	go
ä	father	ī	pie	ô	paw, for

oi	oil	ŭ	cut	zh	vision
ōŏ	book	û	fur	ə	ago, item,
ōō	boot	*th*	the		pencil, atom,
yōō	abuse	th	thin		circus
ou	out	hw	which	ər	butter

un·der·sea | ŭn′dər sē′ | —*adjective* Existing, done, or used under the surface of the sea: *undersea plants and animals.*

un·der·shirt | ŭn′dər shûrt′ | —*noun, plural* **undershirts** A light, close-fitting shirt worn next to the skin under a shirt.

un·der·side | ŭn′dər sīd′ | —*noun, plural* **undersides** The bottom side of something: *There were bugs crawling all over the underside of the boulder.*

un·der·stand | ŭn′dər **stănd′** | —*verb* **understood, understanding**
1. To get or grasp the meaning of: *Do you understand the question? His explanation was too difficult for me to understand.*
2. To be familiar with; know well: *He understands German.* **3.** To be told about; learn: *We understand she got sick on Thanksgiving.*
4. To accept as a fact: *I understood that you were going to be here at five o'clock.* **5.** To be tolerant or sympathetic toward: *She's a good teacher because she understands children. If you can't come to my party, I'll understand.*

un·der·stand·ing | ŭn′dər **stăn′**dĭng | —*noun, plural* **understandings 1.** A grasp of the meaning or intention of something; knowledge: *These exercises will help you get a better understanding of the spelling rules.* **2.** The ability to understand: *Bucky has a good understanding of how engines work.* **3.** A friendly and sympathetic relationship that is based on a knowledge of each other: *There has always been a good understanding between the United States and Canada.* **4.** An agreement, especially after a fight or argument: *After quarreling for an hour we came to an understanding.*
—*adjective* Showing kind or sympathetic feeling: *She gave me an understanding look when I told her I was sad.*

un·der·stood | ŭn′dər **stŏŏd′** | The past tense and past participle of the verb **understand:** *I understood what you said. I had understood you were going to be at the meeting.*

un·der·take | ŭn′dər **tāk′** | —*verb* **undertook, undertaken, undertaking 1.** To decide or agree to do: *We're undertaking a trip across the country.* **2.** To promise to do something: *Who will undertake the task of bringing food to the picnic?*

un·der·tak·en | ŭn′dər **tā′**kən | The past participle of the verb **undertake:** *He has undertaken a most difficult job.*

un·der·tak·er | ŭn′dər tā′kər | —*noun, plural* **undertakers** A person whose job is preparing the bodies of dead people for burial and making funeral arrangements.

un·der·took | ŭn′dər **tŏŏk′** | The past tense of the verb **undertake:** *Yesterday the lawyer undertook three new cases.*

un·der·wa·ter | ŭn′dər **wô′**tər | or | ŭn′dər **wŏt′**ər | —*adjective* Existing, done, or used under the surface of water: *underwater plants; equipment for underwater swimming; underwater oil wells.*
—*adverb* Under the surface of water: *I can swim underwater.*

un·der·wear | ŭn′dər wâr′ | —*noun* Light clothing worn next to the skin and under outer clothes.

un·der·went | ŭn′dər **wĕnt′** | The past tense of the verb **undergo:** *He underwent a serious operation.*

un·did | ŭn **dĭd′** | The past tense of the verb **undo:** *He undid his belt buckle.*

un·dis·turbed | ŭn′dĭ **stûrbd′** | —*adjective* Not bothered or annoyed; calm: *I slept undisturbed even though the radio was playing loud music.*

un·do | ŭn **dŏŏ′** | —*verb* **undid, undone, undoing 1.** To do away

underwater
Divers exploring a part of the ocean

with or reverse something that has already been done: *If you knock over the pitcher of lemonade by mistake, you can't undo the error.* **2.** To untie or loosen: *I finally undid the knot.*

un·do·ing | ŭn dōō′ĭng | —*noun* **1.** Destruction; ruin: *Gambling and alcohol led to his complete undoing.* **2.** The cause of ruin: *That last missed pass was the undoing of our football team.*

un·done | ŭn dŭn′ | The past participle of the verb **undo**: *Billy had undone his shoelaces.*

un·dress | ŭn drĕs′ | —*verb* **undressed, undressing** To remove the clothing of; take one's clothes off: *She undressed the baby and put him to sleep. I undressed and took a bubble bath.*

un·earth | ŭn ûrth′ | —*verb* **unearthed, unearthing** **1.** To dig up out of the ground: *Albert unearthed an old shoe in the garden.* **2.** To discover and reveal; uncover: *The police had not been able to unearth any clues to help them solve the crime.*

un·eas·y | ŭn ē′zē | —*adjective* **uneasier, uneasiest** **1.** Not having a feeling of security; worried; nervous: *I was uneasy about having to go on the airplane by myself.* **2.** Not comfortable; awkward in manner: *I was uneasy standing up in front of the principal.*

un·em·ployed | ŭn′ĕm ploid′ | —*adjective* Not having a job; out of work: *Lionel's been unemployed since the store closed down.*

un·em·ploy·ment | ŭn′ĕm ploi′mənt | —*noun* The fact or condition of not having a job: *Unemployment is one of the most serious problems in the United States.*

un·e·qual | ŭn ē′kwəl | —*adjective* **1.** Not equal; not the same: *He cut the cake into unequal pieces.* **2.** Not fair; not evenly matched: *The basketball game was unequal because all of them are taller than we are.*

un·e·ven | ŭn ē′vən | —*adjective* **unevener, unevenest** **1.** Not straight, level, or smooth: *We couldn't play soccer on the field because the ground was uneven. Could you straighten out that uneven bedspread?* **2.** Not fair or equal: *The game was uneven because our team was a lot better than theirs.*

un·ex·pect·ed | ŭn′ĭk spĕk′tĭd | —*adjective* Not expected; happening without warning: *My cousin paid us an unexpected visit.*

un·fair | ŭn fâr′ | —*adjective* Not fair or right; unjust: *an unfair law. The race was unfair because he started before I did.*

un·fair·ness | ŭn fâr′nĭs | —*noun, plural* **unfairnesses** The condition or quality of being unfair.

un·fa·mil·iar | ŭn′fə mĭl′yər | —*adjective* **1.** Not well known; not easily recognized: *Her face was unfamiliar to me.* **2.** Not acquainted: *My father couldn't help me with the science problem because he was unfamiliar with the subject.*

un·fas·ten | ŭn făs′ən | or | ŭn fä′sən | —*verb* **unfastened, unfastening** To open or untie or become opened or untied: *He unfastened the seat belt. The buckle unfastens easily.*

un·fit | ŭn fĭt′ | —*adjective* **1.** Not fit or suitable for a certain purpose: *The water from the river is unfit to drink.* **2.** In bad or poor health: *He's too unfit to swim across the lake and will never make it.*

un·for·get·ta·ble | ŭn′fər gĕt′ə bəl | —*adjective* Making such a strong impression that it is impossible to forget: *That was the most unforgettable vacation I ever had.*

un·for·giv·a·ble | ŭn′fər gĭv′ə bəl | —*adjective* Not to be forgiven or pardoned: *It was unforgivable to say something like that to your friends.*

un·for·tu·nate | ŭn fôr′chə nĭt | —*adjective* Not fortunate;

ă	pat	ĕ	pet	î	fierce
ā	pay	ē	be	ŏ	pot
â	care	ĭ	pit	ō	go
ä	father	ī	pie	ô	paw, for
oi	oil	ŭ	cut	zh	vision
ŏŏ	book	û	fur	ə	ago, item,
ōō	boot	th	the		pencil, atom,
yōō	abuse	th	thin		circus
ou	out	hw	which	ər	butter

unlucky: *It's unfortunate that it started to rain an hour before the picnic.*

un·friend·ly | ŭn frĕnd′ lē | —*adjective* **unfriendlier, unfriendliest 1.** Not friendly; cold: *The man in the store was unfriendly and kept ignoring me.* **2.** Not liking to meet or talk with others; not sociable; distant: *The new student is unfriendly and doesn't want to help with the class party.* **3.** Hostile; mean: *The unfriendly dog tried to bite me.*

un·grate·ful | ŭn grāt′ fəl | —*adjective* Not grateful; without thanks: *I couldn't believe he was so ungrateful after I helped him carry all his bags home.*

un·hap·pi·ness | ŭn hăp′ ē nĭs | —*noun* The condition or quality of being unhappy: *There was great unhappiness when our team lost the game.*

un·hap·py | ŭn hăp′ ē | —*adjective* **unhappier, unhappiest 1.** Not happy; sad: *He's unhappy because he didn't get what he wanted for his birthday.* **2.** Not pleased or satisfied; upset: *Many people are unhappy with the new law that forbids dogs in the playground.*

un·health·y | ŭn hĕl′ thē | —*adjective* **unhealthier, unhealthiest 1.** In poor health; ill; sick: *an unhealthy puppy.* **2.** Showing poor health: *He has an unhealthy appearance.* **3.** Causing poor health; not wholesome: *Too much sugar can be unhealthy.*

u·ni·corn | yōō′ nĭ kôrn′ | —*noun, plural* **unicorns** An imaginary animal that looks like a white horse and has a long horn in the middle of its forehead.

u·ni·form | yōō′ nə fôrm′ | —*noun, plural* **uniforms** A special suit of clothes worn by the members of a group or organization. It identifies a person as belonging to the group. Soldiers, police, and girl scouts all wear uniforms.
—*adjective* **1.** Always the same; not changing: *All the boards are of uniform length.* **2.** Having the same appearance, form, shape, or color; showing little difference: *The street is lined with uniform brick houses.*

un·im·por·tant | ŭn′ ĭm pôr′ tnt | —*adjective* Not important; having little or no value or interest: *Whether we leave for grandmother's now or in an hour is unimportant as long as we get there by dinner time.*

un·ion | yōōn′ yən | —*noun, plural* **unions 1.** The act of bringing or joining together two or more people or things: *The new school was formed by the union of all the students from two small schools.* **2.** A group of workers who join together to protect their interests and jobs. They do such things as trying to get higher salaries and improving working conditions. **3. the Union a.** The United States of America. **b.** Those states that remained loyal to and fought for the Federal government during the Civil War.

u·nique | yōō nēk′ | —*adjective* **1.** Being the only one of its kind: *Alaska is unique because it's the largest state in the United States.* **2.** Having no equal; rare or unusual: *The artist's painting style is unique.*

u·nit | yōō′ nĭt | —*noun, plural* **units 1.** A single thing, group, or person that is part of a larger group or whole: *The bookcase came in units, which my father put together. The class was divided into units and given different problems to do.* **2.** A defined or fixed quantity that is used for measuring: *A meter is a unit of distance.* **3.** A machine that does a certain job or a part that has a special purpose in a larger machine or device: *A radiator is a heating unit.*

unicorn
A decoration on a building

uniform

The unit that controls the sound in the television is broken. **4.** The first whole number, represented by the numeral 1.

u·nite | yoō nīt′ | —*verb* **united, uniting** **1.** To bring together or join so as to form a whole; make one: *Benjamin Franklin had a plan to unite the colonies under one government. The three Indian tribes united to fight the enemy.* **2.** To become joined or combined into a unit: *All people are united in the desire for peace.*

United Nations An international organization that is made up of members from most of the nations in the world. It was founded in 1945 to promote international understanding, peace, and economic and social development. Its headquarters are in New York City.

United States The United States of America.

United States of America A country in North America. It is made up of fifty states and the District of Columbia. The capital of the United States of America is Washington, D.C. Another name for this country is the **United States.**

u·ni·ver·sal | yoō′nə vûr′səl | —*adjective* **1.** Affecting the whole world; being everywhere: *Sickness and poverty are universal problems.* **2.** Of, for, or shared by everyone: *There was universal sorrow when the war started.*

u·ni·verse | yoō′nə vûrs′ | —*noun, plural* **universes** All things considered as a whole; everything that exists, including the earth, the planets, and space.

u·ni·ver·si·ty | yoō′nə vûr′sĭ tē | —*noun, plural* **universities** A school of higher learning. It is made up of different schools that offer degrees in law, medicine, and other professions, and it also has regular college divisions.

un·just | ŭn jŭst′ | —*adjective* Not just or fair: *unjust punishment.*

un·kind | ŭn kīnd′ | —*adjective* Not kind; harsh or cruel: *That was a very unkind thing to say to him.*

un·known | ŭn nōn′ | —*adjective* Not known or familiar; strange: *The cowboys rode into an unknown town.*

un·law·ful | ŭn lô′fəl | —*adjective* Not lawful or legal; against the law: *Driving over the speed limit is unlawful.*

un·less | ŭn lĕs′ | —*conjunction* Except if: *The snow will melt unless the weather gets colder.*

un·like | ŭn līk′ | —*adjective* Not alike; different: *He and his twin brother are unlike in many ways.*
—*preposition* **1.** Different from; not like: *Unlike her, I love spinach.* **2.** Not typical of: *It's unlike Marney not to call when she's going to be late.*

un·like·ly | ŭn līk′lē | —*adjective* **unlikelier, unlikeliest** **1.** Not likely; not probable or possible: *It's unlikely that we'll be able to go to the movies tonight.* **2.** Not likely to succeed; likely to fail: *The coach considered Brad an unlikely candidate for the football team.*

un·lim·it·ed | ŭn lĭm′ĭ tĭd | —*adjective* Having no limits: *We have unlimited use of the gym at school.*

un·load | ŭn lōd′ | —*verb* **unloaded, unloading** **1.** To remove the load or cargo from: *We unloaded the truck in an hour.* **2.** To remove cargo: *Movers unloaded the furniture from the truck.* **3. a.** To remove the ammunition from a firearm: *Unload your guns, men; the fighting is over.* **b.** To fire or shoot a firearm: *The contestant unloaded his gun at the target.*

un·lock | ŭn lŏk′ | —*verb* **unlocked, unlocking** **1.** To undo or open the lock of: *I had trouble unlocking the car door.* **2.** To

United Nations
The United Nations Building in New York

ă	pat	ĕ	pet	î	fierce
ā	pay	ē	be	ŏ	pot
â	care	ĭ	pit	ō	go
ä	father	ī	pie	ô	paw, for
oi	oil	ŭ	cut	zh	vision
oͦo	book	û	fur	ə	ago, item,
ōo	boot	*th*	the		pencil, atom,
yoō	abuse	th	thin		circus
ou	out	hw	which	ər	butter

become open or unfastened: *The door had been unlocked all day.*
3. To reveal or disclose: *The telescope unlocked many of the mysteries of the stars and planets.*

un·luck·y |ŭn lŭk′ē| —*adjective* **unluckier, unluckiest** Having or causing bad luck: *She must be an unlucky person, since she's always losing things. That unlucky storm washed away all the vegetables we planted.*

un·manned |ŭn mănd′| —*adjective* Without a crew; built to work without a crew: *an unmanned spacecraft.*

un·mis·tak·a·ble |ŭn′mĭ stā′kə bəl| —*adjective* Not able to be mistaken or misunderstood; obvious; clear: *Her southern accent is unmistakable.*

un·nat·u·ral |ŭn năch′ər əl| or |ŭn năch′rəl| —*adjective* Different from what normally occurs or happens in nature; not normal; unusual: *It's unnatural for birds to fly north in the winter.*

un·nec·es·sar·y |ŭn nĕs′ĭ sĕr′ē| —*adjective* Not necessary; not needed: *It's unnecessary to shout; I can hear you.*

un·oc·cu·pied |ŭn ŏk′yə pīd′| —*adjective* Not occupied; vacant or empty: *I took the first unoccupied seat on the bus.*

un·pack |ŭn păk′| —*verb* **unpacked, unpacking 1.** To remove the contents of: *I unpacked both trunks.* **2.** To remove from a container or package: *Will you help me unpack the groceries?*

un·pleas·ant |ŭn plĕz′ənt| —*adjective* Not pleasant; not pleasing: *The cough medicine has an unpleasant taste.*

un·pop·u·lar |ŭn pŏp′yə lər| —*adjective* Not popular; not generally liked or accepted: *an unpopular decision. The unpopular mayor lost the election.*

un·pre·pared |ŭn′prĭ pârd′| —*adjective* **1.** Not prepared; not ready: *I'm unprepared to take the test.* **2.** Done without preparation: *He gave an unprepared speech.*

un·re·al·is·tic |ŭn′rē ə lĭs′tĭk| —*adjective* Not realistic; unlikely to be true or to happen: *It's unrealistic to think you can get everything you want. I think your plan is unrealistic and will never work.*

un·rea·son·a·ble |ŭn rē′zə nə bəl| —*adjective* **1.** Not reasonable; not having or showing good or common sense: *Marcia's fear of dogs is unreasonable.* **2.** Excessive; too high or too great: *The agent was asking an unreasonable amount of money for the house.*

un·re·li·a·ble |ŭn′rĭ lī′ə bəl| —*adjective* Not reliable; not to be depended on or trusted: *I knew he wouldn't be here on time, he's so unreliable.*

un·rest |ŭn rĕst′| —*noun* A condition of agitation; disturbance: *There was unrest in the state when the governor said he was going to raise taxes.*

un·ru·ly |ŭn rōō′lē| —*adjective* **unrulier, unruliest** Hard to discipline or control: *The unruly student was always being kept after school.*

un·safe |ŭn sāf′| —*adjective* Dangerous or risky: *That old bridge is unsafe to drive over.*

un·sat·is·fac·to·ry |ŭn′săt ĭs făk′tə rē| —*adjective* Not good enough; not acceptable; inadequate: *The teacher told Linda that her work in English was unsatisfactory.*

un·self·ish |ŭn sĕl′fĭsh| —*adjective* Not selfish; generous; considerate: *It was unselfish of her to let her younger brother have the last piece of candy.*

un·set·tled | ŭn sĕt′ld | —*adjective* **1.** Not peaceful or orderly; disturbed: *Conditions in the town were unsettled for months after the flood.* **2.** Not decided: *The strike that closed the factory is still unsettled.* **3.** Not paid: *I haven't got enough money to pay all my unsettled bills.* **4.** Not being lived in: *A large part of the southwestern United States is unsettled desert.*

un·skilled | ŭn skĭld′ | —*adjective* **1.** Not having skill or specialized training: *The factory employs many unskilled workers.* **2.** Not needing or requiring special skills: *The boss offered me an unskilled job.*

un·sound | ŭn sound′ | —*adjective* **1.** Not strong or solid: *That old bridge looks pretty unsound to me.* **2.** Not physically sound; unhealthy: *She takes pills for her unsound heart.* **3.** Not based on logic or clear thinking: *Don't ask her for a suggestion; her advice is usually unsound.*

un·sta·ble | ŭn stā′bəl | —*adjective* **unstabler, unstablest** **1.** Not steady or solid: *The table is unstable because one leg is a little shorter than the others.* **2.** Having a tendency to change: *In the last few years the price of oil and gasoline has been unstable.*

un·stead·y | ŭn stĕd′ē | —*adjective* **unsteadier, unsteadiest** **1.** Not steady; shaky or unstable: *I wouldn't climb up the unsteady ladder.* **2.** Shaky or wavering: *an unsteady voice.*

un·tan·gle | ŭn tăng′gəl | —*verb* **untangled, untangling** **1.** To free from tangles or snarls: *It took me fifteen minutes to untangle the telephone cord.* **2.** To resolve or clear up: *The detective was unable to untangle the mystery.*

un·ti·dy | ŭn tī′dē | —*adjective* **untidier, untidiest** Not tidy or neat; messy: *an untidy room.*

un·tie | ŭn tī′ | —*verb* **untied, untying** To loosen or unfasten: *Tim can't untie the knot in his shoelace.*

un·til | ŭn tĭl′ | —*preposition* **1.** Up to the time of: *They danced until dawn.* **2.** Before: *You can't have the bike until tomorrow.* —*conjunction* **1.** Up to the time that: *They danced until it was dawn. We will wait until he arrives.* **2.** Before: *She couldn't go until she finished her work.* **3.** To the point or extent that: *They played football until they were tired.*

un·used —*adjective* **1.** | ŭn yōozd′ | Not in use or never having been used: *Put all that junk in the unused closet upstairs.*
2. | ŭn yōost′ | Not accustomed; not used to: *She didn't want to get a job because she's unused to working.*

un·u·su·al | ŭn yōo′zhōo əl | —*adjective* Not usual, common, or ordinary; rare: *It's unusual for Gus not to eat; he must be sick. What an unusual rock; where did you find it?*

up | ŭp | —*adverb* **1.** From a lower to a higher place: *He threw the ball up. I'll go up in the elevator to the roof of the building.* **2.** In, at, or to a higher position, point, or condition: *Don't look up. He put the books up on the shelves. The temperature is going up this morning. Store prices are going up. The river is up today.* **3. a.** In an erect position; on one's feet: *He is getting ready to stand up.* **b.** Out of bed: *She gets up every morning at eight o'clock.* **4.** Above the horizon: *The sun is up.* **5.** Entirely; thoroughly: *Eat up your sandwich.* **6.** Near: *He came up to say hello.* **7.** Into notice, view, or consideration: *Excuse me for bringing up this unpleasant subject.* **8.** To a higher volume: *Turn the radio up.* —*adjective* **1.** Moving or directed upward: *an up elevator.* **2.** In a high position; not down: *The shades are up.* **3.** Out of bed: *Are*

you up yet? **4.** Active; busy: *He's been up and around for a week.* **5.** Being considered: *Is your house up for sale?* **6.** Finished; over: *Time's up.* **7.** In baseball, at bat: *"You're up," said the coach.*
—*preposition* **1.** From a lower to a higher place or position in or on: *We walked up the hill. The cat climbed up the tree. She walked up the street to the market.* **2.** Toward the source of: *The boat goes up the river.*

    Idioms **up against** Having to fight with; facing: *Their team is up against the champions.* **up to 1.** Busy with; engaged in: *What are you up to?* **2.** Depending upon the action or will of: *The decision is up to him.*

up·hol·ster |ŭp **hōl**′stər| —*verb* **upholstered, upholstering** To provide or fit chairs and other furniture with stuffing, springs, cushions, and a fabric covering.

up·keep |ŭp′kēp| —*noun* The maintenance of something in proper condition or repair: *My father spends a lot of time on the weekends on the upkeep of our house.*

up·on |ə pŏn′| or |ə pôn′| —*preposition* On: *We stopped and sat down upon a flat rock.*

up·per |ŭp′ər| —*adjective* Higher in place or position: *We wanted to rent an apartment on one of the upper floors of the building.*

upper hand A position of control or advantage: *The girls gained the upper hand in the battle when the boys began to run out of snowballs.*

up·right |ŭp′rīt′| —*adjective* **1.** In a vertical position; straight up; erect: *Don't slouch, stand upright. We made a rabbit pen by attaching barbed wire to four upright posts.* **2.** Good or honest; moral: *Upright people do not steal or cheat.*

up·ris·ing |ŭp′rī′zĭng| —*noun, plural* **uprisings** A revolt or rebellion against authority.

up·roar |ŭp′rôr′| or |ŭp′rōr′| —*noun, plural* **uproars** A condition of noisy excitement and confusion: *The fans were in an uproar when our team won the game in the last minute.*

up·root |ŭp **rōot**′| or |ŭp **rŏŏt**′| —*verb* **uprooted, uprooting** **1.** To tear up by the roots; remove a plant from the ground: *The men had to uproot three large trees to make room for the new tennis courts.* **2.** To force to leave a place: *Many people were uprooted from their homes by the fire.*

up·set |ŭp sĕt′| —*verb* **upset, upsetting** **1.** To tip or knock over; overturn: *The cat upset the goldfish bowl.* **2.** To disturb the order or arrangement of; interfere with: *His illness upset our plans to go away for the weekend.* **3.** To disturb or make worried: *The news of his friend's death upset him greatly.* **4.** To make sick: *Onions upset my stomach.* **5.** To defeat unexpectedly in a game or contest: *Everyone was surprised when our team upset the state champions.*
—*noun* |ŭp′sĕt′|, *plural* **upsets** An unexpected defeat or victory in a game or contest: *If I win the race, it will be a real upset.*
—*adjective* |ŭp sĕt′| **1.** Knocked over or overturned: *Look at the upset sailboat.* **2.** Disturbed or worried: *She's still upset by the bad news.* **3.** Sick or ill: *I have an upset stomach.*

upside down A form of the adverb **upside-down.**

up·side-down |ŭp′sīd doun′| —*adjective* With the top part at the bottom: *upside-down letters. Can you read an upside-down page?*
—*adverb* **1.** With the top and bottom parts reversed in position: *She is holding the newspaper upside-down. He turned the table*

upholster

uproot
A tree uprooted by a storm

upside-down

upside-down. **2.** In or into great disorder or confusion: *He turned his room upside-down looking for his wallet.* Another form of this adverb is **upside down.**

up·stairs |ŭp′stârz′| —*adverb* **1.** Up the stairs: *He ran upstairs for a minute.* **2.** On or to an upper floor: *She's upstairs.*
—*adjective* |ŭp′stârz′| On an upper floor: *an upstairs bedroom.*
—*noun* |ŭp′stârz′| (Used with a singular verb.) The upper floor of a building: *He has the whole upstairs for himself.*

up·stream |ŭp′strēm′| —*adverb* In the direction toward the source of a stream or current: *She swam upstream.*
—*adjective* |ŭp′strēm′| At or toward the source of a stream or current: *an upstream current.*

up-to-date |ŭp′tə dāt′| —*adjective* Showing or using the latest improvements or style: *His new suit is really up-to-date.*

up·ward |ŭp′wərd| —*adverb* From a lower to a higher place, level, or condition: *The rocket flew upward and out of sight.* Another form of this adverb is **upwards.**
—*adjective* Moving from a lower to a higher place, level, or condition: *the upward flight of the hawk; an upward glance.*

up·wards |ŭp′wərdz| A form of the adverb **upward.**

u·ra·ni·um |yŏŏ rā′nē əm| —*noun* A heavy, radioactive silver-white metal that is used to produce nuclear energy. Uranium is one of the chemical elements.

U·ra·nus |yŏŏr′ə nəs| or |yŏŏ rā′nəs| —*noun* A planet of our solar system. It is the third largest planet and the seventh in distance from the sun.

ur·ban |ûr′bən| —*adjective* **1.** Of, living in, or located in a city: *urban traffic; urban housing.* **2.** Having to do with a city or city life: *urban problems.*

urge |ûrj| —*verb* **urged, urging 1.** To push or force onward: *He urged on the horse by shouting and cracking the whip.* **2.** To try to convince; plead with: *My parents urged me to go to college.* **3.** To recommend or argue for strongly: *The citizens urged the mayor to build a new hospital in the city.*
—*noun, plural* **urges** A strong desire; an impulse: *I had a sudden urge to go swimming.*

ur·gent |ûr′jənt| —*adjective* Needing immediate action or attention: *There's an urgent message for you.*

u·rine |yŏŏr′ĭn| —*noun* A clear or yellow-colored fluid containing body wastes. It is given off by the kidneys and then discharged by the body.

urn |ûrn| —*noun, plural* **urns 1.** A large vase set on a base. Certain ancient civilizations used them to hold the ashes of the dead. Today they are used for decoration. **2.** A large metal container with a faucet, used to make and serve coffee and tea.
♦ *These sound alike* **urn, earn.**

us |ŭs| —*pronoun* The pronoun **us** is the objective case of **we.** It is used: **1.** As the direct object of a verb: *She saw us on the street.* **2.** As the indirect object of a verb: *He told us the news.* **3.** As the object of a preposition: *Billy left the keys with us.*

US or **U.S.** An abbreviation for **United States.**

USA or **U.S.A.** An abbreviation for **United States of America.**

us·age |yŏŏ′sĭj| or |yŏŏ′zĭj| —*noun, plural* **usages 1.** A way of using something; treatment: *The radio was ruined by rough usage.* **2.** The usual way people use words: *The teacher said I had a problem with the usage of some verbs.*

urn
A coffee urn

ă	pat	ě	pet	î	fierce
ā	pay	ē	be	ŏ	pot
â	care	ĭ	pit	ō	go
ä	father	ī	pie	ô	paw, for

oi	oil	ŭ	cut	zh	vision
ŏŏ	book	û	fur	ə	ago, item,
ōō	boot	*th*	the		pencil, atom,
yŏŏ	abuse	th	thin		circus
ou	out	hw	which	ər	butter

use | yōoz | —*verb* **used, using 1.** To bring or put into service for a particular purpose: *Use the soap when you wash. When was the last time you used the library?* **2.** To do something often; make a habit of employing: *He uses a lot of sugar on his cereal.* **3.** To finish all or most of: *We've used all the clean towels. Did you use up the milk?*
—*noun* | yōos |, *plural* **uses 1.** The act of using: *We climbed up to the roof with the use of a ladder.* **2.** The condition of being used: *The telephone is in use right now.* **3.** The manner or way of using; usage: *Nobody has ever showed me the correct use of an ax.* **4.** The right or privilege of using something: *We were given the use of the basketball court for the whole afternoon.* **5.** The power or ability of using something: *He lost the use of his voice for a week.* **6.** The need to use something: *Do you have any use for this book?*

   Idiom **used to 1.** Accustomed to; familiar with: *It took me awhile to get used to wearing braces.* **2.** Did in the past: *We used to go to that restaurant a lot.*

used | yōozd | —*adjective* Not new; having been used by someone else: *She bought a used car.*

use·ful | yōos′fəl | —*adjective* Capable of being used for some purpose; helpful: *Those tools were useful when I was building the sandbox. Don't just sit there, make yourself useful.*

use·less | yōos′lĭs | —*adjective* **1.** Of little or no worth or help: *Why don't you throw out that useless old typewriter?* **2.** Having no result or effect: *It's useless to talk to her; she's not going to change her mind.*

ush·er | ŭsh′ər | —*noun, plural* **ushers** A person who leads or takes people to their seats in a theater, stadium, or at a wedding or other ceremony.
—*verb* **ushered, ushering** To act as an usher: *She ushered us to our seats in the front of the hall.*

u·su·al | yōo′zhōo əl | —*adjective* Common or ordinary; seen or happening all the time: *There was the usual confusion on the first day of school. It is usual for him to walk to work every day.*

U·tah | yōo′tô′ | or | yōo′tä′ | —*noun* A state in the western United States. The capital of Utah is Salt Lake City.

u·ten·sil | yōo tĕn′səl | —*noun, plural* **utensils** Any tool, device, or container that is used in doing or making something: *We have all the newest cooking utensils.*

u·til·i·ty | yōo tĭl′ĭ tē | —*noun, plural* **utilities 1.** The quality of being useful: *That old lawn mower has no utility anymore.* **2.** A company that provides a public service. Telephone and electric companies are utilities.

ut·most | ŭt′mōst′ | —*adjective* Of the highest or greatest degree or amount: *It is of the utmost importance that we get there on time.*
—*noun* The greatest possible effort or ability: *Jeannie put her utmost into her work and won the first prize.*

ut·ter¹ | ŭt′ər | —*verb* **uttered, uttering 1.** To speak; say: *Joseph uttered the unfamiliar words very slowly.* **2.** To express out loud; give out in a voice that can be heard: *He uttered a sigh as he sat down in the chair.*

ut·ter² | ŭt′ər | —*adjective* Complete or total: *The teacher said there must be utter silence in the room during the test.*

Utah
Utah comes from Ute, the name of an Indian tribe that lived mainly around the region that today includes the state of Utah.

utensil
Kitchen utensils

utter¹, utter²
Utter¹ comes from a Dutch word meaning "to give out, to make known, to reveal." **Utter²** comes from an old English word that originally meant "outer" and later came to mean "extreme." Both words spelled **utter** are related to **out**.

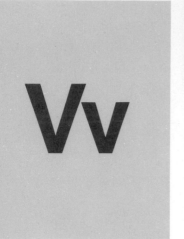

Vv

Phoenician — The letter V comes originally from a Phoenician symbol named *wāw*, which is also the basis for F, U, W, and Y.

Greek — The Greeks borrowed the symbol from the Phoenicians and changed its form. One form they used was called *upsilon*.

Roman — The Romans adapted the letter for carving. They did not always distinguish *u*, *v*, and *w*, so V was the only symbol used.

Medieval — The hand-written form of about 1,200 years ago became the basis of the modern written letter, both capital and small.

Modern — The pointed form of the modern printed capital and small letter was established in modern times.

vaccinate

ă	pat	ĕ	pet	î	fierce
ā	pay	ē	be	ŏ	pot
â	care	ĭ	pit	ō	go
ä	father	ī	pie	ô	paw, for
oi	oil	ŭ	cut	zh	vision
ŏŏ	book	û	fur	ə	ago, item,
ōō	boot	*th*	the		pencil, atom,
yōō	abuse	th	thin		circus
ou	out	hw	which	ər	butter

v or **V** |vē| —*noun, plural* **v's** or **V's** The twenty-second letter of the English alphabet.

va·cant |vā′kənt| —*adjective* **1.** Not occupied or taken; empty: *the vacant seats at the back of the room; a vacant room in a hotel; staring into vacant space.* **2.** Having no expression on the face; blank: *a vacant stare.*

va·ca·tion |vā kā′shən| —*noun, plural* **vacations** A time of rest from school, work, or other regular activities.
—*verb* **vacationed, vacationing** To take or spend a vacation: *They vacationed in the mountains last year.*

vac·ci·nate |văk′sə nāt′| —*verb* **vaccinated, vaccinating** To inoculate with a vaccine as a protection against a disease.

vac·ci·na·tion |văk′sə nā′shən| —*noun, plural* **vaccinations**
1. The act of giving a vaccine to protect against a disease: *the vaccination of children against measles.* **2.** A scar left on the skin where a vaccination was done: *Can you find your vaccination on your left arm?*

vac·cine |văk sēn′| —*noun, plural* **vaccines** Weak or dead disease germs that are injected into a person or animal as a protection against that disease. The injected germs are usually not enough to cause the disease, but can make a body build up a resistance to that disease. Vaccines have been used against diseases such as influenza, measles, and smallpox.

vac·u·um |văk′yōō əm| or |văk′yōōm| —*noun, plural* **vacuums**
1. A space that is so empty that it has nothing in it, not even the smallest bit of air. A perfect vacuum probably does not exist.
2. A space that is almost completely empty. Outer space and the inside of the picture tube of a television are vacuums that are almost perfect. **3.** A vacuum cleaner.
—*verb* **vacuumed, vacuuming** To clean with a vacuum cleaner: *He vacuumed the carpets.*

vacuum cleaner A machine with a kind of electric fan in it that sucks up dirt and dust into a bag or other container. Vacuum cleaners are used for cleaning floors and furniture.

vague |vāg| —*adjective* **vaguer, vaguest** Not clear nor distinct: *a vague description of the thief; a vague outline of a ship; a vague memory of her lost cousin.*

vain |vān| —*adjective* **vainer, vainest** **1.** Without success; of no use: *our vain attempt to save the old library.* **2.** Of no real worth; empty; idle: *his vain bragging about the day he met the football star.* **3.** Thinking too much of oneself or one's appearance: *The vain little man stood looking in the mirror for hours.*

♦ *These sound alike* **vain, vane, vein.**

Idiom **in vain** Without success: *He tried in vain to catch the ball, but it had been thrown too far.*

val·en·tine |văl′ən tīn′| —*noun, plural* **valentines** **1.** A card sent to someone one likes or loves on Valentine's Day. **2.** A person chosen to be one's sweetheart on Valentine's Day. **3.** A figure in the shape of a heart, often used as a symbol of love or affection.

Val·en·tine's Day |văl′ən tīnz′| February 14, a day when people send valentines to their friends and sweethearts.

val·iant |văl′yənt| —*adjective* Acting with or showing courage; brave: *Her valiant effort saved the drowning child.*

val·id |văl′ĭd| —*adjective* **1.** Having facts, evidence, and good judgment as support; sound: *her valid argument that they needed a new leader.* **2.** Able to be accepted according to the law or rules; legal: *Your library card is not valid after the date stamped on it.*

val·ley |văl′ē| —*noun, plural* **valleys** **1.** A long, narrow area of low land between mountains or hills, often with a river running along the bottom. **2.** A large region of land that is drained by one river system.

val·u·a·ble |văl′yōō ə bəl| or |văl′yə bəl| —*adjective* **1.** Worth much money: *a valuable painting; a valuable ring.* **2.** Of great importance, use, or service: *Tim was named the team's most valuable player. Aspirin is valuable for reducing fever.*
—*noun, plural* **valuables** Something one owns that is worth very much: *She keeps her silverware and other valuables locked up.*

val·ue |văl′yōō| —*noun, plural* **values** **1.** What something is worth in exchange for something else: *Those shoes will give you good value for your money.* **2.** The quality that makes something worth having; importance or use: *the value of a good education; a cheap ring that has value only because of the memories it brings to mind.*
—*verb* **valued, valuing** **1.** To give an estimate of how much money something is worth: *The jeweler valued the old watch at $100.* **2.** To consider to be of great worth or importance: *I value your advice.*

valve |vălv| —*noun, plural* **valves** **1.** A device that blocks or uncovers openings to control the flow of liquids, gases, or loose materials through pipes or channels: *He turned the valve to start the sprinkler.* **2.** One of the two parts of the shell of an animal like a clam, oyster, or scallop.

vam·pire |văm′pīr′| —*noun, plural* **vampires** In folk tales and legends, a dead body that is supposed to rise from its grave at night so that it might drink the blood of living people.

van |văn| —*noun, plural* **vans** A covered truck or wagon for moving goods, animals, or furniture. Some vans are also used for camping and for living in while traveling around the country.

vane |vān| —*noun, plural* **vanes** **1.** A thin, flat piece of wood or metal that turns to show the direction the wind is moving. **2.** A

valentine

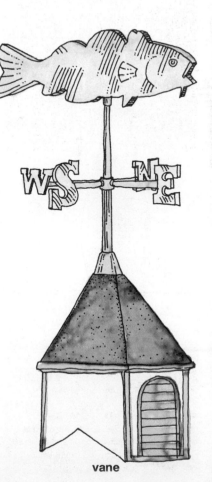

vane

thin, flat blade of a windmill, fan, or other machine.

♦ *These sound alike* **vane, vain, vein.**

va·nil·la |və **nĭl′**ə| —*noun, plural* **vanillas** **1.** A tropical orchid with long seed pods that look like beans. **2.** A flavoring made from the dried seed pods of this plant. Vanilla is used in ice cream, cakes, cookies, puddings, and many other sweets. —*adjective* Having vanilla as the main flavor: *a vanilla pudding; vanilla ice cream.*

van·ish |**văn′**ĭsh| —*verb* **vanished, vanishing** **1.** To disappear; become invisible: *The sun vanished behind a cloud. Her smile vanished when she heard the bad news.* **2.** To stop existing; become extinct: *Dinosaurs vanished many thousands of years ago.*

van·i·ty |**văn′**ĭ tē| —*noun, plural* **vanities** Too much pride in one's looks or ability; conceit: *His vanity makes him think all the girls are in love with him.*

va·por |**vā′**pər| —*noun, plural* **vapors** **1.** Fine particles of matter in the air. Mist, steam, fumes, and smoke are all forms of vapor. **2.** A gas formed from something that is a solid or a liquid at normal temperatures: *Clouds are made of water vapor.*

var·i·a·ble |**vâr′**ē ə bəl| —*adjective* Likely to change or be changed; not staying the same: *a variable climate; her variable moods.* —*noun, plural* **variables** Something that is not always the same: *The weather is one variable that determines whether people go to the park.*

var·i·a·tion |vâr′ē **ā′**shən| —*noun, plural* **variations** **1.** A change from the normal or usual: *This new restaurant is a pleasant variation from the one we always go to. The days were boring, with very little variation.* **2.** Something that is similar to another thing, but with slight changes: *The play is a variation on the fairy tale about a sleeping princess.*

var·ied |**vâr′**ēd| —*adjective* Of many kinds or forms; full of variety: *a varied assortment of candies.*

va·ri·e·ty |və **rī′**ĭ tē| —*noun, plural* **varieties** **1.** An amount of difference or change that keeps things from being dull: *We enjoy variety in our meals.* **2.** A number of different kinds within the same group; an assortment: *a variety of activities; a variety of books to read.* **3.** A kind; type: *diseases of every variety; a small yellow variety of rose.*

var·i·ous |**vâr′**ē əs| —*adjective* **1.a.** Of different kinds: *We were unable to go for various reasons.* **b.** Different; not alike: *flowers as various as the rose, daisy, and carnation.* **2.** More than one; several: *He spoke to various members of the club.*

var·nish |**vär′**nĭsh| —*noun, plural* **varnishes** A kind of paint that dries to leave a thin, hard, shiny, clear surface: *He bought a small can of varnish. The bookcase has a bright varnish.* —*verb* **varnished, varnishing** To cover or coat with a varnish: *Let's varnish the furniture.*

var·y |**vâr′**ē| —*verb* **varied, varying, varies** **1.** To be or become different; change: *The temperature varies from day to day. Prices often vary with the season.* **2.** To make different; give variety to: *She varies the ribbons in her hair to match her dresses.*

vase |vās| *or* |vāz| *or* |väz| —*noun, plural* **vases** A container, usually tall and round, used to hold flowers or to be an ornament. Vases may be made of china, glass, metal, or other materials.

Vas·e·line |**văs′**ə lēn′| *or* |văs′ə **lēn′**| —*noun* A trademark for

vase

ă	pat	ĕ	pet	î	fierce
ā	pay	ē	be	ŏ	pot
â	care	ĭ	pit	ō	go
ä	father	ī	pie	ô	paw, for
oi	oil	ŭ	cut	zh	vision
ōō	book	û	fur	ə	ago, item,
ōō	boot	*th*	the		pencil, atom,
yōō	abuse	th	thin		circus
ou	out	hw	which	ər	butter

a kind of jelly made from petroleum, used for rubbing into the skin, as a base for medicines, and for protecting metal parts in machinery.

vast | văst | or | väst | —*adjective* **vaster, vastest** Very great in area, size, or amount; extremely large: *They were afloat on the vast ocean.*

vat | văt | —*noun, plural* **vats** A large tank or tub used for storing liquids.

vault¹ | vôlt | —*noun, plural* **vaults** A room or compartment with strong walls and good locks, used for keeping valuables safe: *She keeps her jewelry in the bank's vault.*

vault² | vôlt | —*verb* **vaulted, vaulting** To jump or leap over, especially with the help of one's hands or a pole: *She vaulted over the brick fence and ran off.*

—*noun, plural* **vaults** A high leap or jump made with the help of one's hands or a pole: *The athlete set the record for the pole vault.*

veal | vēl | —*noun* The meat of a calf.

veg·e·ta·ble | vĕj′tə bəl | or | vĕj′ĭ tə bəl | —*noun, plural* **vegetables 1.** A plant whose roots, leaves, stems, flowers, or sometimes seeds or pods are used as food. Turnips, cabbage, onions, potatoes, and broccoli are vegetables. Some fruits, such as tomatoes, cucumbers, and squash, are also often called vegetables. **2.** The parts of such plants that are used for food: *He chose peas and carrots for his vegetables.*

—*adjective* **1.** Of or from a plant or plants; not animal nor mineral: *a vegetable oil; vegetable dyes made from roots and bark.* **2.** Made of or containing vegetables: *a bowl of vegetable soup; a vegetable garden.*

veg·e·tar·i·an | vĕj′ĭ târ′ē ən | —*noun, plural* **vegetarians** A person or animal that eats food from plants and does not eat meat: *Rabbits are vegetarians.*

—*adjective* Eating, serving, or made of things from plants: *a vegetarian animal; a vegetarian restaurant; a vegetarian dinner.*

veg·e·ta·tion | vĕj′ĭ tā′shən | —*noun* Plants or plant life: *the thick vegetation of the forest.*

ve·hi·cle | vē′ĭ kəl | —*noun, plural* **vehicles** Anything used for moving people or goods; a means of transportation. Cars, trucks, trains, wagons, bicycles, airplanes, rockets, sleds, and ships are all vehicles.

veil | vāl | —*noun, plural* **veils 1.** A piece of fabric, often fine and thin, worn over the head or face by a woman: *a bridal veil; a hat with a veil.* **2.** Anything that covers or hides like a curtain: *a veil of secrecy; a veil of fog over the city.*

—*verb* **veiled, veiling 1.** To cover with a veil: *In some countries of Asia and Africa, women veil their faces.* **2.** To hide, cover, or disguise as if with a veil: *She could not veil her dislike for the man.*

vein | vān | —*noun, plural* **veins 1.** A blood vessel that carries blood to the heart from other parts of the body. **2.** One of the narrow tubes in an insect's wing or a leaf. **3.** A long deposit of an ore or a mineral in the earth: *a vein of silver ore; a vein of coal.* **4.** A long streak of color in marble, wood, or other material: *pink marble with gray veins.* **5.** A manner or mood: *He spoke in a cheerful vein.*

♦ *These sound alike* **vein, vain, vane.**

ve·loc·i·ty | və lŏs′ĭ tē | —*noun, plural* **velocities** The rate at which something moves in a given direction; speed: *The velocity of*

vault¹, vault²

Vault¹ comes from an old French word that came from a Latin word meaning "something bent or arched." The Latin noun came from a verb that meant "to turn or roll." Vault² originally meant "to leap onto a horse." It can also be traced back through French ("to turn a horse" and "to leap") to Latin ("to turn"). Thus **vault¹** and **vault²** are distant cousins.

vault¹

vault²

veil

vending machine

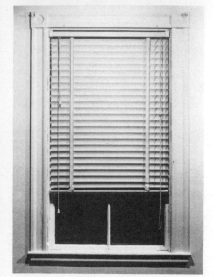

Venetian blind

sound changes depending on what it is passing through.

vel·vet | věl′vĭt | —*noun, plural* **velvets** A soft, smooth cloth with a thick pile. Velvets are made of silk, rayon, nylon, and other materials.

vel·vet·y | věl′vĭ tē | —*adjective* Soft and smooth to touch, taste, or hear: *a velvety fur; a velvety soup; a velvety voice.*

ven·der | věn′dər | —*noun, plural* **venders** A form of the word **vendor.**

vend·ing machine | věn′dĭng | A machine that delivers small items when one or more coins are put into a slot. Vending machines are used to sell drinks, candy, gum, sandwiches, detergents, stamps, and many other things.

ven·dor | věn′dər | —*noun, plural* **vendors** A person who sells goods, sometimes from a cart on wheels; a salesman or peddler: *the hot dog vendor in the park; a newspaper vendor.* Another form of this word is **vender.**

Ve·ne·tian blind | və nē′shən | A window blind with many horizontal slats that can be set at various angles to let in more or less light. The slats can also be raised, lowered, or set at any given height.

ven·om | věn′əm | —*noun, plural* **venoms** The poison that some snakes, spiders, scorpions, insects, or other creatures can transfer through a bite or sting to a person or another animal.

vent | věnt | —*noun, plural* **vents** An opening for gas, liquid, or vapor to escape or for air to enter: *air-conditioning vents in the ceiling.*

—*verb* **vented, venting** To let out; express: *They vented their anger by kicking garbage cans.*

ven·ti·la·tion | věn′tl ā′shən | —*noun* The act or process of causing fresh air to enter or move about: *Windows on three sides of the house provide good ventilation.*

ven·tri·cle | věn′trĭ kəl | —*noun, plural* **ventricles** Either of the two chambers of the heart that pump blood into the arteries.

ven·tril·o·quist | věn **trĭl**′ə kwĭst | —*noun, plural* **ventriloquists** A person who can make sounds with the voice so that they seem to come from somewhere else. Many ventriloquists work with puppets or dummies.

ven·ture | věn′chər | —*noun, plural* **ventures** A task or action that involves risks and possible danger: *astronauts on the first venture to the moon.*

—*verb* **ventured, venturing** **1.** To take a risk with; expose to possible loss or danger: *He ventured all his money on the new business.* **2.** To dare to say: *She ventured an opinion about the new movie.*

Ve·nus | vē′nəs | —*noun* A planet of our solar system. It is the second in order from the sun. Venus is brighter than any other natural object in the sky except the sun and the moon.

ve·ran·dah or **ve·ran·da** | və **răn**′də | —*noun, plural* **verandahs** or **verandas** A porch or balcony with a roof.

verb | vûrb | —*noun, plural* **verbs** Any of a class of words that express state of being or action. For example, the words *be, run,* and *happen* are verbs.

verb·al | vûr′bəl | —*adjective* **1.** Of or having to do with words: *He is a writer with such strong verbal abilities that he can be entertaining on almost any subject.* **2.** Expressed in words; not written; oral: *It was just a verbal agreement, but it has the same*

ă	pat	ĕ	pet	î	fierce
ā	pay	ē	be	ŏ	pot
â	care	ĭ	pit	ō	go
ä	father	ī	pie	ô	paw, for
oi	oil	ŭ	cut	zh	vision
ōŏ	book	û	fur	ə	ago, item,
ōō	boot	*th*	the		pencil, atom,
yōō	abuse	th	thin		circus
ou	out	hw	which	ər	butter

force as if you had written it down. **3.** Of a verb: *verbal endings such as -ed and -ing.*

—noun, plural **verbals** A grammatical construction that contains a verb. A verbal may be a verb or it may be made up of a verb plus other words. For example, in the sentences *It rained, The train arrived late,* and *I locked the car,* the words *rained, arrived late,* and *locked the car* are verbals.

ver·dict | **vûr′**dĭkt′ | *—noun, plural* **verdicts** The decision made by a jury at the end of a trial: *The foreman read the verdict, "Guilty as charged."*

ver·min | **vûr′**mĭn | *—noun, plural* **vermin** An insect or small animal that is annoying or destructive or harmful to health. Cockroaches and rats are vermin.

Ver·mont | vər **mŏnt′** | A state in the northeastern United States. The capital of Vermont is Montpelier.

ver·sa·tile | **vûr′**sə tĭl | or | **vûr′**sə tīl′ | *—adjective* **1.** Able to do many things well: *a versatile athlete who swims, skis, and plays baseball.* **2.** Having many different uses: *Potatoes are versatile vegetables that can be baked and used in stews and salads.*

verse | vûrs | *—noun, plural* **verses** **1.** Words put together with rhythm or rhyme or both; poetry: *That play is written in verse.* **2.** One section or stanza of a poem or song: *The song has three verses, but I know only the first two.* **3.** One line of poetry: *What can I rhyme with the verse "I saw a ship upon the sea"?* **4.** A numbered section of a chapter of the Bible.

ver·sion | **vûr′**zhən | or | **vûr′**shən | *—noun, plural* **versions** **1.** A description or an account from one particular point of view: *Each driver had his own version of the accident.* **2.** A particular translation into another language: *a new English version of the famous Spanish poem.*

ver·te·bra | **vûr′**tə brə | *—noun, plural* **vertebras** Any of the small bones that make up the backbone of a person or animal.

ver·te·brate | **vûr′**tə brāt′ | or | **vûr′**tə brĭt | *—noun, plural* **vertebrates** Any animal that has a backbone. Fish, amphibians, reptiles, birds, and mammals are all vertebrates.

—adjective Having a backbone: *A snake is a vertebrate animal.*

ver·ti·cal | **vûr′**tĭ kəl | *—adjective* Straight up and down; at a right angle to the horizon; upright: *A flagpole is a vertical pole.*

ver·y | **vĕr′**ē | *—adverb* **1.** In a high degree; extremely: *I am very happy. It is very cold today.* **2.** Truly; indeed. Used before the superlative form of an adjective to make its meaning stronger: *the very best coat in the store.* **3.** Exactly: *the very same car we saw.*

—adjective **1.** Absolute: *the very edge of the cliff.* **2.** Exactly the same; identical: *That is the very thing I was about to say.* **3.** Nothing more than; mere: *The very mention of his name frightened the boys.* **4.** Precise; exact: *The tree is in the very center of town.*

ves·sel | **vĕs′**əl | *—noun, plural* **vessels** **1.** A ship or large boat: *The sailors boarded the vessel that would be their home for many months.* **2.** A hollow container, such as a bowl, pitcher, jar, or tank, that can hold liquids. **3.** A narrow tube in a body or a plant through which liquids flow: *Veins and arteries are blood vessels.*

vest | vĕst | *—noun, plural* **vests** A short jacket without sleeves or collar, worn over a shirt or a blouse.

—verb **vested, vesting** To give official power or authority to: *The Constitution vests the President with certain rights and powers.*

vet·er·an | **vĕt′**ər ən | or | **vĕt′**rən | *—noun, plural* **veterans** **1.** A

vest

person who has served in the armed forces: *He was a veteran of two wars.* **2.** A person who has had much experience in a profession or activity: *a veteran of the stage.*

—*adjective* Having had much experience: *a veteran actor.*

vet·er·i·nar·i·an |vĕt′ər ə **nâr**′ē ən| or |vĕt′rə **nâr**′ē ən| —*noun, plural* **veterinarians** A person who is trained and qualified to give medical care to animals.

ve·to |vē′tō| —*noun, plural* **vetoes** **1.** The right or power to keep a proposed law from becoming a law: *The President of the United States has the power of veto.* **2.** The use of this power: *the governor's veto of the bill to raise taxes.*

—*verb* **vetoed, vetoing, vetoes** **1.** To prevent a proposed law from becoming a law by using the power of veto: *The President vetoed the new tax law.* **2.** To refuse to consent to; forbid: *Her parents vetoed her plan to join the circus.*

vi·a |vī′ə| or |vē′ə| —*preposition* By way of: *I went home via the old road. He went home via the shopping center.*

vi·brate |vī′brāt′| —*verb* **vibrated, vibrating** To move or cause to move back and forth rapidly: *Violin strings vibrate to make sounds. He vibrated the string by plucking it.*

vi·bra·tion |vī **brā**′shən| —*noun, plural* **vibrations** A very rapid movement back and forth: *the vibration of a violin's string.*

vice president |vīs| An officer who ranks just below a president and who takes the place of a president who is absent or ill, or who has resigned or died. Another form of this phrase is **vice-president.**

vice-president |vīs′**prĕz**′ĭ dənt| —*noun, plural* **vice-presidents** A form of the phrase **vice president.**

vi·ce ver·sa |vī′sə **vûr**′sə| or |vīs′**vûr**′sə| Just the opposite is true too; the other way around also: *We help our neighbors and vice versa.*

vi·cin·i·ty |vĭ **sĭn**′ĭ tē| —*noun, plural* **vicinities** The nearby or surrounding area or region: *Is there a high school in the vicinity of your house?*

vi·cious |vĭsh′əs| —*adjective* **1.** Full of spite; cruel; mean: *She told vicious lies about her teacher.* **2.** Marked by evil; wicked: *a vicious crime.* **3.** Savage and dangerous: *a vicious shark.*

vic·tim |vĭk′tĭm| —*noun, plural* **victims** **1.** A person or animal that is harmed or killed by another person or animal or by an accident or a disease: *Before a vaccine was developed, many people were victims of polio. The deer became the victim of a hungry lion.* **2.** Someone who suffers or has difficulty because of tricks, cheating, teasing, or a misunderstanding: *She was the victim of a cruel joke. The thief was always looking for a victim.*

Vic·to·ri·a |vĭk **tôr**′ē ə| or |vĭk **tōr**′ē ə| The capital of British Columbia.

vic·to·ri·ous |vĭk **tôr**′ē əs| or |vĭk **tōr**′ē əs| —*adjective* **1.** Being the winner in a war, contest, or struggle: *The victorious team paraded through the town.* **2.** Of or resulting in victory: *a victorious cheer; the army's victorious advance.*

vic·to·ry |vĭk′tə rē| —*noun, plural* **victories** The winning of a war, contest, or struggle against an opponent; triumph: *We were happy about our team's victory in the math contest.*

vid·e·o |vĭd′ē ō| —*noun* The part of a television broadcast or signal that can be seen, not the part that is heard: *We still get the video on our TV set, but the sound is gone.*

ă	pat	ĕ	pet	î	fierce
ā	pay	ē	be	ŏ	pot
â	care	ĭ	pit	ō	go
ä	father	ī	pie	ô	paw, for
oi	oil	ŭ	cut	zh	vision
ŏŏ	book	û	fur	ə	ago, item,
ōō	boot	*th*	the		pencil, atom,
yōō	abuse	th	thin		circus
ou	out	hw	which	ər	butter

video tape A special kind of magnetic recording tape used to record the picture and sound of television programs.

view |vyōō| —*noun, plural* **views 1.** The act of seeing something; sight: *When the ship turned into the harbor, the passengers had their first view of the city.* **2.** A scene: *a lovely view from the window.* **3.** The area that is as far as the eye can see: *The airplane disappeared from view.* **4.** A way of showing or seeing something from a particular position or angle: *The statue looks different from each view.* **5.** An opinion; idea: *She gave us her views on education.*
—*verb* **viewed, viewing 1.** To look at: *They viewed the stars through a telescope.* **2.** To consider; regard: *He viewed her as a nuisance.*

view·er |vyōō′ər| —*noun, plural* **viewers 1.** A person who views or looks at something. **2.** A device used to make photographs or images larger so that they can be easily seen.

view·point |vyōō′point′| —*noun, plural* **viewpoints 1.** A way of thinking about something; point of view: *From my viewpoint, the money spent on an education is worthwhile.* **2.** The place or position from which one looks at something: *From her viewpoint in the tower, she could see the fields and houses all around.*

vig·or |vĭg′ər| —*noun* Physical energy or strength: *a healthy, active girl, full of vigor.*

vig·o·rous |vĭg′ər əs| —*adjective* Full of or done with vigor; lively: *vigorous arguments against nuclear power; vigorous exercise that makes people healthy.*

Vi·king |vī′kĭng| —*noun, plural* **Vikings** One of a group of Scandinavian people from the northwestern coast of Europe who sailed along and raided the coasts of Europe from the ninth to eleventh centuries and who made voyages to the New World.

vil·lage |vĭl′ĭj| —*noun, plural* **villages** A group of houses that make up a community smaller than a town.

vil·lain |vĭl′ən| —*noun, plural* **villains** A person or story character who is wicked or evil: *A wolf is the villain of many fairy tales.*

vine |vīn| —*noun, plural* **vines 1.** A plant with a stem that climbs on, creeps along, twines around, or clings to something for support. **2.** A grapevine.

vin·e·gar |vĭn′ĭ gər| —*noun, plural* **vinegars** A sour liquid that is made from wine, cider, or other liquids that have fermented past the alcohol stage. Vinegar is used in flavoring and preserving foods and in salad dressings, as well as in removing stains and odors.

vine·yard |vĭn′yərd| —*noun, plural* **vineyards** A piece of land on which grapevines are grown.

vi·nyl |vī′nəl| —*noun, plural* **vinyls** Any of several plastics that are tough and shiny and bend easily. Vinyls are used for boots, raincoats, tops of counters, floorings, and phonograph records.

vi·o·la |vē ō′lə| or |vī ō′lə| —*noun, plural* **violas** A stringed musical instrument that is like a violin but larger. A viola has a deeper, mellower tone than a violin.

vi·o·late |vī′ə lāt′| —*verb* **violated, violating** To break; act contrary to; disregard: *He violated the law when he tried to carry a gun onto the airplane. She violated her promise and left without me.*

vi·o·lence |vī′ə ləns| —*noun* **1.** Physical force that can or does cause damage or injury: *crimes of violence; the violence of the*

Viking

vineyard

viola

hurricane. **2.** Breaking the law in a way that causes injury or damage: *Their protests led to violence.*

vi·o·lent | **vī′ə lənt** | —*adjective* **1.** Showing, having, or resulting from great physical force or rough action: *a violent attack; a violent storm.* **2.** Showing or having strong feelings: *a violent temper.*

vi·o·let | **vī′ə lĭt** | —*noun, plural* **violets** **1.** Any of several plants that grow close to the ground and have flowers that are bluish purple or sometimes yellow or white. **2.** A bluish-purple color: *The blouse was a deep violet.*
—*adjective* Bluish purple: *her violet eyes; a violet silk.*

vi·o·lin | **vī′ə lĭn′** | —*noun, plural* **violins** A musical instrument that has four strings and is played with a bow or by plucking with the fingers. A violin has a high, clear sound.

vir·gin | **vûr′ jĭn** | —*adjective* In the original or natural state; not having been used before, touched, or explored: *virgin forests; virgin wool; virgin snow.*

Vir·gin·ia | **vər jĭn′yə** | A state in the eastern United States. The capital of Virginia is Richmond.

vir·tu·al | **vûr′ chōo əl** | —*adjective* In reality; actual; for all practical purposes although not in name or form: *He has virtual control over all sales of ice cream in the area.*

vir·tu·al·ly | **vûr′ chōo ə lē** | —*adverb* For the most part: *The mountain lion is virtually extinct in the eastern states.*

vir·tue | **vûr′ chōo** | —*noun, plural* **virtues** **1.** The state or condition of being morally good: *A leader should be a person of intelligence and virtue.* **2.** A particular example of moral goodness: *Patience is a virtue that few people possess.* **3.** A particular good quality; an advantage: *a machine with the virtue of being attractive as well as useful.*

vi·rus | **vī′rəs** | —*noun, plural* **viruses** A form of living matter that is too small to be seen through an ordinary microscope. Viruses cause diseases in human beings, animals, and plants. Some human diseases caused by viruses are measles, polio, mumps, and the common cold.

vise | **vīs** | —*noun, plural* **vises** A device with a pair of jaws that can be widened or narrowed by turning a screw or moving lever. A vise is used to hold things in position for someone to work on.

vis·i·ble | **vĭz′ə bəl** | —*adjective* **1.** Capable of being seen: *Only one ninth of an iceberg is visible above water.* **2.** Easily noticed; clear: *The child showed visible signs of impatience.*

vi·sion | **vĭzh′ən** | —*noun, plural* **visions** **1.** The sense of sight; the ability to see: *These eyeglasses improve my vision.* **2.** The ability to look ahead into the future; foresight: *The pioneers had the vision to turn the desert into fertile farmland.* **3.** An image in the mind produced by the imagination: *He had visions of being rich and famous.* **4.** Something that is seen, especially something attractive: *She was a vision of beauty in her ballet costume.*

vis·it | **vĭz′ĭt** | —*verb* **visited, visiting** **1.** To go or come to see for a while: *When will you visit your family? He visited his doctor for a checkup.* **2.** To stay with as a guest: *My cousin is visiting us for the summer.* **3.** To talk or chat: *He had to stay after school because he had been visiting too much with his classmates.*
—*noun, plural* **visits** An act or an example of visiting; a short call or stay: *Please stay longer on your next visit.*

vis·i·tor | **vĭz′ĭ tər** | —*noun, plural* **visitors** Someone who visits: *He doesn't live here; he's just a visitor.*

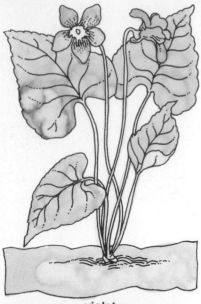

violet

violin

Virginia
Virginia was named for Queen Elizabeth I of England, who was known by her subjects as "the Virgin Queen."

ă	pat	ĕ	pet	î	fierce
ā	pay	ē	be	ŏ	pot
â	care	ĭ	pit	ō	go
ä	father	ī	pie	ô	paw, for
oi	oil	ŭ	cut	zh	vision
ōō	book	û	fur	ə	ago, item,
ōō	boot	*th*	the		pencil, atom,
yōō	abuse	th	thin		circus
ou	out	hw	which	ər	butter

vi·sor | vī′zər | or | vĭz′ər | —*noun, plural* **visors** A part that sticks out in front of a cap or motorcycle helmet to protect the eyes from sun, wind, or rain.

vis·u·al | vĭzh′ōō əl | —*adjective* **1.** Of, for, or serving the sense of sight: *The movie had many unusual visual effects.* **2.** Done with the help of the eyes, but without instruments: *The pilot made a visual landing.* **3.** Designed to communicate through the sense of sight: *The speaker used charts, posters, and other visual aids.*

vi·tal | vīt′l | —*adjective* **1.** Having to do with life or living things: *We thought the animal was dead, but it showed some vital signs.* **2.** Needed for life: *The heart is a vital organ.* **3.** Very important; essential: *Intelligent voting is vital to a democracy.*

vi·ta·min | vī′tə mĭn | —*noun, plural* **vitamins** Any of several substances that are needed for animals to continue living and growing in a normal way. Vitamins are found in food and are also manufactured in pills, liquids, and capsules.

viv·id | vĭv′ĭd | —*adjective* **1.** Bright and distinct; sharp; intense: *The dress was a vivid blue.* **2.** Bringing images to the mind that are very much like real life: *The book gave a vivid description of pioneer life.* **3.** Active: *a vivid imagination.* **4.** Distinct and clear: *her vivid memories of last year's Thanksgiving.*

vo·cab·u·lar·y | vō kăb′yə lĕr′ē | —*noun, plural* **vocabularies** **1.** All the words of a language: *English contains a large vocabulary.* **2.** All the words used by a particular person or group: *She has a large vocabulary for someone her age.* **3.** A list of words and phrases, usually in alphabetical order with definitions: *Does your science book have a vocabulary at the back?*

vo·cal | vō′kəl | —*adjective* **1.** Of or made by the voice: *A cricket's chirps are not vocal; they are made by rubbing the legs.* **2.** Meant to be sung: *vocal music.*

vocal cords | kôrdz | A pair of bands or folds of muscle in the larynx that stretch and vibrate when air from the lungs is forced between them to produce the sound of the voice.

voice | vois | —*noun, plural* **voices** **1.** The particular sounds a person makes by using the mouth and vocal cords in speaking and singing: *Can you recognize my voice on the telephone?* **2.** The ability to produce a sound with the mouth and vocal cords: *He caught a cold and lost his voice. He has a strong voice.* **3.** Expression of feelings or thoughts: *She gave voice to her anger.* **4.** The right or opportunity to express an opinion or choice: *The children had no voice in choosing a place to live.*
—*verb* **voiced, voicing** To give expression to: *At last he had a chance to voice his feelings.*

vol·can·ic | vŏl kăn′ĭk | —*adjective* Of, like, or produced by a volcano: *harsh volcanic smoke; lava and other volcanic materials.*

vol·ca·no | vŏl kā′nō | —*noun, plural* **volcanoes** or **volcanos** **1.** An opening in the crust of the earth through which molten rock, dust, ash, and hot gases are thrown. **2.** A mountain formed by the action of such an opening.

vol·ley·ball | vŏl′ē bôl′ | —*noun, plural* **volleyballs** **1.** A game played between two teams who use their hands to hit a ball back and forth over a net and try not to let the ball touch the ground. **2.** The ball used in this game. A volleyball is a little smaller and lighter than a basketball.

volt | vōlt | —*noun, plural* **volts** A unit of force for measuring an electric current.

visor
On General Douglas MacArthur's hat

volleyball

volt·age | vōl′tĭj | —*noun, plural* **voltages** The amount of force of an electric current, measured in volts.

vol·ume | vŏl′yōom | or | vŏl′yəm | —*noun, plural* **volumes** **1.** A book: *She bought several new volumes of poetry.* **2.** One book of a set: *Look it up in volume four of your encyclopedia.* **3.** The measure or size of how much space an object takes up; the size of a region of space: *A tall, skinny glass may have the same volume as a short, fat glass.* **4.** The force or intensity of sound; quality of being loud: *They insist on playing their radios at high volume.*

vol·un·tar·y | vŏl′ən tĕr′ē | —*adjective* **1.** Made, done, or given of one's own free will; not required: *You may make a voluntary donation to the charity.* **2.** Controlled by the will: *Most of the muscles in the arm are voluntary muscles, but the heart's muscles are not voluntary.*

vol·un·teer | vŏl′ən tîr′ | —*noun, plural* **volunteers** **1.** Someone who does a job or gives service by free will, usually without pay: *Some volunteers record books for blind people. The telephone is answered by volunteers.* **2.** A person who enlists in the armed forces.

—*adjective* Having to do with or made up of volunteers: *volunteer service; a volunteer fire department.*

—*verb* **volunteered, volunteering** To give or offer, usually without being asked: *She volunteered her services to the school library. He volunteered to lead the scout troop. He volunteered an opinion about the new television show.*

vote | vōt | —*noun, plural* **votes** **1.** A choice made in an election: *We will take a vote to see who will be chairman.* **2.** The form in which the choice is made, such as a ballot, show of hands, or other method: *They wanted a secret vote.* **3.** The right to make a choice in an election: *Only members of the team have a vote.*

—*verb* **voted, voting** **1.** To express one's choice by a vote; cast a ballot: *He voted early. She voted for the winner.* **2.** To make available by a vote: *They voted money for flood control.*

vot·er | vō′tər | —*noun, plural* **voters** A person who votes or has a right to vote.

vow | vou | —*noun, plural* **vows** A solemn promise or pledge: *He made a vow to use his invention for the good of humanity.*

—*verb* **vowed, vowing** To make a solemn promise or pledge: *She vowed she would never smoke.*

vow·el | vou′əl | —*noun, plural* **vowels** **1.** A speech sound usually made with the vocal cords vibrating and with the breath passing through the mouth freely, without being cut off or blocked off. A vowel is usually the central or loudest part of a syllable. **2.** A letter that represents such a sound. The vowels in English are *a, e, i, o, u,* and sometimes *y.*

voy·age | voi′ĭj | —*noun, plural* **voyages** A long journey to a distant place, made on a ship, boat, aircraft, or spacecraft: *a voyage across the ocean; a voyage to a distant planet.*

—*verb* **voyaged, voyaging** To make a voyage: *They voyaged for many days before they sighted land.*

vul·gar | vŭl′gər | —*adjective* Having very poor taste or manners; crude; coarse: *He has vulgar table habits. She tells vulgar stories that embarrass people.*

vul·ture | vŭl′chər | —*noun, plural* **vultures** Any of several large birds that usually have dark feathers and a bare head and neck. Vultures feed on the flesh of dead animals.

vulture

ă	pat	ĕ	pet	î	fierce
ā	pay	ē	be	ŏ	pot
â	care	ĭ	pit	ō	go
ä	father	ī	pie	ô	paw, for
oi	oil	ŭ	cut	zh	vision
ŏŏ	book	û	fur	ə	ago, item,
ōō	boot	*th*	the		pencil, atom,
yōō	abuse	th	thin		circus
ou	out	hw	which	ər	butter

Y Phoenician — The letter *W*, like *V*, comes originally from a Phoenician symbol named *wāw*, which is also the basis for *F*, *U*, and *Y*.

V Greek — The Greeks borrowed the symbol from the Phoenicians and changed its form. One form they used was called *upsilon*.

V Roman — The Romans adapted the letter for carving. They did not always distinguish *u*, *v*, and *w*, so *V* was the only symbol used.

ω Medieval — The hand-written form of about 1,200 years ago is a "double *u*." It is the basis of the modern written letter.

Ww Modern — The modern printed capital and small letters are based on the Roman capital *V*.

w or **W** |dŭb′əl yōō′| or |dŭb′əl yŏŏ′| —*noun, plural* **w's** or **W's** The twenty-third letter of the English alphabet.

wad |wŏd| —*noun, plural* **wads** **1.** A small, soft piece of material, such as cotton or chewing gum, pressed into a lump. **2.** A tight roll of paper or paper money: *a wad of ten dollar bills.* —*verb* **wadded, wadding** **1.** To squeeze, roll, or crush into a wad: *She wadded up the paper and threw it in the garbage.* **2.** To plug or stuff with a wad or wads: *He had to wad his ear with cotton.*

wad·dle |wŏd′l| —*verb* **waddled, waddling** To walk with short steps that tilt or sway the body from side to side, as a duck does: *The baby waddled into the kitchen.* —*noun, plural* **waddles** A clumsy or swaying walk.

wade |wād| —*verb* **waded, wading** **1.** To walk in or through water, mud, snow, or any other substance that covers the feet or keeps them from moving freely: *The children waded across the river.* **2.** To move or make one's way through slowly and with difficulty: *She waded through the book.*

wa·fer |wā′fər| —*noun, plural* **wafers** A small, thin, crisp cooky or cracker.

waf·fle |wŏf′əl| —*noun, plural* **waffles** A light, crisp cake made of batter. It is cooked in a griddle or appliance that presses a pattern of little squares into it.

wag |wăg| —*verb* **wagged, wagging** To move, swing, or wave back and forth or up and down: *The dog wagged its tail.* —*noun, plural* **wags** A wagging movement.

wage |wāj| —*noun, plural* **wages** Often **wages** A payment made to a worker for work or services done; salary. —*verb* **waged, waging** To take part in or carry on: *The citizens' group is waging a war against pollution.*

wa·ger |wā′jər| —*noun, plural* **wagers** A bet: *We made a wager on who would win the race.* —*verb* **wagered, wagering** To make a wager; bet: *I wagered him a dollar that I'd sell more magazines than he would.*

wag·on |wăg′ən| —*noun, plural* **wagons** **1.** A large, four-wheeled vehicle. It is pulled by horses and used to carry loads or passengers. **2.** A small cart with wheels that can be pushed or pulled by hand.

wail |wāl| —*verb* **wailed, wailing** To make a long, loud cry

wagon

because of grief, sadness, or pain: *The lost child wailed.*
—*noun, plural* **wails** A long, loud, high-pitched cry or sound: *I was wakened by the wail of the wind through the trees.*

waist |wāst| —*noun, plural* **waists** 1. The part of the human body between the ribs and the hips. 2. The part of a piece of clothing that fits around the waist.
♦ *These sound alike* **waist, waste.**

wait |wāt| —*verb* **waited, waiting** 1. To stay somewhere or stop doing something until someone or something comes: *Wait for me here. You will have to wait until tomorrow to try the new skates.* 2. To stop, pause, or delay: *Wait! I forgot something!* 3. To put off; delay; postpone: *Don't wait lunch for us.* 4. To be put off or delayed: *The meeting had to wait until everybody arrived.* 5. To be patient: *Wait a minute.*

Phrasal verb **wait on** To serve or attend as a waiter, salesclerk, maid, or butler: *The tall salesclerk waited on me.*
—*noun, plural* **waits** A period of time spent in waiting: *I had a short wait at the barber shop.*
♦ *These sound alike* **wait, weight.**

wait·er |wā′tər| —*noun, plural* **waiters** A man who works in a restaurant serving food and drink to people.

wait·ress |wā′trĭs| —*noun, plural* **waitresses** A woman who works in a restaurant serving food and drink to people.

wake¹ |wāk| —*verb* **woke, waked, waking** 1. To stop or cause to stop from sleeping; awaken: *I woke up at seven o'clock. My brother woke me up.* 2. To become or cause to become active: *The book waked my interest in ancient history.*
—*noun, plural* **wakes** A watch kept over the body of a dead person.

wake² |wāk| —*noun, plural* **wakes** The track or path of waves, ripples, or foam left in the water by a moving boat or ship.

wak·en |wā′kən| —*verb* **wakened, wakening** To wake up: *He wakened me at dawn. She wakened early.*

Wales |wālz| A section of the island of Great Britain, in the southwest.

walk |wôk| —*verb* **walked, walking** 1. To move on foot at an easy, steady pace. In walking, a person puts one foot on the ground before lifting the other. 2. To cause to walk: *The jockey is walking the horse around the track.* 3. To go or travel on foot: *I walked to school.* 4. To go over, across, or through on foot; stroll: *We walked the whole length of the town. Let's walk after dinner.* 5. To accompany or escort on foot; walk with: *He walked me to the bus.* 6. In baseball, to allow the batter to go to first base automatically because the pitcher throws four balls.
—*noun, plural* **walks** 1. An act of walking, especially an outing for exercise or pleasure: *We took a walk on the beach.* 2. The distance to be walked: *The walk to school is less than a mile.* 3. A place set apart or designed for walking, such as a sidewalk or path. 4. A way of walking; a pace or gait: *a slow walk.*

wall |wôl| —*noun, plural* **walls** 1. A solid structure that forms a side of a building or room, or that divides two areas. 2. A structure made of brick, stone, wood, or other material that is used to divide, enclose, or protect. Old cities and forts used to be surrounded by a wall to protect them from an attack. 3. Anything that divides, surrounds, or protects like a wall: *We couldn't see the lake through the white wall of fog.*

---

wake¹, wake²
Wake¹ comes from old English words that meant "to be awake" and "to wake someone up." **Wake²** is probably related to a Dutch word that originally meant "a channel made by a boat" and later "a channel in ice."

ă	pat	ĕ	pet	î	fierce
ā	pay	ē	be	ŏ	pot
â	care	ĭ	pit	ō	go
ä	father	ī	pie	ô	paw, for
oi	oil	ŭ	cut	zh	vision
ŏŏ	book	û	fur	ə	ago, item,
ōō	boot	th	the		pencil, atom,
yōō	abuse	th	thin		circus
ou	out	hw	which	ər	butter

—*verb* **walled, walling** To divide, enclose, or protect with or as if with a wall: *Dad walled up the broken window in the attic.*

wal·let | wŏl′ĭt | —*noun, plural* **wallets** A small, flat folding case used for holding money, cards, and photographs.

wall·pa·per | wôl′pā′pər | —*noun, plural* **wallpapers** Heavy paper, printed in colors and patterns, used to cover and decorate walls.

—*verb* **wallpapered, wallpapering** To cover with wallpaper.

wal·nut | wôl′nŭt′ | or | wôl′nət | —*noun, plural* **walnuts** A nut that grows on a tall tree and has a hard, rough shell. Walnuts are good to eat.

wal·rus | wôl′rəs | —*noun, plural* **walruses** or **walrus** A large sea animal that is related to the seals and sea lions and lives in the Arctic. Walruses have tough, wrinkled skin and large tusks.

waltz | wôltz | —*noun, plural* **waltzes** **1.** A smooth, gliding dance done by two people. **2.** The music for this dance.

—*verb* **waltzed, waltzing** To dance a waltz.

wam·pum | wŏm′pəm | or | wôm′pəm | —*noun* Small beads made from polished shells and strung together into necklaces or belts. It was once used by certain North American Indians as money.

wand | wŏnd | —*noun, plural* **wands** A slender rod or stick, especially one used by a magician.

wan·der | wŏn′dər | —*verb* **wandered, wandering** **1.** To move about from place to place with no special purpose or place to go: *We wandered around town looking in store windows.* **2.** To stray or move away from a particular path, place, or group; lose one's way: *One hiker wandered away from the others and got lost.* **3.** To not pay attention; to not be able to think clearly or sensibly: *She didn't hear the question because her mind was wandering.*

wane | wān | —*verb* **waned, waning** **1.** To grow or seem to grow smaller, as the moon does when it passes from full moon to new moon: *The moon is waning this week.* **2.** To become smaller in size, strength, or importance.

want | wŏnt | or | wônt | —*verb* **wanted, wanting** **1.** To have a wish for; desire: *She wants a bicycle. They wanted to play outdoors.* **2.** To have a need for; require: *The grass wants cutting and the flowers want water.*

—*noun, plural* **wants** The condition of needing or the thing needed: *She is in want of a job.*

war | wôr | —*noun, plural* **wars** **1.** Fighting or combat between two or more nations, states, or groups of people. **2.** Any struggle or conflict; an attack: *Many citizens and groups are carrying on a war against pollution.*

—*verb* **warred, warring** To make or take part in a war: *Germany and France have warred against each other many times.*

ward | wôrd | —*noun, plural* **wards** **1.** A section or division of a hospital. It is used to care for a certain group of patients: *a surgery ward.* **2.** A large hospital room shared by a number of patients: *There are ten beds in this ward.* **3.** A division of a city or town, especially an election district. **4.** Someone placed under the care and protection of a guardian or court.

   Phrasal verb **ward off** To stop from striking; avoid being hit: *He tried to punch me but I warded off the blow with my arm.*

war·den | wôr′dn | —*noun, plural* **wardens** **1.** An official who

walnut
Above: Pod and shell *(left)* and leaves *(right)*
Below: Tree

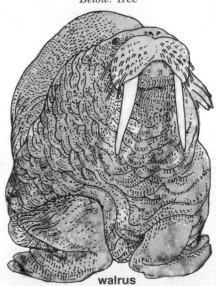

walrus

makes sure that certain laws, such as hunting and fishing laws, are obeyed: *a game warden; a fire warden.* **2.** An official in charge of running a prison.

ward·robe | wôrd′rōb′ | —*noun, plural* **wardrobes** **1.** All of a person's clothing: *Sheila's parents bought her a new wardrobe when she went off to college.* **2.** A large piece of furniture shaped like a closet for hanging or keeping clothes. It may also have drawers.

ware | wâr | —*noun, plural* **wares** **1.** **wares** Goods for sale: *At the fair all the merchants had their wares displayed on tables.* **2.** Pots, vases, and other things made from baked clay; pottery.
♦ *These sound alike* **ware, wear.**

ware·house | wâr′hous′ | —*noun, plural* **warehouses** A large building where merchandise is stored.

war·fare | wôr′fâr′ | —*noun* War or combat.

war·like | wôr′līk′ | —*adjective* **1.** Liking or quick to make war; hostile: *They have always been a warlike people.* **2.** Threatening war: *Shooting at our soldiers was a warlike action.*

warm | wôrm | —*adjective* **warmer, warmest** **1.** Somewhat hot; not cool or very hot: *warm weather. The water was so warm we went swimming.* **2.** Having a feeling of heat: *I felt warm and sweaty after playing basketball.* **3.** Giving off or holding in heat: *I stretched out in the warm sun. This is the warmest sweater I own.* **4.** Friendly, kindly, or enthusiastic: *Everyone likes her because she's such a warm person. When the mayor spoke, he was given a warm reception.*
—*verb* **warmed, warming** To make or become warm or warmer; heat up: *Sit by the fire and it will warm you. The rolls are warming in the oven.*

   Phrasal verb **warm up** **1.** To make or become warm or warmer; heat up: *Will you warm up the soup? I put it on the stove and it's warmed up already.* **2.** To make or become ready to do something, as by practicing beforehand: *The players warmed up for the game by doing exercises.*

warm-blood·ed | wôrm′blŭd′ĭd | —*adjective* Having blood that stays at about the same temperature no matter how much the temperature of the surrounding air or water changes. Birds and mammals are warm-blooded.

warmth | wôrmth | —*noun* **1.** The condition or quality of being warm: *The warmth of the sun felt good.* **2.** The condition or quality of being friendly; kindness: *Alice is a person of great warmth and charm.* **3.** A lively or excited feeling: *Dad spoke about his old childhood friend with warmth.*

warn | wôrn | —*verb* **warned, warning** **1.** To tell of present or coming danger; alert: *The news report on television warned people that the roads were icy.* **2.** To advise or caution: *We warned the children to be careful crossing the street.*
♦ *These sound alike* **warn, worn.**

warn·ing | wôr′nĭng | —*noun, plural* **warnings** A notice of coming danger given beforehand: *Without warning a long snake appeared.*

war·rant | wôr′ənt | or | wŏr′ənt | —*noun, plural* **warrants** **1.** An official written order that gives authority for doing something, such as making an arrest or search: *The police had a warrant to search the warehouse for stolen goods.* **2.** A good reason for doing or thinking something: *There's no warrant for believing you will get a car for your birthday.* **3.** A guarantee: *The salesperson said that*

ă	pat	ĕ	pet	î	fierce
ā	pay	ē	be	ŏ	pot
â	care	ĭ	pit	ō	go
ä	father	ī	pie	ô	paw, for
oi	oil	ŭ	cut	zh	vision
ōō	book	û	fur	ə	ago, item,
ōō	boot	*th*	the		pencil, atom,
yōō	abuse	th	thin		circus
ou	out	hw	which	ər	butter

certainly you don't get a warrant when you buy a used car.
—verb **warranted, warranting** **1.** To earn, merit, or deserve; be a good reason for: *Her work in school warranted her good grades.*
2. To guarantee: *My new watch is warranted for a year.*

war·ri·or |wôr′ē ər| or |wŏr′ē ər| —*noun, plural* **warriors** A fighter or a person who is experienced in fighting battles.

war·ship |wôr′shĭp′| —*noun, plural* **warships** A ship that is built and equipped with weapons for use in battle.

warship

wart |wôrt| —*noun, plural* **warts** A small, hard lump that grows on the skin. It is caused by a virus.

war·y |wâr′ē| —*adjective* **warier, wariest** **1.** Alert to or looking out for danger; on guard: *The robber went out only at night because he was wary of being caught.* **2.** Showing caution; careful: *The wary hiker tested the old wooden bridge before walking across it.*

was |wŏz| or |wŭz| or |wəz| The first and third person singular past tense of the verb **be:** *I was reading all afternoon. She was playing cards.*

wash |wŏsh| or |wôsh| —*verb* **washed, washing** **1.** To clean with water or other liquid and often with soap: *wash dishes; wash your face.* **2.** To clean oneself, clothes, or other things with soap and water: *He washed early today. We wash and iron on Tuesday.* **3.** To carry away or be carried away by moving water: *Rain falls and washes the soil down the hill.*
—noun, plural **washes** **1.** The act or process of washing: *The bathroom sink needs a wash.* **2.** The amount of clothes or linens that are to be or that have just been washed: *He did two washes today.* **3.** A liquid used in cleansing or coating something, such as whitewash or special mixtures to clean the mouth and eyes. **4.** A flow of water or the sound made by it: *We could hear the wash of the river after the storm.*

wash·er |wŏsh′ər| or |wô′shər| —*noun, plural* **washers** **1.** Someone or something that washes, especially a machine used to wash clothes or dishes. **2.** A small flat ring made of metal or rubber. It is placed between a nut and a bolt to reduce friction and give a tighter fit.

wash·ing machine |wŏsh′ĭng| or |wô′shĭng| A machine used for washing clothes and linens.

Wash·ing·ton |wŏsh′ĭng tən| or |wô′shĭng tən| **1.** A state in the northwestern United States. The capital of Washington is Olympia. **2.** The capital of the United States in the District of Columbia.

was·n't |wŏz′ənt| or |wŭz′ənt| A contraction of "was not."

wasp |wŏsp| or |wôsp| —*noun, plural* **wasps** Any of several flying insects that have a narrow middle section. Wasps can give a painful sting.

waste |wāst| —*verb* **wasted, wasting** **1.** To spend, use, or use up foolishly: *They wasted the whole day watching television. Don't waste your money on that cheap toy.* **2.** To fail to use; lose: *She wasted a good opportunity to get a better job.* **3.** To wear away little by little: *The disease wasted the woman's body.* **4.** To destroy completely: *An ice storm had wasted the crops.*
—noun, plural **wastes** **1.** An act or instance of wasting: *Trying to fix that old radio is a waste of time.* **2.** Worthless material that is produced while making something; garbage: *The factory dumps its wastes into the river.* **3.** The material that is left over after food has been digested and is sent out of the body.

Washington
The state of **Washington** was named after George Washington, the first President of the United States. Washington was the only President and, in fact, the only American ever to have a state named for him.

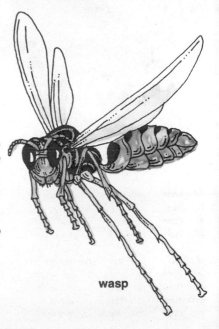

wasp

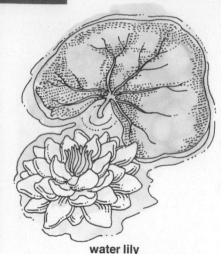

water lily

—*adjective* **1.** Left over or thrown away as worthless or useless: *Dad burned the waste lumber after building the table.* **2.** Of, having to do with, or used for waste: *a waste container; waste paper.*

♦ *These sound alike* **waste, waist.**

waste·bas·ket | wāst′ băs′kĭt | or | wāst′ bä′skĭt | —*noun, plural* **wastebaskets** An open container to hold waste paper or other items to be thrown out.

waste·ful | wāst′ fəl | —*adjective* Spending or using more than is needed: *her wasteful habit of leaving all the lights on in empty rooms.*

waste·land | wāst′ lănd′ | —*noun, plural* **wastelands** A lonely area with few plants or animals living on it; a desert.

watch | wŏch | —*verb* **watched, watching 1.** To look or look at: *People stopped to watch as the parade went by. She likes to watch the clouds.* **2.** To be on the lookout: *Watch for traffic signals. Watch for a green car.* **3.** To keep guard or keep guard over: *Half of us will sleep while the others watch. The dog watches the house.* **4.** To be careful about: *Watch what you are doing.*

—*noun, plural* **watches 1.** A small clock that a person can carry in a pocket or wear on the wrist or on a chain around the neck. **2.** The act of guarding: *The soldiers kept watch over their prisoner.* **3.** Someone who guards or protects: *The day watch came on duty.*

watch·dog | wŏch′ dôg′ | or | wŏch′ dŏg′ | —*noun, plural* **watchdogs** A dog that is trained to guard property.

watch·ful | wŏch′ fəl | —*adjective* On the lookout; alert: *The doctor was watchful for signs that the fever might return.*

watch·man | wŏch′ mən | —*noun, plural* **watchmen** A person whose job is to guard property, especially at night.

wa·ter | wô′ tər | or | wŏt′ ər | —*noun, plural* **waters** A compound of hydrogen and oxygen. Water is the liquid that falls from the skies as rain and is found in rivers, oceans, lakes, and pools.

—*verb* **watered, watering 1.** To sprinkle, wet, or supply with water: *Dad is watering the lawn.* **2. a.** To give water to drink: *The cowboys stopped to water their horses.* **b.** To drink water: *Deer water at the pool.* **3.** To produce a watery liquid, such as tears or saliva: *My eyes water when I cut onions.*

water buffalo A buffalo that lives in Africa and Asia and has large, spreading horns. Water buffaloes can be trained to pull or carry loads.

water color 1. A paint that is made of coloring material mixed with water, not with oil: *She bought a box of water colors.* **2.** A painting done with such paints: *The artist paints water colors.* **3.** The art of painting with water colors.

wa·ter·cress | wô′ tər krĕs′ | or | wŏt′ ər krĕs′ | —*noun* A plant that grows in or near ponds and streams. The leaves of watercress have a strong taste and are used in salads.

wa·ter·fall | wô′ tər fôl′ | or | wŏt′ ər fôl′ | —*noun, plural* **waterfalls** A natural stream of water that falls from a high place.

wa·ter·front | wô′ tər frŭnt′ | or | wŏt′ ər frŭnt′ | —*noun, plural* **waterfronts 1.** Land that is at the edge of a body of water, such as a harbor or a lake: *A cabin at the waterfront made fishing easy.* **2.** The part of a city or town that is at the edge of the water and has wharves where ships and boats dock.

water lily A water plant with broad, floating leaves and showy, colorful flowers.

wa·ter·mel·on | wô′ tər mĕl′ ən | or | wŏt′ ər mĕl′ ən | —*noun,*

watermelon
Above: Fruit and leaves
Below: A slice

ă	pat	ĕ	pet	î	fierce
ā	pay	ē	be	ŏ	pot
â	care	ĭ	pit	ō	go
ä	father	ī	pie	ô	paw, for

oi	oil	ŭ	cut	zh	vision
ōō	book	û	fur	ə	ago, item,
ōō	boot	*th*	the		pencil, atom,
yōō	abuse	th	thin		circus
ou	out	hw	which	ər	butter

plural **watermelons** A very large melon with a hard, thick green rind. The pink or reddish flesh is sweet and watery.

water moccasin A poisonous snake that lives in swamps of the southern United States. Another name for this snake is **cottonmouth.**

wa·ter·proof | wô′tər prōof′ | or | wŏt′ər prōof′ | —*adjective* Capable of keeping water from coming through: *a waterproof raincoat; a waterproof watch.*
—*verb* **waterproofed, waterproofing** To make capable of keeping water from coming through: *They waterproofed the boat.*

wa·ter·shed | wô′tər shĕd′ | or | wŏt′ər shĕd′ | —*noun, plural* **watersheds 1.** A ridge of mountains or other high land that separates two different systems of rivers. **2.** The region from which a river, lake, or other body of water drains its water.

water ski A form of the noun **water-ski.**

wa·ter·ski | wô′tər skē′ | or | wŏt′ər skē′ | —*noun, plural* **water-skis** Either of a pair of broad, short skis used for gliding over water while holding a rope attached to a motorboat. Another form of this noun is **water ski.**
—*verb* **water-skied, water-skiing** To glide over water on water-skis.

wa·ter·way | wô′tər wā′ | or | wŏt′ər wā′ | —*noun, plural* **waterways** A river, canal, or other body of water on which ships and boats travel.

water wheel A wheel that is turned by the power of water falling over it or flowing under it. Water wheels are used to drive machinery.

wa·ter·y | wô′tə rē | or | wŏt′ə rē | —*adjective* **waterier, wateriest 1.** Filled with or containing water or a liquid like water: *The cold wind gave him watery eyes.* **2.** Like water: *a watery blue sky.* **3.** Having too much water: *thin, watery soup; watery mud.*

watt | wŏt | —*noun, plural* **watts** A unit of electrical power.

wave | wāv | —*verb* **waved, waving 1.** To move back and forth or up and down; flap or flutter: *The baby waved her little legs in the air. The flags waved in the breeze.* **2.** To move a hand, arm, or something in the hand back and forth, usually as a signal, greeting, or warning: *She waved her hand to us and called "Hello!" The workers waved us away from the road.* **3.** To fall or cause to fall in gentle curls: *Her long hair waved over her shoulders. She waved her hair by setting it when it was wet.*
—*noun, plural* **waves 1.** A moving high point along the surface of water: *He likes to ride the waves in the ocean.* **2.** A vibrating motion of energy or particles. Light, sound, heat, and x-rays travel in waves. **3.** An act of waving: *She greeted us with a wave of her hand.* **4.** A curve or arrangement of gentle curls: *His hair has a nice wave.* **5.** A sudden increase: *A heat wave kept the city uncomfortable for ten days.*

wa·ver | wā′vər | —*verb* **wavered, wavering 1.** To move or swing back and forth in an uncertain or unsteady way: *The old man's hand wavered as he reached for his medicine.* **2.** To be uncertain; falter: *He wavered as they tried to get him to change his mind.* **4.** To tremble or flicker: *The flame of the candle wavered.*

wav·y | wā′vē | —*adjective* **wavier, waviest** Having waves or curves: *wavy blond hair; a wavy line on the paper.*

wax¹ | wăks | —*noun, plural* **waxes 1.a.** Any of various substances that are solid or soft and sticky, and that melt or become soft when heated. Waxes do not dissolve in water. **b.** A

water-ski

water wheel

wax¹, wax²
Both **wax¹** and **wax²** come from old English words.

substance like wax that is produced by bees; beeswax. **c.** A substance like wax that is found in the ears. **2.** Any of several substances containing wax and used to polish floors, cars, furniture, and many other things.

—*verb* **waxed, waxing** To cover, coat, treat, or polish with wax: *He waxed the car until it shone.*

wax² | wăks | —*verb* **waxed, waxing 1.** To grow or seem to grow larger, as the moon does when it passes from new moon to full moon: *The moon waxes a bit every night, and then it wanes.* **2.** To become or grow: *The seas waxed calm.*

way | wā | —*noun, plural* **ways 1.** A manner or fashion: *A robot moves in a stiff way.* **2.** A method or means; technique: *Do you know a better way to solve the problem?* **3.** A road; route; path: *They took a hidden way through the woods.* **4.** Room enough to pass or go: *Make way for the fire truck.* **5.** The path taken by something that is moving or about to move: *Don't get in the way of a moving car.* **6.** Distance: *Is it a long way to school?* **7.** A direction: *Which way did she go?* **8.** What one wants; a will or wish: *She likes to get her own way.*

—*adverb* Far: *The sweetest apples are way at the top of the tree.*

♦ *These sound alike* **way, weigh.**

-ways A suffix that forms adjectives and adverbs and means "manner, direction, or position": *sideways.*

we | wē | —*pronoun* The pronoun **we** stands for the person who is speaking or writing, together with another person or persons sharing the action of the verb: *We went to the movies. We left the house early.*

♦ *These sound alike* **we, wee.**

weak | wēk | —*adjective* **weaker, weakest 1.** Not having strength, power, or energy: *His muscles are weak after a month in bed. She presented a weak argument. A weak light barely lit the room.* **2.** Likely to fail or break under pressure or stress: *a weak board in the floor; a weak member of the team.*

♦ *These sound alike* **weak, week.**

weak·en | wē′kən | —*verb* **weakened, weakening** To make or become weak or weaker: *Poor food weakened his body. Her hopes weakened as the days passed.*

weak·ly | wēk′lē | —*adjective* **weaklier, weakliest** Feeble; sick; weak: *a weakly baby.*

—*adverb* In a weak way: *The kitten cried weakly.*

♦ *These sound alike* **weakly, weekly.**

weak·ness | wēk′nĭs | —*noun, plural* **weaknesses 1.** The condition or feeling of being weak: *A weakness in his knees causes him to stumble.* **2.** A weak point; fault or flaw; defect: *Her biggest weakness is that she trusts the wrong people.* **3.** A special liking: *He has a weakness for chocolate fudge.*

wealth | wĕlth | —*noun* **1.** A great amount of money, property, or valuable possessions; riches: *The king's wealth was too great to measure.* **2.** A large amount: *He has a wealth of information.*

wealth·y | wĕl′thē | —*adjective* **wealthier, wealthiest** Having wealth; rich: *a wealthy man; a wealthy family.*

weap·on | wĕp′ən | —*noun, plural* **weapons 1.** Any instrument or device used to attack another or defend oneself from attack: *guns, knives, clubs, and other weapons.* **2.** Anything used to overcome, persuade, or defeat: *There is no good weapon against the common cold. His smile was his best weapon.*

weapon
Soldiers carrying weapons

ă	pat	ĕ	pet	î	fierce
ā	pay	ē	be	ŏ	pot
â	care	ĭ	pit	ō	go
ä	father	ī	pie	ô	paw, for

oi	oil	ŭ	cut	zh	vision
ŏŏ	book	û	fur	ə	ago, item,
ōō	boot	th	the		pencil, atom,
yōō	abuse	th	thin		circus
ou	out	hw	which	ər	butter

wear | wâr | —*verb* **wore, worn, wearing** **1.** To have or put on one's body: *He always wears a dark suit and a red tie. She wears lots of make-up and jewelry.* **2.** To have or show: *She wore a sad smile.* **3.** To fit into or look good in: *What size shoe do you wear? Can she wear orange?* **4.** To damage, cut, or remove by rubbing, pressure, or constant use: *The waves are wearing away the cliff.* **5.** To make or become as the result of too much use or rubbing: *He wore a hole in his shoe. The elbows of his jacket wore thin.* **6.** To last even though used: *That fabric wears well.*

   Phrasal verb **wear out** **1.** To use or be used so much that something is no longer useful: *He wore out his shoes. The shoes are wearing out.* **2.** To tire or make exhausted: *Her strength wore out. The long trip wore them out.*

—*noun* **1.** The act of wearing or the condition of being worn: *clothes for evening wear; a coat in constant wear.* **2.** Clothing: *The store sells men's wear.* **3.** Damage that comes from use or age: *The rug shows lots of wear.*

  ♦ *These sound alike* **wear, ware.**

wea·ry | wîr′ē | —*adjective* **wearier, weariest** Needing rest; tired; fatigued: *The weary children went straight to bed.*

—*verb* **wearied, wearying, wearies** To make or become tired: *The hard work wearied them. She wearies quickly.*

wea·sel | wē′zəl | —*noun, plural* **weasels** An animal that has soft fur and a long, narrow body, short legs, and a long tail. Weasels feed on small animals and birds.

weasel

weath·er | wĕth′ər | —*noun* The condition or activity of the atmosphere at a certain time and place. Heat or cold, sunshine, rain and snow, and winds can all be parts of the weather.

—*verb* **weathered, weathering** **1.** To change through exposure to sun, wind, and other elements: *The rocks crumbled as they weathered. Wind and rain had weathered the old barn.* **2.** To pass through in safety; survive: *The old house weathered the storm.*

weather vane A pointer that turns with the wind to show which way the wind is blowing.

weave | wēv | —*verb* **wove, woven, weaving** **1.** To make cloth or other items by passing strands under and over other strands: *She wove the wool into a blanket. He weaves straw baskets.* **2.** To spin a web: *She watched the spider weaving its web.* **3.** *Past tense* and *past participle* **weaved** To move in and out, back and forth, or from side to side: *Our small canoe weaved through the thick plants.*

—*noun, plural* **weaves** A pattern, manner, or method of weaving: *a loose weave; a diagonal weave.*

  ♦ *These sound alike* **weave, we've.**

weather vane

web | wĕb | —*noun, plural* **webs** **1.** A network of fine, silky threads woven by a spider. **2.** Anything made of parts that cross one another in a complicated manner: *a web of highways; the web of life.* **3.** A fold of skin or thin tissue that connects the toes of ducks, frogs, otters, and other animals.

webbed | wĕbd | —*adjective* Having skin or thin tissue that connects the toes: *A goose has webbed feet.*

web-foot·ed | wĕb′foŏt′ĭd | —*adjective* Having feet with webbed toes: *Ducks are web-footed.*

wed | wĕd | —*verb* **wedded, wed** or **wedded, wedding** **1.** To take a person or each other as husband or wife; marry: *She wedded her childhood sweetheart. He is too young to wed. Have they wed yet?* **2.** To unite in marriage: *The minister wedded the young couple.*

we'd |wĕd| A contraction of "we had," "we should," and "we would."
♦ *These sound alike* **we'd, weed.**

wed·ding |wĕd′ĭng| —*noun, plural* **weddings** **1.** A marriage ceremony or celebration: *My sister's wedding will be tomorrow.* **2.** An anniversary of a marriage: *a golden wedding.*

wedge |wĕj| —*noun, plural* **wedges** **1.** A block of wood, metal, or other material that is wide at one end and tapers to a point at the other. Wedges are tools used for splitting things apart, tightening things, lifting, or holding things in place. **2.** Anything shaped like a wedge: *a wedge of cheese.*
—*verb* **wedged, wedging** **1.** To split apart or fix in place with a wedge: *He wedged the logs apart. She wedged the door open.* **2.** To crowd, push, force, or squeeze into a small space: *They all wedged into the little car.*

Wed·nes·day |wĕnz′dē| or |wĕnz′dā′| —*noun, plural* **Wednesdays** The fourth day of the week, after Tuesday and before Thursday.

wee |wē| —*adjective* **weer, weest** **1.** Very little; tiny: *a wee lad; a wee bit afraid.* **2.** Very early: *the wee hours.*
♦ *These sound alike* **wee, we.**

weed |wēd| —*noun, plural* **weeds** Any plant that grows easily where it is not wanted. Weeds are considered to be troublesome, useless, or harmful.
—*verb* **weeded, weeding** To remove or get rid of weeds: *We spent the morning weeding the garden.*
   Phrasal verb **weed out** To remove or eliminate what is not wanted: *He weeded out the worst players from the team.*
♦ *These sound alike* **weed, we'd.**

week |wēk| —*noun, plural* **weeks** **1.** A period of seven days in a row, usually counted from a Sunday through the next Saturday. **2.** The part of that period of seven days during which one works or goes to school: *She works all week and relaxes on weekends.*
♦ *These sound alike* **week, weak.**

week·day |wēk′dā′| —*noun, plural* **weekdays** Any day of the week except Sunday and, usually, Saturday.

week·end |wēk′ĕnd| —*noun, plural* **weekends** The period of time from Friday evening through Sunday evening.

week·ly |wēk′lē| —*adjective* **1.** Happening, appearing, or to be paid once every week: *Our club has weekly meetings.* **2.** For a period of one week: *the weekly sales of cars.*
—*adverb* Every week; once a week: *He writes to me weekly.*
—*noun, plural* **weeklies** A magazine or newspaper that is issued once a week.
♦ *These sound alike* **weekly, weakly.**

weep |wēp| —*verb* **wept, weeping** To shed tears; cry: *She weeps easily. He wept tears of joy.*

wee·vil |wē′vəl| —*noun, plural* **weevils** A beetle with a long snout that curves downward. Weevils do great harm to plants and crops.

weigh |wā| —*verb* **weighed, weighing** **1.** To use a scale or other instrument to determine how heavy something is: *The butcher weighed the chicken.* **2.** To have a weight of: *The boy weighs 45 kilograms, or about 100 pounds.* **3.** To consider in a careful manner; think about: *He weighed his choices before making a*

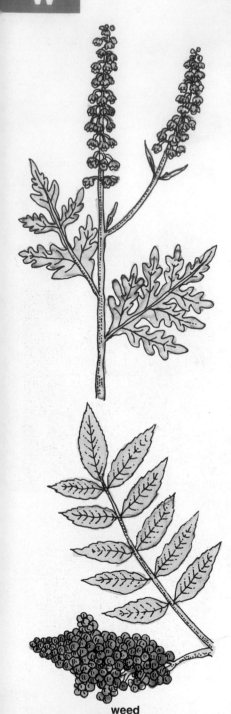

weed
Two kinds of weed

ă	pat	ĕ pet	î fierce
ā	pay	ē be	ŏ pot
â	care	ĭ pit	ō go
ä	father	ī pie	ô paw, for

oi	oil	ŭ cut	zh vision
ŏŏ	book	û fur	ə ago, item,
ōō	boot	*th* the	pencil, atom,
yōō	abuse	th thin	circus
ou	out	hw which	ər butter

decision. **4.** To have an influence; count: *Her mother's opinions weigh a great deal with her.*

   Phrasal verbs **weigh down 1.** To cause to bend under heavy weight: *Snow and ice weighed down the branches of the trees.* **2.** To be a burden to: *Troubles weighed down the family.* **weigh on** or **upon** To be a burden to; oppress: *His bad behavior weighs on his conscience.*

  ♦ *These sound alike* **weigh, way.**

weight | wāt | —*noun, plural* **weights 1.** The measure of how heavy a thing is: *His weight is 45 kilograms, or about 100 pounds.* **2.** The force of gravity pulling on an object: *Your weight on the moon would be less than your weight on earth.* **3.** A unit used for measuring this force: *Grams and kilograms are metric weights.* **4.** A system of units for measuring weight: *How do you express 50 pounds in metric weight?* **5.** An object with a known weight: *He lifts ten-pound weights to strengthen his muscles.* **6.** Something heavy, especially something used to hold objects down: *She used the rock as a weight to keep the papers from flying away.* **7.** A load or burden: *Her illness is a great weight on our minds.* **8.** An ability to convince: *Her brother's opinion has a lot of weight with her.*

  ♦ *These sound alike* **weight, wait.**

weight·less | wāt′lĭs | —*adjective* **1.** Having little or no weight: *as weightless as a feather.* **2.** Experiencing little or no pull of gravity: *a weightless astronaut in space.*

weird | wîrd | —*adjective* **weirder, weirdest 1.** Mysterious and frightening; eerie: *Some weird cries came from the woods.* **2.** Strange, odd, or unusual: *all kinds of weird machines.*

wel·come | wĕl′kəm | —*verb* **welcomed, welcoming 1.** To greet with pleasure, warm feelings, or special ceremony: *We stood at the door to welcome our guests.* **2.** To be willing or grateful to accept: *He welcomed her suggestions.*

  —*noun, plural* **welcomes** The act of greeting or receiving, usually in a warm, friendly manner: *They gave us a lovely welcome.*

  —*adjective* **1.** Greeted, received, or accepted with pleasure: *You are always a welcome guest. We took a welcome vacation.* **2.** Free to or invited to have or use: *You are welcome to anything on the table.* **3.** Under no obligation for a kind act: *When somebody says "Thank you," the polite response is "You're welcome."*

weld | wĕld | —*verb* **welded, welding** To join materials by melting the area that is to be joined and then pressing the materials together.

wel·fare | wĕl′fâr′ | —*noun* **1.** Health, happiness, or prosperity: *He worked for the welfare of his family.* **2.** Money or other kinds of help given to needy or disabled people by a government.

well¹ | wĕl | —*noun, plural* **wells 1.** A deep hole dug or drilled into the ground to get water, oil, gas, or other materials. **2.** A spring or fountain that serves as a natural source of water. **3.** A source: *The dictionary is a well of information.*

  —*verb* **welled, welling** To spring or rise: *Tears of joy welled in his eyes when he learned he had won.*

well² | wĕl | —*adverb* **better, best 1.** In a good or proper way; correctly: *a person who has good posture and holds his body well.* **2.** With skill: *He plays the piano well.* **3.** To a degree that is: **a.** Satisfying or sufficient: *Did you sleep well last night?* **b.** Successful or effective: *How well do you get along with others?* **c.** Suitable or appropriate: *The two teams are well matched.*

weightless
An astronaut in outer space

weld

well¹, well²
Well¹ and **well²** both have their roots in old English words. **Well¹** came from a word meaning "spring of water." **Well²** is related to **wealth**; it originally meant "in a good manner, prosperously."

d. Thorough or complete: *Blend the ingredients well.*
e. Considerable: *It was well after midnight.* **4.** With good reason: *You may well be angry with him.*
—*adjective* **1. a.** In good health; not sick: *We were lucky to stay well last winter.* **b.** Cured or healed: *I will be glad when you are well again.* **2.** All right; in good order: *All is well.*
—*interjection* **1.** A word used to express surprise or other sudden feelings: *Well! I never expected so much company!* **2.** A word used to begin a remark or simply to fill time while one is thinking of what to say: *Well, I'm not sure I agree with you.*

we'll |wĕl| A contraction of "we will" and "we shall."

well-be·ing |wĕl′bē′ĭng| —*noun* Health and happiness; welfare: *They had a sense of well-being in the room.*

well-known |wĕl′nōn′| —*adjective* Known to many people in many places: *a well-known singer.*

went |wĕnt| The past tense of the verb **go**: *We went home.*

wept |wĕpt| The past tense and past participle of the verb **weep**: *The boy wept. She had wept for an hour.*

were |wûr| **1.** The second person singular past tense of the verb **be**: *You were not in your usual seat on the train last night.* **2.** The first, second, and third person plural past tense of the verb **be**: *We were not at home yesterday. You were about to get yourselves into trouble. They were looking for an apartment.*

we're |wîr| A contraction of "we are."

were·n't |wûrnt| or |wûr′ənt| A contraction of "were not."

west |wĕst| —*noun* **1.** The direction from which the sun is seen setting in the evening. **2.** Often **West** A region in this direction. **3. the West** The part of the United States to the west of Wisconsin, Illinois, Kentucky, Tennessee, and Mississippi. **4. the West** The part of the earth west of Asia, especially Europe and North and South America; the Occident.
—*adjective* **1.** Of, in, or toward the west: *the west bank of the river.* **2.** Coming from the west: *a west wind.*
—*adverb* Toward the west: *This river flows west to the sea.*

west·er·ly |wĕs′tər lē| —*adjective* **1.** In or toward the west: *The boat sailed in a westerly direction.* **2.** From the west: *a westerly breeze.*
—*adverb* **1.** In or toward the west: *The boat sailed westerly.* **2.** From the west: *The winds blew westerly.*

west·ern |wĕs′tərn| —*adjective* **1.** Often **Western** Of, in, or toward the west: *the western sky; the western part of the state.* **2.** From the west: *a western wind.* **3.** Often **Western a.** Of, like, or used in the American West: *western settlers; a Western saddle.* **b.** Of the developed countries of Europe and North and South America: *Western civilization; a Western suit and tie.*
—*noun, plural* **westerns** A book, movie, or television or radio program about cowboys or frontier life in the American West.

west·ern·er |wĕs′tər nər| —*noun, plural* **westerners** Often **Westerner** A person who lives in or comes from the west, especially the western United States.

West Vir·gin·ia |vər jĭn′yə| A state in the eastern United States. The capital of West Virginia is Charleston.

west·ward |wĕst′wərd| —*adverb* To or toward the west: *They sailed westward.* Another form of this adverb is **westwards**.
—*adjective* Moving to or toward the west: *the westward movement of the pioneers.*

West Virginia

West Virginia was once the western part of the state of Virginia. The name **Virginia** comes from "the Virgin Queen," the popular name of Queen Elizabeth I of England.

ă	pat	ĕ	pet	î	fierce
ā	pay	ē	be	ŏ	pot
â	care	ĭ	pit	ō	go
ä	father	ī	pie	ô	paw, for
oi	oil	ŭ	cut	zh	vision
ōō	book	û	fur	ə	ago, item,
ōō	boot	*th*	the		pencil, atom,
yōō	abuse	th	thin		circus
ou	out	hw	which	ər	butter

—*noun* A direction or region to the west: *To the westward we could see that the sun was about to set.*

west·wards |wĕst′wərdz| A form of the adverb **westward.**

wet |wĕt| —*adjective* **wetter, wettest 1.** Covered, moist, or soaked with a liquid: *Her clothing was wet from the rain.* **2.** Containing more water than normal: *wet snow; heavy, wet air.* **3.** Rainy: *a week of wet weather.* **4.** Not yet dry or hardened: *wet paint; wet cement.*
—*verb* **wet** or **wetted, wetting** To make wet: *She wet the cloth before ironing it.*

we've |wēv| A contraction of "we have."
♦ *These sound alike* **we've, weave.**

whale |hwāl| or |wāl| —*noun, plural* **whales** Any of several large sea animals that look like fish but are really mammals that breathe air.

whal·er |**hwā**′lər| or |**wā**′lər| —*noun, plural* **whalers 1.** A person who hunts whales or works on a whaling ship. **2.** A ship or boat used in whaling.

whal·ing |**hwā**′lĭng| or |**wā**′lĭng| —*noun* The business or practice of hunting and killing whales for their valuable products.

wharf |hwôrf| or |wôrf| —*noun, plural* **wharves** or **wharfs** A landing place or pier at which ships may tie up and load or unload.

wharves |hwôrvz| or |wôrvz| A plural of the noun **wharf.**

what |hwŏt| or |hwŭt| or |wŏt| or |wŭt| or |hwət| or |wət|
—*pronoun* **1.** Which thing or things: *What are we having for lunch?* **2.** That which; the thing that: *Listen to what I have to say.*
—*adjective* **1.** Which one or ones of several or many: *What train do I take?* **2.** Whatever: *We repaired what damage had been done.* **3.** How great: *What fools we have been!* **4.** How much: *What good will that do?* The adjective **what** belongs to a class of words called **determiners.** They signal that a noun is coming.
—*adverb* How: *What does it matter, after all?*
—*interjection* A word used to express surprise: *What! More snow?*

what·ev·er |hwŏt ĕv′ər| or |hwŭt ĕv′ər| or |wŏt ĕv′ər| or |wŭt ĕv′ər| —*pronoun* **1.** Everything or anything that: *Please do whatever you can to help.* **2.** No matter what: *Whatever you do, come early.*
—*adjective* **1.** Of any number or kind; any: *Whatever troubles you may have, feel free to call on us.* **2.** Of any kind at all: *He was left with nothing whatever.* The adjective **whatever** belongs to a class of words called **determiners.** They signal that a noun is coming.

what's |hwŏts| or |hwŭts| or |wŏts| or |wŭts| A contraction of "what is" and "what has."

wheat |hwēt| or |wēt| —*noun* A kind of grass that bears grain and is grown in many parts of the world as an important source of food. Wheat seeds are ground to make flour.

wheel |hwēl| or |wēl| —*noun, plural* **wheels 1.** A solid disk or a ring with spokes that is attached to an axle to move things or drive machines. **2.** Anything that is like a wheel in its shape or use or that has a wheel as its main part: *a steering wheel on a car; a water wheel; a wheel of cheese.*
—*verb* **wheeled, wheeling 1.** To move or roll on wheels: *Please wheel the cart into the library. The cart wheeled down the hill.* **2.** To turn suddenly and change direction; move in circles: *She wheeled about in anger when the snowball hit her.*

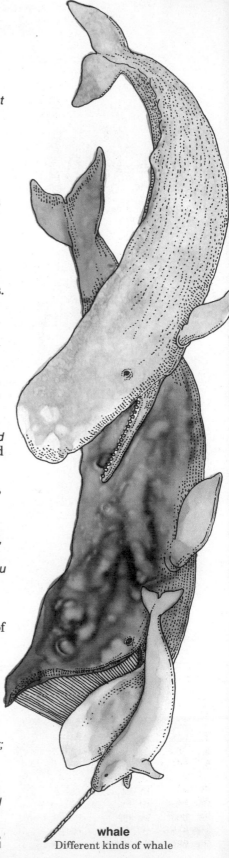

whale
Different kinds of whale

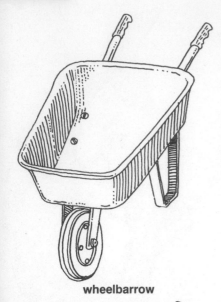

wheelbarrow

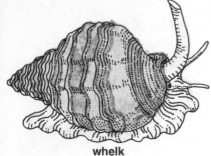

whelk

wheel·bar·row |hwĕl′băr′ō| or |wĕl′băr′ō| —*noun, plural* **wheelbarrows** A small cart that is rolled by hand. A wheelbarrow usually is narrower in front than in back. It has one or two wheels in front and two straight handles at the back.

wheel·chair |hwĕl′châr′| or |wĕl′châr′| —*noun, plural* **wheelchairs** A chair mounted on wheels so that it can be moved about with someone sitting in it. People who are sick or who cannot walk use wheelchairs.

wheeze |hwēz| —*verb* **wheezed, wheezing** To breathe with difficulty, making a hoarse, whistling, or hissing sound.

whelk |hwĕlk| or |wĕlk| —*noun, plural* **whelks** A large sea snail with a pointed spiral shell.

when |hwĕn| or |wĕn| —*adverb* **1.** At what time: *When did you leave?* **2.** At which time: *I know when to leave.*
—*conjunction* **1.** At the time that: *in April, when the snow melts.* **2.** As soon as: *I will call you when I get there.* **3.** Whenever: *He always arrives late when he goes to the library.* **4.** Although: *He's reading comic books when he should be doing his homework.* **5.** Considering that; since: *How are you going to make the team when you won't go to practice?*
—*pronoun* What or which time: *Since when have you been giving the orders around here?*

when·ev·er |hwĕn ĕv′ər| or |wĕn ĕv′ər| —*adverb* When: *Whenever is she coming?*
—*conjunction* **1.** At whatever time that: *We can start whenever you're ready.* **2.** Every time that: *I smile whenever I think of her.*

where |hwâr| or |wâr| —*adverb* **1.** At or in what place, point, or position: *Where is the telephone?* **2.** To what place or end: *Where does this road lead?* **3.** From what place or source: *Where did you get that crazy idea?*
—*conjunction* **1.** At or in what or which place: *I am going to my room, where I can study.* **2.** In or to a place in which or to which: *She lives where the weather is mild. I will go where you go.* **3.** Wherever: *Where there's smoke, there's fire.* **4.** While on the contrary: *Mars has two satellites, where Earth has only one.*
—*pronoun* **1.** What or which place: *Where did they come from?* **2.** The place in, at, or to which: *This is where I found the puppy.*

where·a·bouts |hwâr′ə bouts′| or |wâr′ə bouts′| —*adverb* Where or about where: *Whereabouts did I leave my notebook?*
—*noun* (Used with a singular or plural verb.) The place where someone or something is: *the whereabouts of the stolen jewels.*

where·up·on |hwâr′ə pŏn′| or |hwâr′ə pôn′| or |wâr′ə pŏn′| or |wâr′ə pôn′| —*conjunction* Following which: *Little Pedro fell asleep, whereupon Mrs. Ramirez went downstairs.*

wher·ev·er |hwâr ĕv′ər| or |wâr ĕv′ər| —*adverb* Where; in or to whatever place: *Write these groups of words, using capital letters wherever needed.*
—*conjunction* In or to whatever place or situation: *I'll think of you wherever you go.*

wheth·er |hwĕth′ər| or |wĕth′ər| —*conjunction* **1.** No matter if: *The movie starts at four o'clock whether you are ready or not.* **2.** If: *Have you ever wondered whether animals feel love and grief?*

whey |hwā| or |wā| —*noun* The watery part of milk that separates from the curds when milk turns sour.

which |hwĭch| or |wĭch| —*pronoun* **1.** What one or ones: *Which is your house?* **2.** The one or ones that: *Take those which are*

ă	pat	ĕ	pet	î	fierce
ā	pay	ē	be	ŏ	pot
â	care	ĭ	pit	ō	go
ä	father	ī	pie	ô	paw, for

oi	oil	ŭ	cut	zh	vision
ŏŏ	book	û	fur	ə	ago, item,
ōō	boot	th	the		pencil, atom,
yōō	abuse	th	thin		circus
ou	out	hw	which	ər	butter

yours. **3.** The thing, animal, or person just mentioned: *the movie which was shown later.* **4.** That: *the horse which I bought.*
—*adjective* **1.** What one or ones: *Which coat is yours?* **2.** Being the thing, animal, or person just mentioned: *It started raining, at which point we left the park.* The adjective **which** belongs to a class of words called **determiners.** They signal that a noun is coming.

which·ev·er |hwĭch ĕv′ər| or |wĭch ĕv′ər| —*adjective* Being any one or ones that: *Buy whichever car you like best.* The adjective **whichever** belongs to a class of words called **determiners.** They signal that a noun is coming.
—*pronoun* Any one or ones that: *Buy whichever you like best.*

whiff |hwĭf| or |wĭf| —*noun, plural* **whiffs** A puff or smell carried in the air: *a whiff of smoke; a whiff of fresh popcorn.*

while |hwīl| or |wīl| —*noun* A period of time: *stay for a while.*
—*conjunction* **1.** As long as; during the time that: *It was great while it lasted.* **2.** Although: *Betty is tall while her sisters are short.*
—*verb* **whiled, whiling** To pass or spend pleasantly or in a relaxed way: *He whiled away his free time reading adventure stories.*

whim |hwĭm| or |wĭm| —*noun, plural* **whims** A sudden wish, desire, or idea: *He had a whim to go sailing today.*

whim·per |**hwĭm**′pər| or |**wĭm**′pər| —*verb* **whimpered, whimpering** To cry with weak, broken, whining sounds: *The wet puppy whimpered by the closed door. Stop whimpering.*
—*noun, plural* **whimpers** A low, broken, whining sound.

whine |hwīn| or |wīn| —*verb* **whined, whining** **1.** To make a high, complaining sound or cry: *The child whined after he hurt his foot.* **2.** To complain in a childish, annoying way: *He always whines about having to do his homework.*
—*noun, plural* **whines** A whimpering sound or complaint: *I'm tired of your whines; now go to sleep.*

whin·ny |**hwĭn**′ē| or |**wĭn**′ē| —*noun, plural* **whinnies** A gentle neigh made by a horse: *We heard whinnies from the barn.*
—*verb* **whinnied, whinnying** To make a gentle neighing sound: *The horse whinnied as it ran across the pasture.*

whip |hwĭp| or |wĭp| —*noun, plural* **whips** A rod that bends or that has a lash attached to one end. It is used for driving animals or for striking or beating someone.
—*verb* **whipped, whipping** **1.** To strike, beat, or lash with or as if with a whip: *The jockey whipped his horse to make him go faster.* **2.** To move suddenly and quickly: *I whipped out of the house as fast as I could.* **3.** To beat cream, eggs, or other ingredients into a foam: *He whipped the cream to put on the shortcake.* **4.** To defeat in a fight or contest; beat: *You can't whip our team this year.*

whip·poor·will or **whip-poor-will** |**hwĭp**′ər wĭl′| or |**wĭp**′ər wĭl′| or |hwĭp′ər **wĭl**′| or |wĭp′ər **wĭl**′| —*noun, plural* **whippoorwills** or **whip-poor-wills** A brownish North American bird with a call that sounds like its name.

whir |hwûr| or |wûr| —*verb* **whirred, whirring** To move swiftly with a buzzing or humming sound: *The machines whirred noisily.*
—*noun, plural* **whirs** A buzzing or humming sound.

whirl |hwûrl| or |wûrl| —*verb* **whirled, whirling** **1.** To spin or turn or cause to spin or turn: *The propeller whirled faster and faster. Watch me whirl the baton.* **2.** To turn suddenly, changing directions: *The cat ran across the road, whirled, and ran back again.*
—*noun, plural* **whirls** A quick turn; a whirling, spinning

whippoorwill

whisker
Above: On a seal
Below: On a cat

whistle
On an antique rattle

movement: *The dancer made a whirl and bowed.*

whirl·pool | hwûrl′pōōl′ | or | wûrl′pōōl′ | —*noun, plural* **whirlpools** A current of water that moves rapidly round and round.

whirl·wind | hwûrl′wĭnd | or | wûrl′wĭnd | —*noun, plural* **whirlwinds** A wind or current of air that turns round and round, often violently, as a tornado.

whisk | hwĭsk | or | wĭsk | —*verb* **whisked, whisking** **1.** To brush or sweep with quick, light motions: *He whisked the crumbs off the table.* **2.** To move or carry or cause to move or carry quickly: *He whisked through the halls. Dad whisked me to the dentist's.*

whisk·er | hwĭsk′ər | or | wĭsk′ər | —*noun, plural* **whiskers** **1.** **whiskers** A man's mustache and beard. **2.** A hair on a man's face that has not been shaved. **3.** A stiff, long hair growing near the mouth of certain animals, such as cats, rats, or rabbits.

whis·key | hwĭs′kē | or | wĭs′kē | —*noun, plural* **whiskeys** An alcoholic drink made from corn, rye, barley, or other grains.

whis·per | hwĭs′pər | or | wĭs′pər | —*verb* **whispered, whispering** To speak or say very softly: *She whispered so quietly that I asked her to repeat what she said.*

—*noun, plural* **whispers** A soft, low sound or voice: *We heard whispers coming from the back of the theater.*

whis·tle | hwĭs′əl | or | wĭs′əl | —*verb* **whistled, whistling** **1.** To make a clear, high tone or sound by forcing air out through the teeth or through pursed lips, or by blowing into a whistle: *The boys were whistling as they washed the car.* **2.** To make a sound like this: *The kettle whistled when the water began to boil.* **3.** To signal or call by whistling: *He stood on the corner and whistled for a taxi.* **4.** To make a whistling sound by moving quickly: *The wind whistled through the trees.*

—*noun, plural* **whistles** **1.** A sound or signal made by whistling: *The teams stopped playing when they heard the whistle.* **2.** A device that makes a whistling sound: *The policeman blew his whistle.*

white | hwīt | or | wīt | —*noun, plural* **whites** **1.** The lightest of all colors; the opposite of black; the color of snow. **2.** The white part of something; the light part of something: *the white of an egg.* **3.** A member of a race of people having light-colored skin.

—*adjective* **whiter, whitest** **1.** Of or having the color white: *a white fence.* **2.** Light in color: *I don't like the white meat of the chicken.* **3.** Having little color; pale: *Sam turned as white as a ghost.* **4.** Of or belonging to a race of people having light-colored skin. **5.** Pale gray or silvery, as from age: *My aunt has white hair.* **6.** Snowy: *a white Christmas.*

white blood cell A colorless cell in the blood. Many white blood cells fight against infection by destroying disease germs.

White House, the **1.** The official home of the President of the United States. It is in Washington, D.C. **2.** The President and his staff; the office, authority, or opinion of the President: *The White House announced that the new tax law would be vetoed.*

whit·en | hwī′tən | or | wī′tən | —*verb* **whitened, whitening** To make or become white or whiter: *She added bleach to whiten the clothes. His hair whitened in the sun.*

white·wash | hwīt′wŏsh′ | or | hwīt′wôsh′ | or | wīt′wŏsh′ | or | wīt′wôsh′ | —*noun* A thin liquid used to whiten walls and other surfaces. It is made of a mixture of lime and water.

whit·ish | hwī′tĭsh | or | wī′tĭsh | —*adjective* Somewhat white.

ă	pat	ĕ	pet	î	fierce
ā	pay	ē	be	ŏ	pot
â	care	ĭ	pit	ō	go
ä	father	ī	pie	ô	paw, for
oi	oil	ŭ	cut	zh	vision
ŏŏ	book	û	fur	ə	ago, item,
ōō	boot	*th*	the		pencil, atom,
yōō	abuse	th	thin		circus
ou	out	hw	which	ər	butter

whit·tle |hwĭt′l| or |wĭt′l| —*verb* **whittled, whittling** **1.** To cut small bits or pieces from wood with a knife: *Jim whittled the ends of the sticks.* **2.** To make something in this way: *Sally whittled a wooden doll.*

whiz |hwĭz| or |wĭz| —*verb* **whizzed, whizzing** To move quickly with a buzzing or hissing sound: *The subway train whizzed by.*

who |hōō| —*pronoun* **1.** What or which person or persons: *Who called?* **2.** That: *The boy who came yesterday is now gone.*

who'd |hōōd| A contraction of "who would."

who·ev·er |hōō ĕv′ər| —*pronoun* **1.** Anyone that: *Whoever comes to our school should be welcomed.* **2.** No matter who: *Whoever it was who opened the safe, he was an expert.* **3.** Who: *Whoever could have invented such a thing?*

whole |hōl| —*adjective* **1.** Having all its parts; complete: *This isn't a whole checkers set; two pieces are missing.* **2.** Not divided; in one piece: *He bought a whole acre of land near the beach.* **3.** Well or healthy: *He felt like a whole person again.* **4.** Lasting the full time; entire: *The baby cried during the whole trip.*
—*noun, plural* **wholes** **1.** All of the parts of a thing: *Two halves make a whole.* **2.** A complete group; a system: *The staff as a whole voted to strike.*
♦ *These sound alike* **whole, hole.**

whole number A number that tells how many complete things there are. The numbers 0, 1, 2, 3, 10, 15, and 22 are whole numbers. A number with a fraction, such as 1¼, or a decimal, such as 5.35, are not whole numbers.

whole·sale |hōl′sāl′| —*noun, plural* **wholesales** The sale of goods in large quantities, especially to storekeepers who will then sell them to customers.
—*adjective* Selling goods at wholesale: *a wholesale dealer.*

whole·some |hōl′səm| —*adjective* **1.** Good for the health of mind or body: *a wholesome diet.* **2.** Having or showing good health: *She has a wholesome, rosy color on her cheeks.*

who'll |hōōl| A contraction of "who will."

whol·ly |hō′lē| —*adverb* Entirely or totally; completely: *He did the job wholly by himself.*
♦ *These sound alike* **wholly, holy.**

whom |hōōm| —*pronoun* The pronoun **whom** is the objective case of **who.** It means: **1.** What person: *To whom am I speaking?* **2.** The person that: *This is the girl whom I mentioned yesterday.*

whoop |hōōp| or |hwōōp| or |wōōp| —*noun, plural* **whoops** A loud cry or shout: *Rod gave a whoop of joy.*
—*verb* **whooped, whooping** To shout loudly: *Bill whooped with laughter at the joke.*
♦ *These sound alike* **whoop, hoop.**

whoop·ing crane |hōō′pĭng| or |hwōō′pĭng| or |wōō′pĭng| A large North American bird with long legs and black and white feathers. These birds are now rarely seen.

who's |hōōz| A contraction of "who is" and "who has."
♦ *These sound alike* **who's, whose.**

whose |hōōz| A form of the pronoun **who.** It stands for: Of whom; of which: *I saw the woman whose purse was stolen. Whose car is this? The car whose tires are new is mine.* The pronoun **whose** belongs to a class of words called **determiners.** They signal that a noun is coming.
♦ *These sound alike* **whose, who's.**

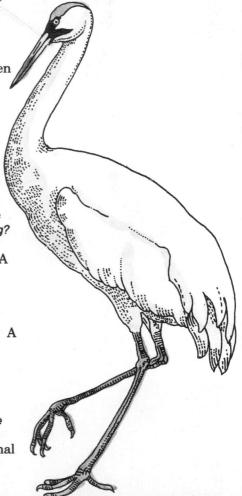

whooping crane

wicker
Wicker baskets

wig
English judges wearing wigs

wigwam

ă	pat	ĕ	pet	î	fierce
ā	pay	ē	be	ŏ	pot
â	care	ĭ	pit	ō	go
ä	father	ī	pie	ô	paw, for

oi	oil	ŭ	cut	zh	vision
ŏŏ	book	û	fur	ə	ago, item,
ōō	boot	th	the		pencil, atom,
yōō	abuse	th	thin		circus
ou	out	hw	which	ər	butter

why | hwī | or | wī | —*adverb* **1.** For what reason or purpose: *Why did you have to leave? Why did you say that?* **2.** Because of which; on account of which: *I wasn't feeling well was the reason why I left. I was angry; that's why I said it.*
—*interjection* A word used to show surprise, pleasure, or doubt: *Why, I'd be glad to help you.*

wick | wĭk | —*noun, plural* **wicks** A cord or piece of twisted thread in a candle or oil lamp. When it is lighted, the wick draws up the melted wax or oil to be burned.

wick·ed | wĭk'ĭd | —*adjective* Evil or morally bad; vicious: *the wicked people who stole food from the poor.*

wick·er | wĭk'ər | —*noun* Thin twigs or branches that bend easily. Wicker is used to make such things as baskets and light outdoor furniture.

wick·et | wĭk'ĭt | —*noun, plural* **wickets** **1.** In the game of cricket, either of the two sets of three stakes that are the target of a player. **2.** In croquet, any of the wire arches through which a player tries to hit his or her ball.

wide | wīd | —*adjective* **wider, widest** **1.** Extending over or covering a large area from side to side; broad: *a wide street.* **2.** Having a certain distance from side to side: *This ribbon is two inches wide.* **3.** Having a large amount or great range: *The store has a wide selection of shirts.* **4.** Landing or found far away from a certain place or goal: *He aimed the rifle but his shot was wide of the target.*
—*adverb* **1.** Over a large area: *He traveled far and wide before he decided to live in Oklahoma.* **2.** To the full extent; completely: *You left the door wide open.*

wid·en | wīd'n | —*verb* **widened, widening** To make or become wide or wider: *The city is widening the river so large ships can sail on it. The road widens after it passes the lake.*

wide·spread | wīd'sprĕd' | —*adjective* **1.** Happening in many places or believed by many people: *The feeling that taxes should be lower is widespread throughout the country.* **2.** Spread out wide; fully open: *The eagle glided above the trees with widespread wings.*

wid·ow | wĭd'ō | —*noun, plural* **widows** A woman whose husband has died and who has not married again.

wid·ow·er | wĭd'ō ər | —*noun, plural* **widowers** A man whose wife has died and who has not married again.

width | wĭdth | or | wĭth | —*noun, plural* **widths** The distance of something from one side to the other: *The width of a basketball court is thirty-five feet.*

wife | wīf | —*noun, plural* **wives** A woman who is married.

wig | wĭg | —*noun, plural* **wigs** A covering for the head that is made of real hair or materials that look like real hair.

wig·gle | wĭg'əl | —*verb* **wiggled, wiggling** To move or cause to move from side to side with short, quick motions: *She wiggled her toes. The goat's ears wiggled.*

wig·wam | wĭg'wŏm' | —*noun, plural* **wigwams** A North American Indian dwelling. It has a frame made of poles in the shape of an arch or cone that is covered with hides, bark, or other material.

wild | wīld | —*adjective* **wilder, wildest** **1.** Growing, living, or found in a natural state; not grown, cared for, or controlled by people: *We picked wild berries in the forest. Wild animals live in the jungle.* **2.** Not having discipline or control: *The teacher yelled at*

the wild boy but he kept throwing his books all over the room.
3. Strange or unusual: *She had a wild idea for a costume party in which people would dress up as animals.*
—*adverb* Not under control; in a wild way: *Flowers grow wild by the lake.*

wild·cat |wĭld′kăt′| —*noun, plural* **wildcats** A lynx, bobcat, or other small to medium-sized animal related to the domestic cat.

wil·der·ness |wĭl′dər nĭs| —*noun, plural* **wildernesses** A wild place or region that is not lived in by people.

wild·life |wĭld′līf′| —*noun* Wild plants and animals, especially wild animals living in their natural surroundings.

will¹ |wĭl| —*noun, plural* **wills** **1.** The power of mind in a person to choose or decide what to do: *Donald is going to be a good businessman because he has a strong will to succeed.* **2.** A wish or decision: *It is the king's will that all the people celebrate his birthday.* **3.** Strong purpose; determination: *The coach told the team they must have the will to win.* **4.** An attitude or feeling toward another person or group: *She's shown ill will to me ever since our team won.* **5.** A legal document that says what a person wants done with property after death.
—*verb* **willed, willing** **1.** To use the power of the mind to choose or decide what to do: *He willed himself to work harder in school.* **2.** To give away one's property or belongings in a will: *The man willed all his money to charity.*

will² |wĭl| —*helping,* or *auxiliary, verb* Past tense **would** As a helping verb **will** is used followed by another verb in the infinitive to show: **1.** An action or state that will take place or exist in the future: *They will come later. She will be twenty on Friday.* **2.** An order: *You will leave now.* **3.** The will to do something: *Will you help me with this? I will too go if I feel like it.*

will·ing |wĭl′ĭng| —*adjective* **1.** Acting or ready to act gladly: *Carole is willing to do anything to help out around the house.* **2.** Ready to tolerate or put up with: *I'm willing to wait.*

wil·low |wĭl′ō| —*noun, plural* **willows** A tree with slender, flexible twigs and narrow leaves.

wilt |wĭlt| —*verb* **wilted, wilting** To become or cause to become limp; droop: *Why did the flowers wilt? The sun wilted them.*

win |wĭn| —*verb* **won, winning** **1.** To get or achieve victory in a game, contest, battle, or competition by doing better than everybody else: *Our soldiers won the fight. I hope our team wins the game. Who is winning the election?* **2.** To gain or get through hard work: *He won fame as one of the best painters of his time.*
—*noun, plural* **wins** A victory or triumph; success: *Our team had five wins before they lost a game.*

wince |wĭns| —*verb* **winced, wincing** To move or pull back quickly from something that is painful, dangerous, or frightening: *Tom winced when I pulled the splinter out of his finger.*

winch |wĭnch| —*noun, plural* **winches** A machine for lifting or pulling something. It is made up of a drum and a long rope or chain with an object attached to it. When the drum is turned, the rope winds around it and lifts the object.

wind¹ |wĭnd| —*noun, plural* **winds** **1.** Air that moves over the earth: *The strong wind knocked over the garbage cans.* **2.** The ability to breathe; breath: *I was out of wind after running.*
—*verb* **winded, winding** To cause to be out of breath: *Moving all that heavy furniture up the stairs winded me.*

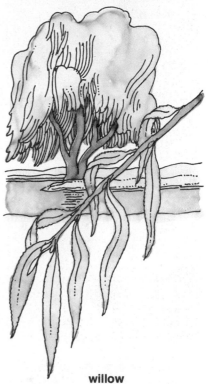
willow
Tree *(above)* and leaves *(below)*

winch

windmill

wind² |wīnd| —*verb* **wound, winding** **1.** To wrap, fold, or place around or on top of something: *She wound the ribbon around her waist.* **2.** To move or cause to move first one way and then another; move in a circular or back-and-forth direction: *The road winds through the valley.* **3.** To cause a clock or other device to work by turning or coiling the spring: *wind a watch.*

wind instrument A musical instrument that is played by blowing through it. Flutes, oboes, trumpets, and clarinets are wind instruments.

wind·mill |wĭnd′mĭl′| —*noun, plural* **windmills** A machine that uses the power of the wind to turn a wheel or a set of vanes. Windmills can be used to grind grain, pump water, and produce electricity.

win·dow |wĭn′dō| —*noun, plural* **windows** An opening in a wall or ceiling that lets in air and light. It is usually made of a frame that surrounds a pane of glass.

win·dow·pane |wĭn′dō pān′| —*noun, plural* **windowpanes** A piece of glass in a window.

wind·pipe |wĭnd′pīp′| —*noun, plural* **windpipes** A tube that goes from the throat to the lungs and carries air to and away from the lungs.

wind·shield |wĭnd′shēld′| —*noun, plural* **windshields** A sheet of glass or plastic at the front of an automobile, motorcycle, or other vehicle. It protects the driver and passengers.

wind·y |wĭn′dē| —*adjective* **windier, windiest** **1.** Having a lot of wind: *a windy day.* **2.** Exposed to the wind: *a windy street.*

wine |wīn| —*noun, plural* **wines** The fermented juice of grapes or other fruits used to make alcoholic beverages.

wing |wĭng| —*noun, plural* **wings** **1.** One of the movable parts of a bird, bat, or insect that it uses to fly. **2.** The structure located on either side of an airplane. Wings lift the plane and support it on air during flight. **3.** A part that is attached to the main part of a structure: *the wing of a house. A new wing for research is being added to the hospital.* **4.** **wings** The area that extends off the main part of a stage and is concealed from the audience: *The actors are waiting in the wings.*
—*verb* **winged, winging** **1.** To fly: *The birds were winging south.* **2.** To wound slightly: *The bullet winged his arm.*

winged |wĭngd| —*adjective* Having wings or parts like wings: *Flies are winged insects.*

wing·spread |wĭng′sprĕd′| —*noun, plural* **wingspreads** The distance between the tip of one wing and the tip of the other when they are spread wide: *the wingspread of an eagle.*

wink |wĭngk| —*verb* **winked, winking** To close and open one eye quickly: *The pretty girl winked at me.*
—*noun, plural* **winks** **1.** The act of winking: *She gave me a wink from across the room when I read her note.* **2.** A very short time: *The job was done in a wink.*

win·ner |wĭn′ər| —*noun, plural* **winners** Someone or something that wins: *The winner of the drawing contest will be announced.*

win·ning |wĭn′ĭng| —*adjective* **1.** Successful or victorious: *the winning team.* **2.** Charming or attractive: *Diana has a winning personality.*
—*noun, plural* **winnings** Something that has been won: *My winnings from the card game amounted to five dollars.*

Win·ni·peg |wĭn′ə pĕg′| The capital of Manitoba.

ă	pat	ĕ	pet	î	fierce
ā	pay	ē	be	ŏ	pot
â	care	ĭ	pit	ō	go
ä	father	ī	pie	ô	paw, for
oi	oil	ŭ	cut	zh	vision
ŏŏ	book	û	fur	ə	ago, item,
ōō	boot	*th*	the		pencil, atom,
yōō	abuse	th	thin		circus
ou	out	hw	which	ər	butter

win·ter | wĭn′tər | —*noun, plural* **winters** The season of the year between fall and spring.

win·ter·green | wĭn′tər grēn′ | —*noun, plural* **wintergreens** **1.** A plant that grows low to the ground and has red berries and evergreen leaves with a spicy smell. **2.** An oil from this plant used in medicine and for flavoring.

win·try | wĭn′trē | —*adjective* **wintrier, wintriest** **1.** Of or like winter; cold: *a bleak wintry day.* **2.** Unfriendly; not cordial: *She answered me in a wintry tone of voice.*

wipe | wīp | —*verb* **wiped, wiping** **1.** To rub, as with a cloth, in order to clean or dry: *Wipe the dishes with a towel. Don't wipe your shoes on the rug.* **2.** To remove as if by rubbing: *She wiped the tears from her face.*

  Phrasal verb **wipe out** To destroy completely: *The hurricane wiped out the entire beach community.*

wire | wīr | —*noun, plural* **wires** **1.** A thin rod or strand of metal. It is made by stretching a piece of metal until it is thin. Wire is usually flexible. **2.** A telegram: *I sent her a wire wishing her a happy birthday.*

—*verb* **wired, wiring** **1.** To join, connect, or fasten with a wire or wires: *He wired the leather bags to the back of the bicycle.* **2.** To install or put in wires for electricity: *The workers are wiring the new house.* **3.** To send a telegram: *He wired me for help.*

wire·less | wīr′lĭs | —*adjective* Not using or having wires. Radio is a form of wireless communication because its signals are sent by waves that move through the air.

—*noun, plural* **wirelesses** A radio.

wir·ing | wīr′ĭng | —*noun* A system of wires that is used to carry electricity: *The lights in the kitchen keep going out, and Mom says there must be a problem in the wiring.*

wir·y | wīr′ē | —*adjective* **wirier, wiriest** **1.** Like wire: *The dog has wiry hair.* **2.** Thin but tough or strong: *The athlete has a wiry body.*

Wis·con·sin | wĭs kŏn′sən | A state in the north-central United States. The capital of Wisconsin is Madison.

wis·dom | wĭz′dəm | —*noun* Intelligence and good judgment in knowing what to do and what is good and bad and right and wrong. A person gains wisdom through learning and experience.

wise | wīz | —*adjective* **wiser, wisest** **1.** Having or showing good judgment, common sense, and intelligence: *wise advice; a wise decision.* **2.** Having knowledge or learning: *a wise man.*

wish | wĭsh | —*noun, plural* **wishes** A strong desire for something: *When she was a child, her wish was to be a veterinarian.*
—*verb* **wished, wishing** **1.** To have or feel a desire; want something: *Your grandparents wish they could see you. I wish I didn't have to go to sleep so early.* **2.** To make a wish: *He blew out the candles and wished for a pony.*

wish·bone | wĭsh′bōn′ | —*noun, plural* **wishbones** A bone that is shaped like the letter Y and is located in front of the breastbone of chickens and many other birds. Many people make wishes on wishbones. One person holds one of the top branches of the bone while another person holds the other end. Each person makes a wish and then they pull the bone till it breaks. The person who gets the longer piece of the bone is supposed to get his or her wish.

wish·ful | wĭsh′fəl | —*adjective* Having or expressing a wish or desire, especially a wish that did not or cannot come true: *Laura*

wintry

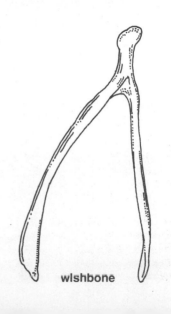

wishbone

Wisconsin
The name **Wisconsin** comes from an Indian word that probably means "at the big river." It seems to be related to a word meaning "place of the beaver."

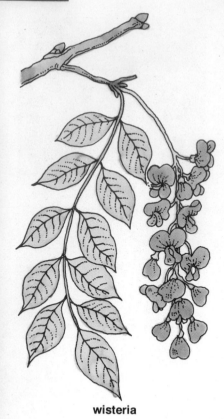

wisteria

would like to travel to Portugal on her vacation but she knows it's only *wishful thinking.*

wis·ter·i·a |wĭ stîr′ē ə| —*noun* A climbing woody vine with bunches of purple or white flowers that droop from the vine.

wist·ful |wĭst′fəl| —*adjective* Full of sad longing: *The boy had a wistful look on his face.*

wit |wĭt| —*noun, plural* **wits 1.** The ability to describe things, people, or situations in a clever, funny way. **2.** A person having this ability: *Jim was the best wit at the party.* **3.** The ability to think and reason clearly: *He kept his wits about him and drove the car to safety.*

witch |wĭch| —*noun, plural* **witches** A woman who practices magic or who is thought to have magical powers.

with |wĭ*th*| or |wĭ*th*| —*preposition* **1.** In the company of: *Come with me.* **2.** Next to: *Walk with him and follow me.* **3.** Having; possessing: *a clown with a red nose.* **4.** On the side of: *I'm with you all the way on this.* **5.** In spite of: *With all that talent, he's got nowhere.* **6.** Against: *He is always looking for a fight with somebody.* **7.** By means of using: *Start the fire with flint and twigs.* **8.** In the spirit of: *He said good-by with great sadness.* **9.** At the same time as; during: *rising with the sun.* **10.** Because of; as a result of: *He was trembling with fear.* **11.** In proportion to: *Many things improve with age.* **12.** From: *She hates to part with money.* **13.** Between: *The company signed a contract with several bookstores.* **14.** In the care of: *You can leave your things with me.* **15.** In regard to: *I'm pleased with her.*

with·draw |wĭ*th* drô′| or |wĭ*th* drô′| —*verb* **withdrew, withdrawn, withdrawing 1.** To take away; remove: *She had to withdraw money from the bank to pay for the car.* **2.** To move back; retreat: *The army withdrew its soldiers from the city.*

with·drawn |wĭ*th* drôn′| or |wĭ*th* drôn′| The past participle of the verb **withdraw:** *He has withdrawn his offer.*
—*adjective* Shy or quiet; timid: *The girl was withdrawn and would rather stay inside and read than go outside and play.*

with·drew |wĭ*th* drŏŏ′| or |wĭ*th* drŏŏ′| The past tense of the verb **withdraw:** *The soldiers withdrew from the town.*

with·er |wĭ*th*′ər| —*verb* **withered, withering** To dry up or cause to dry up; shrivel: *The flowers withered because they hadn't been given enough water. The hot sun withered the grass.*

with·in |wĭ*th* ĭn′| or |wĭ*th* ĭn′| —*preposition* **1.** Inside of: *organs within the body.* **2.** Inside the limits of: *They were within ten miles from home.* **3.** Not going beyond: *within the laws of the land.*
—*adverb* Inside; indoors: *Although it is cold outside, it is warm within.*

with·out |wĭ*th* out′| or |wĭ*th* out′| —*preposition* **1.** Not having; lacking: *She was without money to get home.* **2.** With no or none of: *He built up his company without aid from others.* **3.** Not accompanied by: *There is no smoke without fire.* **4.** On the outside of: *His house is without the city limits.*
—*adverb* On the outside or outdoors: *The house is sturdy within and without.*

with·stand |wĭ*th* stănd′| or |wĭ*th* stănd′| —*verb* **withstood, withstanding** To resist or endure something; not give in to: *That building is strong enough to withstand the shocks from earthquakes.*

with·stood |wĭ*th* stŏŏd′| or |wĭ*th* stŏŏd′| The past tense and past participle of the verb **withstand:** *The army withstood an attack.*

ă	pat	ĕ	pet	î	fierce
ā	pay	ē	be	ŏ	pot
â	care	ĭ	pit	ō	go
ä	father	ī	pie	ô	paw, for
oi	oil	ŭ	cut	zh	vision
ŏŏ	book	û	fur	ə	ago, item,
ōō	boot	*th*	the		pencil, atom,
yōō	abuse	th	thin		circus
ou	out	hw	which	ər	butter

The army had already withstood two attacks.

wit·ness |wĭt′nĭs| —*noun, plural* **witnesses** **1.** Someone who has seen or heard something: *Sam was a witness of the accident.* **2.** A person who is called to testify before a court of law and swears to tell the truth.
  —*verb* **witnessed, witnessing** **1.** To be present at; see: *We both witnessed the robbery.* **2.** To sign a document as a witness: *He witnessed the will.*

wit·ty |wĭt′ē| —*adjective* **wittier, wittiest** Having wit; clever and amusing: *a witty person; a witty remark.*

wives |wīvz| The plural of the noun **wife.**

wiz·ard |wĭz′ərd| —*noun, plural* **wizards** **1.** A person who is thought to have magical powers; magician. **2.** A person who has a very great skill or talent: *He is a wizard at chess.*

wob·ble |wŏb′əl| —*verb* **wobbled, wobbling** To move or cause to move unsteadily from side to side: *This chair wobbles.*

woe |wō| —*noun, plural* **woes** Deep sorrow or suffering; grief: *The drought caused a lot of trouble and woe for the farmers.*

woke |wōk| A past tense of the verb **wake:** *A knock on the door woke me up.*

wolf |wŏŏlf| —*noun, plural* **wolves** An animal related to the dog. Wolves live mostly in northern regions and feed on the flesh of other animals.
  —*verb* **wolfed, wolfing** To eat quickly and greedily: *You'll get sick if you wolf down your food that way.*

wol·ver·ine |wŏŏl′və rēn′| —*noun, plural* **wolverines** An animal with thick, dark fur and a bushy tail. Wolverines live in northern regions and feed on the flesh of other animals.

wolves |wŏŏlvz| The plural of the noun **wolf.**

wom·an |wŏŏm′ən| —*noun, plural* **women** **1.** An adult female human being. **2.** Female human beings in general: *The opportunities for women in society have improved in recent years.*

womb |wŏŏm| —*noun, plural* **wombs** The organ in female mammals in which a baby is developed and nourished before birth.

wom·en |wĭm′ĭn| The plural of the noun **woman.**

won |wŭn| The past tense and past participle of the verb **win:** *We won the game. Who has won first prize?*
  ♦ *These sound alike* **won, one.**

won·der |wŭn′dər| —*noun, plural* **wonders** **1.** A person, thing, or event that is unusual, surprising, or majestic: *The Grand Canyon in Arizona is one of the great wonders of the world made by nature.* **2.** The feeling of awe or admiration caused by something unusual, surprising, or majestic: *I was filled with wonder as I watched the pictures of the astronauts walking on the moon.*
  —*verb* **wondered, wondering** **1.** To feel awe and admiration: *I wondered at the sight of the giant lightning bolts in the sky.* **2.** To be filled with curiosity or doubt: *He wondered why the sun is yellow and the sky is blue.* **3.** To be curious about; want to know: *I wonder what she is doing. We were wondering where you went.*

won·der·ful |wŭn′dər fəl| —*adjective* **1.** Causing wonder; marvelous; impressive: *It must be wonderful to be able to fly like a bird.* **2.** Interesting or enjoyable; very good: *a wonderful movie. I had a wonderful time at the party.*

won't |wōnt| A contraction of "will not."

wood |wŏŏd| —*noun, plural* **woods** **1.** The hard material that

wolf

wolverine

woodchuck

woodpecker

makes up the trunk and branches of trees, bushes, and some plants. It is used for making buildings, furniture, paper, and many other things. **2.** This material cut up. It is used for building, fuel, and other purposes: *Will you bring in some more wood for the fire?* **3. woods** An area where many trees grow close together; forest.

♦ *These sound alike* **wood, would.**

wood·chuck |wŏŏd′chŭk′| —*noun, plural* **woodchucks** A North American animal with brownish fur and short legs. Woodchucks dig burrows in the ground. Also called *ground hog.*

wood·cut·ter |wŏŏd′kŭt′ər| —*noun, plural* **woodcutters** A person whose job is to cut down trees or cut up wood.

wood·ed |wŏŏd′ĭd| —*adjective* Having trees or woods: *I saw a deer in the wooded area behind the barn.*

wood·en |wŏŏd′n| —*adjective* **1.** Made of wood: *wooden shoes; a wooden bridge.* **2.** Stiff or awkward: *the wooden movements of a robot. He had a wooden expression on his face.*

wood·land |wŏŏd′lənd| or |wŏŏd′lănd′| —*noun, plural* **woodlands** Land covered with trees.

wood·peck·er |wŏŏd′pĕk′ər| —*noun, plural* **woodpeckers** Any of several birds with a strong, pointed bill that is used to drill into bark and wood. Woodpeckers also have strong claws for clinging to and climbing trees.

woods·man |wŏŏdz′mən| —*noun, plural* **woodsmen** A person who works, lives, or enjoys spending time in the woods.

wood·wind |wŏŏd′wĭnd′| —*noun, plural* **woodwinds** Any of a group of musical instruments that are played by blowing air into them. In certain woodwinds, such as a clarinet, oboe, or bassoon, the sound is made when the breath causes a reed inside the mouthpiece to vibrate. In others, such as a flute or piccolo, the sound is made by blowing across an opening.

wood·work |wŏŏd′wûrk′| —*noun* Objects made of wood, especially the inside parts of a house, such as doors, window frames, and moldings.

wood·y |wŏŏd′ē| —*adjective* **woodier, woodiest 1.** Made of or containing wood: *woody plants; woody stems.* **2.** Covered with trees; wooded: *a woody hillside.*

wool |wŏŏl| —*noun, plural* **wools 1.** The thick, soft, curly hair of sheep and some other animals. **2.** Yarn, cloth, or clothing made of wool.

wool·en |wŏŏl′ən| —*adjective* Made of wool: *a woolen shirt.*

word |wûrd| —*noun, plural* **words 1.** A sound or group of sounds that have a meaning and that is a unit of speech. **2.** The written or printed letters that represent such a sound. A sentence is made up of words. **3. words** Spoken or written expression; speech or writing: *You must learn how to put your feelings into words.* **4.** A remark or comment: *Let me give you a word of advice.* **5.** A short conversation: *May I have a word with you?* **6. words** Angry remarks made back and forth; a quarrel: *My sister and I had words over who was going to walk the dog.* **7.** A promise or vow: *She always keeps her word.* **8.** News or information; a message: *We sent word of our safe arrival.*

—*verb* **worded, wording** To express in words: *Word your question clearly.*

Idiom **word for word** Without changing or leaving out a word; exactly: *Repeat what he said word for word.*

ă	pat	ĕ	pet	î	fierce
ā	pay	ē	be	ŏ	pot
â	care	ĭ	pit	ō	go
ä	father	ī	pie	ô	paw, for
oi	oil	ŭ	cut	zh	vision
ŏŏ	book	û	fur	ə	ago, item,
ōō	boot	th	the		pencil, atom,
yōō	abuse	th	thin		circus
ou	out	hw	which	ər	butter

word·ing |wûr′dĭng| —*noun* The way something is said or written: *The teacher said she didn't understand what I wanted to know because the wording of my question was not clear.*

word·y |wûr′dē| —*adjective* **wordier, wordiest** Using too many words: *The book was so wordy it was hard to read.*

wore |wôr| or |wōr| The past tense of the verb **wear:** *Did you see the silly hat Dan wore to the party?*

work |wûrk| —*noun, plural* **works** **1.** The effort made to do or make something. Work can be done by the body or the mind: *It was tedious work to paint the house. Solving those arithmetic problems was hard work.* **2.** What a person does to earn money; a job or occupation: *She's been out of work for two months. A doctor's work is to cure disease.* **3.** A task or number of tasks: *There is enough work around the house to keep us busy all day.* **4.** The way in which someone does a task: *The teacher said my work is improving.* **5.** Something that is made or being made: *She stopped sewing and put her work in the basket. The artist says his new painting is his best work.* **6. works** The moving parts of a machine or device: *He had to remove the works of the watch to fix it.*
—*verb* **worked, working** **1.** To put forth effort to do or make something: *We worked hard to finish planting the garden before it got dark.* **2.** To have a job; be employed: *He works for the telephone company.* **3.** To cause or force to do work: *The boss of the store works his employees hard.* **4.** To operate or function the proper way: *The radio isn't working.* **5.** To cause to operate or function the proper way: *I can't work the washing machine unless you show me how.* **6.** To serve a purpose: *The recipe says to use butter, but margarine will work just as well.* **7.** To bring about; accomplish: *The medicine worked and now I feel better.* **8.** To form or shape by applying pressure: *Work the clay with your fingers.* **9.** To be formed or shaped in this way: *Copper works easily.*

Phrasal verb **work out** **1.** To plan or develop: *We are working out a solution to the problem.* **2.** To succeed or prove suitable: *Did everything work out for the picnic? The new assistant my father hired in the store didn't work out.* **3.** To do athletic exercises: *My brother works out for an hour every day.*

work·bench |wûrk′bĕnch′| —*noun, plural* **workbenches** A strong table or bench on which work is done. Workbenches are used by carpenters and other craftsmen.

work·book |wûrk′bŏŏk′| —*noun, plural* **workbooks** A book to help a student or other person study a particular subject. It has exercises and problems that a person works out right on the pages of the book itself.

work·er |wûr′kər| —*noun, plural* **workers** **1.** Someone who works: *There are ten workers in the store. Bill is a fast worker.* **2.** A female ant, bee, or other insect that does most of the work of the colony or hive and that cannot produce offspring.

work·ing |wûr′kĭng| —*adjective* **1.** Of, for, or used in working: *My working hours at the shoe store are from one to five every day after school.* **2.** In operation: *Is the radio working?*

work·man |wûrk′mən| —*noun, plural* **workmen** A person who does some kind of labor with his or her hands or with machines.

work·man·ship |wûrk′mən shĭp′| —*noun* The skill or ability of a workman or the quality of an object that is made: *All of the carpenter's furniture is good because her workmanship is excellent.*

workbench

worker

workout

world
The world seen from outer space

work·out | wûrk′out′ | —*noun, plural* **workouts** Exercise or practice, especially in athletics: *The coach put the team through a workout that lasted two hours.*

work·shop | wûrk′shŏp′ | —*noun, plural* **workshops** **1.** A place, room, or building where work is done: *Dad has a workshop in the garage.* **2.** A group of people studying or working together in a special field or subject: *a workshop on skiing.*

world | wûrld | —*noun, plural* **worlds** **1.** The earth: *I'd like to take a trip around the world.* **2.** A part of the earth: *The United States is in the western world.* **3.** All the people who live on earth: *If we don't control pollution, the world will be in trouble.* **4.** A field or area of interest, activity, or knowledge: *Tom's store was not successful because he doesn't understand the business world.* **5.** A large amount: *The doctor said that resting in the sun would do me a world of good after I'd been sick.*

worm | wûrm | —*noun, plural* **worms** Any of several kinds of animals having a soft, long, rounded body and no backbone. —*verb* **wormed, worming** **1.** To move by or as if by creeping or crawling: *It took me thirty minutes to worm my way through the crowd.* **2.** To get in a sly or sneaky way: *I couldn't worm information out of her.*

worn | wôrn | or | wōrn | The past participle of the verb **wear:** *You have worn that shirt for the last two days.* —*adjective* **1.** Damaged by wear or use: *worn, faded trousers.* **2.** Having a tired look from worry, sickness, or other problems: *He had a pale, worn face after working all night.*

♦ *These sound alike* **worn, warn.**

worn-out | wôrn′out′ | or | wōrn′out′ | —*adjective* **1.** No longer useful or in good condition: *worn-out pants.* **2.** Very tired; exhausted: *I was worn-out after cleaning the house all day.*

wor·ry | wûr′ē | or | wŭr′ē | —*verb* **worried, worrying, worries** **1.** To feel or cause to feel uneasy or anxious: *I'm worried about Dick because he's late. That bad cough of yours worries me.* **2.** To pull or tug at repeatedly: *The kitten worried a ball of yarn.* —*noun, plural* **worries** **1.** An uneasy or troubled feeling; anxiety: *Worry has kept him from sleeping well.* **2.** Something that causes an uneasy feeling or anxiety: *My biggest worry is that the car will break down before I get home.*

worse | wûrs | —*adjective* **1.** The comparative of **bad:** *The situation is even worse than we thought it might be.* **2.** The comparative of **ill:** *Grandpa is worse and we think you should come home.* **3.** More inferior, as in quality, condition, or effect: *These soggy doughnuts are even worse than those.* —*adverb* In a worse way: *You couldn't have sung that worse.* —*noun* Something worse: *Her health has taken a turn for the worse.*

wor·ship | wûr′shĭp | —*noun* **1.** The love and devotion felt for God. **2.** The religious ceremonies and prayers in honor of God: *Churches and synagogues are places of worship.* —*verb* **worshiped** or **worshipped, worshiping** or **worshipping** **1.** To honor and love: *People worship God in their own ways.* **2.** To take part in a religious ceremony: *We worship in church every Sunday.* **3.** To love or be devoted to: *She worships her mother.*

worst | wûrst | —*adjective* **1.** The superlative of **bad:** *He was the worst President we ever had.* **2.** The superlative of **ill:** *This is the worst health he has ever experienced.* **3.** Most inferior, as in quality, condition, or effect: *the worst scrambled eggs I ever tasted.*

ă	pat	ĕ	pet	î	fierce
ā	pay	ē	be	ŏ	pot
â	care	ĭ	pit	ō	go
ä	father	ī	pie	ô	paw, for

oi	oil	ŭ	cut	zh	vision
ōō	book	û	fur	ə	ago, item,
ōō	boot	th	the		pencil, atom,
yōō	abuse	th	thin		circus
ou	out	hw	which	ər	butter

4. Most severe or unfavorable: *the worst winter in years.*
—*noun* Someone or something that is worst: *That apple is the worst of the lot.*

worth |wûrth| —*noun* **1.** The condition or quality that gives a person or thing value or importance: *That antique bowl has great worth because it's over two hundred years old.* **2.** The value of something in money: *That painting's worth is ten thousand dollars.* **3.** The amount that a certain sum of money will buy: *He bought a quarter's worth of chocolate.*
—*adjective* **1.** Good enough to: *This book is worth reading. Your plan is worth trying.* **2.** Having the same value as; equal to: *This old stamp is worth fifty dollars.* **3.** Having wealth that amounts to: *Tom says his father is worth over a million dollars.*

worth·less |wûrth′lĭs| —*adjective* Without worth; not useful, valuable, or important: *I threw out my worthless old shoes. He always breaks his word so his promises are worthless.*

worth·while |wûrth′hwīl′| or |wûrth′wīl′| —*adjective* Valuable enough or important enough to make an effort to do or to spend time and money on: *The old bicycle is still in good shape so it's worthwhile to fix the broken seat.*

wor·thy |wûr′thē| —*adjective* **worthier, worthiest** **1.** Having merit or value; good; useful: *Helping the sick is a worthy cause.* **2.** Deserving or meriting: *Her plan is worthy of consideration.*

would |wŏŏd| The past tense of the verb **will:** *I saw him yesterday, but he would not talk to me.*
♦ *These sound alike* **would, wood.**

would·n't |wŏŏd′nt| A contraction of "would not."

wound¹ |wōōnd| —*noun, plural* **wounds** An injury, especially one in which the skin is broken by cutting.
—*verb* **wounded, wounding** **1.** To injure or hurt by cutting, piercing, or breaking the skin: *The bullet wounded him in the shoulder.* **2.** To hurt another's feelings; cause hurt to another: *Her pride was wounded when her friend didn't invite her to his party.*

wound² |wound| The past tense and past participle of the verb **wind:** *She wound her hair around a finger as she talked. When he had wound the clock, he put it back on the shelf.*

wove |wōv| The past tense of the verb **weave:** *My sister wove me a scarf for my birthday.*

wo·ven |wō′vən| A past participle of the verb **weave:** *The fisherman on the boat said that he had woven all of his own nets.*

wow |wou| —*interjection* A word used to express surprise or excitement: *Wow, did you see how low that plane was flying?*

wrap |răp| —*verb* **wrapped, wrapping** **1.** To cover or enclose by folding or winding something around: *She wrapped a scarf about her shoulders. I have to wrap the baby in a blanket before I take him outside.* **2.** To clasp or wind around: *Wrap your arms around my neck and I'll carry you.* **3.** To put paper around: *She's wrapping birthday presents.*
♦ *These sound alike* **wrap, rap.**

wrap·per |răp′ər| —*noun, plural* **wrappers** A piece of paper or other material that is used to cover or hold something: *Throw the candy wrapper in the garbage.*

wrap·ping |răp′ĭng| —*noun, plural* **wrappings** Paper or other material used for wrapping, covering, or holding something: *She tried not to tear the wrapping so she could use it again.*

wrath |răth| or |räth| —*noun, plural* **wraths** Very great anger;

wreath

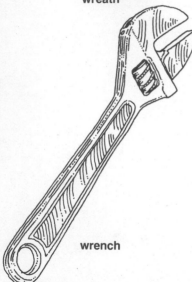

wrench

wrestling

ă	pat	ĕ	pet	î	fierce
â	pay	ē	be	ŏ	pot
â	care	ĭ	pit	ō	go
ä	father	ī	pie	ô	paw, for
oi	oil	ŭ	cut	zh	vision
ōō	book	û	fur	ə	ago, item,
ōō	boot	*th*	the		pencil, atom,
yōō	abuse	th	thin		circus
ou	out	hw	which	ər	butter

rage; fury: *His behavior aroused the teacher's wrath.*

wreath |rēth| —*noun, plural* **wreaths** A circle or ring of leaves, branches, or flowers that are tied together. It is used for decoration: *Christmas wreaths.*

wreck |rĕk| —*verb* **wrecked, wrecking 1.** To ruin or destroy: *The collision wrecked both cars.* **2.** To cause ruin or destruction: *Smoking has wrecked his health.*
—*noun, plural* **wrecks** The remains of something that has been wrecked: *The lot is full of car wrecks.*

wreck·age |rĕk′ĭj| —*noun, plural* **wreckages** The remains of anything wrecked: *the wreckage of a car.*

wren |rĕn| —*noun, plural* **wrens** A small brownish bird that holds its tail pointed upward.

wrench |rĕnch| —*noun, plural* **wrenches 1.** A sudden, hard twist or turn: *I gave the window a wrench and it opened.* **2.** A tool with jaws, used for gripping and turning such things as nuts and bolts.
—*verb* **wrenched, wrenching** To pull or turn suddenly and with force: *He wrenched the nail out of the board.*

wres·tle |rĕs′əl| —*verb* **wrestled, wrestling 1.** To try to force or throw an opponent to the ground by grabbing and struggling with the hands. **2.** To struggle to solve or overcome: *I wrestled with the arithmetic problem for an hour but I couldn't come up with the answer.*

wres·tler |rĕs′lər| —*noun, plural* **wrestlers** A person who wrestles, especially as a sport.

wres·tling |rĕs′lĭng| —*noun* The sport of trying to force or throw an opponent to the ground by grabbing and struggling with the hands.

wretch·ed |rĕch′ĭd| —*adjective* **1.** Very unhappy or unfortunate: *The cold made me feel wretched.* **2.** Evil or wicked: *a wretched thief.*

wri·er |rī′ər| A comparative of **wry.**

wri·est |rī′ĭst| A superlative of **wry.**

wrig·gle |rĭg′əl| —*verb* **wriggled, wriggling 1.** To turn, twist, or move side to side with quick movements: *The snake wriggled along the ground. She told me to stop wriggling in my chair.* **2.** To get into or out of a situation by clever or tricking means: *How did you wriggle out of having to wash the dishes?*

wring |rĭng| —*verb* **wrung, wringing 1.** To twist and squeeze to force water or other liquid out: *She's wringing out the wet clothes.* **2.** To force out liquid by twisting, squeezing, or pressing: *He wrung the water out of the towel.* **3.** To twist with force: *I'd like to wring his neck.* **4.** To get by force: *He said he would wring the answer out of me if I didn't tell him what he wanted to know.* **5.** To hold tightly together and press or twist: *She's been wringing her hands and wondering why Albert has not come home yet.*
♦ *These sound alike* **wring, ring.**

wrin·kle |rĭng′kəl| —*noun, plural* **wrinkles** A small crease, ridge, or fold on a smooth surface, as of skin or cloth: *I ironed the wrinkles out of my dress.*
—*verb* **wrinkled, wrinkling 1.** To make a wrinkle or wrinkles in: *She wrinkled her forehead and tried to remember the message. The rain has wrinkled your suit.* **2.** To show or form wrinkles: *His face wrinkled with a big smile. This shirt wrinkles easily.*

wrist |rĭst| —*noun, plural* **wrists** The joint at which the hand and arm come together.

write | rīt | —*verb* **wrote, written, writing** **1.** To form letters, symbols, or words on a surface with a pencil, pen, or other instrument. **2.** To mark with letters or words: *Please don't write on the walls.* **3.** To compose: *She wrote a book. He writes music.* **4.** To communicate by writing: *She wrote the good news to her friend.* **5.** To send a letter or note to: *I will write to you next month.*

  Phrasal verb **write down** To put into writing: *Please write down the telephone number so you won't forget it.*

♦ *These sound alike* **write, right.**

writ·er | rī′tər | —*noun, plural* **writers** **1.** A person who has written something: *Who is the writer of these letters?* **2.** A person whose job is writing; an author.

writ·ing | rī′tĭng | —*noun, plural* **writings** **1.** Written form: *Put your request in writing.* **2.** Letters or symbols written or printed on a surface: *Whose writing is this?* **3.** **writings** A collection of written works: *the writings of a famous poet.*

writ·ten | rĭt′n | The past participle of the verb **write**: *Have you written a letter to your aunt yet?*

wrong | rông | or | rŏng | —*adjective* **1.** Not correct; mistaken: *a wrong answer to a question.* **2.** Bad; against the law; immoral: *It is wrong to steal.* **3.** Not intended or wanted: *You're heading in the wrong direction to get to town. A wrong telephone number.* **4.** Not fitting or suitable: *This is the wrong time to ask him for money.* **5.** Not working or behaving properly: *Something is wrong with this machine.*

—*adverb* Incorrectly; mistakenly: *You told the story all wrong.*

—*noun, plural* **wrongs** **1.** An unjust or immoral act or condition: *An honorable person will try to make a wrong right.* **2.** The condition of being mistaken or to blame: *You are in the wrong for not telling the truth.*

—*verb* **wronged, wronging** To treat unfairly or unjustly.

  Idiom **go wrong** **1.** To take a wrong turn or course. **2.** To happen or turn out badly: *What went wrong with our plans?*

wrote | rōt | The past participle of the verb **write**: *She wrote me a nice letter thanking me for the gift.*

♦ *These sound alike* **wrote, rote.**

wrung | rŭng | The past tense and past participle of the verb **wring**: *He wrung the water out of his wet shirt. I have wrung out this towel twice and it's still wet.*

♦ *These sound alike* **wrung, rung.**

wry | rī | —*adjective* **wrier** or **wryer, wriest** or **wryest** **1.** Twisted or bent on one side: *a wry smile.* **2.** Twisted in an expression of disapproval or dislike: *She made a wry face when she tasted the medicine.*

♦ *These sound alike* **wry, rye.**

Wy·o·ming | wī ō′mĭng | A state in the western United States. The capital of Wyoming is Cheyenne.

Wyoming
Wyoming comes from an Indian word that means "on the great plain." The name was first used for a valley in Pennsylvania.

Xx

x or **X** |ĕks| —*noun, plural* **x's** or **X's** **1.** The twenty-fourth letter of the English alphabet. **2.** A symbol for a number or quantity that is not known. **3.** A mark made on a map, chart, or other drawing to show a place or location: *X marks the spot where the treasure is buried.*

Xe·rox |zîr ŏks'| —*noun, plural* **Xeroxes** **1.** A trademark for a machine or process that makes photographic copies of written or printed material. **2.** A copy made on a Xerox machine.
—*verb* **Xeroxed, Xeroxing** To copy with a Xerox machine.

X·mas |krĭs'məs| or |ĕks'məs| —*noun, plural* **Xmases** Christmas.

x-ray or **X-ray** |ĕks'rā| —*noun, plural* **x-rays** or **X-rays** **1.** A kind of ray that can go through substances that regular rays of light cannot go through. X-rays are used to take pictures inside the body. Broken bones, tooth cavities, certain tumors, and other things can be located by using x-rays. Certain diseases can also be treated by means of x-rays. **2.** A photograph obtained by the use of x-rays: *A chest x-ray taken yearly is a wise precaution.*
—*verb* **x-rayed** or **X-rayed, x-raying** or **X-raying** To examine, photograph, or treat with x-rays: *The dentist x-rayed his teeth to look for cavities.*

xy·lo·phone |zī'lə fōn'| —*noun, plural* **xylophones** A musical instrument that is made up of two rows of wooden bars of varying lengths. A xylophone is played by striking the bars with small wooden mallets.

xylophone

ă	pat	ĕ	pet	î	fierce
ā	pay	ē	be	ŏ	pot
â	care	ĭ	pit	ō	go
ä	father	ī	pie	ô	paw, for
oi	oil	ŭ	cut	zh	vision
ŏŏ	book	û	fur	ə	ago, item,
ōō	boot	*th*	the		pencil, atom,
yōō	abuse	th	thin		circus
ou	out	hw	which	ər	butter

Y	**Phoenician** — The letter *Y*, like *V*, comes originally from a Phoenician symbol named *wāw*, which is also the basis for *F, U,* and *W*.
Y	**Greek** — The Greeks borrowed the symbol from the Phoenicians and changed its form. One form they used was called *upsilon*.
Y	**Roman** — The Romans took the letter and adapted it for carving into stone. This became the model for our modern printed capital *Y*.
γ	**Medieval** — The hand-written form of about 1,200 years ago became the basis of the modern small letter.
Yy	**Modern** — The modern capital and small letters are based on the Roman capital and later hand-written forms.

y or **Y** |wī| —*noun, plural* **y's** or **Y's** The twenty-fifth letter of the English alphabet.

-y¹ A suffix that forms adjectives and means "full of" or "resembling": *dirty; watery.*

-y² A suffix that forms nouns and means "state or condition": *jealousy.*

-y³ A suffix that forms nouns and means "small or dear one": *kitty; daddy.*

yacht |yät| —*noun, plural* **yachts** A small ship run by sails or a motor and used for pleasure trips or racing.

yak |yăk| —*noun, plural* **yaks** An animal with long hair and horns, found in the mountains of central Asia. Yaks are often tamed and used as work animals and to give milk.

yam |yăm| —*noun, plural* **yams** **1.** The root of a climbing vine that grows in tropical climates. Yams are often eaten as a vegetable or ground into flour. **2.** A reddish sweet potato.

yank |yăngk| —*verb* **yanked, yanking** To pull with a sudden, jerking movement: *The bell rang when I yanked the rope.*
—*noun, plural* **yanks** A sudden, sharp pull; a jerk: *Give the rug a yank and straighten the corner.*

Yan·kee |yăng′kē| —*noun, plural* **Yankees** **1.** A person who was born in or lives in New England. **2.** A person from the northern part of the United States, especially a Union supporter or soldier in the Civil War. **3.** Any person born or living in the United States.

yard¹ |yärd| —*noun, plural* **yards** **1.** A unit of length equal to 3 feet or 36 inches. In the metric system, a yard equals 0.914 meter. **2.** A long pole attached crosswise to a mast to support a sail.

yard² |yärd| —*noun, plural* **yards** **1.** A piece of ground near a house or other building: *I mowed the grass in our back yard. We played ball in the yard by the school.* **2.** An area, often enclosed by a fence, used for a particular kind of work or business: *a coal yard; a lumber yard.*

yarn |yärn| —*noun, plural* **yarns** **1.** Wool or other fibers twisted or spun into long strands and used for knitting, weaving, or mending. **2.** A long tale of adventure, often one that is made up or exaggerated: *a yarn about a haunted sailing ship.*

yawn |yôn| —*verb* **yawned, yawning** **1.** To open the mouth wide

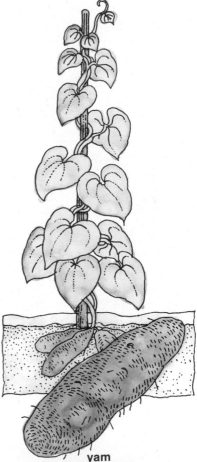

yam
Vine *(above)* and root *(below)*

yard¹, yard²
Yard¹ comes from a word used very long ago by English-speaking people to mean "twig, measuring rod."
Yard² comes from a different old English word that meant "fenced area next to a house, garden."

and breathe in deeply, usually because one is sleepy or bored. **2.** To be open wide as if yawning: *The entrance to the tunnel yawned ahead of them.*

—*noun, plural* **yawns** The act or an instance of yawning: *I think their yawns mean they want us to go home.*

year |yîr| —*noun, plural* **years** **1.** The period of time during which the earth makes one complete revolution around the sun, equal to about 365 days. **2.** Any period of twelve months. **3.** A period of time, sometimes shorter than twelve months, used for a special activity: *the school year.*

year·ly |yîr′lē| —*adjective* **1.** Taking place once a year: *our yearly trip to the country.* **2.** For or during a single year: *yearly earnings; yearly rainfall.*

—*adverb* Once a year or every year: *Oak trees shed their leaves yearly.*

yeast |yēst| —*noun, plural* **yeasts** A substance, often powdered or pressed into small cakes, that is used in baking bread, brewing beer, and for other purposes. Yeast is a tiny plant, or a kind of fungus, that breaks down sugar to produce carbon dioxide and alcohol.

yell |yĕl| —*verb* **yelled, yelling** To shout or cry out loudly, as in excitement, anger, fear, or warning: *The crowd yelled when the team scored. She yelled at me for leaving the door open.*

—*noun, plural* **yells** A loud shout or cry: *Give a yell when you're ready to go.*

yel·low |yĕl′ō| —*noun, plural* **yellows** **1.** The color of ripe lemons, butter, or dandelion blossoms. **2.** Something that has this color: *the yellow of an egg.*

—*adjective* **yellower, yellowest** Of the color yellow: *a yellow rose.*

—*verb* **yellowed, yellowing** To make or become yellow: *The paper yellowed with age.*

yel·low·ish |yĕl′ō ĭsh| —*adjective* Somewhat yellow.

yellow jacket Any of several small wasps having bands of black and yellow around the body.

yen |yĕn| —*noun, plural* **yens** A strong desire; longing: *She had a yen for pizza.*

yes |yĕs| —*adverb* It is true; I agree: *Yes, that is the correct spelling.*

—*noun, plural* **yeses** **1.** An answer that agrees with, approves, or supports: *We'd like you to come, so please say yes.* **2.** A vote or voter that approves of something: *The yeses carried the election.*

yes·ter·day |yĕs′tər dā′| or |yĕs′tər dē| —*noun, plural* **yesterdays** **1.** The day before today: *Yesterday was colder than today.* **2.** The recent past: *The old songs brought back memories of yesterday.*

—*adverb* **1.** On the day before today: *I mailed the letter yesterday.* **2.** In the recent past: *Yesterday she was unknown, but today she's a star.*

yet |yĕt| —*adverb* **1.** At this time; now: *You can't go yet.* **2.** Up to now; so far: *The show hasn't started yet.* **3.** As before; still: *She developed new scientific theories while yet a young student.* **4.** Besides; in addition: *He thought of yet another reason to stay home.* **5.** Even; still more: *That story was sad, but I have a yet sadder one to tell.* **6.** Nevertheless: *She was young yet wise.* **7.** At some future time; eventually: *I haven't solved the problem, but I'll solve it yet.*

yellow jacket

ă	pat	ĕ	pet	î	fierce
ā	pay	ē	be	ŏ	pot
â	care	ĭ	pit	ō	go
ä	father	ī	pie	ô	paw, for
oi	oil	ŭ	cut	zh	vision
ŏŏ	book	û	fur	ə	ago, item,
ōō	boot	*th*	the		pencil, atom,
yŏŏ	abuse	th	thin		circus
ou	out	hw	which	ər	butter

—*conjunction* Nevertheless; and despite this: *He looked calm, yet we knew he had every reason to be very angry.*

yew | yōō | —*noun, plural* **yews** An evergreen tree or shrub that has poisonous, flat dark-green needles and red berries. The tough wood of the yew is used for making archery bows.

♦ *These sound alike* **yew, ewe, you.**

yield | yēld | —*verb* **yielded, yielding 1.** To give forth; produce; provide: *Soybeans yield many useful products.* **2.** To give up; surrender: *We yielded the fort to the enemy when we saw that there was no chance of winning.* **3.** To give in: *We yielded to her arguments when we saw that she was right.* **4.** To give way to pressure or force: *The soft dough yields to your touch.*

—*noun, plural* **yields** An amount yielded or produced: *We used fertilizer to increase our yield of tomatoes.*

yo·gurt | yō′gərt | —*noun, plural* **yogurts** A food that is like custard, made from milk that has been made thick by certain kinds of bacteria. Yogurt has a sharp, slightly sour taste. It is often sweetened and mixed with fruit or flavorings.

yoke | yōk | —*noun, plural* **yokes 1.** A bar with two pieces shaped like U's that fit around the necks of a pair of oxen or other animals that work as a team. **2.** *plural* **yoke** or **yokes** A pair of animals joined by a yoke and working together: *a yoke of oxen.* **3.** Part of a piece of clothing that fits closely around the neck and shoulders or over the hips.

—*verb* **yoked, yoking** To join together with a yoke: *Yoke the oxen and hitch them to the plow.*

♦ *These sound alike* **yoke, yolk.**

yolk | yōk | or | yōlk | —*noun, plural* **yolks** The yellow part inside an egg, especially a chicken's egg.

♦ *These sound alike* **yolk, yoke.**

Yom Kip·pur | yŏm kĭp′ər | The holiest Jewish holiday, celebrated on the tenth day after Rosh Hashanah, the Jewish New Year. Jews fast and pray on Yom Kippur and make up for their sins.

yon·der | yŏn′dər | —*adjective* At a distance but capable of being seen: *The king dwells in yonder castle.*

—*adverb* In, to, or at that place; over there: *The village lies yonder in the valley.*

you | yōō | —*pronoun* **1.** The person or persons spoken to: *You have very little time left. Are you sick?* **2.** A person in general; one; anyone: *You can never be too careful when you drive.* The pronoun **you** is always used with a plural verb, regardless of the fact that it may stand for a singular or a plural noun.

♦ *These sound alike* **you, ewe, yew.**

you'd | yōōd | A contraction of "you had" or "you would."

you'll | yōōl | A contraction of "you will" or "you shall."

♦ *These sound alike* **you'll, Yule.**

young | yŭng | —*adjective* **younger, youngest 1.** Not old or fully grown: *a young girl; a young calf.* **2.** In an early stage of development: *a young company, still trying to get new customers.* **3.** At or near the beginning: *We try to get our work done while the day is young.* **4.** Having the qualities of young people; fresh and vigorous: *She is old in years but young in spirit.*

—*noun* (Used with a singular or plural verb.) People or animals in an early stage of development: *The young of many birds are covered with down when they hatch.*

yew
Above: Needles and berries
Below: Shrub

yoke
Oxen joined by a yoke

young·ster | yŭng′stər | —*noun, plural* **youngsters** **1.** A child or young person: *I loved to roller-skate when I was a youngster.* **2.** A young animal: *The bear bravely protected her youngsters.*

your | yŏŏr | or | yôr | or | yōr | or | yər | —*pronoun* The pronoun **your** is a possessive form of **you.** It means: **1.** Of or belonging to you: *your hat; your house.* **2.** Done or performed by you: *You must finish your chores.* The pronoun **your** belongs to a class of words called **determiners.** They signal that a noun is coming.
—*adjective* **1.** Belonging to you: *Is this your house?* **2.** Done or performed by you: *Here's a list of your duties.*
♦ *These sound alike* **your, you're.**

you're | yŏŏr | or | yər | A contraction of "you are."
♦ *These sound alike* **you're, your.**

yours | yŏŏrz | or | yôrz | or | yōrz | —*pronoun* The pronoun **yours** is a possessive form of **you.** It is used to show that something or someone belongs to you: *I just read a book that is yours. Is she a neighbor of yours? Use my car if yours hasn't been repaired.*

your·self | yŏŏr sĕlf′ | or | yôr sĕlf′ | or | yōr sĕlf′ | or | yər sĕlf′ | —*pronoun, plural* **yourselves** The pronoun **yourself** is a special form of **you.** **1.** It is used: **a.** As the direct object of a verb: *You should not tire yourself.* **b.** As the indirect object of a verb: *Give yourself enough time.* **c.** As the object of a preposition: *Keep it for yourself.* **d.** To call special attention to you: *You yourself admitted you were wrong. You said it yourself.* **2.** The pronoun **yourself** is used to mean "your normal self": *You were not yourself after the accident.*

youth | yōōth | —*noun, plural* **youths** | yōōths | or | yōō*th*z |
1. The condition or quality of being young: *Enjoy your youth while you have it.* **2.** The early time of life before one is an adult: *She has worked hard since her youth.* **3.** A boy or young man: *Her brother is a youth of sixteen.* **4.** (Used with a singular or plural verb.) Young people in general: *a center for the youth of the city.*

youth·ful | yōōth′fəl | —*adjective* **1.** In one's youth; young: *the youthful hero.* **2.** Of or typical of a young person: *a youthful face; youthful impatience.* **3.** Having or giving the look or quality of youth: *a youthful hair style; youthful clothing.*

you've | yōōv | A contraction of "you have."

yo-yo | yō′yō′ | —*noun, plural* **yo-yos** A toy having two disks connected by a short axle. String is wound around the axle and one end is tied to a finger. When the yo-yo is thrown downward, the string unwinds, causing the yo-yo to spin. When the yo-yo reaches the end of the string, its spin causes it to climb back up the string, winding the string around the axle at the same time.

yuc·ca | yŭk′ə | —*noun, plural* **yuccas** A plant that grows in dry regions of western and southern North America. It has stiff, pointed leaves and a large cluster of whitish flowers.

Yule or **yule** | yōōl | —*noun, plural* **Yules** or **yules** Christmas or the Christmas season: *They wished us a happy Yule.*
♦ *These sound alike* **Yule, you'll.**

Yule·tide or **yule·tide** | yōōl′tīd′ | —*noun, plural* **Yuletides** or **yuletides** The Christmas season: *We have a family gathering every Yuletide.*

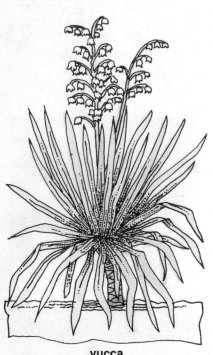

yucca

ă	pat	ĕ	pet	î	fierce
ā	pay	ē	be	ŏ	pot
â	care	ĭ	pit	ō	go
ä	father	ī	pie	ô	paw, for
oi	oil	ŭ	cut	zh	vision
ŏŏ	book	û	fur	ə	ago, item,
ōō	boot	*th*	the		pencil, atom,
yōō	abuse	th	thin		circus
ou	out	hw	which	ər	butter

Z	**Phoenician** — The letter Z comes originally from a Phoenician symbol named *zayin*, which stood for the consonant z.
Z	**Greek** — The Greeks borrowed the symbol from the Phoenicians and changed its name to *zēta*.
Z	**Roman** — The Romans took the letter and adapted it for carving into stone. This became the model for our modern printed capital Z.
z	**Medieval** — The hand-written form of about 1,200 years ago became the basis of the modern small letter.
Zz	**Modern** — The modern capital and small letters are based on the Roman capital and later hand-written forms.

Zz

z or **Z** |zē| —*noun, plural* **z's** or **Z's** The twenty-sixth letter of the English alphabet.

ze·bra |zē′brə| —*noun, plural* **zebras** An African animal that is related to the horse. Its entire body is marked with black and whitish stripes.

ze·nith |zē′nĭth| —*noun, plural* **zeniths** **1.** The point in the sky that is directly above a person. **2.** The highest or most important point: *Being elected President of the United States was the zenith of his political career.*

ze·ro |zîr′ō| or |zē′rō| —*noun, plural* **zeros** or **zeroes** **1.** A number, written 0, that can be added to any other number without changing the value of the other number. **2.** The temperature marked by the numeral 0 on a thermometer. **3.** A point on a scale or other system of measurement that is marked by the numeral 0. **4.** Nothing: *I had zero for lunch today.*
—*adjective* **1.** Of or at zero: *We scored zero points for the third game in a row.* **2.** None at all: *We ought to beat them because they've won zero games this year.*

zig·zag |zĭg′zăg′| —*noun, plural* **zigzags** **1.** A line or course that moves in a series of short, sharp turns from one side or direction to another. **2.** One of a series of short, sharp turns, especially in a road or river: *You have to drive slowly because the street has a lot of zigzags.*
—*verb* **zigzagged, zigzagging** To move in or follow the form of a zigzag: *The trail zigzagged up the mountain.*

zinc |zĭnk| —*noun* A shiny bluish-white metal. It is used for coating iron and in batteries. It is not affected by air and moisture. Zinc is one of the chemical elements.

zin·ni·a |zĭn′ē ə| —*noun, plural* **zinnias** A garden plant with flowers of various colors.

zip |zĭp| —*verb* **zipped, zipping** **1.** To move or do something very fast: *She zipped down the hill on her sled.* **2.** To fasten or close with a zipper: *Zip up your jacket. Does the dress button or zip?*

Zip Code A numeral that identifies a postal delivery area in the United States. It is written right after the address on a letter or package. Zip Codes are supposed to speed up the delivery of mail.

zip·per |zĭp′ər| —*noun, plural* **zippers** A fastener that is made of two rows of teeth on separate edges. The teeth are made to

zebra

zinnia

zither

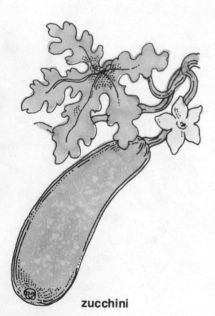

zucchini

lock and unlock by pulling a sliding tab up and down.

zith·er | zĭth′ər | —*noun, plural* **zithers** A musical instrument that is made of a shallow, flat box with thirty to forty strings stretched over it. It is played by plucking the strings.

zo·di·ac | zō′dē ăk′ | —*noun* **1.** An imaginary band in the heavens that extends on both sides of the path traveled by the sun. It includes the paths traveled by the planets and the moon. **2.** The twelve equal parts, called signs of the zodiac, into which this band is divided. Each part has the name of a group of stars.

zom·bie | zŏm′bē | —*noun, plural* **zombies** **1.** In the belief or folklore of some African peoples and others of African origin, a dead body that has been brought to life by magic and is the magician's slave. **2.** A person who looks or acts as if he has no will.

zo·nal | zō′nəl | —*adjective* Of or having to do with a zone or zones: *Time zones make up one of the kinds of zonal divisions of the earth. Zip Codes are part of a zonal system of sorting and delivering mail.*

zone | zōn | —*noun, plural* **zones** **1.** A region or area that is divided or different from another one because of some special reason or use: *In which time zone is Alaska? People must drive slowly in a school zone.* **2.** Any of the five regions into which the surface of the earth is divided according to its climate and latitude.
—*verb* **zoned, zoning** To divide or mark off into zones: *That part of the city was zoned for stores and factories, so no houses can be built there.*

zoo | zoo | —*noun, plural* **zoos** A park or other place where living animals are kept and shown.

zo·o·log·i·cal | zō′ə lŏj′ĭ kəl | —*adjective* Of animals or zoology.

zo·ol·o·gy | zō ŏl′ə jē | —*noun* The scientific study of animals.

zoom | zoom | —*verb* **zoomed, zooming** **1.** To make or move with a loud, low buzzing or humming sound: *The motor zoomed as he started the car. A bee zoomed by.* **2.** To move or climb quickly; move quickly upward or downward: *The rocket zoomed into the sky. I zoomed down the hill on my bicycle.*

zuc·chi·ni | zoo kē′nē | —*noun, plural* **zucchini** A kind of long, narrow squash. Zucchini have a thin dark-green skin.

ă	pat	ĕ	pet	î	fierce
ā	pay	ē	be	ŏ	pot
â	care	ĭ	pit	ō	go
ä	father	ī	pie	ô	paw, for
oi	oil	ŭ	cut	zh	vision
ŏŏ	book	û	fur	ə	ago, item,
ōō	boot	th	the		pencil, atom,
yōō	abuse	th	thin		circus
ou	out	hw	which	ər	butter